SELF CATERING
CATERING
IN BRITAIN

Editor: Penny Hicks
Designers: Ashley Tilleard, Outline Art Services

Gazetteer: Compiled by the Publications Research Unit of the Automobile Association
Maps: Prepared by the Cartographic Services Unit of the Automobile Association

Advertisement Production: Christopher Heard Tel 0256 20123 (ext 2021)
Advertisement Sales Representatives:
North of England and Scotland, Brian Nathaniel Tel 061-338 6498
Wales and Midlands, Arthur Williams Tel 0222 60267
South West England, Bryan Thompson Tel 027-580 3296
London and South East England, Melanie Mackenzie-Aird Tel 0494 40208
Central Southern England, Edward May Tel 0256 20123 (ext 3524) or 0256 67568

Filmset by: Vantage Photosetting Co Ltd, Eastleigh and London
Printed and bound by: William Clowes (Beccles) Ltd, Beccles and London

ISBN 0 86145 138 4

Published by the Automobile Association, Fanum House, Basingstoke, Hampshire RG21 2EA

Contents

4

HOME FROM HOME

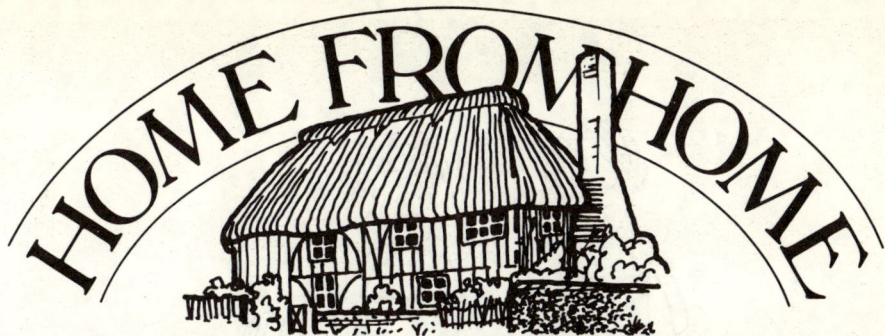

Well, it should be, but with a few vital differences. For a start, your holiday home will be free of all that clutter that has accumulated at home over the years. No danger here of opening a cupboard door and all the contents falling out; no unidentifiable 'cultures' growing at the back of the fridge. You'll move in with a clean slate and it should all be plain sailing . . . .

The trouble is, I know only too well how quickly a family on the loose can create chaos from order, how soon they can make your immaculate holiday home look horribly lived in. Almost before you've turned the key in the lock you'll find bags and baggage, buckets and boots strewn from one end to the other. Children will be leaping from room to room shrieking and more mature troublemakers will be 'gasping for a cup of tea, dear'. Now is the time to call a halt – very loudly and in no uncertain terms.

I'm on holiday too you know!

This stage of the game is called 'putting them in the picture' and is essential if you are all going to get through the holiday in one piece. When they asked me to write an article based on helpful hints for self-caterers, I did a quick survey amongst acquaintances who also go in for this kind of holiday. 'What advice would you give to a first-timer?' I asked. Almost with one voice they replied 'Make sure everyone takes a share of the chores'. This is undoubtedly the single most important factor if you are to make a success of self catering. Babes in arms may be excused duties, but apart from that – get them all organised.

Rules of the House

It might not be necessary to actually pin up a list behind each bedroom door, but it is best to come to a proper understanding right at the beginning. Your stipulations might include the following:

1. Each person to make his/her own bed – if you have very young children, give them sleeping bags instead.
2. Washing/wiping up to be done strictly on a rota – from which mum is exempt.
3. Anyone who *can* cook will do so at least once a week – for this you must, of course, judge your own family's capabilities and the fortitude of your own stomach! Remember, though, that any fool can make some sort of sandwich or drive to the nearest take-away, so this job too can be shared all round.
4. Each person will be responsible for his/her own things – questions such as 'Has anyone seen my piece of string?' will probably not be answered!

You may be able to think of more, but don't get too heavy with the rules and regulations – it is a holiday home, not Colditz! Although it does all sound a bit regimented, you'll find that with everyone working together in this way, all the chores will be done by breakfast time and you will all be free to enjoy the rest of the day together.

Never do today what you can put off until the end of the week

Certain jobs, such as washing up and bedmaking, will have to be tackled every day, but others might best be left until your final grand slam before departing homewards. Floors will obviously not remain spotless, but from bitter experience I know that trying to keep them clean is like painting the Forth Bridge! You can cheat a bit though – pin-point the troublespots (halls and beneath the kitchen sink for instance) and spread newspaper over the floor. It might not look as classy as the Axminster, but you can pick it up and throw it away and all the dirt goes with it.

Dirty linen is another problem – it tends to get thrown into dark corners of bedrooms. With my family the inevitable result is that the pile of dirty clothes in one corner gradually merges with the pile of clean stuff that they've dropped in another. Now I invest in some large bin liners and one goes into each room to catch the dirties. Whether or not they are well-trained enough to use them is another matter, but only the stuff that is in the bag will get washed. It is also a wise request that you get advance warning of the need for a quick washday. There is nothing worse than being all ready to go out for the day when you hear the plaintive cry 'I haven't got any knickers to wear!' I know holidays do allow a certain amount of extra freedom, but on a windy day it isn't worth the risk.

Home Comforts

Our inspectors have made sure that everything you might need is in your holiday home. Nevertheless, there might be a few little things you could take with you to make things run a bit more smoothly. It may seem a bit trivial, but one of the greatest annoyances to me when I am away is trying to peel potatoes with a strange knife or peeler – I am so used to the one I always use at home that nothing else feels quite right. The same might apply to can-openers – if you have ever spent hours, with a packet of Band-aid at your side, fishing out the baked beans one at a time you will know what I mean.

6

Strange bedfellows?

You may have noticed, browsing through the gazetteer that a six-berth house might not necessarily have three doubles. Sometimes you might find three or more beds to a room. This is fine if you are in a family party and don't mind the commune spirit for a couple of weeks, but a group of friends holidaying together might not be so keen – unless they are very good friends, of course. The 'moral' of the story, without being too indelicate, is to check on who you will be sleeping with before you book up.

The lie of the land

Having sorted out the *pied a terre*, the next step in settling in is to cast about the locality, get your bearings and, most important, find all the places you will need during your stay. Shops are always easy to find, but what about a pub with a children's room; a good take-away; a launderette with late opening so that you don't waste valuable daylight hours doing the washing; there might be local events coming up that you would enjoy; what's showing at the local cinema? . . . . The local newspaper is a good source of such information, but failing that, call in at the local and strike up a conversation with the resident 'oracle' (there always is one), or chat to the friendly lady in the village shop. It can save you hours of scouring the neighbourhood and often returning disappointed.

It's Tuesday so it must be the Zoo

How organised do you like to be on holiday? To some people a holiday means retiring into a state of suspended animation for a fortnight, while others might have every second planned out with military precision. Most people fall somewhere between these extremes but of course only you will know what holiday activities your bunch are likely to enjoy. Whether it be lazing on a beach, hiking through the countryside, sightseeing, discos, theatre . . . you can find out just what is available from the Tourist Information Centre in the area you intend to visit. If you phone or write to them in advance you will be able to do a bit of forward planning from the selection of leaflets they will provide, you will learn something about the area and you will get at least some of the arguments out of the way before you set off.

Our companion guides such as *Stately Homes, Museums, Castles and Gardens in Britain* and *Eat Out for around £5* will also be useful to you in planning days out.

Recharging the batteries

Days in might also be planned – after all, it is bound to rain sometime (isn't it?). Of course, there are always places to go on wet days too, but sometimes the family appreciate a quiet day at 'home' – rising at the crack of noon for brunch; spending the afternoon with a good book (a game, or drawing for the children); taking the time to prepare a special meal rather than the rush job which usually follows a tiring day out. It really can set you up for yet another exhausting day on the beach.

So get in there and give it all you've got!

Well, it really is all up to you isn't it. Each member of the family must exchange one home for another without taking the same problems along. Mums and Dads: put aside all thoughts of your jobs, household chores, final demands etc and RELAX; children: well, we all know life is just one long holiday for you anyway(!), but while you are away do try not to fight, break up the happy (rented) home, fall into puddles of mud or get lost (unless specifically instructed to do so!) – and for goodness sake, don't expect to be waited on.

Self catering can be a rest as well as a change, as long as everyone co-operates, and when it works it is one of the best types of holiday outside the millionaire bracket.

Inventory of equipment for self-catering accommodation

Item	Per unit	Per person	Per bed
Ashtrays	2		
Blankets*			3
Bowls/basins, mixing	2		
Bread/chopping board	1		
Bread knife	1		
Bread/cake plate		1	
Broom	1		
Bucket	1		
Butter dish	1		
Carving knife and fork	1		
Casserole dish	1		
Cereal/soup plate		1	
Coat hangers		2	
Colander	1		
Condiment Set	1		
Cooking spoon	2		
Corkscrew and bottle opener	1		
Cup, tea, and saucer		1	
Doormat	1		
Dusters	2		
Dustpan and Brush	1		
Egg-cup		1	
Fish slice	1		
Floor cloth	1		
Food container	2		
Fork, table and dessert		1	
Fruit dish, large	1		
Frying pan	1		
Jugs, large and small	1		
Kettle	1		
Knife, table and dessert		1	
Knife, vegetable	1		
Oven roasting tray	1		
Pillow*		1	
Plate, large and small		1	
Potato peeler	1		
Pot scourer/dish mop	1		
Refuse bin	1		
Saucepans and lids, large med & small	1		
Spoon, dessert and tea		1	
Spoons, table	2		
Sugar basin	1		
Tea caddy	1		
Teapot	1		
Tin opener	1		
Tray	1		
Tumbler		1	
Washing-up bowl	1		

* Bedding must be adequate for the season when the unit is let. Continental quilts are acceptable (one for 2 blankets). Extra pillows to be available, within reason, on request.
Note: A carpet sweeper or equivalent must be readily available.

How to use the gazetteer

The aim of this guide is to provide as much up-to-date information as possible about selected houses, flats, bungalows, chalets, cottages, cabins etc providing self catering accommodation. The use of symbols and abbreviations, keys to which are set out inside the covers, helps to make this possible within a compact gazetteer section.

Gazetteer

Entries are given in one list covering the whole of Great Britain, arranged alphabetically by place name. To find accommodation we suggest you look first at the location atlas or county list, details of which are given below.

County list

Yeddingham
York
Channel Islands
Alderney
Isle of Man
Douglas
Onchan

The present gazetteer order has proved to be most convenient for the majority of people. However, a few people have stated a preference for places to be set out in county order. For this reason, we have compiled a list of all towns and villages appearing in the gazetteer, arranged alphabetically under each county or region. You will find this list on pages 280–284.

Location atlas

For those of you who wish to plan a holiday by area, the atlas gives the location of each town/village heading in the gazetteer. Refer to the Key to Atlas page at the beginning of the map section to find the map you need.

If you find an establishment in the gazetteer first, use the map reference (shown after each town heading) to refer to the location maps. In this way you will see if there are other establishments in the area which may be listed under a different place name.

NB For editorial reasons, the gazetteer is always completed after the atlas pages. Therefore, in some cases, late amendments (either deletions or new entries) do not appear on the atlas. *Always double-check the town/village names appearing on the map with the gazetteer entries.*

AA Inspectors

All establishments with an entry in this guide have been inspected to ensure that premises come up to the required standards. Our inspectors are drawn from accommodation and catering industries, and from experienced staff within the Association. This creates a balance between qualified men and women with specialised knowledge of the industries, and those with expert appreciation of members' needs. The inspectors provide informed and unbiased reports upon which the Self Catering Establishments Committee can base its decisions.

Accommodation types

The entries in this guide cover a wide range of accommodation types, indicated at the beginning of each establishment description by abbreviations. We have accepted the inspectors' definitions of chalet, bungalow, cabin, etc.

9

Booking

All entries contain an address for booking purposes. Where the booking address is different from the establishment address it follows the words *for bookings.*

In the case of multi-units, entries have been consolidated to conserve space. When writing to operators letting more than one unit you should mention this guide and ensure that the unit you book is the one listed in this guide: it is possible that not all units in the property or on the complex may come up to the standard set by the Automobile Association. Self-catering holidays are becoming increasingly popular. It is advisable to book as early in the year as possible to avoid being disappointed.

When writing to book accommodation, it is advisable to include a stamped, self-addressed envelope.

The Tourism (Sleeping Accommodation Price Display) Order 1977 was introduced in February 1978. It compels hotels, motels, guesthouses, inns and self-catering accommodation with four or more letting bedrooms to display in entrance halls the maximum and minimum prices charged for each category of room. This order complements the Voluntary Code of Booking Practice.

Every effort is being made by the AA to encourage the use of the Voluntary Code in appropriate establishments.

Cleaning and vacation of property

Tenants are usually expected to leave the premises clean and vacate the premises by 10am. Incoming tenants may normally arrive from 4pm. Please check these details carefully with the proprietor, since they can vary considerably.

Complaints

Any complaints about services or facilities should be made promptly, giving the proprietor the opportunity to correct matters. If a personal approach fails, members should inform the AA regional office nearest to the establishment concerned.

Deposits

When you make bookings for accommodation, in law you are entering into a contract. You are bound by the conditions which the proprietor stipulates before the contract is made, and the proprietor is equally obliged in law – if he accepts your booking – to give you what you stipulated in the negotiations leading to the confirmation of the booking. If a visitor does not turn up for accommodation, the proprietor must try to relet the accommodation if he can. Illness and accidents preventing a person from taking up the accommodation or obliging the visitor to leave prematurely do not allow the visitor to avoid his commitment to pay the proprietor, although a reasonable proprietor may, as a gesture, accept a lesser sum.

It is common practice to require a deposit, which may purport to be non-returnable in any event. In such a case, if the visitor breaches the contract, the deposit will be lost and the proprietor may still be able to claim for extra losses suffered by him. But if a deposit is paid on such a basis and the proprietor is shown to be in breach of contract, then the deposit may be recovered, as part of the visitor's own claim for damages. (See also 'Insurance').

Gazetteer entries

Description of accommodation type, layout, décor, and sleeping arrangements are as observed at the time of inspection.

Off-season variations in the published conditions and terms of hire, numbers accepted, charges etc may not be covered by the entry. Such matters can often be arranged by private negotiation. Self-catering units are recommended *independently* of any AA rating or classification which may have been applied to the complex or premises in which self-catering units may occasionally be found (*ie* hotels and caravan and camp sites).

Heating

Identification of source of heating in each gazetteer entry follows details of cooking facilities. The source of heating (other than central heating, indicated by a symbol) may be identified as gas, electric, open fires or coal fires. 'Electric' can mean anything from a fan heater to night storage heating.

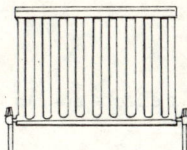

High season

In general this is June, July and August, apart from at winter-sports centres.

Holiday complexes

Some of the holiday complexes included in this publication offer accommodation of various types, differing in sleeping arrangements, settings and prices. Full details are normally available from the operator and the maximum and minimum prices quoted are only a rough guide. It is wise to check details through current brochures.

Insurance

AA Travelsure: Personal Travel Insurance

Enforced cancellation or curtailment of your holiday half-way through can involve you in considerable expense. It is unlikely that your deposit will be refunded and you will often have to pay the full cost of your holiday. In addition, if you were to lose your luggage or money, or were taken ill or met with an accident, this could completely ruin the enjoyment of your holiday.

AA Travelsure is an exclusive policy for holidays and business trips which can help offset the effects of many of the mishaps that may beset the most careful holidaymaker.

Benefits include:
* Loss or damage to luggage.
* Loss of money, including cheques, credit cards etc.
* Medical and additional travelling expenses.
* Reimbursement of costs following cancellation or curtailment.
* Personal accident.
* Personal liability.
* Delay
* Hospital Cash Benefit

Special features:
* Free cover for children under three years of age and 25% reduction for those under 14

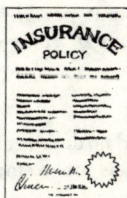

11

* Few exclusions for pre-existing medical conditions
* 24hr English-speaking Emergency Assistance Service.

Also available:
* UK car breakdown cover
* Increased personal accident cover

For full details call in at your local AA office or write to:
AA Insurance Services Ltd,
FREEPOST,
Newcastle-upon-Tyne,
NE99 2RP
(no need to use a stamp)

Licensed clubs
Note that club membership of licensed clubs cannot take effect – nor can a drink be bought – until forty-eight hours after joining.

Linen
When booking check whether linen other than sheets and pillowcases is available (*eg* tea towels etc) and whether charged for. In some cases linen is available to overseas visitors only; this is indicated in the gazetteer entry.

Pets
Many places accept pets, although an additional charge is sometimes made. If you wish to take your pet, please check all relevant details with the proprietor.

Prices
Rentals quoted are normally minimum/maximum per unit per week inclusive of VAT. *Charges are those applicable at the time of going to press.*

Rent Act
Premises included in this guide are for holiday lets only and no details are given of permanent or semi-permanent letting. Holiday lets are exempt from security of tenure.

Restrictions
Some establishments are not let to single persons, nor invalid, infirm or disabled persons. If you fit into one of these categories, please check carefully when making your booking.

Standards of accommodation
When considering applications for listing in this guide the AA insists on standards which it considers are necessary for a comfortable stay. Minimum requirements are shown below under *Accommodation, Furniture, fixtures and fittings, Services, Linen,* and *Inventory of Equipment* but it should be borne in mind that many units offer higher standards.

Accommodation
1 All units to be self contained.
2 *Bedrooms* or sleeping areas to be of reasonable size in relation to the

12

number of occupants; this number to be assessed according to the number of beds (single and double) provided. Convertible settees are acceptable in living rooms as extra bed-space but this should be included in the assessment.

3 *Kitchen/Kitchenettes* may not be sited in bedrooms.

4 *Bath/Shower Rooms and Lavatories:* Each unit to have a private bath or shower room (with washbasin if any bedroom is without washbasin and mirror) and a flush toilet (with disposal bin and toilet paper).

5 *Windows:* Each bedroom to have at least one window of reasonable size, which can be opened. Skylights are acceptable if in keeping with the style of building. All windows in sleeping areas to be fitted with adequate curtains or blinds. All living rooms and kitchens to have windows fitted with adequate curtains or blinds. All living rooms and kitchens to have windows capable of being opened directly into the open air.

6 *Ventilation:* All passages, staircases, communal rooms, bathrooms and lavatories to have adequate ventilation.

7 *Floors:* All areas to have a suitable floor covering or finish.

Furniture, fixtures and fittings

1 *Beds:* To be of comfortable proportions and in good condition, equipped with spring interior or foam mattresses. The following is a guide to minimum sizes: Single: 6' × 2'6" (183 × 76cms). Double: 6' × 4'0" (183 × 122cms). Children's bunks and folding beds: 5'2" × 2' (157 × 61cms).

2 *Furniture:* Adequate for the number of persons accommodated to include at least one dressing table or equivalent and a mirror and adequate wardrobe space equipped with hangers. All furniture to be kept in good condition.

3 *Kitchen fixtures and equipment:* Each kitchen to be equipped with:
   a) Either a gas or electric cooker (or solid fuel cooker where appropriate) with not less than two rings or their equivalent, and a means of grilling or toasting.
   b) A ventilated food-storage cupboard or refrigerator.
   c) An impervious working surface for food preparation.
   d) A sink with draining board.
   e) A pedal bin or other covered refuse container.

4 *Miscellaneous equipment:*
   Each unit to be provided with:
   Adequate dustbins outside the unit
   Adequate ashtrays and waste-paper containers

Services
Each unit supplied with:
   a) Hot, cold and drinking water. Meters acceptable.
   b) Lighting to be adequate in all areas including passages, corridors and staircases. Meters acceptable.
   c) Heating levels to be adequate for the season when the unit is let. Meters acceptable.
   d) Solid fuel (peat, coal etc as appropriate) where no other fuel is available.

Linen
Where linen is provided it must be changed between lets and spare linen should be available for lets of more than one week.

Explanation of a gazetteer entry

The example is fictitious

TOWN NAME
Appears in bold capitals in alphabetical order.

COUNTY NAME
Administrative county names are used (both region and old county names are given for Scotland).

MAP REFERENCE
First figure is map page no. Then follows grid reference: read 1st figure across, (east) 2nd figure vertically (north).

BOOKINGS
Address for bookings.

ALL STRETTON
Shropshire
Map 7 SO49

C The Alders & Corner Cottage
for bookings Mrs E R Allen, Post Office Stores, Alstonefield, Ashbourne, Derbys DE6 2FX ☎Alstonefield(033527)201

This small, white-washed 17th-century cottage comprises bathroom, kitchen, lounge/diner, double and single bedrooms and a good sized, secluded garden. A delightful situation with the Long Mynd as background.

All year   MWB out of season
2 days min, 6 wks max, 1 unit,
1–4 persons ⊚ fridge open fires & storage heaters Elec metered
▣ not provided ☎(1½m) HCE in unit
TV ⊕3 pin square 4P ⊐(1½m)
⊖ ♀(1½m)
Min £40 Max £60 pw

TELEPHONE NUMBER FOR BOOKINGS

CLASSIFICATION
Cottage.

SPECIFIC DETAILS
Letting period, number of units, number of persons accommodated, facilities, terms. See 'Symbols and abbreviations' inside covers.

DESCRIPTION
Description of establishment, sleeping arrangements, setting etc.

Haven Holidays give you so much choice, you should start choosing now.

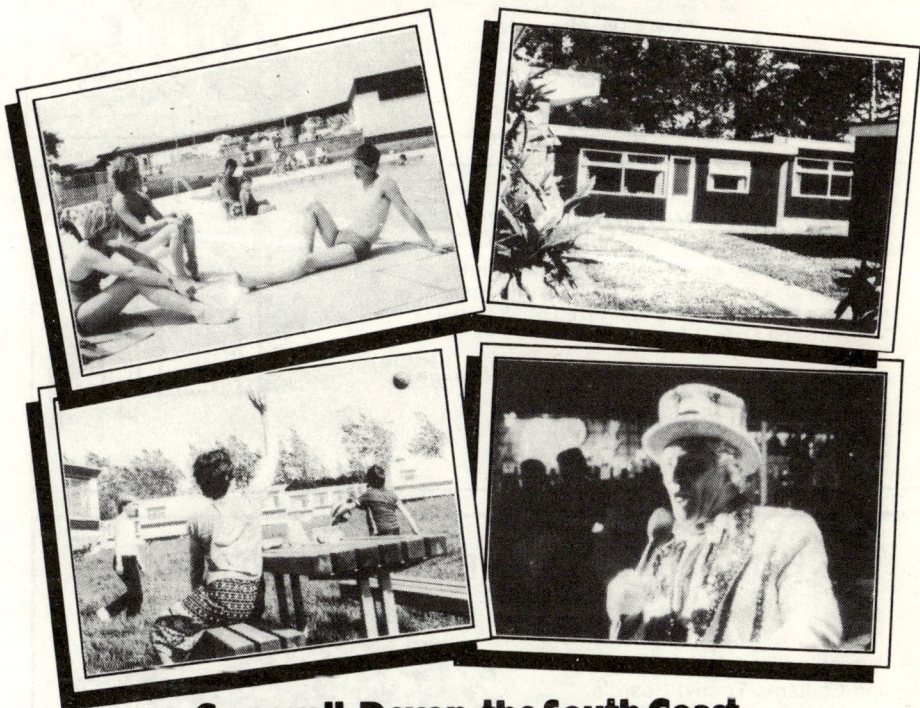

Cornwall, Devon, the South Coast, Dorset, Wales, Yorkshire and Lincolnshire.

Fifteen Parks throughout England and Wales, each with a personality and style of its own.

You'll find chalets or bungalows, villas or luxury caravans.

You can stay on the Park to enjoy our fantastic free entertainment and superb facilities – or explore the beaches or beautiful countryside around.

You can shop in our well stocked supermarkets, or enjoy our delicious restaurant, bar or take-away food.

And if you're tenting or touring, you should still choose Haven. Our facilities for you are equally good, and listed in the AA Guide.

So send for our free colour brochure now and discover how little our holidays will cost you.

☎ **Dial-a-brochure 0726 65432**

Haven Holidays

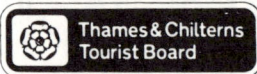

Gazetteer

The gazetteer gives locations and details of AA-listed self catering establishments in England, Wales and Scotland, Channel Islands and Isle of Man.

Details for islands are shown under individual placenames; the gazetteer text also gives appropriate cross-references. A useful first point of reference is to consult the location maps which show where AA-listed establishments are situated. NB *There is no map for Isles of Scilly*

ABBEY DORE
Hereford & Worcester
Map3 SO33

H **Kerrys Gate Farmhouse**
for bookings Mrs M Jenkins, Blackbush Farm, Abbey Dore, Hereford
☎Golden Valley(0981)240281

A modernised, brick-built farmhouse situated in quiet, picturesque village. Consists of lounge, dining room, kitchen/breakfast room, WC with wash hand basin, two double bedrooms, one twin room, one bunk-bedded room and bathroom.

All year MWB out of season 1wk min, 6mths max, 1 unit, 1-8 persons ◊ ◆ ⦿ fridge Electric Elec metered ⌷can be hired ☎(20yds) Airing cupboard in unit Iron in unit HCE in unit ⊕ TV ⊕3 pin square P ♨(4m) ⊖ ☎(2½m)
Min£40 Max£90pw

C **Poplar Cottage**
for bookings Mrs M Jenkins, Blackbush Farm, Abbey Dore, Hereford
☎Golden Valley(0981)240281
Detached brick cottage with its own

garden overlooking surrounding countryside. Comprises lounge, bathroom, kitchen/dining area, two double bedrooms, and a twin-bedded room.

All year MWB out of season 1wk min, 6mths max, 1 unit, 1-6 persons ◊ ◆ ⦿ fridge Electric Elec metered ⌷can be hired ☎(30yds) Airing cupboard in unit Iron in unit HCE in unit ⊕ TV ⊕3 pin square P ♨ ▥ ♨(3m) ⊖ ☎(2m)
Min£35 Max£70pw

ABBOTSHAM
Devon
Map2 SS42

C & B **CC Ref 574L 1-4**
for bookings Character Cottages (Holidays) Ltd, 34, Fore Street, Sidmouth, Devon EX108AQ
☎Sidmouth(03955)77001

Converted farm buildings consisting of three cottages and one bungalow in grounds of Kenwith Castle with marvellous views. Accommodation comprises open plan lounge, kitchen/diner, bathroom and WC. Two cottages sleep four in one double bedroom and one twin-bedded room. The other cottage and bungalow sleeps six in two twin-bedded rooms and one double bedroom. Decorated and furnished to a high standard.

All year MWB out of season 1wk min, 1mth max, 4 units, 1-6 persons ◊ ◆ no pets ⦿ fridge Electric Elec metered ⌷can be hired ☎(1½m) Airing cupboard in unit Iron in unit Ironing board in unit HCE in unit ⊕ CTV ⊕3 pin square 2P ▥ ♨(1½m) ⌁ ⌁Hard ⊖ ☎(1m) ☎(3m)
Min£100 Max£141pw (Low)
Min£109 Max£217pw (High)

ABERDARON
Gwynedd
Map6 SH12

C **Selbiant**

for bookings Miss Hughes-Roberts, Wernol, Edern, Pwllheli, Gwynedd
☎Nefyn(0758)720223

Semi-detached white-painted 17th-century modernised fisherman's cottage situated in the centre of the village adjacent to shops and beach. Accommodation comprises lounge/diner, small rear lobby with kitchen and bathroom/WC. Stairs to landing with one double bedroom and two single bedrooms. From Llanbedrog take B4413, situated 14m from Nefyn.

All year MWB out of season 1wk min, 4wks max, 1 unit, 1-4 persons, nc3 ⦿ fridge Electric Elec metered ⌷not provided ☎(20yds) Airing cupboard in unit Iron in unit Ironing board in unit HCE in unit TV ⊕3 pin square 2P ♨(10yds) ⊖ ☎(200yds)
Min£25 Max£35pw (Low)
Min£65 Max£70pw (High)

ABERDEEN
Grampian *Aberdeenshire*
Map15 NJ90

F Mr J W Runcie **Deeview Holiday Houses** 67 Prospect Terrace, Aberdeen AB12TU ☎Aberdeen(0224)25754

The houses are situated on high ground with some views overlooking the River Dee. Others are sited opposite the owner's house in a grassy quadrangle with rosebeds. Duthie Park and the city centre are easily accessible. All units offer good accommodation of a reasonable standard and comprise two bedrooms, living room, large kitchen and bathroom/WC.

Jul-Sep 1wk min, 15 units, 1-6 persons ◊ no pets ⦿ Electric Elec metered ⌷not provided ☎(20yds) Airing cupboard in unit Iron in unit Ironing board HCE in unit TV ⊕3 pin square P ⊕ ♨(100yds) ⌁Hard ⊖ ☎(1m) ▥(1m) ♫(1m) ▨(1m)
£50pw (Low)
Min£60 Max£65pw (High)

1982 prices quoted throughout gazetteer

ABERDOVEY
Gwynedd
Map**6** SN69

H **Deildre** Gwelfor Road
for bookings Mr J D Menhinick, Prospect Place, Aberdovey, Gwynedd LL35 0EY ☎Aberdovey(065472)595

Two-storey semi-detached house in its own grounds overlooking sea and estuary. On the first-floor there are two bedrooms, bathroom, separate WC, and on the second-floor there are two bedrooms. Also kitchen/diner, sun lounge and separate lounge with gas fire.

All year MWB out of season wkd min, 1mth max, 1unit, 8persons ◐ fridge Gas/Electric Gas/Elec metered ▣not provided ☎(300yds) Iron in unit Ironing board in unit HCE in unit ⊕3pin square P ▥ 🏛(300yds) ⇔ ⛳18 ♀(½m)

Min£115 Max£258pw
See advert on page 17

F **The Eyrie**
for bookings Mr J D Menhinick, Prospect Place, Aberdovey, Gwynedd LL35 0EY ☎Aberdovey(065472)595

Self-contained first-floor flat overlooking sea. Modern furniture. Accommodation consists of one bedroom with double bed (bunk beds available), kitchen/diner, lounge with twin beds, shower and separate WC. Excellent views of estuary, sea and hills.

All year MWB out of season wkd min, 1mth max, 1unit, 4persons ◎ fridge 🔥 Elec metered ▣not provided ☎(200yds) Airing cupboard in unit Iron on premises Ironing board on premises HCE in unit ⊙ ⊕3pin square ▥ 🏛(50yds) ⇔ ⛳18 ♀(20yds)

Min£82 Max£150pw
See advert on page 17

Ch **Plas Panteidal Chaltel**
for bookings Hoseasons Holidays, Sunway House, Lowestoft, Suffolk NR32 3LT ☎Lowestoft(0502)62292

Lying 300ft above sea level, the detached cedarwood chalets stand in 30 acres of wooded hillside facing south over the Dovey estuary. All chalets are detached, with one, two or three bedrooms, lounge/diner, kitchen, bathroom and WC. Restaurant available.

29Mar–25Oct MWB out of season 1day min, 81units, 4–6persons [◇ ◆] ◎ fridge Electric Elec metered ▣inclusive ☎(½m) Iron on premises Ironing board on premises HCE in unit [Launderette on premises] ⊙ TV ⊕3pin square P ▥ 🏛(½m) ⛵ ⇔ ♀(200yds)

F & H **Hafod** Sea Front
for bookings Mr & Mrs C A Bendall, Hafod Sea Front, Aberdovey, Gwynedd LL35 0EB ☎Aberdovey(065472)418

Units consist of one house (Aelfor), one maisonette and seven flats of varying size and design. All are well furnished and newly-decorated and are situated on the seafront.

All year MWB out of season 1wk min, 9units, 2–10persons [◇ ◆ ◆] ◎ fridge 🔥&Electric Elec metered ▣can be hired ☎ Airing cupboard in unit [Iron on premises] Ironing board on premises HCE in unit [Launderette on premises] ⊙ CTV can be hired ⊕3pin square 🏛(10yds) ⛵ 🎾Hard/grass ⇔ ⛳18 ♀(200yds)

Min£30 Max£207pw

ABERFELDY
Tayside *Perthshire*
Map**14** NN84

F ***Tay View*** Home Street
for booking Mrs M Stewart, Prospect House, Home Street, Aberfeldy, Perthshire ☎Aberfeldy(0887)219

A detached three-storey stone house with a small garden. It was built in 1890 and has been modernised and split into three flats. Each flat has a private entrance, is well decorated and has good quality equipment. The house is in a quiet residential street about three minutes' walk from the town centre.

All year 1wk min, 3mths max, 3units 4–6persons [◇] ◆ ◆ no pets ◐ fridge Electric Gas/Elec metered ▣can be hired ☎(100yds) Airing cupboard in unit Iron in unit Ironing board in unit HCE CTV ⊕3pin square 4P 1🏠 ▥ 🏛(100yds) 🎾Hard ⇔ ⛳9 ♀ ▦

ABERPORTH
Dyfed
Map**2** SN25

F ***Highcliffe Apartments***
for bookings Mr & Mrs J V Lee, Highcliffe Hotel, Aberporth, Dyfed ☎Aberporth(0239)810534

Well-appointed apartments in grounds of Highcliffe Hotel. Open-plan sitting/dining room; curtain divider to kitchen. Two bedrooms, double bed in one, twin beds in other. Combined bathroom/WC.

All year MWB out of season 3nights min, 2units, 2–5persons ◇ [◆ ◆] ◎ fridge Electric Elec metered ▣can be hired ☎ Iron in unit Ironing board in unit HCE in unit ⊙ ⊕3pin square P ▥ 🏛(100yds) ⇔ ♀(100yds)

F **Morlan Apartments**
for bookings Mr R M L Morris, Morlan Motel, Aberporth, Cardigan, Dyfed SA43 2EN ☎Aberporth(0239)810611

Purpose-built apartments designed for up to four adults or ideal for families. One room can be divided into two at night by a curtain type divider. Cooking facilities adjoin the dining/sitting area. Double bed/settee and twin beds provide the sleeping accommodation. The apartments are adjacent to the Morlan Motel.

Mar–Oct MWB 1wk min, 23units, 2–4persons ◇ ◆ ◆ ◎ fridge 🔥 Elec inclusive ▣inclusive ☎ HCE in unit [Launderette on premises] ⊙ ⊗ CTV ⊕3pin square 25P 🏛 ⇔ ♀

Min£55 Max£75pw (Low)
Min£80 Max£115pw (High)

ABERSOCH
Gwynedd
Map**6** SH32

B Mrs K Smith **5 Caedu** Abersoch, Gwynedd ☎Abersoch(075881)2955

Detached modern bungalow comprising hall, lounge/diner, bathroom/WC, kitchen, two twin-bedded rooms and a bed-settee in lounge. Set on the right off the Sarn Bach road on the outskirts of Abersoch.

Etr–Oct 1wk min, 4wks max, 1unit, 1–5persons ◆ ◆ no pets ◎ fridge Electric Elec metered ▣not provided ☎(100yds) SD in unit Airing cupboard in unit Iron in unit Ironing board in unit HCE in unit ⊙ CTV ⊕3pin square 2P 🏛(100yds) ⇔ ⛳18(½m) ♀(1m) ▦(1m) ♫(3m)

Min£60 Max£120pw (Low)

B **Spinnakers** Cae-du-Estate
for booking Mrs A E Mardon, Shoreline Villas, 5 Prestwick Drive, Liverpool L23 7XB ☎051–924 6996

Modern, three bedroomed bungalow comprising lounge/diner, kitchen and bathroom/WC. Garden to front and rear.

Etr–Oct MWB out of season 1unit 6persons ◆ no pets ◎ fridge 🔥 Elec metered ▣not provided ☎(200yds) Airing cupboard HCE CTV ⊕3pin square P 🏛(200yds) ⇔ ⛳9(½m) ♀(200yds) ▦(3m)

Min£60 Max£80pw (Low)
Min£90 Max£130pw (High)

B Mrs J Jones **Tynewydd** Sarn Bach, Abersoch, Gwynedd ☎Abersoch(075881)2446

Farm cottage recently modernised throughout. Accommodation consists of lounge/diner, large kitchen, one double bedroom and one sleeping three persons, bathroom/WC. From Abersoch take Sach Bach road, on entering village turn right, cottage on left in private road.

All year MWB 1wk min, 1mth max, 1unit, 1–5persons, ◎ fridge 🔥 Elec metered ▣not provided ☎(½m) [Airing cupboard in unit] Iron in unit Ironing board in unit HCE in unit ⊙ TV ⊕3pin square 2P ▥ 🏛(½m) ⇔ ⛳9(1m) ♀(1m)

Min£50 Max£60pw (Low)
Min£80 Max£95pw (High)

ABERYSTWYTH
Dyfed
Map**6** SN58

F **Ael-y-Don Holiday Flats** Cliff Terrace
for bookings Mrs M Spear, Tidesreach, Borth, Dyfed SY24 5NN
☎Borth(097081)431

Semi-detached house converted into flats and about 50yds from the seafront. All flats with the exception of Flat 6, which has one double bedroom, have twin-bedded rooms. Flat 1 has open-plan kitchen/diner and bathroom/WC. Flat 2 has open-plan kitchen/diner, shower-room and separate WC. Flat 4 has lounge/diner and shower-room/WC. Flat 5 has lounge with bed-settee, kitchen, shower-room and WC. Flat 6 has kitchen/diner and shower-room/WC. Flat 7 and 8 have lounge with bed-settee, shower-room, kitchen and WC.

Jul–Sep MWB 1wk min, 7units, 2–4persons no pets ⚲ & ◙ fridge ♨ Gas/Elec inclusive ⬜can be hired ☎(30yds) Airing cupboard in unit HCE in unit ⊖ CTV ⊕3pin square ▥ ♨(200yds)
↮ ⛾(½m) ⛾(150yds) ▨(½m) ♫(1m) ≋(½m)
Min£35 Max£120pw

C **Esgair Wen** Cwmystwyth
for bookings Mrs T Raw, Tyllwyd, Cwmystwyth, Aberstwyth, Dyfed SY23 4AG
☎Pontrhydygroes(097422)216

Traditional stone and slate cottage set alongside the Devils Bridge—Rhayader mountain road. Accommodation comprises lounge/diner, kitchen, bathroom and WC on ground floor; one double bedded room with extra single bed and one single bedded room on first floor.

All year MWB out of season 1wk min 4wks max 1unit 1–6persons [◇] ◆ no pets ◙ fridge Electric ⬜can be hired ☎(2m) Airing cupboard in unit Iron in unit Ironing board in unit HCE in unit ⊖ ⊕3pin square 3P ♨(2m) Fishing, grouse shooting

H Mrs T Raw **Tyllwyd** Cwmystwyth, Aberstwyth, Dyfed SY23 4AG
☎Pontrhydygroes(097422)216

Part of this 17th-century farmhouse, (once a coaching inn) is decorated to a high standard, comprising lounge/diner, kitchen/breakfast room on ground-floor and two bedrooms and bathroom/WC on first floor.

end May–Sep 1wk min 4wks max 1unit 1–5persons ◇ ◈ ◆ no pets ◙ fridge Elec inclusive ⬜inclusive ☎(2m) Iron in unit Ironing board in unit HCE in unit ⊖ ⊗ TV ⊕3pin square 3P ♨(2m) Fishing, grouse shooting

ABOYNE
Grampian *Aberdeenshire*
Map**15** NO59

F **Kirkton Cottages**
for bookings Aboyne Estates, Estate Office, Old Station, Dinnet, Aboyne, Aberdeenshire AB35LL
☎Dinnet(033985)341

Twelve former poor houses which have been modernised and converted into six holiday flats. Each flat has combined dining area and kitchenette, shower, WC and two bedrooms. This basic but satisfactory accommodation is reasonably priced; the furnishings are minimal but adequate. Ample play area is in front of the cottages.

Close Feb 1wk min, 1mth max, 6units, 1–5persons ◇ ◆ no pets ◙ fridge Electric Elec metered ⬜can be hired ☎(1m) HCE ⊖ ⊕3pin square P ♨(1½m)
↮ ⛾(1½m) ♫(1½m)
Min£46 Max£58pw

ACHNAMARA
Strathclyde *Argyll*
Map**10** NR78

H **Inverlussa House** (200yds from Loch Sween)
for bookings Mr K Fenton, 9 George Street, Hull HU1 3BA ☎Hull(0482)26026

Three-storey stone-built house standing in its own grounds, 200yds from Loch Sween and consisting of kitchen, sitting room, living room, hall, pantry, laundry room, and seven bedrooms.

All year MWB out of season 2wks min, 2wks max, 1unit, 12persons [◇] ◆ ◆ ◙ fridge ♨ Coal & log fires Elec inclusive ⬜inclusive ☎ WM in unit SD in unit TD in unit Airing cupboard in unit Iron in unit Ironing board in unit HCE in unit CTV ⊖ ⊕3pin square P ♨(1m) Fishing & Boating
Min£100 Max£240pw (Low)
Min£280 Max£350pw (High)

AIRTH
Central *Stirlingshire*
Map**11** NS98

H **The Pineapple** Dunmore
for bookings The Landmark Trust, Shottesbrooke Park, Maidenhead, Berks
☎Littlewick Green(062882)3431

The Pineapple House was built by 18th-century stonemasons to celebrate the first pineapple grown in Scotland. A stone gazebo is topped by a pineapple-shaped roof. After restoration, the house has a high standard of décor and fittings, with fine furniture. Bedrooms and bathrooms are not internally linked with lounge and modern kitchen. Situated just N of Airth and reached by ½m long track from the A905/B9124 junction.

All year MWB out of season 1day min, 3wks max, 1unit, 2–4persons ◇ ◆ ◙ fridge Electric & open fires

Elec inclusive ⬜not provided ☎(1m) Iron in unit Ironing board in unit HCE in unit ⊖ ⊕3pin square P ♨(1m) ↮ ⛾(1m)
Max£74pw (Low)
Max£198pw (High)

ALCAIG
Highland *Ross & Cromarty*
Map**14** NH55

B **Cherrytree Cottage**
for bookings H Macduff-Duncan & Co, Alcaig, Conon Bridge, Ross-shire IV78HS ☎Dingwall(0349)61220

A detached, timber-clad bungalow located on Alcaig farm, and situated close to the main building. Pleasantly furnished accommodation comprises lounge/dining room, kitchen, bathroom and three double bedrooms. Small neat garden with extensive views of Cromarty Firth and hills.

May–Sep 1wk min, 1unit, 2–7persons ◇ no cats ◙ fridge Electric & coal fires Elec metered ⬜not provided ☎(1m) WM in unit Iron in unit Ironing board in unit HCE in unit ⊖ ⊕3pin square ⊕3pin round P ▥ ♨(1m)
↮ ⛾(1m) ▨(3m) ≋(3m)
Min£58 Max£86pw

C **Larchtree Cottage** Alcaig farm
for bookings H Macduff-Duncan & Co, Alcaig, Conon Bridge, Ross-shire IV78HS ☎Dingwall(0349)61220

A detached property on farm with pleasant outlook across surrounding countryside towards Wester Ross. Accommodation comprises a ground floor with kitchen, living room and two double bedrooms, one with additional single bed and an attic bedroom reached by a fixed extending ladder.

May–Sep 1wk min, 1unit, 1–6persons ◇ no cats ◙ fridge Electric & open fires Elec metered ⬜not provided ☎(1m) Airing cupboard in unit Iron in unit Ironing board in unit HCE in unit ⊖ ⊕3pin square P ▥ ♨(1m)
↮ ⛿(3m) ⛾(1m)
Min£52 Max£80pw

ALCESTER
Warwickshire
Map**4** SP05

H **Cold Comfort Farm** Ragley Estate
for bookings Heart of England Cottages, Buckland, Broadway, Worcester WR127LY ☎Broadway(0386)853593

Set in a quiet picturesque rural setting this old farmhouse (part of which dates back to the 17th century) comprises sitting room with open fireplace, dining room, games room, large kitchen/diner, utility room, cloakroom with WC. The first floor has three twin and two double →

19

bedrooms, three bathrooms, one with
WC and a separate WC.

All year MWB out of season 3 days min,
6 mths max, 1 unit, 1–10 persons ◇ ◆
◉ fridge 🍴 Elec inclusive 🔲 can be
hired (overseas visitors only) ☎ WM
in unit TD in unit Airing cupboard in
unit Iron in unit Ironing board in unit
HCE in unit CTV 🔥3 pin square 4P
🏠(½m)
↔ ☎(½m)
£245pw

H   Wood Bevington Manor 1 & 2 Wood
Bevington
for bookings Heart of England Cottages,
Buckland, Broadway, Worcester
WR12 7LY ☎Broadway(0386)853593

Ancient manor house steeped in history,
situated at the top of a gentle rise above
the hamlet of Wood Bevington. **Number
One** is the largest and comprises flagged
entrance hall, drawing room, large drawing
room both with open fireplaces, kitchen,
twin-bedded room and bathroom/WC.
Three bedrooms upstairs, two double-
bedded, one twin-bedded and
bathroom/WC. **Number Two** is the
second half of this manor house and
comprises sitting/dining room, kitchen all
on ground floor and upstairs has one
double-bedded room, two twin-bedded
rooms (one with bathroom/WC).

All year MWB out of season 3 days min,
6 mths max, 2 units, 1–8 persons ◇ ◆
◉ fridge 🍴 Elec inclusive 🔲 can be
hired (overseas visitors only) ☎ WM
in unit SD in unit (No 1) Airing cupboard
in unit Iron in unit Ironing board in unit
HCE in unit ⊖ CTV 🔥3 pin square
10P 🏠(½m)
↔ ☎(½m) dishwasher in No 1
£135pw (No 2) £245pw (No 1)

ALDEBURGH
Suffolk
Map **5** TM45

C   44A High Street
for bookings Mrs J Cowan, 9 Crabbe
Street, Aldeburgh, Suffolk IP15 2BW
☎Aldeburgh(072885)2909

Two-storey terraced cottage at rear of
High Street just across from the beach;
access is via a private garden.
Accommodation comprises
kitchen/diner, lounge with put-u-up
settee, one double bedroom with extra
single bed and bathroom/WC.

All year MWB out of season 3 days min,
4 wks max, 1 unit, 1–5 persons no cats
◉ fridge Electric Elec metered
🔲 not provided ☎(100yds) WM in unit
SD in unit Airing cupboard in unit Iron
in unit Ironing board in unit HCE in unit
⊖ ⊛ TV can be hired 🔥3 pin square
1🏠 📺 🏠
↔ 🚿&🚿(1m) ☎(200yds) 📮(400yds)
Min£30 Max£50pw (Low)
Min£65 Max£95pw (High)

ALDERNEY
Channel Islands
Map **16**

Ca   Charity Cottage Pine Springs,
La Vallee
for bookings The Secretary, Pine Springs
c/o Grand Island Hotel, Alderney,
Channel Islands
☎Alderney(048182)2848

Modern and attractive, the
accommodation consists of one
bedroom with double bed, one with bunk
beds, a large sitting room with twin
divans, bathroom and WC and dining
room annexe.

Etr–Nov MWB 1 wk min, 1 unit,
6 persons [◇ ◇ ◆] no pets 🚿
fridge Gas & Electric
Gas/elec inclusive ☎(250yds) Iron in
unit Ironing board in unit HCE in unit
⊖ ⊛ TV 🔥3 pin square P
🏠(450yds)
↔ 🚿(1m) ☎(½m) 📺(½m)
Min£95 Max£202pw

Ca   Faith Cottage Pine Springs,
La Vallee
for bookings The Secretary, Pine Springs
c/o Grand Island Hotel, Alderney,
Channel Islands
☎Alderney(048182)2848

Swedish-style log cabin located in sunny
valley in its own grounds along with three
other units. Faith Cottage is the smallest
unit but is nevertheless spacious and
comfortable. Accommodation comprises
one bedroom with twin beds, a large bed
sitting room with twin divans, bathroom,
WC and well appointed kitchen/dining
room. Small swimming pool.

Etr–Nov MWB 1 wk min, 1 unit,
4 persons [◇ ◇ ◆] no pets 🚿
fridge Gas & Electric
Gas/elec inclusive ☎(250yds) Iron in
unit Ironing board in unit HCE in unit
⊖ ⊛ CTV 🔥3 pin square P
🏠(450yds) 🚼
↔ 🚿(1m) ☎(½m) 📺(½m)
Min£80 Max£165pw

C   Hope Cottage Pine Springs,
La Vallee
for bookings The Secretary, Pine Springs
c/o Grand Island Hotel, Alderney,
Channel Islands
☎Alderney(048182)2848

The largest of four units, the
accommodation comprises one twin-
bedded room, one small single room, one
bedroom with bunk beds, large sitting
room with twin divans, well designed
kitchen, attractive dining room, bathroom
and WC.

Etr–Nov MWB 1 wk min, 1 unit,
7 persons [◇ ◇ ◆] no pets 🚿
fridge Gas & Electric
Gas/Elec inclusive ☎(250yds) Iron in
unit Ironing board in unit HCE in unit

⊖ ⊛ CTV 🔥3 pin square P
🏠(450yds) 🚼
↔ 🚿(1m) ☎(½m) 📺(½m)
Min£100 Max£216pw

C   Trigale Cottage
for bookings The Secretary, Pine Springs,
C/o Grand Island Hotel, Alderney,
Channel Islands
☎Alderney(048182)2848

Stone-built cottage with small
garden/patio, near town centre.
Comprising lounge, kitchen/diner with
open staircase to first floor which has two
double and one single-bedded rooms.

All year MWB 1 wk min, 2 mths max,
1 unit, 5 persons no pets 🚿 ◉ fridge
🍴 Gas/elec inclusive 🔲 can be hired
☎(100yds) Airing cupboard in unit Iron
in unit Ironing board in unit HCE in unit
⊖ ⊛ CTV 🔥3 pin square 1P
🏠(100yds)
↔ 🚿(1m) ☎(100yds) 📮(200yds)
Min£100 Max£216pw

C   Woodmans Cottage Pine Springs,
La Vallee
for bookings The Secretary, Pine Springs
c/o Grand Island Hotel, Alderney,
Channel Islands
☎Alderney(048182)2848

Two-storey Swedish-style log and brick
cottage comprising large bed sitting
room with two divans (on the lower floor)
and kitchen/dining room, bathroom and
WC and a double bedroom with its own
balcony on the first floor.

Etr–Nov MWB 1 wk min, 1 unit,
4 persons [◇ ◇ ◆] no pets 🚿
fridge Gas & Electric
Gas/Elec inclusive ☎(250yds) Iron in
unit Ironing board in unit HCE in unit
⊖ ⊛ CTV 🔥3 pin square P
🏠(450yds) 🚼
↔ 🚿(1m) ☎(½m) 📺(½m)
Min£80 Max£165pw

ALDSWORTH
Gloucestershire
Map **4** SP11

C   V & B Stapleton **Swyre Farm**
Aldsworth, Cheltenham, Gloucester
GL54 3RE ☎Windrush(04514)461

Once the barns of Swyre Farm, these five
cottages are grouped round a charming
walled garden, surrounded by four acres
of fields and orchards. **Apple** sleeps four
persons, while **Bramble** and **Pheasants
Run 1, 2 & 3** Sleep up to six. All have fitted
carpets, and are furnished with pine and
cane.

All year MWB out of season 2 night min,
5 units, 2–6 persons [◇] ◇ ◆ no
dogs except in Bramble ◉ fridge 🍴
Elec metered 🔲 inclusive ☎(½m) WM
in unit (Apple) TD on premises Airing
cupboard in unit (Apple) Iron on
premises Ironing board on premises

HCE in unit ⊙ TV & CTV (in Apple & Bramble) ⊕3pin square 6P ♨(3m) ⇔ ♀(½m)
Min£80 Max£175pw

ALFORD
Grampian *Aberdeenshire*
Map**15** NJ51

H Balfluig Castle
for bookings Mr M I Tennant, 8 New Square, Lincoln's Inn, London WC2A 3QP ☎01–242 4986

A finely restored 16th-century castle which retains much of the original character and is furnished to a high standard throughout. The four-storeyed accommodation has kitchen, dining room and cloakroom/laundry on the ground floor. The great hall makes a spacious lounge on the first floor. There are two bedrooms (one with four-poster bed and one twin-bedded room) and two fully equipped bathrooms on the second floor; two bedrooms (one single and one double) and bathroom (no WC) on the third floor and one double bedroom with washbasin on the fourth floor. A unique opportunity for an ideal holiday in the Scottish Highlands.

All year MWB out of season 1wk min, 1mth max, 1unit, 1–9persons [◇] no pets ◉ fridge Electric & log fires Elec metered ⎕inclusive WM in unit SD in unit Airing cupboard in unit Iron in unit Ironing board in unit HCE in unit ⊙ TV can be hired ⊕3pin square P ▥ ♨(1m)
⇔ ♀(1m)
£250pw

ALMELEY
Hereford & Worcester
Map**3** SO35

C Hawthorne Cottage
for bookings Mr & Mrs D Phillips, Bockleton Farm, Tenbury Wells, Worcester ☎Leysters(056887)238

Detached, white-painted cottage set in gardens and overlooking the surrounding countryside. The accommodation comprises lounge, kitchen/diner, sitting room and three

bedrooms; two doubles, one twin and a bathroom/WC.

All year MWB out of season 1wk min, 1mth max, 1unit, 1–6persons ◆ ◉ fridge Electric & open fires Elec metered ⎕not provided ☎(⅓m) Airing cupboard in unit Iron in unit Ironing board in unit HCE in unit ⊕3pin square 3P 1🕯 ♨(⅓m)
⇔ ♀(⅓m)
Min£45 Max£75pw

ALL STRETTON
Shropshire
Map**7** SO49

C Holly Cottage Gulley Green
for bookings Mr R H Brown, 3 Bell Orchard, Alveley, Bridgnorth, Salop WV16 6NE ☎Quatt(0746)780434

This small, white-washed 17th-century cottage comprises bathroom, kitchen, lounge/diner, double and single bedrooms and a good sized, secluded garden. A delightful situation with the Long Mynd as background.

All year MWB out a of season 2days min, 6wks max, 1unit, 1–4persons ◉ fridge open fires & storage heaters Elec metered ⎕not provided ☎(1⅓m) HCE in unit TV ⊕3pin square 4P ⌐(1⅓m)
⇔ ♀(1⅓m)
Min£40 Max£60pw

ALSTONEFIELD
Staffordshire
Map**7** SK15

C The Alders & Corner Cottage
for bookings Mrs E R Allen, Post Office Stores, Alstonefield, Ashbourne, Derbys DE6 2FX ☎Alstonefield(033527)201

These two recently modernised cottages are set in the centre of the picturesque village of Alstonefield. In each cottage the comfortable accommodation includes two double bedrooms, one small bunk-bedded room, large fitted kitchen/diner and large lounge with

wood-block floor. Both cottages have open fires.

All year MWB 1wk min, 5mths(winter) max, 2units, 1–6persons [◇] ◆ ◆ ◉ fridge ♨ Electric & open fires Elec metered ⎕provided overseas visitors only ☎(50yds) WM in unit SD in unit Airing cupboard in unit Iron in unit Ironing board in unit HCE in unit ⊙ TV ⊕3pin square P ▥ ♨(100yds)
⇔ ♀(150yds)
Min£35 Max£65pw (Low)
Min£75 Max£140pw (High)

H Yew Tree Farm
for bookings Mrs M A Griffin, Coldwall Farm, Okeover, Ashbourne, Derbyshire ☎Thorpe Cloud(033529)249

18th-century stone-built farmhouse, tastefully modernised and retaining much original character; set in its own garden with adjoining field. Situated on the edge of a small and picturesque village with convenient access to the market town of Ashbourne.

All year MWB out of season 2wks max 1unit, 5persons ◆ ◉ fridge Electric & open fires Elec metered ⎕not provided ☎(50yds) Airing cupboard in unit HCE in unit ⊙ TV C⊕3pin square 4P ▥ ♨(60yds)
⇔ ♀(70yds)
Min£50 Max£80pw

ALTON
Staffordshire
Map**7** SK04

H Alton Station Alton Tower
for bookings The Landmark Trust, Shottesbrooke Park, Maidenhead, Berks ☎Littlewick Green(062882)3431

The Station Master's house of the now disused Churnet Valley railway has been carefully preserved and offers fine accommodation for up to seven people. Twin-bedded rooms are on each of the ground, first and second floors. Bathroom/WC are on the ground floor and another WC is in the cloakroom off the hall. There is a lovely lounge furnished with period Victorian and Edwardian pieces from the station's past. A combined kitchen/diner completes the →

accommodation. Two long flights of 18 steps down to the platform makes it difficult for the handicapped person.

All year MWB out of season 1 day min, 3wks max, 1 unit, 1–7 persons ◊ ◆ ◉ fridge Electric Elec inclusive ⌸ not provided ☎(⅓m) Airing cupboard in unit Iron in unit Ironing board in unit HCE in unit ⊖ ⊕3 pin square P ▥ ♨(400yds)

⊷ ☻(400yds)

Max£88pw (Low)
Max£170pw (High)

ALVES
Grampain *Moray*
Map**15** NJ16

H **Four Winds** North Alves
for bookings Moray Estates Development Company, Estates Office, Forres, Moray IV36 0ET ☎Forres(0309)72213

One of four semi-detached farm cottages lying adjacent to caravan park 1m N of A96. The cottage comprises living/dining room, kitchen, bathroom, two double and one single bedrooms.

Apr-Oct MWB out of season 1 wk min, 1 unit, 1–5 persons ◊ ◉ fridge Electric Elec inclusive ⌸ can be hired ☎(100yds) Iron in unit Ironing board in unit HCE in unit [Launderette within 300yds] TV ⊕3 pin round P ▥ ♨(100yds) Burn fishing

Min£92 Max£103.50pw (Low)
Min£115pw (High)

C **Laich View**
for bookings Moray Estates Development Company, Estates Office, Forres, Moray IV36 0ET ☎Forres(0309)72213

One of four semi-detached farm cottages lying adjacent to caravan park, 1m N of A96. Comprising living/dining room with single bedroom, two double bedrooms, kitchen and bathroom.

Apr-Oct MWB out of season 1 wk min, 1 unit, 1–5 persons ◊ ◉ fridge Electric Elec inclusive ⌸ can be hired ☎(100yds) Iron in unit Ironing board in unit HCE in unit [Launderette within 300yds] TV ⊕3 pin square P ▥ ♨(100yds) Burn fishing

Min£92 Max£103.50pw (Low)
Min£115pw (High)

B **Spindle Cottage**
for bookings Moray Estates Development Company, Estates Office, Forres, Moray IV36 0ET ☎Forres(0309)72213

One of four semi-detached farm cottages lying adjacent to caravan park, 1m N of A96. Comprises living/dining room with small double bedroom off, kitchen, bathroom, double room with single room off.

Apr-Oct MWB out of season 1 wk min, 1 unit, 1–5 persons ◊ ◉ fridge Electric Elec inclusive ⌸ can be hired ☎(500yds) Iron Ironing board HCE [Launderette] ⊖ TV ⊕3 pin square P ▥ ♨(1m)

⊷ ☻(1m) Burn fishing

Min£92 Max£103.50pw (Low)
Min£115pw (High)

ALWINTON
Northumberland .
Map**12** NT90

Ch Elizabeth Johnson, **Low Alwinton,** Alwinton, Harbottle, Morpeth, Northd NE65 7BE ☎Rothbury(0669)50224

This is a converted barn, tastefully designed and well furnished. It is situated in a remote valley surrounded by hills and moorland. Accommodation includes a large living room, two double bedrooms on the ground floor and a children's loft room.

All year MWB out of season 1 wk min, 3 wks max, 1 unit, 1–10 persons [◊] ◆ ◉ fridge Electric & open fires Elec metered ⌸ not provided ☎ SD on premises Airing cupboard in unit Iron in unit HCE in unit ⊖ ⊛ TV ⊕3 pin square P ♨(1m)

⊷ ☻(⅓m)

Min£60 Max£80pw (Low)
Min£100 Max£140pw (High)

ALYTH
Tayside *Perthshire*
Map**15** NO24

H **Pictillum**
for bookings Mr & Mrs M H Wilson, Conifers, Blairmore Drive, Rosemount, Blairgowrie, Perthshire ☎Blairgowrie(0250)2961

A newly modernised farmhouse set in open countryside close to Alyth. The accommodation comprises kitchen, dining/sitting room, lounge with convertible settee and double bedroom on ground floor and two bedrooms on the first floor. Located at the end of a long drive.

All year 1 wk min, 1 unit, 1–8 persons ◊ ◆ ◉ fridge 🍴 Elec inclusive ⌸ not provided ☎ WM in unit SD in unit Airing cupboard in unit Iron in unit Ironing board in unit HCE in unit ⊖ TV can be hired ⊕3 pin square 5P 4🏠 ♨(2m)

⊷ ♒(2m) ☻(2m)

Min£65 Max£85pw (Low)
Min£110 Max£130pw (High)

AMBLESIDE
Cumbria
Map**7** NY30

F J D & N B Scott, *Badgers Rake,* Fisherbeck Park, Ambleside, Cumbria LA22 0AL

Modern two-storey building in centre of a small private housing estate ⅓m S of town centre. The building consists of 11 purpose-built flats; four with three bedrooms, four with two bedrooms and three with one bedroom. All are well decorated and well furnished.

All year 1 wk min, 5 mths(winter) max,

---

11 units, 4–7 persons ◊ ◆ no pets ◉ fridge 🍴 Elec metered ⌸ not provided ☎ [WM on premises] [TD on premises] Airing cupboard in unit Iron in unit Ironing board in unit HCE in unit ⊖ CTV ⊕3 pin square 12P 8🏠 ▥ ♨(⅓m)

⊷ ☻(1m) 🚲(⅓m) ♫(⅓m) 🎣(⅓m)

C Mr & Mrs B Counsell, **Balla Wray,** High Wray, Ambleside, Cumbria ☎Ambleside(09663)3308

A local stone-built cottage converted from the stables of Balla Wray House in whose grounds it stands. Set in 2 acres of gardens at the foot of Claife heights overlooking Lake Windermere, with private access by footpath to the lake shore. The accommodation consists of living/dining room (with logfire), kitchen area and bathroom. Spacious first-floor bedroom with one double and two single beds.

All year MWB out of season 1 wk min, 3 mths max, 1 unit, 4 persons ◊ ◆ no pets ◉ fridge 🍴 Elec metered ⌸ not provided ☎ Iron in unit Ironing board in unit HCE in unit ⊖ ⊕3 pin square 1P ▥ ♨(2m) Fishing

⊷ ☻(2m)

Min£50 Max£90pw (Low)
Max£120pw (High)

F T S & J M Willett, **Edenvale Holiday Flats,** Lake Road, Ambleside, Cumbria ☎Ambleside(09663)2313

A converted stone-built Victorian terraced house, with eight flats each sleeping two persons. Seven have double beds. One has twin beds. Very well equipped, furnished and decorated.

All year MWB out of season 1 wk min, 3 wks max, 8 units, 2 persons, nc12 no pets ◔ fridge 🍴 Gas/Elec inclusive ⌸ inclusive ☎(30yds) [Iron on premises] [Ironing board on premises] HCE in unit [Launderette within 300yds] ⊖ TV ⊕3 pin square 8P ♨(200yds)

⊷ ☻(500yds) ☻(700yds)

Min£63 Max£87pw

AMROTH
Dyfed
Map**2** SN10

H **Castle Close**
for bookings Amroth Castle Holiday Centre, Amroth, Dyfed ☎Saundersfoot(0834)813217

Two semi-detached houses, each comprises open-plan lounge/dinette with kitchen leading off; bathroom/WC and three bedrooms.

May-Oct MWB out of season 1 wk min, 2 units, 2–7 persons ◊ no pets ◉ fridge 🍴 Elec metered ⌸ not provided ☎ Airing cupboard in unit Iron in unit Ironing board in unit HCE in unit [Laundry room on premises] ⊖

1982 prices quoted throughout gazetteer

CTV ⊕3pinsquare P ⚙ ⌐
⊖ ⚲

Min£80.50 Max£100.05pw (Low)
Min£204.70 Max£218.50pw (High)

B Shellhaven
for bookings Powells Holidays, High
Street, Saundersfoot, Dyfed
☎Saundersfoot(0834)812791

*Detached bungalow within a few yards of
the beach with panoramic sea views.
Accommodation comprises lounge,
dining room, kitchen, three bedrooms
(one with double bed, dressing room and
bathroom/WC), one with twin beds and
one small double-bedded room.
Bathroom/WC.*

May-Sep MWB out of season 1wk min,
1unit, 1–6persons ◆ nopets ⊚
fridge ▥ Elecinclusive
Ⓛnot provided ☎(200yds) SD in unit
Airing cupboard in unit Iron in unit
Ironing board in in unit HCE in unit ⊖
CTV ⊕3pinsquare 2P 2🛋 ▦
⚫(100yds)

⊖ ⚲(100yds)

Min£99 Max£220pw

___

ANNAN
Dumfries & Galloway *Dumfriesshire*
Map**11** NY16

C Newbie Mill
for bookings Mrs Clarke, Estate Office,
Hoddom & Kinmount Estates, Hoddom,
Lockerbie, Dumfriesshire DG11 1BE
☎Annan(04612)2608

*Semi-detached modernised cottage set
near the banks of the River Annan, about
½m from the public road and 1m from
Annan. Accommodation consists of two
bedrooms, living room, kitchen and
bathroom/WC. A 'short cut' walk is
available to those who wish to visit the
town without taking their car. Price
inclusive of fishing for two rods.*

Feb–Nov 1wk min, 1unit, 1–4persons
◆ ⊚ fridge Gasfire Ⓛnot provided
☎ Airing cupboard in unit HCE in unit
TV ⊕3pinsquare P ▦ ⚫(1m)
fishing

⊖ ⚲(1m) ▨(1m) ▩(1m)
£85pw

___

APPIN
Strathclyde *Argyll*
Map**14** NM94

C Creagan Cottage
for bookings I & S Weir, Dungrianach,
Appin, Argyll PA38 4BQ
☎Appin(063173)287

*Semi-detached cottage with small
garden and views of Loch Creran.
Accommodation comprises one double
bedded room, one small room with bunk
beds, a kitchenette, lounge/diner and
bathroom/WC.*

All year MWB out of season 1wk min,
3wks max, 1unit, 1–4persons [◇] ◆
◆ ⊚ fridge Electric Elecmetered
Ⓛinclusive ☎(2m) Iron in unit Ironing
board in unit ⊖ TV ⊕3pinsquare
1P ⚫(2m) Fishing, dinghies for hire

⊖ ⚲(½m)

CH Dungrianach Chalets
for bookings I & S Weir, Dungrianach,
Appin, Argyll PA38 4BQ
☎Appin(063173)287

*Timber-built bungalows with small
veranda and picture windows giving
superb loch and mountain views.
Accommodation comprises two
bedrooms, (one double, one twin)
bathroom and kitchen/diner/lounge.*

All year MWB out of season 1wk min,
3wks max, 6units, 1–4persons [◇] ◆
◆ ⊚ fridge Electric Elecmetered
Ⓛinclusive ☎(2m) Iron in unit Ironing
board in unit ⊖ TV ⊕3pinsquare
1P ⚫(2m) Fishing, dinghies for hire

⊖ ⚲(½m)

F Kinlochlaich House
for bookings Mr D E Hutchison,
Kinlochlaich House, Appin, Argyll
PA38 4BD ☎Appin(063173)342

*A charming stone-built country house
dating back 300yrs and showing both
Gothic and Georgian influences; it stands
in several acres of its own grounds. The
three flats have been attractively
converted, with tasteful furnishings and
neat décor. Views across Loch Linnhe in*

*the distance. From Appin police station
on the A828 (Oban–Fort William) take a
short private road. Fresh garden produce
available in season. In addition a
maisonette close to the main house,
accommodation includes double
bedroom, lounge/diner/kitchen and
bathroom; first-floor accommodation is
reached by a fairly steep pine staircase.*

Mid Dec–Oct MWB out of season
1wk min, 5wks max, 4units, 1–6persons
[◆] nopets ⊚ fridge Electric
Gas/Elecmetered Ⓛcan be hired ☎
WM on premises TD on premises
Airing cupboard in one unit Iron on
premises Ironing board on premises
HCE in unit ⊖ TV ⊕3pinround P
⚫(½m) Fishing, sailing & skiing

⊖ ⚭(2½m)
Min£30pw (Low)
Min£145pw (High)

C Laich Cottage
for bookings Mr D E Hutchison,
Kinlochlaich House, Appin, Argyll
PA38 4BD ☎Appin(063173)342

*A typical Highland building in its own
grounds several yards from the main
house. Simple but clean and well
maintained accommodation; several
extras such as flower arrangements. Two
bedrooms, one with bunk beds. Tidy
garden. From Appin police station on the
A828 (Oban–Fort William) take a short
private road. Fresh garden produce
available in season.*

Closed Nov–mid Dec MWB out of
season 1wk min, 5wks max, 1unit,
1–6persons [◆] nopets ⚲ fridge
Calorgas Gas/Elecmetered Ⓛcan be
hired ☎ [WM on premises] Airing
cupboard on premises Iron on
premises Ironing board on premises
HCE in unit ⊖ TV ⊕3pinround P
⚫(½m) Fishing, sailing & skiing

⊖ ⚲(2½m)
Min£65pw (Low)
Min£175pw (High)

___

ARDBRECKNISH
Strathclyde *Argyll*
Map**10** NN02

B Bungalow
for bookings Mrs H F Hodge, Rockhill →

Farm, Ardbrecknish, Dalmally, Argyll
PA33 1BH ☎Kilchrenan(08663)218

*A timber frame, shingle clad bungalow
set in grounds of 200-acre livestock farm
overlooking Loch Awe. Accommodation
comprises lounge/diner, large kitchen,
bathroom, two twin-bedded rooms and
one with a double and single bed.
Access via A819 Inveraray – Dalmally
road.*

Closed Xmas wk MWB out of season
1wk min, 1mth max, 1unit, 1–8persons
◊ ◉ fridge Electric Elec metered
▣notprovided ☎ SD in unit Iron in
unit Ironing board in unit HCE in unit
TV ⊕3pin round 4P ▥ ♨(10m)
Fishing

⊕ ☘(2½m)

Min£60pw (Low)
Min£120pw (High)

C Farm Cottage
for bookings Mrs H F Hodge, Rockhill
Farm, Ardbrecknish, Dalmally, Argyll
PA33 1BH ☎Kilchrenan(08663)218

*White-painted two-storey stone cottage
on 200-acre livestock farm overlooking
Loch Awe. The cottage comprises
lounge/diner/kitchen, bathroom,
separate WC and one twin-bedded room
on the ground floor, the first floor
comprises two double-bedded and one
twin-bedded rooms. Access is via A819
Inveraray – Dalmally road.*

Closed Xmas wk MWB out of season
1wk min, 1mth max, 1unit, 1–8persons
◊ ◉ fridge Electric Elec metered
▣notprovided ☎ SD in unit Airing
cupboard in unit Iron in unit Ironing
board in unit HCE in unit ⊖ TV
⊕3pin round 4P ▥ ♨(10m) Fishing

⊕ ☘(2½m)

Min£60pw (Low)
Min£120pw (High)

ARDEN (Loch Lomond)
Strathclyde *Dunbartonshire*
Map 10 NS38

Ca Mr A J Brown, **Lomond Castle Log
Cabins,** Lomond Castle Hotel,
Alexandria, Dunbartonshire G83 8RB
☎Arden(038985)681

*Pine-log cabins set in hotel grounds by
Loch Lomond. Accommodation varies*

Ardbrecknish
—
Ardtornish

*from two to three bedroom units – the
three bedroom units having two double-
bedded rooms and one twin-bedded
while the two bedroom units have one
double-bedded and one twin-bedded
room. All have combined living
room/dinette, kitchen, and bathroom.*

All year MWB 2nights min, 1mth max,
55units, 1–6persons ◊ ◊ ♦
no pets ◉ fridge ♨ Elec metered
▣inclusive ☎ [WM on premises] [SD
on premises] [TD on premises] Iron on
premises Ironing board on premises
HCE in unit ⊖ ⊗ CTV
⊕3pin square 100P ♨ ▱ ⤸Hard
Fishing, shooting & water sports

⊕ ▧(1m) ♫(2m) 🐎
Min£130 Max£275pw

ARDFERN
Strathclyde *Argyll*
Map 10 NM80

**C Teal, Wigeon, Mallard & Eider
Cottages**
for bookings Mr & Mrs R Brown, Galley of
Lorne Hotel, Ardfern, Argyll PA31 8QN
☎Barbreck(08525)284

*Four custom-built white-washed holiday
cottages on the shore of a sheltered tidal
loch close to the Galley of Lorne Hotel.
The focal point of this sprawling village,
the cottages are compact in size and the
furnishings are pleasant and practical.
Each cottage has two bedrooms (with
Continental bedding), living room with
convertible sofa and modern kitchen. The
village and surrounding area is part of
Lunga Estate. Guests are encouraged to
use the sporting facilities available.*

All year MWB out of season 1night min,
1mth max, 4units, 1–4persons ◊ ♦
◉ fridge Electric & open fires
Elec metered ▣inclusive ☎ [WM on
premises] [TD on premises] Iron on
premises Ironing board on premises
HCE in unit TV can be hired
⊕3pin square 8P ♨(½m)

⊕

Min£70pw (Low)
Min£140pw (High)

C Millhouse
for bookings Mrs M C Peterson,
Traighmhor, Ardfern, Lochgilphead,
Argyll ☎Barbreck(08525)228

*Situated in a village and attached to the
small Post Office, this cottage is close to
the shore of Loch Craignish.
Accommodation consists of sitting room,
dining room, large kitchen and four
bedrooms. Ardfern is reached by the
B8002 which leads off the A816.*

All year MWB out of season 1wk min,
4wks max, 1unit, 1–7persons ◊ ♦
no pets ◉ fridge Electric & open
fires Elec metered ▣not provided
☎(100yds) WM in unit SD in unit Iron
in unit HCE in unit [Launderette within
300yds] ⊕3pin square P ♨(½m)

⊕ ☘(200yds)

ARDTORNISH
Highland *Argyllshire*
Map 10 NM64

**F Billiard Room, Garden & 1st Floor
Flats**
for bookings Mr Coyne, Ardtornish
Estate, Morvern, Oban, Argyll
☎Morvern(096784)288

*Three flats located within Ardtornish
House on the Ardtornish estate which
comprises 60 square miles of woodland,
rivers, lochs and coastline. The house
was built nearly 100 years ago as a
Victorian Holiday house with extremely
spacious rooms, fine furniture, marble
floors and fireplaces. The remote location
is opposite the Isle of Mull on the SW
peninsula of Morvern. The Estate is
signposted from the main road.*

All year 1wk min, 5wks max, 3units,
2–8persons [◊ ♦] ◉ fridge
Open fires Elec inclusive
▣not provided ☎(¾m) HCE in unit
⊕3pin square P ♨(2½m) Boat hire,
salmon & trout fishing, stalking & bird
watching

⊕ ☘(2½m)

Min£50 Max£225pw

C Rose & Torrmolach Cottages
for bookings Mr Coyne, Ardtornish
Estate, Morvern, Oban, Argyll
☎Morvern(096784)288

Rose Cottage was originally an estate workers cottage and an ideal location for fishing with the river only 20yds away. Accommodation comprises three twin bedrooms on the first floor and one twin bedroom, bathroom, lounge and kitchen/diner on the ground floor.

Torrmolach Cottage is situated on a hillside on the Ardtornish estate with views of Loch Aune and wooded surroundings. Accommodation comprises three twin bedded rooms, bathroom, lounge and kitchen/diner.

Apr–Oct 1wkmin, 5wksmax, 2units, 2–8persons [◊ ◆] @ fridge Openfires Elecinclusive ⌂notprovided ☎(½m) Airing cupboard in unit HCE in unit ③3pin square P ♨(2½m) Boat hire, salmon & trout fishing
↔ ☎(2½m)
Min£50 Max£130pw

ARDWELL
Dumfries & Galloway *Wigtownshire*
Map**10** NX14

Ch   Ardwell Chalets
for bookings Mrs M McFadzean, Killaser, Ardwell, Stranraer, Wigtownshire
☎Ardwell(077686)294

Six timbered chalets situated on the foreshore at the edge of a tiny village with fine views of the Galloway Hills and Luce Bay. Accommodation comprises living room with bed/couch, two bedrooms (two singles and two bunk beds), kitchenette and bathroom/WC.

All year MWB out of season 1wkmin, 2mthsmax, 6units, 1–4persons [◊] @ fridge Electric Elecmetered ⌂notprovided ☎(200yds) Airing cupboard in unit Iron on premises Ironing board on premises HCE in unit ⊖ TVcan be hired ③3pinsquare P ♨(200yds)
Min£30 Max£100pw

ARNSIDE
Cumbria
Map**7** SD47

F   Mr & Mrs A E & F W Anthony
Hampsfell The Promenade, Arnside, Carnforth, Lancs LA50AD
☎Arnside(0524)761285

Second-floor flat situated within a stone-built semi-detached house standing on the promenade with extensive views of the Kent estuary and the Lakeland Hills. The accommodation comprises one double bedroom, one twin-bedded room, one single-bedded room, lounge, kitchen and bathroom/WC.

All year MWB out of season 3days min, 1unit, 2–5persons, nc5 no pets @ fridge Electric Elecmetered ⌂can be hired ☎ WM in unit Iron in unit Ironing board in unit HCE in unit ⊖ [TV] ③3pinsquare 2P ▥ ♨(100yds)
↔ ♨m(3m) ☎(100yds) ☒(100yds)
Min£35 Max£40pw (Low)
Min£60 Max£77.50pw (High)

Ardtornish
—
Ashcott

F   Mrs A Mitchell, **The Moorings,**
Promenade, Arnside, Carnforth, Lancs LA50AD ☎Arnside(0524)761340

Large, modern, well-furnished and comfortable flat. On first floor of proprietor's stone-built house on the promenade near Arnside centre. Good views across the River Kent estuary to the hills of South Cumbria. The area has many nature trails and is popular with ornithologists.

All year (except Xmas) MWB out of season 1wkmin, 1unit, 5persons ◊ @ fridge ♨ Elecmetered ⌂can be hired ☎(½m) Airing cupboard on premises Iron on premises Ironing board on premises HCE in unit TV ③3pinsquare P ♨(300yds)
↔ ☎(300yds)
£85pw

ARRAN Isle of, see under **Brodick, Dougarie, Lamlash**

ASHBOURNE
Derbyshire
Map**7** SK14

F   This 'n' That, **The Gallery** St John Street
for bookings Mrs J Cannon, 17 Belper Road, Ashbourne, Derbys
☎Ashbourne(0335)2442

In the very centre of Ashbourne, these two recently modernised flats are reached via a narrow cobbled-stoned alley from the south end of the Market Place. The flats are above an attractive bow-windowed shop and have their own entrance alongside. Flat 1 on the first floor has only a single bedroom but the main lounge/diner has a double bed and a single bed. The flats are convenient for the town's amenities and well located for touring Derbyshire and north Staffordshire. Unsuitable for disabled.

All year MWB out of season 1wkmin, 6wksmax, 2units, 1–5persons ◊ @ fridge ♨ Elecmetered ⌂not provided ☎(100yds) Airing cupboard in unit HCE in unit [Launderette within 300yds] ⊖ ③3pinsquare ♨(50yds)
↔ ☎(50yds)

ASHBURTON
Devon
Map**3** SX77

F&H   Apartments 1 & 2, Lent Hill House and The Lodge
for bookings The Manager, The River Dart Country Park Ltd, Holne Park, Ashburton, Newton Abbot, Devon ☎Ashburton(0364)52511

Three self-catering holiday properties set within grounds of the Country Park with the fourth, a large Georgian house across the river. Follow Two Bridges road from

Ashburton, Holne Park signposted on left hand side.
Apartment 1 – Three bedrooms, kitchen, lounge/diner and bathroom.
Apartment 2 – Two bedrooms, kitchen/diner, lounge, bathroom and separate WC both on second floor of country mansion. Electricity is inclusive in summer for the apartments.
Lent Hill House – Detached house with shrubs and woodlands, five double bedrooms, one single, two bathrooms, two WCs, sitting room, TV room, kitchen, dining room, night-storage heaters. A garage is available.
The Lodge – Two twin, one double, twin bunks, two bathrooms, lounge, TV lounge, dining room, kitchen, own garden situated at entrance of park. A garage is available.

All year (Apartments Apr–Sep) MWB out of season 1wkmin, 6mthsmax, 4units, 2–10persons ◊ ◆ @ fridge(3units) ♨ Electric(2units) Elecmetered ⌂can be hired ☎(&1m) WM in Lent Hill House SD on premises Airing cupboard in unit Iron in unit Ironing board in unit HCE in unit ⊖ TV ③3pinsquare ②2pinround P ♨(1m) ⌿ ⌐Hard
↔ ☎(1m) ♫(1m) ▦(1m)
Min£92 Max£184pw (Low)
Min£143 Max£299pw (High)

ASHCOTT
Somerset
Map**3** ST43

C   Coachmans Cottage
for bookings Polden Peak Holiday Cottages, 1A Bath Road, Ashcott, Bridgwater, Somerset TA79QT
☎Ashcott(0458)210627

Converted gardener's cottage dating back to 1865. On the ground floor, there is a large kitchen, separate lounge with beamed ceiling, dining area in kitchen and bathroom and separate WC. An open-tread staircase leads to first-floor bedrooms (one double, one twin and a convertible settee). Set on fringe of village, on A39 to Bath.

Etr–Oct 1wkmin, 1unit, 1–6persons [◊] nopets ◢ fridge ♨ Gas inclusive & Elec metered ⌂can be hired ☎ WM in unit SD in unit TD in unit Airing cupboard in unit Iron in unit HCE in unit ⊖ TV ③3pinsquare P ▥ ♨(¾m)
↔ ☎(500yds)
Min£73 Max£121pw

C   Polden Peak Cottage
for bookings Polden Peak Holiday Cottages, 1A Bath Road, Ashcott, Bridgwater, Somerset TA79QT
☎Ashcott(0458)210627

Stone-built converted coach house. Dining room and separate good sized kitchen, open-tread staircase, shower→

1982 prices quoted throughout gazetteer

room and WC on ground floor. There is a lounge with two put-u-ups, one single and double bedroom. On fringe of village.

Etr–Oct 1wkmin, 1unit, 1–8persons [◊] ◆ nopets 🌑 fridge 🍴 Elecmetered ⬜canbehired ☎ TD on premises SD in unit Iron in unit HCE in unit ⊕ TV ⊕3pinsquare P 🔲 ♨(¾m)

⇔ 🍸(500yds)

Min£75 Max£120pw

ASHREIGNEY
Devon
Map**2**SS61

C   JFH Ref N35C
for bookings John Fowler Holidays, Marlborough Road, Ilfracombe, Devon ☎Ilfracombe(0271)64135

A detached cottage comprising kitchen, sitting room and WC. On first floor there are two bedrooms and a bathroom.

Mar–Oct MWB out of season 3days min, 3wks max, 1unit, 3–5persons ◆ 🌑 fridge Electric Elecinclusive ⬜notprovided ☎(2m) Airing cupboard in unit Iron in unit HCE in unit TV ⊕3pinsquare P 🏠 ♨(2m)

⇔ 🍸(3m)

Min£34 Max£137pw

C   JFH Ref N57B
for bookings John Fowler Holidays, Marlborough Road, Ilfracombe, Devon ☎Ilfracombe(0271)64135

Semi-detached 300-year-old cottage. Accommodation comprises lounge with chintz loose-covered seating and double bed-settee if required, WC, separate kitchen with adequate units and surfaces, first-floor bathroom with H/C washbasin and two bedrooms (a double and a twin).

Mar–Oct MWB out of season 3days min, 3wks max, 1unit, 5–7persons ◆ 🌑 fridge Electric Elecinclusive ⬜not provided ☎(2m) WM in unit Airing cupboard in unit Iron in unit HCE in unit P 🏠 ♨(2m)

⇔ 🍸(3m)

Min£45 Max£160pw

ASHTON
Hereford & Worcester
Map**3**SO56

F   Mrs P Edwards **Ashton Court Farm**
Ashton, Leominster, Herefs ☎Brimfield(058472)245

Two flats which form part of a farmhouse each with its own entrance, one is on the ground floor the other on the first. Each flat contains lounge with double wall bed, one double bedded room, one room with bunk beds and a single bed.

All year MWB in season 2nights min, 1mth max, 2units, 1–10persons ◊ ◆ ◆ 🌑 fridge 🍴 Elecmetered ⬜can be hired ☎(¾m) SD on premises

---

Airing cupboard in unit Iron in unit Ironing board in unit HCE in unit ⊕ CTV ⊕3pinsquare 4P 🔲 ♨(2m) Games room, play area

⇔ 🍸(2m)

ASHURST
Hampshire
Map**4** SU31

C   Foxhills Cottage 211 Lyndhurst Road
for bookings Mrs B M Davidson, 132 Woodlands Road, Ashurst, Southampton, Hants SO4 2AP ☎Ashurst(042129)2309

Attractive red-brick cottage consisting of one double and two twin-bedded rooms, comfortable lounge/diner, kitchen and bathroom. Turn left off the A35 after railway bridge if heading away from Southampton, or right before railway bridge if heading towards Southampton. The road leading to the cottage runs parallel to the A35 for about 300yds.

All year 1wk min, 4mths max, 1unit, 1–6persons ◆ ◑ fridge 🍴 £6.50 charge for Gas/Elec ☎(200yds) Airing cupboard Iron Ironing board HCE ⊕ CTV ⊕3pinsquare P 🔲 ♨(500yds)

⇔ ♨(2m) 🍸(200yds)

Min£50 Max£70pw (Low)
Min£90 Max£150pw (High)

ASTON-ON-CLUN
Shropshire
Map**7** SO38

C   Edge View 3 Broome Marsh
for bookings E P Brown, 'Fairwinds', 16 Station Road, Condover, Shrewsbury, Salop ☎Bayston Hill(074372)2127

A small stone-built semi-detached cottage with pleasant garden. Accommodation consists of a compact kitchen, combined lounge/dining room with large inglenook fireplace on ground floor and upstairs two simply furnished and decorated bedrooms (one twin and one double) and a modern bathroom/WC.

All year MWB out of season 1wk min, 1mth max, 1unit, 4persons 🌑 fridge Electric & open fires Elecmetered ⬜not provided ☎ Airing cupboard in unit Iron in unit HCE in unit ⊕ TV ⊕3pinsquare P 🏠 🔲 ♨(¾m)

⇔ 🍸(¼m) 🄿(2½m) 🎵(2½m)

Min£35 Max£65pw

AUCHENMALG
Dumfries & Galloway *Wigtownshire*
Map**10** NX25

F   Craig Lodge
for bookings The Hon Mrs Agnew, Sweethaws Farm, Crowborough, E Sussex ☎Crowborough(08926)5045

A 19th-century shooting lodge with

---

extension which has been converted into five flats. The flats are decorated and furnished to a high standard and Nos 1 & 2 are particularly spacious. In 2 acres of ground which include a small private stretch of foreshore, about 30yds away.

All year MWB out of season 1wk min, 5units, 1–6persons [◊ ◆] nodogs 🌑 fridge Electric Elecmetered ⬜can be hired ☎ SD in unit Airing cupboard in unit Iron in unit Ironing board in unit HCE in unit ⊕ TV ⊕3pinsquare P 🔲 ♨(7m)

⇔ 🍸(¾m)

Min£35 Max£100pw

AUCHTERARDER
Tayside
Perthshire
Map**11** NN91

F   1–12 Garth Terrace
for bookings Tay Valley Properties (Perth), 230 Oakbank Road, Perth PH1 1DS ☎Perth(0738)27478

Row of 12 modern self-contained flats converted from traditional two-storey stone terrace. Each comprises one or two bedrooms, lounge, kitchen and bathroom. Dining arrangements in either lounge or kitchen. Situated on main road on NE outskirts of town. There is a grassy children's play area to rear, and a lovely outlook across farmland and hills.

Apr–Oct MWB 1wk min, 1mth max, 12units, 1–6persons nopets 🌑 fridge 🍴 Elecmetered ⬜inclusive ☎ Airing cupboard in unit HCE in unit ⊕ TV ⊕3pinsquare P 🔲 ♨(1m)

⇔♨(3m) 🍸(1m) 🄿(1m) 🎵(1m)

Min£50 Max£61pw (Low)
Min£84 Max£107pw (High)

AUCHTERMUCHTY
Fife
Map**11** NO21

C   Orchard Cottage
for bookings Mrs E J Dunlop, 6 Gladgate, Auchtermuchty, Fife KY14 7AY ☎Auchtermuchty(03372)496

19th-century stone cottage which has been carefully renovated to provide modern facilities whilst still retaining much of its original character. Entrance is by outside stairs to the first floor which comprises living room, kitchen, bathroom and three bedrooms, one double, one twin and one single.

All year MWB out of season 1wk min, 8wks max, 1unit, 5persons ◆ nopets ◑ fridge 🍴 Gas/Elec inclusive ⬜inclusive WM in unit TD in unit Airing cupboard in unit Iron in unit Ironing board in unit HCE in unit ⊕ CTV ⊕3pinsquare 🔲 ♨(50yds)

⇔ 🄿(3m) 🍸(100yds)

Min£95pw (Low)
Min£165pw (High)

H   Weavers House 4 Gladgate
for bookings Mrs E J Dunlop, 6 Gladgate, Auchtermuchty, Fife KY14 7AY ☎Auchtermuchty(03372)496

26

A traditional type house standing in own gardens on elevated site in small village. The house is well furnished and offers lounge, dining room, modern kitchen and shower with WC on the ground floor, one bunk-bedded room, one double bedroom, one twin-bedded room and modern bathroom with WC on the first floor. Access from A91 via Crosshills or Gladgate.

All year MWB out of season 1 wk min, 8 mths max, 1 unit, 1–6 persons ◆ no pets ⌀ fridge ▥ Gas/Elec metered ⌷ inclusive ☎ WM in unit SD in unit TD in unit Airing cupboard in unit Iron in unit Ironing board in unit HCE in unit ⊖ CTV ③3 pin square 1P 1🛋 ▥ ♨(200yds) Fishing

⇔ ᕲ(3m) ♀(200yds)
Min£110pw (Low)
Min£175pw (High)

AVIEMORE see also **Carrbridge**
Highland *Inverness-shire*
Map **14** NH81

B Cedar Bungalow
for bookings Inverdruie & Glasnacardoch Properties, Inverdruie House, Inverdruie, Aviemore, Inverness-shire PH22 1QR
☎Aviemore(0479)810357

A cedar-wood bungalow contained in the garden of an 18th-century country house. It has an open-plan living/dining/kitchen, a double bedroom and a room with bunks.

All year MWB out of season 3 nights min, 1 mth max, 1 unit, 1–5 persons ◇ ◆ ◆ ◎ fridge ▥ Elec metered ⌷ can be hired ☎ Airing cupboard in unit Iron in unit Ironing board in unit HCE in unit [Launderette within 300yds] ⊖ TV ③3 pin square 2P ▥ ♨(1m) Childrens play area

⇔ ♀(1m) ☐(1m) ♫(1m) 🛏(1m)
Min£80pw (Low)
Min£160pw (High)

F Freedom Inn Aviemore Centre, Aviemore, Inverness-shire PH22 1PF
☎Aviemore(0479)810781

A modern, low-rise building complex within the Aviemore holiday centre. The main room in each flat is multi-purpose,

---

serving as bedroom, lounge, dining room and kitchenette–only the bathroom is separate. All the facilities of a hotel are available. Rugged highland views over Spey Valley to Cairngorm Mountains.

All year MWB in season 1 night min, 93 units, 1–4 persons ◇ ◆ ◆ ◎(metered) fridge ▥ Elec inclusive ⌷ inclusive ☎ ⊖ ⊛ CTV ③3 pin square P ♨(½m) [☐](200yds) ᕲ

⇔ ♀ ☐ ♫ 🛏(200yds)
Min£80 Max£175pw

F Inverdrui & Glasnacardoch Properties Inverdruie House, Inverdruie, Aviemore, Inverness-shire PH22 1QR
☎Aviemore(0479)810357

18th-century stone-built country house standing in its own grounds and converted into three flats of varying sizes. A lot of space with a high standard of furnishings. Two flats have a dishwasher. Mountain and valley views. Access is from B970.

All year MWB out of season 3 nights min, 1 mth max, 3 units, 4–10 persons [◇] ◆ ◆ ◎ fridge ▥ Elec metered ⌷ can be hired ☎ Airing cupboard in unit Iron in unit Ironing board in unit HCE in unit [Launderette within 300yds] ⊖ TV ③3 pin square 12P ▥ ♨(1½m) Childrens play area

⇔ ♀(1m) ☐(1m) ♫(1m) 🛏(1m)
Min£80 Max£170pw (Low)
Min£150 Max£299pw (High)

C Lynwilg Farm Cottage
for bookings Mrs D H South, Lynwilg, Farm, Aviemore, Inverness-shire PH22 1PZ ☎Aviemore(0479)810286

Situated 1m S of Aviemore, a timber-clad cottage farm building in secluded spot with open views over Spey Valley to Cairngorms. The cottage is neatly decorated and furnished and comprises lounge/dining room/kitchen, bathroom and three bedrooms.

All year MWB out of season 1 wk min, 1 unit, 2–6 persons ◆ no pets ◎

---

fridge ▥(winter only) Elec metered ⌷ not provided ☎(1m) Airing cupboard in unit Iron in unit Ironing board unit HCE in unit ③3 pin square P ▥ ♨(1m)

⇔ ♀(1m) ☐(1m) ♫(1m) 🛏(1m)
Min£75 Max£85pw

Ch & F Speyside Caravan Park & Chalets Craigellachie House, Aviemore, Inverness-shire PH22 1PX
☎Aviemore(0479)810236

Six chalets varying in size and standard from simplicity and compactness to luxury and spaciousness; there is also one flat in the main house. Situated in a sheltered position at the S end of Aviemore village with splendid views over the Spey Valley to the Cairngorm Mountains, within short distance of Aviemore Centre.

All year MWB out of season 2 nights min, 1 mth max, 7 units, 2–7 persons ◆ ⌀ ◎ fridge ▥ Elec metered ☎(50yds) HCE in unit Launderette ⊖ TV ③3 pin square P ♨(500yds)

⇔ ♀(½m) ☐(1m) ♫(1m) 🛏(1m)
Fishing, Bicycle Hire
Min£60 Max£120pw (Low)
Min£100 Max£180pw (High)
See advert on page 28

AXMOUTH
Devon
Map **3** SY29

H CC Ref 776
for bookings Character Cottages (Holidays) Ltd, 34, Fore Street, Sidmouth, Devon EX10 8AQ
☎Sidmouth(03955)77001

House in small attractive village close to the coast. large well-kept garden, next door to pub. Accommodation consisting of kitchen, dining room, lounge, three twin-bedded rooms and bathroom/WC. Older-style décor and furniture in keeping with character of house.

All year MWB out of season 1 wk min, 1 mth max, 1 unit, 1–6 persons ◆ ◎ fridge Electric & open fires →

1982 prices quoted throughout gazetteer

Elec metered ⬛not provided ☎
Airing cupboard in unit Iron in unit
Ironing board in unit HCE in unit ⊙
CTV ③3pin square 2P 🅟 ♨(1m)
⊶ ♀ ♫(1m)
Min£50 Max£106pw (Low)
Min£140 Max£175pw (High)

BACTON
Norfolk
Map**9** TG33

Ch Kimberley & Glendale Chalets
New Zealand Way
for bookings Hoseasons Holidays,
Sunway House, Lowestoft, Suffolk
NR32 3LT ☎Lowestoft(0502)62292

Chalets occupy a level, grassed 5-acre
site and many have sea views. They are
designed to sleep six in two double
bedrooms with double 'put-u-up' in
lounge/kitchen. Well-equipped and of
comfortable size. Small covered patio.
Manager on site.

Apr–Oct 1wk min, 46units,
2–6persons [◇] [◆] ⦿ fridge
Electric Elec metered ⬛inclusive
☎(200yds) Iron on premises ⊙ TV
③3pin square P ♨(200yds)
⊶ ♀(½m) 🅹(2m)

CH New Zealand Bungalows
New Zealand Way
for bookings Hoseasons Holidays,
Sunway House, Lowestoft, Suffolk
NR32 3LT ☎Lowestoft(0502)62292

Detached chalets in quiet location. Each
has two bedrooms (to sleep five) plus
double 'put-u-up' in living room, kitchen,
separate bathroom/WC.

Apr–Oct 1wk min, 9units, 2–7persons
[◇ ◆] ⦿ fridge Electric
Elec metered ⬛inclusive ☎(100yds)
[Iron on premises] ⊙ TV
③3pin square P ♨(100yds)
⊶ ♀(½m) 🅹(2)

BAKEWELL
Derbyshire
Map**8** SK26

C Manor Barn Cottage
for bookings Mrs P M Dabell, Manor
House, Great Longstone, Bakewell,
Derbyshire DE4 1TZ

Axmouth
—
Ballantrae

☎Great Longstone(062987)374

Tastefully converted stone-built barn
standing in its own garden within the
grounds of the proprietors residence.
Accommodation consists of modern
fitted kitchen, lounge/dining room.
Bedrooms consist of one double room
and the second room sleeping three on
one single and two bunk beds,
bathroom/WC. Modern furnishings and
well decorated throughout.

All year MWB out of season 1wk min,
1unit, 5persons ◇ no pets ⦿ fridge
Electric Elec inclusive(heating only)
Elec metered ⬛not provided
☎(100yds) Airing cupboard in unit Iron
in unit Ironing board in unit HCE in unit
⊙ ⦿ CTV ③3pin square 2P 🅟
♨(500yds) ⌇Hard
⊶ ♀(50yds)

BALEROMINDUBH
Isle of Colonsay Strathclyde Argyll
Map**10** 39

C Baleromindubh Cottage
for bookings Mr M C Caldwell Smith,
Managed Estates, 18 Maxwell Place,
Stirling ☎Stirling(0786)62519

Remote cottage situated on the SE side of
the island with views towards Jura. It has
no electricity with lighting by gas and
heating by open fires. The
accommodation is simple and comprises
one double bedded room, one bunk
bedded, sitting room with bed settee and
kitchen/diner.

All year MWB out of season 1wk min
1unit 1–6persons ◇ ◆ ⦿ fridge
open fires Gas/Elec inclusive
⬛not provided ☎(2m) P ♨(2m)
⊶ ♀(2m) 🅹(2m)
Min£70 Max£120pw

BALGEDIE
Tayside Kinross-shire
Map**11** NO10

Ch Mr A Sneddon Eagle Chalets
Stan-ma-Lane, Balgedie, Kinross,
Kinross-shire
☎Scotlandwell(059284)257

A group of 18 chalets set together at the
foot of the Lomond Hills and looking out
over Loch Leven. Each has open plan
kitchen/lounge/dining area and either
two or three bedrooms, one of which may
have bunk beds. The chalets are
compact but modern. Balgedie lies 2m E
of M90 and some 3m NE of Kinross.

All year MWB in season 3days min,
18units, 1–6persons [◇ ◆] no pets
⦿ fridge Electric ⬛can be hired ☎
[WM on premises] [TD on premises]
Iron on premises Ironing board on
premises HCE in unit ⊙ [CTV]
③3pin square P 🅟 Childrens play
area
⊶ ♙(1m) ♀(100yds) 🅹(3m) ♫(3m)
Min£50 Max£70pw (Low)
Min£115 Max£155pw (High)

BALLACHULISH
Highland Argyll
Map**14** NN05

Ch Glenachulish Woodland Chalets
for bookings Barrow & Allen, The House
in the Wood, Glenachulish, Ballachulish,
Argyll ☎Ballachulish(08552)379

Danish-design, timber chalets set in 5¼
acres of rough woodland at the front of
Beinn a Beithir. Nearby are the shores of
Loch Linnie and Ballachulish Bay. The
views are spectacular, and sailing and
hill-walking facilities are available.
Situated on the outskirts of Ballachulish
near the southern approach to road
bridge over Loch Leven on A828.

All year MWB out of season 1wk min,
28days max, 4units, 1–6persons ◇
◆ ⦿ fridge Electric Elec metered
⬛not provided ☎(½m) HCE in unit ⊙
③3pin square P 🅟 ♨(2m)
⊶ ♀(½m)
Min£40 Max£120pw

BALLANTRAE
Strathclyde Argyll
Map**10** NX08

C Carrick, Horsehill & Kyle Cottages
for bookings J & R Stevenson Ltd, Balig,
Ballantrae, Girvan, Ayrshire KA26 0JY
☎Ballantrae(046583)214

Three recently refurbished cottages
200yds from private beach. Modern

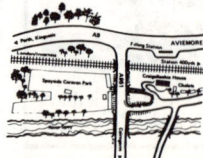

furnishing. 10m S of Girvan on A77.
All year(1 unit) & Mar–Nov(2 units)
MWB 1wk min, 3wks max, 3 units,
1–6 persons [◊] ◊ ◆ ● fridge
Electric Elec metered ☐ not provided
☎(1m) WM in unit SD in unit Airing
cupboard in unit Iron in unit Ironing
board in unit HCE in unit ⊙ CTV
⊕3 pin square 6P 4🏠 ♨(1m)
Shooting & fishing available
↩ ♀(1m) ▦(1m)
Min£50pw (Low)
Min£155.25pw (High)

BALLATER
Grampian *Aberdeenshire*
Map **15** NO39

C **Morvada Cottage**
for bookings Mr & Mrs Nimmo, Morvada
Guest House, Braemar Road, Ballater,
Aberdeenshire ☎Ballater(0338)55501

*Detached two-storey cottage in quiet
setting in garden of Morvada Guest
House. Accommodation comprises two
double bedrooms, lounge with dining
area, kitchen and sun porch. There are
two single bedrooms on the first floor,
ideal for children.*

All year MWB out of season 1wk min,
1 unit, 1–6 persons ◊ ◆ ● fridge
Electric Elec metered ☎(300yds)
Airing cupboard in unit Iron in unit
Ironing board in unit HCE in unit TV
⊕3 pin square 2P ▦ ♨(300yds)
↩ 🏠(½m) ♀(300yds) ▦(300yds)
♫(300yds)
Min£55pw (Low)
Min£75pw (High)

BALLINTUIM
Tayside *Perthshire*
Map **15** NO15

H **Balmachreuchie**
for bookings Miss M Carmichael, White
Lodge, Oxenfoord, Pathhead, Midlothian
EH37 5UD ☎Ford(0875)320241

*A beautifully converted stone-built house
of considerable charm and character.
Large living room with beech floor,
separate well-equipped kitchen; house is
generally tastefully furnished and
decorated and serviced twice yearly. It
is situated on a hillside in the glen E of
Kirkmichael in a quiet spot with superb
views.*

Apr-Oct MWB out of season 1wk min,
1 unit, 1–4 persons, nc5 ● fridge
Electric & Open fires Elec inclusive
☐inclusive (except towels) ☎(1m)
Airing cupboard in unit Iron in unit
Ironing board in unit HCE in unit ⊙
CTV ⊕3 pin square 2P 1🏠 ♨(1m)
↩ ♀(1m)
Min£90 Max£130pw

BALNAIN (Glen Urquhart)
Highland *Inverness-shire*
Map **14** NH43

F **Glenurquhart House**
for bookings Eurecosse Holidays, 7

Ballantrae
—
Banchory

Greenhill Street, Dingwall, Ross-shire
☎Dingwall(0349)62462

*This house, which stands in 5 acres of
grounds and overlooks Lock Meikle, has
been tastefully converted into four flats
which have been furnished and fitted to a
luxury standard. The flats are of varying
size, sleeping four to six people.*

All year MWB out of season 1wk min,
4 units, 1–6 persons ◊ ◆ no pets
● fridge 🍴 Elec inclusive
☐inclusive ☎ WM in unit SD in unit
TD in unit Iron in unit Ironing board in
unit HCE in unit ⊙ CTV
⊕3 pin square 10P ♨(6m) Fishing
available
Min£100.05 Max£200.10pw (Low)
Min£180.55 Max £244.95pw (High)

Ch **Glenurquhart Lodges**
for bookings Eurecosse Holidays, 7
Greenhill Street, Dingwall, Ross-shire
☎Dingwall(0349)62462

*Five spacious Canadian red-cedar
chalets built and equipped to very high
standards. They are situated in the
grounds of Glenurquhart House and all
have fine views of the surrounding area.
Accommodation consists of double, twin
and bunk(full size) bedrooms, open-plan
kitchen/lounge/dining area.*

All year MWB out of season 1wk min,
5 units, 6 persons ◊ ◆ ● fridge
Electric Elec inclusive ☐inclusive ☎
WM in unit SD in unit TD in unit Airing
cupboard in unit Iron in unit Ironing
board in unit HCE in unit ⊙ CTV
⊕3 pin square 12P ♨(6m) Fishing
Min£100.05 Max£170.20pw (Low)
Max£225.40pw (High)

BALTONSBOROUGH
Somerset
Map **3** ST53

H **Corner House**
for bookings Mr & Mrs K P Evans
'Beggars Roost', Glanville Road,
Wedmore, Somerset BS28 4AD
☎Wedmore(0934)712521

*Comfortably furnished semi-detached
stone cottage. Accommodation includes
lounge, fitted kitchen with dining table,
one double and one single bedroom with
extra divan in lounge. Recently
modernised and situated in centre of an
attractive village.*

All year 4 days min, 4wks max, 1 unit,
1–4 persons, no pets ● fridge
Electric & open fire Elec metered
☐not provided ☎(30yds) Airing
cupboard in unit Iron in unit Ironing
board in unit HCE in unit TV
⊕3 pin square 1P ▦ ♨(20yds)
↩ ♀(30yds)
Min£50 Max£55pw (Low)
Min£70 Max£90pw (High)

1982 prices quoted throughout
gazetteer

BALVICAR
Strathclyde *Argyll*
Map **10** NM71

Ch **Balvicar Chalets**
for bookings Mr A Macaskill, Balvicar
Farm, Balvicar, Oban, Argyll PA34 4TE
☎Balvicar(08523)221

*Timber-clad chalets in grass fields on
large stock-rearing farm on the small
island of Seil, some 15m S of Oban and
overlooking the narrow Sound of Seil
(which is in fact the Atlantic Ocean).
A small hump-backed bridge connects
the island with the mainland. Units
comprise kitchenette/living room with
bed-settee, two rather small bedrooms
(one with double bed, the other with twin
beds), and bathroom/WC.*

Apr-Oct MWB out of season 1wk min,
6wks max, 6 units, 1–6 persons ◊
no pets ● fridge Electric
Elec metered ☐not provided ☎(1m)
HCE in unit TV ⊕3 pin square P ▦
♨(1m)
↩ ♀(3m) ▦(3m)
Min£35 Max£110pw

BANAVIE
Highland *Iverness-shire*
Map **14** NN17

Ch **Caledonian Valley Chalets** 14
Muirshearlich
for bookings Mrs D MacKinnon, 1 Blar
Mhor Road, Caol, Fort William, Inverness-
shire ☎Fort William(0397)3356

*Three brick-built chalets lying on open
ground at foot of gently sloping hillside,
close to the Caledonian Canal.
Accommodation comprises lounge with
small kitchen area, bathroom, one double
bedroom and one room with twin bunk
beds. Settee in lounge can be converted
to two single beds. Chalets lie 5m N of
Banavie and have fine views of the Ben
Novic Range.*

May-Oct 1wk min, 3 units, 4–6 persons
◊ ● fridge Electric Elec metered
☐not provided ☎(1m) Airing
cupboard in unit HCE in unit ⊙ TV
⊕3 pin square 4P ▦ ♨(3m)
↩ ♀(3m)
Min£60 Max£70pw (Low)
Min£80 Max£100pw (High)

BANCHORY
Grampian *Kincardineshire*
Map **15** NO69

Ch **Woodend of Glassel** Banchory,
Kincardineshire AB34DB
☎Banchory(03302)2731

*A group of seven timbered chalets
sheltered by woodland on three sides,
facing south and having fine views of
Royal Deeside Valley. Accommodation
comprises open-plan kitchen/living area,
bathroom and bedrooms sleeping up to
five people. The site is situated 3m NW of
Banchory on a minor road signposted
Glassel, Torphins and Lumphanan.* →

All year MWB out of season 1wk min,
7 units, 1–5 persons ◇ ◆ ● fridge
Electric Elec metered ⊡ can be hired
(Overseas visitors only) ☎(1½m) HCE
in unit ⊕ TV ⊕3 pin square P ▥
♨(1½m) cycles for hire

⟷ ♀(3m) ▨(3m)

Min£55 Max£75pw (Low)
Min£80 Max£100pw (High)

BANGOR
Gwynedd
Map 6 SH57

B Coed Vaynol
for bookings Mrs H W Chamberlain, The
Estate Office, Vaynol Park, Bangor,
Gwynedd ☎Bangor(0248)670966

Detached wooden bungalow built as
Pavilion for the Queen when she attended
the Royal Welsh show in 1958. Set in
secluded position on estate and
comprises sitting room, kitchen/diner,
bathroom and three bedrooms; one
double, one twin and one with bunk beds.
Modern pine furniture. 1000 acres of
park, woodland and formal gardens.

All year MWB out of season 2 days min,
8 mth max, 1 unit, 1–6 persons ◇ ◆
● fridge Electric Elec metered
⊡ can be hired ☎ [WM on premises]
[TD on premises] Airing cupboard in
unit Iron in unit Ironing board in unit
HCE in unit CTV ⊕3 pin square 2P
1 🏠 ▥ ♨(2m) Squash

⟷ ♀(1m) ▨(2m)

H The Coach House
for bookings Mrs H W Chamberlain, The
Estate Office, Vaynol Park, Bangor,
Gwynedd ☎Bangor(0248)670966

First and second floor of detached
converted coach house 100yds from
Vaynol Hall. First-floor comprises
spacious kitchen/diner, small sitting
room and bathroom/WC. Second-floor
comprises one double, one twin-bedded
room and one containing two pairs of
bunks; pine furniture throughout. 1000
acres of park, woodland and formal
gardens.

All year MWB out of season 2 days min,
8 mths max, 1 unit, 1–8 persons ◇ ◆
● fridge Electric Elec metered [WM
on premises] [TD on premises] Airing
cupboard in unit Iron in unit Ironing
board in unit HCE in unit CTV
⊕3 pin square 2P ▥ ♨(2m) Squash

⟷ ♀(1m) ▨(3m)

F The Beeches, Lawn Suite, Megans & Snowdon Flats
for bookings Mrs H W Chamberlain, The
Estate Office, Vaynol Park, Bangor,
Gwynedd ☎Bangor(0248)670966

The flats are located within Vaynol Hall
which is situated in a 1000 acres of park,
woodland, lawns and formal gardens.
Accommodation varies and all have
period furniture except The Beeches
which is furnished in pine. Situated on
Bangor side of Portdinorwic.

All year MWB out of season 2 days min,
8 mths max, 4 units, 1–4 persons ◇ ◆
● fridge Electric Elec metered
⊡ can be hired ☎ [WM on premises]
[TD on premises] Airing cupboard in
unit Iron in unit Ironing board in unit
HCE in unit CTV ⊕3 pin square 8P
▥ ♨(2m) Squash

⟷ ♀(1m) ▨(3m)

C E A Jones, *Tynyffridd Holiday Cottages*, Glasinfryn, Bangor, Gwynedd

Beautifully converted cottages in a
picturesque country setting, with
beamed ceilings and open-plan pine
staircase to bedrooms. Separate
bathroom/WC. Open-plan kitchen and
lounge. 3m SE of Bangor off B4409.

Mar-Oct MWB out of season 1wk min,
3 mths max, 6 units, 4–6 persons [◇]
no pets ⌀ (4 cottages)
●(2 cottages) fridge Electric
Gas/Elec metered ⊡ not provided
☎(1m) Airing cupboard in unit HCE in
unit TV ⊕3 pin square P ▥ ♨(1m)

⟷ ♀(2½m) ▨(2½m) ♬(2½m) ▨(2½m)

BANKFOOT
Tayside *Perthshire*
Map 11 NO03

Ca Hunter's Cabins
for bookings Mr B Hunter, Hunters
Lodge, Bankfoot, Perthshire
☎Bankfoot(0324)325

Group of six log cabins on their own in the
grounds of a popular restaurant. Each
comprises lounge/dining area, small
kitchenette, bathroom, a twin bedroom
and one with a single bed and two bunks.
An extra single bed can be set up in the
lounge. The interiors which are fully
timbered, are simple and functional.
Bankfoot is now by-passed by the A9,
which although still conveniently close
makes the environment pleasantly quiet.

MWB out of season 3 nights min, 6 units,
4–6 persons [◇] ◆ ◆ ⌀ fridge
Gas Gas inclusive ⊡ inclusive
☎(50yds) Iron on premises Ironing
board on premises HCE in unit
[Launderette on premises] TV
⊕3 pin square 50P ▥ ♨(200yds)
⯈Hard

⟷

See Dundee section for advert

Ch Mr B Hunter **Hunter's Lodge**
Bankfoot, Perthshire
☎Bankfoot(0324)325

Wing of five compact self-contained
chalets each with its own entrance
attached to restaurant and self-catering
complex. Accommodation comprises
small lounge with two convertible sofas,
small kitchen, twin or double bedroom,
and bathroom. One can eat either in the
lounge or kitchen. Small but comfortable
and ideal for short stays. Maid service on
request at additional charge.

All year MWB out of season 1 night min,
5 units, 1–4 persons ◇ [◆] ◆ ●
fridge ♨ Elec inclusive ⊡ inclusive
☎ Iron on premises Ironing board on
premises HCE in unit [Launderette on
premises] ⊕ ⊛ TV ⊕3 pin square
P ▥ ♨(500yds) ⯈Hard
⟷ ♀

BARMOUTH
Gwynedd
Map 6 SH61

C Glandwr Mill Cottage
for bookings Mrs F J Probert, Glandwr Mill
House, Glandwr, Barmouth, Gwynedd
LL42 1TG ☎Barmouth(0341)280071

17th-century stone mill cottage adjoining
Mill House. Well furnished and equipped
throughout. Accommodation comprising
lounge/dining room, kitchen, two double
bedrooms. Bathroom and WC. Set in
wooded valley overlooking attractive
rock garden. Set just off A496 half way
between Barmouth and Bontddu.

All year MWB out of season 2 days min,
6 wks max, 1 unit, 1–4 persons ◇ ●
fridge ♨ Elec metered ⊡ inclusive
☎ WM on premises SD on premises
TD on premises Airing cupboard in unit
Iron in unit Ironing board in unit HCE in
unit ⊕ ⊛ CTV ⊕3 pin square P 🏠
▥ ♨(2m)

⟷ ♀(2m) ▨(2m) ♬(2m)

Min£85pw Max£95pw

BARNSTAPLE
Devon
Map 3 ST33

F Mrs A M Bryant **Pine Hayes** Harford
Road, Landkey, Barnstaple, Devon
☎Swimbridge(0271)83376

First-floor flat located within modern
detached house set in large garden.
Accommodation comprises
lounge/diner, kitchen, two bedrooms
both with wash hand basins and
bathroom/WC.

6Mar–27Nov MWB out of season
1wk min, 4 wks max, 1 unit, 1–4 persons
[◇] ◆ ◆ no pets ● fridge ♨
Elec metered ⊡ not provided ☎(¼m)
WM on premises SD on premises Iron
on premises Ironing board on
premises HCE on premises ⊕ CTV
⊕3 pin square P ▥ ♨(¼m) Play area

⟷ δ (3m) ♀(3m) ▨(3m) ♬(3m)
▨(3m)

Min£60 Max£140pw

B 21 Walton Way Goodleigh Rise
for bookings Mrs Evans, Fair View,
Acland Cross, Landkey, Barnstaple,
Devon EX32 0LB
☎Swimbridge(0271183)226 due to
change to (0271)830226

Detached bungalow with small front and
rear gardens set on a large estate.
Comprises lounge/diner, kitchen,
bathroom, WC and three bedrooms.

All year MWB out of season 3 days min,
6 wks max, 1 unit, 1–6 persons no pets
● fridge ♨ Elec metered

30

□ not provided ☎(¼m) SD in unit
Airing cupboard in unit Iron in unit
Ironing board in unit HCE in unit ⊖
TV ⊕3pins in square 1P 1🏠 📺 ♨(½m)
⇔ 🛁(3m) ⚲(1½m) 🖵(1½m) ♫(1½m)
🎱(1½m)
Min£50 Max£120pw

BARRA Isle of, see under **Castlebay,
Earsary, Kentangaval**

BASFORD
Staffordshire
Map**7** SJ95

H **Churnet Grange Farm**
for bookings Mrs C M Pickford, Lowe Hill
Farm, Ashbourne Road, Leek, Staffs
☎Leek(0538)383035

*White-painted detached farmhouse in an
elevated position in rural surroundings.
Accommodation comprises lounge,
dining room, large kitchen and small
bedroom, with bunk beds. First floor
comprises a bathroom/WC, a large family
bedroom, a spacious triple-bedded room
and a small double.*

All year MWB out of season 2 days min,
1 unit, 10 persons ◆ ◎ fridge
Electric & open fires Elec metered
□ can be hired ☎ Airing cupboard in
unit Iron in unit Ironing board in unit
HCE in unit ⊖ TV ⊕3pins in square 6P
1🏠 📺 ♨(m)
⇔ ♪(1½m) ⚲(½m) 🖵(3m) 🎱(3m)
Min£50 Max£130pw

BASSENTHWAITE
Cumbria
Map**11** NY23

C Mrs P Trafford **Bassenthwaite Hall
Farm** Bassenthwaite, Keswick, Cumbria
☎Bassenthwaite Lake(059681)393

*A converted cottage adjoining a
farmhouse, on the edge of the village.
Comprising of lounge/diner, with local
stone fireplace, kitchen, one double
bedroom and one family bedroom.*

Etr–Nov MWB 2 days min, 1 mth max,
1 unit, 5 persons [◇] ◆ ◆ no pets
◎ fridge Electric & coal fires
Elec metered □ can be hired
☎(50yds) WM in unit SD in unit Airing
cupboard in unit Iron HCE in unit TV
⊕3pins in square 6P 📺 ♨(m)
⇔ 🛁(3m) ⚲(20yds)
Min£45 Max£75pw (Low)
Min£65 Max£95pw (High)

BEAULIEU
Hampshire
Map**4** SU30

C **Culverley Old Farm Cottage**
for bookings Mrs V M Parker, Culverley
Old Farm House, Beaulieu,
Brockenhurst, Hants
☎Beaulieu(0590)612260

*Small detached country cottage with
own garden, quietly situated in the New
Forest. Accommodation comprises
sitting room with open fireplace, kitchen*

*and dining room, two bedrooms, one
twin, one double-bedded, and bathroom
with WC. Follow Lyndhurst road from
Beaulieu after 2m, cross white-railed
bridge and turn sharp right for gravel
track to cottage and farm. Livery stables
available adjacent to cottage.*

Apr–Nov 1 wk min, 2 mths max, 1 unit,
1–6 persons, nc2 ◎ fridge Electric &
open fires Elec charged for
□ not provided ☎ Airing cupboard in
unit Iron in unit Ironing board in unit
⊖ CTV ⊕3pins in square P ♨(1½m)
🖙Hard
⇔ ⚲(1½m) 🖵(1½m) ♫(1½m)
Min£90 Max£140pw

BEAULY
Highland *Inverness-shire*
Map**14** NH54

Ch **Brackenbrae & Burnbank**
for bookings Mr J MacLennan, Inchrory,
Beauly, Inverness-shire
☎Beauly(0463)782352

*Burnbank and Brackenbrae are two,
almost identical wood chalets in the
attractive grounds of the owner's house.
The chalets are well managed and have
two bedrooms, kitchen/living room,
bathroom and balcony. The site is 1½m
from Beauly overlooking Beauly firth, the
Black Isle and Inverness.*

All year MWB out of season 1 wk(2 wks
Jul & Aug) min, 2 units, 2–6 persons [◆
◆] ◎ fridge Electric □ can be
hired ☎(1m) Iron in unit Ironing board
in unit HCE in unit ⊖ TV
⊕3pins in square P 📺 ♨(1½m) Pony
trekking & fishing
⇔ 🛁(3m) ⚲(1½m)
Min£45 Max£100pw

C **Cuil-na-Caillaich** Mains of Aigas
for bookings Mrs P Masheter, Mains of
Aigas, Beauly, Inverness-shire
☎Beauly(046371)2423

*Fully modernised, stone-built cottage
standing on hillside above farm.
Accommodation comprises lounge,
dining room, kitchen, double bedroom
and bunk-bedded room. There is a
convertible settee in the lounge. Situated
5m W of Beauly on the A831 and then by a
long drive.*

Mar–Nov MWB out of season 1 wk min,
4 wks max, 1 unit, 1–6 persons ◆ ◆
no pets ◎ fridge Electric
Elec metered □ not provided ☎(1½m)
WM on premises SD on premises
Airing cupboard on premises Iron on
premises Ironing board on premises
HCE in unit ⊕3pins in square P 📺
♨(5m)

F **Pond Cottage, Old Dairy & Old
Stable Flats** Mains of Aigas
for bookings Mrs P Masheter, Mains of
Aigas, Beauly, Inverness-shire
☎Beauly(046371)2423

*Three recently converted farm courtyard
flats in an ideal position for use as a
touring base. All flats sleep up to six
persons. Pond Cottage Flat has three
twin- or double-bedded rooms and a
bathroom. Old Dairy and Old Stable have
one double- and one twin-bedded room
and a shower-room. Situated 5m W of
Beauly on A831.*

Mar–Nov MWB out of season 1 wk min,
4 wks max, 3 units, 1–6 persons ◆ ◆
no pets ◎ fridge Electric
Elec metered □ not provided ☎(1½m)
WM in unit SD in unit Airing cupboard
on premises Iron on premises Ironing
board on premises HCE in unit ⊖
⊕3pins in square 10P ♨(5m)

C **Sunny Brae**
for bookings Mr J MacLennan, Inchrory,
Beauly, Inverness-shire
☎Beauly(0463)782352

*A pleasant, stone-built cottage above
and behind the owner's cottage. Three
bedrooms, living room and separate
kitchen with dining area. Extensive views
over the Beauly Valley with the Black Isle
in the distance. 1½m from Beauly on the
A9.*

All year MWB out of season 1 wk min Jul
& Aug, 1 unit, 1–5 persons [◆ ◆] ◎
fridge Electric & coal fires □ can be
hired ☎(1m) Iron in unit Ironing board
in unit HCE in unit ⊖ TV
⊕3pins in square P 📺 ♨(1½m) Pony
trekking & fishing
⇔ 🛁(3m) ⚲(1½m)
Min£45 Max£110pw

BEELEY
Derbyshire
Map**8** SK26

F **The Beeches**
for bookings Mrs J Statham, Brookside,
Beeley, Matlock, Derbyshire
☎Darley Dale(062983)2347

*A ground-floor flat in a modernised stone-
built detached house, alongside a small
brook in the tiny and pleasant village of
Beeley. Décor and furnishings of a good
standard including one twin-bedded
room with bunk beds, lounge with
convertible bed settee, bathroom/WC
and kitchen/dining room.*

All year MWB 3 days min 1 mth max,
1 unit, 1–4 persons, nc5 ◎ fridge
Electric Elec metered □ not provided
☎(100yds) Airing cupboard in unit Iron
in unit Ironing board in unit HCE in unit
⊖ CTV ⊕3pins in square 2P 📺
♨(100yds)
⇔ ⚲(100yds)
Max£75pw

1982 prices quoted throughout
gazetteer

BEMBRIDGE
Isle of Wight
Map 4 SZ68

F Mr & Mrs R L Rowsell **Gainsborough Court** Lane End, Bembridge, Isle of Wight PO35 5SZ
☎Bembridge(098387)2363

Edwardian country house, part of which has been converted into five self-contained apartments with modern fixtures and fittings. Two of the flats have one bedroom, two have two bedrooms (and one has three bedrooms). All units have lounge, kitchen and bathroom/WC. (One has shower instead of bath.) Situated in quiet residential area on eastern side of Bembridge, 250yds from the beach.

All year MWB out of season
1wk (1night winter)min, 6mths max,
5units, 1–8persons ◇ ◇ ◆ ◉
fridge Electric Elecmetered
▣notprovided ☎(½m) SD on
premises Iron in unit Ironing board in
unit HCE in unit ⊖ TV
⊕3pinsquare P ▥ ▟(400yds)
↭ ♀(½m)

Min£62 Max£71pw (Low)
Min£141 Max£151pw (High)

H **Home Cottage** Howgate Road
for bookings Mr & Mrs E I Baker,
3 Beachfield Road, Sandown, Isle of
Wight ☎Sandown(0983)403958

A detached house with rear garden, situated in a quiet area with distant sea views. Accommodation comprises kitchen, breakfast room and lounge on ground-floor, with three bedrooms and bathroom/WC on first-floor.

All year MWB out of season 1wk min,
1mth max, 1unit, 2–5persons ◇
nopets ⌀ fridge ♜ Electric
Gas/Elecmetered ▣inclusive
☎(250yds) Airing cupboard in unit Iron
in unit Ironing board in unit HCE in unit
⊖ TV ⊕3pinsquare P ▟(200yds)
↭ ♀(500yds)

Min£55 Max£65pw (Low)
Min£110 Max£135pw (High)

BERRYNARBOR
Devon
Map 2 SS54

Ch **Sandaway Holiday Park (Chalets)**
for bookings Mr L F Taylor, Sandaway
Holiday Park, Berrynarbor, Ilfracombe,
Devon ☎Combe Martin(027188)3555

These eight chalets of modern design are in 20-acre caravan and chalet park on the coast and close to own private beach. The accommodation consists of two bedrooms, kitchen, bathroom and lounge/diner with double studio couch. Fine views of sea and rolling countryside, with the village of Combe Martin ½m away.

15 Mar-Oct MWB out of season
2nights min, 1mth max, 8units,
2–6persons [◇] ◉ fridge Electric
Elecmetered ▣can be hired
☎(130yds) Airing cupboard in unit
[Iron on premises] Ironing board on
premises HCE in unit [Launderette
within 300yds] ⊖ CTV
⊕3pinsquare P ▟(30yds)
↭ ♀(10yds) ▨(½m) ♫(½m)

BERWICK-UPON-TWEED
Northumberland
Map 12 NT95

H **3 Bowers Crescent**
for bookings Mr E Sutherland-Loveday,
The Old Railway Station, Scremerston,
Berwick-upon-Tweed, Northd
☎Berwick-upon-Tweed(0289)7932

A self-contained house with small garden. Situated in a residential area near the River Tweed and within easy distance of the town centre. Accommodation consists of lounge, with two single beds and kitchen. On the first floor, there is a double bedroom with two single beds (a child's cot can be provided) and bathroom with WC.

All year 1wk min, 7mths max, 1unit,
2–4persons [◇] ◇ ◆ ⌀ fridge
Electric Gas/Elecmetered
▣inclusive ☎(½m) HCE in unit ⊖
TV ⊕3pinsquare ⊕3pin round
▟(300yds)

↭ ▿▨(1m) ♀(1m) ▨(1m) ♫(1m)
▨(1m)

Max£55pw (Low)
Max£75pw (High)

F **Dunrobin Holiday Flats** Main Street,
Spittal
for bookings Mr & Mrs A H Briggs,
Woodville, 139 Main Street, Spittal,
Berwick-upon-Tweed, Northd TD15 1RP
☎Berwick-upon-Tweed(0289)6261

A row of stone-faced cottages in Main Street divided into four ground-floor and four first-floor flats of one and two bedrooms and some having studio couch in the lounge, sleeping from two to six persons. Each unit contains a large living room, bathroom/WC or shower and separate WC and kitchen, or in two flats, lounge/kitchen. Rooms are mostly very spacious and ground-floor flats are suitable for disabled persons. Near beach and river, and ideal base for touring.

All year 1wk min, 2mths max, 8units,
2–6persons ◇ nopets ⌀ ◉
fridge Electric Gas/Elecmetered
▣notprovided ☎(100yds) Airing
cupboard in unit HCE in unit ⊕ TV
⊕3pinsquare ⊕3pin round
▟(30yds) Angling
↭ ▿▨(1½m) ♀(100yds) ▨(1½m)
♫(1½m) ▨(1½m)

Min£25 Max£123pw

C **3 Ivy Place**
for bookings Mr E Sutherland-Loveday,
The Old Railway Station, Scremerston,
Berwick-upon-Tweed, Northd
☎Berwick-upon-Tweed(0289)7932

Small cottage centrally situated. All accommodation is on ground-floor and comprises a twin-bedded room (a child's cot can be provided), lounge with one double bed, kitchen/diner and bathroom.

All year 1wk min, 7mths max, 1unit,
2–4persons [◇] ◇ ◆ ⌀ Electric
Gas/Elecmetered ▣inclusive
☎(150yds) HCE in unit ⊖ TV
⊕3pinsquare ⊕3pin round ▥
▟(60yds)
↭ ▿▨(1m) ♀(1m) ▨(1m) ♫(1m)
▨(1m)

Max£55pw (Low)
Max£75pw (High)

H 9 Palace Street
for bookings Mr E Sutherland-Loveday,
The Old Railway Station, Scremerston,
Northd ☎Berwick-upon-Tweed(0289)7932

A large town house situated in the town centre, offering spacious accommodation. The ground-floor comprises kitchen, dining room and one twin-bedded room. The lounge is on the first-floor along with one twin-bedded room and bathroom. The second-floor has two bedrooms, one with three single beds.

All year 1wk min, 7mths max, 1unit,
2–9persons [◇] ◈ ◆ ◔ fridge
Electric Gas/Elec metered
⬛inclusive ☎(200yds) HCE in unit
☉ TV ⊕3pin square ⊕3pin round
♨(100yds)
↔ ♒(1m) ♀(1m) ⬛(1m) ♫(1m)
🐾(1m)

Max£95pw (Low)
Max£115pw (High)

H 22 The Parade
for bookings Mr E Sutherland-Loveday,
The Old Railway Station, Scremerston,
Berwick-upon-Tweed(0289)7932
☎Berwick-upon-Tweed(0289)7932

A large town house centrally situated in an attractive part of the town. Accommodation comprises kitchen/diner, lounge and one double-bedded room on first-floor. Second-floor has a double-bedded room and one with three single beds, bathroom and separate WC.

All year 1wk min, 7mths max, 1unit,
2–7persons [◇] ◈ ◆ ◔ Electric
Gas/Elec metered ⬛inclusive
☎(250yds) HCE in unit ☉ TV
⊕3pin square ⊕3pin round
♨(125yds)
↔ ♒(1m) ♀(1m) ⬛(1m) ♫(1m)
🐾(1m)

Max£75pw (Low)
Max£95pw (High)

F 95 Ravensdowne
for bookings Mr E Sutherland-Loveday,
The Old Railway Station, Scremerston,
Berwick-upon-Tweed, Northd
☎Berwick-upon-Tweed(0289)7932

A spacious self-contained ground-floor flat, centrally situated. Accommodation comprises a large kitchen/diner, lounge, bathroom/WC and two twin-bedded rooms, lounge has two single beds.

All year 1wk min, 7mths max, 1unit,
2–6persons [◇] ◈ ◆ ◔ fridge
Electric Gas/Elec metered
⬛inclusive ☎(250yds) HCE in unit
☉ TV ⊕3pin square ⊕3pin round
♨(125yds)
↔ ♒(1m) ♀(1m) ⬛(1m) ♫(1m)
🐾(1m)

Max£65pw (Low)
Max£85pw (High)

BEXHILL-ON-SEA
East Sussex
Map5 TQ70

H Quebec Close
for bookings Mrs H Cummings, 171
Cooden Drive, Bexhill-on-Sea, E Sussex
TN393AQ ☎Cooden(042 43)2999

Modern semi-detached house situated in a cul-de-sac, 1m from town centre and sea. Comfortable accommodation comprises lounge/diner, kitchen, WC on first floor.

All year MWB out of season 2wks min,
6mths max, 1unit, 2–7persons no pets
◉ fridge Gas and Electric
Elec metered ⬛can be hired ☎ WM
in unit SD in unit Airing cupboard in
unit Iron in unit Ironing board in unit
HCE in unit ☉ ⊛ CTV
⊕3pin square P ⬛ ⬛ ♨(½m)
↔ ♀(½m) ⬛(1m) ♫(1m) 🐾(1m)

Min£70 Max£100pw (Low)
Min£140 Max£175pw (High)

BICKLEIGH (Nr Tiverton)
Devon
Map3 SS90

C CC Ref 679
for bookings Character Cottages
(Holidays) Ltd, 34, Fore Street, Sidmouth,
Devon EX108AQ
☎Sidmouth(03955)77001

Situated in the west wing of a 16th-century farmhouse. Accommodation comprises a first-floor with large comfortable lounge, one twin-bedded room, one double bedroom and bathroom/WC, and ground-floor with kitchen/diner and a twin-bedded room.

mid May–mid Sep 1wk min, 1mth max,
1unit, 2–6persons ◉ fridge Electric
Elec metered ⬛can be hired ☎ WM
in unit SD in unit Airing cupboard in
unit Iron in unit Ironing board in unit
HCE in unit ☉ TV ⊕3pin square
⊕2pin round P ⬛ ⬛ ♨(½m)
↔ ♀

Min£123 Max£136pw

BICTON
Shropshire
Map8 SJ41

B Inglenook Villa Lane
for bookings Mrs J M Mullineux, Fach-Hir,
Brooks, Welshpool, Powys SY218QP
☎Tregynon(068687)361

A semi-detached bungalow with a small enclosed garden located off the main A5, in a quiet cul-de-sac. The accommodation comprises lounge/dining room, kitchen, two double bedrooms and a bathroom/WC.

All year 1wk min, 3mths max, 1unit,
1–4persons, nc8 no pets ◉ fridge
Electric Elec metered ⬛inclusive
☎(60yds) WM in unit SD in unit Airing
cupboard i1n unit Iron in unit Ironing

board in unit HCE in unit ☉ ⊛ CTV
⊕3pin square 2P 1⬛ ⬛ ♨(⅓m)
↔ ♒(3m) ♀(½m) ⬛(3m) ♫(3m)
🐾(3m)

Min£60 Max£80pw

BIDEFORD
Devon
Map2 SS42

F CC Ref 538E
for bookings Character Cottages
(Holidays) Ltd, 34, Fore Street, Sidmouth,
Devon EX108AQ
☎Sidmouth(03955)77001

First-floor flat in a Georgian residence with good views. Accommodation comprises entrance hall, lounge/diner, kitchen, two twin-bedded rooms and bathroom/WC.

All year MWB out of season 1wk min,
1mth max, 1unit, 2–4persons ◇
no pets ◉ fridge Electric
Elec inclusive ⬛not provided ☎ Iron
in unit Ironing board in unit HCE in unit
TV ⊕3pin square P ⬛ ⬛ ♨(⅓m)
↔ ♒(2m) ♀(1m) ⬛(1m) ♫(1m)
🐾(1m)

Min£65 Max£90pw (Low)
Min£108 Max£128pw (High)

BIGGAR
Strathclyde *Lanarkshire*
Map11 NT03

C Spittal Farm Cottage
for bookings Mrs Murray, Spittal Farm,
Biggar, Lanarks ML126HB
☎Biggar(0899)20039

One semi-detached single storey 19th-century farm cottage built of stone and standing on a minor road at the entrance to the farm. Reached via B7016 Biggar–Broughton road. The cottage comprises sitting room/dining room, a double room, a twin-bedded room, modern kitchen and bathroom.

Apr–Oct MWB out of season 1wk min,
1mth max, 1unit, 1–6persons ◇ ◆
◉ fridge Electric Elec metered
⬛can be hired ☎(1m) SD in unit Iron
in unit Ironing board in unit HCE in unit
TV ⊕3pin square 2P ⬛ ♨(2m)
↔ ♒(2m) ♀(2m) ⬛(2m)

Min£45 Max£60pw

BILBSTER
Highland *Caithness*
Map15 ND25

C Ingimster
for bookings Mrs Adamson, Lealands,
Bilbster, Wick, Caithness
☎Watten(095582)237

Isolated country cottage surrounded by farmland and reached via a rough farm track; access is across a little-used railway line. It comprises kitchen/dining room, lounge with convertible settee, one double-bedded room and one family bedroom. The hamlet of Bilbster borders the A882, 5m W of Wick and Ingimster lies between it and the B874. →

All year MWB 1wk min, 1unit,
1–6persons ◊ ◆ ◉ fridge
Electric Elec metered Ⓛcan be hired
☎(3m) Airing cupboard in unit Iron in
unit Ironing board in unit HCE in unit
TV ⊕3pin square P 🏠 ♨(3m)
⇔ ⚲(3m)
Max£40pw (Low)
Max£60pw (High)

C Roadside Cottage
for bookings Mr N S Miller, The Red
House, Auchingreoch Avenue,
Johnstone, Renfrewshire PA5 0RJ
☎Johnstone(0505)20279

*Neat little cottage situated on the main
Wick to Thurso road 5m W of Wick. It has
a lounge/dining room with small kitchen
leading off, one twin-bedded room, one
double-bedded room and one single-
bedded room. It is set amidst farmland
and has a well-tended garden.*

All year 1wk min, 6mths max, 1unit,
1–5persons no pets ◉ fridge
Electric Elec inclusive Ⓛcan be hired
☎(3m) Airing cupboard in unit Iron in
unit Ironing board on premises HCE in
unit ❂ TV ⊕3pin square P 🔲
♨(3m)
⇔ ⚲(3m)
Min£35 Max£40pw (Low)
Min£45 Max£55pw (High)

BILTON-IN-AINSTY
North Yorkshire
Map **8** SE45

C Lodge Cottage
for bookings Mr G K Raynar, Bilton Hall,
Bilton-in-Ainsty, York YO5 8NP
☎Tockwith(09015)334

*Two-storey cottage with large entrance
hall, attractive lounge, dining room,
kitchen, two twin-bedded rooms,
bathroom/WC. Off the B1224 at the
entrance to the driveway to the Hall.*

All year MWB out of season 1wk min,
4wks max, 1unit, 1–4persons ◆
no pets ◉ fridge Electric
Elec metered Ⓛnot provided ☎(1m)
Airing cupboard in unit Iron in unit
Ironing board in unit HCE in unit TV
⊕3pin square 3P 🏠 🔲 ♨(1½m)
⤵Hard
⇔ ⚲
Min£40 Max£65pw (Low)
Min£70 Max£95pw (High)

BINEGAR
Somerset
Map **3** ST64

F Forecourt & Lawnside
for bookings Mrs A E Rich, Whitnell Farm,
Binegar, Gurney Slade, Bath, Avon
BA3 4UF ☎Oakhill(0749)840277

*Two flats situated in stone farmhouse on a
working farm with fine views of open
countryside. The ground-floor flat sleeps
up to seven, and has a comfortable
beamed lounge with inglenook fireplace,
kitchen with dining area and bathroom.
First-floor flat comprises two bedrooms,*

*lounge, kitchen and bathroom. Use of
garden.*

All year MWB out of season 3days min,
4wks max, 2units, 1–7persons, [◊] ◆
no pets ◉ fridge 🍴 Elec metered
Ⓛcan be hired ☎(1½m) Airing
cupboard in unit Iron in unit Ironing
board in unit HCE in unit ❂ CTV
⊕3pin square 6P 🔲 ♨(2m)
⇔ ♒(3m) ⚲(1½m)
Min£50 Max£90pw (Low)
Min£80 Max£170pw (High)

BIRNAM
Tayside *Perthshire*
Map **11** NO04

C & F Norman Hall-Smith **Erigmore
Caravan Park Ltd** Birnam, Dunkeld,
Perthshire ☎Dunkeld(03502)236

*Six apartments of varying sizes
contained within Erigmore House which
also consists of reception, bar and
restaurant for the caravan site contained
in its grounds. The house has an
interesting history dating from 1823. Also
30yds from Erigmore House is a cottage,
three bedroomed with lounge/dining
room, kitchen. Erigmore House is off the
B898, 300yds from the main A9.*

Apr–Oct 3days min, 6mths max, 7units,
1–5persons ◊ ◆ ◉ fridge
Electric Elec metered (except cottage)
Ⓛcan be hired ☎ HCE in unit
[Launderette on premises] ❂ TV
⊕3pin square P 🔲 ♨(2m) Games
room
⇔ ♒(2½m)
Min£35 Max£75pw (Low)
Min£55 Max£140pw (High)

BISHOP MONKTON
North Yorkshire
Map **8** SE36

C & F Mr & Mrs E C Taylor **Orchard
House** Bishop Monkton, Harrogate, N
Yorks HG3 3QP
☎Bishop Monkton(076581)254

*Orchard Lodge is an 18th-century stone-
built cottage in attractive position and
comprises three double bedrooms, living
room, kitchen and bathroom. Orchard
House Flat is a converted mews type
property with lots of character and set in a
delightful situation and comprises two
bedrooms, living room, kitchen and
bathroom.*

All year MWB out of season 1wk min,
1mth max, 2units, 1–6persons, nc5 in
flat ◉ fridge Electric & Gas
Gas/Elec metered Ⓛcan be hired
☎(100yds) Airing cupboard in unit Iron
in unit Ironing board in unit HCE in unit
TV ⊕3pin square 🔲 ♨(40yds)
⇔ ⚲
Min£85 Max£110pw

BISHOPSTEIGNTON
Devon
Map **3** SB93

F Mr J A Coney **Bishopsteignton
House Holiday Flats** (No's 3, 4 & 5)
Newton Road, Bishopsteignton,
Teignmouth, Devon TQ14 9SD
☎Teignmouth(06267)5270

*Detached manor house in quiet, elevated
position, offering magnificent views
across estuary. Three of five flats
comprising kitchen, bathroom/WC,
lounge/dining room.*

15May-25Sep 1wk min, 1mth max,
3units, 2–8persons, nc4 no pets ◉
fridge Electric Elec inclusive Ⓛcan
be hired ☎ Iron on premises Ironing
board on premises HCE in unit ❂
[TV] ⊕3pin square P 🔲 ♨(300yds)
⇔ ⚲(50yds) ♬(50yds) 🐾(2¼m)
Min£37 Max£56pw (Low)
Min£52 Max£78pw (High)

BISHOPSTONE
Hereford & Worcester
Map **3** SO44

C Church Cottage
for bookings Mrs M Jenkins, Blackbush
Farm, Abbey Dore, Hereford
☎Golden Valley(0981)240281

*Semi-detached brick-built cottage in
rural, peaceful location. Comprises a
lounge, a large dining area, kitchen and
bathroom with WC and wash hand basin.
Upstairs there are two double bedrooms
and one twin-bedded room.*

All year MWB out of season 1wk min,
6mths max, 1unit, 1–6persons ◆ ◆
◉ fridge Electric Elec metered
Ⓛnot provided ☎(½m) Airing cupboard
in unit HCE in unit ❂ TV
⊕3pin square P ♨(1½m)
⇔ ⚲(1½m)
Min£35 Max£70pw

BLACKBOROUGH
Devon
Map **3** ST00

**C Coshes Garden & Cinders
Cottages**
for bookings Mr J L Donnithorne, South
Farm, Blackborough, Cullompton, Devon
☎Hemyock(0823)680483

*A pair of semi-detached, one-storey
cottages converted from farm buildings.
Both have living room/kitchen and
bathroom/WC. Cinders cottage has one
double bedroom, one twin-bedroom and
one bedroom with bunks. Coshes
Garden cottage has one double
bedroom and one twin-bedded room.
They are 7m from M5 motorway junction
28 and 8m from Honiton.*

All year MWB out of season 3days min,
2mths max, 2units, 2–6persons [◊]
◆ ◆ ◉ fridge Electric & Calor gas
Elec metered Ⓛcan be hired ☎(¾m)
Airing cupboard in unit Iron in
unit Ironing board in unit HCE in unit
❂ CTV ⊕3pin square P 🔲 ♨(5m)

⌐(heated) Fishing & pony riding, games room

⊕ ♀(3m)

Min £38 Max £130pw (Low)
Min £140 Max £193pw (High)

B South Farm Bungalow

for bookings Mr J L Donnithorne, South Farm, Blackborough, Cullompton, Devon ☎Hemyock(0823)680483

A modern brick bungalow lying some 75yds from the farmhouse. The accommodation comprises one double bedroom, one twin-bedded room, two bedrooms with bunk beds, large kitchen/diner, living room with open fire and bathroom/WC. It is 7m from M5 motorway junction 28 and 8m from Honiton.

All year MWB out of season 3 days min, 2 mths max, 1 unit, 2–8 persons [◇] ◆ ◆ ⊛ fridge Electric & log fires Elec metered ⎁can be hired ☎ Airing cupboard in unit Iron in unit Ironing board in unit HCE in unit ⊖ CTV ⊕3pin square P ▥ ♨(5m) ⌐(heated) Fishing & pony riding, games room

⊕ ♀(3m)

Min £38 Max £130pw (Low)
Min £140 Max £193pw (High)

BLACKLUNANS
Tayside *Perthshire*
Map **15** NO16

C Drumore Self-catering Blacklunans, Blairgowrie, Perthshire PH10 7LA ☎Blacklunans(025082)218

A terrace of three traditional cottages set in a quiet location 1½m E of A93 on an unclass road signposted 'Drumore & Blacklunans'. The cottages consist of sitting room with convertible couch, kitchen/dining room and two twin bedrooms on the first floor. An ideal location for skiing.

All year MWB out of season 3 days min, 3 units 1–7 persons ◆ ⊛ fridge Electric Elec inclusive up to 100 units ⎁inclusive ☎(½m) Iron in unit Ironing board in unit HCE in unit ⊖ CTV ⊕3pin square 6P ♨(6m) Fishing & pony trekking

⊕ ♀(2m)

Min £58.50 Max £95pw (Low)
Min £76.50 Max £130pw (High)

BLACKPOOL
Lancashire
Map **7** SD33

F Mr & Mrs J R H Battersby **Havelock Court Flats** 117 Coronation Street, Blackpool, Lancs ☎Blackpool(0253)64204 or 23218

Brick-built conversion of former boarding houses situated in a fine position in the centre of town close to the Central Beach and Tower but not on the seafront. The 18 recommended flats have separate kitchens and ten have bathroom/WC and eight have shower/WC.

All year MWB out of season 2 nights min, 18 units, 2–5 persons [◆] [◆] no pets ⊛ fridge ♨ Elec metered ⎁inclusive ☎ Iron on premises Ironing board on premises HCE on premises [Launderette within 300yds] ⊖ CTV ⊕3pin square [P] ♨(20yds)

⊕ ♀(100yds) ▥(100yds) ♫(100yds) ▨(300yds)

Min £35 Max £130pw

BLAIRGOWRIE
Tayside *Perthshire*
Map **11** NO14

Ca,Ch Altamount Chalet Park
Blairgowrie, Perthshire
☎Blairgowrie(0250)3324

Detached, semi-detached timbered chalets and log cabins. All have open-plan lounge/diner with patio windows and kitchen area. The chalets have either two or three bedrooms and showers. The cabins have one bedroom and bathroom. Interiors are natural wood with matching furnishings. Within walking distance of town centre and shielded by pine trees.

All year MWB out of season 2 nights min, 18 units, 1–8 persons [◇ ◆ ◆] ⊛ fridge ♨ Elec metered ⎁can be hired ☎(400yds) Airing cupboard in unit Iron on premises Ironing board on premises HCE in unit ⊖ TV ⊕3pin square P ▥ ♨(400yds) ⤙(Hard ƌ

⊕ ♬(1m) ♀(400yds) ▥(400yds) ▨(400yds)

Min £65 Max £175pw

BLEDINGTON
Gloucestershire
Map **4** SP22

C Chestnut Cottage
for bookings Mrs M Forbes, Chestnuts, Bledington, Oxford, Oxon OX7 6XQ ☎Kingham(060871)308

Small semi-detached cottage with garden, overlooking village green. Accommodation consists of kitchen, lounge and two twin-bedded rooms. Opposite pub.

All year 1 wk min, 3 mths max, 1 unit, 1–4 persons, nc10 no pets ⊛ fridge ♨ Elec metered ⎁not provided ☎(200yds) Airing cupboard in unit Iron in unit Ironing board in unit HCE in unit ⊖ CTV ⊕3pin square 1P ▥ ♨(10yds)

⊕ ♀(10yds)

1982 prices quoted throughout gazetteer

BLOCKLEY
Gloucestershire
Map **4** SP13

C Badgers Den & Moles Cottage
for bookings Robert Greenstock, Lower Farm House, Blockley, Moreton-in-Marsh, Glos.
☎Blockley(0386)700237

Two cottages created from a range of period farm buildings in the natural beauty of the Cotswolds. Each cottage has been furnished in styles incorporating original features, both are similar in design having three bedrooms (one double, one twin and one single bedroom). Kitchen, comfortable sitting room/dining room, bathroom/WC and a second WC downstairs. Serviced twice a week.

All year MWB 2 nights min, 3 mths max, 2 units, 5 persons [◇] ◆ ◆ no pets ⊛ fridge ♨ Elec inclusive ⎁inclusive ☎ WM on premises SD on premises TD on premises Airing cupboard in unit Iron in unit ironing board in unit HCE in unit ⊖ CTV ⊕3pin square 2P ♨(½m)

⊕ ♬ ♀(½m)

Min £195.50 Max £316.25pw

C Toads Hall
for bookings Robert Greenstock, Lower Farm House, Blockley, Moreton-in-Marsh, Glos.
☎Blockley(0386)700237

Attractive and spacious cottage comprising kitchen, comfortable lounge and dining area. Three bedrooms upstairs, one double, one twin and one single, with fitted furniture and beams. Bathroom/WC and a second WC downstairs. Fine views of grounds. Serviced twice a week.

All year MWB 2 nights min, 3 mths max, 1 unit, 6 persons [◇] ◆ ◆ no pets ⊛ fridge ♨ Elec inclusive ⎁inclusive ☎ WM on premises SD on premises TD on premises Airing cupboard in unit Iron in unit Ironing board in unit HCE in unit ⊖ CTV ⊕3pin square 2P ♨(½m)

⊕ ♬ ♀(½m)

Min £195.50 Max £345pw

C Rattys Retreat
for bookings Robert Greenstock, Lower Farm House, Blockley, Moreton-in-Marsh, Glos.
☎Blockley(0386)700237

Designed for two people, open-plan living room with a step to dining room and fitted kitchen. Bedroom forms a gallery with exposed timbers and Victorian half tester and bathroom en suite. Views across the grounds to the brook. Serviced twice a week.

All year MWB 2 nights min, 3 mths max, 1 unit, 2 persons [◇] ◆ ◆ no pets ⊛ fridge ♨ Elec inclusive ⎁inclusive ☎ WM on premises SD on premises TD on premises Airing cupboard in unit Iron in unit Ironing →

board in unit HCE in unit ⊙ CTV ⊕3pin square 2P 🏪(¼m)

⊖ ♂18 ♀(¼m)

Min£115 Max£201.25pw

C Otters Abode & Willow End
for bookings Robert Greenstock, Lower Farm House, Blockley, Moreton-in-Marsh, Glos.
☎Blockley(0386)700237

Spacious cottage featuring a galleried living and dining room separated from the kitchen by a cast-iron spiral staircase, leading upstairs to a double bedroom with timbered roof. Second bedroom is on the ground floor and has twin beds. Bathroom and WC with Shower. Serviced twice a week.

All year MWB 2nights min, 3mths max, 1unit, 4persons [◇] ◆ ◆ no pets ◎ fridge ▦ Elec inclusive ⊡inclusive ☎ WM on premises SD on premises TD on premises Airing cupboard in unit Iron in unit Ironing board in unit HCE in unit ⊙ CTV ⊕3pin square 2P 🏪(¼m)

⊖ ♂18 ♀(¼m)

Min£161 Max£281.75pw

H Old Mill Dene School Lane
for bookings Mrs W V Dare, 61 Kingston Lane, Teddington, Middlesex
☎01-977 2502 or Blockley(0386)700457

Four-hundred-year-old house comfortably furnished and decorated to a high standard, well fitted kitchen with breakfast area, dining room, separate sitting room with open fire. First-floor accommodation with two twin-bedded rooms, bath, WC and shower; second floor with one double-bedded room and a spacious room with bunk beds. The house stands on the edge of the village, has a beautiful garden, fine views and borders a trout pool (dangerous for toddlers) and stream. Additional folding beds available.

All year MWB out of season 1wk min, 1unit, 8–10persons [◇] ◆ ◆ no pets ◎ fridge ▦(metered) Elec inclusive ⊡can be hired ☎ Airing cupboard in unit Iron in unit Ironing board in unit HCE in unit ⊙ TV ⊕3pin square P 🏪(300yds) Play area

⊖ ♀(300yds)

Min£160 Max£260pw

BLOXWORTH
Dorset
Map**3** SY89

C Cottage
for bookings Mr & Mrs S K Chattey, Bloxworth Lodge, Bloxworth, Wareham, Dorset BH20 7EE ☎Morden(092945)360

A delightful thatched cottage set in ¾ acre garden with fine views of country side; 2 miles off A35 Poole to Bere Regis road–2½ miles from Bere Regis. Accommodation comprises of large farmhouse-style kitchen with dining table, two lounges furnished in comfortable style, four bedrooms all with wash-hand basins, well-appointed bathroom.

Etr–Sep 1wk min, 1mth max, 1unit, 1–8persons ◇ ◆ ◆ ◎ fridge ▦ Elec metered ⊡not provided ☎(200yds) WM in unit SD in unit Airing cupboard in unit Iron in unit Ironing board in unit HCE in unit ⊙ CTV ⊕3pin square 3P 1🏠 🏪(2½m)

⊖ ♀(2m)

Min£58 Max£195pw

BOAT OF GARTEN
Highland *Inverness-shire*
Map**14** NH91

H Broom Lodge Drumullie
for bookings Mrs M Hamilton, 3 Maitland Drive, Torrance, Glasgow G64 ☎Torrance(036089)2145

House containing four apartments. One unit listed has a single garage and enclosed garden. Accommodation comprises lounge/dining room with coal fires, modern kitchen, bathroom and two double bedrooms on ground floor. First floor comprises one twin/triple-bedded room. Situated ½m from Boat of Garten on A95 Grantown road.

All year MWB out of season 3days min, 4wks max, 1unit, 1–7persons [◇] ◆ ◆ no pets ◎ fridge Electric & coal fires Elec metered ⊡not provided ☎ WM in unit SD in unit Airing cupboard in unit Iron in unit Ironing board in unit HCE in unit ⊙ TV ⊕3pin square 2P 1🏠 🏪(½m)

⊖ ♂18(½m) ♀(½m)

Min£60 Max£85pw (Low)
Min£95 Max£130pw (High)

BODMIN
Cornwall
Map**2** SX06

B & C Barn Cottage, The Coach House & The Tallet
for bookings J & D Nicholas, 'Washaway your Troubles', Washaway, Bodmin, Cornwall PL30 3AD
☎Bodmin(0208)4951

*Three tastefully converted properties with **The Coach House** comprising one double bedroom and one twin each having shower/WC; kitchen/diner and sitting room. **Barn Cottage** has a large open-plan lounge/kitchen/diner on the ground floor and two bedrooms and bathroom on the first. **The Tallet** is designed for two persons comprising open plan lounge/kitchen/diner on ground floor and one double bedroom with shower room on first floor.*

All year 1wk min, 1mth max, 3units, 1–6persons ◆ ◆ ◎ fridge Electric Elec metered ⊡can be hired ☎(½m) [Iron on premises] Ironing board on premises HCE in unit ⊙ CTV ⊕3pin square P▥ 🏪(3m)

⊖ ▣(3m) ♫(3m) 🎥(3m)

Min£50 Max£80pw (Low)
Min£70 Max£145pw (High)

C Penbugle Cottage
for bookings Mrs Tidy, Penbugle Farm, Bodmin, Cornwall ☎Bodmin(0208)2844

Old farm cottage next to farmhouse. Decorated to a high standard. Accommodation comprises lounge with inglenook, kitchen/diner, bathroom with WC, one double bedroom and another room with twin beds and bunks.

Etr–Oct MWB out of season 1wk min, 1unit, 1–6persons [◇] ◆ ◆ no pets ◎ fridge Wood burning stove Elec metered ⊡not provided ☎(1m) Airing cupboard in unit Iron in unit Ironing board in unit HCE in unit ⊙ TV ⊕3pin square 2P 🏪(1m)

⊖ ♀(1m) ▣(1m) 🎥(1m) Shooting & fishing

Min£40 Max£50pw (Low)
Min£70 Max£100pw (High)

BOGNOR REGIS
West Sussex
Map**4** SZ99

F Glamis House 33 Glamis Street
for bookings Mrs E R Karon, 8 Stocker Road, Bognor Regis, West Sussex PO21 2QF ☎Bognor Regis(0243)861460

Three-storied blue-painted Victorian house which has been converted into self-contained flats all with private entrances. Two flats approached by external stairway. First flat has two bedrooms, bathroom, kitchen and lounge/diner. Second floor flat has one bedroom, bathroom, kitchen, lounge, dining room, and ground-floor flat has two bedrooms, bathroom, kitchen, lounge/diner. All well decorated and comfortable. Situated within easy walking distance of shops, beach and railway station. From High Street, turn into Lyon Street and take first right into Glamis Street.

Spring Bank Holiday–1st wk Sep 1wk min, 3units, 2–8persons [◆] [◆] no pets ◎ fridge Electric Elec metered ⊡not provided ☎(200yds) Iron in unit Ironing board in unit HCE in unit TV ⊕3pin square ▥ 🏪(200yds)

⊖ ♀ ▣ ♫ 🎥

BONCATH
Dyfed
Map**2** SN23

C Madog Fron Fawr
for bookings Mr & Mrs R Cori, Fron Fawr, Boncath, Dyfed ☎Boncath(023974)285

Arranged with all bedrooms on the first floor. One double-bedded room, and two with one or two singles (upper & lower). These beds have been specially designed for Fron Fawr and can be arranged as a single divan by day.

Closed Nov 1wk min, 1unit, 6persons [◇] ◆ ◆ no pets ◎ fridge

Electric Elecmetered ⊟inclusive ☎(½m) SD in unit Airing cupboard in unit Iron in unit Ironing board in unit HCE in unit ⊙ CTV ⊕3pinsquare P ▥ ♨(½m)

⊖ ♀(½m)

Min£109 Max£167pw (Low)
Min£173 Max£334pw (High)

C Merddin Fron Fawr
for bookings Mr & Mrs R Cori, Fron Fawr, Boncath, Dyfed ☎Boncath(023974)285

Delightful décor combining colours, patterns and textiles. Two double bedrooms, third bedroom with one single or two single beds. All three cottages have vanity units and wash basins in the main bedrooms. Fully-tiled, heated bathrooms with drying facilities. Well-fitted kitchens. Thick wool carpets and Continental quilts in all bedrooms.

Closed Nov 1wk min, 1unit, 5persons [◇] ◈ ◆ no pets ◎ fridge Electric Elecmetered ⊟inclusive ☎(½m) SD in unit Airing cupboard in unit Iron in unit Ironing board in unit HCE in unit ⊙ CTV ⊕3pinsquare P ▥ ♨(½m)

⊖ ♀(½m)

Min£104 Max£161pw (Low)
Min£167 Max£328pw (High)

C Talisin Fron Fawr
for bookings Mr & Mrs R Cori, Fron Fawr, Boncath, Dyfed ☎Boncath(023974)285

One of three super cottages, newly-converted from a single huge barn. Each one is luxuriously fitted with particular attention to detail. Sleeping accommodation comprises three bedrooms, one with a double bed and two containing two single beds. One bedroom (with two singles) is situated on the ground floor.

Closed Nov 1wk min, 1unit, 6persons [◇] ◈ ◆ no pets ◎ fridge Electric Elecmetered ⊟inclusive ☎(½m) SD in unit Airing cupboard in unit Iron in unit Ironing board in unit HCE in unit ⊙ CTV ⊕3pinsquare P ▥ ♨(½m)

⊖ ♀(½m)

Min£115 Max£173pw (Low)
Min£178 Max£345pw (High)

BONCHESTER BRIDGE
Borders *Roxburghshire*
Map**12** NT51

Ch Easter Weens Holiday Lodges
for bookings Miss J Bristow, Thorncroft, Lilliesleaf, Roxburghshire TD6 9JD ☎Lilliesleaf(08357)424

Small complex of timber lodges set in the grounds of Easter Weens House. Accommodation comprises open-plan lounge/diner/kitchen with patio windows opening onto small verandah. Shower room, two twin bedrooms and a double bed-settee in lounge. Ideal grounds for children to play in.

All year MWB out of season 1wk min, 1mth max, 8units, 1–6persons [◈] ◎ fridge Electric Elecmetered ⊟can be hired ☎(¼m) Airing cupboard in unit Iron on premises Ironing board on premises HCE in unit ⊙ CTV ⊕3pinsquare 12P ▥ ♨(8m) Trout fishing

⊖ ♀(¼m)

Min£57.50 Max£74.75pw (Low)
Min£115 Max£155.25pw (High)

C Hartshaugh Mill Cottage
for bookings Miss J Bristow, Thorncroft, Lilliesleaf, Roxburghshire TD6 9JD ☎Lilliesleaf(08357)424

A pleasant little two storey semi-detached cottage, comprising sitting/dining room with open fire, kitchen, bathroom and double bedroom on the ground floor, and a twin-bedded and double-bedded room on the first floor. The cottage is situated on a quiet country road about ½m from Bonchester Bridge, in delightful border hill district and beside the shallow Rule Water. The cottage commands good views and behind it is an old church. Trout fishing is available.

All year MWB out of season 1wk min, 2mths max, 1unit, 2–6persons [◈] ◎ fridge Electric & coal fires Elecmetered ⊟can be hired ☎(1m) WM in unit Iron in unit Ironing board in unit HCE in unit ⊙ CTV ⊕3pinsquare ⊕3pinround P ♨(8m)

⊖ ♀(2m)

Min£60.95 Max£74.75pw (Low)
Min£97.75 Max£120.75pw (High)

C Kilknowe Cottage Hobkirk
for bookings Miss J Bristow, Thorncroft, Lilliesleaf, Roxburghshire TD6 9JD ☎Lilliesleaf(08357)424

Former gamekeeper's cottage at the end of a 300yd track set on a hillside overlooking small valley of the River Yule. Accommodation comprises lounge, kitchen/dining room and bathroom on ground floor. First floor comprises one twin and one double bedroom. Also a single divan available in the lounge.

All year MWB out of season 1wk min, 1unit, 1–5persons [◈] ◎ fridge Electric & coal fires Elecmetered ⊟can be hired ☎(1m) Iron in unit Ironing board in unit HCE in unit ⊙ CTV ⊕3pinsquare 2P ♨(8m)

⊖ ♀(1m)

Min£62.10 Max£77.05pw (Low)
Min£103.50 Max£126.50pw (High)

BONTDDU
Gwynedd
Map**6** SH61

B The Cottage Farchynys Court
for bookings Mr J P Propert, 21 Greville Drive, Edgbaston, Birmingham ☎021-440 4040

Late Victorian stone farm buildings recently converted. Front door leading to entrance hall, lounge, kitchen/diner. Bathroom and two bedrooms, one double room and one triple room. From Dolgellau take A496 to Barmouth, passing Bontddu, Farchynys Court is ¾m on left up a short drive.

All year MWB out of season 2days min, 4wks max, 1unit, 1–5persons ◈ ◎ fridge Electric Elecinclusive ⊟not provided ☎(¾m) Airing cupboard in unit Iron in unit Ironing board in unit HCE in unit ⊙ ⊕3pinsquare 3P ♨(¾m)

⊖ ♂(3m) ♀(¾m) ▨(3m)

H The House Farchynys Court
for bookings Mr J P Propert, 21 Greville Drive, Edgbaston, Birmingham ☎021-440 4040

Late Victorian stone farm building recently converted. Front door leading into lounge with kitchen/diner. Stairs from lounge to landing. Three bedrooms, one double, one twin and one with bunks. Two bathrooms. From Dolgellau take A496 from Barmouth, after passing Bontddu, Farchynys Court is about ¾m on left, up a short drive.

All year MWB out of season 2days min, 4wks max, 1unit, 1–6persons ◈ ◎ fridge Electric Elecinclusive ⊟not provided ☎(¾m) Airing cupboard in unit Iron in unit Ironing board in unit HCE in unit ⊙ ⊕3pinsquare 3P ♨(¾m)

⊖ ♂(3m) ♀(¾m) ▨(3m)

BORGUE
Dumfries & Galloway *Kirkcudbrightshire*
Map**11** NX65

C Chapleton Cottage
for bookings G M Thomson & Co, 27 King Street, Castle Douglas, Kirkcudbrightshire ☎Castle Douglas(0556)2701

A comfortable semi-detached stone-built farm cottage. Accommodation comprises a dining/living room, kitchen, bathroom and two bedrooms both with twin beds. Convenient for Carrick and Sandgreen beaches.

All year 1wk min, 6mths max, 1unit, 1–4persons no pets ◎ fridge Electric Elecinclusive ⊟not provided ☎(2m) Ironing board in unit HCE in unit ⊙ TV ⊕3pinsquare P ♨(1m)

⊖ ♀(2m)

Min£45 Max£105pw

C Drum Cottage
for bookings G M Thomson & Co, 27 King Street, Castle Douglas, Kirkcudbrightshire ☎Castle Douglas(0556)2701

Attractive semi-detached farm cottage situated 1m from village. Accommodation consists of a dining/living room, a bathroom, kitchen and three bedrooms, two with twin beds, →

1982 prices quoted throughout gazetteer

and one with two three-quarter-sized bunks.

All year 1wk min, 6mths max, 1 unit, 1–6 persons ⊛ fridge Electric Elec inclusive ⬛ not provided ☎(½m) Ironing board in unit HCE in unit TV ⊕3 pin square P 🅿 ♨(1m)

⊖ ♨(½m)

Min £45 Max £105pw

B Muncraig Shepherds Cottage
for bookings G M Thomson & Co, 27 King Street, Castle Douglas, Kirkcudbrightshire
☎ Castle Douglas(0556)2701

A modern bungalow surrounded by farmland situated near the Solway Firth. Consists of living/dining room, kitchen, bathroom and three bedrooms, one with a double bed, two with a single bed each.

Apr–Oct 1wk min, 6mths max, 1 unit, 1–4 persons, nc12 ⊛ fridge Electric Elec inclusive ⬛ not provided ☎(1m) HCE in unit TV ⊕3 pin round P ♨(2m)

⊖ ♨(1m)

Min £45 Max £105pw

BORTH
Dyfed
Map **6** SN69

C Dovey Cottage High Street
for bookings Mrs M A Davies, Coral Gables, Ynyslas, Borth, Dyfed
☎ Borth(097081)517

Early 18th-century semi-detached fisherman's cottage, in centre of village. Lounge/diner, small kitchen, shower room with separate WC, narrow staircase from lounge leads to twin bedroom.

All year MWB out of season 3 days min, 4 wks max, 1 unit, 1–2 persons, nc16 no pets ⊛ fridge Electric Elec inclusive ⬛ not provided ☎(50yds) HCE in unit ⊖ CTV ⊕3 pin square ♨(30yds)

⊖ 🚬(½m) ♨(100yds)

Min £40 Max £75pw

Borgue
—
Bournemouth & Boscombe

BOSCASTLE
Cornwall
Map **2** SX09

C The Cottage
for bookings Mrs J Weekes, Lundy View, Boscastle, Cornwall
☎ Boscastle(08405)313

A stone-built converted coach house at rear of Lundy View House. Comprising kitchen with modern fittings, lounge/diner and bathroom/WC. Two bedrooms with double bed and single bed. Garden and patio.

All year MWB 3 days min, 4wks max, 1 unit, 1–6 persons ◇ ◆ ⊛ fridge Electric Elec metered ⬛ can be hired ☎(25yds) [WM on premises] Airing cupboard in unit Iron in unit Ironing board in unit HCE in unit ⊖ TV ⊕3 pin square 4P 🅿 ♨(10yds)

⊖ ♨(10yds) 🎵(1m)

Min £30 Max £55pw (Low)
Min £100 Max £140pw (High)

C CC Ref 323 ELP
for bookings Character Cottages (Holidays) Ltd, 34, Fore Street, Sidmouth, Devon EX10 8AQ
☎ Sidmouth(03955)77001

Terraced cottage in picturesque village. Oak beamed living room has original open fireplace dining section, and oak stable door to well-fitted kitchen. Open tread stairs lead to the three bedrooms – two with H/C washbasins.

All year MWB out of season 1wk min, 1 mth max, 1 unit, 2–7 persons ◆ ⊛ fridge Electric Elec metered ⬛ can be hired ☎(½m) Airing cupboard in unit Iron in unit Ironing board in unit HCE in unit ⊖ TV ⊕3 pin square ⊕2 pin round P 🅿 ♨(400yds)

⊖ ♨(400yds)

Min £63 Max £113pw (Low)
Min £132 Max £185pw (High)

C Sarum Paradise Road
for bookings Mr & Mrs Hall, Penrose Burden, St Breward, Cornwall
☎ Bodmin(0208)850277

Split level cottage situated at the top of Boscastle with panoramic views. Accommodation comprises lounge/diner, separate kitchen, bathroom with WC. Sleeping accommodation comprises two double bedrooms and two single bedrooms.

All year 1wk min, 1 unit, 1–6 persons [◇] ◆ no pets ⊛ fridge 🍴 Elec metered ⬛ inclusive ☎(100yds) Airing cupboard in unit Iron in unit Ironing board in unit HCE in unit ⊖ CTV ⊕3 pin square 1P 1🏠 🅿 ♨(50yds)

⊖ ♨(10yds)

Min £75 Max £190pw

BOURNEMOUTH & BOSCOMBE
Dorset
Map **4** SZ09

F Mrs A Curtiss **Azalea Park** 1 & 2 Milner Road, West Cliff, Bournemouth, Dorset BH4 8AD
☎ Bournemouth(0202)761231 or Ascot(0990)24887

Two converted detached superior residences in secluded position on West Cliff, nearby to cliff walks and promenade. Both houses are in extensive and well-kept grounds. Modern and antique furnishings.

All year MWB 1wk min, 15 units, 2–9 persons ◇ ◆ ◆ ⊛ fridge 🍴 Elec metered ⬛ can be hired ☎ Airing cupboard in unit Iron in unit Ironing board in unit HCE in unit ⊖ [CTV] ⊕3 pin square P 🅿 ♨(½m)

⊖ ♨(½m) 🚬(½m) 🎵(½m) 🍴(½m) ♨(½m)

Min £57 Max £92pw (Low)
Min £70 Max £380pw (High)

F Belle Reve Studland Road, Alum Chine
for bookings Mr Callaghan, c/o Riviera Hotel, Burnaby Road, Alum Chine, Bournemouth, Dorset
☎ Bournemouth(0202)765391

Detached building with dormer windows, set in a quiet residential area. Accommodation comprises lounge, kitchen, bathroom/WC, one bedroom and a lounge convertible. The flats are situated on three floors served by a lift.

Courtyard Farm Cottages

Bournemouth
—
& Boscombe

All year MWB out of season 2 days min, 4 wks max, 12 units, 2–7 persons [◊] [♦] ◎ fridge ♨ Elec metered ⊡ inclusive ☎(200yds) Iron on premises HCE in unit ⊕ CTV ⊕3 pin square 12P ⊞ ♨(1m) ⊠&⌂
↝ ♙(3m) ♙ ⊡ ♫ ☏-(2¼m)

F Mr A Bramley **Bermuda Court** 11 Derby Road, Bournemouth, Dorset ☎Bournemouth(0202)22697

Self-contained flats in a large house in the East Cliff area, accommodating up to nine persons. Décor is tasteful and furnishings are modern.

Apr–Sep MWB out of season 1 wk min, 1 mth max, 18 units, 2–9 persons, nc5 [◊ ♦] ◎ fridge Electric Elec metered ⊡ inclusive ☎ Iron on premises Ironing board on premises HCE on premises ⊕ CTV ⊕3 pin square P ⊞ ♨(500yds)
↝ ♙(½m) ⊡(½m) ☏(1m)

Min £80.50 Max £177.50 pw (Low)
Min £115 Max £250 pw (High)

F Mr & Mrs J Brownlow **Carnanton Holiday Apartments** 5A Percy Road, Boscombe, Bournemouth, Dorset BH5 1JF ☎Bournemouth(0202)37838

House converted into apartments. All self-contained, with either double beds or twin beds and extra wall bed in lounge. All with kitchen, dining room and lounge.

Six flats have bathroom/WC and five have shower/WC.

All year MWB out of season 3 days min, 4 wks max, 11 units, 2–6 persons [◊] ◊ ♦ ◎ fridge ♨(4 units) & electric Elec metered ⊡ can be hired ☎ Airing cupboard on premises Iron on premises Ironing board on premises HCE in unit ⊕ CTV ⊕3 pin square P ♨(500yds)
↝ ♙(300yds) ⊡(½m) ☏(1m)

See advert on page 40

F Mr Howard **Chine View Holiday Flats** 5 McKinley Road, West Cliff, Bournemouth, Dorset BH4 8AG ☎Bournemouth(0202)769245

Self-contained flats in a large house, situated in a quiet residential area within walking distance of sea and shops. Flats can accommodate seven persons in well-decorated spacious rooms.

All year MWB out of season 2 nights min, 4 wks max, 6 units, 2–7 persons [◊ ♦] no pets ◎ fridge Electric Elec metered ⊡ can be hired ☎ Airing cupboard in unit Iron on premises Ironing board on premises HCE in units ⊕ CTV ⊕3 pin square 9P ⊞ ♨(½m)
↝ ♙(3m) ⊡(½m) ♫(½m) ☏(1m)

Min £46 Max £74 pw (Low)
Min £178 Max £218 pw (High)

F Mrs T McDade, **Eyeworth Lawn,** West Cliff Gardens, Bournemouth, Dorset BH2 5HL ☎Bournemouth(0202)22228

Fourteen self-contained apartments with balconies overlooking the sea. Décor and furnishings are of a very high standard. One luxury garden flat comprising of two bedrooms (one twin and one double), lounge, kitchen and bathroom/WC.

All year MWB out of season 3 days min, 4 wks max, 14 units, 2–4 persons ◊ ◎ fridge ♨ Elec inclusive (in garden flat only) Elec metered ⊡ inclusive ☎ WM in unit (Garden flat only) [SD on premises] TD in unit (Garden flat only) Iron on premises Ironing board on premises HCE in unit ⊕ TV CTV (Garden flat) ⊕3 pin square ⊞ ♨(½m)
↝ ♙(2m) ♙(200yds) ⊡(200yds) ♫(200yds) ☏(½m)

See advert on page 41

F M G & J C Brodie **Glenhurst Manor Superior Holiday Flats** 44A West Cliff Road, Bournemouth, Dorset ☎Bournemouth(0202)761175 & 708558

Detached, red-brick residence, formerly a private house now converted into flats, standing in its own grounds and approached by a private drive. Located near Durley Chine in quiet and secluded area. Maid service available.

Closed Nov MWB out of season 1 wk min, 6 mths max, 6 units, 2–10 persons ◊ ♦ no pets ◎ →

⓪Bermuda Court

Derby Road, East Cliff, Bournemouth, BH1 3PY
Telephone: 0202 22697

Custom planned holiday suites embodying modern refinements — occupying a fine position amidst the pines of this exclusive quarter, 400 yard level walk to the East Overcliff.
The self-contained suites are one to four rooms (accommodating 2-9), each with tiled bathroom, w.c., fitted kitchenette, refrigerator, shaver points, hot water and colour television.
Equipped for comfort to a superior standard. **Large car park.**
Brochure and tariff on request (stamp only).
Personally supervised by Alan Bramley, who will be pleased to have your enquiries.

fridge ▥ Elec metered ▢ inclusive
☎ WM on premises TD on premises
Iron on premises Ironing board on
premises HCE in unit ⊕ CTV
⊕3pin square P ▥ ♨(½m)
⊛ ☏(½m) ▨(½m) ♫(½m) ☎(1m)
Min£35 Max£130pw (Low)
Min£80 Max£350pw (High)

F Grand Lodge Holiday Flats
for bookings Mr & Mrs R Colman, 14
Grand Avenue, Southbourne,
Bournemouth, Dorset BH6 3SY
☎Bournemouth(0202)420481

*Four flats within a double fronted,
detached, red-brick building located on
a wide avenue in a residential area. All
have lounge/diner with kitchen area and
bathroom/WC. The three first-floor flats
have one bedroom with double bed and
twin bunks with double bed.*

All year MWB out of season 3days min,
1mth max, 4units, 2–4persons ◆ ◆
◉ fridge Electric Elec metered
▢ can be hired ☎ Iron on premises
Ironing board on premises HCE on
premises [Launderette within 300yds]
⊕ TV ⊕3pin square P ▥
♨(250yds)
⊛ ♪(1m) ☏(½m) ▨(2m) ☎(3m)
Min£40 Max£60pw (Low)
Min£70 Max£140pw (High)

**F Mr M Lambert Lyttelton Lodge
Holiday Apartments** 16 Florence Road,
Boscombe, Bournemouth, Dorset
BH5 1HF
☎Bournemouth(0202)33503

*Gabled villa linked to new purpose-built
block, by carpeted reception hall. Five
units in each section, all well equipped. In
a quiet residential road near Boscombe
shops and seafront pier.*

All year MWB out of season 10units,
2–8persons [◇ ◆ ◆] ◉ fridge
▥ & Gas & Electric Gas & Elec metered
▢ can be hired ☎ HCE in unit
Launderette on premises CTV
⊕3pin square P ▥ ♨(200yds)
⊛ ☏(200yds) ▨(300yds) ☎(2m)
Min£37 Max£96pw (Low)
Min£68 Max£286pw (High)

F Mr R O Jones Midchines 14 McKinley
Road, Bournemouth, Dorset BH4 8AQ
☎Bournemouth(0202)764513

*Detached gabled villa located in a quiet
area adjacent to Durley Chine. The Flats
have spacious rooms and are tastefully
decorated.*

All year MWB out of season 1wk min,
2mths max, 5units, 2–8persons ◆ ◆
no pets ◉ fridge ▥ Elec metered
▢ can be hired ☎ Airing cupboard in
unit Iron on premises Ironing board on
premises HCE in units [TV]
⊕3pin square P ▥ ♨(½m)
⊛ ☏(½m) ▨(½m) ♫(½m) ☎(1m)
Min£25 Max£45pw (Low)
Min£100 Max£200pw (High)

F Overcliffe Mansions East Cliff
Holiday Flats, 1–3 Manor Road
for bookings Mrs D Daisley, 17 Clarendon
Road, West Cliff, Bournemouth, Dorset
BH4 8AL
☎Bournemouth(0202)764450

*Detached red-brick block of eight
purpose-built self-contained flats.
Spacious, well equipped and
comfortable. Comprising three double
bedrooms (one double and two twin),
lounge, kitchen/diner, bathroom/WC.
Ideally situated for twon centre.*

All year MWB out of season 3days min,
3mths max, 8units, 1–6persons, nc4
no pets ◢(1unit) ◉(7units) fridge
▥(3units) Electric(5units)
Gas/Elec metered ▢ can be hired
☎(25yds) Airing cupboard in unit
(3units only) Iron on premises Ironing
board on premises HCE in unit ⊕
CTV ⊕3pin square P ▥
♨(500yds)
⊛ ♫ш(2m) ☏(300yds) ▨(300yds)
♫(½m) ☎(1m)
Min£50 Max£250pw

F 3 Portarlington Road West Cliff
for bookings Mr & Mrs F R Peverelle
'White Wings' 4 Mornish Road,
Branksome Park, Poole, Dorset
☎Bournemouth(0202)762149

*A large detached residence in own
grounds with spacious, elegant interior,
converted into six flats. Three flats on
ground floor. All flats have lounge,
kitchen and bathroom/WC. Flat 1 sleeps
five in one bedroom with double bed and
two singles plus a single divan in lounge.
Flat 2 sleeps four comprising of one
double bed and two bunk beds. Flat 3
sleeps four comprising of two double
beds. Two flats on first floor. Both flats
have lounge, kitchen and bathroom/WC.
Flat 4 has two double beds and one
single plus a single in lounge if required.
Flat 5 has two double beds and one
single. One flat on second floor
comprising of lounge/kitchen,
bathroom/WC and two bedrooms each
with double beds and one single plus a
single in lounge.*

All year MWB out of season 1wk min,
4wks max, 6units, 2–6persons ◆ ◢
fridge Electric Elec metered
▢ can be hired ☎ Iron in unit Ironing
board in unit HCE in unit ⊕ CTV
⊕3pin round 10P 3♨ ♨(300yds)
⊛ ♫ш(1½m) ☏(300yds) ▨(1m)
♫(1m) ☎(1m)

F Saltaire Sea Road, Southbourne
for bookings Mr & Mrs D Counter, 'White
Horses,' 47 St Catherine's Road,
Southbourne, Bournemouth, Dorset
BH6 4AQ
☎Bournemouth(0202)420296

*Purpose-built luxury flats on elevated site
overlooking the sea. Southbourne shops
nearby.*

All year MWB out of season
3nights min, 3mths max, 34units,
2–7persons [◇] ◆ ◉ fridge
▥ Elec metered ▢ can be hired ☎
[WM on premises] SD on premises [TD
on premises] Airing cupboard in unit
Iron on premises Ironing board on
premises HCE in unit [Launderette on
premises] ⊕ [CTV] ⊕3pin square
P ▥ ♨(200yds)
⊛ ☏(230yds) ▨(1½m) ♫(1½m)
☎(2m)
Min£42 Max£79pw (Low)
Min£142 Max£264pw (High)
See advert on page 42

F **Salterton**, 17 Warren Edge Road
for bookings Mr & Mrs D Counter, 'White
Horses', 47 St Catherine's Road,
Southbourne, Bournemouth, Dorset
BH6 4AQ
☎Bournemouth(0202)420296

Five new purpose-built holiday
apartments most having sea views and
only 75yds from seafront. Two ground-,
two first- and one second-floor flats, each
with one twin, and one double bedroom
with extra single bed, lounge/diner (with
sofa bed) and bathroom.

Apr–Oct 1wk min, 6wks max, 5units,
2–7persons [◇] [◆ ♦] no pets
◎ fridge ♨ Elec metered Ⓛ can be
hired ☎ [WM on premises] [TD on
premises] [Airing cupboard in unit]
Iron on premises Ironing board on
premises HCE in unit ☉ [CTV]
⊕3pin square 5🅿 🅼 ♨(150yds)
⇔ ♒(2¼m) ♀(200yds) ▣(1¼m)
♫(1¼m) 🐾(2¼m)
Min£75 Max£100pw (Low)
Min£215 Max£264pw (High)

F Mr P Peter **Sheraton Park** 7 Milner
Road, West Cliff, Bournemouth, Dorset
☎Bournemouth(0202)763305

Four flats located within this detached
red-brick residence with bow windows,
standing in own grounds in quiet
residential area. **Flats 1, 2 & 3** are all on
the ground floor and comprise
lounge/diner, separate kitchen;
excepting **Flat 1** which has combined
lounge/kitchen/diner, one double
bedded room plus two divans in lounge
except **Flat 2** which have three divans.
Flat 4 which is on the first floor has
lounge/diner, separate kitchen, two
bedrooms one with a double bed, one
with twin beds, and two divans in lounge.
All have combined bathroom/WC.

All year MWB out of season 1wk min,
4wks max, 4units, 2–6persons ◇ ◆
◎ fridge ♨ Elec metered Ⓛ can be
hired ☎ Airing cupboard in unit Iron in
unit Ironing board in unit HCE in unit
☉ CTV ⊕3pin square P 🅼 ♨(½m)
⇔ ♒(1½m) ♀(½m) ▣(½m) ♫(½m)
🐾(1m)
Min£55 Max£93pw (Low)
Min£145 Max£240pw (High)

Bournemouth — & Boscombe

F Col B A Lipscombe **Stirling Court** 28
Manor Road, East Cliff, Bournemouth,
Dorset BH1 3EZ
☎Bournemouth(0202)26646

Detached villa standing in its own
grounds converted into self-contained
flats. All have tasteful décor and modern
furnishing and comprise either single,
twin or double bedrooms, kitchen/diner,
lounge with fold-up double bed and
bathroom/WC. Located in the East Cliff
area and near to seafront. Laundry room
available.

All year MWB out of season 1wk min,
4wks max, 10units, 2–7persons ◇ ◆
◎ fridge Electric Elec metered
Ⓛ can be hired ☎ Airing cupboard on
premises HCE in unit [Launderette on
premises] ☉ CTV ⊕3pin square
25P 🅼 ♨(½m)
Min£51.75 Max£120.75pw (Low)
Min£110.40 Max£233.45pw (High)

F **Wessex Court Flats** (Wessex Hotel)
West Cliff Road, Bournemouth, Dorset
BH2 5EU
☎Bournemouth(0202)21911

Self-contained flats in detached rambling
villa. Each has lounge, separate kitchen,
bathroom and bedroom(s). Sauna,
billiards and swimming available at
adjacent hotel.

All year MWB 1wk min, 1mth max,
2units, 4–9persons ◇ ◆ ◎ fridge
♨(in first) Electric fires (in second)
Elec metered Ⓛ inclusive ☎ Airing
cupboard on premises Iron in unit
Ironing board in unit HCE in unit ☉
CTV ⊕3pin square P 🅼 ♨(300yds)
⇔ ♀ ▣(100yds) 🐾(1m)
Min£75 Max£210pw

F Mr & Mrs K J Garard **Westbrook
Luxury Holiday Flats** 472/474
Christchurch Road, Boscombe,
Bournemouth, Dorset BH1 4BD
☎Bournemouth(0202)36763 & 34820

Three-storey building comprising 23 flats
adjacent to Boscombe shopping parade.
Accommodation consists of
kitchen/diner or kitchenette,
lounge/bedroom, bathroom/WC and
some have an extra bedroom.

All year MWB out of season 3days min,
8wks max, 23units, 2–6persons [◇]
[◈] [◆] ♨ fridge Gas or Electric
fires Gas/Elec metered Ⓛ can be
hired ☎ Airing cupboard on premises
Iron on premises Ironing board on
premises HCE on premises
[Launderette within 20yds] ☉ CTV
⊕3pin round P 🅼 ♨
⇔ ♀(150yds) ♨(300yds)
♫(300yds) 🐾(1m)
Min£23 Max£62.10pw (Low)
Min£50.60 Max£226.55pw (High)
See advert on page 42

F Mr & Mrs A W Thompson **West Cliff
Lodge** 4 McKinley Road, West Cliff,
Bournemouth, Dorset BH4 8AQ
☎Bournemouth(0202)760925

A detached red-brick villa in 'superior'
quiet residential area. Former private
house converted into flats. Not far from
Durley and Alum Chines. Winter lettings
can be arranged.

Apr–Oct MWB out of season 1wk min,
5units, 2–8persons [◇] [◆] no pets
◎ fridge ♨ Elec metered Ⓛ can be
hired ☎ [SD on premises] [TD on
premises] Iron in unit Ironing board in
unit HCE in unit ☉ [CTV]
⊕3pin square P 🅼 ♨(½m)
⇔ ♀(½m) ▣(½m) ♫(½m) 🐾(½m)
Min£57.50 Max£109.25pw (Low)
Min£126.50 Max£287.50pw (High)
See advert on page 42

F **White Wings** 25 McKinley Road,
West Cliff
for bookings Mr & Mrs F R Peverelle,
White Wings, 4 Mornish Road,
Branksome Park, Poole, Dorset
☎Bournemouth(0202)762149

Large detached house standing in own
grounds, converted into self-contained
flats. Each contains a lounge, kitchen,
bathroom/WC and one or two bedrooms.
A high standard of quality furniture and
spacious elegant rooms.

Apr–Oct MWB out of season 1wk min,
1mth max, 6units, 2–6persons ◇ ♦ →

> 1982 prices quoted throughout
> gazetteer

fridge ⊠ Gas/Elec metered ⊡ can be hired ☎ Airing cupboard in unit Iron in unit Ironing board in unit HCE in unit ⊕ CTV ⊕3pin square ⌂ ▥ ⏧(½m)

↔ ⬡(½m) ▱(½m) ⬛(½m)

F Mr Abrahams **Zena Court Flats**
9 Adeline Road, Boscombe,
Bournemouth, Dorset BH5 1EE
☎Bournemouth(0202)37101

Detached, red-brick gabled villa on corner site in a dense suburban area. Comfortable and well furnished. Near main Boscombe shopping centre.

All year MWB out of season 1wk min, 2mths max, 4units, 2–9persons ◇ ◆ ◆ ◉ fridge Electric Elec metered ⊡inclusive Airing cupboard in unit Iron on premises Ironing board on premises HCE in unit [Launderette within 300yds] ⊕ CTV ⊕3pin square P ⌂ ▥ ⏧(50yds)

↔ ⬡(100yds) ▱(100yds) ♬(100yds) ⬛(1½m)

Min£35 Max£85pw (Low)
Min£80 Max£240pw (High)

BOURTON
Oxfordshire
Map**4** SU28

C **Grange Cottage**
for bookings Mrs M R Benson, Peartree Cottage, Bourton, Swindon, Wiltshire SN6 8HV
☎Swindon(0793)782334

Cottage set in a quiet village, semi-detached and built of stone. Accommodation comprises lounge, kitchen/diner, separate WC on ground floor. Three bedrooms on first floor, two with double beds and two singles and one twin-bedded room. Leaving Swindon on A420 Oxford Road, signposted to Bourton, enter village after passing over railway bridge.

All year MWB out of season 1wk min, 8wks max, 1unit, 2–10persons ◇ ◆ no pets ◉ fridge Electric Elec metered ⊡ can be hired ☎(½m) WM in unit SD in unit Airing cupboard in unit Iron in unit Ironing board in unit HCE in unit ⊕ CTV ⊕3pin square 4P ▥ ⏧(½m)

↔ ⬡(½m) ⬡(½m)

Min£69pw (Low)
Min£92 Max£138pw (High)

BOURTON-ON-THE-HILL
Gloucestershire
Map**4** SP13

C **The Gable**
for bookings Mr & Mrs Schuler, The Warren, 20 Crown Street, Harrow-on-the-Hill, Middx HA2 0HQ
☎01–864 4146

This two-hundred-year-old property has been extensively modernised whilst retaining the character of a traditional Cotswold stone cottage. The large open-plan living and dining room, separated by a pine staircase, leads to the spacious

kitchen and good sized garden. Upstairs are two twin-bedded rooms with built-in cupboards and a carpeted bathroom. The cottage is located on the outskirts of the village.

All year 1wk min, 1mth max, 1unit, 1–4persons, nc13 no pets ⬡ fridge ⊠ Gas inclusive ⊡inclusive ☎ Airing cupboard in unit Iron in unit Ironing board in unit HCE in unit ⊕ ⊕ TV ⊕3pin square 1P ▥ ⏧(½m) Record player, small library and cleaning service

↔ ⬡(½m) ▱(½m)

Min£105 Max£145pw

BOVEY TRACEY
Devon
Map**3** SX87

B **Brancaster** Coombe Cross
for bookings Mr S J Mountford, Glebelands, Coombe Cross, Bovey Tracey, Devon TQ13 9EP
☎Bovey Tracey(0626)832913

Modern bungalow in quiet residential close. Accommodation comprises modern kitchen, dining room, lounge, two twin bedrooms and one double bedroom, bathroom with WC.

3Apr–Oct 1wk min, 6wks max, 1unit, 1–6persons ◇ ◆ no pets except dogs ◉ fridge Log fires & electric Elec inclusive ⊡ can be hired ☎(500yds) Airing cupboard in unit Iron in unit Ironing board in unit HCE in unit [Launderette within 300yds] ⊕ TV ⊕3pin square 2P 1⌂ ▥ ⏧(500yds)

↔ ⬙(3m) ⬡(500yds)

Min£80 Max£140pw

C **Crag Cottage** Fore Street
for bookings C D Harvey, 70 Reddenhill Road, Babbacombe, Devon
☎Torquay(0803)39464

Attractive terraced cottage in main street 500yds from Riverside Inn and River Bovey. Comprises lounge, kitchen, dining room, two double-bedded rooms, one with additional single bed, and bathroom/WC. Well furnished and decorated.

All year MWB out of season 3days min, 6wks max, 1unit, 1–5persons ◇ ◆ ◉ fridge ⊠ Elec metered ⊡inclusive ☎(300yds) Airing cupboard in unit Iron in unit Ironing board in unit HCE in unit ⊕ TV ⊕3pin square ⏧(20yds)

↔ ⬙(3m) ⬡(20yds) ♬(20yds)

Min£45 Max£125pw

B **Merrymeet** Coombe Cross
for bookings Mr S J Mountford, Glebelands, Coombe Cross, Bovey Tracey, Devon TQ13 9EP
☎Bovey Tracey(0626)832913

Fully carpeted modern bungalow set in quiet residential close. Small front garden. Accommodation comprises modern kitchen, dining room, lounge, two double bedrooms and one twin bedroom, bathroom with WC.

3Apr–Oct 1wk min, 6wks max, 1unit, 1–6persons ◇ ◆ no pets except dogs ◉ fridge Log fires & electric Elec inclusive ⊡ can be hired ☎(500yds) Airing cupboard in unit Iron in unit Ironing board in unit HCE in unit [Launderette within 300yds] ⊕ TV ⊕3pin square 2P 1⌂ ⏧(500yds)

↔ ⬙(3m) ⬡(500yds)

Min£80 Max£140pw

C **4 Victoria Terrace**
for bookings Mr S J Mountford, Glebelands, Coombe Cross, Bovey Tracey, Devon TQ13 9EP
☎Bovey Tracey(0626)832913

Red-brick terraced cottage in small row with front garden. Pleasantly modernised, well decorated and furnished. Accommodation consists of lounge/diner, modern kitchen, ground-floor WC. Three bedrooms comprising one single, one twin and one double, bathroom with WC.

3Apr–Oct 1wk min, 6wks max, 1unit, 1–5persons ◆ ◆ ◉ fridge Gas fire Elec inclusive Gas metered ⊡ can be hired ☎(100yds) Airing cupboard in unit Iron in unit Ironing board in unit HCE in unit [Launderette within 300yds] ⊕ TV ⊕3pin square 1P ⏧(50yds)

↔ ⬙(3m) ⬡(100yds)

Min£45 Max£90pw

BRAMPTON
Cumbria
Map**11** NY56

F **Old Gables** 9 High Cross Street
for bookings Mrs E P Bell, The Post Office, Lazonby, Penrith, Cumbria CA10 1BX
☎Lazonby(076 883)437 or 242

A comfortably appointed flat with spacious lounge kitchen/diner, two bedrooms, one double and the other with three single beds. Situated on terrace leading to the Market Square.

All year MWB out of season 3nights min, 6mths max, 1unit, 2–5persons, nc5 no pets ◉ fridge ⊠ Elec inclusive ⊡not provided ☎(100yds) Airing cupboard in unit Iron in unit Ironing board in unit HCE in unit [Launderette within 300yds] ⊕ CTV ⊕3pin square ▥ ⏧(20yds)

↔ ⬙(3m) ⬡(50yds)

Min£65 Max£105pw

1982 prices quoted throughout gazetteer

BRANSCOMBE
Devon
Map **3** SY18

H   Little Seaside
for bookings J A & A S D Hedges,
Westwards, Bickwell Valley, Sidmouth,
Devon
☎Sidmouth(03955)6176

*Delightful 13th-century thatched
residence. Situated 400yds from beach.
Accommodation consists of four oak-
beamed bedrooms, large lounge, stylish
modern kitchen/breakfast room,
separate dining room, study with window
seats and modern bathroom and toilet
facilities. Features include period
furnishings and massive open fireplaces,
large garden.*

All year MWB out of season 1wk min,
6mths max, 1unit, 2–8persons ◊ ◉
fridge Electric Elec inclusive ⊡can
be hired ☎ Wm in unit Airing
cupboard in unit Iron in unit Ironing
board in unit HCE in unit ⊙ CTV
⊕3pin square P 🏠 🖵 ♨(½m)
⊖ ⬤

Min£95 Max£210pw (Low)
Min£225 Max£400pw (High)

BRATTON FLEMING
Devon
Map **2** SS63

C   CC Ref 546 EL
for bookings Character Cottages
(Holidays) Ltd, 34 Fore Street, Sidmouth,
Devon EX10 8AQ
☎Sidmouth(03955)77001

*One of a block of three cottage style
houses of modern design.
Accommodation comprises lounge/diner
on ground floor and one double
bedroom, one twin-bedded room and
tiled bathroom/WC on the first floor.*

All year MWB out of season 1wk min,
1mth max, 1unit, 2–4persons, nc
no pets ◉ fridge 🍴 Elec metered
⊡can be hired ☎(½m) Airing cupboard
in unit Iron in unit Ironing board in unit
HCE in unit TV ⊕3pin square
⊕2pin round 🏠 🖵 ♨(200yds)
⊖ ⬤(½m)

Min£71 Max£106pw

Branscombe
—
Bridgerule

BRECON
Powys
Map **3** SO02

C   Coach House & Stable Cottage
for bookings Mrs F R Harries, The Court,
Cradoc Road, Brecon, Powys
☎Brecon(0874)2028

*The Coach House. An attractive
converted coach house featuring oak
beams and stone arches.
Accommodation comprises
kitchen/dining room on ground floor.
Lounge and three bedrooms on first floor,
one double room, one twin room and one
single room, bathroom with WC. Within
walking distance of the town centre.
Stable Cottage. An old stable block
converted into an attractive stable
cottage with original low wooden beams.
Accommodation comprises large sitting
room with dining area, fitted kitchen with
breakfast table. Two bedrooms upstairs,
one room with double and single beds
and another with twin beds. Bathroom
with WC.*

All year MWB out of season
3nights min, 2units, 2–6persons [◊]
◊ ◆ no pets 🐕(Stable Cottage)
◉(Coach House) fridge 🍴Gas/Elec
inclusive ⊡not provided ☎(300yds)
Airing cupboard in unit Iron in unit
Ironing board in unit HCE in unit
[Launderette within 300yds] ⊙ CTV
⊕3pin square 2P 1🏠 ♨(300yds)
⊖ 🐾(200yds) ⬤(200yds)
🦮(300yds)

Min£45 Max£70pw (Low)
Min£50 Max£140pw (High)

F   Court Flat
for bookings Mrs F R Harries, The Court,
Cradoc Road, Brecon, Powys
☎Brecon(0874)2028

*Converted from a hay loft, the flat with its
panoramic views, stands above the
original cowshed which is now a
veterinary surgeon's premises. It is
comfortable and spacious with
sitting/dining room, kitchen two
bedrooms and bathroom/WC. The flat is*

---

reached by outside stairs.

All year MWB out of season
3nights min, 1unit, 2–4persons [◊]
◊ ◆ no pets ◉ fridge 🍴
Gas/Elec metered ⊡not provided
☎(300yds) Airing cupboard in unit Iron
in unit Ironing board in unit HCE in unit
[Launderette within 300yds] ⊙ CTV
⊕3pin square 2P ♨(½m)
⊖ 🐾 🦮 ⬤(½m) 🐕(½m)

Min£40 Max£60pw (Low)
Min£45 Max£110pw (High)

BRIDGE OF EARN
Tayside *Perthshire*
Map **11** NO11

Ca   River Edge Chalets
for bookings Earn Properties, Old Mill,
Bridge of Earn, Perthshire PH29PS
☎Bridge of Earn(073881)2421/2241

*A recent development of cedar wood log
cabins collectively sited on the banks of
the River Earn situated close to the
village. The cabins each with its own
parking area alongside comprise
living/dining room with convertible
settees, two or three bedrooms, fitted
kitchen and bathroom.*

All year MWB out of season 2days min,
3mths max, 10units, 1–8persons [◊]
◊ ◆ ◉ fridge 🍴 Elec metered
⊡inclusive ☎ WM in unit SD in unit
Airing cupboard in unit Iron on
premises Ironing board in unit HCE in
unit ⊙ CTV ⊕3pin square P
🖵 ♨(100yds) Fishing
⊖ ⬤(50yds) 🎵(½m)

Min£57.50 Max£188pw

BRIDGERULE
Devon
Map **2** SS20

F   The Chancellry
for bookings Mr J Pyper, Glebe House,
Bridgerule, Holsworthy, Devon
EX22 7EW
☎Bridgerule(028881)272

*Situated on the ground floor of Glebe
House with large attractive gardens and
good views. Accommodation comprises
large living room, kitchen/diner, four
bedrooms, two with double beds, one
with four single beds and one with twin*

---

beds. All facilities suitable for the disabled.

mid Feb-mid Nov & mid Dec-mid Jan MWB out of season 2 nights min, 1 unit, 2-10 persons [◇] ◊ ◆ no pets ◎ fridge ⚒ Elec inclusive ⬜inclusive ☎ Airing cupboard in unit Iron on premises Ironing board on premises HCE in unit Launderette on premises ⊙ CTV ⊕3pin square P ▦ ♨(500yds) Games room Croquet lawn
⟷ ♒(3m) ♀(500yds)
Min £160 Max £390pw

C   Coach House, Mews, Granary, Forge, Little Barn & Old Stables Cottages
for bookings Mr J Pyper, Glebe House, Bridgerule, Holsworthy, Devon EX22 7EW
☎Bridgerule(028881)272

A range of converted outbuildings attached to an old Vicarage. Beautifully furnished and decorated, comprising large lounge, kitchen/diner with split level cooker, bathroom/WC and varying sleeping accommodation in two or three bedrooms.

mid Feb-mid Nov & mid Dec-mid Jan MWB out of season 2 nights min, 6 units, 2-6 persons [◇] ◊ ◆ no pets ◎ fridge ⚒ Elec inclusive ⬜inclusive ☎ Airing cupboard in unit Iron on premises Ironing board on premises HCE in unit Launderette on premises ⊙ CTV ⊕3pin square P ▦ ♨(500yds) Games room Croquet lawn
⟷ ♒(3m) ♀(500ds)
Min £80 Max £280pw

BRIDGNORTH
Shropshire
Map **7** SO79

C   Mrs S B Amos **Greensted Cottage** Oldbury, Bridgnorth, Shropshire WV16 5EE
☎Bridgnorth(074 62)3125

A brick-built cottage situated in the grounds of Greensted House, comprising lounge with double divan, a double bedroom, kitchen and bathroom/WC. 1m S of Bridgnorth on B4363.

Bridgerule — Bridlington

All year MWB 2 nights min, 3 wks max, 1 unit, 2-4 persons ◊ ◆ no pets ◎ fridge Electric & log fires Elec metered ⬜can be hired ☎(½m) Airing cupboard in unit Iron in unit HCE in unit ⊛ TV ⊕3pin square 1P ▦ ♨(1m)
⟷ ♒ ♀(1m) ▥(1m) ♫(1m) ☏(1m)
Min £30 Max £80pw

BRIDLINGTON
Humberside
Map **8** TA16

F   22 Belgrave Road
for bookings Mrs D Morgan, 4 Hymers Avenue, Hull, Humberside HU3 1LN
☎Hull(0482)41380

Two self-contained flats on ground and first floors of a semi-detached house situated close to the beach. Sleeping accommodation for up to six people with one double-bedded room, one twin room and a double bed-settee in the lounge is included in each unit. Both flats contain kitchen and bathroom (separate WC in the first-floor flat).

Whit-mid Sep 1 wk min, 1 mth max, 2 units, 1-6 persons ◊ no pets ◊&◎ fridge Gas & Electric fires Gas/Elec metered ⬜not provided ☎(100yds) Airing cupboard in unit HCE in unit TV ⊕3pin square ▦ ♨(200yds)
⟷ ♀(½m) ▥(½m) ♫(½m) ☏(½m)
Min £35 Max £40pw (Low)
Min £45 Max £55pw (High)

F   Marsden Holiday Flats 47 Blackburn Avenue, Bridlington, North Humberside YO15 2ER

Substantially built brick terraced houses converted into 12 self-contained flats, with accommodation for two to six people. Each unit has its own sitting room, separate kitchen and bathroom/WC. Good clean, well ordered flats, but flat no.5 has a kitchen in an internal situation without a window.

May-Oct 1 wk min, 3 mths max, 12 units, 1-6 persons ◊ ◆ no cats ◎ Electric Elec metered ⬜inclusive ☎(200yds) Airing cupboard in unit(2 flats) Iron on premises Ironing board on premises HCE in unit [Launderette within 300yds] TV ⊕3pin square ▦ ♨(200yds) ⌿ ♥Hard ♬
⟷ ♀(200yds) ▥(300yds) ♫(300yds) ☏(300yds)

F   Mrs Ibbotson **Southleigh**
41 Horsforth Avenue, Bridlington, Humberside
☎Bridlington(0262)72552

Second-floor flat comprising one double-bedded room, one room with double bed and ½ bed, lounge with open-plan kitchen and separate bathroom and WC. Situated in a terraced street near to the south bay.

Mar-Oct MWB out of season 1 wk min, 1 mth max, 1 unit, 6 persons ◊ ◆ no pets ⌀ fridge Gas Gas/Elec metered ⬜inclusive ☎(200yds) SD on premises TD on premises Airing cupboard in unit Iron on premises Ironing board on premises HCE in unit [Lauderette within 300yds] TV ⊕3pin square ▦ ♨(100yds) ♬ ⌿ pitch & putt
⟷ ♒ ♀(200yds) ▥(200yds) ♫(200yds) ☏(800yds)
Min £38 Max £50pw (Low)
Min £48 Max £90pw (High)

F   7 Swanland Avenue
for bookings Mrs M Smith, 9 Swanland Avenue, Bridlington, North Humberside YO15 24HH
☎Bridlington(0262)74351

Large Edwardian terraced house, converted into three self-contained flats. The ground-floor flat sleeps five in two bedrooms, the first-floor flat also sleeps five in two bedrooms; and the second floor flat sleeps four with the inclusion of a double studio couch in lounge. Each flat contains lounge, kitchen and bathroom/WC. Situated on the north side of town. →

Etr-Oct 1wk min, 3units, 1–5persons
[◊ ◆] no pets ∅ fridge Gas fires
Gas/Elec metered ⊡ can be hired
☎(300yds) Airing cupboard in unit Iron
on premises Ironing board on
premises HCE in unit [Launderette
within 300yds] CTV ⊕3pin square
1P 2🏠 🔟 ♨(200yds)
⊖ ♀(200yds) ▣(400yds)
♫(500yds) 🍴(300yds)
Min£25 Max£90pw (Low)
Min£95 Max£125pw (High)

BRIDPORT
Dorset
Map3 SY49

F Mrs N Vaughan **Coniston Holiday
Apartments** 69 Victoria Grove, Bridport,
Dorset DT6 3AE
☎Bridport(0308)24049

*Three flats located within detached, red
brick gabled villa in residential road off
A35 through Bridport. The ground floor
flat sleeps 7, first-floor flat sleeps 6 and
second-floor flat sleeps 9. There is a
childrens play area in the grounds of the
house.*

Etr-Oct 1wk min, 1mth max, 3units,
2–9persons [◊] ◊ ◆ ∅ fridge
Electric Elec metered ⊡ not provided
☎(150yds) WM in unit SD in unit
Airing cupboard in unit Iron in unit
Ironing board in unit HCE in unit
[Launderette within 300yds] ⊖ ⊕
CTV ⊕3pin square P 🔟
♨(120yds) ⌒
⊖ ♨(2½m) ♀(120yds) ▣(273yds)
♫(328yds) 🍴(328yds)
Min£40 Max£95pw

F **15 Kingfisher Court** West Bay
for bookings Mr J Fairbrother, 1 Gate
Close, Hawkchurch, Axminster, Devon
EX135TY
☎Hawkchurch(029 77)421

*Modern purpose-built first-floor flat in
two-storey block, with balconies from
bedrooms and lounge looking onto sea.
Comfortable furnishings and fittings.*

All year MWB out of season 1wk min,
3mths max, 1unit, 2–6persons ◎
fridge Electric Elec metered
⊡ not provided ☎(¼m) Airing cupboard
in unit Iron in unit Ironing board in unit
HCE in unit [Launderette within
300yds] ⊖ [TV] ⊕3pin square P
🏠 🔟 ♨
⊖ ♀ ▣ 🍴(2m)
Min£30 Max£75pw (Low)
Max£110pw (High)

F **Flat B, 100 St Andrews Road**
for bookings Mrs N V Strong, Flat A,
Ground Floor, 100 St Andrews Road,
Bridport, Dorset DT6 3BL
☎Bridport(0308)22290

*Located in a red-brick semi-detached
house dated from the late
Victorian/Edwardian period. Within
walking distance of town centre and
approached from the B3066, Beaminster
road, out of Bridport. The flat, which is*

*situated on the upper floor, is on two
levels, the first level comprising
kitchen/breakfast room and lounge with
double put-u-up and the second level
comprising one double bedroom (with
additional bed available) and
bathroom/WC.*

All year MWB out of season 3days min,
2wks max, 1unit, 2–5persons ◊ ◎
fridge Electric Elec metered
⊡ not provided ☎(100yds) Airing
cupboard in unit Iron in unit Ironing
board in unit HCE in unit ⊖ TV
⊕3pin square 🔟 ♨(100yds)
⊖ ♨(2m) ♀(100yds) ▣(½m) 🍴(½m)

BRIGHTON
East Sussex
Map4 TQ30

Ch **East Slope**
for bookings Holiday Lettings Office, The
Refectory, University of Sussex, Falmer,
Brighton, East Sussex BN19QU
☎Brighton(0273)600770

*Twelve split-level red-brick chalets,
situated at one end of the University.
Each unit has modern open-plan
kitchen/diner, shower/WC and varying
sleeping accommodation for six to eight
persons.*

9Jul-17Sep MWB 1wk min,
12wks max, 12units, 6–8persons
no pets ◎ fridge 🍴 Elec inclusive
⊡ not provided ∅ Iron in unit Ironing
board in unit HCE in unit [Launderette
within 300yds] ⊖ ⊕3pin square P
♨(300yds) ⌕Hard Squash, sauna,
tennis & badminton
⊖ ♀(½m) 🍴(1½m)
Max£138pw

BRISTON
Norfolk
Map9 TG03

C **Holly & Ivy Cottages** Edgefield Road
for bookings Mrs R Webb, 33 Blackmores
Grove, Teddington, Middx TW119AE
☎01–977 4197

*Early 19th-century flint and brick
cottages situated on the edge of the
village. They are tastefully modernised
and well-equipped and both have three
bedrooms, living room with storage
heaters for winter use, kitchen/diner and
bathroom/WC. A large garden is
available for the use of both cottages. The
steep staircases make them unsuitable
for the elderly and infirm.*

All year MWB out of season 3days min,
max by arrangement, 2units,
1–6persons [◊] ◊ ◎ fridge
Electric & open fires Elec metered
⊡ not provided ☎(½m) Iron Ironing
board HCE TV can be hired
⊕3pin square P ♨(100yds)
⊖ ♀(½m)
Min£30 Max£89pw

C **2 & 4 Mill Road**
for bookings Mrs R Webb, 33 Blackmores
Grove, Teddington, Middx TW119AE
☎01–9774197

*Modernised and comfortably-appointed
flint and brick cottages situated on the
Briston village green, which is about 4m
W of Holt. No2 has three twin-bedded
rooms, one of which is on the ground-
floor and No4 has four bedrooms, all on
the first-floor. Both have sitting rooms with
solid fuel stoves for winter use, dining
room, kitchen and bathroom/WC. A small
private garden is available for each
cottage in addition to a larger shared
garden. The steep staircases in the
cottages make them unsuitable for
elderly or infirm persons.*

All year MWB out of season 3days min,
max by arrangement, 2units,
1–8persons [◊] ◊ ◎ fridge
Electric & open fires Elec metered
⊡ not provided ☎(½m) Airing
cupboard Iron Ironing board HCE
TV can be hired ⊕3pin square P
⊖ ♀(½m)
Min£30 Max£45pw (Low)
Min£43 Max£103pw (High)

BRIXHAM
Devon
Map3 SX95

Ch Pontin's Ltd **Bayview Holiday
Village** (Types A2 A3 & A5B) Berry Head,
Brixham, Devon TQ59UG
☎Brixham(08045)2279

*Well-situated chalets, some of which are
two-storey. The upper-storey units are
reached by an external stairway and
landing. A central complex contains a
cafeteria, ballroom/bar, games room and
billiards. Also first-aid post, supermarket
and gift shop.*

16May-26Sep MWB out of season
1night min, 5mths max, 241units,
3–7persons ◊ ◆ no pets
No parking by chalets except disabled
◎ fridge Electric Elec metered
⊡ inclusive ☎ [Iron on premises]
Ironing board Launderette on premises
⊖ TV ⊕3pin square P 🔟 ♨ ⌒ ♨
⊖ ♀ ▣ ♫

B **Blue Haven** Cumber Drive
for bookings Mrs M Whittaker, Blue Haze,
43 Petitor Road, Torquay, Devon
TQ1 4QF
☎Torquay(0803)38377

*A modern link bungalow in a residential
area. Accommodation comprises hall,
lounge/diner with double bed-settee,
kitchen, bathroom/WC, one double
bedroom and one twin-bedded room.*

Mar-Oct 1wk min, 8mths max, 1unit
1–6persons ◊ ◆ ◎ fridge
Electric Elec metered ⊡ can be hired
☎(100yds) WM in unit Airing cupboard
in unit Iron in unit Ironing board in unit
HCE in unit TV ⊕3pin square 2P 🔟
♨(1m)
⊖ ♨(3m) ♀(½m) ▣(1m) ♫(1m)
🍴(1m)

F Mr Gooch **Devoncourt Holiday Flats**
Berry Head Road, Brixham, Devon
☎Brixham(08045)3748(am) &
Stoke Gabriel(080428)594(pm)

Beautifully situated, modern block of flats overlooking the southern breakwater of Brixham Harbour. Each flat has its own private balcony. Very well managed and maintained. Good base for walking and motoring tours.

All year MWB out of season 1wk min, 3mths max, 21units, 1–5persons [◈ ◆] ⓦ fridge Electric Elec metered ⌷can be hired ☎ SD on premises Iron on premises Ironing board on premises HCE in unit ⊙ [CTV] ③3pin square P ▥ ♨(300yds) ⌂

⊖ ♀(⅓m) ▤(2m) ♫(3m)

Min£34.50 Max£86.25pw (Low)
Min£94.30 Max£202.10pw (High)

Ch Mr & Mrs B Baker **Fishcombe Cove Holiday Homes** Northfields Lane, Brixham, Devon
☎Brixham(08045)51800

Fifteen detached and five terraced purpose built chalets in pleasant grounds with fine views of Torbay. Each chalet comprises one double and one twin-bedded room, lounge with double put-u-up, kitchen/diner and bathroom.

Mar-Dec MWB out of season 2days min, 20units, 2–6persons ◈ ◆ no pets ⓦ fridge Electric

Elec metered ⌷can be hired ☎(100yds) Airing cupboard in unit Iron on premises Ironing board on premises HCE in unit [Launderette within 300yds] ⊙ TV ③3pin square 20P ♨(100yds) Childrens play area

⊖ ♀(100yds) ♫(100yds)
See advert on page 48

C **Georgian Cottages** Mount Pleasant Road
for bookings Mr J W Griffith, 51 Wall Park Road, Brixham, Devon TG59UF
☎Brixham(08045)2625

Two attractive fishermen's cottages on a hill overlooking the harbour. Each unit comprises lounge with stone fireplace and beamed ceilings, kitchen/dining room, bathroom/WC and four double bedrooms two of which have washbasins.

All year MWB out of season 1wk min, 2units, 3–10persons ◈ ⓦ fridge Storage heaters Elec metered ⌷not provided ☎(200yds) [Airing cupboard in unit] Iron in unit Ironing board in unit HCE in unit [Lauderette within 300yds] ⊙ TV ③3pin square P ▥ ♨(200yds)

⊖ ᗑ(3m) ♀(200yds) ▤(200yds)
Min£60 Max£239pw

F F J & B L Vickery, **Highpoint Flats**
125 Berry Head Road, Brixham, Devon
TQ59AH
☎Brixham(08045)3713

Seven, small, comfortable flats, with sea views from the lounge, located in a Victorian house with modern wings. Flats 3–4 have one bedroom with twin beds, lounge with fold-away double bed and single studio couch, bathroom/WC and hall. Flat 9 comprises one large bedroom with double bed, twin beds and studio couch, large open-plan lounge/diner/kitchen and bathroom/WC. Flats 5–8 are in the new wing and comprise one bedroom with twin beds and a double bunk, lounge with fold-away double bed, kitchen, bathroom/WC and hall.

All year MWB out of season 1wk min, 7units, 1–6persons [◈ ◆] no pets ⓦ fridge Electric Elec metered ⌷can be hired ☎ Airing cupboard in unit Iron in unit Ironing board in unit HCE in unit ⊙ CTV ③3pin square P ▥ ♨(⅓m)

⊖ ᗑ(3m) ♀(300yds) ▤(300yds) ♫(1m)

Min£50 Max£126.50pw

> 1982 prices quoted throughout gazetteer

Ch **Landscove Holiday Village** Berry Head
for bookings Hoseasons Holidays Ltd,
Sunway House, 89 Bridge Road,
Lowestoft, Suffolk NR32 3LT
☎Lowestoft(0502)62292

*117 modern chalets surrounded by
several acres of well laid-out gardens
and grassland on the south-facing side of
Berry Head. Adjoins Berry Head Country
Park.*

Apr-mid Oct MWB out of season
3 days min, 1 mth max, 117 units,
2–6 persons [◇] ◈ ◆ no pets ◎
fridge Electric Elec metered
[⎣inclusive ☎ Airing cupboard in unit
[Iron on premises] [Ironing board on
premises] HCE in unit [Launderette on
premises] ⊖ ⊛ CTV ⊕3 pin square
250P ♨ Licensed clubhouse ♪
⊖ ♒(3m) ♨ ☒ ♫

F Mr D C White *Orchard House*
St Mary's Road, Brixham, Devon
TQ5 9QH
☎Brixham(08045)3590

*Three flats located on the ground and first
floors of modern extension to detached
house in area of St Marys. Each flat has
separate kitchen, bathroom/WC, one
twin-bedded room and lounge/diner with
double put-u-up. Simple traditional
furnishings. Located in residential area
some 700 yds from the sea and 1m from
town centre.*

All year MWB out of season 2 days min,
1 mth max, 3 units, 2–5 persons [◇] ◈
◆ ◎ fridge Electic Elec metered
[⎣not provided ☎ Airing cupboard in
unit Iron in unit HCE in unit
[Launderette within 300 yds] CTV
⊕3 pin square P ▥ ♨(½m)
⊖ ♨(¼m) ☒(1m) ♫(1m) ☻(1m)

Ch Pontin's Ltd, *St Mary's Bay Holiday
Village* (Type A5 & A5B) Mudstone Lane,
St Mary's Bay, Brixham, Devon TQ5 9EL
☎Brixham(08045)2271

*A large camp divided into two sites
100 yds apart. Central complex contains
TV room, ballroom/bar, cafeteria, first-aid
post, gift shop, supermarket and
playroom. Large football/cricket field.
Views over, and access to, St Mary's Bay.
Accommodation for two to eight persons*

Brixham
—
Broad Haven

in four types of chalet.
Mid May-Sep MWB out of season
1 night min, 5 mths max, 124 units,
2–8 persons ◈ ◆ no pets ◎
fridge Electric Elec metered
⎣inclusive ☎ Iron on premises
Ironing board on premises [Launderette
on premises] ⊖ CTV ⊕3 pin square
P ▥ ♨ ⊸ ✔
⊖ ♒ ♨ ☒ ♫

Ch Pontin's Ltd, **Wallpark Holiday
Village** (Type A3) Berry Head, Brixham,
Devon TQ5 9UQ
☎Brixham(08045)2077

*Large, open site with 357 chalets (semi-
detached and terraced). Central
complex containing supermarket,
ballroom, cinema, discothèque, games
room, restaurant, crèche, first-aid centre
and gift shop. Boating pool on site.*

8 May-17 Sep MWB out of season
1 night min, 5 mths max, 357 units,
3–6 persons ◈ ◆ no pets ◎
fridge Electric Elec metered
⎣inclusive ☎(100 yds) [Iron on
premises] [Ironing board on premises]
[Lauderette on premises] ⊖ CTV
⊕3 pin square P ▥ ♨ ⊸
⊖ ♒ ♨ ☒ ♫
Min£51.75 Max£181.70 pw (Low)
Min£149 Max£269.10 pw (High)

F Mrs M Dunsford **Wave Crest Holiday
Flats** 85 Bolton Street, Brixham, Devon
TQ5 9DJ
☎Brixham(08045)3402

*Modern units in colour-washed building
on busy main road. The flats are centrally
located and within easy walking distance
of the shops and harbour.*

Mar-Oct 1 wk min, 1 mth max, 4 units,
2–8 persons ◈ ◆ ◎ fridge
Electric Elec metered ⎣inclusive
☎(100 yds) Iron in unit Ironing board in
unit HCE in unit [Launderette within
300 yds] ⊖ [TV] ⊕3 pin square P
▥ ♨
⊖ ♨(500 yds) ☒(700 yds) ♫(800 yds)
Min£30 Max£50 pw (Low) /
Min£65 Max£95 pw (High)

H **Winkle Cottage** Roseacre Terrace
For bookings Mr J W Griffith, 51 Wall Park
Road, Brixham, Devon TQ5 9UF
☎Brixham(08045)2625

*Georgian cottage only ⅓m from town
centre and ½m from St Mary's Bay.
Accommodation comprises lounge with
put-u-up, separate kitchen and dining
area. One double bedroom and one room
with bunk beds. Bathroom with
washbasin and WC. Street parking. Out
of town centre into Bolton Street, left into
Rea Barn Road, terrace on the right.*

All year MWB out of season 1 wk min,
6 mths max, 1 unit, 1–6 persons, nc6 ◎
fridge Electric Elec metered
⎣not provided ☎(200 yds) Airing
cupboard in unit Iron in unit Ironing
board in unit HCE in unit [Launderette
within 300 yds] ⊖ TV ⊕3 pin square
▥ ♨(300 yds)
⊖ ♒(3m) ♨(¼m) ☒(¼m)
Min£40 Max£169 pw

BROAD HAVEN
Dyfed
Map 2 SM81

F Mr & Mrs J Thirkettle, **Seaview
Apartment** 47 Croft Road, Broadhaven,
Dyfed SA62 3HY
☎Broadhaven(043783)441

*Small apartment adjacent to proprietors'
home. Convenient walking distance to
the beach and facilities in Broadhaven.
Accommodation comprises an entrance
hall with utility area, concealed shower
unit, kitchen/dining room, sitting room
with a double bed-settee. The only
bedroom has a double and single bed.
Separate WC. Approaching Broadhaven
from Haverfordwest, Croft Road is signed
to the right.*

All year MWB out of season 3 days min,
1 unit, 2–4 persons [◇] ◈ ◎ fridge
▦ Elec inclusive ⎣can be hired
(overseas visitors only) ☎(400 yds)
WM in unit SD in unit Iron in unit
Ironing board in unit HCE in unit ⊖
TV ⊕3 pin square 1P ▥ ♨(½m)
⊖ ♒(½m) ♨(500 yds)
Min£79 Max£155 pw

BROADHEMBURY
Devon
Map**3** ST10

C **CC Ref 637 ELP**
for bookings Character Cottages
(Holidays) Ltd, 34 Fore Street, Sidmouth,
Devon EX10 8AQ
☎Sidmouth(03955)77001

*Picturesque detached cottage, situated
on outskirts of village. Accommodation
comprises lounge, fitted kitchen/diner,
modern bathroom and WC, three
bedrooms with exposed beams and
good interior-sprung beds. Ample
wardrobe space.*

All year MWB out of season 1wk min,
6mths max, 1 unit, 2–6 persons ◇ ◉
fridge Electric Elec metered ⌷ can be
hired ☎(300yds) Airing cupboard in
unit Iron in unit Ironing board in unit
HCE in unit ⊙ TV ⊕3pin square P
▥ ♨(200yds)
↔ ♀(200yds)

Min£47 Max£65pw (Low)
Min£88 Max£128pw (High)

BROADWAY
Hereford & Worcester
Map**4** SP03

C **Bibsworth Lodge**
for bookings Heart of England Cottages,
Buckland, Broadway, Worcester
☎Broadway(0386)853593

*An attractive two-storey lodge standing
by the entrance to Bibsworth House. It
has its own small garden. The
accommodation comprises lounge,
dining room, kitchen and bathroom/WC
on the ground floor and one twin-bedded
room and one double bedroom on the
first floor. Camp beds are also available.*

All year MWB out of season 3days min,
6mths max, 1 unit, 1–4 persons ◇ ◉
no pets ◉ fridge Electric
Elec metered ⌷ can be hired ☎ Airing
cupboard in unit HCE in unit TV
⊕3pin square 2P ▥ ♨(¾m) Putting
↔ ♀(¾m)
Max£120pw

C **Pear Tree Cottage**
for bookings Heart of England Cottages,
Buckland, Broadway, Worcester
☎Broadway(0386)853593

*A 100-year-old two-storey Cotswold
stone cottage comprising kitchen/diner,
lounge with open fireplace and a divan
bed. The first floor comprises one double
and one single bedroom and
bathroom/WC.*

All year MWB out of season 3days min,
6mths max, 1 unit, 1–5 persons ◇ ◈
◆ no cats ◢ fridge ♨
Gas/Elec metered ⌷ can be hired
☎(100yds) Airing cupboard Iron
Ironing board HCE Launderette ⊙
TV ⊕3pin square 1P ▥ ♨(1m)
↔ ♀
Max£125pw

BROADWINDSOR
Dorset
Map**3** ST40

C **Hursey Farm Cottages**
for bookings Mrs Poulton, Hursey Farm,
Hursey, Broadwindsor, Beaminster,
Dorset DT8 3LN
☎Broadwindsor(0308)68323

*Three stone-built cottages set in quiet
rural countryside. First cottage
comprises ground-floor lounge/diner,
separate kitchen. Two bedrooms (one
double and one twin), combined
bathroom/WC on first floor. Also double
bed-settee in lounge. Middle cottage
consists of ground-floor lounge/diner,
separate kitchen, combined
bathroom/WC. Two bedrooms on first
floor comprising one double-bedded
room and one with three single beds.
Third cottage consists of ground-floor
accommodation only, lounge,
kitchen/diner, combined bathroom/WC,
two bedrooms (one double and one twin),
additional single bed available if
required.*

All year MWB out of season 3days min,
6wks max, 3 units, 2–6 persons [◇] ◈
◉ fridge Electric Elec metered
⌷ can be hired ☎(¼m) Iron in unit
Ironing board in unit HCE in unit ⊙
TV ⊕3pin square 2P ▥ ♨(¼m)
↔ ♀(¼m)
Min£35 Max£98pw

BRODICK
Isle of Arran, Strathclyde *Bute*
Map**10** NS03

C **Altbeg Corriegills**
for bookings Altbeg Cottages, Room 355,
93 Hope Street, Glasgow, Strathclyde
☎041–884 2706 & Brodick(0770)2386

*Detached traditional two-storey stone
cottage with its own little garden and
adjacent pleasant lawns situated in quiet
little hamlet. On the ground floor there is a
lounge, dining room, kitchen and
bedroom with bunk beds. Upstairs there
are two twin bedrooms. The cottage is
attractively decorated and furnished, and
equipped to a high standard. Corriegills
lies 250ft above sea level 1m from
Brodick Pier.*

All year 1wk min, 1mth max, 1 unit,
2–6 persons, nc7 no pets ◉ fridge
Electric Elec metered ⌷ not provided
☎(1m) SD on premises Iron in unit
Ironing board in unit HCE in unit ⊙
TV ⊕3pin square P ▥ ♨(1½m)
↔ ♒(2m) ♀(1m)
Min£35 Max£130pw

1982 prices quoted throughout
gazetteer

BRONYDD
Powys
Map**3** SO24

C **Rose Cottage**
for bookings Mrs H Williams, Cabalva
Farmhouse, Whitney on Wye, Hereford
☎Clifford(04973)324

*Traditional white-painted stone cottage
on hillside with views of Wye Valley and
Black Mountains. Accommodation
comprises lounge/diner, bathroom/WC,
kitchen. First floor comprises one double
and one twin-bedded room.*

All year MWB out of season 3days min,
4wks max, 1 unit, 1–5 persons ◇ ◆
◉ fridge Electric & gas fires
Gas/Elec inclusive ⌷ inclusive
☎(1m) Airing cupboard in unit Iron in
unit Ironing board in unit HCE in unit
⊙ CTV ⊕3pin square 2P ▥
♨(2m) Fishing
↔ ♀(½m) ♒(2m)
Min£90 Max£125pw

BROUGHTON-IN-FURNESS
Cumbria
Map**7** SD28

F **The Coach House**
for bookings Mrs D V Walker, High
Duddon Guest House, Broughton-in-
Furness, Cumbria LA20 6ET
☎Broughton-in-Furness(06576)279

*Two spacious, modern, well-equipped
flats in what used to be the old coach
house. Set in 7½ acres of woodlands,
grounds and gardens, the sleeping
accommodation consists of one double
and one twin bedroom or one double and
two twins plus a double convertible bed-
settee in lounge. Convenient position for
access to coast and Lake District.*

All year MWB out of season 1wk min,
1mth max, 2 units, 4–8 persons ◇ ◆
◉ fridge Electric Elec metered
⌷ inclusive ☎ Airing cupboard in unit
Iron in unit Ironing board in unit HCE in
unit ⊙ TV ⊕3pin square P ▥
♨(1½m)
↔ ♀(25yds)
Min£50 Max£70pw (Low)
Min£85 Max£135pw (High)

BRYHER
Isles of Scilly (No Map)

F P W Philpott **Hell Bay Hotel** Bryher,
Isles of Scilly
☎Scillonia(0720)22947

*Modern units comprising one or two
bedrooms, lounge with convertible bed,
chairs and kitchen area, shower/WC. The
units are grouped around a lawn in front
of the hotel bar, restaurant and television
lounge. Situated beside beautiful rocky
coast ½m from village.*

Feb–Nov MWB 1day min, 4wks max,
10 units, 2–4 persons ◈ no pets ◢
fridge ♨ Elec inclusive ⌷ inclusive
☎ [WM on premises] [SD on
premises] Airing cupboard on
premises Iron on premises Ironing →

49

board on premises   HCE on premises
⊖   ♨(⅓m)
⇔   ⚲

BRYNCIR
Gwynedd
Map **6** SH44

H   Derwin Fawr
for bookings Mrs E W Roberts, Cae-
Canol, Criccieth, Gwynedd LL52 0NB
☎Criccieth(076671)2351

Well converted 18th-century farmhouse
set in 280 acres with fishing and shooting
available. Accommodation comprises
lounge, dining room, kitchen and
breakfast room. There are three double
bedrooms, one single bedroom,
bathroom and separate shower. Views of
mountains and countryside. Approx 5m
from Criccieth and approached by long
cement drive off the A487.

All year   MWB out of season   1unit,
1–6persons ◇ ◆ no pets ◎
fridge ♨ Elec metered
⎍not provided   ☎(⅓m) Airing cupboard
in unit Iron in unit HCE in unit ⊖ TV
⊕3pin square 6P ♨(⅓m)

⇔ ঌ ⚲(⅓m)

BUCKIE
Grampian *Banffshire*
Map **15** NJ46

C   Oystercatcher, Sandpiper & Tern
4/5/8 Bowie's Lane, Buckpool
for bookings Blantyre Holiday Homes
Ltd, West Bauds, Findochty, Buckie,
Moray AB5 2EB
☎Buckie(0542)31773

Three completely renovated early 19th-
century fishermen's cottages on the
seafront of the Moray Firth fishing town.
The accommodation is all on the ground
floor and comprises lounge/diner with
bed-settee, one double bedroom, one
twin-bedded room, modern kitchen and
bathroom. Off the A92 on Buckpool road.

All year   MWB out of season   1wk min,
3wks max, 3units, 1–6persons [◇ ◇
◆] ◎ fridge Electric Elec metered
⎍can be hired ☎(⅓m) Airing cupboard
in unit Iron in unit Ironing board in unit
HCE in unit ⊖ CTV ⊕3pin square P
Children's play area

⇔ ঌ(2m) ⚲(100yds) ♫(2m)
♨(1½m)

BUCKFASTLEIGH
Devon
Map **3** SX76

**F & C   Mrs J Ford Longwood Court
Holiday Apartments** Fore Street,
Buckfastleigh, Devon
☎Buckfastleigh(03644)3332

Five flats situated within large period
house and comprising lounge/diner,
bathroom/WC and sleeping one–eight
persons. The cottage is to the rear of the
house and comprises
lounge/diner/kitchen with double bed
settee, large double bedroom with en
suite bathroom and WC.

Apr–Sep   1night min, 6wks max, 6units,
1–8persons [◇ ◇ ◆] ◎
Electric Elec metered ⎍can be hired
☎ Airing cupboard in unit Iron in unit
Ironing board in unit HCE in unit ⊖
[CTV] ⊕3pin square P ♨ ▥
♨(20yds)

⇔ ⚲ ▨

Min£33 Max£55pw (Low)
Min£85 Max£140pw (High)

BUCKINGHAM
Buckinghamshire
Map **4** SP63

B   The Bungalow Church End,
Hillesden
for bookings Mrs S Goodall, Home farm,
Hillesden, Buckingham, Bucks
MK18 4DB
☎Steeple Claydon(029673)256

Modern bungalow with two bedrooms.
Surrounded by garden and facing the
village church.

All year   1wk min, 1unit, 2–6persons
[◇] ◇ ◆ ◎ fridge Electric
Elec metered ⎍inclusive ☎(100yds)
SD on premises Airing cupboard in
unit Iron in unit Ironing board in unit
HCE in unit ⊖ TV ⊕3pin square 2P
1♨ ▥ ♨(1m) Trout lake, river fishing

⇔ ঌ(3m) ⚲(1m) ♫(3m)

Min£60 Max£90pw (Low)
Min£130 Max£168pw (High)

C   4 Church End Hillesden
for bookings Mrs S Goodall, Home Farm,
Hillesden, Buckingham, Bucks
MK18 4DB
☎Steeple Claydon(029673)256

Modernised semi-detached cottage with
three bedrooms and lounge/diner. Close
to village church.

All year   1wk min, 1unit, 2–6persons
[◇] ◇ ◆ ◎ fridge Electric
Elec metered ⎍inclusive ☎(100yds)
SD on premises Airing cupboard in
unit Iron in unit Ironing board in unit
HCE in unit ⊖ TV ⊕3pin square 2P
1♨ ▥ ♨(1m) Trout lake, river fishing

⇔ ঌ(3m) ⚲(1m) ♫(3m)

Min£60 Max£90pw (Low)
Min£130 Max£168pw (High)

H   Lower Farm House Hillesden
for bookings Mrs S Goodall, Home Farm,
Hillesden, Buckingham, Bucks
MK18 4DB
☎Steeple Claydon(029673)256

Luxurious and spacious period
farmhouse with five large bedrooms and
three bathrooms. Set in peaceful
surroundings with lovely views
overlooking countryside.

All year   1wk min, 1unit, 2–14persons
[◇] ◇ ◆ ◎ fridge ♨
Elec inclusive ⎍can be hired ☎(⅓m)
WM in unit SD in unit Airing cupboard
in unit Iron in unit Ironing board in unit

HCE in unit ⊖ CTV ⊕3pin square
6P 2♨ ▥ ♨(1m) Trout lake, river
fishing

⇔ ঌ(3m) ⚲(1m) ♫(3m)
Min£100 Max£190pw (Low)
Min£240 Max£328pw (High)

BUCKS CROSS
Devon
Map **2** SS32

Ch   Bideford Bay Holiday Village
for bookings Hoseasons Holidays,
Sunway House, Lowestoft, Suffolk
NR32 3LT
☎Lowestoft(0502)62292

Blocks of semi-detached stone and
timber chalets. Two bedrooms each for
two persons ie double and twin. Good
units and wardrobes. Lounge/diner with
'put-u-up'. Kitchen area. Separate
bathroom with WC and washbasin. All
furnished in contemporary style. Clean
and well-maintained.

3May–17Sep   1wk min, 162units,
1–6persons [◇ ◇] [◆] ◎ fridge
Electric Elec metered ⎍inclusive ☎
HCE in unit [Launderette on premises]
TV ⊕3pin square P ♨ Games
room Children's play area

⇔ ⚲ ▨

BUDE
Cornwall
Map **2** SS20

H   CC Ref 319 ELP
for bookings Character Cottages
(Holidays) Ltd, 34 Fore Street, Sidmouth,
Devon EX10 8AQ
☎Sidmouth(03955)77001

Semi-detached house ½m from main
beach with small hall, sitting room,
modestly furnished dining room, bright
kitchen and three bedrooms (one double,
one single and one family room) and
modern bathroom/WC.

All year   MWB out of season   1wk min,
1mth max, 1unit, 2–6persons ◇ ◆
fridge Electric Elec inclusive ⎍can
be hired ☎(200yds) Airing cupboard
in unit Iron in unit Ironing board in unit
HCE in unit ⊖ TV ⊕3pin square
⊕2pin round P ♨ ♨(⅓m)

⇔ ⚲ ▨
Min£50 Max£69pw (Low)
Min£84 Max£117pw (High)

F   Chapter House Burn View
for bookings Mr J D Linnard, Hideaway,
Maiden Street, Stratton, Bude, Cornwall
EX23 9DQ
☎Bude(0288)2743

Purpose-built flat with picture windows
set above a furniture repository, between
a golf course and shopping centre and
within walking distance of beaches.
Access is via an outside stairway.

Jan–Nov   MWB out of season   1wk min,
3mths max, 1unit, 1–4persons ◇ ◆
◎ fridge Electric Elec metered
⎍can be hired ☎(100yds) Airing
cupboard in unit Iron in unit Ironing

board in unit HCE in unit [Launderette within 300yds] ⊙ [TV]
⊕3pin square 1P Ⅲ ♨(100yds)
⟷ ♿(100yds) ☎(100yds) ⌷(100yds)
♫(100yds) ▨(100yds)

Min£40 Max£70pw (Low)
Min£95 Max£105pw (HIgh)

F Endeavour Self-Catering Flats
Summerleaze Crescent
for bookings Mr R R Powell, 9 Summerleaze Crescent, Bude, Cornwall
☎Widemouth Bay(028885)517

Four flats situated overlooking the harbour and beach. All flats have lounge with double bed-settee, kitchen/diner and bathroom/WC. Flat 4 has one double bedroom and Flat 5 has one double and one twin-bedded room.

All year MWB out of season 1wk min, 1mth max, 2units, 1–6persons ◇ ◆ no pets ◎ fridge Electric Elec metered ⌸inclusive ☎(20yds) Airing cupboard in unit Iron in unit Ironing board in unit HCE in unit [Launderette within 300yds] ⊙ TV ⊕3pin square P ⌂ Ⅲ ♨(100yds)
⟷ ♿(¼m) ♿(¼m) ⌷(¼m) ♫(¼m) ▨(¼m)

Min£35 Max£55pw (Low)
Min£90 Max£130pw (HIgh)

H Ferndale 1 Victoria road
for bookings Mrs J E Carilll, 1A Victoria Road, Bude, Cornwall EX23 8RJ
☎Bude(0288)3070

Semi-detached house with small front garden, close to beach. Accommodation comprises kitchen, dining room, lounge, bathroom/WC. Four bedrooms, one family room with double and two bunk beds, one single bedroom and two double bedrooms. Separate WC.

All year MWB out of season 3days min, 3mths max, 1unit, 1–9persons ◇ ◢ fridge Electric & gas fires Gas/Elec metered ⌸not provided ☎(100yds) Iron Ironing board HCE ⊙ CTV ⊕3pin square ♨(100yds)
⟷ ♿(100yds) ♿(¼m) ⌷(¼m) ♫(¼m) ▨(¼m)

Min£50 Max£100pw (Low)
Min£120 Max£150pw (High)

F Flexbury Chimes Flexbury park Road
for bookings Mrs A T Price, Hideaway, Maiden Street, Stratton, Bude, Cornwall EX23 9DQ
☎Bude(0288)2743

A spacious first-floor flat in large terraced house situated in quiet residential area, overlooking golf course with short walk to beach and shops.

All year MWB out of season 1wk min, 1mth max, 1unit, 2–10persons ◇ ◆ ◎ fridge Electric Elec metered ⌸inclusive Airing cupboard in unit Iron in unit Ironing board in unit HCE in unit [Launderette within 300yds] ⊙ TV ⊕3pin square ⊕2pin round Ⅲ ♨(100yds) ⌁ ♿ ♿

⟷ ♿(100yds) ⌷(100yds) ♫(100yds) ▨(100yds)

Min£35pw (Low)
Min£40 Max£120pw (High)

F Gellalin House Victoria road
for bookings Mrs A T Price, Hideaway, Maiden Street, Stratton, Bude, Cornwall EX23 9DQ
☎Bude(0288)2743

First-floor maisonette of a terraced house, which sleeps up to six people. Within walking distance of Crooklets Beach and shops.

All year MWB out of season 1wk min, 1mth max, 1unit, 2–9persons ◇ ◆ ◎ fridge Elec metered ⌸inclusive ☎(200yds) Airing cupboard in unit Iron in unit Ironing board in unit HCE in unit [Launderette within 300yds] ⊙ TV ⊕3pin square ⊕3pin round ⊕2pin round Ⅲ ⌁ ♿ ♿

⟷ ♿(200yds) ⌷(200yds) ♫(200yds) ▨(200yds)

Min£35 Max£55pw (Low)
Min£60 Max£100pw (High)

F 8 Granville Terrace
for bookings Miss J Ball, 13 Belle Vue, Bude, Cornwall
☎Bude(0288)3780(day)
Widemouth Bay(028885)311(evening)

Two flats situated within a brick-built end of terrace house. The ground floor comprises lounge/diner with single convertible settee, kitchen, bathroom/WC, one twin-bedded room and one double bedroom. The other flat is located on the first and second floors and comprises kitchen/diner, lounge with double convertible settee, bathroom/WC on the first floor and one double bedroom and one small bedroom both with washbasins on the upper floor. For access enter the Strand and keep left of Lloyds Bank for Granville terrace on the right.

May–Sep 1wk min, 6mths max, 2units, 2–5persons ◇ ◎ fridge Electric Elec metered ⌸can be hired ☎(50yds) Iron in unit Ironing board in unit HCE in unit [Launderette within 300yds] TV ⊕3pin square Ⅲ ♨
⟷ ♿ ♿ ⌷ ♫ ▨

BUDLEIGH SALTERTON
Devon
Map 3 SY08

F Mr & Mrs Skelding Cliff House Flat
Cliff House, Budleigh Salterton, Devon EX9 6JY
☎Budleigh Salterton(03954)2432

First-floor flat with private entrance, situated in quiet residential road. Accommodaaion comprises kitchen/diner, lounge with double bed-settee, one double bedroom, one with bunk beds and wash hand basin,

---

bathroom and WC. Well furnished and decorated. Beach 200yds.

All year MWB out of season 1wk min, 6wks max, 1unit, 1–6persons [◇] ◎ fridge ⋈ Elec inclusive ⌸can be hired ☎(220yds) Airing cupboard in unit Iron in unit Ironing board in unit HCE in unit ⊙ CTV ⊕3pin square 1P Ⅲ ♨(100yds)
⟷ ♿(¼m) ♿ ⌷ ♫ ▨

C CC Ref 681E
for bookings Character Cottages (Holidays) Ltd, 34 Fore Street, Sidmouth, Devon EX10 8AQ
☎Sidmouth(03955)77001

Large cottage in grounds of country house estate. Good tarmac approach. Porch, attractive lounge, styled fireplace dining room, fitted kitchen, three twin bedrooms. Expensive and modern furnishings.

All year MWB out of season 1wk min, 1mth max, 1unit, 2–6persons ◇ no pets ◎ fridge Electric Elec metered ⌸not provided ☎ WM in unit SD in unit TD in unit Airing cupboard in unit Iron in unit Ironing board in unit HCE in unit ⊙ CTV ⊕3pin square ⊕2pin round P Ⅲ ♨(¼m)
⟷ ♿(1m)

Min£67 Max£120pw (Low)
Min£175 Max£250pw (High)

F CC Ref 690
for bookings Character Cottages (Holidays) Ltd, 34 Fore Street, Sidmouth, Devon EX10 8AQ
☎Sidmouth(03955)77001

Flat in semi-detached house in residential area of seaside resort in secluded position. Two twin-bedded rooms, lounge, kitchen, dining room. All modern furnishings and equipment.

All year MWB out of season 1wk min, 6wks max, 1unit, 2–4persons [◇] ◆ no pets ◢ fridge ⋈ Gas/Elec metered ⌸can be hired ☎(100yds) Airing cupboard in unit Iron in unit Ironing board in unit HCE in unit ⊙ TV ⊕3pin square ⊕2pin round P ⌂ Ⅲ ♨(100yds)
⟷ ♿(1m) ♿

Min£71 Max£104pw (Low)
Min£117 Max£149pw (High)

H CC Ref 6034
for bookings Character Cottages (Holidays) Ltd, 34 Fore Street, Sidmouth, Devon EX10 8AQ
☎Sidmouth(03955)77001

A modern, brick-built, detached residence with a large garden. On the ground floor is a large lounge, dining room, kitchen, WC and one double bedroom. On the first floor are two double bedrooms and a bathroom/WC. →

┌─────────────────────────────┐
│ 1982 prices quoted throughout │
│ gazetteer │
└─────────────────────────────┘

All year MWB out of season 1wk min, 6mths max, 1unit, 2–6persons ◊ ◿ fridge Electric & gas
Gas/Elec inclusive ⬡can be hired ☎
Airing cupboard in unit Iron in unit
Ironing board in unit HCE in unit
[Launderette within 300yds] ⊕ TV
⊕3pin square ⊕2pin round P ♨ ▥
↔ ◊ʀ(1¼m) ♀(½m) ▨(½m)
Min£97 Max£110pw (Low)
Min£155 Max£220pw (High)

F   Ocean House
for bookings C L Prior (T A Prior Marine Charters), Ocean House, Fore Street, Budleigh Salterton, Devon
☎Budleigh Salterton(03954)3252

Two flats located in brick-built building over a main street shop approached via an iron staircase at the rear of 'Ocean House', off the A376. The accommodation consists of a first floor with kitchen, dining room and a spacious lounge. The second floor has two double bedrooms, one twin-bedded room and a bathroom/WC. Both have lawned garden and sea views.

All year 1wk min, 6mths max, 2units, 2–6persons [◊ ◆] ⊛ fridge
Electric Elec metered ☎ Airing cupboard in unit Iron in unit Ironing board in unit HCE in unit [Launderette on premises] ⊕ [TV] ⊕3pin square
▥ ♨
↔ ◊ʀ(1m) ♀(50yds) ▨(1m)

BUILTH WELLS
Powys
Map3 SO05

C   Cottage & Extension Nant-yr-Arian
for bookings Mr & Mrs A H Beater, Teme House, Lancing College, Lancing, Sussex BN15 0RW
☎Shoreham by Sea(07917)2219

Stone-built terraced cottage comprising lounge, separate open-plan dining room, kitchen. On the first floor there are two twin-bedded rooms and one single, bathroom and WC. The Extension has a separate front door, studio room with bed-settee, breakfast bar with cooking facilities, balcony bedroom with twin-beds and shower/WC.

All year MWB out of season wkd min, 6mths max, 2units, 2–5persons ⊛ fridge Electric Elec heating inclusive
Elec metered ⬡not provided ☎(½m)
SD in unit Airing cupboard in unit Iron in unit Ironing board in unit HCE in unit TV ⊕3pin square P ▥ ♨(½m)
↔ ◊ʀ(½m) ♀(½m) ▨(½m)
Min£28 Max£110pw

BURFORD
Oxfordshire
Map4 SP21

C & F   Widford Farm Cottages
for bookings Mrs E Buxton, Widford Manor, Burford, Oxford OX8 4DU
☎Burford(099382)2152

Five cottages and one flat all built of Cotswold stone. All have lounge/dining room, well equipped kitchens, bathroom and WC. Widford Manor Flat is self-contained and has one double bedroom. Whitehill cottage is semi-detached with three bedrooms, two twin-bedded rooms and one with bunk beds, plus an additional folding bed. Clock House is converted from farm buildings with two twin-bedded rooms and one room with bunk beds plus a double bed-settee in lounge. Shepherd's Cottage has two twin-bedded rooms and one room with three single beds plus a folding bed. Gardeners Cottage has one double bedroom and another room with three single beds plus a folding bed. Widford End, self-contained ground-floor accommodation with two bedrooms, one double room and the other having bunk beds plus a convertible bed-settee in lounge. Each unit has its own garden. 2m E of Burford on unclassified road.

All year 1wk min, 6units, 2–8persons [◊] ◊ ◆ no pets except dogs ⊛ fridge Electric & open fires
Elec metered ⬡can be hired ☎ WM on premises SD on premises TD on premises Airing cupboard in unit Iron in unit Ironing board in unit HCE in unit ⊕ ⊛ TV ⊕3pin square
⊕3pin round 30P ♨ ▥ ♨(2m)
⤷Hard Trout fishing, table tennis & bicycles for hire
↔ ◊ʀ(2m) ♀(1m)
Min£60 Max£90pw (Low)
Min£85 Max£150pw (High)

BURGH CASTLE
Norfolk
Map5 TG40

Ch   Waveney Valley Holiday Village
Butt lane
for bookings Hoseasons Holidays, Sunway House, Lowestoft, Suffolk NR32 3LT
☎Lowestoft(0502)62292

One hundred units with small patios. Designed to sleep four in two bedrooms plus double put-up in lounge/diner, they are set in a quiet rural location.

Etr–mid Sep MWB out of season 1wk min, 100units, 2–6persons [◊ ◆] ⊛ fridge Electric Elec metered ⬡inclusive ☎(½m) HCE in unit ⊕ TV ⊕3pin square P ♨(½m)
↔ ♀(1m) ▨(2m)

BURNHAM-ON-SEA
Somerset
Map3 ST34

Ch   Pontin's Brean Sands Holiday Village Burnham-on-Sea, Somerset TA8 2RJ
☎Brean Down(027875)203

Well-spaced, purpose-built chalets with various sleeping accommodation for up

---

to eight persons. Modern or traditional furnishings with fitted carpets throughout. Ideal family holiday situation offering all the usual amenities and attractions, under good management and supervision. (72 Type A1 do not conform to basic requirements.)

3Apr–2Nov MWB 1day min, 641units, 2–8persons ◊ ◆ no pets ⊛ fridge Electric Elec metered
⬡inclusive ☎ Ironing board on premises HCE in unit [Launderette on premises] ⊕ CTV ⊕3pin square P ♨ ▣ ▵ ⤷Hard ♪
↔ ♀ ▨ ♬ ♨

BURNMOUTH
Borders Berwickshire
Map12 NT95

H   Bayview
for bookings Mrs M Spouse, Harbour View, Burnmouth, Eyemouth, Berwickshire TD14 5ST
☎Ayton(03902)213

House converted from an old coastguard station situated on hillside overlooking the harbour and North Sea. Accommodation comprises three bedrooms, sitting room, kitchen/diner, shower and WC.

All year MWB out of season 1wk min, 1mth max, 1unit, 2–8persons ◊ ◆ ⊛ fridge Electric & Coal fires
Elec metered ⬡not provided
☎(200yds) SD un unit Iron in unit Ironing board in unit HCE in unit TV ⊕3pin square P ♨(200yds)
↔ ♀(200yds) ▨(2m)
Min£35 Max£45pw (Low)
Max£50pw (High)

BURTON BRADSTOCK
Dorset
Map3 SY48

H   CC Ref 811 ELP
for bookings Character Cottages (Holidays) Ltd, 34 Fore Street, Sidmouth, Devon EX10 8AQ
☎Sidmouth(03955)77001

Three bedroomed house (one double, one twin, one single) with lounge kitchen/diner, cloakroom, bathroom and WC. In a recently built terrace, a quiet cul-de-sac on perimeter of charming unspoilt Burton Bradstock village.

All year MWB out of season 1wk min, 1mth max, 1unit, 2–8persons ◊ ◆ no cats ⊛ fridge ♨ Elec inclusive
⬡can be hired ☎(500yds) SD un unit Airing cupboard in unit Iron in unit Ironing board in unit HCE in unit ⊕ TV ⊕3pin square ♨ ▥ ♨(500yds)
↔ ◊ʀ(1½m) ♀(500yds) ▨(½m)
♬(2m) ♨(2m)
Min£39 Max£75pw (Low)
Min£97 Max£142pw (High)

1982 prices quoted throughout gazetteer

BUTE, Isle of see under **Rothesay**

BUTTERSTONE
Tayside *Perthshire*
Map**15** NO04

Ca **Butterstone Log Cabins Ltd**
Butterstone, Dunkeld, Perthshire
☎Butterstone(03504)234/205

A group of ten sturdy Scandinavian spruce log cabins lying in sheltered wooded clearing by small burn. Each has three bedrooms – a double, one with two single beds and a bunk bed above each and one room with bunk beds. There is a living/dining room with small open-plan kitchen area, a bathroom with bath and shower (hand). Butterstone village is 5m E of Dunkeld on A923 amidst loch and mountain scenery.

All year MWB out of season 1wk min, 1mth max, 10units, 1–8persons ◊ @ fridge Electric Elec inclusive ▣inclusive ☎(200yds) Airing cupboard HCE ⊕ CTV ⊕3pin square 2P ▥ ♨(4m) Fishing
Min£125 Max£230pw

BUXTON
Derbyshire
Map**7** SK07

C **Jenny's Cottage** 47 West Road
for bookings Mrs R Draper, Avilda, 43 West Road, Buxton, Derbyshire SK17 6HQ
☎Buxton(0298)5831

A low-roofed, local stone cottage set in a row of houses. Attractive, 'old world' charm with low oak beams and quaint old stairways. Situated on south side of town close to Pavilion Gardens.

All year MWB out of season 7days min, 14days max, 1unit, 2–4persons, nc5 no pets @ fridge Electric Elec inclusive ▣not provided ☎(50yds) Airing cupboard in unit Iron in unit Ironing board in unit HCE in unit ⊕ TV can be hired ⊕3pin square P ♨(15yds)
↦ ☕(50yds) ▨(¼m) ▤(¼m)
Min£70 Max£90pw

BYRNESS
Northumberland
Map**12** NT70

C **Rose Cottage**
for bookings Mr R H Armstrong, Border Park Service Station, Byrness, Otterburn, Newcastle upon Tyne NE19 1TR
☎Otterburn(0830)20271

Single-storey cottage converted from a village school room. Accommodation comprises living room, two twin-bedded rooms with two additional bunk beds in one, modern kitchen and bathroom/WC. Sun porch and ample parking space.

All year MWB out of season 1wk min, 3mths max, 1unit, 1–6persons ◊ @ fridge ☰ Elec metered ▣not provided ☎(¼m) WM in unit SD in unit Iron in unit Ironing board in unit HCE in unit ⊕ TV ⊕3pin square P ♨(60yds)
↦ ☕(100yds)
Min£25 Max£95pw
See advert on page 54

CADBURY
Devon
Map**3** SS90

F **East & North Wing Flats**
for bookings Mrs C Fursdon, Fursdon House, Cadbury, Thorverton, Exeter, Devon EX5 5JS
☎(0392)860860

Flats situated in two wings of a delightful country mansion in total seclusion amidst its large estate. Accommodation varies with **North Wing** *having one bedroom with four-poster and one with bunk-beds and* **East Wing** *with two twin-bedrooms and one single. Both offer fine views over the estate.*

All year MWB out of season 3days min, 4wks max, 2units, 1–5persons ◊ ◊ ◆ no pets ◢ fridge ☰ & open fires Gas & Elec inclusive(lighting) Elec metered(heating) ▣can be hired Airing cupboard in unit Iron in unit Ironing board in unit HCE in unit ⊕ CTV ⊕3pin square P ▥ ♨(2m)

↦grass Croquet Table tennis
↦ ☕(2m)
Min£38 Max£55pw (Low)
Min£60 Max£110pw (High)

H **Lime House**
for bookings Mrs C Fursdon, Fursdon House, Cadbury, Thorverton, Exeter, Devon EX5 5JS
☎Exeter(0392)860860

Detached stone-built house set in a garden within the grounds of Fursdon House. Accommodation includes kitchen, dining room, lounge, five bedrooms, bathroom/WC and separate WC.

All year MWB out of season 3days min, 4wks max, 1unit, 1–8persons no pets @ fridge Electric & open fires Elec metered ▣can be hired Airing cupboard in unit Iron in unit Ironing board in unit HCE in unit ⊕ CTV ⊕3pin square P ▥ ♨(2m) ↦grass Croquet Table tennis
Min£35 Max£50pw (Low)
Min£70 Max£120pw (High)

H **East Wing,** Fursdon Barton
for bookings Mrs C Fursdon, Fursdon House, Cadbury, Thorverton, Exeter, Devon EX5 5JS
☎(0392)860860

Wing of old stone farmhouse located within the grounds of a large estate. Accommodation comprises kitchen/diner with Rayburn, lounge, three bedrooms, bathroom and WC. Delightful position and good standard of furnishings and fittings.

All year MWB out of season 3days min, 4wks max, 1unit, 1–6persons no pets @ fridge Electric & wood burning stove Elec metered ▣can be hired Airing cupboard in unit Iron in unit Ironing board in unit HCE in unit ⊕ CTV ⊕3pin square P ▥ ♨(2m) ↦grass Croquet Table tennis
↦ ☕(2m)
Min£35 Max£50pw (Low)
Min£70 Max£120pw (High)

CADGWITH
Cornwall
Map **2** SW71

C **CC Ref 307 EL**
for bookings Character Cottages
(Holidays) Ltd, 34 Fore Street, Sidmouth,
Devon EX10 8AQ
☎Sidmouth(03955)77001

*Stone-built cottage with patio and five
steps to beach. The accommodation
consists large lounge and modern
kitchen and an open-tread staircase to
two double and two single bedrooms and
a bathroom/WC.*

All year MWB out of season 1wk min,
1mth max, 1 unit, 2–6 persons ◇ ◆
◉ fridge Electric Elec metered
Ⓛcan be hired ☎(50yds) Airing
cupboard in unit Iron in unit Ironing
board in unit HCE in unit ⊙ TV
⊕3pin square ⊕2pin round P ▥
♨(50yds)
⊕ ♀

Min£77 Max£118pw (Low)
Min£136 Max£177pw (High)

F **CC Ref 316 EL (1, 2 & 3)**
for bookings Character Cottages
(Holidays) Ltd, 34 Fore Street, Sidmouth,
Devon EX10 8AQ
☎Sidmouth(03955)77001

*Three maisonettes located in a block and
timber building near to the sea. Numbers
one and three have a ground floor with
one twin and one single bedroom and a
first floor with living room, well appointed
kitchen, double bedroom and
bathroom/WC. Flat two also has two
floors comprising two twin-bedded
rooms, one double-bedded room, 'L'
shaped living room with an open ceiling,
kitchen/diner, bathroom and separate
WC.*

All year MWB out of season 1wk min,
1mth max, 3 units, 2–6 persons ◇ ◆
no pets ◉ fridge ♨ Elec inclusive
Ⓛcan be hired ☎(50yds) Airing
cupboard in unit Iron in unit Ironing
board in unit HCE in unit ⊙ TV
⊕3pin square ⊕2pin round P ▥ ♨
⊕ ♀

1982 prices quoted throughout
gazetteer

Min£59 Max£83pw (Low)
Min£110 Max£159pw (High)

CAERNARFON
Gwynedd
Map **6** SH46

Ch **Glan Gwna Private Riverside
Chalets**
for bookings Mr P G Hill Turner, Bron
Eifion, South Road, Caernarfon,
Gwynedd LL55 2HP
☎Caernarfon(0286)2565

*Wooden and slate chalets:
accommodation comprises an open-
plan kitchen/diner, lounge, two or three
bedrooms and combined bathroom/WC.
Bed-settee in lounge.*

5 Mar-Oct MWB out of season
1mth max, 6units, 1–8 persons [◇ ◆
◆] ◉ fridge Electric Elec metered
Ⓛinclusive ☎(200yds) Airing
cupboard in unit HCE in unit
[Launderette within 300yds] ⊙ CTV
⊕3pin square P ♨(200yds) ⌂
⊕ ♨(3m) ♀(200yds) ▩(3m)
Min£46 Max£185pw

CAIRNRYAN
Dumfries & Galloway *Wigtownshire*
Map **10** NX06

Ch **Cairnryan Caravan & Chalet Park**
Cairnryan, Stranraer, Wigtowns
☎Cairnryan(05812)231

*Six chalets within a caravan site that
overlooks Loch Ryan. Five of the chalets
comprise open-plan kitchen and
lounge/dining area with convertible
settee, two twin-bedded rooms and
shower/WC. The sixth chalet is one of a
row of terraced wooden chalets and
sleeps two people in bed-sitter-type
accommodation with WC and shower (no
bath).*

Apr-Oct MWB out of season 6units,
1–6 persons ◇ ◆ ◉ fridge
Electric Elec metered Ⓛcan be hired
☎ Iron in unit Ironing board in unit
HCE in unit Launderette on premises

⊙ ⊕3pin square 7P ♨ ⌂
Children's play area TV room
⊕ ♀ ▨
Min£50 Max£120pw

CALCETHORPE
Lincolnshire
Map **8** TF28

C **Lincolnshire Wolds Cottages
(Swift & Swallow)**
for bookings C V Stubbs & Sons, Manor
Farm, Calcethorpe, Louth, Lincs
LN11 0RF
☎Louth(0507)604219

*A pair of semi-detached, two-storey,
brick-built, farm workers' cottages dating
from the 1920s standing in a quiet
country lane in the midst of the
Lincolnshire Wolds. Situated off the
A157, about 5m W of Louth. The
accommodation comprises one double
bedroom, lounge/diner and kitchen on
the ground floor and one single-bedded
room and one twin-bedded room on the
first floor.*

All year MWB out of season 1wk min,
2 units, 5 persons ◇ ◉ fridge
Electric Elec metered except heating
Ⓛcan be hired ☎(1½m) Airing
cupboard in unit Iron in unit Ironing
board in unit HCE in unit TV
⊕3pin square P ♨(3m)
⊕ ♀(3m)
Min£57.50 Max£97.75pw

CALIFORNIA
Norfolk
Map **9** TG51

Ch **California Sands Estate** Beach
Road
for bookings Hoseasons Holidays,
Sunway House, Lowestoft, Suffolk
NR32 3LT
☎Lowestoft(0502)62292

*Four hundred and three chalets situated
on a grass site 500yds from the beach.
Chalets have two or three bedrooms, with
a double convertible settee, and sleep up
to eight. All but three chalets have
bathrooms, the others have a shower.*

ROSE COTTAGE

Rose Cottage is situated in the Border Forest Park amid the Cheviot Hills and is a good base for walking, touring in the Borders or just relaxing.

The cottage is completely modern and fully furnished to a high standard — it consists of sun porch, kitchen with dining area, two bedrooms, bathroom, living room with TV, also a store room and there is parking space for a car in the garden. The premises are centrally heated and there is an electric cooker, washer, and fridge in the kitchen. In one bedroom there are two single beds and in the other, two single beds and a double bunk bed, a cot and a 'Z' bed are also available, a maximum of 6 persons is requested.

It is a quarter of a mile south of Byrness village and is adjacent to the main Jedburgh — Edinburgh (A68) road, the Pennine Way and the Forest Scenic Route are nearby.

The charge per week depending on the season is from £25 to £85 — you would require your own linen, and a deposit of £15 per week is payable on booking.

The cottage keys are available from 2pm on the Saturday at the Border Park Service Station, Byrness. Otterburn, Newcastle on Tyne. Telephone (0830) 20271

Whit–24Sep 1wk min, 403units,
2–8persons [◇ ◆] no pets ◎
fridge Electric Elec metered
⌷inclusive ☎ [TD on premises]
Airing cupboard in unit [Iron on
premises] HCE in unit [Launderette
within 300yds] ⊕ TV ⊕3pin square
P ♨
⊛ ♀ ▦

CALLANDER
Central *Perthshire*
Map**11** NN60

H **The Eagle** 38A Main Street
for bookings Mr & Mrs D R Scott,
Whitecroft, East Calder, West Lothian
EH53 0ET
☎Mid Calder(0506)881810

*An attractive and comfortable house
situated on the main street, comprising
kitchen, lounge and panelled dining
room, and four bedrooms. Well furnished
and decorated.*

All year MWB out of season 1unit,
1–10persons ◇ ◆ no pets ◎
fridge Electric Elec metered
⌷not provided ☎(100yds) WM in unit
SD in unit Airing cupboard in unit Iron
in unit Ironing board in unit HCE in unit
[Launderette within 300yds] ⊕ TV can
be hired ⊕3pin square 1P ♨(20yds)
⊛ ⌑(1m) ♀(50yds) ▦(100yds)
Min£100 Max£120pw

B **Trean Lodge**
for bookings Mrs A Denholm, Boghall,
Thornhill, Stirlingshire
☎Thornhill(078685)621

*A modern chalet style bungalow on farm
ground commanding a view to Ben Ledi.
It comprises two twin-bedded rooms, one
single room, lounge, dining room,
kitchen, bathroom and additional
separate WC.*

All year MWB out of season 1wk min,
6mths max, 1unit, 1–5persons ◇
no dogs ◎ fridge ▦ Elec metered
⌷can be hired ☎ Airing cupboard in
unit Ironing board in unit HCE in unit
⊕ TV can be hired ⊕3pin square P
♨ ♨(½m)
⊛ ⌑(1m) ♀(½m) ▦(½m) ♫(½m)

California
—
Camelford

Min£22.50 Max£50.50pw (Low)
Min£85 Max£115pw (High)

CALVINE
Tayside *Perthshire*
Map**14** NN87

C **Cuildaloskin Cottage**
for bookings Mrs Wendy Stewart,
Clachan of Struan, Calvine, Pittlochry,
Perthshire PH18 5UB
☎Calvine(079683)207

*Quaint little detached former shepherd's
cottage surrounded by grazing land.
Accommodation comprises living room
(with double bed-settee), dining room,
kitchen and upstairs a twin bedroom, a
bedroom with one double and one
single bed and bathroom. Décor
furnishings and fitments are simple but
the cottage is not without charm or
character. Lies just off B847 close to the
River Errochty 1½m W of Calvine, which
itself is on the A9 12m N of Pitlochry.*

Etr–Oct 1wk min, 1unit, 1–5persons
◇ ◆ ◎ fridge Electric
Elec metered ⌷can be hired ☎(1½)
Airing cupboard in unit Iron in unit
Ironing board in unit HCE in unit ⊕
⊕3pin square P ♨(1½m)
⊛ ♀(1½m)

CAMBER
East Sussex
Map**5** TQ91

Ch **Camber Sands Leisure Park** Lydd
Road, Camber, Rye, E. Sussex TN31RT
☎Rye(0797)225555

*Fifty-seven chalets set in a large complex
of 297 units with extensive recreational
facilities. Small units with simple clean
décor and furniture. Accommodation
comprises two bedrooms, lounge,
kitchen and bathroom/WC. Sea and
sands within walking distance.*

21May–Sep MWB out of season
3nights min, 11mths max, 57units,
1–6persons [◇ ◆] no dogs
Electric Elec metered ⌷inclusive ☎

HCE [Launderette on premises] ⊕
[TV] ⊕3pin square P ♨ ▱ ♪
⊛ ♀ ▦ ♫
Min£52 Max£90pw (Low)
Min£110 Max£175pw (High)

CAMBRIDGE
Cambridgeshire
Map**5** TL45

F Mrs & Mrs S J Wilson **Whitehouse
Holiday Apartments** Conduit Head
Road, Cambridge CB3 0EY
☎Cambridge(0223)67110 or
Caxton(09544)436

*A luxury block of eight flats on two floors
each comprising one double and one
single bedded room, lounge with double
bed settee, kitchen and bathroom. Maid
service is available at extra cost. Located
1½m from the centre of Cambridge just off
the A1303.*

All year MWB 2days min, 42days max,
8units, 1–5persons [◇] ◆
⌬ (3units) ◎(5units) fridge ▦
Gas/Elec inclusive ⌷inclusive ☎ Iron
in unit Ironing board in unit HCE in unit
[Launderette on premises] ⊕ CTV
⊕3pin square 25P ▱ ♨(1m)
⊛(2m) ♀(½m) ▦(1m) ♫(1m)
♨(1m)
Min£81 Max£96.60pw

CAMELFORD
Cornwall
Map**2** SX18

B **Grey Park**
for bookings Mrs R C Biscombe, Trevia
Coombe, Camelford, Cornwall
☎Camelford(08402)3373

*Detached bungalow close to town centre
on moderately busy road.
Accommodation comprises large
lounge, kitchen/diner, bathroom/WC, two
double bedrooms and one twin bedroom.*

All year MWB out of season 1wk min,
8wks max, 1unit, 1–6persons ◆ ◎
fridge Electric Elec metered
⌷not provided ☎(200yds) Airing
cupboard in unit Iron in unit Ironing →

---

board in unit HCE in unit ⊙ TV ⊕3pin square 2P 1🏠 ▥ ⛼(400yds)

⊖ ♁18(3m) ♀(½m)

C **Stables A & B** Trethin Farm
for bookings Cornish Farm Holidays, Homeleigh, Chapel Amble, Wadebridge, Cornwall
☎Wadebridge(020881)2388

Completely modernised old stone farm building comprising open-plan lounge/kitchen/diner. Two twin bedrooms (double bed available if requested), and bathroom with shower/WC. On the A39 Wadebridge/Stratton road. Follow signs to Advent Church.

Mar–Dec MWB out of season 1wk min, 6wks max, 2units, 1–4persons [◇] ◆ ◆ no pets ◎ fridge Electric Elec metered ⊡inclusive ☎ [WM on premises] [TD on premises] Airing cupboard in unit Iron in unit Ironing board in unit ⊙ CTV ⊕3pin square 20P ▥ ⛼(1¾m) Fishing, games room

⊖ ♀(1¾m)

Min£28.75 Max£184pw

C **Barn A & B** Trethin Farm
for bookings Cornish Farm Holidays, Homeleigh, Chapel Amble, Wadebridge, Cornwall
☎Wadebridge(020881)2388
Barn A. *An old stone farm building which has been modernised throughout and comprises open-plan lounge/kitchen/diner, two twin bedrooms (double available if requested), bath/shower and WC.* ***Barn B.*** *A converted barn which has been thoroughly modernised and comprises open-plan lounge/kitchen/diner, one double bedroom, and one large bedroom containing twin beds and bunks. On the A39 Wadebridge/Stratton road. Follow signs to Advent Church.*

Mar–Dec MWB out of season 1wk min, 6wks max, 2units, 1–6persons [◇] ◆ ◆ no pets ◎ fridge Electric Elec metered ⊡inclusive ☎ [Wm on premises] [TD on premises] Airing couborad in unit Iron in unit Ironing board in unit ⊙ CTV ⊕3pin square 20P ▥ ⛼(1¾m) Fishing, games room

⊖ ♀(1¾m)

Min£28.75 Max£184pw

C **Coachhouse A & B** Trethin Farm
for bookings Cornish Farm Holidays, Homeleigh, Chapel Amble, Wadebridge, Cornwall
☎Wadebridge(020881)2388

Modernised Coach house with a lounge/diner, separate kitchen, two twin-bedded rooms and bathroom/WC. On the A39 Wadebridge/Stratton road. Follow signs to Advent Church.

Mar–Dec MWB out of season 1wk min, 6wks max, 2units, 1–4persons [◇] ◆ ◆ no pets ◎ fridge Electric Elec metered ⊡inclusive ☎ [WM on premises] [TD on premises] Airing cupboard in unit Iron in unit Ironing board in unit ⊙ CTV ⊕3pin square 20P ▥ ⛼(1¾m) Fishing, games room

⊖ ♀(1¾m)

Min£28.75 Max£184pw

C **Cottage** Trethin Farm
for bookings Cornish Farm Holidays, Homeleigh, Chapel Amble, Wadebridge, Cornwall
☎Wadebridge(020881)2388

Converted old farm building comprising open-plan lounge/diner, three bedrooms, one double-bedded room and two twin-bedded rooms, bathroom/WC with facilities for the handicapped. Ideal for children. On the A39 Wadebridge/Stratton road. Follow signs to Advent Church.

Mar–Dec MWB out of season 1wk min, 6wks max, 1unit, 1–6persons [◇] ◆ ◆ no pets ◎ fridge Electric Elec metered ⊡inclusive ☎ [WM on premises] [TD on premises] Airing cupboard in unit Iron in unit Ironing board in unit ⊙ CTV ⊕3pin square 20P ▥ ⛼(1¾m) Fishing, games room

⊖ ♀(1¾m)

Min£28.75 Max£211.60pw

C **Old Mill A, B & C** Trethin Farm
for bookings Cornish Farm Holidays, Homeleigh, Chapel Amble, Wadebridge, Cornwall
☎Wadebridge(020881)2388

Mill A. *A modernised old stone farm building, comprising open-plan lounge/kitchen/diner, two twin bedrooms and bathroom/shower and WC.* ***Mill B & C.*** *Modernised mill consisting of open-plan lounge/kitchen/diner, two twin bedrooms and bathroom/WC with facilities for the handicapped. Excellent décor throughout. On the A39 Wadebridge/Stratton road. Follow signs to Advent Church.*

Mar–Dec MWB out of season 1wk min, 6wks max, 3units, 1–4persons [◇] ◆ ◆ no pets ◎ fridge Electric Elec metered ⊡inclusive ☎ [WM on premises] [TD on premises] Airing cupboard in unit Iron in unit Ironing board in unit ⊙ CTV ⊕3pin square 20P ▥ ⛼(1¾m) Fishing, games room

⊖ ♀(1¾m)

Min£28.75 Max£184pw

CAMROSE
Dyfed
Map**2** SM92

B Mrs N Tudor-Williams **The Fold**
Cleddau Lodge, Camrose, Haverfordwest, Dyfed
☎Camrose(043784)226

Modern, spacious bungalow with own sitting-out area. Fitted to a high standard throughout. Bedroom 1 has three sets of bunk beds and bedrooms 2 and 3 have double and single beds. Large lounge/dining room. Fitted kitchen. Good bathroom. Take Camrose road from Haverfordwest.

Apr–Oct MWB out of season 1wk min, 1mth max, 1unit, 2–12persons ◆ no pets ◎ fridge ▦ Elec metered ⊡not provided ☎(1m) SD in unit Airing cupboard in unit Iron in unit Ironing board in unit HCE in unit ⊙ TV ⊕3pin square P ▥ ⛼(1m) Home produce, fresh fruit & veg in season Private fishing Garden & woodlands

⊖ ♀ 🎥

Min£80 Max£100pw (Low)
Min£120 Max£150pw (High)

CANTERBURY
Kent
Map**5** TR15

H **University of Kent**
for bookings The Conference Officer, Cornwallis South, University of Kent, Canterbury, Kent CT2 7NF
☎Canterbury(0227)66822

Clustered around informal quadrangles, these units comprise of two-storey apartments each containing either four bedrooms (one twin-bedded) and a lounge; or five single bedrooms. All have kitchen/diner and shower/WC.

2Jul–Sep MWB in season 1wk min, 3mths max, 40units, 2–5persons [◆] no pets ⌀ fridge ▦ Gas/Elec inclusive ⊡inclusive except towels ☎ Airing cupboard in unit Iron in unit Ironing board in unit HCE in unit [Launderette within 300yds] ⊙ ⊕3pin square 1P ⛼(½m) ⚲Hard Squash, badminton & library

⊖ ♁18(3m) ♀(½m) ▧(3m) ♫(3m) 🎥(3m)

Min£110pw (Low)
Min£133.40 Max£144.90pw (High)

CANWELL
Staffordshire
Map**4** SK10

H **White Owl Farmhouse**
for bookings Mrs P J H Packwood, Rookery Farm, Brockenhurst, Canwell, Sutton Coldfield, W. Midlands
☎021–308 1039

Brick-built farmhouse standing in its own garden overlooking the surrounding countryside and comprises kitchen, dining room, lounge with open fire, bathroom/WC and three bedrooms.

All year MWB 1night min, 3wks max, 1unit, 1–7persons [◇] ◆ ◆ no pets ◎ fridge Electric Elec metered ⊡can be hired ☎(1m) WM in unit SD in unit Iron in unit

1982 prices quoted throughout gazetteer

Ironing board in unit   HCE in unit   ⊕
CTV   ⊕3pin square   4P   ⚎(1m)
⊖   ⚑(2½m)
Min£45 Max£65pw (Low)
Min£60 Max£75pw (High)

CAPEL BANGOR
Dyfed
Map**6** SN68

H   Bron-Llangwrda Penllwyn
for bookings Mr T & Mr S Hulme, 7
Bwthyn, Cefnllwyd, Capel Dewi,
Aberstwyth, Dyfed
☎Capel Bangor(097084)465

*Re-decorated and refurbished 17th-
century farmhouse standing at the end of
a lane 300yds from the A44. The main
entrance door leads into a sun lounge,
through to hall and lounge with feature
stone fireplace, there is a beamed
kitchen/diner, bathroom/WC and a
ground floor bedroom with double and
single beds. The first floor comprises a
single, twin and family bedroom plus a
room containing two sets of bunks.*

All year   MWB out of season   3 days min,
6wks max, 1unit, 1–13persons   ◇   ◎
fridge   Electric   Elec metered
Ⓛinclusive   ☎   WM in unit   Airing
cupboard in unit   Iron in unit   Ironing
board in unit   HCE in unit   ⊕   TV
⊕3pin square   6P   ⚎(300yds)
⊖   ⚑(300yds)

CAPEL ISSAC
Dyfed
Map**2** SN52

H   Coachhouse
for bookings Mr & Mrs C E Roberts,
Maesteilo Mansion, Capel Isaac,
Llandeilo, Dyfed
☎Dryslwyn(05584)510

*An old stone-built traditional building with
a slate roof. Accommodation consists of
dining room, entrance hall, sitting room,
kitchen, bathroom and two bedrooms
(one is twin-bedded and the other has a
double bed). There is a space in one of
the bedrooms for a third bed. This
property lies within the 16-acre country
estate of Maesteilo Mansion.*

All year   MWB out of season   1wk min,
1mth max, 1unit, 2–4persons, nc8   ◎

---

fridge   Electric & log fires
Elec metered   Ⓛcan be hired
☎(on request)   WM in unit   SD in unit
Airing cupboard in unit   Iron in unit
Ironing board in unit   HCE in unit   ⊕
CTV   ⊕3pin square   P   🏠   ⚎(1½m)
▭   Games room
⊖   ⚑(1½m)

CARBOST
Isle of Skye, Highland *Inverness-shire*
Map**13** NG33

H   Old School House
for bookings Mrs E R Wakefield,
Glendrynoch Lodge, Carbost, Isle of
Skye IV47 8SX
☎Carbost(047842)209

*Stone, school house with neat garden
area and splendid views. House offers
combined sitting room/dining
room/kitchen, two ground-floor twin
bedrooms and one first-floor room
sleeping four. Served by bathroom/WC.
Directions from owner at Glendrynoch
Lodge which is situated at junction on
A863 and A8009 Carbost Road.*

All year   MWB out of season   2wks min,
3mths max, 1unit, 2–8persons   ◇   ◎
fridge   Electric & open fires
Elec metered   Ⓛnot provided   ☎(½m)
Airing cupboard in unit   Iron in unit
Ironing board in unit   HCE in unit   TV can
be hired   ⊕3pin square   P   ⚎(½m)
Games room

H   Park House
for bookings Mrs E R Wakefield,
Glendrynoch Lodge, Carbost, Isle of
Skye IV47 8SX
☎Carbost(047842)209

*Traditional white-painted, two-storey
Scottish house standing on hillside, just
out of village centre. House surrounded
by garden area featuring pines and
shrubs. A neat standard in décor and
furnishings. Three first-floor bedrooms,
sitting room, combined dining room and
kitchen, modern bathroom and separate
WC. Situated north end of Carbost village
near distillery. Splendid views of Loch
Harport and Cuillin Hills.*

All year   MWB out of season   2wks min,
3mths max, 1unit, 2–5persons   ◇   ◎
fridge   Electric & open fires
Elec metered   Ⓛnot provided   ☎(½m)
Airing cupboard in unit   Iron in unit
Ironing board in unit   HCE in unit   ⊙   TV
can be hired   ⊕3pin square   P   ⚎(½m)

CARDIGAN
Dyfed
Map**2** SN14

F   Coach House (Flats)
for bookings Mr & Mrs Hobbs,
Cilbronnau, Mansion, Llangoedmor,
Cardigan, Dyfed SA43 2LP
☎Llechryd(023987)254

*Two flats located within a converted
coach house, the **Ground**-floor flat
comprises two bedrooms, lounge with
bed-settee, kitchen/diner, shower and
WC. The **First**-floor flat has lounge with
convertible settee, one double-bedded
room, kitchen/diner and bathroom/WC.
1m E of Cardigan on B4570.*

All year   MWB out of season
3 nights min, 2units, 4–6persons   ◇   ◆
◎   fridge   Electric   Elec metered
Ⓛcan be hired   (400yds)   WM on
premises   SD on premises   Iron on
premises   Ironing board on premises
HCE in unit   ⊙   TV   ⊕3pin square   4P
⚎(2m)
⊖   ᗑ(4m)   ⚑(1½m)   🚌(2m)
Min£35 Max£85pw (Low)
Min£80 Max£135pw (High)

C   River Hill Cottages (St Dogmaels)
1m W off B4546)
for bookings Hoseason's Holidays,
Sunway House, Lowestoft, Suffolk
NR32 3LT
☎Lowestoft(0502)62292

*Semi-detached cottages with lounge,
kitchen, bathroom/WC and bedrooms
(sleeping from three to five persons).
Furnishings include modern lightwood
furniture, fitted wardrobes in bedrooms
and coloured suite in bathroom. Kitchen
is separated from lounge by
pine-screening.*

All year   MWB out of season   1wk min,
26units, 3–5persons   [◇   ◆   ●]
fridge   Electric   Elec metered
Ⓛinclusive   ☎   Airing cupboard in unit →

57

Iron on premises Ironing board on premises ⊖ TV ⊕3pinsquare P
🎦 ♨

↭ ♨(200yds) ▨(2m) 🐾(2m)

C Tycanol (Middle House) Trenewydd Holiday Cottages, St Dogmaels (1m W off B4546)
for bookings Mrs Y Davies, Trenewydd Farm, St Dogmaels, Cardigan, Dyfed
☎Cardigan(0239)612370

The second of the cottages on this 12-acre smallholding. Ideal for a family of five, there are two bedrooms, one with a double bed and one single and the other with two single beds. Also there are a combined bathroom and WC, sitting room and kitchen.

All year MWB out of season 3nights min, 1unit, 5persons ◇ ◆ ◎ fridge 🍴
Electric Elec metered 🔌can be hired (overseas visitors only) ☎(1½m) WM in unit SD in unit Airing cupboard in unit Iron in unit Ironing board in unit HCE in unit ⊖ CTV ⊕3pinsquare P
♨(1½m)

↭ ♨(1½m) 🐾(3m)

Min£50 Max£140pw
See advert on page 57

C Tymawr (Big House) Trenewydd Holiday Cottages, St Dogmaels, (1m W off B4546)
for bookings Mrs Y Davies, Trenewydd Farm, St Dogmaels, Cardigan, Dyfed
☎Cardigan(0239)612370

One of three attractive cottages of modern design converted from old farm buildings, in quiet situation a short distance from National Park. Set out on two levels, there is a double-bedded room, a twin-bedded room and a further room with bunks on the ground floor, and a pleasant sitting room and kitchen/diner, combined bathroom and WC on the first floor.

All year MWB out of season 3nights min, 1unit, 6persons ◇ ◆ ◎
fridge 🍴 Electric Elec metered 🔌can be hired (overseas visitors only) ☎(1½m) WM in unit SD in unit Airing cupboard in unit Iron in unit Ironing board in unit HCE in unit ⊖ CTV ⊕3pinsquare P ♨(1½m)

↭ ♨(1½m) 🐾(3m)

Min£50 Max£145pw
See advert on page 57

C Tytwt (Small House) Trenewydd Holiday Cottages, St Dogmaels (1m W off B4546)
for bookings Mrs Y Davies, Trenewydd Farm, St Dogmaels, Cardigan, Dyfed
☎Cardigan(0239)612370

Compact and nicely appointed two-bedroomed cottage with lounge/diner, separate kitchen and combined bathroom and WC. 3m from historic town of Cardigan and less than 2¼ from the glorious expanse of Poppit Sands.

All year MWB out of season 3nights min, 1unit, 4persons ◇ ◆ ◎
fridge 🍴 Electric Elec metered

🔌can be hired (overseas visitors only) ☎(1½m) WM in unit SD in unit Airing cupboard in unit Iron in unit Ironing board in unit ⊖ CTV
⊕3pinsquare P ♨(1½m)

↭ ♨(1½m) 🐾(3m)

Min£50 Max£135pw
See advert on page 57

CARDINHAM
Cornwall
Map**2** SX16

F Courtyard, Coachhouse, Hayloft & Stable Flats
for bookings Mrs A M Kerslake, Cardinham House, Cardinham, Bodmin, Cornwall
☎Cardinham(020882)297

*Four recently converted flats within wing of Cardinham House. All comprise lounge, kitchen/diner, bathroom/WC (except **Hayloft** which has shower/WC) one or two bedrooms and a bed-settee in lounge. There is a pet pony.*

All year MWB out of season 1wk min, 4units, 1–6persons [◇ ◆ ◆]
no pets except dogs ◎ fridge
Electric Elec metered 🔌not provided (except for overseas visitors)
☎(200yds) Airing cupboard in unit Iron in unit Ironing board in unit HCE in unit
⊖ TV ⊕3pinsquare P 🎦 ♨(2m)
👶

↭ ♨(3m)

Min£40 Max£125pw

CAREY
Hereford & Worcester
Map**3** SO53

C Mrs D B Lawson *Mews Cottage*
Carey Court, Carey, Ballingham, Hereford
☎Carey(043270)644

A small stone cottage located behind Carey Court with its own gate and driveway, overlooks fields and a valley. On the ground floor there is a kitchen/diner, large comfortable lounge with open-plan staircase and bathroom/WC. The first-floor has a double and a twin-bedded room. For access from the A49 follow the Hoarwithy road through Carey, passing the 'Cottage of Content' Inn then take first turning on left.

Mar–Oct 1wk min, 4wks max, 1unit, 1–4persons, nc5 ◎ fridge 🍴
Elec metered 🔌not provided ☎(½m)
WM in unit SD in unit Iron in unit Ironing board in unit HCE in unit ⊖
◎ TV ⊕3pinsquare 2P 🎦 ♨(5m)

↭ ♨(½m)

CARLISLE
Cumbria
Map**11** NY35

C Millstone Cottage Blackhall Wood

---

for bookings Country Farm Holidays, The Place, Horn Lane, Powick, Worcester
☎Worcester(0905)830899

A converted farm building in a tranquil setting within easy reach of the Borders the Lake District and the Pennines. Well furnished accommodation comprising kitchen/diner, lounge, two twin-bedded rooms, one double-bedded room and bathroom/WC. 3m S off unclassified road between M6 Junction 42 and Dalston.

All year MWB out of season 3days min, 3mths max, 1unit, 2–8persons ◆ ◆
no pets ◎ fridge 🍴& Electric
Elec metered 🔌can be hired ☎ WM in unit SD in unit Airing cupboard in unit Iron in unit Ironing board in unit HCE in unit CTV ⊕3pinsquare 2P 🎦
♨(2½m) Fishing & shooting

↭ ♨(1½m)

Min£60 Max£140pw

CARNWATH
Strathclyde *Lanarkshire*
Map**11** NS94

C Lintmill Cottage
for bookings Miss J Bristow, Thorncroft, Lilliesleaf, Roxburghshire TD6 9JD
☎Lilliesleaf(08357)424

Secluded farm cottage situated about 1m from Carnwath, sheltered by small hillocks and adjacent to a meandering river (fishing available free of charge). This small unit offers sitting/dining room, one double bedroom, kitchen and bathroom downstairs and two bedrooms (one family and one twin) upstairs. Neat standard of décor and furnishings.

Apr–Oct MWB out of season 1wk min, 2mths max, 1unit, 2–7persons [◆] ◎
fridge Electric & coal fires
Elec metered 🔌can be hired ☎(½m)
Iron in unit Ironing board in unit HCE in unit TV ⊕3pinround P ♨

↭ ♨(1½m)

Min£50 Max£62pw (Low)
Min£78 Max£95pw (High)

C Millridge Cottage
for bookings Miss J Bristow, Thorncroft, Lilliesleaf, Roxburghshire TD6 9JD
☎Lilliesleaf(08357)424

Country cottage with views over farmlands, situated approx 4m from Carnwath. Accommodation consists of sitting/dining room with studio couch which converts to single bed, kitchen, bedroom with one double and one single bed, bedroom with two single beds, and bathroom/WC. There is a small, fenced garden and parking area for two cars.

Apr–Oct MWB out of season 1wk min, 2mths max, 1unit, 2–5persons [◆] ◎
fridge Electric & coal fires
Elec metered 🔌can be hired ☎(1¼m)
Iron in unit Ironing board in unit HCE in unit TV ⊕3pinsquare
Min£45 Max£50pw (ow)
Min£65 Max£75pw (High)

1982 prices quoted throughout gazetteer

58

CARRBRIDGE
Highland *Iverness-shire*
Map **14** NH82

B Major & Mrs Dunlop **Fairwinds**
(Bungalows), Carrbridge, Inverness-shire
PH23 3AA
☎Carrbridge(047 984)240

These timber alpine bungalows are
situated just off the A9 in secluded
grounds on the outskirts of the village of
Carrbridge. Neatly spaced within 3 acres
of tree-studded land overlooking an
artificial pond. The well-equipped
bungalows are modern and offer
excellent accommodation with two
bedrooms, lounge/diner, kitchenette and
bathroom.

All year MWB 1wk min, 3units,
2–5persons ◇ ◆ ◉ fridge
Electric Elec metered ⬛inclusive
☎(30yds) Iron on premises Ironing
board on premises HCE in unit ⊙ TV
⊕3pin square P ⓐ 🅣 ♨(200yds)
⊖ 🅟(200yds) 🅩(200yds) 🎵(200yds)
Min£75 Max£135pw

F Major & Mrs Dunlop **Fairwinds**
(Flats), Carrbridge, Inverness-shire
PH23 3AA
☎Carrbridge(047 984)240

Two self-contained flats located in
Fairwinds House containing sitting room,
kitchen/dinette, and modern bathroom.
The larger flat has three twin-bedded
rooms, and the smaller one has two
double bedrooms with adjoining single
bedroom. They have direct access from
main road through Carrbridge Village.

All year MWB 1wk min, 2units,
1–7persons ◇ ◆ ◉ fridge 🍴
Elec metered ⬛inclusive ☎ TD on
premises Airing cupboard in unit Iron
on premises Ironing board on
premises HCE in unit ⊙ TV
⊕3pin square P ⓐ 🅣 ♨(200yds)
Cycle & ski hire
⊖ 🅟(200yds) 🅩(200yds)
Min£75 Max£150pw

Ch Manager **Lochanhully Lodges**
Carrbridge, Inverness-shire (or any AA
Travel Agency)
☎Carrbridge(047 984)234

Fifty timber-constructed Finnish chalets
with south-facing views. They are set
amidst birch trees ½m E of Carrbridge and
A9 on the A938 Grantown road. Each
chalet consists of a double-bedded
room, bunk-bedded room, bathroom,
large living room (with double bed-
settee, pine table, seating, french
windows and balcony) and kitchen area.

Closed 5 Nov-16 Dec MWB 5wks max,
50units, 1–6persons ◇ ◆ ◉
fridge Electric Elec inclusive
⬛inclusive ☎ Airing cupbaord in unit
Iron on premises Ironing board in unit
HCE in unit Launderette on premises
⊙ CTV ⊕3pin square P ⓐ 🖳
⊖ ♨(½m) 🅟 🅩(½m)
Min£120 Max£260pw

Ca **Pineacre** Station Road
for bookings Mrs F R McArthur,
3 Laurelhill Place, Stirling, Stirlingshire
FK8 2JN
☎Stirling(0786)2053

One modern well-equipped pine and
cedarwood log cabin offering open-plan
lounge/dining room/kitchen area with
bedrooms to accommodate eight and
bathroom. The cabin stands on ½ acre of
level ground and there is a tree-studded
hill at the rear.

All year 1wk min, 1mth max, 1unit,
2–8persons ◇ ◆ ◉ fridge 🍴
Elec metered ⬛not provided ☎ WM
in unit SD in unit Airing cupboard in
unit Iron in unit Ironing board in unit
HCE in unit ⊙ TV ⊕3pin square P
♨(½m)
⊖ 🅟(½m) 🅩(½m)
Min£85 Max£100pw (Low)
Min£120 Max£140pw (High)

C Mrs M Sinclair **Slochd Cottages**
Carrbridge, Inverness-shire
☎Carrbridge(047 984)666

Situated 4m N of Carrbridge just off the
A9, three stone-built cottages in a
clearing surrounded by hills with distant
views over the Cairngorms.
Accommodation consists of two
bedrooms, lounge, kitchen and
shower/WC.

All year MWB out of season 1wk min,
3wks max, 3units, 2–6persons ◇ ◉
fridge Calor gas & open fires
Gas metered ⬛not provided ☎ Iron
on premises Ironing board on
premises HCE in unit P ⓐ(4m)
Min£58 Max£60pw (Low)
Max£72pw (High)

CARRICK CASTLE
Strathclyde *Argyll*
Map **10** NS19

Ch Mrs T Murray **Darroch Mhor Chalet
& Water Sports Centre** Carrick Castle,
Lochgoilhead, Argyll PA24 8AF
☎Lochgoilhead(030 13)249 & 348

Cedar chalets with two bedrooms and
combined living room and kitchen.
Situated on the shores of Loch Goil with
good views. Water sports orientated,
dinghy or day cruiser hire; winter rates
are higher because of fishing season.
Very well maintained.

All year MWB in season 2nights min,
3wks max, 5units, 1–6persons ◇ ◆
◉ fridge Electric Elec metered
⬛not provided ☎(20yds) SD Iron on
premises [Ironing board on premises]
HCE in unit ⊙ ⊕3pin square 5P 🅣
♨(20yds) Boat & bicycle hire, fishing
tackle shop
⊖ 🅟(20yds)
Min£40 Max£70pw (Low)
Min£85 Max£110pw (High)

CARTMEL
Cumbria
Map **7** SD37

F Mrs B Smith **Aynsome Manor Park**
Cartmel, Grange-over-Sands, Cumbria
LA11 6HH
☎Cartmel(044 854)433

A collection of stone-built buildings which
used to form part of the old manor house
(now a hotel) and set within 8 acres of
land which includes a dairy farm and a
lake. One flat was the coachman's
quarters the other four were converted
from an old barn. The conversion has
been tastefully carried out and provides
comfortable accommodation.

All year MWB out of season 5units,
2–4persons, nc11 ◉ fridge 🍴 →

Church Town House
Market Square, Cartmel

This is a listed property in a conserved village
2 miles from Grange-over-Sands and about
6 miles from Lake Windermere affording a high-
class holiday flat with four windows fronting
the Square.
Accommodation comprises kitchen (modern
cooker & fridge); lounge/dining room (colour
TV); two twin-bedded rooms; and
bathroom/WC. Fire precautions taken. All linen
etc found. £125, including VAT, Saturday to
Saturday. Electricity on pre-payment meters. No
pets or young children please.
Further details Westbourne Hotel Ltd,
Lake Road, Lytham St Annes, Lancs FY8 1BE.
Telephone Lytham 734-736 Code (0253).

Elec metered ⬚can be hired ☎ Airing cupboard in unit Iron on premises Ironing board on premises HCE in unit ⊙ TV ⊕3pin square 10P ♨(½m)

⊖ ♠(2m) ♀(½m) ▨(½m)

F Church Town House Market Square *for bookings* Westbourne Hotel, 10 Lake Road, Lytham St Annes, Lancs ☎Lytham(0253)734736

A well-furnished flat occupying the top-floor level of a three-storey early 19th-century town house, situated in the main square of the delightful village of Cartmel. Accommodation comprises two twin-bedded rooms, kitchen, lounge and bathroom. 2m from the coast and in a good position for touring the Lake land.

All year except Xmas 1wk min, 4wks max, 1unit, 2–4persons, nc12 no pets ◉ fridge Electric & open fires Elec metered ⬚inclusive ☎ Iron in unit Ironing board in unit HCE in unit ⊙ CTV ⊕3pin square ▥ ♨(10yds)

⊖ ♠(1½m) ♀(10yds)

Max£115pw
See advert on page 59

F Mr & Mrs J R S Wilkie **Longlands** Cartmel, Grange-over-Sands, Cumbria ☎Cartmel(044 854)475

Large stone-built Georgian country house part of which has been converted into four spacious flats. Decorated, furnished and equipped to a high standard. The house stands in four acres of ground off the Cartmel/Newby Bridge road in the Cartmel Valley 1m N of Cartmel village.

All year MWB out of season 2days min, 4units, 2–7persons ◈ ◆ ◗ ◉ fridge Electric Gas/Elec metered ⬚can be hired ☎(300yds) [TD on premises] Iron on premises Ironing board on premises HCE in unit ⊙ TV ⊕3pin square P ♨(½m)

⊖ ♀(½m)

Min£45 Max£65pw (Low)
Min£90 Max£175pw (High)

Cartmel — Castle Douglas

CASTLEBAY
Isle of Barra Western Isles *Inverness-shire*
Map**13** NL69

C 149 Brevig
for bookings Dr C Bartlett, 1 The Green, Frimley Green, Camberley, Surrey ☎Deepcut(02516)5123

Small converted croft situated at the edge of Brevig Bay. The accommodation comprises two double bedrooms, one single bedroom on first floor, kitchen/dining room, sitting room and bathroom/WC on ground floor. It is adequately and comfortably furnished, with linoleum floor coverings.

All year 1wk min, 5wks max, 1unit, 1–10persons ◈ ◆ ◉ fridge Electric & coal fires Elec inclusive ⬚can be hired ☎(2m) Iron HCE ⊕3pin square P ♨(2m)

⊖ ♀(2½m) ▨(2½m)

Min£38 Max£62pw (Low)
Min£85 Max£100pw (High)

C 12 Leanish
for bookings Dr C Bartlett, 1 The Green, Frimley Green, Camberley, Surrey ☎Deepcut(02516)5123

Two-storey cottage set on high ground by Brevig bay. Accommodation comprises three bedrooms, kitchen/dining room, sitting room, children's playroom and bathroom/WC. The cottage is situated about 150yds from the road along a rough pathway.

All year 1wk min, 5wks max, 1unit, 1–8persons ◈ ◆ ◉ fridge Electric & coal fires inclusive ⬚can be hired ☎(2m) WM in unit Iron Ironing board HCE ⊕3pin square P ♨(2¼m)

⊖ ♀(2½m)

Min£38 Max£62pw (Low)
Min£85 Max£100pw (High)

C 1 Shore Cottage Horve
for bookings Mr G Campbell, 26 Bentangaval, Castlebay, Isle of Barra, Inverness-shire
☎Castlebay(08714)328

Close to water's edge at Kentangaval Bay, this two-storey cottage consists of three bedrooms, kitchen, dining room, sitting room and shower room/WC. Adequate furnishings and equipment.

All year MWB out of season 1wk min, 5wks max, 1unit, 1–8persons ◈ ◉ fridge Electric & open fires Electric inclusive ⬚can be hired ☎(1m) ⊕3pin square ♨(½m)

⊖ ♀(½m) ▨(½m)

Min£40 Max£65pw (Low)
Min£80 Max£95pw (High)

C 2 Shore Cottage Horve
for bookings Mr G Campbell, 26 Bentangaval, Castlebay, Isle of Barra, Inverness-shire
☎Castlebay(08714)328

A small renovated croft, standing by Kentangaval Bay, and backed by council houses. Cars have to be left at roadside 30yds away. Accommodation comprises kitchen, dining/living room with convertible settee, one large family bedroom and shower room/WC. Furnishings are satisfactory with linoleum-covered floors.

All year MWB out of season 1wk min, 5wks max, 1unit, 1–5persons ◈ ◉ fridge Electric & open fires ⬚can be hired ☎(1m) Iron HCE ⊕3pin square ♨(½m)

⊖ ♀(½m) ▨(½m)

Min£30 Max£45pw (Low)
Min£60 Max£75pw (High)

CASTLE DOUGLAS
Dumfries & Galloway *Kirkcudbrightshire*
Map**11** NX76

B 1 & 2 Ardencaple
for bookings G M Thomson & Co, 27 King Street, Castle Douglas, Kirkcudbrightshire DG7 1AB ☎Castle Douglas(0556)2701

Two units of a divided bungalow in a quiet residential part of the town centrally situated just off town centre, near hospital. Both have double-bedded and twin-bedded rooms. No 1 has dining/living room with bed-settee, compact modern kitchen, shower and WC. No 2 has small sitting room with

bed-settee, compact basic kitchen (calor gas cooking) bathroom and WC.

Apr–Oct 1wkmin, 2units, 1–6persons
◆ nopets noball games ◎ fridge Electric Elecinclusive ⬜notprovided ☎(200yds) Airing cupboard in one unit HCE in unit TV ③3pinsquare P ⬛ ♨(200yds)

⇔ ♒(200yds) ♀(200yds) ▦(200yds) ♫(200yds) ⛫(200yds)

Min£40 Max£105pw

C Ellislade
for bookings G M Thomson & Co,
27 King Street, Castle Douglas,
Kirkcudbrightshire DG7 1AB
☎Castle Douglas(0556)2701

A comfortable stone-built cottage with three acres of grounds set in attractive farmland. It is situated 3m from Castle Douglas on B795. The cottage sleeps up to five and comprises two double rooms, dining room, sitting room with bed-settee, kitchen and bathroom.

All year 1wkmin, 1unit, 1–5persons
◎ fridge ♨ Elecinclusive
⬜notprovided ☎ Iron in unit Ironing board in unit HCE in unit ⊕ CTV ③3pinsquare P ⬛ ♨(3m)

⇔ ♒(3m) ♀(3m) ⛫(3m)

Min£50 Max£115pw

C Livingstone Cottage Balmaghie
for bookings G M Thomson & Co,
27 King Street, Castle Douglas,
Kirkcudbrightshire DG7 1AB
☎Castle Douglas(0556)2701

Traditional country cottage in own grounds reached by a winding rough track. Accommodation is all on the ground floor and includes two twin-bedded rooms, sitting room/dining room, compact kitchen and bathroom. Access via B795 towards Laurieston. Turn right after crossing Glenlocher Bridge. After 2m cottage is signposted on the left

All year 1wkmin, 1unit, 1–4persons
◎ fridge Electric & open fires Elecinclusive ⬜notprovided ☎(2½m) Airing cupboard in unit Iron in unit Ironing board in unit HCE in unit TV ③3pinsquare P ♨(5m)

Min£45 Max£105pw

H Livingstone House
for bookings G M Thomson & Co,
27 King Street, Castle Douglas,
Kirkcudbrightshire DG7 1AB
☎Castle Douglas(0556)2701

A fine 18th-century country house on three floors with spacious accommodation; dining room, sitting room, large kitchen, games room, WC, two bathrooms and five bedrooms sleeping a total of eight people. Large twenty-four acre garden beside River Dee. Access via B795 towards Laurieston. Turn right after crossing Glenlochar Bridge. After 2m house on right.

All year 1wkmin, 1unit, 1–8persons
◆ ◎ fridge Electric & open fires Elecinclusive ⬜notprovided ☎ Wm in unit SD in unit Airing cupboard in unit Iron in unit Ironing board in unit HCE in unit ⊕ TV ③3pinsquare P ♨(5m) Fishing

Min£95 Max£235pw

CASTLE SWEEN
Strathclyde Argyll
Map **10** NR77

Ch 1&2 Chalets, Castle Sween Holiday Centre
for bookings Castle Sween Agency, The Booking Office, Ellary, Lochgilphead, Argyll PA31 8PB
☎Ormsary(088 03)232

Attractive wooden chalets with small verandahs, on the shores of Loch Sween, situated at the far end of the caravan park. Accommodation comprises one double bedroom and one with bunk beds, living room with fold-away settee, kitchenette and shower/WC.

Mar–Oct MWB out of season 1wkmin, 2units, 1–6persons ◆ ◎ fridge Electric Elecmetered ⬜notprovided ☎(½m) [WM on premises] [TD on premises] Iron on premises Ironing board on premises HCE in unit [Launderette on premises] ⊕ TV ③3pinsquare P ♨

Min£60pw (low)
Min£120pw (High)

CASWELL BAY
West Glamorgan
Map **2** SS58

F 309–310 Redcliffe Apartments
for bookings Mr & Mrs B & M Davis. Bar Marc Holiday Properties, 7A Redcliffe, Caswell Bay, Swansea, W Glam ☎Swansea(0792)69169

Situated in an apartment block at the water's edge. Accommodation comprises purpose-built units of open plan design with large lounge (and double bed-settee), balcony, double bedroom and shower room/WC.

All year 1wkmin, 3mths max, 2units, 2–4persons ◆ nopets ◎ fridge Electric Elecmetered ⬜notprovided ☎ HCE in unit ⊕ TV ③3pinsquare P ♨(⅓m)

⇔ ♀(⅓m)

Min£70 Max£81pw (Low)
Min£108 Max£140pw (High)

CAULKERBUSH
Dumfries & Galloway Kirkcudbrightshire
Map **11** NX95

H Oakbank
for bookings G M Thomson & Co,
27 King Street, Castle Douglas,
Kirkcudbrightshire DG7 1AB
☎Castle Douglas(0556)2701

A modern house commanding magnificent views of Solway Firth. It accommodates six persons in a double-bedded room, a twin-bedded room and a bunk-bedded room. There is a modern kitchen, a living room and a bathroom.

All year 1wkmin, 6mths max, 1unit, 1–6persons ◆ ◎ fridge Elecinclusive ⬜notprovided ☎(½m) SD in unit Ironing board in unit HCE in unit CTV ③3pinsquare P ♨(½m)

⇔ ♒(3m) ♀(3m)

Min£65 Max£160pw

CAVENDISH
Suffolk
Map **5** TL84

C 1&2 Newman's Cottages
for bookings Suffolk Holiday Cottages, Depden, Bury St Edmunds, Suffolk IP29 4BY
☎Chevington(0284)850606

A pair of modernised Tudor cottages, one sleeping four and the other sleeping two. Good kitchens, modern bathrooms and a sitting room. A rear garden and patio is shared by both.

All year MWB 1wkmin, 2units, 1–4persons ◆ ◆ ◎ fridge Electric Elecmetered ⬜can be hired ☎ Airing cupboard Iron Ironing board HCE ⊕ CTV ③3pinsquare P ⬛ ♨(100yds)

⇔ ♀(100yds)

Min£40 Max£75pw (Low)
Min£55 Max£100pw (High)

C 1&2 Peacock Ley Cottages
for bookings Suffolk Holiday Cottages, Depden, Bury St Edmunds, Suffolk IP29 4BY
☎Chevington(0284)850606

A pair of modernised 16th-century cottages in a quiet location close to the village green. No 1 is larger, sleeping five in three rooms with an extra bed on the large landing. No 2 sleeps four plus an extra bed on landing. Both cottages are well equipped and share a rear garden.

All year MWB out of season 1wkmin, 2units, 1–6persons ◆ ◆ ◎ fridge ♨ Elecmetered ⬜can be hired ☎ Airing cupboard in unit Iron in unit Ironing board in unit HCE in unit ⊕ CTV ③3pinsquare P ♨ ⬛ ♨(½m)

⇔ ♀(½m)

Min£65 Max£100pw (Low)
Min£90 Max£125pw (High)

C Pentlow Hall Cottage
for bookings Suffolk Holiday Cottages, Depden, Bury St Edmunds, Suffolk IP29 4BY
☎Chevington(0284)850606

A fully modernised cottage with two double bedrooms, (one with washbasin) on first floor. Separate dining and sitting rooms plus kitchen and bathroom on ground floor. The cottage has a small garden and backs onto a private park with front views over open countryside. →

All year MWB out of season 1 wk min,
1 unit, 1–4 persons ◆ ◆ ◉ fridge
Electric Elec metered Ⓛ can be hired
☎ Airing cupboard in unit Iron in unit
Ironing board in unit HCE in unit ⊖
CTV ⊕3 pin square ⊕3 pin round P
Ⅲ ♨(½m)

Min £70 Max £105 pw

CHAGFORD
Devon
Map 3 SX78

H Belaire Cottisbourne
for bookings Mrs P Phemister,
2 St Peters Square, London W6
☎01-748 3409

Large, white detached house in pleasant
garden with stream. Accommodation
comprises large kitchen/diner, lounge,
twin bedroom with bathroom en suite.
The first floor consists of one double
bedroom, one double-bedded room with
single bed, one twin-bedded room, one
single-bedded room and a bathroom.

Etr-Oct MWB 1 wk min, 1 mth max,
1 unit, 1–8 persons no pets ◉ fridge
♥ Gas & Elec inclusive Ⓛ inclusive
☎ Airing cupboard on premises Iron
on premises Ironing board on
premises HCE on premises ⊖
⊕3 pin square ⊕3 pin round 3P 1☗
Ⅲ ♨(50yds)

⊖ ♿(2m) ⚲(50yds)

**C Coach House, Granary & Tackery
Cottages**
for bookings Mr Bennie, Beechlands
Farm, Chagford, Newton Abbot, Devon
☎Chagford (064 73)3313

Converted from stables these attractive
cottages have been well decorated and
carpeted throughout. All comprise
kitchens, bathroom/WC and open-plan
lounge/diner with additional sofa bed.
Tackery has one double-bedded room,
Coach House has two double and one
twin-bedded and Granary has one
double, one double with single bed and
one twin.

Mar-Dec 3 days min, 6 wks max, 3 units,
1–7 persons ◆ ◉ fridge Electric
Elec metered Ⓛ can be hired ☎(½m)
Airing cupboard in unit Iron in unit
Ironing board in unit HCE in unit ⊖
CTV ⊕3 pin square 6P Ⅲ ♨(½m)
Fishing

⊖ ♿(2m) ⚲(½m)

Min £45 Max £80 pw (Low)
Min £90 Max £170 pw (High)

B CC Ref 542 ELP
for bookings Character Cottages
(Holidays) Ltd, 34 Fore Street, Sidmouth,
Devon EX10 8AQ
☎Sidmouth (03955)77001

A newly constructed block building with
Tyrolean finish. Accommodation
comprises lounge/diner, one bedroom,
one single bedroom, lounge with french
windows to patio, cloakroom and
washbasin and bathroom/WC.

All year MWB out of season 1 wk min,
1 mth max, 1 unit, 2–6 persons ◆ ∂
fridge ♥ Electric Gas/Elec inclusive
Ⓛ can be hired ☎(½m) Airing cupboard
in unit Iron in unit Ironing board in unit
HCE in unit ⊖ CTV ⊕3 pin square
⊕2 pin round P ☗ Ⅲ ♨(½m)

⊖ ⚲(½m)

Min £71 Max £97 pw (Low)
Min £117 Max £153 pw (High)

CHALLABOROUGH BAY
Devon TQ7 4JB
Map 2 SX64

B Mr & Mrs B Carter **Beachdown
Holiday Bungalows** Challaborough
Bay, Bigbury-on-Sea, Kingsbridge,
Devon TQ7 4JB
☎Kingsbridge (0548)2282

Situated in a valley with direct access to
beach in an area of some 2¼ acres
adjacent to a complex of holiday
caravans. Each unit has one double- and
one twin-bedded room plus double put-
u-up in lounge/diner, kitchen and
bathroom/WC.

All year MWB out of season 3 days min,
13 units, 2–8 persons [◆] [◆] ◉

fridge Electric Elec metered
⌷not provided ☎ Iron on premises
Ironing board on premises HCE in unit
[Launderette within 300yds] ⊕ TV
⊕3pin square 25P ♨(250yds)
Children's play area

↤ ♨a(½m) ☎(300yds) ♫(300yds)

Min£39 Max£71pw (Low)
Min166 Max£189pw (High)

CHANNEL ISLANDS
Map **16**
See Alderney

CHARMOUTH
Dorset
Map **3** SY39

H **Char View** Catherston Lane
for bookings A Loosmore, Manor Farm,
Charmouth, Bridport, Dorset DT6 6QL
☎Charmouth(0297)60226

*Semi-detached modern house situated
on outskirts of village. Accommodation
comprises two double and one twin-
bedded room, kitchen/diner, lounge,
bathroom, two separate toilets. Located
off A35 on east side of Charmouth.*

All year MWB out of season 1wk min,
3wks max, 1unit, 2–6persons [◇ ◆]
◉ fridge Electric Elec metered
⌷not provided ☎(200yds) Airing
cupboard in unit Iron in unit Ironing
board in unit HCE in unit [Launderette
within 300yds] ⊕ TV ⊕3pin square
3P ♨(200yds)

↤ ♨a(2½m) ☎(250yds) ♫(3m)
🐾(3m)

Min£90 Max£110pw (Low)
Min£120 Max£155pw (High)

B **Holcombe Pine** Catherston Lane
for bookings A Loosmore, Manor Farm,
Charmouth, Bridport, Dorset DT6 6QL
☎Charmouth(0297)60226

*Detached modern bungalow situated in
own grounds. Accommodation
comprises kitchen/diner, lounge, two
double-bedded rooms, one twin
bedroom, bathroom and separate WC.
Located off A35 on east side of
Charmouth.*

All year MWB out of season 1wk min,
3wks max, 1unit, 2–6persons [◇ ◆]
◉ fridge Electric Elec metered
⌷not provided ☎(200yds) Airing
cupboard in unit Iron in unit Ironing
board in unit HCE in unit [Launderette
within 300yds] ⊕ TV ⊕3pin square
3P ♨(200yds)

↤ ♨a(2½m) ☎(250yds) ♫(3m)
🐾(3m)

Min£105 Max£135pw (Low)
Min£150 Max£200pw (High)

H **Park View** Catherston Lane
for bookings A Loosmore, Manor Farm,
Charmouth, Bridport, Dorset DT6 6QL
☎Charmouth(0297)60226

Challaborough Bay
—
Cheddar

*Semi-detached house situated on
outskirts of village. Accommodation
comprises kitchen/diner, lounge, two
double-bedded rooms, one twin-bedded
room, bathroom and two separate WC's.
Located off A35 on east side of
Charmouth.*

All year MWB out of season 1wk min,
3wks max, 1unit, 2–6persons [◆ ◆]
◉ fridge Electric Elec metered
⌷not provided ☎(100yds) Airing
cupboard in unit Iron in unit Ironing
board in unit HCE in unit [Launderette
within 300yds] ⊕ TV ⊕3pin square
3P 1🏠 ♨(100yds)

↤ ♨a(2½m) ☎(250yds) ♫(3m)
♫(3m) 🐾(3m)

Min£90 Max£110pw (Low)
Min£120 Max£155pw (High)

CHATHILL
Northumberland
Map **12** NU12

C Miss R Barber **Cottage No 6**
Newham Hall, Chathill, Northd
☎Chathill(066 589)234

*Stone-built terraced cottage in a rural
situation north of Alnwick and 3m E of the
A1. It has one double-bedded room and
one twin-bedded room on the first-floor
and a living room, kitchen and
bathroom/WC on the ground floor.*

All year MWB out of season 1wk min,
1mth max, 1unit, 2–4persons no pets
◉ fridge Electric Elec metered ⌷not
provided ☎(1m) HCE in unit TV can
be hired ⊕3pin square P 🏠 ♨(3m)

↤ ♨a(3m) ☎(2m) ♫(3m) ♫(3m)

Min£30 Max£45pw (Low)
Min£50 Max£65pw (High)

F **Flat A**
for bookings Mrs N M Barrett, Tuggal
Hall, Chathill, Northd NE67 5EW
☎Chathill(066 589)229

*A first-floor flat located within a 17th-
century stone-built country house in a
tranquil setting 2m from the sea. Close to
a sandy beach, golf course and the Farne
Island bird sanctuary. Only 2m from
Seahouses on the B1340. Sleeping
accommodation comprises three double
bedrooms.*

All year MWB out of season 1wk min,
2mths max, 1unit, 6persons [◇] ◆
no pets ◉ fridge Electric
Elec metered ⌷can be hired ☎(¼m)
Airing cupboard on premises HCE on
premises ⊕ ⊕3pin square
⊕3pin round P ♨(2m)

↤ ♨a(½m) ☎(2m) ♫(2m) ♫(2m)

C **The Cottage**
for bookings Mrs N M Barrett, Tuggal
Hall, Chathill, Northd NE67 5EW
☎Chathill(066 589)229

---

*In a countryside setting this stone-built
cottage is within the grounds of Tuggal
Hall, close to beaches, golf course and
Farne Islands. Accommodation
comprises sitting room, kitchen/diner,
bathroom and twin-bedded room on the
ground floor with one twin and one
double-bedded room on first-floor.*

All year MWB out of season 3days min,
5mths max, 1unit, 2–6persons [◇ ◆
◆] ◉ fridge Electric & coal fires
Elec metered ⌷not provided ☎(½m)
[WM on premises] Airing cupboard in
unit Iron in unit Ironing board in unit
HCE in unit TV ⊕3pin square 2P 🏠
♨(2m)

↤ ♨a(3m) ☎(1½m) ♫(3m)

CHEDDAR
Somerset
Map **3** ST45

H **Clouds Hill** Barrows Road
for bookings Mrs M Earle, The Old
Manse, Barrows Croft, Cheddar,
Somerset BS27 8BH
☎(0934)742496

*Detached post war house in residential
area with garden and garage.
Accommodation comprises four
bedrooms two single, one twin and one
double, kitchen/dining area and lounge
with put-u-up.*

All year MWB out of season 1wk min,
4wks max, 1unit, 1–7persons ♨
fridge 🔥 Gas/Elec inclusive
⌷inclusive ☎(¼m) Airing cupboard in
unit Iron in unit Ironing board in unit
HCE in unit TV ⊕3pin square 1P
1🏠 🏠 ♨(½m)

↤ ☎(¼m) ♫(1m)

Min£60 Max£80pw (Low)
Min£90 Max£110pw (High)

C Mrs S Blakeney Edwards **Stable &
Orchard Cottages** Fairlands House,
Cheddar, Somerset
☎Cheddar(0934)742629

*Semi-detached stone cottages
converted from old stables, set in large
orchard with views of Mendip Hills and
Cheddar Gorge. Accommodation
comprises open-plan
lounge/kitchen/diner; first-floor has two
bedrooms, one with a double bed and the
other with twin bunks, and a shower room
with WC.*

All year 1wk min, 3wks max, 2units,
4–6persons ◇ ◆ ◆ no pets ◉
fridge Electric Elec metered
⌷inclusive ☎(200yds) Airing
cupboard in unit Iron in unit Ironing
board in unit HCE in unit [Launderette
within 300yds] ⊕ TV ⊕3pin square
2P 🏠 ♨(150yds)

↤ ☎(200yds) ♫(½m)

Min£60 Max£150pw

1982 prices quoted throughout
gazetteer

CHERITON BISHOP
Devon
Map 3 SX79

H   **CC Ref 478**
for bookings Character Cottages
(Holidays) Ltd, 34 Fore Street, Sidmouth,
Devon EX108AQ
☎Sidmouth(03955)77001

*A converted farm cottage in secluded
position, with access along farm road.
Set on hillside with garden area and
parking, overlooking woods. There is a
kitchen with modern fittings, rear
entrance and cloakroom with WC and
hand basin and large lounge. On the
first-floor there is a bathroom, two double
bedrooms, one room with three singles.*

All year MWB out of season 1wk min,
6wks max, 1unit, 1–7persons ◊ @
fridge Electric Elec inclusive Ⓛcan
be hired ☎(1m) WM in unit SD in unit
Airing cupboard in unit Iron in unit
Ironing board in unit HCE in unit ☺
CTV ⊕3pin square P ♨(1m)
⊖ ♟(1m)

Min£59 Max£89pw (Low)
Min£110 Max£158pw (High)

H   **Furze Cottage** West Beer
for bookings Mr & Mrs R G Reynolds,
West Beer Holidays, Cheriton Bishop,
Exeter, Devon EX66HF
☎Cheriton Bishop(064724)260

*A converted hayloft adjacent to farm.
Accommodation comprises a ground-
floor with kitchen, spacious living room
and enclosed staircase and first-floor
with one double bedroom, two twin-
bedded rooms, one single-bedded
room, WC and shower room. There is an
integral car port.*

Etr-Oct 1wk min, 1mth max, 1unit,
2–7persons ◊ @ fridge Electric
Elec metered Ⓛinclusive ☎(20yds)
Airing cupboard in unit Iron in unit
Ironing board in unit HCE in unit ☺
CTV ⊕3pin square ⊕2pin round P
🏠 ♨(2m) Table tennis
⊖ ♟(2m)

Min£55 Max£85pw (Low)
Min£90 Max£120pw (High)

CHESWICK
Northumberland
Map 12 NU04

C   **Garden Cottage**
for bookings Lt Col H Crossman,
Cheswick House, Berwick-upon-Tweed,
North d TD15 2RL
☎Berwick-upon-Tweed(0289)87234

*A semi-detached cottage in the grounds
of Cheswick House, ⅓m from the A1. The
ground-floor accommodation comprises
lounge, kitchen, bathroom/WC and one
twin-bedded room and first floor has two
twin-bedded rooms.*

Apr–mid Oct 1wk min, 1mth max, 1unit,
2–6persons [◊] ◊ ◆ ◁ fridge
Electric & coal fires Gas/Elec metered
Ⓛinclusive ☎(¼m) HCE in unit ☺
TV ⊕3pin square 1P 🔟 ♨(5m)
⊖ ☒(½m)

Min£25 Max£65pw

H   **West Lodge**
for bookings Lt Col H Crossman,
Cheswick House, Berwick-upon-Tweed,
North d TD15 2RL
☎Berwick-upon-Tweed(0289)87234

*Single-storey stone-built lodge in the
grounds of the Victorian mansion,
Cheswick House. Accommodation
consists of two twin-bedded rooms, living
room, bathroom/WC and kitchenette. 5m
from Berwick and 1m from the sea.*

Apr–mid Oct 1wk min, 1mth max, 1unit,
1–5persons ◊ ◆ fridge Electric
and open fires Elec metered
Ⓛinclusive ☎(400yds) Airing
cupboard in unit HCE in unit ☺ TV
⊕3pin square P ♨(5m)
⊖ ♒(1m) ♟(1m)

Min£20 Max£65pw

CHEW MAGNA
Avon
Map 3 ST56

B   **Bailiffs House**
for bookings Mrs S E Lyons, Chew Hill
Farm, Chew Magna, Bristol BS18 8QP
☎Chew Magna(027 589)2496

*A modern, detached, pebble dashed,
dormer bungalow in grounds of a
farmhouse. Situated in a rural setting with
open views from an elevated position.
Accommodation comprises a ground
floor with dining room, kitchen, lounge
and WC and first floor with twin-bedded
room, two single-bedded rooms and
bathroom/WC. Access from the A38,
Bristol to Bridgwater road, or A37, Bristol
to Shepton Mallet road, then by B3130 to
Dundry Hill.*

All year MWB out of season 1wk min,
4wks max, 1unit, 2–4persons @
fridge Electric Elec metered
Ⓛinclusive ☎(2½m) Airing cupboard in
unit Iron in unit Ironing board in unit
HCE in unit ☺ TV ⊕3pin square P
🔟 ♨(2½m)

Min£75 Max£105pw (Low)
Min£130 Max£160pw (High)

B   **East Lodge** Chew Hill
for bookings Mrs S E Lyons, Chew Hill
Farm, Chew Magna, Bristol BS18 8QP
☎Chew Magna(027589)2496

*A modern, detached, colour washed,
dormer bungalow in a quiet, rural,
elevated setting with open views across
to the valley and lake. Accommodation
comprises lounge, dining room, kitchen
and WC on the ground floor and one
twin-bedded room, two single bedrooms
and bathroom/WC on the first floor.
Access from the A38 Bristol to Bridgwater
road, or A37, Bristol to Shepton Mallet
road, thence by B3130 to Dundry Hill.*

All year MWB out of season 1wk min,
4wks max, 1unit, 2–4persons @
fridge Electric Elec metered
Ⓛinclusive ☎(1m) Airing cupboard in
unit Iron in unit Ironing board in unit
HCE in unit ☺ TV ⊕3pin square P
🏠 🔟 ♨(1m)

Min£75 Max£105pw (Low)
Min£130 Max£160pw (High)

H   **West Lodge** Limeburn Hill
for bookings Mrs S E Lyons, Chew Hill
Farm, Chew Magna, Bristol BS18 8QP
☎Chew magna(027589)2496

*A colour washed, stone-built, Victorian
lodge standing at entrance to grounds
along private drive to farm house in a*

quiet, rural setting with good views. The ground floor comprises dining room, lounge, kitchen and bathroom/WC. The first floor comprises one twin and two single bedrooms. Access from A38 Bristol to Bridgwater road or A37, Bristol/Shepton Mallet road, thence by B3130 Limeburn Hill.

All year MWB out of season 1wkmin, 4wks max, 1 unit, 2–4 persons ◉ fridge Electric Elec metered ⬜inclusive ☎(2½m) Airing cupboard in unit Iron in unit Ironing board in unit HCE in unit ⊖ TV ⊕3 pin square P ⌂ ▥ ♨(2½m)

Min£70 Max£100pw (Low)
Min£115 Max£130pw (High)

CHILLENDEN
Kent
Map**5** TR25

C **Whitehorn**
for bookings The Cottage Secretary, Knowlton Estate Office, Knowlton Court, Wingham, Canterbury, Kent CT31PT
☎Sandwich(0304)617344

Small comfortable cottage in the village of Chillenden. Accommodation comprises one twin-bedded and one bunk-bedded room, dining room, kitchen, sitting room and bathroom/WC. Private garden.

All year MWB out of season 1wk min, 1 unit, 1–4 persons [◇] ◆ ◉ fridge Electric Elec metered ⬜can be hired ☎(½m) Airing cupboard Iron Ironing board HCE ⊖ TV ⊕3 pin square ▥ ♨(1m)

⊖ ♨(½m)

Min£42.50 Max£47.50pw (Low)
£100pw (High)

CHILLINGTON
Devon
Map**3** SX74

H **The House**
for bookings Mrs L M McIntosh, 13 Mead Lane, Thurlestone, Devon TQ7 3PB
☎Thurlestone(054857)613

Modern semi-detached house in quiet cul-de-sac, two miles from Torcross and four miles from Kingsbridge. The accommodation sleeps two to six persons in one double bedded room, one single and single bed settee in lounge. Small rear garden.

All year MWB out of season 3 days min, 1 mth max, 1 unit, 2–6 persons [◇] ◆ ◆ no pets ◉ fridge Electric Elec metered ⬜not provided ☎(150yds) Airing cupboard in unit Iron in unit Ironing board in unit HCE ⊖ ◉ TV ⊕3 pin square 2P 1⌂ ▥ ♨(½m)

⊖ ♨(½m)

Min£55 Max£138pw

1982 prices quoted throughout gazetteer

CHILTON POLDEN
Somerset
Map**3** ST33

B **The Bungalow** 12 Willmott's Close
for bookings Mrs I M Smith, Polden Peak House, 1A Bath Road, Ashcott, Bridgwater, Somerset TA7 9QT
☎Ashcott(0458)310627

Bungalow in residential close with small garden to front and a large one to rear. Accommodation comprises lounge/diner, kitchen, one double bedded room and two singles, bathroom and separate WC.

All year MWB out of season 1wkmin, 2mths max, 1 unit, 6 persons [◇ ◆] no pets ◉ fridge 🍴 Elec inclusive ⬜can be hired ☎ Wm in unit SD in unit Airing cupboard in unit Iron in unit Ironing board in unit HCE in unit ◉ CTV ⊕3 pin square 1P 2⌂ ▥ ♨(50yds)

⊖ ♨(½m)

CHITTLEHAMPTON
Devon
Map**3** SS62

C **Cleave Farm**
for bookings Mrs H Falkner, Cleave Farm, Chittlehampton, Umberleigh, Devon
☎Chittlehamholt(07694)361

Once farm buildings now converted into two stone-built cottages. Interior has pinewood doors, oak beams and Scandinavian log burners. Each cottage has three bedrooms, lounge/diner, kitchen/diner, bathroom and WC. Leave B3226 at Clapworthy on unclassed road heading N, Cleave Farm is on the left.

Mar–Nov MWB out of season 1wk min, 6 wks max, 2 units, 2–8 persons ◇ ◆ ◆ ◉ fridge Electric Elec metered ⬜not provided ☎ WM in unit SD in unit Airing cupboard in unit Iron in unit Ironing board in unit HCE in unit ⊖ TV ⊕3 pin square ⊕2 pin round P ♨(4m) Games room

⊖ ♨(3m)

Min£35 Max£75pw (Low)
Min£85 Max£143.75pw (High)

H **South Cottage**
for bookings Mrs Falkner, Cleave Farm, Chittlehampton, Umberleigh, Devon
☎Chittlehamholt(07694)361

Semi-detached converted wing of farmhouse with lounge/diner, kitchen, four bedrooms comprising various sleeping accommodation including two cots, bathroom/WC and separate WC.

Mar–Nov & Xmas MWB out of season 1wk min, 1mth max, 1 unit, 1–11 persons ◇ ◆ ◆ ◉ fridge Electric Elec metered ⬜not provided ☎ WM SD Airing cupboard in unit Iron in unit Ironing board in unit HCE in unit ⊖ TV ⊕3 pin square P ♨(4m) Games room

⊖ ♨(3m)

Min£35 Max£75pw (Low)
Min£85 Max£172.50pw (High)

CHRISTOW
Devon
Map**3** SX88

C **CC Ref 436 EL**
for bookings Character Cottages (Holidays) Ltd, 34 Fore Street, Sidmouth, Devon EX108AQ
☎Sidmouth(03955)77001

A luxurious, detached, brick-built cottage dating from the Elizabethan period with modern extension. Accommodation comprises 'L' shaped lounge with dining area, kitchen, bathroom/WC, separate WC, utility room, twin-bedded room, one room with bunk beds and one double bedroom en suite on the first floor.

All year MWB out of season 1wk min, 1mth max, 1 unit, 2–6 persons ◆ no pets ◉ fridge 🍴 Elec metered ⬜can be hired ☎ WM in unit SD in unit Airing cupboard in unit Iron in unit Ironing board in unit HCE in unit ⊖ CTV ⊕3 pin square ⊕2 pin round P ▥ ♨(1m)

⊖ ♨(1m)

Min£140 Max£218pw (Low)
Min£327 Max£363pw (High)

C **CC Ref 446 ELP**
for bookings Character Cottages (Holidays) Ltd, 34 Fore Street, Sidmouth, Devon EX108AQ
☎Sidmouth(03955)77001

One of five cottages comprising lounge with put-u-up, one double bedroom, twin-bedded room, WC, bathroom and kitchen diner. It lies in a beauty spot.

All year MWB out of season 1wk min, 1mth max, 1 unit, 2–6 persons ◆ ◉ fridge Electric & Calor gas Elec metered ⬜can be hired ☎ Iron on premises Ironing board on premises HCE on premises ⊖ TV ⊕3 pin square ⊕2 pin round P ▥ ♨(200yds)

⊖ ♨(1m) ▨ ♫

Min£40 Max£78pw (Low)
Min£73 Max£118pw (High)

CHUDLEIGH
Devon
Map**3** SX87

C **CC Ref 441**
for bookings Character Cottages (Holidays) Ltd, 34 Fore Street, Sidmouth, Devon EX108AQ
☎Sidmouth(03955)77001

Period stone-built cottage of which the accommodation consists of ground floor lounge, kitchen, twin-bedded room and WC. On the first floor, two single rooms, twin-bedded room, bathroom and WC.

Jul–Sep 1wk min, 1mth max, 1 unit, 2–6 persons ◉ fridge Electric Elec metered ⬜can be hired Airing cupboard in unit Iron in unit Ironing →

65

board in unit HCE in unit ⊙ TV
⊕3pin square ⊕2pin round P 🏠(2m)
↤ 🅿(2m) 🅰(2m) 🎵(2m)
Min£78 Max£110pw (Low)
Min£132 Max£162pw (High)

CHUDLEIGH KNIGHTON
Devon
Map**3** SX87

C CC Ref 427 ELP
for bookings Character Cottages
(Holidays) Ltd, 34 Fore Street,Sidmouth,
Devon EX10 8AQ
☎Sidmouth(03955)77001

*Wing of period farmhouse comprising
lounge, kitchen/diner and bathroom/WC
on ground floor. On first floor a double
bedroom, a twin-bedded room and room
with bunk beds and a 'Z' bed.*

Jun–Sep 1wk min, 1mth max, 1unit,
2–7persons [◇] ◆ ◉ fridge
Electric Elec inclusive 🔲can be hired
Iron in unit Ironing board in unit HCE on
premises TV ⊕3pin square
⊕2pin round P 📺 🏠(1m)
↤ δ🔥(2m) 🅿(2m) 🅰(2m) 🎵(2m)
Min£55 Max£65pw (Low)
Min£80 Max£117pw (High)

CHULMLEIGH
Devon
Map**3** SS61

H Mrs Stevens **Hollacombe Barton**
Chulmleigh, Devon
☎Winkleigh(083783)385

*Large farmhouse on a working farm near
the small village of Hollacombe; well
decorated accommodation.*

All year MWB out of season 4days min,
4wks max, 1unit, 2–10persons ◇ ◆
◆ ◉ fridge Electric Elec inclusive
🔲inclusive ☎(½m) WM in unit SD in
unit TD in unit Airing cupboard in unit
Iron in unit Ironing board in unit HCE in
unit ⊙ ⊗ TV ⊕3pin square 2P
1🏠 📺 🏠(2m) Rough shooting
↤ δ🔥(3m) 🅿(2m)
Min£57.50 Max£138pw

CHURCHILL
Avon
Map**3** ST45

H The Farm House
for bookings Mrs J A Sacof, Churchill
Green Farm, Churchill, Avon
☎Churchill(0934)852438

*Traditional old farmhouse set amidst 25
acres in quiet setting facing wooded
slopes of Mendip Hills. Accommodation
comprises lounge, kitchen/diner; four
bedrooms (two double, two twin),
bathroom/WC on the first floor and two
twin-bedded rooms on the second floor.
Traditionally furnished with one bedroom
having an antique canopied double bed.*

Sep–Jun MWB out of season 1wk min,
6mths max, 1unit, 2–12persons ◆
no pets Aga fridge 🍴 Elec metered
🔲inclusive ☎(½m) Airing cupboard
Iron Ironing board HCE in unit ⊙ TV

⊕3pin square 🏠(⅓m) ⊐
↤ 🅿(⅓m) 🅰(2m) 🎵(2m)

B The Pool House
for bookings Mrs J A Sacof, Churchill
Green Farm, Churchill, Avon
☎Churchill(0934)852438

*Stone-built bungalow set alongside
swimming pool in peaceful setting,
comprising lounge/diner, kitchen, two
bedrooms (one twin, one three single
beds plus lounge settee) bathroom/WC.*

All year MWB out of season 1wk min,
6mths max, 1unit, 2–6persons ◆
no pets ◉ fridge 🍴 Elec metered
🔲inclusive ☎(½m) HCE in unit ⊙
CTV ⊕3pin square P 🏠(½m) ⊐
↤ 🅿 🅰(½m) 🎵(2m)

CHURCHINFORD
Somerset
Map**3** ST21

C Ivy Cottage Moor Lane
for bookings Mrs C A Barnard, The Mill,
Preston Bower, Milverton, Taunton,
Somerset TA4 1PH
☎Milverton(0823)400650

*Double-fronted, stone-built ivy-clad
cottage close to village centre. It
comprises lounge, dining room, small
kitchen and bathroom. First floor
comprises one twin-bedded room and
one double bedroom with washbasin.*

All year 1wk min, 1mth max, 1unit,
1–5persons ◆ ◉ fridge Electric
Elec metered 🔲can be hired
☎(90yds) Airing cupboard in unit Iron
in unit HCE in unit TV ⊕3pin square
🏠(90yds)
↤ 🅿(80yds)
Min£30 Max£75pw

CHURCH STOKE
Powys
Map**7** SO29

C Bwthyn Bach & Todleth Cottages
Todleth Hill
for bookings Sir Michael & Lady Pollock,
The Ivy House, Churchstoke,
Montgomery, Powys SY15 6DU
☎Churchstoke(05885)426

*Two Welsh hill cottages on open grass
and bracken hillside reached by 600yds
of rough track. 1m off A489.* **Bwthyn
Bach** *offers kitchen/breakfast room,
sitting room with twin bedroom off, and a
second bedroom and bathroom/WC on
the first floor.* **Todleth** *comprises
kitchen/breakfast room, bathroom and
separate WC, sitting room. Two
bedrooms on the first floor. The cottages
are 50yds apart.*

Mar–Dec MWB out of season 1wk min,
2wks min in winter, 2units, 1–5persons
◆ ◉ Propane 🔥 fridge Gas & open
fires 🔲not provided ☎(1m) Iron in
unit Ironing board in unit HCE in unit
⊙ ⊕3pin square 3P 🏠(1m)

↤ 🅿(1m)
Min£40 Max£60pw (Low)
Min£80 Max£105pw (High)

CHURCH STRETTON
Shropshire
Map**7** SO49

C The Old Cobblers Shop High Street
for bookings Mrs S A Woolston, 29 Broad
Street, Ludlow, Salop SY8 1NJ
☎Ludlow(0584)3554

*A converted terraced cottage with
exposed beams (once a cobbler's shop)
comprising lounge, kitchen/diner, an
outside WC; upstairs comprises three
bedrooms, one double, one twin-bedded
and one with bunk beds and a
shower/WC.*

All year 2nights min, 2mths max, 1unit,
1–7persons ◇ ◆ no pets ◉
fridge 🍴 Elec metered 🔲inclusive
except towels ☎(½m) Airing cupboard
in unit Iron in unit Ironing board in unit
HCE in unit ⊙ TV ⊕3pin square 2P
🏠(100yds)
↤ δ🔥(1½m) 🅿(100yds) 🅰(100yds)
🎵(100yds)
Min£65 Max£95pw

CHURSTON FERRERS
Devon
Map**3** SX95

B CC Ref 403E
for bookings Character Cottages
(Holidays) Ltd, 34 Fore Street, Sidmouth,
Devon EX10 8AQ
☎Sidmouth(03955)77001

*Modern split-level, semi-detached
bungalow, 1½m from seafront with views
over Torbay. There are three double
bedrooms, lounge/diner, kitchen,
bathroom and WC.*

All year MWB out of season 1wk min,
6ths max, 1unit, 2–6persons ◆
no pets ◉ fridge 🍴
Gas/Elec metered 🔲not provided
☎(150yds) SD in unit Airing cupboard
in unit Iron in unit Ironing board in unit
HCE in unit ⊙ TV ⊕3pin square
⊕2pin round P 🏠 📺 🏠(150yds)
Sailing

↤ 🅿(1m) 🅰(1m) 🎵(2m) 🐴(2m)
Min£91 Max£117pw (Low)
Min£155 Max£207pw (High)

CHWILOG
Gwynedd
Map**6** SH43

H Mrs C Jones *Chwilog Fawr* Chwilog
Pwllheli, Gwynedd
☎Chwilog(076688)506

*This south-facing wing, part of an 18th-
century stone farmhouse in elevated
position, comprises lounge, dining room,
kitchen, two double-bedded rooms, one
twin-bedded, and bathroom/WC. 1½m
from village.*

Etr–Sep 1wk min, 4wks max, 1unit,
1–6persons ◇ ◆ ◆ no pets ◉
fridge 🍴 Elec metered

🛏notprovided ☎(400yds) [WM on premises] [SD on premises] Iron in unit Ironing board in unit HCE in unit ⊖ CTV ⊕3pinsquare 3P 🎦 ♨(1m)
⊷ Ᏸ(3m) ♀(1m) 🔲(3m)

Ch Wernol Farms Caravan Park
for bookings Mrs C Jones, Chwilog Fawr, Chwilog, Pwlheli, Gwynedd
☎Chwilog(076688)506

Six purpose-built timber chalets on quiet caravan site adjacent to beaches and mountains. Five of the units have lounge/diner, kitchen, one twin-bedded room, one double and one with bunk beds, bathroom/WC. The other has lounge/kitchen/diner, bathroom/WC and two bedrooms, one with twin beds, the other with double.

Mar–Oct MWB MWB out of season 1wk min, 4wks max, 6units, 1–6persons ◊ ◆ ◿ fridge Electric Elec metered 🛏can be hired ☎(200yds) Airing cupboard in unit Iron in unit Ironing board in unit HCE in unit CTV ⊕3pinsquare 2P 🎦 ♨(1m)
⊷ Ᏸ(3m) ♀(1m) 🔲(3m)
Min£40 Max£95pw

CILGERRAN
Dyfed
Map**2**SN14

H Cilanne
for bookings Dr & Mrs Kramer, Cilfair, Cilgerran, Cardigan, Dyfed SA432SN
☎Cardigan(0239)614222

A mature house in the village of Cilgerran which stands above the wooded gorge of the River Teifi. On the ground floor there are two sitting rooms each of which will, if necessary, sleep two adults, kitchen, dining room, conservatory and WC. On the first-floor there are bedrooms with double, twin and bunk beds. Combined bath/WC. Lawned garden.

All year MWB out of season 3days min, 1unit, 10persons ◆ ◆ ◎ fridge Electric Elec metered 🛏can be hired ☎(4m) WM in unit SD in unit Airing cupboard in unit Iron in unit Ironing board in unit HCE in unit TV ⊕3pinsquare P 🎦 ♨(½m)
⊷ ♀(½m)
Min£30 Max£135pw

H Cilddewi
for bookings Dr & Mrs Kramer, Cilfair, Cilgerran, Cardigan, Dyfed SA432SN
☎Cardigan(0239)614222

A small but particularly attractive former farmhouse adapted for a high degree of comfort, but retaining many of its attractive features. Accommodation comprises dining room with Victorian cast-iron range, kitchen, study/bedroom, and a short staircase leading to a gallery sitting room with good views. There are two bedrooms and a small bathroom on the first-floor.

All year MWB out of season 3days min, 1unit, 8persons ◆ ◎ fridge Electric Elec metered 🛏can be hired

---

☎(½m) WM in unit SD in unit Iron in unit Ironing board in unit HCE in unit ⊖ TV ⊕3pinsquare P 🎦 ♨(½m)
⊷ ♀(½m)
Min£30 Max£135pw

C Rose Cottage
for bookings Dr & Mrs Kramer, Cilfair, Cilgerran, Cardigan, Dyfed SA432SN
☎Cardigan(0239)614222

A most attractive cottage in the village. To the rear is a balcony with a superb view of the wooded Gorge of the Teifi and Cilgerran Castle. Kitchen/dining room. Bedroom 1 has a double bed and a cot with a child's bed if required. Bedroom 2 has single or bunk bed if required. Shower room, WC and sitting room with studio couch for two. Below the balcony is a single study bedroom with separate access.

All year MWB out of season 3days min, 1unit, 4–5persons ◆ ◆ ◎ fridge Electric Elec metered 🛏can be hired SD in unit ☎(½m) Airing cupboard in unit Iron in unit Ironing board in unit HCE in unit ⊖ TV ⊕3pinsquare P 🎦 ♨(½m)
⊷ ♀(½m)
Min£25 Max£115pw

CLACHAN-SEIL
Strathclyde *Argyll*
Map**10**NM71

C Seil Island Cottages
for bookings Mr M Murray, Kilmahumaig, Crinan, Lochgilphead, Argyll
☎Crinan(054683)238

Three modern detached cottages set on a hillside on Seil Island. Each cottage contains living/dining room with two divans, double bedroom, room with bunks and kitchen. The properties are 5m from the A816 on the B844 and are reached by crossing the famous 'Bridge over the Atlantic'.

All year MWB out of season 4days min, 3units, 1–6persons ◆ nopets ◎ fridge Electric Elec metered 🛏notprovided ☎(250yds) Airing cupboard in unit Iron in unit Ironing board in unit HCE in unit ⊖ ⊕3pinsquare P ♨(5m)
Min£40 Max£120pw

CLACTON-ON-SEA
Essex
Map**5**TM11

Ch Highfield Holiday Park London Road
for bookings Hoseasons Holidays Ltd, Sunway House, Lowestoft, Suffolk NR323LT
☎Lowestoft(0502)62292

A holiday park approx 2m from the seafront with good recreation facilities and children's amusements. Caribbean chalets comprise two double bedrooms,

---

living room, kitchen & bathroom. Simple but functional.

Etr wknd & 15May–11Sep 1wk min, (High season) 1night min (low season) 68units, 1–6persons [◆ ◆]nopets ◎ fridge 🍴 Elec metered 🛏inclusive ☎ Airing cupboard in unit Iron on premises Ironong board on premises [Launderette within 300yds] ⊖ CTV ⊕3pinsquare 500P ♨(200yds) ⌒ Children's play area
⊷ Ᏸ(3m) 🔲 ♫ 🎣(2¼m)

CLEETON ST MARY
Shropshire
Map**7**SO67

F Cleeton Court Farm (Flat)
foo bookings Mr C E Pearce, Cleeton Court Farm, Cleeton St Mary, Cleobury Mortimer, Kidderminster, Worcestershire
☎Stoke St Milborough(058475)288

Traditionally-decorated flat with fitted carpets, adjoining a farmhouse situated ½m N of the village. Accommodation comprises one double- and one twin-bedded room, kitchen, lounge/diner and bathroom/WC. Extensive views of surrounding countryside.

All year MWB out of season 4wks max, 1unit, 1–5persons ◊ ◆ ◆ nopets ◎ fridge Electric Elec metered ☎(½m) Airing cupboard in unit Iron in unit HCE in unit ⊖ TV ⊕3pinsquare P ♨(3m)
⊷ ♀(3m)
Min£30 Max£64pw

CLEY NEXT THE SEA
Norfolk
Map**9**TG04

C 1,2,3 & 4 Bank Cottages High Street
for bookings Mrs S M Finch, The Mill House, Little Braxted, Witham, Essex
☎Witham(0376)513008

Situated in a village on A149, these two-storey terraced cottages are fully furnished and have a small communal garden. All have two first-floor bedrooms. Area famous for its bird-watching.

All year 1mth max, 4units, 1–6persons [◊] ◆ nopets ◎ fridge 🍴 Elec metered 🛏notprovided ☎(20yds) Airing cupboard in unit Iron in unit Ironing board in unit HCE in unit ⊖ CTV ⊕3pinsquare P ♨(50yds)
⊷ ♀(100yds)
Min£50 Max£80pw (Low)
Min£100 Max£140pw (High)

CLIPPESBY
Norfold
Map**9**TG41

B Arbroath & Tiree
for bookings Clippesby Holidays, Clippesby, Gt Yarmouth, Norfolk NR293BJ
☎Fleggburgh(049377)367

Two semi-detached bungalows overlooking fields on perimeter of the Holiday Centre. Each has two double →

bedrooms and a double fold-up bed in the lounge/diner. Well equipped, comfortable accommodation, quietly located, but with every on-site amenity.

21May–Sep MWB out of season 1wk min, 3wks max, 2units, 1–6persons [◇ ◆ ◆] ◎ fridge Electric Electric Elecmetered ⬜inclusive ☎ Airing cupboard in unit [Iron on premises] [Ironing board on premises] HCE in unit [Launderette on premises] ⊕ TV ③pinsquare P 🅼 ♨ ⌂ 🌿Grass ♦

⊖ 🕿

Min£62.10 Max£103.50pw (Low)
Min£100.05 Max£128.80pw (High)

F Banff & Nairn

for bookings Clippesby Holidays, Clippesby, Gt Yarmouth, Norfolk NR29 3BJ
☎Fleggburgh(049 377)367

Two two-bedroomed flats, both on the first-floor. Each contains one double bedroom and one with two bunk beds, separate bathroom and kitchen. Decorated and equipped to good standard, the flats face onto the former courtyard of the old Hall. Ideal for family holidays.

21May–Sep MWB out of season 1wk min, 3wks max, 2units, 1–4persons [◇ ◆ ◆] ◎ fridge Electric Elecmetered ⬜inclusive ☎ [Iron on premises] [Ironing board on premises] HCE in unit [Launderette on premises] ⊕ TV ③pinsquare P 🅼 ♨ ⌂ 🌿Grass ♦♦

⊖ 🕿

Min£56.35 Max£86.25pw (Low)
Min£94.30 Max£106.95pw (High)

B Glenross & Galbraith

for bookings Clippesby Holidays, Clippesby, Gt Yarmouth, Norfolk NR29 3BJ
☎Fleggburgh(049 377)367

Two detached bungalows backing onto woodland and overlooking fields on the perimeter of the Centre which is set in some 30 acres. Each has three double bedrooms, large lounge/diner, separate kitchen and bathroom. Ideal touring area.

21May–Sep MWB out of season 1wk min, 2wks max, 2units, 1–6persons [◇] ◆ ◆ ◎ fridge Electric Elecmetered ⬜inclusive ☎ Airing cupboard in unit [Iron on premises] [Ironing board on premises] HCE in unit [Launderette on premises] ⊕ TV ③pinsquare P 🅼 ♨ ⌂ 🌿Grass ♦

⊖ 🕿

Min£80.50 Max£115pw (Low)
Min£128.80 Max£139.15pw (High)

B Grampian

for bookings Clippesby Holidays, Clippesby, Gt Yarmouth, Norfolk NR29 3BJ
☎Fleggburgh(049 377)367

Clippesby
—
Clynnog Fawr

Large two-storey property, well-equipped and designed to sleep eight in four twin-bedded rooms. One bedroom with double bed is situated on the ground floor along with bathroom, spacious lounge/diner and kitchen.

21May–Sep MWB out of season 1wk min, 3wks max, 1unit, 1–8persons [◇ ◆ ◆] ◎ fridge Electric Elecmetered ⬜inclusive ☎ Airing cupboard in unit [Iron on premises] [Ironing board on premises] HCE in unit [Launderette on premises] ⊕ TV ③pinsquare P 🅼 ♨ ⌂ 🌿Grass ♦

⊖ 🕿

Min£69 Max£118.45pw (Low)
Min£115 Max£144.90pw (High)

F Lewis, Montrose & Angus

for bookings Clippesby Holidays, Clippesby, Gt Yarmouth, Norfolk NR29 3BJ
☎Fleggburgh(049 377)367

Three comfortable flats ('Lewis' on ground-floor, other two on first-floor), each with a twin-bedded room and a fold-down double bed in lounge/diner. Well-fitted kitchen and bathroom. All within converted complex of units originally forming the old Hall and auxiliary buildings.

21May–Sep MWB out of season 1wk min, 3wks max, 3units, 1–4persons [◇ ◆ ◆] ◎ fridge Electric Elecmetered ⬜inclusive ☎ Airing cupboard in unit [Iron on premises] [Ironing board on premises] HCE in unit [Lauderette on premises] ⊕ TV ③pinsquare P 🅼 ♨ ⌂ 🌿Grass ♦

⊖ 🕿

Min£43.70 Max£77.05pw (Low)
Min£74.75 Max£98.90pw (High)

C Lomond

for bookings Clippesby Holidays, Clippesby, Gt Yarmouth, Norfolk NR29 3BJ
☎Fleggburgh(049 377)367

Two-storey chalet with spacious lounge/diner with fold-down double bed, bathroom and kitchen on ground-floor and two bedrooms equipped to sleep four on the first-floor. Overlooks spacious lawns.

21May–Sep MWB out of season 1wk min, 3wks max, 1unit, 1–6persons [◇ ◆ ◆] ◎ fridge Electric Elecmetered ⬜inclusive ☎ [Iron on premises] [Ironing board on premises] HCE in unit [Launderette on premises] ⊕ TV ③pinsquare P 🅼 ♨ ⌂ 🌿Grass ♦

⊖ 🕿

Min£62.10 Max£103.50pw (Low)
Min£100.05 Max£128.80pw (High)

F Mendip & Cheviot

for bookings Clippesby Holidays, Clippesby, Gt Yarmouth, Norfolk NR29 3BJ
☎Fleggburgh(049 377)367

Two attractive and spacious flats converted from part of the auxiliary buildings attached to the former old Hall. Each has three twin-bedded rooms, lounge/diner, separate bathroom and kitchen. Very suitable for family holiday.

22May–Sep MWB out of season 1wk min, 3wks max, 2units, 1–6persons [◇] [◆] ◎ fridge Electric Elecmetered ⬜inclusive ☎ [Iron on premises] [Ironing board on premises] HCE in unit [Launderette on premises] ⊕ TV ③pinsquare P 🅼 ♨ ⌂ 🌿Grass ♦

⊖ 🕿

Min£69 Max£106.95pw (Low)
Min£115 Max£133.40pw (High)

F Moray & Oban

for bookings Clippesby Holidays, Clippesby, Gt Yarmouth, Norfolk NR29 3BJ
☎Fleggburgh(049 377)367

Two flats each with two twin-bedded rooms, a fold-down bed in a spacious lounge/diner, good bathroom and kitchen. Comfortable and well-equipped accommodation.

21May–Sep MWB out of season 1wk min, 3wks max, 2units, 1–6persons [◇ ◆ ◆] ◎ fridge Electric Elecmetered ⬜inclusive ☎ Airing cupboard in unit [Iron on premises] [Ironing board on premises] HCE in unit [Launderette on premises] ⊕ TV ③pinsquare P 🅼 ♨ ⌂ 🌿Grass ♦

⊖ 🕿

Min£62.10 Max£103.50pw (Low)
Min£100.05 Max£128.80pw (High)

CLYNNOG FAWR
Gwynedd
Map **6** SH44

F Flat 3, St Beuno's Court

for bookings Mr J Smith, 15 Birch Grove, Alveley, Bridgnorth, Salop WV15 6NE
☎Quatt(0746)780609

School house converted into flats. The unit consists of a lounge/diner, separate kitchen, bathroom/WC, twin-bedded room and double room. On A499 Pwllheli–Caernarfon road.

All year MWB out of season 1wk min, 1unit, 4persons no pets ◎ fridge Electric Elecmetered ⬜not provided ☎(50yds) Airing cupboard in unit HCE in unit ⊕ TV ③pinsquare 1P 1🏠 ♨(50yds) Sea fishing

⊖ 🕿(50yds)

Min£50 Max£84pw

Clynnog Fawr — Coll (Isle of)

C 3 Ty Canol
for bookings Rev D T Hadley, St Augustine's Vicarage, Tonge Moor, Bolton, Lancs BL2 2QW
☎Bolton(0204)23899

Victorian mid terrace cottage with front door leading straight into lounge/diner, stairs from lounge to one twin-bedded, one double-bedded room and bathroom/WC. Well equipped modern kitchen. In centre of village off A499 Pwllheli–Caernarfon road.

Allyear MWB out of season 3days min, 1mth max, 1unit, 4–5persons, no pets ◎ fridge Electric Elec metered 🅻not provided ☎(20yds) [Airing cupboard in unit] Iron in unit Ironing board in unit HCE in unit ⊙ ⊕3pin square ♨(20yds)

⊖ ♀(100yds) ♫(100yds)

Min£30 Max£35pw (Low)
Min£40 Max£70pw (High)

COLATON RALEIGH
Devon
Map**3** SY09

C Mrs Jean Daniels, **Drupe Farm Cottages (No's 1–7 & 9–15)** Drupe Farm, Colaton Raleigh, Sidmouth, Devon
☎Colaton Raleigh(0395)68838

Fourteen delightful cottages converted from old farmhouse and outbuildings, set around a courtyard. Each has a lounge/diner with kitchen area, and sleeping accommodation which varies with either two or three bedrooms. Excellent standard of furnishings and fittings.

Allyear MWB out of season 1wk min, 3mths max, 14units, 1–7persons [◇] ◆ ◎ fridge ⧉ Elec inclusive 🅻inclusive ☎ Iron in unit Ironing board in unit HCE in unit [Launderette on premises] ⊙ CTV ⊕3pin square P 6🏠 ▥ ♨(¼m) Games room & childrens play area

⊖ ♂18(3m) ♀(¼m)

Min£40 Max£50pw (Low)
Min£155 Max£220pw (High)

1982 prices quoted throughout gazetteer

COLCHESTER
Essex
Map**5** TM02

F University House Avon Way
for bookings University of Essex, Catering & Accommodation Office, PO Box 23, Wivenhoe Park, Colchester, Essex CO4 3SQ
☎Colchester(0206)862286 ext 2008

Modern flats in three-storey buildings. Each flat consists of four or six bedrooms, bathroom and kitchen. One bedroom can be converted into a small lounge if required. All campus facilities are available to guests. Flats situated 1½m from town centre and University campus.

9Jul–10Sep 1wk min, 9wks max, 85units, 2–6persons ◆ ◎ fridge ⧉ Elec inclusive 🅻inclusive ☎ WM on premises SD on premises Airing cupboard on premises Iron on premises Ironing board on premises HCE in unit TV can be hired ⊕3pin square P ▥ ♨(150yds)

⊖ ♂18 ♀ ▣ ♫ ▚

Min£115 Max£133pw

COLDINGHAM
Borders *Berwickshire*
Map**12** NT96

***Ch* The Chalet** Press Castle
for bookings Miss Bristow, Thorncroft, Lilliesleaf, Roxburghshire TD6 9JD
☎Lilliesleaf(08357)424

Finnish chalet in secluded setting within the grounds of Press Castle, comprising open-plan lounge/diner, kitchen and shower/WC. There are two small bedrooms, with two single beds each, also available is a single and double bed settee in the lounge.

Allyear MWB out of season 1wk min, 1unit, 4–6persons [◆] ◎ fridge Electric Elec metered 🅻inclusive ☎(1m) Iron on premises HCE TV ⊕3pin square 2P ▥ ♨(3m)

⊖ ♀(3m)

Min£63.25 Max£86.25pw (Low)
Min£109.25 Max£138pw (High)

F Press Castle Flats
for bookings Miss J Bristow, Thorncroft, Lilliesleaf, Roxburghshire TD6 9JD
☎Lilliesleaf(08357)424

This country mansion has been converted into six small and two large flats comprising either one or two twin/double bedrooms, sitting/dining room, kitchen or kitchenette and bathroom. There is also a single and double bed-settee in each sitting room for aditional occupancy if required.

Allyear MWB out of season 1wk min, 8units, 4–7persons [◆] ◎ fridge Electric Elec metered 🅻inclusive ☎(1m) Iron on premises HCE in unit CTV ⊕3pin square 8P ▥ ♨(3m)

⊖ ♀(3m)

Min£57.50 Max£86.25pw (Low)
Min£89.70 Max£138pw (High)

COLL (ISLE OF)
Strathclyde *Argyll*
Map**13** NM25

F Malin & Hebrides Arinagour
for bookings Mrs C K M Stewart, Estate Office, Isle of Coll, Argyll PA78 6TB
☎Coll(08793)339

Situated approximately ¼m from Coll pier in the small coastal settlement of Aringour, these two modernised first-floor flats are situated above the local shop. Both offer neatly-furnished lounge/dining room, modern kitchen and bathroom/WC, Malin has one twin and two single bedrooms and Hebrides contains one double, one single and one family room. Superb views over loch and islands. Accommodation unsuitable for invalids.

Allyear MWB out of season 1wk min, 1mth max, 2units, 2–8persons [◆ ◆] ◎ fridge Electric & open fires Gas/Elec metered 🅻can be hired ☎(100yds) Airing cupboard HCE [Launderette] ⊙ ⊕3pin square 1P ♨(20yds)

⊖ ♂ ♀ ▣

Min£55 Max£110pw

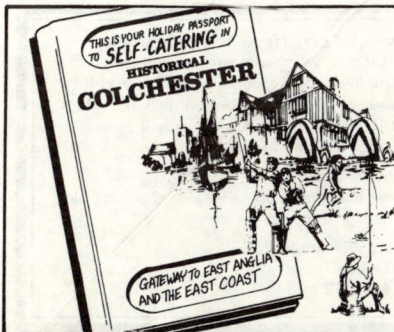

B **Minches** Arinagour
for bookings Mrs C K M Stewart, Estate Office, Isle of Coll, Argyll PA78 6TB
☎Coll(08793)339

Cedar-clad bungalow situated approximately ½m from Coll pier. Modern décor and furnishings. Accommodation comprises lounge/dining room with double bed-settee, modern kitchen, two bedrooms (one double and one bunk-bedded) and bathroom/WC. Splendid views over loch and islands. Accommodation unsuitable for invalids.

All year MWB out of season 1wk min, 1mth max, 1unit, 2–6persons [◊ ◆] ⌑ fridge Electric & open fires Gas/Elec metered ⌷ can be hired ☎(100yds) TD Airing cupboard HCE [Launderette] ⊖ ⊕3pin square 1P ♨(20yds) ℥

⊖ ℥ ☺ ▥

Min£55 Max£70pw (Low)
Min£75 Max£100pw (High)

B **Stronvar** Breachacha Bay
for bookings Mrs C K M Stewart, Estate Office, Isle of Coll, Argyll PA78 6TB
☎Coll(08793)339

Large, timber-built bungalow with splendid views of sandy beach, Breachacha Bay, and two castles (one 14th and one 18th-century). Spacious accommodation comprises kitchen, sitting/dining room, four bedrooms (one double, one twin, one single and one with bunk beds) all with wash basins and bathroom/WC. Accommodation unsuitable for invalids.

Apr–Oct MWB out of season 1wk min, 1mth max, 1unit, 2–8persons [◊ ◆] ⌑ fridge Electric & open fires Gas/Elec metered ⌷ can be hired ☎(100yds) Airing cupboard HCE [Launderette] ⊖ ⊕3pin square 2P ♨(5m) Loch fishing

⊖ ℥ ☺ ▥

Min£65 Max£88pw (Low)
Min£90 Max£120pw (High)

COLONSAY Isle of, see under **Kilchattan, Kiloran, Kiloran Bay & Scalasaig.**

COLWELL BAY
Isle of Wight
Map**4** SZ38

F A & V S Dobson ***Solent Court Holiday Flats*** Colwell Bay, Isle of Wight PO40 9NP
☎Wootton Bridge(0983)883477

Fourteen flats on two floors; twelve two-bedroomed (one double and one twin), and two with one double bedroom. All have kitchen, bathroom/WC and lounge/diner with studio couch. Situated 200yds from sandy beach.

All year MWB 1wk min, 6mths max, 14units, 1–6persons ◊ ◆ no pets ◉ fridge Electric Elec metered ⌷ can be hired ☎ Airing cupboard in unit Iron on premises Ironing board on premises HCE on premises ⊖ CTV ⊕3pin square P ▥ ♨(⅓m) ℥

⊖ ℥(200yds) ▨(2m) ♫(2m)

COLWYN BAY
Clwyd
Map**6** SH87

F **Spindrift** 16 Mostyn Road
for bookings R W Gibson, Bryniau, Vicarage Road, Llandudno, Gwynedd
☎Llandudno(0492)79228

Three flats located within semi-detached Edwardian house in residential area. They all contain kitchen/diner, lounge with double bed, bathroom/WC and sleep up to seven people. Simple furniture and décor.

Apr–Oct MWB out of season 1wk min, 6wks max, 3units, 1–7persons [◊] ◉ fridge Electric Elec metered ⌷ can be hired ☎(100yds) Airing cupboard in unit Iron in unit Ironing board in unit HCE in unit TV ⊕3pin square 3P ▥ ♨(100yds)

⊖ ♒(2m) ℥(100yds) ▨(1m) ♫(1m) ▦(200yds)

1982 prices quoted throughout gazetteer

COLYTON
Devon
Map**3** SY29

H CC Ref 631 EP
for bookings Character Cottages (Holidays) Ltd, 34 Fore Street, Sidmouth, Devon EX10 8AQ
☎Sidmouth(03955)77001

Modern semi-detached house with three bedrooms (two double, one single), living room with folding doors to dining room, kitchen and modern bathroom. Situated 3m from sea.

All year MWB out of season 1wk min, 6mths max, 1unit, 2–5persons ◊ ◉ fridge Electric Elec metered ⌷ not provided ☎(100yds) Airing cupboard in unit Iron in unit Ironing board in unit HCE in unit ⊖ TV ⊕3pin square ⊕2pin round P ▤ ▥

⊖ ℥(3m) ♫(3m)

Min£53 Max£93pw (Low)
Min£122 Max£144pw (High)

COMBE MARTIN
Devon
Map**2** SS54

F **Bay View**
for bookings Mr & Mrs B Brook, Bay View, Woodlands, Combe Martin, Devon EX34 0AT
☎Combe Martin(027 188)2522

First- and second-floor flats in end terrace house on main road on edge of village. Flat comprises kitchen/diner, two bedrooms ie doubles and double with additonal single bed. Lounge, bathroom/WC/washbasin. Flat No 1 has washbasins in all bedrooms. Comfortably furnished.

All year MWB out of season 4wks max, 2units, 2–6persons ◊ ◊ ◆ no pets ⌑ fridge Gas Gas metered ⌷ inclusive ☎(400yds) Airing cupboard Iron Ironing board HCE [Lauderette within 300yds] ⊖ TV ⊕3pin square P ▥ ♨(400yds)

⊖ ♒(2½m) ℥(200yds) ▨(¼m) ♫(¼m)

Min£30 Max£60pw (Low)
Min£70 Max£120pw (High)

B   Beachside
for bookings Mrs P J Norman, Waters
Edge, Newberry Road, Combe Martin,
Devon EX34 0AP
☎Combe Martin(027 188)3321

*Modern semi-detached bungalow
situated on the seaward side of the main
road to the W of the village. Within 100yds
of the beach and close to the sea. The
accommodation is spacious and well-
furnished and consists of two bedrooms,
lounge/diner, kitchen and bathroom/WC.
There is a completely fenced rear yard.*

Mar-Nov   MWB   3days min, 6wks max,
1unit, 2–5persons   [◇ ◆ ◆] ◿
fridge   Electric   Elec inclusive
Gas metered   ⬛inclusive   ☎(300yds)
Iron in unit   Ironing board in unit   HCE in
unit   [Launderette within 300yds]   ⊖
TV   ⊕3pin square
⊸ ♀(300yds)   ▣(300yds)   ♫(1m)
Min£55 Max£135pw

H   Channel View
for bookings Mrs P J Norman, Waters
Edge, Newberry Road, Combe Martin,
Devon EX34 0AP
☎Combe Martin(027 188)3321

*A Victorian semi-detached house in a 'no
through road', close to shops and beach.
The lounge and three of the four
bedrooms have a sea view. A kitchen,
and bathroom/WC completes the
accommodation.*

Mar-Nov   MWB out of season
3days min, 6wks max, 1unit,
2–10persons   [◇ ◆] ◿ fridge
Gas metered
⬛inclusive   ☎(300yds)   Iron in unit
Ironing board in unit   HCE in unit
[Launderette within 300yds]   ⊖   TV
⊕3pin square   P   🔲   ♿(200yds)
⊸ ♀(300yds)   ▣(300yds)   ♫(1m)
Min£85 Max£200pw

F   Drake Flat Boronga Road
for bookings Mrs P J Norman, Waters
Edge, Newberry Road, Combe Martin,
Devon EX34 0AP
☎Combe Martin(027 188)3321

*Attractive cottage style flat located above
a gift shop, 100yds from the sea. Beamed
entrance hall, living room with kitchen off,
two bedrooms and bathroom/WC. Car
parking on payment in garage opposite
or public car park, 100yds.*

Mar-Nov   MWB out of season
3days min, 1mth max, 1unit,
1–4persons   [◇ ◆ ◆] ◿ fridge
Electric   Elec metered   ⬛inclusive
☎(50yds)   Airing cupboard in unit   Iron
in unit   Ironing board in unit   HCE in unit
[Launderette within 300yds]   ⊖   TV
⊕3pin square   🔲   ♿

⊸ ♿(2½m)   ♀(50yds)   ▣(50yds)
♫(½m)
Min£60 Max£125pw

Ch   Mr M H Knight **Glenavon Park
(Bungalows)** Combe Martin, Devon
EX34 0AS
☎Combe Martin(027 188)2563

*Comfortable bungalows, built of wood
and stone in wooded and secluded
grounds near sea and beach.
Accommodation comprises
kitchenette/living room with double
studio couch, bathroom/WC and two
bedrooms (one double and one twin).*

15Mar-Nov   MWB out of season
1wk min, 18units, 1–6persons   [◇ ◆
◆]   no pets(in summer)   ◎   fridge
Electric   Elec inclusive   ⬛inclusive
☎(100yds)   Iron on premises   Ironing
board on premises   HCE in unit
[Launderette on premises]   ⊖   CTV
⊕3pin square   P   🔲   ♿   ⌂
⊸ ▣(1m)

F   Flat No 1 (Coach House)
for bookings Mr M H Knight, Glenavon
Park, Combe Martin, Devon EX34 0AS
☎Combe Martin(027 188)2563

*Once the senior groom's flat, this
attractive first-floor accommodation
comprises kitchen, bathroom, well
appointed lounge and three bedrooms.* →

71

Combe Martin

All year MWB out of season 1wk min,
1mth max, 1unit, 1–6 persons [◇] ◆
◆ no pets (in summer) ◉ fridge
Electric Elec inclusive ⬜inclusive
☎(100yds) Airing cupboard in unit Iron
in unit Ironing board in unit HCE in unit
[Launderette within 300yds] ⊕ CTV
⊕3pin square 2P ▥ ♨(300yds) ⌐
↬ ♒(3m) ⚲(½m) ▨(1m) ♫(1m)
Min£81 Max£207pw

F Mr M H Knight Glenavon Park (Flats)
Combe Martin, Devon EX34 0AS
☎Combe Martin (027 188)2563

Flats in a Victorian-style house situated in
wooded area with views of Combe Martin
Bay. Two flats have one bedroom with
studio couch in lounge; one has two
bedrooms, while the sleeping
accommodation of the other two is a
divan and a studio couch in the lounge.
All have bathroom and kitchen or
kitchenette.

All year MWB out of season 1wk min,
5units, 1–8 persons [◇ ◆ ◆]
no pets ◉ fridge ♨ Elec inclusive
⬜inclusive ☎ Iron on premises
Ironing board on premises HCE in unit
[Launderette on premises] ⊕ CTV
⊕3pin square P ▥ ♨ ⌐
↬ ⚲ ▨(1m)

C Gorwell Cottage Upper Rows Close
for bookings Mr M H Knight, Glenavon
Park, Combe Martin, Devon EX34 0AS
☎Combe Martin (027 188)2563

Attractive stone cottage in peaceful
position with views over Combe. Small TV
lounge and a part beamed lounge/diner,
kitchen, bathroom and sleeping up to
eight people.

All year MWB out of season 1wk min,
4wks max, 1unit, 1–8 persons [◇ ◆
◆] ◉ fridge Electric Elec inclusive
⬜inclusive ☎(300yds) WMin unit SD
in unit Airing cupboard in unit Iron in
unit Ironing board in unit HCE in unit
[Launderette within 300yds] ⊕ CTV
⊕3pin square 3P ▥ ♨(200yds)
↬ ♒(3m) ⚲(200yds) ▨(300yds)
♫(300yds)
Min£92 Max£225pw

H The Horizon
for bookings Mrs P J Norman, Waters
Edge, Newberry Road, Combe Martin,
Devon EX34 0AP
☎Combe Martin (027 188)3321

Semi-detached Victorian house in a 'no
through road' between beach and main
road, in a good position for shops. It
consists of kitchen, dining room,
bathroom/WC, lounge and four
bedrooms. Fine sea views from lounge
and two of the bedrooms.

Mar-Nov MWB 3days min, 6wks max,
1unit, 2–10 persons [◇ ◆ ◆] ⌐
fridge Electric Elec inclusive

Gas metered ⬜inclusive ☎(300yds)
Airing cupboard in unit Iron in unit
Ironing board in unit HCE in unit
[Launderette within 300yds] ⊕ TV
⊕3pin square P ▥ ♨(200yds)
↬ ⚲(300yds) ▨(300yds) ♫(1m)
Min£95 Max£225pw

F The Flat
for bookings Lion Inn, Victoria Street,
Combe Martin, Devon EX34 0LZ
☎Combe Martin (027 188)2485

First-floor flat located within a public
house comprising three bedrooms,
lounge/diner with a double put-u-up,
kitchen area and shower room with WC.

Feb-Nov MWB out of season
4days min, 1mth max, 1unit,
1–8 persons [◇] ◆ ◆ no pets ◉
fridge Electric Elec metered
⬜not provided ☎(5yds) Iron on
premises Ironing board on premises
HCE in unit ⊕ TV ⊕3pin square 2P
▥ ♨(½m)
↬ ⚲ ▨(½m) ♫(½m)
Min£85 Max£145pw

C 1 Mimosa & 2, Roseus Cottages
for bookings Lion Inn, Victoria Street,
Combe Martin, Devon EX34 0LZ
☎Combe Martin (027 188)2485

A pair of semi-detached, pebble dashed
cottages converted from stables.
Mimosa comprises open-plan
lounge/diner and kitchen area divided
off, with open-plan stairway leading to

two bedrooms and shower room/WC.
Roseus has kitchen/diner on ground-floor with open-plan stairway leading to first-floor lounge with bed settee, two bedrooms and shower room/WC.

Feb-Nov MWB out of season
4 days min, 1 mth max, 2 units,
1–6 persons [◇] ◈ ◆ ◉ fridge
Electric Elec metered ▣ not provided
☎ Iron on premises Ironing board on premises HCE in unit ⊕ TV
⊕ 3 pin square 4P ▥ ♨(¼m)
↔ ☕ ▨(½m) ♫(½m)

Min£65 Max£125pw

C Lyncliff Cross Street
for bookings Mrs P J Norman, Waters Edge, Combe Martin, Ilfracombe, Devon EX34 0AP
☎ Combe Martin (027 188) 3321

Small, semi-detached cottage style property comprising lounge/diner, kitchen, two bedrooms and bathroom/WC.

Mar-Nov MWB out of season
3 days min, 1 mth max, 1 unit,
1–4 persons [◇] ◈ ◆ ◉ fridge
Electric Elec metered ▣ inclusive
☎(50yds) Airing cupboard in unit Iron in unit Ironing board in unit HCE in unit [Launderette within 300yds] ⊕ TV
⊕ 3 pin square 2P ▥ ♨(20yds)
↔ ☖(3m) ☕(50yds) ▨(50yds)
♫(½m)

Min£65 Max£140pw

Ch Moory Mead Sea Close
for bookings Mrs P J Norman, Waters Edge, Combe Martin, Devon EX34 0AP
☎ Combe Martin (027 188) 3321

This neat little detached chalet of older design, clad in wood, is tucked away behind shops, on the seaward side of the main road through village about 150yds from the beach. The furnishings are traditional and the accommodation comprises two bedrooms, lounge and shower unit with WC.

Mar-Nov MWB 3 days min, 6 wks max,
1 unit, 2–4 persons [◇] ◈ ◆ ◉
fridge Electric Elec metered
▣ inclusive ☎(20yds) Iron

Ironing board HCE [Launderette] ⊕
TV ⊕ 3 pin square P ▥ ♨(20yds)
↔ ☕(300yds) ▨(300yds) ♫(300yds)
Min£45 Max£100pw

H Sea Close
for bookings Mrs P J Norman, Waters Edge, Newberry Road, Combe Martin, Devon EX34 0AP
☎ Combe Martin (027 188) 3321

A detached Victorian house with fine views of coast, close to shops and beach. The accommodation consists of lounge, dining room, kitchen, four bedrooms, bathroom and WC. Traditionally furnished and well equipped.

Mar-Nov MWB 3 days min, 6 wks max,
1 unit, 2–10 persons [◇] ◈ ◆ ◢
fridge Electric Elec inclusive Gas metered ▣ inclusive ☎(300yds) Iron in unit Ironing board in unit HCE in unit [Launderette within 300yds] ⊕ CTV
⊕ 3 pin square P ▥ ♨(200yds)
↔ ☕(300yds) ▨(300yds) ♫(1m)

Min£85 Max£200pw

F Seaside Flat Borough Road
for bookings Mrs P J Norman, Waters Edge, Newberry Road, Combe Martin, Devon EX34 0AP
☎ Combe Martin (027 188) 3321

A first-floor flat over shops in main road through village. About 60yds from the sea with good views of the beach and cliffs from the lounge. The accommodation, which has fitted carpets throughout, comprises two bedrooms with washbasins, lounge/dining room with foldaway bed, kitchen, shower unit and WC.

Mar-Nov MWB 3 days min, 6 wks max,
1 unit, 2–7 persons [◇] ◈ ◆ ◉
fridge Electric Elec metered
▣ inclusive ☎(100yds) Iron
Ironing board HCE [Launderette within 300yds] ⊕ TV ⊕ 3 pin square ▥
♨(20yds)
↔ ☕(300yds) ♫(300yds)
Min£50 Max£140pw

F Sundora Flats 1, 2 & 3 Cross Street
for bookings Mrs P J Norman, Waters Edge, Newberry Road, Combe Martin, Devon EX34 0AP
☎ Combe Martin (027 188) 3321

One ground and two first-floor flats, all comprise kitchen, lounge/dining room, bathroom and WC. Ground-floor has three bedrooms and sleeps up to seven, the others have two bedrooms. 100yds from the sea.

Mar-Nov MWB out of season
3 days min, 1 mth max, 3 units,
1–7 persons [◇] ◈ ◆] no pets in first floor flats ◉ fridge Electric
Elec metered ▣ inclusive ☎(50yds)
Airing cupboard in unit Iron in unit
Ironing board in unit [Launderette within 300yds] ⊕ CTV
⊕ 3 pin square 4P ♨(30yds)
↔ ☖(3m) ☕(50yds) ▨(50yds)
♫(½m)

Min£60 Max£130pw (Low)
Min£100 Max£180pw (High)

F Sunray Holiday Flats Moory Meadow, Seaside
for bookings Mrs K R Wood, Moory Lodge, Moory Meadow, Combe Martin, Devon EX34 0DG
☎ Combe Martin (027 188) 2325

Eight flats in detached brick-built property situated in village centre, 150yds from beach and close to shops and facilities. Well-maintained units of varying sizes, some with sea views.

All year MWB out of season 2 days min,
8 units, 2–8 persons [◇] ◈ ◆] ◉
fridge Electric Elec metered ▣ can be hired ☎(30yds) Iron in unit Ironing board in unit HCE in unit [Launderette within 300yds] ⊕ TV ⊕ 3 pin square P ▥ ♨(20yds)
↔ ☕(25yds) ▨(50yds) ♫(1m)

Min£45 Max£72pw (Low)
Min£65 Max£122pw (High)

COMBE ST NICHOLAS
Somerset
Map **3** ST31

B CC Ref 816 EL
for bookings Character Cottages
(Holidays) Ltd, 34 Fore Street, Sidmouth,
Devon EX10 8AQ
☎Sidmouth(03955)77001

*A modern bungalow, consisting of large
kitchen, two double bedrooms, one
single bedroom, separate WC and
bathroom. Front patio with garden
furniture. Situated in quiet area off village
green.*

All year MWB out of season 1wk min,
8mths (4wks summer)max, 1unit,
1–5persons ◆ no pets ◎ fridge
♨ Electric Elec inclusive ⬜can be
hired ☎(40yds) WM in unit SD in unit
Airing cupboard in unit Iron in unit
Ironing board in unit HCE in unit CTV
⊕3pin square P 🏛 ♨(100yds)
↝ ☍(300yds) ☷(3m) ♫(3m)
Min£71 Max£100pw (Low)
Min£119 Max£148pw (High)

CONICAVEL
Grampian *Moray*
Map **14** NH95

C Ryecot Darnaway Estate
for bookings Moray Estates Development
Co, Estates Office, Forres, Moray
IV36 0ET
☎Forres(0309)72213

*A comfortable compact cottage behind
the Post Office and General Store in a
small hamlet. Accommodation is all on
the ground floor and consists of a double
bedroom, living/room, kitchen and
bathroom. Ideal for two people.*

Apr–Oct MWB out of season 1wk min,
1unit, 1–2persons ◆ no pets ◎
fridge Electric Elec inclusive ⬜can
be hired ☎(10yds) Iron in unit Ironing
board in unit HCE in unit ⊙ TV
⊕3pin square P 🏛 ♨(10yds) Burn
fishing
Min£74.75 Max£86.25pw (Low)
Min£97.75pw (High)

CONISTON
Cumbria
Map **7** SD39

F East Wing Apartment
for bookings R & K Smith, Low Bank
Ground, Coniston, Cumbria LA21 8AA
☎Coniston(09664)314

*A maisonette containing two twin-
bedded rooms, one double and one with
bunks. Located east of Coniston Water
with views across to surrounding hills.
Furnished, decorated and equipped to a
high standard.*

All year MWB 1wk min, 1mth max,
1unit, 8persons ◆ ◎ fridge ♨
Elec metered ⬜not provided ☎(1½m)
Airing cupboard in unit Iron in unit
Ironing board in unit HCE in unit ⊙
⊕3pin square P 🏛 ♨(1½m)

↝ ☍(1½m) ☷(1½m)
Min£130 Max£160pw

F Highfield Flats
for bookings R & K Smith, Low Bank
Ground, Coniston, Cumbria LA21 8AA
☎Coniston(09664)314

*Four flats, each with one double-bedded
room and one twin-bedded room, on the
ground and first floors of a house
standing in 30 acres of grounds and
gardens, which stretch to the shore of
Coniston Water. Each flat has views
across the lake to Coniston village and
the hills beyond. Warm, comfortable,
well-equipped and well-furnished
accommodation. Licensed dining-room.*

All year MWB 1wk min, 1mth max,
4units, 4persons ◆ ◎ fridge ♨
Elec metered ⬜not provided ☎(1½m)
Airing cupboard in unit Iron in unit
Ironing board in unit HCE in unit ⊙
⊕3pin square P 🏛 ♨(1½m)
↝ ☍(1½m) ☷(1½m)
Min£65 Max£80pw

CONNEL
Strathclyde *Argyll*
Map **10** NM93

C Cruachan & Linnhe View Cottages
South Ledaig
for bookings Mr A McIntyre, Eilean Beag,
South Ledaig, Connel, Argyll
☎Connel(063 171)597

*Renovated farm building now two semi-
detached cottages each with kitchen,
sitting room, one double, one twin
bedroom and bathroom. Shared large
garden, Cruachen has a terrace. Two
miles from Connel on main A828 to Fort
William.*

Apr–Oct MWB out of season 1wk min,
4wks max, 2units, 1–4persons ◆ ◆
no pets ◎ fridge Electric
Elec metered ⬜can be hired ☎(1m)
Iron in unit Ironing board in unit HCE in
unit ⊙ CTV ⊕3pin square 20P
♨(2m) Rough shooting, pony trekking &
gliding
↝ ☍(1m)
Max£50pw (Low)
Max£125pw (High)

C Diarmid Cottage Tigh-na-Mara
for bookings Alexander Dawson, Estate
Agents, 120 George Street, Oban, Argyll
PA34 5NT
☎Oban(0631)63901/62056

*Single-storey cottage with its own lawn
sloping down to the sea. Accommodation
consists of a fitted kitchen, front facing
dining room with access to lawn, back
lounge with fireplace, and three
bedrooms sleeping up to six people.
Heating is included in the rental.*

All year MWB out of season 1wk min,
3mths max, 1unit, 1–6persons no pets
◎ fridge Electric Elec metered
⬜not provided ☎(½m) Airing cupboard

---

in unit Iron in unit HCE in unit CTV
⊕3pin square P ♨(½m)
↝ ☍(2½m) ☍(2½m) ☷(2½m)
♫(2½m) ☎(2½m)
Min£62 Max£92pw (Low)
Min£150 Max£211pw (High)

B Fairfield Connel North
for bookings Alexander Dawson, Estate
Agents, 120 George Street, Oban, Argyll
PA34 5NT
☎Oban(0631)63901/62056

*Modern two-floor bungalow overlooking
Loch Etive and Ben Cruachan. Access off
A85, over Connel Bridge, right on road to
Bonawe–2m. It comprises large
lounge/diner, kitchen, and four
bedrooms each sleeping two people.
Heating is included in rental.*

All year MWB out of season 1wk min,
3mths max, 1unit, 1–8persons no pets
◎ fridge Elec metered
⬜not provided ☎ Airing cupboard in
unit Iron in unit Ironing board in unit
HCE in unit ⊙ CTV ⊕3pin square P
♨(2½m)
↝ ☍(1m) ☷(2½m)
Min£62 Max£122pw (Low)
Min£150 Max£234pw (High)

H Fingal House Tigh-na-Mara
for bookings Alexander Dawson, Estate
Agents, 120 George Street, Oban, Argyll
PA34 5NT
☎Oban(0631)63901/62056

*Elegant house forming the main part of
Tigh-na-Mara House. A lounge, kitchen,
dining room, double-bedded room with
dressing room, double room, single
room, and two bathrooms with WC forms
the accommodation. Heating included in
rental.*

All year MWB out of season 1wk min,
3mths max, 1unit, 1–7persons, nc15
no pets ◎ fridge Elec metered
⬜not provided ☎ Airing cupboard in
unit Iron in unit Ironing board in unit
HCE in unit ⊙ CTV ⊕3pin square P
♨(½m)
↝ ☍(2½m) ☷(2½m) ♫(2½m) ☎(2½m)
Min£95 Max£125pw (Low)
Min£188 Max£235pw (High)

C Somerled Cottage Tigh-na-Mara
for bookings Alexander Dawson, Estate
Agents, 120 George Street, Oban, Argyll
PA34 5NT
☎Oban(0631)63901/62056

*A cottage on two floors being the central
section of Tigh-na-Mara House. The
ground floor comprises an entrance hall,
central dining room, lounge, modern
kitchen, bathroom/WC, separate WC and
a large double bedroom with a dressing
room. Upstairs has a further two
bedrooms. Heating included in rental.*

All year MWB out of season 1wk min,
3mths max, 1unit, 1–6persons no pets
◎ fridge Elec metered
⬜not provided ☎(½m) Airing cupboard
in unit Iron in unit Ironing board in unit
HCE in unit ⊙ CTV ⊕3pin square P
🏛 ♨(½m)

⊖ ♿(2½m) ☎(2½m) ▨(2½m)
♫(2½m) 🛏(2½m)

Min£69 Max£99pw (Low)
Min£166 Max£218pw (High)

CONTIN
Highland *Ross & Cromarty*
Map **14** NH45

Ch Craigdarroch Chalets
for bookings R E Hendry, Craigdarroch
Drive, Contin, Strathpeffer, Ross-shire
☎Strathpeffer(09972)584

*Ten attractive detached chalets
containing two bedrooms, bathroom and
lounge/kitchen with convertible settee.
The chalets are grouped together at the
end of a driveway that runs from A832,
1m NW of Contin.*

Apr–Oct 4 days min, 10 units,
1–6 persons ◎ fridge 🍳
Elec metered 🔌inclusive ☎(100yds)
Airing cupboard in unit Iron in unit
Ironing board in unit HCE in unit ⊖
CTV ⊕3 pin square P 🚿(1m) Horse
riding & fishing

⊖ ♿(3m) ♀(100yds) ▨(3m)

Min£96.60 Max£128.50pw (Low)
Min£154.10 Max£181.70pw (High)

COPMANTHORPE
North Yorkshire
Map **8** SE54

C Mr J Hughes Holiday Cottages
Copmanthorpe Grange, Copmanthorpe,
York YO23TN
☎Appleton Roebuck(090484)318

*Restored and converted farm building,
previously a specialist stud-farm set in
attractive rural surrounds of open farm
land, 4m S of York. These twelve units
sleep from 1–6 people with either
bathroom/WC or shower room/WC and
combined lounge/dining room and
kitchen.*

All year MWB 3 days min, 6 mths max,
12 units, 1–6 persons [◇] ◆ ● ◎
fridge Electric Elec inclusive
🔌inclusive ☎(1m) Iron on premises
Ironing board in unit HCE in unit ⊖
CTV ⊕3 pin square 20P ▥ 🚿(1m)
Games room, restaurant & bar

⊖ ♿ ♀

Min£38 Max£168pw

COPPLESTONE
Devon
Map **3** SS70

H Mr Saunders Ash Bullayne
Copplestone, Crediton, Devon
☎Copplestone(03634)215

*Part of large farmhouse with separate
front door to hallway,
kitchen/diner/lounge. Two large
bedrooms and bathroom/WC on first
floor.*

All year 1 wk min, 3 wks max, 1 unit,
2–7 persons ◆ ● ◎ fridge
Electric Elec inclusive 🔌not provided
☎(2m) Iron in unit Ironing board in
unit HCE in unit ⊖ TV

⊕3 pin square 10P ▥ 🚿(1½m)

⊖ ♀(3m)

CORNHILL
Grampian *Banffshire*
Map **15** 55

C Bogroy Croft
for bookings J & J Palphramand,
Knockdurn Croft, Portsay, Banffshire
☎Portsoy(02614)3821

*A most attractively modernised cottage
with bright and roomy kitchen/dining
room, sitting room with open fire and two
bedrooms. 4m S of Portsoy.*

All year MWB out of season 1 wk min,
1 unit, 1–4 persons ◎ fridge Electric &
open fires Elec metered 🔌can be
hired ☎(1½m) Airing cupboard in
premises HCE on premises ⊖ TV
⊕3 pin square 4P 🚿(1½m)

⊖ ♀(1½m)

Min£58 Max£135pw

CORNWOOD
Devon
Map **2** SX65

C CC Ref 4023
for bookings Character Cottages
(Holidays) Ltd, 34 Fore Street, Sidmouth,
Devon EX10 8AQ
☎Sidmouth(03955)77001

*Originally a barn, now converted to a high
standard and comprising lounge,
kitchen/diner, bathroom and three
bedrooms. Decorated to a high standard.*

All year MWB out of season 3 days min,
1 unit, 1–6 persons ◇ ◆ ◎ fridge
Electric Elec metered 🔌not provided
☎(½m) Airing cupboard in unit Iron in
unit Ironing board in unit HCE in unit
⊖ TV ⊕3 pin square P ▥ 🚿(1m)

⊖ ♀(1m)

Min£73 Max£98 pw (Low)
Min£117 Max£149pw (High)

CORPACH
Highland *Inverness-shire*
Map **14** NN07

C Victoria Cottage
for bookings Mr & Mrs Sutton, Tigh-na-
Ha, Corpach, Fort William, Inverness-
shire
☎Corpach(03977)376

*Traditional Highland cottage in village
centre with views of Ben Nevis and Loch
Linnhe. Lounge, dining room, two
bedrooms (one double, one bunk-
bedded; in lounge additional double
lounge settee and put-u-up), kitchen and
bathroom. Take A830 Mallaig road from
A82 2m N of Fort William.*

Etr–Sep 1 wk min, 1 mth max, 1 unit,
2–8 persons ◎ fridge Electric
Elec inclusive 🔌inclusive ☎(100yds)
WM in unit SD in unit Iron in unit
Ironing board in unit HCE in unit TV
⊕3 pin square 3P 🚿

⊖ ♿(3m) ♀(100yds) ▨(3m) ♫(3m)

Min£95 Max£170pw

CORSOCK
Dumfries & Galloway *Kirkcudbrightshire*
Map **11** NX77

C Mr N Gray Caldow Lodge Holiday
Cottages Caldow House, Corsock,
Castle Douglas, Kirkcudbrightshire
DG7 3EB
☎Corsock(06444)286

*A row of renovated farm cottages set
amidst Galloway Hills. Each unit
comprises of kitchen/dining room/living
area, with bed-settee, bath or shower,
and either one or two bedrooms. Off
A712, 3m W of Corsock.*

All year MWB out of season 1 wk min,
1 mth max, 6 units, 1–6 persons [◆ ◆]
◎ fridge 🍳 Elec metered 🔌can be
hired ☎(3m) SD in unit Airing
cupboard in unit Iron in unit Ironing
board in unit HCE in unit ⊖ TV
⊕3 pin square 10P 🚿(3m) Pony
trekking & fishing

⊖ ♀(3m)

Min£30 Max£86pw

CORWEN
Clwyd
Map **6** 04

H Waen-Yr-Hŷdd Faerdref, Cynwyd
for bookings C J E B Day, 7 Cotham
Road, Cotham, Bristol, Avon BS6 6DG
☎Bristol(0272)741107

*Traditional Welsh stone barn recently
modernised and converted; plus a 17th-
C stone farmhouse fully modernised yet
retaining old world charm. Situated in
tranquil setting and quite isolated.*

All year MWB out of season 1 wk min,
6 wks max, 2 units, 1–6 persons [◇] ◆
◆ no pets ◎ fridge Electric Elec
inclusive in farmhouse Elec metered in
Barn 🔌can be hired ☎(1m) Airing
cupboard in unit Iron in unit Ironing
board in unit HCE in unit ⊖ TV
⊕3 pin square 3P 🚿(2m)

⊖ ♀(2m)

Min£65 (Low)
Max£105pw (High)

COSHESTON
Dyfed
Map **2** SM90

H West Farm
for bookings Powells Holidays, High
Street, Saundersfoot, Dyfed
☎Saundersfoot(0834)812791

*Large modern detached house set in
quiet lane with good views over estuary.
Comprises lounge, dining room, large
kitchen, one double bedroom, one with
double and a single bed and one single
bedroom, bathroom/WC and
shower/WC.* →

1982 prices quoted throughout
gazetteer

May–Sep 1wk min, 1unit, 1–6persons
◊ no pets ◉ fridge ⚏
Elec inclusive ⊡ not provided ☎(2m)
Airing cupboard in unit Iron in unit
Ironing board in unit HCE in unit ⊙
CTV ⊕3pin square 2P ⊞ ♨(1m)
⊖ ☗(1m)
Min£75 Max£218pw

COULMORE
Highland *Inverness-shire*
Map**14** NH64

C **Coulmore House Cottage**
for bookings Highland Coastal Estates,
Estate Office, Coulmore, Kessock,
Inverness IV11XB
☎Kessock(046373)212
*A semi-detached cottage containing
sitting room, kitchenette/dining room,
double bedroom and two twin-bedded
rooms. Access is via the estate road off
the shore road from North Kessock.*
end May–Sep 1wk min, 1unit,
1–6persons [◊] ◉ fridge Electric
Elec metered ⊡can be hired ☎(3m)
Airing cupboard in unit HCE in unit TV
⊕3pin round P ♨(3m) Boating &
canoeing
⊖ ☗(3m)
Min£51.17 Max£91.35pw

C **Ploverfield Cottage**
for bookings Highland Coastal Estates,
Estate Office, Coulmore, Kessock,
Inverness IV11XB

Cosheston — Coventry

☎Kessock(046373)212
*A stone-built cottage having living room
with convertible settee, kitchen, double
room, and a room with three single beds.
Access is via an unclass road off B9161
4m from North Kessock.*
end May–Sep 1wk min, 1unit,
1–6persons [◊] ◉ fridge Electric
Elec metered ⊡can be hired ☎(4m)
Airing cupboard in unit HCE in unit TV
⊕3pin round P ♨(4m) Boating &
canoeing
Min£51.17 Max£108.67pw

C **Ross & Wood Cottages**
for bookings Highland Coastal Estates,
Estate Office, Coulmore, Kessock,
Inverness IV11XB
☎Kessock(046373)212
*Two adjoining stone-built cottages
containing kitchenette, living/dining
room, sun lounge, one double bedroom
and one twin-bedded room. There is also
a convertible settee. Access is by the
estate road of the North Kessock road.*
end May–Sep 1wk min, 2units,
1–6persons [◊] ◉ fridge Electric
Elec metered ⊡can be hired ☎(3m)
Airing cupboard in unit HCE in unit TV
⊕3pin round P ♨(3m) Boating &
canoeing
⊖ ☗(3m)
Min£51.17 Max£91.35pw

COVENTRY
West Midlands
Map**4** SP37

Hurst & Redfern Flats
for bookings Vacation Flats
Administrator, Vacation Flats Office,
Rootes Hall, University of Warwick,
Gibbet Hill Road, Coventry, West
Midlands.
☎Coventry(0203)24011 ext2507
*Modern blocks of flats set in extensive
landscaped grounds on the University
campus. Each comprises kitchen/dining
area, bathroom, WC and five or six single
bedrooms all with wash hand basins.
Bedrooms can be converted into twin
rooms upon request. Ideal for sports
enthusiast.*
mid Jul–mid Sep MWB 2days min,
8wks max 50units 1–7persons [◊]
no pets ♂ fridge ⚏
Gas&Elec inclusive ⊡inclusive ☎
Iron HCE in unit [Launderette within
300yds] ⊕3pin square 70P ⊞
♨(300yds) ⊠ ⚲Hard&grass ♭
Sports centre, sauna & croquet
⊖ ♫ᴙ(3m) ☗ ⊡ ♫ ☗
Min£120.80 Max£157.02pw

1982 prices quoted throughout
gazetteer

COWFOLD
West Sussex
Map**4** TQ22

C ***Laneswood Cottage*** 7 Church Path *for bookings* R A H Clarke, Corner Park House, Church Road, Snitterfield, Warwicks CV37 0LE
☎Stratford-upon-Avon(0789)730212

Small terraced cottage set within St Peter's Church grounds. Well-modernised, the accommodation consists of lounge/dining room, modern kitchen on ground-floor; master bedroom and good-sized modern bathroom on first-floor; two single bedrooms on top-floor. Steep stairs to top-floor rooms make them unsuitable for elderly people or young children. Situated in small Sussex village, 6m from Horsham and 17m from Brighton.

All year 1wk min, 25wks max, 1unit, 2–5persons, nc5 no pets ◎ fridge Electric Elec metered except heating ▣inclusive ☎ WM in unit Airing cupboard in unit Iron in unit Ironing board in unit HCE in unit ⊕3pin square ⊕3pin round ▥ ♨(50yds)

⊖ ♀(15yds)

C ***Westcoe Cottage*** 6 Church Path *for bookings* R A H Clarke, Corner Park House, Church Road, Snitterfield, Warwicks CV37 0LE
☎Stratford-upon-Avon(0789)730212

A small, comfortably furnished two-storey, terraced cottage overlooking church in centre of village. Comprises lounge/diner, nicely furnished modernised kitchen, one twin-bedded room and a bathroom/WC.

All year 1wk min, 25wks max, 1unit, 1–2persons, nc5 ◎ fridge ⅏ Elec metered except heating ▣not provided ☎ Iron in unit Ironing board in unit HCE in unit ⊕3pin round ▥ ♨(50yds)

⊖ ♂18(3m) ♀(15yds)

CRACKINGTON HAVEN
Cornwall
Map**2** SX19

B **CC Ref 331 P**
for bookings Character Cottages (Holidays) Ltd, 34 Fore Street, Sidmouth, Devon EX10 8AQ
☎Sidmouth(03955)77001

Semi-detached bungalow with integral garage situated in corner of cul-de-sac. Accommodation comprises small hall, cloakroom/WC, living room, modern kitchen/diner, two bedrooms (one with double bed, one with twin beds), modern bathroom and WC. Good position, just over 1m from beach.

All year MWB out of season 1wk min, 1mth max, 1unit, 2–4persons ◆ ◎ fridge Electric Elec metered ▣not provided ☎(½m) Airing cupboard in unit Iron in unit Ironing board in unit HCE in unit ⊙ TV ⊕3pin square ⊕2pin round P ⌂ ♨(1½m)

⊖ ♀(1½m)

Min£39 Max£104pw (Low)
Min£129 Max£155pw (High)

C **East & West Emetts**
for bookings Mr & Mrs A Cummins, Mineshop, St Gennys, Bude, Cornwall EX23 0NR
☎St Gennys(08403)338

A pair of cottages (one of them thatched, the other slated), about a mile from the Haven. Accommodation comprises open-plan living room and kitchenette; upstairs one double and one single in same bedroom and twin-bedded room, bathroom and WC. One of the cottages has a pair of bunk beds instead of the twin beds, one double bedroom and studio couch in lounge. Leave A39 at Wainhouse Corner, follow signs to Crackington Haven; at the post office the cottages can be seen on the right.

All year MWB out of season 1wk min, 1mth max, 2units, 2–6persons ◆ ◎ fridge Electric Elec metered ▣not provided ☎(300yds) Airing cupboard in unit Iron in unit Ironing board in unit HCE in unit TV ⊕3pin square P ▥ ♨

⊖ ♀(1½m)

Min£46 Max£64.40pw (Low)
Min£90.85 Max£135.70pw (High)

CRANTOCK
Cornwall
Map**2** SW76

B **Halwyn Farm Bungalow** West Pentire
for bookings J A & P A Eastlake, Treago Farm, Crantock, Newquay, Cornwall
☎Crantock(0637)830277

Detached bungalow comprising double bedroom, twin-bedded room, single-bedded room, lounge, conservatory, breakfast room, kitchen, separate bathroom and WC. Large south-facing garden at back, front lawn overlooks beach, 2½m off A3075 Newquay–Redruth road at West Pentire.

All year MWB 1wk min, 3mths max, 1unit, 1–5persons ◆ ◎ fridge Electric Elec inclusive ▣not provided ☎(½m) Airing cupboard in unit Iron in unit Ironing board in unit HCE in unit ⊙ TV ⊕3pin square P ▥ ♨(½m)

⊖ ♂18(2m) ♀(2m) ▣(2m) ♫(2m) 🎥(2m)

Min£92 Max£126.50pw (Low)
Max£178.25pw (High)

C **Halwyn Farm Cottage** West Pentire
for bookings J A & P A Eastlake, Treago Farm, Crantock, Newquay, Cornwall
☎Crantock(0637)830277

Semi-detached stone cottage overlooking Crantock Beach. Comprising large family bedroom, lounge, dining room, kitchen and separate bathroom/WC. All rooms have sea views, 2½m off A3075 Newquay–Redruth road at West Pentire.

All year MWB 1wk min, 3mths max, 1unit, 1–5persons ◆ ◎ fridge Electric Elec inclusive ▣not provided ☎(½m) Airing cupbaord in unit Iron in unit Ironing board in unit HCE in unit ⊙ TV ⊕3pin square P ▥ ♨(½m)

⊖ ♂18(2m) ♀(2m) ▣(2m) ♫(2m) 🎥(2m)

Min£92 Max£126.50pw (Low)
Max£178.25pw (High)

C **Malt House**
for bookings J A & P A Eastlake, Treago Farm, Crantock, Newquay, Cornwall
☎Crantock(0637)830277

Malt House is a modern purpose-built holiday cottage on the site of an old malthouse and backs onto the farm courtyard. Accommodation comprises lounge, open-plan kitchen with breakfast bar, dining area, three bedrooms (two double-bedded rooms and one twin-bedded room), bathroom and separate WC.

All year MWB 1wk min, 3mths max, 1unit, 6persons ◆ ◆ no dogs ◎ fridge Electric Elec metered ▣not provided ☎(100yds) Airing cupboard in unit Iron in unit Ironing board in unit HCE in unit ⊙ TV ⊕3pin square 1P ▥ ♨(200yds)

⊖ ♂18(3m) ♀(2m) ▣(2m) ♫(2m) 🎥(2m)

Min£92 Max£126.50pw (Low)
Max£178.25pw (High)

C **Scantlebury Cottage** West Pentire
for bookings J A & P A Eastlake, Treago Farm, Crantock, Newquay, Cornwall
☎Crantock(0637)830277

Terraced stone-built cottage adjoining farmhouse; specially converted and comprising two double bedrooms, bedroom with two bunk beds. Large lounge/diner, kitchen. Separate bathroom and WC. Modern furnishings and fittings. 2½m off A3075 Newquay–Redruth road at West Pentire.

All year MWB 1wk min, 3mths max, 1unit, 1–6persons ◆ ◎ fridge Electric Elec inclusive ▣not provided ☎(½m) Airing cupboard in unit Iron in unit Ironing board in unit HCE in unit ⊙ TV ⊕3pin square P ▥ ♨(½m)

⊖ ♂18(2m) ♀(2m) ▣(2m) ♫(2m) 🎥(2m)

Min£92 Max£126.50pw (Low)
Max£178.25pw (High)

C **Treago Cottage**
for bookings J A & P A Eastlake, Treago Farm, Crantock, Newquay, Cornwall
☎Crantock(0637)830277

Stone-built, beamed ceiling. Accommodation comprises one double bedroom, one twin-bedded room, landing bedroom, lounge/diner. Separate kitchen, bathroom and WC. SW of Crantock village centre. →

All year MWB 1wk min, 3mths max, 1unit, 1–5persons ◆ ● fridge Electric Elec inclusive ☐not provided ☎(½m) Airing cupboard in unit Iron in unit Ironing board in unit HCE in unit ⊖ TV ③3pin square P 📺 in unit ☎(½m)

↩ ☄(2m) ♀(2m) 🗔(2m) ♫(2m) 🐕(2m)

Min£75.90 Max£103.50pw (Low) Max£140.30pw (High)

C Trevalsa Cottage West Pentire
for bookings J A & P A Eastlake, Treago Farm, Crantock, Newquay, Cornwall ☎Crantock(0637)830277

Semi-detached stone-built cottage, especially converted and comprising a twin-bedded room and two double bedrooms, lounge, kitchen/diner. Separate bathroom and WC. Modern furnishings and fittings. 2¼m off A3075 Newquay–Redruth road at West Pentire.

All year MWB 1wk min, 3mths max, 1unit, 1–6persons ◆ ● fridge Electric Elec inclusive ☐not provided ☎(½m) Airing cupboard in unit Iron in unit Ironing board in unit HCE in unit ⊖ TV ③3pin square P 📺 ☎(½m)

↩ ☄(2m) ♀(2m) 🗔(2m) 🐕(2m)

Min£92 Max£126.50pw (Low) Max£178.25pw (High)

CRESSELLY
Dyfed
Map**2** SN00

H Newton Grange
for bookings Powell's Holidays, High Street, Saundersfoot, Dyfed ☎Saundersfoot(0834)812791
Modern detached house. Accommodation consists of lounge, dining/sitting room, kitchen; on the first floor there are three double-bedded rooms, one double-bedded family room with twin beds. Separate bathroom/WC.

May–Oct 1wk min, 4wks max, 1unit, 2–12persons [◇] ◆ ● fridge Electric Elec inclusive ☐not provided ☎(100yds) Airing cupboard in unit Iron in unit Ironing board in unit HCE in unit ⊖ CTV ③3pin square P 📺 ☄(½m)

↩ ♀(½m)

Min£63 Max£168pw

CRESSING
Essex
Map**5** TL72

C 1 & 2 Red Lion Cottages Lanham Green Road
for bookings Mrs M Ratcliffe, Ashes Farm, Cressing, Braintree, Essex CM7 8DW ☎Silver End(0376)83236

Two small country cottages with exposed beams, each with lounge/dining room, two bedrooms, bathroom and kitchen. There are good views of surrounding open countryside and the cottages, which have been converted from an old country pub, are only 2m from the Essex Market town of Braintree.

All year MWB out of season 2units, 2–5persons, nc7 no pets ● fridge Electric Elec inclusive ☐can be hired ☎ Airing cupboard in unit Iron in unit Ironing board in unit HCE in unit ⊖ TV can be hired ③3pin square P 📺 ☄(3m) Bicycle hire

↩ ♀(½m) 🗔(3m) ♫(3m) 🐕(3m)

Min£50 Max£65pw

CRICCIETH
Gwynedd
Map**6** SH43

B Bro Eifion
for bookings Mr & Mrs G Lloyd Jones, Bro Dewi, Ynys, Criccieth, Gwynedd, LL52 0NT ☎Garn Dolbenmaen(076675)334

18th-century store recently converted to a single storey dwelling of high standard throughout. Accommodation comprises of lounge, kitchen/diner, two double and one twin-bedded room. Take B4411 from Criccieth.

All year MWB out of season 1wk min, 6wks max, 1unit, 1–6persons ◇ ◆ ◆ ● fridge Electric Elec metered ☐not provided ☎(2m) [Airing cupboard in unit] Iron on premises Ironing board on premises HCE in unit ⊖ CTV ③3pin square 3P 📺 ☄(3m) Rough shooting

↩ ♀(2m)

Min£45 Max£65pw (Low) Min£85 Max£110pw (High)

F Mr A Murray Clifton House 27 Marine Terrace, Criccieth, Gwynedd LL52 0EL ☎Criccieth(076671)2220

Located on the seafront 400yds from village centre. Two flats (2 & 3) are on different levels comprising two bedrooms, one with double and single beds, one with twin beds, lounge/dining room, kitchen, bathroom/WC. Both flats have a bed-settee in the lounge/dining room. In addition there is a third-floor flat consisting of lounge with double bed-settee, well equipped kitchen, bedroom with double and single bed and bathroom/WC.

Apr–Oct MWB out of season 1wk min, 1mth max, 3units, 3–6persons ◆ ◆ no pets ● fridge Electric Elec metered ☐inclusive ☎(100yds) HCE in unit [Launderette within 300yds] ⊖ TV ③3pin square 📺 ☄(100yds)

↩ ♀(½m) 🗔(½m)

Min£49 Max£120pw

F Ty Clyd Pwhelli Road
for bookings Mrs Stanton, Abereistedd, West Parade, Criccieth, Gwynedd ☎Criccieth(076671)2710

Large Victorian house divided into three spacious flats each having hallway,

lounge, one double bedroom plus bunk beds and one bedroom with twin beds, kitchen, bathroom and WC. On edge of Criccieth off the A497 Pwllheli road.

All year MWB out of season 1day min, 6wks max, 3units, 2–6persons [◇] ◆ ◆ no pets ● fridge Electric Elec inclusive ☐inclusive ☎(150yds) SD in unit Iron in unit Ironing board in unit HCE in unit [Launderette within 300yds] ⊖ CTV ③3pin square 6P 📺 ☄(400yds)

↩ ☄(½m) ♀(½m)

Min£50 Max£90pw (Low) £150pw (High)

F Mrs Broadley Vista Marina 30 Marine Terrace, Criccieth, Gwynedd ☎Criccieth(076671)2139

Very well run and clean flats in a town house which faces S over the beach and Cardigan Bay. To the W is a green and another sea view. Within walking distance of twon centre. Flat 1B has a shower instead of a bath.

All year MWB out of season 4units, 3–8persons ◆ ● fridge Electric Elec metered ☐can be hired ☎(200yds) SD in unit Airing cupboard in unit Iron in unit Ironing board in unit HCE in unit TV ③3pin square P 📺 ☄(½m)

♀(300yds)

Min£48 Max£77pw (Low) Min£72 Max£125pw (High)

F Mrs Y E Davies Windsor Flats 12 Marine Terrace, Criccieth, Gwynedd ☎Criccieth(076671)2856

1st, 2nd and 3rd floor flats in single fronted Victorian mid-terraced house on sea front. Bright and airy kitchen/diner, seafront lounge with bed settee and french bed, double bedroom with wash basin. 1st and 3rd floor flats have bathroom/WC while the 2nd floor has shower/WC. Neatly furnished and decorated throughout. Direct access to beach.

Apr–Oct MWB out of season 3days min, 6wks max, 3units, 1–4persons ◆ ● fridge Electric Elec metered ☐can be hired ☎ Airing cupboard in unit Iron on premises Ironing board on premises HCE in unit ⊖ TV ③3pin square 🔔 📺 ☄(25yds)

↩ ♿(½m) ♀(100yds)

Min£35 Max£50pw (Low) Min£60 Max£85pw (High)

C Yr Hen Feudy Muriau
for bookings Mrs E A Williams-Ellis, 65 Warwick Square, London SW1 ☎01–834 5634

Modernised 18th-century cottage in its own grounds. Accommodation comprises of living/dining room, kitchen, two double-bedded rooms, two single-bedded rooms and bathroom/WC. ½m from town centre.

Etr–Oct 1wkmin, 1mthmax, 1unit,
6persons ◎ fridge Electric
Elecmetered ⬛notprovided ☎(½m)
Airing cupboard in unit Iron in unit
Ironing board in unit HCE in unit
[Launderette within 300yds] ☎
⊕3pinsquare P ⛽ ▥ ▲(½m)
↵Hard
⊖ ♒(2m) ☖(½m)

CRIEFF
Tayside *Perthshire*
Map11 NN82

H Craigeuan
for bookings Mrs J S Scott, Easter
Dowald, Crieff, Perthshire PH7 3QX
☎Crieff(0764)3285

*A large secluded farmhouse with
panoramic views situated 100yds off
A85, 2m E of Crieff. It comprises large
living room, one double bedroom, WC
and shower room/WC on ground floor,
with four bedrooms and bathroom on firs
floor.*

14Mar–14Nov MWB out of season
1wkmin, 1unit, 1–12persons ◈
nopets ◎ fridge Electric
Elecmetered ⬛can be hired
☎(100yds) Airing cupboard in unit Iron
in unit Ironing board in unit HCE in unit
⊖ TV ⊕3pinround 6P 1⛽ ▲(2m)
⊖ ♒(2m) ☖(100yds) ▣(2m)
Min£92 Max£149.50pw

Ch Mr A A Colquhoun **Loch
Monzievaird Chalets** Ochtertyre, Crieff,
Perthshire
☎Crieff(0764)2586

*Norwegian chalets spaciously grouped
in secluded mature parkland below
hillside and overlooking Loch
Monzievaird. Accommodation varies,
nine chalets having two bedrooms and
three having four. All have open-plan
lounge/diner, kitchenette and bathroom
plus one chalet with sauna. They are
completely pine panelled with matching
furnishings and are finished to a high
standard. 2m W of Crieff off A85. Three
ponies are available to Chalet occupants
with previous riding experience.*

All year MWB 1nightmin, 13units
1–8persons ◈ ◆ ◎ fridge
🍴 Elecinclusive ⬛inclusive ☎ Iron
in unit Ironing board in unit HCE in unit
[Launderette on premises] ⊕ CTV
⊕3pinsquare P ▥ ▲(2m) Trout
fishing and sailing instruction available
⊖ ♒(400yds) ▣(2m)
♫(2m) ▣(2m)
Min£65pw (Low)
Min£110pw (High)

1982 prices quoted throughout
gazetteer

CRINAN
Strathclyde *Argyll*
Map10 NR89

F Kilmahumaig Barns
for bookings Mr M Murray, Kilmahumaig,
Crinan, Lochgilphead, Argyll
☎Crinan(054683)238

*A recently converted barn containing
three flats situated ½m E of Crinan on
B841. Two of the flats have open-plan
kitchen/living area with two divans on the
ground-floor and a double-bedded
gallery bedroom upstairs. The larger unit
has separate living room, kitchen/dining
area downstairs and two gallery
bedrooms. All have a steep spiral
staircase.*

All year MWB out of season 3days min,
3mths max, 3units, 1–6persons ◈ ◆
nopets ◎ fridge Electric
Elecmetered ⬛notprovided ☎(½m)
Airing cupbaord in unit HCE in unit ⊖
⊕3pinsquare P ▲(½m)
⊖ ☖(½m)
Min£36 Max£75pw (Low)
Min£54 Max£120pw (High)

CROCKETFORD
Dumfries & Galloway *Dumfries-shire*
Map11 NX77

C **Stable & Byre Cottages**
for bookings A W & M M S McDonald, →

Brandedleys, Crocketford, Dumfries
DG28RG
☎Crocketford(055669)250

*Two semi-detached converted farm
cottages set in a yard by a farmhouse.
Access is from the A75, W of Crocketford.
Loch views. It comprises an open-plan
kitchen/dining room/lounge with bed-
settee (Byre cottage has a separate
kitchen and an additional twin-bedded
room), patio, shower room/WC and a
double room with extra folding bed.
Games room.*

All year MWB out of season 3 days min,
3 mths max, 2 units, 1–7 persons ◈ ◆
◉ fridge ♨ Elec metered
🅛not provided ☎(50yds) HCE in unit
[Launderette on premises] ⊕ CTV
⊕3 pin square 2P 🅿(50yds) ⌒
⤙Hard

⊖ ♀ 🅿(½m)

Min£55 Max£90pw (Low)
Min£95 Max£150pw (High)

CROSSGATES
Powys
Map6 SO06

Ch **Park Motel Chalets** Park Motel,
Crossgates, Llandrindod Wells, Powys
☎Penybont(059787)201

*Modern brick-built chalets; all have
kitchen/diner (with bed-settee if
required), twin-bedded room and
combined shower/WC. Daily maid
service available.*

All year MWB 1 night min, 7 units,
4 persons ◈ ◆ ♨ fridge ♨
Gas inclusive 🅛inclusive ☎(20yds)
HCE in unit ⊕ TV can be hired
⊕3 pin square P 🅿(400yds) ⌒
Licensed restaurant and bar.

⊖ 🅿(3m)

Min£58.60 Max£76.80pw (Low)
£96pw (High)

CROSSMICHAEL
Dumfries & Galloway *Kirkcudbrightshire*
Map11 NX76

H **Culgruff Lodge**
for bookings G M Thomson & Co, 27 King
Street, Castle Douglas,
Kirkcudbrightshire DG7 1AB
☎Castle Douglas(0556)2701

*A pleasant detached stone-built house
situated off the drive to Culgruff House
Hotel and containing sitting room,
kitchen/diner and three bedrooms
sleeping up to seven people.*

All year 1 wk min, 1 unit, 1–7 persons
◉ fridge Electric & open fires
Elec inclusive 🅛not provided
☎(400yds) Iron in unit Ironing board in
unit HCE in unit CTV ⊕3 pin square
P 🅿(1m) Coarse fishing on Woodhall
Loch.

⊖ ♀(1m)

Min£50 Max£115pw

H **Dane Vale Stable Court** Dane Vale
Park
for bookings G M Thomson & Co, 27 King
Street, Castle Douglas,
Kirkcudbrightshire DG7 1AB
☎Castle Douglas(0556)2701

*A comfortable house situated in the
courtyard of Dane Vale Stables on the
banks of the River Dee. Dane Vale Park is
situated on the A713 3m from Castle
Douglas. The house offers spacious
accommodation with a dining room,
sitting room, kitchen, two bathrooms, two
twin-bedded rooms and a double
bedroom.*

All year 1 wk min, 6 mths max, 1 unit,
1–6 persons ◈ no pets Aga ◉
fridge Electric & open fires
Elec inclusive 🅛not provided ☎(1m)
HCE in unit TV ⊕3 pin square P
🅿(1m)

⊖ 🅿(3m) ♀(3m) Fishing
Min£55 Max£130pw

H **Kirkbrae**
for bookings G M Thomson & Co, 27 King
Street, Castle Douglas,
Kirkcudbrightshire DG7 1AB
☎Castle Douglas(0556)2701

*Semi-detached two-storey house in the
main street opposite the church. A
double room, a twin-bedded room,
dining room/living room with bed-settee
and kitchen are included in this small
compact house.*

All year 1 wk min, 6 mths max, 1 unit,
1–6 persons ◈ no pets ◉ fridge
Electric Elec inclusive 🅛not provided
☎(200yds) WM in unit SD in unit
Airing bupboard in unit Iron in unit
Ironing board in unit HCE in unit ⊕
CTV ⊕3 pin square P 🅿(20yds)

⊖ 🅿(3m) ♀(20yds) 🅿(3m) ♫(3m)
🗑(3m)

Min£45 Max£105pw

H **Station Cottage**
for bookings G M Thomson & Co, 27 King
Street, Castle Douglas,
Kirkcudbrightshire DG7 1AB
☎Castle Douglas(0556)2701

*A former two-floor railway office and
house standing by the former railway
track. Accommodation comprises a
sitting room with bed-settee, combined
kitchen/dining room, a double bedroom,
a family room with a double and two
single beds and a modern bathroom.
Central heating charged for separately.*

Apr-Oct 1 wk min, 1 mth max, 1 unit,
1–8 persons no pets ◈ ◉ fridge ♨
& open fires Elec inclusive
🅛not provided ☎(200yds) WM in unit
SD Airing cupboard in unit Iron in unit
Ironing board in unit HCE in unit ⊕
TV ⊕3 pin square P 🅿(100yds)

⊖ 🅿(3m) ♀(20yds) 🅿(3m) ♫(3m)
🗑(3m)

Min£55 Max£130pw

CRYMMYCH
Dyfed
Map2 SN13

B **Brengast, Hafan & Hafod**
for bookings Mr & Mrs E Rees,
Esgairordd Farm, Crymych, Dyfed
SA41 3SQ
☎Crymych(023973)275

*Three bungalows facing the Preseli Hills.
'Brengast' has spacious lounge with
patio doors onto a terrace, modern
kitchen/diner, bathroom and separate
WC. Two double bedrooms and one with
twin beds (a convertible settee in lounge
if required) completes the
accommodation. The other two
bungalows are semi-detached and have
good sized lounges, kitchen, dining area,
one double bedroom, one twin bedroom,
bathroom and separate WC. Wide
windows give full advantage of the hill
views.*

All year MWB out of season
3 nights min, 3 units, 4–8 persons ◈ ◆
◉ fridge ♨(inclusive) Elec metered
🅛not provided ☎(1½m) Airing
cupboard in unit Iron in unit Ironing
board in unit HCE in unit ⊕ TV
⊕3 pin square 2P 1🏠 🅿 🅿(1½m)
Trout fishing

⊖ ♀(1½m)

Min£57.50 Max£132pw

CULBROKIE
Highland *Ross & Cromarty*
Map14 NH65

Ch **Chalets at 'Wester Brae'**
for bookings Mrs E M Phillips, Wester
Brae, Balblair, Conon Bridge, Ross-shire
☎Culbokie(034987)609

*Two neat, compact chalets situated in
grassy field on owners small-holding,
backed by woodland. They comprise
open-plan lounge/kitchen, one double-
bedded room and one with twin bunks,
bathroom/WC. Superb views across
Cromarty Firth and distant mountains;
approach via B9169.*

Mar-Nov 1 wk min, 2 units, 1–4 persons
◈ no pets ◉ fridge Electric
Elec inclusive 🅛inclusive ☎(2m)
Airing cupboard in unit Iron in unit
Ironing board in unit HCE in unit ⊕
TV ⊕3 pin square 4P 🅿 🅿(3m)

⊖ ♀(3m)

Min£45 Max£95pw

CULKEIN
Highland *Sutherland*
Map14 NC03

Ch **Bayview & Brisbane**
for bookings Mrs V Macleod, 7 Mount
Stuart Road, Largs, Ayrshire KA30 9ES
☎Largs(0475)672931

*Two modern timber chalets in a beautiful
and isolated position, on foreshore of
Culkein Bay overlooking Sandy Bay.
Bayview comprises
lounge/diner/kitchen, shower/WC, one
twin-bedded room, one double and one*

with bunk beds. **Brisbane** has lounge/diner/kitchen, shower/WC and two bedrooms, one twin- and one double-bedded.

Etr-Oct MWB 1wkmin, 4wks max, 2units, 2–8persons ◇ ◆ ◎ fridge Electric Elec inclusive ⊑ not provided ☎(1m) SD in unit Airing cupboard in unit Iron in unit HCE in unit ⊖ TV ⊕3pin square 4P ♨(3m)

Min£70 Max£135pw

Ch Burnside Chalet
for bookings Mrs V MacLeod, 7 Mount Stuart Road, Largs, Ayrshire KA30 9ES
☎Largs(0475)672931

Chalet on stilts facing sandy bay where Atlantic rollers break. There are two bedrooms, open-plan lounge and kitchen, bathroom and verandah.

Etr-Oct MWB 1wkmin, 1unit, 1–6persons ◇ ◆ ◎ fridge Electric Elec inclusive ⊑ not provided Airing cupboard in unit Iron in unit HCE in unit ⊖ ⊕3pin square P ♨(3m)

Min£70 Max£135pw

CULLEN
Grampian *Banffshire*
Map**15** NJ56

C Burnside Lintmill
for bookings J & J Palphramand, Knockdurn Croft, Portsoy, Banffshire
☎Portsoy(02614)3821

Situated just outside the small village of Lintmill, 1m from Cullen, this detached cottage comprises of kitchen/diner, lounge and sitting room on the ground floor and two bedrooms on the first. There is a large enclosed garden to the rear.

Apr-Oct MWB out of season 1wkmin, 1unit, 1–4persons ◎ fridge Electric Elec metered ⊑ can be hired ☎(200yds) Airing cupboard in unit HCE in unit ⊖ TV ⊕3pin square 1P ▥ ♨(1m)
⊖ ᛄ(1m) 🔋(1m)

Min£58 Max£135pw

H Fulmar 58 Seafield Street
for bookings Blantyre Holiday Homes Ltd, West Bauds, Findochty, Buckie AB5 2EB
☎Buckie(0542)31773

Small, two-storied house standing under old unused railway viaduct on main road through town. Accommodation comprises sitting room/dining room, with bed-settee, twin-bedded room, modern kitchen and bathroom, all on ground-floor. On the first-floor, there is a double-bedded room, with bay window giving views of local coastline.

All year MWB out of season 1wkmin, 3wks max, 1unit, 1–6persons [◇ ◇] [◆] ◎ fridge Electric Elec metered ⊑ can be hired ☎(200yds) Airing cupboard in unit Iron in unit Ironing board in unit HCE in unit ⊖ CTV

⊕3pin square ♨(50yds) Pony trekking & fishing
⊖ ᛄ(⅓m) 🔋(200yds) ♫(1m)

CULLIPOOL
Isle of Luing Strathclyde *Argyll*
Map**10** NM71

F Miss A Stone **Cluain Flats** Cullipool, Isle of Luing, Oban, Argyll
☎Luing(08524)209

Two flats in a Victorian, stone-built house with superb views over Firth of Lorn. The ground-floor flat has two twin-bedded rooms and a fifth bed is provided in the sitting room. Each has kitchen/dining room and modern bathroom. Deep freeze in each unit.

All year MWB out of season 1wkmin, 6mths max, 2units, 2–6persons ◇ ◎ fridge ▦ Elec metered ⊑ inclusive ☎(⅓m) SD on premises Iron in unit Ironing board in unit HCE in unit ⊖ ⊕3pin square P ♨(100yds)

Max£60pw (Low)
Min£80 Max£120pw (High)

CULLODEN MOOR
Highland *Inverness-shire*
Map**14** NH74

F Cherry Tree Flat
for bookings Clava Lodge Hotel, Culloden Moor, Inverness IV12 EJ
☎Culloden Moor(0463)790228

Charming flat situated on the top of a country house with use of facilities, if required. The hotel stands in its own grounds, close to Culloden Moor battlefield and within 15 minutes' drive of Inverness. Good standard of accommodation.

All year 1wkmin, 6mths max, 1unit, 1–4persons ◇ ◆ no pets ◎ fridge Electric Elec metered ⊑ can be hired ☎ Iron in unit Ironing board in unit HCE in unit ⊖ TV ⊕3pin square 2P ♨(5m) Fishing

Min£30 Max£40pw (Low)
Min£55 Max£65pw (High)

CULVER DOWN
Isle of Wight
Map**4** SZ68

C Old Coastguard Cottages
for bookings Mrs A Cheverton, 18 Ranelagh Road, Sandown, Isle of Wight PO36 8NT
☎Sandown(0983)406193

Five coastguard cottages with superb views overlooking Sandown and Shanklin Bay. Some have four bedrooms, the others have three, all with a lounge, kitchen, bathroom/WC. Adequately furnished accommodation.

All year MWB out of season 1wkmin, 3mths max, 5units, 2–8persons [◆] [◆] ◎ fridge Electric Elec metered ⊑ not provided ☎ Iron in unit Ironing

board in unit HCE in unit ⊖ ⊛ TV ⊕3pin square P ▥ ♨(4m) Fishing ⊖ 🔋

Min£76 Max£120pw (Low)
Min£115 Max£195pw (High)

CURY
Cornwall
Map**2** SW62

B Mr & Mrs Mills **Franchis Holiday Bunglaows** Cury Cross Lanes, Helston, Cornwall
☎Mullion(0326)240301

Modern bungalows located in a secluded position at the edge of 10acres of private woodland, adjacent to a select rural camping site. They are well appointed and furnished and comprise of two twin-bedded rooms, lounge/diner and kitchenette, shower room with WC. Additional folding bed available. Pleasant location off A3083 6m S of Helston.

Mar-Oct MWB out of season 1wkmin, 5units, 1–5persons ◇ ◆ no pets ◑ fridge Gas fires Gas/Elec inclusive ⊑ inclusive ☎(1m) Iron in unit Ironing board in unit HCE in unit ⊖ CTV ⊕3pin square P ♨
⊖ ᛄ(3m) 🔋(1m) ▨(1m) ♫(1m)

DALBEATTIE
Dumfries & Galloway *Kirkcudbrightshire*
Map**11** NX86

C Ernglass
for bookings Mrs R Hanbury, Drumstinchall, Dalbeattie, Kirkcudbrightshire DG5 4PD
☎Southwick(038778)279

Whitewashed ex-fisherman's cottage, about 160 years old, standing in own grounds; comprises lounge, bathroom, kitchen and four bedrooms (two on the ground-floor – two on the upper-floor, reached by a loft ladder). 5½m from Dalbeattie

Apr-mid Nov MWB out of season 1wkmin, 1unit, 1–8persons [◇] ◆ ◎ fridge Electric Elec metered ⊑ not provided ☎(2m) Airing cupboard in unit Iron in unit HCE in unit TV can be hired ⊕3pin round 3P ♨(2m) ᛄHard Trout fishing available
⊖ ᛄ(2m) 🔋(2m)

Min£40 Max£75pw (Low)
Min£80 Max£122pw (High)

DALE
Dyfed
Map**2** SM70

F Blue Anchor Wood
for bookings Powells Holidays, High Street, Saundersfoot, Dyfed
☎Saundersfoot(0834)812791

Ground-floor flat located in modern detached house comprising small lounge/dining room, breakfast bar/kitchen, two double bedrooms with additional bed. →

Apr-Oct 1wk min, 1mth max, 1unit,
4–6persons [◇] ◈ ◆ no pets ◉
fridge ⴹ Elec inclusive Ⓛinclusive
☎(50yds) Airing cupboard in unit Iron
in unit Ironing board in unit HCE in unit
⊝ CTV ⊕3pin square 2P Dinghy
available
⊷ ♀(200yds) ♫(200yds)in summer
Min£63 Max£168pw

DALRY (St John's Town of)
Dumfries & Galloway *Kirkcudbrightshire*
Map **11** NX68

C **Cleuchbrae Cottage**
for bookings Mrs Fergusson, Barlaes
Farm, Dalry, Castle Douglas,
Kirkcudbrightshire DG7 3TZ
☎Dalry(064 43)251

*A solitary two-storey stone-built roadside
cottage situated off the B7000 in an
elevated moorland position. 3m N of
Dalry. It is simply-furnished
accommodation comprising three
bedrooms, kitchen/living room and
bathroom, with its own back yard. The
position offers excellent views across the
Ken Valley to the Rinns of Kells.*

May-Oct 2wks min, 1unit, 1–6persons
◈ ◉ fridge Electric & coal fires
Elec metered Ⓛnot provided HCE in
unit TV ⊕3pin square P ♨(3m)
⊷ ♀(3m) Fishing
Min£46 Max£65pw

C **Grennan Cottages** Grennan Farm
for bookings Mrs E Gordon, Glenlee
Holiday Houses, New Galloway, Castle
Douglas, Kirkcudbrightshire DG7 3SF
☎Dalry(064 43)445

*Two renovated farm cottages amidst
farmland overlooking River Ken.
Accommodation comprises comfortable
sitting room, well-equipped kitchen, twin-
bedded room with good outlook and
ample storage. Modern fitted bathroom.
Access off the A713 1m S of St John's
town of Dalry.*

28Mar-Oct 1wk min, 4units,
1–2persons ◉ fridge Electric & open
fires Elec metered Ⓛnot provided
☎(1m) SD in unit HCE in unit ⊝
TV can be hired ⊕3pin square P 🅿
♨(1m)
⊷ ♨(2m) ♀(1m)

C **Grennan Mill Cottage**
for bookings Miss S Harrison,
Grennan Mill, Dalry, Castle Douglas,
Kirkcudbrightshire DG7 3XQ
☎Dalry(064 43)297

*Single-storey post-war cottage
peacefully situated behind the main
house and enjoying its 20 acres of
wooded grounds. The cottage is simply
decorated and furnished but has many
items of objets d'art which give it a
homely, charming atmosphere. There are
two bedrooms, living room and compact
kitchen. The rocky Garpel Burn and
Water Mill, which is now in working order,
are just a few yards from the cottage. A
most delightful setting. The cottage's own*

---

*donkeys and peacocks augment the
area's bird and wildlife.*

Apr-Nov MWB out of season 1wk min,
1unit, 1–6persons ◆ ◉ fridge
Electric & open fires Elec metered
Ⓛnot provided ☎(½m) WM in unit Iron
in unit Ironing board in unit HCE in unit
⊝ ⊕3pin square P ♨(½m) Trout
fishing
⊷ ♨(2m) ♀(2m)
Min£45 Max£65pw (Low)
Min£85 Max£125pw (High)

DARLEY DALE
Derbyshire
Map **8** SK26

C **Spring Cottage** Bent Lane, Off
Whitworth Road
for bookings Mrs J Statham, Brookside,
Beeley, Matlock, Derbyshire
☎Darley Dale(062 983)2347
(evenings & weekends only)

*Modernised, stone-built cottage in quiet
lane in an elevated postiion with good
views across the valley. It comprises two
bedrooms (one of which has bathroom en
suite), lounge, combined kitchen/dining
area and bathroom/WC.*

All year 1wk min, 1unit, 1–4persons,
nc5 no pets 🐕 fridge
Gas/Elec metered Ⓛnot provided
☎(½m) Iron in unit Ironing board in unit
HCE in unit ⊝ ⊕3pin square 2P 🅿
♨(½m)
⊷ ♀(1m)
Min£85 Max£100pw

DARTMOUTH
Devon
Map **3** SX85

F **No 1 Clare Court** 2 Newport Street
for bookings Mr & Mrs G Powell, 20 South
Town, Dartmouth, Devon
☎Dartmouth(080 43)2638

*Ground-floor flat in modern block
situated opposite the market in town
centre. Large lounge, one double and
one twin-bedded room, neat galley-type
kitchen and separate bathroom.*

All year MWB out of season 2day min,
3mths max, 1unit, 2–4persons [◆]
[◆] ◉ fridge Electric Elec metered
Ⓛnot provided ☎(50yds) Iron in unit
Ironing board in unit HCE in unit
[Launderette within 300yds] ⊝ TV
⊕3pin square 1P ♨(10yds)
⊷ ♨(3m) ♀(50yds) ♫(200yds)
Min£30 Max£42pw (Low)
Min£55 Max£88pw (High)

C **The Cottage** The Old Bakehouse
for bookings Mrs S R Ridalls,
7 Broadstone, Dartmouth, Devon
TQ6 9NR
☎Dartmouth(080 43)4585

*Compact 'olde worlde' style terraced
cottage, with beamed ceilings and stone-
fireplace, adjacent to town centre. On the*

---

*ground-floor is lounge, kitchenette and
double bedroom, first-floor has another
bedroom and bathroom/WC.*

All year MWB out of season 3days min,
6wks max, 1unit, 2–6persons [◇] ◈
◆ ◉ fridge Electric Elec metered
Ⓛcan be hired ☎(800yds) Iron in unit
Ironing board in unit HCE in unit ⊝
TV ⊕3pin square 🅿 ♨(200yds)
Boat for hire
⊷ ♀(200yds) ♫(200yds)
Min£45 Max£50pw (Low)
Min£60 Max£130pw (High)

F **Second Flat** The Old Bakehouse
for bookings Mrs S R Ridalls The Old
Bakehouse, 7 Broadstone, Dartmouth,
Devon TQ6 9NR
☎Dartmouth(080 43)4585

*Ground-floor flat forming part of the Old
Bakehouse comprising lounge/dining
room with beamed ceiling, kitchenette,
one double and one twin bedroom,
shower room/WC.*

All year MWB out of season 3days min,
6wks max, 1unit, 2–4persons [◇] ◈
◆ ◉ fridge Electric Elec metered
Ⓛcan be hired ☎(800yds) Iron in unit
Ironing board in unit HCE in unit ⊝ TV
can be hired ⊕3pin square 🅿
♨(200yds) Boat for hire
⊷ ♀(200yds) ♫(200yds)
Min£40 Max£45pw (Low)
Min£55 Max£125pw (High)

F Mrs A Day **Redwalls (Flats 1–3 &
5–8 & 10)** Townstal Road, Dartmouth,
Devon TQ6 9HT
☎Dartmouth(080 43)4222

*Large detached residence, well
converted to self-contained apartments.
Standing in 1-acre of garden on high-
ground above Dartmouth, with views of
estuary. All flats have double bedrooms,
double wall beds, lounge, kitchenette
and shower room (three have dining
area). Flat 5 has a separate kitchen but no
bedroom (double wall bed in lounge).*

Feb-Nov MWB out of season
3days min, 2mths max, 8units,
2–4persons ◉ fridge Electric
Elec metered Ⓛcan be hired ☎ Iron
in unit Ironing board in unit HCE in unit
⊝ TV ⊕3pin square 8P 🅿 ♨(½m)
Boats for hire
⊷ ♀(½m) ♫(½m)
Min£27 Max£61pw (Low)
Min£69 Max£149pw (High)

DAWLISH
Devon
Map **3** SX97

H **Arncliffe**
for bookings Mr & Mrs R J Richmond, Oak
Park Holiday Flats and Houses, Oak Park
Cottage, Old Gatehouse Road, Dawlish,
Devon EX7 0DG
☎Dawlish(0626)863113

*Two-storey detached house in quiet
situation. Own garden, garage and
forecourt parking. Four bedrooms, dining
room/lounge, kitchen. Two WCs,*

bathroom and shower room. Comfortably furnished and well equipped. Access to Oak Park House amenities.

All year MWB out of season 7 days min in season, shorter breaks in low season, 8 mths max, 1 unit, 9 persons ◆ ◆ no pets ◎ fridge ▥ Elec inclusive ⬜inclusive ☎(50yds) Airing cupboard in unit Iron in unit Ironing board in unit HCE in unit [Launderette within 100yds] ⊖ TV ⊕3 pin square ⊕3pin round P ▥ ⬚(150yds)

⇔ ⅋(3m) ⚲(400yds) ⬚(½m) ♫(1m)

Min £86 Max £203pw (Low)
Max £247pw (High)

H Clematis
for bookings Mr & Mrs R J Richmond, Oak Park Holiday Flats and Houses, Oak Park Cottage, Old Gatehouse Road, Dawlish, Devon EX7 0DG
☎Dawlish (0626) 863113

Two-storey detached house with garage and forecourt parking and secluded garden with lawn. Four bedrooms, kitchen/diner, lounge, bathroom, downstairs cloakroom. Furnished and decorated to high standard. Comfortable and well equipped. Access to Oak Park House amenities.

All year MWB out of season 7 days min in season, shorter breaks in low season, 8 mths max, 1 unit, 10 persons ◆ ◆ no pets ◎ fridge ▥ Elec inclusive ⬜inclusive ☎(50yds) Airing cupboard in unit Iron in unit Ironing board in unit HCE in unit [Launderette within 100yds] ⊖ TV ⊕3 pin square P ▥ ⬚(50yds)

⇔ ⅋(3m) ⚲(400yds) ⬚(½m) ♫(1m)

Min £96 Max £225pw (Low)
Max £274pw (High)

H Coach House
for bookings Mr & Mrs J Patrick-Mitchinson, Edencliffe, Holcombe Drive, Holcombe, Dawlish, Devon EX7 0JW
☎Dawlish (0626) 863171
Converted coach house with private path to the beach 300yds away. Accommodation comprises three double bedrooms, lounge with convertible settee, kitchen/diner, bathroom and glass-covered patio.

All year MWB out of season 1 wk min, 1 mth max, 1 unit, 2–8 persons [◇] ◆ no pets ◎ fridge ▥ Electric ⬜can be hired ☎(300yds) [WM on premises] [SD on premises] [TD on premises] Iron on premises Ironing board on premises HCE on premises ⊖ CTV ⊕3 pin square P ▥ ⬚(½m) ⇔ ⚲(½m) ⬚(1½m) ♫(1½m) ⬚(1½m)

Min £54 Max £113pw (Low)
Min £125 Max £194pw (High)

F Edencliffe
for bookings Mr & Mrs J Patrick-Mitchinson, Edencliffe, Holcombe Drive, Holcombe, Dawlish, Devon EX7 0JW
☎Dawlish (0626) 863171

Flat in house rebuilt in 1928 from John

Nash's plans for original 19th-century house. Impressive views overlooking Lyme Bay towards Babbacombe, beach 300yds. Accommodation comprises two bedrooms (one large double, one small child's room), lounge/diner, kitchen and bathroom.

Apr–Oct 1 wk min, 1 unit, 4 persons [◇] [◆] no pets [◎] fridge ▥ Elec inclusive ⬜can be hired ☎(300yds) WM on premises SD on premises TD on premises Iron on premises Ironing board on premises HCE in unit ⊖ CTV ⊕3 pin square P ▥ ⬚(½m)

⇔ ⚲(½m) ⬚(1½m) ♫(1½m) ⬚(1½m)

Min £52 Max £91pw (Low)
Min £98 Max £155pw (High)

F 1 Park Road (The Flat)
for bookings I & J Bulpin, Little Down, Breakneck Hill, Teignmouth, Devon TQ14 9NZ
☎Teignmouth (06267) 6040
First-floor flat in shopping/residential area of Dawlish, ½m from the seafront. Two bedrooms, one with double and bunk beds, one with bunk beds, lounge/diner with double put-u-up, kitchen and shower/WC.

All year 1 wk min, 8 mths max, 1 unit, 2–8 persons ◆ ◆ ◎ fridge Electric Elec metered ⬜can be hired ☎(120yds) SD in unit [Airing cupboard in unit] Iron in unit Ironing board in unit HCE in unit [Launderette within 300yds] CTV ⊕3 pin square 2P ⬚(20yds)

⇔ ⅋(2m) ⚲(20yds) ⬚(½m) ♫(½m)

Min £48 Max £95pw (Low)
Min £100 Max £115pw (High)

F 28 Park Road (Flats 1 & 2)
for bookings I & J Bulpin, Little Down, Breakneck Hill, Teignmouth, Devon TQ14 9NZ
☎Teignmouth (06267) 6040

First- and second-floor flats over shop in Dawlish shopping area, ½m from seafront. Both flats have lounge with put-u-up or divan, two bedrooms with either double, twin and single/bunk beds, separate kitchen and shower room/WC.

All year 1 wk min, 8 mths max, 2 units, 2–7 persons ◆ ◆ Electric Elec metered ⬜can be hired ☎(100yds) SD in unit Airing cupboard in unit Iron in unit Ironing board in unit HCE in unit [Launderette within 300yds] CTV ⊕3 pin square ⬚(20yds)

⇔ ⅋(2m) ⚲(20yds) ⬚(½m) ♫(½m)

Min £55 Max £95pw (Low)
Min £100 Max £125pw (High)

F Mr & Mrs R A Potter **Gaycourt Holiday Flats** 8 Marine Parade, Dawlish, Devon EX7 9DJ
☎Dawlish (0626) 862846

Five flats of varied accommodation. One has double bedroom, kitchen/diner, lounge with convertible and bathroom. Two have family bedroom, lounge with convertible, kitchen/diner and bathroom. Of the other two, one has two family bedrooms and the other one family bedroom, both with lounge/diner with convertible, kitchen and bathroom.

All year MWB out of season 1 wk min, 6 mths max, 5 units, 2–8 persons [◇] ◆ ◆ ◎ fridge ▥ Gas & Electric Gas/Elec metered ⬜can be hired ☎(100yds) Airing cupboard in unit Iron in unit Ironing board in unit HCE in unit [Launderette within 300yds] ⊖ TV ⊕3 pin square P ▥ ⬚(200yds) ⇔ ⅋(2½m) ⚲(100yds) ⬚(100yds) ♫(100yds)

Min £65 Max £120pw (Low)
Min £112 Max £160pw (High)

F High Trees
for bookings Mr & Mrs R J Richmond, Oak Park Holiday Flats and Houses, Oak Park Cottage, Old Gatehouse Road, Dawlish, Devon EX7 0DG
☎Dawlish (0626) 863113

Eleven self-contained flats in pleasantly converted hotel. All have lounge/diner with double convertible bed-settee, kitchen and bathroom with shower attachment (except Flat 18, see description). The sleeping accommodation is as follows: Flat 12: two bedrooms, one with double, one twin-bedded room and bunk bed. Flats 14, 15, 16 and 19: one bedroom with double and bunk bed. Flat 17: two bedrooms, one with double and single plus shower and basin, one with two single beds. Flat 18: bed-sitter for two people, kitchen/diner, bathroom and lounge with superior bed-settee. Flat 20: one bedroom with four single beds. Double wall bed in lounge and breakfast bar in kitchen. Flat 21: spacious two bedroom flat, one with double and bunk bed, one with two single beds and bunk bed. Flat 22: one bedroom with double bed and bunk beds which convert to two singles. Flat 23: one bedroom with two singles and bunk bed.

All year MWB out of season 7 days min in season, shorter breaks in low season, 8 mths max, 11 units, 1–8 persons ◆ ◆ no pets ◎ fridge ▥ Elec metered (except lighting) ⬜inclusive ☎ Airing cupboard in unit Iron in unit Ironing board in unit HCE in unit [Launderette within 100yds] ⊖ TV ⊕3 pin square P ▥ ⬚ ⇔ ⅋(3m) ⚲(400yds) ⬚(½m) ♫(1m)

Min £48 Max £162pw (Low)
Min £137 Max £197pw (High)

1982 prices quoted throughout gazetteer

F Mr & Mrs R A Potter, **Lisburne Holiday Flats** Westcliffe, Dawlish, Devon EX7 9DN
☎Dawlish(0626)863385

Three-storey building in an elevated position overlooking Marine Parade and sea. First, second and third-floor flats, some with sea views. Five of the flats each have kitchen, lounge, double beds and studio couch in lounge. Four with shower, one with bath. Another three flats on the second floor have lounge with studio couch, bedroom with bunk beds, double bedroom, kitchen and bathroom with WC.

All year MWB out of season 1 wk min, 6 mths max, 8 units, 2–6 persons [◇] ◇ ◆ no pets ◎ fridge Electric Elec metered ⌷can be hired ☎(100yds) Iron on premises Ironing board on premises HCE on premises [Launderette within 300yds] ⊙ TV ⊕3 pin square P 🏠 🕮 🏛(200yds)

↔ δ▥(1½m)

Min£60 Max£110pw (Low)
Min£100 Max£140pw (High)

H **The Lodge**
for bookings Mr & Mrs A A Jameson, Shell Cove House, Old Teignmouth Road, Dawlish, Devon
☎Dawlish(0626)862523

Detached property in grounds of Shell Cove House. Accommodation comprises lounge, separate kitchen, and one single bedroom on the ground floor; one double bedroom and one twin-bedded room on the first floor; also separate bathroom/WC. Off the A379 Dawlish to Teignmouth road.

All year MWB 1 wk min, 5 mths max, 1 unit, 1–5 persons [◇] [◇ ◆] no pets ⋄ fridge Gas & Electric fires Gas/Elec inclusive ⌷inclusive ☎Airing cupboard in unit Iron on premises Ironing board on premises HCE in unit [Launderette on premises] ⊙ TV ⊕3 pin square 2P 1🏠 🕮 🏛(½m) ≈(heated) ➤Hard Badminton, croquet lawn, games room

↔ δ▥(2½m) 🚲(½m) 🖾(½m) ♫(½m) 🚌(3m)

Min£50 Max£224pw

B **The Lodge**
for bookings Mr & Mrs J Patrick-Mitchinson, Edencliffe, Holcombe Drive, Holcombe, Dawlish, Devon EX7 0JW
☎Dawlish(0626)863171

Self-contained bungalow built over coach house, with own garden and private path to the beach. There are two double bedrooms, lounge/diner with double studio couch, kitchen and bathroom.

All year MWB out of season 1 wk min, 1 unit, 6 persons [◇] [◆] no pets ⋄ fridge 🍳 Elec metered ⌷can be hired ☎(300yds) WM on premises SD on premises TD on premises Iron on premises Ironing board on premises HCE on premises ⊙ CTV ⊕3 pin square P 🕮 🏛(½m)

↔ 🚲(½m) 🖾(1½m) ♫(1½m) 🚌(1½m)

Min£54 Max£113pw (Low)
Min£125 Max£190pw (High)

F **Oak Park House**
for bookings Mr & Mrs R J Richmond, Oak Park Holiday Flats and Houses, Oak Park Cottage, Old Gatehouse Road, Dawlish, Devon EX7 0DG
☎Dawlish(0626)863113

Nine self-contained flats in converted hotel on ground- and first-floor levels. Accommodation as follows: Flat 1 two bedrooms, one with double and single beds with shower/WC en suite, one with two singles and bunk bed, kitchen, bathroom and lounge/diner with bed-settee. Flat 2 two bedrooms, one with double bed and one with two single beds, kitchen, bathroom and lounge/diner with bed-settee. Flat 5 one bedroom with double and bunk bed, kitchen, bathroom and lounge/diner with convertible. Flat 6 one bedroom with double bed and two single beds, bathroom and large lounge/kitchen/diner. Flat 7 three bedrooms, one with double bed and shower/WC en suite, one with two singles and bunk bed and one with a 4ft double, kitchen, bathroom and lounge/diner with convertible. Flat 8 two bedrooms, one with two singles, one with three singles,
kitchen, bathroom and lounge/diner. Flat 9 two bedrooms, one with double and single, one with bunk beds, kitchen, bathroom and lounge/diner. Flat 10 three double bedrooms, one with double and en suite shower room, one with two singles and vanity unit and one with bunk beds, kitchen, bathroom and lounge/diner with double bed-settee. Flat 11 one bedroom with three singles, kitchen, bathroom and lounge/diner with two divans. All flats have baths and showers.*

All year MWB out of season 7 days min in season, shorter breaks in low season, 8 mths max, 9 units, 1–9 persons ◇ ◆ no pets ◎ fridge 🍳 Elec metered (except lighting) ⌷inclusive ☎Airing cupboard in unit Iron in unit Ironing board in unit HCE in unit [Launderette on premises] ⊙ TV ⊕3 pin square P 🕮 🏛 Children's play area

↔ δ▥(3m) 🚲(400yds) 🖾(½m) ♫(1m)

Min£43 Max£165pw (Low)
Min£125 Max£202pw (High)

H **Shell Cove Cottage**
for bookings Mrs A A Jameson, Shell Cove House, Old Teignmouth Road, Dawlish, Devon EX7 0LA
☎Dawlish(0626)862523

A late 19th-century house within the grounds of Shell Cove House and sharing all amenities. Accommodation comprises one bedroom, bathroom, sitting room and kitchen on ground floor and three bedrooms on first floor.

All year MWB out of season 1 wk min, 5 mths max, 1 unit, 7 persons [◇] ◇ ◆ ◎ fridge 🍳 Elec metered ⌷inclusive ☎ [WM on premises] SD on premises TD on premises Airing cupboard on premises Iron on premises Ironing board on premises HCE on premises ⊙ TV ⊕3 pin square P 🕮 🏛 ≈ ➤Hard Badminton, croquet, games room

↔ 🚲(½m) 🖾(1m) ♫(1m) 🚌(2½m)

Min£50 Max£228pw

F **Shell Cove House Flats**
for bookings Mrs A A Jameson, Shell Cove House, Old Teignmouth Road, Dawlish, Devon EX7 0LA
☎Dawlish(0626)862523

Large Georgian house with new wing. Situated within six acres of grounds, with a secluded beach. All units are comfortably furnished and decorated to the same standards, varying only in the number of persons accommodated. Each unit contains living room, 1–3 bedrooms, kitchen and bathroom/WC. Communal TV lounge, games room and laundry room.

All year MWB 3days min, 5mths max, 10units, 2–7persons [◇] ◆ ◆ ⌀ fridge ♨ Gas/Elec inclusive ⌴inclusive ☎ [WM on premises] TD on premises SD on premises Airing cupboard on premises Iron on premises Ironing board on premises HCE in unit ⊙ TV ③3pin square P 𝕞 ♨ ⌁ ⌁Hard Badminton, croquet, games room

↔ ⚲(½m) ⌷(1m) ♫(1m) ⌖(2½m)

Min£49 Max£244pw

DAWLISH WARREN
Devon
Map3 SX97

F   Lee Cliff Park Dawlish Warren, Dawlish, Devon EX7 0NE
☎Dawlish(0626)862269

Modern, purpose-built, two- and three-storey blocks of flats with ground-floor patios and upper balconies. All units comprise kitchenette/lounge with drop-down bed, bathroom/WC; 31 units have two bedrooms and the remaining two have three.

Dawlish — Denford

Mar–Oct MWB out of season
3mths max, 33units, 2–8persons [◈] ♨ fridge Electric Elec metered ⌴can be hired ☎(100yds) SD on premises [TD on premises] Airing cupboard in unit Iron on premises Ironing board on premises HCE in unit [Launderette within 300yds] ⊙ TV ⊕3pin square 62P ♨(100yds)

↔ ☌(200yds) ⚲(200yds) ⌷(200yds) ♫(400yds) Children's play area

Min£19 Max£45pw (Low)
Min£69 Max£158pw (High)

DEGANWY
Gwynedd
Map6 SH77

F   Berklay Court Marine Crescent
for bookings Mr & Mrs J Williams, Clova, 20 Marine Crescent, Deganwy, Aberconwy, Gwynedd
☎Deganwy(0492)83464

Three-storey house containing three flats, each comprising two bedrooms, kitchen, lounge, bathroom, WC and separate shower room. On seafront 400yds from village centre.

All year MWB out of season 1wk min, 1mth max, 3units, 4persons ♨ fridge Electric Elec inclusive ⌴inclusive ☎

Airing cupboard in unit Iron on premises Ironing board on premises HCE in unit Launderette on premises ⊙ ⊛ CTV ③3pin square P 𝕞 ♨(750yds)

↔ ⌁(750yds) ⚲(750yds) ⌷(750yds)

Min£95 Max£125pw (Low)
£150pw (High)

DENFORD
Staffordshire
Map7 SJ95

C   2 & 5 Hollybush Cottages
for bookings Mrs P J Sewell, Mount Pleasant, Mount Road, Leek, Staffs
☎Leek(0538)383894

Two of a row of six Victorian terraced cottages in a peaceful location alongside Cauldon Canal approx 3m W of Leek. They both comprise lounge, kitchen/diner, bathroom/WC, one twin-bedded room and one double and No 5 has a bed-settee in the lounge. Good standard of décor and furnishings.

All year MWB wkds min, 2units, 2–5persons ♨ fridge Electric & open fires (coal provided) Elec metered ⌴not provided ☎(60yds) SD in unit(No2) Airing cupboard in unit HCE in unit TV(No5) CTV(No2) ⊕3pin square 2P 𝕞 ♨(1m) →

⊖ ⛳(2m) 🍷(60yds) 🎥(3m)
Min£45 Max£60pw (Low)
Min£80 Max£100pw (High)

DENHOLM
Borders *Roxburghshire*
Map **12** NT51

B Mrs D J Ingliss **Denholm Hill**
Denholm, Roxbourghshire TD9 8PA
☎Denholm (045 087) 226

This bungalow forms part of a 600-acre mixed farm on the outskirts of a small village. Set amongst tree-studded, rolling countryside, it has panoramic views of five counties, the Minto and Eildon Hills. It is secluded and pleasantly furnished. 1m S off unclass. road.

May-Sep 2wks min, 1mth max, 1unit, 4persons ◈ ◆ ◎ fridge Electric Elec metered ◻not provided ☎ WM in unit Iron in unit HCE in unit TV ⊕3pin square P ▥ 🛒(1m)

⊖ 🍷(1m) ▨(1m)

Min£55 Max£65pw

DERVAIG
Isle of Mull, Strathclyde *Argyll*
Map **13** NM45

Ch Mr J G King **Glen Houses** Dervaig, Isle of Mull, Argyll PA75 6QJ
☎Dervaig (06884) 270 & Tobermory (0688) 2422

Ten modern wood-framed chalets with Skye chip rendering and concrete tile roofs set on a terraced site. Each offers an open-plan lounge/dining room/kitchen with twin convertible settee, two bedrooms with twin or bunk beds, and a modern bathroom. Three chalets are fitted with low level cookers and oven for the disabled. Good views, ½m from Dervaig on unclass road to Salen.

Mar-Oct MWB out of season 3days min, 5wks max, 10units, 1–5persons [◇] ◈ ◆ £8 charge for dogs ◎ fridge Electric Elec metered ◻inclusive ☎(¼m) Airing cupboard in unit HCE in unit ⊙ ⊕3pin square P 🛒(½m) Trout fishing, sea fishing, pony trekking & birdwatching

⊖ 🍷(½m) ▨(½m) ♬(½m) 🎥(½m)

Min£75 Max£155pw

C **The Shieling**
for bookings Mrs G U Richardson, Torr a'Ahlachain, Dervaig, Isle of Mull, Argyll PA75 6QR
☎Dervaig (068 84) 229

Timber-clad single-floor cottage, with combined sitting room, dining room with fold down single bed, attractively furnished modern kitchen, two twin-bedded rooms and a heated bathroom. Situated on west of island, about 1m out of village.

Mar-Nov MWB out of season 1wk min, 1mth max, 1unit, 1–5persons, nc10 no cats ◎ fridge Electric Elec metered ◻not provided ☎(1m) Airing cupboard in unit Iron in unit Ironing board in unit HCE in unit ⊕3pin square P 🛒(1m)

⊖ 🍷(1m) ▨(1m) ♬(1m) 🎥(1m)

Min£45 Max£70pw (Low)
Min£80 Max£100pw (High)

DERWEN
Clwyd
Map **6** SJ05

C Mrs P A Houlton, ***Aberclwyd Mews***
Aberclwyd, Derwen, Corwen, Clwyd
☎Clawdd Newydd (08245) 639

Originally a stable, now converted into a semi-detached cottage; accommodation comprises (on the ground-floor) kitchen, lounge (and bed-settee), WC, separate bathroom, dining room. On the first-floor there is a bedroom with a single and two bunks and a double with single beds and cot.

All year MWB out of season 4wks max, 1unit, 1–6persons [◇] ◈ ◆ ◎ fridge ▦ Elec metered ◻can be hired ☎(100yds) Iron in unit Ironing board in unit HCE in unit ⊙ ⊛ TV ⊕3pin square 2P 2🏠 ▥ 🛒(100yds) Fishing & sailing

⊖ 🍷(1m) ▨(3m) ♬(3m) 🎥(3m)

DESS
Grampian *Aberdeenshire*
Map **15** NJ50

H **Lewiston**
for bookings Aboyne Estates, Estate Office, Old Station, Dinnet, Aberdeenshire AB3 5LL
☎Dinnet (033 985) 341

A former farmhouse with two double bedrooms, bathrooms and combined kitchen and living room. Simple, but pleasant accommodation. Fine views across Deeside Valley. Situated about 4m E of Aboyne, near the old Dess Station and reached by a short farm track.

end Feb-Oct 1wk min, 1mth max, 1unit, 1–6persons ◈ ◆ ◎ fridge Electric & coal fires Elec inclusive ◻can be hired ☎(3m) Airing cupboard in unit HCE in unit ⊕3pin square P 🏠 🛒(3m)

⊖ 🍷(3m)

Max£90pw (Low)
Max£105pw (High)

DIDDLEBURY
Shropshire
Map **7** SO58

C ***Glebe Cottage***
for bookings Mrs M J Wilkes, Glebe Farm, Diddlebury, Craven Arms, Salop
☎Munslow (058 476) 221

A comfortable modernised stone-cottage in the village centre, facing the church and a ford. A lawn separates if from the owner's farm.

Apr-Nov 3nights min, 2wks max, 1unit, 1–5persons ◎ fridge Electric Elec metered ◻not provided ☎(½m) Iron in unit HCE in unit ⊙ TV can be hired ⊕3pin square P ▥ 🛒(2m)

⊖ 🍷(1m)

DINGWALL
Highland *Ross & Cromarty*
Map **14** NH55

C&H **East & West Cottages** (2m W off A834)
for bookings Mr I R McCrae, Fodderty Lodge, Dingwall, Ross-shire IV15 9UE
☎Strathpeffer (09972) 207

A cottage and a house attached to proprietors residence, originally built as a country Manse in 1730. The gardens surrounding the cottages contain many shrubs and trees bordered by lawns. The house (West cottage) has two bedrooms, one on the ground-floor, the other in a loft style area overlooking the living room and reached by an open wooden staircase. The cottage has three bedrooms, one on the ground-floor and two reached by a steep staircase.

Mar-Oct 1wk min, 5wks max, 2units, 1–7persons ◎ fridge Electric Elec metered ◻not provided ☎(2m) Airing cupboard in unit Iron on premises Ironing board on premises HCE in unit ⊙ TV can be hired ⊕3pin square P 🛒(2½m) Pony trekking, fishing

⊖ ⛳(2m) 🍷(2m) ▨(2m) 🎥(2½m)

Min£57.50pw (Low)
Min£130pw (High)

F **East & West Flats** Fodderty Lodge (2m W off A834)
for bookings Mr I R McCrae, Fodderty Lodge, Dingwall, Ross-shire IV15 9UE
☎Strathpeffer (09972) 207

Two recently modernised flats attached to owner's house. East flat has an open plan living room/kitchen and one twin-bedded room on the ground-floor and one double bedroom on the first-floor. West flat has a living room and kitchen/dinette on the ground-floor, one double bedroom with additional single bed on the first-floor and one twin-bedded room on the second-floor.

Mar-Oct 1wk min, 5wks max, 2units, 1–5persons ◎ fridge Electric Elec metered ◻not provided ☎(2m) Airing cupboard in unit Iron on premises Ironing board on premises HCE in unit ⊙ TV/CTV can be hired ⊕3pin square P 🛒(2½m) Pony trekking Fishing

⊖ ⛳(2m) ▨(2m) 🎥(2½m)

Min£57.50pw (Low)
Min£130pw (High)

1982 prices quoted throughout gazetteer

DINMORE
Hereford & Worcester
Map3 SO45

C Mrs S R Aubrey **Kipper Knowle Farm** Dinmore, Wellington, Herefs
☎Canon Pyon(043271)287

Two-storey, semi-detached farm cottage comprising kitchen, pantry, lounge, dining room, bathroom and WC on the ground floor. There are two bedrooms (one twin and one double) on the first-floor. Going south, turn right off A49 signed Dinmore Manor, proceed for 1m through parkland; farm is signed right, cottage is adjacent to farmhouse. A car is essential for this establishment.

All year MWB out of season 3days min, 3wks max, 1unit, 1–6persons ◉ fridge Electric & open fires Elec metered ⊡inclusive ☎ Airing cupboard in unit HCE in unit TV ⊕3pin square
Min£30 Max£40pw (Low)
Min£50 Max£55pw (High)

DOCKLOW
Hereford & Worcester
Map3 SO55

H **Brimstone House**
for bookings Mrs M R M Brooke, Nicholson Farm, Docklow, Leominster, Herefs HR6 0SL
☎Steens Bridge(056882)269

A detached house with its own private garden. Comprises larder, kitchen, dining room, lounge plus utility room, WC and integral garage on ground-floor. Bathroom with WC, one twin-bedded room, one double and one room with a double/single bed.

All year MWB out of season 3days min, 4wks max, 1unit, 2–8persons ◈ ◉ fridge ♨ Elec metered ⊡can be hired ☎(1m) Airing cupboard in unit Iron on premises HCE in unit ⊖ TV ⊕3pin square P 🅿 🎬 ♨(2m) Fishing
⊶ 🍴(1m)

B **Cedars**
for bookings Mrs M R M Brooke, Nicholson Farm, Docklow, Leominster, Herefs HR6 0SL
☎Steens Bridge(056882)269

A remarkable conversion from a former poultry house, this is a modern cedar-built bungalow with generous accommodation. Comprising large modern kitchen/diner and lounge, two bedrooms, each with double beds, the larger room having two additional single beds. Combined bathroom/WC.

All year MWB out of season 1wk min, 1unit, 1–8persons [◇] ◈ ◉ fridge Electric & open fires Elec metered ⊡can be hired ☎(1½m) WM in unit Airing cupboard in unit Iron in unit HCE in unit ⊖ TV ⊕3pin square P ♨(1½m) Trout lake
⊶ 🍴(1m)

C Mr & Mrs M Ormerod **Docklow Manor** Docklow, Leominster, Herefordshire
☎Steens Bridge(056882)643

These cottages were originally ancillary buildings to the manor house, they are constructed of local stone and grouped around a walled pond. Set in 10 acres of garden and grounds. Each cottage is differently furnished, all to a high standard, several with wood burning stoves. Cottages cater for two, four or six people.

All year MWB out of season 2days min, 6wks max, 10units, 1–6persons [◇] ◈ ◆ no dogs ◉ fridge Electric Elec inclusive ⊡inclusive ☎ Airing cupboard in unit Iron on premises Ironing board on premises HCE in unit [Launderette on premises] ⊖ CTV ⊕3pin square P ♨(5m) Croquet lawn
⊶ 🍴(½m)

B **Firs**
for bookings Mr & Mrs M R M Brooke, Nicholson Farm, Docklow, Leominster, Herefs HR6 0SL
☎Steens Bridge(056882)269

Modern cedar built bungalow comprising lounge, kitchen/diner, bathroom/WC, one single and a double bedded room.

All year MWB out of season 2nights min, 3wks max, 1unit, 1–6persons ◈ ◆ ◉ fridge Electric Elec metered ⊡can be hired ☎(2m) WM in unit Airing cupboard in unit Iron in unit HCE in unit ⊖ TV ⊕3pin square 5P ♨(1¾m) Trout fishing
⊶ 🍴(1m)

DOLLERIE
Tayside *Perthshire*
Map11 NN92

H **Dollerie Annexe**
for bookings Mr A G Murray, Dollerie House, Crieff, Perthshire PH7 3NX
☎Crieff(0764)3234

Annexe to Lairds mansion, on two floors. Entrance hall/games room, shower room with WC, kitchen with breakfast bar and dishwasher, sitting room, dining room, with serving hatch, grandfather clock, small neat little study/single bedroom with TV and writing desk, heated bathroom. Separate twin bedroom with own access stair. Other set of stairs leads to family room with washbasin and attractively decorated twin room.

15Mar–15Nov MWB out of season 1wk min, 1unit, 1–8persons [◇] ◈ no cats ◉ fridge Electric & open fires Elec metered ⊡not provided ☎(2½m) WM in unit SD in unit TD in unit Iron in unit Ironing board in unit HCE in unit ⊖ TV ⊕3pin square P 🅿 🎬 ♨(2½m)

⊶ ♨ₘ(2½m) 🍴(2½m) 🖥(2½m) 🎵(2½m) ☎(2½m)
Min£66 Max£116pw (Low)
Min£132 Max£160pw (High)

C **Dollerie Cottage**
for bookings Mr A G Murray, Dollerie House, Crieff, Perthshire PH7 3NX
☎Crieff(0764)3234

Second-floor converted coach house situated by main house. Accommodation comprises attractive lounge/dining room with open fireplace, and one tiny single bedroom leading off. Kitchen with dishwasher and bathroom. Upstairs two sizeable double-bedded rooms, one of which leads off the other. 2½m E of Crieff on secondary road to Perth via Madderty.

15Mar–15Nov MWB out of season 1wk min, 1unit, 1–6persons [◈ ◆] no cats ◉ fridge Electric & open fires Elec metered ⊡not provided ☎(2½m) SD in unit Iron in unit Ironing board in unit HCE in unit ⊖ ⊕3pin round P 🅿 🎬 ♨(2½m)

⊶ ♨ₘ(2½m) 🍴(2½m) 🖥(2½m) 🎵(2½m) ☎(2½m)
Min£55 Max£93pw (Low)
Min£110 Max£132pw (High)

H **Dollerie Lodge**
for bookings Mr A G Murray, Dollerie House, Crieff Perthshire PH7 3NX
☎Crieff(0764)3234

Detached stone cottage with its own garden nestling at the end of one of the avenues to the estate. Accommodation is all on one level and comprises spacious sitting room with dining area, open fireplace and occasional bed/divan, sizeable kitchen with dishwasher, twin and family room.

15Mar–15Nov MWB out of season 1wk min, 1unit, 1–6persons [◈ ◆] no cats ◉ fridge Electric & open fires Elec metered ⊡not provided ☎(2½m) SD in unit Iron in unit Ironing board in unit HCE in unit ⊖ ⊕3pin round P 🅿 🎬 ♨(2½m)

⊶ ♨ₘ(2½m) 🍴(2½m) 🖥(2½m) 🎵(2½m) ☎(2½m)
Min£55 Max£93pw (Low)
Min£110 Max£132pw (High)

C **East Tuckethill**
for bookings Mr A G Murray, Dollerie House, Crieff, Perthshire PH7 3NX
☎Crieff(0764)3234

Small farm cottage on little country road, stone faced with slate roof. Single-floor accommodation comprising comfortable lounge/dining room with occasional bed, and open fireplace. Small, well-equipped kitchen with dishwasher, attractively-decorated small double bedroom, twin bedroom and heated bathroom.

15Mar–15Nov MWB out of season 1wk min, 1unit, 1–5persons [◈ ◆] no cats ◉ fridge Electric & open fires Elec metered ⊡not provided ☎(2½m) SD in unit Iron in unit Ironing board in unit HCE in unit ⊖ ⊕3pin square P 🅿 🎬 ♨(2½m) →

☺ ♨(2½m) ♀(2½m) 📺(2½m)
♫(2½m) ✆(2½m)
Min£44 Max£83pw (Low)
Min£93 Max£110pw (High)

C Muir of Dollerie Farm Cottage
for bookings Mr A G Murray, Dollerie
House, Crieff, Perthshire PH7 3NX
☎Crieff(0764)3234

Detached, single-storey farm cottage
with garden, in peaceful setting with open
outlook at extremity of estate. Reached
by private farm road. Accommodation
comprises lounge/dining room with open
fireplace, twin-bedded room leading off,
a family bedroom and kitchen with
dishwasher.

15Mar–15Nov MWB out of season
1wk min, 1unit, 1–5persons [◆ ◆]
☎ fridge Electric & open fires
Elec metered ⌷not provided ☎(3½m)
SD in unit Airing cupboard in unit Iron
in unit Ironing board in unit HCE in unit
☺ ☺3pin square P ♨ ♨(3m)
Min£44 Max£83pw (Low)
Min£93 Max£110pw (High)

H Muir of Dollerie Farmhouse
for bookings Mr A G Murray, Dollerie
House, Crieff, Perthshire PH7 3NX
☎Crieff(0764)3234

Substantial two-storey stone farmhouse
not far from the farm cottage. Peaceful
setting with fine views to the north and a
large well-maintained garden in front.
The ground-floor accommodation
comprises sitting room with open
fireplace, double bedroom with antique
canopy bed, large kitchen/dining room
with door leading to twin-bedded room
(dishwasher in kitchen) and double
bedroom above. The first floor has two
twin bedrooms and bathroom.

15Mar–15Nov MWB out of season
1wk min, 1unit, 1–10persons [◆ ◆]
no cats ◉ fridge Electric & open
fires Elec metered ⌷not provided
☎(3½m) WM in unit SD in unit TD in
unit Airing cupboard in unit Iron in unit
Ironing board in unit HCE in unit ☺
TV ☺3pin square P ♨ ♨(3½m)
Min£77 Max£126pw (Low)
Min£155 Max£182pw (High)

DOLPHINTON
Strathclyde *Peeblesshire*
Map**11** NT14

H Mrs Hunter Garvald Farm Cottages
Garvald Farm, Dolphinton, West Linton,
Peebles-shire
☎Dolphinton(09688)238

Two adjoining houses with grassy area
located within small farm complex which
lies one mile off A702 amidst pleasant
wooded countryside. The houses are
comfortable and have either two or three
bedrooms.

2Apr–29Oct MWB out of season
1wk min, 2units, 2–5persons ◆
no pets ◉ fridge Electric & open
fires Elec metered ⌷can be hired

Dollerie
—
Dougarie

☎(1½m) Airing cupboard in unit Iron on
premises Ironing board on premises
HCE in unit TV ☺3pin square 4P
♨(1½m)
☺ ♀(3m)
Min£40 Max£60pw (Low)
Min£70 Max£80pw (High)

DOLTON
Devon
Map**2**
SS51

C The Nook Chapel Street
for bookings P W Gomersall, 17
Wordsworth Walk, London NW11 6AL
☎01–4559490

Charming double-fronted cottage with
thatched roof next to Baptist Chapel, in
quiet village. Lounge has open log fire,
and leads off to kitchen area. On the first
floor, there is a well-fitted bathroom, small
bedroom with bed which converts to two
singles or a double, and a master
bedroom with double bed.

Apr–Oct 1wk min, 2wks max, 1unit,
2–4persons no pets ◉ fridge
Electric & open fires Elec metered
⌷not provided ☎(120yds) Airing
cupboard in unit Iron in unit Ironing
board in unit HCE in unit ☺ ☺ TV
☺3pin square P ♨(50yds)
☺ ♀(50yds)
Min£60 Max£100pw

DORNOCH
Highland *Sutherland*
Map**14** NH78

B Mrs Bailey **Heatherwood Park**
Dornoch, Sutherland
☎Dornoch(086 281)596

A select development of thirteen
Norwegian style bungalows, set in six
acres of natural woodland some distance
form the town. All offer modern
lounge/diner/kitchen, two bedrooms
(one double, one twin bedded) and
bathroom/WC.

All year MWB out of season 1wk min,
6wks max, 13units, 2–7persons ◆ ◉
fridge 🐕 Elec metered ⌷can be
hired ☎(30yds) SD in unit Airing
cupboard in unit Iron in unit Ironing
board in unit HCE in unit ☺ TV
☺3pin square 20P ♨(1m)
☺ ♨(1½m) ♀(1½m) 📺(1½m) ♫(1½m)

Ca Mrs E M Grant **Pitgrudy Farm**
Holidays, The Cabins Pitgrudy Farm,
Dornoch, Sutherland IV25 3HY
☎Dornoch(086 281)291

Two timber-framed cabins comprising
wood-panelled lounge/dining room,
modern kitchen, two bedrooms and
shower/WC. Modern well-maintained
equipment. Beautiful views of Kyle of
Sutherland and Ross-shire hills beyond.

All year MWB out of season 1wk min,
2units, 2–6persons ◆ ◉ fridge
Electric Elec metered ⌷not provided
☎(1½m) HCE in unit [Launderette
within 300yds] CTV ☺3pin square P
📺 ♨(1m)
☺ ♀(1m) 📺(1m) ♫(1m)
Min£57.50 Max£74.75pw (Low)
Min£86.25 Max£103.50pw (High)

C Mrs E M Grant **Pitgrudy Farm**
Holidays, The Cottages Pitgrudy Farm,
Dornoch, Sutherland IV25 3HY
☎Dornoch(086 281)291

Pitgrudy Farm is situated approx 1m from
the historic burgh of Dornoch and enjoys
panoramic views of the Kyle of
Sutherland and Ross-shire hills beyond.
There are four modern cottages, each
comprising lounge/dining room with
breakfast bar, two bedrooms with
modern furniture and a convertible settee
is available and modern bathroom/WC.

All year MWB out of season 1wk min,
4units, 2–6persons ◆ ◉ fridge
Electric Elec metered ⌷not provided
☎(1½m) Airing cupboard in
unit [Launderette within 300yds] CTV
☺3pin square P 📺 ♨(1m)
☺ ♀(1m) 📺(1m) ♫(1m)
Min£57.50 Max£74.75pw (Low)
Min£86.25 Max£103.50pw (High)

Ca Mrs E M Grant **Pitgrudy Farm**
Holidays, The Log Cabin Pitgrudy Farm,
Dornoch, Sutherland IV25 3HY
☎Dornoch(086 281)291

Log cabin situated near to the farm
house, with panoramic views of the Kyle
of Sutherland and Ross-shire hills.
Accommodation of open-plan layout,
comprises bathroom, lounge/kitchen
with bed-settee and heavy curtains to
bedroom area with bunk beds.

All year MWB out of season 1wk min,
1unit, 2–5persons ◆ ⌀ Calor gas
heating Gas/Elec metered
⌷not provided ☎(1½m) HCE in unit
[Launderette within 300yds] CTV P
📺 ♨(1m)
☺ ♨(½m) ♀(1m) 📺(1m) ♫(1m)
Min£51.75 Max£63.25pw (Low)
Min£69 Max£86.25pw (High)

DOUGARIE
Isle of Arran, Strathclyde *Bute*
Map**10** NR83

H Boatman's House High Dougarie
for bookings S C Gibbs, Dougarie Estate
Office, Dougarie, Isle of Arran, Bute
☎Machrie(077 084)259 & 229

Small, detached traditional stone house
adjacent to farm set in elevated position
2m from the coast road and with
delightful views out across Machrie Bay.
Accommodation comprises sitting room,
dining/living room and kitchen. Upstairs
there are a twin, a double and two single
bedrooms. Décor and furnishings are
simple and functional. The estate lies on
the west coast of Arran; fine coastal
scenery beach nearby.

26Mar–Oct 1wkmin, 1mthmax, 1unit, 1–6persons ◎ fridge Electric Elecmetered ◻notprovided ☎(2m) HCE in unit ⊕3pinsquare P ♨(6m)

⊖ ♨(2m)

Min£85 Max£140pw

H **Druid House**
for bookings S C Gibbs, Dougarie Estate Office, Dougarie, Isle of Arran, Bute ☎Machrie(077 084)259 & 229

Detached, traditional two-storey house with rear courtyard and outhouses. Accommodation compriises sitting room/dining room, kitchen and twin bedroom. Upstairs are two twin bedrooms. Situated about ½m from coast road.

26Mar–Oct 1wkmin, 1mthmax, 1unit, 1–6persons ◎ fridge Electric Elecmetered ◻notprovided ☎ Airing cupboard in unit HCE in unit ⊕3pinsquare P ⌂ ♨(6m)

⊖ ♨(2m)

Min£75 Max£130pw

C **Garden Cottage**
for bookings S C Gibbs, Dougarie Estate Office, Dougarie, Isle of Arran, Bute ☎Machrie(077 084)259 & 229

Detached, traditional stone roadside cottage, situated by the sea. Sitting/dining room, bathroom and one bedroom downstairs. Two attic bedrooms upstairs.

26Mar–Oct 1wkmin, 1mthmax, 1unit, 1–6persons ◎ fridge Electric Elecmetered ◻notprovided ☎ Ironing board in unit HCE in unit ⊕3pinsquare P ⌂ ♨(6m)

⊖ ♨(2m)

Min£75 Max£130pw

H **Rockmount** Auchencar
for bookings S C Gibbs, Dougarie Estate Office, Dougarie, Isle of Arran, Bute ☎Machrie(077 084)259 & 229

Small detached traditional stone house adjacent to smallholding and craft shop. On the ground floor there is a sitting/dining room, kitchen and twin bedroom with two bedrooms upstairs. ½m from coast road.

26Mar–Oct 1wkmin, 1mthmax, 1unit, 1–6persons ◎ fridge Electric Elecmetered ◻notprovided ☎(2m) HCE in unit ⊕3pinsquare P ♨(6m)

⊖ ♨(2m)

Min£75 Max£130pw

DOUGLAS
Isle of Man
Map**6** SC37

H **2 Albany Street**
for bookings Mr & Mrs G S & J P Shimmin, 3 Tennis Road, Douglas, Isle of Man ☎Douglas(0624)5469

A large end-terraced house situated at the end of a quiet surburban road. The property comprises a kitchen/diner, lounge, bathroom/WC plus five separate bedrooms (one with WC and wash basin en suite).

Allyear MWB out of season 7daysmin, 1unit, 11persons ◆ ◆ ◊ fridge Electric & Calor Gas Elecmetered ◻inclusive ☎(100yds) WM in unit SD in unit Airing cupboard in unit Iron in unit Ironing board in unit HCE in unit CTV ⊕3pinsquare ▥ ♨(100yds)

⊖ ♀(100yds) ▨(½m) ♞(½m)

Min£30 Max£60pw (Low)
Min£45 Max£200pw (High)

F Mr & Mrs C D Scully **Griffindale House** Brunswick Road, Douglas, Isle of Man
☎Douglas(0624)3203

Six flats located in a detached house with newer extension to the rear. The accommodation is of modern design and each flat has one bedroom with double bed, shower room and WC. Extra child's bed is available. Suitable for a couple or a couple with one child.

Allyear MWB out of season 1wkmin, 6units, 2–4persons ◆ ◆ ◎ fridge Electric Elecmetered ◻inclusive ☎ Airing cupboard in unit Iron on premises Ironing board on premises HCE in unit [Launderette on premises] ⊙ CTV ⊕3pinsquare P ⌂ ▥ ♨(100yds) ⚘Hard/grass

⊖ ♀(100yds) ▨(300yds) ♬(½m) ♞(½m)

Min£45 Max£120pw

F Mr & Mrs G S & J P Shimmin **3 Tennis Road** Douglas, Isle of Man
☎Douglas(0624)5469

Large flats situated in a detached house in pleasant residential area. The five flats have two bedrooms (one with double bed and one with single) plus studio bed in lounge. The house is adequately furnished and close to shops.

Allyear MWB out of season 7daysmin, 5units, 2–6persons ◆ ◆ 1◊ 4◎ fridge Electric Gas/Elecmetered ◻inclusive ☎(100yds) [WM on premises] [SD on premises] Airing cupboard in unit Iron on premises Ironing board on premises HCE on premises ⊙ CTV ⊕3pinsquare 9P ▥ ♨(100yds)

⊖ ♀(100yds) ▨(½m) ♬(½m) ♞(½m)

Min£28 Max£48pw (Low)
Min£95 Max£140pw (High)

DOWNDERRY
Cornwall
Map**2** SX25

C **CC Ref 306 ELP**
for bookings Character Cottages (Holidays) Ltd, 34 Fore Street, Sidmouth, Devon EX10 8AQ
☎Sidmouth(03955)77001

Converted coastguard house with a garden, adjacent to beach. Accommodation comprises three small bedrooms, lounge, kitchen/diner, bathroom and WC.

Allyear MWB out of season 1wkmin, 1mthmax, 1unit, 2–7persons ◆ ◎ fridge Electric Elecmetered ◻can be hired ☎ Airing cupboard in unit Iron in unit Ironing board in unit HCE in unit ⊙ CTV ⊕3pinsquare ⊕2pinround P ▥ ♨(200yds)

⊖ ♀(200yds) ▨(200yds)

Min£66 Max£100pw (Low)
Min£125 Max£195pw (High)

B **Downderry Beach Holiday Village**
for bookings John Fowler Holidays, Marlborough Road, Ilfracombe, Devon ☎Ilfracombe(0271)64135

Small site of 35 units situated close to beach. Accommodation comprises sitting/dining room with bed-settee, kitchen, three bedrooms (one double, two twin), bath/WC.

Mar–Oct MWB out of season 1wkmin, 2wksmax, 35units, 2–6persons [◇] [◆] ◎ fridge Electric Elecmetered ◻notprovided ☎ Iron in unit Ironing board in unit HCE in unit ⊙ CTV ⊕3pinsquare P ▥ ♨(100yds) Children's play area

⊖ ♀(½m) ▨(1m) ♬(1m)

Min£56 Max£194pw

Ch **Downderry Beach Holiday Village**
for bookings John Fowler Holidays, Marlborough Road, Ilfracombe, Devon ☎Ilfracombe(0271)64135

Small semi-detached or terraced chalets with kitchenette, sitting/dining room with put-u-up. Double- or twin-bedded rooms. Bathroom/WC. Bathrooms contain hipbaths only. 100yds from beach.

Mar–Oct MWB out of season 1wkmin, 2wksmax, 8units, 2–4persons [◇] [◆] [◆] ◎ fridge Electric Elecmetered ◻notprovided ☎(200yds) SD on premiises Airing cupboard in unit Iron in unit Ironing board in unit HCE in unit ⊙ CTV ♨(100yds) Children's play area

⊖ ♀(½m) ▨(1m) ♬(1m)

Min£45 Max£148pw

DREWSTEIGNTON
Devon
Map**3** SX79

C **CC Ref 506 LP A & B**
for bookings Character Cottages (Holidays) Ltd, 34 Fore Street, Sidmouth, Devon EX10 8AQ
☎Sidmouth(03955)77001

Two semi-detached thatched cottages in rural surroundings, recently restored and modernised. Accommodation comprises two double bedrooms, oak-beamed lounge, large fitted kitchen/diner and combined bathroom and WC. →

1982 prices quoted throughout gazetteer

All year MWB out of season 1wk min, 6mths max, 2units, 2-4persons ◇ ◉ fridge Electric Elecmetered ⌷ can be hired ☎(200yds) Airing cupboard in unit Iron in unit Ironing board in unit HCE in unit ⊙ TV ⊕3pinsquare ⊕2pinround P ⊞

↔ ⚑(2m)

Min£42 Max£63pw (Low)
Min£73 Max£90pw (High)

B Old Mill Bungalow
for bookings Mrs A E Watkins, Weir Mill, Drewsteignton, Exeter, Devon
☎Cheriton Bishop(064 724)223

New detached bungalow standing in grounds of old mill. Entrance hall, lounge/diner, patio and two large bedrooms. Entrance along private road signed Weir Mill.

All year MWB out of season 1wk min, 6mths max, 1unit, 2-5persons, nc12 nopets ◉ fridge Electric Elecmetered ⌷notprovided ☎(2½m) Iron in unit Ironing board in unit HCE in unit ⊙ CTV ⊕3pinsquare ⊕2pinround P ⛉ ⊞ ▦(2½m) [Fishing]

↔ ⚑(2½m)

Min£30 Max£50pw (Low)
Min£70 Max£90pw (High)

DRIMNIN
Highland *Argyll*
Map**13**NM55

C An Camas & Suidhe Cottages
for bookings R A M Coyne, Garden Cottage, Ardtornish, Morvern, Oban, Argyll PA34 5UZ
☎Morvern(096 784)234

An Camas is a 150 year old semi-detached cottage 10yds from a small beach which is sandy at low tide. Completely renovated to a high standard it comprises lounge, pine clad kitchen/dining room, one twin-bedded room and bathroom on ground-floor with three bedrooms on the first. Suidhe is a modern cottage on a hillside some 70yds from the sea. It comprises large lounge/diner/kitchen and bathroom with three bedrooms on the first-floor.

All year MWB out of season 1wk min, 5wks max, 2units, 1-8persons ◇ ◆

Drewsteignton — Duirinish

Rayburn fridge Electric & log fires Elec inclusive(except heating) ⌷notprovided ☎(½m) SD in unit Iron in unit(An camas) Ironing board in unit(An Camas) HCE in unit ⊙ ⊕3pinsquare 4P ⊞ ▦(10m) Dinghy for hire

Min£45 Max£170pw

DROITWICH
Hereford & Worcester
Map**3**SO86

C The Cottage Newland Common Road
for bookings Heart of England Cottages, Buckland, Broadway, Worcs
☎Broadway(0386)853593

Originally a pair of 18th-century cottages, this is now a large, two-storey cottage with gardens. On the ground-floor there is a lounge, dining room, kitchen, utility room and separate WC, and on the first-floor, there are two twin bedrooms, one single bedroom and a double bunk bedroom. All decorated to a high standard.

All year MWB out of season 1wk min, 3mths max, 1unit, 1-8persons ◇ ◆ ◉ fridge Electric & open fires Elecmetered ⌷can be hired (overseas visitors only) ☎(½m) WM in unit Airing cupboard in unit Iron in unit Ironing board in unit HCE in unit ⊙ ⊛ TV 3pinsquare 2P 1⛉ ▦(1½m) ↜Grass ↔ ⚑(1m)

£130pw Max

DRUMNADROCHIT
Highland *Inverness-shire*
Map**14**NH53

Ch Mrs E Mackintosh Achmony Chalets Drumnadrochit, Inverness-shire IV36UX
☎Drumnadrochit(045 62)357

Superbly situated chalets on different levels of the hillside, overlooking Drumnadrochit, S to Lewiston and Glen Urquhart, and E to Loch Ness. Comfortable and meticulously cleaned

---

and maintained by owner. Steep narrow access road.

Apr-Oct MWB out of season 1wk min, 8units, 2-6persons ◇ no pets ◉ fridge Electric Elecmetered ⌷notprovided ☎(½m) Airing cupboard in unit Iron in unit HCE in unit ⊙ CTV ⊕3pinsquare P ▦(½m) Pony trekking & bowling

↔ ⚑(½m)

Min£45 Max£70pw (Low)
Min£65 Max£135pw (High)

DRYBURGH
Borders *Roxburghshire*
Map**12**NT53

H Rose Cottage
for bookings Miss J Bristow, Thorncroft, Lilltiesleaf, Roxburghshire TD6 9JD
☎Lilliesleaf(083 57)424

Spacious detached house with garden set high above the River Tweed in the small but well known village of Dryburgh. Comprising comfortable sitting room, dining room, small kitchen and double bedroom on the ground-floor. Upstairs there is a family bedroom, single bedroom and the bathroom. The village lies on the east side of the River Tweed approx 4m by road from the A68. Parking arrangements can be made with owner who lives nearby.

All year MWB out of season 1wk min, 1unit, 1-6person [◇] ◉ fridge Electric & open fires Elecmetered ⌷can be hired ☎(100yds) Iron in unit Ironing board in unit HCE in unit CTV ⊕3pinsquare ⊞ ▦(4m)

↔ ⚑(¼m)

Min£63.25 Max£85.10pw (Low)
Min£109.25 Max£132.25pw (High)

DUIRINISH
Highland *Ross & Cromarty*
Map**13**NG73

Ch Allt Duirinish Chalets
for bookings Duirinish Lodge Holidays, Dept. AA, Duirinish, Kyle, Ross-shire IV40 8BE
☎Plockton(059 984)325

A group of six well laid out chalets situated on the edge of mature

woodlands. *All have open-plan kitchen/lounge/dining room, two twin-bedded rooms and a bunk-bedded room. Located on an unclassed road some ½m E of Duirinish.*

28Mar–Oct MWB out of season 1wk min, 5wks max, 6units, 1–6persons
◆ ♦ ◎ fridge Electric
Elec metered ⚡can be hired ☎(⅓m)
SD in unit Iron in unit Ironing board in unit HCE in unit ⊙ TV can be hired
⊕3pin square P ♨(2m)
⇔ ☎(2m)

F The Flat
for bookings Duirinish Lodge Holidays, Dept. AA, Duirinish, Kyle, Ross-shire IV40 8BE
☎Plockton(059 984)325

This property is attached to the proprietor's own house set amidst a wooded area and commanding a pleasant view. The accommodation comprises lounge/diner and kitchen on the ground floor, and two single bedrooms and a twin-bedded room on the first floor. The Lodge is on an unclass road some ½m S of Duirinish.

All year MWB out of season 1wk min, 5wks max, 1unit, 1–4persons, nc8 no pets ◎ fridge Electric
Elec inclusive ⚡can be hired ☎(⅓m)
SD in unit Iron in unit Ironing board in unit HCE in unit TV can be hired
⊕3pin square P ♨(2m)
⇔ ☎(2m)

DUISKY
Highland *Inverness-shire*
Map **14** NN07

Ch Old School Chalet
for bookings Mrs J Cox, The Old School Duisky, Fort William, Inverness-shire
☎Kinlocheil(039 783)227

A log chalet built in the grounds of owner's cottage on the south side of Loch Eil, on the A861. It has a verandah and a private garden area. Accommodation comprises two bedrooms, bathroom/WC and open plan kitchen and living room.

All year MWB out of season 1wk min, 1unit, 6persons ◆ ◎ fridge
Electric Elec metered ⚡can be hired
☎(1m) Airing cupboard in unit Iron in unit Ironing board in unit HCE in unit
⊙ ⊕3pin square P ♨(13m) Boat for hire
Min£45 Max£70pw (Low)
Min£80 Max£120pw (High)

DULNAIN BRIDGE
Highland *Moray*
Map **14** NH92

C The Cottage
for bookings Mr P I MacGregor, Skye of Curr Hotel, Skye of Curr Road, Dulnain Bridge, Grantown-on-Spey, Morayshire PH26 3PA
☎Dulnain Bridge(047 985)345

A two-floor cottage standing in hotel grounds. The ground floor comprises lounge/diner, kitchen with Aga cooker, one bedroom with three single beds, one twin-bedded room, shower room, bathroom and separate WC. On the first floor there is a very large seven-bedded room and a double bedroom with separate WC. It lies 13m NE of Aviemore and 3m SW of Grantown-on-Spey.

All year MWB out of season 1wk min, 3mths max, 1unit, 1–15persons
Aga cooker fridge Electric
Elec metered ⚡not provided
☎(100yds) Iron in unit Ironing board in unit HCE in unit ⊙ TV
⊕3pin square P ▥ ♨(100yds)
⇔ ♒(3m) ☎
Min£100 Max£200pw

C Mrs G M Whittle Easter Laggan Cottage Dulnain Bridge, Grantown-on-Spey, Moray PH26 3NT
☎Dulnain Bridge(047 985)283

The white stone cottage, which dates from 1786, is situated in a secluded spot about ⅓m from the A95, Aviemore to Grantown-on-Spey road, at the end of a private farm road 1m from the village. It stands in 5 acres of hilly land with fine views over the River Spey and across the Forest of Abernethy to the Cairngorm mountains. The accommodation consists of three bedrooms, sitting room which contains a piano and a wood stove, kitchen, cloakroom/WC and bathroom/WC. The fittings and furniture are of good standard and the décor is clean but simple.

All year 1wk min, 1unit, 2–6persons
◆ ◎ no pets ◎ fridge ♨
Elec metered ⚡not provided ☎ WM in unit SD in unit Airing cupboard in unit Iron in unit ⊙ [TV]
⊕3pin square P ♨(1m)
⇔ ☎(2m)
Min£50 MAx£100pw

DULOE
Cornwall
Map **2** SX25

C Trefanny Hill Cottages St Mary Manor
for bookings Mr & Mrs D E Slaughter, St Mary Manor, Trefanny Hill, Duloe, Liskeard, Cornwall PL14 4QF
☎Lanreath(0503)20622

Fifteen cottages which are converted from buildings of stone and slate with own gardens and lawns. All cottages are well furnished and decorated. Leave Duloe by unclassified road opposite telephone kiosk, turn left at crossroads, first right leads to St Mary Manor.

All year MWB 1wk min, 3mths max, 15units, 2–6persons [◇] ◆ ◎
fridge Electric Elec metered
⚡inclusive ☎(100yds) Iron in unit

Ironing board in unit HCE in unit ⊙
CTV ⊕3pin square ◎2pin round P
▥ ♨(1½m) ⊇ Solarium
⇔ ☎(1½m) ▨(3m) ♫(3m)
Min£78 Max£102pw (Low)
Min£237 Max£417pw (High) ·

DUNBAR
Lothian *East Lothian*
Map **12** NT67

F East Wing
for bookings Mrs Moira Marrian, Bourhouse, Dunbar, E Lothian EH42 1RE
☎Dunbar(0368)62293

Part of a 19th-century mansion house converted to a modern nicely decorated spacious flat. First-floor level comprises double bedroom, a twin bedroom, open-plan lounge/dining room (with double bed-settee), large kitchen and a bathroom. The ground floor has a generous hall area, single bedroom and a WC. 2m S of Dunbar.

All year MWB out of season 1unit, 6–8persons ◎ fridge Electric
Elec metered ⚡can be hired ☎(2m)
Iron on premises Ironing board on premises HCE in unit ⊕3pin square
2P ▥ ♨(2½m)
⇔ ♒(3m) ☎(2m)
Min£60 Max£80pw (Low)
Min£100 Max£150pw (High)

C Laundry Cottage
for bookings Mrs Moira Marrian, Bourhouse, Dunbar, E Lothian EH42 1RE
☎Dunbar(0368)62293

Converted from the former laundry, adjacent to the mansion house, this small building has been attractively re-designed to give lots of character. Living/dining room (with double bed-settee) and kitchen on split level, one twin bedroom, one with two single bunks and a bathroom.

All year MWB out of season 1unit, 4–6persons ◎ fridge Electric
Elec metered ⚡can be hired ☎(2m)
Iron on premises Ironing board on premises HCE in unit ⊕3pin square
2P ▥ ♨(2½m)
⇔ ♒(3m) ☎(2m)
Min£45 Max£60pw (Low)
Min£75 Max£120pw (High)

C Mr W M Henderson Pleasants
Dunbar, E Lothian EH42 1RE
☎Dunbar(0368)63737

Small, single-storey red-sandstone detached cottage situated at farm. Comprises lounge/diner, one twin and one double bedroom, kitchen and bathroom. Very fine views over the Firth of Forth towards Fife. →

Hunters Lodge & Cabins

BANKFOOT, PERTH
Telephone: 073 887 325

The cabins sleep up to 6 persons, the lodge sleeps 4. All units are fully equipped and linen is provided, each unit has heaters in the lounge and bedrooms, fuel by meter, TV provided. These privately owned units (6 cabins, 5 lodges) are situated in the grounds of the Hunters Lodge Hotel in this beautiful part of Scotland.

An ideal centre for touring, the area offers excellent sporting facilities and the famous golf courses of Gleneagles, Carnoustie and St Andrews are within easy reach.

The nearby village of Bankfoot will supply your shopping requirements, and if you wish to enjoy a drink or a meal there are first class facilities in the Hunters Lodge Hotel, plus a games room. The restaurant serves good Scottish fayre, bar snacks are a speciality (Winner of the BBC's Best Pub Grub Award).

The ideal location for touring, golf and fishing.

Children most welcome in the hotel.

See gazetteer entry under Bankfoot.

All year 1wk min, 1mth max, 1unit,
4–5persons no pets ◎ fridge
Electric Elec metered ☐not provided
☎(1m) WM in unit Airing cupboard in
unit Iron in unit Ironing board in unit
HCE in unit TV ⊕3pin square P ▣
⊞ ▟(3m)
↩ ♀ ▨ ♫
£57.50pw (Low)
Min£63.25 Max£74.75pw (High)

DUNDEE
Tayside *Angus*
Map**11** NO33

F *Peterson House* 25 Roseangle
for bookings Mr J G Houston,
Accommodation Office, University of
Dundee, 3 Cross Row, Dundee DD1 4HN
☎Dundee(0382)23181 ext250/440

*Purpose-built flats in quiet location
surrounded by attractive gardens, within
the University precinct. Close to the town
centre and river. There is single-
bedroomed accommodation for each
person and additional University facilities
are available at moderate prices.*

Jul–mid Sep MWB in season 20units,
2–6persons ◆ no pets ◎ fridge
🍴 Elec inclusive ☐inclusive ☎ [Iron
on premises] [Ironing board on
premises] [HCE on premises]
[Launderette on premises] ⊕ TV can
be hired ⊕3pin square 30P ⊞
▟(200yds) Sports centre
↩ ▟(2m) ♀(200yds) ▨(400yds)
♫(400yds) 🐾(400yds)

F *Wimberley House* Glamis Drive
for bookings Mr J G Houston,
Accommodation Office, University of
Dundee, 3 Cross Row, Dundee DD1 4HN
☎Dundee(0382)23181 ext250/440

*Purpose-built two-storey flats situated in
a residential area on high ground amidst
most attractive gardens overlooking Firth
of Tay. Single bedrooms (within units) are
available for each person and the
fitments are of modern design.*

Jul–mid Sep MWB in season 20units,
4–7persons ◆ no pets ◎ fridge
🍴 Elec inclusive ☐inclusive ☎ [WM
on premises] [TD on premises] Iron in
unit Ironing board in unit HCE in unit
⊕ TV can be hired ⊕3pin square
50P ⊞ ▟(½m)
↩ ▟(2m) ♀(½m) ▨(2m) ♫(2m)
🐾(2m) Sports centre

DUNNING
Tayside *Perthshire*
Map**11** NO01

H **Coachman & Gean Tree Cottages**
for bookings Mrs J R Marshall, Duncrub
Park, Dunning, Perth PH2 0QR
☎Dunning(076 484)368

*Two semi-detached and recently
modernised stone houses forming part of
the old stable block which belong to
Duncrub House. The larger house sleeps
eight in three twin and one double
bedrooms; the smaller house has one*

bedroom with double and single beds
plus bed settee in the lounge.

All year MWB out of season 1wk min,
2units, 1–8persons ◆ ◆
◎ & solid fuel fridge Electric & open
fires Elec inclusive ☐inclusive ☎
WM in unit SD in unit TD in larger unit
only Airing cupboard in larger unit only
Iron in unit Ironing board in unit HCE in
unit ⊕ CTV ⊕3pin square 6P
▟(½m)
↩ ▟(½m) ♀(½m)
Min£69 Max£207pw

H **Thorntree Villa**
for bookings Mrs D M Howie, Millhouse,
Dunning, Perthshire
☎Dunning(076 484)233

*A detached, completely renovated, 18th-
century stone villa, converted from the
former village slaughterhouse situated in
the heart of farming land. The ground
floor comprises kitchen with dining area,
lounge and one double bedroom. The
first floor comprises one family bedroom
and three single beds and two bunks,
one twin-bedded room and a bathroom.
The house is pleasantly furnished and
decorated and to the side is a pebbled
drive and a spacious garage.*

All year MWN out of season 1wk min,
1unit, 1–8persons ◆ ◆ ◎
🍴 Elec metered ☐can be hired ☎
WM in unit SD in unit Airing cupboard
in unit Iron in unit Ironing board in unit
HCE in unit ⊕ CTV ⊕3pin square
2P 1▣ ⊞ ▟(100yds)
↩ ▟(200yds) ♀(100yds)

C **Townhead Cottage**
for bookings Mrs D M Howie, Millhouse,
Dunning, Perthshire
☎Dunning(076 484)233

*Former dairyman's cottage situated in a
quiet cul-de sac within a pleasant
country village amidst farmland.
Accommodation comprises two double
bedrooms, one with additional single
bed, lounge/diner, kitchen and
bathroom/WC.*

All year MWB out of season 1wk min,
1unit, 1–5persons ◆ ◆ ◎ fridge
Electric Elec metered ☐can be hired
☎ WM in unit SD in unit Airing
cupboard in unit Iron in unit Ironing
board in unit HCE in unit ⊕ TV
⊕3pin square 2P ⊞ ▟(300yds)
↩ ▟(400yds) ♀(300yds)

DUNNINGTON
North Yorkshire
Map**8** SE65

C **Woodlea** Intake Lane
for bookings Mrs K M Sykes, Lime Field
Farm, Scoreby, Gate Helmsley, York
YO4 1NR
☎York(0904)489224

*Semi-detached cottage with views of
surrounding countryside.*

*Accommodation comprises a family
room with a double and a single bed,
double-bedded room and single room.
Ground-floor bathroom, separate WC,
kitchen and pantry. ½m from village and
shops.*

All year MWB out of season 1wk min,
1mth max, 1unit, 1–6persons ◆ ◆
no pets ◎ fridge Electric
Elec metered ☐inclusive ☎(½m)
Airing cupboard in unit Iron in unit
Ironing board in unit HCE in unit TV
⊕3pin square P ⊞ ▟(½m)
↩ ▟(3m) ♀(½m)
Min£30 Max£40pw (Low)
Min£60 Max£85pw (High)

DUNPHAIL
Grampian *Moray*
Map**14** NJ04

H **Relugas Mill,** Logie
for bookings Moray Estate Development
Company, Estate Office, Forres, Moray
IV36 0ET
☎Forres(0309)72213

*Detached two-storey house, recently
modernised, in beautiful countryside.
Accommodation comprises comfortable
lounge, large kitchen/dining area and
twin-bedded room, and separate WC on
ground-floor. On the first-floor there are
two double bedrooms and one single
bedroom, bathroom and WC. All fittings
and furnishings to a high standard. 8m S
of Forres on B9007 2m from A940.*

Apr-Oct MWB out of season 1wk min,
1unit, 1–7persons 🍴 ◢ fridge 🍴
Gas/Elec inclusive ☐not provided ☎
Iron in unit HCE in unit ⊕ TV
⊕3pin square P ▟(2m) Burn fishing
↩ ♀(3m)
Min£103.50 Max£115pw (Low)
£126.50pw (High)

DUNS TEW
Oxfordshire
Map**4** SP42

C Mr R F Moffatt **Daisy Hill Farm** Duns
Tew, Oxford, Oxfordshire
☎Steeple Aston(0869)40293

*Eight converted cottage-type units set in
a picturesque Cotswold village. The
accommodation varies, with one having
one bedroom, five having two bedrooms
and two having three bedrooms. All have
open-plan kitchen with dining area,
sitting room and bathroom with WC.
Modern furniture and equipment.*

All year MWB out of season
3nights min, 4wks max, 8units,
2–6persons ◆ ◆ no pets ◎
fridge 🍴 Electric Elec inclusive
☐inclusive ☎(10yds) Airing cupboard
in unit Iron on premises Ironing board
on premises HCE in unit Launderette
on premises ⊕ CTV ⊕3pin square
10P ⊞ ▭ →

1982 prices quoted throughout
gazetteer

93

⊖ ♀

Min£80 Max£150pw (Low)
Min£140 Max£240pw (High)

DUNSYRE
Strathclyde *Lanarkshire*
Map**11** NT14

C **Mount View Cottage**
for bookings Lee & Carnwath Estates, Estate Office, Carnwath, Lanark ML11 8JY
☎Carnwath(055 584)273

Small, single-storey, stone cottage built in 1820 and modernised in 1974, it has its own pleasant garden offering superb views of Black Mount and Medwin Valley. Accommodation comprises lounge with open log-fire (logs provided), modern kitchen/dinette, two twin-bedded rooms and a bathroom/WC.

All year 1wk min, 1mth max, 1unit, 2–4persons [◈ ◆] ◉ fridge Electric & log fires Elec inclusive ◫not provided ☎(50yds) Airing cupboard in unit Iron in unit Ironing board in unit HCE in unit ⊙ ✪3pin square P ⛪(3m) Fishing

Min£70pw (Low)
Min£150pw (High)

C **Westhall Cottage**
for bookings Lee & Carnwath Estates, Estate Office, Carnwath, Lanark ML11 8JY
☎Carnwath(055 584)273 & Dolphinton(096 88)254

Single-storey cottage built in 1830, recently extended and modernised. Three bedrooms (two double and one twin-bedded), charming sitting room with adjoining patio, modern kitchen/diner and bathroom. On unclassified road from Newbigging to Dunsyre.

All year 1wk min, 1mth max, 1unit, 1–6persons [◈] [◆] ◉ fridge Electric Elec inclusive ◫can be hired Airing cupboard in unit Iron in unit Ironing board in unit HCE in unit ⊙ TV ✪3pin square 3P ⛪(5m)

Min£100pw (Low)
Min£170pw (High)

DUNVEGAN Isle of Skye
Highland *Inverness-shire*
Map**13** NG24

F **Roskhill Barn Flats**
for bookings Mrs I E Beevers, Roskhill Guest House, Roskhill, Dunvegan, Isle of Skye IV55 8ZD
☎Dunvegan(047 022)317

Two self-contained flats in a recently converted barn. Each has lounge/dining room/kitchen and bathroom. Ground-floor flat has one double bedroom with a single folding bed in lounge. First-floor flat has two double bedrooms plus a double bed-settee in lounge.

1982 prices quoted throughout gazetteer

Mar-Dec 1wk min, 5wks max, 2units, 2–6persons no pets ◉ fridge Electric Elec metered ◫inclusive ☎(350yds) Airing cupboard in unit Iron in unit Ironing board in unit HCE in unit TV ✪3pin square P ⛪(2½m)

⊖ ♀(2½m) ▣(2½m)

DUNWICH
Suffolk
Map**5** TM47

F Mrs M Stone ***Grey Friars Flat*** Grey Friars, Dunwich, Saxmundham, Suffolk
☎Westleton(072 873)327

Self-contained luxury flat, adjoining the main house in peaceful location. Accommodation includes one twin-bedded room, separate lounge/diner which gives uninterrupted views of landscaped garden and sea. Convertible settee/armchairs can sleep two extra. Access off Dunwich road from Westleton just past turning signed Minsmere.

All year MWB out of season 3days min, 4wks max, 1unit, 1–4persons, nc5 no pets ◉ fridge ⚿ Elec metered ◫inclusive ☎(¼m) Airing cupboard in unit Iron in unit Ironing board in unit HCE in unit ⊙ CTV ✪3pin square P ⌂ ⛪(1½m)

⊖ ♀(¼m)

EARSARY Isle of Barra,
Western Isles *Inverness-shire*
Map**13** NL79

C **Harbour Cottage** Allt
for bookings Dr C Bartlett, 1 The Green, Frimley Green, Camberley, Surrey
☎Deepcut(02516)5123

A two-storey cottage close to the sea and to a small creek which is used as a harbour for small boats. Backed by hill and moorland, the cottage offers open-plan living room on ground-floor with three bedrooms, small lounge and bathroom/WC on first-floor. Furnishings are adequate. Car park beside the house.

All year 1wk min, 5wks max, 1unit, 1–10persons ◈ ◊ fridge Electric, gas & open fires Gas/Elec inclusive ◫can be hired ☎(¼m) WM Iron Ironing board HCE ✪3pin square ⛪(4m)

⊖ ♀(1½m)

Min£45 Max£74pw (Low)
Min£95 Max£110pw (High)

C **South Bank Cottage** Allt
for bookings Dr C Bartlett, 1 The Green, Frimley Green, Camberley, Surrey
☎Deepcut(02516)5123

Small renovated croft sited in a quiet pleasant spot on the E of the island, with views over sandy inlets towards Skye and the mainland. Accommodation comprises family room, bathroom/WC and kitchen/living room with convertible settee. Adequately furnished and compact.

All year 1wk min, 5wks max, 1unit, 1–5persons ◈ ◉ fridge Electric & open fires Elec inclusive ◫can be hired ☎(¼m) HCE ✪3pin square ⛪(4m)

⊖ ♀(1½m)

Min£32 Max£48pw (Low)
Min£65 Max£80pw (High)

EASDALE
Strathclyde *Argyll*
Map**10** NM71

Ch **The Chalet**
for bookings Mrs B Nathan, The Old Inn, Easdale, Oban, Argyll
☎Balvicar(085 23)209

This cedar-wood chalet stands in a grassed area at the back of the owner's house on the island of Seil (access to mainland by bridge). Location is 15¾m S of Oban in a picturesque village nestling under a rock face. Ferry service is available to the Easdale island. Accommodation comprises two bedrooms, shower and WC and open plan living/dining/kitchen area. It is adequately furnished and has a small private garden.

26Mar-7Oct 1wk min, 1mth max, 1unit, 1–4person ◈ no pets ◉ fridge Electric Elec metered ◫can be hired ☎(200yds) Airing cupboard in unit Iron on premises Ironing board on premises HCE in unit ⊙ ✪3pin square P ▥ ⛪(200yds)

⊖ ♀(¼m)

Min£35 Max£75pw

C **The Cottage**
for bookings Mrs B Nathan, The Old Inn, Easdale, Oban, Argyll
☎Balvicar(085 23)209

A two-storey cottage attached to the owner's house, in the same picturesque location as 'The Chalet'. An ideal location for sea and countryside. Well furnished accommodation comprises living room, modern kitchen and bathroom on the ground-floor and two bedrooms on the first-floor.

26Mar-7Oct 1wk min, 1mth max, 1unit, 1–6persons ◈ no pets ◉ fridge Electric Elec metered ◫can be hired ☎(200yds) Airing cupboard in unit Iron on premises Ironing board on premises HCE in unit ⊙ ✪3pin square P ▥ ⛪(200yds)

⊖ ♀(¼m)

Min£40 Max£80pw

EASTBOURNE
East Sussex
Map**5** TV69

C **1 Barden Road**
for bookings Mrs H Pulleng, 6 Barden Road, Eastbourne, E Sussex BN22 7ED
☎Eastbourne(0323)763922

Small modernised end of terrace town cottage, with two bedrooms and comfortable lounge.

All year MWB out of season 1wk min, 28 days max, 1 unit, 1–4 persons, nc6 🔲 fridge 🍴 Elec metered 🔲inclusive ☎(300yds) Airing cupboard in unit Iron in unit Ironing board in unit HCE in unit [Launderette within 300yds] ⊖ TV ⊕3pin square 🔲 ♨(100yds)

⇔ 🚿(3m) 🛒(100yds) 🅿(200yds) 🎵(200yds) 🐕(300yds)

Min £40 Max £65pw (Low)
Min £70 Max £110pw (High)

F Beach House 34 Beach Road
for bookings Mrs K E Jones, The Spinney, Downs View Lane, East Dean, Eastbourne, Sussex BN20 0DS
☎East Dean(032 15)3230

A semi-detached late 19th-century fisherman's house skilfully converted into two flats, each comprising two bedrooms, lounge, kitchen and bathroom/WC. Set in quiet suburban area of Eastbourne. 500yds from eastern end of seafront.

All year MWB out of season 8 mths max, 2 units, 1–5 persons 🔲 ◆ no pets ⊚ fridge Electric Elec metered 🔲inclusive ☎(300yds) Airing cupboard in unit Iron on premises Ironing board on premises HCE in unit ⊖ ⊛ TV ⊕3pin square P [🏠] 🔲 ♨(50yds) 〰Hard ♿

⇔ 🛒(½m) 🅿(½m) 🎵(1m) 🐕(1m)

Min £40 Max £60pw (Low)
Min £50 Max £135pw (HIgh)

F Mr R H Brooker, Holiday Flats 3 Jevington Gardens, Eastbourne, East Sussex BN21 4HR
☎Eastbourne(0323)29998

Part of a terraced house, situated in quiet residential part of town 300yds from Winter Gardens. Two of the three flats have one bedroom (four single beds) plus a large lounge with two folding beds. The other flat is small with just two folding beds in the lounge. All have modern furnishings, fittings and fitted carpets. Large bathroom/WC.

All year MWB out of season 1wk min, 6 mths max, 3 units, 1–6 persons 🔲 ◆ no pets ⊚ fridge 🍴 Elec metered 🔲inclusive ☎(10yds) Iron on premises Ironing board on premises HCE in unit ⊖ ⊛ CTV ⊕3pin square 🔲 ♨(200yds)

⇔ 🛒(250yds) 🅿(300yds) 🎵(300yds) 🐕(1m)

Min £27 Max £45pw (Low)
Min £55 Max £135pw (High)

F 1 Jevington Gardens
for bookings Mr & Mrs J N Weaver, Meads Holiday Flats, 6 Jevington Gardens, Eastbourne, East Sussex BN21 4HR
☎Eastbourne(0323)27895

Detached house skilfully converted into four self-contained flats. Decorated and furnished to a high standard. Ideally situated in one of the best parts of Eastbourne.

Apr–Nov MWB out of season 1wk min, 4 wks max, 4 units, 2–4 persons [◊ ◆] ⊚ fridge 🍴(inclusive) Elec metered 🔲can be hired ☎ Iron on premises Ironing board on premises HCE on premises ⊖ ⊛ TV ⊕3pin square 🔲 ♨(200yds)

⇔ 🚿(2m) 🛒(200yds) 🅿(200yds) 🎵(½m) 🐕(600yds)

Min £52.90 Max £64.40pw (Low)
Min £101.20 Max £143.75pw (High)

F 6 & 8 Jevington Gardens
for bookings Mr & Mrs J N Weaver, Meads Holiday Flats, 6 Jevington Gardens, Eastbourne, East Sussex BN21 4HR
☎Eastbourne(0323)27895

Five-storey Edwardian building which has been renovated and converted into fourteen modern flats. Situated in quiet residential part of Eastbourne, 400yds from sea and Devonshire Park. Units comprise kitchenette, bathroom/WC or shower/WC, one bedroom and lounge with one or two fold-away beds.

All year MWB out of season 1wk min, 1mth max, 14 units, 1–4 persons [◊ ◆] ⊚ fridge Electric Elec metered 🔲can be hired ☎ Iron on premises Ironing board on premises HCE on premises ⊖ ⊛ TV ⊕3pin square 🔲 ♨(100yds)

⇔ 🚿(1m) 🛒(200yds) 🅿(½m) 🎵(½m) 🐕(1m)

Min £41.40 Max £57.50pw (Low)
Min £80.50 Max £161pw (High)

F Mowbray Court Lascelles Terrace, Eastbourne, East Sussex BN21 4DJ
☎Eastbourne(0323)642693

Eight self-contained flats; each having a twin-bedded room, with a third bed in the lounge; combined bathroom and WC. One flat sleeps four including two beds in lounge; shower and WC.

Mar–Oct 1wk min, 4 wks max, 8 units, 1–4 persons, nc7 no pets ⊚ fridge Electric Elec metered 🔲can be hired ☎ Airing cupboard in unit Iron on premises Ironing board on premises HCE on premises ⊖ ⊛ CTV ⊕3pin square 🔲 ♨(100yds)

⇔ 🛒 🅿 🎵 🐕

Min £38.26 Max £61.23pw (Low)
Min £101.03 Max £114.80pw (High)

F Netherby Holiday Flats 17 Cambridge Road, Royal Parade
for bookings Mrs M J McHugh, Field Place, Huggetts Lane, Willingdon, Eastbourne, East Sussex BN22 0LH
☎Eastbourne(0323)52142

An end terraced house, 100yds from sea, converted into six flats. All have one bedroom (double or twin beds) plus fold-away beds in the lounge. Top two flats sleep three, remainder four. Two flats have separate kitchen, remainder have combined lounge/diner/kitchenette. Modern equipped kitchen. Five flats have showers, the other has a bath.

All year MWB out of season 6 mths max, 6 units, 1–4 persons ◊ ⊚ fridge Electric Elec metered 🔲can be hired ☎(10yds) HCE on premises [Launderette within 300yds] ⊖ ⊛ TV ⊕3pin square P 🏠 🔲 ♨(300yds) ♿

⇔ 🛒(30yds) 🅿(1m) 🎵(½m) 🐕(½m)

Min £30 Max £45pw (Low)
Min £46 Max £112pw (High)

F Mr & Mrs F Maull Travancore Wilmington Gardens, Eastbourne, East Sussex
☎Eastbourne(0323)23770

Six-storeyed building, converted into self-catering units. Resident proprietors. Situated just off seafront, opposite Congress Theatre, shop on premises others 100yds. Units serviced by passenger lift. All have separate kitchen/diner, bathroom, WC, one double bedroom and three single beds in lounge. Modern, clean and well appointed. Only six of the 21 units meet our requirements.

All year MWB out of season 2 days min, 6 units, 1–5 persons, nc3 ◊ ⊚ fridge Electric Elec metered (power points only) 🔲inclusive ☎ Iron on premises Ironing board on premises HCE in unit ⊖ ⊛ CTV ⊕3pin square P 🏠 🔲 ♨(100yds) 🔲

⇔ 🛒(100yds) 🅿(200yds) 🎵(½m) 🐕(1½m)

Min £46 Max £92pw (Low)
Max £155.25pw (High)

EAST DEAN
East Sussex
Map 5 TV59

B Birlingdean 81 Micheldene Road
for bookings Miss P G Elkins, 26 Lymington Court, All Saints Road, Sutton, Surrey SM1 3DE
☎01-644 7271

Lying ⅓m N of East Dean village off A259, this recently built three-bedroomed detached chalet-bungalow stands in a quiet residential ground on elevated ground with extensive views of the downs and sea (1½m). The accommodation consists of three double bedrooms (one on ground floor with cloak room), lounge/dining room, kitchen, bathroom, hall and garage.

All year MWB out of season 1wk min, 5 mths max, 1 unit, 1–6 persons ◊ ◆ ⊚ fridge 🍴 Elec metered 🔲can be hired ☎(½m) SD in unit Airing cupboard in unit Iron in unit Ironing board in unit HCE in unit ⊖ ⊛ TV →

⊕3pin square P 🔥 ♨(¾m)

↤ ☎(1m) 📺(3m) ♫(3m) 🛏(3m)

Min£40 Max£60pw (Low)
Min£85 Max£180pw (High)

EAST PORTLEMOUTH
Devon
Map**3** SX73

F Mr L Richards **Gara Rock Hotel** East
Portlemouth, Salcombe, Devon
☎Salcombe(054 884)2342

*Nineteen self contained flats within this
hotel complex which was once a
coastguard station and consequently
affords fine views. Thirteen flats are
purpose built and stand in the hotel
grounds while six form part of the main
hotel building.*

All year MWB out of season 1wk min,
3mths max, 19units, 2–6persons ◇
◇ ◆ ◉ fridge Electric
Elec metered ⬛inclusive ☎(20yds)
WM on premises TD on premises Iron
on premises Ironing board on
premises HCE in unit ⊖ CTV
⊕3pin square 100P 📺 ♨(2m)
Games room

↤ ☎(20yds) ♫(20yds)

Min£50.50 Max£115pw (Low)
Min£184 Max£258.75pw (High)

EAST PRESTON
West Sussex
Map **4** TQ00

C **Kingston Corner Cottage**
for bookings Kingston Corner, Kingston
Gorse, East Preston, W Sussex
☎Rustington(09062)2723

*Modern detached cottage on quiet,
private residential estate within easy
reach of the beach. Accommodation
comprises one double and one twin-
bedded room, both en suite, one situated
on ground floor, the other on first floor, a
comfortably furnished lounge/diner and
kitchen. 2m E of East Preston on
unclassified road.*

Mar–Oct 1wk min, 1unit, 1–4persons,
nc7 no pets ♦ fridge ♨
Gas inclusive Elec metered
⬛inclusive ☎(½m) Airing cupboard in
unit Iron in unit Ironing board in unit
HCE in unit ⊖ ◉ TV ⊕3pin square
2P 1🔥 📺 ♨(1m)

↤ 🛏(1½m) ☎(1m) 📺(3m) ♫(3m)

Min£100 Max£110pw (Low)
Min£130pw (High)

EASTRY
Kent
Map**5** TR35

C **1 & 2 Tickenhurst Cottages**
for bookings The Cottage Secretary,
Knowlton Estate Office, Knowlton Court,
Wingham, Canterbury, Kent CT3 1PT
☎Sandwich(0304)617344

*A pair of cottages set in rural
surroundings. One has three bedrooms,
large sitting room/dining room, kitchen*

East Dean
—
Edinburgh

*and two bathrooms. The other has two
bedrooms, sitting room, dining room,
kitchen and bathroom.*

All year MWB out of season 1wk min,
8mths max, 2units, 1–6persons [◇]
◇ ◆ ◉ fridge ♨ Electric
Elec metered ⬛inclusive ☎(1m)
Airing cupboard in unit Iron in unit
Ironing board in unit HCE in unit ⊖
TV ⊕3pin square P 📺 ♨(1m)

↤ ☎(1m)

Min£42.50 Max£50pw (Low)
Min£80 Max£125pw (High)

EAST WORLINGTON
Devon
Map**3** SS71

C **Tweenmoors**
for bookings Mr & Mrs Hosegood,
Yeatheridge farm, East Worlington,
Crediton, Devon
☎Tiverton(0884)860330

*An attractive white-stone cottage with
small rear garden; accommodation
comprises kitchen, lounge, dining room,
shower room/WC, all on ground floor and
one twin-bedded room, one double-
bedded and one double with bunk beds
and bathroom/WC on first floor. Well
furnished and in good decorative order.*

All year MWB out of season 1wk min,
3mths max, 1unit, 1–8persons ◆
no pets ◉ fridge ♨ Elec metered
⬛not provided ☎(1m) Airing
cupboard in unit Iron in unit Ironing
board in unit HCE in unit ⊖ CTV
⊕3pin round P 1🔥 ♨(1m)

↤ ☎(1½m)

ECKINGTON
Hereford & Worcester
Map**3** SO94

C **Japonica & Juniper Cottages**
for bookings Mrs L Leyland, The Manor
House, Manor Road, Eckington,
Pershore, Worcs
☎Evesham(0386)750315

*A Victorian stable block converted into
two cottages each providing
accommodation of a very high standard.
Each comprises two bedrooms,
Japonica's are on the 1st floor and
Junipers on the ground floor. There is a
large lounge with open fire (logs
supplied), kitchen/diner and
bathroom/WC.*

All year MWB 2days min, 6mths max,
2units, 1–5persons [◇ ◇] ◉
fridge ♨ & Open fires Elec inclusive
⬛inclusive ☎ Airing cupboard in unit
Iron in unit HCE in unit [Launderette on
premises] ⊖ CTV ⊕3pin square
4P 📺 ♨(½m) ↦Hard ♂ Croquet
lawn, fishing & sailing

↤ ☎(½m)

Min£95 Max£140pw (Low)
Min£155 Max£195pw (High)

EDALE
Derbyshire
Map**7** SK18

F **Flat 3** Edale Mill
for bookings The Landmark Trust,
Shottesbrooke, Maidenhead, Berkshire
☎Littlewick Green(062 882)3431

*A self-contained flat on the second-floor
of a renovated 18th-century cotton mill.
Accommodation comprises two
bedrooms with twin beds and two folding
beds. Situated in the very pleasant village
of Edale, it features original oak beams.*

All year MWB out of season 1day min,
3wks max, 1unit, 2–6persons ◉
fridge ♨ Elec inclusive
⬛not provided ☎(100yds) Airing
cupboard in unit Iron in unit Ironing
board in unit HCE in unit ⊖
⊕3pin square P 📺 ♨100yds)

↤ ☎(1m)

Max£81pw (Low)
Max£167pw (High)

EDERN
Gwynedd
Map**6** SH23

B Mr & Mrs G Owen **Glanrhyd Holiday
Bungalows** Edern, Pwllheli, Gwynedd
☎Nefyn(0758)720288

*Three groups of converted RAF
Mess/living quarters which vary from two
to four bedded units; the larger ones
offering a separate dining room, the
smaller a lounge/diner. Both have large
kitchen and bathroom/WC. From Pwllheli
take A497 to Nefyn, follow road to Morfa
Nefyn turning left on to B4417. In Morfa
turn left, approx 1m to bungalow.*

6Mar–Oct MWB out of season 1wk min,
6wks max, 17units, 2–9persons [◇]
[◆] ◉ fridge Electric Elec metered
⬛not provided ☎(1m) [Airing
cupboard in unit] Iron in unit Ironing
board in unit ⊖ TV ⊕3pin square
2P 📺 ♨(1m) Bicycles for hire

↤ 🛏(2m) ☎(1m) 📺(2m) ♫(2m)

EDINBURGH
Lothian *Midlothian*
Map**11** NT27

F Controller of Catering & Residences
Heriot-Watt University Riccarton,
Currie, Edinburgh EH14 4AS
☎031–449 5111 ext2178

*Ideal self-contained flatlets in three
modern blocks on the University
Campus. Each flat has a
lounge/kitchenette, with twin- and single-
bedded rooms, shower and WC. Full
campus amenities available.*

Jul–24Sep 1wk min, 3mths max, 36units,
3–6persons ◉ fridge Elec inclusive
⬛inclusive ☎ Iron in unit Ironing
board in unit HCE in unit [Launderette
on premises] ⊖ ⊕3pin square P ♨
↦Hard Sports complex

↤

Min£89.70 Max£138pw

96

F Mr P Glazik **Keyplan** 21–31 Causewayside, Edinburgh EH9 1QR ☎031–667 7500

Nine units, part of a complex of 27 apartments in a newly renovated development of self-catering flats located in a four-storey Victorian tenement block. Each comprises lounge, kitchen, bathroom, and double or single beds. Daily servicing of the flats is included in the rental.

All year MWB 1 day min, 9 units, 1–3 persons [◊] ◆ ◆ ⚲ fridge ⁍ Gas/Elec inclusive ⬜inclusive ☎ Airing cupboard in unit Iron on premises Ironing board on premises [Launderette within 300 yds] ⊙ CTV ⊕3 pin square 10P ♨(100 yds) ⊖ ♪ (1m) ♀(100 yds) ▨(½m) ♫(½m) ▉(½m)

Min£44 Max£180pw

F Vacation Accommodation (Box AA) **Pollock Halls of Residence** 18 Holyrood Park Road, Edinburgh, Midlothian EH16 5AY ☎031–667 1971

Student flats within Halls of Residence and Conference Centre, set in extensive grounds on S side of city. Each is self-contained and comprises two twin bedrooms with wash hand basins, a third bedroom with single bed, used as a dining room, bathroom, WC and small kitchen with two ring cooker.

Edinburgh
—
Ellary

---

2 Jul–24 Sep 1 wk min, 6 units, 1–5 persons ⊛ fridge Electric Elec inclusive ⬜inclusive ☎(100 yds) [WM on premises] [TD on premises] Iron on premises Ironing board on premises HCE in unit ⊕3 pin square ⊕3 pin round 12P ▦ ♨(½m) Squash courts ⊖ ♪(½m) ♀(½m) ▨(1m) ♫(1m) ▉(1m)

Min£46 Max£132pw

ELGIN
Grampian *Moray*
Map **15** NJ26

Ch Lossie Holiday Homes Palmers Cross *for bookings* Miss J Bristow, Thorncroft, Lilliesleaf, Roxburghshire ☎Lilliesleaf(08357)424

Self-contained modern chalets standing in grounds of Georgian country house which has a fine setting by the banks of the River Lossie on the outskirts of Elgin. Accommodation ranges from one to three bedrooms, depending on type of unit, with open-plan living/dining/kitchen area. Access to palmers Cross is via B9010 road to Dallas.

Apr–Sep 1 wk min, 3 wks max, 10 units, 4–8 persons ◊ ⊛ fridge Electric Elec metered ⬜inclusive ☎(150 yds) Airing cupboard in unit HCE ⊙ CTV ⊕3 pin square P ▦ ♨(1m) ⊖ ♪₈(1m) ♀(2m) ▨(1m) ♫(1m) ▉(1m)

Min£86.25 Max£129.95pw (Low)
Min£97.75 Max£184pw (High)

ELLARY
Strathclyde *Argyll*
Map **10** NR77

C Holiday Homes at Ellary *for bookings* The Booking Office, Castle Sween Bay (Holidays) Ltd, Ellary, Lochgilphead, Argyll PA31 8PA ☎Ormsary(088 03)232 or 209

Four traditional cottages of varying size situated on the shores of Loch Caolisport. They range from a spacious three bedrooms, sitting room, dining room plus convertible settee, to a smaller two-bedroomed cottage.

All year MWB out of season 1 wk min, 4 units, 1–8 persons [◊] ⊛ fridge Electric Elec metered ⬜not provided ☎(3m) HCE in unit TV ⊕3 pin square ⊕3 pin round P ▦ ♨(11m)

Min£73 Max£94pw (Low)
Min£145 Max£187pw (High)

> 1982 prices quoted throughout gazetteer

F   Holiday Homes at Ellary

for bookings The Booking Office, Castle Sween Bay (Holidays) Ltd, Ellary, Lochgilphead, Argyll PA31 8PA
☎Ormsary(088 03)232 or 209

Two spacious flats located within Ellary House each comprising one double and two twin-bedded rooms, lounge/dining room, small kitchen and bathroom/WC. Situated in elevated position with magnificent views.

All year   MWB out of season   1wk min, 2units, 1–7persons   ◈   ⌖ fridge   Electric & coal fires   Elec metered   ⌑not provided   ☎(3m)   HCE in unit   TV   ⊕3pin square   P   ▥   ♨(11m)

Min£60 Max£85pw (Low)
Min£120 Max£174pw (High)

C   Holiday Homes at Ellary

for bookings The Booking Office, Castle Sween Bay (Holiday) Ltd, Ellary, Lochgilphead, Argyll PA31 8PA
☎Ormsary(088 03)232 or 209

Modernised farm cottage with out-buildings, close to sheltered private beach. Comprises lounge with fireplace, open wooden staircase leading to two bedrooms. The bathroom has older fittings with modern décor.

All year   MWB out of season   1wk min, 1unit, 1–6persons   ◈   ⌖ fridge   Electric & coal fires   Elec metered   ⌑not provided   ☎(3m)   HCE in unit   TV   ⊕3pin square   P   2▥   ▥   ♨(11m)

Min£60 Max£85pw (Low)
Min£120 Max£174pw (High)

ELRIG
Dumfries & Galloway *Wigtownshire*
Map **10** NX34

H   The Anchorage

for bookings Mr J H Korner, House of Elrig, Port William, Wigtownshire DG8 9RF
☎Port William(098 87)242

Detached two-storey traditional stone house in small rural hamlet. On the ground-floor there is a small sitting room, dining room, double bedroom, bathroom and modern kitchen. Upstairs are three twin-bedded rooms and additional bathroom.
A neat homely house. Elrig is located in the heart of pleasant farming countryside but still only 10 minutes' drive from the sea.

Apr-Nov   MWB out of season   1wk min, 1unit, 1–8persons   ◈   ⌖ fridge   ▥ & open fire   Elec metered   ⌑not provided   ▥   WM in unit   Iron in unit   Ironing board in unit   HCE in unit   ⊕   CTV   ⊕3pin square   P   ▥   ♨(3m)   ✎Hard   Fly-fishing

⊛   ♨(3m)

Min£80 Max£110pw (Low)
Min£130pw (High)

C   Mr J H G Korner **Lochside of Elrig**
Port William, Wigtownshire DG8 9RF
☎Port William(098 87)242

Restored gamekeeper's cottage, situated almost on the edge of Loch Elrig only 2m from the sea. One double, one twin and one single bedroom, two bathrooms (one with shower), lounge, kitchen and dining room. Boathouse.

All year   MWB out of season   1unit, 1–5persons   [◇]   ◈   ⌖ fridge   ▥ & open fire   Elec metered   ⌑not provided   ☎(1m)   WM in unit   Iron on premises   Ironing board on premises   HCE on premises   ⊕   CTV   ⊕3pin square   6P   1▥   ▥   ♨(4m)   ✎Hard

Min£75 Max£105pw (Low)
£125pw (High)

ELSDON
Tyne & Wear
Map **12** NY99

C   Bilsmoor Foot Farm

for bookings Mrs M Carruthers, Dunns Farm, Elsdon, Newcastle upon Tyne, NE19 1EL
☎Rothbury(0669)40219

A two-storey stone-built farm cottage with one twin bedroom, two double bedrooms, bathroom/WC on first-floor. On ground-floor a lounge, kitchen/diner. Situated in the Coquet Valley on the B6341 Rothbury-Otterburn road.

All year   MWB out of season   3nights min, 3mths max, 1unit, 1–6persons   ◈   ⌖ fridge   Elec metered   ⌑can be hired   ☎(1m)   Airing cupboard in unit   Iron in unit   HCE in unit   HCE in unit   ⊕   TV   ⊕3pin square   P   ♨(4m)   Fishing

⊛   ♨(3m)

Min£30 Max£40pw (Low)
Min£50 Max£100pw (High)

EPPERSTONE
Nottinghamshire
Map **8** SK64

C   The Cottage

for bookings Mrs S Santos, Eastwood Farm, Hagg Lane, Epperstone, Notts NG14 6AX
☎Lowdham(060 745)2218 due to change to Nottingham(0602)663018

Two-storey 150year-old cottage adjoining proprietors' own farmhouse. Accommodation comprises one double and one single-bedded room on first-floor, a lounge/dining room on ground-floor, small, but adequately-equipped kitchen with larder, and a combined bathroom/WC with wash hand basin. Simple but clean décor and furnishings. Situated 10m NE of Nottingham. Leave A6097 (Doncaster/Leicester) opp a garage and head for Epperstone village. Turn left at T junc and right into Hagg Lane. Eastwood Farm is ⅓m on the left hand side.

All year   1wk min, 1unit, 3–4persons   ◇   ◈   ◆   ⦿ fridge   ▥ & electric   Elec metered   ⌑can be hired   ☎(⅓m)   Iron in unit   Ironing board in unit   HCE in unit   ⊕   TV   ⊕3pin round   P   ▥   ♨(1m)

⊛   ♨(1m)

Min£45 Max£48pw (Low)
Min£58 Max£68pw (High)

F   The Mews

for bookings Mrs S Santos, Eastwood Farm, Hagg Lane, Epperstone, Notts NG14 6AX
☎Lowdham(060 745)2218 due to change to Nottingham(0602)663018

First-floor accommodation over garage and outbuildings comprising one double and one twin-bedded room, small lounge/dining room, small kitchen providing basic essentials, combined bathroom/WC and wash hand basin.

All year   1wk min, 1unit, 5persons   ◇   ◈   ◆   ⦿ fridge   ▥ & open fires   Elec metered   ⌑can be hired   ☎(⅓m)   Airing cupboard in unit   Iron in unit   Ironing board in unit   HCE in unit   ⊕   TV   ⊕3pin square   P   ▥   ♨(1m)

⊛   ♨(1m)

Min£45 Max£48pw (Low)
Min£58 Max£68pw (High)

ERMINGTON
Devon
Map **2** SX65

C   CC Ref 412 LP

for bookings Character Cottages (Holidays) Ltd, 34 Fore Street, Sidmouth, Devon EX10 8AQ
☎Sidmouth(039 55)77001

16th-century detached cottage with large garden in rural setting. Accommodation consists of large kitchen, small dining room, lounge, ground-floor bathroom, separate WC, three bedrooms, one with bunk beds, one double room and one room with three beds. WC on first floor. Very well decorated and furnished.

All year   MWB out of season   1wk min, 6wks max, 1unit, 1–7persons   [◇]   ◈   ◆   ◔ fridge   ▥   Gas inclusive   Elec metered   ⌑can be hired   ☎   Airing cupboard in unit   Iron in unit   Ironing board in unit   HCE in unit   ⊕   TV   ⊕3pin square   4P   ▥   ♨(1½m)

⊛   ♨(½m)

Min£65 Max£110pw (Low)
Min£133 Max£166pw (High)

EVANTON
Highland *Ross & Cromarty*
Map **14** NH66

H   Calas & Tamh

for bookings Mr & Mrs A H Munro, Balconie, Evanton, Ross-shire IV16 9XG
☎Evanton(0349)830218

Two large stone-built houses located in pleasant spot by the River Skiack overlooking the Cromarty Firth. Both are on two levels and contain kitchen,

lounge/diner, one double and two twin bedrooms. A pitch and putt course and games room are nearby. Access from A9 at Evanton on an unclass road.

May–Oct MWB out of season 1wk min, 4wks max, 2units, 1–6persons ◈ ◎ fridge Electric [Elec] ☐not provided ☎(½m) Iron in unit Ironing board in unit HCE in unit ⊙ TV/CTV can be hired ⊕3pin square P ⌂ ♨(½m) Hard ♪ Games room, Fishing

⇔ ⛳(3m) ♀(½m)

C Sonas & Fasgadh
for bookings Mr & Mrs A H Munro, Balconie, Evanton, Ross-shire IV16 9XG
☎Evanton(0349)830218

Two attractive, neighbouring, white painted cottages situated in pleasant farmland, ¼m from village centre. Both have lounge/diner and kitchen but Fasgadh has three bedrooms on two levels, while Sonas has two bedrooms at ground level.

May–Oct MWB out of season 1wk min, 4wks max, 2units, 1–6persons ◈ ◎ fridge Electric [Elec] ☐not provided ☎(½m) Iron in unit Ironing board in unit HCE in unit ⊙ ⊕3pin square P ⌂ ♨(½m) Hard ♪ Games room, fishing

⇔ ⛳(3m) ♀(½m)

EXBOURNE
Devon
Map**2** SS60

***C* CC Ref 518 EP**
for bookings Character Cottages (Holidays) Ltd, 34 Fore Street, Sidmouth, Devon EX10 8AQ
☎Sidmouth(039 55)77001

Detached thatched cottage in a peaceful setting comprising two bedrooms (one double, one twin-bedded), sitting room, dining room, kitchen, and bathroom/WC.

All year MWB out of season 1wk min, 1mth max, 1unit, 2–4persons ◎ fridge Electric Elec inclusive ☐can be hired ☎(200yds) Airing cupboard in unit Iron in unit Ironing board in unit HCE in unit ⊙ TV ⊕3pin square ⊕2pin round P ▥ ♨(1m)

⇔ ♀

Min£47 Max£75pw (Low)
Min£79 Max£104pw (High)

EXETER
Devon
Map**3** SX99

***H* 72 Barrack Road**
for bookings Exeter Holiday Homes, Barnfield End, 4 Spicer Road, Exeter EX1 1SX
☎Exeter(0392)71668

Modern link house in residential area of Exeter 1m from city centre. On the ground floor there is a lounge, separate dining room and modern fitted kitchen. On the first floor there is one double, one twin and one bunk-bedded room, and separate bathroom/WC/wash hand basin.

All year MWB out of season 1wk min, 6mths max, 1unit, 2–8persons [◇] ◈ ◎ fridge 🂠 Elec metered ☐can be hired Airing cupboard in unit Iron in unit Ironing board in unit HCE in unit ⊙ CTV ⊕3pin square ▥ ♨(½m)

⇔ ⛳18(2m) ♀(½m) ▣(1m) ♫(1m) 🎥(1m)

Min£66 Max£96pw (Low)
Min£84 Max£140pw (High)

***F* 1 Denmark Road**
for bookings Exeter Holiday Homes, Barnfield End, 4 Spicer Road, Exeter, Devon EX1 1SX
☎Exeter(0392)71668

Two flats, one on each floor of an end-of-terrace house in a relatively peaceful street very near the centre of Exeter. In excellent condition and ably managed by owner who lives 100yds away and is constantly on call.

All year MWB out of season 7days min, 6mths max, 2units, 1–10persons ◈ ◆ ◎ fridge Electric Elec metered ☐can be hired ☎ Airing cupboard in unit Iron in unit Ironing board in unit HCE in unit [Launderette within 300yds] ⊙ ⊛ TV ⊕3pin square ⌂ ▥ ♨(150yds)

⇔ ♀ ▣ ♫ 🎥

Min£56 Max£96pw (Low)
Min£72 Max£160pw (High)

***F* 18 Watermore Court** Pinhoe Road
for bookings Exeter Holiday Homes, Barnfield End, 4 Spicer Road, Exeter, Devon EX1 1SX
☎Exeter(0392)71668

A modern flat on the second floor of a purpose-built block ¾m from city centre ideal touring base for Devon. In immaculate condition; owner on call ½m away.

All year MWB out of season 7days min, 6mths max, 1unit, 1–5persons ◈ ◆ ◎ fridge Electric Elec metered ☐can be hired ☎ Airing cupboard in unit Iron in unit Ironing board in unit HCE in unit ⊙ ⊛ CTV ⊕3pin square P ▥ ♨(50yds)

⇔ ♀(50yds) ▣(½m) ♫(1m) 🎥(½m)

Min£60 Max£84pw (Low)
Min£72 Max£96pw (High)

EXFORD
Somerset
Map**3** SS83

F Mr & Mrs J Edwards **Westermill Farm** Exford, Minehead, Somerset TA24 7NJ
☎Exford(064 383)238

Purpose-built flat being an extension of a 17th-century farmhouse of modern design. Well appointed and furnished. Three bedrooms (two twin, one bunk beds), separate kitchen–modern and well equipped–fitted bathroom and dining/sitting room, overlooking river. From Exford take Porlock road, in ¼m take left fork and continue for 2½m.

All year MWB out of season 1day min, 3wks max, 1unit, 1–6persons [◇] [◈] [◆] ◎ fridge Electric Elec metered ☎ Airing cupboard in unit Iron in unit Ironing board in unit HCE in unit CTV ⊕3pin square P ▥

⇔ ♀(2½m)

Min£69 Max£85pw (Low)
Min£138 Max£166pw (High)

C Mr & Mrs J Edwards **Westermill Log Cottages** Westermill Farm, Exford, Minehead, Somerset TA24 7NJ
☎Exford(064 383)238

Four Scandinavian log cottages of very high quality. They comprise two or three bedrooms, one with bunk beds plus one or two with twin beds, all have wash basin, living room, open plan kitchen and bathroom with WC and shower. From Exford take Porlock road and in ¼m fork left; continue for 2½m and fork left again at Westermill sign.

15Mar–15Jan MWB out of season 1wk min, 10mths max, 4units, 4–6persons [◇] [◈ ◆] ◎ fridge Electric Elec metered ☐not provided ☎(50yds) Airing cupboard in unit HCE in unit ⊙ CTV ⊕3pin square 8P ♨(50yds)

⇔ ♀(2½m)

Min£57 Max£69pw (Low)
Min£137 Max£166pw (High)

EXMOUTH
Devon
Map**3** SY08

***C* Athelstan Cottage** St John's Road, Withycombe
for bookings J A & A S D Hedges, Westwards, Bickwell Valley, Sidmouth, Devon
☎Sidmouth(039 55)6176

Pretty, tastefully-decorated thatched cottage in a secluded position. Accommodation comprises two bedrooms (one double, twin divans), lounge with french windows to garden, oak-beamed dining room, two bedrooms, kitchen with breakfast bar and modern bathroom and WC. Garden.

All year MWB out of season 1wk min, 1mth max, 1unit, 2–4persons ◈ ◎ fridge Electric Gas/Elec inclusive ☐can be hired ☎ WM in unit Airing cupboard in unit Iron in unit Ironing board in unit HCE in unit [Launderette within 300yds] ⊙ CTV ⊕3pin square P ▥ ♨(100yds) →

1982 prices quoted throughout gazetteer

◈ ♨(400yds) ▨(400yds)
♬(400yds) ⚌(400yds)

Min£70 Max£100pw (Low)
Min£150 Max£200pw (High)

B 22 & 24 Bradham Lane

for bookings Exmouth Holiday Homes,
123 Hulham Road, Exmouth, Devon
EX8 4QZ
☎Exmouth(03952)4119 & 75304

*Two modern detached bungalows 1 m
from town centre in quiet residential area.
Both bungalows have three double
bedrooms, lounge, kitchen and
bathroom/WC.*

All year MWB out of season 3 days min,
3 mths max, 2 units, 2–6 persons [◆]
[◆] ◉ fridge Electric Elec metered
Ⓛcan be hired ☎(250yds) Airing
cupboard in unit Iron in unit Ironing
board in unit HCE in unit TV
⊕3 pin square P ▥ ♨(200yds)
◈ ♨(½m) ▨(1½m) ♬(1½m) ⚌(1½m)

H 3 Brooklands Road

for bookings Exmouth Holiday Homes,
123 Hulham Road, Exmouth, Devon
EX8 4QZ
☎Exmouth(03952)4119 & 75304

*Semi-detached house in a residential
area. Accommodation comprises
entrance hall, lounge, dining room,
kitchen, two double bedrooms, one twin-
bedded room and bathroom/WC. For
access from the A376 turn right into
Bradham Lane then take the second
turning on right.*

All year MWB out of season 1 wk min,
8 mths max, 1 unit, 2–6 persons [◆]
[◆] ◉ fridge Electric Elec metered
Ⓛcan be hired ☎(25yds) Airing
cupboard in unit Iron in unit Ironing
board in unit HCE in unit ⊖ [TV]
⊕3 pin square ⊕2 pin round ▥
♨(300yds) ♪
◈ ♨ ▨ ♬ ⚌

C CC Ref 764L Littleham (2m E off
A376)

for bookings Character Cottages
(Holidays) Ltd, 34 Fore Street, Sidmouth,
Devon EX108AQ
☎Sidmouth(03955)77001

*Attractive thatched terraced cottage in
rural position, with views of Exmouth
Estuary. Accommodation consisting of
dining room, kitchen, lounge with
inglenook, bathroom and WC. Two
bedrooms, one double room and one
twin room. Very pretty and modern. 2m
from sandy beach.*

All year MWB out of season 1 wk min,
1 mth max, 1 unit, 1–4 persons ◆ ◉
fridge Electric Elec metered
Ⓛnot provided Airing cupboard in unit
Iron in unit Ironing board in unit HCE in
unit ⊖ CTV ⊕3 pin square 1P ▥
♨(½m)
◈ ♨₁₈(3m) ♨(½m) ▨(½m) ♬(½m)
⚌(½m)

Min£84 Max£110pw (Low)
Min£142 Max£185pw (High)

F Essington Court Flats 3/7 Mount
Pleasant Avenue

for bookings Exmouth Holiday Homes,
123 Hulham Road, Exmouth, Devon
EX8 4QZ
☎Exmouth(03952)4119 & 75304

*Purpose-built, self-contained flats on first
floor of a new construction set in quiet
suburban area. Each comprises two
double bedrooms, lounge, kitchen and
bathroom/WC. Modern furnishings.*

All year MWB out of season 3 days min,
3 mths max, 2 units, 2–4 persons [◆]
[◆] ◉ fridge Electric Elec metered
Ⓛcan be hired ☎(½m) [SD in unit]
Airing cupboard in unit Iron in unit
Ironing board in unit HCE in unit TV
⊕3 pin square P ▦ ▥ ♨(½m)
◈ ♨(1½m) ▨(1½m) ♬(1½m) ⚌(1½m)

F 88 Exeter Road Flats 1 & 2

for bookings Exmouth Holiday Homes,
123 Hulham Road, Exmouth, Devon
EX8 4QZ
☎Exmouth(03952)4119 & 75304

*Two flats in a terraced house near the
town centre. The ground-floor flat has two
double bedrooms, the first-floor flat has
two double and two single bedrooms;
with lounge, kitchen and bathroom/WC in
each unit.*

All year MWB out of season 3 days min,
3 mths max, 2 units, 2–8 persons [◆]
[◆] ◉ fridge Electric Elec metered
Ⓛcan be hired ☎(200yds) Airing
cupboard in unit Iron in unit Ironing
board in unit HCE in unit TV
⊕3 pin square ▦ ▥ ♨(200yds)
◈ ♨(500yds) ▨(½m) ♬(½m)
⚌(500yds)

F Flats 1,2 & 3 112 Exeter Road

for bookings Exmouth Holiday Homes,
123 Hulham Road, Exmouth, Devon
EX8 4QZ
☎Exmouth(03952)4119 & 75304

*Three flats located within converted
Victorian house close to town centre on
main road. Flats 1 & 2 are on the ground
and first-floor and comprise large
lounge/diner, kitchen, bathroom/WC and
two twin bedrooms. Flat 3 is on the
second-floor and has lounge/diner,
kitchen, bathroom/WC and one twin
bedroom. All are well equipped with
modern furniture and décor.*

All year MWB out of season 8 mths max,
3 units, 2–4 persons [◆ ◆]
fridge Electric Elec metered Ⓛcan be
hired ☎(10yds) Airing cupboard in
unit Iron in unit Ironing board in unit
HCE in unit ⊖ TV ⊕3 pin square P
▥ ♨(10yds)
◈ ♨₁₈(3m) ♨(50yds) ▨(½m) ♬(½m)
⚌(½m)

H&F 61 & 61A/B Featherbed Lane

for bookings Exmouth Holiday Homes,
123 Hulham Road, Exmouth, Devon
EX8 4QZ
☎Exmouth(03952)4119 & 75304

*Two flats located in detached house and
two semi-detached houses, situated in
quiet suburb. The flats have three
bedrooms, one double and two twins,
lounge, bathroom/WC and kitchen. The
houses have one double-bedded room,
one twin-bedded room and one single
bedroom, lounge, bathroom/WC and
kitchen.*

All year MWB out of season 1 wk min,
8 mths max, 4 units, 2–7 persons [◆ ◆]
◉ fridge Electric Elec metered
Ⓛcan be hired ☎(250yds) Airing
cupboard in unit Iron in unit Ironing
board in unit HCE in unit TV
◈ ♨(½m) ▨(1½m) ♬(1½m) ⚌(1½m)

F The Flat Savoy Buildings, Rolle Street

for bookings J A & A S D Hedges,
Westwards, Bickwell Valley, Sidmouth,
Devon
☎Sidmouth(03955)6176

*Second-floor flat in office block above the
main shopping street in Exmouth.
Accommodation comprises kitchen,
utility room, bathroom, lounge/diner,
separate WC, three bedrooms, two are
double-bedded rooms and the other is a
twin-bedded room. Well decorated and
carpeted. In the same block as Savoy
cinema.*

All year MWB out of season 1 wk min,
1 unit, 1–6 persons no pets ⚁ fridge
Electric Gas & Elec inclusive
Ⓛnot provided ☎(100yds) Airing
cupboard in unit Iron in unit Ironing
board in unit HCE in unit ⊖ CTV
⊕3 pin square ♨
◈ ♨₁₈(3m) ♨(10yds) ▨(½m) ♬(½m)
⚌(10yds)

Min£55 Max£85pw (Low)
Min£100 Max£125pw (High)

F 37 Halsdon Road Flat 2

for bookings Exmouth Holiday Homes,
123 Hulham Road, Exmouth, Devon
EX8 4QZ
☎Exmouth(03952)4119 & 75304

*Self-contained flat in a semi-detached
house near to the town centre.
Accommodation comprises one double
bedroom, lounge, kitchen and
bathroom/WC.*

All year MWB out of season 3 days min,
3 mths max, 2 units, 2–4 persons [◆]
[◆] ⚁ ◉ fridge Electric
Gas/Elec metered Ⓛcan be hired
☎(½m) Airing cupboard in unit Iron in
unit Ironing board in unit HCE in unit
[Launderette within 300yds] TV
⊕3 pin square ▥ ♨(500yds)
◈ ♨(½m) ▨(½m) ♬(½m) ⚌(½m)

F Mrs P M Voisey **Isca House Flats (No's 1,2,4,5 & 6)** Isca Road, Exmouth, Devon
☎Exmouth(03952)3747

First- and second-floor flats in converted hotel set in quiet residential area close to sea front, 1m from town centre. Each comprise lounge, kitchen/diner, bathroom and WC, with either one double bedroom or one double and one twin-bedded room.

Etr-Nov MWB out of season 3days min, 4wks max, 5units, 2–6persons ◈ ◉ fridge ▦ Electric Elec metered ⊡inclusive ☎(½m) Iron on premises Ironing board on premises HCE in unit [Launderette within 300yds] ⊙ CTV ⊕3pin square 12P ▥ ♨(½m)

⇔ ♁18(3m) ♀(½m) ▨(½m) ♬(½m) ▩(½m)

Min£35 Max£100pw (Low)
Min£65 Max£145pw (High)

H **Lovering Farm Cottage** Marley Road
for bookings Eagle Holiday Flats, Eagle House, The Strand, Exmouth, Devon EX8 1AL
☎Exmouth(03952)71661

Detached farm cottage situated 1½m from town centre. Accommodation offers lounge with two folding beds, dining room, kitchen, two twin and one single bedroom, and bathroom/WC.

Mar-Oct 1wk min, 1mth max, 1unit, 1–7persons ◉ fridge Electric Elec metered ⊡not provided ☎(½m) Airing cupboard in unit Iron in unit Ironing board in unit HCE in unit ⊙ TV ⊕3pin square 2P 1⌂ ▥ ♨(½m)

⇔ ♁18(3m) ♀(1m) ▨(1½m) ♬(1½m) ▩(1½m)

Min£50 Max£81pw

F **23 Moreton Crescent, Flats 1,3 & 4**
for bookings Eagle Holiday Flats, Eagle House, The Strand, Exmouth, Devon EX8 1AL
☎Exmouth(03952)71661

Three flats situated in a Victorian brick-built seafront residence. Number 1 is on the second-floor and comprises two twin-bedded rooms, one double-bedded room with additional single bed, kitchen/diner, bathroom/WC and lounge with convertible settee. Number 3 is a spacious flat on the ground-floor and comprises lounge with three folding beds, one double bedroom with additional single bed, one twin-bedded room, kitchen, bathroom and separate WC. Number 4 is a basement flat and comprises lounge with two convertible beds, one bedroom with three single beds, one double bedroom and one single bedroom, kitchen/diner and bathroom/WC. Approach the seafront by Victoria Road for Morton Crescent on the right, facing the sea.

Apr-Oct 1wk min, 1mth max, 3units, 1–11persons ◉ fridge Electric Elec metered ⊡not provided ☎(100yds) Airing cupboard in unit Iron in unit Ironing board in unit HCE in unit ⊙ TV ⊕3pin square 1P ▥ ♨(200yds)

⇔ ♁18(3m) ♀(200yds) ▨(½m) ♬(½m) ▩(½m)

Min£50 Max£105pw

F **32 The Parade (Flats 2,3 & 4)**
for bookings Eagle Holiday Flats, Eagle House, The Strand, Exmouth, Devon EX8 1AL
☎Exmouth(03952)71661

Three flats in a brick building above shops. They have comfortably furnished lounges all with the exception of Flat 4, having folding beds, bathroom and WC. Flats 4, 3 & 2 have one double bedroom, one twin-bedded room and one single bedroom. Approach from the rear of the shops.

Mar-Oct 1wk min, 1mth max, 3units, 2–7persons [◈] [◆] ♁ ◉(1unit) fridge Electric Gas/Elec metered ⊡not provided ☎(100yds) Airing cupboard in unit Iron in unit Ironing board in unit HCE in unit [Launderette] TV ⊕3pin square ⊕2pin round ▥ ♨

⇔ ♁9 ♀ ▨ ♬ ▩

Min£35 Max£60pw

F ***100 St Andrew's Road*** Flats 1,2 & 3
for bookings Exmouth Holiday Homes, 123 Hulham Road, Exmouth, Devon EX8 4QZ
☎Exmouth(03952)4119 & 75304

Flats situated in terraced house, all with lounge, dining room, bathroom/WC and kitchen. Flats 2 and 3 have one twin-bedded room and one single-bedded room. Flat 1 has two twin-bedded rooms. St Andrews Road is at the western end of the Esplanade, near to the harbour.

All year MWB out of season 3days min, 3mths max, 3units, 2–4persons [◈] [◆] ◉ Fridge Electric Elec metered ⊡can be hired ☎(100yds) Airing cupboard in unit Iron in unit Ironing board in unit HCE in unit ⊙ TV ⊕3pin square ⊕2pin round P ▥ ♨(100yds)

⇔ ♁9(½m) ♀ ▨ ♬ ▩

F ***49 Salisbury Road*** Flats 1 & 2
for bookings Exmouth Holiday Homes, 123 Hulham Road, Exmouth, Devon EX8 4QZ
☎Exmouth(03952)4119 & 75304

Self-contained flat on the ground-floor of an end of terrace house, situated near the town centre. Accommodation comprises three double bedrooms (one with double bed, two with single beds), lounge/diner, kitchen and bathroom/WC. Also, first-floor flat is available with two bedrooms.

All year MWB out of season 3days min, 3mths max, 2units, 2–6persons [◈] [◆] ◉ fridge Electric Elec metered ⊡can be hired ☎(½m) [SD in unit] Airing cupboard in unit Iron in unit Ironing board in unit HCE in unit [Launderette within 300yds] TV ⊕3pin square P ▥ ♨(300yds)

⇔ ♀(½m) ▨(½m) ♬(½m) ▩(½m)

F **Templetown Lodge** The Sea Front
for bookings Eagle Holiday Flats, Eagle House, The Strand, Exmouth, Devon EX8 1AL
☎Exmouth(03952)71661

Four flats, three of which are at the rear of large house on sea front, each with lounge/diner, kitchen, two bedrooms, double sofa bed in lounge and bathroom/WC.

Apr-Oct 1wk min, 1mth max, 4units, 1–6persons ♁ fridge Electric Gas metered ⊡not provided ☎(100yds) Airing cupboard in unit Iron in unit Ironing board in unit HCE in unit ⊙ TV ⊕3pin square 1P 1⌂ ▥ ♨(200yds)

⇔ ♁18(3m) ♀(100yds) ▨(½m) ♬(½m) ▩(½m) Beach nearby

Min£46 Max£94pw

FALMOUTH
Cornwall
Map **2** SW83

F Mr & Mrs J Morgan **Anchorage Apartments** Gyllyngvase Road, Gyllyngvase Beach, Falmouth, Cornwall TR11 4DJ
☎Falmouth(0326)312164

Nine one- and two-bedded apartments adjacent to Gyllyngvase Beach and within a few minutes' walk of town centre and famous subtropical gardens. Each offers a high standard of facilities comprising separate lounges and adjoining well-equipped fitted kitchens, luxury bathroom//WC.

All year MWB out of season 1wk min, 2wks max, 9units, 1–7persons [◇] [◈] ◉ fridge Electric Elec metered ⊡inclusive ☎ Airing cupboard in unit Iron in unit Ironing board in unit HCE in unit ⊙ CTV ⊕3pin square 1P ▥ ♨(½m)

⇔ ♁18(2m) ♀(½m) ▨(½m) ♁18(½m) ▩(½m)

Min£45 Max£60pw (Low)
Min£110 Max£145pw (High)

F J C P Thomas **Courtenay Holiday Flats** Swanpool Beach, Falmouth, Cornwall
☎Falmouth(0326)311416

Purpose-built blocks of flats in a secluded position. Good standard of furnishings. Picutre windows with good views from most units of sea and Swanpool.

Feb-Nov MWB out of season 1wk min, 4wks max, 24units, 2–6persons [◈] [◆] ♁ ◉ fridge Electric Gas inclusive Elec metered ⊡can be →

hired ☎ Iron on premises Ironing board on premises HCE in unit ⊙ TV ⊕3 pin square ⊘2 pin round P 🅼 ♨(½m) ♾

⊖ ♨ ♀(2m) 🅿(2m) 🛉-(2m)

Min£35 Max£55pw (Low)
Min£66 Max£96pw (High)

F Crossways Holiday Flats Pennance Road
for bookings S A Higgs, Lamorva House, Woodland Crescent, Falmouth, Cornwall ☎Falmouth(0326)313985

Complex of five flats situated within a former hotel in convenient position at corner of Pennance Road and Sea View Road, north-west of Gyllyngvase Beach. Flat 1 on the ground-floor comprises one bedroom with twin beds, lounge with double folding bed, bathroom/WC and kitchen area. Flat 3, also on the ground-floor, comprises two bedrooms, one with double bed and one with bunk beds, lounge with bed-settee, separate kitchen and shower/WC. Flat 4 is located on the first-floor with two bedrooms, one double with bunk beds, the other with a single bed, lounge with bed-settee, separate kitchen and shower/WC. Flat 5 is also on the first-floor with lounge/kitchen, separate double bedroom and bathroom. Flat 6 is on the second-floor with twin-bedded room, kitchen, bathroom and large partitioned lounge with twin beds and bed-settee.

Mar – Nov MWB out of season 1 wk min, 1 mth max, 5 units, 1–6 persons, nc5 no pets ◉ fridge Electric Elec metered ⊑ inclusive ☎(300yds) Iron on premises Ironing board on premises HCE in unit ⊙ CTV ⊕3 pin square P 🅼 ♨(400yds) ⊖ ♨(1m) ♀(300yds) 🅿(½m) 🎵(1m) 🛉-(1m)

Min£49.45pw (Low)
Min£109.25 Max£184pw (High)

F Falmouth Hotel Falmouth, Cornwall TR11 4NZ
☎Falmouth(0326)312671

Two delightfully situated, purpose-built blocks of flats. They are situated behind the hotel but linked to it by a covered corridor. The hotel's facilities are available to self-catering guests.

All year (except 20 Dec – 3 Jan) MWB 24 units, 1–6 persons ◈ ◆ ◉ fridge Electric Elec metered ⊑ inclusive ☎ Airing cupboard in unit Iron on premises Ironing board on premises HCE in unit ⊙ TV ⊕3 pin square ⊘2 pin round P 🏠 🅼 ♨(200yds) ⚓ ♾ Ballroom Games room

⊖ ♀ 🅿 🎵 🛉-

Min£50 Max£120pw (Low)
Min£140 Max£220pw (High)

F 21 Green Bank
for bookings Mr P M Turner, 7 Stratton Place, Falmouth, Cornwall
☎Falmouth(0326)314066 or 315686

Two flats in converted terraced house built around 1808. First flat with ground-floor entrance to two bedrooms (one double, one twin), lounge/kitchen, bathroom and separate WC. Fully centrally heated. Second flat is reached by eleven internal steps to front door then fifteen steps to accommodation of two bedrooms (one double, one twin), lounge/kitchen, separate bathroom and WC.

All year MWB out of season 1 wk min, 2 units, 1–4 persons ◉ fridge Electric Elec metered ⊑ inclusive ☎(100yds) Airing cupboard in unit Iron in unit Ironing board in unit HCE in unit ⊙ CTV ⊕3 pin square 🅼 ♨(200yds) ⊖ ♨(2m) ♀(50yds) 🅿(200yds) 🎵(200yds) 🛉-(200yds)

Min£40 Max£50pw (Low)
Min£45 Max£125pw (High)

B Mr B F Smales Maenheere Holiday Bungalows Maineere Hotel, Grove Place, Falmouth, Cornwall TR11 4AU
☎Falmouth(0326)312009

Modernised conventionally built bungalows in attractive devleopment close to harbour, each with private lawn or patio. Situated in quiet mews-like area behind hotel. The accommodation which has fitted carpets and comfortable conventional furnishings, comprises large sitting room with convertible-settee,

twin bedroom, double room, children's bedroom with twin bunk beds, bathroom/WC and kitchen. All bedrooms have hand basin and an additonal single bed is also available.

All year MWB out of season 1 wk min, 5 units, 1–9 persons ◈ ◆ no dogs ◉ fridge Electric Elec metered ⊑ inclusive ☎ Airing cupboard Iron Ironing board HCE ⊙ TV ⊕3 pin square P 🅼 ♨(300yds)

⊖ ♀ 🅿 🎵 🛉-

Min£66.70 Max£79.35pw (Low)
Min£125.35 Max£141.45pw (High)

F Mr B F Smales Maenheere Holiday Flats Maenheere Hotel, Grove Place, Falmouth, Cornwall TR11 4AU
☎Falmouth(0326)312009

The flats are located in a purpose-built block behind the hotel. Accommodation consists of a twin bedroom, double bedroom, large lounge with dining alcove, kitchen/breakfast room and bathroom/WC. The flats have fitted carpets and comfortable, conventional furnishings. All bedrooms have wash basins.

All year MWB out of season 1 wk min, 5 units, 8 persons ◈ ◆ no dogs ⌀ ◉ fridge Electric Gas/Elec metered ⊑ inclusive ☎ Iron ⊙ TV ⊕3 pin square P 🅼 ♨(300yds)

⊖ ♀ 🅿 🎵 🛉-

Min£64.40 Max£70.15pw (Low)
Min£123.05 Max£131.10pw (High)

F Mr P Turner 7 Stratton Place Falmouth, Cornwall
☎Falmouth(0326)314066 or 315686

Three flats, Flat 1 has two bedrooms (one twin, one double), lounge, kitchen, bath shower and two WCs; this flat has 20 internal steps to front door. Flat 2 has one double bedroom, lounge (with convertible), dining room, bathroom and WC; this flat has six steps to front door. Flat 3 has two bedrooms (one double, one twin), kitchen/living area with internal spiral staircase. Flat 1 is fully centrally heated, and Flats 1 & 2 have a telephone.

All year MWB out of season 1 wk min, 3 units, 1–4 persons ◉ fridge Electric Elec metered ⊑ inclusive ☎

Iron in unit Ironing board in unit HCE in
unit ⊖ CTV ⊕3pin square P 🕾
🏠(200yds)

↔ 🕭(2m) 🌳(50yds) 🏊(200yds)
🎵(200yds) 🍴(200yds)

Min£40 Max£50pw (Low)
Min£45 Max£125pw (High)

F Mr E B May **Treslothan Hotel Flats**
Spernen Wyn Road, Falmouth, Cornwall
TR113EH
🕾Falmouth(0326)312676

*A converted hotel in a residential area
and 400yds from Gyllyngvase Beach.
Exterior décor, furnishings and
equipment of good standard.*

All year MWB out of season 1wk min,
1mth max, 14units, 2–6persons, nc5
◉ fridge Electric Elec metered
🅸inclusive ☎ HCE on premises ⊖
TV can be hired ⊕3pin square
⊕2pin round P 🏠 🏠(200yds) 🌳 🐾

↔ 🌳(½m) 🏊(½m) 🎵(½m) '🍴(½m)

Min£40 Max£72pw (Low)
Min£65 Max£120pw (High)

FENITON
Devon
Map**3** SY09

C Adders Hole
for bookings J A & A S D Hedges,
Westwards, Bickwell Valley, Sidmouth,
Devon
🕾Sidmouth(039 55)6176

*Attractive stone-built thatched cottage in
small village. Accommodation comprises
on the ground floor a beamed lounge with
open fireplace, separate dining room,
modern kitchen, bathroom with WC and
wash hand basin. On the first floor there is
one bedroom with twin beds and wash
basin, one bedroom with double bed and
one bedroom with bunk beds. Garden.*

All year MWB out of season 1wk min,
6mths max, 1unit, 7persons ◈ ◆
fridge 🍴& open fires Elec inclusive
🅸can be hired ☎ WM in unit SD in
unit Airing cupboard in unit Iron in unit
Ironing board in unit HCE in unit ⊖
CTV ⊕3pin square P 🏠 🕾 🏠(½m)

↔ 🕭(3m) 🌳(½m)

Min£85 Max£135pw (Low)
Min£200 Max£250pw (High)

H CC Ref 673 E
for bookings Character Cottages
(Holidays) Ltd, 34 Fore Street, Sidmouth,
Devon EX108AQ
🕾Sidmouth(039 55)77001

*Front part of large farmhouse, facing
south. Walled garden in front. Entrance
and porch. Spacious living room with
fireplace. Large dining room, modern
kitchen. Four double bedrooms, two with
twin beds. Good bathroom facilities.
Separate WC.*

All year MWB out of season 1wk min,
6mths max, 1unit, 2–8persons ◈
no pets ◉ fridge Electric
Elec inclusive 🅸not provided ☎(1m)
WM in unit SD in unit Airing cupboard

in unit Iron in unit Ironing board in unit
HCE in unit ⊖ TV ⊕3pin square
⊕2pin round P 🏠 🏠(1m)

↔ 🌳(1m) 🏊(1m)

Min£68 Max£95pw (Low)
Min£115 Max£154pw (High)

C CC Ref 6072 ELP Sherwood
for bookings Character Cottages
(Holidays) Ltd, 34 Fore Street, Sidmouth,
Devon EX108AQ
🕾Sidmouth(039 55)77001

*A delightful white stucco cottage with
thatched roof. Beamed lounge/dining
area with quality furniture and canopy log
fire. Large modern fully-fitted kitchen,
open tread staircase to twin and double
bedrooms. Bathroom/WC/wash hand
basin, ground floor twin-bedded room
with adjacent cloakroom and WC. High
standard throughout.*

All year MWB out of season 1wk min,
6wks max, 1unit, 1–6persons ◈ ◉
fridge Electric & Aga Elec metered
🅸can be hired ☎ Airing cupboard in
unit Iron in unit Ironing board in unit
HCE in unit ⊖ TV ⊕3pin square P
🏠 🕾 🏠(½m)

↔ 🌳(½m)

Min£94 Max£175pw (Low)
Min£207 Max£275pw (High)

FENNY BENTLEY
Derbyshire
Map**7** SK14

B Drysdale
for bookings Mrs B Herridge, Bent Farm,
Tissington, Ashbourne, Derbys
🕾Parwich(033 525)214

*This brick built bungalow stands just off
the A515 and overlooks the surrounding
countryside from the rear bedrooms and
lounge. It comprises kitchen with
Rayburn, WC, lounge/dining room,
bathroom/shower/WC, one double
bedded room, one twin and one bunk
bedded room.*

All year MWB out of season 3days min,
3mths max, 1unit, 1–6persons ◈ ◉
fridge 🍴 Elec metered 🅸inclusive
(except towels) ☎(½m) Airing
cupboard in unit HCE in unit ⊕ CTV
⊕3pin square P 🕾 🏠(2m)

↔ 🕭 🌳

Min£40 Max£90pw

FILEY
North Yorkshire
Map**8** TA18

F Flats A & B 27 Hope Street
for bookings Mr & Mrs K Swann, 81
Wooldale Drive, Filey, N Yorks
🕾Scarborough(0723)513228

*Two flats in a small shopping street in
town centre. Flat A. Has one twin-bedded
room and one room with double and
single bed, shower and WC. Flat B. Three*

*double-bedded rooms one of which also
contains a single bed, bathroom and WC.*

All year 1wk min, 1mth max, 2units,
1–7persons [◈] ◈ fridge 🍴
Gas/Elec metered 🅸not provided
☎(100yds) Airing cupboard in unit Iron
in unit Ironing board in unit HCE in unit
[Launderette within 300yds] ⊖ [TV]
⊕3pin square 🕾 🏠(10yds) 🐾

↔ 🌳(10yds) 🏊(100yds) 🎵(100yds)
🍴(200yds)

Min£40 Max£75pw

F Mrs E Cutts **Fern-Lee Holiday Flat** 15
Rutland Street, Filey, N Yorks YO149JA
🕾Scarborough(0723)512696

*Well-maintained flat on the top floor of a
three storey terraced house.
Accommodation consists of two
bedrooms (one large room with a double
and a single bed, the other a double
room), kitchen, lounge and
bathroom/WC. Within easy reach of the
town centre and beach.*

May–Oct MWB out of season 1wk min,
2wks max, 1unit, 2–6persons ◈ ◆
no pets ◉ fridge 🍴Gas & Electric
Gas/Elec metered 🅸not provided
☎(250yds) Airing cupboard in unit
HCE in unit TV ⊕3pin square 🕾
🏠(200yds) 🌳Hard/grass

↔ 🌳(100yds) 🏊(200yds)
🎵(200yds) 🍴(½m)

Min£30 Max£50pw (Low)
Min£67 Max£70pw (High)

FINDOCHTY
Grampian *Banffshire*
Map**15** NJ46

C 3 Station Road
for bookings Scott Holiday Homes, 8
Markethill Road, Turriff, Morayshire
🕾Turriff(088 82)3524

*A pleasant little cottage close to the
harbour. Accommodation comprises of
lounge, kitchen, bathroom and double
bedroom on the ground floor, and one
twin and one double bedroom on the first.*

All year MWB out of season 1wk min,
1unit, 1–6persons ◈ ◉ fridge
Electric Elec metered 🅸not provided
☎ WM in unit SD in unit Iron in unit
Ironing board in unit HCE in unit ⊖
CTV ⊕3pin square 2P 🏠(70yds)

↔ 🕭(1m) 🌳(3m)

Min£40 Max£100pw

FINSTOWN
Orkney
Map**16** HY31

B, F & H Firth Bay Bungalows
for bookings Mrs K Reid, Boat House,
Finstown, Orkney
🕾Finstown(085 676)397

*Located right off A965 entering Finstown
from Kirkwall, a neatly-planned crescent
of five bungalows, two flats and an →*

1982 prices quoted throughout
gazetteer

---

upside-down (roof is an upturned boat) 'boathouse' set between the road and sea. All provide a high standard of facilities, including a small sauna in one of the flats.

All year MWB out of season 1wk min, 8units, 1–8persons ◇ ◎ fridge Electric Elec metered ⬚inclusive ☎(100yds) [WM on premises] Airing cupboard in unit HCE in unit ⊖ CTV ⊕3pin square P 🔟 ♨(100yds) ⌣ Fishing

FINTRY
Central *Stirlingshire*
Map **11** NS68

Ch Culcreuch Castle Fintry, Stirlingshire
☎Fintry(036 086)228

Eight cedar chalets sited in nearly 2,000 acre grounds of 14th/15th-century Culcreuch Castle. Each offers lounge/diner/kitchen, bathroom, one double, one twin and one bunk-bedded room. Situated on outskirts of Fintry, access from B822.

5Mar–29Oct MWB out of season 3days min, 1mth max, 8units, 1–6persons [◇] [◆] no pets ◎ fridge 🍴 Elec inclusive ⬚inclusive ☎(½m) WM in unit Airing cupboard in unit HCE in unit ⊖ ⊕3pin square 16P ♨(½m) Coarse & game fishing, climbing & squash

↫ ♀(½m) 🔟(½m)

Min£75 Max£224.25pw

FISHGUARD
Dyfed
Map **2** SM93

F Garden Guest Wing 6 Feidr Dylan, Pen-y-Aber
for bookings Mr L Rees, Cerbid Holiday Cottages, Solva, Haverfordwest, Dyfed
☎Croesgoch(034 83)240

Compact modern guest wing adjoining a private property, but independent. There is an attractive living room with adjoining dining section, integral kitchen and french windows leading to a patio. A wrought iron staircase leads to gallery bedroom with twin beds; a 'Z' bed and cot is also provided. Combined shower/WC.

All year MWB out of season 2days min, 1unit, 1–3persons [◇] ◇ ◆ ◎ fridge Electric Elec inclusive ⬚inclusive ☎(400yds) SD in unit Iron in unit Ironing board in unit HCE in unit ⊖ CTV ⊕3pin square P 🔟 ♨(300yds)

↫ ♀(300yds) 🐾(300yds)

Min£69 Max£161pw

FLICHITY
Highland *Inverness-shire*
Map **14** NH62

C Balvoulin Brin Estate
for bookings Mr J Trotter, Brin Holiday Homes, Flichity, Inverness-shire IV1 2XE
☎Farr(08083)211

This stone-built cottage of considerable character, commands magnificent views over Loch Ruthven and the hills to the S, and stands close to Loch Choire. Fully-modernised, the accommodation comprises large sitting room with open fire, dining area, kitchen, drying area, three double bedrooms (one with bunk beds) and bathroom/WC. Restaurant, bar and craft shop.

Apr–Oct 1wk min, 1unit, 1–6persons [◇] ◆ ◎ fridge Electric & open fires Elec inclusive [Elec metered in winter] ⬚inclusive ☎ Airing cupboard in unit Iron in unit Ironing board in unit HCE in unit [Launderette on premises] ⊖ TV ⊕3pin square P ♨(3m) Games room

Min£60 Max£220pw

Ca Bradan, Breac, Beithe & Broc, Log Cabins Brin Estate
for bookings Mr J Trotter, Brin Holiday Homes, Flichity, Inverness-shire IV1 2XE
☎Farr(08083)211

Situated on a hillside amongst silver birch trees, with superb views of Loch Ruthven, these four log cabins are of two types: two sleep four people and two sleep six. Full sporting facilities of the estate are available to visitors. Restaurant and craft shop.

Apr–Oct 1wk min, 4units, 1–6persons [◇] [◆] ◎ fridge Electric Elec inclusive ⬚inclusive ☎(1m) Airing cupboard in unit Iron in unit Ironing board in unit HCE in unit [Launderette on premises] ⊖ TV ⊕3pin square P ♨(3m) Games room

Min£55 Max£200pw

B Feadag & Guilbneach Brin Estate
for bookings Mr J Trotter, Brin Holiday Homes, Flichity, Inverness-shire IV1 2XE
☎Farr(08083)211

Feadag and Guilbneach are two modern bungalows with extensive views across farmland to the river and hills beyond. All modern amenities are available including TV, and drying facilities. Restaurant, bar and craft shop.

Apr–Oct 1wk min, 2units, 1–6persons [◇] ◆] ◎ fridge Electric Elec inclusive [Elec metered in winter] ⬚inclusive ☎(1m) Airing cupboard in unit Iron in unit Ironing board in unit HCE in unit [Launderette on premises] ⊖ TV ⊕3pin square P ♨(3m) Games room

Min£55 Max£200pw

C Ruthven Lodges Brin Estate
for bookings Mr J Trotter, Brin Holiday Homes, Flichity, Inverness-shire IV1 2XE
☎Farr(08083)211

Five lodges housed in an attractively converted and modernised farm steading, set on the hillside. Each varies between one and three bedrooms and all are equipped to a high standard.

Overlooks Loch Ruthven and providing superb views of the surrounding hills. Restaurant, bar and craft shop.

Apr–Oct 1wk min, 5units, 1–6persons [◇ ◆] ◎ fridge Electric Elec inclusive ⬚inclusive ☎(1m) Airing cupboard in unit Iron in unit Ironing board in unit HCE in unit [Launderette on premises] ⊖ TV ⊕3pin square 6P ♨(3m) ⛸Hard 🏊 Games room, golf practise net.

↫ ♀(1m)

H Tullich Lodge Brin Estate
for bookings Mr J Trotter, Brin Holiday Homes, Flichity, Inverness-shire IV1 2XE
☎Farr(08083)211

A modernised two-storey stone-built house in an elevated position, looking down on Loch Ruthven. Accommoadation includes living room, dining room and four bedrooms, two bathrooms and WC. Décor and furnishings are pleasant. Restaurant, bar and craft shop.

Apr–Oct 1wk min, 1unit, 1–8persons [◇] [◆] ◎ fridge Electric & open fires Elec inclusive [Elec metered in winter] ⬚inclusive ☎ Airing cupboard in unit Iron in unit Ironing board in unit HCE in unit [Launderette on premises] ⊖ TV ⊕3pin square P ♨(3m) Games room

Min£80 Max£230pw

FORT WILLIAM
Highland *Inverness-shire*
Map **14** NN17

See also **Banavie** *and* **Corpach**

Ch E A Cameron & Co **Glen Nevis Holiday Chalets** Glen Nevis, Fort William, Inverness-shire PH33 6SX
☎Fort William(0397)2191

Brick-built chalets situated in Glen Nevis, with splendid views of Ben Nevis. Tastefully furnished accommodation comprises two bedrooms, open plan lounge and kitchen and bathroom/WC. Set beside caravan park with shopping facilities and Licensed restaurant. 2½m from Fort William.

19Feb–7Nov MWB out of season 2nights min, 1mth max, 12units, 1–6persons [◇] ◆ ◎ fridge 🍴 Elec inclusive ⬚can be hired ☎(100yds) Airing cupboard in unit Iron in unit Ironing board in unit HCE in unit [Launderette on premises] ⊖ CTV ⊕3pin square P ♨

↫ ♀(3m) 🔟(3m) 🎵(3m)

Min £105 Max£210pw

Ch Great Glen Holidays Torlundy
for bookings Lochaber Estate Agents, 53 High Street, Fort William, Inverness-shire
☎Fort William(0397)3015

1982 prices quoted throughout gazetteer

Eight Scandinavian timber chalets set in pine woods on the 6,000-acre Great Glen Cattle Ranch. They are well spread out and secluded. Their interior fittings are modern and of good standard. The Great Glen is bordered by mountains, dominated by Ben Nevis. The chalets are situated 3m N of Fort William and just off the A82.

Apr–Nov MWB out of season 1wk min, 3mths max, 8units, 4–6persons [◊]
🌀 fridge Electric Elec inclusive
🔲 can be hired ☎(1m) HCE in unit ⊙
CTV ⊕3pin square P 🅟 ♨(3m)
Pony trekking
⊖ ♪(1m) ♟(3m) 🖾(3m) 🎵(3m)
🐾(3m)

Min£86.25 Max£184pw

FOWEY
Cornwall
Map2 SX15

Ch Mr I G McLeod, **Foye Holiday Village** Fowey, Cornwall
☎Fowey(072 683)2228

Fifteen modern single storey units of recent construction. Accommodation consists of large bedsitting room, kitchen, some with bathroom/WC and some with shower/WC. Nine units have a double and a single bed. Two units have a double bed and a twin bedroom. Four units have twin beds, one double bedroom and another bedroom with twin beds.

Etr–Sep MWB out of season
3days min, 15units, 1–6persons [◊]
🌀 fridge Electric Elec inclusive
🔲 can be hired ☎ Iron on premises
Ironing board on premises HCE in unit
[Launderette on premises] ⊙
⊕3pin square 40P 🅟 ♨ ⌣
⊖ ♟ 🖾

FOXHOLES
Humberside
Map8 TA07

C Whitehouse Farm Cottages .
for bookings Mrs R Rivio, Rarey Farm, Weaverthorpe, Malton, N Yorks
☎West Lutton(094 43)627

Three self-contained farm cottages in

Fort William
—
Fylingdales

Foxholes village on the B1249 10m N of Driffield. Number one has sleeping for nine in three double-bedded rooms, one of which has two bunk beds and another an extra single bed. Number two sleeps seven in a double-bedded room with an extra single bed and two rooms each having two bunk beds. Number three sleeps six in a large room with two double beds and a room with two single beds.

end May–Sep 1wk min, 1mth max, 3units, 1–8persons ◊ ◆ 🌀 fridge
🍴 Elec metered 🔲 not provided
Airing cupboard in unit Iron in unit HCE in unit ⊙ TV ⊕3pin round P
🖾 except Sun ♨(⅓m)
⊖ ♟(3m)

Min£50 Max£60pw (Low)
Min£70 Max£80pw (High)

FRESHWATER BAY
Isle of Wight
Map4 SZ38

F Mrs M K Traverse **Cameron House**
Terrace Lane, Freshwater Bay, Isle of Wight PO40 9QE
☎Freshwater(0983)752788

Cream-painted, brick-built 19th-century house with distant views of the bay, now converted into four self-contained flats. Each unit sleeps four persons although one ground-floor flat is suitable only for two adults and two children. All have lounge/diner and bathroom and WC.

Mar–Oct MWB out of season 1wk min, 3mths max, 4units, 2–4persons [◊
◆] 🌀 fridge Electric Elec metered
🔲 can be hired ☎(300yds) Airing cupboard in unit Iron in unit Ironing board in unit HCE in unit TV
⊕3pin square P 🅟 ♨(100yds)
⊖ ♟(100yds) 🖾(1m) 🎵(2m)

Min£45 Max£65pw (Low)
Min£62 Max£70pw (High)

FYLINGDALES
North Yorkshire
Map8 NZ90

C Billira Cottage
for bookings Mr & Mrs J Thornton, 10 West Park Avenue, Newby, Scarborough, N Yorks YO12 6HH
☎Scarborough(0723)62682

Detached self-contained two-storey ex-gamekeeper's cottage in a secluded moorside location, containing a double-bedded room, a twin-bedded room and a single room. On the ground floor, separate bathroom, pleasantly restored and modernised. Sitting room and well-equipped dining kitchen plus utility room/washhouse and surrounding rough gardens. Situated halfway between Scarborough and Whitby off the A171. Close to the Flask Inn.

Apr–Oct 1wk min, 1unit, 1–5persons
◊ no pets 🌀 fridge Electric
Elec inclusive 🔲 inclusive ☎(⅓m)
Airing cupboard in unit Iron in unit →

Ironing board in unit HCE in unit TV
⊕3pin square P ♨(½m)

⊷ ☎(½m) ▨(½m) ♫(½m)

Min£88 Max£125pw (Low)
Min£145 Max£185pw (High)

GAIRLOCH
Highland *Ross & Cromarty*
Map **14** NG87

F Mr Howie *Gairloch Sands*
Apartments Gairloch, Ross-shire
IV21 2BJ
☎Gairloch(0445)2131

Eight self-contained apartments
attractively converted from bedrooms in
the Gairloch Sands Hotel.
Accommodation consists of either one or
two twin bedrooms, lounge/dining room
with convertible sofa, kitchen and
bathroom.

Etr–midOct MWB out of season
1wk min, 8units, 1–6persons ◊ ◆
◉ fridge Electric Elec metered
⊡inclusive ☎ WM on premises SD on
premises Iron in unit Ironing board in
unit HCE in unit ⊖ ⊗ CTV
⊕3pin square 50P ♨(200yds)
Fishing & tennis

⊷ ♨o(½m) ☎ ♫ 🐾

F *Millcroft Hotel* Gairloch, Wester
Ross, Ross-shire
☎Gairloch(0445)2376

Seven self-contained apartments set
within and forming part of this hotel. They
sleep four or six in two or three bedrooms
and comprise lounge/diner, kitchenette,
bathroom with bath, shower, WC and
bidet. A daily maid service is included in
the rental.

All year MWB out of season 3days min,
7units, 4–6persons [◊] ◉ fridge
♨ Elec inclusive ⊡inclusive ☎ TD in
unit Iron in unit Ironing board in unit
HCE in unit CTV ⊕3pin square 20P
♨(20yds) Sailing, fishing, dingies for
hire

⊷ ♨o(1½m) ☎
Min£69 Max£220pw

GARTHMYL
Powys
Map **7** SO19

Ch **Brynllwyn Luxury Cabins**
for bookings Mr W J H Black, Brynllwyn
Farm, Garthmyl, Powys
☎Garthmyl(068 685)269

Eleven scandanavian style wooden
chalets set on low density wooded
hillock. All have verandahs, natural pine
clad walls and furnished to a high
standard. They vary in size and sleep
up to seven people.

1982 prices quoted throughout
gazetteer

Fylingdales
—
Gatehouse of Fleet

All year MWB out of season 2days min,
6wks max, 11units, 1–7persons [◊]
◊ ◆ ◉ fridge ♨ Elec metered
⊡not provided ☎(½m) Iron in unit
Ironing board in unit HCE in unit ⊖
⊗ CTV ⊕3pin square 8P ♨(1m)

⊷ ☎(1m)

C Mr W J H Black **Wain House Cottage**
Brynllwyn Farm, Garthmyl, Powys
☎Garthmyl(068 685)269

Recently converted barn retaining much
original character, situated at entrance to
the farm, overlooking the lake. It
comprises of lounge with woodburning
stove, open-plan kitchen off with
breakfast bar, one double-bedded room
and shower/WC; stairs lead to a loft
beamed twin-bedded room. Furnished
and decorated to a high standard.

All year MWB out of season 2days min,
6wks max, 1unit, 1–4persons [◊] ◊
◆ ◉ fridge ♨ Elec metered
⊡not provided ☎(½m) Iron in unit
Ironing board in unit HCE in unit ⊖
⊗ CTV ⊕3pin square 2P ♨(1m)
Fishing

⊷ ☎(1m)

GARTLY
Grampian *Aberdeenshire*
Map **15** NJ53

C **Station Holiday Cottages**
for bookings Mr J T Cosgrove, 118
Kidmore End Road, Emmer Green,
Reading RG4 8SL
☎Reading(0734)472524

Two modernised cottages, which still
retain their original character, situated at
the village centre close to the Railway
crossing. The cottages adjoin and share
a garden and one has two bedrooms, the
other has one double.

All year MWB out of season 1wk min,
2units, 1–6persons [◊] ◉ fridge
Electric & open fires Elec inclusive
⊡can be hired ☎(200yds) WM on
premises SD on premises Airing
cupboard in unit Iron in unit Ironing
board in unit HCE in unit ⊖
⊕3pin square 2P ♨(100yds) Fishing
& shooting, bicycle for hire

⊷ ☎(100yds)
Min£50 Max£100pw

GARVAN
Highland *Inverness-shire*
Map **14** NM97

H **Garvan House**
for bookings Mrs J Cox, The Old School,
Duisky, Fort William, Inverness-shire
☎Kinlocheil(039 783)227

A stone-built former gamekeeper's
cottage in a pleasant location on the S
side of Loch Eil, 200yds along a farm
track from the A861. Water has to be
pumped daily from the nearby river and

---

instructions on use of pump are given.
The rooms are spacious and there is a
pleasant sun lounge at the rear. Ideal as a
touring centre, for children and dog
owners.

All year MWB out of season 1wk min,
1unit, 10persons ◊ ◉ fridge
Electric Elec metered ⊡can be hired
☎(1m) Iron in unit Ironing board in
unit HCE in unit ⊖ ⊕3pin square P
♨(10m) Boat for hire

Min£55 Max£90pw (Low)
Min£105 Max£155pw (High)

GATEHOUSE OF FLEET
Dumfries & Galloway *Kirkcudbrightshire*
Map **11** NX55

H **Barrhill Lodge**
for bookings G M Thomson & Co, 27 King
Street, Castle Douglas,
Kirkcudbrightshire
☎Castle Douglas(0556)2701

Attractive stone-built lodge house
furnished to a high standard and situated
on the periphery of Fleet Forest.
Accommodation consists of a double-
bedded room and twin-bedded room,
modern fitted kitchen, bathroom and
living/dining room. The Lodge is W of
Gatehouse of Fleet on rural road off A75.

All year 1wk min, 6mths max, 1unit,
1–4persons ◉ fridge Electric
Elec inclusive ⊡not provided ☎(3m)
Ironing board in unit HCE in unit TV
⊕3pin square P ♨(2m)

⊷ ♨o(3m) ☎(3m)

Min£55 Max£130pw

F Mrs Morton **Dalavan House (Flat)**
Fleet Forest, Gatehouse of Fleet,
Kirkcudbrightshire
☎Gatehouse(05574)291 or
Bishops Stortford(0279)813223

Modern, fully-furnished flat with separate
entrance situated within Forestry
Commission's land. Consists of kitchen,
dining room with a double divan bed, a
bedroom with two single beds, shower
room with wash basin and WC.

All year MWB out of season 1wk min,
6mths max, 1unit, 1–4persons no pets
◉ fridge Electric Elec metered
⊡not provided ☎(3m) HCE in unit
⊖ TV ⊕3pin square P ♨(½m)

⊷ ♨o(3m) ☎(½m)

Min£35 Max£50pw (Low)
Min£60 Max£80pw (High)

C **Drumwall**
for bookings G M Thomson & Co, 27 King
Street, Castle Douglas,
Kirkcudbrightshire
☎Castle Douglas(0556)2701

Detached farm cottage commanding
spectacular views over the Fleet Estuary
and surrounding hills. Accommodation
comprises kitchen, living/dining room,
bathroom and three bedrooms, two with a
double bed and one with two single beds.
⅓m E of Gatehouse of Fleet off A75.

All year 1wk min, 6mths max, 1unit,
1–6persons ◊ ◉ fridge Electric &
open fires Elec inclusive
⌺notprovided ☎(3m) HCE in unit
TV ⊕3pin round ☎ ▥ ▦(2m)
↩ ♨(3m) ☖(3m)
Min£45 Max£105pw

H 30 High Street
for bookings G M Thomson & Co, 27 King
Street, Castle Douglas,
Kirkcudbrightshire
☎Castle Douglas(0556)2701

Spacious stone-built terraced house on
main street. Consists of two bedrooms,
with twin beds and two single beds, a
kitchen, two bathrooms, cloakroom,
dining room and sitting room.

All year 1wk min, 6mths max, 1unit,
1–6persons ◊ nopets ◉ fridge
🍴 open fire Elec inclusive
⌺notprovided ☎(200yds) Ironing
board in unit HCE in unit TV
⊕3pin square P ▥ ▦(10yds)
↩ ♨ ☖ ▨ ♫
Min£50 Max£115pw

GAZELEY
Suffolk
Map5 TL76

C April Cottage Needham Street
for bookings Mrs E Turner, Needham
Hall, Gazeley, Newmarket, Suffolk
☎Newmarket(0638)750275

A delightful, detached cottage standing
in its own garden on the green of the tiny
hamlet of Needham Street, with views
over the surrounding countryside. It
comprises of lounge, dining room, open-
plan kitchen and a bedroom with two
single beds washhand basin/WC. The
first-floor comprises two twin-bedded
rooms and bathroom/WC.

All year 1wk min, 1mth max, 1unit,
1–6persons ◊ ♦ ◉ fridge
Electric Elec metered ⌺can be hired
☎(¾m) Airing cupboard in unit Iron in
unit Ironing board in unit HCE in unit
⊕ CTV ⊕3pin square 3P ▦(¾m)
↩ ☖(¾m)
Min£80 Max£120pw (Low)
Min£100 Max£140pw (High)

GELSTON
Dumfries & Galloway Kirkcudbrightshire
Map11 NX75

F 1–6 Courtyard Cottages
for bookings Gelston Castle Estate,
Orchardton Mains, Palnackie, Castle
Douglas, Kirkcudbrightshire DG7 1QH
☎Palnackie(055660)268

Converted stable block with surrounding
courtyard in extensive grounds of
Gelston Castle Estate. Six flats, five of
which comprise three twin-bedded
rooms, kitchen and bathroom, four have
cloakrooms. Flats 1–4 have spacious
sitting rooms (dining room in No 3, and
additional bathroom in No. 1). No 5 is on
first-floor and has living/dining room. Flat
6 has two twin-bedded rooms,

sitting/living room, kitchen and
bathroom. Access by B736 about 2½m S
of Castle Douglas on right past lodge
house up rough private road.

Apr-Oct 1wk min, 6units, 1–6persons
◊ ◉ fridge Electric & open fires
Elec inclusive ⌺notprovided ☎ WM
on premises Airing cupboard in unit
Iron in unit Ironing board in unit HCE in
unit TV ⊕3pin square P ▥
▦(2½m) ⌲ ↯Hard
↩ ♨(3m) ☖(3m) ▨(3m) ♫(3m)
🐾(3m)
Min£55 Max£75pw (Low)
Min£145 Max£170pw (High)

F Gelston House
for bookings Gelston Castle Estate,
Orchardton Mains, Palnackie, Castle
Douglas, Kirkcudbrightshire DG7 1QH
☎Palnackie(055660)268

Former Dower House of the Gelston
Castle Estate dating back to the 18th-
century, this spacious two-floor building
offers four twin-bedded rooms (all with
their own bathroom), large kitchen, utility
room, large sitting room, large dining
room, and entrance hall. Access by
B736, about 2½m S of Castle Douglas, on
right.

Apr-Oct 1wk min, 1unit, 1–8persons
◊ ◉ fridge 🍴 Elec inclusive
⌺notprovided ☎ WM on premises
Airing cupboard in unit Iron in unit
Ironing board in unit HCE in unit TV
⊕3pin square P ▥ ▦(2½m) ↯Hard
↩ ♨(2½m) ☖(2½m) ▨(2½m)
♫(2½m) 🐾(2½m)
Min£100 Max£250pw

C Motte Brae No 3
for bookings G M Thomson & Co, 27 King
Street, Castle Douglas,
Kirkcudbrightshire DG7 1AB
☎Castle Douglas(0556)2701

A semi-dated cottage with a large
grassed garden, situated off a quiet road
3m W of Castle Douglas. It contains
living/dining room, kitchen and three
bedrooms.

All year 1wk min, 1unit, 1–8persons
◊ ◉ fridge Electric & open fires
Elec inclusive ⌺notprovided ☎(1m)
Iron in unit Ironing board in unit HCE in
unit CTV ⊕3pin square P ▥ ▦
▦(3m)
↩ ♨(3m) ☖(3m) 🐾(3m)
Min£45 Max£105pw

GILLING EAST
North Yorkshire
Map8 SE67

C Sunset Cottages
for bookings Mr R J Kelsey, Grimston
Manor Farm, Gilling East, York YO6 4HR
☎Brandsby(03475)654

Three cottages converted from a farm
granary in the rual surroundings of the

Howardian Hills. Ground floor
accommodation comprises
lounge/dining/kitchen all combined and
tastefully designed. The first-floor has a
double- and a twin-bedded room and
bathroom/WC.

Mid Mar-Oct & Xmas-New Year
7days min, 6wks max, 3units,
1–4persons ◊ nopets ◉ fridge
Electric Elec metered ⌺inclusive
☎(1½m) HCE in unit ⊕ TV
⊕3pin square 10P ▥ ▦(3m)
↩ ♨ ☖(1½m)
Min£70 Max£80pw (Low)
Min£125 Max£130pw (High)

GILSLAND
Northumberland
Map12 NY66

F Hill Farmhouse The Hill, Gilsland,
Carlisle, Cumbria CA6 7DA
☎Gilsland(06972)214

Three units located in recently converted
farmhouse built around a courtyard. All
flats have two twin-bedded rooms,
bathroom/WC and kitchen. In addition,
the ground-floor flat has a single
convertible bed in the lounge and the
first-floor flat and other flat, which is on
two levels, have two convertible beds in
the lounge.

All year MWB out of season
3nights min, 3units, 4–6persons [◊]
[◊] ◉ fridge Electric Elec metered
⌺inclusive ☎ [Iron on premises]
[Ironing board on premises] HCE in
unit [Launderette on premises] ⊕
TV ⊕3pin square P ▥ ▦(1m)
Games room
↩ ♨(2m) ☖(1m)
Min£38 Max£48pw (Low)
Min£70 Max£100pw (High)

GIRVAN
Strathclyde Ayrshire
Map10 NX19

F 52 Dalrymple Street
for bookings Mrs M M Hay, Bon Accord,
50 Dalrymple Street, Girvan, Ayrshire
KA26 9BT
☎Girvan(0465)4421

A first-floor modernised flat with own
entrance situated above shop in main
shopping centre of coastal town. The
accommodation comprises
lounge/diner, kitchen, bathroom and two
bedrooms.

All year MWB out of season 1wk min,
1mth max, 1unit, 2–4persons ◊ ♦
nopets ◉ fridge Electric
Elec metered ⌺inclusive ☎(150yds)
Iron in unit Ironing board in unit HCE in
unit [Launderette within 300yds] CTV
⊕3pin square ▦
↩ ♨(¾m) ☖(100yds) ▨(100yds)
♫(100yds) 🐾(50yds)
Min£75 Max£120pw

GLAN CONWY
Gwynedd
Map **6** SH87

H Mr & Mrs M Slater **Cromlech Farm**
Glan Conwy, Colwyn Bay, Clwyd
☎Glan Conwy(049268)274

A semi-detached farmhouse consisting of dining room with an Aga cooker, kitchen, lounge. On the first-floor there is a twin-bedded room with two folding single beds and one double-bedsed room. Bathroom/WC combined.

Etr-Oct 1wk min, 1mth max, 1unit, 6persons ◇ ◆ no pets Aga fridge Electric Elec metered ⬚ not provided ☎(½m) SD in unit Airing cupboard in unit Iron in unit Ironing board in unit HCE in unit ⊖ TV ⊕3pin square P ⬚(2m)
⊖ 🚰(2m)
Min65pw (Low)

GLASGOW
Strathclyde *Lanarkshire*
Map **11** NS56

F Maclay Hall Office **Maclay Hall** 18 Park Terrace, Glasgow G3 6BX
☎041-332 5056

Early Victorian three-storey city mansion overlooking Kelvingrove Park, and with fine views of the city. The flats vary in size and all have been modernised in keeping with the traditonal design of the house.

10Aug-Sep MWB 3dqys min, 3mths max, 5units, 1–10persons ⊛ fridge 🍴 Elec inclusive ⬚ inclusive Airing supboard on premises Iron on premises Ironing board on premises HCE on premises [Launderette on premises] ⊖ ⊕3pin square 🔥 ⬚(500yds)
⊖ 🚰(½m) 🚿(½m) 🛁(½m)
Min£27pw

F Mr J Ferguson **White House** 11–13 Cleveden Crescent, Glasgow G12 0PA
☎041-339 9375

Modernised, two-storey terraced houses in West End residential crescent opposite a small park. Suites of mixed sizes, and degrees of luxury. Attractively converted property in pleasant surroundings.

All year MWB 1night min, 32units, 1–4persons ◇ [◇] ◆ no pets ⊛ fridge Electric Elec inclusive ⬚ inclusive ☎ Iron on premises Ironing board on premises HCE in unit [Launderette within 300yds] ⊖ ⊛ CTV ⊕3pin square 🔥 📺 ⬚(1¾m)
⊖ 🍴(3m) 🚰(½m) 🚿(1m) 🛁(1m)

> 1982 prices quoted throughout gazetteer

GLENBORRODALE
Highland *Argyll*
Map **13** NM66

B&H **Lochside Holidays,** 14 Beltane Drive, London SW19 5JR
☎01-946 9779

The Kennels and The Cottage are two semi-detached bungalows and Glen House is a larger attractive stone house. All are situated to the east of Glenborrodale Castle Hotel accessible by a private road in 23 acres of uncultivated hillside with small lawns around houses.

All year MWB 7days min, 3units, 1–10persons [◇] ◇ ◆ ⊛ fridge Electric Elec inclusive(over 300KWH charged) ⬚ inclusive WM in unit TD in unit Airing cupboard in unit Iron in unit Ironing board in unit HCE in unit ⊖ ⊕3pin square P
⊖ 🚰(200yds)

Min£90 Max£220pw (Low)
Min£240 Max£360pw (High)

Ch Mrs G A Hunter **Log Chalet** Hunterscolt, Glenborrodale, Acharacle, Argyll PH36 4JP
☎Glenborrodale(09724)219

Modern, pine-log chalet situated on hillside overlooking Loch Sunart. Accommodation comprises two small bedrooms, lounge with convertible settee, kitchenette and bathroom.

2Apr-29Oct 1wkmin, 5wksmax, 1unit,
1–5persons ◆ ◎ fridge Electric
Elecmetered ⬓notprovided ☎(½m)
Iron on premises Ironing board on
premises HCE in unit ⊙
⊕3pinsquare P ♨(10m)
↔ ♀(½m)
Min£50 Max£95pw

GLENGAIRN
Grampian *Aberdeenshire*
Map**15**NO39

H Candacraig
for bookings Aboyne Estates, Estate
Office, Old Station, Dinnet, Aboyne,
Aberdeenshire AB35LL
☎Dinnet(033985)341
*Granite house, fully modernised and
furnished to a high standard. Large
comfortable rooms, pleasantly
decorated. Separate lounge, dining room
and kitchen with Rayburn cooker and
electric rings. Four bedrooms (double,
twin, single and bunks).*
Mar-3rd wk July 1wkmin, 1mthmax,
1unit, 1–7persons ◆ ◎ fridge
Electric & open fires Rayburn
Elec inclusive ⬓canbehired ☎ WM
Iron Ironing board HCE ⊙
⊕3pinsquare P ♨ ⊞ ♨(2m)
Fishing
↔ ♀(3m)
Max£95pw (Low)
Max£128pw (High)

C Morven West
for bookings Aboyne Estates, Estate
Office, Old Station, Dinnet, Aboyne,
Aberdeenshire AB35LL
☎Dinnet(033985)341
*Small, semi-detached cottage in a
delightful glen surrounded by hills and
beside the River Gairn. Comfortable
accommodation with small, separate
kitchen, living room, two double
bedrooms, shower and WC. Ground-floor
accommodation and easy access
making the cottage suitable for elderly
people.*
Mar-Oct 1wkmin, 1mthmax, 1unit,
1–4persons ◆ ◆ ◎ fridge
Electric Elec inclusive ⬓can be hired
☎(2m) HCE in unit ⊕3pinsquare P

Glenborrodale
—
Glenshee

⊞ ♨(2m) Trout fishing
↔ ♀(3m) ▨(3m)
Max£75pw (Low)
Max£85pw (High)

H Glengairn Old School
for bookings Mr I G Mackenzie, Upper
Kingshill, Kingswells, Aberdeens
AB18QB
☎Aberdeen(0224)740454
*Ideal family accommodation, this old
greystone schoolhouse is set amidst
woodlands in a secluded glen. The house
is well equipped, with radiogram, books
and games. Accommodation comprises
living room with parquet flooring, kitchen,
bathroom/shower and two single
bedrooms (also with parquet flooring) on
the ground floor, and two bedrooms (one
double and one room with four beds) on
the first-floor. Dishwasher.*
May-Nov MWB out of season
2wksmin, 1unit, 1–7persons ◎
fridge Electric & open fires
Elecmetered ⬓notprovided ☎ WM
in unit SD in unit Airing cupboard in
unit Iron in unit Ironing board in unit
HCE in unit ◈ TV ⊕3pinsquare
⊕3pinround 6P ♨(6m)
Min£105 Max£120pw

GLENISLA
Tayside *Perthshire*
Map**15**NO26

C Altaltan
for bookings Mrs M Everett, Inchley,
Alyth, Blairgowrie, Perthshire
☎Alyth(08283)2469
*Quaint country cottage of charm and
character in rural setting surrounded by
garden and a small burn flowing into
River Isla nearby. There is a living room
with small bedroom off, kitchen with
adjacent dinette and double bedroom, a
bedroom with three beds and fine
bathroom. The cottage lies on the B951
and is best approached by way of the
A93 from Blairgowrie.*
Apr-Oct MWB out of season 1wkmin,
1unit, 1–7persons ◆ ◆ ◎ fridge

Electric & open fires Elecmetered
⬓can be hired ☎(1m) Airing
cupboard in unit Iron in unit Ironing
board in unit HCE in unit
⊕3pinsquare P ♨ ♨(1½m)
↔ ♀(3m)

H Little Forter
for bookings Mrs M Everett, Inchley,
Alyth, Blairgowrie, Perthshire
☎Alyth(08283)2469
*Stone farmhouse giving delightful outlook
down the Glen. There is a sitting room,
dining room, spacious kitchen, utility
room, shower/WC, and upstairs, three
double bedrooms and two singles, with
two bathrooms either of which can
connect to a bedroom. The house is in
good order throughout.*
All year MWB out of season 1wkmin,
1unit, 1–8persons ◇ ◆ ◆ ◎
fridge 🍴 & log fires Elecmetered
⬓can be hired ☎(1m) Airing
cupboard in unit Iron in unit Ironing
board in unit HCE in unit ⊙
⊕3pinsquare P ♨ ♨(½m)
↔ ♀(3m)

GLENSHEE (SPITTAL OF)
Tayside *Perthshire*
Map**15**NO16

C Dalmunzie Ltd (Cottages) Spittal of
Glenshee, Blairgowrie, Perthshire
PH107QG
☎Glenshee(025085)226
*Four cottages located on the Dalmunzie
Estate. 'Glenlochsie' is a former
shepherd's cottage comprising small
kitchen with dining alcove, lounge,
bathroom and two twin-bedded rooms.
'Dower' is the largest property with
lounge, dining room, two twin-bedded
rooms on ground-floor and two
bathrooms. 'Lochsie' has a
lounge/bedroom (double), dining room,
small kitchen and large porch. 'Leanach'
has a lounge, kitchen, double bedroom
and is reached by a steep driveway.*
All year MWB 4units, 1–12persons
◇ ◆ ◎ fridge Electric
Elec inclusive ⬓inclusive
☎(400yds), Logie 1½m) Iron in unit →

Ironing board in unit   HCE in unit
⊕3pin square   P   ▥   ▥(20m)
↪Hard   Trout fishing

↩   ▱(6m)   ♨(400yds)

C   Easter & Wester Caiplich
for bookings Mrs Burke & Mrs Cameron,
Dalnaglar Castle, Glenshee, Blairgowrie,
Perthshire
☎Blacklunans(025082)232

*Semi-detached cottages converted from
original coachhouse and stables. Easter
has a large living room with open beamed
ceiling and gallery (which can be used as
additional sleeping accommodation),
kitchen, bathroom and three bedrooms.
Wester has a living room with additonal
bedroom over (loft access), kitchen,
bathroom and two double bedrooms.
Traditional furnishings and simple décor.*

All year   MWB   2 days min, 2 units,
1–6 persons   ◇   ◎   fridge   Electric &
open fires   Elec metered   ▣ can be
hired   ☎(3m)   Iron on premises   Ironing
board on premises   HCE in unit   ⊕
CTV   ⊕3pin square   2P   ▥(8m)   Trout
fishing

↩   ♨(3m)

Min£45 Max£95pw

F   Mount Blair Tower
for bookings Mrs Burke & Mrs Cameron,
Dalnaglar Castle, Glenshee, Blairgowrie,
Perthshire
☎Blacklunans(025082)232

*Self-contained apartment in east wing of
castellated mansion. Access is by
outside spiral staircase to first floor of
building (alternative access for luggage
is permitted). At this level is the entrance
hall with cloakroom and WC. Upstairs
there is a large kitchen, dining room with
french doors out onto a balcony, two twin
bedrooms, one double bedroom and a
bathroom. On the top floor there is an
architect-designed and converted
studio/living room with beamed ceiling,
panelled walls and panoramic views.*

All year   MWB   2 days min, 1 unit,
1–6 persons   ◇   ◎   fridge   ▥
Elec metered   ▣ can be hired   ☎(3m)
Iron on premises   Ironing board on
premises   HCE in unit   ⊕   CTV
⊕3pin square   2P   ▥(8m)   Trout fishing

↩   ♨(3m)

Min£75 Max£95pw (Low)
Min£110 Max£125pw (High)

F   East Wing
for bookings Mrs Burke & Mrs Cameron,
Dalnaglar Castle, Glenshee, Blairgowrie,
Perthshire
☎Blacklunans(025082)232

*Self-contained apartment set in
castellated mansion. Accommodation
comprises drawing room, dining room,
kitchen and WC on 1st-floor. 2nd-floor
consists of large master bedroom with
private bathroom, two twin-bedded
rooms, one double-bedded room and
bathroom.*

All year   MWB   2 days min, 1 unit,
1–9 persons   ◇   ◎   fridge   ▥

Glenshee
—
Godolphin Cross

Elec metered   ▣ can be hired   ☎(3m)
Iron on premises   Ironing board on
premises   HCE in unit   ⊕   CTV
⊕3pin square   2P   ▥(8m)   Trout fishing

↩   ♨(3m)

Min£100 Max£135pw (Low)
Min£150 Max£175pw (High)

C   Keeper's Cottage
for bookings Mrs Burke & Mrs Cameron,
Dalnaglar Castle, Glenshee, Blairgowrie,
Perthshire
☎Blacklunans(025082)232

*Detached two-storey cottage offering
lounge/dining room with kitchen off, one
double- and one twin-bedded room and
bathroom, all on ground-floor. A twin- and
single-bedded room in the attic.*

All year   MWB   2 days min, 1 unit,
1–9 persons   ◇   ◎   fridge   Electric &
open fires   Elec metered   ▣ can be
hired   ☎(3m)   Iron on premises   Ironing
board on premises   HCE in unit   ⊕
CTV   ⊕3pin square   2P   ▥(8m)   Trout
fishing

↩   ♨(3m)

Min£45 Max£65pw (Low)
Min£80 Max£95pw (High)

C   Tower House
for bookings Mrs Burke & Mrs Cameron,
Dalnaglar Castle, Glenshee, Blairgowrie,
Perthshire
☎Blacklunans(025082)232

All year   MWB   2 days min, 1 unit,
1–6 persons   ◇   ◎   fridge   Electric &
open fires   Elec metered   ▣ can be
hired   ☎(3m)   Iron on premises   Ironing
board on premises   HCE in unit   ⊕
CTV   ⊕3pin square   2P   ▥(8m)   Trout
fishing

↩   ♨(3m)

Min£45 Max£60pw (Low)
Min£75 Max£90pw (High)

GLEN TROOL
Dumfries & Galloway *Kirkcudbrightshire*
Map**10** NX48

H   Glentrool Village
for bookings Forest Holiday Bookings,
Forestry Commission, 231 Corstorphine
Road, Edinburgh, EH12 7AT
☎031-334 0066

*Eight two-storey semi-detached former
forestry workers' houses set in Forestry
Commission village. Simple but
comfortable accommodation comprising
lounge/diner, kitchen, bathroom and
single bedroom on the ground-floor and
two twin-bedded rooms on the 1st-floor.
Access is from A714 Newton
Stewart/Girvan road; at Bargrennan
follow unclass road to Glentrool/Straiton.*

1982 prices quoted throughout
gazetteer

All year   MWB out of season   1 wk min,
1 mth max, 8 units, 1–5 persons   ◇   ◆
◆   ◎   fridge   Electric   Elec metered
▣ not provided   ☎(100yds)   Airing
cupboard in unit   HCE in unit
⊕3pin round   11P   ▥(100yds)   Fishing

↩   ♨(½m)

GLOUCESTER
Gloucestershire
Map**3** SO81

F   The Limes 96 Barnwood Road
for bookings Mrs J Limbrick, Alfords
Farm, Upleadon, Newent, Glos GL18 1EF
☎Newent(0531)820578

*These self-contained flats are housed
within a large detached property which is
set in its own grounds and situated in a
pleasant residential area of Gloucester.
Each flat comprises lounge/diner (except
for one which has a separate dining
room), kitchen, bathroom and separate
WC. All have one bedroom with either
double or twin beds.*

All year   3 days min, 3 mths max, 9 units,
2 persons   ◇   ◆   ◎   fridge   Electric
Elec metered   ▣ can be hired
☎(50yds)   Airing cupboard in unit   Iron
in unit   Ironing board in unit   HCE in unit
⊕   TV   ⊕3pin square   9P   ▥(200yds)

↩   ▱(1½m)   ♨(200yds)   ▨(1½m)
♫(1½m)   ▦(1½m)

Min£35 Max£50pw (Low)
Min£40 Max£55pw (High)

F   Mrs R I Yorke **Upton Knoll, 1st &
2nd Floor Apartment** Upton Hill, Upton St
Leonards, Glos GL4 8DB
☎Gloucester(0452)67192

*Two flats in a country house of distinction,
furnished and equipped to a high
standard. Both flats have modern
bathroom and kitchen. One flat has
lounge/diner and three bedrooms, a
double, a twin and a family room with
double and single beds. The other flat
has one twin bedroom with en suite
bathroom and lounge/diner with bed-
settee.*

All year   MWB out of season   1 wk min,
2 units, 2–7 persons, nc5   no pets   ◎
fridge   ▥   Elec inclusive   ▣ can be
hired   ☎(1½m)   Airing cupboard in one
unit   Iron in unit   Ironing board in unit
HCE in unit   ⊕   TV   ⊕3pin square   P
▥   ▥(½m)

↩   ♨(¼m)

Min£45pw (Low)
Min£60 Max£100pw (High)

GODOLPHIN CROSS
Cornwall
Map**2** SW63

B   9 Forth Vean
for bookings Mr & Mrs G N F Broughton,
Orchard House, 26 Wall Rd, Gwinear,
Hayle, Cornwall TR27 5HA
☎Leedstown(073685)201

*Detached, modern bungalow situated on
a very small private site in a rural location
approx. 4m NW of Heston. This well*

appointed property comprises of lounge with open fire, kitchen with breakfast bar and dining area, two twin-bedded rooms and one double and a bathroom/WC.

All year 1wk min, 1 units, 6 persons ◇ ◆ ◎ fridge ♨ Elec inclusive Ⓛcan be hired ☎(100yds) Airing cupboard in unit Iron in unit Ironing board in unit HCE in unit ⊙ CTV ③3pin square 1P 1🏠 Ⓜ ♨(100yds)
⇔ 🛁(100yds)

GODSHILL
Isle of Wight
Map4 SZ58

C Bank Cottage High Street
for bookings Mrs & Mrs Applin, Kareley Cottage, High Street, Godshill, Ventnor, Isle of Wight
☎Godshill(098 389)402

A small period cottage in a pretty village. The accommodation includes two bedrooms, sitting room, dining room, large bathroom and kitchen. The cottage is 5m from Shanklin and is in pleasant surroundings overlooking countryside.

All year MWB out of season 1wk min, 1mth max, 1 unit, 2–5 persons ◇ ◆ ⌀ fridge ♨ Electric Elec & Gas inclusive Ⓛinclusive ☎(200yds) SD in unit Airing cupboard in unit Iron in unit Ironing board in unit HCE in unit ⊛ CTV ③3pin square P Ⓜ ♨(200yds)
⇔ 🛁(300yds)
Min£60 Max£110pw

GOLSPIE
Highland *Sutherland*
Map14 NH89

Ca Log Cabin Backies
for bookings Mr J M L Scott, The Old Rectory, Tinwell, Stamford, Lincolnshire
☎Stamford(0780)3365

A modern, pine log cabin offering holiday accommodation in a peaceful setting, with splendid views. There are three bedrooms, lounge/diner, kitchen and bathroom.

Godolphin Cross
—
Goodnestone

Mar–Dec 1wk min, 1mth max, 1 unit, 1–5 persons no pets ◎ fridge Electric & open fires Elec metered Ⓛnot provided ☎(100yds) Airing cupboard in unit Iron in unit Ironing board in unit HCE in unit ⊙ TV can be hired ③3pin square P 🏠 ♨(1½m)
⇔ 🛁(1½m) 🛁(1½m) 📺(1½m)
Min£35 Max£45pw (Low)
Min£55 Max£80pw (High)

GOODNESTONE
Kent
Map5 TR25

C 8 Lower Rowling
for bookings The Estate Office, Knowlton Court, Wingham, Canterbury, Kent CT3 1PT
☎Sandwich(0304)617344

Country cottage sleeping six people. Well-furnished accommodation comprises three bedrooms, sitting room, dining room, kitchen and bathroom/WC. Garage and garden.

All year MWB out of season 1wk min, 8mths max, 1 unit 1–6 persons [◇] ◆ ◆ ◎ fridge Electric Elec metered Ⓛcan be hired ☎(1m) Airing cupboard Iron Ironing board HCE ⊙ TV ③3pin square 🏠 Ⓜ ♨(1m)
⇔ 🛁(1m)
Min£45 Max£50pw (Low)
Min£75 Max£110pw (High)

C 3 & 4 Meadow Cottages Lower Rowling
for bookings The Estate Office, Knowlton Court, Wingham, Canterbury, Kent CT3 1PT
☎Sandwich(0304)617344

Two cottages with communicating door through the kitchens, can be let separately or together, each sleeping six in two twin-bedded rooms and one with a pair of bunks, bathroom, kitchen and sitting room well-furnished, retaining a farm cottage atmosphere.

All year MWB out of season 2 units, 1–12 persons [◇] ◆ ◆ ◎ fridge Electric Elec metered Ⓛcan be hired ☎(1m) Airing cupboard Iron Ironing board HCE ⊙ TV ③3pin square ♨(1m)
⇔ 🛁(1m)
Min£40 Max£45pw (Low)
Min£60 Max£90pw (High)

C Rowling Court Cottage Rowling
for bookings The Estate Office, Knowlton Court, Wingham, Canterbury, Kent CT3 1PT
☎Sandwich(0304)617344

Semi-detached cottage having extensive views of countryside with driveway to garage and garden. Accommodation comprises kitchen, dining room, sitting room, three bedrooms, one double room, one twin-bedded room, one room with bunks, and bathroom/WC.

All year MWB out of season 1wk min, 8mths max, 1–6 persons [◇] ◆ ◎ fridge Elec metered Ⓛcan be hired ☎ Airing cupboard in unit Iron in unit Ironing board in unit HCE in unit ⊙ TV ③3pin square 1🏠 ♨(1m)
⇔ 🛁
Min£45 Max£50pw (Low)
Min£75 Max£110pw (High)

C Southview No 1 Lower Rowling
for bookings The Estate Office, Knowlton Court, Wingham, Canterbury, Kent CT3 1PT
☎Sandwich(0304)617344

Farm cottage in rural setting 9m from Canterbury. Accommodation comprises four twin-bedded rooms, kitchen, dining room, two sitting rooms and bathroom/WC.

All year MWB out of season 1wk min, 8mths max, 1 unit, 1–8 persons [◇] ◆ ◆ ◎ fridge Electric Elec metered Ⓛcan be hired ☎ Airing cupboard Iron Ironing board HCE ⊙ TV ③3pin square Ⓜ ♨(1m)
⇔ 🛁(1m)
Min£45 Max£50pw (Low)
Min£75 Max£110pw (High)

GOONHAVERN
Cornwall
Map 2 SW75

C **Beech, Cedar, Larch & Pine Cottages**
for bookings L D & J A Reynolds, Oak Ridge Farm, Goonhavern, Truro, Cornwall
☎Zelah(087 254)379

Four delightful holiday cottages converted from 200-year-old former stables and granary. Set in unspoilt farmland with beautiful views of the sea.
Beech *and* ***Larch*** *are first-floor cottages comprising one double-bedded room, one twin-bedded room, separate lounge with bed-settee, kitchenette, shower and WC.* ***Pine*** *cottage comprises one double room, one twin-bedded room, separate lounge with bed-settee, kitchenette and bathroom/WC.* ***Cedar*** *cottage comprises of two double bedrooms, one room with bunk beds, separate lounge with bed-settees, kitchenette, bathroom/WC.*

Mar-Oct MWB out of season 4 units, 1–7 persons [◇] ◇ ◆ ◷ fridge Gas Gas/Elec inclusive ⎣not provided ☎ WM on premises SD on premises Iron on premises Ironing board on premises HCE on premises ⊙ TV ⊕3 pin square 1P ▥ ♨(1m)
↔ ♨▣(3m) ♨(1m) 🅿(3m) ♫(3m)
Min£50 Max£105pw (Low)
Min£120 Max£170pw (High)

GOOSEHAM
Cornwall
Map 2 SS21

C **Glen Elm Cottage**
for bookings Mrs B A Jones, Glen Elm, Gooseham, Morwenstow, Bude, Cornwall EX23 9PG
☎Morwenstow(028 883)269

A detached cottage surrounded by lawns. Accommodation comprises entrance hall, lounge/diner with put-u-up, kitchen, one double bedroom, one twin-bedded room and bathroom/WC. For access from the A39 follow sign Morwenstow and Bush Inn. Turn right at Gooseham sign then third left.

Mar-Nov MWB out of season 1 wk min, 1 mth max, 1 unit, 2–6 persons ◇ ◆ ◷ fridge Calor gas & Electric Gas inclusive Elec metered ⎣can be hired ☎ WM on premises Airing cupboard in unit Iron in unit Ironing board in unit HCE in unit ⊙ CTV ⊕3 pin square ♨2 pin round P ♨(1m)
↔ ♨(1m)
Min£45 Max£75pw (Low)
Max£85pw (High)

F **Wild Goose Cottage Flats 1 & 2**
for bookings Mrs D H Young, Little Orchard, 26 Clive Road, Esher, Surrey KT10 8PS
☎Esher(0372) 64514

A detached stone cottage converted into two flats. The first flat is approached by

an outside stairway of stone steps and comprises one double bedroom, one twin-bedded room, one bedroom with twin bunks, kitchen/diner and lounge. The ground-floor flat comprises lounge with two divans, one twin-bedded room, kitchen/diner and has a lawned garden. For access from the A39 turn into the Eastcott road for Wildgoose, on the right before entering the hamlet of Gooseham.

All year MWB out of season 4 days min, 6 mths max, 2 units, 2–6 persons ◇ ◷ fridge ♨ Elec metered ⎣not provided ☎(1m) WM in one unit SD in one unit Airing cupboard in unit Iron in unit Ironing board in unit HCE in unit ⊙ CTV ⊕3 pin square P ♨(1m)
↔ ♨(1¼m)
Min£25 Max£65pw (Low)
Min£70 Max£115pw (High)

GORING-ON-THAMES
Oxfordshire
Map 4 SU68

H Mr L J M Weaver **Cleeve Mill** Goring-on-Thames, Reading, Berks RG8 9DB
☎Goring-on-Thames(0491)872624

Three modern and delightful units created by converting part of a watermill on the River Thames.

All year 1 wk min, 6 mths max, 3 units, 2–5 persons, nc5, no pets ◷ fridge ♨ Elec inclusive ⎣inclusive ☎ Iron in unit Ironing board in unit HCE in unit ⊙ CTV ⊕3 pin square ▥
♨(500yds) Rowing boats available
Min£127.65 Max£190.09pw (Low)
Min£166.75 Max£239.20pw (High)

GOSFORTH
Cumbria
Map 11 NY00

C **The Cottage**
for bookings Mr & Mrs P Richardson, Haverigg Moorside, Gosforth, Seascale, Cumbria
☎Gosforth(09405)410

Modern, comfortable, well-equipped cottage, constructed from a stone-built barn and hayloft, adjacent to the proprietor's farmhouse. There are two twin-bedded rooms and one double. Set in rural surroundings ½m from Gosforth and approximately 3m from the beach.

Mar-Oct 1 wk min, 1 mth max, 1 unit, 6 persons ◇ ◷ fridge Electric & open fires Gas/Elec metered ⎣inclusive ☎(½m) Airing cupboard in unit Iron in unit HCE in unit ⊙ ⊕3 pin square ♨(½m)
↔ ♨(½m)
Min£60 Max£100pw

1982 prices quoted throughout gazetteer

H **3 Hardinghill Cottage**
for bookings Mrs P Lawson, High Boonwood Farm, Gosforth, Seascale, Cumbria
☎Gosforth(09405)423

A middle terraced house situated on the edge of the village near to coast and mountains. There are two bedrooms on the first-floor and a shower room and an open-plan ground-floor of good design.

Etr-Oct MWB in season 7 days min, 1 unit, 2–6 persons ◇ ◆ ♨ fridge Electric Elec metered ⎣not provided ☎(200yds) Airing cupboard in unit Iron in unit HCE in unit CTV ⊕3 pin square ▥ ♨(200yds)
↔ ♨▣(3m) ♨(200yds)
Min£50 Max£110pw

GRAMPOUND
Cornwall
Map 2 SW94

C **Golden Keep**
for bookings Mr & Mrs Perry, Golden Manor, Grampound, Cornwall TR2 4DF
☎Tregony(087253)500

Attractive furnished stone cottage set in large gardens of a beautiful hamlet. Comprises lounge/diner, ktichen, two double bedrooms and bathroom/WC.

Apr-Sep 1 wk min, 3 mths max, 1 unit, 1–4 persons [◇] ◇ ♨ fridge Electric Elec metered ⎣inclusive ☎(2m) TD in unit Airing cupboard in unit Iron in unit Ironing board in unit HCE in unit ⊙ CTV ⊕3 pin square 2P ▥ ♨(2m)
↔ ♨(2m)
Min£65 Max£135pw (High)

GRANGE-OVER-SANDS
Cumbria
Map 7 SD47

F Mrs R Bowyer **Berkeley** Kents Bank Road, Grange-over-Sands, Cumbria
☎Grange-over-Sands(044 85)2065

Two comfortable, spacious flats on the first- and second-floors of a large stone-built terraced house, built in 1875. One flat has a twin and double bedroom and the other has a family bedroom. The house is set on the main coast road just S of the town centre and has good views of Morecambe Bay.

All year MWB 2 units, 3–4 persons ◇ ♨ fridge Elec metered ⎣can be hired ☎ Airing cupboard in unit HCE in unit ⊙ TV ⊕3 pin square P ♨(100yds)
↔ ♨(300yds)
Min£54 Max£72pw

F Mrs M Shrigley **Granville Holiday Flats** Granville, Methven Terrace, Kents Bank Road, Grange-over-Sands, Cumbria LA11 7DP
☎Grange-over-Sands(044 85)2509

Two large, comfortable and well-equipped flats in a stone-built terraced house, on the coast road west of the town

centre. Both flats have good views across
Morecambe Bay and are convenient for
visiting the Lake District.

All year 1wk min, 1mth max, 2units,
4–6persons, nc4 ◉ fridge Electric
Elec metered ⌂ inclusive ☎ Airing
cupboard in unit Iron on premises
Ironing board on premises HCE in unit
☉ TV ③3pin square ▥ ♨(½m)

⊖ ♀(300yds) ▨(½m)

Min£45 Max£48pw (Low)
Min£50 Max£55pw (High)

F *Kentholme* Kents Bank Road
for bookings Mrs Poole, The Coach
House, Seawood, Grange-over-Sands,
Cumbria
☎Grange-over-Sands(04484)3235

*Spacious and comfortable
accommodation over a ladies'
hairdressing salon comprising a
maisonette with two family bedrooms and
a flat with one twin bedroom and double
bed-settee. Situated on the main road
close to the town centre and shops, a
good base for touring the southern Lake
District.*

All year 1wk min, 2mths max, 2units,
4–7persons ◈ ♨ ◉ fridge
Electric Gas/Elec metered
⌂ not provided ☎(100yds) Airing
cupboard in unit Iron on premises
Ironing board on premises HCE in unit
[Launderette within 300yds] ☉ TV
③3pin square ▥ ♨(50yds)

⊖ ♀(100yds)

GRANSMOOR
Humberside
Map**8** TA15

C *Fold Cottage*
for bookings Mrs S R Barry, Gransmoor
Lodge, Gransmoor, Driffield,
Humberside YO25 8HY
☎Burton Agnes(026 289)340

*Self-contained single-storey converted
farm cottage (once a barn) situated
behind a country house in quiet rural
position. Accommodation comprises
kitchen/diner, shower/WC with bidet, two
bedrooms, one with double bed, one with
bunk beds and a bed-settee in the
lounge.*

All year MWB out of season 1wk min,
6mths max, 1unit, 1–6persons ◇
no pets ◉ fridge ♨ Elec metered
⌂ inclusive ☎ Airing cupboard in unit
Iron in unit Ironing board in unit HCE in
unit ☉ TV ③3pin square 2P
♨(3m) Croquet, table tennis

⊖ ♀(3m)

C *Gamekeeper's Cottage*
for bookings Mrs S R Barry, Gransmoor
Lodge, Gransmoor, Driffield,
Humberside YO25 8HY
☎Burton Agnes(026 289)340

*The cottage is attached to a secluded old
farmhouse surrounded by rural scenery.
Accommodation comprises kitchen,
dining room and sitting room on the
ground-floor. On the first-floor there is a*

---

*bathroom/WC, two bedrooms with a
double and a single bed and a room with
bunk beds.*

All year MWB out of season 1wk min,
1unit, 1–8persons ◇ ◈ ◆ no pets
◉ fridge Open & electric fires
Elec metered ⌂ inclusive ☎ Airing
cupboard in unit Iron in unit Ironing
board in unit HCE in unit TV
③3pin square P ♨(4m) Croquet

GRANTOWN-ON-SPEY
Highland *Moray*
Map**14** NJ02

H Mr J W Walker **Dunvegan Cottage**
Dunvegan Hotel, Heathfield Road,
Grantown-on-Spey, Inverness-shire
☎Grantown-on-Spey(0479)2301

*Two-storey modern house next door to
the hotel and with views of Crondale Hills;
5 minutes walk from River Spey.
Accommodation comprises
sitting/dining room, kitchen, and a single
bedroom and bathroom on the ground-
floor with one double, one twin-bedded
room on the first-floor.*

Etr–Oct 7days min, 2wks max, 1unit,
1–5persons ◈ ◆ ◉ fridge ♨
Elec metered ⌂ can be hired ☎ WM
in unit SD in unit Airing cupboard in
unit Iron in unit Ironing board in unit
☉ TV ③3pin square 2P ▥ ♨(½m)

⊖ ♨(200yds) ♀ ▨(1m) ♫(½m)

Min£85.75 Max£115pw

GRASMERE
Cumbria
Map**11** NY30

F **Beck Allans Self-Catering
Apartments**
for bookings Mr B G Yates, Beck Allans
Cottage, Grasmere, Ambleside, Cumbria
LA22 9SZ
☎Grasmere(09665)329

*Six flats located in an attractive stone-
built house in the heart of Grasmere
Village. They vary in size sleeping 2–5
persons and are all very well appointed
and comfortable.*

All year MWB out of season 3days min,
6units, 1–5persons ◇ ◆ ◉ fridge
Electric Elec metered ⌂ inclusive ☎
HCE in unit ☉ CTV ③3pin square
12P ▥ ♨(300yds)

⊖ ♀(½m) ♫(½m)

Min£80 Max£145pw (Low)
Min£110 Max£200pw (High)

F Mr & Mrs A D Bateman **Helm Cragg
Flat** Meadow Brow, Grasmere, Cumbria
LA22 9LR
☎Grasmere(09665)275

*First floor wing of house luxuriously
converted to a self-contained flat. It
comprises entrance hall with seating
area, open-plan kitchen/living room
leading to balcony with deck chairs; two
bedrooms, one twin, one double and*

---

shower/WC.

All year MWB out of season 2wks min,
3wks max, 1unit, 2–5persons ◈ ◆
no pets ◉ fridge Electric
Elec metered ⌂ inclusive ☎ SD on
premises Iron on premises Ironing
board on premises HCE in unit ☉
CTV ③3pin square 1P ▥ ♨(1m)

Min£55 Max£80pw (Low)
Min£100 Max£150pw (High)

C Mr & Mrs A D Bateman **The Cottage**
Meadow Brow, Grasmere, Cumbria
LA22 9LR
☎Grasmere(09665)275

*A modernised stone built cottage in the
grounds of the main house. It comprises
of ground floor lounge/diner and kitchen
with two bedrooms and shower/WC on
the first floor.*

All year MWB out of season
2nights min, 3wks max, 1unit,
3–5persons ◆ no pets ◉
fridge Electric Elec metered
⌂ inclusive ☎ SD on premises Iron on
premises Ironing board on premises
HCE in unit ☉ CTV ③3pin square
1P ▥ ♨(1m)

⊖ ♀(1m)

Min£50 Max£90pw (Low)
Min£110 Max£140pw (High)

F *Wood Close* How Head Lane
for bookings Mrs E A Simmons, 10 Tower
Road, Branksome Park, Poole, Dorset
☎Bournemouth(0202)762222

*A traditional lakeland country house
divided into seven self-contained flats.
The house stands in its own secluded 2½
acre grounds on the slopes of Rydal Fell
and is within walking distance of
Grasmere.*

All year 1wk min, 6wks max, 7units,
2–9persons ◈ ◆ fridge ♨
Elec metered ⌂ not provided ☎ WM
available SD in two units TD Airing
cupboard in unit Iron in unit HCE in
unit ☉ TV ③3pin square
③3pin round P ▥(in season) ♨(1m)

⊖ ♀(1m)

GREAT
Placenames incorporating the word
'Great' such as Gt Malvern and Gt
Yarmouth will be found under the actual
placename, *ie* Malvern, Yarmouth

GREENLAW
Borders *Berwickshire*
Map**12** NT74

C **Dean Cottage** Greenlaw
for bookings Miss J Bristow, Thorncroft,
Lilliesleaf, Roxburghshire TD6 9JD
☎Lilliesleaf(08357)424

*Pleasant cottage with garden, standing
adjacent to farm property, ½m from the
border town of Greenlaw.
Accommodation consists of sitting room
with open-range-type fire, kitchen/dining
room, bathroom, one double bedroom* →

and one room with two double beds.
Clean, fresh décor and neat standards in
fittings and furniture.

Mar–Oct MWB out of season 1wk min,
2mths max, 1 unit, 2–6 persons [◊] ◉
fridge Electric & coal fires
Elec metered Ⓛcan be hired
☎(100yds) WM in unit Iron in unit
Ironing board in unit HCE in unit TV
☺3 pin round P ♨(1m) Fishing

↦ ☗(1m)

Min£48 Max£55pw (Low)
Min£70 Max£85pw (High)

GREWELTHORPE
North Yorkshire
Map8 SE27

B Allendale
for bookings Mrs T Mould, Sunnydale,
Ilton Road, Grewelthorpe, Ripon, N Yorks
HG43DF
☎Kirkby Malzeard(076 583)389

Self-contained semi-detached bungalow
near the village centre. Sleeping
accommodation for five in a double-
bedded room, a room with three single
beds and a bed-settee in the lounge.
Separate kitchen and bathroom with WC.

All year MWB out of season 1wk min,
3mths max, 1 unit, 1–5 persons ◊ ◉
fridge ♨ Elec metered Ⓛcan be
hired ☎(150yds) WM in unit SD in
unit Airing cupboard in unit Iron in unit
Ironing board in unit HCE in unit ☺
☻ TV ☺3 pin square P ♨ ▥
♨(150yds)

↦ ☗(150yds)

Min£40 Max£55pw (Low)
Min£65pw (High)

C Heckfall Mount
for bookings Mrs T Mould, Sunnydale,
Ilton Road, Grewelthorpe, Ripon, N Yorks
☎Kirkby Malzeard(076 583)389

Self-contained two-storey stone-built
cottage in the village centre. Sleeping
accommodation for four, three single-
bedded room and three single beds in
another room (two make a double bed),
separate small kitchen and bathroom
with WC.

All year MWB out of season 1wk min,
1 unit, 1–4 persons ◊ ◉ fridge
Electric Elec metered Ⓛcan be hired
☎(200yds) WM in unit SD in unit
Airing cupboard in unit Iron in unit
Ironing board in unit HCE in unit ☺
☻ TV ☺3 pin round 2P 1♨ ▥
♨(25yds)

↦ ☗(20yds)

Min£40 Max£55pw (Low)
Min£65pw (High)

1982 prices quoted throughout
gazetteer

GWINEAR
Cornwall
Map2 SW53

C Mr & Mrs D B & J E Busfield Wall
Farm Gwinear, Hayle, Cornwall
☎Leedstown(073685)506

Three modern cottages adjacent to the
farmhouse which dates back to the 18th
century. Each accommodation
comprises of lounge with bed-settee,
kitchen/diner, one double bedroom with
additional single bed and one twin-
bedded room, bathroom/WC. The farm is
situated in the quiet hamlet of Wall, 3m W
of Camborne.

All year MWB out of season 1wk min,
1mth max, 3 units, 1–6 persons ◊ ◆
◉ fridge Electric Elec inclusive
Ⓛcan be hired ☎(400yds) Airing
cupboard in unit Iron in unit Ironing
board in unit HCE in unit ☺ CTV
☺3 pin square 1P 1♨ ▥ ♨(400yds)

↦ ☗(½m) ▥(½m)

Min£30 Max£140pw

GWITHIAN
Cornwall
Map2 SW54

F B R Staker **Sandbank Holiday Flats**
Gwithian, Hayle, Cornwall TR27 5BJ
☎Falmouth(0326)311063

Located off the B3301 Gwithian to Hayle
road, the flats are in two blocks of eight
surrounded by lawns and shrubbery, and
within walking distance of beaches. The
flats have one or two bedrooms and all
have bathroom/WC, kitchen/diner/
lounge with convertible settee.

Apr–Nov MWB out of season 1wk min,
1mth max, 18 units, 1–6 persons ◊
no pets ◉ fridge Electric
Elec metered Ⓛcan be hired ☎ Airing
cupboard in unit Iron on premises
Ironing board on premises HCE in unit
☺ CTV ☺3 pin square 1P ♨(50yds)

↦ ☗(½m) ▥(1m) ♫(1m) 🛥(1m)

Min£35 Max£155pw

HAPPISBURGH COMMON
Norfolk
Map9 TG32

B St Michael Mead
for bookings Mrs E Sharples, Orchard
Cottage, Great Melton, Norwich NR9 3BQ

Modern brick-built bungalow situated in
quiet position about 1m from the sea and
off B1159 ½m from village.
Accommodation comprises
lounge/diner, one double-bedded room,
one twin and one with bunk beds.

All year MWB out of season 4days min,
1mth max, 1 unit, 1–6 persons ◊ ◆
no pets ◉ fridge ♨ Elec inclusive
Ⓛnot provided ☎(100yds) WM in unit
SD in unit Airing cupboard in unit Iron

---

in unit Ironing board in unit HCE in unit
☺ TV ☺3 pin square 2P ▥ ♨(½m)

↦ ☗ ▥

Min£96pw (Low)
Min£100 Max£140pw (High)

HARLECH
Gwynedd
Map6 SH53

C Moel View
for bookings Mrs A Stumpp, Bron Haul,
Harlech, Gwynedd

Mid-terrace Welsh stone cottage
comprising lounge, dining room, kitchen,
bathroom/WC and three bedrooms (one
double, two single). On A496, the
Maentwrog side of Harlech.

Mar–Nov 1wk min, 4wks max, 1 unit,
1–4 persons, nc3 no pets ◉ fridge
Electric Elec metered Ⓛnot provided
☎ [Airing cupboard in unit]
[Launderette] ☺ ☺3 pin square 1P
▥ ♨(½m)

↦ δ(½m) ☗(½m)

Min£33 Max£43pw (Low)
Min£58 Max£68pw (High)

HARPFORD
Devon
Map3 SY09

C CC Ref 604L
for bookings Character Cottages
(Holidays) Ltd, 34 Fore Street, Sidmouth,
Devon EX10 8AQ
☎Sidmouth(039 53)77001

Thatched country cottage with attractive
garden, situated near coast. Comfortably
furnished and tastefully decorated, the
accommodation comprises small well-
equipped kitchen, large living room with
open fireplace and bread oven, two
bedrooms (one double and one twin)
plus cot, and bathroom/WC.

All year MWB out of season 1wk min,
6mths max, 1 unit, 4–5 persons ◊ ◉
fridge ♨ Elec inclusive Ⓛcan be
hired ☎ Airing cupboard in unit Iron in
unit Ironing board in unit HCE in unit
☺ TV P ♨ ♨(1m) ⌐

↦ ☗(1m) ▥(1m) ♫(1m)

Min£52 Max£80pw (Low)
Min£97 Max£142pw (High)

HARROGATE
North Yorkshire
Map8 SE35

C Bothy Cottage
for bookings Rudding Park Holiday
Cottages, Rudding Park, Follifoot,
Harrogate. N. Yorks HG3 1DT
☎Harrogate(0423)871350

A recently renovated old stone cottage
within Rudding Park which was formerly a
keepers cottage and has a small private
garden. All rooms are spacious and
tastefully furnished.

All year 1wk min, 3mths max, 1 unit,
1–7 persons ◊ ◆ ◉ fridge ♨

Elec metered ⌂can be hired ☎(30yds) WM in unit Airing cupboard HCE ⊖ CTV ③3pin square 4P 1🏠 🎲 ♿(30yds)

↩ ♒(1½m) ⚲(1½m) ✉(3m)

Min£60 Max£70pw (Low)
Min£110 Max£150pw (High)

F 104 Dragon Parade
for bookings Mrs G E Wood, Aarons, 54 Electric Avenue, Harrogate, N Yorks HG12BB
☎Harrogate(0423)502581

Two flats located within a stone-built, end of terrace house near the North Stray. Flat 2 has one family bedroom and a double folding bed in the lounge. Flat 3 has one double-bedded room, one bunk-bedded room and a single folding bed in the lounge.

All year MWB 1wk min, 2units, 1–5persons, nc4 no pets ⊚ fridge Electric Elecmetered ⌂inclusive ☎(200yds) Airing cupboard in unit Iron in unit Ironong board in unit HCE in unit [Launderette within 300yds] ⊗ TV ③3pin square ♿(150yds)

↩ ♒(1m) ⚲(150yds) 📷(150yds) 🎵(900yds) ✉(900yds)

Min£55pw Max£85pw

F Flats 1,2 & 4 25 St Mary's Avenue
for bookings Mrs G E Wood, 54 Electric Avenue, Harrogate, N Yorks HG12BB
☎Harrogate(0423)502581

These flats are located within an Edwardian terraced house near the town centre. They comprise kitchen, bathroom/WC, lounge and sleep 1–5. Bed-settee in lounge.

All year MWB 3days min, 3mths max, 3units, 1–5persons, nc4 no pets ⊚ fridge Electric Elecmetered ⌂inclusive Iron in unit Ironing board in unit HCE in unit [Launderette within 300yds] TV ③3pin square 1P ♿(100yds)

↩ ⚲(30yds) 📷(30yds) ✉(½m)

Min£55pw Max£90pw

C Keepers Cottage
for bookings Rudding Park Holiday Cottages, Rudding Park, Follifoot, Harrogate, N Yorks HG31DT
☎Harrogate(0423)871350

A large stone cottage in a quiet and secluded location standing in it's own garden with a small orchard and surrounded to the south and west by open fields. There are three bedrooms, two lounges, large kitchen, bathroom/WC and separate WC.

All year 1wk min, 3mths max, 1unit, 1–7persons ◆ ◆ ⊚ fridge Electric Elecmetered ⌂can be hired ☎(½m) Airing cupboard in unit HCE in unit TV ③3pin square 4P 🎲 ♿(½m)

↩ ♒(1½m) ⚲(1½m) ✉(3m)

Min£60 Max£70pw (Low)
Min£100 Max£160pw (High)

C North Lodge
for bookings Rudding Park Holiday

Cottages, Rudding Park, Follifoot, Harrogate, N Yorks HG31DT
☎Harrogate(0423)871350

This cottage occupies a very pleasant position, being the lodge cottage at the north entrance to Rudding Park, adjacent to camp site. It overlooks the Crimple valley and the park gardens. There are two bedrooms, kitchen/breakfast room and two ground-floor sitting rooms.

All year MWB out of season 1wk min, 3mths max, 1unit, 1–5persons ◆ ◆ ⊚ fridge Electric & solid fuel Elecmetered ⌂ can be hired ☎(60yds) Airing cupboard in unit Iron in unit Ironing board in unit [Launderette within 300yds] ⊖ CTV ③3pin square 4P 1🏠 🎲 ♿(60yds)

↩ ♒(1m) ⚲(1m) ✉(3m)

Min£50 Max£60pw (Low)
Min£90 Max£130pw (High)

C Peacock Cottage
for bookings Rudding Park Holiday Cottages, Rudding Park, Follifoot, Harrogate. N Yorks HG31DT
☎Harrogate(0423)871350

A spacious wing of Rudding House, retaining all the character of mansion living set in a quiet, elevated position with superb views over extensive lawns and parkland. The cottage is all on one level with two bedrooms and is suitable for wheelchair bound disabled.

All year 1wk min, 3mths max, 1unit, 1–4persons ◆ ◆ ⊚ fridge Electric Elecmetered ⌂can be hired ☎(½m) Iron in unit Ironing board in unit HCE in unit [Launderette within 300yds] CTV ③3pin square 6P 🎲 ♿(½m)

↩ ♒(2m) ⚲(2m) ✉(3m)

Min£50 Max£60pw (Low)
Min£90 Max£140pw (I ligh)

C Rock Cottage
for bookings Rudding Park Holiday Cottages, Rudding Park, Follifoot, Harrogate. N Yorks HG31DT
☎Harrogate(0423)871350

Charming stone cottage situated in the centre of the picturesque village of Follifoot. The rooms are small and cosily furnished, with original low beamed ceilings in ground-floor rooms.

All year 1wk min, 3mths max, 1unit, 1–4persons ◆ ◆ ◇ fridge Electric Gas inclusive Elecmetered ⌂can be hired ☎(100yds) Iron in unit Ironing board in unit HCE in unit CTV ③3pin square 2P 🎲 ♿(25yds)

↩ ♒(1m) ⚲(30yds) ✉(3m)

Min£50 Max£60pw (Low)
Min£90 Max£120pw (High)

HARTINGTON
Derbyshire
Map**7** SK16

F Mrs E Gould **Croft Cottage** (Flat 2) Mill Lane, Hartington, Derbys
☎Hartington(029884)307

An old two-storey cottage built of limestone, which has been modernised to a high standard, situated opposite the Charles Cotton Hotel in village centre. The first-floor is occupied by the proprietor and the ground-floor is occupied by the proprietor and the ground-floor with a separate entrance is the holiday flat. Accommodation comprises kitchen with dining table and chairs, lounge, bathroom with WC and a double-bedded room.

All year MWB out of season 1wk min, 1mth max, 1unit, 2persons no pets ⊚ Electric Elecmetered ⌂not provided ☎(500yds) Airing cupboard in unit HCE in unit ③3pin square 2P 🎲 ♿(500yds)

↩ ⚲(300yds)

Min£30pw Max£40pw

HASTINGS
East Sussex
Map**5** TQ80

F 9 Strongs Passage The Old Town
for bookings The House of Brandon-Bravo Ltd, Beauport Park, The Ridge, Hastings, East Sussex TN37 7PP
☎Hastings(0424)53207

A modern ground-floor flat in old town. Accommodation comprises lounge, kitchen and double bedroom with double bed. Fitted carpets and modern furnishings throughout.

All year 3days min, 3wks max, 1unit, 2persons, nc ⊚ fridge 🍴 Elec inclusive ⌂not provided ☎(300yds) Airing cupboard in unit Iron in unit Ironing board in unit HCE in unit [Launderette within 300yds] ⊗ CTV ③3pin square P 🎲 ♿(300yds)

↩ ♒(3m) ⚲(200yds) 📷(½m) 🎵(½m) ✉(½m)

Min£74.75 Max£109.25pw

HATHERLEIGH
Devon
Map**2** SS50

C Motcombe Cottage 23 Bridge Street
for bookings Mrs P M Sutton, Jubilee Cottage, Exbourne, Okehampton, Devon EX203RX
☎Exbourne(083785)292

Delightfully modernised cottage in olde-worlde village with lounge/diner (inglenook fireplace), well-equipped kitchen, two bedrooms, one with three singles and one with two. Bathroom and WC. Enter Hatherleigh by A386 from Okehampton, Motcombe Cottage is on right.

Apr-Oct MWB out of season 1wk min, 1mth max, 1unit, 2–5persons, [◇] ◆ ◆ ⊚ fridge Electric Elecmetered ⌂can be hired ☎(50yds) WM in unit SD in unit Airing cupboard in unit Iron in unit Ironing board in unit HCE in unit →

⊕ TV ⊕3pinsquare ⊕2pinround
P ▥ ⚉

⊛ ♀ ▤ ♫

Min£50pw Max£65pw (Low)
Min£75pw Max£80pw (High)

HATTON
Derbyshire
Map**8** SK23

H Hoon Hay Manor Hoon
for bookings Mrs A Hollis, Newton Park,
Newton Solney, Burton-on-Trent, Staffs
☎Burton-on-Trent(0283)703952

An outstanding 200-year-old Manor
Farmhouse, set amidst 250 acres of open
farmland in the Dove Valley with gardens,
lawns and a summerhouse. Fishing and
rough shooting are available on the
estate. Accommodation comprises four
bedrooms, three double, one single,
large sitting room, dining room and
kitchen with breakfast area.

Apr-Oct 1wkmin, 2wks max, 1unit,
1–8persons ◇ ◆ ⊚ fridge ▥ &
Electric Elecmetered ⊡inclusive ☎
Airing cupboard in unit Iron in unit
Ironong board in unit HCE in unit ⊕
⊛ CTV ⊕3pinsquare ⊕3pinround
4P ⚉(¾m)

⊛ ♀

Min£90pw Max£140pw

HAUGH OF URR
Dumfries & Galloway Kirkcudbrightshire
Map**11** NX86

B Kabria
for bookings G M Thomson & Co, 27 King
Street, Castle Douglas,
Kirkcudbrightshire DG7 1AB
☎Castle Douglas(0556)2701

Modern bungalow with its own garden
and garage. The accommodation
comprises two double bedrooms, one
twin-bedded room, large comfortable
lounge with dining area, spacious kitchen
and bathroom with shower attachment.
Situated in village which lies E of Castle
Douglas on A75. For access take A710
towards Dalbeattie and at crossroads in
village turn left for property on left.

All year 1wkmin, 1unit, 1–7persons
◆ ⊚ fridge ▥ & open fire
Elec inclusive ⊡not provided
☎(50yds) SD in unit Airing cupboard in
unit Iron in unit Ironing board in unit
HCE in unit ⊕ TV ⊕3pinsquare
⊕3pinround P ⚐ ⚉(100yds)

⊛ ♀(200yds)

Min£60 Max£145pw

HAVERFORDWEST
Dyfed
Map**2** SM91

F Apple Loft
for bookings Mr J E Lloyd, Rosemoor
Estate, Walwyn's Castle, Haverfordwest,
Dyfed
☎Broad Haven(043 783)326

Situated within Rosemoor Estate of which
20 of the 34 acres have become a nature
reserve and a 5-acre lake has been
created as the habitat for migratory and
breeding birds. This exciting project is
ranked as of major regional importance
and there are reserved rights of access
for visitors to Rosemoor cottages. The
Apple Loft is a spacious flat reached by a
stone staircase. The accommodation is
finished in pinewood and retains some of
the original features of the 1700's. Roomy
open plan area for sitting and dining with
well appointed kitchen area at one end.
There is a family bedroom, a double
bedroom, a further room to take a single
bed or bunks as required and a
bathroom/WC.

All year MWB out of season 1night min,
1unit, 2–7persons [◇] ◆ ⊚ fridge
▥ Elec metered ⊡inclusive (except
towels) WM on premises SD on
premises TD on premises Airing
cupboard in unit Iron in unit Ironing
board in unit HCE in unit ⊕ CTV
⊕3pinsquare P ▥ ⚉(2m) Play area

⊛ ♀(2m)

Min£24.15pw (Low)
Min£44.85 Max£209.10pw (High)

C Coach House
for bookings Mr J E Lloyd, Rosemoor
Estate, Walwyn's Castle, Haverfordwest,
Dyfed
☎Broad Haven(043 783)326

For details of Rosemoor Estate see Apple
Loft. The Coach House is a detached,
red-sandstone cottage overlooking a
large walled garden with fruit trees. The
accommodation is all on the ground-floor
and is suitable for the disabled. It
comprises a pretty, open-plan living
area, dining area with fitted kitchen, one
double-bedded room, one twin-bedded
room, one single bedroom with provision
of an extra bed if required and bathroom
with shower and bidet.

All year MWB out of season 1night min,
1unit, 2–6persons [◇] ◆ ⊚
fridge Elec metered ⊡inclusive
(except towels) ☎ WM on premises
SD on premises TD on premises Airing
cupboard in unit Iron in unit Ironing
board in unit HCE in unit ⊕ CTV
⊕3pinsquare P ▥ ⚉(2m) Play area

⊛ ♀(2m)

Min£24.15pw (Low)
Min£57.50 Max£241.50pw (High)

C First Cottage
for bookings Mr J E Lloyd, Rosemoor
Estate, Walwyn's Castle, Haverfordwest,
Dyfed
☎Broad Haven(043 783)326

For details of Rosemoor Estate see Apple
Loft. A single-storey courtyard cottage
built on modern lines on one level and
suitable for the disabled. There are two
family bedrooms, but unwanted beds
can be removed, lounge/diner, fitted

open-plan kitchen and bathroom/WC.
Opens onto south facing grassed
garden.

All year MWB out of season 1night min,
1unit, 2–7persons [◇] ◆ ⊚
fridge ▥ Elec metered ⊡inclusive
(except towels) ☎ WM on premises
SD on premises TD on premises Airing
cupboard in unit Iron in unit Ironing
board in unit HCE in unit ⊕ CTV
⊕3pinsquare P ▥ ⚉(2m) Play area

⊛ ♀(2m)

Min£24.15pw (Low)
Min£43.70 Max£179.40pw (High)

C Gardeners Cottage
for bookings Mr J E Lloyd, Rosemoor
Estate, Walwyn's Castle, Haverfordwest,
Dyfed
☎Broad Haven(043 783)326

For details of Rosemoor Estate see Apple
Loft. A detached, red sandstone cottage
offering compact, attractively laid out
accommodation. The ground floor
comprises a pretty, open-plan area with
lounge seating, dining area and well-
fitted kitchen. On the first floor there is a
double-bedded room, a single bedroom
and a bathroom/WC. There is space for a
bunk bed or additional single bed if
required.

All year MWB out of season 1night min,
1unit, 2–4persons [◇] ◆ ⊚
fridge ▥ Elec metered ⊡inclusive
(except towels) ☎ WM on premises
SD on premises TD on premises Airing
cupboard in unit Iron in unit Ironing
board in unit HCE in unit ⊕ CTV
⊕3pinsquare P ▥ ⚉(2m) Play area

⊛ ♀(2m)

Min£24.15pw (Low)
Min£42.55 Max£161pw (High)

C Mr & Mrs J D Rees **North Rogeston
Cottages** North Rogeston, Portfield
Gate, Haverfordwest, Dyfed
☎Broad Haven(043 783)373

A charming conversion from farm
buildings, the cottages are equipped to a
high standard with maximum use made
of natural materials. They comprise open-
plan timbered living/dining area with
kitchen, pine clad shower room with WC,
one twin bedded room with continental
quilts. A bed settee is available if
required. Each unit has a patio.

Mar–Jan MWB out of season
3nights min, 5units, 2persons [◇] ◆
◆ no pets ⊚ fridge ▥
Elec inclusive ⊡inclusive ☎(1m)
Airing cupboard in unit Iron in unit
Ironing board in unit HCE in unit
[Launderette on premises] ⊕ CTV
⊕3pinsquare 10P ⚉(2m)

⊛ ♀(1½m)

F Mr & Mrs J D Rees **Old Granary
Apartments** North Rogeston, Portfield
Gate, Haverfordwest, Dyfed
☎Broad Haven(043 783)373

Spacious, bright, comfortable

apartments on ground and 1st floor level. Sitting/dining room, kitchen and three bedrooms and bathroom/WC. Private patio with each unit. Delightful views.

All year MWB out of season 3 nights min, 2 units, 2–6 persons [◇] ◊ ♦ no pets ◉ fridge ♨ Elec inclusive ⊑ inclusive ☎(1m) Airing cupboard in unit Iron in unit Ironing board in unit HCE in unit [Launderette on premises] ⊙ CTV ⊕3pin square 10P ♨(2m) ⇔ ♀(1½m)

C Orchard Cottage
for bookings Mr J E Lloyd, Rosemoor Estate, Walwyn's Castle, Haverfordwest, Dyfed
☎Broad Haven (043783) 326

For details of Rosemoor Estate see Apple Loft. An attractive courtyard cottage on two levels, overlooking a large walled garden with fruit trees. The ground floor comprises a pretty living room with open-plan pine-fitted kitchen. The first floor comprises one double bedroom, one twin-bedded room, one single-bedded room with provision for additional single bed and bathroom/WC.

> 1982 prices quoted throughout gazetteer

Haverfordwest

All year MWB out of season 1 night min, 1 unit, 2–6 persons [◇] ◊ ♦ ◉ fridge ♨ Elec metered ⊑ inclusive (except towels) ☎ WM on premises SD on premises TD on premises Airing cupboard in unit Iron in unit Ironing board in unit HCE in unit ⊙ CTV ⊕3pin square P ▥ ♨(2m) Play area ⇔ ♀(2m)

Min £24.15pw (Low)
Min £51.75 Max £193.20pw (High)

F Peace Cottage
for bookings Mr J E Lloyd, Rosemoor Estate, Walwyn's Castle, Haverfordwest, Dyfed
☎Broad Haven (043783) 326

For details of Rosemoor Estate see Apple Loft. An attractive courtyard flat which opens onto a south-facing grassed garden and would be suitable for disabled guests. There is an attractive sitting room with dining area, open-plan kitchen, two double bedrooms, one other bedroom which can be furnished to requirement and a bathroom/WC.

All year MWB out of season 1 night min, 1 unit, 2–6 persons [◇] ◊ ♦ ◉ fridge ♨ Elec metered ⊑ inclusive

(except towels) ☎ WM on premises SD on premises TD on premises Airing cupboard in unit Iron in unit Ironing board in unit HCE in unit ⊙ CTV ⊕3pin square P ▥ ♨(2m) Play area ⇔ ♀(2m)

Min £24.15pw (Low)
Min £46 Max £218.50pw (High)

C Rose Cottage
for bookings Mr J E Lloyd, Rosemoor Estate, Walwyn's Castle, Haverfordwest, Dyfed
☎Broad Haven (043783) 326

For details of Rosemoor Estate see Apple Loft. An attractive single-storey courtyard cottage with its own tiny, south-facing garden. It is all on one level and suitable for the disabled or infirm. The well-designed interior comprises sitting room with dining area, well-fitted kitchen and one double bedroom with bathroom en suite. There are two day beds in the sitting room if required.

All year MWB out of season 1 night min, 1 unit, 2–4 persons [◇] ◊ ♦ ◉ fridge ♨ Elec metered ⊑ inclusive (except towels) ☎ WM on premises SD on premises TD on premises Airing cupboard in unit Iron in unit Ironing board in unit HCE in unit ⊙ CTV ⊕3pin square P ▥ ♨(2m) Play area →

◷ ⚲(2m)
Min£24.15pw (Low)
Min£41.40 Max£115pw (High)

C Rosemoor Lodge
for bookings Mr J E Lloyd, Rosemoor
Estate, Walwyn's Castle, Haverfordwest,
Dyfed
☎Broad Haven(043 783)326

*For details of Rosemoor Estate see Apple
Loft. A small four-bedroomed cottage
with open-plan kitchen, double
bedrooms and a twin-bedded room,
cottage-style sitting room/diner,
bathroom/WC. A steepish open stairway
leads to two dormer rooms with twin beds
suitable for children and teenagers.*

All year MWB out of season 1 night min,
1 unit, 8 persons [◇] ◆ ✦ ◎
Calor gas, Electric & log fires
Elec metered ⌸ inclusive (except
towels) ☎ WM on premises SD on
premises TD on premises Airing
cupboard on premises Iron in unit
Ironing board in unit HCE in unit ◷
CTV ⊕3 pin square P ▥ ♨(2m)
◷ ⚲(2m)
Min£25pw (Low)
Min£39 Max£170pw (High)

C Spring Cottage
for bookings Mr J E Lloyd, Rosemoor
Estate, Walwyn's Castle, Haverfordwest,
Dyfed
☎Broad Haven(043 783)326

*For details of Rosemoor Estate see Apple
Loft. Attractive, two-storey cottage
overlooking a large walled garden with
fruit trees. The ground floor comprises
one room with open-plan sitting room,
dining area and pine-fitted kitchen. The
first floor comprises one double-bedded
room, one bedroom which can be used
as a single or fitted with bunk beds and a
bathroom/WC.*

All year MWB out of season 1 night min,
1 unit, 2–4 persons [◇] ◆ ✦ ◎
fridge ♨ Elec metered ⌸ inclusive
(except towels) ☎ WM on premises
SD on premises TD on premises Airing
cupboard in unit Iron in unit Ironing
board in unit HCE in unit ◷ CTV
⊕3 pin square P ▥ ♨(2m) Play area
◷ ⚲(2m)

Min£24.15pw (Low)
Min£48.30 Max£165.60pw (High)

C Woodsend Granary
for bookings Mr J E Lloyd, Rosemoor
Estate, Walwyn's Castle, Haverfordwest,
Dyfed
☎Broad Haven(043 783)326

*For details of Rosemoor Estate see Apple
Loft. Woodsend Granary is ideal for two
people requiring an away from it all
setting in a sheltered valley. The compact
cottage has its own private patio
overlooking a stream, pond and garden.
Equipment and furnishings are new.
Accommodation comprises an open-
plan sitting room with well-fitted kitchen
and dining area, one double-bedded
room and well-appointed shower room
with WC.*

Apr–Oct 1 night min, 1 unit, 2 persons
[◇] ◆ ✦ ◿ fridge Electric
Gas/elec metered (winter only)
⌸ inclusive (except towels) ☎(½m)
WM(½m) SD(½m) TD(½m) Airing
cupboard in unit Iron in unit Ironing
board in unit HCE in unit ◷ CTV
⊕3 pin square P ▥ ♨(2m) Play area
◷ ⚲(2m)
Min£36 Max£75pw

HAWES
North Yorkshire
Map 7 SD88

C Mrs B A Stott Brunskill Cottage
Shaw Ghyll Farm, Simonstone, Hawes,
N Yorks DL8 3LY
☎Hawes(09697)359

*Stone-built 17th-century cottage. Two
bedrooms, each with a double and a
single bed. Ground floor; bathroom/WC,
small living room and separate kitchen.
Authentic beam and low ceilings. Stone
staircase. Quiet position in rural
surroundings at head of Wensleydale.
Horse riding within ½m.*

All year MWB out of season 1 wk min,
1 mth max, 1 unit, 1–6 persons ◆ ✦
◎ fridge Electric Elec metered
⌸ can be hired ☎(500yds) SD in unit
Airing cupboard in unit Iron in unit
Ironing board in unit HCE in unit ◷
TV ⊕3 pin square P ▥ ♨(2m)
◷ ⚲(½m) ▨(2m)
Min£50pw Max£95pw

H High Shaw Farmhouse
for bookings Mrs B A Stott, Shaw Ghyll
Farm, Simonstone, Hawes, N Yorks
DL8 3LY
☎Hawes(09097)359

*An 18th-century detached stone built
farmhouse which has been completely
modernised, set in open countryside with
views across Stags Fell. Accommodation
comprises four bedrooms with various
combinations of beds, kitchen, dining
room and a pleasant lounge complete
with piano.*

All year MWB out of season 3 days min,
1 unit, 2–11 persons ◆ ✦ ◎ fridge
Electric Elec metered ⌸ can be hired
☎(½m) WM in unit SD in unit Airing
cupboard Iron Ironing board HCE
◷ TV ⊕3 pin square 4P ▥ ♨(2m)
◷ ⚲(2m)
Min£75 Max£145pw

**H, C Mirk Pot Farmhouse & West
Cottage**
for bookings Mrs C J Kemp, Tow Hill,
Snaizeholme, Hawes, N Yorks DL8 3NB
☎Hawes(0450)303

*Converted farmhouse and cottage on the
slopes of Snaizeholme Fell, overlooking a
secluded valley and facing Dodd Fell.
Mirk Pot farmhouse has sitting room,
dining room and kitchen, also two double
bedrooms, two twin-bedded rooms and
one single bedroom, West Cottage has
sitting room and kitchen/dining room,
also one double and one twin bedroom.
There is also a double bed-settee in the
sitting room.*

┌─────────────────────────────┐
│ 1982 prices quoted throughout │
│   gazetteer   │
└─────────────────────────────┘

All year MWB out of season 1wk min,
4mths max, 2units, 1–10persons ◇
◉ fridge Electric & oil Elec metered
🗠not provided ☎(½m) WM in unit
Airing cupboard in unit Iron in unit
Ironing board in unit HCE in unit ⊖
[TV] ⊕3pin square P ⚊(4m) Fishing

HAWICK
Borders *Roxburghshire*
Map **12** NT51

C Broadhaugh Cottage
for bookings Miss J Bristow, Thorncroft,
Lilliesleaf, Roxburghshire TD6 9JD
☎Lilliesleaf(08357)424

A converted shepherd's cottage in a
secluded position by the River Teviot.
Good view of border hill country. Pleasant
décor and furnishings. Ground floor
comprises sitting/dining room, kitchen
and one double bedroom. First floor has a
double bedroom, one twin-bedded room
and a bathroom. Fishing by permit in the
River Teviot can be arranged. Situated
about 4m S of Hawick and reached via a
narrow road off the A7.

Apr–Oct MWB out of season 1wk min,
2mths max, 1unit, 2–6persons [◇] ◉
fridge Electric & coal fires
Elec metered 🗠can be hired ☎(4m)
Iron in unit Ironing board in unit HCE in
unit TV ⊕3pin square P ⚊(4m)
Fishing
⊖ ♀(3m)
Min£57.50 Max£71.30pw (Low)
Min£89.70 Max£109.25pw (High)

C Chapelhill Cottage
for bookings Miss J Bristow, Thorncroft,
Lilliesleaf, Roxburghshire TD6 9JD
☎Lilliesleaf(08357)424

Semi-detached stone cottage with
simple but adequate standard of facilities
and fittings. All rooms on one level,
comprising sitting/dining room, studio
couch, double bedroom, twin-bedded
room, kitchen and bathroom. Lies in
isolated position on farm with sweeping
views S: over Teviotdale and the Cheviot
Hills. Reached off A7 3m S of Hawick via a
½m-long earthen track.

Apr–Oct MWB out of season 1wk min,
2mths max, 1unit, 2–5persons [◇] ◉
fridge Open fires Elec metered 🗠can
be hired ☎(4m) Iron in unit Ironing
board in unit HCE in unit TV
⊕3pin square P ⚊(4m)
⊖ ♀(3m)
Min£55.20 Max£63.25pw (Low)
Min£80.50 Max£97.75pw (High)

C Goldielands Cottage
for bookings Miss J Bristow, Thorncroft,
Lilliesleaf, Roxburghshire TD6 9JD
☎Lilliesleaf(08357)424

Detached stone cottage in secluded
position on wooded hillside. It comprises
lounge/dining room, double bedroom,
kitchen and bathroom on ground floor
and one twin and one family bedroom on
first floor. Off A7 about 3m S of Hawick,
access by unmetalled track.

Mar–Oct MWB out of season 1wk min,
2mths max, 1unit, 2–7persons [◇] ◉
fridge Electric & coal fires
Elec metered 🗠can be hired ☎(4m)
Iron in unit Ironing board in unit HCE in
unit CTV ⊕3pin square P ⚊(4m)
⊖ ♀(3m)
Min£59.80 Max£73.60pw (Low)
Min£94.30 Max£115pw (High)

C Hassendean Cottage
for bookings Miss J Bristow, Thorncroft,
Lilliesleaf, Roxburghshire TD6 9JD
☎Lilliesleaf(08357)424

Semi-detached cottage comprising
lounge/dining room, twin and double
bedroom, kitchen, shower/WC. Situated
5m NE of Hawick, via B6359.

All year MWB out of season 1wk min,
1unit, 1–4persons [◇] ◉ fridge
Electric Elec metered 🗠can be hired
☎(3m) Iron in unit Ironing board in
unit HCE in unit CTV ⊕3pin square
2P ⚊(3m)
⊖ δ☞(3m) ♀(3m)
Min£55.20 Max£63.25pw (Low)
Min£80.50 Max£97.75pw (High)

HAWKSHEAD
Cumbria
Map **7** SD39

H&F Rogerground House
for bookings Mrs I G Mackie, 2
Rowanside, Prestbury, Macclesfield,
Cheshire SK10 4BE
☎Prestbury(0625)828624

Rogerground house is made up of six
separate parts. There is the original 16th-
century cottage, a late 17th-century
house and, built onto the house, a studio
flat in the attic and a ground-floor garden
room plus a detached 17th-century barn
which has been converted into two flats.
All are well furnished and they are
situated on high ground, ⅓m from
Hawkshead village. There are fine views
from the property.

All year 1wk min, 6units, 2–8persons
◇ ◆ ◉ fridge ⛲ Elec metered
🗠not provided ☎(½m) SD on
premises HCE in unit TV can be hired
⊕3pin square 9P ⊞ ⚊(½m)
⊖ ♀(½m)
Min£55 Max£190pw

Ch Mrs Evans Ramsteads Coppice
(1m E B5286) Outgate, Hawkshead,
Ambleside, Cumbria LA22 0NH
☎Hawkshead(09666)583 & 051-
428 2605

Six timber-clad chalets of good design in
15 acres of mature deciduous woodland,
2m N of Hawkshead. Three of the chalets
have two bedrooms while the other three
chalets have three bedrooms. They all
have lounge, kitchen and bathroom.

Mar-Oct 1wk min, 6units, 2–6persons
no pets Calor gas fridge Electric

Gas/Elec inclusive 🗠not provided
☎(½m) HCE in unit ⊖ ⊕3pin square
P 1⚪ ⚊(2m)
Min£68 Max£96pw (Low)
Min£98 Max£146pw (High)

HAWORTH
West Yorkshire
Map **7** SE03

C Cobbler's Cottage 64 Sun Street
for bookings Mr & Mrs G C Pickard,
Sandfield House, Sandfield Avenue,
Leeds LS6 4DZ
☎Leeds(0532)752977

Attractive, restored weaver's cottage with
beamed ceilings set in a row of three. The
unit contains lounge, kitchen and two
bedrooms (one with bunk beds and one
double bed). Situated in the heart of
Brontë country with many attractions
nearby.

All year MWB 1wk min, 3mths max,
1unit, 1–5persons [◇] no cats ◉
fridge Gas & Elec Gas/Elec metered
🗠not provided ☎(250yds) Iron in unit
Ironing board in unit HCE in unit ⊖
TV ⊕3pin square ⊞ ⚊(20yds)
☞Hard δ☞
⊖ ♀(200yds) 🖾(3m) ♫(3m) ⛴(3m)
Min£65 Max£80pw

H 5 Stanbury
for bookings Mrs H M Holroyd,
Greenacres, Moorhouse Lane,
Oxenhope, Keighley, W Yorks BD22 9RY
☎Haworth(0535)42787

A solid stone-built semi-detached house
with very good furnishings throughout.
There are four bedrooms, one double,
two twins and one single, a bathroom and
WC, lounge and kitchen.

All year MWB out of season 7days min,
1unit, 2–7persons ◇ no pets ♩
fridge ⛲ Gas/Elec metered
🗠inclusive ☎(½m) WM in unit Iron in
unit Ironing board in unit HCE in unit
⊖ TV ⊕3pin square I⚪ ⊞
⚊(200yds)
⊖ δ☞(2m) ♀(100yds) ♫(2m)
Min£50 Max£70pw (Low)
Min£65 Max£80pw (High)

H 55 & 57 Sunstreet Haworth, W Yorks
for bookings Mrs Sunderland, Moor
House, Oxenhope, nr Keighley, W Yorks
☎Haworth(0535)42421

Both are single fronted, two-storey,
middle terraced houses situated close to
village amenities. Each accommodation
comprises living room leading to small
rear garden, kitchen, one twin-bedded
and one single or bunk bedroom, as
required and bathroom/WC. Ideal for
touring Brontë country.

All year MWB out of season 1wk min,
2units, 2–4persons ◇ ◆ ◉ fridge
⛲ Elec metered 🗠inclusive ☎
Airing cupboard in unit Iron in unit
Ironing board in unit HCE in unit TV
⊕3pin square ⊞ ⚊(200yds) →

119

⊖ ♀(100yds)
Min£35pw (Low)
Min£50 Max£80pw (High)

HAYLE
Cornwall
Map**2** SW53

Ch Mr Trenchard **Beachside Leisure Holidays Ltd** Hayle, Cornwall TR27 5AW
☎Hayle(0736)753080

These stone-built chalets are in blocks of four, each comprise two bedrooms separated by a sun patio from the lounge/kitchen/diner with studio couch and bathroom/WC. The chalets are sited among sand dunes on the N side of Hayle facing the sea, with a private walk to the beach, and are separated from the adjoining caravan park by Spanish-type walling. The furnishings and décor are good.

Etr-Sep 1wkmin, 20wksmax, 60units, 2–6persons ◆ nopets ◎ fridge Electric Elecmetered ⊡inclusive ☎(100yds) Airing cupboard in unit Iron on premises Ironing board on premises HCE in unit ⊙ TV ⊕3pinsquare ⊕2pinround P ▦ ⛟ ⌂(heated)

⊖ ♀ ▣(1m) ♫(1m) ▣(1m)

Ch **St Ives Bay Chalet & Caravan Park** Upton Towans, Hayle, Cornwall TR27 5BH
☎Hayle(0736)752274

Pleasantly grouped, pine-wood chalets located within a holiday centre of some 45 acres in undulating grassland and sand dunes. Accommodation comprises two bedrooms, lounge/kitchen and bathroom/WC. The full facilities of the holiday centre are available. Located just off the A30, Redruth to St Ives road.

May-Sep MWB out of season 1wkmin, 3mths max, 130units, 1–4persons [◇] [◆] [◆] ◎ fridge Electric Elecmetered ⊡inclusive ☎ [Iron on premises] Ironing board on premises HCE in unit [Launderette on premises] ⊙ CTV ⊕3pinsquare P ⛟ Games room & children's playground

⊖ ⛳18(2m) ♀ ▣ ♫ ▣(1m)

Min£23 Max£115pw (Low)
Min£92 Max£161pw (High)

HAYLING ISLAND
Hampshire
Map**4** SZ79

B ***Rowlingsea*** 7 Sea Front Estate
for bookings Mrs J Noone, 'Elmwood', 9A Sea Front Estate, Hayling Island, Hants PO11 9JJ

Small brick-built bungalow in quiet residential area, consisting of one double bedroom, small lounge with put-u-up, dining room, separate bathroom and WC and small, nicely-equipped kitchen.

Etr-Sep 1wkmin, 1mthmax, 1unit, 1–6persons ◆ ◆ ◎ fridge Electric Elecmetered ⊡notprovided ☎(25yds) Iron in unit Ironing board in unit HCE on premises [Launderette within 300yds] TV ⊕3pinsquare ⛟(25yds)

⊖ ⛳18(2m) ♀(200yds) ▣(200yds) ♫(200yds)

HEBDEN
North Yorkshire
Map**7** SE06

H **Cruck Rise**
for bookings Mrs J M Joy, Jerry and Bens, Hebden, Skipton, N Yorks BD23 5DL
☎Grassington(0756)752369

Cruck Rise is on the converted barn of Jerry and Ben's (it takes its name from William Riley's novel) and is situated 100yds up the hill from the main property. Sleeping accommodation for up to six persons consists of one double bedroom, a room with bunk beds and a bed-settee in the lounge.

Allyear MWB out of season 1wkmin, 1unit 1–6persons ◇ ◆ ◎ fridge ▦ Elecmetered ⊡can be hired ☎ [WM on premises SD on premises] Airing cupboard on premises Iron on premises Ironing board on premises HCE in unit TV ⊕3pinsquare P ▦(summer only) ⛟(½m)

⊖ ♀(1½m) ▣(1½m)

Min£66.70 Max£80.50pw (Low)
Min£94.30 Max£112.70pw (High)

F **High Close**
for bookings Mrs J M Joy, Jerry and Ben's, Hebden, Skpton, N Yorkshire DB23 5DL
☎Grassington(0756)752369

Jerry and Ben's five furnished properties and a converted barn, is sited on a privately-owned estate in Hebden Gill with its rocky crags, deciduous trees and picturesque waterfalls. High Close is one of the units and sleeps seven to nine persons in a double bedroom, bunk-bedded room and loft bedroom with three single beds. Other accommodation consists of open-plan and sitting area with bed-settees, kitchen, bathroom and WC.

Allyear MWB out of season 1wkmin, 1unit, 1–9persons, ◇ ◆ ◎ fridge Electric Elecmetered ⊡can be hired ☎ WM on premises SD on premises Iron on premises Ironing board on premises HCE in unit TV ⊕3pinsquare P ▦(summer only) ⛟(½m)

⊖ ♀(1½m) ▣(1½m)

Min£75.90 Max£87.40pw (Low)
Min£108.10 Max£121.90pw (High)

1982 prices quoted throughout gazetteer

C **Mamie's Cottage**
for bookings Mrs J M Joy, Jerry & Ben's, Hebden, Skipton, N Yorks BD23 5DL
☎Grassington(0756)752369

This cottage comprises kitchen, dining room/sun lounge, sitting room with wood burning stove, bathroom/WC and three double bedrooms plus bed-settee in sitting room.

Allyear MWB out of season 1wkmin, 1unit, 1–8persons ◇ ◆ ◎ fridge Electric Elec inclusive ⊡can be hired ☎ WM on premises SD on premises Airing cupboard on premises Iron on premises Ironing board on premises HCE in unit ⊙ TV ⊕3pinsquare P ▦(summer only) ⛟(½m)

⊖ ♀(1½m) ▣(1½m)

Min£80.50 Max£92pw (Low)
Min£112.70 Max£128.80pw (High)

F **Paradise End**
for bookings Mrs J M Joy, Jerry and Ben's, Hebden, Skipton, N Yorks BD23 5DL
☎Grassington(0756)752369

Paradise End, another property in Jerry and Ben's, sleeping up to six people in a double bedroom, twin-bedded room and two single bed-settees in lounge. Satisfactory accommodation.

Allyear MWB out of season 1wkmin, 1unit, 1–6persons ◇ ◆ ◎ fridge Electric Elecmetered ⊡can be hired ☎ [WM on premises SD on premises] Airing cupboard on premises Iron on premises Ironing board on premises HCE in unit TV ⊕3pinsquare P ▦(summer only) ⛟(½m)

⊖ ♀(1½m) ▣(1½m)

Min£57.50 Max£64.40pw (Low)
Min£82.80 Max£96.60pw (High)

F **Robin Middle**
for bookings Mrs J M Joy, Jerry and Ben's, Hebden, Skipton, N Yorks BD23 5DL
☎Grassington(0756)752369

Robin Middle is the middle section of Jerry and Ben's sleeping six people in a double bedroom, twin-bedded room and two single bed-settees in lounge. Clean and adequate accommodation with good views.

Allyear MWB out of season 1wkmin, 1unit, 1–6persons ◇ ◆ ◎ fridge Electric Elecmetered ⊡can be hired ☎ [WM on premises SD on premises] Airing cupboard on premises Iron on premises Ironing board on premises HCE in unit TV ⊕3pinsquare P ▦(summer only) ⛟(½m)

⊖ ♀(1½m)

Min£57.50 Max£64.40pw (Low)
Min£82.80 Max£96.60pw (High)

HELLANDBRIDGE
Cornwall
Map**2** SX07

B **Bungalows 1–5**
for bookings Mr & Mrs A Goggs,

Silverstream, Hellandbridge, Bodmin,
Cornwall
☎Bodmin(0208)4408

*Five attractive cedar-wood bungalows in
idyllic surroundings by River Camel.
Accommodation comprises
lounge/diner, kitchen, bathroom and
separate WC. Three bungalows have two
bedrooms with one double and one twin-
bedded room. The other two have three
bedrooms comprising one double, one
twin-bedded, and one with bunks.*

18Mar-18Nov MWB out of season
1wkmin, 1mthmax, 5units, 1–6persons
[◇ ◆] ◉ fridge Electric
Elecmetered 🔲can be hired ☎(1m)
Airing cupboard in unit Iron on
premises Ironing board in unit HCE in
unit ⊕ TV ⊛3pinsquare 2P 🅟
♨(1½m) Private trout fishing
↔ ♀(2½m)
Min£45 Max£80pw (Low)
Min£90 Max£130pw (High)

F R W Firth **The Grange** Helland,
Bodmin, Cornwall
☎Bodmin(0208)2249

*Ten flats, nine of which are on the ground
and first-floors of a converted barn, the
other is part of the Grange House.
Haywain 1 & 2, Linney 1 & 2 and Croft
Cottage Lower Mews & Upper Mews
comprise kitchen, lounge/diner,
bathroom/WC, one double bedroom and
one with either bunk or twin beds. The
Loft has lounge, kitchen/diner,
shower/WC and one double bedroom.
Wain Cottage has lounge, kitchen/diner,
shower/WC and one double bedroom,
one double with bunk beds and a further
room with bunks. Grange Flat comprises
lounge/diner, kitchen, shower/WC and a
twin bedded room. Midway between A3
and Hellandbridge.*

Feb-Nov MWB out of season 1wkmin,
8wks max, 10units, 1–8persons ◇ ◆
◉ fridge Electric Elecmetered
🔲can be hired ☎(100yds) Airing
cupboard in unit Iron on premises
Ironing board on premises HCE in unit
⊕ CTV ⊛3pinsquare P 🅟 ♨(2m)
Children's play area, paddling pool
↔ ♀ 🐾(3m)

C **Horseshoe Cottage**
for bookings Mr & Mrs A Goggs,
Silverstream, Hellandbridge, Bodmin,
Cornwall
☎Bodmin(0208)4408

*Attractive stone cottage in idyllic setting
in rural area on the banks of River Camel.
Accommodation comprises kitchen,
lounge/diner with open fire, bathroom
with separate WC, two bedrooms, one
double and one twin-bedded.*

All year MWB out of season 1wkmin,
1mth max, 1unit, 1–4persons [◇ ◆]
◉ fridge 🍳(oil) Electric & open fires
Elecmetered 🔲can be hired ☎(1m)
Airing cupboard in unit Iron on
premises Ironing board in unit HCE in
unit ⊕ TV ⊛3pinsquare 2P 🅟

♨(1½m) Private trout fishing
Min£55 Max£90pw (Low)
Min£110 Max£140pw (High)

HELSTON
Cornwall
Map2 SW62

F **44A, 44B & 44C Church Street**
for bookings Mr & Mrs P I Mollard, 44
Church Street, Helston, Cornwall
TR138TQ
☎Helston(03265)3606

*Three flats of character situated in what
was once an old coaching inn. The
accommodation varies in size and they
sleep from one to six persons. Located in
mainly residential area close to town
centre.*

Apr–Sep MWB out of season 1wkmin,
3units, 1–6persons [◇] ◇ ⚴
fridge Electric & gas fires
Gas/Elec inclusive 🔲inclusive
☎(100yds) Iron on premises Ironing
board on premises HCE in unit ⊕ TV
⊛3pinsquare 1P 🅟 ♨(100yds)
↔ ♀(100yds) 🅿(100yds)
♫(100yds) 🐾(300yds)

B Mr G R Goodere **Greenacres
Holiday Bungalows** Clodgey Lane,
Helston, Cornwall TR138PN
☎Helston(03265)2620 /
Mullion(0326)240666

*Twelve semi-detached bungalows of
conventional design. Secluded site with
lawns, trees and shrubs. Each contains
one twin and one double bedroom,
lounge with studio couch, large diner
(comfortable furnishings and good
décor), kitchen area, bathroom and WC.
Clean and modern accommodation.*

Etr–Sep MWB in season 3days min,
1mth max, 12units, 2–6persons ◇ ◆
◉ fridge Electric Elecmetered
🔲inclusive ☎ Iron in unit Ironing
board in unit HCE in unit ⊕ TV
⊛3pinsquare ⊛2pinround P 🅟
♨(200yds) ♒(400yds)
↔ ♀(400yds) 🅿(400yds)
♫(400yds) 🐾(400yds)
Min£36 Max£55pw (Low)
Min£150 Max£175pw (High)

HEMSBY
Norfolk
Map9 TG41

Ch **Belle Aire Chalet Site** Beach Road
for bookings Hoseasons Holidays,
Sunway House, Lowestoft, Suffolk
NR323LT
☎Lowestoft(0502)62292

*Richmond, Ascot and Belle Aire are three
different types of chalet on this site which
lies on sloping grassland 700yds from the
beach. Units have two or three
bedrooms, sleeping up to five, with an
additional double convertible settee in
the lounge. All chalets have a*

---

*shower/WC. Beach Road is off the B1159
in the village which is some 6m N of Great
Yarmouth.*

May–Oct MWB 1wkmin, 130units,
2–7persons [◇] [◆] ◉ fridge
Electric Elec inclusive 🔲inclusive
☎(300yds) [Iron on premises]
[Launderette within 300yds] TV
⊛3pinsquare P 🅟(200yds)
↔ ♀(300yds) 🅿(300yds)

Ch **Excelsior, Sundowner Holiday
Park** Newport Road, Newport Beach
for bookings Hoseasons Holidays,
Sunway House, Lowestoft, Suffolk
NR323LT
☎Lowestoft(0502)62292

*Purpose-built timber chalets, with
accommodation comprising a two bunk-
bedded room, a double room, a compact
lounge/kitchen/dining room, shower with
washbasin and separate WC.*

Apr–Oct MWB out of season
3days min, 2units, 2–6persons [◇]
[◆] ◉ fridge Electric Elecmetered
🔲inclusive ☎ Airing cupboard in unit
[Iron on premises] HCE in unit ⊕ TV
⊛3pinsquare P 🅟(200yds) 🔲
↔ ♀(½m) 🅿(½m) ♫(1m)

Ch **Haiti, Sundowner Holiday Park**
Newport Road, Newport Beach
for bookings Hoseasons Holidays,
Sunway House, Lowestoft, Suffolk
NR323LT
☎Lowestoft(0502)62292

*Timber and brick built semi-detached
chalets with two twin-bedded rooms, one
double, kitchen, lounge, bathroom/WC.*

Apr–Oct MWB out of season
3days min, 12units, 2–8persons [◇]
[◆] ◉ fridge Electric Elecmetered
🔲 inclusive ☎ Airing cupboard in unit
[Iron on premises] HCE in unit ⊕ TV
⊛3pinsquare P 🅟(200yds) 🔲
↔ ♀(½m) 🅿(½m) ♫(1m)

Ch **Hemsby Beach Chalet Centre**
Beach Road
for bookings Hoseasons Holidays,
Sunway House, Lowestoft, Suffolk
NR322LT
☎Lowestoft(0502)62292

*Spacious chalet park extending over 14
acres of lawns and only 300yds from the
beach. Chalets are designed to sleep two
to six people in either one or two
bedrooms; all have a double studio
couch in lounge area and shower/WC.*

Etr–Sep MWB 3days min, 224units,
2–6persons [◇] [◆] ◉ fridge
Electric Elec inclusive 🔲inclusive ☎
WM on premises SD on premises [Iron
on premises] [Ironing board on
premises] HCE on premises
Launderette on premises TV
⊛3pinsquare P 🅟
↔ ♀ 🅿(1m) ♫(1m)

Ch **Pontin's Holiday Village** Beach
Road, Hemsby, Gt Yarmouth, Norfolk
NR294HL
☎Gt Yarmouth(0493)730698 →

121

Purpose-built chalets within a holiday complex 6m N of Gt Yarmouth and ½m from the beach. Chalets have either one or two bedrooms, living area, an open-plan kitchen/dining area and bathroom.

22May–15Oct MWB out of season
1day min, 520units, 2–7persons ◇
◇ ◆ no pets ◉ fridge Electric
Elec metered ☐inclusive ☎ [Iron on premises] Ironing board on premises
HCE in unit [Launderette on premises]
⊙ TV ③3pin square P ▥ ▩
◪(heated) ↩Hard ໂ

⇔ ♨ ⍔ ♫

Min£57 Max£69pw (Low)
Min£181 Max£210pw (High)

Ch J A Gillespie & Son **Sea Dell Chalets** Sea Dell Estate, Beach Road, Hemsby, Gt Yarmouth, Norfolk NR29 4HS
☎Gt Yarmouth(0493)730238

Purpose-built brick/timber chalets, all detached and situated on a site of 150 chalets. Well-furnished accommodation comprising two bedrooms (one twin, one double), lounge/kitchen area, and combined bathroom/WC. Turn right off B1159 signed Hemsby Beach: site is ½m along beach road on the right side.

Etr–Sep 1wk min, 3wks max, 30units, 2–6persons [◇ ◆] no pets ◉
fridge Electric Elec metered ☐can be hired ☎ Airing cupboard in unit Iron in unit HCE in unit ⊙ [CTV]TV ③3pin square 60P ▩(200yds) ໂ
Children's play area

⇔ ♨(⅓m) ▥(⅓m) ♫(⅓m)

Min£40 Max£60pw (Low)
Min£95 Max£110pw (High)

Ch **Sunbeam & Sunrise, Sundowner Holiday Park** Newport Road, Newport Beach
for bookings Hoseasons Holidays, Sunway House, Lowestoft, Suffolk NR32 3LT
☎Lowestoft(0502)62292

Timber and brick-built semi-detached chalets on a well-maintained site. Accommodation has one twin and one double room. Lounge/kitchen, combined bathroom/WC and small patio area.

Apr–Oct MWB out of season
3days min, 90units, 2–6persons [◇]
[◆] ◉ fridge Electric Elec metered
☐inclusive ☎ Airing cupboard in unit
[Iron on premises] HCE in unit ⊙ TV
③3pin square P ▩(200yds) ▣

⇔ ♨(⅓m) ▥(⅓m) ♫(1m)

HEMYOCK
Devon
Map**3** ST11

***H* CC Ref 684**
for bookings Character Cottages (Holidays) Ltd, 34 Fore Street, Sidmouth, Devon EX10 8AQ
☎Sidmouth(03955)77001

An attractive modernised farmhouse in an isolated position close to Hemyock village. A high standard of furnishing.

Accommodation comprises kitchen, utility room, children's playroom, dining room, lounge, shower room, two bathrooms/WCs and five dbl bedrooms.

All year MWB in season 1wk min, 2mths max, 1unit, 10persons ◇ ◆
no pets ◉ fridge ▥ Elec inclusive
except heating ☐not provided ☎ WM in unit SD in unit Airing cupboard in unit Iron in unit Ironing board in unit
HCE in unit ⊙ TV ③3pin square P
▥ ▩(2m)

⇔ ♨(2m)

Min£90 Max£130pw (Low)
Min£140 Max£260pw (High)

HEREFORD
Hereford & Worcester
Map**3** SO54

F Mr & Mrs C Powell **Munstone House** Munstone, Hereford, Herefordshire HR1 3AH
☎Hereford(0432)267122

Two flats on ground and upper floors of old brick and stone-built house. Both have lounge, kitchen, double bedroom, shower, WC; the WC of the upper flat is reached down a small flight of stairs. On unclass road in village 2m N of Hereford.

Etr–Nov 3days min, 3wks max, 2units, 1–5persons no pets ◉ fridge
Electric Elec metered ☐not provided
☎(100yds) Iron in unit Ironing board in unit HCE in unit ⊙ ③3pin square P
▥ ▩(2m)

⇔ ♨(200yds) ▥(2m) ♫(2m) ✿(2m)

Min£35 Max£74

C Mr D Beaumont **Poolspringe Cottage** Much Birch, Hereford, Herefordshire
☎Golden Valley(0981)540355

Recently modernised two-storey cottage with lounge/dining area, bathroom and kitchen on the ground floor and one twin bedroom with washbasin and a second bedroom with three single beds on the first floor. Use of pool and sauna.

All year MWB out of season 3days min, 6wks max, 1unit, 1–6persons ◇ ◆
◉ fridge Electric Elec metered
☐can be hired ☎(1m) [WM on premises] [SD on premises] [TD on premises] Iron in unit Ironing board in unit HCE in unit ⊙ ⍟ CTV
③3pin square P ▥ ▩(1m) ▣
sauna

⇔ ♨(1m)

Min£45 Max£115pw

HERODSFOOT
Cornwall
Map**2** SX15

C **Keepers Cottage**
for bookings Mrs J I Hawke, Woodlay Farm Holidays, Herodsfoot, Liskeard, Cornwall

---

☎Lanreath(0503)20221

A conversion of a detached, stone-built keepers cottage situated behind a farmhouse in a beautiful wooded valley amidst an orchard of about 5½ acres. Accommodation comprises one family bedroom, one double bedroom, entrance hall, kitchen/diner, walk in larder, lounge and bathroom/WC. A carport is available. For access leave the A390 at East Taphouse onto the B3359 for the farmhouse 3m on right. Coarse fishing is available in two ponds.

Mar–Dec MWB out of season
3days min, 3mths max, 1unit, 1–5persons [◇] ◇ ◆ no pets ◉
fridge ▥ Elec inclusive
☐not provided ☎ Airing cupboard in unit Iron in unit Ironing board in unit HCE in unit [Launderette on premises]
⊙ CTV ③3pin square 2P 1✿ ▥
▩(2m)

⇔ ໂ(3m) ♨(3m)

Min£70 Max£160pw (Low)
Min£170 Max£210pw (High)

F **Woodley Farm Flats**
for bookings Mrs J I Hawke, Woodlay Farm Holidays, Herodsfoot, Liskeard, Cornwall
☎Lanreath(0503)20221

Eight flats located on three floors of a stone-built converted 18th-century barn set in a beautiful wooded valley amidst an orchard of about 5½ acres. All are tastefully furnished to a high degree and have lounge/diner, kitchen area and bathroom/WC. Two flats have three double bedrooms, three have two double bedrooms and three have one double bedroom. Coarse fishing is available from two ponds. For access leave the A390 at East Taphouse onto the B3359 for the farmhouse in 3m on right.

Mar–Dec MWB out of season
3days min, 3mths max, 8units, 1–6persons [◇] ◇ ◆ no pets ◉
fridge ▥ Elec inclusive
☐not provided ☎ Airing cupboard in unit Iron in unit Ironing board in unit
HCE in unit [Launderette on premises]
⊙ CTV ③3pin square P ▥ ▩(2m)

⇔ ໂ(3m) ♨(3m)

Min£50 Max£160pw (Low)
Min£115 Max£210pw (High)

HESKET NEWMARKET
Cumbria
Map**11** NY33

***H* Haltcliffe House**
for bookings Mrs M A Ridley, Lonning Head, Hesket Newmarket, Wigton, Cumbria CA7 8JU
☎Caldbeck(06998)619

A large 18th-century stone farmhouse built by a prominent local Quaker family. The accommodation is spacious with old-fashioned but serviceable furnishings. There are two double-bedded rooms, two family rooms and a modern kitchen. Modernised bathroom.

All year MWB out of season 1wk min,
1 unit, 10 persons ◇ ◉ fridge
Electric Gas/Elec metered
⬜ not provided ☎(150yds) Airing
cupboard in unit Iron in unit Ironing
board in unit HCE in unit ⊕ CTV
⊕ 3 pin square P ♨(2m)
⊷ ☻(½m)
Min£70pw Max£90pw

HEYSHAM
Lancashire
Map**7** SD46

B Heysham Head Leisure Park
Barrows Lane, Heysham, Lancashire
LA3 2RR
☎Heysham(0524)52391

*These 76 modern villas are set on a
headland overlooking Morecambe Bay
and at the edge of the 29-acre Heysham
Head Leisure Park with its
comprehensive range of facilities.*

22May–17Sep MWB out of season
7 days min, 76 units, 2–8 persons ◇ ◆
◉ fridge Electric Elec metered
⬜ inclusive ☎ Iron on premises
Ironing board on premises HCE in unit
[Launderette on premises] ⊕ TV
⊕ 3 pin square 100P ♨ ⌐
⊷ ♒(1m) ☻ ♫ ☏(3m)
Min£40 Max£55pw (Low)
Min£90 Max£135pw (High)

HIGHAMPTON
Devon
Map**2** SS40

C Mrs J Caudwell **Warren Farm
(Cottage)** Highampton, Beaworthy,
Devon
☎Hatherleigh(083781)209

*Semi-detached farm cottage in a quiet
location. Accommodation comprises
kitchen/diner, utility room, large lounge,
one double, one single and twin
bedrooms, bathroom.*

All year MWB out of season 3 days min,
1 unit, 1–7 persons [◇] ◇ ◆ ◉
fridge Electric Elec metered
⬜ not provided ☎(1½m) Airing
cupboard in unit Iron in unit Ironing
board in unit HCE in unit ⊕ CTV
⊕ 3 pin square 3P ▥ ♨(3m) ⌐
⊷ ☻(1m)
Min£60 Max£150pw

HIGH LORTON
Cumbria
Map**11** NY12

C Midtown Cottages
for bookings Mr N G Hunter, 12 Derwent
Street, Keswick, Cumbria CA12 5AN
☎Keswick(0596)74392

*A row of cottages in High Lorton, a tiny
village in the Buttermere Valley. Each
comprises two twin ground-floor
bedrooms and bathroom/WC, whilst the
kitchen, lounge and dining alcove are on
the first floor.*

Hesket Newmarket
—
Hindringham

All year MWB out of season
2 nights min, 4 units, 2–4 persons ◇ ◆
◉ fridge ☖ Elec inclusive
⬜ inclusive Iron in unit Ironing board in
unit HCE in unit ⊕ CTV
⊕ 3 pin square 4P ▥ ♨(300yds)
⊷ ☻(100yds)
Min£45 Max£100pw (Low)
Min£110 Max£150pw (High)

HILLBERRY
Nr Douglas, Isle of Man
Map**6** SC37

B & F Meadowview Bungalow & The
Apartment
for bookings Glen Dhoo Camping Site,
Hillbery, Onchan, I.O.M.
☎Douglas(0624)21254

The Apartment *is situated above the
camp site shop in a converted stone
building central to all campsite facilities.
It comprises lounge, dining room,
kitchen, shower/WC and two twin
bedded rooms plus studio couch in
lounge. **Meadowview** bungalow situated
near the main building on the camping
site in rural surroundings.
Accommodation comprises lounge,
kitchen, two twin bedded rooms,
shower/WC and studio couch in lounge.
Guests can use camp site facilities.*

All year MWB out of season 1wk min,
1 mth max, 2 units, 1–persons ◇ ◆
◉ fridge Electric Elec metered
⬜ inclusive ☎ Airing cupboard in unit
Iron in unit Ironing board in unit HCE in
unit [Launderette within 300yds] ⊕
CTV ⊕ 3 pin square 2P ▥ ♨
Games room
⊷ ♒(1m) ☻(1m) ▨(2½m) ☏(2½m)
☎(2½m)
Max£30pw (Low)
Min£40 Max£98pw (High)

HINDRINGHAM
Norfolk
Map**9** TF93

C Banes Cottage
for bookings Major G Bowlby, English
Country Cottages, Claypit Lane,
Fakenham, Norfolk NR21 8AS
☎Fakenham(0328)51155

*A pretty flint and pantile cottage standing
in approx ⅓-acre of lawn and garden in
very quiet and secluded location. Fully-
modernised and furnished in cottage
fashion, accommodation comprises
diner/kitchen, sitting room with put-u-up,
one double bedroom and one twin-
bedded room.*

Apr–Oct 1wk summer, 1 unit,
1–5 persons ◇ ◉ fridge Electric
Elec metered ⬜ inclusive ☎(1m)
Airing cupboard in unit Iron in unit
Ironing board in unit HCE in unit TV
⊕ 3 pin square 2P ♨(1m)
⊷ ☻(1m)
Min£96 Max£162pw

F East Wing Flat Hindringham Hall
for bookings Major G Bowlby, English
Country Cottages, Claypit Lane,
Fakenham, Norfolk NR21 8AS
☎Fakenham(0328)51155

*A large ground-and first-floor flat forming
part of the beautiful 16th-century hall,
approached by bridge across the moat.
Accommodation is well-equipped, with
antique furniture, and includes a
spacious drawing room and two
bedrooms (one on the ground floor and
one on the first floor) altogether sleeping
five. Part of the garden is reserved for
guests. Rural location some 5m S of
Blakeney.*

Apr–Oct 1wk summer, 1 unit, 5 persons
◇ no pets ◉ fridge ☖
Elec inclusive ⬜ inclusive ☎(1m)
Airing cupboard in unit HCE in unit TV
⊕ 3 pin square 1P ♨(1m)
⊷ ☻(1m)
Min£96 Max£162pw

C 58 & 60 Lower Green
for bookings Mrs P Forrest, 195 East End
Road, London N2 0LZ
☎01–8838137

*Semi-detached traditional brick and flint
cottages partly dating from the 17th
century. Accommodation comprises: No
58– downstairs lounge, kitchen and
bathroom with WC and wash-basin,
upstairs one double-bedded room with
wash-basin, one twin-bedded room; No
60– downstairs lounge, kitchen and
cloakroom with WC and wash-basin,
upstairs one double-bedded room, one
twin-bedded room with wash-basin, one
bunk-bedded room and bathroom with
WC and wash-basin.*

All year MWB out of season 3 days min,
6 mths max, 2 units, 1–6 persons [◇]
◇ ◉ fridge Electric heating
included Elec metered
⬜ not provided ☎(½m) Airing cupboard
in unit HCE in unit ⊕ 3 pin square P
♨(1½m) Children's playhouse
⊷ ☻(1½m)
Min£45 Max£75pw (Low)
Min£80 Max£155pw (High)

C Well Cottage 22 Home Lane
for bookings Major G Bowlby, English
Country Cottages, Claypit Lane,
Fakenham, Norfolk NR21 8AS
☎Fakenham(0328)51155

*Brick and pantile cottage in quiet,
secluded position with hedged garden.
Fully-modernised and prettily-furnished
accommodation with separate sitting and
dining rooms and one double bedroom
and one twin bedroom equipped to sleep
four. This quiet and unspoilt village lies
5m NE of Fakenham and about 5m from
the sea at Blakeney.*

All year 1wk summer, 1 unit, 5 persons
◇ ◉ fridge Electric Elec metered →

1982 prices quoted throughout
gazetteer

⊡inclusive ☎(1m) Airing cupboard in unit Iron in unit Ironing board in unit HCE in unit TV ⊕3pin square 2P ♨(1m)
⇔ ♀(1m)
£78pw (Low)
Min£96 Max£162pw (High)

H The Windmill Mill Lane
for bookings Mrs P Forrest, 195 East End Road, London N2 0LZ
☎01–8838137

A tower mill which has been carefully restored and converted so that externally it resembles a working mill without sails and has a Norfolk boat shaped cap. On the first floor there is a dining room, kitchen and cloakroom. On the second floor, a lounge, and on the third, one double bedroom and a bathroom. On the fourth floor there is one twin-bedded room, a bunk-bedded room on the fifth, and one single bedroom on the sixth. Located on outskirts of village.

All year MWB out of season 3 days min, 6mths max, 1unit, 1–8persons [◇] ◆ ◉ fridge Electric Elec metered ⊡not provided ☎(½m) Airing cupboard in unit HCE in unit ⊕ ⊕3pin square P ♨(1½m)
⇔ ♀(1½m)
Min£60 Max£95pw (Low)
Min£105 Max£215pw (High)

HOLBETON
Devon
Map**Q** SX65

F Garden & Orchard Flat
for bookings Mr K W Wilson, Fairfield, Fore Street, Holbeton, Plymouth, Devon PL8 1NE
☎Holbeton(075530)366

Two semi-detached purpose-built ground-floor flats each comprising large open-plan lounge/kitchen/diner with french windows, bathroom/WC, one double bedroom and one bedroom with twin beds. Well decorated and furnished.

14Mar–14Jan MWB out of season 3 days min, 6wks max, 2units, 1–5persons [◇] ◆ no pets ◉ fridge Electric Elec metered ⊡inclusive ☎(100yds) Airing cupboard in unit Iron in unit Ironing board in unit HCE in unit ⊕ CTV ⊕3pin square P ▥ ♨(100yds)
⇔ ♀(100yds)
Min£45 Max£65pw (Low)
Min£70 Max£120pw (High)

HOLLINGTON
Staffordshire
Map**7** SK03

C Hollybush Cottage
for bookings Mrs F R Clayton, Hollybush House, Hollington, Tean, Stoke-on-Trent, Staffs
☎Hollington(088926)314

This stone-built former gamekeeper's house is attached to the rear of the

original farmhouse and set in open countryside. There is a well appointed lounge/dining room with open fire (logs provided), a small kitchen, bathroom/WC, a room with both a double and single bed and an outside WC. A fold-away bed is also available. The cottage is midway between Tean and Hollington; turn opposite the nursery.

All year MWB out of season wkds min, 1mth max, 1unit, 2persons ◇ ◆ ◉ fridge open fire Elec inclusive ⊡can be hired (overseas visitors only) ☎(1¼m) Iron on premises Ironing board on premises HCE in unit ⊕ TV ⊕3pin square P ♨(1¼m)
⇔ ♀
Min£40 Max£70pw

HOLLOCOMBE
Devon
Map**3** SS60

H Wood Terrill (Farmhouse)
for bookings Mrs Cowle, Westfield, Hollocombe, Chulmleigh, Devon
☎Winkleigh(083783)330

Isolated stone farmhouse comprising lounge, dining room, kitchen, three double rooms with extra single beds, one twin-bedded room and bathroom/WC. Modest furnishing.

Apr-Oct MWB 1unit, 1–11persons ◆ ◉ fridge Electric Elec metered ⊡not provided ☎(½m) Airing cupboard in unit Iron in unit Ironing board in unit HCE in unit ⊕ TV ⊕3pin square P ▥ ♨(2m)
⇔ ♀(2m)
Min£55 Max£70pw (Low)
Min£115 Max£165pw (High)

F Woodtrill (Flat)
for bookings Mr J Cowle Westfield, Hollocombe, Chumleigh, Devon EX18 7QG
☎Winkleigh(083783)330

Flat located within an old farmhouse in secluded position. It has kitchen/diner, lounge with bed-settee, one large bedroom with one double bed and twin bunks, and shower/WC. For access leave the B3220 at Berners Cross, north of Winkleigh, and follow Hollocombe signs, then take second turning on left.

Apr-Oct MWB 1wk min, 1mth max, 1unit, 2–6persons ◆ ◉ fridge Electric Elec metered ⊡not provided ☎(½m) Airing cupboard in unit HCE in unit ⊕ TV ⊕3pin square ⊕2pin round P ▥ ♨(2m)
⇔ ♀(2m) ▣(3m) ♫(3m)
Min£28 Max£50pw (Low)
Min£55 Max£105pw (High)

HOLLYBUSH
Strathclyde *Ayrshire*
Map**10** NS31

H Holiday Homes Skeldon Caravan Park
for bookings Mrs K Pickles, Skeldon Caravans, Hollybush, by Ayr, Ayrshire KA6 7EB
☎Dalrymple(029256)202

Local hall for former woollen mill village, converted into two self-contained units. Accommodation comprises two bedrooms (one double, one with three single beds), lounge with two convertible settees, kitchenette and shower unit. At centre of small caravan site but on banks of River Doon and in heart of farmland.

Apr-Sep MWB out of season 1wk min, 2units, 1–6persons ◇ ◆ ◉ Electric Elec inclusive ⊡not provided ☎(¾m) Iron in unit Ironing board in unit HCE in unit ⊕ ⊕3pin square P ▥ ♨(100yds)
⇔ ♀(1m)
Min£60 Max£90pw (Low)
Min£140 Max£170pw (High)

HOLNEST
Dorset
Map**3** ST60

F&C A J & A F Claypole **Manor Farm Country House** Holnest Park, Holnest, Sherborne, Dorset DT9 6HA
☎Holnest(096321)474

*Three flats located in the east and west wings of a modernised Georgian farmhouse. The **Summerlea**, a ground-floor flat in the east wing, comprises lounge with kitchen annexe and studio couch, one double bedroom, one twin-bedded room and bathroom/WC **Grooms Cottage**, a ground-floor flat in the west wing, comprises lounge with twin put-u-up, one double-bedded room, one twin-bedded room, kitchen/diner and bathroom/WC. **Park View** is a first-floor flat in the east wing and comprises lounge with twin put-u-up, one double-bedded room, one twin-bedded room and bathroom/WC. Approach is from the Dorchester to Sherborne road and is signposted. There is also a detached Lodge. The single-storey accommodation comprises lounge, two twin-bedded rooms, a double bedroom, kitchen/diner and bathroom/WC.*

Apr-Oct MWB in season 4units, 4–8persons ◇ ◆ ◉ fridge ▦ Elec metered ⊡not provided ☎(100yds) Iron on premises Ironing board on premises HCE in unit ⊕ CTV ⊕3pin square P ♨(5m)
⇔ ♀(100yds) Games room
Min£68 Max£125pw

HOLSWORTHY
Devon
Map**2** SS30

B Ashcroft Pyworthy (2m SW unclass road)

for bookings Mr & Mrs G Emmons, Beechwood, The Coombe, Streatley, Reading, Berks
☎Goring-on-Thames(0491)872395

A modern, block-built, cement-rendered bungalow situated in a quiet and unspoilt Devon village. It has a large lounge, three double bedrooms, kitchen/diner and bathroom/WC. A patio is available outside the lounge window. From Holsworthy follow unclass twisting road in a westerly direction for Pyworthy for 3m.

All year MWB out of season 1wkmin, 4wksmax, 1unit, 2–6persons ◊ ◆ ◉ fridge Electric Elecmetered ⌸notprovided ☎(200yds) Airing cupboard in unit Iron in unit Ironing board in unit HCE in unit ⊙ CTV ⊕3pinsquare ⊕2pinround P ▥ ⚐(200yds)
⊶ ♨(3m) ♨(200yds)
Min£40 Max£120pw

C No's 1 & 2 North Arscott Cottages
Lufflands
for bookings Mrs T A Bartlett, North Arscott Farm, Holsworthy, Devon
☎Bradworthy(040924)391

Two modernised cottages set in comparative isolation approx. 3 miles from Holsworthy. Accommodation comprises kitchen/breakfast room, dining room, lounge and three double bedrooms. Large garden.

Etr-Oct 1wkmin, 2units, 1–7persons ◊ ◉ fridge Electric & open fires Elecmetered ⌸notprovided ☎(200yds) Airing cupboard in unit Iron in unit Ironing board in unit HCE in unit ⊙ TV ⊕3pinsquare 1P 1⚐ ⚐(200yds)
⊶ ♨(3m) ♨(3m)

HOLT
Norfolk
Map**9** TG03

C 1–8 Carpenters Cottages,
Carpenters Close, Norwich Road
for bookings Mr J P Siddall, Fell Dyke Cottage, 54 Well Street, Langham, Oakham, Leicestershire LE15 7JS
☎Oakham(0572)56515

Early 18th-century terraced cottages built in traditional flint. Accommodation comprises lounge/kitchen, double-bedded room, single-bedded room and bathroom with WC. Located on edge of village.

All year MWB out of season 3days min, 6wks max, 8units, 1–6persons ◊ ◉ fridge ♨ Elecmetered ⌸can be hired ☎(400yds) SD in unit Airing cupboard in unit Iron in unit Ironing board in unit HCE in unit [Launderette within 300yds] ⊙ CTV ⊕3pinsquare P ▥ ⚐(100yds)
⊶ ♨(100yds)
Min£55 Max£65pw (Low)
Min£140 Max£170pw (High)

HOPESAY
Shropshire
Map**7** SO38

F Hesterworth Holidays
for bookings Mr & Mrs Richards, Hesterworth, Hopesay, Craven Arms, Shropshire
☎Little Brampton(05887)487

Seven flats, three of which are located within a section of this Victorian house, whilst four are located within a converted Victorian coach house and stable building. Aston comprises two single bedrooms, kitchen, lounge with a folding double wall bed. Burrow comprises three bedrooms, sitting/dining room, kitchen and bathroom. Hopesay comprises two double bedrooms, sitting room with wall bed, dining room, kitchen and bathroom. Clee comprises living room, kitchen, one double bedroom and bathroom. Clunbury comprises living room with bed-settee, kitchen, one double bedroom and bathroom. Long Mynd comprises living room with bed-settee, two double bedrooms and bathroom. Wenlock comprises sitting room, kitchen, one double and one single bedroom and bathroom.

All year MWB 3days min, 5mths max, 7units, 1–8persons [◊] ◊ ◉ fridge ♨ Electric Elecmetered ⌸can be hired ☎ Airing cupboard in unit Iron on premises Ironing board on premises HCE in unit ⊙ TV ⊕3pinsquare 50P ▥ ⚐(½m)
⊶ ♨
Min£35 Max£55pw (Low)
Min£80 Max£125pw (High)

HORNING
Norfolk
Map**9** TG31

Ch Ferry Marina Chalets Ferry Boat
Yard Ltd, Ferry Road
for bookings Blakes Chalet Holidays, Wroxham, Norwich, Norfolk NR12 8DH
☎Wroxham(06053)2917

Five cedar-wood Swiss/Scandinavian style chalets in a peaceful location, within the confines of Ferry Marina, which provides all facilities and amenities for boating activities. Two double bedrooms on first-floor and one twin-bedded room on ground-floor. Combined bathroom/WC on the ground-floor and one separate WC on first-floor. Good quality furnishings and equipment throughout.

Mar-mid Oct MWB out of season 1wkmin, 5units, 6persons [◊] [◆] ◉ fridge Electric Elecmetered ⌸inclusive ☎(200yds) Airing cupboard in unit HCE in unit ⊙ CTV ⊕3pinsquare P ▥ ⚐(50yds) Boats for hire

---

♨ (100yds)
Min£69 Max£132pw (Low)
Min£168 Max£182pw (High)

HORNS CROSS
Devon
Map**2** SS32

H CC Ref 517 ELP
for bookings Character Cottages (Holidays) Ltd, 34 Fore Street, Sidmouth, Devon EX10 8AQ
☎Sidmouth(039 55)77001

Houses stylishly converted from an old Victorian school, architecturally designed. Accommodation comprises two bedrooms (one twin-bedded, one single), lounge with studio couch, kitchen/diner and bathroom.

All year MWB out of season 1wkmin, 1mth max, 1unit, 2–5persons ◊ ◉ fridge ♨ Elecinclusive ⌸can be hired ☎ Airing cupboard in unit Iron in unit Ironing board in unit HCE in unit ⊙ TV ⊕3pinsquare ⊕2pinround P ⚐(5m) Riding & fishing
⊶ ♨
Min£39 Max£79pw (Low)
Min£111 Max£162pw (High)

HORTON
West Glamorgan
Map**2** SS48

B 3 Westernside Farm
for bookings Mr G R Macpherson, 75 Sketty Road, Uplands, Swansea SA2 0EN
☎Swansea(0792)298512

A brick-built bungalow situated on a small development of holiday homes in rural surroundings. Accommodation comprises open-plan lounge/diner/kitchen area, two bedrooms (one with double and one with twin beds) and bathroom/WC. A bed-settee is available in the lounge.

Mar-Oct MWB out of season 2nights min, 1unit, 2–6persons [◊ ◆] ◉ fridge Electric Elecmetered ⌸can be hired (overseas visitors only) ☎(200yds) Airing cupboard in unit Iron in unit HCE in unit ⊙ TV ⊕3pinsquare 1P ⚐(200yds)
⊶ ♨(1m)
Min£40 Max£150pw

HOVETON ST JOHN
Norfolk
Map**9** TG31

C Broadland View 28 Horning Road
for bookings Mrs S M Reynolds, 30 Horning Road, Hoveton St. John, Norwich NR12 8JN
☎Horning(0692)630055

Located on the outskirts of Hoveton this semi-detached cottage comprises kitchen, lounge, hall and dining area on the ground-floor and three bedrooms and bathroom/WC on the first-floor.

All year 1wkmin, 1mth max, 1unit, 1–5persons ◊ ◆ ◉ fridge ♨ →

125

Elec metered ☐inclusive ☎ WM in
unit Airing cupboard in unit Iron in unit
Ironing board in unit HCE in unit ⊕
CTV ⊕3pin square 4P ▥ ♨(1m)
Bicycle and boat available
⊶ ⚲(1m)

Min£72 Max£136pw

H **Little Broad House**
for bookings Mrs S M Reynolds, 30
Horning Road, Hoveton St. John,
Norwich, NR12 8JN
☎Horning(0692)630055

This delightful, secluded, four bedroom,
wooden house stands in over an acre of
ground, overlooking the broads. It
comprises dining room, lounge, kitchen
and WC; with three bedrooms and a
bathroom/WC on the first-floor.

All year 1wk min, 1mth max, 1unit,
1–5persons ◊ ◆ ◉ fridge
Electric Elec metered
☐inclusive(except towels) ☎ Airing
cupboard in unit Iron in unit Ironing
board in unit HCE in unit ⊕ CTV
⊕3pin square 4P ▥ ♨(1m) Bicycle
& boat available
⊶ ⚲(1½m)

Min£80 Max£150pw (Low)
Min£130 Max£218pw (High)

HOW CAPEL
Hereford & Worcester
Map**3** SO63

F **Rugden Granary Flat**
for bookings Mrs J Cross, Rugden
House, How Caple, Hereford
☎How Caple(098 986)224

Situated on a fruit farm this first-floor flat
forms part of an old stone farm building
and comprises lounge/kitchen,
bathroom and sleeps up to six persons.

Apr-Oct MWB in season 2nights min,
1mth max, 1unit, 1–6persons ◆
no pets ◉ fridge Gas & electric
heaters Gas/Elec metered ☐can be
hired ☎(½m) Airing cupboard in unit
Iron in unit Ironing board in unit HCE in
unit ⊙ TV ⊕3pin square 4P
♨(½m) ⤷Hard
⊶ ⚲(1m)

HUNSTANTON
Norfolk
Map**9** TF64

Ch **Manor Park** Manor Road
for bookings Hoseasons Holidays,
Sunway House, Lowestoft, Suffolk
NR32 3LT
☎Lowestoft(0502)62292

Chalets situated on a caravan site each
accommodating six persons. There are
two bedrooms (one double, the other has
twin bunk beds), lounge, kitchen and
bathroom/WC.

Etr-Sep 3days min, 6wks max, 25units,
1–6persons ◆ [◆] ◉ fridge
Electric Elec metered ☐inclusive ☎
Airing cupboard in unit HCE in unit ⊙
TV ⊕3pin square P ♨(20yds) ⌂

Hoveton St John
—
Ilfracombe

⊶ ⚲(100yds) ▨(100yds) ▤(½m)

B **Sandringham Bungalows** Old
Hunstanton Road
for bookings Hoseasons Holidays,
Sunway House, Lowestoft, Suffolk
NR32 3LT
☎Lowestoft(0502)62292
Wooden bungalows situated adjacent to
the Lodge Hotel, and 1m from the sea.
Accommodation comprises two
bedrooms (one double, one twin-
bedded), lounge/kitchen and
bathroom/WC.

Mar-Oct MWB 3days min, 3mths max,
30units, 1–6persons [◆] [◆] ◉
fridge Electric Elec metered
☐inclusive ☎(150yds) [Iron on
premises] [Ironing board on premises]
HCE in unit TV ⊕3pin square P
♨(150yds)
⊶ ⚲(100yds) ▨(1½m) ♫(1½m)
▤(1½m)

IDEN GREEN
Kent
Map**5** TQ83

C **Tudor Farmhouse Cottage**
for bookings Mrs A C Grant, Campion
House, Iden Green, Cranbrook, Kent
TN17 4LB
☎Benenden(058082)617

Period cottage adjoining 15th-century
Tudor farmhouse containing two
bedrooms, bathroom/WC and ground-
floor foyer lounge. South facing with
outstanding country views over the
Weald and sharing 1¼ acres of private
garden.

All year MWB out of season 1day min,
28days max, 1unit, 1–6persons ◊ ◆
◆ ◉ fridge ♨ Elec metered
☐inclusive ☎(¾m) WM in unit SD in
unit Airing cupboard in unit Iron on
premises Ironing board on premises
HCE in unit ⊙ TV ⊕3pin square 3P
▥ ♨(¾m)

Min£30 Max£81pw (Low)
Min£85 Max£108pw (High)

ILCHESTER
Somerset
Map**3** ST52

F Mrs W T C Hawkes **Flats 3 & 4** Bos
House, Limington Road, Ilchester,
Somerset BA22 8LX
☎Ilchester(0935)840507

Two self-contained flats with own
entrance. Ground-floor flat comprises
kitchen/diner, lounge, bathroom with WC
and two twin-bedded rooms. First-floor
has dining unit in lounge, kitchen,
bathroom/WC and two twin-bedded
rooms. Situated on B3151 at southern
end of town.

All year MWB out of season 1wk min,
8wks max, 2units, 1–4persons [◊] ◆
◆ ♪ fridge Electric Gas inclusive
Elec metered ☐can be hired ☎ WM
on premises SD on premises [TD on
premises] Airing cupboard in unit Iron
in unit Ironing board in unit ⊕ CTV
⊕3pin square ▥ ♨(100yds)
⊶ ⚲(100yds)

Min£55 Max£72pw (Low)
£88pw (High)

ILFRACOMBE
Devon
Map**2** SS54

C **1 & 2 Dean Cottages**
for bookings Mrs A & Miss J Hookway,
Dean Farm, West Down, Ilfracombe,
Devon EX30 8NT
☎Ilfracombe(0271)63915

Attractive, whitewashed semi-detached
farm cottages with front lawn, situated
close to working farm. Both comprise
lounge, kitchen/diner, bathroom and one
with two bedrooms the other with three.
On A361 at Dean Cross, 1½m S of
Mullacott Cross.

All year MWB out of season 4days min,
4wks max, 2units, 1–5persons ◊ ◆
no pets ◉ fridge Elec metered
☐can be hired(overseas visitors only)
☎(1m) Iron in unit Ironing board in
unit HCE in unit TV ⊕3pin square
2P ▥ ♨(1m)
⊶ ♨(3m) ⚲(½m) ▨(3m) ♫(3m)
▤(3m)

Min£40 Max£55pw (Low)
Min£70 Max£110pw (High)

B Mr James Meanley **Golden Coast
Holiday Bungalows** Worth Road,
Ilfracombe, Devon
☎Ilfracombe(0271)63543

Sixteen holiday bungalows set in 1½ acres
of pleasant wooded and lawned estate
affording views of sea and cliffs.
Accommodation, equipped for six,
comprises two bedrooms (one double,
one twin-bedded), lounge with
convertible double bed, kitchen,
bathroom and WC.

15Mar-15Jan MWB out of season
3days min, 1mth max, 16units,
2–6persons [◊] ◆ ◆] ◉ fridge
Electric Elec metered ☐not provided
☎(50yds) [WM on premises SD on
premises] Airing cupboard in unit Iron
on premises Ironing board on
premises HCE in unit ⊙ CTV
⊕3pin square 16P ♨(200yds)
⊶ ♨(2m) ⚲(1m) ▨(1m) ♫(1m)
▤(1m)

Min£30 Max£59pw (Low)
Min£75 Max£189pw (High)

F Mrs E V Brookman **High Gables** St
Brannocks Road, Ilfracombe, Devon
☎Ilfracombe(0271)62861

Two maisonettes attached to large
Victorian house set in its own attractive
gardens and overlooking Bicclescombe

Park and woodlands. One maisonette consists of two bedrooms, kitchen, bathroom and lounge/diner with convertible settee. Excellent views from all units with town centre ½m away.

4Apr-24Oct 1wkmin, 1mthmax, 2units, 2–7persons [◆] nocats ◎ fridge Electric Elecmetered ⊡notprovided ☎(200yds) Iron in unit Ironing board in unit HCE in unit ⊙ TV ⊕3pinsquare ⊕3pinround P ⌂ ▥ ⛭(¼m)

⊕ ⛳18(2m) ♀(½m) ⊡(1m) ⛭(1m)

Min£35 Max£85pw (Low)
Min£80 Max£145pw (High)

B&C **Ilfracombe Holiday Village**
for bookings John Fowler Holidays, Marlborough Road, Ilfracombe, Devon
☎Ilfracombe(0271)64135

Compact neat units of varying sizes accommodating up to eight persons. All have lounge/diner, kitchen area, bathroom/WC and either one, two or three bedrooms. Use of varied facilities within this holiday complex including sauna, solarium and licensed club/restaurant.

Mar-Oct MWB out of season 1nightmin, 3wks max, 190units, 1–8persons [◇ ◆] ◎ fridge Electric Elecmetered ⊡can be hired ☎ Airing cupboard in unit Iron on premises HCE in unit ⊙ CTV ⊕3pinsquare P ⛭ ⌓(heated) ♿

⊕ ⛳18(2m) ♀(300yds) ⊡(300yds) ♫(300yds) ⛭(¾m)

Min£45 Max£205pw

F **Ilfracombe Holiday Village**
for bookings John Fowler Holidays, Marlborough Road, Ilfracombe, Devon
☎Ilfracombe(0271)64135

Modern units comprising kitchen, breakfast bar and stools, large lounge with double bed and comfortable settee, all fully carpeted. There is a licensed restaurant/club, sauna, solarium and childrens play area all within the holiday village.

Mar-Oct MWB out of season 1nightmin, 3wks max, 20units, 1–3persons [◇ ◆] ◎ fridge Electric Elecmetered ⊡can be hired ☎ Airing cupboard in unit Iron in unit HCE in unit ⊙ CTV ⊕3pinsquare P ⛭(50yds) ⌓(heated) ♿

⊕ ⛳18(2m) ♀(300yds) ⊡(300yds) ♫(300yds) ⛭(¾m)

Min£45 Max£205pw

F **7 Larkstone Terrace**
for bookings Mr & Mrs P J Brook, Bay View, Woodlands, Combe Martin, N Devon
☎Combe Martin(027 188)2522

Three flats located in terraced house on road to town centre. View of the sea from rear rooms. Two of the flats have two bedrooms with one double and one single bed, lounge with put-u-up and dining table, kitchen and bathroom/WC. The other flat has a bedroom with double bed, lounge, kitchen/diner and bathroom/WC. Two flats have high-chairs available.

All year MWB out of season 1wkmin, 4wks max, 3units, 1–5persons ◆ ◆ no pets ♨ fridge Gas Gas/Elec metered ⊡inclusive ☎(100yds) Airing cupboard in unit Iron in unit Ironing board in unit HCE in unit TV ⊕3pinsquare ⛭(¼m)

⊕ ⛳18(1½m) ♀(500yds) ⊡(½m) ♫(½m) ⛭(½m)

Min£30 Max£60pw (Low)
Min£70 Max£120pw (High)

F **Marine View Holiday Flats** 18 Montpellier Terrace
for bookings Mrs J Kingston, Imperial Hotel, Ilfracombe, Devon
☎Ilfracome(0271)62536

Flats situated on four floors of a modernised, terraced Georgian building located on a rise at the edge of town. The ground-floor flat has a large kitchen/diner with foldaway bed if required, one double bedroom, one twin-bedded room and shower room/WC. The first-, second- and third-floor flats have kitchen/diner, one double bedroom, one with three single beds and a bathroom/WC. All bedrooms have wash-basins.

Apr-Oct 1wkmin, 1mthmax, 4units, 1–6persons ◆ ◆ no pets ◎ fridge Electric Elecmetered ⊡can be hired ☎(200yds) Iron in unit Ironing board in unit HCE in unit [Launderette within 300yds] ⊙ CTV ⊕3pinsquare P ⛭(200yds)

⊕ ⛳18(2m) ♀(300yds) ⊡(500yds) ♫(500yds) ⛭(500yds)

Min£45 Max£80pw (Low)
Min£65 Max£105pw (High)

F Mrs P Thomas & Mr I Todd **Rovanda** 12 Hillsborough Terrace, Ilfracombe, Devon EX34 9NR
☎Ilfracombe(0271)64011

Two flats within three-storey Georgian-style terraced house, on main Combe Martin to Ilfracombe road. Each has two bedrooms, kitchen, lounge/diner. Modern-style furnishings and décor. Good views overlooking sea and Ilfracombe.

Mar-Oct 1wkmin, 4wks max, 2units, 2–5persons ◆ no pets ◎ fridge Electric Elecmetered ⊡inclusive ☎(350yds) Iron in unit Ironing board in unit HCE in unit [Launderette within 300yds] ⊙ TV ⊕3pinsquare 2P ▥ ⛭(300yds) ⊟ ⛳Hard Putting

⊕ ♀(600yds) ⊡(600yds) ♫(600yds) ⛭(½m)

Min£52 Max£120pw

1982 prices quoted throughout gazetteer

F Mr & Mrs W A Elliott ***Silver Surf Holiday Flats*** 7 Oxford Park, Ilfracombe, Devon EX34 9JS
☎Ilfracombe(0271)63539

Four self-contained flats, three of which comprise two or three bedrooms, lounge with convertible settee, and kitchen/diner, bathroom/shower unit and WC. The other sleeps two people in lounge with double foldaway bed, kitchen and bathroom/WC.

Apr-Oct MWB out of season 1wkmin, 4units, 2–8persons [◇] ◆ ◆ ◎ fridge Electric Elecmetered ⊡can be hired ☎ Airing cupboard in unit Iron on premises Ironing board on premises HCE in unit [Launderette within 300yds] ⊙ [TV] ⊕3pinsquare P ▥ ⛭(200yds)

⊕ ♀(500yds) ⊡(500yds) ♫(500yds) ⛭(500yds)

C **Sunningdale** Cheglinch, West Down
for bookings Mr W A J Hewitt, Leonard House, Sampford Peverell, Tiverton, Devon EX16 7EL
☎Tiverton(0884)820677

Semi-detached cottage in quiet lane with fine views. Accommodation comprises small lounge, dining room, kitchen and breakfast room, two double bedrooms, one twin and bathroom. Pleasant cottage furniture.

Apr-Oct 1wkmin, 4wks max, 1unit, 1–6persons ◆ ◆ ◎ fridge Electric Elecmetered ⊡not provided ☎(1m) WM in unit Airing cupboard in unit Iron in unit Ironing board in unit HCE in unit ⊙ ⊛ TV ⊕3pinsquare 2P 1⌂ ▥ ⛭(1½m)

⊕ ⛳18(3m) ♀(1m) ⊡(3m) ♫(3m) ⛭(3m)

Min£65 Max£75pw (Low)
Min£90 Max£110pw (High)

INKBERROW

Hereford & Worcester
Map**4** SP05

C **Rose Cottage**
for bookings Mr & Mrs C V Collingford, Bramley House, Withybed Lane, Inkberrow, Worcs. WR7 4JJ
☎Inkberrow(0386)792956

This detached listed cottage has great charm and character and is set within the conservation area of this Worcestershire village. There is a neatly kept small flower garden with a well and sitting area. Accommodation comprises kitchen/dining room, large lounge, two double bedrooms on the 1st floor and two double bedrooms on the 2nd floor.

All year MWB out of season 3daysmin, 1mthmax, 1unit, 1–9persons [◇] ◆ ◆ ◎ fridge ₩ Elecmetered ⊡can be hired (overseas visitors only) ☎(200yds) WM in unit SD in unit Airing cupboard in unit Iron in unit Ironing board in unit HCE in unit ⊙ CTV ⊕3pinsquare 3P ▥ ⛭(10yds)→

⊖ ♀(150yds) ☑(200yds)
Min£60 Max£110pw (Low)
Min£85 Max£130pw (High)

INVERGARRY
Highland *Inverness-shire*
Map**14** NH30

Ca Mrs G Swann **High Garry Lodges**
Ardgarry Farm, Faichem, Invergarry,
Inverness-shire
☎Invergarry(08093)226

*Solid round-log lodges situated on a
small working farm with animals and
panoramic views. Each offers a modern,
spacious, well furnished
lounge/diner/kitchen, two double and
one twin-bedded bedroom and
bathroom. Set on A87 Invergarry/Kyle
road 1m W of junction A87/A82.*

All year MWB out of season 1wk min,
1mth max, 4units, 2–6persons [◊] ◆
[Dogs accepted on lead] ◎ fridge
🍴 Elec metered ⌷inclusive ☎(1m)
Airing cupboard in unit HCE in unit ⊖
CTV ☼3pin square 8P ♨(½m)

⊖ ♀(1m)
Min£74.75 Max£97.75pw (Low)
Min£138 Max£253pw (High)

INVERKEILOR
Tayside *Angus*
Map**15** NO65

C Mr I Stuart **Ethie Mains** Inverkeilor,
Arbroath, Angus DD11 5SN
☎Inverkeilor(02413)258

*Six pleasant two or three bedroomed
cottages on a 460-acre arable farm which
is located on a hilltop at the southern end
of the sandy Lunan Bay. These stone-
built cottages have been modernised
and are pleasantly furnished throughout.
A popular base for golfers with a number
of famous courses within 30m.*

Mar–16Oct MWB out of season
1wk min, 6units, 1–6persons [◊] ◎
fridge Electric & open fires
Elec metered ⌷not provided ☎(2½m)
Iron in unit Ironing board in unit HCE in
unit ☼3pin round 12P 🝙 ♨(4m)
⤙Hard

⊖ ♀(3m)
Min£45 Max £34w (Low)
Min£72 Max£90pw (High)

C Mrs Mathieson **Lawton Mill Cottage**
Lawton Mill, Inverkeilor, Arbroath, Angus
D11 4RU
☎Inverkeilor(02413)246

*A conversion of two former mill workers'
stone cottages in an attractive setting in
the grounds of Lawton Mill, a private
house which lies adjacent.
Accommodation consists of a large living
room, kitchen, bathroom, one twin-
bedded room, one bedroom with bunk
beds and a single bed. lies 1½m W of
Inverkeilor off the B965.*

All year MWB out of season 1wk min,
1unit, 1–5persons ◊ ◎ fridge 🍴&

open fire Elec metered ⌷can be
hired ☎(1½m) Airing cupboard in unit
HCE in unit TV ☼3pin square P ▥
♨(1½m)

⊖ ♀(1½m)
Min£25 Max£55pw (Low)
£85pw (High)

INVERMORISTON
Highland *Inverness-shire*
Map**14** NH41

C **Altruadh, Farm, Farmburn,
Homewood & Levishie Cottages**
for bookings Estate Office, Glenmoriston
Estates Ltd, Glenmoriston, Inverness
IV36YA
☎Glenmoriston(0320)51202

*Five individual cottages at varying
locations in an 8m section of
Glenmoriston. Although beautiful, the
locations are often isolated, making a car
a necessity. Each cottage provides
suitable accommodation for the sporting
enthusiast and tourist alike. Sleeping up
to 10 people, the cottages offer privacy
and peacefulness.*

5Mar–29Oct MWB out of season
1–2wks min, 5units, 1–10persons [◊]
No tents or caravans ◎ fridge
Electric Elec metered ⌷can be hired
☎(½m) Iron in unit Ironing board in unit
HCE in unit ☼3pin square P ▥
♨(½m) Fishing

⊖ ♀(½m)
Min£36 Max£98pw (Low)
Min£118 Max£174pw (High)

Ch **Bhiaraidh Chalets**
for bookings Estate Office, Glenmoriston
Estates Ltd, Glenmoriston, Inverness
IV36YA
☎Glenmoriston(0320)51202

*Four chalets, one with three bedrooms,
remainder with twin-bedded rooms, in a
secluded spot on the banks of the River
Moriston some 3m W of Invermoriston
along the A887 Skye road. Parking is no
problem and the area offers good
facilities for fishing.*

5Mar–29Oct MWB out of season
1–2wks min, 4units, 1–8persons [◊]
No tents or caravans ◎ fridge
Electric Elec metered ⌷can be hired
Iron in unit Ironing board in unit HCE in
unit CTV ☼3pin square P ▥
♨(½m) Fishing

⊖ ♀ ☑
Min£46 Max£99pw (Low)
Min£99 Max£142pw (High)

Ch **Dalcattaig Chalets**
for bookings Estate Office, Glenmoriston
Estates Ltd, Glenmoriston, Inverness
IV36YA
☎Glenmoriston(0320)51202

*One three-bedroomed and seven two-
bedroomed chalets situated in a wooded
area backed by the forested hill of Stron*

na Muich, facing the River Moriston and
only a short walk from the village. Various
combinations of sleeping arrangements
are available and furnishings are simple
but compact.*

5Mar–29Oct MWB out of season
1–2wks min, 8units, 1–8persons [◊]
No tents or caravans ◎ fridge
Electric Elec metered ⌷can be hired
Iron in unit Ironing board in unit HCE in
unit CTV ☼3pin square P ▥
♨(½m) Fishing

⊖ ♀ ☑
Min£36 Max£142pw

Ch **Sian Drochit Chalets**
for bookings Estate Office, Glenmoriston
Estates Ltd, Glenmoriston, Inverness
IV36YA
☎Glenmoriston(0320)51202

*Eight cedar-wood chalets situated close
to the River Moriston and ½m from the
village. Each unit comprises living room,
kitchen, two bedrooms and
bathroom/WC.*

5Mar–29Oct MWB 1–2wks min,
8units, 1–6persons [◊] No tents or
caravans ◎ fridge Electric
Elec metered ⌷can be hired Iron in
unit Ironing board in unit HCE in unit
☼3pin square P ▥ ♨(½m) Fishing

⊖ ♀ ☑
Min£36 Max£76pw (Low)
Min£89 Max£118pw (High)

INVERNESS
Highland *Inverness-shire*
Map**14** NH64

B **Fulnary Cottage** 10A Culduthel
Road
for bookings Scottish Highland Holiday
Homes, 26 Station Square, Inverness
IV11VE
☎Inverness(0463)222820

*Traditional detached bungalow situated
in its own garden, 10 minutes' walk from
the town centre. It comprises sitting room
with views across the town, small dining
room, kitchen, bathroom/WC and three
bedrooms, one with bunk beds. Street
parking only but no restrictions.*

May–Sep MWB out of season 1wk min,
1unit, 1–6persons ◎ fridge 🍴◎
Elec metered ⌷not provided ☎
Airing cupboard in unit Iron in unit
Ironing board in unit HCE in unit TV
☼3pin round ▥ ♨(½m)

**⊖ 🚲(3m) ♀(100yds) ☑(½m)
♫(½m) 🐕(½m)**
Min£60 Max£80pw (Low)
Min£70 Max£95pw (High)

C **Ivy Cottage** 58 Argyle Street
for bookings Scottish Highland Holiday
Homes, 26 Station Square, Inverness
IV11VE
☎Inverness(0463)222820

*A converted Mews Cottage in small
courtyard, close to town centre,
comprising sitting room/dining area with
open-plan kitchen. Two bedrooms and
bathroom/WC upstairs.*

May–Sep MWB out of season 1wk min, 1unit, 1–4persons [◇] ◎ fridge Electric Elec metered ⬛not provided ☎(25yds) WM in unit Airing cupboard in unit Iron in unit Ironing board in unit HCE in unit ⊕3pin square 1P ▥ ♨(100yds)

⇔ ♒(3m) ♀(100yds) ⊡(½m) ♫(½m) 🐾(½m)

Min£75 Max£95pw

IPSTONES
Staffordshire
Map7 SK05

C Clough Head Farm
for bookings Mrs Leeson, Crow Gutter Farm, Ipstones, Staffs ST102ND
☎Ipstones(053871)428

Two cottages approximately 150 years old situated on a farm with pleasant rural views, in a quiet picturesque area ½m SE of Ipstones village. One unit comprises lounge/diner, kitchen, bathroom and WC, one large family bedroom, one double and one twin-bedded room. The second unit comprises lounge, dining area in kitchen, bathroom and WC. It has one family bedroom, one twin-bedded room and a double bed-settee in lounge.

Apr–Sep MWB out of season 1wk min, 1mth max, 2units, 2–7persons ◆ ◎ fridge ♏ Electric & open fires Elec metered ⬛not provided ☎(½m) Airing cupboard in unit HCE in unit CTV ⊕3pin square 6P ♨(½m)

⇔ ♒ ♀(½m)

Min£40 Max£90pw

F Mrs J Brindley Glenwood House Farm Ipstones, Stoke-on-Trent, Staffordshire ST102JP
☎Ipstones(053871)294

Two ground-floor flats in a sandstone-built former Cow Shed at the side of the farmyard. Each has a kitchen, compact lounge, two bedrooms, one having twin beds in flat 1 and a single bed in flat 2. Both have shower and WC. The farm lies at the end of a ½m track just ½m W of Ipstones on the Cheddleton road.

Mar–Nov, Xmas & New Year MWB out of season 2nights min, 1mth max, 2units, 1–6persons ◆ ◆ ◎ fridge Electric Elec metered ⬛can be hired (overseas visitors only) ☎(1½m) WM on premises SD on premises [Iron on premises] [Ironing board on premises] HCE ⊙ CTV ⊕3pin square P ▥ ♨(1½m) Games room, children's play area

⇔ ♀(1½m)

Min£40 Max£50pw (Low)
Min£75 Max£80pw (High)

C Low Top Cottage
for bookings Mrs A Bates, The Cottage, Park Lane, Ipstones, Stoke-on-Trent, Staffordshire
☎Ipstones(053871)409

This stone built detached cottage occupies an elevated position overlooking the surrounding countryside and villages. The accommodation comprises lounge with oak beams and large open fireplace, kitchen, bathroom/WC all on ground floor and two twin bedded rooms on the first floor.

All year MWB out of season 3days min, 3mths max, 1unit, 1–4persons [◇] ◆ ◆ ◎ fridge Electric Elec metered ⬛can be hired ☎(½m) WM in unit SD in unit Airing cupboard in unit Iron in unit Ironing board in unit HCE in unit ⊙ TV ⊕3pin square 2P ▥ ♨(½m)

⇔ ♀(½m) ⊡(½m)

Min£45 Max£90pw

ISLANDS
Details for islands are listed under the name of the island e.g. **Skye** (Isle of Skye), **Wight** (Isle of Wight) etc., then follows a list of towns or villages on the island which have AA-listed self-catering establishments; these places appear in alphabetical order throughout the gazetteer text and give full details. A useful first point of reference is to consult the location maps which show where AA-listed establishments are situated.
N.B. There is no map for Isles of Scilly.

ISLAY, ISLE OF
Strathclyde *Argyll*
Map10 NR
See Port Charlotte, Port Ellen

ISLE ORNSAY
Isle of Skye, Highland *Inverness-shire*
Map13 NG61

B Culleag
for bookings Miss M M Fraser, Post Office House, Isle Ornsay, Isle of Skye
☎Isle Ornsay(047 13)201

A modern slate-roofed bungalow standing on elevated site with hill backdrop and magnificent views, over the Sound of Sleat and Mouth of Loch Hourn. A well decorated and furnished unit with one twin bedroom and one family room (double and single bed) sitting room/dining room/kitchen and modern bathroom. From A851 turn into village, then right on Camberscross Road Bungalow next to post office.

All year 1wk min, 1mth max, 1unit, 2–5persons ◆ ◎ fridge Electric Elec metered ⬛not provided ☎(200yds) Airing cupboard in unit Iron in unit Ironing board in unit HCE in unit ⊙ ⊕3pin square P ♨(3m) Fishing

⇔ ♀(200yds) ⊡(200yds)

Min£45pw (Low)
Min£70pw (High)

IVYBRIDGE
Devon
Map2 SX65

C Keaton Cottages 1, 2 & 3 Keaton (1m S B3211)
for bookings Mrs S Day, Keaton House, Ivybridge, Devon
☎Ivybridge(07554)2576

A row of three cottages converted to a very high standard. Each has its own entrance to ground-floor lounge with very fine furnishings and stone fireplace, dining area and modern fully fitted kitchen. Open tread staircase to two bedrooms, one double and one bunk-bedded, and bathroom/WC/washbasin.

Mar–Sep MWB out of season 1wk min, 4wks max, 3units, 1–4persons ◆ ◆ no pets ◎ fridge Electric, calor & open fires Elec metered ⬛inclusive ☎(½m) Airing cupboard in unit Iron in unit Ironing board in unit HCE in unit ⊙ CTV ⊕3pin square P ♨(½m) Fishing

⇔ ♀(½m) ⊡(1½m) ♫(1½m)

C Power House (1m S B3211)
for bookings Mrs S Day, Keaton House, Ivybridge, Devon
☎Ivybridge(07554)2576

Delightfully converted farm property with split-level living room/dining area, and granite fireplace, modern kitchen, one double, one twin and one bunk-bedded room. There is also a separate bathroom, WC and washbasin.

Mar–Sep MWB out of season 1wk min, 4wks max, 1unit, 2–6persons ◆ ◆ no pets ◎ fridge Electric & open fires Elec metered ⬛inclusive ☎(½m) Airing cupboard in unit Iron in unit Ironing board in unit ⊙ CTV ⊕3pin square P ♨(½m) Fishing

⇔ ♀(½m) ⊡(1½m) ♫(1½m)

C Witheridge One & Two Keaton (1m S B3211)
for bookings Mrs S Day, Keaton House, Ivybridge, Devon
☎Ivybridge(07554)2576

Two cottages situated 1½ from Ivybridge. Each has an attractive ground-floor lounge with dining area, separate kitchen, cloakroom with washbasin, and bathroom/WC. Witheridge One has one double room and one twin-bedded room. The larger cottage (Witheridge Two) has four bedrooms; two double and two twin-bedded.

Mar–Sep MWB out of season 1wk min, 4wks max, 2units, 2–8persons ◆ ◆ no pets ◎ fridge Rayburn cooker Electric & open fires Elec metered ⬛inclusive ☎(½m) Airing cupboard in unit Iron in unit Ironing board in unit HCE in unit ⊙ CTV ⊕3pin square P ♨(½m) Fishing

⇔ ♀(½m) ⊡(1½m) ♫(1½m)

1982 prices quoted throughout gazetteer

JEDBURGH
Borders *Roxburghshire*
Map **12** NT62

C   Upper Samieston
for bookings Mrs C V Dagg, Woodhead,
Jedburgh, Roxburghshire TD8 6TY
☎Ancrum(083 53)205

Two cottages, part of a 600-acre farm,
about 6m from Jedburgh. Very good
standard of décor and furnishings.
Pleasant views over Border country.

Mar–Nov MWB out of season 1 wk min,
2 mths max, 2 units, 1–5 persons ◊ ◆
◉ fridge Electric Elec metered
⬜not provided ☎(2m) Airing
cupboard in unit Iron in unit Ironing
board in unit HCE in unit ⊕ TV
⊕3 pin round P ♿(6m)

Min£60 Max£90pw

JEFFRESTON
Dyfed
Map **2** SN00

C   Hanbury Cottages
for bookings Saundersvale Holiday
Estate Ltd, Valley Road, Saundersfoot,
Dyfed SA6 9RT
☎Saundersfoot(0834)812310

Four recently-modernised cottages set in
a very pleasant rural area.
Accommodation in each comprises
good-sized lounge/dining room with
studio couch (forming a double bed),
kitchen, modern bathroom/WC, one
double bedroom and one room with three
beds.

All year MWB out of season
2 nights min, 4 units, 2–7 persons [◊]
◊ ◆ ◉ fridge Electric
Elec inclusive ⬜can be hired
☎(300yds) Airing cupboard in unit Iron
in unit Ironing board in unit HCE in unit
⊕ TV ⊕3 pin square P 🅟
♿(300yds)

↫ ♀(500yds)

Min£30 Max£100pw (Low)
Min£60 Max£190pw (High)

H   Hanbury Lodge
for bookings Saundersvale Holiday
Estate Ltd, Valley Road, Saundersfoot,
Dyfed SA6 9RT
☎Saundersfoot(0834)812310

Set in open countryside this lodge offers
spacious accommodation for eight
persons in three bedrooms, one of which
is on the ground floor. A very modern unit
containing large lounge with dining
facilities, fully fitted kitchen and
bathroom/WC. Ideal situation for those
who prefer a peaceful holiday.

All year MWB out of season
2 nights min, 2 units, 2–8 persons ◊ ◊
◆ ◉ fridge Electric Elec inclusive
⬜can be hired ☎(300yds) Airing
cupboard in unit Iron in unit Ironing
board in unit HCE in unit ⊕ CTV
⊕3 pin square P 🅟 ♿(300yds)

↫ ♀(500yds)

Min£40 Max£210pw

KEESTON
Dyfed
Map **2** SM82

B   The Bungalows
for bookings Mr B Caulfield Giles,
Keeston Hall, Keeston, Haverfordwest,
Dyfed
☎Camrose(0437)710482

Two-bedroomed bungalows, all have
fully equipped kitchens, spacious living
room with dining area, bathroom and WC.

All year MWB 2 nights min, 8 units,
4–7 persons [◊] ◊ ◆ ◉ fridge
Electric Elec metered ⬜inclusive
☎(25yds) SD in unit Airing cupboard in
unit Iron in unit Ironing board in unit
HCE in unit ⊕ TV ⊕3 pin square P
🅟 ♿(¾m) ⌂

↫ ♀(1m) ♫(2m)

Min£60 Max£230pw

C   Keeston Hall
for bookings Mr B Caulfield Giles,
Keeston Hall, Keeston, Haverfordwest,
Dyfed
☎Camrose(0437)710482

Four cottages in the heart of the
Pembrokeshire countryside. All have
lounge, bathroom/WC and kitchen, one
with kitchen/diner and either two or three
bedrooms.

All year MWB 2 nights min, 4 units,
2–7 persons [◊] ◊ ◆ ◉ fridge
Electric Elec metered ⬜inclusive
☎(25yds) SD in unit Airing cupboard in
unit Iron in unit Ironing board in unit
HCE in unit ⊕ TV ⊕3 pin square P
🅟 ♿(¾m) ⌂

↫ ♀(1m) ♫(2m)

Min£60 Max£230pw

KEINTON MANDEVILLE
Somerset
Map **3** ST53

C   'Ingledene' Castle Street
for bookings Mr W J Duncan, Church
Farm, Compton Dundon, Somerton,
Somerset TA11 6PE
☎Somerton(0458)72927

Stone-built, semi-detached cottage in
centre of small village. Accommodation
comprises lounge, kitchen/diner, three
bedrooms (two with double beds and one
children's room with bunk beds),
bathroom/WC.

Apr–Sep 1 wk min, 3 wks max, 1 unit,
1–6 persons ◉ fridge Electric
Elec metered ⬜inclusive ☎(300yds)
SD in unit Airing cupboard in unit Iron
in unit Ironing board in unit HCE in unit
TV ⊕3 pin square 2P 🅟 ♿(50yds)

↫ ♀(200yds)

Min£75 Max£95pw

1982 prices quoted throughout
gazetteer

KELSO
Borders *Roxburghshire*
Map **12** NT73

F   Mr P Halley **Maxmill Park** Station
Road, Kelso, Roxburghshire
☎Kelso(0573)24468

Studio and garden flats forming part of an
extention to the owner's house.
Accommodation comprises open-plan
lounge/diner/kitchen area, with Baby
Belling cooker, small double bedroom
and bathroom. Additional bed settee in
each flat. One flat has two adjoining
bedrooms which may be made available
at extra charge. They overlook spacious
gardens with ducks and hens. Access via
B6352 then take last drive on left out of
Kelso.

All year MWB 1 wk min, 3 units,
1–4 persons [◊] ◊ ◉ fridge
Electric Elec metered ⬜can be hired
☎(1m) WM on premises SD on
premises Airing cupboard on
premises Iron on premises Ironing
board on premises HCE on premises
TV/CTV can be hired ⊕3 pin square P
🅟 ♿(120yds)

↫ 🚲 ♀(100yds) 📮(1m) ♫(1m)

Min£45 Max£65pw (Low)
Min£55 Max£130pw (High)

KEMERTON
Hereford & Worcester
Map **3** SO93

F   Coach House
for bookings Mr H W Herford, Upper
Court, Kemerton, Tewkesbury, Glos.
☎Overbury(038 689)351

Within the estate of Upper Court Manor
House with its own stream and trout
fishing lake. The accommodation is on
the first floor and comprises a spacious
beamed living room, with dining area,
one double bedroom, two twin-bedded
rooms, kitchen and bathroom/WC.

All year MWB out of season
2 nights min, 3 mths max, 1 unit,
1–6 persons [◊] ◊ ◆ ◉ firdge
Electric Elec metered ⬜inclusive ☎
[WM on premises] [SD on premises]
Airing cupboard in unit Iron in unit
Ironing board in unit HCE in unit ⊕
CTV ⊕3 pin square 4P ♿(300yds)
⌂ ⛵Hard Croquet, fishing & boating
↫ ♀(300yds)

F   Courtyard Cottage
for bookings Mr H W Herford, Upper
Court, Kemerton, Tewkesbury, Glos.
☎Overbury(038 689)351

Within the estate of Upper Court Manor
House with its own stream and trout
fishing lake. The front door is the archway
to a courtyard and accommodation is on
two floors. It comprises an open-plan
living room with pine kitchen area, dining
room, three-bedded room, and
bathroom/WC. In addition a sofa is
available which converts into a double
bed.

130

All year MWB out of season
2nights min, 3mths max, 1 unit,
1–8persons [◇] ◈ ◆ ◎ fridge
Electric Elec metered ◻inclusive ☎
[WM on premises] [SD on premises]
Airing cupboard in unit Iron in unit
Ironing board in unit HCE in unit ⊙
CTV ⊕3pin square 4P ♨(300yds)
⇌ Hard Croquet, fishing & boating
⇔ ♀(300yds)

C *The Gallery*
for bookings Mr H W Herford, Upper Court, Kemerton, Tewkesbury, Glos.
☎Overbury(038 689)351

Part of a converted coachhouse this ground floor cottage comprises large open plan lounge/diner/kitchen area, one bedroom with twin beds and shower/WC leading off. There is a bed settee in the lounge.

All year MWB out of season
2nights min, 3mths max, 1 unit,
1–4persons [◇] ◈ ◆ ◎ fridge
Electric Elec metered ◻inclusive ☎
[WM on premises] [SD on premises]
Airing cupboard in unit Iron in unit
Ironing board in unit HCE in unit ⊙
CTV ⊕3pin square 4P ♨(300yds)
⇌ Hard Croquet, fishing & boating
⇔ ♀(300yds)

C *The Stables*
for bookings Mr H W Herford, Upper Court, Kemerton, Tewkesbury, Glos.
☎Overbury(038 689)351

Part of a converted coachhouse comprising large lounge with two bed settees, kitchen and shower. The first floor has two double bedrooms, one with double, one with twin beds.

All year MWB out of season
2nights min, 3mths max, 1 unit,
1–4persons [◇] ◈ ◆ ◎ fridge
Electric Elec metered ◻inclusive ☎
[WM on premises] [SD on premises]
Airing cupboard in unit Iron in unit
Ironing board in unit HCE in unit ⊙
CTV ⊕3pin square 4P ♨(300yds)
⇌ Hard Croquet, fishing & boating
⇔ ♀(300yds)

KENDAL
Cumbria
Map **7** SD59

C 22 Castle Cresent
for bookings Mrs B Stainton, Exchange Garage, Old Shambles, Kendal, Cumbria LA9 4TA
☎Kendal(0539)20331

An old stone-built terraced cottage in a quiet setting overlooking a small park and the River Kent. Simple accommodation of two double and one single bedroom, lounge, kitchen, and bathroom/WC, all on the first floor. The cottage is in the centre of town and is a good base from which to tour the Lake District.

All year MWB out of season 1wk min,
1 unit, 5persons ◈ ◎ fridge
Gas & Electric Gas/Elec metered
◻inclusive ☎(500yds) WM in unit
Airing cupboard in unit Iron in unit
Ironing board in unit HCE in unit ⊙
TV ⊕3pin square ◫ ♨(100yds)
⇔ ♀(150yds) ◫(½m) ◫(½m)
Min£60 Max£65pw (Low)
Min£70 Max£90pw (High)

C Garth Cottage 36 Castle Garth
for bookings Mrs E Steele, 53 Burton Road, Kendal, Cumbria LA9 7JA
☎Kendal(0539)23400

Stone-built end terraced cottage set in a quiet area on the N side of town. The accommodation comprises two bedrooms, one room with a double and single bed and the other with twin beds. Extra folding bedspace is also available in lounge. There are two lounges, kitchen/diner and modern bathroom and WC.

All year MWB out of season 1wk min,
1 unit, 2–5persons ◈ no pets ◎
fridge Electric & gas fires
Gas/Elec metered ◻not provided
☎(400yds) Airing cupboard in unit Iron in unit Ironing board in unit HCE in unit
[Launderette within 300yds] ⊙ TV
⊕3pin square P ◫ ♨(200yds)
⇔ ₁₈(1½m) ♀(200yds) ◫(½m)
♫(½m) ◫(½m)
Min£35pw

F Mr S N J North ***The Flat*** 56 Gillingate, Kendal, Cumbria LA9 4JB
☎Kendal(0539)22208

This compact first-floor flat is situated in a stone-built end terraced house set in a side road but convenient to the town centre. It comprises lounge, kitchen, bathroom and bedroom containing a double bed.

May–Sep 1wk min, 1 unit, 2persons, nc
no pets ◎ fridge Electric
Elec metered ◻can be hired
☎(50yds) Airing cupboard in unit Iron in unit Ironing board in unit HCE in unit
⊙ ⊛ TV ⊕3pin square ◫
♨(50yds)
⇔ ₁₈(½m) ♀(50yds) ◫(50yds)
♫(50yds) ◫(½m)

F Plumgarths Holiday Flats
Plumgarths
for bookings Mr & Mrs Jonathan Somervell, Braithwaite, Crook, Kendal, Cumbria LA8 8LE
☎Staveley(0539)821325

A 17th-century country house carefully converted into five spacious flats with the original character being retained. Situated in 3 acres of gardens on B5284 between Windermere and Kendal. The flats are of various sizes each having a living room, kitchen and bathroom.

All year MWB out of season 3days min,
3mths max, 5units, 1–6persons [◈]
[◆] no cats ◎ fridge ⋈ Electric & open fires Elec metered ◻provided
(overseas visitors only) ☎ [WM on premises] [TD on premises] Airing cupboard in unit Iron in unit Ironing board in unit HCE in unit ⊙ TV
⊕3pin square P ◫ ♨(2m)
⇔ ₁₈(2m) ♀(2m) ◫(2m) ◫(2m)
Min£53 Max£75pw (Low)
Min£117 Max£164pw (High)

KENTALLEN
Highland *Argyllshire*
Map **14** NN05

Ch Loch Linnhe Chalets
for bookings Loch Linnhe Chalets, 31 Acorn Road, Newcastle-upon-Tyne NE2 2DT
☎Newcastle-upon-Tyne(0632)815744

Purpose built timber chalets situated at the Lochside all with superb views. Comfortably furnished with modern pine furnishings and quality equipment. Situated 4 miles west of Ballachulish.

All year MWB out of season 7days min,
8units, 1–6persons [◇] ◈ ◆ ◊
fridge ⋈ Elec inclusive ◻inclusive
☎(50yds) Airing cupboard in unit Iron on premises Ironing board on premises HCE in unit [Launderette on premises] ⊙ CTV ⊕3pin square
8P ♨(50yds) Sea fishing, boats for hire
⇔ ♀(3m) ◫(3m)
Min£103.50 Max£126.50pw (Low)
Min£155.25 Max£224pw (High)
See advert on page 132

KENTANGAVAL
Isle of Barra Western Isles *Inverness-shire*
Map **13** NL69

Ch Monte Fracelma
for bookings Mr G Campbell, 26 Bentangaval, Castlebay, Isle of Barra
☎Castlebay(087 14)328

This Norwegian-designed timber-clad dwelling is well furnished and contains central heating and double glazing. Spacious accommodation consists of three bedrooms, large living room with convertible settee, modern kitchen, bathroom and WC. Views of Castle Bay can be enjoyed from this centrally-situated unit.

All year MWB out of season 1wk min,
5wks max, 1 unit, 1–10persons ◈ ◎
fridge ⋈ Elec inclusive Elec metered in winter ◻inclusive ☎(½m) Airing cupboard in unit Iron in unit Ironing board in unit HCE in unit TV
⊕3pin square P ♨(½m)
⇔ ♀(½m) ◫(½m)
Min£45 Max£70pw (Low)
Min£85 Max£110pw (High)

KENTCHURCH
Hereford & Worcester
Map **3** SO42

C Park Gate Cottage
for bookings Cooke & Arkwright, Berrington House, Hereford, Herefordshire HR4 0BG →

☎Hereford(0432)267213

Recently modernised, this secluded cottage sits on the edge of a large country estate. Accommodation comprises kitchen/diner, dining room, lounge, one double and two twin bedrooms.

Apr–Oct 1wk min, 4wks max, 1 unit, 1–6persons ◊ ◆ ◎ fridge Electric & open fires Elec inclusive ☐not provided ☎(2¼m) Airing cupboard in unit Iron in unit Ironing board in unit HCE in unit ⊕3pin square P 🅿 ♨(4m) Fishing

↩ ☕(2¼m)

Min£80.50 Max£97.75pw (Low)
Min£97.75 Max£115pw (High)

KENTISBEARE

Devon
Map**3**ST00

H CC Ref 638 EP

for bookings Character Cottages (Holidays) Ltd, 34 Fore Street, Sidmouth, Devon EX10 8AQ
☎Sidmouth(039 55)77001

Detached farmhouse situated in village. House has been modernised but still retains its olde-worlde charm with oak beams and open fireplace. Large dining room with Queen Anne furnishings. Four bedrooms, all well furnished. Ample

Kentchurch
—
Kentisburyford

wardrobe space, bedside lights, tables and chairs. Bathroom and WC. Kitchen has Rayburn cooker.

All year MWB out of season 1wk min, 6mths max, 1 unit, 2–8persons no pets ◎ fridge ⍾ Elec inclusive ☐can be hired ☎(20yds) Airing cupboard in unit Iron in unit Ironing board in unit HCE in unit ⊙ TV ⊕3pin square ⊕2pin round P 🅿 ♨

↩ ☕

Min£91 Max£162pw

B CC Ref 682

for bookings Character Cottages (Holidays) Ltd, 34 Fore Street, Sidmouth, Devon EX10 8AQ
☎Sidmouth(039 55)77001

A detached brick-built bungalow with a lawned garden. Accommodation comprises two twin-beddeded rooms, one double-bedded room, kitchen, dining room and lounge. Approaching on M5 leave motorway at junction 28. Take first left to Bradfield and the bungalow is on the right at the junction.

All year MWB out of season 1wk min, 6mths max, 1 unit, 2–6persons ◊ ◎ fridge Open fire Elec metered ☐can

be hired ☎(1m) Airing cupboard in unit Iron in unit Ironing board in unit HCE in unit TV ⊕3pin square P ♨(1½m)

↩ ☕(1½m) 🅿(1½m)

Min£38 Max£57pw (Low)
Min£85 Max£110pw (High)

KENTISBURYFORD

Devon
Map**2**SS64

Ch Mr P J Floyd **No's 1–22 Kentisbury Grange** Kentisburyford, Barnstaple, Devon
☎Combe Martin(027 188)3421

Twenty two modern detached chalets in the grounds of Kentisbury Grange. Comprises open-plan lounge/kitchen/diner with double bed-settee, one twin and one double bedroom, bathroom and WC. Fully carpeted. Situated on A39.

15Mar–15Jan MWB out of season 1 day min, 6wks max, 22units, 1–6persons [◊ ◆] ◎ fridge Electric Elec metered ☐not provided ☎ Iron on premises [Launderette on premises] ⊙ CTV ⊕3pin square P 🅿 ♨ ⌕ Filmshows in the Grange Club Children's playground and games room.

↩ ☕ 🖼 🎵

132

Min£57.50 Max£86.25pw (Low)
Min£103.50 Max£189.75pw (High)

KENTON
Devon
Map**3** SX98

H CC Ref 474
for bookings Character Cottages
(Holidays) Ltd, 34 Fore Street, Sidmouth,
Devon EX10 8AQ
☎Sidmouth(039 55)77001

*Semi-detached, two-storey period house
comprising entrance hall to lounge,
large, well-appointed kitchen, dining
room, four bedrooms, one with twin beds
and wash-basin, one double-bedded
room with wash-basin, well fitted
bathroom and separate WC, a further
double bedroom and children's room
with three single and double bunk beds.
Small front garden.*

All MWB out of season 1 wk min,
6 wks max, 1 unit, 1–9 persons ◆ ◉
fridge Electric Elec inclusive ⬜can
be hired ☎ Airing cupboard in unit
Iron in unit Ironing board in unit HCE in
unit ⊖ TV ⊕3 pin square P 🅼
🛏(3m)
⊖ ⚲(3m)

Min£83 Max£138pw (Low)
Min£177 Max£220pw (High)

KESSINGLAND
Suffolk
Map**5** TM58

Ch Sea View Chalet Park Kessingland
Beach, Green Lane
for bookings Hoseasons Holidays,
Sunway House, Lowestoft, Suffolk
NR32 3LT ☎Lowestoft(0502)62292

*Well equipped and furnished chalets on
site overlooking the sea. Accommodation
comprises three bedrooms, one double,
two singles, lounge and kitchen. Divan in
lounge converts to sleep two extra
people. Leave A12 signposted
Kessingland Beach, turn left into Green
Lane upon entering village.*

Apr–Oct MWD out of season 1 wk min,
3 wks max, 39 units, 1–6 persons [◆]

Kentisburyford
—
Keyhaven

[◆] ◉ fridge Electric Elec inclusive
⬜inclusive ☎(¼m) Airing cupboard in
unit HCE in unit ⊕3 pin square P 🅼
🛏(¼m)
⊖ ⚲(¼m)

KESWICK
Cumbria
Map**11** NY22

F Brigham Farm Flats Low Brigham
for bookings B & C Burn, High Melbecks,
Bassenthwaite, Keswick, Cumbria
CA12 4QX
☎Bassenthwaite Lake(059 681)211

*Six flats located in a quiet cul-de-sac. ½m
from the town centre. First-floor flat
comprises one double bedroom,
bathroom with shower and WC,
lounge/diner/kitchen with a single
convertible bed-settee in the lounge. One
ground and one first-floor flat comprise
kitchen/diner, shower/WC and lounge
with convertible twin bed-settees. Two
flats on ground- and first-floors
comprising one double-bedded room,
shower/WC, kitchen/diner and lounge
with single bed-settee. A ground-floor flat
comprising one double-bedded room,
one twin bedroom each with wash hand
basin, lounge, kitchen/diner and
bathroom with shower and WC.*

All year MWB 2 nights min, 6 units,
2–4 persons ◆ ◆ ◉ fridge
Electric Elec metered ⬜inclusive ☎
Airing cupboard in unit Iron on
premises Ironing board on premises
HCE in unit [Launderette within
300yds] ⊖ CTV ⊕3 pin square 1P
🅼 🛏(¼m)
⊖ ♨(3m) ⚲(50yds) 🛒(¼m) 🍴(¼m)

Min£50 Max£100pw (Low)
Min£75 Max£140pw (High)

F Dunkley Court 25 Helvellyn Street
for bookings Mrs I Davies, 23 Helvellyn
Street, Keswick, Cumbria CA12 4EN
☎Keswick(0596)73491

*Three modern well-maintained spacious
flats forming the first and second floors*

---

*above the premises of the proprietor's
taxi business; each containing one twin-
and two double-bedded rooms, plus a
double bed-settee. The flats, which are in
a side street close to town centre, provide
a good base for touring the Lake District.*

All year 1 wk min, 3 units, 8 persons ◆
◉ fridge Electric Elec metered
⬜inclusive ☎ Airing cupboard in unit
Iron in unit Ironing board in unit HCE in
unit [Launderette within 300yds] ⊖
TV ⊕3 pin square 🅼 🛏(100yds)
⊖ ⚲(300yds) 🚲(¼m) 🎵(¼m) 🛒(¼m)

KEYHAVEN
Hampshire
Map**4** SZ39

*C Mr B Trehearne Fishers Mead
Cottages* Keyhaven, Lymington, Hants
SO4 0TP
☎Milford-on-Sea(059 069)2047

*These cottages are situated near the sea
in a quiet location about 1m E of Milford-
on-Sea. The well furnished
accommodation comprises lounge/diner
with two divans, two bedrooms, kitchen,
bathroom and WC.*

All year MWB out of season 1 wk min,
5 wks max, 2 units, 1–6 persons ◇ [◆]
◆ ♨ fridge 🍴 Gas/Elec inclusive
⬜can be hired ☎(150yds) HCE in
unit ⊖ TV ⊕3 pin square P 🅼
🛏(1m) ⌂
⊖ ⚲(150yds)

Min£35 Max£45pw (Low)
Min£140 Max£205pw (High)

F Mr B Trehearne Fishers Mead Flats
Keyhaven, Lymington, Hants SO4 0TP
☎Milford-on-Sea(059 069)2047

*Terraced ground-floor flats in quiet rural
surroundings. Three flats with one
bedroom and a bed-sitting room,
kitchen/diner, bathroom and WC.*

All year MWB out of season 1 wk min,
5 wks max, 3 units, 1–6 persons ◇ [◆]
◆ ♨ fridge 🍴 Gas/Elec inclusive
⬜can be hired ☎(150yds) Airing →

---

cupboard in unit HCE in unit ⊙ TV ⊕3pin square 10P ▥ 🛒(1m)

⊖ 🏠(150yds)

Min£36 Max£45pw (Low)
Min£140 Max£205pw (High)

KILCHATTAN Isle of Colonsay, Strathclyde *Argyll*
Map **10** NR39

***C* Alister Annies**
for bookings Mrs E McNeill, Machrins Farm, Isle of Colonsay, Argyll
☎Colonsay(09512)312

Painted pebbledash cottage on small hilltop overlooking Loch Fada. Accommodation comprises kitchen/diner, lounge with sofa bed and bathroom on ground-floor and two attic bedrooms, one double, one twin which are reached by steep ladder type staircase. The cottage is set back from single road that encircles the island.

All year MWB out of season 1wk min, 1unit, 1–5persons ◆ ⌀ fridge Calor gas & open fires Gas/Elec inclusive ▢not provided ☎(3m) ⊕3pin round P 🛒(3m)

⊖ ⛳(1m) 🏠(3m) ▨(3m)

Min£65 Max£110pw

***C* Cnoc Na Ban**
for bookings Mrs E McNeill, Machrin's Farm, Isle of Colonsay, Argyll
☎Colonsay(09512)312

Croft-style cottage with attic bedrooms, access at each end of the cottage by narrow staircase. Also one double bedroom on ground-floor. Sitting room has attractive stone fireplace, and compact kitchen and bathroom leading off. Reached by a short rough track, the cottage is on W side of island.

All year MWB out of season 1wk min, 1unit, 1–6persons ◆ ⌀ fridge Calor gas & open fires Gas/Elec metered ▢not provided ☎(3m) HCE in unit ⊕3pin round 2P 🛒(3m)

⊖ ⛳(1m) 🏠(3m) ▨(3m)

Max£80.50pw (Low)
Max£138pw (High)

***C* Cnoc-na-Fad**
for bookings Mrs E McNeill, Machrins Farm, Isle of Colonsay, Argyll
☎Colonsay(09512)312

White painted stone cottage half way between Loch Fada and Port Mhor on island road. Accommodation is all on the ground floor and comprises sitting room, kitchen/diner, bathroom, three bedrooms, one double, one twin and one bunk-bedded room.

All year MWB out of season, 1wk min, 1unit, 1–6persons ◆ ⌀ fridge Calor gas & open fires Elec inclusive ▢not provided ☎(3m) ⊕3pin round 1P 🛒(3m)

⊖ ⛳(1m) 🏠(3m) ▨(3m)

Min£70 Max£120pw

***C* Garta Ghoban**
for bookings Mrs E McNeill, Machrins Farm, Isle of Colonsay, Argyll
☎Colonsay(09512)312

Two-storey stone cottage situated on west side of island. Comprising sitting/dining room/kitchen with open fire. There is a double bedroom and bathroom on the ground floor with two twin-bedded rooms on the first floor.

All year MWB out of season 1wk min, 1unit, 1–6persons ◆ ⌀ fridge Calor gas & open fires ▢not provided ☎(3m) HCE in unit ⊕3pin round 2P 🛒(3m)

⊖ ⛳(1m) 🏠(3m) ▨(3m)

Max£80.50pw(Low)
Max£138pw (High)

***C* Port Mhor**
for bookings Mrs E McNeill, Machrins Farm, Isle of Colonsay, Argyll
☎Colonsay(09512)312

Stone cottage comprising living room, kitchen with adjoining bathroom and a double-bedded room all on the ground-floor. There are two twin-bedded rooms in the attic.

All year MWB out of season 1wk min, 1unit, 1–6persons ◆ ⌀ fridge Calor gas & open fires ▢not provided ☎(3m) HCE in unit ⊕3pin round 2P 🛒(3m)

⊖ ⛳(1m) 🏠(3m) ▨(3m)

Max£80.50pw (Low)
Max£138pw (High)

***C* School & Sgreedan Cottages**
for bookings Mrs E McNeill, Machrins Farm, Isle of Colonsay, Argyll
☎Colonsay(09512)312

Both cottages overlook Loch Fada and are set back from the single road that circuits the island. They comprise of sitting/dining room with open fire, kitchen, bathroom and double bedroom. The first-floor has two twin attic bedrooms reached by a steep staircase.

All year MWB out of season 1wk min, 2units, 1–6persons ◆ ⌀ fridge Calor gas & open fires ▢not provided ☎(3m) HCE in unit ⊕3pin round 4P 🛒(3m)

⊖ ⛳(1m) 🏠(3m) ▨(3m)

Max£80.50pw (Low)
Max£138pw (High)

KILGETTY
Dyfed
Map **2** SN01

Powell's Holidays High Street, Saundersfoot, Dyfed
☎Saundersfoot812791
Powell's Holidays have a total of ten AA inspected properties in Kilgetty. Of these, five are cottages, two are bungalows, two are houses and one is a flat.

An entry for one of each type of property follows. For information on the other properties contact Powell's Holidays.

***C* Ivy Chimney Cottage** Ivy Chimney Ln
for bookings Powell's Holidays (address as above)
☎Saundersfoot(0834)812791

Detached cottage with beamed and feature stone interior walls. It comprises of lounge/diner, bathroom, WC and three bedrooms. 1½m from Saundersfoot and ¼m from Kilgetty.

Whit–Sep 1wk min, 1unit, 6persons ◆ no pets ◎ fridge Electric Elec inclusive ▢not provided ☎(¾m) Airing cupboard in unit Iron in unit Ironing board in unit HCE in unit TV ⊕3pin square 1P ▥ 🛒(¾m)

⊖ 🏠(¾m) ▨(1½m) ♫(1½m)

Min£63 Max£153pw

***F* The Pebbles** Begelly
for bookings Powell's Holidays (address as above)
☎Saundersfoot(0834)812791

A new flat on first floor above shop with fitted carpets and comfortable modern furnishings. Accommodation comprises kitchen/diner, lounge, two double-bedded rooms, one with additional beds and bathroom/WC.

Jan–Nov MWB out of season 1wk min, 6wks max, 1unit, 1–6persons ◆ ◆ no pets ◎ fridge Electric Elec inclusive ▢can be hired ☎(¼m) Iron in unit Ironing board in unit HCE in unit TV ⊕3pin square 2P ▥ 🛒

⊖ 🏠(½m) ▨(2½m) ♫(2½m)

Min£48 Max£118pw

***B* Rhoslyn** Ash Park
for bookings Powell's Holidays (address as above)
☎Saundersfoot(0834)812791

Modern, detached bungalow in quiet cul-de-sac. Comprising lounge/dining area and kitchen, three bedrooms, bathroom and WC. Off A477 at Kilgetty, 2½m from Saundersfoot and 5½m from Tenby.

Etr–Sep 1wk min, 4wks max, 1unit, 2–5persons [◇] ◆ ◎ fridge Electric Elec inclusive ▢can be hired ☎(100yds) WM in unit SD in unit Airing cupboard in unit Iron in unit Ironing board in unit HCE in unit CTV ⊕3pin square 2P ▥ 🛒(100yds)

⊖ 🏠(200yds) ▨(2m) ♫(2m)

Min£51 Max£123pw

***H* Shaldon** 5 Fir Grove
for bookings Powell's Holidays (address as above)
☎Saundersfoot(0834)812791

An attractive semi-detached dormer bungalow in quiet cul-de-sac just off the A478 at the northern end of the village. The comfortably furnished accommodation comprises lounge/diner, lounge, kitchen, bathroom/WC, one double bedroom on

ground floor, one double bedroom with
wash-basin and one twin-bedded room
on the first floor.

May–Aug MWB out of season 1wk min,
1 unit, 6 persons [◇] ◆ no pets ◉
fridge Electric Elec inclusive
▭ not provided ☎(½m) Airing cupboard
in unit Iron in unit Ironing board in unit
HCE in unit ⊕ CTV ⊕3pin square
2P 🅿 ☕(½m)

↔ ♀(½m)

Min £51 Max £135pw

KILKERRAN
Strathclyde *Ayrshire*
Map **10** NS30

H   Glenton Kilkerran Estate
for bookings Blairquhan Estate Office,
Straiton, Maybole, Ayrshire KA19 6LX
☎Straiton(065 57)239

*Detached stone-built farmhouse
overlooking the Girvan Valley. There are
four bedrooms (two on the ground floor,
two on the first floor), bathroom and open-
plan kitchen and living room.*

All year MWB out of season 1wk min,
6wks max, 1 unit, 1–8 persons ◆ ◆
◉ fridge Electric & coal fires
Elec metered ▭ not provided ☎ Iron
in unit HCE in unit ⊕ ⊕3pin square
6P 2🅿 ▦ ☕(1m) Fishing

↔ ♀(3m)

Min £43.25 Max £81.45pw (Low)
Min £93.40 Max £143.75pw (High)

KILLIECRANKIE
Tayside *Perthshire*
Map **14** NN96

F, C Mr & Mrs T B Milne **Druimuan**
Killiecrankie, Pitlochry, Perthshire
PH16 5LG
☎Pitlochry(0796)3214

*The four flats adjoining the main house,
and the cottage linked to the stables,
have distinctive Highland cottage
features. Guests have access to
excellent, well-maintained gardens.
Situated in the scenic Pass of
Killiecrankie, just off the A9. Pitlochry is
4m S.*

All year MWB out of season 1wk min,
5 units, 2–4 persons ◆ ◉ fridge
Electric Elec metered ▭ can be hired
☎(200yds) Iron in unit Ironing board in
unit HCE in unit TV ⊕3pin square
⊕3pin round P ☕(200yds) Putting
green, croquet

↔ ♀(½m)

Min £54 Max £85pw (Low)
Min £70 Max £125pw (High)

Ch Mrs E P Stephen **Old Faskally
House Chalets** Killiecrankie, Pitlochry,
Perthshire PH16 5LR
☎Pitlochry(0796)3436

*Situated 4 miles N of Pitlochry, these
recently constructed chalets are
pleasantly sited amongst conifers and
comprise lounge/dining room with
double bed settee, two bedrooms, one*

---

*twin, one double bedded and an open
kitchen area.*

All year MWB out of season 1wk min,
5 units, 1–6 persons [◇ ◆] ◉
fridge Electric Elec inclusive
▭ inclusive ☎(½m) WM on premises
TD on premises Airing cupboard in unit
Iron on premises Ironing board on
premises HCE in unit ⊕ TV can be
hired ⊕3pin square 12P ▦ ☕(½m)

↔ ☍(3m) ♀(½m)

Min £63.25 Max £195.50pw

KILLINGTON
Cumbria
Map **7** SD68

C   Upper Ghyll Style Cottage
for bookings Mr & Mrs C M Kevan, Ghyll
Style Cottage, Killington, Sedbergh,
Cumbria LA10 5EH
☎Sedbergh(0587)20628

*A stone-built cottage standing in an
elevated position overlooking terraced
gardens which run down to the wooded
Priestfield Beck. Good views. It
comprises two bedrooms (one twin-
bedded and one double) modern
bathroom, lounge and kitchen. Situated
near A684 from Sedbergh.*

All year MWB out of season 1wk min,
1 unit, 2–6 persons ◆ no cats ◉
fridge 🍴 & open fire Elec metered
▭ not provided ☎(200yds) WM in unit
Airing cupboard in unit Iron in unit
Ironing board in unit HCE in unit TV
⊕3pin square P ☕(3m)

↔ ♀(1m)

Min £45 Max £55pw (Low)
Min £90 Max £120pw (High)

KILMARNOCK
Strathclyde *Ayrshire*
Map **10** NS43

F   Stable Flats Carnell, Hurlford (3m SE
off A719)
for bookings Blakes Holidays Ltd,
Wroxham, Norwich, Norfolk NR12 8DH
☎Wroxham(060 53)2917

*Two converted stable flats are on the
ground floor, one on the first. Each has a
twin-bedded room, a double bedroom,
dining room, lounge, kitchen, bathroom
and WC. ½m from A719 within the Carnell
Estate.*

28Mar–Oct 1wk min, 1mth max, 2 units,
1–4 persons ◆ ◆ ◉ fridge Electric
& open fires Elec metered ▭ can be
hired ☎(1½m) Airing cupboard in unit
HCE in unit TV ⊕3pin square P ▦
☕(4m)

↔ ♀(3m)

Min £68 Max £109pw (Low)
Min £103 Max £129pw (High)

1982 prices quoted throughout
gazetteer

KILMELFORD
Strathclyde *Argyll*
Map **10** NM81

C   Ardenstur Cottages Ardenstur
Estate
for bookings Woodside Park Estates,
Park Avenue, Hartlepool TS26 0EA
☎Kilmelford(085 22)240 (out of season
Hartlepool(0429)67266

*Detached stone building forming three
modernised self-contained cottages, in a
sheltered hillside position. Each
comprise of a lounge/diner with open-
plan kitchenette, one twin bedroom and a
bathroom in two cottages, the other
having a shower. Situated off the A816 at
the head of Loch Melford.*

All year 1wk min, 5wks max, 3 units,
1–4 persons [◇] ◆ ◉ fridge
Electric & open fires Elec metered
▭ inclusive ☎(3m) Airing cupboard in
unit Iron in unit Ironing board in unit
HCE in unit ⊕ ⊕3pin square P
☕(3m) Fishing, sailing & deer stalking

↔ ♀(3m)

Min £75 Max £100pw

C   Beechwood Cottages
for bookings Loch Melfort Estate, Melfort
House, Kilmelford, Oban, Argyll
PA34 4XD
☎Kilmelford(085 22)257

*Detached two-storey substantial stone
cottage with fenced garden. On the
ground floor there is a kitchen, dining
room, lounge and upstairs two twin
bedrooms and a bathroom. Furnishings
are of good standard.*

All year MWB out of season 1wk min,
1 unit, 1–6 persons [◇] ◆ ◉ fridge
Electric & open fires Elec inclusive
▭ inclusive ☎(1m) Iron in unit Ironing
board in unit HCE in unit ⊕
⊕3pin square P ☕(1½m) Games
room, pony trekking, fishing, sailing

↔ ♀(2½m)

Min £100 Max £120pw (Low)
Min £130 Max £200pw (High)

C   Farm Cottages 1 & 2
for bookings Loch Melfort Estate, Melfort
House, Kilmelford, Oban, Argyll
PA34 4XD
☎Kilmelford(085 22)257

*Two farm cottages at gabled ends of
two-storey 'L' shaped stone building
situated near the working area of Melfort
Farming Estate. Both cottages have small
gardens. Cottage No 1 consists of
lounge, dining room, kitchen, bathroom,
bedroom with two sets of bunk beds and
two twin bedrooms with adjacent box
room containing single bed. Cottage No
2 has dining room with small open plan
kitchen and lounge with two convertible
single easy chairs, two twin bedrooms
and bathroom. Furnishing of a good
standard.*

All year MWB out of season 1wk min,
2 units, 1–7 persons [◇] ◆ ◉
fridge Electric & open fires
Elec inclusive ▭ inclusive ☎(1m) Iron →

135

in unit Ironing board in unit HCE in unit
⊕3pin square P ⚙(1½m) Games
room, pony trekking, sailing & fishing
⊖ ⚑(2½m)

Min£110 Max£125pw (Low)
Min£135 Max£220pw (High)

C Melfort Lodge
for bookings Loch Melfort Estate, Melfort
House, Kilmelford, Oban, Argyll
PA34 4XD
☎Kilmelford(085 22)257

*Two-storey cottage-style building with its
own small garden area. Ground-floor
lounge with two convertible easy chair
beds, dining room and small kitchen with
bathroom leading off. Upstairs is a
double and a twin bedroom. Furnishings
of a high standard.*

All year MWB out of season 1wk min,
1unit, 1–8persons [◇] ◆ ⊚ fridge
Electric & open fires Elec inclusive
ⓁInclusive ☎(1m) Iron in unit Ironing
board in unit HCE in unit
⊕3pin square P ⚙(1½m) Games
room, pony trekking, sailing & fishing
⊖ ⚑(2½m)

Min£110 Max£125pw (Low)
Min£135 Max£220pw (High)

H Pier Houses
for bookings Loch Melfort Estate, Melfort
House, Kilmelford, Oban, Argyll
PA34 4XD
☎Kilmelford(085 22)257

*This detached, two-storey stone building
has been fully modernised and
converted into two self-contained houses
situated by quiet roadside near old pier
with pleasant views. Each house has
spacious lounge and dining room with
open-plan kitchen on the ground floor.
Upstairs are three twin bedrooms and
bathroom. Good overall standard of
furnishings.*

All year MWB out of season 1wk min,
2units, 1–8persons [◇] ◆ ⊚
fridge Electric & open fires
Elec Inclusive ⓁInclusive ☎(1m) Iron
in unit Ironing board in unit HCE in unit
⊙ ⊕3pin square P ⚙(1½m) Games
room, pony trekking, sailing & fishing
⊖ ⚑(2½m)

Min£115 Max£140pw (Low)
Min£135 Max£220pw (High)

C Weighbridge Cottage
for bookings Loch Melford Estate, Melfort
House, Kilmelford, Oban, Argyll
PA34 4XD
☎Kilmelford(085 22)257

*L-shaped single-storey building with its
own small garden to the rear.
Accommodation comprises lounge (with
two convertible single easy chair beds),
dining room with combined kitchen area,
and bathroom with shower. Furnishings
of a good standard.*

All year MWB out of season 1wk min,
1unit, 1–4persons [◇] ◆ ⊚ fridge
Electric & open fires Elec inclusive
ⓁInclusive ☎(1m) Iron in unit Ironing

board in unit HCE in unit
⊕3pin square P ⚙(1½m) Games
room, pony trekking, sailing & fishing
⊖ ⚑(2½m)

Min£100 Max£120pw (Low)
Min£115 Max£140pw (High)

KILMORACK
Highland *Inverness-shire*
Map **14** NH44

C Mr I Mackay 12 Torgormack
Kilmorack, Beauly, Inverness-shire
☎Beauly(0463)782296

*Simple accommodation in rural
surroundings, built in 1973 and
attractively situated amongst birch trees,
just off the A831 near the River Beauly
and facing up Strathglass. Salmon lifts on
the river.*

All year MWB out of season 1wk min,
3mths max, 3units, 2–7persons ◆ ⊚
fridge Electric Elec metered
ⓁInclusive ☎(½m) Iron in unit Ironing
board in unit HCE in unit ⊗ TV
⊕3pin square ⊕2pin round P ▥
⚙(3m) Pony trekking
⊖ ⚑(3m)

Min£25 Max£35pw (Low)
Min£80 Max£100pw (High)

KILMORE
Strathclyde *Argyllshire*
Map **10** NM82

C Barnacarry Cottage
for bookings Mrs C Hodge, Barnacarry
Farm, Kilmore, Oban, Argyll
☎Kilmore(063 177)210

*Stone-built white painted cottage
situated on 15,000-acre farm and
comprising one large and two small
bedrooms, lounge and large kitchen.
Located 4¼ miles South of Oban off A816.*

Etr-Oct MWB out of season 1wk min,
3mths max, 1units, 1–6persons ◆ ◆
no pets ⊚ fridge Electric
Elec metered ⓁNot provided ☎(1m)
Airing cupboard in unit Iron in unit
Ironing board in unit HCE in unit ⊙
⊕3pin square P ⚙(4m) Fishing
⊖ ⚑(1m)

B The Bungalow
for bookings Mrs C Hodge, Barnacarry
Farm, Kilmore, Oban, Argyll
☎Kilmore(063 177)210

*A small timber-built bungalow painted
green and situated at Barnacarry Farm
which is 4¼ miles south of Oban off A816.
The Bungalow can sleep four persons but
is more suited for two. Simple, clean
accommodation.*

Etr-Oct MWB out of season 1wk min,
3mths max, 1unit, 1–4persons ◆ ◆
no pets ⊚ fridge Electric
Elec metered ⓁNot provided ☎(1m)
Airing cupboard in unit Iron in unit

Ironing board in unit HCE in unit ⊙
⊕3pin square P ⚙(4m) Fishing
⊖ ⚑(1m)

Min£50 Max£70pw (Low)
Min£80 Max£105pw (High)

C Kilmore Cottage
for bookings Mrs C Hodge, Barnacarry
Farm, Kilmore, Oban, Argyll
☎Kilmore(063 177)210

*Stone-built white painted cottage
situated on Kilmore farm which adjoins
Barnacarry farm and between them these
two hill farms cover 1500 acres. Located
4¼ miles south of Oban off A816. The
cottage is neatly maintained with lounge,
kitchen, bathroom and two bedrooms.*

Etr-Oct MWB out of season 1wk min,
3mths max, 1unit, 1–6persons ◇ ◆
no pets ⊚ fridge Electric
Elec metered ⓁNot provided ☎(1m)
Airing cupboard in unit Iron in unit
Ironing board in unit HCE in unit ⊙
⊕3pin square P ⚙(4m) Fishing
⊖ ⚑(1m)

Min£60 Max£80pw (Low)
Min£90 Max£135pw (High)

KILMORY
Strathclyde *Argyll*
Map **10** NR77

B Holiday Homes at Kilmory
for bookings The Booking Office, Estate
Office, Ellary, Lochgilphead, Argyll
PA31 8PB
☎Ormsary(088 03)232 or 209

*Five modern chalet-style bungalows in an
isolated location, with magnificent views
overlooking the Sound and Isle of Jura.
Accommodation comprises three
bedrooms, lounge, kitchen, bathroom
and verandah. All units are fitted to a high
standard.*

All year MWB out of season 1wk min,
5units, 1–6persons ◆ ⊚ fridge
Electric Elec metered ⓁNot provided
☎(½m) HCE in unit TV ⊕3pin square
P ⚙(2½m)

Min£87 Max£174pw

KILNINVER
Strathclyde *Argyll*
Map **10** NM82

C Alpein Cottage
for bookings D R Kilpatrick, Kilninver,
Oban, Argyll PA43 4UT
☎Kilninver(08526)272 (before 9pm)

*Single-storey cottage beautifully situated
overlooking loch towards the Island of
Mull, 8 miles south of Oban off A816 –
road signed Kilninver/Easdale. The
accommodation consists of two
bedrooms, lounge/dining room, kitchen
and bathroom. There is also a garage
with a table tennis table.*

20Mar-20Nov 1wk min, 1unit,
1–4persons ◆ ◆ no pets ⊚
fridge Electric Elec inclusive
ⓁNot provided ☎ SD in unit TD in unit
Iron in unit Ironing board in unit HCE in

unit CTV ⊕3pinsquare 2P ▥
♨(8m) Loch fishing & boat available
Min£110 Max£195pw

C Dairy Cottage
For bookings D R Kilpatrick, Kilninver,
Oban, Argyll PA34 4UT
☎Kilninver(085 26)272 (before 9pm)

A farm cottage with views across the
fields to the sea loch. Accommodation
comprises two bedrooms (one double
bed, folding single bed and two bunk
beds), living room with convertible
settee, kitchen, bathroom/WC. The barn
has been converted into a playroom, and
a 12ft sailing boat is included in the rental.

20Mar-20Nov 1wkmin, 1unit,
1–6persons ◊ ◆ ◎ fridge
Electric Elec inclusive Ⓛnot provided
☎(75yds) SD TD Iron
Ironing board HCE in unit CTV
⊕3pinsquare P ▥ ♨(8m) Loch
fishing
Min£100 Max£195pw

H Home Farm
for bookings D R Kilpatrick, Kilninver,
Oban, Argyll PA43 4UT
☎Kilninver(08526)272 (before 9pm)

Modern detached house in own grounds
on hillside with splendid views
northwards towards Island of Mull, 8
miles south of Oban on A816.
Accommodation comprises sitting room,
dining room, kitchen, four bedrooms, one
double, one twin, one family room and a
single-bedded room. There is also a bed-
settee in the sitting room, a separate
games room and bathroom/WC plus
additional WC.

20Mar-20Nov 1wkmin, 1unit,
1–9persons ◊ ◆ ◎ fridge
Electric Elec inclusive Ⓛnot provided
☎ SD in unit TD in unit Airing
cupboard in unit Iron in unit Ironing
board in unit HCE in unit CTV
⊕3pinsquare 6P ▥ ♨(8m) Fishing
Min£115 Max£225pw

H The Old Kirk
for bookings D R Kilpatrick, Kilninver,
Oban, Argyll PA34 4UT
☎Kilninver(08526)272 (before 9pm)

18th-century kirk converted into a holiday
home with pine-panelled interior, situated
on a rocky knoll with fine views across
Loch Feochan. Accommodation
comprises open-plan kitchen/living area,
three twin bedrooms, bathroom/WC. A
children's playroom has been built into
the loft, with two beds and one folding
bed.

20Mar-20Nov 1wkmin, 1unit,
1–9persons ◊ ◆ ◎ fridge
Electric Elec inclusive Ⓛnot provided
☎(200yds) SD in unit TD in unit Iron in
unit Ironing board in unit HCE in unit
⊙ CTV ⊕3pinsquare P ▥ ♨(8m)
Loch fishing
Min£125 Max£230pw

1982 prices quoted throughout
gazetteer

Kilninver
—
Kingsbridge

KILORAN Isle of Colonsay,
Strathclyde Argyll
Map **10** NR39

C Avenue Cottage
for bookings Mrs E McNeill, Machrins
Farm, Isle of Colonsay, Argyll
☎Colonsay(09512)312

Single-storey cottage in gardens of
Colonsay House, comprising lounge with
open fire, kitchen/diner, two twin and one
double bedroom, fourth bedroom with
bunks, and bathroom/WC.

All year MWB out of season 1wk min.
1 unit, 1–6persons ◊ ◎ fridge
Calor gas, Rayburn cooker & open fires
Ⓛnot provided ☎(½m) HCE in unit
⊕3pinround 2P ♨(3m) Tennis court
at Colonsay House
⟋ ♿(3m) ☎(3m) ▨(3m)
Max£80.50pw (Low)
Max£138pw (High)

F Colonsay House Flats
for bookings Mrs E McNeill, Machrins
Farm, Isle of Colonsay, Argyll
☎Colonsay(09512)312

Nine self-contained flats forming a wing
of Colonsay House and set on either
ground, first or second floor level. They
vary in size but each has sitting/dining
room, kitchen, bathroom and one to three
bedrooms.

All year MWB out of season 1wkmin,
9units, 2–6persons ◊ ◎ fridge
Calor gas or solid fuel fires
Ⓛnot provided ☎ HCE in unit
⊕3pinround 20P ♨(3m) ⚲
⟋ ♿(3m) ☎(3m) ▨(3m)
Min£74.75 Max£80.50pw (Low)
Min£115 Max£138pw (High)

H Farm House
for bookings Mrs E McNeill, Machrins
Farm, Isle of Colonsay, Argyll
☎Colonsay(09512)312

Largest house on the estate situated
adjacent to entrance of Colonsay House
garden, and backing onto Kiloran Farm.
Comprises lounge with open fire,
kitchen/diner, one double bedroom and
two bathrooms downstairs and three
twin-bedded rooms and one double-
bedded room upstairs.

All year MWB out of season 1wkmin,
1unit 10–12persons ◊ ◎ fridge
Calor gas, oil fired Rayburn & open fires
Ⓛnot provided ☎(½m) HCE in unit
⊕3pinround 6P ♨(3m) Tennis at
Colonsay House
⟋ ♿(3m) ☎(3m) ▨(3m)
Max£184pw

KILORAN BAY Isle of Colonsay,
Strathclyde Argyll
Map **10** NR39

C Uragaig & Kiloran Bay Cottages
for bookings Mrs E McNeill, Machrins

Farm, Isle of Colonsay, Argyll
☎Colonsay(09512)312

Two cottages overlooking Kiloran Bay,
close to sandy beaches. Each comprises
lounge/diner with open fire, kitchen and
double bedroom on ground-floor plus
two twin attic bedrooms reached by steel
staircase. No electricity, lighting by calor
gas.

All year MWB out of season 1wkmin,
2units, 1–6persons ◊ ♿ fridge
Calor gas & open fires Ⓛnot provided
☎(3m) HCE in unit 6P ♨(3m) Tennis
at Colonsay House
⟋ ♿(1m) ☎(3m) ▨(3m)
Max£80.50pw (Low)
Max£138pw (High)

KILSYTH
Strathclyde Stirlingshire
Map **11** NS77

C Shawend & Woodend Cottages
for bookings Mrs Chalmers, Woodend
Farm, Kilsyth, Glasgow G65 0PZ
☎Kilsyth(0236)822201

Two farm cottages offering simple
accommodation; **Woodend** which
adjoins the farmyard, has one double
bedroom, living room with studio beds,
kitchen and bathroom. **Shawend** which
is situated ½ mile away, comprises two
bedrooms, living room with couch bed,
kitchen and bathroom. Both are situated
on the eastern outskirts of Kilsyth, off
A803.

Apr-Sep MWB 1wkmin, 4wks max,
2units, 1–5persons ◊ no pets ◎
fridge Electric Elec metered
Ⓛnot provided ☎(1m) Iron in unit
Ironing board in unit HCE in unit TV
⊕3pinsquare 6P ▥ ♨(1m)
⟋ ♿(1m) ☎(1m)
Min£60 Max£75pw (Low)
Max£100pw (High)

KINGSBRIDGE
Devon
Map **3** SX74

C CC Ref 450 EL
for bookings Character Cottages
(Holidays) Ltd, 34 Fore Street, Sidmouth,
Devon EX10 8AQ
☎Sidmouth(039 55)77001

Two stone and slate-built cottages 150
years old situated on the Kingsbridge to
Salcombe road. Each has a
kitchen/diner, lounge, bathroom with
WC, and two bedrooms. A cot is
available.

All year MWB out of season 1wkmin,
2units, 2–5persons ◊ no pets ◎
fridge Electric Elec metered Ⓛcan be
hired ☎(1m) Airing cupboard in unit
Iron in unit Ironing board in unit HCE in
unit TV ⊕3pinsquare P ♨(2m)
⟋ ♿(3m) ☎(½m) ▨(2m) ♫(2m)
Min£59 Max£78pw (Low)
Min£110 Max£149pw (High)

KING'S CAPLE
Hereford & Worcester
Map **3** SO52

F Captain & Mrs J F Cockburn
Pennoxstone Court King's Caple,
Herefordshire HR1 4TX
☎Carey(043270)284

A first-floor flat in a Georgian mansion on a fruit farm. The accommodation comprises a kitchen/diner, bathroom, two bedrooms and a lounge which can also serve as an additional bedroom. There are extensive grounds open to guests. Situated about ½m W of the village.

All year 1wk min, 4wks max, 1 unit,
1–7 persons ◊ ◆ ◉ fridge
Electric Elec metered ▣ can be hired
☎(¼m) Airing cupboard on premises
Iron in unit Ironing board in unit HCE in
unit ⊖ CTV ⊕3pin square P ⊞
▨(5½m) Fishing
⊖ ♨(¼m)
Min£40 Max£54pw (Low)
Min£65 Max£89pw (High)

KING'S NYMPTON
Devon
Map **3** SS61

H **Sletchcott**
for bookings Mrs D H Young, Little
Orchard, 26 Clive Road, Esher, Surrey
KT10 8PS
☎Esher(0372)64514

Farmhouse of historical interest set in 3 acres of gardens and orchard. Study, drawing room, kitchen/diner, one bedroom all on ground floor. On the first floor there are four bedrooms, all with oak beams and bathroom. Special features are inglenook fireplaces and an old bread oven. Electricity paid to caretaker. Leave A377 at King's Nympton railway station on to B3226. Turn right in 1m to King's Nympton.

All year MWB out of season 4days min,
6mths max, 1 unit, 2–10 persons [◊]
◊ ◆ ◉ fridge Storage heaters
▣ not provided ☎(1½m) WM in unit SD
in unit Airing cupboard in unit Iron in
unit Ironing board in unit HCE in unit

⊖ ◉ CTV ⊕3pin square P ▨(1½m)
⊖ ♨(1½m)
Min£45 Max£110pw (Low)
Min£130 Max£200pw (High)

KINGSTON DEVERILL
Wiltshire
Map **3** ST83

F Mrs R A Brown **Kingston House**
Kingston Deverill, Warminster, Wilts
BH12 7HE
☎Maiden Bradley(098 53)448

Ground and first floor flats in a large stone-built country house dating from the 17th Century and standing in 2½m acres of grounds. Ground floor comprises two bedrooms (both with a double and single bed), lounge/diner, large kitchen and bathroom/WC. One of the first floor flats comprise kitchen/lounge/diner, bathroom/WC and two bedrooms (both with double and single bed). The other has kitchen/diner, lounge, bathroom/WC and two bedrooms (one twin-bedded and one with a double and single bed).

All year 1wk min, 6mths max, 3 units,
1–6 persons [◊] ◊ ◆ ◉ fridge
Electric Elec metered ▣inclusive ☎
Airing cupboard in unit HCE in unit
[Launderette on premises] ⊖ CTV
⊕3pin square 3P ▨(200yds)
⊖ ♨(3m)
Min£50 Max£66pw (Low)
Min£65 Max£135pw (High)

C **Rose Cottage**
for bookings Mrs R A Brown, Kingston
House, Kingston Deverill, Warminster,
Wilts BH12 7HE
☎Maiden Bradley(098 53)448

Self-contained cottage with own entrance attached to country house in 2½ acres of gardens. Accommodation comprises kitchen/diner, lounge and bathroom/WC. Two first floor bedrooms each with a double and single bed.

All year MWB out of season 1wk min,
6mths max, 1 unit, 1–6 persons [◊] ◊

◉ fridge Electric Elec metered
▣inclusive ☎ Airing cupboard in unit
Iron in unit Ironing board in unit HCE in
unit [Launderette on premises] ⊖ ◉
CTV ⊕3pin square 3P 1▨
▨(200yds)
⊖ ♨(3m)
Min£54 Max£75pw (Low)
Min£82 Max£135pw (High)

KINGSTON UPON THAMES
Greater London
Map **4** TQ16

F Hotel Antoinette Ltd **26 Beaufort
Road** Kingston upon Thames, Surrey
KT1 2TQ
☎01–546 1044

Two flats situated near an excellent shopping centre, and with good train services to London. Accommodation comprises either one or two bedrooms (twin-bedded), lounge, kitchen and bathroom.

All year MWB 1 night min, 8mths max,
2 units, 1–6 persons [◊] ◊ ◆ ◢
◉ fridge ⛽ Gas/Elec inclusive
▣inclusive ☎ Iron in unit Ironing
board in unit HCE in unit ⊖ CTV can
be hired ⊕3pin square P ⊞
▨(100yds)
⊖ ♨(¼m) ▣(¼m) ♫(¼m) ▨(¼m)
Min£90 Max£120pw

KINLOCHEWE
Highland *Ross & Cromarty*
Map **14** NH06

Ch Mr P Macdonald **Kinlochewe
Holiday Chalets** Kinlochewe,
Achnasheen, Ross-shire IV22 2PA
☎Kinlochewe(044 584)256

Holiday chalets in ideal setting near a river and situated behind the Kinlochewe Hotel just off the A832. The three types of chalet accommodation comprise, in the main, two twin-bedded rooms, lounge with convertible settee, kitchen and bathroom. Ideal base for a fishing holiday.

All year MWB out of season 1wk min,
6 units, 1–6 persons ◊ ◉ fridge
Electric Elec metered ▣inclusive

≅(150yds) HCE in unit ⊕3pin square
P ♨(100yds) Fishing
⊛ ☎(50yds)
Max£60pw (Low)
Max£80pw (High)

KINLOCHLEVEN
Highland *Argyll*
Map **14** NN16

Ca Log Cabin
for bookings Mrs E Bush, Mamore Lodge,
Kinlochleven, Inverness-shire
☎Kinlochleven(08554)213

*Log cabin of modern design situated on a
hillside within the grounds of Mamore
Lodge and commands a spectacular
view over the town some 800ft below. The
cabin is on one level and offers
lounge/diner/kitchen, two twin-bedded
rooms and shower/WC. Access is by a
1m drive from the B863 on the North
Lochside road just out of Kinloch Leven.*

All year MWB out of season 1wk min,
3mths max, 1unit, 2–6persons [◇] ◆
◆ Dogs charged for ◎ fridge
Elec metered ⊡inclusive ☎(330yds)
Airing cupboard in unit HCE in unit
[Launderette on premises] ⊖ TV
⊕3pin square 2P ♨(2m) Games
room, fishing
⊛ ☎(400yds)
Min£70 Max£100pw (Low)
Min£150 Max£200pw (High)

H Mamore Farmhouse
for bookings Mrs E Bush, Mamore Lodge,
Kinlochleven, Inverness-shire
☎Kinlochleven(08554)213

*The farmhouse is situated in the grounds
of Mamore Lodge and comprises large
lounge/diner, kitchen, four bedrooms
and WC all on ground floor level plus two
separate showers and one bathroom all
with WCs on lower ground floor. Access
is by a 1m drive from the B863 on the
North Lochside Road just out of
Kinlochleven.*

All year MWB out of season 1wk min,
3mths max, 1unit, 2–10persons [◇]
◆ ◆ Dogs Charged for ◎ fridge
Electric Elec metered ⊡inclusive

Kinlochewe
—
Kinloch Rannoch

≅(330yds) Airing cupboard in unit
Iron in unit Ironing board in unit HCE
in unit [Launderette on premises] ⊖
TV ⊕3pin square 3P ♨(2m) Games
room, fishing
⊛ ☎(330yds)
Min£70 Max£100pw (Low)
Min£180 Max£200pw (High)

F Mrs E Bush **Mamore Lodge (Flats)**
Kinlochleven, Inverness-shire
☎Kinlochleven(08554)213

*Large, white-painted shooting lodge
dating from 1902 standing 800ft above
sea level in 45,000-acre estate.
Magnificent views. The house has been
converted into two ground-floor and three
first-floor flats and offers good standard
in décor and modern furniture. Three of
the flats have three bedrooms sleeping
six and two have accommodation to
sleep eight. The house is situated on a
steep hillside with a 1m drive from the
B863 on the North Lochside Road just out
of Kinlochleven.*

All year MWB out of season wkds min,
5units, 6–8persons ◆ ◆ Dogs
charged for ◎ fridge Elec metered
⊡inclusive ⊛ Airing cupboard in unit
Iron on premises Ironing board on
premises HCE in unit [Launderette on
premises] ⊖ TV ⊕3pin square 50P
𝄞 ♨(1m) Games room, fishing
⊛ ☎ ⊠(1m) ♫(1m) ☰(1m)
Min£70 Max£100pw (Low)
Min£150 Max£200pw (High)

KINLOCH RANNOCH
Tayside *Perthshire*
Map **14** NN65

F West Tempar Flat
for bookings Mrs Nicol, West Tempar,
Kinloch Rannoch, Perthshire
☎Kinloch Rannoch(08822)338

*A pleasant two-bedroomed flat with
sitting room and kitchen, attached to
West Tempar Lodge which is set in its
own grounds on this 2,500-acre estate at
the foot of Schiehallion.*

All year MWB out of season 1wk min,
1unit, 1–5persons ◎
fridge Electric Elec metered
⊡not provided ☎(1½m) Airing
cupboard in unit Iron in unit Ironing
board in unit HCE in unit
⊕3pin square 3P ▥ ♨(1½m) Fishing
⊛ ☎(1½m)

H West Tempar Lodge
for bookings Mrs Nicol, West Tempar,
Kinloch Rannoch, Perthshire
☎Kinloch Rannoch(08822)338

*An attractive and spacious lodge only 2
miles from the village, situated on a 2,500
acre estate at the foot of Schiehallion.
Accommodation comprises four
double/twin and two single bedrooms on
the first floor and five ground-floor public
rooms.*

All year MWB out of season 1wk min,
1unit, 1–10persons ◆ no pets ⊘
fridge 🔥 Gas/Elec metered
⊡inclusive ☎ WM in unit SD in unit
Iron in unit Ironing board in unit HCE in
unit ⊕3pin square 6P ▥
♨(1½m) Fishing
⊛ ☎(1½m)

H West Tempar Estate
for bookings Mrs Nicol, West Tempar,
Kinloch Rannoch, Perthshire
☎Kinloch Rannoch(08822)338

*Part of a large and attractive farmhouse
with its own entrance comprising three
bedrooms, one double-bedded, one twin
and one large room with three single
beds and a large lounge/dining room on
the ground floor.*

All year MWB out of season 1wk min,
1unit, 1–7persons ◆ no pets ◎
fridge Electric Elec metered
⊡not provided ☎(1½m) WM in unit
Iron in unit Ironing board in unit HCE in
unit ⊕3pin square 2P ▥ ♨(1½m)
Fishing
⊛ ☎(1½m)

C West Tempar Estate (Cottages)
for bookings Mrs Nicol, West Tempar,
Kinloch Rannoch, Perthshire →

1982 prices quoted throughout
gazetteer

Kinloch Rannoch — Kirkby Malham

☎Kinloch Rannoch(088 22)338

Four comfortable farm cottages of varying size set on a large estate at the foot of Schiehallion. The cottages have been modernised and offer a good standard of décor and furnishings.

All year MWB out of season 1wk min, 4units, 1–7persons ◊ no pets ⏚or◉ fridge Electric Gas/Elec metered ▢not provided ☎(1½m) Iron in unit Ironing board in unit HCE in unit ⊕3pin round 8P ▥ ♨(1½m) Fishing ⊛ ⚑(1½m)

KINVER
Staffordshire
Map7 SO88

C **Nailmakers Cottage** 15/16 High Street
for bookings Mr & Mrs Harding, Glaslyn, Foley Street, Kinver, Stourbridge, W Midlands DY7 6EP
☎Kinver(038 483)3033

Originally two tiny cottages, now one, it is believed to be the only remaining example of an 18th-century nailmaker's home. In a secluded position, immediately behind a 15th-century building, there is an attractive garden which extends to the River Stour. Beautifully modernised, the ground-floor consists of two bedrooms, fully-fitted kitchen and dining area. The lounge and an area that can be divided off to form a third bedroom, are on the first-floor. Bathroom is on mezzanine floor.

All year 7days min, 6mths max, 1unit, 1–6persons [◊] ◊ ◆ no pets ⏚ fridge ♨ Gas/Elec metered ▢inclusive ☎ Airing cupboard in unit Iron in unit Ironing board in unit HCE in unit [Launderette within 300yds] ⊙ TV ⊕3pin square ⚓ ▥ ♨(100yds) ⊛ ♒(3m) ⚑(50yds) ▨(½m) ♫(½m) Min£60 Max£100pw

KIPPFORD
Dumfries & Galloway *Kirkcudbrightshire*
Map11 NX85

C **Brackenbank**
for bookings Mrs I Galt, Hillend,

Kinloch Rannoch — Kirkby Malham

Auldgirth, Dumfriesshire DG2 0UB
☎Auldgirth(038774)246

Detached cottage facing west, overlooking the Urr estuary and Galloway Hills. Two-storied accommodation, on the ground-floor are living room, dining room and spacious well-equipped kitchen, on the first-floor are double bedroom with washbasin, a twin-bedded room and a bathroom. Kippford is a popular yachting centre.

3 Apr-Oct 1wk min, 1unit, 1–4persons ◊ ◆ ◉ fridge ♨ Elec inclusive ▢inclusive ☎(200yds) WM in unit Iron in unit Ironing board in unit HCE in unit ⊙ CTV ⊕3pin square P ⚓ ▥ ♨(200yds) ⊛ ⚑(½m)

KIRBY HILL
North Yorkshire
Map12 NZ10

F **Old Grammar School**
for bookings The Landmark Trust, Shottesbrooke Park, Maidenhead, Berkshire
☎Littlewick Green(062 882)3431

Converted 16th-century grammar school adjacent to village church. Accommodation is on first- and second-floors above the small community hall and includes sitting room, combined bathroom/WC, two twin-bedded rooms plus a folding bed for a fifth person.

All year MWB out of season 1day min, 3wks max, 1unit, 1–5persons ◉ fridge Electric Elec inclusive ▢inclusive ☎(50yds) Airing cupboard in unit Iron in unit Ironing board in unit HCE in unit ⊙ ⊕3pin square ▥ ♨(½m) ⊛ ⚑(50yds)
£81pw (Low) £157pw (High)

1982 prices quoted throughout gazetteer

Kirkby Lonsdale

KIRKBY LONSDALE
Cumbria
Map7 SD67

H **Biggin Court** High Biggins
for bookings Mrs J T & S Mansergh, Kellet Farm, Silecroft, Millom, Cumbria LA18 4NU
☎Millom(0657)2727

House within the hamlet of High Biggin. It has four bedrooms; two with double beds and two with twin beds. Ideally situated for Yorkshire Dales and Lake District.

Apr-Oct MWB out of season 1wk min, 1mth max, 1unit, 2–8persons ◊ ◆ no pets ◉ fridge [Calor gas ♨] Elec metered ▢not provided ☎(½m) WM in unit SD in unit Airing cupboard in unit Iron in unit Ironing board in unit HCE in unit CTV ⊕3pin square P ▥ ♨(1m) ⊛ ♒(2m) ⚑(1m)
Max£80pw (Low)
Max£150pw (High)

F Mrs B Bayley **1 & 2 Durham Ox Holiday Flats** Old Town, Kirkby Lonsdale, Carnforth, Lancs LA6 2EP
☎Kirkby Lonsdale(0468)71689

Two modern well-equipped flats in part of stone-built property in the centre of the tiny village of Old Town. Good views across the valley to Barbon and Middleton Fells. Flat 1 has two twin-bedded rooms, one with twin bunks and a double bed-settee. Flat 2 has two twin-bedded rooms supplemented by fold-away twin bunks and a double bed-settee.

Apr-Oct(Flat1)24May-Sep(Flat2) 1wk min, 1mth max, 2units, 4–8persons ◊ no pets ◉ fridge ♨ Elec inclusive ▢not provided ☎(200yds) Airing cupboard in unit Iron on premises HCE in unit ⊙ TV ⊕3pin square 2P 2⚓ ♨(3m) ⊛ ♒(3m) ⚑(3m)

KIRKBY MALHAM
North Yorkshire
Map7 SD86

C&F Mr & Mrs G Durham **Scalegill** Kirkby Malham, Skipton, N Yorks

---

BD23 4BN
☎Airton(07293)293

Scalegill consists of a water mill converted into five modern flats and a row of three stone-built cottages which were previously for the mill workers. They are of varying sizes sleeping from two to six people. Set in 5½ acres of secluded grounds to the east of the village.

All year MWB out of season 3 days min, 3wks max, 8units, 2–6persons ◆ no pets(in flats) ◉ fridge Electric Elec metered ⌷not provided ☂ Airing cupboard in unit Iron on premises Ironing board on premises HCE in unit ⊕ TV ③pin square 12P ▥ ♨(2m) Fishing
↭ ⚲(1m)

Min£45 Max£70pw (Low)
Min£80 Max£130pw (High)

KIRKCUDBRIGHT
Dumfries & Galloway *Kirkcudbrightshire*
Map**11** NX65

H Bombie Glen Farm House
(3m E unclass)
for bookings G M Thomson & Co, 27 King Street, Castle Douglas, Kirkcudbrightshire DG7 1AB
☎Castle Douglas(0556)2701

Beautifully situated rustic farmhouse consisting of a large kitchen, breakfast room, dining room, sitting room, laundry room, four twin-bedded rooms and two bathrooms. Access via B727 E of Kirkcudbrightshire. At edge of town keep right for Dundrennan, after crossing Buckland Bridge the house is signposted on the left.

All year 1wk min, 1unit, 1–8persons ◉ fridge Electric & open fires Elec inclusive ⌷not provided SD in unit Airing cupboard in unit Iron in unit Ironing board in unit HCE in unit ⊕ TV ③pin square P ♨(3m) Games room, fishing

Min£80 Max£195pw

H Cumstoun Coachman's House
for bookings G M Thomson & Co, 27 King Street, Castle Douglas, Kirkcudbrightshire DG7 1AB
☎Castle Douglas(0556)2701

A former stable recently converted to form an ideal family house overlooking the rose garden and parkland of Cumstoun House Estate. It contains kitchen/diner, living room, and four bedrooms sleeping seven. 2m from Kirkcudbright off A762.

All year 1wk min, 1unit, 1–7persons ◆ ◉ fridge Electric & wood burning stove Elec inclusive ⌷not provided ☎(2m) Iron in unit Ironing board in unit HCE in unit ⊕ CTV ③pin square P ♨(2m) ⤺Hard Dinghy & canoe available
↭ ♌(3m) ⚲(2m)

Min£70 Max£170pw

C Cumstoun Cottage Cumstoun House
for bookings G M Thomson & Co, 27 King Street, Castle Douglas, Kirkcudbrightshire DG7 1AB
☎Castle Douglas(0556)2701

A wing of Cumstoun House which has recently been converted to provide one double bedroom, one twin-bedded room, kitchen, bathroom, WC and living/dining room with a view.

All year 1wk min, 1unit, 1–4persons ◆ ◉ fridge ♨ & wood burning stove Elec inclusive ⌷not provided Iron in unit Ironing board in unit HCE in unit ⊕ TV ③pin square P ♨(2m) ⤺Hard Dinghy & canoe available
↭ ♌(3m) ⚲(2m)

Min£55 Max£130pw

F Fludha Flat
for bookings Mr J Beattie, Fludha, Tongland Road, Kirkcudbright, Kirkcudbrightshire DG6 4UU
☎Kirkcudbright(0557)30208

First-floor flat comprising three bedrooms, lounge/diner and kitchen. This spacious accommodation forms part of the owner's 19th-century two-storey stone-built house. Set back off the main road on the N outskirts of Kirkcudbright, overlooking the Dee estuary.

All year 1wk min, 1unit, 1–6persons ◆ ◉ fridge Electric & coal fires Elec metered ⌷not provided ☎(1m) Airing cupboard in unit Iron on premises Ironing board on premises HCE in unit ⊕ TV ③pin square P ♨(1m)
↭ ⚲(1m) ▨(1m)

Min£40 Max£70pw (Low)
Min£80 Max£90pw (High)

C Laundry Cottage (St Mary's Isle)
for bookings G M Thomson & Co, 27 King Street, Castle Douglas, Kirkcudbrightshire DG7 1AB
☎Castle Douglas(0556)2701

Attractive, recently modernised cottage formerly a laundry to the estate house. Access via A711 Dundrennan road. Keep right, through gates, past lodge and down private road. All accommodation is on the ground-floor and comprises three bedrooms sleeping six, modern kitchen, living room and bathroom.

All year 1wk min, 1unit, 1–6persons ◆ no pets ◉ fridge ♨ & open fire Elec inclusive ⌷not provided ☎ WM in unit Airing cupboard in unit Iron in unit Ironing board in unit HCE in unit CTV ③pin square P ♨(1½m)
↭ ♌(1½m) ⚲(1½m) ▨(1½m) ♫(1½m)

Min£60 Max£145pw

C Mrs I M Blacklock **Little Sypland Farm (Cottages)** Kirkcudbright, Kirkcudbrightshire DG6 4XS
☎Kirkcudbright(0557)30592

Three attractive detached, bungalow style farm cottages with hill views. Two contain two bedrooms, the remainder, one, all have bathroom and kitchen. From Castle Douglas follow A745 for six miles, turn right at Gelston sign and proceed approx 3m to farm which is on the B727.

Mar-Nov 1wk min, 1mth max, 3units, 1–6persons ◆ ◆ ◉ fridge Electric & open fires Elec metered ⌷can be hired ☎(2½m) WM in unit SD in unit Airing cupboard in unit Iron in unit Ironing board in unit HCE in unit TV ③pin square(Cott.1) ③pin round(Cott.2&3) 24P ♨(3½m) Fishing and pony trekking

Min£40 Max£50pw (Low)
Min£45 Max£90pw (High)

KIRKHILL
Highland *Inverness-shire*
Map**14** NH54

F Garden Flat
for bookings Mr M R Fraser, Reelig House, Kirkhill, Inverness-shire IV5 7PR
☎Drumchardine(046 383)208

A conversion of a farm building providing a large hallway, kitchen, living room with convertible studio couch and three bedrooms. The estate is reached by an unclass road leading from A9.

26Mar-5Nov MWB out of season 1wk min, 1unit, 1–9persons [◇] [◆] ◉ fridge Electric Elec metered ⌷can be hired ☎ Airing cupboard in unit Iron in unit Ironing board in unit HCE in unit [Launderette on premises] ⊕ [TV] ③pin square P ▥ ♨(5m) ⤺Hard ♌ Fishing, Croquet, Games room
↭ ⚲(2m)

Min£61 Max£87pw (Low)
Min£116 Max£141pw (High)

C Gate Lodge
for bookings Mr M R Fraser, Reelig House, Kirkhill, Inverness-shire IV5 7PR
☎Drumchardine(046 383)208

Stone-built cottage standing at estate entrance by hump backed bridge ⅓m from A9. It contains a kitchen/diner, living room with convertible studio couch, and two twin-bedded rooms.

All year MWB out of season 1wk min, 1unit, 1–8persons [◇] [◆] ◉ fridge Electric Elec metered ⌷can be hired ☎ Airing cupboard in unit Iron in unit Ironing board in unit HCE in unit [Launderette on premises] ⊕ [TV] ③pin square P ▥ ♨(5m) ⤺Hard ♌ Fishing, Croquet, Games room
↭ ⚲(2m)

Min£56 Max£84pw (Low)
Min£109 Max£138pw (High)

B Hardies Byre
for bookings Mr M R Fraser, Reelig
House, Kirkhill, Inverness-shire IV5 7PR
☎Drumchardine(046 383)208

A converted stone-built byre standing in estate woodlands. It contains lounge/dining room with convertible studio couch, kitchen and three twin bedded rooms. The estate is reached by unclass road leading from A9.

All year   MWB out of season   1wk min,
1 unit, 1–8 persons   [◊]   [♦]   ◉
fridge Electric Elec metered ⌷ can be
hired ☎ Airing cupboard in unit Iron in
unit Ironing board in unit HCE in unit
[Launderette on premises] ⊙ [TV]
⊕3pin square P ▥ ▲(5m) ⚲Hard
♪ Fishing, croquet, games room
↔ ♟(2m)
Min£65 Max£90pw (Low)
Min£120 Max£146pw (High)

C Mill House
for bookings Mr M R Fraser, Reelig
House, Kirkhill, Inverness-shire IV5 7PR
☎Drumchardine(046 383)208

A modernised stone-built cottage standing in estate woodlands. It contains kitchen, dining room, sitting room with convertible studio couch and three bedrooms. The estate is reached by unclass road leading from A9.

All year   MWB out of season   1wk min,
1 unit, 1–8 persons   [◊]   [♦]   ◉

---

fridge Electric Elec metered ⌷ can be
hired ☎ Airing cupboard in unit Iron in
unit Ironing board in unit HCE in unit
[Launderette on premises] ⊙ [TV]
⊕3pin square P ▥ ▲(5m) ⚲Hard
♪ Fishing, Croquet, games room
↔ ♟(2m)
Min£65 Max£90pw (Low)
Min£120 Max£146pw (High)

Ch Reelig Glen Chalets
for bookings Mr M R Fraser, Reelig
House, Kirkhill, Inverness-shire IV5 7PR
☎Drumchardine(046 383)208

Twelve cedar wood chalets all having pleasant views. They are either two or three-bedroomed, and have open plan kitchen/sitting room. Some have a fixed fold-down bed. The estate is reached by unclass road leading from A9.

26Mar–5Nov   MWB in season   1wk min,
12 units, 1–8 persons   [◊]   [♦]   ◉
fridge Electric Elec metered ⌷ can be
hired ☎ Airing cupboard in unit Iron in
unit Ironing board in unit HCE in unit
[Launderette on premises] ⊙ [TV]
⊕3pin square P ▥ ▲(5m) ⚲Hard
Fishing, croquet, games room
↔ ♟(2m)
Min£56 Max£87pw (Low)
Min£109 Max£141pw (High)

C Tigh Faire
for bookings Mr M R Fraser, Reelig
House, Kirkhill, Inverness-shire IV5 7PR
☎Drumchardine(046 383)208

A stone-built cottage standing in woodland above the estate house on a hillside. It contains three bedrooms, kitchen and sitting room with convertible studio couch. The house stands on an unclass road off A9.

26Mar–5Nov   MWB out of season
1wk min, 1 unit, 1–7 persons   [◊]   [♦]
◉ fridge Electric Elec metered
⌷ can be hired ☎ Airing cupboard in
unit Iron in unit Ironing board in unit
HCE in unit [Launderette on premises]
⊙ [TV] ⊕3pin square P ▥ ▲(5m)
⚲Hard ♪ Fishing, croquet, games
room
↔ ♟(3m)
Min£65 Max£90pw (Low)
Min£120 Max£146pw (High)

KIRKMICHAEL
Tayside *Perthshire*
Map 15 NO06

Cs Balloch & Crievie Lodges Glen
Derby
for bookings Miss M K Crossley, Redhu
House, Kirkmichael, Blairgowrie, Perths
PH10 7NX
☎Strathardle(025 081)340

These Norwegian log cabins, with natural wood interiors and furnishings to blend,

are set in 150 acres of moorland with pine
trees and are part of a community of 18
log cabins, of which only one other is let.
The accommodation consists of three
bedrooms, an open plan living area,
bathroom and terrace. Two of the
bedrooms have wash-basins and there is
an open fire in the living area.

Apr–Oct MWB out of season 1wk min,
6wks max, 2units, 6persons [◊] ◆
◆ No camping & caravanning
equipment ● fridge ♨
Elec inclusive ⌷inclusive ☎(1½m)
Airing cupboard in unit Iron in unit
Ironing board in unit HCE in unit ☉
TV ⊕3pin square P ♨ ⚓(1½m)
⊶ ♀(½m) ▨(½m)
Min£115 Max£145pw

C Mr & Mrs A J Scaife **The Cottage**
c/o Macdonalds Store, Main Street,
Kirkmichael, Blairgowrie, Perthshire
PH107NT
☎Strathardle(025081)256

*Situated in the centre of the village, this
former bakehouse was converted into a
cottage in 1980. It consists of two
bedrooms and open plan
kitchen/lounge/dining room with
convertible settee. 14 miles south of the
Glenshee ski slopes.*

All year MWB out of season 3day min,
1unit, 1–6persons [◊] ◊ ◆ ●
fridge Electric Elec inclusive
⌷inclusive ☎(100yds) Airing
cupboard in unit Iron in unit Ironing
board in unit HCE in unit ☉ CTV
⊕3pin square 2P 2♨ ▥ ⚓(20yds)
⊶ ♀(100yds)
Min£60 Max£110pw

KIRKPATRICK DURHAM
Dumfries & Galloway *Kirkcudbrightshire*
Map**11** NX87

B **Walton Park Farm Cottage**
for bookings G M Thomson & Co, 27 King
Street, Castle Douglas,
Kirkcudbrightshire DG/1AB
☎Castle Douglas(0556)2701

*Modern, fully-furnished bungalow on
quiet farmland near the River Urr. It has
two double-bedded rooms, each with a
single bed and a twin-bedded room.
There is also a modern kitchen, a
bathroom and a living room. Situated just
off the B784 towards Corsock.*

All year 1wk min, 6mths max, 1unit,
1–8persons ◊ no pets ● fridge
Open & electric fires Elec inclusive
⌷notprovided ☎(2m) WM in unit SD
in unit Ironing board in unit HCE in unit
TV ⊕3pin square P ▥ ⚓(2m)
Fishing in private loch and use of boat
Min£60 Max£145pw

KIRKTON MANOR
Borders *Peeblesshire*
Map**11** NT23

C **Glenrath Farm Cottages,**
for bookings Mrs J P Campbell, Glenrath
Farm, Kirkton Manor, Peebles
☎Kirkton Manor(072 14)221

Kirkmichael — Knucklas

*Situated in rolling-border hill country
approximately 6½m from Peebles. The
three brick and stone cottages, built thirty
years ago, form part of a large farm
complex. They are well decorated and
pleasantly furnished and sited close to
the main farm buildings. The cottages
have small garden areas and stand in
tree-studded surroundings. Electric
charged separately.*

All year MWB out of season 1wk min,
1mth max, 3units, 2–8persons ◊ ◆
● fridge Electric & open fires
⌷notprovided ☎(4m) Ironing board in
unit HCE in unit ⊖(2units) CTV
⊕3pin square P ⚓(7m) Fishing
Min£50 Max£80pw (Low)
Min£100 Max£135pw (High)

KIRTON
Suffolk
Map**5** TM23

C **2 Church Lane**
for bookings W R Dellar, Stratton Hall,
Levington, Ipswich, Suffolk
☎Nacton(047388)218

*This white painted terraced cottage with
its own small garden is located in the
peaceful village of Kirton.
Accommodation comprises lounge,
bathroom/WC, dining room, kitchen and
three bedrooms.*

All year MWB out of season 4days min,
5mths max, 1unit, 1–6persons ◊ ◆
● fridge Electric Elec metered ⌷can be
hired ☎(100yds) Airing cupboard in
unit Iron in unit Ironing board in unit
HCE in unit CTV ⊕3pin square 2P
▥ ⚓(100yds)
⊶ ♀(½m)
Min£52.94 Max£129.41pw

C **Dweeny & Lee Cottages** Falkenham
Road,
for bookings W R Dellar, Stratton Hall,
Levington, Ipswich, Suffolk
☎Nacton(047388)218

*Modernised semi-detached cottages
located in the peaceful village of Kirton.
Accommodation comprises lounge,
kitchen/dining room, two bedrooms and
bathroom/WC.*

All year MWB out of season 4days min,
5mths max, 2units, 1–4persons ◊ ◆
● fridge Electric Elec metered ⌷can be
hired ☎(½m) Airing cupboard in unit
Iron in unit Ironing board in unit HCE in
unit CTV ⊕3pin square 2P ▥
⚓(10yds)
⊶ ♀(½m)
Min£52.94 Max£129.41pw

1982 prices quoted throughout
gazetteer

KNIGHTON
Powys
Map**7** SO27

C Mrs G Pugh **Treburvaugh Cottage**
Knighton, Powys LD7 1SG
☎Llangunllo(054781)257

*Part of a Black and White Tudor Manor
Farm set in heart of wooded countryside.
Comprises lounge and large kitchen on
the ground floor; two connecting large
double bedrooms and bathroom/WC on
1st floor and two connecting large double
bedrooms on second floor.*

All year MWB out of season 6mths max,
1unit, 1–8persons [◊] ◊ ● fridge
Electric & open fires Elec metered
⌷inclusive ☎ Airing cupboard in unit
Iron in unit Ironing board in unit HCE in
unit ☉ TV ⊕3pin square 3P
⚓(2½m)
⊶ ♀(3m)
Min£25 Max£50pw (Low)
Min£40 Max£70pw (High)

KNIVETON
Derbyshire
Map**8** SK25

H **Merryfields Farm**
for bookings Mrs E J Harrison, Little Park
Farm, Okeover, Ashbourne, Derbyshire
☎Thorpe Cloud(033529)341

*A detached pebbledash and tiled house
just 100yds off the B5035
Ashbourne/Wirksworth Road
(signposted Kniveton Wood). The
accommodation consists of two double
bedrooms and one single, kitchen, dining
room, lounge, bathroom/WC and
separate WC. Places of interest in the
north Staffordshire and Derbyshire
border accessible, but own transport is a
necessity.*

Apr–Oct 1wk min, 3wks max, 1unit,
1–5persons, nc2 ● fridge Electric &
coal fires Elec metered
⌷not provided ☎(½m) Airing cupboard
in unit HCE in unit TV ⊕3pin square
P ⚓(2m)
⊶ ♀(½m)
Min£50 Max£80pw

KNUCKLAS
Powys
Map**7** SO27

H **Lower Rhas-y-Garth**
for bookings Mrs G M Vogel, Craig-y-
Don, Knucklas, Knighton, Powys
LD7 1PH
☎Knighton(0547)528438

*Detached house of modern type. Three
bedroomed, with two family rooms.
Bathroom/WC combined and large
lounge and modern kitchen. Situated 2m
from town off the Knighton-Newtown
road.*

All year MWB out of season 1wk min,
1mth max, 1unit, 8persons ◊ ◊ ◆
● fridge Electric Elec metered
⌷can be hired ☎(1½m) SD in unit
Airing cupboard in unit Iron in unit →

143

Ironing board in unit HCE in unit ☺
✿ TV ⊕3pin square P 🏠 🛖
🛁(1½m)
⊖ 🐾(1½m) 🍴(1½m) 🖬(1½m)
Min£35 Max£45pw (Low)
Min£50 Max£65pw (High)

LAIRG
Highland *Sutherland*
Map**14** NC50

F   The Apartment
for bookings Sutherland Arms Hotel,
Lairg, Sutherland IV27 4AT
☎Lairg(0549)2291

*A first-floor apartment in the hotel and
with separate entrance to rear. Two
bedrooms, one double and one twin-
bedded, lounge/diner with bed-settee,
kitchen and bathroom.*

midApr–midOct MWB out of season
1wk min, 1unit, 2–6persons, ◊ ◆ ◎
fridge Electric Elec metered
🗌inclusive ☎(in hotel) Iron in unit
Ironing board in unit HCE in unit ☺
✿ CTV ⊕3pin square P
🛁(200yds) Fishing, deer stalking, pony
trekking
⊖ 🍴

Min£60 Max£85pw (Low)
Min£125 Max£185pw (High)

C   The Cottage
for bookings Sutherland Arms Hotel,
Lairg, Sutherland IV27 4AT
☎Lairg(0549)2291

*Single-storey cottage in grounds of hotel
with views over Loch Shin. Two
bedrooms, one twin and one double-
bedded, lounge/diner with convertible
settee, well equipped kitchen and
modern bathroom.*

All year MWB out of season 1wk min,
1unit, 2–6persons ◊ ◆ ◎ fridge
Electric Elec metered 🗌inclusive
☎(75yds) Iron in unit Ironing board in
unit HCE in unit ☺ CTV
⊕3pin square P 🛁(200yds) Fishing,
deer stalking, pony trekking
⊖ 🍴(75yds)

Min£60 Max£85pw (Low)
Min£125 Max£185pw (High)

Knucklas
—
Landshipping

LAMLASH Isle of Arran
Strathclyde *Bute*
Map**10** NS03

Ch   Dyemill Chalets
for bookings Mr & Mrs J T Cowie, The
Dyemill, Lamlash, Brodick, Isle of Arran
KA27 8NU
☎Lamlash(077 06)419

*Six pinewood chalets of Finnish design
set in woodland, with beautiful views,
close to the Mona Mohr burn.
Accommodation comprises two
bedrooms (one double, one twin-
bedded), lounge/diner, kitchenette and
bathroom/WC.*

Apr–Oct 1wk min, 1mth max, 6units,
1–4persons [◆] ◎ fridge Electric
Elec metered 🗌inclusive ☎(1m)
Airing cupboard in unit Iron on
premises Ironing board on premises
HCE in unit ☺ ⊕3pin square P 🖬
🛁(1m)
⊖ 🍴(1m) 🖬(1m) 🎵(1m)

Min£63.25 Max£89.70pw (Low)
Min£103.50 Max£138pw (High)

H   Dyemill House
for bookings Mr & Mrs J T Cowie, The
Dyemill, Lamlash, Brodick, Isle of Arran
KA27 8NU
☎Lamlash(07706)419

*A two-storey country house which is an
extension to the owner's house making a
self-contained unit, beside the Mona
Mohr burn in rural setting with good
views. The house is spacious with three
bedrooms (one double, twin-bedded and
a single), sitting room, dining
room/kitchen and bathroom.*

All year MWB 1wk min 1unit,
1–5persons [◆] [◆] ◎ fridge
Electric Elec metered 🗌inclusive
☎(1m) Airing cupboard in unit Iron on
premises Ironing board on premises
HCE in unit ⊕3pin square P 🖬
🛁(1m)
⊖ 🍴(1m) 🖬(1m) 🎵(1m)

Min£69 Max£112pw (Low)
Min£120 Max£142.60pw (High)

LAMPLUGH
Cumbria
Map**11** NY02

H   Barn & Main House Apartments
Lowmillgillhead
for bookings Lady Moon, 79 Woodstock
Road, Oxford OX2 6HL
☎Oxford(0865)57687(after 6pm)

*Two houses, one a converted barn
adjoining a large 17th-century
farmhouse, the other making up part of
the farmhouse, which stands in two acres
of attractive grounds and gardens in
quiet rural surroundings a few hundred
yards from the A5086, 7m S of
Cockermouth. The Barn Apartment
comprises one twin-bedded room and
one room with two singles and twin
bunks. Main House Apartment consists
of two bedrooms, one with a double bed
and one twin-bedded, and a further two
with twin bunks and a single bed.*

All year 2 days min, 1mth max, 2units,
1–9persons ◊ no pets ◎ fridge
🍴 Elec inclusive(1unit)
Elec metered(1unit) 🗌not provided
☎(⅓m) WM in unit(1unit) SD in
unit(1unit) TD in unit(1unit) Airing
cupboard in unit Iron in unit Ironing
board on premises HCE in unit
TV(1unit) CTV(1unit) ⊕3pin square
P 🖬 🛁(7m)
⊖ 🍴(⅓m)

Min£75 Max£100pw (Low)
Min£85 Max£120pw (High)

LANDSHIPPING
Dyfed
Map**2** SN01

C   Beggars Reach Coed-Can-Las
for bookings Powell's Holidays, High
Street, Saundersfoot, Dyfed
☎Saundersfoot(0834)812791

*Attractive detached four-bedroomed
cottage with large garden in secluded
country area, accommodation also
consists of small lounge, dining room and
kitchen. From Carmarthen- Haverfordwest.*

road (A40) (near Canaston Bridge) take
A4075 southwards (signpost Tenby) for
½m then turn right (unclass) and in 3m
right again for Landshipping.

May-Sep MWB out of season 1wk min,
3wks max, 1 unit, 8 persons [◊] ◆
no pets Aga cooker ◎ fridge
Elec inclusive ⊡ can be hired ☎
Airing cupboard in unit Iron in unit
Ironing board in unit HCE in unit ☉
CTV ⊕3pin square P ♨(1m)
⊖ ♀(1m) ▨(2½m) ♫(2½m)
Min£63 Max£168pw

H Woodhouse Grange
(1m S Landshipping Quay)
for bookings Powell's Holidays, High
Street, Saundersfoot,
☎Saundersfoot(0834)812791

An interesting 17th-century farmhouse
standing in extensive grounds alongside
the estuary of the River Cheddau. Small
boats can be launched. The
Landshipping pottery is situated in the
grounds and visitors are welcome. There
are five bedrooms, several with good
views, a drawing room, sitting room,
dining room, kitchen, conservatory,
garden and also a bar.

May-Sep MWB out of season 1wk min,
6wks max, 1 unit, 2–8 persons ◆
no pets Aga cooker & ◎ fridge ♨
Elec inclusive ⊡ can be hired ☎ WM
in unit Iron in unit Ironing board in unit
HCE in unit ⊖ CTV ⊕3pin square
P ♨(1½m) Fishing
⊖ ♀(1m)
Min£111 Max£318pw

LANGHOLM
Dumfries & Galloway Dumfriess-shire
Map11 NY38

C Burngrains Cottage Bush Farm,
Ewes
for bookings Miss J Bristow, Thorncroft,
Lilliesleaf, Roxburghshire
☎Lilliesleaf(08357)424
Converted and modernised stone croft in
isolated country location.
Accommodation comprises sitting room,
kitchen, bathroom, shower-room and one
family bedroom on the ground-floor; one

---

twin-bedded room and one with a double
bed and a single bed on the first-floor.
Situated off the A7, 5m N of Langholm.

Mar-Oct MWB out of season 1wk min,
3mths max, 1 unit, 2–9 persons ◆ ◎
fridge Electric & coal fires
Elec metered ⊡ can be hired ☎(2m)
WM in unit SD in unit TD in unit Airing
cupboard in unit Iron in unit Ironing
board in unit HCE in unit ☉
⊕3pin square 4P ♨(6m)
Min£92 Max£115pw (Low)
Min£149.50 Max£189.75pw (High)

C Cleuchfoot Cottages
for bookings Miss J Bristow,
Lilliesleaf, Roxburghshire
☎Lilliesleaf(08357)424
Two semi-detached cottages, standing
on grassy bank at the side of Logan
Water. Accommodation consists of
sitting/dining room, kitchen, bathroom
and one double bedroom all on ground-
floor, whilst the first-floor comprises two
twin-bedded rooms. Cottages are in
isolated position ½m from the
Langholm/Lockerbie road and 4m from
Langholm.

Mar-Dec MWB out of season 1wk min,
3mths max, 2 units, 2–8 persons [◊]
◎ fridge Electric & coal fires
Elec metered ⊡ can be hired ☎(3½m)
Airing cupboard in unit Iron in unit
Ironing board in unit HCE in unit CTV
⊕3pin square 6P ♨(3½m)
Min£60.95 Max£74.75pw (Low)
Min£97.75 Max£120.75pw (High)

C Rashiel Cottage
for bookings Mrs J Bristow, Thorncroft,
Lilliesleaf, Roxburghshire
☎Lilliesleaf(08357)424
Converted stone farming croft in a quiet
location, with exceptional hill views.
There are four bedrooms sleeping nine
persons (one double, and one family
room upstairs, one double and one twin-
bedded room downstairs), lounge/diner,
kitchen and bathroom. There is an extra
WC on first-floor.

Mar-Dec MWB out of season 1wk min,
2mths max, 1 unit, 2–9 persons [◊] ◎
fridge freezer Electric & coal fires
Elec metered ⊡ can be hired ☎(3m)
WM in unit TD in unit Airing cupboard in
unit Iron in unit Ironing board in unit
HCE in unit TV ⊕3pin square P ♨
♨(3m)
⊖ ♀(3m)
Min£92 Max£115pw (Low)
Min£149.50 Max£189.75pw (High)

C Wauchope School House Cottage
for bookings Miss J Bristow, Thorncroft,
Lilliesleaf, Roxburghshire
☎Lilliesleaf(08357)424

Old country school house which has
been modernised to make a holiday
cottage in a peaceful spot with good
views. Accommodation comprises three
bedrooms (one double, one with three
singles, and one with a double and a
single bed), sitting room, kitchen/diner
and bathroom.

Mar-Oct MWB out of season 1wk min,
2mths max, 1 unit, 2–8 persons [◊] ◎
fridge Electric & coal fires
Elec metered ⊡ can be hired ☎(3½m)
Iron in unit Ironing board in unit HCE in
unit TV ⊕3pin square P ♨ ♨(3m)
⊖ ♀(3m)
Min£62.10 Max£77.05pw (Low)
Min£103.50 Max£126.50pw (High)

LANGTREE
Devon
Map2 SS41

F, C CC Ref 586 Higher Lakes
for bookings Character Cottages
(Holidays) Ltd, 34 Fore Street, Sidmouth,
Devon EX10 8AQ
☎Sidmouth(03955)77001

Barn converted into three units, one flat
on first-floor and two cottages on the
ground-floor. The first-floor flat consists of
open-plan lounge, kitchen and diner,
three bedrooms, two with bunk beds and
one with a double bed. Shower and WC.
Two ground-floor units comprising open- →

> 1982 prices quoted throughout
> gazetteer

---

plan lounge, kitchen, diner, shower and WC, one double bedroom and one room with bunk beds. Good décor and furnishings.

All year MWB out of season 1wk min, 1mth max, 3 units, 1–6 persons ◆ no pets ● fridge Electric Elec metered ⬜ not provided ☎(1m) Airing cupboard in unit Iron on premises Ironing board on premises HCE in unit ⊙ TV ⊕3pin square 2P ⑩ ♨(2m)
↝ ♀(1m)
Min£30 Max£70pw (Low)
Min£65 Max£120pw (High)

LANREATH
Cornwall
Map 2 SX15

F Mr & Mrs Toothill **The Old Rectory**
Lanreath, Looe, Cornwall PL13 2NU
☎Lanreath(0503)20247
Seven well converted and attractively furnished flats in large rectory on outskirts of village. Two flats on ground-floor, comprising kitchen, lounge/diner, one twin and one double bedroom with interconnecting bathroom. Four flats on first-floor, comprisng kitchen, lounge/diner with either one or two double bedrooms, bathroom and WC. One flat on second-floor, comprisng kitchen, lounge/diner with twin sofa bed, two twin-bedded rooms and bathroom/WC.

All year MWB 1wk min, 7 units, 1–6 persons [◇ ◆] no pets ● fridge Electric Elec metered ⬜ can be hired ☎(60yds) Airing cupboard in unit Iron on premises Ironing board on premises HCE in unit ⊙ [TV] ⊕3pin square 1P ⑩ ♨(2m) Croquet lawn
↝ ♀(60yds)
Min£30 Max£50pw (Low)
Min£48 Max£108pw (High)

LAUDER
Borders *Berwickshire*
Map 12 NT54

C Upper **Blainslie Cottage** Upper Blainslie Farm

Langtree
—
Lazonby

for bookings Miss J Bristow, Thorncroft, Lilliesleaf, Roxburghshire TD6 9JD
☎Lilliesleaf(08357)424
Situated on a farm just 3m SW of Lauder, this one of three adjoining stone farm cottages, is spacious and offers sitting room with open fire, and bed-settee, kitchen/dining room with walk-in pantry, bathroom and two bedrooms (one double and one twin-bedded) all on the ground floor. Peaceful setting with views across valley.

Apr–Oct 1wk min, 6mths max, 1 unit, 2–6 persons [◆] ● fridge Coal fires & Electric Elec metered ⬜ can be hired ☎(1½m) Airing cupboard in unit Iron in unit Ironing board in unit HCE in unit TV ⊕3pin round P ♨(3m)
↝ ♀(3m) ▦(3m)
Min£55.20 Max£63.25pw (Low)
Min£80.50 Max£97.75pw (High)

LAUGHARNE
Dyfed
Map 2 SN31

B **Penthouse & Playboy** Broadway
for bookings Powell's Holidays, High Street, Saundersfoot, Dyfed
☎Saundersfoot(0834)812791
Two detached bungalows both three bedroomed with kitchen/dining area, lounge, bathroom and WC. In rural setting 4m from Pendine Beach.

Jan–Nov MWB out of season 1wk min, 4wks max, 2 units, 2–6 persons [◇] ◆ ◆ ● fridge ♨ Elec metered ⬜inclusive (Penthouse) ⬜not provided (Playboy) ☎(20yds) WM in unit Airing cupboard in unit Iron in unit Ironing board in unit HCE in unit ⊙ ⊕ CTV ⊕3pin square P ⑩ ♨(½m)
↝ ▦(½m) ♫(½m)
Min£105 Max£267pw

1982 prices quoted throughout gazetteer

LAUNCESTON
Cornwall
Map 2 SX38

F Mrs E Paul **Dunheved View** (Flat) Chapple, Launceston, Cornwall PL15 7EH
☎Launceston(0566)2066
One half of bungalow set in small garden on the outskirts of Launceston. Sun porch entrance, lounge/diner, kitchen, shower/WC and two double bedrooms. There is also a double sofa bed in lounge.

All year MWB out of season 3days min, 6wks max, 1 unit, 1–6 persons ◇ ◆ no pets ● fridge Electric Elec metered ⬜inclusive ☎(100yds) WM on premises Iron in unit Ironing board in unit ⊙ TV ⊕3pin square 3P ⑩ ♨(½m)
↝ ♿(½m) ♀(½m) ▦(½m) ♫(½m)
♨(½m)
£40pw (Low)
Min£100 Max£150pw (High)

LAZONBY
Cumbria
Map 12 NY53

C **Edengrove Holiday Cottages**
for bookings Mrs E P Bell, The Post Office, Lazonby, Penrith, Cumbria CA10 1BX
☎Lazonby(076 883)242 & 437
A row of late 19th-century cottages in the rural village of Lazonby. Each has a lounge/diner, spacious kitchen and three bedrooms. Two cottages have two twin-and one single-bedded rooms, the other two have one double, one twin and one room with bunk beds. Bedrooms and bathrooms are all on the first floor.

All year MWB out of season 5days min, 6mths max, 4 units, 5–6 persons ◆ ◆ no pets ● fridge Electric Elec metered ⬜not provided ☎(½m) Airing cupboard in unit Iron in unit Ironing board in unit HCE in unit ⊙ TV ⊕3pin square P ⑩ ♨(½m)
↝ ♀(½m)
Min£45 Max£55pw (Low)
Min£65 Max£105pw (High)

LEA

Hereford & Worcester
Map **3** SO62

C   Barn End Cottage The Lea
for bookings Mr & Mrs A T Ewens, Lea
Hall, The Lea, Ross-on-Wye,
Herefordshire HR9 7LQ
☎Lea(098 981)249

*Stone-built cottage comprising hall,
kitchen, lounge, three bedrooms and
bathroom. The cottage is ideally situated
for touring and close to the Forest of
Dean. It stands in the grounds of Lea Hall
just off A40, 200yds beyond New Lea
Garage and has its own private drive and
garden with open loggia.*

21 May–15 Oct   1 wk min, 1 unit,
1–5 persons ◇ ◆ no pets ●
fridge   Electric   Elec metered
▢not provided   ☎(300yds)   Airing
cupboard in unit   Iron in unit   Ironing
board in unit   HCE in unit   TV
⊕3 pin square   P ● ▥ ♨(300yds)
↔ ♀(200yds)
Min£50 Max£70pw

C   Castle End Cottage
for bookings Captain M R Lowe, Castle
End, Lea, Ross-on-Wye, Herefordshire
☎Lea(098 981)276

*A stone-built cottage comprising
kitchen/dining room, bathroom/WC,
lounge, two single and one double
bedrooms. The accommodation is simply
but comfortably furnished and guests
have use of garden.*

Apr–Oct   MWB out of season
2 days min, 4 wks max, 1 unit,
1–4 persons [◇] ◇ ◆ ● fridge
Electric & open fires   Elec metered
▢not provided   ☎(½m)   Airing cupboard
in unit   Iron in unit   Ironing board in unit
HCE in unit   TV ⊕3 pin square   P ▥
♨(½m) ➔ ✒Hard
↔ ♀(½m)
£20pw (Low)
Min£35 Max£75pw (High)

Lea
—
Leckmelm

LEADBURN

Borders *Peeblesshire*
Map **45** NT25

H   Easter Deans Farmhouse
for bookings Mrs J P Campbell, Glenrath
Farm, Kirkton Manor, Peebles, Peeblesshire
☎Kirkton Manor(072 14)221

*This farmhouse is on the last farm in
Tweeddale and is only 12 miles from
Edinburgh, with Peebles 9 miles to the
south. It is 1 mile off the A703 and ideally
situated for touring the Borders. The
accommodation includes large kitchen,
two lounges, three bedrooms and
bathroom.*

mid May–mid Nov   1 wk min, 1 mth max,
1 unit, 2–8 persons ◇ ● fridge
Electric & open fires   Elec metered
▢can be hired   ☎(1½m)   Iron in unit
Ironing board in unit   HCE in unit ⊖
CTV ⊕3 pin square   3P ♨(4m)
↔ ♀(1½m)
Min£100 Max£175pw

LEAMINGTON SPA (ROYAL)

Warwickshire
Map **4** SP36

F   Ettington House 13 Radford Road,
for bookings Mrs Reader, 4 Offchurch
Lane, Radford Semele, Leamington Spa,
Warwickshire
☎Leamington Spa(0926)24801

*Early 19th-C town house at southern end
of town, divided into ground, first and
second floor flats plus a maisonette. The
accommodation comprises kitchen,
lounge/dining room, bathroom/WC and
bedroom with twin beds. The lounges
have either a studio couch or bed settee.*

All year   MWB   1 wk min, 3 mths max,
4 units, 1–6 persons nc5, no pets ●
fridge   Electric   Elec inclusive
▢inclusive (except towels)   ☎   Airing
cupboard in unit   Iron in unit   Ironing
board in unit   HCE in unit   [Launderette
within 300yds]   ⊖ ⊛ CTV

⊕3 pin square   6P ▥ ♨(100yds)
↔ ♫ ♀(200yds) ▨(½m) ♪(½m)
▩(½m)
Min£50 Max£130pw

LECKMELM

Highland *Ross & Cromarty*
Map **14** NH19

C   The Cabin
for bookings The Manager, Leckmelm
Holiday Cottages, Loch Broom, Garve,
Ross-shire IV23 2RL
☎Ullapool(0854)2471

*Wood-built cabin commanding fine views
of Loch Broom. Accommodation consists
of kitchen, lounge/dining room, double
bedroom, single bedroom and a third
bedroom containing bunks. Sited
adjacent to the Loch Broom Restaurant
3½m E of Ullapool on the A835.*

Apr–mid Oct   MWB in season
3 days min, 4 wks max, 1 unit,
1–6 persons ◇ ◆ ● fridge
Electric   Elec metered   ▢can be hired
☎   [WM on premises]   [SD on
premises]   Airing cupboard in unit   Iron
in unit   Ironing board in unit   HCE in unit
⊖   TV ⊕3 pin square   ♨(3½m)
Fishing, shooting & rowing boat available
↔ ♀
Max£70pw (Low)
Min£90 Max£120pw (High)

C   Campbeltown Cottages
for bookings The Manager, Leckmelm
Holiday Cottages, Loch Broom, Garve,
Ross-shire IV23 2RL
☎Ullapool(0854)2471

*Substantial stone building housing six
cottages, all containing kitchen,
living/dining room, twin or double-
bedded room and a bedroom with full-
size bunks. Set some 300yds from A835
3m E of Ullapool.*

All year   MWB   3 days min, 4 wks max,
6 units, 1–6 persons ◇ ◆ ● fridge
▮ coal fires   Elec metered   ▢can be
hired   ☎(½m)   [WM on premises]   [SD
on premises]   Airing cupboard in unit
Iron in unit   Ironing board in unit   HCE in
unit   ⊖ ⊕3 pin square   P ♨(3m)
Fishing, shooting & rowing boat available →

⊖ ⚲(½m)
Min£50 Max£60pw (Low)
Min£70 Max£95pw (High)

C Lochside Cottages
for bookings The Manager, Leckmelm
Holiday Cottages, Loch Broom, Garve,
Ross-shire IV23 2RL
☎Ullapool(0854)2471

Attractive modern cottages on the slope
of Loch Broom adjacent to the Leckmelm
Farm. Two of the units are semi-detached
and all contain kitchens, sitting/dining
rooms, double or twin bedrooms. 300yds
from main A835.

All year MWB 3days min, 4wks max,
3units, 1–6persons ◊ ◆ ◎ fridge
🍴 coal fire Elec metered ⌷can be
hired ☎(½m) [WM on premises] [SD
on premises] Airing cupboard in unit
Iron in unit Ironing board in unit HCE in
unit ☉ ⊕3pin square P ⚑(3m)
Fishing, shooting & rowing boat available

⊖ ⚲(¾m)
Min£60 Max£70pw (Low)
Min£90 Max£120pw (High)

LEDBURY
Hereford & Worcester
Map3 SO73

F Mr A R Hanshaw *Heathfield Flat*
Heathfield Guest House, Ross Road,
Ledbury, Hereford HR8 2LE
☎Ledbury(0531)2829

Self-contained flat on first floor at rear of
house, comprising kitchen/dining room,
a large lounge with studio couch,
bedroom and bathroom. Extensive views
of the gardens and surrounding
countryside, the flat is located 1½m SW of
Ledbury off the A449.

All year 1wk min, 3wks max, 1unit,
1–6persons ◊ ◆ ◎ fridge
Electric Elec metered ⌷inclusive ☎
Airing cupboard in unit Iron on
premises Ironing board on premises
HCE in unit TV ⊕3pin square P 🆄
⚑(1½m)

⊖ ⚲(1½m)

LEEBOTWOOD
Shropshire
Map7 SO49

C Sunnyside Comley
for bookings Mr & Mrs T W E Corbett,
Home Farm, Leebotwood, Church
Stretton, Shropshire
☎Leebotwood(069 45)231

A white painted detached cottage
located on a hillside in the heart of the
countryside. Accommodation consists of
bathroom/WC, kitchen, dining room and
lounge with exposed beams. The first
floor has one double bedroom, two twin
bedrooms and a roof patio.

Apr–Oct 1wk min, 1mth max, 1unit,
1–6persons ◎ fridge Electric & open
fires Elec metered ⌷not provided
☎(1¼m) Airing cupboard in unit HCE in
unit TV ⊕3pin square 3P 1⚑
⚑(1¼m)

⊖ ☒(3m) ⚲(1¼m)

LEEDS
West Yorkshire
Map8 SE33

F Flats 1 & 3
for bookings Mr & Mrs G C Pickard,
Sandfield House, Sandfield Avenue,
Leeds LS6 4DZ
☎Leeds(0532)752977

Stone-built detached house in 1 acre at
the end of cul-de-sac in pleasant suburb
of Leeds. One ground floor and one first
floor flat, each with two bedrooms – one
has double bed and the other has
singles. Separate lounge and kitchen.

All year MWB 3days min, 6mths max,
2units, 1–6persons ◊ ♂ ◎ fridge
Gas & Electric Gas/Elec metered
⌷can be hired ☎(100yds) Iron in unit
Ironing board in unit HCE in unit
[Launderette within 300yds] TV can be
hired ⊕3pin round P 🆄 ⚑(100yds)

⊖ ☒(2m) ⚲(½m) ▯(½m) ♫(½m)
🅿(½m)

Min£65 Max£80pw

LEEK
Staffordshire
Map7 SJ95

H Fould Farm Leekfrith (3m N)
for bookings Mrs G Heath, Red Earth
Farm, Rudyard, Leek, Staffordshire
☎Rudyard(053833)639

Two units, one with one double and two
twin-bedded rooms, the other with one
double and one family rooms, in a large,
early 17th-century farmhouse set in
elevated position in peaceful,
picturesque surroundings. The house
has been renovated and refurbished to a
high standard and provides spacious,
comfortable accommodation in fully fitted
kitchens, lounges, separate dining
rooms, modern bathrooms and WCs. 2m
NE of Leek on Meerbrook road.

All year MWB out of season 1wk min,
1mth max, 2units, 5–6persons ◊ ◆
◎ fridge 🍴 Elec inclusive
⌷not provided ☎ WM in unit SD in
unit Airing cupboard in unit Iron in unit
Ironing board in unit HCE in unit ☉
CTV ⊕3pin square P ⚑ 🆄 ⚑(1¼m)

⊖ ☒(2m) ⚲(1m) ▯(2m) ♫(2m)
🅿(2m)

Min£45 Max£100pw

C Lowe Hill Cottage No 1, Lowe Hill
Farm, Ashbourne Road, Leek,
Staffordshire
☎Leek(0538)383035

At the end of a row of three stone-built
terraced cottages (approximately 200
years old), in fairly peaceful location. ¾
mile S of Leek just off A523. The cottage
has been tastefully modernised and has
simple but clean décor with
accommodation comprising
kitchen/diner, lounge with exposed
ceiling beam and natural stonework.
Upstairs there is a family bedroom, a
small double bedroom and
bathroom/WC.

All year MWB 2days min, 1unit,
5persons ◎ no pets ◎ fridge
Electric & open fires Elec metered
⌷can be hired ☎(¼m) Airing
cupboard Iron in unit Ironing board in
unit HCE in unit TV ⊕3pin square
3P 🆄 ⚑(½m) ⌂ 🐾 🐕

⊕ ♂(2m) ♀(¼m) 🖥(1m) 🐾(1m)
Min£35 Max£45pw (Low)
Min£55 Max£85pw (High)

LEGBOURNE
Lincolnshire
Map 9 TF38

C Millers Cottage Mill Lane
for bookings Mr R B Hutchinson, Coach
Road End, Burton, Lincoln, Lincolnshire
LN1 2RB
☎Lincoln(0522)22556

*Fully modernised, two-storey cottage on
the opposite bank of the mill race to
Legbourne Mill, just a walk away from the
village pub. Well equipped, the cottage
has a sitting room, separate
kitchen/diner, two double bedrooms, one
single bedroom, bathroom and shower
room.*

All year MWB out of season 1wk min,
1unit, 1–5persons [◇] ◆ ◆ ◉
fridge 🍴 Elec metered ⬜can be
hired ☎ Airing cupboard in unit Iron in
unit Ironing board in unit HCE in unit
CTV can be hired ⊕3pin square 2P
⚓(¼m) Trout fishing
⊕ ♂(3m) ♀(¼m)

LEIGHTON
Shropshire
Map 7 SJ60

C Garmston Farm Cottage
for bookings Mr R B Henderson,
Garmston Farm, Leighton, Shrewsbury,
Shropshire
☎Cressage(095289)246

*Two-storey, brick-built cottage with
beautiful rural views at front, situated on
the proprietor's farm. The ground floor
comprises lounge and kitchen, while on
the first floor there are three bedrooms,
one double, one twin and one single, and
a bathroom with WC.*

10Apr–10Sep 1wk min, 1mth max,
1unit, 5persons ◇ no pets ◉ fridge
🍴 Elec inclusive ⬜inclusive ☎
Airing cupboard in unit Iron in unit
Ironing board in unit HCE in unit ⊙
CTV ⊕3pin square 2P 🖥 ⚓(2½m)
Fishing available
⊕ ♀(¼m)

LELANT
Cornwall
Map 2 SW53

Ch Trust House Forte Leisure Ltd **St
Ives Holiday Village** Lelant, St Ives,
Cornwall TR26 3HX
☎Hayle(0736)752000

*This holiday village consists of stone and
cedar-clad chalets each with two
bedrooms, lounge/kitchen, bathroom
and WC. The chalets are well furnished
and well sited in woodland.*

26Mar–29Oct MWB out of season
4wks max, 300units, 2–6persons ◇
◆ no pets ◉ fridge Electric
Elec metered ⬜inclusive ☎ Airing
cupboard in unit [Iron on premises]
[Ironing board on premises]
[Launderette on premises] ⊙ ⊛
CTV ⊕3pin square ⊕2pin round
300P ⚓ 🖂
⊕ ♀
Min£35 Max£52pw (Low)
Min£170 Max£200pw (High)

LENDALFOOT
Strathclyde *Ayrshire*
Map 10 NX19

C Gull Cottage
for bookings Mrs M M Hay, Bon Accord,
50 Dalrymple Street, Girvan, Ayrshire
KA26 9BT
☎Girvan(0465)4421

*Modernised stone-cottage located on the
foreshore with splendid views over Firth
of Forth and Ailsa Craig. Attractive
beamed split-level lounge/diner with
open stairway leading to two twin bedded
rooms. Modern kitchen and bathroom on
ground floor.*

All year 1wk min, 1mth max, 1unit,
2–4persons ◇ ◆ ◉ fridge
Electric Elec metered ⬜not provided
☎(150yds) Iron in unit Ironing board in
unit HCE in unit ⊛ ⊕3pin square
3P ⚓(150yds)
Min£75 Max£140pw

B Meidlum Holiday Site
for bookings Manager, Meidlum
Holidays, 40 Manor Close, Sherston,
Malmesbury, Wilts SN16 0NS
☎Sherston(066649)694

*Four small bungalows each comprising
sitting room with bed-settee, kitchen,
bathroom and two bedrooms. On A77 7m
S of Girvan 100 yards from shore.*

Mar–Oct MWB out of season
wknd min, 4mths max, 3units,
1–6persons [◇] [◆] ◉ fridge
Electric Elec metered ⬜inclusive
☎(200yds) Airing cupboard in unit
HCE in unit ⊙ CTV ⊕3pin square P
🖥 ⚓(200yds)
Min£57.50 Max£69pw (Low)
Min£184 Max£201.25pw (High)

LENTRAN
Highland *Inverness-shire*
Map 14 NG54

Ch Pine Chalets Newton Hill
for bookings Mr A Chisholm, 'Fernlea',
Kirkhill, Inverness, Inverness-shire
☎Drumchardine(046383)619

*Five wooden chalets set amongst mature
trees with panoramic views. Units
comprise kitchen, living/dining room with
two narrow convertible beds, two
double/twin bedrooms and bathrooms.
Reached by unclassified road from A9.*

Mar–Oct MWB out of season 1wk min,
5units, 1–6persons ◇ ◆ ◉ fridge
Electric Elec metered ⬜inclusive
☎(1m) Airing cupboard in unit Iron in
unit Ironing board in unit HCE in unit
⊙ TV ⊕3pin square 12P ⚓(5m)
⊕ ♀(1m)
Min£50 Max£70pw (Low)
Min£80 Max£120pw (High)

LEOMINSTER
Hereford & Worcester
Map 3 SO45

F Stable House
for bookings The Lady Cawley, Bircher
Hall, Leominster, Herefordshire
☎Yarpole(056885)218

*A recently modernised stable block
comprising a reception hall and WC with
wash hand basin on the ground-floor,* →

and a twin-bedded room, a single-bedded room; bathroom, kitchen and lounge on the first floor.

All year 1wk min, 6mths max, 1unit, 1–3 persons no dogs ⊚ fridge ▥ & wood burning stove Elec metered ⌸ can be hired ☎ WM SD Airing cupboard Iron HCE ⊖ TV can be hired ③3pin square 2P ♨(1½m)

↤ ♀(1½m)

Min£40 Max£100pw

F West Wing
for bookings The Lady Cawley, Bircher Hall, Leominster, Herefordshire
☎Yarpole(056885)218

A fully modernised unit set within the confines of Bircher Hall. It has a private entrance leading into a lobby, with WC and wash hand basin, kitchen/diner, lounge. The first floor comprises three twin bedrooms and large bathroom.

All year 1wk min, 6mths max, 1unit, 1–6 persons, nc6 ◆ ◇ ⊚ fridge ▥ Elec metered ⌸ can be hired ☎(1m) SD in unit Airing cupboard in unit Iron in unit Ironing board in unit HCE in unit ⊖ TV can be hired ③3pin square 2P ♨(1m)

↤ ♀(1½m)

Min£30 Max£90pw

Leominster
—
Lerags

LERAGS
Strathclyde Argyll
Map 10 NM82

B Mr S Woodman **Cologin Homes Ltd**
Lerags, Oban, Argyll
☎Oban(0631)64501

Modern timber clad bungalows, eleven detached and four semi-detached, located in small glen south of Oban amidst highland scenery. The eleven detached bungalows comprise one twin, one double-bedded room, kitchen/lounge/diner (with sofa bed) and bathroom. The other four comprise one twin-bedded room, shower/WC and lounge/diner/kitchen, with additional sofa bed in the lounge. There is a bar with all day buffet, games room and farm animals on site.

All year MWB out of season 1day min, 5wks max, 15units, 1–7 persons [◇] ◆ ◆ ⊚ fridge Electric Elec inclusive ⌸ inclusive ☎ Airing cupboard in unit Iron on premises Ironing board on premises HCE in unit [Launderette on premises] ⊖ CTV ③3pin square P ♨ Bicycles, fishing & boating

↤ ᴥ(3m) ♀ ▣ ♫(3m) ▨(3m)

Min£62 Max£172pw

Ch Mr & Mrs D Wren **Lag-na-Keil Chalets (Oban) Ltd** Lerags, Oban, Argyll PA34 4SE
☎Oban(0631)62746

Four different types of chalet, all with either bath or shower and separate or open-plan kitchen/living room as required. Pleasant situation on sloping ground with picturesque views of hills and Loch Feochan in the distance. Reached by heading south of Oban on the A816 for 2m, then turning right (signposted Lerags) along a single track road for 1½m.

Mar-Oct MWB out of season 1wk min, 4wks max, 19units, 1–8 persons ◆ ⊚ fridge Electric Elec metered ⌸ can be hired ☎ Airing cupboard in unit Iron on premises HCE ⊖ TV ③3pin square P ▥ ♨

↤ ♀(3m) ▣(3m) ▨(3m)

Min£69 Max£115pw (Low)
Min£103.50 Max£149.50pw (High)

F Miss E Lees-Whittick **Larags Beag**
Lerags, Oban, Argyll PA34 4SE
☎Oban(0631)62450

Large flat on first-floor of owner's cottage. Consists of a sitting room, dining room, two double bedrooms (one with extra divan), two single bedrooms, two bathrooms and kitchen. The flat is tastefully furnished and commands fine views across Loch Feochan. Set in the grounds of Lerags House, 3m down a

---

*single-track road 2m S of Oban on A816.
Additional charge made for central
heating.*

All year MWB out of season wknd min,
1 unit, 1–7 persons ◇ ◆ no pets ◉
fridge ♨ Elec metered ⌷ can be
hired ☎(1½m) [WM on premises]
Airing cupboard in unit Iron in unit
Ironing board in unit HCE in unit ⊕
CTV can be hired ③3 pin round P
♨(5m)

⊖ ♀(2m)

Min£40pw Max£150pw

LESNEWTH
Cornwall
Map **2** SX19

C   Courtyard Cottages
for bookings Mr & Mrs A Tomkinson, The
Courtyard Farm, Lesnewth, Boscastle,
Cornwall
☎ Otterham Station(084 06)256

*The cottages are conversions from old
farm and mill buildings some 200 years
old, built of Cornish stone and slate round
an attractive courtyard. There are seven
cottages of varying sizes, most of which
have panoramic views to the sea. Follow
B3266 from Boscastle towards
Camelford, turn left after Tredorh farm,
follow signs to Lesnewth. Courtyard Farm
is near church.*

All year MWB out of season wknd min,
1 mth max, 7 units, 2–9 persons [◇] ◆
◆ no pets ◉ fridge
Electric(heating free) Elec metered
⌷ can be hired ☎ [WM on premises]
[SD on premises] [TD on premises]
Airing cupboard in unit Iron in unit
Ironing board in unit HCE in unit ⊕
CTV ③3 pin square ②2 pin round P
▥ ♨(2½m) ♪

⊖ ♀ Games room, badminton court &
riding

Min£60 Max£100pw (Low)
Min£170 Max£250pw (High)

LETHEN
Highland *Nairn*
Map **14** NH95

C   1,2,3 & 4 Braeside Cottages
for bookings The Factor, Estate Office,
Lethen, Nairn IV12 5PR
☎ Nairn(0667)52247

*Row of cottages situated on Lethen
Estate with magnificent views of the
Moray Firth and surrounding mountains.
Cottages sleep between four and six
persons in twin-bedded rooms with
lounge (with bed-settee), kitchen and
bathroom.*

Apr-Sep MWB out of season 1 wk min,
4 units, 1–6 persons [◆] ◉ fridge
Electric Elec metered ⌷ not provided
☎(1m) Iron in unit Ironing board in
unit HCE in unit ⊕ ③3 pin square P
♨(3m)

⊖ ♀(3m)

Min£27 Max£40pw (Low)
Min£55 Max£70pw (High)

Lerags
—
Leysmill

C   Dulsie Cottage
for bookings The Factor, Estate Office,
Lethen, Nairn IV12 5PR
☎ Nairn(0667)52247

*Cottage ideally situated for a fishing
holiday, with two twin-bedded rooms,
lounge with a bed-settee, kitchen and
bathroom.*

Apr-Sep MWB out of season 1 wk min,
1 unit, 1–6 persons [◇] ◉ fridge
Electric Elec metered ⌷ not provided
☎ Iron in unit Ironing board in unit
HCE in unit ③3 pin square P ♨(6m)
Fishing

Min£45 Max£50pw (Low)
Min£75 Max£95pw (High)

C   Easter Clune & Garrowstrype
for bookings The Factor, Estate Office,
Lethen, Nairn IV12 5PR
☎ Nairn(0667)52247

*Two small cottages set in quiet secluded
part of estate amidst wood and farmland
with fine views across rolling countryside
to Moray Firth. Both have two bedrooms,
lounge with bed-settee, kitchen and
bathroom (shower in* **Easter Clune***).*

Apr-Sep MWB out of season 1 wk min,
2 units, 4–6 persons ◆ ◉ fridge
Electric & coal fires Elec metered
⌷ not provided ☎(1½m) Iron in unit
Ironing board in unit HCE
③3 pin square 2P ♨(3m)

⊖ ♀(3m)

H   Lethen Mill House
for bookings The Factor, Estate Office,
Lethen, Nairn IV12 5PR
☎ Nairn(0667)52247

*Large house with simple but spacious
accommodation comprising three
bedrooms, one on the ground-floor, living
room, kitchen with dining area, bathroom.
The house lies at a country road junction
near to the Estate's small saw mill.*

Apr-Sep MWB out of season 1 wk min,
1 unit, 1–6 persons ◆ ◉ fridge
Electric & coal fires Elec metered
⌷ not provided ☎(100yds) Airing
cupboard in unit Iron in unit Ironing
board in unit HCE in unit
③3 pin square 2P 1♨ ♨(3m)

⊖ ♀(3m)

LEVINGTON
Suffolk
Map **5** TM23

H   Bridge Farm
for bookings W R Dellar, Stratton Hall,
Levington, Ipswich, Suffolk
☎ Nacton(047 388)218

*Wing of a large farmhouse occupying an
isolated position overlooking a meadow
and wooded area. It forms part of a
private stable yard with accommodation
comprising lounge, kitchen, dining room
and bathroom/WC. There are three
bedrooms on the first-floor.*

All year MWB out of season 4 days min,
5 mths max, 1 unit, 1–5 persons ◆ ◉
fridge ♨ Elec metered ⌷ can be
hired ☎(1½m) Airing cupboard in unit
Iron in unit Ironing board in unit HCE in
unit TV ③3 pin square 2P ▥
♨(1½m) Horse riding

⊖ ♀(1½m)

Min£52.94 Max£129.41pw

C   1 & 2 Heath Cottages
for bookings W R Dellar, Stratton Hall,
Levington, Ipswich, Suffolk
☎ Nacton(047 388)218

*These brick-built semi-detached
cottages are situated behind a small
coppice in a 100-acre agricultural block,
300yds from the main A45. Each
comprises three bedrooms,
bathroom/WC, kitchen/diner and lounge.
Cottage no 1 has a double bedroom on
the ground-floor.*

All year MWB out of season 4 days min,
5 mths max, 2 units, 1–6 persons ◆ ◉
fridge Electric & open fires
Elec metered ⌷ can be hired ☎(1½m)
Airing cupboard in unit Iron in unit
Ironing board in unit HCE in unit TV
③3 pin square 6P ▥ ♨(1½m)

⊖ ♀(1½m)

Min£52.94 Max£129.41pw

C   Stratton Hall Cottages
for bookings W R Dellar, Stratton Hall,
Levington, Ipswich, Suffolk
☎ Nacton(047 388)218

*Semi-detached cottages standing in the
heart of a rural area overlooking the
surrounding countryside to the River
Orwell. Accommodation comprises
lounge, kitchen, dining room and
bathroom/WC; three bedrooms on the
first-floor (one double, one twin and one
single-bedded).*

All year MWB out of season 4 days min,
5 mths max, 3 units, 1–5 persons ◆ ◉
fridge Electric Elec metered ⌷ can be
hired ☎(1½m) Airing cupboard in unit
Iron in unit Ironing board in unit HCE in
unit TV ③3 pin square 2P ▥
♨(1½m)

⊖ ♀(1½m)

Min£52.94 Max£129.41pw

LEYSMILL
Tayside *Angus*
Map **15** NO64

C   Quarry House
for bookings Mrs A M Ephraums,
Damside, Leysmill, Arbroath, Angus
DD11 4RS
☎ Friockheim(024 12)226

*Detached two-storey stone cottage in the
grounds of a private house. There is a
living/dining room, kitchen, sitting room
with single convertible settee, bathroom,
a twin-bedded room and a room with
bunks or single beds. There is a
woodland garden and a paved patio. →*

1982 prices quoted throughout
gazetteer

All year 1wk min, 1unit, 1–5persons
◆ no pets ◉ fridge Electric & open
fires Elec inclusive ⌷can be hired
☎(400yds) WM in unit SD in unit
Airing cupboard in unit Iron in unit
Ironing board in unit HCE in unit ☺
TV can be hired ⊕3pin square P ♠
▥ ♨(2m)
⊷ ♀(2m)
Min£25 Max£35pw (Low)
Min£65 Max£85pw (High)

LISKEARD
Cornwall
Map2 SX26

B Rosecraddoc Manor Holiday Bungalows
for bookings Mrs G Poole, 45 Dillotford
Avenue, Stivichall, Coventry, W Midlands
☎Coventry(0203)415364

Three bungalows set in the grounds of a
small country house estate, the gardens
of which are thought to have been laid out
by Capability Brown. No11 is semi-
detached and comprises lounge/diner
and kitchen, one double bedroom and
another room with a single bed and bunk
beds, bathroom/WC. No33 has
lounge/diner, kitchen, one double
bedroom, one twin bedroom and
bathroom/WC. No34 has lounge/diner
and kitchen, one double bedroom, one
room with twin and bunk beds and
bathroom/WC. Nos 11, 33 & 34 each have
a bed-settee.

Mar-Dec MWB out of season 6wks min,
3units, 1–6persons ◆ ◆ ◉ fridge
Electric Elec metered ⌷not provided
☎ SD in unit Airing cupboard in unit
Iron in unit Ironing board in unit ☺
CTV ⊕3pin square 1P ♨(2m)
⊷ ♀(2m) ▥(2m) ♫(2m)
Min£50 Max£140pw

LITTLE COMPTON
Warwickshire
Map4 SP23

C B J Coleman The Barn Cottage
Grey Goose, Little Compton, Moreton-in-
Marsh, Gloucestershire
☎Barton-on-the-Heath(060874)310

120-year-old detached cottage standing
in own grounds with pleasant views over
surrounding countryside. Ground-floor
comprises sitting room and separate
kitchen/diner; first-floor, one double
bedroom, one twin, one single and
bathroom/WC.

Mar-Dec 1unit, 2–5persons [◇] ◉
fridge ♨ Elec metered
⌷not provided Airing cupboard in unit
Iron in unit Ironing board in unit HCE in
unit TV ⊕3pin square P ♨(4m)
⊷ ♀(200yds)

Leysmill
—
Little Longstone

LITTLEHAM
Devon
Map2 SS42

C 1 Boundstone Cottage
for bookings Mrs R M Stevens,
Panoramic House, Littleham, Bideford,
Devon
☎Bideford(02372)4382

Modern cottage in terrace of three with
small front and large rear garden. Good
plain décor and modern furnishings
comprising lounge/diner, large kitchen,
three bedrooms, one with bunks and one
single, one double room and one double
plus a single. Bathroom with WC and a
separate WC on ground floor.

All year MWB out of season 3days min,
3mths max, 1unit, 1–8persons [◇] ◆
◆ no pets ◉ fridge ♨ & Log fire
Elec metered ⌷not provided
☎(20yds) Airing cupboard in unit Iron
in unit Ironing board in unit HCE in unit
☺ TV ⊕3pin square 2P 1♠ ▥
♨(½m)
⊷ ♀(200yds) ♫(3m)
Min£40 Max£90pw (Low)
Min£115 Max£160pw (High)

H Boundstone Farmhouse
for bookings Mrs R M Stevens,
Panoramic House, Littleham, Bideford,
Devon
☎Bideford(02372)4382

Pleasant, well-kept house adjacent to
farm in rural surroundings.
Accommodation comprises lounge and
dining room with traditional furniture, two
kitchens with good units, bathroom and
WC plus outside WC. Two single
bedrooms, one double bedroom, and
two bedrooms each with a double and
single bed.

All year MWB out of season 2wks min,
8wks max, 1unit, 1–12persons [◇] ◆
◆ no pets ◉ fridge Log & electric
fires Elec metered ⌷not provided
☎(60yds) Airing cupboard in unit Iron
in unit Ironing board in unit HCE in unit
TV ⊕3pin square ⊕3pin round P
♠ ▥ ♨(800yds)
⊷ ♀(2½m)
Min£40 Max£90pw (Low)
Min£115 Max£170pw (High)

C Cherry Tree Cottage
for bookings Mrs R M Stevens,
Panoramic House, Littleham, Bideford,
Devon
☎Bideford(02372)4382

Well-maintained 18th-century cottage.
Ground floor comprises lounge/dining
room (with beamed ceiling, traditional
furniture and open log fire), kitchen with
modern units, double bedroom, separate
bathroom and WC. First floor comprises
twin-bedded room, double-bedded room
with extra single bed and single
bedroom.

All year MWB out of season 2wks min,
8wks max, 1unit, 1–8persons [◇] ◆
◆ no pets ◉ fridge Log & electric
fires Elec metered ⌷can be hired
☎(30yds) Airing cupboard in unit Iron
Ironing board HCE TV ⊕3pin round
P ▥ ♨(500yds)
⊷ ♀(2½m)
Min£30 Max£65pw (Low)
Min£85 Max£130pw (High)

LITTLEHAMPTON
West Sussex
Map4 TQ00

Ch Mr J A Sinclair Canadian Village
Rope Walk, Littlehampton, W Sussex
BN17 5DE
☎Littlehampton(09064)3816

Eighteen modern, one, two or three
bedroomed chalets with lounge/diner,
kitchen, bathroom and WC. (One other
chalet on site does not conform to AA
requirements.) Near to golf course,
twelve minutes' walk from beach and
town centre. On the west bank of the
River Arun off the A259.

All year MWB 18units, 1–6persons
◆ ◆ no pets ◉ fridge Electric
Elec metered ⌷can be hired ☎ Iron
in unit Ironing board in unit HCE in unit
☺ TV ⊕3pin square P ▥
♨(600yds)
⊷ ♨ ♀(300yds) ▧(2½m) ♫(2½m)
Min£36 Max£60pw (Low)
Min£48 Max£175pw (High)

LITTLEHAVEN
Dyfed
Map2 SM81

F Haven Court
for bookings Mr K H Walters, Haven
Court, Little Haven, Haverfordwest,
Dyfed SA62 3UP
☎Broad Haven(043783)264

Well-facilitated holiday flats in sheltered
position in village. Three-bedroomed
maisonettes and two-bedroomed flats.
All have open-plan lounge, dining room,
kitchen and bathroom.

May–2 Oct MWB out of season
1 wk min 21 units 2–10persons [◇]
[◆] [◆] no pets ◉ fridge ♨
Electric Elec metered ⌷inclusive ☎
Airing cupboard in unit Iron on
premises Ironing board on premises
HCE in unit Launderette on premises
CTV ⊕3pin square P ▥
♨(200yds) Recreation room
⊷ ♀(100yds)
Min£55.20 Max£95.45pw (Low)
Min£170.20 Max£216.20pw (High)

LITTLE LONGSTONE
Derbyshire
Map7 SK17

C Leverets
for bookings Mrs H D Longsdon, The
Manor, Little Longstone, Bakewell,
Derbyshire
☎Great Longstone(062987)215

A typical Derbyshire stone cottage, in centre of village, with parking behind the cottage. There is a lounge, dining room and kitchen on the ground floor; three bedrooms (one double, one twin and a single) and bathroom with WC on the first floor.

All year MWB only 1wk min, 1 unit, 1–5 persons no pets ⊚ fridge ♨ plus Electric & open fires Elec metered ⊡ not provided ☎ Airing cupboard in unit Iron in unit Ironing board in unit HCE in unit CTV ⊕3pin square 2P 🛏 ♨(¾m) ↔ ♿(3m) ♀(100yds) Min£60 Max£130pw

LITTON
Derbyshire
Map 7 SK17

C Dale Cottage
for bookings Mrs A Barnsley, Dale House Farm, Litton, Buxton, Derbys SK17 8QL ☎Tideswell(0298)871309

An end stone-built cottage with accommodation on first floor level. Compact, with lounge (which has convertible), separate kitchen, two bedrooms off lounge (one double and one single). Good situation for touring the Peak District.

Mar–Sep MWB out of season 1wk min, 1mth max, 1 unit, 2–4 persons no pets ⬭ fridge Gas & Electric Gas/Elec metered ⊡ not provided ☎(¼m) Airing cupboard in unit Iron in unit HCE in unit ⊙ TV ⊕3pin square P 🛏 🛏 ♨(¼m) ↔ ♀(¼m)

LIZARD
Cornwall
Map 2 SW71

F Mr K Williams Penmenner House Hotel The Lizard, Cornwall TR12 7NR ☎The Lizard(0326)290370

Flats 1, 2 & 3 are adjacent to the hotel and comprise lounge, kitchen, bath and WC, two double (apart from the third flat which only has one), and one twin-bedded room. Use of hotel gardens and facilities.

Apr–Oct MWB out of season 1wk min,

3 units, 1–6 persons [◇] ◈ ◆ ◎ fridge Electric Elec metered ⊡ not provided ☎ Airing cupboard in unit Iron in unit Ironing board in unit HCE in unit ⊙ TV ⊕3pin square 1P 🛏 ♨(¼m) ⬭ ↔ ♀(¼m) ⊠(¼m) Min£50 Max£130pw

LLANDANWG
Gwynedd
Map 6 SH52

B Mordan Llandanwg Caravan Park
for bookings J & P G Conolly, 10 Frampton Way, Great Barr, Birmingham B43 7UH ☎021–360 8199

Semi-detached bungalow overlooking Tremadog Bay, consisting of one double bedroom, one twin with wash hand basin, kitchen/diner and bathroom/WC. 1½m from Harlech on A496.

6 Mar–22 Oct 1wk min, 1mth max, 1 unit, 4–6 persons no pets ⊚ fridge Electric Elec metered ⊡ not provided ☎(30yds) Airing cupboard in unit Iron in unit ⊙ ⊕3pin square P 🛏 ↔ ♨(1½m) ♀(1½m) ⊠(1½m) Min£32 Max£50pw (Low) Min£54 Max£89pw (High)

LLANDUDNO
Gwynedd
Map 6 SH78

F Mr N Robinson Augusta Holiday Flats 5–11 Augusta Street, Llandudno, Gwynedd ☎Llandudno(0492)78330

Town house converted into holiday flats near to town centre. Ample parking in forecourt. Residential manageress.

Apr–Oct MWB out of season 2 days min, 3mths max, 39 units, 1–8 persons [◇] ◈ ◆ No large School groups ⊚ fridge Electric Elec metered ⊡ inclusive ☎ Airing cupboard in unit Iron on premises Ironing board on premises [Launderette within 300yds] ⊙ CTV

⊕3pin square 14P 🛏(50yds) ↔ ♨(1m) ♀(50yds) ⊠(400yds) ♫(400yds) 🐾(300yds) Min£30 Max£64pw (Low) Min£69 Max£145pw (High)

F Conway Court Vaughan Street
for bookings Mr G Robinson, Flat 8, Conway Court, Vaughan Street, Llandudno, Gwynedd LL30 1AH ☎Llandudno(0492)83884

Six luxury self-contained holiday flats in the town centre consisting of kitchen/diner, separate lounge with bed-settee or pulldown bed, bathroom and WC. Four flats have two bedrooms, each with double and single beds, while two flats have one room with a double and a single bed.

All year MWB Etr only 6 units, 5–8 persons ◈ ◆ ◎ fridge Electric Elec metered ⊡ inclusive ☎ Airing cupboard in unit HCE in unit [Launderette within 300yds] ⊙ CTV ⊕3pin square 🛏(5yds) ↔ ♨(2m) ♀(10yds) ⊠(¼m) ♫(¼m) 🐾(¼m) Min£55 Max£80pw (Low) Min£115 Max£160pw (High)

H Waters Edge West Parade, West Shore
for bookings Mr E J Carter, The Pines, Brokencote, Chaddesley Corbett, Kidderminster, Worcs ☎Chaddesley Corbett(056 283)210

A detached house overlooking the bay on the west shore. There is a separate TV lounge, WC and kitchen/diner on the ground floor and WC, separate bathroom, one twin-bedded room and two bedrooms with one double and a single bed. ¾m from town centre.

Mar–Oct 1wk min, 3wks max, 1 unit, 8 persons ◎ no pets ⊚ fridge ♨ Gas inclusive Elec metered ⊡ not provided ☎(300yds) Airing cupboard in unit [Launderette within 300yds] ⊙ CTV ⊕3pin square P 🛏 🛏(300yds) ↔ ♨(¼m) ♀(300yds) ⊠(¾m) 🐾(¾m) Min£75 Max£100pw (Low) Min£150 Max£200pw (High)

153

LLANDUDNO JUNCTION
Gwynedd
Map **6** SH87

C Castle Keep & Gwyrfai Cottages
Glan Conwy Corner
for bookings Mr A E Mardon, Gateway
Cottages, 5 Prestwick Drive, Liverpool
L23 7XB
☎051–924 6996

*Two architect-designed conversions of
typical Welsh cottages.* **Castle Keep**
*comprises open-plan lounge/kitchen,
three bedrooms, one double and two
twin-bedded and bathroom/WC.*
Gwyrfai *has lounge, kitchen, two
bedrooms with twin beds and
bathroom/WC. Both have views across
the River Conwy.*

All year MWB out of season 2 units,
4–6 persons no pets in Gwyrfai ⊚
fridge ᕯ Gas/Elec metered
⬛not provided ☎(½m) Airing cupboard
in unit HCE in unit CTV
⊕3 pin square P ▥ ♨(½m)
⊛ ♀(½m) ▨(3m)

Min£50 Max£80pw (Low)
Min£80 Max£130pw (High)

LLANDWROG
Gwynedd
Map **6** SH45

C 1 Tyn-y-Maes Cesarea
for bookings Rev E Plaxton, St John's
Vicarage, Belmont Rise, Belmont, Sutton,
Surrey SM2 6EA
☎01–642 2363

*Semi-detached stone-built cottage
comprising lounge, dining room, kitchen,
bathroom/WC. There are two double-
bedded rooms and a loft suitable for
children with two single beds. From
Caernarfon follow A487 Porthmadog
road through Bontewydd, then take first
turning left, signposted Rhostryfan,
Rhosgadfan and Cesarea. Turn left at
Cesarea village green after PO, pass
school on right and chapel on left. Last
house on left set back from road.*

All year MWB out of season 1 wk min,
4 wks max, 1 unit, 4–6 persons ◇ ⊚
fridge Electric & open fires
Elec metered ⬛not provided ☎ SD in
unit Airing cupboard in unit Iron in unit

Ironing board in unit HCE in unit TV
⊕3 pin square P ▨ ▥ ♨(200yds)
⊛ ♀(300yds)
Min£45 Max£55pw (Low)
Min£60 Max£85pw (High)

LLANDYFRYDOG
Gwynedd
Map **6** SH48

C Ty Refail Capel Parc
for bookings Mrs M A Riley, 34 Redland
Crescent, Chorlton-cum-Hardy,
Manchester M21 2DL
☎061–881 8045

*Traditional early 18th-century stone
cottage with own gardens comprising
kitchen/diner, childrens play room,
lounge with open fire,
bathroom/shower/WC, and one double,
one family bedroom on the ground-floor;
one twin-bedded room on the first-floor.*

Etr–midOct 1 wk min, 4 wks max, 1 unit,
1–8 persons [◇] ◇ ◆ ⊚ fridge
Electric Elec metered ⬛not provided
Iron on premises Ironing board on
premises HCE on premises ⊛ TV can
be hired ⊕3 pin square 4P ▥ ♨(2m)
⊛ ♀(2m)
Min£90 Max£140pw

LLANDYSSUL
Dyfed
Map **2** SN44

H The Castell & Granary Llwyndafydd
Road
for bookings Mr B Williams, Aston Street,
Shifnal, Shropshire
☎Telford(0952)460056

*Two houses quietly set in an unspoilt
valley with a trout stream and 14 acres of
private woodland. The Castell is an
interesting old stone building restored to
a high standard with large lounge
containing log-burning stove, well-fitted
kitchen, breakfast bar, two twin-bedded
rooms and two double-bedded rooms,
bathroom/shower and WC. The Granary
is a unique house with a particularly large
sitting room (also containing log-burning*

---

*stove), separate dining room and large
well-fitted kitchen and open staircase
from the sitting room leads to two family
bedrooms, a double bedroom and
bathroom/WC.*

All year MWB out of season 3 days min,
2 units, 2–8 persons ◇ ◆ no pets
⊚ fridge Electric & log stove
Elec metered ⬛inclusive ☎(200yds)
WM in unit SD in unit Airing cupboard
in unit Iron in unit Ironing board in unit
HCE in unit ⊕ CTV ⊕3 pin square P
♨(½m)
⊛ ♀(½m)

LLANENGAN
Gwynedd
Map **6** SH32

C Tyn Don Holiday Cottages Tyn Don
Farm
for bookings Mrs M J Bailey, 18 Russell
Drive, Riverslea, Christchurch, Dorset
☎Bournemouth(0202)486630

*Five self-contained cottages with
spacious rooms, beamed ceilings, open-
plan pine staircase and modern
furnishings including pine tables and
chairs. Four of the cottages have showers
the other a bathroom.*

Feb–Nov MWB out of season wknd min,
5 units, 5–8 persons ◇ ◆ ⊚ fridge
Electric Elec metered ⬛not provided
☎(1m) Airing cupboard in unit Iron in
unit Ironing board in unit HCE in unit
⊕ TV ⊕3 pin square P ▥ ♨(1m)
⊛ ♀(1m)

Min£46 Max£58pw (Low)
Min£130 Max£155pw (High)

LLANFAIRFECHAN
Gwynedd
Map **6** SH67

C, Ch, F Mrs E Kenyon **Queens House**
Llanfairfechan, Gwynedd
☎Llanfairfechan(0248)680509

*Two wood-built chalets and six stone-
built units (two flats, two cottages and two
maisonettes). All units have lounge/diner
with bed-settee, kitchenette or separate
kitchen, bathroom/WC except the
maisonettes which have a lounge with
bed-settee, kitchen/diner and
bathroom/WC.*

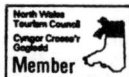

All year(Chalet 1 & 2 Mar-Nov) MWB out of season 4 days min, 8 units, 4–6 persons [◇] ◈ ◆ ◉ fridge Electric Elec metered ⊡inclusive ☎ Airing cupboard on premises Iron on premises Ironing board on premises HCE in unit [Launderette within 300 yds] TV ⊕3 pin square P ▥ ▲(100 yds)

⊖ ♿(100 yds)

Min£40 Max£75 pw (Low)
Min£60 Max£113 pw (High)

F   Yenton Holiday Flats Promenade
for bookings Mr Bordoni, The Windsor, Promenade, Llanfairfechan, Gwynedd
☎Llanfairfechan(0248)680075

Two detached houses on the promenade facing the beach which provide six flats with lounge/diner, shower and WC, combined and sleeping accommodation for four, a 'Z' bed is available for the lounge.

All year MWB out of season 1 wk min, 6 units, 2–4 persons [◇] ◈ ◆ ◉ fridge Electric Elec metered ⊡inclusive ☎ Airing cupboard in unit HCE on premises [Launderette within 300 yds] TV ⊕3 pin square ▥ ▲(20 yds)

⊖ ♿(¼m) ♟(200 yds) 🎫(200 yds) ♫(200 yds)

LLANFAIR WATERDINE
Shropshire
Map**7** SO27

C   Myrtle Cottage
for bookings Mrs A Gwilt, Rose Villa, Llanfair Waterdine, Knighton, Powys
☎Knighton(0547)528511

Semi-detached, stone-built cottage next to the post office. Accommodation comprises lounge, bathroom/WC and kitchen/diner on the ground-floor and two twin-bedded rooms and one double bedroom on the first-floor. Wood-burning stove. Situated in centre of small country village.

All year MWB out of season 1 wk min, 1 mth max, 1 unit, 6 persons [◇] ◈ ◉ fridge Electric Elec inclusive ⊡inclusive ☎ SD in unit Airing cupboard in unit Iron in unit Ironing board in unit HCE in unit TV ⊕3 pin square P ⌂ ▲ Fishing

⊖ ♟(10 yds)

Min£30 Max£40 pw (Low)
Min£50 Max£60 pw (High)

*H   Mrs J M Morgan **Selley Hall*** Llanfair Waterdine, Knighton, Powys LD7 1TR
☎Knighton(0547)528429

A wing of a farmhouse comprising a separate lounge, kitchen/diner, two double-bedded rooms, one twin-bedded room, bathroom and WC. There is also a bed-settee in the lounge.

All year MWB out of season 1 wk min, 1 mth max, 1 unit, 1–6 persons [◇] no pets ◉ fridge Electric Elec metered ⊡not provided ☎(3½m) SD in unit Airing cupboard in unit Iron

Llanfairfechan — Llangrove

in unit Ironing board in unit HCE in unit ☉ TV ⊕3 pin square P ▥ ▲(3½m)

⊖ ♟(2m)

Min£35 Max£70 pw

LLANFYLLIN
Powys
Map**6** SJ11

H   Tyddyn-y-Sais Bwlch-y-Cibau
for bookings Mrs B Evans, Waen Uchaf, Bwlch-y-Cibau, Llanfyllin, Powys
☎Llanfyllin(069 184)577

Traditional Welsh black and white working farmhouse in rural setting. Accommodation comprises two sitting rooms, kitchen/diner, twin bedrooms, shower and WC on ground-floor. Situated on A490 Welshpool-Llanfyllin road.

All year MWB out of season 1 wk min, 6 wks max, 1 unit, 1–9 persons ◈ no pets ◉ fridge Electric & open fires Elec metered ⊡inclusive ☎(100 yds) Airing cupboard in unit Iron in unit Ironing board in unit HCE in unit Launderette on premises ☉ ☯ CTV ⊕3 pin square 4P ▲(100 yds) Free riding available, fishing

⊖ ♟(100 yds) 🎫(3m) ♫(3m)

Min£90 pw (Low)
Min£125 Max£155 pw (High)

LLANGARRON
Hereford & Worcester
Map**3** SO52

C   Langstone Cottage
for bookings Mrs P Amos, Oaklands, Llangarron, Ross-on-Wye, Herefordshire HR9 6NZ
☎Llangarron(098 984)277

A stone-built, semi-detached, two-storey cottage overlooking the surrounding countryside; the ground-floor comprises the kitchen, bathroom, dining room, and lounge. The first-floor has two double bedrooms and one room with three single beds.

All year 3 days min, 8 mths max, 1 unit, 1–7 persons ◈ ◉ fridge ♨ Elec metered ⊡can be hired ☎(1m) WM in unit Airing cupboard in unit Iron in unit Ironing board on premises HCE in unit TV ⊕3 pin square P ▲(1m)

⊖ ♟(1½m)

Min£25 Max£40 pw (Low)
Min£45 Max£115 pw (High)

C   Owls Nest Cottage & The Barn House
for bookings Mrs P Amos, Oaklands, Llangarron, Ross-on-Wye, Herefordshire HR9 6NZ
☎Llangarron(098 984)277

Recently re-built cottages in stone, adjoining farmlands. Both comprise WC, kitchen, lounge and dining room on the ground-floor and one double, one twin, one single bedroom and bathroom on first floor. Fully modernised.

All year 3 days min, 8 mths max, 2 units, 1–6 persons ◈ ◉ fridge ♨ Elec metered ⊡can be hired ☎(400 yds) WM in unit Airing cupboard in unit Iron in unit Ironing board in unit HCE in unit ☉ TV ⊕3 pin square P ⌂ ▥ ▲(700 yds)

⊖ ♟(1m)

Min£25 Max£115 pw

LLANGERNYW
Clwyd
Map**6** SH86

Ch   Mr W Morgan-Jones *Elwy Valley Lodges Ltd* Tu Hwnt Lr Afon, Llangernyw, Abergele, Clwyd LL22 8PH
☎Llangernyw(074 576)216

Modern purpose-built Finnish Lodges. Furnishings and fittings of a high standard. Accommodation comprises lounge/diner, well-equipped kitchen, two twin-bedded rooms, bathroom with separate WC, bed-settee in lounge. From Abergele take A548 to Llanrwst, lodges well signed about 1m from Llangernyw.

Closed Nov MWB out of season 1 wk min, 6 wks max, 15 units, 1–6 persons [◇] ◈ ◆ no pets ◉ fridge ♨ Elec inclusive ⊡inclusive ☎(100 yds) Airing cupboard in unit Iron on premises Ironing board on premises HCE in unit Launderette on premises ☉ ⊕3 pin square 2P ▥ ▲ Salmon fishing

⊖ ♟(2m)

LLANGROVE
Hereford & Worcester
Map**3** SO51

C   The Elms
for bookings Mrs P Amos, Oaklands, Llangarron, Ross-on-Wye, Herefordshire
☎Llangarron(098 984)277

Detached cottage recently modernised to a high standard. There is a large rear garden and patio. Accommodation comprises kitchen, dining room, lounge and WC on the ground-floor, and one single bedroom, one twin, and a double bedroom with combined bathroom on the first floor.

All year 3 days min, 8 mths max, 1 unit, 1–6 persons ◈ ◆ ◉ fridge ♨ Elec metered ⊡can be hired ☎(¼m) WM in unit Airing cupboard in unit Iron Ironing board HCE ☉ [TV] ⊕3 pin square 4P ▥ ▲(¼m)

⊖ ♟(¼m)

Min£40 Max£140 pw

C   Holly Cottage
for bookings Mrs A C Williams, The Nurseries, Llangrove, Ross-on-Wye, Herefordshire
☎Llangarron(098 984)252 →

Two-storey stone-built cottage situated in a quiet undisturbed position. Compact and well-furnished, the accommodation comprises kitchen, bathroom/WC, one single one twin-bedded and two double bedrooms (one with a cot).

All year 1wk min, 4wks max, 1 unit, 1–7 persons ◊ ◎ fridge Electric & open fires Elec metered ⬛not provided ☎(200yds) WM in unit SD in unit Airing cupboard in unit Iron in unit Ironing board in unit HCE in unit TV can be hired ⊕3pin square ⊕3pin round P 🅃 🏛(200yds)

↩ ♀(450yds)

Min£34 Max£97pw

B Valley View
for bookings Mrs A C Williams, The Nurseries, Llangrove, Ross-on-Wye, Herefordshire
☎Llangarron(098 984)252

Leave the A40 (Ross-on-Wye–Monmouth road) at the exit signposted to Whitchurch. On entering the village turn left at signpost for Llangrove. Continue along the lane for 2m and the bungalow is on the left, adjacent to the Nurseries. The pleasantly furnished accommodation consists of kitchen/dining room, lounge, bathroom and WC, one three-bedded room and one double room. Large garden with superb views of the Wye Valley.

All year 1wk min, 4wks max, 1 unit, 1–7 persons ◊ ◎ fridge 🍳 Electric Elec metered ⬛not provided ☎(200yds) Airing cupboard in unit Iron in unit Ironing board in unit HCE in unit TV can be hired ⊕3pin square P 🅃 🏛(200yds)

↩ ♀(450yds)

Min£34 Max£97pw

LLANGUNLLO
Powys
Map**7** SO27

F Mrs B Morgan **Lower Cefnsuran**
Llangunllo, Knighton, Powys LD7 1SL
☎Llangunllo(054 781)219

Self-contained wing of an old farmhouse, situated in its own grounds. Lounge/diner, separate kitchen, large

---

Llangrove
—
Llanrhaeadr-ym-Mochnant

bathroom/WC, family room, one double and one small double room. 4½m off A488, the Knighton–Llandrindod road.

All year MWB out of season wknd min, 1 mth max, 1 unit, 8 persons ◊ ◊ ◆ ◎ fridge 🍳 Elec metered ⬛can be hired ☎ SD in unit TD in unit Airing cupboard in unit Iron in unit Ironing board in unit HCE in unit TV ⊕3pin square P 🏛(1½m) Games room

Min£50 Max£100pw

C 1 Valley View
for bookings Mrs A Deakins, Rhinlas, Llangunllo, Knighton, Powys
☎Llangunllo(054 781)256

Red brick semi-detached signalman's cottage adjacent to Shrewsbury–Swansea line at Llangunllo station, where trains stop on request only. Accommodation consists of two bedrooms, bathroom/WC on first floor and lounge/diner with kitchen off and separate WC on ground floor.

All year MWB out of season 3 days min, 6 wks max, 1 unit, 1–4 persons [◊] ◊ ◆ ◎ fridge 🍳 Elec metered ⬛can be hired ☎(½m) SD in unit Airing cupboard in unit HCE in unit ⊕3pin square 4P 🏛(1½m)

↩ ♀(1½m)

Min£50 Max£75pw

LLANGYBI
Gwynedd
Map**6** SH44

C Gernant
for bookings Mr E J Carter, The Pines, Brokencote, Chaddesley Corbett, Kidderminster, Worcs
☎Chaddesley Corbett(056 283)210

Three-bedroomed semi-detached cottage in country surroundings. Accommodation consists of lounge, kitchen/diner, bathroom/WC. 1m from village.

Mar–Oct 1wk min, 3wks max, 1 unit, 6 persons ◊ ◎ fridge Electric Elec metered ⬛not provided

---

☎(300yds) Airing cupboard in unit Iron in unit Ironing board in unit HCE in unit ⊙ CTV ⊕3pin square 🅃 🏛(1m)

↩ ♀(1m)

LLANGYNIDR
Powys
Map**3** SO11

F Mrs P James **Flats 1 & 2** Penlan, Forge Road, Llangynidr, Crickhowell, Powys
☎Bwlch(0874)730461

Modern, ground and first floor flats with lovely views of river, countryside and mountains beyond. Both comfortable and well maintained. Ground floor flat sleeps two people the first floor sleeps up to six.

All year 1wk min, 2 units, 2–6 persons [◊] ◊ ◆ ◎ fridge Electric Elec metered ⬛can be hired ☎(100yds) SD in unit Iron in unit Ironing board in unit HCE in unit ⊙ TV ⊕3pin square 2P 🏛(100yds)

↩ ♀(½m)

LLANRHAEADR-YM-MOCHNANT
Powys
Map**6** ST12

C No 3 Aber-Rhaeadr Cottage
for bookings Mr M Lucas, 52 Palmerston Road, London SW14
☎01–878 2365

End-of-terrace stone cottage with front door leading directly onto the B4396. The accommodation comprises kitchen/diner, sitting room, two bedrooms (one double- and one twin-bedded) and bathroom/WC. There is a small garden leading down to a stream.

All year 1wk min, 4mths max, 1 unit, 2–5 persons [◊] ◊ ◎ fridge Electric Elec metered ⬛not provided ☎(1m) SD in unit [Airing cupboard in unit] Ironing board in unit HCE in unit CTV ⊕3pin square 1P 🅃 🏛(1m)

↩ ♀(1m)

Min£39 Max£84pw

Llanrug
—
Llawr-y-Glyn

LLANRUG
Gwynedd
Map **6** SH56

F   The Secretary **Bryn Bras Castle**
Llanrug, Caernarfon, Gwynedd LL55 4RE
☎Llanberis(0286)870210

These nine charming flats are located within the imposing castellated wall, turrets and towers of Bryn Bras Castle. This 19th-century building stands amidst graceful gardens and woodlands, pools and statuary, on the foothills of Snowdon, covering a total of 32 acres. Accommodation ranges from three one-bedroomed flats sleeping two to five persons, four two-bedroomed flats sleeping four to five persons and two four-bedroomed flats sleeping five to six. Each flat has its own unique characteristic and all are tastefully furnished and decorated. The Flag Tower has a four-poster bed.

All year   MWB out of season
2 nights min, 1 mth max, 9 units,
2–6 persons   ◇   [◆]   ◎   fridge
Electric   Elec metered   ▣ not provided
☎   HCE in unit   TV   ⊕3pin square   P
▥   ♨(½m)
↭   ♀(½m)
Min£57.50 Max£224.25pw

B   **4 & 5 Craig-y-Dinas**
for bookings Mrs W Williams, 2 Craig-y-Dines Llanrug, Gwynedd
☎Llanberis(0286)870643

Two semi-detached white painted bungalows each having small hall, kitchen, lounge/diner, one double bedroom and one twin-bedded room. Bathroom with coloured suite. Patio area with small rockery garden. Good views of Snowdon. Along A4086 from Llanberis, right on entering Llanrug over two hump backed bridges, turn right.

All year   MWB out of season   1 wk min,
6 wks max, 2 units, 4 persons   ◆   ◆
🛁(no5)   ◎(no4)   fridge   Electric & open fire   Elec metered   ▣ can be hired
☎(½m)   HCE in unit   ⊕   TV
⊕3pin square   2P   ▥   ♨(½m)
↭   ♨(3m)   ♀(½m)   🐾(3m)
Min£35pw (Low)
Min£50 Max£110pw (High)

LLANSANTFFRAID YM MECHAIN
Powys
Map **7** SJ21

C   **Tan-y-Bryn** Deythur
for bookings Mrs M E Jones, Glanvyrnwy Farm, Llansantffraid ym Mechain, Powys
☎Llansantffraid(069 181)258

Modern detached cottage situated 1m off B4393 opposite Glanvyrnwy Farm and comprising lounge, kitchen/diner, three bedrooms sleeping up to eight, a bathroom/WC and separate WC.

All year   MWB 1 wk min, 2 wks max, 1 unit,
8 persons   ◆   🛁   fridge   Electric & log fires   Elec metered   ▣ not provided
☎(1m)   WM in unit   Airing cupboard in unit   Iron in unit   Ironing board in unit

HCE in unit   TV   ⊕3pin square   P   ▥
♨(1m)
↭   ♨(3m)   ♀(3m)
Min£75 Max£90pw (Low)
Min£100 Max£120pw (High)

LLANSTEPHAN
Dyfed
Map **2** SN31

Ch   **Elmrise Park Holiday Village**
for bookings Hoseasons Holidays, Sunways House, Lowestoft, Suffolk NR32 3LT
☎Lowestoft(0502)62292

Situated on elevated terraces, each well-decorated cedar wood chalet has two or three bedrooms. A lounge and kitchen/dining area.

All year   MWB out of season   3 days min,
4 mths max, 95 units, 2–6 persons
[◇   ◆   ◆]   ◎   fridge   Electric
Elec inclusive   ▣ inclusive   ☎   Airing cupboard in unit   Iron in unit   Ironing board in unit   HCE in unit   [Launderette on premises]   ⊕   TV   CTV can be hired   ⊕3pin square   P   ♨   ⌐
↭   ♀

LLANTEG
Dyfed
Map **2** SN11

H   **Garness Farm**
for bookings Powell's Holidays, High Street, Saundersfoot, Dyfed
☎Saundersfoot(0834)812791

Two flats in a large farmhouse, situated in 34 acres of pastureland within view of the sea. A trout stream provides fishing. One has a lounge, dining area, kitchen and three bedrooms, the dining area, kitchen and three bedrooms, the other has a kitchen, lounge/diner and two bedrooms. Both have sun decks.

May-Sep   MWB out of season   1 wk min,
6 wks max, 2 units, 2–8 persons   ◇   ◆
◆   no pets   ◎   fridge   🍴
Elec inclusive   ▣ provided
(overseas visitors only)   ☎   Airing cupboard in unit   Iron in unit   Ironing board in unit   HCE in unit   ⊕   ◎(1unit)
CTV   ⊕3pin square   P   ▥   ♨(4m)
↭   ♀(½m)
Min£99 Max£240pw

C   **Llanteglos Cottage**
for bookings Johnson & Swingler, Llanteglos Hamlet, Llanteg, Amroth, Narberth, Dyfed SA67 8PU
☎Llanteg(083 483)677

Cottage situated in the grounds of Llanteglos holiday hamlet, with club facilities nearby. Accommodation comprises two family bedrooms, lounge, dining room, kitchen, bathroom/WC and garden.

Mar-Oct   MWB out of season   1 unit,
2–6 persons   [◇]   ◆   ◆   ◎   fridge
Electric   Elec metered   ▣ not provided

☎   Airing cupboard in unit   HCE in unit
⊕   TV
⊕3pin square   P   ▥   ♨   ⤶Hard
↭   ♀   ▨(2m)
Min£40 Max£136pw

C   **Llanteglos Hamlet**
for bookings Johnson & Swingler, Llanteglos Hamlet, Llanteg, Amroth, Narberth, Dyfed SA67 8PU
☎Llanteg(083 483)677

High quality architect-designed modern cottages located amidst trees and shrubs in the grounds of an estate. Each unit has lounge/diner/kitchen with three bedrooms (one double, one twin, one bunk beds) and bathroom.

Mar-Oct   MWB out of season   1 wk min,
24 units, 2–6 persons   [◇   ◆]   ◎
fridge   Electric   Elec metered
▣ not provided   ☎   Airing cupboard in unit   HCE in unit   ⊕   TV
⊕3pin square   P   ▥   ♨   ⤶Hard
↭   ♀   ▨(2m)
Min£40 Max£136pw

LLANWRTYD WELLS
Powys
Map **3** SN84

C, F   **Kite I & II and Raven Barn**
for bookings Mrs C Johnson, Trallwm, Abergwesyn, Llanwrtyd Wells, Powys
☎Llanwrtyd Wells(05913)229

A converted 18th-century stone-barn make up these two cottages and one flat. All comprise two twin-bedded rooms, lounge/diner, with bed-settee, kitchen and bathroom/WC.

All year   MWB out of season   1 day min,
4 wks max, 3 units, 1–6 persons   [◇]   ◆
◆   no pets   ◎   fridge   Electric (Kite I & II have wood burning stoves)
Elec inclusive   ▣ inclusive except towels   ☎(1½m)   Airing cupboard in unit   Iron in unit   Ironing board on premises   HCE in unit   ⊕
⊕3pin square   P   ♨(1½m)   Fishing
Min£60 Max£70pw (Low)
Min£75 Max£110pw (High)

LLAWR-Y-GLYN
Powys
Map **6** SN99

C   **Penypound Cottage**
for bookings Mr J R Plater, 5 Tan-yr-Eglwys, Tregynon, Newtown, Powys
☎Tregynon(068 687)527

Semi-detached stone-built cottage on the banks of the River Trannon in the centre of the village, containing lounge/diner with bed-settee, kitchen, bathroom/WC, and further sleeping accommodation for four. A cot is also available.

Apr-Oct   MWB in season   1 wk min,
1 mth max, 1 unit, 6 persons   ◆   ◎
fridge   Electric   Elec metered
▣ not provided   ☎(50yds)   SD in unit
Airing cupboard in unit   Iron in unit
Ironing board in unit   HCE in unit   ⊕
TV   ⊕3pin square   P   ♨(150yds)   →

⊖ ♀(2m)
Min£30 Max£42pw (Low)
Min£48 Max£69pw (High)

LLWYNGWRIL
Gwynedd
Map **6** SH50

B **Golwg-y-Bae**
for bookings Mrs M A Bareham, The Hill
Cottage, Bausley, Crew Green,
Shrewsbury, Shropshire SY5 9BP
☎Halfway House(074 378)320

*Recently constructed bungalow set
down 14 steps from A493 with extensive
views over Cardigan Bay.
Accommodation comprises lounge with
kitchen off, one twin, one double-bedded
room and shower/WC.*

All year MWB out of season 2 days min,
6wks max, 1 unit, 1–4 persons ◊ ◆
⊛ fridge ▥ Elec metered
⊡ not provided ☎(⅓m) Airing cupboard
in unit Iron in unit Ironing board in unit
HCE in unit ⊕ TV ⊕3pin square 2P
▥ ♨(⅓m)
⊖ ♀(1m)
Min£70 Max£80pw (Low)
Min£85 Max£100pw (High)

LLWYNDAFYDD
Dyfed
Map **2** SN35

C Mr & Mrs M Headley **Neuadd Farm
Holiday Cottages** Llwyndafydd,
Llandysul, Dyfed
☎Newquay(0545)560324

*Nine luxurious holiday cottages set in 16
acres of land overlooking the lovely Cwm
Tydu Valley and situated near the coast.
They have been artistically converted
from old farm buildings and form a most
attractive south facing courtyard. The
cottages vary in size and sleep from 2–8
persons.*

All year MWB out of season 9 units,
2–8 persons [◊] ◊ ◆ ⊛ fridge
▥ Elec inclusive ⊡ inclusive except
towels ☎(500yds) WM on premises
SD on premises TD on premises Airing
cupboard in unit Iron in unit Ironing
board in unit HCE in unit ⊕ CTV
⊕3pin square P ▥ ♨(500yds)
Barbecue facilities

Llawr-y-Glyn
—
Loddiswell

⊖ ♀(500yds)
Min£80 Max£120pw (Low)
Min£125 Max£310pw (High)

LOCHEAD
Strathclyde *Argyll*
Map **10** NR77

C, Ch **Holiday Homes at Lochead**
for bookings The Booking Office, Estate
Office, Ellary, Lochgilphead, Argyll
PA31 8PB
☎Ormsary(088 03)232

*Four wooden chalets overlooking the
tidal shore of Loch Caolisport. Three units
comprise two double bedrooms with
bunk beds, living room with convertible
settee, kitchenette, shower/WC. The
fourth chalet is more spacious. Also
available is lochead cottage with three
double bedrooms, living room, kitchen
and bathroom. Only 2m from Ellary
holiday homes.*

All year MWB out of season 5 units,
1–6 persons ◊ ⊛ fridge Electric
Elec metered ⊡ not provided ☎(1m)
HCE in unit TV ⊕3pin square P ▥
♨(12m)
Min£66 Max£87pw (Low)
Min£132 Max£174pw (High)

LOCHEARNHEAD
Central *Perthshire*
Map **11** NN52

Ch **Lochearn Lodges**
for bookings Mrs R Peattie, Glenogle
Tweeds, Lochearnhead, Perthshire
☎Lochearnhead(056 73)240

*Six pleasantly furnished wooden chalets
well spaced on hillside above the village
with magnificent views south over Loch
Earn. Ideally situated just off the A85, a
good base for winter sports (Glencoe
1 hour) and touring.*

All year MWB out of season
2 nights min, 6 units, 1–6 persons ◊ ◆
no camping gas or paraffin on premises
⊛ fridge Electric Elec inclusive
⊡ inclusive except towels ☎(⅓m)
Airing cupboard in unit Iron in unit
Ironing board in unit HCE in unit ⊕

CTV ⊕3pin square 15P ♨(⅓m)
Water sports centre
⊖ ♀(⅓m) ▨(⅓m)

LOCHINVER
Highland *Sutherland*
Map **14** NC02

Ch **Lochinver Holiday Lodges**
33 Strathan, Lochinver, Sutherland
IV27 4LR
☎Lochinver(05714)282

*Scandinavian lodges with double glazed
doors and windows set in secluded bay
with tree lined back-drop and splendid
sea views. Accommodation comprises
modern lounge/diner, kitchen, one
double and one twin bedroom, modern
bathroom. All lodges have balconies.
Access from Lochinver (harbour) via
unclassified scenic coast road to
Ullapool 1½m.*

All year MWB out of season 1wk min,
5wks max, 7 units, 1–6 persons ◊
no pets ⊛ fridge ▥ Elec metered
⊡ inclusive ☎ Airing cupboard in unit
Iron on premises Ironing board on
premises HCE in unit [Launderette
within 300yds] ⊕ CTV
⊕3pin square 14P ♨(1½m) Sea &
Loch fishing
⊖ ♀(1½m) ▨(1½m)
Min£50 Max£305pw

LODDISWELL
Devon
Map **3** SX74

F D E Pethybridge, **Reads Farm**
Loddiswell, Kingsbridge, Devon TQ7 4RT
☎Loddiswell(054 855)317

*Flat on two floors, part of old farmhouse,
consisting of two bedrooms, one with
double bed and the other with double
bed plus two single beds, bathroom with
WC, on first floor. Ground-floor
kitchen/lounge/diner with TV. Own
entrance from small private garden with
fine views of Avon Valley. Turn left in
Loddiswell off B3196 travelling S.*

All year MWB out of season 1wk min,
4wks max, 1 unit, 1–6 persons ◊ ◆
⊛ fridge Electric Elec metered
⊡ not provided ☎(⅓m) Airing cupboard
in unit Iron in unit Ironing board in unit

HCE in unit ⊙ TV ⊕3pin square 3P
♨(½m)
⊕ ♀(½m)
Min£57.50 Max£92pw

F&B Mr & Mrs B Clayton **Woolston House** Loddiswell, Kingsbridge, Devon TQ7 4DU
☎Loddiswell(054 855)341

In an estate of 30 acres, self-contained flats and one bungalow of character and style. Accommodation is varied, Garden, Cloudsmoor, and Penthouse, although set in a Georgian house, all have own private entrance. Stable Corner, Coach House and Swallows have been tastefully converted from the stone outbuildings. These are set around a paved courtyard with troughs of flowers but have their own secluded entrances. The Old Dairy is a modern detached bungalow, built on the site of an old dairy. On B3196, 4m N of Kingsbridge.

All year MWB 2 days min, 5 mths max, 7 units, 2–8 persons [◇] ◆ no pets ◎ fridge Elec metered Ⓛinclusive ☎ SD in unit Airing cupboard in unit Iron in unit Ironing board in unit HCE in unit ⊙ TV ⊕3pin square P ▥ ♨(1m) ⌣(heated) ⌣Hard
⊕ ♀(1m) ▨(2½m)
Min£56 Max£110pw (Low)
Min£125 Max£230pw (High)

LOGIE-BUCHAN
Grampian *Moray*
Map **14** NH95

C   Easter & Wester Oaks Darnaway Estate
for bookings Moray Estates Development Co, Estate Office, Forres, Moray IV36 0ET
☎Forres(0309)72213

Semi-detached farm cottages set within Darnaway Estate, completely renovated and modernised. Each has living/dining room, compact kitchen, double bedroom and bathroom on ground floor, and upstairs two twin bedrooms.

Apr–Oct MWB out of season 1 wk min, 2 units 1–6 persons ◆ no pets ◎ fridge Electric Elec inclusive Ⓛcan be hired ☎(2m) Iron in unit Ironing board in unit ⊙ TV ⊕3pin square P ▥ ♨(2m) Burn fishing
Min£97.75 Max£109.25pw (Low)
Min£120.75pw (High)

LOGIE-COLDSTONE
Grampian *Aberdeenshire*
Map **15** NJ40

C   Redburn
for bookings Aboyne Estates, Estate Office, Old Station, Dinnet, Aberdeenshire AB35LL
☎Dinnet(033 985)341

A former gamekeeper's cottage beautifully situated on the edge of heathland with a fine view of the Deeside Valley about 4½m N of Dinnet. Three bedrooms, lounge/diner and separate kitchen. Comfortable, modern furnishings, except old, but satisfactory bathroom fittings. Provision for wood or coal fires.

Mar–Oct 1 wk min, 1 mth max, 1 unit, 1–6 persons ◆ ◆ no pets ◎ fridge Electric & open fires Elec inclusive Ⓛcan be hired ☎(3m) HCE ⊕3pin square P ♨(3m)
⊕ ♀(3m)
Min£90 Max£105pw

LONDON Greater London Map **4**

Places within the London postal area are listed below in postal district order commencing North, South and West. Other places within the county of London are listed under their respective place names and are keyed to maps **4 & 5.**

159

N6 HIGHGATE

F Mrs E Stein, *75 Hornsey Lane Gardens*, Highgate, London N6 5PA
☎01–3409684

Edwardian house in tree-lined road, converted into self-contained flats. The holiday flat available has one lounge with settee and two armchairs, large double bedroom, small kitchen and bathroom/WC. Maid service.

All year MWB 1mth min, 3mths max, 1unit, 2–3persons ◈ no pets ◎ fridge ♨ Elec inclusive ▣inclusive ☎ Iron Ironing board HCE [Launderette within 300yds] ⊕ CTV ⊕3pin square ▥ ♨(300yds)

⊛ ☊(200yds) ▨(1m) ♫(1m) ☙(1m)

NW1 St Marylebone; *Regent's Park*

F **21 Park Road**
for bookings Alexanders & Co, 34 Ivor Place, London NW1
☎01–4020066

Three well-maintained luxury apartments in a narrow Georgian terraced house. Accommodation consists of lounge/diner, kitchen, bathroom and twin-bedded room. One of the apartments contains two twin-bedded rooms which are reached by a spiral staircase.

All year MWB 4wks min, 8mths max, 3units, 1–5persons [◈] [◆] no pets ◎ fridge ♨ Elec inclusive ▣inclusive ☎ Airing cupboard in unit Iron in unit Ironing board in unit HCE in unit [Launderette within 300yds] ⊕ CTV ⊕3pin square ▥ ♨(75yds)

⊛ ☊(75yds) ▨(300yds) ♫(100yds) ☙(200yds)

Min£100pw (Low)
Min£200 (High)

NW3 Swiss Cottage

F **51 Belsize Park Gardens**
for bookings Alexanders & Co. 34 Ivor Place, NW1
☎01–4020066

A large Victorian house in Swiss Cottage,

---

skilfully converted into seven self-contained units, three of which conform to basic requirements. The flats have two twin-bedded rooms, sitting/dining room, kitchen and bathroom.

All year MWB 4wks min, 8mths max, 3units, 1–5persons [◈] [◆] no pets ◎ fridge ♨ Elec metered ▣inclusive ☎ Airing cupboard in unit Iron in unit Ironing board in unit HCE in unit [Launderette within 300yds] ⊕ ♨ TV CTV can be hired ⊕3pin square ▥ ♨(20yds)

⊛ ☊(300yds) ▨(300yds)
♫(300yds) ☙(½m)

Min£60 Max£250pw (Low)
Min£75 Max£350pw (High)

SW1 Westminster

F Dolphin Square Furnished Apartments Dolphin Square Trust Ltd, Dolphin Square, London SW1 3LX
☎01–8349134

Seventy-eight two-room apartments situated in large block of flats consisting of twin-bedded room, separate well-furnished lounge, kitchen and bathroom with WC

All year MWB 1night min, 6mths max, 78units, 1–2persons ◈ ◆ no pets ◎ fridge ♨ Elec inclusive ▣inclusive ☎ Iron in unit Ironing board in unit HCE in unit [Launderette within 300yds] ⊕ ♨ CTV ⊕3pin square ⊕3pin round ⊕2pin round ♨ ▥ ▣ [Sauna, squash, tennis]

⊛ ☊ ▨(½m) ♫(½m)

Min£180 Max£540pw

F Dolphin Square Furnished Apartments Dolphin Square Trust Ltd, Dolphin Square, London SW1V 3LX
☎01–8349134

Thirty-four three-room apartments in large block consisting of some with one double and one single bedroom, and some with two double bedrooms. Separate lounge, modern and

---

comfortably furnished. Modern, well-equipped kitchen. Bathroom/WC.

All year MWB 1night min, 6mths max, 34units, 3–4persons ◈ ◆ no pets ◎ fridge ♨ Elec inclusive ▣inclusive Iron in unit Ironing board in unit HCE in unit [Launderette within 300yds] ⊕ ♨ CTV ⊕3pin square ⊕3pin round ⊕2pin round ♨ ▥ ♨ ▣ [Sauna, squash, tennis]

⊛ ☊ ▨(½m)

Min£180 Max£540pw

F Dolphin Square Furnished Apartments Dolphin Square Trust Ltd, Dolphin Square, London SW1V 3LX
☎01–8349134

A four-room apartment consisting of three twin-bedded rooms with modern divan beds and furniture, a well appointed lounge/diner, separate well equipped kitchen and two separate bathrooms and WCs. Situated in large block of flats off the Embankment, in residential area.

All year MWB 1night min, 6mths max, 1unit, 6persons ◈ ◆ no pets ◎ fridge ♨ Elec inclusive ▣inclusive Iron in unit Ironing board in unit HCE in unit [Launderette within 300yds] ⊕ ♨ CTV ⊕3pin square ⊕3pin round ⊕2pin round ♨ ▥ ▣ [Sauna, squash, tennis]

⊛ ☊ ▨(½m) ▨(½m) ☙(½m)

Min£180 Max£540pw

F 4 Lower Sloane Street
for bookings Mrs H Hoyer, 42 Lower Sloane Street, London SW1 W8BP
☎01–7305766 Telex(Ref2979)24224

Four luxurious flats with very comfortable amenities in residential area near Sloane Square. All flats have lounge, kitchen and bathroom with the larger flats having two bathrooms.

All year MWB 1wk min, 3mths max, 4units, 1–7persons ◈ ◆ ◎ fridge ♨ Elec metered ▣inclusive ☎ Airing cupboard in unit Iron in unit Ironing board in unit HCE in unit [Launderette within 300yds] ⊕ CTV ⊕3pin square ▥ ♨(10yds)

⊛ ☊(100yds) ▨(100yds)
♫(500yds) ☙(500yds)

Min £168 Max £266pw (Low)
Min £196 Max £294pw (High)

F 11 Sloane Gardens
for bookings Mrs H Hoyer, 42 Lower
Sloane Street, London SW1W8BP
☎01–7305766 Telex (Ref2979)24224

A four-storey block of flats set in a
residential area; two with three
bedrooms, four with two bedrooms and
one with one bedroom. All have separate
lounge, kitchen and bathroom (three
bedroom flats have two bathrooms). Well
maintained with fitted carpets
throughout.

All year MWB 1wk min, 7units,
1–6persons ◈ ◉ fridge ⋈
Elec metered ⊡inclusive ☎ Airing
cupboard in unit Iron in unit Ironing
board in unit [Launderette within
300yds] ⊙ CTV ⊕3pin square ⊞
♨(300yds)

⇔ ⚲(¼m) ⊠(¼m) ♫(¼m) ⋈-(¼m)
Min £133 Max £326pw (Low)
Min £147 Max £378pw (High)

SW3 Chelsea

F Clifton Lodge 45 Egerton Gardens,
London SW3 2DD
☎01–5840099

Eight out of twelve flats in a modernised
Victorian terraced house a short distance
from Harrods. The flats have a good sized
lounge/dining room, concealed well-
equipped kitchenette, pull down single or
double bed, single or twin bedrooms and
modern bathroom.

All year MWB 1night min, 8units,
2–4persons, nc 11 no pets ◉ fridge
⋈ Elec inclusive ⊡inclusive ☎ Iron
on premises Ironing board on
premises HCE on premises
[Launderette within 300yds] ⊙ CTV
⊕3pin square ⊞ ♨(20yds)

Min £200 Max£ ▪▪ pw

▪▪▪▪ ar M ▪▪▪▪ Kensington
for ▪▪▪ the ma ▪▪▪ Gardens Kensington
▪▪▪▪ servations Dept, Travel
Apartments Ltd, 138 Sloane Street,
Knightsbridge, London SW1X 9AY
☎01–7305121

Five-storey Victorian terraced house
close to West London air terminal and
Earls Court divided into one, two and
three-bedroom flats, some with two
bathrooms, containing lounge, open-
plan kitchen and breakfast bar. Serviced
daily.

All year MWB 1wk min, 12units,
1–8persons ◈ ◆ no pets ◉
fridge ⋈ Elec inclusive ⊡inclusive
☎ Iron in unit Ironing board in unit
HCE on premises [Launderette within
300yds] ⊙ CTV ⊕3pin square ⊞
♨(300yds)

⇔ ⚲(20yds) ⊠(3m) ♫(3m) ⋈-(3m)

F The Manager **Grenback Court** 32
Trebovir Road, London SW5
☎01–3704938

Twenty-eight one-bedroomed flats;
lounge, double bedroom, bathroom and
kitchen. All units are serviced daily and
there is a resident housekeeper. In a
quiet street, 100yds from shops and Earls
Court underground, also central for
places of interest.

All year MWB 1wk min, 28units,
1–4persons ◈ ◆ ◉ fridge ⋈
Gas/Elec inclusive ⊡inclusive ☎ Iron
on premises Ironing board on
premises HCE on premises
[Launderette within 300yds] ⊙ CTV
⊕3pin square ♨(50yds)

⇔ ⚲(100yds) ⊠(100yds)
♫(100yds) ⋈-(¼m)
Min £112 Max£182pw (Low)
Min £156 Max£210pw (High)

SW7 South Kensington

F Mr M Raphael **45 Ennismore
Gardens** Knightsbridge SW7 1AQ
☎01–5844123

In a quiet street within walking distance of
Knightsbridge and Hyde Park. A
Victorian terraced house divided into 10
flats with lift to all floors. All flats are
cleaned daily and consist of
lounge/bedroom, kitchen/diner and
bathroom.

All year MWB 1wk min, 6mths max,
10units, 2persons no pets ◉ fridge
⋈ Elec inclusive ⊡inclusive ☎ Iron
in unit Ironing board in unit HCE on
premises ⊙ CTV ⊕3pin square ⊞
♨(200yds)

⇔ ⚲(100yds) ⊠(1m) ♫(3m) ⋈-(1m)
Min £140 Max£145pw (Low)
Min £160 Max£165pw (High)

W1 West End; Mayfair, St Marylebone

F Mr M A S Terry **47 Park Street**
Mayfair, London W1Y 4EB
☎01–4917282

Six-storey Georgian-style mansion
situated in the heart of Mayfair. There are
four types of accommodation comprising
two and three-room apartments and
communicating two-room apartments of
one and two bedrooms (some have
breakfast room). All apartments are
serviced daily.

All year MWB 1wk min, 54units,
1–6persons [◇] ◈ ◆ ◉ fridge
⋈ ⊡inclusive ☎ Iron on premises
Ironing board on premises HCE on
premises ⊙ CTV ⊕3pin square ⊞
♨(200yds)

⇔ ⚲(200yds) ⊠(2m) ♫(2m) ⋈-(¼m)
Min £645.75 Max£1980.30

F 3 York Street
for bookings Alexander & Co, 34 Ivor
Place, London NW1
☎01–4020066

Victorian terraced house situated ½m from
Marble Arch and Hyde Park. Flats consist
of studio room, kitchen and bathroom.

All year MWB 4wks min, 8mths max,
14units, 1–4persons [◈ ◆] no pets
◉ fridge ⋈ Elec inclusive
⊡inclusive ☎ Airing cupboard in unit
Iron in unit Ironing board in unit HCE in
unit Launderette within 300yds ⊙ ⊛
TV CTV can be hired ⊕3pin square
⊞ ♨(100yds)

⇔ ⚲(¼m) ⊠(¼m) ♫(¼m) ⋈-(¼m)
Min £50pw (Low)
Min £75pw (High)

W4 Chiswick

F Miss Innes **60 Flanders Road,**
Bedford Park, Chiswick, London W4 1NG
☎01–9942561

A first floor two-room flatlet in private
house situated in a residential area, with
railway line at end of garden. The rooms
are not large but adequate for two
persons. Good decorative order and
reasonably furnished. Modern double
bed. Small lounge/dinette with easy
chairs and single bed-settee.

All year MWB 1mth min, 5mths max,
1unit, 1–2persons, nc no pets ⌕
fridge Gas fires Gas metered
⊡inclusive Iron in unit Ironing board in
unit HCE in unit [Launderette within
300yds] TV can be hired
⊕3pin square ⊞ ♨(300yds) ⋈Hard

⇔ ⚲(¼m) ⊠(1½m) ♫(1½m) ⋈-(¼m)
Min £36 Max£40pw

W8 Kensington

F Clearlake Hotel 18–19 Prince of
Wales Terrace, Kensington, London
W8 5PQ
☎01–9373274

Four flats in a four-storey Victorian
terraced house adjacent to hotel. One flat
has a lounge, the others have a
lounge/diner. Each has a fitted kitchen
and bathroom/WC. Three flats have two
double bedrooms the other has only one.
Situated in a quiet street off Kensington
High Street.

All year MWB 1night min, 1mth max,
4units, 1–6persons ◇ ◈ ◆ ⌕ ◉
fridge ⋈ Gas/Elec inclusive
⊡inclusive ☎ Iron in unit Ironing
board in unit HCE in unit [Launderette
within 300yds] ⊙ ⊛ CTV
⊕3pin square ⊞ ♨(200yds)

⇔ ⚲(20yds) ⊠(300yds) ♫(300yds)
⋈-(¼m)
Min £169.05 Max£212.75pw (Low)
Min £241.50 Max£299pw (High)

W13 West Ealing

F 94 Gordon Road Ealing
for bookings Mr W G Smith, 1 Park Road
East, Uxbridge, Middx UB10 0AQ
☎Uxbridge(0895)33365

Large Edwardian house containing two
studio flats with large living area, kitchen, →

1982 prices quoted throughout
gazetteer

161

separate shower and WC, two flats with double bedroom, lounge, kitchen, shower and WC. The other two flats in an annexe have lounge, two bedrooms, kitchen and bathroom. Central London is a twenty minute underground ride away.

All year MWB 1wk min, 3mths max, 6units, 2–6persons ◆ no pets ⌀ ◉ fridge ♨ Electric Gas/Elec metered ⊑inclusive ☎ HCE [Launderette] ⊙ TV can be hired ⊕3pin square ▥ ♨(100yds) ⌫Hard

⊷ ☏(300yds) ♫(¼m) ☖(¼m)

Min£50 Max£140pw (Low)
Min£60 Max£175pw (HIgh)

LONGBOROUGH
Gloucestershire
Map**4** SP12

C The Bothy & Garden Cottages
Windy Ridge
for bookings Longborough Properties Ltd, The Crook, Longborough, Moreton-in-Marsh, Glos GL56 0QY
☎Stow-on-the-Wold(0451)30327
(9am–5pm weekdays)

A pair of cottages unobtrusively set in attractive gardens both compact and on one floor. They comprise one twin bedded room, cosy sitting room, kitchen and combined bathroom/WC.

All year MWB 1wk min, 2units, 2persons ◇ ◆ no pets ◉ fridge ♨ Elec metered ⊑can be hired ☎(¼m) Airing cupboard in unit Iron in unit Ironing board in unit HCE in unit [Launderette on premises] ⊙ CTV ⊕3pin square 1P ▥ ♨(¼m) ⌫Hard ⊷ ☏(200yds)

Min£149.50 Max£178.25pw

C Crook Cottage Windy Ridge
for bookings Longborough Properties Ltd, The Crook, Longborough, Moreton-in-Marsh, Glos GL56 0QY
☎Stow-on-the-Wold(0451)30327
(9am–5pm weekdays)

Country cottage with own garden within beautifully maintained Windy Ridge Estate; cloakroom/WC, kitchen, dining room and sitting room with open fires. Bathroom/WC, bedroom with bunk beds, 2 double bedrooms.

All year MWB 3days min, 1unit, 1–7persons [◇] ◆ ◉ fridge ♨ & open fire Elec metered ⊑ ☎ WM in unit SD in unit Airing cupboard in unit Iron in unit Ironing board in unit HCE in unit ⊙ CTV ⊕3pin square P ▥ ♨(¼m) ⌫ ⌫Hard

⊷ ☏(100yds)

Min£166.75 Max£178.25pw (Low)
£218.50pw (High)

F Stable Cottage Windy Ridge
for bookings Longborough Properties Ltd, The Crook, Longborough, Moreton-in-Marsh, Glos GL56 0QY
☎Stow-on-the-Wold(0451)30327
(9am–5pm weekdays)

Also located on Windy Ridge Estate, a small attractive unit within a thatched stable block consists of an upstairs flat with spacious sitting room with put-u-up, fitted kitchen with dining area, single bedroom with cot available, twin-bedded room, bathroom and WC.

All year MWB 1unit, 1–4persons [◇] ◆ ◆ ◉ fridge ♨ Elec metered ⊑inclusive ☎ WM SD Airing cupboard in unit Iron in unit Ironing board in unit HCE in unit ⊙ CTV ⊕3pin square P ▥ ♨(¼m) ⌫ ⌫Hard

⊷ ☏(100yds)

£149.50pw (Low)
£200.75pw (High)

C Windy Ridge Cottage
for bookings Longborough Properties Ltd, The Crook, Longborough, Moreton-in-Marsh, Glos GL56 0QL
☎Stow-on-the-Wold(0451)30327
(9am–5pm weekdays)

A very attractive cottage with its own garden within Windy Ridge estate with views of the Cotswolds. Very well appointed and most comfortable. Spacious sitting room with open fire, dining room, fully fitted kitchen, utility room, three bedrooms, a double, a twin, and a further double bedded room with two additional bunk beds. Bathrooms ground and first floor.

All year MWB 1wk min, 1unit, 2–9persons ◇ ◆ ◆ ◉ fridge ♨ Elec metered ☎ WM in unit SD in unit TD in unit Airing cupboard in unit Iron in unit Ironing board in unit HCE in unit ⊙ CTV ⊕3pin square P ▥ ♨(¼m) ⌫ ⌫Hard

⊷ ☏(100yds)

Min£178.25 Max£189.75pw (Low)
£243pw (High)

LONGNOR
Staffordshire
Map**7** SK06

C Brund Mill Cottage
for bookings Mrs J Humphries, Brund Mill, Sheen, Longnor, Derbys
☎Hartington(029 884)383

A stone built detached cottage with a fully modernised interior, the accommodation comprising of downstairs kitchen/dining room and a lounge with open fire and upstairs, two bedrooms, one with twin beds, one with two single beds and bathroom/WC. 3m S off B5053.

All year except Xmas & New Year MWB out of season 2nights min, 3mths max, 1unit, 1–4persons ◆ ◆ ◉ fridge Electric Elec metered ⊑not provided ☎(1m) Airing cupboard in unit HCE in unit ⊕3pin square 2☖ ♨(1m) Fishing

⊷ ☏(1¼m)

Min£50 Max£65pw (Low)
Min£75 Max£105pw (High)

C 4 & 5 Chapel Street
for bookings Mrs J Humphries, Brund Mill, Sheen, Longnor, Buxton, Derbyshire
☎Hartington(029 884)383

Two terraced cottages converted into one, fully modernised throughout, the downstairs accommodation has a lounge/dining room, separate kitchen. Upstairs is a bathroom/WC, one single bedroom, one twin bedroom and a bedroom with two single beds. 3m
B5053.

All year except Xmas & New Ye~~~ out of season 2nights min, 3m~~~ 1unit, 1–4persons ◇ ◆ ◉ fridge Electric & open fires Elec metered ⊑not provided ☎(200yds) Airing

cupboard in unit HCE in unit ⊕
⊕3pin square 🏠(25yds)
⊖ ☎(50yds)
Min£50 Max£65pw (Low)
Min£75 Max£105pw (High)

F No7 Chapel Street
*for bookings Mrs J Humphries, Brund
Mill, Sheen, Longnor, Buxton, Derbys
☎Hartington(029 884)383
Located above a tea room in the centre of
this quiet village; a modernised flat
comprising of lounge/diner, open plan
kitchen, bathroom/WC and three
bedrooms, two twin-bedded rooms and
one with a single bed. 3m S off B5053.*

All year except Xmas & New Year MWB
out of season 2 nights min, 3 mths max,
1 unit, 1–5 persons ◊ ◆ ⊚ fridge
Electric Elec metered ⎁ not provided
☎ Airing cupboard in unit HCE in unit
⊕ ⊕3pin square 6P 🏠(25yds)
⊖ ☎(50yds)
Min£50 Max£65pw (Low)
Min£75 Max£105pw (High)

C Lawley Cottage
*for bookings Mr & Mrs T W E Corbett,
Home Farm, Leebotwood, Church
Stretton, Shropshire
☎Leebotwood(06945)231
A detached modernised stone cottage
enjoying superb views across to the Long
Mynd and is set in ⅓rd-acre of garden and
orchard. It comprises lounge/kitchen
with dining facilities including
dishwasher on ground-floor and one
double, two single bedrooms on first-
floor.*

Apr-Oct 1 wk min, 1 mth max, 1 unit,
1–6 persons ⊚ fridge Electric & open
fires Elec metered ⎁ not provided
☎(1¾m) Airing cupboard in unit HCE in
unit ⊕ TV ⊕3pin square 4P

C Sunnyside Holiday Cottages
*for bookings Mr & Mrs G W Fox,
Sunnyside, Church Street, Longnor,
Buxton, Derbys
☎Longnor(029 883)496
These stone-built semi-detached
cottages, separated by a covered
passageway, are in a quiet street in the
tiny village of Longnor, 6m S of Buxton.
The ground-floor comprises two single*

Longnor — Looe

*bedrooms, one double and
bathroom/WC. The first-floor has kitchen,
living/dining room and one or two
bedrooms.*

All year MWB out of season 1 day min,
1 mth max, 2 units, 1–7 persons ◊ ◆
⊚ fridge Electric & wood stove
Elec metered ☎(10yds)
Airing cupboard HCE ⊕ CTV
⊕3pin square 4P 🏠(150yds)
⊖ ☎(200yds)
Min£55 Max£100pw (Low)
Min£85 Max£140pw (High)

LOOE
Cornwall
Map **2** SX25

F Bay, Blyth & Pilchard Cottages East
Looe
*for bookings Mrs A Lean, Trelean, West
Looe Hill, Looe, Cornwall PL13 2HW
☎Looe(050 36)2530
Five holiday homes converted from a
400-year-old harbour warehouse and fish
store. Units with modern interiors, consist
of two bedrooms (one double and one
twin-bedded), lounge and convertible
settee, dining area, kitchenette and
bathroom.*

All year MWB out of season 1 wk min,
1 mth max, 5 units, 6 persons ◊ ◆ ◔
fridge Electric Gas/Elec metered
⎁ can be hired ☎(100yds) Iron in unit
Ironing board in unit HCE in unit
[Lauderette within 300yds] ⊕ CTV
⊕3pin square 🏠(100yds)
⊖ ☎(¼m) 🖥(¼m) ♫(¼m)
Min£40 Max£100pw

F Belfry & Haven 1 Chapel Court
*for bookings Mrs L E Ross, The Old Hall,
Chapel Court, Shutta Road, Looe,
Cornwall PL13 1HW
☎Looe(050 36)3700
Attractive conversion of old chapel into
two flats, reached by a wide pine
staircase. Each has a lounge/diner and
well equipped kitchen. One has two
large bedrooms, one with twin divans, the
other with two pairs of full-size bunk beds.
Turn left at the Globe Inn, then first right*

*into Shutta Road. (This thoroughfare is
one-way and narrow).*

All year MWB out of season 1 wk min,
4 mths max, 2 units, 2–8 persons [◊]
no pets ⊚ fridge 🍳 Elec metered
⎁ not provided ☎(75yds) Airing
cupboard in unit Iron in unit Ironing
board in unit HCE in unit ⊕ CTV
⊕3pin square P 📺 🖥 🏠(50yds)
⊖ 🚸(3m)
Min£30 Max£80pw (Low)
Min£100 Max£195pw (High)

F Island Cottages 1 & 2 Church Street,
West Looe
*for bookings Mrs W J M Collings, Brook
Cottage, Longcombe Lane, Polperro,
Cornwall PL13 2PL
☎Polperro(0503)72274
17th-century residence carefully
converted into two flats, one at ground-
floor level, the other at first and second-
floor levels. Both have stone fireplaces in
the lounge.*

All year MWB out of season 1 wk min,
1 mth max, 2 units, 2–7 persons ◊ ⊚
fridge Electric Elec metered ⎁ can be
hired ☎(200yds) Airing cupboard in
unit Iron in unit Ironing board in unit
HCE in unit [Launderette within
300yds] ⊕ CTV ⊕3pin square
⊕2pin round P 📺 🏠
⊖ ♫(1½m) 📺 ♫ 🚸
Min£40 Max£175pw

B, F Mr D C West **Milendreath Holiday
Village** Milendreath, Looe, Cornwall
☎Looe(050 36)3281
*One hundred and thirty-seven
comfortable, well-equipped units. All
within easy reach of the beach; some
accommodation overlooks Milendreath
Valley and some are at the base of the
valley, the remainder overlook the beach.
Comprehensive water sports centre.*

Jun-Sep MWB out of seson 1 wk min,
1 mth max, 137 units, 2–6 persons [◊]
◆ ⊚ fridge Electric Elec metered
⎁ inclusive ☎(100yds) Airing
cupboard in unit HCE in unit →

1982 prices quoted throughout
gazetteer

[Launderette within 300yds] ⊙ TV
⊕3pin square ⊕2pin round P
🏠(100yds) ✍Hard Squash
⇔ ⚓ 🍴 ♪

Min£35 Max£45pw (Low)
Min£159 Max£185pw (High)

F Penpont Holiday Flats 8 Trelawney Terrace
for bookings Mrs V Weber, Springfort, Langreek Road, Polperro, Cornwall PL132PW
☎Polperro(0503)72580

Large 1920s end-of-terrace house converted into three flats. Flat 1 is on the second-floor with access over the bridge at rear to the kitchen. Accommodation comprises lounge/diner, bathroom/WC and two bedrooms one with double bed, bunks and wash hand basin, the other having double bed and wash hand basin. Flat 2 is on the first-floor and comprises open-plan lounge/kitchen/diner, bathroom/WC and two bedrooms, one double room and one with one double bed and bunk beds. Flat 3 is on the ground-floor, comprisng lounge/diner, separate kitchen, bathroom/WC and one family room with double bed, bunk beds and one double bedroom all with washbasins. 200yds from Looe Bridge.

Apr-Nov MWB out of season 1wk min, 4wks max, 3units, 1–6persons ◊ ◆
◉ fridge Electric Elec metered
⊡not provided ☎(90yds) Airing cupboard in unit Iron in unit Ironing board in unit HCE in unit ⊙ CTV
⊕3pin square ♪ 🏠(50yds)
⇔ 🛁(3m) ⚓(300yds) 🎿(300yds)
♪(1m) 🏄(½m)

Min£60 Max£158pw

F Plaidy Beach Holiday Apartments
for bookings Mr H Milne, Plaidy Beach Holiday Hotel, Plaidy, Looe, Cornwall
☎Looe(05036)2044

Three flats, flat 2 being situated on the first-floor consisting of kitchen/diner, lounge with double sofa bed, single room with bunk beds and two double with washbasin, also bathroom and separate WC. Flats 4 and 5, one on the first- and the other on the second-floor, both having kitchen/diner, lounge with double bed-settee, double room with bunks, bath or

shower with WC. Leave A38 at roundabout at Trerlefeut follow signs to Looe, bear left opposite St Margarets Church, take first left into Hay Lane; Plaidy Hotel on left.

All year MWB out of season 3days min, 28days max, 3units, 1–7persons [◊]
◊ ◆ no pets ◉ fridge Electric Elec metered ⊡can be hired ☎ Airing cupboard in unit Iron on premises Ironing board on premises HCE in unit ⊙ CTV ⊕3pin square 3P ♪ 🏠(½m)
⇔ 🛁(2m) ⚓ ♪(1m)

H Spindrift Cottage Downs View Road
for bookings Mrs W J M Collings, Brook Cottage, Longcombe Lane, Polperro, Cornwall PL132PL
☎Polperro(0503)72274

Modern detached house with views of river, harbour and quays. Accommodation consists of lounge, kitchen/dining room, four bedrooms, three with double beds, one with single bed, and washbasin. Bathroom/WC.

All year MWB out of season 1wk min, 6mths max, 1unit, 7persons ◊ ◆ ◆
◉ fridge Electric Elec metered ⊡can be hired ☎(250yds) Airing cupboard in unit Iron in unit Ironing board in unit HCE in unit ⊙ CTV ⊕3pin square P ♪ 🏠(½m)
⇔ 🛁(3m) ⚓(200yds) 🎿(200yds)
♪(200yds)

Min£60 Max£175pw

F Mrs A Nisbett *Stoneleigh Villa* Plaidy Beach, Looe, Cornwall PL131LG
☎Looe(05036)2538

Superbly located maisonette in elevated position, overlooking Plaidy Beach. The maisonette is well furnished with accommodation comprising two bedrooms, lounge with bed-settee, kitchen and bathroom. Steps lead to a concrete patio in the front. The approach is by private road.

All year MWB out of season 1wk min, 5mths max, 1unit, 2–6persons ◊ [◆]
♨ fridge Gas Gas metered ⊡can be

hired ☎ SD in unit TD on premises Iron in unit Ironing board in unit HCE in unit ⊙ [CTV] ⊕3pin square ⊕2pin round P ♪ 🏠(⅓m)
⇔ ⚓(¼m) 🎿(¼m) ♪(¼m)

F Stonerock Holiday Flats Portruan Road, Hannafore
for bookings, Mr & Mrs R M C Hore, Green Borders, Marine Drive, Looe, Cornwall PL132DH
☎Looe(05036)2928

Once a hotel, now converted into nine well-maintained flats with one, two and three bedrooms. Close to shops and about 150yds from Hannafore Beach and the western seafront.

All year MWB out of season 1wk min, 1mth max, 9units, 2–9persons [◆]
no cats ◉ fridge Electric Elec metered ⊡can be hired ☎(150yds) Airing cupboard in unit Iron in unit Ironing board in unit HCE in unit ⊙ CTV ⊕3pin square ⊕2pin round 🏠 🏠(½m) 🏄 ♒
⇔ ⚓ 🎿 ♪

Min£30 Max£70pw (Low)
Min£60 Max£155pw (High)

Ch Treble 'B' Holiday Centre Ltd Polperro Road, Looe, Cornwall
☎Looe(05036)2425

Near to beach, these two chalets are well decorated and modestly furnished; one is cedar-wood and the other block-built both adjacent to Treble 'B' Caravan Park.

mid May-Sep MWB out of season 2nights min, 2units, 2–6persons [◆ ◆] no pets ◉ fridge Electric Elec metered ⊡can be hired ☎(60yds) Airing cupboard in unit HCE in unit [Launderette] [TV] ⊕3pin square P 🏠(60yds)

Min£60 Max£110pw (Low)
Min£140 Max£180pw (High)

F Treble 'B' Holiday Centre Ltd Polperro Road, Looe, Cornwall
☎Looe(05036)2425

Purpose-built flats of concrete with stucco finish situated adjacent to a large camping park. They are well appointed and furnished and have access to all the facilities of the holiday centre.

mid May-Sep MWB out of season 2nights min, 6units, 2–6persons [◇ ◆] no pets ◎ fridge 🛏 Elec metered 🄻can be hired ☎(60yds) Airing cupboard in unit HCE in unit [Launderette] [TV] ⊕3pin square P 🏠 🏪(60yds) ⛵

Min£60 Max£110pw (Low)
Min£140 Max£180pw (High)

C, F Mrs P Duff ***Tregertha Court & Captains Cottage*** Station Road, Looe, Cornwall
☎Looe(05036)2014

A large stone-built house, previously a hotel, but now converted into flats. A further accommodation unit is a detached cottage adjacent to the main building. There is a reception, lounge, bar, small dance floor and a heated swimming pool. Good views. Each of the 13 flats comprises a compact kitchen, bathroom with WC, lounge with folding wall bed and a separate bedroom. They sleep from one to seven people depending on each flat. The Captains Cottage sleeps four people and has a lounge with a folding double wall bed, a twin-bedded room, kitchen and bathroom. Tregertha Court is situated on the left upon entering East Looe.

9Apr-Oct MWB out of season 3days min, 1mth max, 14units, 1–7persons ◇ [◇] [◆] no pets ◎ fridge Electric Elec metered 🄻inclusive ☎ SD on premises [TD on premises] Iron on premises Ironing board on premises HCE in unit [Launderette] ⊙ [TV] ⊕3pin square ⊕2pin round P 🏠 🏪(100yds) ⛵ Games room

⊖ ♂18(3m) 🍷 ⊡ ♬ 🎥

F Trelawney Flat & Trelawney Maisonette 6 Trelawney Terrace
for bookings Mrs V Weber, Springford, Lengreek Road, Polperro, Cornwall PL13 2PW
☎Polperro(0503)72580

Large 1920s terraced house converted into two apartments. The flat is on the ground-floor with a lounge/diner/kitchen, shower/WC and two double bedrooms with wash hand basin. The maisonette has a ground-floor entrance. Accommodation comprises lounge/kitchen/diner, bathroom/WC and one double bedroom with wash hand basin on the first-floor. On the second-floor there are three double bedrooms, one with bunk beds, all with washbasins. 200yds from Looe Bridge.

Apr-Nov MWB out of season 1wk min, 4wks max, 2units, 1–10persons ◇ ◆ ◎ fridge Electric Elec metered 🄻not provided ☎(90yds) Airing cupboard in unit Iron in unit HCE in unit ⊙ CTV ⊕3pin square ▥ 🏪(50yds)

⊖ ♂18(3m) 🍷(300yds) ⊡(300yds) ♬(1m) 🎥(½m)

Min£50 Max£70pw (Low)
Min£136 Max£246pw (High)

***F* Up-Aloft** The Quay, West Looe
for bookings Mrs A Lean, Trelean, West Looe Hill, Looe, Cornwall PL13 2HW
☎Looe(05036)2530

Self-contained flat with magnificent views of the harbour and East Looe. Accommodation comprises three bedrooms (two double and one twin-bedded), lounge with double studio couch, kitchen and bathroom. Parking is difficult.

All year MWB out of season 1wk min, 1mth max, 1unit, 8persons ◇ ◆ ◎ fridge Electric Elec metered 🄻can be hired ☎(50yds) Iron in unit Ironing board in unit HCE in unit ⊙ CTV ⊕3pin square ▥ 🏪(50yds)

⊖ 🍷(½m) ⊡(½m) ♬(½m)

Min£50 Max£130pw

LOWESTOFT
Suffolk
Map**5** TM59

***Ch* Broadsedge, Broadland Chalets**
Oulton Broad
for bookings Hoseasons Holidays, Sunway House, Lowestoft, Suffolk NR32 3LT
☎Lowestoft(0502)62292

Brick-built chalets accommodating up to eight persons in three bedrooms (one double, one with two singles and another with bunk beds). There is a studio couch in the living room. Access opposite St Mark's Church and alongside the railway bridge off A146 at Oulton Broad.

Mar–Oct MWB out of season 2days min, 1mth max, 6units, 6–8persons [◇] [◆] no dogs ◎ fridge Electric Elec metered 🄻inclusive ☎(½m) [Iron on premises] [Ironing board on premises] HCE in unit ⊙ TV ⊕3pin square P 🏠 🏪 Fishing & boats for hire

⊖ ♂18(2m) 🍷 ⊡(½m) 🎥(2m)

***Ch* Broadshaven, Broadland Chalets**
Oulton Broad
for bookings Hoseasons Holidays, Sunway House, Lowestoft, Suffolk NR32 3LT
☎Lowestoft(0502)62292

Brick-built chalets comprising two bedrooms, one with double bed and the other with two-tiered single beds. Living room has a divan which converts to a single bed.

Mar–Oct MWB out of season 2days min, 1mth max, 17units, 4–5persons [◇] [◆] no dogs ◎ fridge Electric Elec metered 🄻inclusive ☎(½m) [Iron on premises] [Ironing board on premises] HCE in unit ⊙ TV ⊕3pin square P 🏠 🏪 Fishing & boats for hire

⊖ ♂18(2m) 🍷 ⊡(½m) 🎥(2m)

***Ch* Broadside, Broadland Chalets**
Oulton Broad
for bookings Hoseasons Holidays, Sunway House, Lowestoft, Suffolk NR32 3LT
☎Lowestoft(0502)62292

Brick-built chalets containing one double bedroom plus studio couch in living room. There is a verandah leading off living room.

Mar–Oct MWB out of season 2days min, 1mth max, 18units, 2–4persons [◇] [◆] no dogs ◎ fridge Electric Elec metered 🄻inclusive ☎(½m) [Iron on premises] [Ironing board on premises] HCE in unit ⊙ TV ⊕3pin square P 🏠 🏪 Fishing & boats for hire

⊖ ♂18(2m) 🍷 ♬(½m) 🎥(2m)

***Ch* Broadsmead, Broadland Chalets**
Oulton Broad
for bookings Hoseasons Holidays, Sunway House, Lowestoft, Suffolk NR32 3LT
☎Lowestoft(0502)62292

Large brick-built chalets comprising two bedrooms, one with double bed and the other with two singles. Living room has a studio couch which converts into a double or two single beds.

Mar–Oct MWB out of season 2days min, 1mth max, 19units, 4–6persons [◇] [◆] no dogs ◎ fridge Electric Elec metered 🄻inclusive ☎(½m) [Iron on premises] [Ironing board on premises] HCE in unit ⊙ TV ⊕3pin square P 🏠 🏪 Fishing & boats for hire

⊖ ♂18(2m) 🍷 ♬(½m) 🎥(½m)

***B* 251 Gorleston Road** Oulton (2m W)
for bookings Mr J E Platford, 21 Cambridge Road, Lowestoft, Suffolk NR32 1TE
☎Lowestoft(0502)82607

A semi-detached bungalow with a garage, front and rear gardens, situated in a residential area on the northern side of Lowestoft. 2m from the sea and 1m from Oulton Broad, A1117 road. Accommodation comprises two double-bedded rooms (extra bed is available), sitting room, dining/living room, kitchen and bathroom.

All year MWB 1wk min, 12wks max, 1unit, 1–5persons ◎ fridge Coal or Electric Elec metered 🄻can be hired ☎(100yds) Airing cupboard in unit Iron in unit Ironing board in unit HCE in unit ⊙ ⊛ [CTV] ⊕3pin square P 🏠 ▥ 🏪(½m)

⊖ 🍷(½m) ⊡(2m) ♬(2m) 🎥(2m)

Min£30 Max£40pw (Low)
Min£50 Max£60pw (High)

1982 prices quoted throughout gazetteer

H Whittington House 58 Colville Road, Oulton Broad
for bookings Mr D Hodge, 56 Colville Road, Oulton Broad, Lowestoft, Suffolk NR339QT
☎Lowestoft(0502)65710

Spacious two-storey house with ½-acre garden, occupying a corner position within a 6-acre market garden. Situated about 15 minutes' walk from the sea and 10 minutes' from the Broads. Adequately equipped, with large recreation room, the accommodation sleeps up to nine people in four bedrooms.

Allyear MWB out of season 1wkmin, 4wks max, 1unit, 2–9persons ◇ ◎ fridge Electric Elecmetered ⬓inclusive ☎ Airing cupboard in unit Iron in unit Ironing board in unit HCE in unit ⊙ TV ⊕3pinsquare P 🖿 ▲(200yds)

� 🍴(½m) 📺(½m)
Min£55 Max£110pw

LOW HESKET
Cumbria
Map**11** 44

C Barrock Park Ltd, **The Manor**
Barrock Park, Low Hesket, Carlisle, Cumbria CA40JS
☎Southwaite(06993)681

The outbuildings of this 18th-Century manor house have been tastefully converted into fourteen luxury cottages offering one, two or three bedrooms, superb kitchens, bathrooms and extremely comfortable living rooms. Situated off the A6 at the end of a mile long tree lined drive.

Allyear MWB out of season 3nightsmin, 1mthmax, 14units, 2–7persons ◇ [◆ ◆] ◊ fridge 🍴 Gas/Elecmetered ⬓inclusive ☎ Iron on premises Ironing board on premises HCE in unit [Launderette on premises] ⊙ CTV ⊕3pinsquare 14P 🖿 ▲(1½m) ✒Hard

� 🍴(1½m)
Min£60 Max£75pw (Low)
Min£80 Max£275pw (High)

LOXBEARE
Devon
Map**3** SS81

H Mrs E G Arney *East Sidborough Farm* Loxbeare, Tiverton, Devon EX168DA
☎Tiverton(0884)2172

This establishment is half of a farmhouse which dates from the 16th century. Accommodation includes a kitchen/diner, lounge/diner, bathroom and WC, and three double bedrooms approached by a 16th-century winding staircase. Leave B3221 at fork between Leigh and Leigh Barton, 1m W of Calverleigh, the farm is just under a mile.

Allyear 1wkmin, 3mthsmax, 1unit, 2–6persons [◇] ◆ ◆ ◎ fridge Electric & open fires Elecmetered ⬓notprovided ☎ Airing cupboard in

---

unit Iron in unit Ironing board in unit HCE in unit ⊙ TV ⊕3pinsquare ⊕2pinround P ♠ 🖿 ▲(1½m) Pony riding

� 🍴(1½m) 📺(3m)

LUDCHURCH
Dyfed
Map**2** SN11

B Windermere
for bookings Powell's Holidays, High Street, Saundersfoot, Dyfed
☎Saundersfoot(0834)812791

Modern four-bedroomed bungalow with lounge/diner, kitchen, dining/breakfast area, bathroom and WC. In quiet country area with open views across rural countryside. 2½m from Amroth Beach. Off A477 Pembroke/Camarthen road, signposted Ludchurch.

Jan–Nov MWB out of season 1wkmin, 4wks max, 1unit, 2–8persons ◇ ◆ nopets ◎ fridge 🍴 Elecinclusive ⬓notprovided ☎(½m) Airing cupboard in unit Iron in unit Ironing board in unit HCE in unit ⊙ CTV ⊕3pinsquare P 🖿 ▲(3m)

� 🍴(1½m)
Min£63 Max£168pw

LUDGVAN
Cornwall
Map**2** SW53

B, C, F, H Mr & Mrs Richards **Nanceddan Farm** Ludgvan, Penzance, Cornwall TR208AW
☎Cockwells(0736)740238

Fully-equipped modern holiday homes situated on working farm and holiday complex conveniently positioned within easy reach of many famous beauty spots surrounding the Cornish peninsula. Location midway between St Ives and Penzance approx 1m off A30 and 2½m from sea.

Mar–Oct MWB out of season 1wkmin, 15units, 1–8persons ◇ nopets ◎ fridge Electric Elecmetered ⬓can be hired ☎(onsite) Airing cupboard in unit [Iron on premises] [Ironing board on premises] HCE in unit [Launderette on premises] ⊙ CTV ⊕3pinsquare 2P 1♠ 🖿 ▲(onsite)

� ♿(3m) 🍴(½m) 📺(3m) 🎵(3m) 📺(3m)
Min£35 Max£70pw (Low)
Min£90 Max£190pw (High)

LUMPHANAN
Grampian *Aberdeenshire*
Map**15** NJ50

C Cottar House
for bookings Mr David Gracie, The Old Manse, Glenbuchat, Strathdon, Aberdeenshire AB38TR
☎Glenkindie(09753)222

Detached, one-storey cottage which has been modernised, with good standard of décor. There are two bedrooms (one twin-bedded, the other bunk-bedded), lounge/diner, kitchen, bathroom and WC.

Apr–Oct MWB out of season 1wkmin, 1mthmax, 1unit, 1–5persons ◆ ◎ fridge Electric & open fires Elecmetered ⬓notprovided ☎(2m) Airing cupboard in unit Iron in unit HCE in unit ⊙ ⊕3pinsquare P

� 🍴(2m)
Min£55 Max£110pw

H Croft House
for bookings Mr David Gracie, The Old Manse, Glenbuchat, Strathdon, Aberdeenshire AB38TR
☎Glenkindie(09753)222

Spacious detached house standing on a hillside overlooking Deeside. There are three bedrooms (one double, one twin-bedded and one bunk-bedded room), lounge, kitchen, store room, bathroom and WC.

Apr–Oct MWB out of season 1wkmin, 1mthmax, 1unit, 1–7persons ◆ ◎ fridge Electric, coal & calor gas fires Elecmetered ⬓notprovided ☎(2m) Airing cupboard in unit HCE in unit ⊕3pinsquare P ▲(2m)

�
Min£65 Max£130pw

C St Finans Cottage & Barn
for bookings Mrs T M Collier, St Finans House, Lumphanan, Aberdeenshire
☎Lumphanan(033983)622

*Two modernised stone built cottages on the outskirts of Lumphanan ½mile north of town on A980. **The Barn** is the largest and has open plan living room/kitchen and three bedrooms all on ground floor. **St Finans** comprises kitchen, sitting room and a twin bedded room on ground floor plus two double bedrooms on the first floor.*

Allyear MWB 1wkmin, 2units, 1–8persons ◆ ◎ fridge 🍴 Elecmetered ⬓notprovided ☎(½m) Airing cupboard in unit Iron in unit Ironing board in unit HCE in unit ⊙ TV can be hired ⊕3pinsquare 4P 🖿 ▲(½m)

� ♿(2m) 🍴(½m)
Min£60 Max£85pw (Low)
Min£90 Max£115pw (High)

LUSTLEIGH
Devon
Map**3** SX78

C Becka, Fingle & Holne Cottages
East Wray, Barton Court Cottages
for bookings Mrs V J Procter, Clennon Estates Ltd, Alston Farm, Alston Lane, Churston, Brixham, Devon

An old barn, converted into three delightful cottages whilst preserving old-world charm. All comprise kitchen/diner, lounge, bathroom and WC. Becka and Fingle sleep four people whilst Holne sleeps six. Situated to rear of East Wray

166

Barton Hotel on Moretonhampstead-Bovey Tracey road, A382.

Mar–Oct MWB out of season
3 nights min, 3 units, 4–6 persons ◇ ◆
◉ fridge Electric Elec metered
Ⓛcan be hired ☎(1m) Iron in unit
Ironing board in unit HCE in unit ⊕
TV ⊕3 pin square 50P Ⓜ ♨(1m)

⊖ ♒(2m) ♀(1m) ♨(2m)

Min£40 Max£75pw (Low)
Min£90 Max£120pw (High)

LYDFORD
Devon
Map **2** SX58

F   Mr & Mrs I McCardle, **Gorge House**
Lydford, Okehampton, Devon EX20 4BH
☎Lydford(082 282)224

Three spacious self-contained flats in an attractive country house built on the design of a mid-European castle with 2 acres of grounds overlooking Lydford Gorge. The flats accommodate two to four persons in single or twin-bedded rooms. Each has a living room, kitchen and bathroom.

All year MWB out of season 1 wk min,
3 units, 2–4 persons ◇ ◆ no pets
◉ fridge Electric Elec metered
Ⓛcan be hired ☎(400yds) Airing
cupboard in unit Iron in unit Ironing
board in unit HCE in unit TV
⊕3 pin square P Ⓜ ♨(400yds)
Croquet Lawn, fishing

⊖ ♀(400yds)

Min£35 Max£75pw (Low)
Min£50 Max£85pw (High)

F   Mr R J Parker **Larrick House (Flat)**
Lydford, Okehampton, Devon EX20 4BJ
☎Lydford(082 282)205

Self contained ground floor flat in small country house which is situated in 3¼ acres of natural woodland and lawns on the edge of Lydford Gorge. Accommodation comprises lounge/diner with wood-burning stove, kitchen, bathroom and two bedrooms, one double the other with bunk beds.

All year 1 wk min, 6 wks max, 1 unit,
1–4 persons ◇ ◆ no pets ◉
fridge Electric & woodburning stove
Elec metered Ⓛnot provided
☎(100yds) WM in unit SD in unit
Airing cupboard in unit Iron in unit
Ironing board in unit HCE in unit ⊕
TV ⊕3 pin square 2P Ⓜ ♨(1½m)

⊖ ♀(1½m)

Min£35 Max£85pw

LYDLINCH
Dorset
Map **3** ST71

B   **The Cottage**
for bookings Mrs Wingate-Saul, Holbrook Farm, Lydlinch, Sturminster Newton, Dorset
☎Hazelbury Bryan(025 86)348

Lustleigh
—
Lympstone

Modern detached bungalow located in the beautiful Blackmoor Vale. Accommodation comprises two twin-bedded rooms, plus one with bunk beds, lounge, kitchen/diner, separate bath and WC. Situated 1m from centre of village, off A357 Blandford/Wincanton road. No through road beyond church.

Apr–Oct 1 wk min, 1 mth max, 1 unit,
2–6 persons ◇ ◆ ◉ fridge
Electric Elec metered Ⓛcan be hired
☎ Airing cupboard in unit Iron in unit
Ironing board in unit HCE in unit ⊕
TV ⊕3 pin square 4P 1🛏 ♨(1m)

⊖ ♀(1m)

Min£60 Max£80pw (Low)
Min£85 Max£120pw (High)

LYDSTEP
Dyfed
Map **2** SS19

C   **Giltar Grove Cottage** Giltar Grove Farm
for bookings Powell's Holidays, High Street, Saundersfoot, Dyfed
☎Saundersfoot(0834)812791

Stone-built cottage with separate kitchen/diner, lounge, two bedrooms one with double bed, one with twin beds, bathroom and WC.

May–Dec MWB out of season 1 wk min,
1 unit, 4 persons, nc13 no pets ◉
fridge Rayburn Elec inclusive
Ⓛnot provided ♒ Airing cupboard in
unit Iron in unit Ironing board in unit
HCE in unit ⊕ TV ⊕3 pin square P
Ⓜ ♨(1m) ⌂ ⏖Hard

⊖ ♒(2m) ♀(½m) ▨(1½m) ♫(1½m)
▧(1½m)

Min£57 Max£150pw

C   **Vinlen Cottage**
for bookings Powell's Holidays, High Street, Saundersfoot, Dyfed
☎Saundersfoot(0834)812791

Detached cottage comprising three bedrooms, lounge, kitchen, dining room, bathroom and WC.

Jun–Sep MWB out of season 1 wk min,
1 unit, 8 persons ◇ ◉ fridge 🍴
Gas inclusive Ⓛnot provided
☎(100yds) Airing cupboard in unit Iron
in unit Ironing board in unit HCE in unit
⊕ TV ⊕3 pin square Ⓜ ♨(100yds)

⊖ ♒(2m) ♀(100yds) ▨(2½m)
♫(2½m) ▧(2½m)

Min£69 Max£175pw

LYME REGIS
Dorset
Map **3** SY39

C   Mr & Mrs Blackshaw, ***Coram Towers Cottage*** Pound Road, Lyme Regis, Dorset
☎Lyme Regis(029 74)2012

Detached stone cottage comprising lounge, kitchen/diner, bathroom/WC and three bedrooms, one double-bedded and twin-bedded and one single-bedded room.

Apr–Oct MWB out of season 1 wk min,
4 wks max, 1 unit, 2–5 persons [◇ ◆]
◉ fridge Electric Elec metered
Ⓛcan be hired ☎(20yds) Airing
cupboard in unit Iron on premises
Ironing board on premises HCE in unit
⊕ TV ⊕3 pin square 1P ♨(½m)

⊖ ♒(1m) ♀(½m) ▨(½m) ♨(½m)

LYMINGTON
Hampshire
Map **4** SZ39

B   **33, 36, 37 Rodbourne Close** Everton
for bookings Mr R H Warton, Forfeits, Lymore Lane, Keyhaven, Lymington, Hants
☎Milford on Sea(059 069)2093

Three linked bungalows with modern furnishings, lounge/diner, two bedrooms, modern bathroom with shower. Enclosed garden and garage. 2¾m west of Lymington on A337. Rodbourne Close is a right hand turn coming from Lymington off A337 on W side of Everton.

All year MWB out of season 1 wk min,
6 mths max, 3 units, 2–6 persons [◇]
◇ ◆ ◉ fridge 🍴 Elec inclusive (in
summer) Elec metered (in winter)
Ⓛinclusive ☎(300yds) Airing
cupboard in unit Iron in unit Ironing
board in unit HCE in unit ⊕ CTV
⊕3 pin square 3P 3🛏 Ⓜ ♨(300yds)

⊖ ♒(3m) ♀(300yds) ▨(3m)

Min£60 Max£75pw (Low)
Min£120 Max£150pw (High)

LYMPSTONE
Devon
Map **3** SX98

C   **CC Ref 658**
for bookings Character Cottages (Holidays) Ltd, 34 Fore Street, Sidmouth, Devon EX10 8AQ
☎Sidmouth(039 55)77001

Well-built fisherman's cottage overlooking water front on River Exe with views of Haldon Hills from sun parlour. Accommodation comprises two twin-bedded rooms, lounge/kitchen/diner, and a library; all tastefully furnished. Leave A376 at Sadler's Arms and proceed to far end of village to rivers edge.

All year MWB out of season 1 wk min,
6 mths max, 1 unit, 2–4 persons no pets
◉ fridge Electric Elec inclusive
Ⓛnot provided ☎(100yds) Airing
cupboard in unit Iron in unit Ironing
board in unit HCE in unit ⊕ TV
⊕3 pin square ⊕2 pin round Ⓜ
♨(100yds)

⊖ ♀

Max£111pw (Low)
Min£120 Max£150pw (High)

C CC Ref 6030 L
for bookings Character Cottages
(Holidays) Ltd, 34 Fore Street, Sidmouth,
Devon EX108AQ
☎Sidmouth(039 55)77001

*Double terraced cottage, on River Exe,
with three bedrooms (one twin and two
single beds), lounge, dining room,
kitchen, bathroom and WC. Leave A376
at Sadlers Arms Inn, proceed through
village to Globe Inn, cottage opposite.*

All year MWB out of season 1wk min,
6mths max, 1unit, 2–4persons [◇] ◆
no pets ◢ fridge Electric
Gas inclusive Elec metered ⌴can be
hired ☎($\frac{1}{4}$m) Airing cupboard in unit
Iron in unit Ironing board in unit HCE in
unit ⊕ TV ③3pin square
②2pin round ▥ ♨

↩ ♀
Min£50 Max£129pw

LYNDON
Leicestershire
Map**4** SK90

H Honeysuckle Cottage 5 Church
Road
for bookings Sir John Conant Bt, Lyndon
Hall, Oakham, Leics LE158TU
☎Manton(057 285)275

*Semi-detached house in quiet and
attractive country village. It has its own
small garden area. Downstairs there is a
lounge, kitchen/dining area and upstairs
two twin-bedded rooms and a bathroom
with WC and washbasin.*

Apr–Oct 3days min, 4mths max, 1unit,
1–4persons [◇] ◆ ◆ no pets ◎
fridge Electric Elec metered ⌴can be
hired ☎(25yds) Airing cupboard in
unit HCE in unit TV ③3pin square P
▥ ♨ ⌱ ⌴Hard

↩ ♀(1$\frac{1}{2}$m)
Min£40 Max£50pw (Low)
Min£55 Max£70pw (High)

C Rose Cottage 12 Post Office Lane
for bookings Sir John Conant Bt, Lyndon
Hall, Oakham, Leics LE158TU
☎Manton(057 285)275

*Attractive, stone-built cottage standing in
its own grounds at end of cul-de-sac in
quiet country village. Upstairs there is
one twin-bedded room, and a double
room, downstairs there are a sitting room,
kitchen/dining area and bathroom with
WC and wash basin.*

Apr–Oct 3days min, 4mths max, 1unit,
1–4persons [◇] ◆ no pets ◎
fridge Electric Elec metered ⌴can be
hired ☎(75yds) Airing cupboard in
unit HCE in unit ⊕ TV
③3pin square P ⌂ ▥ ♨(1$\frac{3}{4}$m) ⌱
⌴Hard

↩ ♀($\frac{1}{4}$m)
Min£45 Max£55pw (Low)
Min£60 Max£75pw (High)

LYONSHALL
Hereford & Worcester
Map**3** SO35

C Offa's Cottage
for bookings Mrs M A Eckley, The Holme,
Lyonshall, Kington, Hereford
☎Lyonshall(054 48)216

*A modernised, 17th-century stone-built
cottage built on Offa's Dyke. There are
three bedrooms, a double on the ground
floor, two doubles upstairs with two
double children's bunk beds, a lounge,
dining room, kitchen and bathroom.
Situated at the end of a lane, surrounded
by rich farmland and with views across to
Radnor Forest, own transport is essential.*

Etr–Oct 2days min, 1mth max, 1unit,
1–8persons ◇ ◆ ◎ fridge Electric
& open fires Elec metered
⌴not provided ☎($\frac{1}{4}$m) Airing cupboard
in unit Iron in unit Ironing board in unit
HCE in unit TV ③3pin square P
♨($\frac{1}{4}$m)

↩ ◔◭(3m) ♀(1m)
Min£60 Max£80pw

LYTHAM ST ANNES
Lancashire
Map**7** SD32

F E & D Bitar Argyll Holiday Flats 336
Clifton Drive North, St Annes, Lytham St
Annes, Lancashire FY82PB
☎St Annes(0253)721810

*Tall, semi-detached, stone-fronted
house, containing four well-designed
and spacious flats. Standing to the N of St
Anne's square opposite Ashton Park and
gardens, the flats are conveniently
placed for the town's amenities, with the
beach and pier only a short walk away.*

All year MWB out of season 1wk min,
4units, 2–7persons ◇ ◆ ◎ fridge
Electric Elec metered ⌴inclusive
☎(100yds) Airing cupboard in unit
HCE in unit CTV ③3pin square P ▥
♨(100yds) ⌴Grass

↩ ♀(100yds) ⌷(3m) ⌷(3m) ⌸($\frac{1}{4}$m)
Min£35 Max£50pw (Low)
Min£55 Max£145pw (High)

F Beach Holiday Flats 362/364 Clifton
Drive North
for bookings Mr Norton, Beach Cottage,
364 Clifton Drive North, St Annes, Lytham
St Annes, Lancashire
☎St Annes(0253)727915

*Flats standing in own small grounds, near
to sea. All well furnished and fully self-
contained. Six flats have three bedrooms,
six have one bedroom and one has two
bedrooms with various combinations of
beds. Extra bed space in some by means
of wall-beds in lounge.*

All year MWB out of season 1wk min,
13units, 2–8persons ◆ ◆
◢(4units) ◎(9units) fridge Electric
Gas/Elec metered ⌴inclusive ☎

Airing cupboard in unit Iron in unit
Ironing board in unit HCE in unit ⊕
TV(2units) CTV(11units)
③3pin square 16P 3⌂ ▥
♨(200yds)

↩ ◔◭($\frac{1}{2}$m) ♀(100yds) ⌷(100yds)
⌰($\frac{1}{2}$m) ⌸($\frac{1}{4}$m)

Min£41 Max£98pw (Low)
Min£70 Max£170pw (High)

F Claremont Court Flats 43 South
Promenade
for bookings Lindum Hotel, 65–67 South
Promenade, St Annes, Lytham St Annes,
Lancashire
☎St Annes(0253)725226

*Six flats within a three-storey house, each
flat has lounge with convertible settee,
kitchen and bedroom with two single
beds.*

All year MWB out of season 3day min,
6units, 2–5persons [◆ ◆] ◎
fridge ♨(Oct-May) Electric(Jun-Sep)
Elec inclusive ⌴can be hired
☎(100yds) Airing cupboard in unit Iron
in unit Ironing board in unit HCE in unit
Launderette within 300yds ⊕ TV
③3pin square 12P ▥ ♨($\frac{1}{4}$m)

↩ ◔◭($\frac{1}{2}$m) ♀(200yds) ⌷($\frac{1}{4}$m)
⌰($\frac{1}{2}$m) ⌸($\frac{1}{4}$m)

**F Mrs N Kember Fern Bank Holiday
Flats** 28 St Thomas' Road, St Annes,
Lytham St Annes, Lancashire FY81EN
☎St Annes(0253)725155

*Well-designed flats in a three-storey
building next to a bakery; on the south
side of the town opposite a Baptist
Church and conveniently placed for
shops.*

All year MWB out of season 7days min,
3units, 2–7persons ◆ ◆ ◢ ◎
fridge Electric & Gas
Gas/Elec metered ⌴inclusive ☎ Iron
on premises Ironing board on
premises HCE on premises
[Launderette within 300yds ⊕ TV
③3pin square P ▥ ♨(20yds)

↩ ♀($\frac{1}{4}$m) ⌷($\frac{1}{4}$m) ⌸($\frac{1}{4}$m)

Min£30 Max£50pw (Low)
Min£45 Max£85pw (High)

F Mrs W Ettenfield Greenaways
7 Victoria Road, St Annes, Lytham St
Annes, Lancashire FY81LE
☎St Annes(0253)726204

*A clean and comfortable ground-floor flat
in a Victorian house with large double
bedroom, lounge with foldaway double
bed, kitchen, bathroom and WC. The
house is situated in quiet side road, $\frac{1}{2}$m
from sea, beach and sand dunes.*

May-Sep 1wk min, 1mth max, 1unit,
1–5persons ◇ ◆ ◢ no pets ◢
fridge Electric & Gas fires
Gas/Elec metered ⌴inclusive ☎ SD
on premises Iron in unit Ironing board
in unit HCE in unit [Launderette within
300yds] ⊕ CTV ③3pin square 6P
▥ ♨($\frac{1}{4}$m)

⇔ ♀(½m) ▣(2m) ♬(2m) ♜(¾m)

Min£42 Max£52pw (Low)
Min£45 Max£55pw (High)

F Mrs E Crowther ***Harcourt Holiday Flats*** 22 Victoria Road, St Annes, Lytham St Annes, Lancashire FY8 1LE
☎St Annes(0253)720659

Well-maintained and well-furnished flats in brick-built, semi-detached house. Located south of town centre in a quiet tree-lined road a short distance from the seafront. Pleasant small garden in front and parking facilities at rear.

Etr-Oct MWB out of season 7days min, 3units, 4–6persons [◇] ◈ ◆ no pets ◎ fridge Electric Elec metered ◫inclusive ☎ Iron on premises Ironing board on premises HCE in unit ⊙ TV ⊕3pin square P ▥ ♨(100yds)

F **Sandgate** 352/254 Clifton Drive North
for bookings Mr Norton, 364 Clifton Drive North, St Annes, Lytham St Annes, Lancashire
☎St Annes(0253)727915 & 737389

Ten flats, two are three bedroomed, four are two bedroomed, and four are one bedroomed. Some of the flats also have wall beds for extra bed space. On main A584 Blackpool road close to Ashton Garden and St Annes Square and beach.

All year MWB out of season 1wk min, 10units, 2–8persons ◈ ◆ ◎ fridge Electric Elec metered ◫inclusive ☎ Airing cupboard in unit Iron in unit Ironing board in unit HCE in unit ⊙ TV(2units) CTV(8units) ⊕3pin square 8P ▥ ♨(200yds)

⇔ ⛳(½m) ♀(100yds) ▣(100yds) ♬(½m) ♜(½m)

Min£50.50 Max£93pw (Low)
Min£90 Max£162pw (High)

F F R & M T Hoyle **Trevelyn House** 23 Fairhaven Road, St Annes, Lytham St Annes, Lancashire
☎St Annes(0253)727871

A large three-storey, semi-detached, brick-built house situated in a quiet side road just off the Promenade. Five units, all with one or two bedrooms with extra bed space within the lounges (wall beds). Adequately furnished. Proprietor lives on premises.

All year MWB out of season 1wk min, 5units, 2–6persons ◈ ◆ ◎ fridge Electric Elec metered ◫inclusive Airing cupboard in unit Iron in unit Ironing board on premises HCE in unit [Launderette within 300yds] ⊙ CTV ⊕3pin square P ▥ ♨(200yds) ⛳ Putting

⇔ ♀(200yds) ▣(200yds) ♬(200yds) ♜(½m)

Min£40 Max£55pw (Low)
Min£65 Max£98pw (High)

MADLEY
Hereford & Worcester
Map **3** SO43

B Mrs L G M Coppock **Swinmore Bungalow** Pan'rama, Canon Bridge Road, Madley, Hereford
☎Golden Valley(0981)250486

On entering village of Madley on B4352 turn left at signpost Canon Bridge. Continue for ½m and the bungalow is on the left, set in a private garden with extensive views of surrounding countryside. The accommodation consists of lounge/diner, kitchen, bathroom/WC and three double bedrooms.

All year MWB 2days min, 2wks max, 1unit, 1–6persons ◈ no pets ◎ fridge Electric & open fires Elec metered ◫not provided ☎(½m) Iron in unit Ironing board in unit HCE in unit TV ⊕3pin square 2P ♨(½m)

⇔ ♀(½m)

Min£35 Max£70pw

MALHAM
North Yorkshire
Map **7** SD86

F, C **Gordale Court Holiday Flats**
for bookings Mrs S F Marston, Calton Hall, Calton, Airton, Skipton, N Yorkshire BD23 4AD
☎Airton(07293)285

Two barns and a coach house. Flat 1 on the ground-floor (with patio) sleeps six in a double-bedded room, a twin-bedded room and a small room with bunk beds. Flat 2 is above with the same accommodation. Flat 6 has a double room and a twin room plus sun balcony. Cottages 3, 4 & 5 have one bedroom. All have a bathroom, WC, kitchen and lounge.

All year MWB out of season 2days min, 6units, 1–6persons ◈ ◆ ◎ fridge Electric Elec metered ◫can be hired ☎(50yds) Airing cupboard in unit HCE in unit ⊙ TV ⊕3pin square 10P ▥ ♨(50yds)

⇔ ♀

Min£30 Max£51pw (Low)
Min£73 Max£120pw (High)

MALVERN, GREAT
Hereford & Worcester
Map **3** SO74

C Mr & Mrs M G Allen **Hartlands** Evendine Lane, Colwall, Malvern, Worcestershire WR13 6DT
☎Colwall(0684)40658

A modernised 17th-century thatched cottage with a large garden, orchard and brook. The stone-built cider house and outbuildings, also sheep, chickens and goat, give it a farm-like atmosphere. It is situated on the sunny, west slopes of the Malvern Hills and is a good centre for walking and touring.

All year MWB out of season 1night-wknds min, 4wks max, 1unit, 1–4persons ◇ ◈ ◆ ◎ fridge Electric Elec metered ◫can be hired ☎(½m) SD in unit Airing cupboard in unit Ion in unit Ironing board in unit HCE in unit ⊙ TV ⊕3pin square P ▥ ♨(½m)

⇔ ♀(½m)

Min£38.50 Max£60pw (Low)
Min£82.50 Max£105pw (High)

H **4 West Malvern Road**
for bookings Mrs J Lewis, 6 West Malvern Road, North Malvern, Malvern, Worcestershire
☎Malvern(068 45)4407 →

Gordale Court Holiday Accommodation

The cottages and flats are situated near the centre of Malham behind The Buck Inn. They occupy a peaceful position with open views over fields and fells. There is ample private car parking and space for children to play. Pets are welcome. Close at hand are two old world inns offering a wide choice of meals.

Cottages and flats are tastefully furnished and carpeted, are all electric, with fridge, cooker, electric fires, night storage heaters, shaving points and a 625 line TV. Electricity, storage radiators only are included in the price. No linen provided.

For Bookings: Mrs S MARSTON
CALTON HALL, CALTON, Nr. AIRTON,
SKIPTON, NORTH YORKSHIRE BD23 4AD.
TEL. AIRTON 285/257.

Terraced three-storey house with extensive views over Worcestershire. Accommodation comprises kitchen/dining area, lounge and first-floor twin bedroom and double bedroom. On the second-floor there are two bedrooms (one double and one single) with bath/WC/washbasin. Pets are allowed, but will be charged for.

All year 2days min, 3mths max, 1unit, 1–7persons [◇] ◆ ◉ fridge Electric Elec metered ⚡can be hired ☎ Airing cupboard in unit Iron in unit Ironing board in unit HCE in unit ⊕ ⊕3pin square Ⓜ ♨(100yds)

↤ δ☖(2½m) ☁(100yds) ▨(1m) ♫(½m) 🐾(1m)

Min£38 Max£48pw (Low)
Min£58 Max£68pw (High)

C Mr & Mrs P Bennett **Whitewells Farm** Ridgeway Cross, Malvern, Worcestershire WR135JS
☎Ridgeway Cross(088 684)607

Converted Tudor-style cottages (previously an old stable and milking parlour, barn and a kiln) featuring many fine floors and oak beams. Accommodation includes double and twin-bedded rooms, lounge/dining room, kitchen and bathroom. Located on A4103 Worcester–Hereford road at Ridgeway Cross.

All year MWB out of season 3days min, 6mths max, 5units, 1–6persons [◇] ◆ ◆ ◉ fridge Elec metered apart from lighting and kitchen use ⚡inclusive ☎ Airing cupboard in unit Iron in unit Ironing board in unit HCE in unit [Launderette on premises] ⊕ CTV ⊕3pin square P Ⓜ ♨(¼m)

Min£80.50 Max£258.75pw

MALVERN WELLS
Hereford & Worcester
Map**3** SO74

F **Blackmore House** 215–217 Wells Road
for bookings Mrs J Limbrick, Alfords Farm, Upleadon, Newent, Gloucestershire GL18 1EF
☎Newent(0531)820578

Converted old five-storey house, approx 2½m from Great Malvern centre. Accommodation comprises a kitchen, lounge/dining room and either one, two or three bedrooms with either single, double or twin beds.

All year 1wk min, 6mths max, 5units, 1–6persons ◆ ◆ ◉ fridge Electric Elec metered ⚡can be hired ☎(100yds) WM in unit SD in unit Airing cupboard in unit Iron in unit Ironing board in unit HCE in unit ⊕ TV ⊕3pin square Ⓜ ♨(100yds) ⌒

↤ δ (1m) ☁(½m) ▨(2m) ♫(2m) 🐾(2m)

Min£35 Max£90pw

1982 prices quoted throughout gazetteer

MAMHEAD
Devon
Map**3** SX98

B **CC Ref 404 P**
for bookings Character Cottages (Holidays) Ltd, 34 Fore Street, Sidmouth, Devon EX108AQ
☎Sidmouth(039 55)77001

Spacious, detached bungalow in open country facing S. Entrance hall, large lounge with picture windows giving fine views, sun room with extra bed, large well-equipped kitchen with bright décor, and two large bedrooms with H/C washbasin. One double and one twin-bedded. Modern bathroom/WC and separate WC.

All year MWB out of season 1wk min, 1mth max, 1unit, 2–6persons ◆ ◉ fridge Elec inclusive ⚡not provided ☎ Airing cupboard in unit Iron in unit Ironing board in unit HCE in unit ⊕ TV ⊕3pin square ⊕2pin round P ♨(2½m)

↤ ☁(2½m)

Min£62 Max£91pw (Low)
Min£122 Max£155pw (High)

MAN, ISLE OF
Map**6** SC
see DOUGLAS, ONCHAN, RAMSEY

MANESTY
Cumbria
Map**11** NY21

B **High Seat**
for bookings Mrs S J Leyland, Youdale Knot, Manesty, Keswick, Cumbria CA125UG
☎Borrowdale(059 684)663

Modern newly-built bungalow situated in the ground of the proprietor's residence, sleeps five persons in one double and one family bedroom. Breathtaking views across the Borrowdale Valley to the hills beyond. Only 5m from Keswick.

All year 1wk min, 1mth max, 1unit, 5persons, nc5 no pets ◉ fridge Electric Elec metered (hot water inclusive) ⚡not provided ☎(½m) HCE in unit ⊕ ⊕3pin square P Ⓜ ♨(½m)

↤ ☁(1m)

Min£65 Max£75pw (Low)
Max£100pw (High)

MANORBIER
Dyfed
Map**2** SS09

C **Coach House** Tarr Farm
for bookings Powell's Holidays, High Street, Saundersfoot, Dyfed
☎Saundersfoot(0834)812791

Retaining the old arched entrance of the Coach House, this detached cottage with character is set in the grounds of a farm. It

has an open plan lounge with dining area and kitchen. There are two bedrooms on the first floor.

Apr–Oct MWB out of season 1wk min, 6wks max, 1unit, 2–4persons ◇ ◆ ◆ no pets ⚴ fridge Electric Gas/Elec inclusive ⚡provided (overseas visitors only) ☎ Iron in unit HCE in unit ⊕ TV ⊕3pin square P Ⓜ ♨(150yds)

↤ ☁(150yds)

Min£57 Max£150pw

C **Coachmans Cottage** Sunnyhill Farm, The Ridgeway
for bookings Powell's Holidays, High Street, Saundersfoot, Dyfed
☎Saundersfoot(0834)812791

Renovated detached cottage, two bedrooms, lounge, kitchen/diner, bathroom and WC. 2½m from Manorbier.

Jan–Nov MWB out of season 1wk min, 1unit, 5persons [◇] ◆ ◉ fridge 🍴 Elec inclusive ⚡not provided ☎(30yds) Airing cupboard in unit Iron in unit Ironing board in unit HCE in unit CTV ⊕3pin square P ♨(1½m)

↤ ☁(1½m)

Min£51 Max£135pw

H **Slade Farm** Lydstep Road
for bookings Powell's Holidays, High Street, Saundersfoot, Dyfed
☎Saundersfoot(0834)812791

Large detached house consisting of four bedrooms, lounge, dining room, kitchen/diner, bathroom and WC. 1m from Lydstep Beach.

May–Oct MWB out of season 1wk min, 1unit, 10persons [◇] ◆ ◉ fridge 🍴 Elec inclusive ⚡not provided ☎(½m) WM in unit Airing cupboard in unit Iron in unit Ironing board in unit HCE in unit CTV ⊕3pin square P Ⓜ ♨(2m)

↤ δ☖(2m) ☁(2½m) ▨(2½m) ♫(2½m)

Min£105 Max£267pw

C **Tarr Cottage** Tarr Farm
for bookings Powell's Holidays, High Street, Saundersfoot, Dyfed
☎Saundersfoot(0834)812791

A newly adapted detached cottage within the grounds of a farm. The accommodation consists of an open plan lounge with dining area and kitchen. There are two bedrooms.

Apr–Nov MWB out of season 1wk min, 6wks max, 1unit, 2–4persons ◇ ◆ ◆ no pets ⚴ fridge Electric Gas/Elec inclusive ⚡provided (overseas visitors only) ☎ Iron in unit HCE in unit ⊕ TV ⊕3pin square P Ⓜ ♨(150yds)

↤ ☁(150yds)

Min£57 Max£150pw

F **Tarr Farmhouse (Flat 1)**
for bookings Powell's Holidays, High Street, Saundersfoot, Dyfed
☎Saundersfoot(0834)812791

A first-floor flat within Tarr Farmhouse, comprising lounge/diner, kitchen, shower/WC and two bedrooms one with double bed and one with twin beds.

May–Sep MWB out of season 1wk min, 6wks max, 1unit, 2–4persons ◇ ◆ ◆ no pets ◎ fridge Electric Elec inclusive ⬜can be hired (overseas visitors only) ☎ Iron in unit Ironing board on premises HCE in unit ⊕ TV ⊛3pin square 2P ▥ ⚏(100yds)
⇥ ⚲(100yds)
Min£51 Max£135pw

MAPLEDURHAM
Oxfordshire
Map **4** SU67

C   No 1 The Almshouse
for bookings Mapledurham Estate Office, Mapledurham, Reading, Berkshire RG4 7TP
☎Kidmore End(0734)723350
Completely modernised 17th-century Almshouse in Mapledurham village, with four bedrooms, two on ground floor and two on first floor. Lounge with open fire, kitchen/diner, bathroom and WC. There is an enclosed rear garden.

All year 1wk min, 1unit, 2–6persons ◇ ◆ ◎ fridge Elec metered ⬜can be hired ☎ Airing cupboard Iron Ironing board HCE TV ⊛3pin square 1P ⚏(3m)
⇥ ⚲
Min£55pw (Low)
Min£80.50 Max£119.75pw (High)

C   The Bothy & Bottom Farm Cottage
for bookings Mapledurham Estate Office, Mapledurham, Reading, Berkshire RG4 7TP
☎Kidmore End(0734)723350
Two period cottages with exposed beams, one with two bedrooms, the other with three. Set in rural location.

All year 1wk min, 2units, 2–6persons ◇ ◆ ◎ fridge ♨ Elec metered ⬜can be hired ☎(½m) Airing cupboard on premises Iron on premises Ironing board on premises HCE on premises TV ⊛3pin square 1P 1▥ ⚏(3m)
⇥ ⚲ ▨
Min£45pw (Low)
Min£69 Max£119.75pw (High)

C   Longcross Cottage Chazey Heath
for bookings Mapledurham Estate Office, Mapledurham, Reading, Berkshire RG4 7TP
☎Kidmore End(0734)723350
Secluded cottage surrounded by open farm land. Accommodation comprises large living room, kitchen, bathroom, WC and three bedrooms.

All year 1wk min, 1unit, 2–6persons ◇ ◆ ◎ fridge Rayburn Elec metered ⬜can be hired ☎ Airing cupboard Iron Ironing board HCE TV ⊛3pin square ⊛3pin round 2P ⚏(2m)

⇥ ⌀�a(3m) ⚲(3m) ▨(3m) ♫(3m) ▩(3m)
Min£45pw (Low)
Min£69 Max£109.25pw (High)

H   No 3 New Farm Cottage
for bookings Mapledurham Estate Office, Mapledurham, Reading, Berkshire RG4 7TP
☎Kidmore End(0734)723350
A spacious cottage situated close to New Farm, ½m from Mapledurham village. The cottage has four bedrooms (one double, one twin and two single rooms), bathroom and WC. The ground floor comprises lounge, dining room, kitchen and WC.

All year 1wk min, 1unit, 2–6persons ◇ ◆ ◎ fridge Electric & open fires Elec metered ⬜can be hired ☎(½m) Airing cupboard on premises Iron on premises Ironing board on premises HCE on premises TV ⊛3pin square 2P ⚏(3½m)
⇥ ⚲(2m)
Min£45pw (Low)
Min£69 Max£109.25pw (High)

MARAZION
Cornwall
Map **2** SW53

H   Roselea
for bookings Mr J A A Lambert, Rose Hill, Marazion, Penzance, Cornwall
☎Penzance(0736)710461
Detached studio-type house with wonderful views of Mounts Bay. Accommodation comprises three good sized bedrooms (two family and one double), modern kitchen, dining room and bathroom and WC.

Mar–Nov MWB out of season 1wk min, 1mth max, 1unit, 2–8persons ◇ ◎ fridge ♨ Elec metered ⬜can be hired ☎(300yds) SD in unit Airing cupboard in unit Iron in unit Ironing board in unit HCE in unit ⊕ CTV ⊛3pin square 2P 1▥ ▥ ⚏ ⌫
⇥ ⚲(3m) ▨(3m) ♫(3m) ▩(3m)
Min£60 Max£95pw (Low)
Min£105 Max£180pw (High)

H   Rosemount (1, 2, 3, 4)
for bookings Mr J A A Lambert, Rose Hill, Marazion, Penzance, Cornwall
☎Penzance(0736)710461
Four houses in grounds of period house. A modern well-equipped kitchen, large sunny lounge with good sea views, two good-sized bedrooms with divan beds, one double, one twin, bunk bedroom and bathroom/WC.

Mar–Nov MWB out of season 1wk min, 1mth max, 4units, 2–6persons ◇ ◎ fridge Electric Elec metered ⬜can be hired ☎(300yds) SD in unit Airing cupboard in unit Iron in unit Ironing board in unit HCE in unit ⊕ CTV ⊛3pin square P ▥ ⚏(300yds) ⌫

⇥ ⚲(3m) ▨(3m) ♫(3m) ▩(3m)
Min£42 Max£80pw (Low)
Min£95 Max£160pw (High)

MARGATE
Kent
Map **5** TR37

F   Mr & Mrs Mather **39 Prices Avenue**
Cliftonville, Margate, Kent CT9 2NT
Two flats on the ground floor of a Victorian house occupying a corner position ½m from seafront. Both flats have lounge, dining room, kitchen and bathroom/WC, with two bedrooms in one flat and one in the other. The proprietor's flat is on the first floor.

Feb–Oct MWB out of season 3days min, 3mths max, 2units, 2–6persons ◇ ◎ fridge Electric Elec metered ⬜can be hired ☎(100yds) Iron in unit Ironing board in unit HCE in unit [Launderette within 300yds] ⊕ ❀ TV ⊛3pin square ▥ ⚏(100yds)
⇥ ⚲(200yds) ▨(½m) ♫(½m) ▩(½m)
Min£35 Max£70pw (Low)
Min£40 Max£90pw (High)

MARLDON
Devon
Map **3** SX86

F   Mr D Best **Little Westerland**
Marldon, Paignton, Devon
☎Paignton(0803)557898
Flat in unspoilt country with own entrance via eight steps. Accommodation comprises double bedroom plus two divans in a comfortable lounge, kitchen/diner, bath and separate WC. ¾m from village of Marldon just off A3022 Torquay/Brixham road.

May–Dec 1wk min, 1mth max, 1unit, 1–4persons ◇ no pets ◎ fridge Electric Elec metered ⬜can be hired ☎(½m) Airing cupboard in unit Iron in unit HCE in unit ⊕ CTV ⊛3pin square P ▥ ⚏(½m)
⇥ ⌀�a(2½m) ⚲(½m) ▨(2½m) ♫(2½m) ▩(2½m)
Min£50 Max£100pw

MARNHULL
Dorset
Map **3** ST71

F   The Flat
for bookings Mr & Mrs R G Gorton, Walton Elm House, Marnhull, Sturminster Newton, Dorset DT10 1QG
☎Marnhull(0258)820553
A country residence of the late 19th-century of which the outbuilding and cottages have been converted into self-catering units. There is also an upstairs flat in the owner's house which has a separate outside stairs access. The flat has sitting room with divider, kitchen, bathroom with WC, two separate bedrooms (one double and 2 single beds). →

All year MWB out of season 1wk min, 6mths max, 1unit, 2–4persons, nc10 no pets ◉ fridge ♨ Elec inclusive Ⓛinclusive ☎(¾m) Iron on premises Ironing board on premises HCE in unit [Launderette on premises] ⊕ TV ⊕3pin square P Ⅲ ♨ ⌂ Recreation rooms Croquet

⊷ ♀(1m)

Min£74.25 Max£99pw (Low)
Min£132pw (High)

C   Lodge Cottage
for bookings Mr & Mrs R G Gorton, Walton Elm House, Marnhull, Sturminster Newton, Dorset DT10 1QG
☎Marnhull(0258)820553

Two-storey, three bedroomed cottage in grounds of main house, with living room, open-plan kitchen, bathroom, and WC. There is also a put-u-up.

All year MWB out of season 1wk min, 6mths max, 1unit, 2–6persons, nc10 no pets Aga cooker fridge Electric & log fires Elec inclusive Ⓛinclusive ☎(¾m) Iron on premises Ironing board on premises HCE in unit [Launderette on premises] ⊕ TV ⊕3pin square P Ⅲ ♨ ⌂ Recreation rooms Croquet

⊷ ♀(1m)

Min£132pw (Low)
Min£154 Max£176pw (High)

C   Pavilion Cottage
for bookings Mr & Mrs R G Gorton, Walton Elm House, Marnhull, Sturminster Newton, Dorset DT10 1QG
☎Marnhull(0258)820553

Two-bedroomed cottage in grounds of main house, with living room, open-plan kitchen, bathroom with WC, one double bed and two single beds, and an additonal put-u-up.

All year MWB out of season 1wk min, 6mths max, 1unit, 2–6persons, nc10 no pets ◉ fridge ♨ Elec inclusive Ⓛinclusive ☎(¾m) Iron on premises Ironing board on premises HCE in unit [Launderette on premises] ⊕ TV ⊕3pin square P Ⅲ ♨ ⌂ Recreation rooms Croquet

⊷ ♀(1m)

Min£74.25 Max£99pw (Low)
Min£132pw (High)

C   Pool Cottages
for bookings Mr & Mrs R G Gorton, Walton Elm House, Marnhull, Sturminster Newton, Dorset DT10 1QG
☎Marnhull(0258)820553

Three adjoining cottages, each having living room, open-plan kitchen, shower with WC, a double bedroom and single bed-settee in the living room.

All year MWB out of season 1wk min, 6mths max, 3units, 2–3persons, nc10 no pets ◉ fridge ♨ Elec inclusive Ⓛinclusive ☎(¾m) Iron on premises Ironing board on premises HCE in unit [Launderette on premises] ⊕ TV ⊕3pin square P Ⅲ ♨ ⌂ Recreation rooms Croquet ♿

⊷ ♀(1m)

Min£49.50 Max£76pw (Low)
Min£88 Max£98pw (High)

C   Wing Cottage
for bookings Mr & Mrs R G Gorton, Walton Elm House, Marnhull, Sturminster Newton, Dorset DT10 1QG
☎Marnhull(0258)820553

Cottage extension wing of the main house with ground-floor accommodation of three double bedrooms (plus bed-settee), living room, kitchen, bath and WC.

All year MWB out of season 1wk min, 6mths max, 1unit, 2–6persons, nc10 no pets Aga cooker fridge Electric & log fires Elec inclusive Ⓛinclusive ☎(¾m) Iron on premises Ironing board on premises HCE in unit [Launderette on premises] ⊕ TV ⊕3pin square P Ⅲ ♨ ⌂ Recreation rooms Croquet ♿

⊷ ♀(1m)

Min£132pw (Low)
Min£154 Max£176pw (High)

MASHAM
North Yorkshire
Map**8** SE28

Ch, C   Charlcot Estate Ltd Charlcot, Masham, Ripon, N Yorkshire
☎Ripon(0765)89335

Six excellent Norwegian chalets and two detached self-contained cottages standing in 30 acres of parkland. Chalet accommodation comprises open-plan kitchen, dining room with partition to lounge, two bedrooms (one twin-bedded, the other with bunk beds). There is also a convertible bed-settee in the lounge. Cottage accommodation comprises lounge/dining room, open-plan kitchen, with bedrooms containing either twin beds or bunk beds (one sleeps six, the other sleeps eight). Attractive Norwegian décor and furniture. An ideal situation for the country lover.

All year 1wk min, 4wks max, 8units, 5–8persons [◇] ◆ no pets ◉ fridge Electric Elec inclusive Ⓛinclusive ☎(1m) Airing cupboard in unit Iron on premises Ironing board on premises HCE in unit TV can be hired ⊕3pin square P Ⅲ ♨(3½m)

⊷ ♀(2½m)   Private fishing

Min£80 Max£110pw (Low)
Min£178 Max£201pw (High)

F   The Coach House
for bookings Mrs J Airton, Sunnyside, Red Lane, Masham, Ripon, N Yorkshire HG4 4HH
☎Ripon(0765)89327

First-floor accommodation in a converted stone-built coach house and stable, within the grounds of Sunnyside House. Restored to a good standard with

---

two twin-bedded rooms, lounge/diner and well-fitted kitchen. Semi rural and wooded surroundings near the village centre.

All year MWB out of season 3days min, 1unit, 1–6persons ◇ ◆ no pets ◉ fridge ♨ Elec inclusive Ⓛinclusive Elec inclusive Ⓛinclusive ☎(300yds) Iron in unit Ironing board in unit HCE in unit [Launderette on premises] ⊕ CTV ⊕3pin square 2P Ⅲ ♨(200yds) Pony trekking, fishing & bowling green

⊷ ♿ ♀(400yds) 🅿(400yds)

Min£85 Max£95pw (Low)
Min£125 Max£160pw (High)

C   Nelson Cottage Market Square
for bookings Mrs J Airton, Sunnyside, Red Lane, Masham, Ripon, N Yorkshire HG4 4HH
☎Ripon(0765)89327

Two-storey stone-built cottage converted from outbuildings inside the pub yard. Sitting room/kitchen on the ground-floor with convertible bed-settee. A double-bedded room and a twin-bedded room on the first-floor with bathroom and shower unit/WC. Entrance is through the archway facing the village square. Self-contained with private entrance.

All year MWB out of season 3day min, 1unit, 1–6persons ◇ ◆ no pets ◉ fridge ♨ Elec inclusive Ⓛinclusive ☎(60yds) Airing cupboard in unit Iron in unit Ironing board in unit HCE in unit ⊕ CTV ⊕3pin square Ⅲ ♨(50yds) Fishing, pony trekking, bowling green

⊷ ♿(1m) ♀(50yds)

Min£85 Max£95pw (Low)
Min£125 Max£160pw (High)

F   Nelson House Market Square
for bookings Mrs J Airton, Sunnyside, Red Lane, Masham, Ripon, N Yorkshire HG4 4HH
☎Ripon(0765)89327

Three-storey stone-built converted 18th-century public house, comprising four self-contained flats. Three flats have a common entrance. Accommodation for two of them includes one double-bedded room plus one twin-bedded room, a combined kitchen/lounge, bathroom and shower unit/WC. The third flat has kitchen/lounge, double bedroom and shower room. The fourth flat has a separate entrance, and accommodation consists of one double-bedded room, one twin-bedded room, lounge/kitchenette and bathroom/shower/WC.

All year MWB out of season 3days min, 4units, 2–6persons ◇ ◆ no pets ◉ fridge ♨ Elec inclusive Ⓛinclusive ☎(60yds) Airing cupboard in unit Iron in unit Ironing board in unit HCE in unit ⊕ CTV ⊕3pin square Ⅲ ♨(50yds) Fishing, pony trekking, bowling green

⊖ δ₉(1m) ☎(60yds)
Min£65 Max£75pw (Low)
Min£85 Max£120pw (High)

C Sunnyside Cottage
for bookings Mrs J Airton, Sunnyside,
Red Lane, Masham, Ripon, N Yorkshire
HG4 4HH
☎Ripon(0765)89327

*Detached cottage situated on the
outskirts of the town not far from the small
local brewery. Ground floor comprises
lounge, dining room and kitchen. First
floor comprises one twin-bedded room,
one family room with double and single
bed, one double-bedded room,
bathroom and WC.*

All year MWB out of season 3days min,
3mths max, 1unit, 1–8persons [◇] ◆
no pets ◎ fridge ♨ & gas fire
Gas/Elec inclusive ⬛inclusive
☎(400yds) Airing cupboard in unit Iron
in unit Ironing board in unit HCE in unit
[Launderette on premises] ⊖ CTV
⊕3pin square 1P ▥ ♨(200yds)
Fishing, pony trekking & bowling green

⊖ δ₉ ☎(400yds) ▨(400yds)
Min£90 Max£100pw (Low)
Min£130 Max£173pw (High)

MATLOCK
Derbyshire
Map**8** SK25

C Coach House Clifton Road
for bookings Mrs D M Derr, 1 Dale Road,
Matlock, Derbyshire
☎Matlock(0629)3683

*Tastefully converted former coach house
accommodation comprises double and
single-bedded room, lounge,
kitchen/diner and bathroom. 100yds off
main A6 close to New Bath Hotel.*

Apr-Nov 1wk min, 1unit, 3persons ◆
no pets ◔ fridge ♨& gas fires
Gas inclusive ⬛not provided ☎(½m)
Airing cupboard in unit Iron in unit
Ironing board in unit HCE in unit CTV
⊕3pin square 4P ▥ ♨(½m)

⊖ δ₈(2m) ☎(200yds) ▨(2m)
♫(2m) ♨(2m)
Min£60 Max£95pw

MAWGAN PORTH
Cornwall
Map**2** SW86

F Europa Court International
for bookings Mr N Maine-Tucker, 4 Mylor
Downs, Falmouth, Cornwall TR11 5UN
☎Truro(0872)863450

*Two-storey block of luxury holiday villas,
with either patio or balcony, in a
protected position overlooking Mawgan
Porth beach. Accommodation comprises
two bedrooms (one double, one twin-
bedded), lounge/diner with twin studio
divans, kitchen and bathroom/WC.*

Mar-Nov MWB out of season 1wk min,
8mths max, 18units, 1–7persons ◆
◆ no pets ◎ fridge Electric
Heating inclusive (Sep-May)
Elec metered ⬛inclusive ☎ Airing

cupboard in unit Launderette on
premises ⊖ CTV ⊕3pin square P
▥ ♨(100yds) ♭

⊖ ☎(100yds) ▨(¼m)
Min£65 Max£110pw (Low)
Min£120 Max£195pw (High)

**Ch Mr & Mrs A S Wood Mawgan Porth
Holiday Park** Mawgan Porth, Newquay,
Cornwall TR8 4BD
☎St Mawgan(063 74)322

*Chalet bungalows set in 22 acres of rural
countryside, close to the sea.
Accommodation comprises two
bedrooms (one double, one with twin
beds), lounge/diner with bed-settee,
kitchenette and bathroom/WC. All have
good quality modern furniture and
fittings.*

Apr-Oct MWB out of season 1wk min,
12units, 1–6persons ◆ ◆ no pets
◔ fridge Electric
Gas/Elec metered ⬛not provided ☎
Airing cupboard in unit Iron in unit
Ironing board in unit HCE in unit
Launderette on premises ⊖ CTV
⊕3pin square P ▥ ♨(¼m) ◿

⊖
Min£45 Max£185pw

F Sandy Court
for bookings Mr J Dinsdale, 36 Pentire
Crescent, Newquay, Cornwall
☎Newquay(063 73)3183

*Purpose built, two-storey holiday houses
situated directly on the beach.
Constructed in 1972, each unit has a
comfortable lounge with a put-u-up
settee, spacious kitchen, diner,
bathroom and two bedrooms. A patio
overlooks the beach.*

Etr-Sep MWB out of season 4days min,
8units, 6–7persons ◆ ◆ no pets
◔ fridge Electric Gas inclusive
Elec metered ⬛not provided
☎(200yds) Airing cupboard in unit Iron
in unit Ironing board in unit HCE in unit
⊖ TV ⊕3pin square P ▥
♨(200yds) δ

⊖ ☎ ▨ ♫ ♨
Min£60 Max£80pw (Low)
Min£90 Max£200pw (High)

MEIGLE
Tayside *Perthshire*
Map**11** SO24

**Ch Mr A J G Brown Kings of Kinloch
Holiday Lodges** Meigle, Blairgowrie,
Perthshire PH12 8QX
☎Meigle(082 84)273

*Small, complex of five modern Finnish
timbered lodges, individually sited in
tree-studded setting in the grounds of a
country hotel. Each has large living room
with open-plan kitchen, a twin-bedded
room and a bedroom with four bunk
beds. There is also a verandah.*

All year MWB out of season 1wk min,
3wks max, 5units, 1–6persons ◇ ◆
◎ fridge Electric Elec inclusive
⬛inclusive ☎ Airing cupboard in unit
Iron in unit Ironing board in unit HCE in
unit ⊖ CTV ⊕3pin square 2P ▥
♨(1m)

⊖ δ₉(3m) ☎(100yds)
Min£85 Max£105pw (Low)
Min£125 Max£160pw (High)

MELLON UDRIGLE
Highland *Ross & Cromarty*
Map**14** NG89

Ch Ceol Na Mara Chalets
for bookings M E Tew, Ceol Na Mara Ltd,
South Kenwood, Kenton, Exeter, Devon
☎Mamhead(062 688)672

*Five timber framed chalets set on edge of
a fir wood only yards from the sea and
beach; commanding superb coastal and
mountain views. Mellon Udrigle is a small
hamlet set in quiet location 3 miles off
A832. Dinghy and outboard motor with
each chalet.*

26Mar–5Nov MWB out of season
1wk min, 5units, 1–6persons ◇ ◎
fridge ♨ Elec metered ⬛can be
hired ☎(⅓m) Airing cupboard in unit
Iron in unit Ironing board in unit HCE in
unit ⊖ TV ⊕3pin square P ♨(3m)
Sauna

⊖ ☎(3m)
Min£69 Max£115pw (Low)
Min£172.50 Max£201.25pw (High)

MELROSE
Borders *Roxburghshire*
Map**12** NT53

C Lilac Cottage Darnick by Melrose,
Roxburghshire
for bookings Miss J Bristow, Thorncroft,
Lilliesleaf, Roxburghshire, TD6 9JD
☎Lilliesleaf(083 57)424

*Cottage in centre of small village one mile
from historic Melrose. Accommodation
comprises compact lounge/dining room
with small modern kitchen leading to
garden at rear, twin and bunk bedrooms,
bathroom and separate WC.*

All year MWB out of season 1wk min,
1unit, 1–4persons [◇] no pets ◎
fridge Electric Elec inclusive (during
summer) ⬛can be hired ☎(50yds)
Iron in unit Ironing board in unit HCE in
unit TV ⊕3pin round ▥ ♨(1m)

⊖ δ₉(2m) ☎(200yds)
Min£48 Max£55pw (Low)
Min£70 Max£85pw (High)

MELVICH
Highland *Caithness*
Map **14** NC86

Ch   63 Melvich
for bookings Mrs J Ritchie, Tigh-na-
Clash, 81 Melvich, Thurso, Caithness
KW14 7YJ
☎Melvich(064 13)262

*Four holiday chalets containing lounge
with kitchen area, a double room, a twin-
bedded room and shower/WC. There is a
bed-settee in the lounge. The chalets are
close to the beach and have an open
outlook across moorland. Situated off
A836 on the eastern outskirts of Melvich.*

Apr–Sep   MWB out of season   1wk min,
4wks max, 4units, 1–6persons   ◉
fridge   Electric   Elec metered
⌷inclusive   ☎(1m)   Iron in unit   Ironing
board in unit   ⊙   ⊕3pin square   P   ⊞
⚲(1m)   Fishing, pony trekking
⟿   ⚱(1m)
Min£40 Max£50pw (Low)
Min£55 Max£65pw (High)

MENHENIOT
Cornwall
Map **2** SX26

H   Deerpark Farm
for bookings Mrs H Sneyd, Coldrenick,
Menheniot, Liskeard, Cornwall
☎Widegates(05034)261

*Stone-built farmhouse situated on a large
estate in its own valley. Accommodation
comprises a very large lounge, a second
lounge on ground floor for children. Small
kitchen, separate dining room and
outside utility room. On first floor there are
three bedrooms and bathroom/WC. Off
A38 Liskeard–Plymouth road take first
turning to Menheniot.*

Apr–Sep   MWB in season   1wk min,
1unit, 8persons   [◇]   ◈   ◆   no pets
◉   fridge   Electric   Elec metered
⌷not provided   ☎(¾m)   Airing cupboard
in unit   Iron in unit   Ironing board in unit
HCE in unit   ⊙   ⊕3pin square   4P
⚲(¾m)
⟿   ⚱(¾m)

C   Higher Lodge
for bookings Mrs H Sneyd, Coldrenick,
Menheniot, Liskeard, Cornwall
☎Widegates(05034)261

*Old lodge at entrance to a large estate
with lovely views over the farmland.
Accommodation comprises
kitchen/breakfast room, separate
lounge, with three bedrooms and
bathroom/WC on first floor. Off A38
Liskeard–Plymouth road, turn right after
entering village.*

Apr–Sep   MWB in season   1wk min,
1unit, 6persons   [◇]   ◈   ◆   no pets
◉   fridge   Electric   Elec metered
⌷not provided   ☎(200yds)   Airing
cupboard in unit   Iron in unit   Ironing
board in unit   HCE in unit   ⊙
⊕3pin square   4P   ⚲(1¼m)   ⚓Hard
⟿   ⚱(1¼m)

MEOUL
Dumfries & Galloway *Wigtownshire*
Map **10** NX05

C   Fuchsia Cottage
for bookings Mr & Mrs E Davis, Carlton,
South Crescent, Portpatrick,
Wigtownshire
☎Portpatrick(077 681)253

*A modernised and extended single
storey cottage in own grounds standing
on elevated site with views towards North
Channel. Cottage offers combined
lounge/diner, one double bedded room
and one single, kitchen and shower
room.*

Etr–Oct   MWB in season   1wk min,
1mth max, 1unit, 2–4persons   ◉
fridge   Electric   Elec inclusive
⌷inclusive   ☎(2m)   Airing cupboard in
unit   HCE in unit   TV can be hired
⊕3pin square   2P   ⚲(4m)
⟿   ⚱(3m)

METCOMBE
Devon
Map **3** SY09

C   CC Ref 632 EP
for bookings Character Cottages
(Holidays) Ltd, 34 Fore Street, Sidmouth,
Devon EX10 8AQ
☎Sidmouth(03955)77001

*Detached country cottage 4m from
Sidmouth with secluded garden. Small
well-furnished sitting room,
kitchen/breakfast room with fitted units,
three double bedrooms (two with double
divan beds and third with twin bunks).*

All year   MWB out of season   1wk min,
6mths max, 1unit, 6persons   ◈   ◉
fridge   Electric   Elec inclusive
⌷not provided   ☎   Airing cupboard in
unit   Iron in unit   Ironing board in unit
HCE in unit   ⊙   TV   ⊕3pin square
⊕2pin round   P   ⊞   ⚲(4m)
⟿   ⚱(1m)
Min£70 Max£101pw (Low)
Min£129 Max£171pw (High)

MEVAGISSEY
Cornwall
Map **2** SX04

B   Altamira Tregoney Hill
for bookings Mr D E Howells, 49 Port
Mellon Park, Portmellon, Mevagissey,
St Austell, Cornwall
☎Mevagissey(0726)843679

*Delightful stone bungalow with views of
sea, beautifully decorated and furnished,
with parking for two cars in driveway.
Accommodation comprises lounge,
dining room, kitchen, two bedrooms (one
with double and one with two single
beds), bathroom and cloakroom/WC.*

1982 prices quoted throughout
gazetteer

All year   MWB out of season   1wk min,
2wks max, 1unit, 1–4persons   ◈   ◆
no pets   ☎   fridge   Electric
Elec metered   ☎(½m)   SD in unit   Airing
cupboard in unit   Iron in unit   Ironing
board in unit   HCE in unit   TV   ⊞
⚲(½m)
⟿   ⚱(½m)   ⊡(½m)
Min£60 Max£120pw

MIDDLETON-ON-SEA
West Sussex
Map **4** SU90

**B   Mr B E Moyler Sussex Holiday
Village (Bungalows)** Manor Way, Elmer
Sands, Middleton-on-Sea, Bognor Regis,
W Sussex PO22 6LA
☎Middleton-on-Sea(024 369)2641

*Thirty brick-built bungalows comprising
one double bedroom, one bedroom with
bunk beds, lounge, dining room, kitchen
area in same room and bathroom/WC.
On a holiday estate with private beach
and heated swimming pool.*

All year   MWB   1day min, 6mths max,
30units, 4–6persons   ◈   no pets   ◉
fridge   Electric   Elec metered   ⌷can be
hired   ☎(30yds)   Iron on premises
Ironing board on premises   HCE in unit
⊙   CTV   ⊕3pin square   P   ⤢
⟿   ⚱(3m)
Min£57.50 Max£115pw (Low)
Min£87.50 Max£175pw (High)

**F   Mr B E Moyler Sussex Holiday
Village (Flats)** Manor Way, Elmer Sands,
Middleton-on-Sea, Bognor Regis,
W Sussex PO22 6LA
☎Middleton-on-Sea(024 369)2641

*Situated in grounds of holiday centre,
these fourteen flats are on the ground and
first floor levels. Accommodation
consists of one double bedroom, lounge
with convertible sofa, kitchen/diner,
bathroom/WC. The holiday centre has its
own private beach and heated swimming
pool.*

All year   MWB   1day min, 6mths max,
14units, 2–4persons   ◈   no pets   ◉
fridge   Electric   Elec metered   ⌷can be
hired   ☎(30yds)   Iron on premises
Ironing board on premises   HCE in unit
⊙   CTV   ⊕3pin square   P   ⤢   ẟ
⟿   ⚱(3m)
Min£57.50 Max£115pw (Low)
Min£87.50 Max£175pw (High)

MILBORNE ST ANDREW
Dorset
Map **3** SY89

B   No 2 Bladen View
for bookings Mr & Mrs W Bagwell,
Delcombe Farm, Milton Abbas,
Blandford, Dorset
☎Milton Abbas(0258)880215

*Detached modern bungalow in
residential area in centre of village. It
comprises large kitchen/diner, lounge,
bathroom/WC and three bedrooms, two
doubles and one single.*

Apr–Oct 1wkmin, 1mthmax, 1unit, 1–5persons nc5 nopets ◎ fridge Electric Elecinclusive ▢notprovided ☎(300yds) SD in unit Iron in unit Airing cupboard in unit HCE in unit ⊙ TV ⊕3pinsquare 1P 1🏠 ♨(300yds)
⊷ ♀(500yds)
Min£80 Max£100pw

MINIONS
Cornwall
Map2 SX27

F Mrs P M Hart **Cheesewring Farm**
Minions, Liskeard, Cornwall
☎Rilla Mill(0579)62200

Detached stone-built barn modernised and converted to a one-bedroomed flat with lounge/diner, kitchen, bathroom and WC. Steps to entrance hall. Good views of Kit Hill and Tamar Valley. Leave Liskeard by B3254, continue to Upton Cross, turn left, sharp right before Minions village.

Mar–Dec MWB out of season wknd min 1mthmax, 1unit, 2–4persons [◇] ◆ ◆ ◎ fridge Electric Elecmetered ▢notprovided ☎ Airing cupboard in unit HCE in unit ⊙ TV ⊕3pinsquare P ♨(1m)
⊷ ♀(1m) ♫(1m)
Min£50 Max£70pw

MITCHELDEAN
Gloucestershire
Map3 SO61

H Wilderness 29 Baynham Road
for bookings Mrs V Locks, Fairfield, Higham, Gloucester, Gloucestershire GL28DY
☎Gloucester(0452)417512

Modern, semi-detached house on an estate in an elevated position on the outskirts of the town. Accommodation comprises lounge, dining room, kitchen, three bedrooms and bathroom/WC.

All year MWB out of season 4nights min, 1unit, 6persons [◇] ◎ fridge 🍴 Elecmetered ▢can be hired ☎(½m) WM in unit SD in unit Airing cupboard in unit Iron in unit Ironing board in unit HCE in unit ⊙ TV ⊕3pinsquare 1P 1🏠 🎏 ♨(½m)
⊷ ♀(½m)
Min£75 Max£95pw

MIXTOW
Cornwall
Map2 SX15

C Michaelstow Cottage
for bookings Mr & Mrs Hall, Penrose Burden, St Breward, Cornwall
☎Bodmin(0208)850277

Attractive modernised cottage with one twin and one double bedroom, lounge/diner, kitchen, bathroom/WC, plus separate WC, balcony, patio and private quay.

All year 1wkmin, 1unit, 1–4persons ◊ ◆ ◎ fridge 🍴 Elecmetered ▢inclusive ☎ Airing cupboard in unit Iron in unit Ironing board in unit HCE in unit ⊙ CTV ⊕3pinsquare 1P 🍴 ♨(2m)
⊷ ♀(1m)
Min£75 Max£190pw

MOCHRUM
Dumfries & Galloway Wigtownshire
Map10 NX34

F Auchengaillie Farm
for bookings Mr J H G Korner, House of Elrig, Port William, Wigtownshire DG89RF
☎Port William(098 87)242

The ground-floor of this 19th-century farmhouse, has been converted into two self-contained flats, only one of which is available. There are three bedrooms, sitting room and kitchen with dining area. The flat is simply decorated and furnished but the kitchen has modern equipment. Auchengaillie is a working farm, and some noise from farm machinery should be expected during the day. The farm lies on a country road 1½m from the village of Mochrum. →

All year MWB out of season 1wk min
(2wks Dec–Mar) 1unit, 1–6persons
◆ ◎ fridge Electric & open fires
Elec metered ▣not provided ☎(1m)
WM in unit Ironing board in unit Iron
in unit Airing cupboard in unit HCE in unit
⊙ TV ③3pin round P ▥ ▦(1¼m)
⤙Hard Fly fishing
⊖ ♀

Min£53 Max£75pw (Low)
Max£100pw

MONMOUTH
Gwent
Map**3** SO51

H Mr J Hoddell **Lewstone Farmhouse**
Ganarew, Monmouth, Gwent NP53SS
☎Symonds Yat(0600)890292

*The self-contained wing of this
Elizabethan farmhouse consists of
kitchen, dining room, lounge and four
bedrooms, three of which have own
washbasins; most rooms have exposed
beams. There is a large walled garden for
the use of visitors, and the farmhouse is at
the centre of a working mixed farm. Turn
left off A40, 2m beyond Whitchurch,
follow signs to Lewstone; the farmhouse
is the second house on the right ½m from
A40.*

All year 1wk min, 1unit, 1–8persons
◆ no pets ◎ fridge Electric & open
fires Elec metered ▣not provided
☎(½m) WM in unit SD in unit Airing
cupboard in unit Iron in unit Ironing
board in unit HCE in unit TV
③3pin square P ▦(1m)

⊖ ♀(½m)

Min£20 Max£50pw (Low)
Min£40 Max£100pw (High)

MONTCOFFER
Grampian *Banffshire*
Map**15** NJ66

C **Eastgate, Westgate & Cottage**
for bookings Mrs Dean, Montcoffer,
Banff, Banffshire AB4 3LJ
☎Banff(026 12)2597

*Situated in a quiet position south of Banff
overlooking the River Deveron, these
cottages, one detached and two semi-
detached, stand slightly apart from the*

Mochrum
—
Morecambe

*main farmhouse. Furnishings and décor
are in good condition.*

All year MWB out of season 1wk min,
3units, 1–6persons ◆ ◆ ◎ fridge
Electric & coal fires Elec metered
▣not provided ☎(2m) Airing
cupboard in unit Iron in unit Ironing
board in unit HCE ⊙ ③3pin square
P ▥ ▦(3m)

⊖ ♀(3m) ▨(3m)
Min£30 Max£55pw

MONTGOMERY
Powys
Map**7** SO29

H **Castle Terrace**
for bookings Mrs J N Corfield, Castle
Terrace House, Montgomery, Powys
☎Montgomery(068 681)481

*Three-storey terraced house built in the
mid 17th century on a hillside. First floor
comprises one double and one single
room. The second floor comprises one
single room, one double bedroom and
bathroom/WC. The living room and
kitchen are on the ground floor. 50 yards
from Market Square.*

May–Sep 3days min, 4wks max, 1unit,
1–6persons [◇] ◆ ◆ no pets ◎
fridge Electric Elec metered ▣can be
hired ☎(50yds) SD in unit Airing
cupboard in unit Iron in unit Ironing
board in unit HCE in unit ⊙ CTV
③3pin square 3P ▥ ▦(50yds)

⊖ ♀(50yds)

Min£60 Max£90pw

MORECAMBE
Lancashire
Map**7** SD46

F **The Anchorage** 19 Clarence Street
for bookings Mrs M Woodcock, 99
Regent Road, Morecambe, Lancashire
LA3 1AF
☎Morecambe(0524)413466

*Detached stone-built house divided into
double-bedded flats. Good quality
accommodation, very reasonably priced.
One minute's walk from promenade.*

Etr–Oct 1wk min, 2wks max, 3units,
2–4persons nc6 no pets ◎ fridge
Electric Elec metered ▣inclusive
☎(200yds) Airing cupboard in unit
HCE in unit [Launderette within 300yds]
⊙ TV ③3pin square ▦(30yds)

⊖ ♀(100yds) ▨(250yds)
♫(250yds) ▧(½m)

Min£38 Max£46pw (Low)
Min£48 Max£60pw (High)

F **Delamere Flats** 366 Marine Road
for bookings Mr A Willoughby, 7 Scafell
Avenue, Morecambe, Lancashire
☎Morecambe(0524)416858

*Two spacious, well equipped and
comfortable flats on the ground and first
floors of a stone-built terraced property,
on the seafront. Each flat has a family
bedroom plus a studio couch in the
lounge.*

All year MWB out of season 1wk min,
2units, 5persons ◆ ◆ ◔ fridge
Electric & Gas Gas/Elec metered
▣inclusive ☎(100yds) Iron in unit
Ironing board in unit HCE in unit ◈
TV ③3pin square P ▦(500yds)

⊖ ♀(200yds) ▨(200yds) ♫(200yds)
▧(1m)

F **Delamere Flats** 10 Skipton Street
for bookings Mrs A Willoughby, 7 Scafell
Avenue, Morecambe, Lancashire
☎Morecambe(0524)416858

*Three compact flats, each comprising
lounge with bed–settee, bedroom with
double and single divans, bathroom and
kitchen. Stands in small street just off
Marine Rd Central near to the Central
Pier, Winter Gardens and most other
amenities of this seaside resort. Although
street parking is restricted public car
parks are within easy reach.*

All year MWB out of season 1wk min,
3units, 4persons ◆ ◆ no pets ◔
fridge Electric & Gas
Gas/Elec metered ▣inclusive
☎(100yds) Iron in unit Ironing board in
unit HCE in unit [Launderette within
300yds] ◈ TV ③3pin square
▦(50yds)

⊖ ♀(20yds) ▨(200yds) ♫(2m)
▧(500yds)

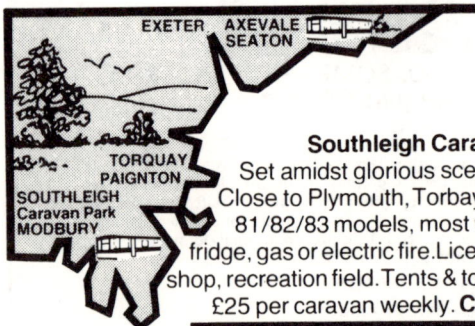

F Mr M J Donnelly *Eden Vale Holiday Flats* 338 Marine Road, Morecambe, Lancashire
☎Morecambe(0524)415544

Stone-built Georgian terraced house overlooking Morecambe Bay, converted into flats. The flat has a double bedroom and additional double bed-settee. Conveniently situated for access to all amenities of this seaside resort.

All year 1wk min, 1unit, 2–4persons, nc9 no pets ⊚ fridge Electric ⊡inclusive ☎ HCE in unit [Launderette within 300yds] CTV ⊕3pin square P ▥ ♨(½m)
⇔ ⚑(150yds) ▨(1m) ♫(2m) ☎(1½m)

F 301 Marine Road Central
for bookings Mrs Charnley, Clarkson Farm, Moss Lane, Thurnham, Lancaster
☎Galgate(0524)751411

Two compact flats located on the first and second floors of terraced property over shops. Each has a family bedroom plus fold-away bed in the lounge. Close to the pier and sea.

25Jun–Sep 1wk min, 2units, 5persons [◆ ◆] no pets ⊚ fridge Electric Elec metered ⊡inclusive ☎(200yds) Airing cupboard in unit Iron in unit Ironing board in unit HCE in unit [Launderette within 300yds] TV ⊕3pin square ⊕3pin round ♨(400yds)
⇔ ♒(1m) ▨(200yds) ▨(500yds) ♫(2m) ☎(1m)

Min£48 Max£50pw

F Mrs Christine Crabtree, *The Wateredge* 71–72 Sandylands Promenade, Morecambe, Lancashire LA3 1DW
☎Morecambe(0524)410389

Formerly a hotel, this large terraced, stone, four-storey building has been converted into eight flats, each supplemented by a double bed-settee in lounge. Located on south side of town overlooking Morecambe Bay, within reach of all amenities.

All year MWB out of season 7days min, 8units, 2–6persons, nc3 ⊚ fridge Electric Elec metered ⊡inclusive ☎ HCE in units Launderette within 300yds ⊕ CTV ⊕3pin square ▥
⇔ ♒(2m) ⚑(50yds) ▨(50yds) ♫(½m) ☎(1m)

MORTEHOE
Devon
Map**2** SS44

C Priors Cottage
for bookings Mr & Mrs J Notley, 9 Willoway Lane, Braunton, Devon EX33 1AS
☎Braunton(0271)813885

Cottage converted from an old chapel, retaining the original pine-block flooring throughout most of the ground floor area.

There are three bedrooms (two double beds, one twin-bedded), lounge, kitchen and bathroom/WC. There are good views of the sea and National Trust hills beyond Mortehoe.

Mar–Oct 1wk min, 1mth max, 1unit, 2–6persons ◆ ◆ ◔ fridge Gas inclusive Elec metered ⊡not provided ☎(300yds) Airing cupboard in unit Iron in unit Ironing board in unit HCE in unit CTV ⊕3pin square P ▥ ♨(200yds)
⇔ ⚑(200yds) ▨(1½m) ♫(1½m) ☎(1½m)

Min£75 Max£150pw

MOSSDALE
Dumfries & Galloway *Kirkcudbrightshire*
Map**11** NX67

H Airds of Kells Cottage Airds of Kells Farm
for bookings G M Thomson & Co, 27 King Street, Castle Douglas, Kirkcudbrightshire DG7 1AB
☎Castle Douglas(0556)2701

Former keeper's house recently modernised and standing in farmland. It has a dining room, sitting room with double bed-settee, kitchen and bathroom and two twin-bedded rooms. The Airds of Kells are on the A762 at Mossdale. Most peaceful situation.

All year 1wk min, 6mths max, 1unit, 1–6persons ◆ ⊚ fridge Electric Elec inclusive ⊡not provided ☎(1m) HCE in unit TV ⊕3pin round P ▥ ♨(1m)

Min£50 Max£115pw

B Bellvue Airds of Kells
for bookings G M Thomson & Co, 27 King Street, Castle Douglas, Kirkcudbrightshire
☎Castle Douglas(0556)2701

Attractive, modern bungalow situated on farmland. Accommodation comprises dining/living room, kitchen, bathroom, and three bedrooms, one with a double bed, one with a three-quarter sized double bed and one with twin beds. Situated off the A726.

All year 1wk min, 6mths max, 1unit, 1–6persons ◆ no pets Oil fired cooker fridge ⊞ Elec inclusive ⊡not provided ☎(½m) WM in unit Ironing board in unit HCE in unit TV ⊕3pin square P ♨(½m) Fishing

Min£55 Max£130pw

B Drumwhill
for bookings G M Thomson & Co, 27 King Street, Castle Douglas, Kirkcudbrightshire DG7 1AB
☎Castle Douglas(0556)2701

Self-contained wing of a modern newly-built house at the head of Woodhall Loch. The accommodation which is all on the ground floor, comprises two twin and one

single-bedded room, sitting room, diner, kitchen with breakfast table, bathroom and utility room. Access via A762 N from Laurieston for 2½m. Take left turn for Slogarie then next left.

All year 1wk min, 1unit, 1–5persons, nc3 no pets ⊚ fridge ⊞ & open fires Elec inclusive ⊡not provided ☎(2m) Airing cupboard in unit Iron in unit Ironing board in unit HCE in unit ⊕ TV ⊕3pin square P ▦ ♨(2m)
⇔ ⚑(3m)

Min£55 Max£130pw

MUASDALE
Strathclyde *Argyll*
Map**10** NR63

F Upper & Lower Muasdale House
for bookings Mr & Mrs R Semple, Rhonadale, Muasdale, Tarbert, Argyll PA29 6XD
☎Glenbarr(058 32)234

Late 19th-century two-storey house now converted into two self-contained flats—one on the ground floor to the rear and one first-floor flat to the front. Lower Muasdale has two bedrooms, living room with double bed-settee, kitchenette and bathroom. Upper Muasdale has three bedrooms, living room (with sea views), kitchen and bathroom. Décor and furnishings are practical and apart from the small kitchens, the flats are spacious. Situated 50yds from sandy beach.

All year MWB out of season 1wk min, 1mth max, 2units, 1–6persons ◆ ⊚ fridge Electric Elec metered ⊡can be hired ☎(100yds) Iron in unit Ironing board in unit HCE in unit ⊕ TV can be hired ⊕3pin square 4P ▥ Sea fishing & boat for hire
⇔ ⚑(100yds)

MUIR OF ORD
Highland *Ross & Cromarty*
Map**14** NH55

H Mrs Ann B G Fraser Gilchrist Farm Muir of Ord, Ross-shire IV6 7RS
☎Muir-of-Ord(0463)870243

A white semi-detached house standing in the farmyard, 1½m outside Muir of Ord off A832. There is a kitchen, living/dining room, two double and one twin-bedded room.

2Apr–Oct 1wk min, 4wks max, 1unit, 1–7persons ◆ ⊚ fridge Electric & open fires Elec metered ⊡inclusive ☎(1½m) WM in unit SD in unit Airing cupboard in unit Iron in unit Ironing board in unit HCE in unit TV ⊕3pin square P ▥ ♨(1½m) Pony trekking, boating
⇔ ♒(1½m) ⚑(1½m) ▨(1½m)

Min£35 Max£45pw(Low)
Min£60 Max£80pw (High)

C Croft Ardnagrask
for bookings Mrs McLean, 43 Riccarton
Mains Road, Currie, Midlothian EH14 5NF
☎031–449 2448

Detached country cottage in peaceful
setting, amidst open farmland with fine
views across to Beauly Firth.
Accommodation comprises kitchen,
sitting/dining room, bathroom and one
double bedroom on the ground floor
whilst the first floor has a double and a
twin bedroom.

Apr–Oct 1wk min, 1unit, 1–6persons
◊ ◎ fridge Electric Elec metered
⬚not provided ☎ WM in unit Iron in
unit Ironing board in unit HCE in unit
⊕3pin square 3P ♨(1m)

⊖ ᗱ(2m) ♀(1m)

Min£35 Max£70pw

MULL, ISLE OF
Strathclyde Argyll
Map **13** NM
See Dervaig, Tobermory, Torloisk

MULLION
Cornwall
Map **2** SW61

B, C & F J O & L N Jaine Ltd **Trenance
Farm** Mullion, Helston, Cornwall
☎Mullion (0326) 240639

Trenance is a coastal farm situated
midway between the village of Mullion
and Polurrian Cove. The properties vary
and include five modern bungalows, one
cottage, being part of the farmhouse yet
self-contained and two flats which are
contained within the farmhouse, parts of
which date back to the 12th century. Well
appointed accommodation of character.

Feb–Oct MWB out of season 1wk min,
8units, 1–8persons ◊ ◆ ◎ fridge
Electric Elec metered ⬚can be hired
☎(⅓m) Airing cupboard in unit Iron in
unit Ironing board in unit HCE in unit
⊙ TV ⊕3pin square P ▥ ♨(⅓m)

⊖ ᗱ(2m) ♀(1m) ▨(2m)

Min£45 Max£170pw

B Pedn-y-ke Holiday Bungalows
for bookings Mr L R Francis, Polurrian
Hotel Ltd, Mullion, Helston, Cornwall
☎Mullion (0326) 240421

Six purpose built bungalows located
approx. 100yds from hotel and situated
with their own small private rear gardens.
Each comprises one double and one twin
bedded room, lounge/diner, kitchenette
and bathroom/WC. Full use of hotel
amenities.

Apr–Oct MWB 3days min, 6units,
1–4persons [◊] ◊ ◆ ◎ fridge
Electric Elec metered ⬚inclusive ☎
Airing cupboard on premises Iron on
premises Ironing board on premises
HCE in unit [Launderette on premises]
⊙ CTV ⊕3pin square 1P ▥
♨(½m) ⌐ ⚲Hard ⚡

⊖ ᗱ(2m) ▨ ♫

Min£67.50 Max£175pw (Low)
Max£220pw (High)

C & F F A & Mrs D J Heywood
Treveglos Self-Catering Holidays
Lender Lane, Mullion, Helston, Cornwall
TR12 7RJ
☎Mullion (0326) 240713

Treveglos is in the centre of Mullion, the
complex includes six cottages and four
flats each named after coves and
beaches in the area. Each unit has living
room/kitchen and bathroom. Two flats
have one double bedroom and one with
two single beds. A third flat has a double
bedroom, one with single beds and
another with bunks. The fourth flat has a
double bedroom and a bedroom with
bunks. Three cottages have a double
bedroom and one bedroom with single
beds. A fourth has one double bedroom.
Of the remaining two cottages one has
one bedroom with single beds, the other
has two bedrooms one with singles the
other bunk beds.

Apr–Sep MWB out of season 1wk min,
10units, 2–6persons [◊] ◊ ◆ ◎
fridge Electric Elec metered
⬚inclusive ☎(70yds) Airing cupboard
on premises Iron on premises Ironing

board on premises HCE in unit
[Launderette within 300yds] ⊙ CTV
⊕3pin square 12P ♨(50yds)

⊖ ᗱ(2m) ♀(50yds) ▨(½m) ♫(⅓m)

Min£86.25 Max£138pw (Low)
Min£126.50 Max£270.25pw (High)

MUMBLES
West Glamorgan
Map **2** SS68

F 3a Chapel Street
for bookings Mumbles & Gower Holiday
Homes, 3 Chapel Street, Mumbles,
Swansea, W Glamorgan
☎Swansea (0792) 61160

A spacious first and second-floor flat
consisting of lounge/dining room, fitted
kitchen, bathroom, separate WC and
three bedrooms capable of sleeping nine
persons.

Jul–Sep 1wk min, 1unit, 2–9persons
◊ ◎ fridge ⋈ Electric
Elec metered ⬚not provided
☎(400yds) Airing cupboard in unit Iron
in unit Ironing board in unit HCE in unit
CTV ⊕3pin square P ▥ ♨

⊖ ♀ ▨(3m)

Min£120 Max£140pw

F Highcliff Court
for bookings Langland Court Hotel,
Langland Court Road, Langland Bay,
Mumbles, Swansea, W Glamorgan
☎Swansea (0792) 68505

Spacious purpose-built flats with balcony
and good sea views. Large sitting/dining
room and well fitted kitchen. One twin and
one double bedroom, shower/bathroom
and separate WC.

All year MWB out of season 2units,
4–6persons [◊] [◆] ⌀ fridge ⋈
Elec inclusive ⬚inclusive ☎ Airing
cupboard in unit Iron in unit Ironing
board in unit HCE in unit [Launderette
on premises] ⊙ TV ⊕3pin square
P ▤ ▥ ♨(½m) ⚲Hard

⊖ ᗱ ♀(50yds) ▨(100yds)
♫(100yds)

Min£90 Max£150pw (Low)
Min£95 Max£170pw (High)

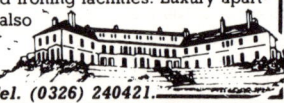

B 19 Limeslade Drive

for bookings Mr & Mrs B & M Davies, Bar Marc Holiday Properties, 7A Redcliffe, Caswell Bay, Swansea, W Glamorgan
☎Swansea(0792)69169

Modern brick-built bungalow with large lounge, two bedrooms (double and twin), kitchen and bathroom/WC.

Feb–Nov 1wk min, 3mths max, 1unit, 2–4persons ◆ ◉ fridge Electric Elec metered ⬚not provided ☎(¼m) Airing cupboard in unit HCE in unit ⊖ TV ⊕3pin square P ▥ ♨(¼m)

⊛ ⚲(1m) ⛟(3m)

Min£70 Max£81pw (Low)
Min£108 Max£140pw (High)

B 4 Sealands Drive Limeslade

for bookings Mumbles & Gower, Holiday Homes, 3 Chapel Street, Mumbles, Swansea, W Glamorgan
☎Swansea(0792)61160 (daytime)
Swansea(0792)62337 (evenings)

Modern, semi-detached brick bungalow, with two double bedrooms, lounge, bathroom/WC and open-plan kitchen. Situated above Limeslade Beach five minutes' walk from the pier and 14 minutes' walk from the village of Mumbles.

Jul–Sep 1wk min, 10mths max, 1unit, 6persons ◆ ◉ fridge Electric Elec metered ⬚not provided ☎(¼m) Airing cupboard in unit HCE in unit ⊖ TV ⊕3pin square P ▥ ♨(1m)

⊛ ⚲(¼m) ▨(¼m)

Min£30 Max£45pw (Low)
Min£90 Max£105pw (High)

B 10 Sealands Drive

for bookings Mr & Mrs B & M Davies, Bar Marc Holiday Properties, 7A Redcliff, Caswell Bay, Swansea, W Glamorgan
☎Swansea(0792)69169

Modern brick-built bungalows with large lounge, two bedrooms (double and twin), kitchen and bathroom/WC.

Feb–Nov 1wk min, 3mths max, 1unit, 2–4persons ◆ ◉ fridge Electric Elec metered ⬚not provided ☎(¼m) Airing cupboard in unit HCE in unit ⊖ TV ⊕3pin square P ▥ ♨(¼m)

Mumbles — Nantlle

⊛ ⚲(1m) ⛟(3m)

Min£70 Max£81pw (Low)
Min£108 Max£140pw (High)

B 11 Sealands Drive

for bookings Mr & Mrs B & M Davies, Bar Marc Holiday Properties, 7A Redcliffe, Caswell Bay, Swansea, W Glamorgan
☎Swansea(0792)69169

Brick-built bungalow sleeping up to four persons. Modern accommodation comprises large lounge, two bedrooms (one double and one twin), kitchen and bathroom/WC.

Feb–Nov 1wk min, 3mths max, 1unit, 2–4persons ◆ ◉ fridge Electric Elec metered ⬚not provided ☎(¼m) TV

⊛ ⚲(1m) ⛟(3m)

Min£70 Max£81pw (Low)
Min£108 Max£140pw (High)

F Woodridge Court

for bookings Langland Court Hotel, Langland Court Road, Langland Bay, Mumbles, Swansea, W Glamorgan
☎Swansea(0792)68505

Ten purpose-built units, each with a balcony overlooking the beach. Spacious lounge/diner, kitchenette, shower/WC and one small double bedroom, plus convertible bed-settee in the lounge.

All year MWB out of season 10units, 2–4persons [◆] [◆] ◉ fridge ♨ Elec inclusive ⬚inclusive ☎ Airing cupboard in unit Iron in unit Ironing board in unit HCE in unit [Launderette on premises] ⊖ CTV ⊕3pin square P ▤ ▥ ♨(¼m) ⚘Grass

⊛ ♨(50yds) ▨(100yds) ♫(100yds)

Min£65 Max£95pw (Low)
Min£120 Max£170pw (High)

1982 prices quoted throughout gazetteer

MUNDESLEY-ON-SEA
Norfolk
Map9 TG33

C 17 Victoria Road

for bookings Mr & Mrs Duniam, 52 Trelawney Road, Barkingside, Hainault, Essex
☎01–5003907

This terraced two-storey cottage backs onto the village green and is situated at the end of a cul-de-sac about 300yds from the beach. Accommodation comprises two bedrooms, lounge/dinette, kitchen and bathroom/WC. It is fully-carpeted and has good quality furniture.

All year MWB 2wks min, 4wks max, 1unit, 1–5persons, nc6 ◆ no pets ◊ fridge ♨ Gas/Elec inclusive ⬚not provided ☎(100yds) Airing cupboard in unit Iron in unit Ironing board in unit HCE in unit [Launderette within 300yds] ⊖ ⊗ TV ⊕3pin square ▥ ♨(100yds) ♪

⊛ ⚲(220yds) ▨(220yds) ♫(220yds)

Min£45 Max£60pw

NANTLLE
Gwynedd
Map6 SH55

C Dol Gwydion & Plas Bach
Baladeulyn

for bookings Mr H D Roberts, Gwynant, 31 Cefn Coed Road, Cyncoed, Cardiff
☎Cardiff(0222)751879 or Penygroes(028681)676

Two cottages by Nantlle Lake, both two-bedroomed with kitchen, bathroom and WC. One cottage has lounge/diner the other lounge with bed-settee.

All year 1wk min, 4wks max, 2units, 5persons ◆ ◉ fridge Electric Elec metered ⬚not provided ☎(20yds) Airing cupboard in unit Iron in unit Ironing board in unit HCE in unit ⊖ TV ⊕3pin square P ▥ ♨(100yds) Fishing

⊛ ⚲(2m)

Min£50 Max£70pw (Low)
Min£90 Max£110pw (High)

H **Dol Pebin** Baladeulyn
for bookings Mr H D Roberts, Gwynant,
31 Cefn Coed Road, Cyncoed, Cardiff
☎Cardiff(0222)751879 or
Penygroes(028681)676

*Detached house near Nantlle Lake
consisting of lounge/diner, TV lounge
and another separate lounge, large
modern kitchen, three bedrooms,
bathroom and WC. Views of lake and
mountains.*

All year 1wk min, 4wks max, 1unit,
5persons ◈ ◎ fridge Electric
Elec metered ⬛not provided ☎
Airing cupboard in unit Iron in unit
Ironing board in unit HCE in unit ⊖
CTV ⊕3pin square P ▥
♨(100yds) Fishing

◈ ☏(2m)

Min£70 Max£150pw

NARBERTH
Dyfed
Map**2** SN11

**Powell's Holidays, High Street,
Saundersfoot, Dyfed**
☎**Saundersfoot (0834) 812791**
**Powell's Holidays have a total of
thirteen AA Inspected properties in
Narberth. Of these seven are houses,
four are bungalows and two are
cottages. An entry for one of each type
of property follows. For information on
the other properties contact Powell's
Holidays.**

B **The Briars**
for bookings Powell's Holidays
(address as above)
☎Saundersfoot(0834)812791

*A new, detached bungalow located in a
rural area with pleasant views.
Accommodation comprises lounge,
kitchen/diner, bathroom, separate WC
and two double bedrooms with unit
furniture.*

Jun–Sep 1wk min, 6wks max, 1unit,
1–4persons ◈ ◎ fridge ♨
Electric Elec inclusive ⬛not provided
☎(150yds) Airing cupboard in unit Iron
in unit Ironing board in unit HCE in unit
TV ⊕3pin square 3P ▥ ♨(1m)

◈ ☏(100yds)

Min£51 Max£135pw

H **Burwood Lodge** Bethesda Road
for bookings Powell's Holidays
(address as above)
☎Saundersfoot(0834)812791

*A luxurious house with garden in rural
setting. Well furnished and carpeted,
comprising large lounge, dining room,
breakfast room, luxury fitted kitchen
including dishwashing machine and
micro-wave oven. There are four
bedrooms, one double, one twin and two
single bedded, bathroom/WC and
shower plus a separate WC.*

Nantlle
—
Nethy Bridge

May–Sep 1wk min, 1unit, 6persons
[◇] ◈ ◆ no pets ◎ fridge ♨
Elec inclusive ⬛not provided Airing
cupboard in unit Iron in unit Ironing
board in unit HCE in unit ⊖ TV & CTV
⊕3pin square 2P ▥ ♨(4m)

Min£69 Max£159pw

H **Glanrhyd Farm** Lampeter Velfrey
for bookings Powell's Holidays
(address as above)
☎Saundersfoot(0834)812791

*Farmhouse situated within 50 acres of
pasture land. Accommodation
comprises comfortably furnished lounge,
dining room, well-equipped kitchen,
study/playroom, two bathrooms/WC one
of which is outside, three double
bedrooms with wash basins and two twin-
bedded rooms.*

Jan–Nov MWB out of season 1wk min,
6wks max, 1unit, 2–10persons [◇] ◈
◆ ◎ fridge Electric Elec inclusive
⬛not provided ☎(1m) Airing
cupboard in unit Iron in unit Ironing
board in unit HCE in unit ⊖ TV
⊕3pin square 6P ▥ ♨(4m)

◈ ☏(1m)

Min£69 Max£174pw

C **Mews Cottage** Upper Coxhill Farm
for bookings Powell's Holidays
(address as above)
☎Saundersfoot(0834)812791

*Cottage, adjacent to farm.
Accommodation comprises lounge,
kitchen/diner, one double bedroom and
one double-bedded room with additional
single bed. There is a bathroom with
shower and WC on the first floor and a
separate WC with washbasin on the
ground floor.*

Jun–Sep 1wk min, 6wks max, 1unit,
2–5persons ◈ ◎ fridge ♨
Elec metered ⬛not provided ☎(½m)
Airing cupboard in unit Iron in unit HCE
in unit ⊖ TV ⊕3pin square 4P ▥
♨(½m)

◈ ☏(½m)

Min£42 Max£108pw

NETHER WASDALE
Cumbria
Map**11** NY10

C **Church How Cottage**
for bookings Mr Friend, 77 Leslie Road,
Dorking, Surrey
☎Dorking(0306)886199

*Traditional lakeland stone building
situated within the grounds of the Old
Vicarage. Built approx. 150 years ago,
the cottage has been extensively
modernised and refurbished yet retains
old world character. There are three
bedrooms, large living/dining room,
kitchen and bathroom.*

All year MWB out of season 3days min,
1unit, 2–7persons [◈ ◆] no pets

◔ fridge ♨ Gas inclusive
Elec metered ⬛inclusive (except
towels) ☎(100yds) WM in unit Airing
cupboard in unit Iron in unit Ironing
board in unit HCE in unit ⊖ ⊗ TV
⊕3pin u are 4P ▥ ♨(4m)

◈ ☏(100yds)

Min£82.50 Max£165pw

NETHY BRIDGE
Highland *Inverness-shire*
Map**14** NJ02

C **Badanfhuarain**
for bookings Mr & Mrs J Fleming, Dell of
Abernethy, Nethy Bridge, Inverness-
shire PH23 3DL
☎Nethybridge(047 982)643

*Small cottage containing living room,
kitchen two twin-bedded rooms and a
small single room suitable for a child.
Views of Cairngorms. Access is by a
400yd driveway 1m from Nethy Bridge on
an unclass road leading from the centre
of the village.*

Etr–Nov 1wk min, 4wks max, 1unit,
1–5persons [◈] [◆] ◎ fridge
Electric Elec metered ⬛not provided
☎(½m) Airing cupboard in unit Ironing
board in unit HCE in unit ⊖
⊕3pin square P ♨(½m) ⚘ Riding

◈ ♘(1m) ☏(1m) ▨(1m)

Min£50 Max£90pw(Low)
Min£80 Max£110pw (High)

H **Byna & Creggan** The Causar
for bookings Mr & Mrs J B Patrick,
1 Chapelton Place, Forres, Moray
☎Forres(0309)72505

*Two modern bungalow type houses
containing kitchen, lounge, one twin-
bedded room, a room with bunks and a
double room with an additional single
bed.*

All year MWB out of season
2nights min, 2units, 1–7persons [◆]
◎ fridge Elec metered ⬛can be hired
☎(150yds) Airing cupboard in unit Iron
in unit Ironing board in unit HCE in unit
⊖ CTV ⊕3pin square P ♨(100yds)

◈ ♘(400yds) ☏(400yds)

Min£66 Max£83pw (Low)
Min£89 Max£156pw (High)

F Mr & Mrs L D Gavin **Culreach**
Grantown-on-Spey, Nethybridge,
Morayshire
☎Nethybridge(047 982)269

*Two small flats forming a modern
extention to main croft farmhouse
situated 1¼ miles from Nethybridge. Both
are compact with the larger flat
comprising one bedroom with twin beds,
bathroom, kitchen and lounge/diner. The
other has bathroom, kitchen/diner and
lounge with furnishings which adapt to
either twin or a double bedded room.*

All year MWB out of season
2nights min, 2mths max, 2units,
1–2persons ◎ fridge Electric
Elec metered ⬛not provided ☎(1½m)
Airing cupboard in one unit Iron in unit

Ironing board in unit   HCE in unit   ⊙
TV   ⊕3pin square   P   1🛏   🔲   ♨(1½m)
⊖ ♨ (1½m)   ☎(1½m)   ☒(3m)   ♬(3m)
Min£45 Max£50pw

H   Derraid Dell Road
for bookings Mr & Mrs J B Patrick,
1 Chapelton Place, Forres, Moray
☎Forres(0309)72505

This bungalow-type house has kitchen,
lounge, a twin-bedded room, a double
room, and a room with bunks.

All year   MWB out of season
2 nights min, 1 unit, 1–6 persons   [◈]
⊛   fridge   Elec metered   🔲 can be
hired   ☎(300yds) Airing cupboard in
unit   Iron in unit   Ironing board in unit
HCE in unit   ⊙   CTV   ⊕3pin square   P
♨(300yds)
⊖ ♨(900yds)   🍴(200yds)
Min£66 Max£77pw (Low)
Min£79 Max£127pw (High)

C   Near Dell & Far Dell
for bookings Mr & Mrs J Fleming, Dell of
Abernethy, Nethy Bridge Inverness-shire
PH25 3DL
☎Nethybridge(047 982)643

Modern cottages located in the 2¼ acres
of tree-studded grounds of Dell Lodge,
on the outskirts of Nethy Bridge. They are
well decorated and furnished, Near Dell
having three bedrooms, sitting room,
kitchen/dining room and bathroom and
Far Dell two twin bedrooms, one single
bedroom with double bunk, living
room/diner, kitchenette and bathroom.
They are set in a secluded spot with views
of the mountains.

All year   MWB out of season   1 wk min,
4 wks max, 2 units, 2–8 persons   [◈]   ⊛
fridge   Electric   Elec included (in
summer)   🔲 included   ☎(½m) Airing
cupboard in unit   Ironing board in unit
HCE in unit   ⊙   TV can be hired
⊕3pin square   P   🔲   ♨(1m)   ⚲ Pony
trekking, bowling green
⊖ ♨(1m)   🍴(½m)   ☒(1m)
Min£65 Max£113pw (Low)
Min£95 Max£155pw (High)

H   Old Smithy The Causar *for bookings*
Mr & Mrs J B Patrick, 1 Chapelton Place,
Forres, Moray
☎Forres (0309) 72505

Converted blacksmith's shop with many
original features maintained. It contains
open-plan living/dining/kitchen area and
four bedrooms sleeping up to nine,
bathroom and shower room.

All year   MWB out of season
2 nights min, 1 unit, 1–9 persons   [◈]
⊛   fridge   Elec metered   🔲 can be
hired   ☎(150yds)   Airing cupboard in
unit   Iron in unit   Ironing board in unit
HCE in unit   ⊙   CTV   ⊕3pin square   P
♨(100yds)   ⊖ ♨(400yds)   🍴(400yds)
Min£94 Max£122pw (Low)
Min£129 Max£185pw (High)

H   Straanmore Dell Road   *for bookings*
Mr & Mrs J B Patrick, 1 Chapelton Place,
Forres, Moray
☎Forres (0309) 72505

Modern house with garden in a quiet
village location. Dell Road runs off B970
and is close to the River Nethy. It contains
kitchen, lounge, two twin-bedded rooms,
bathroom and shower room with WC and
a room with two sets of bunks.

All year   MWB out of season
2 nights min, 1 unit, 1–8 persons   [◈]
⊛   fridge   Electric & open fires
Elec metered   🔲 can be hired
☎(300yds)   Airing cupboard in unit   Iron
in unit   Ironing board in unit   HCE in unit
⊙   CTV   ⊕3pin square   P
♨(300yds)
⊖ ♨(900yds)   🍴(400yds)
Min£77 Max£83pw (Low)
Min£89 Max£156pw (High)

C   West Dell, South Dell & Little Dell
for bookings Mr & Mrs J Fleming, Dell of
Abernethy, Nethy Bridge, Inverness-
shire PH25 3DL
☎Nethybridge(047 982)643

Modernised cottages located in the
wings of Dell Lodge, a Georgian house
dating from 1775. West Dell and South
Dell have three bedrooms, living

room/diner, kitchenette and bathroom.
Little Dell has two bedrooms, sitting room
with diner/kitchenette and bathroom. All
have good standard of décor and fittings.

All year   MWB out of season   1 wk min,
4 wks max, 3 units, 1–7 persons   [◈]   ⊛
fridge   Electric   Elec inclusive
(in summer)   🔲 inclusive   ☎(½m)   Airing
cupboard in unit   Ironing board in unit
HCE in unit   ⊙   TV can be hired
⊕3pin square   P   🔲   ♨(1m)   ⚲ Pony
trekking, Bowling green
⊖ ♨(1m)   🍴(½m)   ☒(1m)
Min£65 Max£113pw (Low)
Min£95 Max£155pw (High)

NETLEY MARSH
Hampshire
Map 4 SU31

F   Holiday Flat   *for bookings* Mrs J
Puttock, The Old Vicarage, Netley Marsh,
Southampton, Hants SO4 2GX
☎Southampton (0703) 869444

A first-floor self-contained flat within a
wing of the Old Vicarage comprising
kitchen/diner, lounge, one twin-bedded
and one double-bedded room,
shower/WC. The Old Vicarage is located
on the A336 in Netley Marsh, next to the
church.

All year   1 wk min, 3 mths max, 1 unit,
1–6 persons   [◇]   ◈   ⊛   fridge
Electric   Elec metered   🔲 not provided
☎(200yds)   SD in unit   Iron in unit
Ironing board in unit   HCE in unit   ⊙
⊛   CTV   ⊕3pin square   2P   🔲
Badminton
⊖ ♨(3m)   🍴(200yds)   ☒(2m)   ♬(2m)
Max£65pw (Low)
Min£80 Max£100pw (High)

NEWBRIDGE
Isle of Wight
Map 4 SZ48

D   Greytiles   *for bookings* Mrs M E J
Morris, Three Gables, Newbridge,
Yarmouth, Isle of Wight PO41 0TU
☎Calbourne (098 378) 371 →

Small bungalow in centre of quiet village about 4m from Yarmouth. The accommodation consists of four bedrooms (two double, two twin), large kitchen, lounge, bathroom/WC and separate WC. Well maintained and plainly furnished.

All year MWB 1wk min, 8mths max, 1unit, 2–8persons ◊ no pets ◉ fridge Electric Elec metered ⬜can be hired ☎(100yds) Airing cupboard in unit Iron in unit Ironing board in unit HCE in unit ◐ TV ⊕3pin square P 🏠 ⛟(50yds)
⇔ 🍴(1m)

Min£40 Max£100pw (Low)
Min£130 Max£180pw (High)

H   1 & 2 Oamar Cottages for bookings Mrs M E J Morris, Three Gables, Newbridge, Yarmouth, Isle of Wight PO41 0TU
☎Calbourne (098 378) 371

Two semi-detached modern houses each with three bedrooms, separate lounge and kitchen/diner.

All year MWB 1wk min, 1mth max, 2units, 2–8persons ◊ ◆ no pets ◉ fridge Electric Elec metered ⬜can be hired ☎(300yds) Airing cupboard in unit Irin in unit Ironing board in unit [HCE in unit] ⊕ ◐ [TV] ⊕3pin saure 4P 📺 ⛟(300yds)
⇔ 🍴(1m)

Min£40 Max£100pw (Low)
Min£130 Max£180pw (High)

**Newbridge
—
New Galloway**

NEWBY BRIDGE
Cumbria
Map**6** SD38

F   Stock Park Mansion
for bookings Manager Holidays in Lakeland, Stock Park Estate, Newby Bridge, Cumbria LA12 8AY
☎Newbybridge(0448)31549

Ten spacious flats, decorated, furnished and equipped to an exceptionally high standard, on the ground, first and second floors of an attractive mansion standing in 120 acres of beautiful grounds, stretching to the W shore of Lake Windermere. Flats range from one with three bedrooms, six with two bedrooms, and three with one bedroom.

Mar–Oct 1wk min, 10units, 2–6persons ◊ ◆ no pets ◉ fridge 🍴 Elect metered ⬜inclusive ☎ WM on premises SD on premises TD on premises Airing cupboard in unit Iron on premises Ironing board on premises HCE in unit ⊕ CTV ⊕3pin square P 📺 ⛟(3m) ♿ fishing & games room
⇔ 🍴(1m) 🚲(1½) 🎵(1½m)

Min£50 Max£80pw (Low)
Max£200pw (High)

NEW FOREST
Hampshire
Map**4**

For details of AA-listed self-catering establishments in this area see **Ashurst, Beaulieu, Netley Marsh, and Woodlands**

NEW GALLOWAY
Dumfries & Galloway Kirkcudbrightshire
Map**11** NX67
C   Barlay & Woodland Cottages
for bookings Mrs C M Collison, Barlay, Balmaclellan, New Galloway, Kirkcudbrightshire DG7 3QW
☎New Galloway (064 42) 284

Two cottages standing in 16 acre estate in secluded and peaceful location. **Barlay** comprises two twin-bedded rooms, lounge/diner, kitchen and bathroom, all on ground floor. **Woodland** which is a two storey cottage, offers similar accommodation.

All year MWB out of season 1wk min 3wks max 2units 2–6persons ◊ ◆ ◉ fridge 🍴in Barlay Electric in Woodland Elec inclusive in Woodland Elec metered in Barlay ⬜can be hired ☎(2m) Airing cupboard in Barlay Iron in unit Ironing board in unit HCE in unit ⊕ CTV ⊕3pin square 4P ⛟(2m) ⋅🚶Hard
⇔ 🍴(3m)

Max£55pw (Low)
Min£130 Max£140pw (High)

C **Glenlee Cottage**
for bookings Mrs E Gordon, Glenlee Holiday Houses, New Galloway, Castle Douglas, Kirkcudbrightshire DG7 3SF
☎Dalry (06443) 445

Former farm and sawmill buildings, well converted into five linked cottages, forming a pleasant courtyard. The cottages have plenty of space and furnishings are of a good standard. They lie within Glenlee Estate, not far from the River Ken Valley, 2m N of New Galloway.

28Mar–Oct 1wk min, 5units, 1–8persons [◆ ◆] ◎ fridge Electric & open fires Elec metered ☐not provided SD in unit Airing cupboard in unit Iron in unit Ironing board in unit HCE in unit ⊙ TV can be hired ⦿3pin square 10P ♨(2m) Fishing

⊖ ♂9(2½m) ♀(2m) ▣(2m)

H **Makkevet Bor** Main Street
for bookings G M Thomson & Co, 27 King Street, Castle Douglas, Kirkcudbrightshire DG7 1AB
☎Castle Douglas (0556) 2701

Spacious newly built three-storey house with garden standing back from the main street, it has a living room, kitchen/dining room, utility room, and bedrooms sleeping upto ten people.

All year 1wk min, 1unit, 1–10persons ◆ ◎ fridge ▦& open fire Elec inclusive ☐not provided ☎(200yds) WM in unit SD in unit Airing cupboard in unit Iron in unit Ironing board in unit HCE in unit TV ⦿3pin square P ▥ ♨(100yds)

⊖ ♂9(100yds) ♀(100yds)

Min£85 Max£175pw

C Mrs I G Maclaren **Meadowbank Lodge** New Galloway, Kirkcudbrightshire DG7 3RU
☎New Galloway (06442) 282

Modernised lodge cottage standing at entrance to main house. Accommodation is all on the ground floor and comprises living room with dining area and open plan kitchen, two twin-bedded and one bunk-bedded room and bathroom. Situated at S end of High Street on A762.

Mar–Oct 1wk min, 1mth max, 1unit, 1–6persons [◆ ◆] no pets ◎ fridge ▦ Elec inclusive ☐not provided ☎(200yds) Airing cupboard in unit Iron in unit Ironing board in unit HCE in unit ⊙ TV ⦿3pin square 2P ♨(100yds)

⊖ ♂9(150yds) ♀(150yds) ▣(150yds)

Min£50 Max£120pw

NEWICK
East Sussex
Map**5** TQ42

B **Netherall Cottage**
for bookings Mrs P Welfare, 1 Netherall Cottages, Fletching Common, Newick, Lewes, E Sussex
☎Newick (082 572) 2713

Small bungalow set at the rear of cottages in quiet rural surroundings. Accommodation is one double bedroom, small lounge with bed settee, kitchen/diner and bathroom. 1¼ miles from the village.

All year MWB out of season 1wk min, 1mth max, 1unit, 1–4persons ◆ ◆ ◎ ▦ Elec metered ☐inclusive Iron in unit Ironing board in unit HCE in unit ⊙ TV ⦿3pin square ⦿2pin round 3P ▥ ♨(1¼) ⊇

⊖ ♂18(2m) ♀(1m) ▣(1m) ♬(1m)

Max£80pw (Low)
Max£110pw (High)

C **2 Netherall Cottages**
for bookings Mrs P Welfare, 1 Netherall Cottages, Fletching Common, Newick, Lewes, E Sussex
☎Newick (082572) 2713

Late Victorian semi-detached cottage with modern extension, accommodation includes two double-bedded rooms, one twin and one single, large lounge, separate dining room, kitchen, two bathrooms and WCs. Garden includes heated pool. 1m from Newick village.

All year MWB out of season 1wk min, 1mth max, 1unit, 1–8persons ◇ ◆ ◆ no pets ◎ fridge ▦ Elec metered ☐inclusive ☎ WM in unit SD in unit TD in unit Airing cupboard in unit Iron in unit Ironing board in unit HCE in unit ⊙ ⊛ CTV ⦿3pin square P ⌂ ▥ ♨(1m) ⊇

⊖ ♂18 ♂9(2m) ♀(1m)

Min£95 Max£160pw

NEWLAND
Gloucestershire
Map**3** SO50

F **Newland House**
for bookings Mr G Bird, 39 Murray Road, Wimbledon, London SW19 4PD
☎01-947 1478

Large Georgian house on the edge of the old world village of Newland which is situated between the Wye valley and the Royal Forest of Dean.
The house has been converted into spacious flats on three floors. Flat 1 is on the ground floor and sleeps five in two bedrooms (one double and one twin) and an extra divan in the lounge. Flats 2 & 3, on the ground floor, sleep up to six and seven persons respectively. Flat 2 comprises lounge (includes double divan) with part-oak panelling, and bow window with French door to garden, two bedrooms, one double and one twin, kitchen/diner and bathroom/WC. Flat 3 has three bedrooms, one with double bed, one with twin beds and one with three single beds. Flats 4, 6, 7, and 9 sleep five persons per unit. Flats 4 and 6 are on the first floor and flats 7 and 9 are second-floor flats. All have lounge, kitchen/diner and bathroom/WC. Flat 8 is a second floor flat with extra twin divans in the spacious living room, two bedrooms (one double and one twin with optional single foldaway bed), kitchen/diner and bathroom/WC.

Etr–Dec MWB out of season 1wk min, 6mths max, 8units, 5–7persons ◎ fridge Electric Elec metered ☐included ☎(250yds) Iron on premises Ironing board on premises HCE on premises ⊙ [CTV] 3pin round P ⌂ ▥ ♨(200yds) ▭ ⸙Grass & hard Croquet

⊖ ♀(200yds)

Min£50 Max£80pw (Low)
Min£98 Max£146pw (High)

NEW MILTON
Hampshire
Map**4** SZ29

Ch **Bashley Park Ltd** Sway Road, New Milton, Hampshire BH25 5QR
☎New Milton (0425) 612340

Twenty-five chalets with modern furnishings, part of a large holiday complex with chalets and static and touring caravans. In open rural surrounding on the fringe of the New Forest 12m E of Bournemouth on the B3055.

Mar-Oct MWB in season 1wk min, 1mth max, 25units, 2–6persons ◆ ◆ ◎ fridge Electric Elec metered ☐not provided ☎(10yds) Airing cupboard on premises [Iron on premises] Ironing board on premises HCE on premises [Launderette within 300yds] TV can be hired ⦿3pin square P ▥ ♨ ⊇ ⸙Hard Licensed clubroom, Restaurant ♂ ▣ ♬

Min£30 Max£55pw (Low)
Min£90 Max£135pw (High)

F & Ch **Naish Estate & Caravan Park** Christchurch Road, New Milton, Hampshire BH25 7RE
☎Highcliffe (04252) 3586

192 wooden chalets and 8 two storey maisonettes. All sleep 2–6 people and have kitchen, lounge/dining area, two bedrooms and bathroom. The site is situated on the edge of the New Forest, close to the sea and provides many facilities.

Mar-Oct MWB out of season 1wk min, 3wks max, 200 units, 2–6persons [◆ ◆] ◎ fridge Electric Elec metered ☐can be hired ☎ Airing cupboard in unit HCE in unit [Launderette on premises] ⊙ TV ⦿3pin square P ♨ ⊇ ⸙Hard ♂

⊖ ♂18(1m) ♀ ▣ ♬

Min£45 Max£55pw (Low)
Min£120 Max£140pw (High)

1982 prices quoted throughout gazetteer

NEW POLZEATH
Cornwall
Map2SW97

F Mrs B N Tait **Polzeath Court** New Polzeath, Polzeath, Cornwall
☎Trebetherick(020886)2270

Attractive flats with lounge, kitchen/diner, one double and one twin bedroom, bathroom and WC (lounge has double sofa-bed).

All year MWB 1wkmin, 1mthmax, 8units, 1–6persons [◇] ◆ ◆ nopets ◎ fridge Electric Elecmetered ⌴can be hired ☎ Airing cupboard in unit Iron in unit Ironing board in unit [Launderette on premises] ⊕ CTV ⊕3pinsquare 8P ▥ ♨(1m) Children's play area ⇔ ♒(3m) ♀(1m)

Min£60 Max£200pw

NEWPORT
Dyfed
Map2SN03

F **Sunnymeade Holiday Apartments**
for bookings Mr & Mrs Joseph, Sunnymeade, Parrog, Newport, Dyfed SA42 0RW
☎Newport(0239)820301

Two flats in a building located on a coastal path, where it skirts the old harbour and beach at Parrog on Newport Bay. Flat one is a first-floor flat with one twin-bedded room, an open plan living area, fitted kitchen, dining area and bathroom/WC. Flat two is a large flat on two floors and comprises a second-floor with lounge/diner, double bedroom, bathroom/WC and well equipped kitchen and third floor with two doubles and one twin-bedded room. All bedrooms have wash basins. Restaurant on premises.

All year MWB out of season 2units, 2–10persons [◇] ◆ ◆ nopets ◎ fridge ♨ Electric Elecinclusive ⌴inclusive ☎ Airing cupboard in unit HCE in unit ⊕ TV ⊕3pinsquare ▥ ♨(30yds) ⇔ ♒(3m) ♀

Min£50 Max£130pw (Low)
Min£75 Max£180pw (High)

NEWQUAY
Cornwall
Map2SW86

F **The Anchorage** Porthway, Porth
for bookings Mrs P S Schofield, High Cove Farm, Trenance, Mawgan Porth, Newquay, Cornwall TR8 4B2
☎St Mawgan(06374)567

Four modern apartments within small complex of flats, positioned in secluded cul de sac approx 300 yards from Porth Beach. Each comprises of one double-bedded and one twin-bedded rooms, lounge/diner with double bed-settee, kitchen & bathroom/WC.

All year MWB out of season 1wkmin, 4units, 1–6persons ◆ nopets ◎ fridge ♨ Electric Elecmetered ⌴can be hired ☎(400yds) [SD in unit] Airing cupboard in unit Iron on premises Ironing board on premises HCE in unit ⊕ TV ⊕3pinsquare 1P 1▥ ▥ ♨(300yds) ⇔ ♀(⅓m) ▦(⅓m) ♫(⅓m) ☃(⅓m)

Min£40 Max£50pw (Low)
Min£120 Max£180pw (High)

H **The Barn**
for bookings Mrs J Schofield, Hendra Paul Farm, St Columb Minor, Newquay, Cornwall
☎Newquay(06373)4695

Converted from its former farm use to its present condition of a lovely open beamed four bedroomed house. The accommodation comprises of a large living/dining room, one four poster bedroom and washbasin, one four poster bedroom together with single bed and washbasin, a further two bedrooms off the sitting room, one with a four poster double bed and the other containing twin beds. Shower room and WC available. Steps from sitting room lead to garden. This character property offers accommodation in a picturesque rural setting. Located off the A3059 St Columb Major to Newquay road approx 5 miles NE of Newquay.

All year MWB out of season 1wkmin, 1unit,¹1–8persons ◆ ◆ ◎ fridge Electric Elecmetered ⌴can be hired ☎ WM in unit SD in unit Airing cupboard in unit Iron in unit Ironing board in unit HCE in unit ⊕ CTV ⊕3pinsquare 2P ▥ ♨(2m) Maid service ⇔ ♀(2m) ▦(3m) ♫(3m)

Min£40 Max£250pw

F **The Orchard** Porth Way
for bookings Mrs J L M Rickard, Poldistra, 7 Riverside Avenue, Pentire, Newquay, Cornwall TR7 1PL
☎Newquay(06373)3412

Attractive three-storey, purpose-built flats with modern furnishings. In residential area 170yds from Porth Beach.

All year MWB out of season 3days min, 1mthmax, 6units, 2–6persons ◆ ◎ fridge ♨ Elecmetered ⌴can be hired ☎(100yds) Airing cupboard in unit Iron in unit Ironing board in unit HCE in unit CTV ⊕3pinsquare P ▥ ♨(100yds) ⇔ ♀ ▦ ♫ ☃

Min£45 Max£65pw (Low)
Min£90 Max£185pw (High)

F **Porthcova Holiday Flats** Beach Road (2m E B3276)
for bookings Mrs J Schofield, Hendra Paul Farm, St Columb Minor, Newquay, Cornwall
☎Newquay(06373)4695

Sited in their own grounds each with its own garage parking space, approx 150 yards from Porth beach. Each apartment comprises of one double and one twin-bedded room, lounge with double bed-settee separate kitchenette and modern bathroom/WC.

All year MWB out of season 1wkmin, 3units, 1–6persons ◆ ◆ ◎ fridge Electric Elecmetered ⌴can be hired ☎(150yds) Airing cupboard in unit Iron in unit Ironing board in unit HCE in unit ⊕ CTV ⊕3pinsquare 1P 1▥ ▥ ♨(500yds) ⇔ ♒(3m) ♀(200yds) ▦(2m) ♫(2m) ☃(2m)

Min£35 Max£170pw

F **Porth Sands Holiday Flats 1–6** Porth
for bookings Mr R Gerrell, Gerrells Holidays, 24 Trevemper Road, Newquay, Cornwall
☎Newquay(06373)5127

Modern purpose built flats situated at the edge of the beach with good sea views. The flats vary in size and sleep from two to eight persons some having bed-settee's in the lounge.

All year MWB out of season 1wkmin, 6units, 2–8persons ◆ ◆ nopets ◎ fridge Electric Elecmetered ⌴not provided ☎(100yds) Iron in unit Ironing board in unit HCE in unit ⊕ CTV ⊕3pinsquare 6P ▥ ♨(100yds) ⇔ ♒(2m) ♀(100yds) ▦(⅓m) ♫(⅓m) ☃(⅓m)

B **Sandy Reaches** 16 Trethewey Way, Tregunnel
for bookings H L & Mrs D O Mayne, 'Riverways', 11 Trethewey Way, Tregunnel, Newquay, Cornwall
☎Newquay(06373)5079

Detached bungalow in quiet residential location approx 1 mile from the town centre. Accommodation consists of one double-bedded room and single bed, one twin bedroom and a third bedroom with bunks, lounge, dining room, kitchen, bathroom and WC.

May-Oct 1wkmin, 1unit, 1–7persons ◎ fridge ♨ Elecmetered ⌴not provided ☎(500yds) Airing cupboard in unit Iron in unit Ironing board in unit HCE in unit ⊕ TV ⊕3pinsquare 2P 1▥ ▥ ♨(⅓m) ⇔ ♒(2m) ♀(1m) ▦(1m) ♫(1m) ☃(1m)

B **Tidal View** 13 Trethewey Way, *for bookings* Mr & Mrs K E Appleford, 2 Chyverton Close, Tregunnel, Newquay, Cornwall TR7 2AR
☎Newquay(06373)5967

Modern, detached bungalow in a quiet residential area close to town and beaches, positioned with commanding views of the tidal River Gannel. The property is well furnished and comprises of one double-bedded room, one double with additional single bed and one small

double bedroom; lounge with adjacent dining area, separate kitchen and bathroom/WC.

All year MWB out of season 1wk min, 1unit, 1–7persons [◇ ◆] ⊚ fridge ⋈ Gas/Elec metered ⊔ not provided ☎(500yds) WM in unit SD in unit Airing cupboard in unit Iron in unit Ironing board in unit HCE in unit ⊝ TV ⊕3pin square ⊕2pin round 2P 1⌂ ▥ ⛟(½m)

⇔ ᚐ(½m) ♀(½m) ☑(½m) ♬(½m) ☛(½m)

Min£75 Max£140pw

F Tides Reach Holiday Homes Porth Way
for bookings Mr P Renault, Kiandra, Trencreek, Newquay, Cornwall
☎Newquay(06373)2479

A three-storey block of purpose built flats and maisonettes in a secluded residential area. Each unit comprises of two double bedrooms, bathroom, kitchenette and lounge/diner with wall bed. Positioned close to the beach.

All year MWB out of season 2wks min, 6units, 1–6persons ◇ no pets ⊚ fridge ⋈ Elec metered ⊔ can be hired ☎(300yds) Iron on premises Ironing board on premises HCE in unit ⊝ CTV ⊕3pin square 1⌂ ⛟(300yds)

⇔ ᚐ(2m) ♀(½m) ☑(2m) ♬(2m) ☛(2m)

F Mr & Mrs R W Pearce Trevelga Flats 3 Lusty Glaze Road, Newquay, Cornwall
☎Newquay(06373)2527

Flats in a large villa situated in an elevated position overlooking the sea. Accommodation varies with one or two double bedrooms but in the larger units there is an additional pair of bunk beds. Each unit has a kitchen, breakfast room, bathroom/WC and living room with foldaway bed.

Mar-Oct MWB out of season 1wk min, 4wks max, 11units, 1–8persons [◇] no pets ⊚ fridge Electric Elec metered ⊔ not provided ☎ Airing cupboard in unit HCE in unit ⊝ CTV ⊕3pin square P ⌂ ⛟(200yds)

⇔ ♀(200yds) ☑(100yds)
♬(100yds) ☛(100yds)

Min£45 Max£55pw (Low)
Min£70 Max£148pw (High)

F White Surf Flats Pentire
for bookings Mr Robson, Robson Self-Catering Holidays, Morfa Hall, Cliff Road, Newquay, Cornwall
☎Newquay(06373)3649

Purpose-built, two-storey blocks of flats. Reception office, resident warden. Luxury furnishings. On cliff top overlooking Newquay beaches.

Etr-Oct MWB out of season 3days min, 6mths max, 2–8persons ◆
◆ ⊚ fridge Electric ⊔ can be hired ☎ Airing cupboard in unit Iron in unit Ironing board in unit HCE in unit ⊝ CTV ⊕3pin square ⊕2pin round 50P ▥ ⛟(300yds) ⌿ ᚐ(½m) ᚒ

⇔ ♀ ☑(½m) ♬(½m) ☛(½m)

NEWTON
Highland Inverness-shire
Map **14** NH30

C Mrs Oliver Calbarian Newton, Invergarry, Inverness-shire
☎Fort Augustus(0320)6270

Four semi-detached cottages dating from 1868, on the A82 (busy in summer). Furnishing is simple but adequate. Cooking is by Calor Gas. Kitchen and living room combined.

May-Sep 1wk min, 4units, 1–4persons no pets Electric Elec metered Calor ⌀ Gas inclusive ⊔ can be hired ☎(1m) HCE in unit P ▥ ⛟(3¼m)

Min£50 Max£55pw

NEWTONMORE
Highland Inverness-shire
Map **14** NN79

B Ballathie Station Road
for bookings Mrs H Hilton, Marlow Cottage, Laggan Road, Newtonmore, Inverness-shire
☎Newtonmore(05403)426

Modern detached bungalow located ¼ mile from town centre on road to Newtonmore Station. It comprises large lounge, kitchen/diner, bathroom, two good sized bedrooms and a small childs room with bunk beds.

All year MWB out of season 7days min, 6mths max, 1unit, 1–6persons ⊚ fridge Electric & woodburning stove Elec metered ⊔ not provided ☎(¼m) Airing cupboard in unit Iron in unit Ironing board in unit HCE in unit ⊝ CTV ⊕3pin square P ▥ ⛟(½m)

⇔ ᚐ(½m) ♀(½m) ☑(½m)

Ch Crubenmore Chalet Crubenmore (5m S on A9)
for bookings Blakes Holidays Ltd, Wroxham, Norwich, Norfolk NR12 8DH
☎Wroxham(06053)2917

Chalet situated within the grounds of Crubenmore Lodge, just off the A9 between Dalwhinnie and Newtonmore. Accommodation comprises a large wood panelled sitting room, twin-bedded rooms and two single bedrooms, also wood-panelled, kitchen and bathroom. Cots and high chairs to be requested at time of booking.

May-Oct 1wk min, 6mths max, 1unit, 1–6persons ◇ ◆ ⊚ fridge Electric Elec metered ⊔ can be hired Iron in unit Ironing board in unit HCE in unit ⊕3pin square P ⛟(5m) Fishing

Min£80 Max£128pw (Low)
Min£121 Max£152pw (High)

H Crubenmore Lodge Crubenmore (5m S on A9)
for bookings Blakes Holidays Ltd, Wroxham, Norwich, Norfolk NR12 8DH
☎Wroxham(06053)2917

An attractive stone-built hunting lodge located 5m from Newtonmore on the A9. It has five bedrooms; two double and three twin-bedded rooms; large dining room, sitting room, two bathrooms and two WCs. Trout and salmon fishing is available to guests. Cots and high chairs have to be requested at time of booking. →

1982 prices quoted throughout gazetteer

GLENTRUIM ESTATE

Glentruim' is a private estate close to the A9 in the very centre of the Highlands. It is an ideal place for those who wish to see as much as possible of the Highlands. For those who prefer a quieter holiday, Glentruim offers traditional Highland buildings, formerly occupied by estate staff which are comfortable, well equipped and situated in private woods and farmland. Fishing is included and other recreations available include swimming, riding, canoeing, gliding, skiing, sailing and golf. Phone Newtonmore 221.

May–Oct 1wk min, 6mths max, 1 unit,
1–10 persons ◊ ◆ ◉ fridge
Electric Elec metered Ⓛ can be hired
☎(5m) Iron in unit Ironing board in
unit HCE in unit ⊕3 pin square P
♨(5m) Fishing

Min£123 Max£197pw (Low)
Min£180 Max£233pw (High)

F Crubenmore Wing Crubenmore (5m
S on A9)
for bookings Blakes Holidays Ltd,
Wroxham, Norwich, Norfolk NR12 8DH
☎Wroxham(06053)2917

*A fully modernised flat in the wing of
Crubenmore Lodge located 5m from
Newtonmore on the A9. Accommodation
comprises one double and two twin-
bedded rooms, kitchen and living room.
Cots and high chairs have to be
requested at the time of booking.*

May–Oct 1wk min, 6mths max, 1 unit,
1–6 persons ⌀ (Calor) fridge 🍳
Gas inclusive Elec metered Ⓛ can be
hired ☎(5m) Airing cupboard in unit
Iron in unit Ironing board in unit HCE in
unit ⊕3 pin square P ♨(5m) Fishing

Min£74 Max£95pw (Low)
Min£111 Max£139pw (High)

C Mrs E Macpherson **Glentruim**
Newtonmore, Inverness-shire
☎Newtonmore(05403)221

*The cottages, which were originally
occupied by staff from the castle estate,
vary in size and have traditional décor
and furnishings. Situated in a quiet tree-
studded location in extensive estate
grounds 3m S of Newtonmore; the rivers
Spey and Truim are a short distance
away.*

All year MWB out of season 1wk min,
3mths max, 3 units, 2–8 persons ◇ ◆
◆ ◉ fridge Electric & open fires
Elec metered Ⓛ not provided
☎(100yds) HCE in unit TV can be
hired ⊕3 pin square P ♨(3m)
Fishing

↔ 🍴(3m) 🚻(3m)

Min£46 Max£69pw (Low)
Min£80.50 Max£126.50pw (High)

See advert on page 185

1982 prices quoted throughout
gazetteer

Newtonmore — Neyland

F Ralia Flats 1 & 2 Ralia Estate
for bookings Blakes Holidays Ltd,
Wroxham, Norwich, Norfolk NR12 8DH
☎Wroxham(06053)2917

*Situated within a large country house, 4m
off the A9 on the B970, 1m S of
Newtonmore. Flat 1 comprises a very
large kitchen, three twin-bedded rooms
all with wash basins, sitting room and
bathroom. Flat 2 comprises three
bedrooms with wash basins, two
bathroom/WCs, lounge and kitchen and
is located on the first and ground floors.
Both flats offer fine views across
Mondhliath Mountains. Cots and high
chairs have to be requested at time of
booking.*

May–Oct 1wk min, 6mths max, 2 units,
1–6 persons ◊ ◆ ⌀ (Calor) fridge
Electric Gas/Elec inclusive Ⓛ can be
hired ☎(1m) Airing cupboard in unit
Iron in unit Ironing board in unit HCE in
unit ⊕3 pin round P 🚻 ♨(1m)
Fishing

Min£75 Max£118pw (Low)
Min£134 Max£139pw (High)

NEWTON STEWART
Dumfries & Galloway *Wigtownshire*
Map**10** NX46

Ch Mr & Mrs I S Lowth *Conifers
Leisure Park* Newton Stewart,
Wigtownshire DG8 6AN
☎Newton Stewart(0671)2107

*Twenty-four timber chalets of Finnish
design in an elevated position in a pine
wood. High standard of furnishings.
Secluded position, although there is an
hotel conveniently situated in the same
grounds. 1m E of Newton Stewart off A75.*

All year MWB out of season 2 days min,
24 units, 1–6 persons ◊ ◆ ◉
fridge Electric Elec inclusive Ⓛ can
be hired ☎(½m) Iron on premises
Ironing board on premises HCE in unit
⊖ TV ⊕3 pin square 50P 🚻 ♨(1m)

↔ 🍴(½m)

NEWTOWN ST BOSWELLS
Borders *Roxburghshire*
Map**12** NT53

C Chesterhall West Cottage
Chesterhall
for bookings Miss J Bristow, Thorncroft,
Lilliesleaf, Roxburghshire TD6 9JD
☎Lilliesleaf(08357)424

*Semi-detached cottage at foot of the
Eildon Hills. Accommodation offers
sitting/dining room, twin bedroom,
kitchen with adjoining bathroom, upstairs
a spacious family bedroom. The cottage
lies within a farm estate approx 1½m W of
Newtown St Boswells.*

All year MWB out of season 1wk min,
1 unit, 1–5 persons [◊] ◉ fridge
Electric Elec metered Ⓛ can be hired
☎(2m) Iron in unit Ironing board in
unit HCE in unit CTV ⊕3 pin round
2P ♨(1½m)

↔ 🍴(3m) 🍴(1½m)

Min£57.50 Max£71.30pw (Low)
Min£89.70 Max£109.25pw (High)

NEYLAND
Dyfed
Map**2** SM90

B Haven View 4 Woodland Park (off
Gothic Road)
for bookings Powell's Holidays, High
Street, Saundersfoot, Dyfed
☎Saundersfoot(0834)812791

*A modern detached bungalow set in
landscaped garden overlooking the
River Cleddau. It contains a large lounge,
and sleeping accommodation for six
people. A cot is also available. From
Honeyborough Road into Kensington
Road, signed Neyland. After ⅓m turn into
Charles Street then left into Gothic Road.
Haven View is at the bottom of the hill.*

May–Oct MWB out of season 1wk min,
1mth max, 1 unit, 2–6 persons ◊
no pets ◉ fridge [🍳] Elec inclusive
Ⓛ can be hired ☎(350yds) SD in unit
Airing cupboard in unit Iron in unit
Ironing board in unit HCE in unit ⊖
CTV ⊕3 pin square 🅰 🚻 ♨(½m)

↔ 🍴(½m) 🚻(½m) 🎵(½m)

Min£57 Max£150pw

NITON
Isle of Wight
Map **4** SZ57

C **Bluebell Cottage** Church Street
for bookings Mrs P Rogers, 30 Leyborne
Park, Kew Gardens, Surrey
☎ 01–9400293

*Attractive fully-modernised stone cottage
situated in middle of village. Upstairs
there are two bedrooms (one a double-
bedded room and the other a twin-
bedded room); one has bathroom/WC en
suite, the other has a wash basin.
Downstairs area comprises lounge,
separate dining room and kitchen. Good
quality solid furnishings. Second WC
outside back door.*

All year except Xmas 1wk min,
3mths max, 1 unit, 2–4 persons ◇ ◎
fridge ▥ Elec metered
⌧ not provided ☎ (200yds) Iron in unit
Ironing board in unit HCE in unit CTV
⊕ 3pin square ▥ ♨ (200yds)
◒ ♀ (200yds) ♫ (200yds)
Min£50 Max£60pw (Low)
Min£65 Max£75pw (High)

NORTHAM
Devon
Map **2** SS42

H **JFH Ref RG 68A**
for bookings John Fowler Holidays,
Marlborough Road, Ilfracombe, Devon
☎ Ilfracombe(0271)64135

*Semi-detached house with gardens both
front and rear. Accommodation
comprises lounge with settee and put-u-
up, dining room, well-equipped kitchen,
bathroom, separate WC and three well-
furnished bedrooms (one double and two
twins).*

Mar–Oct MWB out of season
3 days min, 3 wks max, 1 unit,
2–8 persons ◇ ◆ ◆ ◢ fridge
Electric Gas/Elec metered
⌧ not provided ☎ (500yds) Airing
cupboard in unit Iron in unit Ironing
board in unit HCE in unit [Launderette
within 300yds] TV ⊕ 3pin square P
▥ ♨ (500yds)
◒ ♀ (500yds) ▨ (½m) ▩ (2m)
Min£56 Max£182pw

B **JFH Ref SB 46C**
for bookings John Fowler Holidays,
Marlborough Road, Ilfracombe, Devon
☎ Ilfracombe(0271)64135

*Chalet bungalows adjacent to beach.
Each comprises lounge/diner with
double put-u-up and contemporary
furnishings, kitchen area off lounge using
divider, bathroom/WC and one double
and one twin-bedded room.*

Mar–Oct MWB out of season
3 days min, 3 wks max, 10 units,
2–6 persons [◇] [◆] [◆] ◎
fridge Electric Elec metered
☎ (200yds) Airing cupboard in unit Iron
on premises HCE in unit ⊕ TV
⊕ 3pin square P ♨ (½m) Children's
playground, horse riding

◒ ☋ (½m) ▨ (½m) ♫ (½m) ▩ (2½m)
Min£34 Max£137pw

Ch **Lenwood Country Club** Lenwood
Road, Northam, Bideford, Devon
EX39 3PN
☎ Bideford(023 72)4372

*Brick and cedarwood chalets set in
wooded area 1½m from Bideford.
Accommodation comprises two, three or
four bedrooms, lounge/dining room with
separate kitchen area, bathroom and
WC. Club facilities include restaurant,
squash, bar billiards, games room and
skittle alley.*

3 Apr–5 Nov MWB out of season
3 days min, 6 wks max, 59 units,
4–10 persons [◇] [◆] ◎ fridge
Electric Elec metered ⌧ can be hired
☎ (100yds) Airing cupboard Iron in
unit Ironing board in unit HCE in unit
[Launderette within 300yds] ⊕ TV
⊕ 3pin square P ▥ ♨ (200yds) ⌚
▱ Hard ☋

◒ ♀ (200yds) ▨ (1½m) ♫ (1½m)
▩ (1½m)
Min£30 Max£165pw

NORTH BERWICK
Lothian *East Lothian*
Map **12** NT58

H **8 West Bay Road**
for bookings Mrs E M MacDonald, Blake
Holt, Brownsea View Avenue, (Lilliput),
Poole, Dorset BH14 8LQ
☎ Canford Cliffs(0202)707894

*Small semi-detached house with garden,
in quiet road in holiday resort town. Three
bedrooms. Furnishings are a little dated
but of reasonable appearance and
comfort.*

All year MWB out of season 1wk min,
8 mths max, 1 unit, 6 persons ◆
no pets ◢ fridge Electric & coal fires
Elec metered ⌧ not provided ☎ WM
SD Airing cupboard in unit Iron in unit
Ironing board in unit HCE in unit ⊕
⊕ 3pin square P ▥ ♨ (½m) ⌚ ☋
Min£45 Max£135pw

NORTHBOURNE
Kent
Map **5** TR35

C **1 & 2 Longdane Cottages**
for bookings Mr & Mrs R W Stiles,
Parsonage House, Northbourne, Deal,
Kent
☎ Deal(030 45)5826

*Two modernised farm cottages in the
small village of Northbourne. Each
comprises a dining room, sitting room,
kitchen, bathroom and two bedrooms
each with twin beds.*

All year MWB out of season 1wk min,
3 mths max, 2 units, 4 persons ◇ ◎
fridge Electric Elec inclusive

⌧ inclusive ☎ (125yds) SD in unit
Airing cupboard in unit Iron in unit
Ironing board in unit HCE in unit ⊕
TV ⊕ 3pin square 2P ▥ ♨ (125yds)
◒ ☋ (4m) ♀ (125yds)
Min£70 Max£100pw

NORTH CREAKE
Norfolk
Map **9** TF83

C **Crossways Cottage**
for bookings Major G Bowlby, English
Country Cottages, Claypit Lane,
Fakenham, Norfolk
☎ Fakenham(0328)51155

*A typically early 19th-century farmhouse
in isolated position. Clean and simple but
adequately equipped to sleep six
persons in three bedrooms, all
accommodation being on the first floor.*

All year 1wk min, 1 unit, 1–6 persons
◇ ◎ fridge ▥ Elec metered
⌧ not provided ☎ (1m) Iron in unit
Ironing board in unit HCE in unit TV
⊕ 3pin square 2P ♨ (½m)
◒ ♀ (½m)
Max£63pw (Low)
Min£75 Max£114pw (High)

NORTH ELMHAM
Norfolk
Map **9** TF92

C **The Cottage** Eastgate
for bookings Major G Bowlby, English
Country Cottages, Claypit Lane,
Fakenham, Norfolk
☎ Fakenham(0328)51155

*A very quiet and secluded large flint and
brick family cottage standing in an acre of
hedged, well-kept garden. Pretty and
comfortable furnishings in dining room,
large drawing room and four bedrooms
(to sleep six). The village lies midway
between the A1067 and A47 some 8m S
of Fakenham.*

Apr–Oct 1wk(summer), 1 unit,
1–6 persons ◇ ◎ fridge Electric
Elec metered ⌧ inclusive ☎ (100yds)
Airing cupboard in unit Iron in unit
Ironing board in unit HCE in unit TV
⊕ 3pin square 3P 1♨ ♨ (100yds)
Coarse fishing available
◒ ♀ (150yds) ▩ (3m)
Min£114 Max£222pw

OAKFORD
Dyfed
Map **2** SN45

C **Oakford Country Cottages**
for bookings Anne Rushton, Neuadd
Coach House, Oakford, Llanarth, Dyfed
☎ Llanarth(054 554)696

***Barn Owl, Cobnut, Oak Apple** and **Pear
Tree** cottages are all equipped and
maintained to a very high standard. Each
has a well-designed open plan living
room, kitchen and bathroom. Sleeping
accommodation varies, Oak Apple
cottage having three bedrooms, the →*

others have two. They have maintained an individual charm and have been tastefully furnished to suit their character.

All year MWB out of season 4 units, 2–8 persons ◊ ◆ no pets ⊚ fridge ♨ Elec inclusive ⊡ inclusive (except towels) ☎(½m) SD in unit Airing cupboard in unit Iron in unit Ironing board in unit HCE in unit ⊙ CTV ⊕3 pin square P ▥ ♨(1m) Barbecue area

⊷ ⚲(2m)

Min£100 Max£125pw (Low)
Min£225 Max£350pw (High)

OAKHAM
Leicestershire
Map 4 SK80

C   Birch Cottage
for bookings Mrs R S C Abel-Smith, Old Hall Cottage, 36 Burley Road, Langham, Oakham, Leicestershire LE15 7JE
☎Oakham(0572)2964(evenings)

Two-storey stone-built cottage overlooking the village 14th-century church. On the ground floor there is a lounge with simple, clean décor, and a kitchen which provides basic requirements, dining area. Upstairs there is a bathroom/WC with washbasin, one double room, one twin and one with full-size bunks.

All year MWB out of season wknd min, 2 mths max, 1 unit, 8 persons ◊ ⊚

---

fridge Gas & electric fires
Gas/elec metered ⊡not provided ☎(150yds) HCE in unit ⊙ TV ⊕3 pin square P ▥ ♨(150yds)

⊷ ⚲(200yds) ▨(200yds) ♬(2m) ▩(2m)

Min£60 Max£87pw (High)

F   The Old Hall (Garden Flat)
for bookings Mrs R S C Abel-Smith, Old Hall Cottage, 36 Burley Road, Langham, Oakham, Leicestershire LE15 7JE
☎Oakham(0572)2964(evenings)

This garden flat is a modernised wing of the Old Hall comprising of lounge, dining room, kitchen, bathroom/WC, one double bedroom, a single bedroom and a child's room. All on one level. 2m NW on A606.

All year MWB out of season wknds min, 6 mths max, 1 unit, 1–4 persons ◊ ◆ ⚲ fridge ♨ Gas/Elec metered ⊡can be hired ☎ Airing cupboard in unit Iron in unit Ironing board in unit HCE in unit CTV ⊕3 pin square 4P ▥ ♨(150yds)

⊷ ⚲(200yds) ▨(2m) ♬(2m) ▩(2m)

Min£60 Max£87pw (High)

1982 prices quoted throughout gazetteer

C   Stable Cottage
for bookings Mrs R S C Abel-Smith, Old Hall Cottage, 36 Burley Road, Langham, Oakham, Leicestershire LE15 7JE
☎Oakham(0572)2964(evenings)

Two-storey cottage in part of stone-built stable block. On the ground floor is a lounge/dining room and kitchen. Upstairs there is a large double room, one single and one room with twin beds. Bathroom with wash hand basin and separate WC.

All year MWB out of season 1 wk min, 2 mths max, 1 unit, 5 persons ◊ ⚲ fridge Gas & electric fires Gas/Elec metered ⊡not provided ☎(150yds) Airing cupboard in unit HCE in unit ⊙ TV ⊕3 pin square P ▥ ♨(150yds)

⊷ ⚲(200yds) ▨(200yds) ♬(2m) ▩(2m)

Min£60 Max£87pw (High)

OBAN
Strathclyde Argyll
Map 10 NM82

B   Braes of Ganavan Ganavan (2m along unclass road beside Oban Bay) for bookings Alexander Dawson, Estate Agents, 120 George Street, Oban, Argyll PA34 5NT
☎Oban(0631)63901 or 62056

Modern single-floor bungalow in superb hillside position with own garden. It

ESPLANADE COURT OBAN

Purpose built holiday apartments beautifully situated overlooking the sea and surrounding islands. Each apartment completely self-contained with central heating throughout. Bed linen and all equipment provided.

Colour TV in each lounge. Elevator to all floors.
Laundry rooms with automatic equipment. Private parking free.
Special off-season terms.

For brochure and tariff write, with S.A.E.:
Mr NICOLSON,
Esplanade Court, The Esplanade, OBAN — Argyll.
Or telephone: Oban (0631) 62067.

comprises two twin-bedded rooms, one
double and one single bedroom,
bathroom/WC, separate WC, kitchen with
hatch into dining area and large lounge
with splendid sea views.

All year MWB out of season 1wk min,
3mths max, 1unit, 1–7persons no pets
fridge Electric Elec inclusive
⊡not provided ☎(500yds) Airing
cupboard in unit Iron in unit Ironing
board in unit HCE in unit ⊕ CTV
⊕3pin square P 🏠 🏛(500yds)
⊛ ⚲(2m) ⬚(2m) ♫(2m)
🐾(2m)

Min£90 Max£120pw (Low)
Min£165 Max£210pw (High)

F Mr I Nicholson **Esplanade Court**
Corran Esplanade, Oban, Argyll
☎Oban(0631)62067

*Purpose-built flats of good standard.
Each flat has at least one room
overlooking Oban Bay to the islands of
Kerrera and Mull. The esplanade is right
in the heart of the town, but private
parking is available.*

12Mar–6Nov 1wk min, 1mth max,
14units, 1–7persons ◇ ◆ no pets
⊚ fridge 🍴 Elec metered
⊡inclusive ☎ [WM on premises] [SD
on premises] [TD on premises] Airing
cupboard in unit Iron on premises
Ironing board on premises HCE in unit
⊕ CTV ⊕3pin square P 🏠
🏛(100yds) ▭ ⊁Hard 🐾

⊛ ⚲ ▭ ♫ 🐾

Min£63 Max£152pw (Low)
Min£155 Max£200pw (High)

OLD STORRIDGE
Hereford & Worcester
Map**3** SO75

C **Nestledown Cottage**
for bookings Mrs Sadler, Wyvern
Cottages, 60 East Road, Stoney Hill,
Bromsgrove, Worcestershire
☎Bromsgrove(0527)73734

*A delightfully preserved black and white
cottage set in the grounds of the owner's
home. The accommodation comprises
lounge/dining room, kitchen and
bathroom, with one double-bedded room
and one single-bedded room on the first
floor.*

Etr–Sep 1wk min, 3wks max, 1unit,
1–4persons [◇] ◆ no pets Aga
fridge 🍴 Elec metered
⊡not provided ☎(2m) Airing
cupboard in unit Iron in unit HCE ⊕
TV ⊕3pin square 2P 🏛(2m)

⊛ ⚲(2m)

Min£65 Max£90pw

ONCHAN
Isle of Man
Map**6** SC37

F **8 Belgravia Road**
for bookings Mrs E Casey, Halcyon Rise,
54 Ballachurry Avenue, Onchan, Isle of
Man
☎Douglas(0624)24827

*Stone-built terraced house in residential
area of Onchan, short walk from sea front.
House comprises of three modestly
furnished flats; the ground-floor flat has
one bedroom with double beds, first and
second floor flats have two bedrooms
with double beds. All flats have lounge
with studio couch, well-equipped
kitchen/diner and modern bathroom.*

Mar–Oct MWB out of season 1wk min,
3units, 2–8persons ◇ no pets ⊚
fridge Electric Elec metered
⊡inclusive ☎(200yds) Airing
cupboard in unit Iron in unit Ironing
board in unit HCE in unit TV
⊕3pin square ▦ 🏛(200yds)

⊛ 🐾(1m) ⚲(200yds) ⬚(300yds)
♫(300yds) 🐾(2m)

Min£45 Max£110pw

C **The Cottages** Groundle Glen,
Onchan, Douglas, Isle of Man
☎Douglas(0624)23075

*A village of 35 modern cottages set in a
pleasant glen leading to a small cove. All
are well furnished and each has three
bedrooms (one with double bed, one with
two singles and one with two bunks).*

All year MWB out of season 1wk min,
2wks max, 35units, 2–6persons [◇]
[◆] no pets ⊚ fridge 🍴(12units)
Electric Elec metered (inclusive in
summer) ⊡inclusive ☎ Airing
cupboard in unit Iron on premises HCE
in unit TV [CTV] ⊕3pin square P
▦ 🏛 ♿

⊛ ⚲(3m) ⬚(3m) ♫(3m) 🐾(3m)

Min£45 Max£160pw

ONICH
Highland *Inverness-shire*
Map**14** NN06

R & Ch **Inchree Holiday Village**
for bookings Mrs K J Heron, Rosapenna,
Onich, Fort William, Inverness-shire
☎Onich(08553)287

*Four bungalows and five chalets set in
natural surroundings with views of Loch
and hills. The Bungalows comprise one
double and one twin bedded room while
chalets have one double and two twin
bedded rooms. Situated about ½ mile off
the A82, signed 'Inchree'.*

All year MWB out of season 3days min,
9units, 1–6persons ◇ ◆ ⊚ fridge
Electric Elec inclusive(lighting)
Elec metered(power) ⊡inclusive
☎(100yds) Airing cupboard on
premises [Iron on premises] Ironing
board on premises HCE in unit
[Launderette on premises] ⊕ CTV
⊕3pin square P 🏛(½m) Children's
play area

⊛ ⚲(½m) ⬚(½m)

Min£40 Max£190pw

ORKNEY
Map**16**
See Finstown, Orphir, Stenness

ORMSARY
Strathclyde *Argyll*
Map**10** NR77

Ch **Camas Log Cabins**
for bookings Lithgows Rural
Management Ltd, Estates Office,
Ormsary, Lochgilphead, Argyll PA31 8PE

*Modern timber-framed chalets lying
together in natural surroundings,
overlooking Loch Coalisport.
Accommodation comprises three
bedrooms (one double, one twin and one
room with bunk beds), living room, open-
plan fitted kitchen and bathroom.*

All year MWB out of season 1wk min,
6wks max, 13units, 1–6persons ◇ ⊚
fridge Electric Elec inclusive
⊡provided ☎(2½m) Airing cupboard in
unit HCE in unit ⊕ ⊕3pin square P
🏛(12m) Rowing boats for hire

Min£51.75 Max£69pw (Low)
Min£155.25 Max£212.75pw (High)

ORPHIR
Orkney
Map**16** HY30

H **Waterslap**
for bookings Mrs V Pirie, Orakirk, Orphir,
Orkney KW17 2RE
☎Orphir(085681)328

*Modern four-bedroomed house set in
close proximity to the A964, and 8m from
Stromness which it faces to the W across
Hoy Sound. The house is well maintained
with a spacious and comfortable living
room. Transport is recommended. Ideally
located for sea and countryside.*

All year 1wk min(winter),
2wks min(summer), 1unit, 1–8persons
◇ no pets ⊚ fridge Electric
Elec metered ⊡not provided ☎(4m)
Airing cupboard in unit Iron in unit
Ironing board in unit HCE in unit ⊕
CTV ⊕3pin square P ▦ 🏛(3m)

Min£55 Max£70pw (Low)
Min£65 Max£80pw (High)

ORSETT
Essex
Map**5** TQ68

C **The Cottage**
for bookings Mrs M A Wordley, Lorkin's
Farm, Orsett, Essex RM16 3EL
☎Grays Thurrock(0375)891439

*Small Victorian terraced cottage in quiet
cul-de-sac. Spacious and well-
decorated family accommodation.
Situated in the village of Orsett just off the
main A128.*

All year MWB wknd min, 7mths max,
1unit, 2–5persons ◇ ◆ no pets
fridge 🍴 Elec inclusive ⊡inclusive
☎ WM in unit SD in unit Airing
cupboard in unit Iron in unit Ironing
board in unit HCE in unit ⊕ ⊛ CTV
⊕3pin square 2P ▦ 🏛(300yds) →

189

⊖ ♿ ♀ 🛋️
Min£85 Max£120pw (Low)
Min£125 Max£145pw (High)

OTTERTON
Devon
Map **3** SY08

H **CC Ref 645 EP**
for bookings Character Cottages
(Holidays) Ltd, 34 Fore Street, Sidmouth,
Devon EX10 8AQ
☎Sidmouth(039 55)77001

*Delightful old farmhouse with spacious
oak-beamed rooms. Accommodation
comprises hall, attractive lounge with
open fireplace, cloakroom with WC and
H/C washbasin, dining room with period
furnishings, four large bedrooms (two
twin bedded, two doubles) and
bathroom/WC.*

All year MWB out of season 1 wk min,
1 mth max, 1 unit, 2–8 persons ◆ ◉
fridge Electric Elec metered ⌷ can be
hired ☎ Airing cupboard in unit Iron in
unit Ironing board in unit HCE in unit
TV ⊕3pin square ⊕2pin round P
🏠 Ⅲ ♨️
⊖ ♀(200yds) 🅿(1m)
Min£129 Max£162pw (Low)
Min£225 Max£327pw (High)

OTTERY ST MARY
Devon
Map **3** SY19

H **CC Ref 757 L**
for bookings Character Cottages
(Holidays) Ltd, 34 Fore Street, Sidmouth,
Devon EX10 8AQ
☎Sidmouth(039 55)77001

*Modern terraced house on small
attractive estate. Accommodation is
comprised of lounge/diner, fully
equipped separate kitchen,
bathroom/WC, and two bedrooms (one
with a double bed and the other having
bunk beds).*

All year MWB out of season 1 wk min,
4wks max, 1 unit, 1–6 persons ◆
no pets ◉ fridge 🍴 Elec inclusive
⌷ can be hired ☎(500yds) WM in unit
Airing cupboard in unit Iron in unit
Ironing board in unit HCE in unit ⊖
TV ⊕3pin square 1P 1🏠 Ⅲ ♨️(½m)
⊖ ♀(½m) 🅿(1m) 🎵(1m)
Min£75 Max£88pw (Low)
Min£119 Max£163pw (High)

OWLPEN
Gloucestershire
Map **3** ST79

C **The Court House**
for bookings Mr & Mrs N Mander, Owlpen
Manor, Owlpen, Dursley,
Gloucestershire GL11 5BZ
☎Dursley(0453)860261

*A charming building, fundamentally
Stuart period, situated within the Manor
estate. Ground floor includes small
kitchen, bathroom and dining area
leading to garden. Living room and*

*double bedded room on the first floor and
two rooms in the loft, one with twin beds
and one with double beds. Comfortably
furnished.*

All year MWB 2 nights min, 1 unit,
3–6 persons ◆ ◆ ◉ fridge 🍴
Elec inclusive ⌷ inclusive ☎ Iron in
unit Ironing board in unit HCE in unit
⊖ CTV ⊕3pin square 2P ♨️(1m)
⊖ ♿(2m) ♀(1m)
Min£110 Max£161pw (Low)
Min£184 Max£276pw (High)

H **Grist Mill**
for bookings Mr & Mrs N Mander, Owlpen
Manor, Owlpen, Dursley,
Gloucestershire GL11 5BZ
☎Dursley(0453)860261

*A listed building which provides
essentially modern accommodation of
unrivalled character and charm, features
of the working mill have been retained.
Open plan dining/living room, pine fitted
kitchen, on the first floor there is a double
bedded room with four poster bed and a
twin bedded room, bathroom and WC.
The second floor is reached by narrow
stairs giving access to a large open area
with a double and three single beds.*

All year MWB 2 nights min, 1 unit,
4–9 persons ◆ ◆ ◗ fridge 🍴
Gas/elec inclusive ⌷ inclusive ☎
Airing cupboard in unit Iron in unit
Ironing board in unit HCE in unit ⊖
CTV ⊕3pin square P ♨️(1m)
⊖ ♿(3m) ♀(1m)
Min£121 Max£196pw (Low)
Min£213 Max£374pw (High)

H **Manor Farm**
for bookings Mr and Mrs N Mander,
Owlpen Manor, Owlpen, Dursley,
Gloucestershire GL11 5BZ
☎Dursley(0453)860261

*Modern house comprising living/dining
room with open fireplace, kitchen, one
double and one twin bedded room, and
shower room with WC.*

All year MWB 2 nights min, 1 unit,
4 persons [◆ ◆] ◉ fridge 🍴
Elec inclusive ⌷ inclusive ☎ WM in
unit Airing cupboard in unit Iron in unit
Ironing board in unit HCE in unit ⊖
CTV ⊕3pin square P ♨️(1m)
⊖ ♿(3m) ♀(1m)
Min£98 Max£150pw (Low)
Min£173 Max£242pw (High)

C **Marling's End Cottage**
for bookings Mr & Mrs N Mander, Owlpen
Manor, Owlpen, Dursley, Gloucester
GL11 5BZ
☎Dursley(0453)860261

*Attractive cottage in pleasant valley
setting. Accommodation consists of
comfortable sitting room, dining room,
kitchen, cloakroom/WC, double and twin*

*bedrooms with a smaller room containing
bunk beds and bathroom/WC.*

All year MWB 2 nights min, 1 unit,
2–6 persons [◆ ◆] ◉ fridge 🍴
Elec inclusive ⌷ inclusive ☎ Airing
cupboard in unit Iron in unit Ironing
board in unit HCE in unit ⊖ CTV
⊕3pin square 2P ♨️(½m)
⊖ ♿(2m) ♀(1m)
Min£110 Max£173pw (Low)
Min£178 Max£316pw (High)

H **Overcourt**
for bookings Mr & Mrs N Mander, Owlpen
Manor, Owlpen, Dursley, Gloucestershire
GL11 5BZ
☎Dursley(0453)860261

*Adjoining the Manor Farm this attractive
small cottage comprises sitting room,
kitchen, bathroom/WC and three
bedrooms, one of which is a small childs
room.*

All year MWB 1 unit, 2–5 persons [◇]
◆ ◆ no pets ◉ fridge 🍴
Elec inclusive ⌷ inclusive ☎ WM in
unit SD in unit Airing cupboard in unit
Iron in unit Ironing board in unit HCE in
unit ⊖ CTV ⊕3pin square 2P Ⅲ
♨️(1m)
⊖ ♿(2m) ♀(1m)
Min£98 Max£150pw (Low)
Min£173 Max£242pw (High)

C **Summerfield Cottage**
for bookings Mr & Mrs N Mander, Owlpen
Manor, Owlpen, Dursley,
Gloucestershire GL11 5BZ
☎Dursley(0453)860261

*A small charming cottage with open
views, situated a few minutes from the
Manor House Estate. Accommodation
includes sitting room, double bedroom,
kitchen and bathroom, patio sitting area.*

All year MWB 2 nights min, 1 unit,
2 persons ◆ ◆ ◉ fridge 🍴
Elec inclusive ⌷ inclusive ☎ Airing
cupboard in unit Iron in unit Ironing
board in unit HCE in unit ⊖ CTV
⊕3pin square 2P ♨️(1m)
⊖ ♿(2m) ♀(1m)
Min£92 Max£127pw (Low)
Min£150 Max£190pw (High)

OXTON
Borders *Berwickshire*
Map **12** NT45

C **Laverock Bank Cottage**
for bookings Miss J Bristow, Thorncroft,
Lilliesleaf, Roxburghshire TD6 9JD
☎Lilliesleaf(083 57)424

*Secluded cottage in a peaceful situation
with views over the Lammermuir Hills.
Accommodation comprises
sitting/dining room, kitchen, bathroom
and three bedrooms sleeping up to ten
persons.*

Apr–Oct MWB out of season 1 wk min,
2 mths max, 1 unit, 2–10 persons [◆]
◉ fridge Electric & coal fires
Elec metered ⌷ can be hired ☎(2m)
Iron in unit Ironing board in unit HCE in

unit CTV ⊕3pin round P 🏠 🗔
🛁(3m)

⇔ ♀(3m)

Min£60.95 Max£74.75pw (Low)
Min£97.75 Max£120.75pw (High)

OXWICH
West Glamorgan
Map 2 SS58

B 12 & 14 Oxwich Leisure Park
for bookings Mr MacPherson, 75 Sketty
Road, Uplands, Swansea, W Glamorgan
☎Swansea(0792)298512

*Two bungalows situated on an estate of
holiday homes where the facilities
include a licensed club and general
shop. The units are compact and well
maintained, comprising sitting/dining
room, kitchen, two bedrooms, one with a
double bed and one with bunks/small
twin beds. One has bathroom/WC and
the other has a shower/WC, there is also a
bed-settee in the lounge if required.*

Mar – Oct MWB out of season
2 nights min, 2 units, 2 – 6 persons
[◆ ◆] ◎ fridge Electric
Elec metered 🔲can be hired (overseas
visitors only) ☎(100yds) Airing
cupboard in unit Iron in unit HCE in
unit TV ⊕3pin square 2P 🛁(100yds)

⇔ (100yds)

PADSTOW
Cornwall
Map 2 SW97

C Martinette & St Martins Trevone
for bookings Mrs S Edwards, 76
Somerset Place, Stoke, Plymouth, Devon
☎Plymouth(0752)53594

*Two modernised stone cottages in small
terrace with orchard to rear. Martinette
comprises kitchen/diner, lounge,
bathroom/WC, with large twin bedroom
on the first floor. St Martins has
kitchen/diner, lounge and two double
bedrooms and bathroom/WC. 300yds
from beach. Turning to Trevone off A39
coast road, Padstow – Newquay.*

Mar – Nov 1 wk min, 2 units, 2 – 4 persons
◆ ◎ fridge Electric Elec metered
🔲not provided ☎(15yds) Airing
cupboard in unit Iron in unit Ironing

board in unit HCE in unit ⊙ TV can be
hired ⊕3pin square 2P 🗔 🛁(15yds)

⇔ 🚿(2m) ♀(100yds)

Min£45 Max£150pw

PAIGNTON
Devon
Map 3 SX86

F Mr & Mrs A L Wilson Ashdene Cliff
Park Road, Paignton, Devon
☎Paignton(0803)558397

*Six flats located on ground and first floor
of this detached modern villa-style
property. Each comprises lounge/diner,
bathroom/WC, kitchen, large bedroom
with double and bunk beds. Flat 4 has
two bedrooms.*

All year MWB out of season 2 days min,
5 mths max, 6 units, 2 – 4 persons ◇
[◆] ◎ fridge Electric Elec metered
🔲can be hired ☎(400yds) Iron in unit
Ironing board in unit HCE in unit ⊙
CTV ⊕3pin square 10P 🗔
🛁(400yds)

⇔ 🚿(2m) ♀(200yds) 🖾(1½m)
🎵(1½m) 🐾(1½m)

Min£45 Max£65pw (Low)
Min£75 Max£168pw (High)

F Mr & Mrs R Bewley Casa Marina
2 Keysfield Road, Paignton, Devon
TQ4 6EP
☎Paignton(0803)558334

*Flats located in a skilfully-converted
Victorian house in a pleasant residential
area which climbs up from the
promenade and seafront. They are of
varied design, five having shower units
and the remainder baths. The furnishings
are comfortable and modern and all units
have fitted carpets and bright décor.*

All year MWB out of season 9 units,
1 – 6 persons ◇ ◆ no pets fridge
Electric Elec metered 🔲can be hired
☎ Iron on premises Ironing board on
premises HCE on premises ⊙ CTV
⊕3pin square P 🗔 🛁(400yds)

⇔ ♀ 🖾 🎵 🐾

F Mr & Mrs T S Gabbott Cranmore
Lodge 45 Marine Drive, Paignton, Devon
TQ3 2NS
☎Paignton(0803)556278

*Cranmore Lodge is a detached property
standing in ¼ acre of ground on the
seafront. There are five apartments which
sleep up to five people with a lounge and
bed-settee, bedroom (except flat 5 which
has two bedrooms), kitchen area and
bathroom with WC.*

Etr – Oct MWB out of season
3 days min, 1 mth max, 5 units,
2 – 5 persons, nc8 ◎ fridge
Electric Elec metered 🔲provided (for
overseas visitors only) ☎(80yds)
Airing cupboard on premises HCE in
unit [Launderette within 300yds] ⊙
CTV ⊕3pin square P 🛁(250yds)

⇔ ♀(250yds) 🖾(¼m) 🎵(½m) 🐾(¼m)

Min£55 Max£143pw (Low)
Min£93 Max£189pw (High)

F Mrs S M Dixon Flat 1 Elmore
8 Leighon Road, Paignton, Devon
☎Churston(0803)842236

*Ground-floor flat in three-storeyed
terraced house built in the 1920s.
Accommodation comprises lounge/diner
and kitchen area. Double bedroom with
shower cubicle and separate WC.
Situated in a cul-de-sac, two minutes'
walk from the seafront.*

All year MWB out of season 3 days min,
3 wks max, 1 unit, 2 persons, nc2 ◇ ◆
no pets ◎ fridge Electric
Elec metered 🔲inclusive ☎ Iron on
premises Ironing board on premises
HCE in unit ⊙ TV ⊕3pin square 🗔
🛁(¼m)

⇔ 🚿(3m) ♀(400yds) 🖾(800yds)
🎵(800yds) 🐾(¼m)

Min£35 Max£80pw (Low)
Min£60 Max£90pw (High)

> 1982 prices quoted throughout
> gazetteer

F Mr B Lock **The Inn on the Green**
27 Esplanade Road, Paignton, Devon
TQ4 6BG
☎Paignton(0803)557841

*Nineteen of these flats are located within
a converted hotel whilst 60 are purpose-
built flats centred around the green at the
back of the hotel. They vary in size and
sleep from two to six people. They are all
well appointed with a good standard of
furnishings and décor. The hotel is
located on seafront opposite open green
and the sea.*

19Mar–Nov MWB out of season
2days min, 1mth max, 79units,
2–6persons [◇] ◇ ◆ no pets No
groups of under 18's ◔&◎ fridge
Electric Gas/Elec inclusive ⌷can be
hired ☎ Airing cupboard in 60 units
Iron on premises(hotel flats only) Ironing
board on premises(hotel flats only) HCE
in unit [Launderette on premises] ⊕
CTV ⊕3pin square 85P ▥
♨(500yds) Games room, music room,
maid service available, wine bar
↔ ☟(3m) ♀ ▨ ♫ ▮(½m)

Min£40 Max£250pw

F Mrs S M Dixon **Redlands** (Flat 1)
18 Broadsands Park Road, Paignton,
Devon TQ3 3JP
☎Churston(0803)842236

*First-floor self-contained flat with its own
entrance off communal stairs, with two
double bedrooms, kitchen/dinette, small
lounge with double bed-settee, shower
room and separate WC. Going W on
A379 Paignton–Brixham road, turn left
near the end of the dual carriageway into
Broadsands Park Road, Redlands is on
the right.*

All year MWB out of season 3days min,
3wks max, 1unit, 2–6persons ◇ ◆
no pets ◎ fridge Electric
Elec metered ⌷inclusive ☎(½m) Iron
in unit Ironing board in unit HCE in unit
⊕ TV ⊕3pin square P ▥ ♨(½m)
↔ ☟(1m) ♀(1m) ▨(2m) ♫(2m)
▮(2m)

Min£35 Max£80pw (Low)
Min£90 Max£135pw (High)

Ch **South Sands Holidays, Type A &
B**
for bookings I F & J L Glover, South Sands
Holidays, Goodrington Beach Holiday
Estate, Cliff Park Road, Paignton, Devon
☎Torquay(0803)22517

*Types A & B are purpose-built chalets
built in a square around a car park.
Accommodation for up to six persons
comprising living room with double bed-
settee, two bedrooms (one double and
one twin), kitchen and bathroom. All 16
units are situated within 500yds of
beautifully laid-out recreation grounds
and a few seconds' walk from the beach.*

Mar–Oct MWB out of season
2days min, 16units, 2–6persons [◇]
[◇ ◆] no pets ◔ fridge Electric &
gas fires Gas & Electric inclusive

⌷can be hired ☎ Iron in unit Ironing
board in unit HCE in unit [Launderette
within 300yds] ⊕ TV ⊕3pin square
P ♨(20yds)
↔ ☟(1m) ♀(½m) ▨(½m) ♫(½m)
▮(½m)

Min£45 Max£87.50pw (Low)
Min£80 Max£135pw (High)
See advert on page 191

Ch **South Sands holidays, Type C & D**
for bookings I F & J L Glover, South Sands
Holidays, Goodrington Beach Holiday
Estate, Cliff Park Road, Paignton, Devon
☎Torquay(0803)22517

*Types C & D have sitting room with bed-
settee, three bedrooms (one double, one
twin and one with bunk beds), kitchen
and bathroom or shower, in each unit.
There are 14 units.*

Mar–Oct MWB out of season
2days min, 14units, 2–8persons [◇]
[◇ ◆] no pets ◔ fridge Electric &
Gas fires Gas & Elec inclusive ⌷can
be hired ☎ Iron in unit Ironing board
in unit HCE in unit [Launderette within
300yds] ⊕ TV ⊕3pin square P
♨(20yds)
↔ ☟(1m) ♀(½m) ▨(½m) ♫(½m)
▮(1½m)

Min£45 Max£87.50pw (Low)
Min£80 Max£145pw (High)

B **South Sands Holidays, Type E**
for bookings I F & J L Glover, South Sands
Holidays, Goodrington Beach Holiday
Estate, Cliff Park Road, Paignton, Devon
☎Torquay(0803)22517

*Type E sleeps up to six persons in two
bedrooms (one double and one twin) and
double settee in living room. Each of the
seven units also contains small kitchen,
bathroom and sun balcony.*

Mar–Oct MWB out of season
2days min, 7units, 2–6persons [◇]
[◇ ◆] no pets ◔ fridge Electric &
gas fires Gas & Elec inclusive ⌷can be
hired ☎ Iron in unit Ironing board in
unit HCE in unit [Launderette within
300yds] ⊕ TV ⊕3pin square P
♨(20yds)
↔ ☟(1m) ♀(½m) ▨(½m) ♫(½m)
▮(1½m)

Min£47.50 Max£92pw (Low)
Min£84 Max£141.75pw (High)

F Mr & Mrs K E Watts **Top House**
21 Sandringham Gardens, Preston,
Paignton, Devon TQ3 1JA
☎Paignton(0803)522481

*Extensively modernised large old house
with views of the bay. Flat 3 (two other
flats are not up to required standard) is on
two floors, with lounge with double wall
bed, kitchen/diner, WC and shower room
on the first level. There are two double
bedrooms on the second level.*

All year MWB out of season 1 night min,
8mths max, 1unit, 4–8persons ◇ ◆
◆ ◎ fridge Electric Elec metered

⌷can be hired ☎(100yds) Airing
cupboard in unit Iron in unit HCE in
unit ⊕ [TV] ⊕3pin square P ▣
▥ ♨(100yds) ♬
↔ ♀(½m) ▨(½m) ♫(½m) ▮(1½m)
Min£30 Max£90pw (Low)
Min£105 Max£135pw (High)

F **Tregarth Flats 2 & 3**
for bookings Mrs J L Jackman, Tregarth,
2 Cliff Park Road, Goodrington, Paignton,
Devon TQ4 6NB
☎Paignton(0803)550382

*A chalet bungalow 'Tregarth', built in
1927, converted into two units.
Accommodation comprises two
bedrooms, lounge/kitchen, bathroom
and WC. Five other units in grounds,
three not up to required standards.*

Apr–Oct MWB out of season 1wk min,
4wks max, 2units, 2–6persons ◇ [◆
◆] ◎ fridge Electric Elec metered
⌷can be hired ☎(150yds) SD on
premises Iron in unit Ironing board in
unit HCE in unit ⊕ CTV
⊕3pin square P ▥ ♨(100yds)
↔ ♀(100yds) ▨(½m) ♫(½m) ▮(1m)
Min£50 Max£158pw

B, Ch **Tregarth Holiday Bungalow &
Family Chalet**
for bookings Mrs J L Jackman, Tregarth,
2 Cliff Park Road, Goodrington, Paignton,
Devon TQ4 6NB
☎Paignton(0803)550382

*Two units in the grounds of 'Tregarth',
sleeping five and six persons
respectively. Accommodation in the
recently built bungalow comprises
kitchen, living room with convertible
couch (double), bedroom with one
double and one single bed and
bathroom/WC. The chalet comprises
living room/kitchen with studio couch,
two bedrooms (one double and one
single bed in each room) and
shower/WC.*

Apr–Oct MWB out of season 1wk min,
4wks max, 2units, 2–6persons ◇ ◆
◔(1unit) ◎(1unit) fridge Electric
Gas/Elec metered ⌷can be hired
☎(150yds) SD on premises Iron in
unit Ironing board in unit HCE in unit
⊕ CTV ⊕3pin square P ▥
♨(100yds)
↔ ♀(100yds) ▨(½m) ♫(½m) ▮(1m)
Min£40 Max£140pw

PANT-Y-LLYN
Dyfed
Map **2** SN61

C **Brynderi Cottage**
for bookings Mrs D M Ridout,
19 St Edyths Road, Seamills, Bristol
BS9 2EP
☎Bristol(0272)681967

*Rurally situated small cottage comprising
pine furnished dining room, small sitting
room with twin daybeds, kitchen and WC.
The first floor comprises two bedrooms,
one with a double and single bed, the
other with a double bed. 2m NW of
Llandybie.*

All year MWB out of season
4 nights min, 1 unit, 2–7 persons ◆
no pets ⊚ fridge Electric
Elec metered Ⓛinclusive ☎(25yds)
WM in unit SD in unit Iron in unit
Ironing board in unit HCE in unit TV
⊕3pin square 3P ♨(½m)
↩ ☕(2m)
Min£70 Max£80pw

PARC
Gwynedd
Map **6** SH83

F Flatlets 1 & 3
for bookings Mr & Mrs Ellis Davies, Cyffdy
Farm, Parc, Bala, Gwynedd LL23 7YU
☎Llanuwchllyn(06784)271

Stone-built Tudor-style farmhouse
converted into two units comprising
kitchen/diner, bathroom/WC and one
family room. Both units have a convertible
settee. There is a nature trail and rare
breeds to be seen on the farm. Situated
1½m from A494.

All year MWB out of season 2 days min,
2 wks max, 2 units, 4–6 persons [◇ ◆ ◆]
⊚ fridge 🍴(inclusive) Elec metered
Ⓛcan be hired ★ [WM in unit] [SD in
unit] Iron in unit Ironing board in unit
HCE in unit ⊕ TV ⊕3pin square P
♨(3m) Playground, shooting, fishing &
horse riding
↩ ⚘(2½m) ☕(3m)
Min£30 Max£40pw (Low)
Min£90 Max£110pw (High)

PARKHAM
Devon
Map **2** SS42

C CC Ref 507 ELP
for bookings Character Cottages
(Holidays) Ltd, Fore street, Sidmouth,
Devon EX10 8AQ
☎Sidmouth(03955)77001

Originally a granary, now converted to a
delightful studio cottage. Steps lead to
modern living room with picture window
and through modern room divider to
attractive kitchen. A flight of stairs leads
down to two bedrooms, one with double
bed and one with bunks, and shower
room with WC.

All year MWB out of season 1 wk min,
1 mth max, 1 unit, 2–4 persons ◆ ◇
fridge Electric Elec metered Ⓛcan be
hired ☎ Airing cupboard in unit Iron in
unit Ironing board in unit HCE in unit
⊕ TV ⊕3pin square ⊕2pin round
P ▥ ♨(½m)
Min£44 Max£60pw (Low)
Min£79 Max£112pw (High)

PARTON
Dumfries & Galloway Kirkcudbrightshire
Map **11** NX66

H Nether Ervie Farmhouse
for bookings G M Thomson & Co, 27 King
Street, Castle Douglas,
Kirkcudbrightshire
☎Castle Douglas(0556)2701

Pant-y-Llyn
—
Peasenhall

Former farm house near the shore of Loch
Ken in ideal position. It has a dining room,
sitting room, kitchen, bathroom, bedroom
with double bed, and two twin-bedded
rooms. There is also a small bedroom
with a cot. 10m N of Castle Douglas on
A713.

All year 1 wk min, 6 mths max, 1 unit,
1–7 persons ◆ ⊚ fridge Rayburn,
Electric & open fires Elec inclusive
Ⓛnot provided ☎(3m) HCE in unit
TV ⊕3pin round P ♨(3m)
Boat available
Min£70 Max£170pw

PARWICH
Derbyshire
Map **8** SK25

H No 1 Nethergreen House
for bookings Mrs J Wayne, No 2
Nethergreen House, Parwich,
Ashbourne, Derbys DE6 1QL
☎Parwich(033525)268

Part of a pleasant stone-built house
(proprietor lives in other part) standing in
peaceful Peak District village of Parwich
approx 7m N of Ashbourne.
Accommodation comprises one double
and one family bedroom on the first-floor
with bathroom/WC and lounge,
kitchen/diner on the ground-floor. Good
décor and furniture.

All year MWB out of season 1 wk min,
3 wks max, 1 unit, 5 persons ◇ ◆ ◆
⊚ fridge 🍴& Electric Elec metered
Ⓛnot provided ☎(400yds) Airing
cupboard in unit HCE in unit ⊕ TV
⊕3pin square 3P ▥ ♨(450yds)
↩ ☕(200yds)
Min£40 Max£75pw

PATELEY BRIDGE
North Yorkshire
Map **7** SE16

C Curlew, Robins Rest & Throstle
Nest Cottages Highfold, Glasshouses
(1m SE off B6165)
for bookings Mr G Poole, The Cloisters,
Harefield Hall, Pateley Bridge,
Harrogate, N Yorkshire HG3 5QE
☎Harrogate(0423)711328

An 18th-century three-cottage terrace
with oak beams situated in pleasant rural
surroundings. The largest cottage
(Curlew) has a lounge, dining room, three
bedrooms (sleeping eight), kitchen and
bathroom with WC and shower unit. Both
the other cottages have lounge/diners, a
kitchen and WC with either a shower or
bath. Robin's Rest has one bedroom with
a double and a single bed and a bed-
settee in the lounge. Throstle Nest has
two bedrooms on the first-floor, one a
double, one with twin beds. A further
single bed may also be available.

┌─────────────────────────────┐
│ 1982 prices quoted throughout │
│ gazetteer   │
└─────────────────────────────┘

All year MWB out of season 1 wk min,
1 mth max, 3 units, 1–8 persons ◆
◑(2 units) ⊚(1 unit) fridge Gas &
Electric Gas/Elec metered Ⓛcan be
hired ★(½m) Iron in unit Ironing board
in unit HCE in unit ⊖(1 unit)
⊕(2 units) TV ⊕3pin square P
▥(½m) Fishing
↩ ☕(½m) ▨(2m) ♫(2m)
Min£27 Max£107pw

PEASENHALL
Suffolk
Map **5** TM36

C New Inn Cottage for bookings
The Landmark Trust, Shottesbrooke,
Maidenhead, Berks
☎Littlewick Green(062882)3431

The end cottage of a delightfully restored
former 15th-century inn, with walled rear
garden and parking, situated in attractive
village. The cottage is equipped with
period furniture and sleeps six in three
bedrooms, with separate lounge and
living room.

All year MWB out of season 1 day min,
3 wks max, 1 unit, 1–6 persons ◆ ⊚
fridge 🍴 Elec inclusive
Ⓛnot provided ☎(400yds) Airing
cupboard in unit Iron in unit Ironing
board in unit HCE in unit ⊖
⊕3pin square P ▥ ♨
↩ ☕(½m)
Max£81pw (Low)
Max£154pw (High)

C Peasenhall High End
for bookings The Landmark Trust,
Shottesbrooke, Maidenhead, Berks
☎Littlewick Green(062882)3431

Fully-restored period cottage with
entrance off the Wool Hall, which formed
part of a 15th-century inn. Equipped with
period furniture, the cottage has two first-
floor bedrooms (sleeps five) and
attractive sitting room, separate
kitchen/diner and well-fitted bathroom.

All year MWB out of season 1 day min,
3 wks max, 1 unit, 1–5 perons ◆ ⊚
fridge 🍴 Elec inclusive
Ⓛnot provided ☎(400yds) Iron in unit
Ironing board in unit HCE in unit ⊖
⊕3pin square P ▥ ♨
↩ ☕(½m)
Max£81pw (Low)
Max£160pw (High)

C Peasenhall Low End
for bookings The Landmark Trust,
Shottesbrooke, Maidenhead, Berks
☎Littlewick Green(062882)3431

Attractive cottage equipped with fine
furniture, but with all modern facilities.
Accommodation comprises two first-floor
bedrooms to sleep four and ground-floor
lounge plus kitchen/diner.

All year MWB out of season 1 day min,
3 wks max, 1 unit, 1–4 persons ◆ ⊚
fridge 🍴 Elec inclusive
Ⓛnot provided ☎(400yds) Iron in unit →

Ironing board in unit   HCE in unit   ⊕
⊕3pin square   P   🅟   ♨

↩   ♀(½m)

Max£81pw (Low)
Max£173pw (High)

PEEBLES
Borders *Peeblesshire*
Map **11** NT24

F **Thistles** 7 Graham Street
for bookings Mrs Inglis, Quenon, 16
Kingsmeadows Gardens, Peebles,
Peeblesshire
☎Peebles(0721)20648
*Small first-floor flat in a two-storey house
at W end of border town. Lounge/diner,
kitchen, one double room and a small
bunk-bedded room, shower with
washbasin and separate WC. Access
from A72 at Young Street, second left at
St Andrews Road and left again into
Graham Street.*

Etr-Oct   1wk min, 1mth max, 1unit,
1–5persons   ◆   ◆   ∅   fridge   🍳
Gas metered   Ⓛnot provided   ☎   Iron in
unit   Ironing board in unit   HCE in unit
⊕   TV   ⊕3pin square   2P   🅟
♨(150yds)

↩   ♐(½m)   ♀(300yds)

Min£45 Max£70pw

PELYNT
Cornwall
Map **2** SX25

C **Blacksmiths Cottage** Tremaine
Green
for bookings John Jolliff, Pendower Farm,
Tremaine Green, Pelynt, Looe, Cornwall
PL13 2LS
☎Lanreath(0503)20333
*Stone- and slate-built Cornish-style
cottage comprising two bedrooms
(double-bedded, twin divans and Z bed),
lounge/diner with good décor, well-
equipped modern kitchen, bathroom and
WC. Well appointed. Leave Pelynt village
in northerly direction on B3359.*

All year   1wk min, 6mths max, 1unit,
2–5persons   [◇]   ◆   ◆   ◎   fridge
Electric   Elec metered   Ⓛprovided   ☎
Airing cupboard in unit   Iron in unit
Ironing board in unit   . HCE in unit   ⊕
CTV   ⊕3pin square   ⊕2pin round   P
🏠   🅟   ♨(1½m)   ↪

↩   ♀(1m)   🚲(1m)   ♫(1m)

Min£70 Max£260pw

C Mr & Mrs J Ward **Cartole Farm
(Cottages)** Pelynt, Looe, Cornwall
PL13 2QH
☎Lanreath(0503)20486
*Six self-contained cottages converted
from old barns with mellow stone walls
and slate roofs and designed to retain
their traditional cornish character.
Modern style furnishings; the cottages
offer one or two bedrooms (duvets
provided), lounge/dining room, kitchen
(some open-plan) and a laundry room is
provided on site. Farm animals can be*

---

*fed, such as ducks, hens and lambs in
spring.*

All year   MWB out of season   3days min,
6wks max, 6units, 1–5persons   [◇]   ◆
◆   ◎   fridge   🍳   Elec metered
Ⓛinclusive   ☎(½m)   Airing cupboard in
unit   Iron in unit   Ironing board in unit
HCE in unit   [Launderette on premises]
⊕   CTV   ⊕3pin square   10P   🅟
♨(⅓m)

↩   ♀(1m)

Min£55 Max£110pw (Low)
Min£105 Max£210pw (High)

C **Cobblers & Gamekeepers
Cottages** Tremaine Green
for bookings John Jolliff, Pendower Farm,
Tremaine Green, Pelynt, Looe, Cornwall
PL13 2LS
☎Lanreath(0503)20333
*Stone- and slate-built Cornish cottages
with two bedrooms (one double, one twin,
divans in both), lounge/diner, modern
kitchen, and well equipped bathroom
and WC. Leave Pelynt village in northern
direction on B3359.*

All year   MWB out of season   1wk min,
6mths max, 2units, 2–4persons   [◇]
◆   ◆   ◎   fridge   Electric
Elec metered   Ⓛprovided   ☎   Airing
cupboard in unit   Iron in unit   Ironing
board in unit   HCE in unit   ⊕   CTV
⊕3pin square   ⊕2pin round   P   🏠   🅟
♨(1m)

↩   ♀(1m)   🚲(1m   ♫(1m)

Min£68 Max£250pw

C **Farmhouse** Tremaine Green
for bookings John Jolliff, Pendower Farm,
Tremaine Green, Pelynt, Looe, Cornwall
PL13 2LS
☎Lanreath(0503)20333
*Stone- and slate-built in Cornish-style
comprising three bedrooms (one with
antique brass bed, one with three divans
and one with bunk beds), kitchen/diner,
well-equipped comfortable lounge,
bathroom and WC.*

All year   MWB out of season   1wk min,
6mths max, 1unit, 2–6persons   [◇]   ◆
◆   ◎   fridge   Electric   Elec metered
Ⓛprovided   ☎   Airing cupboard in unit
Iron in unit   Ironing board in unit   HCE in
unit   CTV   ⊕3pin square
⊕2pin round   P   🏠   🅟   ♨(1m)   ↪

↩   ♀(1m)   🚲(1m)   ♫(1m)

Min£74 Max£270pw

C **Jasmin Cottage** The Green
for bookings Mrs J W M Collings, Brook
Cottage, Longcombe Lane, Polperro,
Cornwall PL13 2PL
☎Polperro(0503)72274
*Previously village carpenters, this stone-
built cottage is adjacent to the village
green and has oak beams and shuttered
windows. Accommodation includes a
lounge, kitchen/diner, combined
bathroom/WC, a bedroom with a double*

---

*bed and a single bed and another
upstairs room with double bed.*

All year   MWB out of season   1wk min,
1mth max, 1unit, 2–5persons   ◆   ◎
fridge   Electric   Elec metered   Ⓛcan be
hired   ☎(200yds)   Airing cupboard in
unit   Iron in unit   Ironing board in unit
HCE in unit   ⊕   CTV   ⊕3pin square   P
♨(100yds)

↩   ♐(2m)   ♀(½m)   🚲   ♫

Min£55 Max£145pw

C **Mariners & Carpenters Cottages**
Tremaine Green
for bookings John Jolliff, Pendower Farm,
Tremaine Green, Pelynt, Looe, Cornwall
PL13 2LS
☎Lanreath(0503)20333
*Stone- and slate-built Cornish-style
cottages having one bedroom with
antique beds, lounge/diner and well-
equipped kitchen.*

All year   MWB out of season   1wk min,
6mths max, 2units, 2persons   [◇]   ◆
◆   ◎   fridge   Electric   Elec metered
Ⓛprovided   ☎   Airing cupboard in unit
Iron in unit   Ironing board in unit   HCE in
unit   ⊕   CTV   ⊕3pin square
⊕2pin round   P   🏠   🅟   ♨(1½m)   ↪

↩   ♀(1m)   🚲(1m)   ♫(1m)

Min£60 Max£140pw

C **Ploughman's Cottage** Tremaine
Green
for bookings John Jolliff, Pendower Farm,
Tremaine Green, Pelynt, Looe, Cornwall
PL13 2LS
☎Lanreath(0503)20333
*Cornish-style cottage comprising three
bedrooms (a twin-bedded room, a room
with a four-poster bed, and the third with
two divans), lounge/diner comfortably
furnished with easy armchairs, modern
kitchen and well-equipped bathroom and
WC.*

All year   MWB out of season   1wk min,
6mths max, 1unit, 2–6persons   [◇]   ◆
◆   ◎   fridge   Electric   Elec metered
Ⓛprovided   ☎   Airing cupboard in unit
Iron in unit   Ironing board in unit   HCE in
unit   ⊕   CTV   ⊕3pin square
⊕2pin round   P   🏠   🅟   ♨(1m)   ↪

↩   ♀(1m)   🚲(1m)   ♫(1m)

Min£72 Max£264pw

PENCOYD
Hereford & Worcester
Map **3** SO52

C **1 The Ark**
for bookings Mrs Sadler, Wyvern
Cottages, 60 East Road, Stoney Hill,
Bromsgrove, Worcestershire
☎Bromsgrove(0527)73734
*A semi-detached 18th-century stone
cottage with a small rear garden. The
accommodation comprises
lounge/dining room, kitchen,
bathroom/WC and a twin-bedded room.
The first-floor consists of a double
bedroom and a single.*

194

All year MWB out of season 1wk min,
3wks max, 1 unit, 1–5 persons ◇ ◉
fridge Electric Elec metered
🔲 not provided ☎(½m) Airing cupboard
in unit Iron in unit Ironing board in unit
HCE in unit ⊙ TV ⊕3 pin square 2P
1🏠 ♒(2m)
⇔ ♀ ▨(2m) ♫(2m)
Min£35 Max£88pw

PENCRAIG
Hereford & Worcester
Map 3 SO52

F Mrs W Ing **Mount Craig Hall**
Pencraig, Ross on Wye, Herefordshire
HR9 6HP
☎ Llangarron(098 984)476

*These flats are located to the rear of
Mount Craig Hall, formerly a hotel, and
they form part of the converted old
coachhouse and stables. They vary in
size and all are well decorated and
comfortably furnished.*

All year MWB out of season
2 nights min, 6 mths max, 7 units,
1–7 persons ◇ ◆ ◉ fridge
Electric Elec metered 🔲 can be
hired (overseas visitors only) ♒ WM on
premises SD on premises Iron in unit
Ironing board in unit HCE in unit ⊙
TV ⊕3 pin square 10P 4🏠 ♒(½m)
⇔ ♀(1m) ▨(1½m)
Min£45 Max£75pw (Low)
Min£55 Max£120pw (High)

PENDINE
Dyfed
Map 2 SN20

F **Brook Mill** Brook
for bookings Powell's Holidays, High
Street, Saundersfoot, Dyfed
☎ Saundersfoot(0902)812791

*On ground-floor part of a modern split
level bungalow offering woodland and
sea views. Accommodation: lounge,
dining/kitchen, bathroom/WC and two
bedrooms sleeping up to six people.
Patio and garden.*

Jan-Nov MWB out of season 1wk min,
4wks max, 1 unit, 2–6 persons [◇] ◇
◆ ◉ fridge ♨ Elec inclusive
🔲 inclusive ☎ Iron in unit Ironing
board in unit HCE in unit ⊙ CTV
⊕3 pin square P ▥ ♒(1m) ⌐
⇔ ♀(1m) ♫(2m)
Min£111 Max£321pw

PENNAL
Gwynedd
Map 6 SH70

Ch **Cedar Wood Lodges**
for bookings Llugwy Lodge Estates Ltd,
Pennal, Machynlleth, Powys
☎ Pennal(065 475)228/622

*Cedar wood chalets set on high ground in
rural surroundings overlooking the valley.
Accommodation comprises of
kitchen/diner, lounge with bed-settee,
three bedrooms, one with bunk beds and
two family rooms.*

Pencoyd
—
Pennal

Mar-Nov 1wk min, 3wks max, 14 units,
6–8 persons [◇ ◇ ◆] ◉ fridge
Electric Elec metered 🔲 inclusive
☎(20yds) , Iron on premises Ironing
board on premises HCE in unit ⊙ TV
⊕3 pin square 14P ▥ ♒(1½m)
Fishing & shooting
⇔ ♀(400yds) ♫(3m)
Min£50 Max£95pw (Low)
Min£100 Max£190pw (High)

F **Coach House**
for bookings Llugwy Lodge Estates Ltd,
Pennal, Machynlleth, Powys
☎ Pennal(065 475)228/622

*A coach house converted into two flats
comprising lounge, kitchen, two
bedrooms, one with twin beds and a
family room, bathroom/WC. The units
retain much original character.*

Mar-Nov MWB 1wk min, 3wks max,
2 units, 1–5 persons [◇ ◇ ◆] ◉
fridge Electric Elec metered
☎(20yds) Iron on premises Ironing
board on premises HCE in unit ⊙
[TV] ⊕3 pin square P ▥ ♒(1½m)
Fishing & shooting
⇔ ♀(100yds) ♫(3m)
Min£50 Max£95pw (Low)
Min£100 Max£190pw (High)

F **Mews Flats**
for bookings Llugwy Lodge Estates Ltd,
Pennal, Machynlleth, Powys
☎ Pennal(065 475)288/622

*Stone-built upper-storey mews flats
comprising kitchen/diner, lounge,
bathroom/WC and three bedrooms (two
double, one twin). Entrance at the side of
the hotel 1 mile from Pennal village.*

Mar-Nov 1wk min, 3wks max, 3 units,
1–6 persons [◇ ◇ ◆] ◉ fridge
Electric Elec metered 🔲 inclusive
☎(10yds) Iron on premises Ironing
board on premises HCE in unit ⊙ TV
⊕3 pin square P ▥ ♒(1½m) Fishing
& shooting
⇔ ♀(10yds) ♫(3m)
Min£50 Max£95pw (Low)
Min£100 Max£190pw (High)

B **No 7 Plas Talgarth**
for bookings Mr P Beaumont, 35
Briarsyde Close, Fellsyde Park,
Whickham, Tyne & Wear NE16 5UQ
☎ Newcastle-upon-Tyne(0632) 884572

*A pleasant detached brick-built
bungalow with white-painted elevations
and bay windows. Situated on the well-
laid-out Plas Talgarth Estate, within the
Snowdonia National Park approx 3m from
Machynlleth on the A493 Aberdovey
road. Accommodation comprises
lounge, kitchen with dining area,
bathroom and two bedrooms.*

1982 prices quoted throughout
gazetteer

All year MWB out of season 1wk min,
6wks max, 1 unit, 1–5 persons ◉
fridge ♨ Elec inclusive ☎(50yds)
Airing cupboard in unit ⊙ CTV
⊕3 pin square 1P ▥ ♒(½m) ⌐
♒Hard Restaurant, children's play area
& croquet
⇔ ♀ ▨(2m) ♫(2m)
Min£65 Max£185pw

B, H The Manager **Plas Talgarth
Country Club** Pennal, Machynlleth,
Powys SY20 9JY
☎ Pennal(065 475)273

*Nine luxury bungalows and 15 houses of
exceptionally high standard: all very
modern, clean and spacious. Located
within Snowdonia National Park, enjoying
magnificent views in all directions and
overlooking the Dyfi Valley.*

Feb-Dec MWB out of season 1wk min,
6wks max, 24 units, 1–6 persons ◇ ◇
◆ ◉ fridge ♨ Elec metered
🔲 inclusive ☎ Airing cupboard in unit
Iron in unit Ironing board in unit HCE in
unit [Launderette on premises] ⊙ ⊛
CTV ⊕3 pin square P ▥ ♒(½m) ⌐
♒Hard Croquet
⇔ ♀ ▨(2m) ♫(2m)

B **11 Plas Talgarth** Pennal
for bookings Mr & Mrs Thorndyke, Graig-
y-Morfa, Pennal, Machynlleth, Powys
☎ Pennal(065 475)685

*Situated in a private, wooded estate in
Snowdonia National Park, enjoying
magnificent views of the Cader Idris
range and Snowdonia. Comprises three
bedrooms (two with double beds and one
with two bunk beds), luxury bathroom,
spacious living room, large kitchen.
Approximately 3m from Machynlleth on
the A493 Aberdovey road.*

All year MWB out of season 1wk min,
6wks max, 1 unit, 1–6 persons ◉
fridge ♨ inclusive Elec metered
🔲 inclusive ☎(50yds) Airing cupboard
in unit Iron in unit Ironing board in unit
HCE in unit [Launderette on premises]
CTV ⊕3 pin square 1P ▥ ♒(½m)
⌐ ♒Hard
⇔ ♀ ▨(2m) ♫(2m)
Min£69 Max£213pw

H **Stable House**
for bookings Llugwy Lodge Estates Ltd,
Pennal, Machynlleth, Powys
☎ Pennal(065 475)228/622

*Converted, stone-built stable house
comprising of lounge, kitchen,
bathroom/WC and three bedrooms, one
with bunk beds.*

Mar-Nov 1wk min, 3wks max, 1 unit,
1–6 persons [◇ ◇ ◆] ◉ fridge
Electric Elec metered 🔲 inclusive
☎(30yds) Iron on premises Ironing
board on premises HCE in unit ⊙ TV
⊕3 pin square 1P ▥ ♒(1½m) Fishing
& shooting
⇔ ♀(30yds) ♫(3m)
Min£50 Max£95pw (Low)
Min£100 Max£190pw (High)

C Wayne House Cottages
for bookings Llugwy Lodge Estates Ltd,
Pennal, Machynlleth, Powys
☎Pennal(065475)228/622

Well converted stone-built cottages
situated in the hotel grounds.
Accommodation consists of lounge,
kitchen, two bedrooms, one family room
and one with beds.

Mar-Nov 1wkmin, 3wksmax, 2units,
1–6persons [◇ ◈ ◆] ⊚ fridge
Electric Elec metered ⊡inclusive
☎(300yds) Iron on premises Ironing
board on premises HCE in unit ⊙ ⊛
TV ⊕3pin square P 🔟 ⚏(1½m)
Fishing & shooting

⊕ ⚲(300yds) ♫(3m)

Min£50 Max£95pw (Low)
Min£100 Max£190pw (High)

PENRHYNDEUDRAETH
Gwynedd
Map**6** SH63

C Portmeirion Ltd, Angel Cottage
Portmeirion, Penrhyndeudraeth,
Gwynedd
☎Penrhyndeudraeth(0766)770228

Rounded cottage merging into shops in
the centre of the village, comprising
lounge, kitchen, bathroom with WC and
four bedrooms sleeping six.

Etr-Oct 1wkmin, 6wksmax, 1unit,
1–6persons [◇] ◈ ◆ ⊚ fridge
Electric Elec inclusive ⊡inclusive ☎
Iron in unit Ironing board in unit HCE in
unit ⊙ CTV ⊕3pin square 2P 🔟
⚏(½m) ⌿ ↳Hard Golf

⊕ ♨(3m) ⚲(100yds) ☏(3m)

Min£150pw (Low)
Min£280pw (High)

C Portmeirion Ltd Battery Cottage
Portmeirion, Penrhydeudraeth, Gwynedd
☎Penrhyndeudraeth(0766)770228

Detached cottage with large balcony on
edge of village. Comprises kitchen/diner,
lounge, three bathrooms/WCs and three
bedrooms for a total of five people.

Etr-Oct 1wkmin, 6wksmax, 1unit,
1–5persons [◇] ◈ ◆ ⊚ fridge
Electric Elec inclusive ⊡inclusive ☎
Iron in unit Ironing board in unit HCE in
unit ⊙ CTV ⊕3pin square 2P 🔟
⚏(½m) ⌿ ↳Hard Golf

⊕ ♨(3m) ⚲(100yds) ☏(3m)

Min£150pw (Low)
Min£260pw (High)

C Portmeirion Ltd, Chantry Cottage
Portmeirion, Penrhyndeudraeth,
Gwynedd
☎Penrhyndeudraeth(0766)770228

Three-storey stone-built cottage in an
elevated position with the following
accommodation: large lounge/diner,
kitchen, shower/WC, two bathrooms with
WC, a separate WC and six rooms
sleeping eight people.

Etr-Oct 1wkmin, 6wksmax, 1unit,
1–8persons [◇] ◈ ◆ ⊚ fridge
🕯 Elec inclusive ⊡inclusive ☎ Iron

in unit Ironing board in unit HCE in unit
⊙ CTV ⊕3pin square 2P 🔟
⚏(½m) ⌿ ↳Hard Golf

⊕ ♨(3m) ⚲(100yds) ☏(½m)

Min£230pw (Low)
Min£330pw (High)

C Portmeirion Ltd Dolphin Cottage
Portmeirion, Penrhyndeudraeth,
Gwynedd
☎Penrhyndeudraeth(0766)770228

Detached cottage in an elevated
position, comprising kitchen/diner,
lounge, separate WC/shower all on the
ground-floor, two twin-bedded rooms
and bathroom/WC on the first-floor.

Etr-Oct 1wkmin, 6wksmax, 1unit,
1–4persons [◇] ◈ ◆ ⊚ fridge
Electric Elec inclusive ⊡inclusive
Iron in unit Ironing board in unit HCE in
unit ⊙ CTV ⊕3pin square 2P 🔟
⚏(½m) ⌿ ↳Hard Golf

⊕ ♨(3m) ⚲(100yds) ☏(3m)

Min£150pw (Low)
Min£230pw (High)

C Portmeirion Ltd Gatehouse Cottage
Portmeirion, Penrhyndeudraeth,
Gwynedd
☎Penrhyndeudraeth(0766)770228

Detached cottage in an elevated position
with a balcony. Lounge, dining room,
kitchen, bathroom/WC, separate WC,
two single rooms and twin-bedded room
forms this compact property.

Etr-Oct 1wkmin, 6wksmax, 1unit,
1–4persons [◇] ◈ ◆ ⊚ fridge
Electric Elec inclusive ⊡inclusive ☎
Iron in unit Ironing board in unit HCE in
unit ⊙ CTV ⊕3pin square 2P 🔟
⚏(½m) ⌿ ↳Hard Golf

⊕ ♨(3m) ⚲(100yds) ☏(3m)

Min£150pw (Low)
Min£255pw (High)

C Portmeirion Ltd, Government House
Portmeirion, Penrhyndeudraeth,
Gwynedd
☎Penrhyndeudraeth(0766)770228

Elevated cottage set amongst others with
views of the estuary. It has a large lounge,
dining room, kitchen, and sleeping
accommodation for up to eight people.

Etr-Oct 1wkmin, 6wksmax, 1unit,
1–8persons [◇] ◈ ◆ ⊚ fridge
Electric Elec inclusive ⊡inclusive ☎
Iron in unit Ironing board in unit HCE in
unit ⊙ CTV ⊕3pin square 2P 🔟
⚏(½m) ⌿ ↳Hard Golf

⊕ ⚲(100yds) 3m)

Min£230pw (Low)
Min£330pw (High)

1982 prices quoted throughout
gazetteer

C Portmeirion Ltd Telfords Tower
Portmeirion, Penrhyndeudraeth,
Gwynedd
☎Penrhyndeudraeth(0766)770228

Spiral cottage with view over village.
Ground floor, kitchen/diner, lounge (with
single divan), shower room/WC. Spiral
staircase to bedrooms and bathroom.
The property sleeps up to four people.

Etr-Oct 1wkmin, 6wksmax, 1unit,
1–4persons [◇] ◈ ◆ ⊚ fridge
Electric Elec inclusive ⊡inclusive ☎
Iron in unit Ironing board in unit HCE in
unit ⊙ CTV ⊕3pin square 2P 🔟
⚏(½m) ⌿ ↳Hard Golf

⊕ ♨(3m) ⚲(100yds) ☏(3m)

Min£100pw (Low)
Min£220pw (HIgh)

C Portmeirion Ltd Toll House
Penrhyndeudraeth, Gwynedd
☎Penrhyndeudraeth(0766)770228

Detached cottage with a balcony in the
centre of the village. Comprising
lounge/diner, kitchen and sleeping
accommodation for six (including a
single in an attic room). Two twin-bedded
rooms with bathroom and separate WC.

Etr-Oct 1wkmin, 6wksmax, 1unit,
1–6persons [◇] ◈ ◆ ⊚ fridge
Electric Elec inclusive ⊡inclusive ☎
Iron in unit Ironing board in unit HCE in
unit ⊙ CTV ⊕3pin square 2P 🔟
⚏(½m) ⌿ ↳Hard Golf

⊕ ♨(3m) ⚲(100yds) ☏(3m)

Min£150pw (Low)
Min£290pw (High)

C Portmeirion Ltd White Horses
Portmeirion, Penrhyndeudraeth,
Gwynedd
☎Penrhyndeudraeth(0766)770228

Detached cottage near water's edge on a
private road, consisting of lounge with
two bunk beds, kitchen, bathroom/WC
and two twin-bedded rooms.

May–Oct 1wkmin, 6wksmax, 1unit,
1–6persons [◇] ◈ ◆ ⊚ fridge
Electric Elec inclusive ⊡inclusive ☎
Iron in unit Ironing board in unit HCE in
unit ⊙ CTV ⊕3pin square 2P 🔟
⚏(½m) ⌿ ↳Hard Golf

⊕ ♨(3m) ⚲(100yds) ☏(3m)

Min£260pw (Low)
Min£280pw (High)

PENTON
Cumbria
Map**12** NY47

C Mr & Mrs J Sissons Bessiestown
Farm Penton, Carlisle, Cumbria CA6 5QP
☎Nicholforest(022877)219

Three stone cottages converted from an
old barn and stable in farmhouse
courtyard, comprising open plan
lounge/diner/kitchen on the first floor
which affords panoramic views of the
Borders and Solway countryside. All
have three double bedrooms (additional
bunk beds on request) and a
bathroom/WC on ground floor.

All year MWB out of season
3 nights min, 3 units, 4–6 persons ◇ ◆
◉ fridge Electric Elec metered
🔲 not provided ☎(100yds) Airing
cupboard in unit HCE in unit TV
⊕3 pin square 20P 🚿(100yds) ⌐
Games room, horse riding

↔ 🍴(1m)
Min£40 Max£60pw (Low)
Min£100 Max£130pw (High)

B Mr & Mrs J E Newton **Liddel Park**
Penton, Carlisle, Cumbria
☎Nicholforest(022877)317

*Formerly a block of brick-built stables
now converted into three terraced
bungalows with courtyard at rear.
Modernised and equipped to a very high
standard. Two units have one twin
bedded room and a double room while
the third has two twins. In addition each
has two single foldaway beds. Set in very
quiet rural surroundings in an area used
by the Forestry Commission, with views of
Scottish hills.*

All year 3 units, 6 persons [◇] ◆ ◆
◉ fridge ♨ Elec inclusive
🔲 inclusive ☎(¼m) [WM on premises]
[SD on premises] [TD on premises] Iron
on premises Ironing board in unit HCE
in unit ⊕ TV ⊕3 pin square P 🅼
🚿(¼m)

↔ 🍴(1m) 🖵(1m)
Min£59 Max£79pw (Low)
Min£97 Max£111pw (High)

PENZANCE
Cornwall
Map 2 SW 43

H **CC Ref 313 ELP**
for bookings Character Cottages
(Holidays) Ltd, 34 Fore Street, Sidmouth,
Devon EX108AQ
☎Sidmouth(03955)77001

*Comfortable terraced house on the
seafront with views of St Michael's Mount.
Unit includes front garden, glazed porch,
entrance hall, sitting room with sea view,
dining room, well equipped
kitchen/breakfast room and three
bedrooms (one with bunk beds, two with
divans). Good bathroom and WC.*

All year MWB out of season 1 wk min,
1 mth max, 1 unit, 2–6 persons ◇ ◉
Electric Elec metered 🔲 can be hired
☎(100yds) WM on premises Airing
cupboard in unit Iron in unit Ironing
board in unit HCE in unit [Launderette
within 300yds] ⊕ TV ⊕3 pin square
⊕2 pin round 🚿 🅼 🚿
↔ 🍴(200yds) 🖵(200yds)
🎵(200yds) 🐾(200yds)
Min£68 max£110pw (Low)
Min£129 Max£199pw (High)

F **Carne House** Newlyn, Penzance,
Cornwall
for bookings Mr P Thomas, Tolcarne
Holidays, 'Porthcressa', The Lidden,
Penzance, Cornwall
☎Penzance(0736)5740

---

*Two flats, the first-floor flat containing two
twin-bedded rooms, open plan kitchen
with breakfast bar to lounge, luxury
bathroom with shower, bath & WC, whilst
the ground-floor flat has one twin-bedded
room, lounge and dining room, kitchen,
separate bathroom and WC and garage.
Each have one double bedroom with
washbasin and are exceptionally
appointed with quality furnishing.*

All year MWB out of season 3 days min,
6 wks max, 2 units, 1–6 persons [◆ ◆]
◉ fridge Electric Elec metered
🔲 can be hired ☎(100yds) Iron in unit Ironing
board in unit HCE in unit [Launderette
within 150yds] ⊕ CTV
⊕3 pin square 3P 1🚿 🚿
🚿(200yds) 🐾(Hard), bowls & riding
↔ 🍴(200yds) 🖵(¼m) 🎵(¼m) 🐾(¼m)
Min£40 Max£70pw (Low)
Min£50 Max£150pw (High)

B **Hawkesland** Alexandra Road
for bookings J A & A S D Hedges,
Westwards, Bickwell Valley, Sidmouth,
Devon
☎Sidmouth(03955)6176

*Spacious bungalow situated in Penzance
within walking distance of seafront.
Accommodation consists of entrance
porch, sunny lounge, dining room,
modern kitchen with stainless steel sink
unit and fitted cupboards, utility room
with door to secluded garden, three
bedrooms, one with bathroom en suite.
All well appointed with double divans.
Also modern bathroom and WC.*

All year MWB out of season 1 wk min,
6 mths max, 1 unit, 6 persons ◇ 🌢
fridge ♨ Gas/Elec inclusive 🔲 can be
hired ☎ WM in unit Airing cupboard in
unit Iron in unit Ironing board in unit
HCE in unit [Launderette within 300yds]
⊕ [CTV] ⊕3 pin square P 🅼
🚿(200yds) 🐾 Grass
↔ 🍴 🖵 🎵
Min£85 Max£135pw (Low)
Min£200 Max£250pw (High)

H **Hawks Farm** Averton Road
for bookings J A & A S D Hedges,
Westwards, Bickwell Valley, Sidmouth,
Devon
☎Sidmouth(03955)6176

*Thatched house of great historical
interest situated in Penzance.
Accommodation comprises entrance hall
with window seats, study with Ercol
furniture and good décor, dining room
with large stone fireplace, three good
bedrooms with kidney-shaped dressing
tables and divan beds, kitchen and
modern equipped bathroom and WC.
Attractive garden.*

All year MWB out of season 1 wk min,
6 mths max, 1 unit, 2–6 persons ◆ ◉
fridge Electric Elec inclusive 🔲 can
be hired ☎ WM in unit Airing
cupboard in unit Iron in unit Ironing

---

board in unit HCE in unit [Launderette
within 300yds] ⊕ CTV
⊕3 pin square P 🚿 🅼 🚿 ⌐
🐾 Grass

↔ 🍴(¼m) 🖵(¼m) 🎵(¼m)
Min£85 Max£135pw (Low)
Min£200 Max£250pw (High)

H **Lynrose** 12 Kenstella Road, Newlyn
(2m SW A3077)
for bookings Mrs M Eddy, Boleigh Farm,
Lamorna, Penzance, Cornwall
☎St Buryan(073672)305

*Semi-detached twon house situated
within a residential area overlooking
Newlyn harbour and town centre.
Located within the village of Newlyn just
off B3315. It includes two double rooms,
one single-bedded room, lounge,
kitchen, dining room and bathroom with
WC.*

Apr–Xmas MWB out of season
1 wk min, 1 mth max, 1 unit, 1–5 persons
nc3 no pets ◉ fridge Gas
Gas/Elec metered 🔲 not provided
☎(400yds) Airing cupboard in unit Iron
in unit Ironing board in unit HCE in unit
[Launderette within 300yds] ⊕ TV
⊕3 pin square 🚿(400yds)
↔ 🍴(¼m) 🖵(¼m) 🎵(¼m) 🐾(¼m)
Min£50 Max£130pw

C **28 & 29 Queen Street**
for bookings Mrs P A Buckingham, 8
Higher Lariggan, Penzance, Cornwall
☎Penzance(0736)4182

*Two terraced stone built cottages
situated in the hearR of Penzance. Each
comprise lounge, kitchen/diner,
bathroom, WC, and two bedrooms.*

All year MWB out of season 1 wk min,
3 mths max, 2 units, 1–6 persons ◇ ◆
◉ fridge Electric Elec metered
🔲 inclusive ☎(100yds) Airing
cupboard in unit Iron in unit Ironing
board in unit HCE in unit ⊕ TV
⊕3 pin square 🚿(50yds)
○↔ 🐾(3m) 🍴(200yds) 🖵(200yds)
🎵(200yds) 🐾(200yds)
Max£40pw (Low)
Min£110 Max£115pw (High)

F **Seacrest Flats A, B & C** 19 Regent
Terrace
for bookings Mr T G Lommel, Fir Cones,
Alexandra Road, Penzance, Cornwall
☎Penzance(0736)66262

*Three flats within a Regency period
terraced property overlooking seafront
within easy access of town centre. One
flat first and second floor with two double
bedrooms, lounge, kitchen, bathroom
and WC. Two flats at ground level, one
with two double bedrooms and the other
one double bedroom. Both with lounge,
bathroom, WC and kitchen.*

All year MWB out of season 3 days min,
3 mths max, 3 units, 2–6 persons ◇ ◆
◉ fridge Electric Elec metered
🔲 inclusive ☎(100yds) Airing
cupboard in unit Iron in unit Ironing
board in unit HCE in unit ⊕ TV
⊕3 pin square P 🅼 🚿(100yds) →

⊖ ⚲(200yds) ⊠(200yds) ♫(200yds) ⬟(800yds)

Min£34 Max£50pw (Low)
Min£98 Max£125pw (High)

C 11 Tolcarne Terrace Newlyn
for bookings Mr P Thomas, Tolcarne
Holidays, 'Porthcressa', The Lidden,
Penzance, Cornwall
☎Penzance(0736)5740

*Small stone terraced property consisting
of one double and one twin-bedded room
both with washbasin, one single
bedroom, lounge, dining room, kitchen,
bathroom and WC. Enclosed court yard
at rear.*

All year MWB out of season 1wk min,
1 unit, 1–5 persons [◊ ◆] ◎ fridge
🍴 Elec metered Ⓛ can be hired
☎(100yds) Airing cupboard in unit Iron
in unit Ironing board in unit HCE in unit
[Launderette within 150yds] ⊙ CTV
⊕3pin square 2P ⬟ ♨(200yds)
⅄(Hard), bowls & riding

⊖ ⚲(20yds) ⊠(½m) ♫(½m) ⬟(½m)

Min£40 Max£60pw (Low)
Min£55 Max£130pw (High)

F Tremayne Holiday Flats C, D & E
Alexandra Road
for bookings M & R O'Brien, St Dorothy's
Nurseries, Crowlas, Penzance
☎Cockwells(0736)740334

*Three flats situated in a late Victorian
terraced house. Flat C is on the second
floor and consists of one twin and one*

double-bedded room, small lounge,
kitchenette, bathroom and WC. *Flat D is*
on the ground floor with one double-
bedded room and one single bed in
lounge, small kitchen, shower and WC.
*Flat E occupies the lower-ground floor
and comprises one twin-bedded room,
one small double-bedded room, and a
single bed in the lounge. There is a
kitchen, shower room and WC.*

All year MWB out of season 1wk min,
2 mths max, 3 units, 2–5 persons ◊ ◆
no pets ◎ fridge Electric
Elec heating inclusive Elec metered
Ⓛ inclusive ☎(150yds) Iron on
premises Ironing board on premises
HCE in unit ⊙ CTV ⊕3pin square
⬟ ♨(400yds)

⊖ ♨(3m) ⚲(½m) ⊠(½m) ♫(½m)
⬟(½m)

Min£40 Max£55pw (Low)
Min£95 Max£140pw (High)

PERRANPORTH
Cornwall
Map2 SW75

C Myrtle Cottage Cox Hill
for bookings J A & A S D Hedges,
Westwards, Bickwell Valley, Sidmouth,
Devon
☎Sidmouth(039 55)6176

*Detached pretty olde-worlde cottage in
secluded valley 1m from coast. Attractive
living room with old fireplace (and bread
oven) and oak beams, dining room,
modern bathroom and WC, two
bedrooms with good beds and ample
wardrobe space. One bedroom has a
washbasin. All in good decorative order.
Garden.*

All year MWB out of season 1wk min,
6 mths max, 1 unit, 2–4 persons ◊ ◎
fridge Electric Elec inclusive Ⓛ can
be hired ☎ WM in unit Airing
cupboard in unit HCE in unit ⊙ CTV
⊕3pin square 2pin round P ⬟
♨(1m)

⊖ ⚲(1m) ⊠(1m) ♫(1m)

Min£75 Max£120pw (Low)
Min£150 Max£200pw (High)

B, Ch Leycroft Holidays
Perrancombe, Perranporth, Cornwall
TR6 0JQ
☎Perranporth(087 257)3044

*Ten bungalows and ten chalets
constructed of wood located in a small
holiday park within a very picturesque
valley. Each has two bedrooms, lounge
with bed-settee, kitchen/diner, and
bathroom with WC. They sleep from one
to six persons.*

26 Mar–Oct 1wk min, 3 mths max,
20 units, 1–6 persons ◊ ◆ no pets
(Jul & Aug) ◎ fridge Electric
Elec metered Ⓛ not provided SD on

premises TD on premises Iron on premises Ironing board on premises HCE in unit ⊙ TV ⊛3pin square P 📺 🅿️

⟷ 🛁(2m) 📶(2m) 🎵(2m)

Min£30 Max£145pw (Low)
Min£80 Max£165pw (High)

F Marine Court Holiday Flats

for bookings R T & S Rilstone, Marine House, Perranporth, Cornwall TR6 0BJ
☎Perranporth(087 257)2157

Twelve purpose-built holiday flats comprising two double-bedded rooms (one with additional bunks), open plan lounge, with bed-settee, kitchen and separate bathroom and WC.

All year MWB out of season 3mths max, 12units, 6–7persons [◇] ◆ ◉ fridge Electric Elec metered ⬜can be hired ☎(50yds) Airing cupboard in unit Iron in unit Ironing board in unit HCE in unit [Launderette within 300yds] ⊙ CTV ⊛3pin square P 📺 ♨️(50yds)

⟷ 🛁(1½m) ☏(100yds) 📶(100yds) 🎵(100yds)

Min£45 Max£130pw

B Ocean View Somerville Road

for bookings Mrs J E Muskett, Goodwins, Somerville Road, Perranporth, Cornwall TR6 0HE
☎Perranporth(087 257)3391

Detached modern bungalow situated in an elevated position with good views of Perranporth beach and coastline, close to the town. Accommodation comprises one double bedded room, one twin bedded, small lounge, spacious breakfast room and kitchen. Located off the B3284, ½ mile S of Perranporth.

All year 1wk min, 1mth max, 1unit, 4persons [◇ ◆] no pets ◉ fridge Electric Elec metered ⬜can be hired ☎(100yds) Airing cupboard in unit Iron in unit Ironing board in unit HCE in unit [Launderette within 300yds] ⊙ TV ⊛3pin square 2P 📺 ♨️(½m)

⟷ 🛁(1m) ☏(½m) 📶(½m) 🎵(½m)

Min£35 Max£130pw

F St Davids Hill Flats 1–3 Tywarnhayle Road

for bookings Mr & Mrs A J Brook, Tinkers Lodge, Golla Water, Penhallow, Truro, Cornwall TR4 9LY
☎Perranporth(087 257)2230

Three flats in a large converted villa set above Perranporth with views over the town. Flats 1 and 2 have three bedrooms (all with washbasins), lounge, large hall that can be used as a dining area, kitchen and bathroom/WC. Flat 3 is smaller with two bedrooms (with washbasins), lounge/dining room, kitchen and bathroom.

All year MWB out of season 2wks (1wk winter) min, 3units, 1–7persons ◆ no pets ◉ fridge Electric Elec inclusiva ⬜inclusive ☎(½m) Airing cupboard in unit Iron in unit Ironing board in unit HCE in unit

⊙ TV ⊛3pin square 📺 ♨️(½m)
⟷ ☏(½m) 📶(½m) 🎵(½m)

Min£65 Max£75pw (Low)
Min£120 Max£145pw (High)

PLYMOUTH
Devon
Map 2 SX45

F Hoeside Flats 1A, 2A & 3A 10 Athenaeum Street, The Hoe

for bookings Mrs D L Seymour, 170 Beacon Park Road, Beacon Park, Plymouth PL2 2QS
☎Plymouth(0752)53504

Three maisonettes, each set on two floors, conveniently situated within walking distance of Plymouth Hoe. Flat 1A comprises two twin-bedded rooms, lounge with bed-settee, kitchenette with breakfast bar and combined bathroom/WC. High chairs are provided in flat. Flat 2A has one twin-bedded room, lounge with bed-settee, kitchenette with fridge and breakfast bar, and combined bathroom. Flat 3A consists of one double bedroom, one twin and bunk-bedded room, lounge with bed-settee, modern fitted kitchen with breakfast bar and fridge.

All year MWB out of season 1wk min, 1mth max, 3units, 2–9persons ◆ ◉ Electric Elec metered ⬜inclusive ☎(100yds) Airing cupboard in unit Iron in unit Ironing board in unit HCE in unit [Launderette within 300yds] ⊙ CTV ⊛3pin square ⊛2pin round P ♨️(10yds) ⌒ ✈Hard/grass ✦

⟷ ☏ 📶 🎵 🐾

Min£50 Max£100pw (Low)
Min£100 Max£140pw (High)

F Mr I Gordon *27 Milehouse Road*

Milehouse, Plymouth, Devon PL3 4AD
☎Plymouth(0752)51527

Situated on the first-floor of a brick built semi-detached house in residential area consisting of lounge with put-u-up, a double bedroom, kitchen, bathroom and separate toilet.

All year 1wk min, 1mth max, 1unit, 2–5persons no pets ◉ fridge 🍳 Electric Elec metered ⬜inclusive Airing cupboard in unit Iron in unit Ironing baord in unit HCE in unit [Launderette within 300yds] ⊙ ⊛3pin square ⊛2pin round 📺 ♨️(100yds)

⟷ ☏(100yds) 📶(1m) 🎵(1m) 🐾(1m)

PLYMTREE
Devon
Map 3 ST00

C CC Ref 662

for bookings Character Cottages (Holidays) Ltd, 34, Fore Street, Sidmouth, Devon EX10 8AQ
☎Sidmouth(03955)77001

End of farmhouse with oak beams and white décor, 16th-century cottage with southerly aspect. One twin bedroom, one family room, kitchen/diner, lounge and modern bathroom/WC comprise this cottage. Fitted carpets.

All year MWB out of season 1wk min, 6mths max, 1unit, 2–5persons [◇] ◆ ◉ fridge Electric Elec metered ⬜can be hired ☎ Airing cupboard in unit Iron in unit Ironing board in unit HCE in unit ⊙ TV ⊛3pin square ⊛2pin round P 📺 ♨️(1m)

Min£35 Max£55pw (Low)
Min£73 Max£108pw (High)

POLPERRO
Cornwall
Map 2 SX25

C Beville Cottage The Coombes

for bookings Mrs N J Blake, Sunways, The Coombes, Polperro, Cornwall
☎Polperro(0503)72485

Old terraced cottage comprising lounge/diner, kitchen, two double bedrooms (one with an additional single bed), and bathroom. Parking by arrangement.

All year MWB out of season 1wk min, 2wks max, 1unit, 1–5persons, nc7 no pets ◉ fridge Electric Elec metered ⬜not provided Airing cupboard in unit Iron in unit Ironing board in unit HCE in unit ⊙ TV ⊛3pin square 📺 ♨️(100yds)

⟷ ☏

Min£38 Max£68pw (Low)
Min£78 Max£135pw (High)

C Bwthyn Cernywaldd Little Laney

for bookings Mrs N J Blake, Sunways, The Coombes, Polperro. Cornwall
☎Polperro(0503)72485

Old terraced cottage extensively modernised with open staircase, lounge, dining room, kitchen, two double hedrooms, a single bedroom and bathroom. Close to harbour. Car parking by arrangement.

All year MWB out of season 1wk min, 2wks max, 1unit, 5persons, nc10 no pets ◉ fridge Electric Elec metered ⬜not provided ☎(300yds) Airing cupboard in unit Iron in unit Ironing board in unit HCE in unit ⊙ TV ⊛3pin square 📺 ♨️(100yds)

⟷ ☏(300yds)

Min£38 Max£68pw (Low)
Min£78 Max£135pw (High)

C Crumplehorn Cottages 1 & 2

for bookings Mrs W J M Collings, Brook Cottage, Longcombe Lane, Polperro, Cornwall PL13 2PL
☎Polperro(0503)72274 →

Two stone-built cottages in a terrace of three situated at the entrance of this Cornish fishing village. One has lounge/diner with kitchen area, bathroom and WC, and one family bedroom sleeping three. The other cottage has a kitchen/diner, lounge with open fireplace, two bedrooms, bathroom and WC.

All year MWB out of season 1wk min, 1mth max, 2 units, 2–5 persons ◆ ◎ fridge Electric(1unit) Elec metered ⌷ can be hired ☎ Airing cupboard in unit Iron in unit Ironing board in unit HCE in unit ☉ ⊕(1unit) CTV ⊕3pin square ⊕2pin round P ▥ ♨(100yds)

⊖ ♒(3m) ♀ ▱(½m) ♫(½m)
Min£50 Max£145pw

C Hael-a-Gwynt Little Laney
for bookings Miss L G Blake, Sunways, The Coombes, Polperro. Cornwall
☎Polperro(0503)72485

Well modernised old terraced cottage with two double bedrooms, lounge/diner, kitchenette and bathroom. Car parking by arrangement. Close to harbour.

All year MWB out of season 1wk min, 2wks max, 1unit, 2–4persons, nc7 no pets ◎ fridge Electric Elec metered ⌷ not provided ☎(300yds) Airing cupboard in unit Iron in unit Ironing board in unit HCE in unit ☉ TV ⊕3pin square ▥ ♨(100yds)

Polperro
—
Polzeath

⊖ ♀(300yds)
Min£38 Max£68pw (Low)
Min£75 Max£135pw (High)

POLYPHANT
Cornwall
Map2 SX28

C CC Ref 318 ELP The Stables
for bookings Character Cottages (Holidays) Ltd, 34, Fore Street, Sidmouth, Devon EX108AQ
☎Sidmouth(03955)77001

Semi-detached cottage in tastefully converted 18th-century coach house on edge of the village green. Slate-cobbled yard to entrance, attractive sitting room, cloakroom, kitchen/diner with modern pine wood fittings and breakfast bar, two bedrooms each with a double and a single bed. Cot available.

Jun–Dec 1wk min, 1mth max, 1unit, 2–6persons ◆ ◎ fridge ♨ Gas/Elec inclusive ⌷ can be hired ☎(40yds) Airing cupboard in unit Iron in unit Ironing board in unit HCE in unit ☉ TV ⊕3pin square ⊕2pin round P ▥ ♨(2m)

⊖ ♀(2m)
Min£64 Max£85pw (Low)
Min£114 Max£155pw (High)

POLZEATH
Cornwall
Map2 SW97

C The Cottage
for bookings The Manager, Polzeath Holiday Apartments, Polzeath, Cornwall
☎Trebetherick(020 886)2371

Detached white cottage with marvellous views, adjacent to flats. Accommodation comprises lounge/diner with convertible sofa bed, separate kitchen, one double bedroom and one double bedroom with bunk beds. Bathroom and separate WC. Situated on Polzeath road, 300yds from the beach.

Mar–1Jan MWB out of season 3days min, 4wks max, 1unit, 1–6persons [◆ ◆] ◎ fridge Electric Elec metered ⌷ not provided ☎ Iron on premises Ironing board on premises HCE in unit [Launderette on premises] ☉ CTV ⊕3pin square P ▥ ♨(300yds)

⊖ ♒(2½m) ♫
Min£55 Max£88pw (Low)
Min£100 Max£165pw (High)

F Flats 1–9
for bookings The Manager, Polzeath Holiday Apartments, Polzeath, Cornwall
☎Trebetherick(020 886)2371

Old hotel converted into nine flats with views over beach and cliffs. Flats 1, 3, 4 &5 comprise lounge/diner/kitchen with

*double sofa bed, one separate double bedroom and bathroom/WC. Each sleeps four persons. **Flats 6 & 7** comprise lounge/kitchen/diner with double sofa bed, one double room and one double room with bunk beds. Bathroom/WC. Each sleeps eight persons. **Flats 2, 8 & 9** comprise lounge/kitchen/diner with double sofa bed, one twin room and one double room. Bathroom/WC. Each sleeps six persons. Situated on the Polzeath road, 300yds from the beach.*

.Mar-1Jan MWB out of season
3days min, 4wks max, 9units,
1–8persons [◆ ◆] no pets ◉
fridge Elec Elec metered
🔲 not provided ☎ Iron on premises
Ironing board on premises HCE in unit
[Launderette on premises] ☉ CTV
⊕3pin square 200P 🔳 ♨(300yds)
↮ ⌑(2½m) ♪

Min£32 Max£85pw (Low)
Min£100 Max£180pw (High)

B, C, F Mr & Mrs Beale **Pinewood Flats**
Old Polzeath, Wadebridge, Cornwall
PL27 6TQ
☎Trebetherick(020886)2269

This property, originally Polzeath Lodge has now been converted into self-catering accommodation set in 2¼ acres of natural wooded grounds, high on the north Atlantic coast above the village of Polzeath. The flats are on various levels, the majority having sea/beach views. Close to village and safe bathing area of Polzeath and Daymer Bay.

Apr-Oct MWB out of season 1wk min,
1mth max, 12units 1–8persons [◇]
◆ ◆ ◉ fridge Electric
Elec metered 🔲 can be hired ☎ HCE
in unit [Launderette on premises] ☉
TV & CTV ⊕3pin square P 🔳
♨(200yds)
↮ ⌑(2m) ♀(100yds)

Min£40 Max£75pw (Low)
Min£65 Max£195pw (High)

PONTESBURY
Shropshire
Map**7** SJ40

H **Gatten Home Farmhouse** Gatten
for bookings Mr & Mrs R Hulton-Harrop,
Gatten Lodge, Pontesbury, Shropshire
☎Shrewsbury(0743)790265

White painted farmhouse forming part of a traditional farmyard near the centre of the Gatten Estate. Accommodation comprises of lounge/diner, kitchen/breakfast room and three bedrooms, one with a brass bedstead.

All year MWB 2nights min, 3mths max,
1unit, 1–7persons [◇] ◆ ◆ ◉
fridge 🍴 Elec inclusive 🔲 can be
hired ☎(5m) Airing cupboard in unit
Iron in unit Ironing board unit HCE in
unit ☉ TV ⊕3pin square 4P
♨(5m) Fishing
↮ ♀(3m)

F **Rear Wing** Gatten Lodge, Gatten
for bookings Mr & Mrs R Hulton-Marrop,
Gatten Lodge, Pontesbury, Shropshire
☎Shrewsbury(0743)790265

Flat occupying the rear wing of Gatten Lodge standing near the centre of the Gatten Estate amidst some 2000 acres of woods, moors and farmland. Ground-floor comprises of utility room and cloakroom with WC. The first-floor has lounge/diner, kitchen, bathroom with WC and two twin bedrooms.

All year MWB 2nights min, 3mths max,
1unit, 1–4persons [◇] ◆ ◆ ◉
fridge 🍴 Elec inclusive 🔲 can be
hired ☎(5m) Airing cupboard in unit
Iron in unit Ironing board in unit HCE in
unit ☉ TV ⊕3pin square 4P
♨(5m) Fishing
↮ ♀(3m)

PONTFAEN
Dyfed
Map**2** SN03

F **Foel Eryr**
for bookings Powell's Holidays, High
Street, Saundersfoot, Dyfed
☎Saundersfoot(0834)812791

Converted from a farm out-building this flat comprises open-plan lounge/diner/kitchen combined, one twin-bedded room, one double-bedded and one with bunk beds (also a bed-settee in the lounge) and bathroom/shower/WC. Signed 'Cmw Gwaune' off B4313 from New Inn.

Apr-Sep MWB out of season
3days min, 1unit, 6–8persons ◇ ◆
◆ ◉ fridge Electric Elec inclusive
🔲 can be hired ☎ WM on premises
SD on premises TD on premises Airing
cupboard in unit Iron on premises
Ironing board on premises HCE ☉
CTV ⊕3pin square P ♨(4m) ⌑
↮ ♀

Min£69 Max£195pw

POOLE
Dorset
Map**4** SZ09

F **Aern House** 93 Tatnam Road
for bookings Mrs P Broad, 63 Springdale
Road, Broadstone, Dorset BH189BN
☎Broadstone(0202)698957

An individually designed purpose-built block of two flats in a quiet residential area. Each fully-equipped unit has two twin-bedded rooms, hall, lounge, kitchen and bathroom/WC. Tatnam Road lies off the A349 Wimborne Road.

All year MWB out of season 3days min,
1mth max, 2units, 2–4persons ◇ ◆
no pets ◉ fridge Electric
Elec metered 🔲 inclusive ☎(½m)
Airing cupboard in unit Iron in unit
Ironing board in unit HCE in unit

[Launderette within 300yds] ☉
⊕3pin square 🅿 🔳 ♨(½m)
↮ ⌑(2m) ♀(½m) 🖼(½m) ♪(½m)
🛏(½m)
Min£60 Max£160pw

F **Ardmair Holiday Apartments**
Balmoral Road, Lower Parkstone
for bookings Mrs B Mills, 90 Blandford
Road, Hamworthy, Poole, Dorset
BH15 4BD
☎Poole(02013)5457

Semi-detached brick villa in quiet residential area, a short distance from Parkstone shopping area, having a ground-floor and a first-floor flat. Each comprises double bedroom, lounge with bed-settee, kitchen and bathroom/WC. Turn off A35 along Sandcotes Road, over railway and take second right along Balmoral Road. The apartments are on the right.

Mar-Sep MWB out of season 1wk min,
1mth max, 2units, 2–4persons ◇ ◆
no pets ∅ fridge Gas
Gas/Elec metered 🔲 can be hired
☎(½m) Airing cupboard in unit Iron on
premises Ironing board on premises
HCE in unit [TV] ⊕3pin square P 🔳
♨(½m)
↮ ⌑(1½m) ♀(½m) 🖼(½m) ♪(½m)
🛏(½m)

F Mr & Mrs L C Greenham **Crosby
Court** 50 Kings Avenue, Parkstone,
Poole, Dorset BH14 9QJ
☎Bournemouth(0202)744626

Three flats located within a detached brick gabled house standing in ½-acre of grounds situated in quiet residential area. Two of the flats are on the first-floor, the other on the second, they vary in size one having three bedrooms the others have two, all have a bed-settee in the lounge.

All year MWB out of season 1wk min,
4wks max, 3units, 2–10persons [◇]
◆ ◆ no pets ∅ fridge
Electric/Gas Gas/Elec metered 🔲 can
be hired ☎ SD in unit Airing cupboard
in two units, Iron in unit Ironing board in
unit HCE in unit CTV ⊕3pin square
9P 🔳 ♨(½m)
↮ ⌑(½m) ♀(1m) 🖼(1m) ♪(1m)
🛏(3m)

F **Four Jayes** 6 Windsor Road,
Parkstone
for bookings Mr J D Whatley, 75 Uppleby
Road, Parkstone, Poole, Dorset
BH123DD
☎Parkstone(0202)747310

Victorian house divided into five flats. Adequate standard, mixed furniture. In residential area of Parkstone near railway station. The house is on sloping ground with distant views of Poole Harbour. →

1982 prices quoted throughout
gazetteer

201

All year 1wk min, 5mths max, 5units, 5–7persons ◊ ◆ ◉ fridge ♨ Elec metered ▣ not provided ☎(325yds) Iron on premises Ironing board on premises HCE on premises ⊙ TV ⊕3pin square P ♨(350yds)

⊛ ⚲(320yds) ♫(1½m)

F 16 Windsor Road Parkstone
for bookings Mr G Parsons, 16 Windsor Road, Parkstone, Poole, Dorset BH148SF
☎Broadstone(0202)692927

Detached suburban villa in quiet residential area, converted into self-contained flats with all basic requirements.

May-Sep MWB out of season 1wk min, 1mth max, 5units, 4–8persons [◊] ◉ fridge Electric Elec inclusive ▣not provided ☎(500yds) Airing cupboard in unit HCE in unit TV ⊕3pin square P ▥ ♨

⊛ ⚲(½m) ☕(3m)

Min£60 Max£80pw (Low)
Min£120 Max£150pw (High)

F R B James **Woodlea Holiday Flats** 24 Tower Road, Branksome Park, Poole, Dorset BH136HX
☎Bournemouth(0202)763692

Four flats in detached red-brick gabled villa standing in own grounds and located in a quiet residential suburb. Two first-floor flats, one second-floor flat (sleeps six). Each with two bedrooms (one double and one twin) plus lounge convertible. The ground-floor flat has one twin bedroom and convertible in lounge. Lounge/diner, separate kitchen and bathroom/WC. All with good quality furnishings and fittings.

Apr-Sep MWB out of season 1wk min, 1mth max, 4units, 2–6persons [◊ ◆] no pets ◉ fridge ♨ Elec metered ☎ SD on premises Airing cupboard in unit Iron on premises Ironing board on premises HCE in unit ⊙ CTV ⊕3pin square 6P ▥ ♨(½m)

⊛ ♪(1½m) ⚲(½m) ▨(2½m) ♫(2½m) ☕(2½m)

Min£69 Max£103.50pw (Low)
Min£126.50 Max£195.50pw (High)

PORT APPIN
Strathclyde *Argyll*
Map**14** NM94

C Mr B Harper, **Pier House,** Port Appin, Argyllshire PA384QE
☎Appin(063173)302

Quaint 19th-century renovated cottage, situated beside the old pier affording fine sea views. The ground-floor has one twin-bedded room, together with lounge/diner, kitchenette, utility room and bathroom. Two bedrooms form the first-floor. Adjacent to the tea room and craft shop.

May-Oct 1wk min, 1mth max, 1unit, 1–6persons Calor ♨ fridge Electric Gas inclusive Elec metered ▣inclusive ☎(200yds) Airing

cupboard in unit HCE in unit ⊙ TV ⊕3pin square P ♨(200yds) Fishing, pony trekking, boat trips

⊛ ⚲(½m)

Min£90 Max£120pw

C Spring Cottage
for bookings D E Hutchison, Kinlochlaich House, Appin, Argyll PA384BD
☎Appin(063173)342

Set in its own, rough garden which runs down to the shore of Loch Creran offering magnificent views over Loch Linnhe to Lismore, Morven and Mull. Accommodation comprises lounge/diner, kitchen, one twin-bedded room and two bunk-bedded rooms. It stands 1m S of Port Appin on an unclass road.

May-Oct 1wk min, 5wks max, 1unit, 1–8persons ◊ no pets ◉ fridge Electric Elec inclusive ▣not provided ☎(1m) SD in unit Airing cupboard in unit Iron in unit HCE in unit ⊙ ⊕3pin square P ♨(1m)

⊛ ⚲(1m)

Min£60pw(Low)
Min£175pw (High)

PORT CHARLOTTE Isle of Islay
Strathclyde *Argyll*
Map**10** NR25

H An Cala House
for bookings Lady Wilson, Cala Na Ruadh, Port Charlotte, Islay, Argyll PO487TS
☎Port Charlotte(049685)289

A two-storey white fronted house, looking across Loch Indaal. Comprises a large living room, large kitchen/dining room with oil-fired stove, bedrooms (two with bunk beds) and bathroom and WC. Extras include piano and books.

All year MWB out of season 1wk min, 1mth max, 1unit, 1–8persons ◆ fridge Open fire & Electric Elec metered ▣not provided ☎(200yds) Airing cupboard in unit Iron in unit Ironing board in unit HCE in unit ⊕3pin square P ♨(200yds)

⊛ ⚲(200yds) ▨(200yds)

Min£20 Max£85pw

F The Annexe An Cala
for bookings Lady Wilson, Cala Na Ruadh, Port Charlotte, Islay, Argyll PO487TS
☎Port Charlotte(049685)289

Very small unit, comprising a bedsitting room, separate bathroom leading off from a small scullery. Simply but pleasantly furnished. Bed-settees, bookcase, attrative picture window. Pleasantly situated in fishing village.

All year MWB out of season 1wk min, 1mth max, 1unit, 1–2persons ◉ fridge Electric Elec metered

▣not provided ☎(200yds) HCE in unit ⊕3pin square P ♨(200yds)

⊛ ⚲(200yds) ▨(200yds)
Min£12 Max£20pw (Low)
Min£35 Max£50pw (High)

F The Flat An Cala
for bookings Lady Wilson, Cala Na Ruadh, Port Charlotte, Islay, Argyll PO487TS
☎Port Charlotte(049685)289

First-floor flat in delightful fishing village overlooking Loch Indaal, to blue hills of Jura. Accommodation comprises a living room with piano, open fire, bed-settee and storage heater; combined kitchen and living room; bathroom and WC; double bedroom, all on first-floor. A steep staircase leads to a second-floor, with two large bedrooms. One doubles as a playroom.

All year MWB out of season 1wk min, 1mth max, 1unit, 1–8persons ◉ fridge Open fires & Electric Elec metered ▣not provided ☎(2r0yds) Airing cupboard in unit Iron in unit Ironing board in unit HCE in unit ⊕3pin square P ♨(200yds)

⊛ ⚲(200yds) ▨(200yds)
Min£20 Max£35pw (Low)
Min£60 Max£75pw (High)

PORT DINORWIC
Gwynedd
Map**6** SH56

H 44 Ffordd Garnedd Menai Marina
for bookings Mrs W M Gillibrand, 7 Rutland Road, Ellesmere Park, Eccles, Manchester M309FA
☎061–789 2966

Modern house on large privately owned marina development, comprising one double and two twin bedrooms, bathroom/WC, lounge/diner with balcony, open-plan kitchen, deep freezer and dishwasher. Take A487 from Caernarfon to Bangor at far end of Port Dinorwic the marina is on the left.

All year MWB out of season 1wk min, 6wks max, 1unit, 1–6persons no pets ◉ fridge Electric Elec metered ▣can be hired ♨(½m) Airing cupboard in unit Iron in unit Ironing board in unit HCE in unit [Launderette within 300yds] ⊙ ⊛ CTV ⊕3pin square 2P ▥ ♨(½m) Sailing dinghy

⊛ ⚲(½m)

Min£60 Max£80pw (Low)
Min£105 Max£142pw (High)

F 61 Ffordd Garnedd Menai Marina
for bookings Mrs W M Gillibrand, 7 Rutland Road, Ellesmere Park, Eccles, Manchester M309FA
☎061–789 2966

First-floor flat on large privately owned marina development comprising two twin bedrooms, one bedroom with bunk beds, bathroom/WC, lounge/diner and open-plan kitchen. Take A487 from Caernarfon to Bangor at far end of Port Dinorwic the marina is to be found on the left.

All year MWB out of season 1 wk min,
6wks max, 1unit, 1–6persons no pets
⊛ fridge Electric Elec metered
⌴can be hired ☎(½m) Airing cupboard
in unit Iron in unit Ironing board in unit
HCE in unit [Launderette within 300yds]
☺ ⊙ CTV ③3pin square 2P ⊞
♨(½m) Sailing dinghy
⇔ ♀(½m)

Min£50 Max£68pw (Low)
Min£89 Max£121pw (High)

PORTH
Cornwall
Map**2** SW86

F Coastline Court Holiday Flats
for bookings Mr Robson, Robson Self
Catering Holidays, Morfa Hall, Cliff Road,
Newquay, Cornwall
☎Newquay(06373)3649

*Purpose-built holiday flats situated on
cliff road with views over Newquay and
the sea. The exterior is decorated in white
stucco. The furniture and fittings are of
modern design. A large car park is
located at the rear of the building.*

Etr-Oct MWB out of season 3 days min,
6mths max, 26units, 2–7persons ⊛
fridge Electric Elec metered ⌴can be
hired ☎ Airing cupboard in unit Iron in
unit Ironing board in unit HCE in unit
⊙ CTV ③3pin square ②2pin round
36P ⊞ ♨(300yds) ⌲
⇔ ♀(½m) ▦(½m) ♫(½m) ▦-(½m)

PORTHLEVEN
Cornwall
Map**2** SW62

F Harbourside Holiday Flats (1–3)
for bookings E M Stoyles, 7 Church Hill,
Ludgvan, Penzance, Cornwall
☎Cockwells(0736)740793

*Former Cornish cannery converted into
flats adjacent to harbour, in the heart of
the village. Flats 1 & 3 on the first-floor
have lounge/diner, one double bedroom,
one twin bedroom, kitchen, bathroom
and WC. Flat 2 on the second-floor has a
double bedroom, twin bedroom, a fold-
away single bed, lounge/diner, ktichen,
bathroom and WC.*

All year MWB out of season 1wk min,
3units, 1–5persons ◇ ◆ ◆
no pets ⊛ fridge Electric
Elec metered ⌴can be hired
☎(100yds) Airing cupboard in unit Iron
in unit Ironing board in unit HCE in unit
[Launderette within 300yds] ⊙ TV
③3pin square 1P ⊞ ♨(100yds)
⇔ ♨(2m) ♀(100yds) ▦(2m) ♫(2m)
Min£60 Max£120pw

PORT ISAAC
Cornwall
Map**2** SW98

H CC Ref 314E
for bookings Character Cottages
(Holidays) Ltd, 34 Fore Street, Sidmouth,
Devon EX10 8AQ
☎Sidmouth(03955)77001

Port Dinorwic
—
Port Navas

*Georgian-type house in secluded
position with terraced garden.
Accommodation includes 'L' shaped
living room with bow window, three
bedrooms (two singles, one twin) all
newly furnished, modern bathroom and
toilet facilities.*

3Apr-28Aug 1wk min, 1mth max, 1unit,
2–5persons ◇ ⊛ fridge ⟐
Elec inclusive ⌴can be hired
☎(200yds) Airing cupboard in unit Iron
in unit Ironing board in unit HCE in unit
⊙ TV ③3pin square ②2pin round
P ⌂ ⊞ ♨
⇔ ♀

Min£78 Max£93pw (Low)
Min£113 Max£369pw (High)

PORTKNOCKIE
Grampian *Banffshire*
Map**15** NJ56

C 30 Church Street
for bookings Scott Holiday Homes, 8
Markethill Road, Turriff, Morayshire
☎Turriff(088 82)3524

*Attractively modernised cottage on main
street of little fishing village.
Accommodation comprises one double
and one triple bedroom, lounge,
kitchen/dining room and bathroom.*

All year MWB out of season 1wk min,
1unit, 1–5persons ◇ ⊛ fridge
Electric Elec metered ⌴not provided
☎(200yds) WM in unit SD in unit Iron
in unit Ironing board in unit HCE in unit
⊙ CTV ③3pin square 2P
♨(200yds)
⇔ ♨(1m) ♀(600yds)
Min£40 Max£100pw

H Cormorant & Gannet 23/25 Pulteney
Street
for bookings Blantyre Holiday Homes
Ltd, West Bauds, Findochty, Buckie,
Moray AB5 2ED
☎Buckie(0542)31773

*Two semi-detached houses both of
which offer comfortable accommodation
of living room (with bed-settee), modern
kitchen, bathroom, twin and double-
bedded rooms. In quiet street above
harbour. Pulteney Street runs parallel to
main street off A92.*

All year MWB out of season 1wk min,
3wks max, 2units, 1–6persons [◇]
[◆] [◆] ⊛ fridge Electric
Elec metered ⌴can be hired
☎(300yds) Airing cupboard in unit Iron
in unit Ironing board in unit HCE in unit
⊙ CTV ③3pin square ♨(200yds)
⇔ ♨(2m) ♀(300yds) ▦(2m) ▦-(3m)

1982 prices quoted throughout
gazetteer

C 12 & 14 Pulteney Street
for bookings Scott Holiday Homes, 8
Markethill Road, Turriff, Morayshire
☎Turriff(088 82)3524

*Two adjoining modernised cottages on
quiet street, smaller property comprises
lounge, double and triple bedrooms,
kitchen/diner. The larger property
lounge, dining room, kitchen, bathroom,
double bedroom on the ground floor and
double and twin bedrooms on the first
floor.*

All year MWB out of season 1wk min,
2units, 1–8persons ◇ ⊛ fridge
Electric Elec metered ⌴not provided
☎ WM in unit SD in unit Iron in unit
Ironing board in unit HCE in unit ⊙
CTV ③3pin square 2P ♨(200yds)
⇔ ♨(1m) ♀(600yds)
Min£40 Max£115pw

PORT NAVAS
Cornwall
Map**2** SW72

C Mr B R Roper Pons-a-Verran Farm
Apartments Port Navas, Falmouth,
Cornwall TR11 5RL
☎Constantine(0326)40542

*Converted old Cornish farm buildings
located in an elevated rural position
facing S and commanding magnificent
views of Port Navas creek. These
properties vary in character and size and
all are well-appointed and traditionally
furnished.*

All year MWB out of season 1wk min,
6units, 1–6persons [◇] ◇ ⊛
fridge Electric Elec metered
⌴not provided ☎(300yds) [SD on
premises] [TD on premises] Airing
cupboard in unit Iron on premises
Ironing board on premises HCE in unit
⊙ [TV] ③3pin square 1P ⊞
♨(400yds) Sailing
⇔ ♨(1m) ♀(½m) ▦(½m)
Min£35 Max£190pw

F Mr B R Roper Pons-a-Verran
Apartments Port Navas, Falmouth,
Cornwall TR11 5RL
☎Constantine(0326)40542

*Pons-a-Verran was previously a hotel and
has now been converted into five self-
contained apartments each with a lounge
affording magnificent views of Port Navas
creek. The accommodation varies in size
and character.*

All year MWB out of season 1wk min,
5units, 1–6persons [◇] ◇ ⊛
fridge Electric Elec metered
⌴not provided ☎(300yds) [SD on
premises] [TD on premises] Airing
cupboard in unit Iron on premises
Ironing board on premises HCE in unit
⊙ [TV] ③3pin square 1P ⊞
♨(400yds) Sailing
⇔ ♨(1m) ♀(½m) ▦(½m)
Min£40 Max£190pw

PORT OF MENTEITH
Central *Perthshire*
Map **11** NN50

Ch Mrs J Nairn **Lochend Chalets**
Lochend House, Port of Menteith,
Kippen, Stirlingshire FK8 3JZ
☎Port of Menteith(087 75)268

*Attractive cedar wood 'A' frame chalets
situated on the banks of the Lake of
Menteith with its island priory where
Mary, Queen of Scots was once held.
Most of the chalets have a view of the lake
through foliage. They comprise open-
plan kitchen, dining/lounge area and all
have verandahs. On the B8034.*

All year MWB out of season 6mths max,
14 units, 1–7 persons [◇] ◆ no pets
⦿ fridge Electric Elec metered
⬜inclusive ☎ [SD on premises] [TD
on premises] Iron on premises Ironing
board on premises HCE in unit ⊙
CTV can be hired ⊕3pin square 30P
🎞 ♨(5m) Games room, sailing &
fishing
⊸ ♨(1m)
Min£57.50 Max£230pw

PORTREE
Isle of Skye Highland *Inverness-shire*
Map **13** NG44

B **Beechwood Holiday Homes**
Woodpark, Dunvegan Road
for bookings Hugh Murray Ltd, Dunvegan
Road, Portree, Isle of Skye
☎Portree(0478)2634

*Five modern, timber-frame concrete
block bungalows set in tree-studded
area on outskirts of town. The bungalows
offer up to date fittings and modern
furniture. One bedroom with three single
beds, one double-bedded room,
combined lounge/dining area with
convertible settee sleeping two. A very
well-equipped kitchen with dishwasher
and modern bathroom. On reaching
Portree, turn left on A856 Dunvegan road.
Access to bungalows on right.*

All year MWB out of season 1wk min,
5wks max, 5units, 2–7 persons ◇ ⦿
fridge Electric & open fires
Elec metered ⬜can be hired ☎(½m)
Airing cupboard in unit HCE in unit ⊙
CTV ⊕3pin square P 🎞 ♨(½m)
⊸ ♨(½m) 🎞(½m) 🎵(½m)
Min£62.25 Max£166.75pw

B **Chracaig** Straffin Road
for bookings Mr & Mrs Burgess, East
House, Fort Haven, Shoreham-by-Sea,
W Sussex BN4 5HL
☎Shoreham-by-Sea(079 17)3632

*Detached modern bungalow situated on
the Staffin road 1m from town centre. The
bungalow contains a living room,
kitchen/diner and two twin-bedded
rooms. There is also a conservatory.*

May–Sep 2wks min, 4wks max, 1unit,
1–4 persons ⦿ fridge Electric
Elec metered ⬜not provided ☎(1m)
Airing cupboard in unit HCE in unit ⊙

TV ⊕3pin square P 🎞 ♨(1m)
⊸ ♨(1m)
Min£65 Max£80pw

PORTSONACHAN
Strathclyde *Argyll*
Map **11** NN02

B **Blarghour Bungalow**
for bookings Mrs E Crawford, Blarghour
Farm, Dalmally, Argyll PA33 1BW
☎Kilchrenan(086 63)246

*A compact bunglaow sitting in its own
grounds close to the roadside and with a
burn and waterfall nearby. There is a
living/dining room, kitchen, double
bedroom, twin bedroom and bunk
bedroom. Fully double glazed. The
bungalow lies 7m S of Portsonachan and
1m before Blarghour Farm.*

Mar–Nov 1wk min, 1unit, 1–6 persons
◇ ◆ no pets ⦿ fridge Electric
Elec metered ⬜not provided ☎(5m)
SD in unit Airing cupboard in unit Iron
in unit Ironing board in unit HCE in unit
⊙ TV ⊕3pin square P ♨(16m)
Boats for hire
Min£52 Max£110pw (Low)
Min£160 Max£195pw (High)

H **Burnside House**
for bookings Mr & Mrs A A Rose,
Sonachan House, Portsonachan,
Dalmally, Argyll PA33 1BN
☎Kilchrenan(086 63)240

*Detached two-storey house with small
stream running at the back, situated
adjacent to, and to the rear of Sonachan
House. Pleasant accommodation
consisting of kitchen, living room, three
bedrooms and bathroom. Freedom to
roam in relative safety makes this an ideal
holiday location for children.*

Apr–Oct 1wk min, 1unit, 1–8 persons
◇ ◆ ⦿ fridge Electric
Elec metered ⬜not provided ☎
[WM on premises] Airing cupboard on
premises Iron in unit Ironing board in
unit HCE in unit ⊕3pin square
⊕3pin round P 🏠 ♨(11m)
⊸ ♨(½m)
Min£55.20 Max£103.50pw (Low)
Min£138 Max£207pw (High)

Ch **Sonachan House Chalets**
for bookings Mr & Mrs A A Rose,
Sonachan House, Portsonachan,
Dalmally, Argyll PA33 1BN
☎Kilchrenan(086 63)240

*Three timbered chalets with superb
views across Loch Awe to Cruachan,
situated in the grounds of Sonachan
House. Units comprise of either two or
three bedrooms, living room, kitchen and
bathroom.*

Mar–Oct 1wk min, 3units, 1–6 persons
◇ ◆ ⦿ fridge Electric
Elec metered ⬜not provided ☎
[WM on premises] Airing cupboard on

premises Iron in unit Ironing board in
unit HCE in unit ⊙ ⊕3pin square P
🏠 ♨(11m)
⊸ ♨(½m)
Min£55.20 Max£100.05pw (Low)
Min£134.55 Max£193.20pw (High)

F **Sonachan House Flats**
for bookings Mr & Mrs A A Rose,
Sonachan House, Portsonachan,
Dalmally, Argyll PA33 1BN
☎Kilchrenan(086 63)240

*Sonachan House is a country mansion
set on the SE bank of Loch Awe with
grounds sloping down to a small pier on
the Loch. Part of the house has been
converted into six spacious flats on first
and second floors. Each unit contains
kitchen, sitting room and either two or
three bedrooms. Decorative appearance
is pleasant and furnishings functional.*

Apr–Oct 1wk min, 6units, 1–8 persons
◇ ◆ no pets ⦿ fridge Electric
Elec metered ⬜not provided ☎
[WM on premises] Airing cupboard on
premises Iron in unit Ironing board in
unit HCE in unit ⊙ ⊕3pin square
⊕3pin round P 🏠 ♨(11m)
⊸ ♨(½m)
Min£55.20 Max£106.95pw (Low)
Min£134.55 Max£213.90pw (High)

H **Upper Blarghour House** Blarghour
Farm
for bookings Mrs E Crawford, Blarghour
Farm, Dalmally, Argyll PA33 1BW
☎Kilchrenan(086 63)246

*This recently-built architect designed
holiday house is situated in an elevated
position on hillside above Blarghour
Farm, and commands magnificent
panoramic views across Loch Awe. On
the ground floor, there is a living/dining
room with sun lounge area and twin
bedroom. Upstairs is the main bedroom
(double bed) leading on to balcony
overlooking the Loch, and twin bedroom
also with bunk beds. Blarghour Farm is
set on eastern shores of Loch Awe 8m S
of Portsonachan.*

Mar–Nov 1wk min, 1unit, 1–8 persons
◇ ◆ no pets ⦿ fridge Electric &
open fires Elec metered
⬜not provided ☎(5m) WM in unit SD
in unit [TD on premises] Airing
cupboard in unit Iron in unit Ironing
board in unit HCE in unit ☎ TV
⊕3pin square P ♨(16m) Boats for
hire
Min£70 Max£133pw (Low)
Min£188 Max£220pw (High)

PORTSOY
Grampian *Banffshire*
Map **15** NJ56

C J & J Palphramand **Knockdurn Croft**
Portsoy, Banffshire
☎Portsoy(026 14)3821

*A nicely restored and extended cottage
with high standards throughout
comprising sitting room with sun lounge,
kitchen and two bedrooms.*

All year MWB out of season 1wk min,
1unit, 1–3persons, nc6 no pets ⌀
fridge Electric & woodburning stove
Elec metered ⬜can be hired ☎(1½m)
HCE in unit ⊙ TV ⊕3pin square 4P
♨(1½m)
⊸ ☏(1½m)
Min£95 Max£150pw

PORTWRINKLE
Cornwall
Map2 SX35

F **Whitsand Bay Hotel** Portwrinkle,
Torpoint, Cornwall PL11 3BU
☎St Germans(0503)30276

*Accommodation comprises 6 units
located in the grounds of the hotel, and
one flatlet on the 2nd floor of the hotel
itself. They are spacious and well
furnished, have ample wardrobe space
and good décor. The grounds are
surrounded by an 18 hole golf course.
There are panoramic sea and cliff views
with distant views of the Eddystone
lighthouse.*

All year MWB out of season 1wk min,
6mths max, 6units, 2–8persons [◇]
[◇] [◆] ⊚ fridge Electric
Elec metered ⬜can be hired ☎ HCE
in unit Launderette within 300yds ⊙
⊕3pin square ⊕2pin round P ▥
♨(200yds)
⊸ ♿ ☏
Max£80pw (Low)
Min£85 Max£207pw (High)

POUNDSTOCK
Cornwall
Map2 SX29

B **Cancleave**
for bookings Mr & Mrs A Cummins,
Mineshop, St Gennys, Bude, Cornwall
EX23 0NR
☎St Gennys(084 03)338

*A concrete block constructed bungalow
with a slate roof. Leave A39 at Box's shop
for Widomouth Bay. Turn left following the
cliff road to 1m W of Millook Haven. It is
then on the right. Accommodation
includes two double rooms one with twin
beds, a room with bunks, a lounge/dining
room, kitchen and combined bathroom
and WC.*

Portsoy
—
Powburn

All year MWB out of season 1wk min,
1mth max, 1unit, 2–9persons ◇ ⊚
fridge Electric Elec metered
⬜not provided ☎(2m) Airing
cupboard in unit Iron in unit Ironing
board in unit HCE in unit TV
⊕3pin square P ♨(3½m)

Min£54.05 Max£69pw (Low)
Min£116.15 Max£184pw (High)

C Little Millook
for bookings Mr & Mrs A Cummins,
Mineshop, St Gennys, Bude, Cornwall
EX23 0NR
☎St Gennys(084 03)338

*Stone- and slate-construction with two
bedrooms (one double, one four-
bedded) lounge with open fireplace and
bread oven, kitchen/diner and combined
bathroom and WC. Leave A39 at Box's
shop for Widemouth Bay. Turn left
following the cliff road westwards to
Millook Haven. The cottage is on the left
before the beach.*

All year MWB out of season 1wk min,
1mth max, 1unit, 2–6persons ◇ ⊚
fridge Electric Elec metered
⬜not provided ☎(3m) Airing
cupboard in unit Iron in unit Ironing
board in unit HCE in unit TV
⊕3pin square P ♨(2½m)
⊸ ☏(3m)
Min£48.30 Max£70.15pw (Low)
Min£100.05 Max£154.10pw (High)

C Millook House
for bookings Mr & Mrs A Cummins,
Mineshop, St Gennys, Bude, Cornwall
EX23 0NR
☎St Gennys(084 03)338

*A cottage of Cornish stone with a slate
roof provides accommodation for up to
eight with three bedrooms, lounge with
open fireplace, dining room,
kitchen/diner, bathroom with WC and
separate WC. Leave A39 at Box's shop
for Widemouth Bay. Turn left following the
cliff road westward to Millook Haven.*

All year MWB out of season 1wk min,
1mth max, 1unit, 2–8persons ◇ ⊚
fridge Electric Elec metered
⬜not provided ☎(3m) Airing
cupboard in unit Iron in unit Ironing
board in unit HCE in unit TV
⊕3pin square P ♨(2½m)
⊸ ☏(3m)

Min£54.05 Max£69pw (Low)
Min£116.15 Max£184pw (High)

POWBURN
Northumberland
Map12 NU01

C *The Cottage*
for bookings Mrs S R Stephenson, The
Old Rectory, Ingram, Powburn, Alnwick,
Northumberland NE66 4LT
☎Powburn(066 578)236

*A quaint cottage at the rear of the
Rectory, surrounded by gardens.
Sleeping accommodation for four in two
double bedrooms on first-floor. Ground-
floor comprises lounge/diner, kitchen,
bathroom and WC.*

All year MWB out of season 1wk min,
3mths max, 1unit, 2–4persons ◇ ◆
no pets ⊚ fridge Electric
Elec metered ⬜not provided
☎(500yds) Airing cupboard in unit Iron
in unit Ironing board in unit HCE in unit
⊙ ⊕3pin square 6P ▥ ♨(100yds)
⤸Grass
⊸ ♿ ☏(3m)

F Mrs S R Stephenson *The Old
Rectory* Ingram, Powburn, Alnwick,
Northumberland NE66 4LT
☎Powburn(066 578)236

*Rambling stone-built house situated at
the head of the Ingram Valley. There are
two flats within the house. Ground-floor
flat sleeps four in one double bedroom
and a double convertible in the lounge.
The other flat is on the second-floor
sleeping six, having an additional double
bedroom.* →

Etr-Sep MWB out of season 1wk min,
3mths max, 2units, 2–6persons ◊ ◆
no pets ◎ fridge Electric
Elec metered ⬛not provided
☎(500yds) Airing cupboard in unit Iron
in unit Ironing board in unit HCE in unit
⊖ ⊕3pin square 6P ⬚ ♨(100yds)
⚓Grass Games room
⟷ ♀(3m)

PRESTATYN
Clwyd
Map6 SJ08

F Pontin's Ltd, *Prestatyn Sands
Holiday Village,* Central Beach,
Prestatyn, Clwyd LL19 7LA
☎Prestatyn(07456)2267

*Flats sleeping up to eight persons,
situated in a holiday village with all
amenities. Accommodation comprises
one or two bedrooms, kitchen/diner
(which can convert into an extra
bedroom) and bathroom/WC.*

2Apr-5Oct MWB in season 1night min,
1mth max, 964units, 4–8persons ◊
◊ ◆ no pets ◎ fridge Electric
Elec metered ☎inclusive [Iron on
premises] [Ironing board on premises]
⊖ TV ⊕3pin square P ⬚ ♨ ⬛
Games room
⟷ ▨ ♫ 🕮

F Pontin's Ltd **Tower Beach Holiday
Village** Prestatyn, Clwyd
☎Prestatyn(07456)2244

*Two-storey blocks of flats forming a
holiday village. They include several
different types of property and sleep from
four to eight people. Each has
lounge/diner with settee or wall bed,
kitchen or kitchen area and
bathroom/WC. 1m from town centre.*

Apr-Oct MWB in season 3days min,
6wks max, 350units, 2–6persons
[◊ ◊ ◆] no pets ⚱(108units)
◎(242units) fridge Electric
Gas/Elec metered ⬛inclusive
☎(250yds) [Iron] Ironing board HCE
in unit [Launderette on premises] ⊖
CTV ⊕3pin square P ♨(250yds)
⬛ ⚓Hard Restaurant
⟷ ♬(2m) ♀ ▨ ♫ 🕮

PRESTEIGNE
Powys
Map7 SO36

C The Lodge
for bookings Mrs B L Gibbons, Middle
Moor, Presteigne, Powys
☎Presteigne(054 44)412

*Old gardener's lodge surrounded by
lawns. The accommodation comprises a
lounge and dining room, both with open
fires, shower room, kitchen, WC and
storage room. Upstairs are two twin-
bedded rooms. Located on unclass road
between Presteigne and Lower Kinsham
1m NE of Presteigne.*

Apr-Sep 3days min, 6mths max, 1unit,
1–5persons ◊ ◆ ◎ fridge
Electric Elec metered ⬛can be hired

Powburn
—
Pwllheli

☎(1m) Airing cupboard in unit Iron in
unit HCE in unit TV can be hired
⊕3pin square P ⚱ ⬚ ♨(1m)
Fishing
⟷ ♀(1m)

Min£20 Max£30pw (Low)
Min£50 Max£70pw (High)

F Middle Moor
for bookings Mrs B L Gibbons, Middle
Moor, Presteigne, Powys
☎Presteigne(054 44)412

*Self-contained part of country house.
Upstairs there is a large sitting room, a
single bedroom with wash basin, a
double bedroom, bathroom and
separate WC. Downstairs there is an
entrance hall, small dining room and
kitchen. Located on unclass road
between Presteigne and Lower Kinsham,
1m NE of Presteigne.*

Apr-Sep 3days min, 6mths max, 1unit,
1–5persons, nc8 no pets ◎ fridge
Electric Elec metered ⬛can be hired
☎(1m) Airing cupboard in unit Iron in
unit HCE in unit ⊖ ⊕ TV
⊕3pin square P ⬚ ♨(1m) Fishing
⟷ ♀(1m)

Min£20 Max£30pw (Low)
Min£50 Max£70pw (High)

PRIMROSE VALLEY
North Yorkshire
Map8 TA17

Ch Primrose Valley Holiday Estate
for bookings Leisure Caravan Parks Ltd,
25 Stephyn's Chambers, Bank Court,
Hemel Hempstead, Herts HP11DA
☎Hemel Hempstead(0442)51244

*Modern brick chalets on a large seaside
complex. Each of the 170 chalets sleeps
two to six people in three bedrooms (two
with bunk beds and one with a double
bed). The estate has shops, a cinema,
hairdressers and a large theatre with bar
(giving variety performances), plus a
range of other holiday amenities.*

Etr-Oct MWB 4days min, 4wks max,
170units, 1–6persons [◊ ◆]
no pets ◎ fridge Electric
Elec metered ⬛can be hired ☎ Airing
cupboard HCE in unit [Launderette on
premises] ⊖ TV ⊕3pin square
166P ♨ ⬛ Putting green
⟷ ♬(2m) ♀ ▨ ♫ 🕮

Min£28 Max£82pw (Low)
Min£102 Max£133pw (High)

Ch Primrose Valley Holiday Estate
for bookings Leisure Caravan Parks Ltd,
25 Stephyn's Chambers, Bank Court,
Hemel Hempstead, Herts HP11DA
☎Hemel Hempstead(0442)51244

*Twenty-three brick chalets on large
seaside complex, with spacious
lounge/kitchen, two double bedrooms
and one with bunk beds, bathroom with
shower and WC.*

Etr-Sep MWB 4days min, 4wks max,
23units, 1–6persons ◊ no pets ◎
fridge Electric Elec inclusive ⬛can
be hired ☎ Airing cupboard in unit
HCE in unit ⊖ CTV ⊕3pin square
23P ♨ ⬛ ♀ ▨ ♫ 🕮

Min£42 Max£74pw (Low)
Min£128 Max£192pw (High)

PURLEY
Greater London
Map4 TQ36

F 163–165 Brighton Road
for bookings Gillian Mitchell,
Ravenscroft, Coulsdon Lane, Coulsdon,
Surrey CR3 3QG
☎01–660 8167

*Eight units in two converted adjoining
houses, situated on A23 London-
Brighton road. There are three different
types of unit one or two bedrooms with
lounge, kitchen, bathroom, plus studio
units which have combined
bedroom/lounge, kitchen, bath or
shower. Four of the units have automatic
washing machines.*

All year 1wk min, 6mths max, 8units,
1–7persons [◊] ◊ ♨ fridge ♨
Gas/Elec metered ⬛inclusive
☎(200yds) Airing cupboard in unit Iron
in unit Ironing board in unit HCE in unit
⊖ CTV ⊕3pin square 9P ⬚ ♨(⅓m)
⟷ ♬(1m) ♀(300yds) ▨(300yds)
♫(300yds) 🕮(1m)

Min£95 Max£210pw

PWLLHELI
Gwynedd
Map6 SH33

H Mrs A F Jones **Gwindy** Abererch,
Pwllheli, Gwynedd
☎Pwllheli(0758)2074

*Part of a detached house converted to
spacious modern holiday
accommodation with lounge, dining
room, kitchen, bathroom, WC, three
double rooms (one with a cot) and one
room with three single beds. 2m from
Pwllheli and ⅓m off A497.*

Etr-Oct 3days min, 1unit, 9persons
[◊] ◊ no pets ◎ fridge Electric
Elec metered ⬛not provided ☎
Airing cupboard in unit Iron in unit
Ironing board in unit HCE in unit ⊖
TV ⊕3pin square P ⬚ ♨(100yds)
⟷ ♬(2m) ♀(2m) 🕮(2m)

Min£50 Max£60pw (Low)
Min£65 Max£75pw (High)

F Mrs J M Underwood **Seaview &
Studio Flats** Heathside, South Beach,
Pwllheli, Gwynedd LL53 5AL
☎Pwllheli(0758)3414

*Seaview Flat occupies the first-floor of
this late Victorian, four-storey, seafront
terrace. Spacious lounge/diner, kitchen,
one double, one triple bedroom both with
washbasin, separate bathroom/WC.*

Studio Flat *situated on second- and third-floors, large lounge with seaview, kitchen, triple bedroom and bathroom/WC, upstairs offers three single and one double bedroom with separate WC.*

May–Aug(Studio Flat Jul & Aug only) 1wkmin, 4wks max, 2units, 1–8persons [◊] [◆] no pets ◔ (Studio) ◎(Seaview) fridge Electric Gas/Elecmetered ⨆not provided ☎(100yds) SD in unit Iron in unit Ironing board in unit HCE in unit ⊖ TV ⊕3pinsquare ▥ ♨(100yds)

⊖ ♨(¼m) ♀(100yds) ▥(¼m)

Min£50 Max£95pw (Low)
Min£90 Max£150pw (High)

QUARNFORD
Derbyshire
Map**7** SK06

C Colshaw Cottage
for bookings Mrs J Riley, Sycamore Bank, Colshaw, Quarnford, Buxton, Derbyshire
☎Buxton(0298)3909

One of two typical Derbyshire cottages situated in a remote area S of Buxton. A car is essential for this cottage and is reached by leaving A53 at 'Traveller's Rest' and taking the first turning left. A simply decorated cottage with two bedrooms (one with two double beds), kitchen/diner, lounge and bathroom/WC. Truly splendid views across a very narrow, steep-sided valley to the River Dove.

All year MWB out of season 1wkmin, 1mthmax, 1unit, 1–5persons ◆ no pets ◎ fridge Electric Elecmetered ⨆not provided ☎(1½m) Airing cupboard in unit HCE TV ⊕3pinsquare P ♨(1m)

⊖ ♀(1m)

RAFFORD
Grampian *Moray*
Map**15** NJ05

Ch Tulloch Lodges
for bookings Mrs Du Boulay, Tulloch Holiday Lodges, Rafford, Forres, Moray IV360RU
☎Forres(0309)73311

A group of four attractive cedar wood lodges lying in a peaceful setting, off B9010, 4m S of Forres. Each contains an open-plan kitchen/dining area, lounge with convertible settee, two bedrooms and a modern bathroom.

All year MWB out of season 3nights min, 3wks max, 4units, 1–6persons [◊] ◆ ◆ ◎ fridge ▥ Elecmetered ⨆inclusive ☎ Airing cupboard in unit Iron on premises Ironing board on premises HCE in unit ⊖ CTV ⊕3pinsquare P ▥ ♨(4m) Fishing

Min£50 Max£115pw (Low)
Min£135 Max£145pw (High)

1982 prices quoted throughout gazetteer

RAGLAN
Gwent
Map**3** SO40

H Ty Newydd Farm
for bookings Mr G W Watkins, New House Farm, Clytha, Abergavenny, Gwent
☎Gobion(087 385)341

Quietly located stone-built farmhouse with its own garden. Accommodation consists of spacious kitchen and separate breakfast/dining room, small lounge and a further ground-floor room which may be used as a bedroom, two twin-bedded rooms and a double-bedded room, and spacious combined bathroom/WC. Just off the A40 near Clytha.

All year MWB out of season 4days min, 1unit, 2–6persons ◆ ◎ fridge Electric & open fires ⨆can be hired by overseas visitors ☎ WM in unit SD in unit Airing cupboard in unit Iron in unit Ironing board in unit HCE in unit ⊖ TV ⊕3pinsquare P 1♨ ▥ ♨(2m) Riding available

⊖ ♀(¼m)

RAMSEY
Isle of Man
Map**6** SC49

B & C Ballacarmel Ballure Road,
Ramsey, Isle of Man
☎Ramsey(0624)812012

Nine modern bungalows and one cottage located in 40 acres of hillside with superb views over Ramsey Bay. Each bungalow is furnished to a very high standard including leather Chesterfields. Three bedrooms (one double, two twins). The cottage comprises lounge, kitchen, bathroom and two double bedrooms, all furnished to a high standard.

All year 1wkmin, 10units, 2–7persons ◆ ◎ fridge ▥ Electric & open fires in cottage Elecmetered ⨆inclusive Airing cupboard in unit Iron in unit Ironing board in unit HCE in unit ⊖ CTV ⊕3pinsquare P ▥ ♨(½m) ⤷Grass

⊖ ♨(1m) ♀(1m) ▥(1m) ♫(1m)

Min£92 Max£126.50pw (Low)
Min£161 Max£184pw (High)

F Mrs G Procter Mannix Court
Mooragh Promenade, Ramsey, Isle of Man
☎Ramsey(0624)813840

Flats in a four-storey stone-built terraced property overlooking Ramsey Bay. All well furnished and fully equipped. Accommodation comprises two bedrooms (one double and two singles with bunks). Extra bed can be provided. Lounge, kitchen and bathroom of a good standard.

All year MWB out of season 1wkmin, 10units, 2–5persons ◊ ◆ no pets ◎ fridge Electric Elecmetered ⨆inclusive ☎(200yds) Iron on premises Ironing board on premises HCE on premises TV can be hired ⊕3pinsquare ▥ ♨(250yds)

⊖ ♨(1m) ♀(100yds) ▥(1m)
♫(250yds)

Min£40 Max£70pw

RATFORD BRIDGE
Dyfed
Map**2** SM81

C Mr & Mrs T A Poole Solbury Mountain Farm Cottages Tiers Cross,
Ratford Bridge, Haverfordwest, Dyfed SA623SB
☎Haverfordwest(0437)5368

Five attractive cottages located within farm complex the décor and furnishings are of a good standard; they vary in size sleeping up to five persons.

Mar–Oct & Dec MWB out of season 3days min, 5units, 2–5persons ◊ ◆ ◆ no pets ◎ fridge Electric & open fires Elec inclusive (Heating) Elecmetered ⨆inclusive ☎(1m) WM on premises SD on premises TD on premises Airing cupboard in unit Iron on premises Ironing board on premises HCE in unit ⊖ CTV ⊕3pinsquare 8P ♨(1m)

⊖ ♨(3m) ♀(3m) ▥(3m)

Min£40 Max£100pw (Low)
Min£60 Max£155pw (High)

RATHILLET
Fife *Fife*
Map**11** NO32

H Creich Farmhouse
for bookings Mr A Wedderburn, Mountquhanie Holiday Homes, Cupar, Fife KY154QJ
☎Gauldry(082624)252

A traditional Scottish Lowland stone farmhouse standing back off the road. Via A914 and at Rathillet turn left for 1m. The house offers five first-floor bedrooms (two singles, two twins and one double), two extra beds can be supplied, sitting room, dining room with grand piano, large modernised kitchen and bathroom.

All year MWB out of season 1wkmin, 1mthmax, 1unit, 2–10persons ◆ ◎ fridge ♫ Elecinclusive ⨆can be hired ☎ WM in unit TD in unit Iron in unit Ironing board in unit HCE in unit CTV ⊕3pinround P ▥ ♨(5m) Tennis, pigeon shooting and fishing

⊖ ♀

F Dairy House
for bookings Mr A Wedderburn, Mountquhanie Holiday Homes, Cupar, Fife KY154QJ
☎Gauldry(082624)252

Converted and modernised ground-floor flat situated in a large mansion which stands in an extensive estate. The flat offers two twin-bedded rooms, one →

double-bedded room, sitting room,
kitchen/diner and bathroom with bidet.
1½m NW of Rathillet, take turning off A914
to Newburgh.

All year MWB out of season 1wk min,
1mth max, 1unit, 2–6persons ◆ ◉
fridge ♨ Elec inclusive ⬜can be
hired ☎ Airing cupboard in unit Iron in
unit Ironing board in unit HCE in unit
[Launderette on premises] ⊖ CTV
⊕3pin square P ▥ ♨(5m) ✆Hard
Pigeon shooting, agate hunting
⊖ ♀

C Drummond Cottages
for bookings Mr A Wedderburn,
Mountquhanie Holiday Homes, Cupar,
Fife KY15 4QJ
☎Gauldry(082 624)252

Converted semi-detached stone farm
cottages on hill position commanding
good views each consisting of two twin-
bedded rooms, combined sitting
room/lounge, kitchen and bathroom. Via
A914 to Rathillet then turn left and drive
for 1m.

All year MWB out of season 1wk min,
1mth max, 2units, 2–4persons ◆ ◉
fridge ♨(log fired stove)
Elec inclusive ⬜can be hired
☎(100yds) Iron in unit Ironing board in
unit HCE in unit ⊖ CTV
⊕3pin square P ▥ ♨(5½m) ✆Hard
Pigeon shooting and agate hunting
⊖ ♀

F Gillespie House
for bookings Mr A Wedderburn,
Mountquhanie Holiday Homes, Cupar,
Fife KY15 4QJ
☎Gauldry(082 624)252

Converted and modernised ground-floor
flat in a large mansion standing in an
extensive estate. It comprises three twin-
bedded rooms, sitting/dining room,
kitchen and bathroom with bidet. 1m
down a left turn from Rathillet and A914.

All year MWB out of season 1wk min,
1mth max, 1unit, 2–6persons ◆ ◉
fridge ♨ Elec inclusive ⬜can be
hired ☎ Iron in unit Ironing board in
unit HCE in unit [Launderette on
premises] ⊖ CTV ⊕3pin square P
▥ ♨(5m) ✆Hard Pigeon shooting,
agate hunting
⊖ ♀

Rathillet
—
Restronguet

H The Lodge
for bookings Mr A Wedderburn,
Mountquhanie Holiday Homes, Cupar,
Fife KY15 4QJ
☎Gauldry(082 624)252

Stone lodge standing at a minor entrance
to the Mountquhanie Estate. The Lodge
offers three twin-bedded rooms,
sitting/dining room, kitchen and
bathroom. Via A914 to Rathillet, then turn
left for 1m.

All year MWB out of season 1wk min,
1mth max, 1unit, 2–6persons ◆ ◉
fridge ♨ Elec inclusive ⬜can be
hired ☎ Iron in unit Ironing board in
unit HCE in unit [Launderette within
300yds] ⊖ CTV ⊕3pin round P ▥
♨(5m) ✆Hard Pigeon shooting, agate
hunting
⊖ ♀

REDSTONE
Grampian *Moray*
Map**14** NH95

C Shipples Darnaway Estate
for bookings Moray Estates Development
Co, Estate Office, Forres, Moray IV36 0ET
☎Forres(0309)72213

A detached cottage lying by a quiet
country road in the estate hamlet of
Redstone. On the ground floor is a double
bedroom, living/dining room, kitchen,
bathroom and upstairs is a twin and a
single bedroom.

Apr–Oct MWB out of season 1wk min,
1unit, 1–5persons ◆ no pets ◉
fridge Electric Elec inclusive ⬜can
be hired ☎(¼m) Iron in unit Ironing
board in unit HCE in unit ⊖ TV
⊕3pin square P ▥ ♨(¼m) Burn
fishing

Min£92 Max£103.50pw (Low)
Max£115pw (High)

REIGHTON GAP
North Yorkshire
Map**8** TA17

Ch Reighton Sands Holiday Village
5, 10 & 16 Sands Close
for bookings Mrs J M Callingham, Kiwi

Lodge, 11 Temple Close, Welton,
Brough, N Humberside HU15 1NX
☎Hull(0482)667969

Three modern privately owned chalets
situated on the edge of a holiday village.
No 5 sleeps seven persons in a double-
bedded room, single room and a room
with bunk beds. Also a bed-settee in
lounge. Nos 10 and 16 sleep up to eight
persons in each with one double-bedded
room, bed-settee and a room with four
bunk beds.

Etr–Oct MWB out of season
2nights min, 3mths max, 3units,
1–8persons ◆ ◉ fridge Electric
Elec metered ⬜not provided
☎(50yds) HCE in unit [Launderette
within 300yds] ⊖ TV ⊕3pin square
♨(300yds)
⊖ ♀(300yds) ▨(300yds) ▮(300yds)
Min£34 Max£58pw (Low)
Min£64 Max£98pw (High)

RESTRONGUET
Cornwall
Map**2** SW83

H Marlow
for bookings Mr P Watson, Restronguet,
Falmouth, Cornwall TR11 5ST
☎Penryn(0326)72722

Semi-detached house with access to
moorings for boats. There is a tastefully
decorated lounge, modern kitchen,
dining room, cloakroom and shower and
WC, three good sized bedrooms and
combined bathroom/WC. Lawn and well
kept gardens.

All year MWB out of season 1unit,
1–7persons [◆] ◉ fridge ♨
Elec metered ⬜not provided ☎ WM
SD Airing cupboard in unit ☎
Ironing board HCE in unit ⊖ CTV
⊕3pin square P ▥ ♨(1m)
⊖ ♀(100yds)
Min£92 Max£225pw (Low)
Min£230 Max£384pw (High)

H Oyster Shell Nos 1 & 2
for bookings Mr P Watson, Restronguet,
Falmouth, Cornwall TR11 5ST
☎Penryn(0326)72722

Two semi-detached houses with lawned
garden overlooking Fal Estuary and
private beach. Number 1 has a kitchen,

---

lounge/diner, and bathroom with shower/WC. Number 2 has a kitchen, lounge and dining room and a bathroom/WC on the ground floor. Upstairs there are three bedrooms two of which are family rooms. In Number 1 the third bedroom has a single bed whilst in Number 2 the third bedroom has a double bed. Both houses have a bathroom/WC upstairs.

All year MWB out of season 2units, 1–8persons [◊] ◎ fridge Electric Elecmetered ⬜notprovided ☎ WM Airing cupboard in unit Iron in unit Ironing board HCE ⊙ CTV ⊕3pinsquare SD P ▥ ♨(1m)

↩ ☘(100yds)

Min£92 Max£216pw (Low)
Min£227 Max£360pw (High)

RHANDIRMWYN
Dyfed
Map3 SN74

C Mrs I T Williams **Gelly Farm Cottage** Galltybere, Rhandirmwyn, Llandovery, Dyfed SA20 0PH
☎Rhandirmwyn(05506)218

Situated near the head of the valley this small old Welsh farm cottage has a peaceful setting. Downstairs there is a lounge, dining room, kitchen, bathroom/shower with WC and a double bedroom. Upstairs a bedroom with bunks and a single bed, also a room with double bed and cot.

All year 1wkmin, 1unit, 2–8persons ◊ ◆ nopets ◎ fridge Electric & open fires Elecmetered ⬜notprovided ☎(½m) Airing cupboard in unit Iron in unit Ironing board in unit HCE in unit ⊙ ⊕3pinsquare P ▥ ♨(2m) Pony trekking, fishing

↩ ☘(2m)

Min£30 Max£100pw

RHAYADER
Powys
Map6 SN96

H **Garreg Lwyd** Llangurig Road
for bookings Mrs A J Hampshire, 57 Parkside Road, Reading, Berkshire RG32BT
☎Reading(0734)57990

Detached house in isolated position at the end of a drive, set high above A470 with extensive views over the Wye Valley. Accommodation comprises lounge with open fire, kitchen/breakfast room and a twin bedded room. First floor has two twin bedded rooms and bathroom/WC.

Mar–Oct 1wkmin, 6wksmax, 1unit, 1–6persons ◆ nopets ◎ fridge ♨ Elecinclusive ⬜can be hired ☎(2m) SD on premises Airing cupboard on premises Ironing board on premises HCE on premises ◉ ⊕3pinsquare P ♨(4m)

Min£50 Max£90pw

RHOSGOCH
Powys
Map3 SO14

H **The North**
for bookings Mrs N M Griffiths, Hondon, Rhosgoch, Builth Wells, Powys LD23JT
☎Painscastle(04975)219

Isolated farmhouse set in beautiful countryside 2m from Rhosgoch. Accommodation comprises three bedrooms (one twin and two double rooms), bathroom/WC, kitchen and lounge/dining room.

Mar–Nov 1wkmin, 3wksmax, 1unit, 6persons nopets ◎ fridge Electric Elecmetered ⬜can be hired ☎(400yds) WM in unit HCE in unit ✪ ⊕3pinsquare P ♨(7m)

RHYL
Clwyd
Map6 SJ08

B, Ch Mr Marshall **Stafford Park Holiday Chalets** 108 Marsh Road, Rhyl, Clwyd
☎Rhyl(0745)4948

Small and compact site of nine bungalows and eight chalets. The property is partly bordered by trees, backs on to a grass play area, and is beside large holiday camp. Within walking distance of main shopping area.

May–Oct MWB out of season 26wksmax, 17units, 4–6persons ◆ ◎ Electric Elecinclusive ⬜can be hired ☎ Airing cupboard in unit [Iron on premises] [Launderette within 300yds] [TV] ⊕3pinsquare P ♨(½m) ⌒

↩ ☘(50yds) ▣(50yds) ♫(50yds) ▆(50yds)

Min£35 Max£80pw

RINGFORD
Dumfries & Galloway Kirkcudbrightshire
Map11 NX65

C **Meadow Park**
for bookings G M Thomson & Co, 27 King Street, Castle Douglas, Kirkcudbrightshire
☎Castle Douglas(0556)2701

Old stone-built cottage renovated and furnished, and conveniently placed for the beaches. Consists of a living room, kitchen, two bathrooms, two twin-bedded rooms and a bedroom with bunk beds. On the A726 towards New Galloway.

All year 1wkmin, 6mths max, 1unit, 1–6persons ◆ Rayburn fridge Electric & open fires Elecinclusive ⬜not provided ☎(2m) HCE in unit TV ⊕3pinsquare P ♨(2m)

Min£50 Max£115pw

ROBERTSBRIDGE
East Sussex
Map5 TQ72

F Mr & Mrs R B Wiseman **Glottenham Manor** Robertsbridge, E Sussex
☎Robertsbridge(0580)880212

A large country manor house situated in the peace and quiet of the Sussex countryside offering six flats each affording accommodation for two people. These small cosy flats have a combined lounge and diner/kitchenette – one has a separate kitchen.

Etr–Oct MWB 1wkmin, 4wks max, 6units, 1–2persons nopets ◎ fridge ♨ Elecinclusive ⬜inclusive ☎(1m) Iron on premises HCE on premises ⊙ TV 3pinsquare P ♨(1m)

↩ ☘(1m)

£105pw

ROCK
Hereford & Worcester
Map7 SO76

F Mr & Mrs Maidment **The Flat** Rockmoor, Rock, Kidderminster, Worcestershire
☎Clows Top(029922)214

A beautifully preserved converted 16th-century black and white farmhouse set amid 100 acres of farmland. Comprises on the ground floor a lounge/diner, fully equipped kitchen and separate WC. The first floor has a modern bathroom/WC, twin bedroom, single bedroom and a bedroom with two bunks.

Apr–Oct MWB out of season 1wkmin, 4wks max, 1unit, 1–5persons ◊ ◆ ◎ fridge Electric & open fires Elecinclusive ⬜can be hired ☎ WM on premises SD on premises Iron on premises Ironing board on premises HCE in unit ⊙ CTV ⊕3pinsquare P ♨(2m) Riding stables

↩ ☘(½m)

ROCKCLIFFE
Dumfries & Galloway Kirkcudbrightshire
Map11 NX85

H **Boreland of Colvend Farm House** (off A75)
for bookings G M Thomson & Co, 27 King Street, Castle Douglas, Kirkcudbrightshire DG71AB
☎Castle Douglas(0556)2701

White faced stone built two-storey farmhouse with spacious accommodation of large kitchen/dining room, two sitting rooms, two bathrooms, utility room, spacious hall and three bedrooms, sleeping six people. Good views.

All year 1wkmin, 1mthmax, 1unit, 1–6persons ◆ ◎ fridge Electric & open fires Elecinclusive ⬜not provided ☎(1m) Airing cupboard in unit Iron in unit Ironing →

board in unit TV ⊕3pin round P ▥ ⛫(1m)

⊖ ♁(1½m) ♀(2m)

Min£55 Max£130pw

ROSEDALE ABBEY
North Yorkshire
Map**8** SE79

F Mrs R Buckle **Mill Bungalow Flat** Rosedale Abbey, Pickering, N Yorkshire ☎Lastingham(07515)272

Spacious, first floor luxury flat comprising 'L' shaped lounge/diner with pine clad ceiling, two bedrooms, one double and one twin bedded, kitchen and shower/WC.

All year MWB 3nights min, 1mth max, 1unit, 1–4persons, nc5 ◎ fridge ⊞ Elec inclusive ⊡inclusive ☎(100yds) [WM on premises] SD on premises [TD on premises] Airing cupboard in unit Iron in unit Ironing board in unit HCE in unit [Launderette within 300yds] ⊙ CTV ⊕3pin square 4P ⌂ ▥ ⛫(50yds)

⊖ ♁(500yds) ♀(200yds)

Min£70 Max£130pw

ROSS-ON-WYE
Hereford & Worcester
Map**3** SO52

C **Corner House** Wilton
for bookings Mrs A M Collett, 11 Broad Street, Ross-on-Wye, Herefordshire ☎Ross-on-Wye(0989)62559

This three storey, white painted house, forms part of a group of early 18th-century listed buildings and has its own small garden and patio. It comprises of lounge/dining room with open fire and exposed beams, and kitchen. There is one family bedroom and one bunk bedded room on the first floor with one twin bedded room and bathroom/WC on the second floor. Logs provided at extra cost.

All year MWB out of season 3days min, 6mths max, 1unit, 1–6persons [◇] ◈ ◆ ◎ fridge Electric Elec metered ⊡can be hired ☎(20yds) Airing cupboard in unit Iron in unit Ironing board in unit HCE in unit TV ⊕3pin square ⛫(10yds)

⊖ ♀ ▨ ♬ ▪

Min£55 Max£80pw

C **Great Howle Farm Cottage** Howle Hill
for bookings Heart of England Cottages, Buckland, Broadway, Worcester WR12 7LY
☎Broadway(0386)853593

The cottage is attached to the farm buildings and comprises of hall, bathroom/WC, kitchen, living/dining room, one double bedroom, one twin and one single bedroom. All on the ground floor.

All year MWB out of season 3days min, 6mths max, 1unit, 1–5persons ◎ fridge Electric Elec inclusive ⊡can be hired (overseas visitors only) ☎ Iron in unit Ironing board in unit HCE in unit ⊙ CTV ⊕3pin square 4P ▥ ⛫(3m)

⊖ ♀(½m) ▨(3m) ♬(3m) ▪(3m)

Max£110pw (High)

C **Hildersley Farm Cottage**
for bookings Mrs D Boynton, Hildersley Farm, Ross-on-Wye, Herefordshire HR9 7NW
☎Ross-on-Wye(0989)62095

A low, single-storey cottage of stone and tile behind the main farmhouse. The farm is situated on the A40 Gloucester – Ross-on-Wye road. Smaller than average, the accommodation consists of a kitchen, utility room, lounge/dining room, two bedrooms (the double room can only be reached by passing through the twin-bedded room), and bathroom/WC.

All year MWB out of season 3days min, 4wks max, 1unit, 1–4persons ◈ no pets ◐ fridge Electric & coal fires Gas/Elec metered ⊡not provided ☎(½m) HCE in unit ⊕3pin square 2P ▥ ⛫(1m)

⊖ ♀(1m) ▨(1m) ♬(1m) ▪(1m)

Min£40 Max£46pw

C **Howle Green Lodge** Howle Hill
for bookings Heart of England Cottages, Buckland, Broadway, Worcester WR12 7LY
☎Broadway(0386)853593

Modernised semi-detached stone cottage, situated 680ft above sea level and offering excellent views across the surrounding countryside. The accommodation comprises a ground floor with entrance hall, cloakroom/WC, large kitchen, laundry room, bathroom with WC and shower, dining room and large lounge with divan bed. Upstairs there are three bedrooms, two double, one with bathroom en suite, and one with twin beds, sun lounge with divan bed and a bathroom/WC. Dishwasher & freezer.

All year MWB out of season 3days min, 6mths max, 1unit, 1–8persons ◎ fridge Electric Elec inclusive ⊡can be hired (overseas visitors only) ☎ WM in unit SD in unit Airing cupboard in unit Iron in unit Ironing board in unit HCE in unit ⊙ CTV ⊕3pin square 5P ▥ ⛫(¾m)

⊖ ♀(¾m) ▨(3m) ♬(3m) ▪(3m)

Max£235pw

H Ms H Smith **Old Kilns** Howle Hill, Ross-on-Wye, Herefordshire HR9 5SP
☎Ross-on-Wye(0989)62051

The accommodation is located in one half of a neat, cement rendered house and consists of three double bedrooms, WC, lounge with convertible settee, kitchen/diner, and bathroom. Second WC and washroom upstairs. The rooms are large and the furnishings are new. Very nice accommodation. It is situated some 2m W of Ross-on-Wye near the Crown public house and opposite the tiny village church.

All year MWB 1night min, 1unit, 8persons [◇ ◈] ◆ ◎ fridge Electric Elec metered ⊡can be hired ☎ [SD on premises] [TD on premises] Airing cupboard in unit Iron in unit Ironing board in unit HCE in unit ⊙ ⊛ CTV ⊕3pin square P ▥ ⛫(1½m)

⊖ ♀(200yds) ♬(2m) ▪

C **Vine Cottage** Church Street
for bookings Mrs D Y Watson, 15a Alton Street, Ross-on-Wye, Herefordshire
☎Ross-on-Wye(0989)62302

Formerly an old stable, this recently-redesigned cottage in the centre of the town has been completely modernised and is well-furnished and fully carpeted. The ground-floor comprises lounge, bathroom/WC, dining room, kitchen and open staircase leading to a twin-bedded room and a single room with wash basin.

All year 1wk min, 3mths max, 1unit, 1–5persons ◈ ◐ fridge ⊞ Gas/Elec metered ⊡can be hired(overseas visitors only) ☎(200yds) Airing cupboard in unit Iron in unit Ironing board in unit HCE in unit [Launderette within 300yds] ⊙ TV ⊕3pin square 4P ⛫(50yds)

⊖ ♀(½m) ▨(½m) ♬(½m) ▪(½m)

C **The Vineyard** Howle Hill (2m S)
for bookings Heart of England Country Cottages, Buckland, Broadway, Worcestershire
☎Broadway(0386)853593

The cottage is an old farmhouse converted throughout. Good views of the surrounding countryside. Downstairs is a large kitchen, cloakroom/WC, dining room, sitting room, sun lounge and bathroom with WC. On the first-floor there is one room with a double and two single beds, and the second bedroom has twin beds. Each has a dressing room and fitted wardrobes.

All year MWB out of season 3days min, 6mths max, 1unit, 1–6persons ◎ fridge Electric Elec inclusive ⊡can be hired(overseas visitors only) ☎ Airing cupboard in unit Iron in unit Ironing board in unit HCE in unit ⊙ CTV ⊕3pin square 4P 1⌂ ▥ ⛫(½m)

⊖ ♀(½m) ▨(3m) ♬3m) ▪(3m)

Max£175pw

ROTHESAY Isle of Bute,
Strathclyde *Bute*
Map**10** NS06

F Mrs J McIntosh **Beechwood Holiday Flats** 11 Bishop Terrace, Rothesay, Bute PA20 9HF
☎Rothesay(0700)3999

Flats in a two-storey stone-built house on a cliff top overlooking the harbour, pier and town. The units vary in size, the largest sleeping a maximum of six

people, with toilet facilities shared by tenants on each floor.

All year MWB out of season 2 days min, 9 units, 1–6 persons [◊] [◆] [♦] no pets ◔ ◑ fridge Electric or gas Gas/Elec metered ⌷ can be hired ☎ Iron on premises Ironing board on premises HCE on premises TV ⊕3 pin square ⊕2 pin round P ▥ ♒(½m) ⌷ ↝Hard

↤ ≈ ♀(½m) ⊠(½m) ☏(½m)

Min£30 Max£80pw (Low)
Min£40 Max£120pw (High)

ROY BRIDGE
Highland *Inverness-shire*
Map **14** NN28

Ch Mr W A McCallum **Bunroy Holiday Chalets** Roy Bridge, Inverness-shire PH31 4AG
☎Spean Bridge(039 781)332

Secluded and well laid out site of mainly level grass and birch trees. The A-frame, detached timber chalets are very compact with effective décor and fittings. Views over grassland to River Spean and the Nevis range of mountains with Ben Nevis just screened by Aonach Mhor.

Apr–midOct MWB out of season 1 wk min, 1 mth max, 8 units, 2–4 persons ◔ fridge Electric Elec metered ⌷not provided ☎(400yds) HCE in unit ⊕ TV can be hired ⊕3 pin square P ▥ ♒(600yds) Trout fishing

↤ ♀(500yds) ⊠(500yds)

Min£50 Max£80pw

RUDYARD
Staffordshire
Map **7** SJ95

C **Reacliffe Cottage**
for bookings Mrs C J Gee, Reacliffe Farm, Rudyard, Leek, Staffordshire
☎Rudyard(053 833)276

A self-contained two-storey unit adjoining the proprietor's stone-built farmhouse. In a rural setting approx 1m from Rudyard. It comprises one family bedroom, one double room, lounge with convertible settee, kitchen/diner and a modern bathroom/WC.

May–Sep MWB 1 wk min, 1 unit, 6 persons ◊ ◆ ◑ fridge ♨&Elec fires Gas/Elec metered ⌷ can be hired ☎(1m) Iron in unit Ironing board in unit HCE in unit ⊕ TV ⊕3 pin square P ▥ ♒(1m)

↤ ♀(1m) ⊠(1m) ☏(1m) ☏(3m)

Min£60 Max£65pw (Low)
Max£80pw (High)

RUMFORD
Cornwall
Map **2** SW87

C Mr A R Horwood **St Ervan Country House** St Ervan, Rumford, Wadebridge, Cornwall PL27 7TA
☎Rumford(084 14)255

Rothesay
—
St Andrews

*A former rectory situated in four acres. The cottages arranged around the courtyard once served the rectory as Coach House, Stables and Bakery and have been converted into luxurious self-catering cottages. **Coach House, Stable and Cloam Cottages** each consist of one double-bedded room, one twin and one double bed-settee in the lounge, separate fitted kitchen and modern bathroom/WC. The **Coach** and **Stable** are situated on two floors, whereas **Cloam Cottage** is a ground-floor residence. Use of adjoining hotel facilities including lounge bar and games room.*

Mar–Dec MWB out of season 1 wk min, 1 mth max, 3 units, 1–6 persons ◊ ◆ ◑ fridge Electric Elec metered ⌷ can be hired ☎ Airing cupboard in unit Iron on premises Ironing board on premises HCE in unit [Launderette on premises] ⊕ CTV ⊕3 pin square 2P ▥ ♒(½m)

↤ ≈(3m) ♀ ⊠(3m) ☏(3m)

Min£55 Max£100pw (Low)
Min£160 Max£175pw (High)

RYDE
Isle of Wight
Map **4** SZ59

F Mr R W J Cawdell **Eastfield House** 33 Dover Street, Ryde, Isle of Wight
☎Ryde(0983)883629 & 63594

A large Victorian house on three floors, with distant views of the sea, converted into eight flats, four of which are for letting. All flats are spacious, three have one double bedroom, lounge with kitchen in corner. The other flat has two bedrooms and separate kitchen. Convertible settees are available.

All year MWB out of season 1 wk min, 1 mth max, 4 units, 2–7 persons ◊ no pets ◔ fridge 2 Gas, 2 Electric Elec inclusive Gas metered ⌷inlusive ☎ Iron on premises HCE in unit [Launderette within 200yds] TV ⊕3 pin square P ▥ ♒(200yds) ⌐

↤ ♀(200yds ⊠(½m) ☏(½m) ☏(½m)

Min£70 Max£150pw (Low)
Min£75 Max£160pw (High)

C, F Mrs M Hines **Solent House** Playstreet Lane, Ryde, Isle of Wight PO33 3LJ
☎Ryde(0983)64133

Two self-contained flats within a two-storey Victorian stately home, and one modernised cottage, set in three acres of secluded grounds. Well appointed units with spacious comfortable rooms. They are either two or three bedroomed.

    1982 prices quoted throughout
    gazetteer

All year 1 wk min (2 wks min, Jul&Aug), 6 mths max, 3 units, 2–8 persons ◆ no pets ◑ fridge Electric Elec metered ⌷not provided ☎(1m) [WM on premises] [SD on premises] Airing cupboard in unit Iron in unit Ironing board in unit HCE in unit ⊕ CTV ⊕3 pin square P ▥ ♒(400yds)

↤ ♀(½m) ⊠(1m) ☏(1m) ☏(1m)

£90pw

SAGESTON
Dyfed
Map **2** SN00

H **Ashleigh House**
for bookings Powell's Holidays, High Street, Saundersfoot, Dyfed
☎Saundersfoot(0834)812791

This is a large detached stone house with five bedrooms, a lounge, separate dining room, breakfast room and kitchen. A child's bed is also available.

May–Sep MWB out of season 1 wk min, 2 wk max, 1 unit, 2–11 persons ◊ ◑ fridge Electric Elec inclusive ⌷not provided ☎ Airing cupboard in unit Iron in unit Ironing board in unit HCE in unit ⊕ CTV ⊕3 pin square P ▥ ♒(1m)

↤ ♀(50yds) ⊠(3m) ☏(3m)

Min£69 Max£195pw

ST AGNES
Cornwall
Map **2** SW75

C **Trevenys**
for bookings A S D & J A Hedges, Westwards, Bickwell Valley, Sidmouth, Devon
☎Sidmouth(03955)6176

A traditional detached olde worlde thatched cottage with a large garden situated on the St Agnes – Perranporth coast road. Accommodation comprises beamed lounge with fireplace, study/bedroom, large farmhouse style kitchen/diner, one double and one twin-bedded room, bathroom/WC.

All year MWB out of season 1 wk min, 6 mths max, 1 unit, 2–6 persons [◊] ◆ ◑ fridge ♨ Elec inclusive ⌷ can be hired ☎ WM in unit SD in unit Airing cupboard in unit Iron in unit Ironing board in unit HCE in unit ⊕ CTV ⊕3 pin square 2P 1◭ ▥ ♒(½m)

↤ ≈(3m) ♀(1m) ⊠(1m) ☏(1m) ☏(1m)

Min£75 Max£130pw (Low)
Min£165 Max£225pw (High)

ST ANDREWS
Fife *Fife*
Map **12** NO51

F **Albany Park** St Mary's St
for bookings The Bursar of Residences, College Gate, St Andrews, Fife KY16 9AJ
☎St Andrews(0334)76161(Ext547)

A student housing complex by the shore, south of the harbour. The 44 units are →

in blocks of 4–8 and consist of a kitchen/dinette, six single rooms, WC, lounge and shower/WC. Recently built and well maintained, they are ideal for families and sailing enthusiasts because of their position.

27Jun-23Sep 1wkmin, 3mths max, 44units, 1–6persons no pets ⊚ fridge ♨ Elecmetered(hot water free) Ⓛinclusive ☎(100yds) Iron in unit Ironing board in unit HCE in unit [Launderette within 300yds] ⊕ TV can be hired ⊕3pin square 100P ▥ ⚏(200yds)

Min£70 Max£85pw (Low)
Min£120pw (High)

H Fife Park Strathkinnes High Road for bookings The Bursar of Residences, College Gate, St Andrews, Fife KY169AJ
☎St Andrews(0334)76161(Ext547)

Student accommodation in a pleasant, quiet area at the west end of town. There are 42 units. The two-storey houses each consists of six single bedrooms and a kitchen/dining area. Double beds can be arranged. No lounge.

27Jun-23Sep 1wkmin, 3mths max, 42units, 1–6persons no pets ⊚ fridge Electric Elecmetered (except hot water) Ⓛinclusive ☎(100yds) Iron in unit Ironing board in unit HCE in unit [Launderette within 300yds] TV ⊕3pin square 100P ▥ ⚏(1m)

⊖ ⚲(1½m) ▣(1½m) ♫(1½m) ⚼(1½m)

Min£65 Max£80pw (Low)
Min£110pw (High)

Ca Kincaple House St Andrews, Fife KY169SH
☎Strathkinness(033485)217 & 511

Nine log cabins with two twin-bedded rooms with washbasins, modern living area with kitchen, and bathroom. Set in the landscaped grounds of the 18th-century Kincaple House which offers outdoor pool, tennis, croquet, picture gallery and fine views over the Eden Estuary, 3m NW of St Andrews ½m off A91.

All year MWB 2nights min, 9units, 2–5persons ◇ no pets ⊚ fridge Electric Elecinclusive Ⓛinclusive ☎(100yds) Airing cupboard in unit

Iron in unit Ironing board in unit HCE in unit (Launderette on premises] ⊕ TV ⊕3pin square P ▥ ⚏(1m) ⌐ ⇘Hard

⊖ ⚎(2½m) ⚲(2½m) ♫(2½m) ⚼(2½m)

F 133 South Street for bookings Mrs S D Room, Woodriffe, 44 Buchanan Gardens, St Andrews, Fife KY169LX
☎St Andrews(0334)72253

Four flats located in one of the main shopping streets. Three flats sleeping two to four persons in one double-bedded room and one twin-bedded room, lounge/dining area, modern kitchen and bathroom. The one remaining flat sleeps two to six persons in one double and two twin-bedded rooms also with lounge/dining area, modern kitchen and bathroom.

18Jun-Sep 1wkmin, 3wks max, 4units, 2–6persons ◇ ◈ ◆ no pets ⊚ fridge Electric Elecinclusive Ⓛnotprovided ☎ WM on premises TD on premises Airing cupboard in unit Iron in unit Ironing board in unit HCE in unit [Launderette within 800yds] ⊕ CTV ⊕3pin square ⚏

⊖ ⚎(½m) ⚲(100yds) ▣(½m) ♫(100yds) ⚼(400yds)

Min£80 Max£135pw

ST ANTHONY IN ROSELAND
Cornwall
Map2 SW83

C Cellars Cottage Place Estate for bookings Mr Grant Dalton, Place Manor Hotel, St-Anthony-in-Roseland, Portscatho, Truro, Cornwall
☎Portscatho(087258)447

Stone-built cottage of character in a secluded position on the edge of a sandy beach, opposite the famous fishing village of St Mawes. Accommodation consists of four bedrooms, all of which have sea views a pine-panelled sitting room with log fire, and two bathrooms.

Mar-Oct MWB out of season 1wk min, 1unit, 8persons ◇ ◆ ◁ fridge ♨ Gas/Elecinclusive Ⓛinclusive ☎(½m) Airing cupboard in unit Iron in unit Ironing board in unit HCE in unit ⊕ TV ⊕3pin square 4P ⚏(½m)

⊖ ⚲(½m) ▣(½m) ⚼(½m)

Min£225 Max£490pw

ST AUSTELL
Cornwall
Map2 SX05

B, C & Ch Mr & Mrs A A Milln **Bosinver Farm & Holiday Centre** St Austell, Cornwall
☎St Austell(0726)2128

A well screened complex of seven chalets, three cottages and seven bungalows set in thirty acres of wooded meadowland. All units are comfortable and well equipped; the number of persons accommodated in each unit is dependent on which type of accommodation is selected. For further information contact booking address.

All year (3 units) Apr–Oct(14units) MWB out of season 1wk min, 17units, 2–7persons [◇] [◆] ⊚ fridge Electric & solid fuel Elecmetered Ⓛcan be hired ☎(½m) [WM TD] Airing cupboard in unit Iron on premises Ironing board on premises HCE in unit [Launderette on premises] ⊕ CTV ⊕3pin square P ▥ ⚏(½m) ⌐ ⇘ δ Children's play area, sauna & solarium

⊖ ⚎(½m) ⚲(1m) ▣(1½m) ⚼(1½m)

Min£23 Max£65pw (Low)
Min£60 Max£170pw (High)

Ch Duporth Bookings Manager **Duporth Holiday Resort** PO Box 8, St Austell Bay, Cornwall PL266AJ
☎St Austell(0726)65551

Duporth Holiday Resort has many amenities and lively entertainments. The 100 self-catering suites, or similar types, are in two-storey buildings of modern style. Accommodation consists of lounge/kitchenette with convertible bed, bathroom/WC and one or two bedrooms.

14May–23Sep MWB out of season
3days min, 3wks max, 100units
1–6persons ◇ [◇ ◆] no pets ◎
fridge Electric Elec metered ⌂ can be
hired ☎ [Iron on premises] [Ironing
board on premises] HCE in unit
[Launderette on premises] ⊙ TV can
be hired ⊕3pin square 40P ⊞ ♨
⌱ ⚲Hard Crazy Golf

⊖ ♒(1m) ♀ ⧈ ♫

Min£77 Max£117pw (Low)
Min£201 Max£267pw (High)

ST BREWARD
Cornwall
Map2 SX17

F Glenview Flats 1–5
for bookings S A McLeod, Dunvegan
Holidays, Ryland, St Breward, Bodmin,
Cornwall
☎Bodmin(0208)850528

*Five flats in a converted old house with
fine views across Bodmin Moor. Two split
level flats, one comprising kitchen/diner,
lounge one double and one twin
bedroom, bathroom with WC, the other is
on two floors with bathroom and WC,
open plan lounge/kitchen/diner and
double bedroom. Two further flats one
with lounge, kitchen/diner, one double
and one three-bedded room, bathroom
and WC, other flat sleeps up to six
persons. Also an attic flat comprising
lounge, kitchen/diner, one single, one
double and one three-bedded room, plus
bathroom and WC.*

All year MWB out of season 3days min,
3mths max, 5units, 1–6persons [◇]
◆ ◆ ◎ fridge Electric
Elec metered ⌂ not provided
☎(100yds) [WM on premises] [SD on
premises] [TD on premises] Airing
cupboard in unit Iron on premises
Ironing board on premises HCE on
premises ⊙ TV ⊕3pin square P ⊞
♨(100yds)

⊖ ♀(1m)

Min£35 Max£135pw

C Jingles, Snappers & Linney
for bookings Mr & Mrs Hall, Penrose
Burden, St Breward, Cornwall PL30 4LZ
☎Bodmin(0208)850277

*Three traditional single level cottages,
renovated to a very high standard,
comprising open plan lounge,
kitchen/diner, bathroom with WC, two
double bedrooms, nicely furnished and
decorated. Suitable for the disabled.*

All year 1wk min, 3units, 1–5persons
[◇] ◆ ◆ ◎ fridge Wood burning
stove & electric Elec metered
⌂inclusive (except towels) ☎(1m)
Airing cupboard in unit Iron in unit
Ironing board in unit HCE in unit ⊙
CTV ⊕3pin square 6P ⊞ ♨(1m)
Barbeque in each unit, private fishing

⊖ ♀(1m)

Min£60 Max£185pw

1982 prices quoted throughout
gazetteer

C 2 & 3 Mount Pleasant
for bookings S A McLeod, Dunvegan
Holidays, Ryland, St Breward, Bodmin,
Cornwall
☎Bodmin(0208)850528

*Two adjacent cottages close to centre of
small village on Bodmin Moor. Pleasantly
furnished, each comprising open plan
lounge/kitchen/diner with open fire, one
double bedroom, bathroom and WC.*

All year MWB out of season 3days min,
3mths max, 2units, 1–2persons [◇]
◆ ◆ ◎ fridge Electric & open fire
Elec metered ⌂ not provided
☎(150yds) [WM on premises] [SD on
premises] [TD on premises] Airing
cupboard in unit Iron in unit Ironing
board in unit HCE in unit ⊙ TV
⊕3pin square P ⊞ ♨(150yds)

⊖ ♀(1m)

Min£35 Max£80pw

ST CLETHER
Cornwall
Map2 SX28

Ch Blue Moor, Dogwood, Tor Grass & Woodrush
for bookings Mr G W Pope, Ta Mill
Holidays, St Clether, Launceston,
Cornwall PL15 8PS
☎Otterham Station(084 06)381

*Four attractive wooden chalets in quiet
isolated spot, with good views.
Accommodation consists of a large
lounge/kitchen/diner with double sofa
bed, one double bedroom, one with
bunks and bathroom/WC.*

Mar–Oct MWB out of season
3days min, 8mths max, 4units,
1–4persons ◆ ◆ ◎ fridge
Electric Elec metered ⌂ not provided
☎ Airing cupboard in unit Iron on
premises Ironing board on premises
HCE in unit ⊙ TV ⊕3pin square P
⊞ ♨ Fishing

⊖ ♀

Min£55 Max£162pw

C Forge, Millers, Pump & Watermill Cottages
for bookings Mr G W Pope, Ta Mill
Holidays, St Clether, Launceston,
Cornwall PL15 8PS
☎Otterham Station(084 06)381

*Four tastefully converted stone farm
buildings in peaceful west country
setting. Forge and Watermill Cottages
offer one double and two twin bedrooms,
Pump Cottage has one double and one
twin bedroom, and Millers Cottage
comprises of one double room. All are
furnished pleasantly throughout.*

All year MWB out of season 3days min,
8mths max, 4units, 1–6persons ◆ ◆
◎ fridge Electric Elec metered ☎
Airing cupboard in unit Iron on
premises Ironing board on premises
HCE in unit ⊙ TV ⊕3pin square P

⊞ ♨ Trout Lake, fishing

⊖ ♀

Min£50 Max£55pw (Low)
Min£136 Max£202pw (High)

ST DAVIDS
Dyfed
Map2 SM72

F St Davids Apartments Flats 1, 2, 3, 10, 11 & 12
for bookings G & D Lloyd, Warpool Court
Hotel, St Davids, Dyfed
☎St Davids(0437)720300

*Twelve well-maintained luxury
apartments on two levels each reached
from first floor balcony, which overlooks a
courtyard. Six are open plan, the others
comprise kitchen/diner, lounge with
convertible divans on first floor and a
twin-bedded room, one double bedroom
and bathroom on second floor.
Attractively furnished.*

All year 2days min, 12units,
2–6persons [◇] ◆ ◆ ◎ fridge
⋈ Elec metered ⌂inclusive ☎ WM
in unit SD in unit TD in unit Iron in unit
Ironing board in unit HCE in unit ⊙
CTV ⊕3pin square 14P Free use of
swimming pool at Warpool Hotel

⊖ ♒ ♀(¼m)

Min£55 Max£95pw (Low)
Min£125 Max£220pw (High)

ST ERTH
Cornwall
Map2 SW53

C 14 Chenhalls Close
for bookings Mr & Mrs G N Broughton,
Orchard House, 26 Wall Road, Gwinear,
Hayle, Cornwall TR27 5HA
☎Leedstown(073685)201

*Modern terraced cottage on a small
private site in a rural and isolated
position. It is well appointed and
furnished comprising one double
bedded room on the ground floor and
one twin bedded, one bunk bedded on
the first floor. There is a spacious lounge,
kitchen/diner and bathroom/WC. Quality
furnishings and décor.*

All year MWB 1wk min, 1unit,
6persons ◆ ◆ ◎ fridge Electric
Elec inclusive ⌂can be hired ☎(1m)
Airing cupboard in unit Iron in unit
Ironing board in unit HCE in unit ⊙
TV ⊕3pin square 1P 1♨ ⊞ ♨(1m)

⊖ ♀(2m)

ST FLORENCE
Dyfed
Map2 SN00

H The Ark
for bookings Powell's Holidays, High
Street, Saundersfoot, Dyfed
☎Saundersfoot(0834)812791

*Brick built corner house with open plan
lounge/diner, separate kitchen,
bathroom/WC, one double, one single,
one twin-bedded room, and another
room with a double bed.* →

May–Oct MWB out of season 1wk min,
1unit, 7persons ◊ ◉ fridge
Electric Elec inclusive ⬛not provided
☎(½m) Airing cupboard in unit Iron in
unit Ironing board in unit HCE in unit
TV ⊕3pin square P 🅿 ♨(10yds)
⇔ ♀(10yds)

Min£63 Max£168pw

C, H Court Vale & Court Vale Cottage
for bookings Powell's Holidays, High
Street, Saundersfoot, Dyfed
☎Saundersfoot(0834)812791

One house and one cottage adjoining
each other set in the centre of the village.
The converted malthouse has a
lounge/diner, kitchen, and four
bedrooms sleeping up to eight people.
The stone-built cottage has an open-plan
lounge/kitchen/diner and two bedrooms
accommodating four persons.

May–Oct MWB out of season 1wk min,
2units, 4–8persons [◇] ◊ no pets
◉ fridge Electric, gas or coal fires
Elec inclusive ⬛not provided ☎
Airing cupboard in unit Iron in unit
Ironing board in unit HCE in unit ⊖
CTV ⊕3pin square P 🅿 ♨(10yds)
⇔ ♨(3m) 𝄞(3m) 🎿(3m)

Min£48 Max£174pw

C Ranch Cottage East Tarr Farm
for bookings Powell's Holidays, High
Street, Saundersfoot, Dyfed
☎Saundersfoot(0834)812791

Detached stone-built cottage in the
grounds of a riding school, comprising
lounge/diner with kitchen area, bath/WC
and sleeping accommodation for five.

Apr–Sep MWB out of season 1wk min,
4wks max, 1unit, 2–5persons [◇] ◊
♦ ◉ fridge Electric Elec metered
⬛can be hired ☎(50yds) Airing
cupboard in unit Iron in unit Ironing
board in unit HCE in unit ⊖ TV
⊕3pin square P ♨(½m)
⇔ ♨(2½m) ♀(½m) 🅿(2½m) 𝄞(2½m)
🎿(2½m)

Min£57 Max£150pw

ST GENNYS
Cornwall
Map2 SX19

Ca Mineshop Bungalows
for bookings Mr & Mrs A Cummins,
Mineshop Holiday Cottages, Mineshop,
St Gennys, Bude, Cornwall EX23 0NR
☎St Gennys(084 03)338

Canadian cedar-wood cabins situated in
a peaceful wooded valley 1½m E of
Crackington Haven by road and 1m by
footpath. They have open-plan living
rooms with wall beds, one twin bedroom
and one with two bunk beds, kitchenette,
bathroom and WC. The furnishings are
modern and comfortable and the décor
of good standard.

Mar–Oct MWB out of season
7days min, 6units, 1–6persons ◊ ◉
fridge Electric Elec metered ⬛can be
hired Airing cupboard in unit Iron on

St Florence
—
St Ives

premises Ironing board on premises
HCE in unit TV ⊕3pin square P 🅿
♨(1½m)
⇔ ♀(1½m)

Min£36.80 Max£52.90pw (Low)
Min£80.50 Max£120.75pw (High)

C Old Shippon
for bookings Mr & Mrs A Cummins,
Mineshop Holiday Cottages, Mineshop,
St Gennys, Bude, Cornwall EX23 0NR
☎St Gennys(084 03)338

Part white-washed one-storey cottage
overlooking a stream and woodland in a
peaceful valley. The accommodation
comprises one double and two twin
bedrooms, open-plan living area with
bed-settee, kitchenette, bathroom and
WC. French door leads to a stone-paved
patio.

All year MWB out of season 7days min,
1unit, 1–8persons ◊ fridge Electric
Elec metered ⬛can be hired Airing
cupboard in unit Iron on premises
Ironing board on premises HCE in unit
TV ⊕3pin square P 🅿 ♨(1½m)
⇔ ♀(1½m)

Min£50.60 Max£64.40pw (Low)
Min£75.90 Max£141.45pw (High)

C Old Smithy
for bookings Mr & Mrs A Cummins,
Mineshop Holiday Cottages, Mineshop,
St Gennys, Bude, Cornwall EX23 0NR
☎St Gennys(084 03)338

One-storey cottage converted from the
old blacksmith's shop standing on the
banks of a stream, in a peaceful wooded
valley. Accommodation consists of one
double bedroom and one with two bunk
beds, open-plan living area with studio
couch, kitchenette, bathroom and WC. A
patio paved in traditonal 'blue' Cornish
slate, and private lawn with the original
blacksmith's granite water trough still in
place are addtional features.

All year MWB out of season 7days min,
1unit, 1–6persons ◊ ◉ fridge
Electric Elec metered ◊ ⬛can be hired
Airing cupboard in unit Iron on
premises Ironing board on premises
HCE in unit TV ⊕3pin square P 🅿
♨(1½m)
⇔ ♀(1½m)

Min£47.15 Max£67.85pw (Low)
Min£95.45 Max£141.45pw (High)

ST ISHMAEL (Nr Kidwelly)
Dyfed
Map2 SN41

Ch Carmarthen Bay Holiday Village
Kidwelly, Dyfed
☎Ferryside(026 785)511

Chalets situated in a natural dune area
and comprising three bedrooms (one
double, one twin and one single), large
lounge with open dining and kitchen
area. Furnished and decorated to a high

standard. Wide variety of sporting
facilities and entertainments available.
Prices vary according to type of
accommodation.

29May–25Sep MWB 154units,
2–6persons [◊] [♦] ◉ fridge
Electric Elec metered ⬛inclusive ☎
Airing cupboard in unit [Iron on
premises] [Ironing board on premises]
HCE in unit [Launderette on premises]
⊖ TV ⊕3pin square P 🅿 ⌒
Fishing and boat hire
⇔ ♀ 🎨
Min£31 Max£180pw

ST IVES
Cornwall
Map2 SW54

Ch Ayr Holiday Park
for bookings Mr R D Baragwanath, Ayr
Holiday Park, St Ives, Cornwall TR26 1EJ
☎Penzance(0736)795855

There are 16 units, each accommodating
4–6persons. Twelve are compact
Western Red Cedar timber chalets with a
lounge, kitchen, two bedrooms,
bathroom and a separate WC. The
remainder are traditionally-built, single-
storey holiday homes giving extra
comfort and space, with a sitting room,
kitchen, two bedrooms and a bathroom.
The location gives magnificent views
over Porthmeor Beach and the North
Cornish coastline. Three sandy beaches,
the harbour and the town are all within 1m
of the Park.

Apr-Oct MWB 1wk min, 16units,
4–6persons ◊ ◉ fridge Electric
Elec inclusive ⬛not provided
☎(on site) [Iron] HCE [Launderette
on premises] ⊖ TV ⊕3pin square
P 🅿
⇔ ♀(½m) 🎨(½m) 𝄞(½m) 🎿(½m)
Min£50 Max£69pw (Low)   •
Min£155 Max£240pw (High)

F Mr & Mrs Blackburn Berachah
Holiday Flats Wheal Whidden, Carbis
Bay, St Ives, Cornwall TR26 2QX
☎Penzance(0736)795966

Two holiday flats situated in one wing of
the owner's house. Magnificent views
through garden of sea and coastline.
Flat A comprises lounge, dining room,
kitchen, one double and one single
bedroom, separate shower room and WC
on first-floor. Flat B is on ground-floor
comprising lounge, kitchen, one double
and twin bedroom, bathroom with WC.
Access to Carbis Bay Beach through
Carbis Valley.

All year MWB out of season 1wk min,
2mths max, 2units, 1–5persons ◊
no pets ◉ fridge Electric
Elec metered ⬛not provided ☎
Airing cupboard in unit Iron in unit
Ironing board on premises HCE in unit
⊖ CTV ⊕3pin square 1P 🅿
♨(200yds)

```
1982 prices quoted throughout
gazetteer
```

⊖ ⌂(1m) ☎(1m) ⌷(½m) ♫(1m)
🏠(1½m)

Min£55 Max£88pw (Low)
Min£90 Max£135pw (High)

C Carnstabba Holiday Cottages
Carnstabba Farm, Steeple Lane
for bookings Mr & Mrs Blackburn,
Berachah, Wheal Whidden, Carbis Bay,
St Ives, Cornwall TR26 2QX
☎Penzance(0736)795966

*Four recently constructed cottages in
rural surroundings just outside St Ives.
Accommodation consists of lounge, two
bedrooms, kitchen, bathroom and WC.
Elevated position overlooking St Ives and
Carbis Bay.*

Mar-Oct MWB out of season 1wk min,
2mths max, 4units, 1–6persons ◆
no pets ◉ fridge Electric
Elec metered ⌷not provided
☎(20yds) Airing cupboard in unit
CTV ⊕3pin square P ⊞ ⌂(½m)

⊖ ⌂(2m) ☎ ⌷(½m) ♫(½m) 🏠(½m)

Min£55 Max£85pw (Low)
Min£90 Max£135pw (High)

B Mr & Mrs Williams **Casa Bella
Holiday Apartments** Hain Walk, St Ives,
Cornwall
☎Penzance(0736)795427

*Modern house situated in a commanding
position overlooking St Ives Bay. Two-
bedroomed (one double, one twin-
bedded room which has separate area
with bunk beds), lounge, kitchen/dining
room, bathroom/WC. Private patio with
sun beds. Adjacent to B3306 Carbis Bay
to St Ives road approx ½m from town
centre.*

All year 3mths max, 1unit, 1–6persons
◆ ◉ fridge Electric Elec metered
⌷inclusive ☎(200yds) Airing
cupboard in unit Iron in unit Ironing
board in unit HCE in unit ⊕ TV
⊕3pin square P ⊞ ⌂(250yds)

⊖ ⌂(2m) ⌷(½m) ♫(½m) 🏠(½m)

F Mr A Luke **Cheriton House** Market
Place, St Ives, Cornwall TR26 1RZ
☎Penzance(0736)795083

*Situated in town centre within half a
minute's walk of harbour and beaches
these seven self-contained units are*

*neatly furnished and well decorated
throughout. All flats have bath or shower,
and kitchen/dinette, some have lounges.*

Mar-Nov MWB out of season 1wk min,
3wks max, 6units, 4persons [◇] [◆]
◉ fridge Electric Elec metered
⌷can be hired ☎(50yds) Iron HCE in
unit [Launderette within 300yds] ⊕
[◉] TV ⊕3pin square P ⊞ ⌂
↪Hard/Grass ♪

⊖ ☎(100yds) ⌷(100yds)
♫(100yds) 🏠(100yds)

Min£40 Max£70pw (Low)
Min£90 Max£150pw (High)

H Hayeswood & Rocky Close Higher
Ayr
for bookings Mr R D Baragwanath, Ayr
Holiday Park, St Ives, Cornwall TR26 1EJ
☎Penzance(0736)795855

*Two houses of individual character, each
standing in own grounds of ¾ acre with
views of St Ives and Porthmeor Beach.
Hayeswood is somewhat more spacious
then Rocky Close and each enjoys
private, quiet surroundings. Lots of
character; comfortable furnishings.*

All year MWB out of season 1wk min,
2units, 8persons no pets ◉ fridge
Electric Elec metered ⌷inclusive
Airing cupboard in unit Iron in unit
Ironing board in unit HCE in unit
[Launderette on premises] ⊕ TV
⊕3pin square P ⌂

⊖ ☎(1m) ⌷(1m) ♫(1m) 🏠(1m)

Min£85 Max£150pw (Low)
Min£250 Max£280pw (High)

H 2 & 3 Higher Boskerris Carbis Bay
for bookings F W Smith, Lamorna, St Ives
Road, Carbis Bay, St Ives, Cornwall
☎Penzance(0736)797229

*Two terraced properties both comprising
one double, one twin and one bunk-
bedded room, dining room, kitchen
breakfast bar, bathroom and WC. Good
stanadard of décor and equipped with
modern furnishings. 50yds off St Ives
road (A3074) SW of Carbis Bay. High
chair provided in No2.*

All year MWB out of season 1wk min,
3mths max, 2units, 1–6persons ◇ ◆
no pets ◉ fridge Electric
Elec metered ⌷not provided
☎(50yds) Airing cupboard in unit
Iron in unit Ironing board in unit HCE in
unit [Launderette within 300yds] ⊕
CTV ⊕3pin square P ⊞ ⊞
⌂(200yds)

⊖ ⌂(½m) ☎(100yds) ⌷(200yds)
♫(200yds) 🏠(2m)

Min£40 Max£70pw (Low)
Min£80 Max£140pw (High)

B Holiday Bungalows Polwithen
Drive, Carbis Bay
for bookings Mr & Mrs Blackburn
Berachah, Wheal Whidden, Carbis Bay,
St Ives, Cornwall TR26 2QX
☎Penzance(0736)795966

*Three modern bungalows situated at
Carbis Bay approx 1½m from St Ives.
Each bungalow has lounge/dining area
(with studio couch), two double
bedrooms (one with addtional single
bed), kitchen, bathroom and WC.*

Mar-Oct MWB out of season 1wk min,
2mths max, 3units, 1–5persons ◆
no pets ◉ fridge Electric
Elec metered ⌷not provided ☎(1m)
Airing cupboard in unit Iron in unit
Ironing board in unit HCE in unit ⊕
CTV ⊕3pin square P ⌂(½m)

⊖ ⌂(1m) ⌷(1m) ♫(1m) 🏠(1m)

Min£55 Max£85pw (Low)
Min£90 Max£135pw (High)

F Palm Court, Chyangweal
for bookings F W Smith, Lamorna, St Ives
Road, Carbis Bay, St Ives, Cornwall
☎Penzance(0736)797229

*Two-storey semi-detached cottage flats
(c1750). Comprises two bedrooms,
lounge/dining room, kitchen, and
bathroom/WC. Cottage-style interior and
older furnishings but comforortable.
Situated on the St Ives road (A3074)
approx 1m from St Ives and overlooking
Carbis Bay.*

All year MWB out of season 1wk min,
1mth max, 2units, 1–6persons ◆
no pets ◉ fridge Electric
Elec metered ⌷not provided →

☎(50yds) Airing cupboard in unit Iron in unit Ironing board in unit HCE in unit TV ⊕3pinsquare P ▥ ♨(50yds)

↩ ჽ▨(½m) ☎(50yds) ▨(½m) ♫(½m) 🐾(1m)

Min£30 Max£60pw (Low)
Min£70 Max£120pw (High)

F S B Rains **Rockcliffe Holiday Flats**
(Nos 2, 3, 4, 5 & 6) Island Road, St Ives,
Cornwall TR26 1NS
☎Penzance(0736)797165

A former net factory, converted to flats, situated in the old part of town. All flats have lounge, kitchen and bathroom/WC. Two have family bedrooms and three have one double and one family bedroom. Modern in style and décor. Drying cabinets in units.

All year MWB out of season 1wk min, 5units, 2–8persons ◈ ◆ ◉ fridge Electric Elec metered ⊑can be hired ☎ (100yds) Airing cupboard in unit Iron in unit Ironing board in unit HCE in unit [Launderette within 300yds] ⊙ TV ⊕3pinsquare ▥ ♨(50yds)

↩ ჽ▨(3m) ☎(½m) ▨(½m) ♫(½m) 🐾(½m)

Min£40 Max£70pw (Low)
Min£106.50 Max£174pw (High)

F Mr & Mrs S O Scott **Talland House Holiday Flats (1–5)**, St Ives, Cornwall
☎Penzance(0736)796368

Five luxury flats located in spacious detached residence in an acre of well-kept gardens overlooking St Ives Bay. Each flat is fully carpeted with comfortable lounge, kitchen dinette and bathroom/WC. The bedrooms have hot and cold water. Flats 1 and 4 have two bedrooms with principal bedroom incorporating lounge with balcony, and Flat 5 has three bedrooms with divan bed.

All year MWB out of season 1wk min, 6mths max, 5units, 1–6persons ◈ no pets ◉ fridge Electric Elec metered ⊑can be hired ☎(½m) Airing cupboard on premises Iron on premises Ironing board on premises HCE in unit ⊙ TV ⊕3pinsquare 1P ▥ ♨(300yds)

↩ ჽ▨(2m) ☎(½m) ▨(½m) ♫(½m) 🐾(½m)

F Mr I Johnson Polley **Tol Pedn**
Headland Road, Carbis Bay, St Ives,
Cornwall TR26 2NS
☎Penzance(0736)797219

Attractive holiday flats providing a high standard of accommodation. They are modern and comfortable, and the administration and maintenance aspects are excellent. In a quiet spot about six minutes' walk from the beach.

Apr–Sep MWB out of season 1wk min, 1mth max, 18units, 6persons ◈ no pets ◉ fridge Electric(heating inclusive) Elec metered ⊑inclusive ☎ Airing cupboard in unit Iron on premises Ironing board on premises

HCE in unit ⊙ CTV ⊕3pinsquare 19P ▥ ♨(½m)

↩ ჽ▨(1m) ▨(200yds) ▨(½m) ♫(½m)

ST JUST
Cornwall
Map 2 SW33

H **Chy-an-Eglos**
for bookings Tregeseal Holiday Cottages, Wharf Road, Penzance, Cornwall
☎Penzance(0736)2008

Delightful house situated opposite the old church in St Just. The house is spacious and offers accommodation for up to ten people in four bedrooms, lounge, dining room and kitchen.

All year MWB 1wk min, 1unit, 1–10persons ◈ ◉ fridge Electric Elec metered ⊑can be hired ☎(100yds) Airing cupboard in unit Iron in unit Ironing board in unit HCE in unit [Launderette within 300yds] ⊙ TV ⊕3pinsquare 2P ▥ ♨(100yds)

↩ ☎(100yds)

Min£52 Max£69pw (Low)
Min£75 Max£207pw (High)

F **Foundry House Flats 1 & 2**
Tregeseal Valley
for bookings Tregeseal Holiday Cottages, Wharf Road, Penzance, Cornwall
☎Penzance(0736)2008

Two flats in a converted cottage ½m E of St Just. The ground-floor flat has two double bedrooms and an extra single bed whilst the first-floor flat has one double room and another room with three single beds. Each have a lounge, kitchen, bathroom and WC.

All year MWB 1wk min, 2units, 1–5persons ◈ ◉ fridge Electric Elec metered ⊑can be hired ☎(200yds) Airing cupboard in unit Iron in unit Ironing board in unit HCE in unit ⊙ TV ⊕3pinsquare 1P ▥ ♨(½m)

↩ ☎(½m)

C **Glen** Tregeseal Valley
for bookings Tregeseal Holiday Cottages, Wharf Road, Penzance, Cornwall
☎Penzance(0736)2008

Traditional granite cottage standing in its own grounds ½m E of St Just. It comprises of a lounge, sun patio, bathroom/WC and four bedrooms including a double bedroom with bathroom en suite on the ground floor.

All year MWB 1wk min, 1unit, 1–8persons ◈ ◉ fridge Electric Elec inclusive ⊑inclusive ☎(200yds) Airing cupboard in unit Iron in unit Ironing board in unit HCE in unit CTV ⊕3pinsquare 3P ▥ ♨(½m)

↩ ☎(½m)

Min£70 Max£95pw (Low)
Min£104 Max£228pw (High)

C **Labour-in-Vain (1–4)** Lafrowda Common
for bookings Tregeseal Holiday Cottages, Wharf Road, Penzance, Cornwall
☎Penzance(0736)2008

Four stone-built semi-detached properties in a quiet location on Lafrowda Common 1m SE of St Just off A3071. Each has one double room, and another with bunk beds, lounge/diner, kitchen, bathroom and WC.

All year MWB 1wk min, 4units, 1–4persons ◈ ◉ fridge Electric Elec metered ⊑can be hired ☎(½m) Airing cupboard in unit Iron in unit Ironing board in unit HCE in unit ⊙ TV ⊕3pinsquare 2P ♨(½m)

↩ ☎(½m)

Min£35 Max£69pw (Low)
Min£75 Max£127pw (High)

C **Mill House Cottage** Tregeseal Valley
for bookings Tregeseal Holiday Cottages, Wharf Road, Penzance, Cornwall
☎Penzance(0736)2008

Delightful Cornish cottage in peaceful surroundings ½m E of St Just. It comprises lounge with low beamed ceiling, a double-bedded room, a twin-bedded room, and a separate shower bathroom and WC. There is car parking at the front and a garden behind the property.

All year MWB 1wk min, 1unit, 1–4persons ◈ ◉ fridge Electric Elec metered ⊑can be hired ☎(½m) Airing cupboard in unit Iron in unit Ironing board in unit HCE in unit ⊙ TV ⊕3pinsquare 1P ♨(½m)

↩ ☎(½m)

Min£35 Max£69pw (Low)
Min£80 Max£115pw (High)

C **Princess Street Cottage** Princess Street
for bookings Tregeseal Holiday Cottages, Wharf Road, Penzance, Cornwall
☎Penzance(0736)2008

Terraced granite Cornish cottage situated within the heart of St Just comprising one double room, one twin-bedded and one with bunks, lounge, dining room, toilet and shower.

All year MWB 1wk min, 1unit, 1–6persons ◈ ◉ fridge Electric Elec metered ⊑can be hired ☎(½m) Airing cupboard in unit Iron in unit Ironing board in unit HCE in unit [Launderette within 300yds] ⊙ TV ⊕3pinsquare 1P ▥ ♨(½m)

↩ ☎(½m)

Min£35 Max£69pw (Low)
Min£80 Max£115pw (High)

┌─────────────────────────────┐
│ 1982 prices quoted throughout │
│ gazetteer │
└─────────────────────────────┘

C **Wesley Cottage,** North Row
for bookings Mr & Mrs Smith, 8 Rosemary Court, Coombe Road, Paignton, Devon TQ32RS
☎Paignton(0803)553875 & 557268

Two cottages converted into one self-contained establishment, fully modernised and comfortably furnished. Comprising one double and one twin bedroom, lounge, kitchen/diner, bathroom with WC, and small garden to rear. Located in heart of St Just village about 6m from Penzance.

May–Oct 1wk min, 1unit, 1–4persons no pets ◉ fridge Electric Elec metered ⊡not provided ☎(100yds) SD in unit Airing cupboard in unit Iron in unit Ironing board in unit HCE in unit [Launderette within 300yds] ⊙ TV ⊕3pin square 2P ⊞ ▲(100yds)
⊖ ☺(200yds)

Min£45 Max£65pw (Low)
Min£80 Max£95pw (High)

ST KEVERNE
Cornwall
Map**2** SW72

C & H **St James Court Holiday Cottages & Tregowris Farmhouse**
for bookings F J H & A E Bray, 2 Glenview, Tregonning Park, St Keverne, Helston, Cornwall
☎St Keverne(0326)280459

Small complex of character cottages in rural location approx 2m NW of St Keverne village. **Cottages 1, 2 & 7** *are ideal for two adults and three children.* **Cottage 6** *is for two adults plus small child and* **Cottages 3, 4 & 5** *sleep up to seven people.* **The Farmhouse** *is a large stone and cob property located opposite the cottages and sleeps up to ten persons.*

Etr–Oct MWB out of season 1wk min, 8units, 1–10persons ◈ ◆ ◉ fridge Electric Elec metered ⊡not provided ☎ Airing cupboard in unit Iron in unit Ironing board in unit HCE in unit ⊙ CTV ⊕3pin square P ▲(1½m)
⊖ ☺(2m)

ST KEW
Cornwall
Map**2** SX07

H **Lower Tregellist Farm**
for bookings Mrs S J D Harris, Kelly Green, St Kew Highway, St Kew, Bodmin, Cornwall
☎Bodmin(0208)850275

Rebuilt farmhouse in modern style in secluded position with pretty garden. Modern, well-equipped kitchen, dining room, lounge and four bedrooms (one with double and single beds, two doubles, one with twin beds). Leave St Kew in north-westerly direction, at T junction turn right. First turning left to Tregellist.

St Just
—
St Mary's

All year MWB out of season 1wk min, 1mth max, 1unit, 2–9persons ◈ ◆ no pets ◉ fridge Electric Elec metered ⊡can be hired ☎ Airing cupboard in unit Iron in unit Ironing board in unit HCE in unit ⊙ TV ⊕3pin square ⊕2pin round P ⊞ ▣(3m)
⊖ ☺(1½m)

Min£50 Max£100pw (Low)
Min£150 Max£190pw (High)

ST LAWRENCE
Isle of Wight
Map**4** SZ57

F Mrs P A Knight **La Falaise** Undercliffe Drive, St Lawrence, Ventnor, Isle of Wight PO38 1XF
☎Ventnor(0983)853440

Two flats in a large detached house, comprising two double bedrooms with double and twin beds, lounge/diner/kitchen and bathroom with WC. Comfortably furnished. 1½m W of Ventnor.

All year MWB out of season 1wk min, 2units, 1–6persons ◈ ◉ fridge Electric Elec metered ⊡inclusive ☎(25yds) Airing cupboard in unit Iron in unit Ironing board in unit HCE in unit ⊙ TV ⊕3pin square 4P ⊞ ▲(50yds)
⊖ ᵟ♂(1½m) ☺(50yds) ▨(1½m) ☺(1½m)

Min£30 Max£60pw (Low)
Min£100 Max£130pw (High)

ST MARY'S
Isles of Scilly
No map

Ch **The Chalet, Seaways Farm Holiday Flats**
for bookings Mrs R C May, Seaways Flower Farm, St Mary's, Isles of Scilly
☎Scillonia(0720)22398

Chalet situated in grounds of large house near sea. Comprises one twin-bedded room and one room with three beds. Adequately furnished living room and kitchen. Shower/WC.

All year MWB 1wk min, 1mth max, 1unit, 5persons ◈ ◆ no pets ◉ fridge Elec metered ⊡inclusive Iron in unit Ironing board in unit HCE in unit ⊙ TV can be hired ⊕3pin square ⊞ ▲(1m)
⊖ ᵟ♂(½m) ☺(1m)

Min£86.25 Max£110.55pw (Low)
Max£178.25pw (High)

F **The Flatlet, Seaways Farm Holiday Flats**
for bookings Mrs R C May, Seaways Flower Farm, St Mary's, Isles of Scilly
☎Scillonia(0720)22398

Smaller flatlet in converted farm building overlooking harbour, and comprising

living room, kitchen, shower/WC and one twin-bedded room.

All year MWB 1wk min, 1mth max, 1unit, 2persons ◈ ◆ no pets ◉ fridge Electric Elec metered ⊡inclusive Iron in unit Ironing board in unit HCE in unit ⊙ TV can be hired ⊕3pin square ⊞ ▲(1m)
⊖ ᵟ♂(½m) ☺(1m)

Min£80.50 Max£120.75pw

F Mr Gregory **Moonrakers Holiday Flats** Garrison Lane, St Mary's, Isles of Scilly TR21 0JF
☎Scillonia(0720)22717

Six self-contained flats comfortably furnished and well-equipped in an attractive detached building adjacent to the Garrison Gateway in an elevated position overlooking town harbour and sea views over numerous rocky islets.

8Mar–9Nov MWB in season 1wk min, 1mth max, 6units, 1–6persons, nc4 no pets ◉ fridge Electric Elec metered ⊡inclusive ☎(100yds) Airing cupboard in unit Iron in unit Ironing board in unit HCE in unit ⊙ TV ⊕3pin square P ⊞ ▲(200yds)
⊖ ☺(100yds)

Min£59 Max£327pw (Low)
Min£137 Max£225pw (High)

F **The Patio, Seaways Farm Holiday Flats**
for bookings Mrs R C May, Seaways Flower Farm, St Mary's, Isles of Scilly
☎Scillonia(0720)22398

An attractive flat in converted farm buildings overlooking harbour. Accommodation comprises two bedrooms (a double and a single with bunk beds). Comfortable living room and well-equipped kitchen.

All year MWB 1wk min, 1mth max, 1unit, 5persons ◈ ◆ no pets ◉ fridge Electric Elec metered ⊡inclusive Iron in unit Ironing board in unit HCE in unit ⊙ TV can be hired ⊕3pin square ⊞ ▲(1m)
⊖ ᵟ♂(½m) ☺(1m)

Min£92 Max£207pw

F **Summerhouse, Seaways Farm Holiday Flats**
for bookings Mrs R C May, Seaways Flower Farm, St Mary's, Isles of Scilly
☎Scillonia(0720)22398

Attractive flat in converted farm buildings overlooking harbour. Accommodation comprises two bedrooms on lower level including one double, one single and bunk beds, well-equipped kitchen and lounge, shower/WC. Situated in Porthloo Lane adjacent to golf course on western coast of island.

All year MWB 1wk min, 1mth max, 1unit, 5persons ◈ ◆ no pets ▩ fridge Electric Elec metered ⊡inclusive Iron in unit Ironing board in unit HCE in unit ⊙ TV can be hired ⊕3pin square ⊞ ▲(1m) →

⊖ δ☊(¼m) ☏(1m)
Min£86.25 Max£110.55pw (Low)
Max£178.25pw (High)

ST MARY'S BAY
Kent
Map5 TR02

B The Bungalow
for bookings Mr & Mrs J Sweeney The
Grange, Hadlow Down, Uckfield, East
Sussex TN22 4HH
☎Hadlow Down(082 585)643

Well-equipped bungalow with large
garden, situated at the end of a private
road, close to the sea. The property can
accommodate up to 10 persons, offering
four bedrooms, and is especially suitable
for children.

All year MWB out of season 2 days min,
3wks max, 1 unit, 2–10 persons ◇ ◆
◉ fridge Electric Elec metered ⊡not
provided ☎(350yds) SD in unit Airing
cupboard in unit Iron in unit Ironing
board in unit HCE in unit CTV
⊕3pin square 3P 🎦 ♨(320yds)

ST MELLION
Cornwall
Map2 SX36

F Mrs W A J Dark *Hillcrest* St Mellion,
Cornwall
☎St Dominick(0579)50403

A first-floor flat, over a farm shop,
reached by an external spiral staircase
and comprises two twin-bedded rooms,
combined bathroom/WC, kitchen/diner
and a lounge. Follow A388 from Saltash
towards Callington and the property can
be found on the left in St Mellion.

All year 1wk min, 1mth max, 1unit,
2–4persons, nc12 no pets ◉ fridge
Electric Elec metered ⊡not provided
☎ Airing cupboard in unit Iron in unit
Ironing board in unit HCE in unit ⊙
TV ⊕3pin square ⊕2pin round P
🎦 ♨

⊖ δ☊(¼m) ☏ 🖾

ST MINVER
Cornwall
Map2 SW97

**Ch Four & Five Star Chalets, St
Minver House Holiday Estate**
for bookings The Booking Manager, PO
Box 8, St Austell Bay, Cornwall
☎St Austell(0726)65551

Single storey half wood, half concrete-
constructed chalets. Accommodation
comprises lounge/diner, kitchen and
bathroom/WC. Sleeping is arranged in
two twin-bedded rooms in twenty-three
chalets and one double room and one
twin-bedded room in three chalets.

Etr–Sep MWB out of season
3days min, 3wks max, 26units,
1–6persons [◇ ◆] no pets ◉
fridge Electric Elec inclusive in Five
Star Elec metered ⊡can be hired ☎
[Iron on premises] Ironing board on
premises HCE in unit [Launderette on

St Mary's
—
St Tudy

premises] ⊙ CTV in Five Star TV can
be hired ⊕3pin square 50P 🎦 ♨
⊐

⊖ ☏ 🖾 ♫
Min£69 Max£88pw (Low)
Min£154 Max£207pw (High)

ST NEWLYN EAST
Cornwall
Map2 SW85

C 12 & 12A Station Road
for bookings Mrs F Gibbs, 24 St Michaels
Road, Ponsanooth, Truro, Cornwall
☎Devoran(0872)864279

A pair of semi-detached cottages located
in the village of St Newlyn East about 5
miles from Newquay. **No 12** comprises a
small lounge with adjacent kitchen/diner
and one twin bedded room on the ground
floor and two bedrooms, one double, one
twin bedded on the first floor, bathroom
and WC. **No 12A** comprises three
bedrooms, one double, one twin bedded
with additional twin bedded room leading
directly off (ideal for childrens room).
There is also a dining room, lounge and
kitchen, bathroom and WC. Use of small
gardens at rear.

May–Sep 1wk min, 2units,
1–6persons ◇ ◉ fridge Electric
Elec inclusive ⊡inclusive ☎(400yds)
Iron in unit Ironing board in unit HCE in
unit ⊙ TV ⊕3pin square 2P
♨(400yds)

⊖ ☏(400yds)

ST SAVIOUR'S
Guernsey, Chanel Islands
Map16

C L'Atlantique Cottages L'Atlantique
Hotel, Perelle Bay, St Saviour's,
Guernsey, Channel Islands
☎Guernsey(0481)64056

Three blocks of modern cottages
situated in grounds of hotel. All
comfortably furnished with lounge/diner,
fitted kitchen, two bedrooms and
bathroom/WC. Hotel facilities are
available and discount is offered on main
meals.

All year MWB 1wk min, 10units,
4persons [◇ ◇ ◆] no pets
Sunbeam multi cooker fridge 🍳
Elec metered ⊡inclusive ☎ Iron in
unit Ironing board in unit HCE in unit
⊙ CTV ⊕3pin square P 🎦
♨(100yds) ⊐

⊖ ☏
Min£60 Max£95pw (Low)
Min£160 Max£230pw (High)

ST THOMAS
Cornwall
Map2 SX28

H Mr & Mrs Graham-Jones *Tredidon* St
Thomas, Launceston, Cornwall PL15 8SJ
☎Pipers Pool(056 686)288

The self-contained wing of a beautiful
period farmhouse with attractive
gardens, amidst rural surroundings on a
200-acre farm reached by a narrow road
leading N from the A395. The very
spacious accommodation consists of a
large entrance hall, living room, master
bedroom, three double bedrooms, one
single bedroom with adjoining bathroom
and WC on each floor. There are many
interesting features including a
parliament clock set above the Georgian
stairway, a barrel ceiling in the master
bedroom, which together with the living
room is of stately home proportions.
Provides an opportunity to experience
gracious living at moderate cost.

Mar–Oct 1wk min, 1mth max, 1unit,
1–9persons ◇ ◇ ◆ no pets ◉
fridge Electric & log fires
Elec inclusive ⊡not provided ☎(3m)
Airing cupboard in unit Iron in unit
Ironing board in unit HCE in unit ⊙
⊕3pin square P 🎦 ♨(3m) Fishing &
games room

⊖ ☏(3m)

ST TUDY
Cornwall
Map2 SX17

F Mr J R Hill *Hengar Manor* St Tudy,
Cornwall
☎Bodmin(0208)850382

Five flats located within old manor house
set in 35 acres of lovely grounds. The flats
enjoy the charm of the house itself but are
fully modernised and self contained, they
have either one or two bedrooms, and
offer accommodation for up to six people.

26Mar–Oct MWB out of season
3days min, 4wks max, 5units,
1–6persons [◇ ◆] ◉ fridge
Electric Elec metered ⊡can be hired
☎ Iron on premises Ironing board on
premises [Launderette on premises]
⊙ TV ⊕3pin square 5P 🎦 ♨ ⊐
🏊Hard Children's playground

⊖ ☏ 🖾 ♫
Min£42.55 Max£49.45pw (Low)
Min£96.60 Max£124.20pw (High)

Ch 44–102 Woodland Bungalows
for bookings Mr J R Hill, Hengar Manor, St
Tudy, Cornwall
☎Bodmin(0208)850382

Well-constructed brick and wood semi-
and detached chalets set in 35 acres of
woodland, comprising lounge,
kitchen/diner, bathroom with WC, one
double and one single bedroom with
bunks and single bed. Follow signs from
B3266.

26Mar–Oct MWB out of season
3days min, 4wks max, 59units,
1–5persons [◇ ◆] ◉ fridge

Electric Elecmetered ◻can be hired ☎ [WM on premises] [SD on premises] [TD on premises] [Iron on premises] [Ironing board on premises] [Launderette on premises] ⊙ TV ⊕3pin square 1P(per unit) ⛼ ⛱ Hard ⚲ ▥ ♫

Min£34.50 Max£51.75pw (Low)
Max£186.30pw (High)

SALCOMBE
Devon
Map**3** SX73

F **Flats 1 & 2**
for bookings Mr G E Ware, Grafton Towers Hotel, Salcombe, Devon
☎Salcombe(054 884)2882

Both flats situated in modern bungalow in hotel grounds overlooking estuary and South Sands. Nicely maintained, comprising modern well-equipped kitchen, lounge/diner, bathroom, one double and one twin bedroom. Flat 1 sleeps up to six persons.

All year MWB out of season 2days(1wk min, in season) 1mth max, 2units, 2–6persons [◇] ◆ ◆ no pets ◊ fridge ⚡ & electric Gas/elec inclusive ◻inclusive ☎(10yds) [WM on premises] [SD on premises] [TD on premises] Airing cupboard in unit Iron in unit Ironing board in unit HCE in unit ⊙ CTV ⊕3pin square 2P ▥ ⛼(1m) Hotel facilities, restaurant, bar, gardens & laundry available

⊖ ⚲(10yds) ▥(1m)

Min£80 Max£110pw(Low)
Min£160 Max£210pw (High)

SALEN
Highland *Argyllshire*
Map**13** NM66

Ch Mrs D H McEwan **Tigh-na-Creagan (Chalets)** Salen, Acharacle, Argyllshire PH36 4JN
☎Salen(096 785)270(summer) & Chelmsford(0245)421106(winter)

Two Scandinavian pine chalets standing in 1½ acres of trees and shrub-studded land with views over Loch Sunart. Each comprises two twin-bedded rooms, open-plan lounge (with double convertible)/diner/kitchen and bathroom. From Salen follow Kilchoan road (B8007) for ½m.

Apr–Oct 1wk min, 3wks max, 2units, 2–6persons ◆ ◆ ◎ fridge Electric Elecmetered ◻inclusive ☎(½m) Airing cupboard in unit Iron on premises Ironing board on premises HCE in unit ⊕3pin square 4P ⛼(½m) Fishing & boating

⊖ ⚲(½m)

Min£50 Max£140pw

F Mrs D H McEwan **Tigh-na-Creagan (Flat)** Salen, Acharacle, Argyllshire PH36 4JN
☎Salen(096 785)270(summer) & Chelmsford(0245)421106(winter)

Flat with balcony adjoining owner's house, situated on edge of Loch Sunart, with good views. Accommodation comprises twin bedroom, lounge/diner/kitchen and bathroom. From Salen follow Kilchoan road, B8007 for ½m.

Apr–Oct 1wk min, 3wks max, 1unit, 2persons, nc no pets ◊ fridge Electric Gas/Elec inclusive ◻inclusive ☎(½m) Iron on premises Ironing board on premises HCE in unit ⊙ ⊕3pin square 1P ⛼(½m) Fishing & boating

⊖ ⚲(½m)

£75pw

SANDHAVEN
Grampian *Aberdeenshire*
Map**15** NJ96

C ***Broomhills Holiday Cottages***
for bookings Mrs M Milne, Broomhills Farm, Sandhaven, Fraserburgh, Aberdeenshire
☎Rosehearty(034 67)235

Two of three adjoining farm cottages surrounded by fields within the grounds of Broomhills Farm. Each has living/dining room with convertible settee, kitchen, bathroom, and two double bedrooms. The farm lies just west of Sandhaven and has uninterrupted views out to sea.

Apr–Nov 1wk min, 4wks max, 2units, 1–6persons ◆ ◆ no pets ◎ fridge Electric & open fires Elecmetered ◻inclusive ☎(1m) WM in unit SD in unit Airing cupboard in unit Ironing board in unit HCE in unit TV ⊕3pin square P ▥ ⛼(1m)

⊖ ⚲(1m) ▥(1m)

SANDYHILLS
Dumfries & Galloway *Kirkcudbrightshire*
Map**11** NX85

Ch **Barend Farm**
for bookings Barend Properties Ltd, 15 Barend, Sandyhills, Dalbeattie DG5 4NU
☎Southwick(038 778)663

Two-storey Scandinavian-style timbered chalets. Facilities and décor of very high standard. The chalets are in an elevated position overlooking a man-made loch, and set in the grounds of a farm ½m N of Sandyhills and the Solway Firth.

All year MWB out of season 3days min, 4wks max, 50units, 2–12persons [◇] [◆ ◆] ◊ fridge ⚡ Gas inclusive ◻inclusive ☎ Iron on premises Ironing board on premises HCE in unit [Launderette on premises] ⊙ CTV ⊕3pin square P ⛼(½m) Riding school & pony trekking

⊖ ⛳(½m) ⚲

Min£80 Max£92pw (Low)
Min£207 Max£253pw (High)

SANDY LANE
Wiltshire
Map**3** ST96

C **CC Ref 807 EP**
for bookings Character Cottages (Holidays) Ltd, 34 Fore Street, Sidmouth, Devon EX10 8AQ
☎Sidmouth(039 55)77001

A detached stone-built thatched cottage with magnificent views over the Wiltshire Downs, set in a hamlet of similarly styled cottages. The completely modernised interior comprises kitchen/dining room, →

living room, bath/shower, two WC's and three bedrooms.

All year MWB out of season 1wk min, 3mths max, 1unit, 2–4persons ◇ ◆ ⌂ fridge Electric Gas inclusive in summer ⬜not provided ☎(1m) Airing cupboard in unit HCE in unit ⊖ TV ⊕3pin square P ♨(5m)
⊖ ☏(1m)

Min£59 Max£84pw (Low)
Min£97 Max£147pw (High)

C CC Ref 808 EP
for bookings Character Cottages (Holidays) Ltd, 34 Fore Street, Sidmouth, Devon EX10 8AQ
☎Sidmouth(03955)77001

A picturesque, modernised thatched cottage set in a hamlet of similar cottages, with accommodation comprising kitchen/dining room, two bedrooms, bathroom/WC.

All year 1wk min, 3mths max, 1unit, 4persons ◇ ◆ ⌂ fridge Electric Gas/Elec inclusive in summer ⬜not provided ☎(½m) Airing cupboard in unit HCE in unit ⊖ TV ⊕3pin square P ♨(5m)
⊖ ☏(1m)

Min£68 Max£97pw (Low)
Min£124 Max£178pw (High)

C CC 809 EP
for bookings Character Cottages (Holidays) Ltd, 34 Fore Street, Sidmouth, Devon EX10 8AQ
☎Sidmouth(03955)77001

Detached cottage comprising lounge, kitchen/diner, three bedrooms (two double, one single), bathroom/WC. Within an all-thatched hamlet in peaceful country setting.

All year 1wk min, 3mths max, 1unit, 2–5persons ◇ no cats ◉ fridge Electric Elec inclusive ⬜not provided Airing cupboard in unit Iron in unit Ironing board in unit HCE in unit ⊖ TV ⊕3pin square P ▥ ♨(3m)
⊖ ঌ(3m) ☏(½m) ▨(3m)

Min£48 Max£75pw (Low)
Min£90 Max£138pw (High)

SAUNDERSFOOT
Dyfed
Map 2 SN 10

F Holmlea, The Strand
for bookings Mrs J Griffiths, Sea Breezes, The Strand, Saundersfoot, Dyfed SA69 9EX
☎Saundersfoot(0834)812617

Situated on the harbour edge with direct access to the beach. The flats are on the ground and first floor, with one or two bedrooms, there are also convertible beds in some flats. The flats are comfortable and well-equipped.

Apr-Nov MWB out of season 2nights min, 4units, 3–8persons ◇ ◆ ◉ fridge Electric Elec inclusive ⬜can be hired (overseas visitors only) ☎(300yds) Airing cupboard in unit Iron

---

in unit HCE in unit [Launderette within 300yds] ⊖ CTV ⊕3pin square 4P ▥
⊖ ঌ(3m) ☏(100yds) ▨(100yds) ♫(100yds) ▨(3m)

B Mrs J M Rogers Homecroft (Bungalows) Saundersfoot, Dyfed
☎Saundersfoot(0834)813249

Pair of recently converted bungalows with pleasant garden outlook. Comprising lounge/dining room, family bedroom (double bed and bunk beds, and double bedroom). Fitted kitchen and bathroom.

Etr-Oct MWB out of season 1wk min, 2units, 2–7persons [◇] ◆ ◉ fridge Electric Elec metered ⬜not provided ☎(½m) Airing cupboard in unit Iron in unit Ironing board in unit HCE in unit ⊖ CTV ⊕3pin square P ▥ ♨(½m)
⊖ ☏(1m)

Min£50 Max£70pw (Low)
Min£95 Max£125pw (High)

H Mrs J M Rogers Homecroft (House)
Saundersfoot, Dyfed
☎Saundersfoot(0834)813249

A former guesthouse with garden, now self-catering accomodation comprising lounge, dining room, five bedrooms, bathroom, kitchen and ground-floor shower room.

Etr-Oct MWB out of season 1wk min, 1unit, 1–14persons [◇] ◆ ◉ fridge Electric Elec metered ⬜not provided ☎(½m) SD in unit Airing cupboard in unit Iron in unit Ironing board in unit HCE in unit ⊖ CTV ⊕3pin square P ▥ ♨(½m)
⊖ ☏(1m)

Min£165 Max£200pw

F Seaward Court Flats Wogan Terrace
for bookings Saundersvale Holiday Estate Ltd, Valley Road, Saundersfoot, Dyfed SA69 9BT
☎Saundersfoot(0834)812310

Satisfactory family accommodation in block of six modern, purpose-built flats. Each unit contains lounge/dining room with double studio couch, small kitchen, two bedrooms (one double, with small balcony off and one twin) and bathroom/WC.

All year MWB out of season 2nights min, 6units, 2–6persons [◇] ◆ ◉ fridge Electric Elec inclusive ⬜can be hired ☎(200yds) Airing cupboard in unit Iron in unit Ironing board in unit [Launderette within 300yds] ⊖ CTV ⊕3pin square ▥ ♨(100yds) ঌ
⊖ ☏(10yds) ▨(50yds) ♫(50yds)

Min£30 Max£100pw (Low)
Min£50 Max£190pw (High)

F Squibbs Holiday Flats (A, B & C)
3 Cambrian Terrace
for bookings Mrs M M Hughes, 1 Napleton Place, Warren Street, Tenby, Dyfed
☎Tenby(0834)2109 (4109 after 6pm)

Flat A is a first-floor flat with lounge/dining room, with double put-u-up, a twin-bedded room with washbasin, double bedroom, kitchen and combined bathroom/WC. Flat B is a ground-floor flat with sitting room/diner with put-u-up, kitchen, double and twin bedrooms, and combined bath/WC. Flat C has sea views, a comfortable lounge with bed-settee, double bedrooms, a twin-bedded room, kitchen and bathroom/WC.

All year MWB out of season 7days min, 1mth max, 3units, 2–6persons ◇ no pets ◉ fridge Gas & electric Gas inclusive Elec metered ⬜not provided ☎(25yds) Airing cupboard in unit Iron in unit Ironing board in unit HCE in unit Launderette within 300yds ⊖ TV ⊕3pin square ▥ ♨(20yds)
⊖ ☏(200yds) ▨(200yds) ▨(3m)

Min£50 Max£70pw (Low)
Min£95 Max£125pw (High)

B Valley Close Bungalows Valley Road
for bookings Saundersvale Holiday Estate Ltd, Valley Road, Saundersfoot, Dyfed SA69 9BT
☎Saundersfoot(0834)812310

Group of eight semi-detached bungalows with compact family accommodation. Each unit comprises lounge with studio couch (forming a double bed), kitchen/dining room, one family bedroom (one double and bunk beds) and bathroom/WC. Large families can be accommodated by use of adjoining doors to next unit.

All year MWB out of season 2nights min, 8units, 2–6persons [◇] ◆ ◉ fridge Electric Elec inclusive ⬜can be hired ☎(300yds) Airing cupboard in unit Iron in unit Ironing board in unit HCE in unit [Launderette within 300yds] ⊖ TV ⊕3pin square P ♨(300yds)

Min£30 Max£90pw (Low)
Min£40 Max£190pw (High)

H Valley Grove Villas Valley Road
for bookings Saundersvale Holiday Estate Ltd, Valley Road, Saundersfoot, Dyfed SA69 9BT
☎Saundersfoot(0834)812310

Ten compact villas, each with patio. Modern accommodation comprises two bedrooms (one double and one twin), sitting/dining room with double bed-settee, kitchen and bathroom/WC.

All year MWB out of season 2nights min, 10units, 2–6persons [◇] ◆ ◉ fridge Electric Elec inclusive ⬜can be hired ☎(200yds) Iron in unit Ironing board in unit HCE in unit [Launderette within 300yds] ⊖ CTV ⊕3pin square P ♨(200yds)

➔ ⚲ (200yds)
Min£40 Max£100pw (Low)
Min£50 Max£200pw (High)

F   Waters Edge The Strand
for bookings Mrs J Griffiths, Sea Breeze,
The Strand, Saundersfoot, Dyfed
SA69 9EX
☎Saundersfoot(0834)812617

*Spacious well-maintained units available
on four levels with good views and direct
access to the beach. Flats have one or
two bedrooms and some also have sofa
beds, and all flats have balcony.
Magnificent views from the higher floors.*

All year   MWB out of season
2 nights min, 14 units, 2–7 persons ◆
◉ fridge Electric Elec inclusive
🖵can be hired(overseas visitors only)
☎(300yds) Airing cupboard in unit Iron
in unit HCE in unit [Launderette within
300yds] ⊕ CTV ⊕3pin square 14P
🏧 ♨
➔ ♿(3m) ⚲(100yds) 🚻(100yds)
♬(100yds) 🍴(3m)

Powell's Holidays High Street,
Saundersfoot, Dyfed
☎Saundersfoot(0834)812791

**Powell's Holidays have a total of
sixtyseven AA-inspected properties in
Saundersfoot. Of these, twenty seven
are bungalows, fifteen are flats, twenty
one are houses and four are cottages.
An entry for one of each type of
property follows. For information on
the other properties contact Powell's
Holidays.**

B **Chantry** Twy Cross, Redberth
for bookings Powell's Holidays (address as Page 221)
☎Saundersfoot(0834)812791
This three-bedroomed modern detached bungalow has a stone fireplace in the lounge, a dining area and a well fitted kitchen.

Apr-Oct MWB out of season 1wk min, 6wks max, 1unit, 2–6persons ◆ no pets ◊ fridge ♨ Gas/elec inclusive ☐not provided ☎(50yds) Airing cupboard in unit Iron in unit Ironing board in unit HCE in unit ⊙ CTV ⊕3pin square P ▥ ♨(50yds)

⊖ ♂(3m) ♀(50yds) ▣(1m) ♫(1m) ▩(2m)

Min£69 Max£195pw

C **Inkerman House** Wogan Terrace
for bookings Powell's Holidays (address as page 221)
☎Saundersfoot(0834)812791
Semi-detached cottage, recently converted, near to the beach in the centre of the village. Accommodation comprises a lobby, kitchen/diner, one double bedroom, lounge with steep, open stairs leading to one twin-bedded room, one double-bedded room with additional bunk beds and bathroom/WC with shower.

Jun-Oct MWB out of season 1wk min, 6wks max, 1unit, 1–8persons ◆ no pets ◎ fridge Electric Elec inclusive ☐can be hired ☎(¼m) Airing cupboard in unit Iron in unit Ironing board in unit HCE in unit TV ⊕3pin square ⊕3pin round ⊕2pin round 2P ▥ ♨(½m)

⊖ ♀(½m) ▣(½m) ♫(½m)

Min£63 Max£168pw

H **Joketa** The Ridgeway
for bookings Powell's Holidays (address as page 221)
☎Saundersfoot(0834)812791
Large detached house close to beach with sea views. Accommodation comprises lounge, dining room, kitchen and three bedrooms (one double, one twin-bedded and one with a double and single bed). There is a bathroom/WC and two shower rooms.

May-Sep MWB out of season 1wk min, 1unit, 6–7persons no pets ◎ fridge ♨ Elec inclusive Iron in unit Ironing board in unit CTV

Min£75 Max£216pw

H **Kantara** 77 Ridgeway Close
for bookings Powell's Holidays (address as page 221)
☎Saundersfoot(0834)812791
An attractive modern detached house in an elevated position in a quiet cul-de-sac only a few minutes' walk from the harbour. Accommodation comprises a kitchen, dining room and lounge on the ground floor and two double bedrooms, one bedroom with two bunk beds and a bathroom/WC on the first-floor.

Jul-Sep 1wk min, 6wks max, 1unit, 2–6persons ◆ ◆ ◎ fridge Electric & coal fires Elec inclusive ☐inclusive ☎(¼m) Airing cupboard in unit Iron in unit Ironing board in unit HCE in unit ⊙ CTV ⊕3pin square 2P ▥ ♨(½m)

⊖ ♀(½m) ▣(½m) ♫(½m)

Min£63 Max£174pw

B **Peace Haven**
for bookings Powell's Holidays (address as page 221)
☎Saundersfoot(0834)812791
A split-level bungalow of unusual design overlooking village. There is a pleasant patio and small terraced garden. Accommodation comprises breakfast kitchen, spacious lounge/diner, two double bedrooms, one twin-bedded room, one room with bunk beds and bathroom/WC with shower. There is an additional WC outside.

Mar-Oct MWB out of season 1wk min, 1unit, 1–8persons ◆ ◆ no pets ◎ fridge ♨ Elec inclusive ☐can be hired ☎(½m) Airing cupboard in unit Iron in unit Ironing board in unit HCE in unit TV ⊕3pin square 3P ▥ ♨(½m)

⊖ ♂(2½m) ♀(½m) ▣(½m) ▩(2½m)

Min£69 Max£174pw

F **Watlands Flat** Valley Road
for bookings Powell's Holidays (address as page 221)
☎Saundersfoot(0834)812791
A small, first-floor unit approached by steep open-tread staircase. Accommodation comprises one double-bedded room, bathroom/WC and kitchen/diner. Fifteen minutes' walk to the sea and harbour.

May-Sep MWB out of season 1wk min, 6wks max, 1unit, 2persons no pets ◆ ◆ ◎ fridge Electric Elec inclusive ☐can be hired ☎(300yds) Airing cupboard in unit Iron in unit Ironing board in unit HCE in unit Launderette within 300yds TV ⊕3pin square 1P ▥ ♨(½m)

⊖ ♀(2½m)

Min£30 Max£84pw

SCALASAIG
Isle of Colonsay Strathclyde *Argyll*
Map**10** NR39

H **Baleruminmhor Farmhouse** Cable Bay
for bookings Mrs E McNeill, Machrins Farm, Isle of Colonsay, Argyll
☎Colonsay(09512)312
Stone farmhouse in superb position overlooking islands of Jura and Islay. It has three bedrooms and a bathroom on the first floor. On the ground floor there is one lounge and a large kitchen/diner. Additional bathroom, cloakroom and double bedroom on ground floor. Calor gas lighting. Facilities are modest. Very rough approach road of 1m.

Mar–Oct MWB out of season 1wk min, 1unit, 1–11persons ◆ ◊ fridge Calor gas & open fires Gas inclusive ☐not provided ☎(3m) Airing cupboard in unit HCE in unit P ♨(3m) Loch & sea fishing, boat for hire

⊖ ♂(3m) ♀(3m) ▣(3m)

Max£195.50pw

C **Glen Cottage**
for bookings Mrs E McNeill, Machrins Farm, Isle of Colonsay, Argyll
☎Colonsay(09512)312
Small white painted stone cottage located close to Scalasaig Pier comprising kitchen, sitting room, bathroom and one double bedded room on the ground floor. A steep staircase leads to two twin bedded attic bedrooms.

All year MWB out of season 1wk min, 1unit, 1–6persons ◆ ◊ fridge Calor gas & open fires Gas/Elec inclusive ☐not provided ☎(200yds) ⊕3pin round P ♨(200yds)

⊖ ♀(¼m) ▣(¼m)

Min£70 Max£120pw

SCARBOROUGH
North Yorkshire
Map**8** TA08

F **Adelaide House** St Martins, Scarborough, N Yorkshire YO11 2DQ
☎Scarborough(0723)60928
On south cliff overlooking open garden close to large shopping area, and bus services. Large garden with swings available to guests and their children. Three self-contained flats in a large three-storey house. Flats 4 and 6 have a double bed and two bunk beds in only one bedroom and a double bed in the sitting room. Separate kitchens, bathrooms/WC. Flat 7 also sleeps six but with double bed and twin beds in one room and a double bed in the other. Separate kitchen, shower and WC.

All year MWB out of season 1wk min, 1mth max, 3units, 1–6persons ◆ ◆ no pets ◎ fridge ♨ Elec metered ☐can be hired ☎(50yds) Iron on premises Ironing board on premises HCE in unit [Launderette within 300yds] ⊙ ⊛ ⊕3pin square ▥ ♨(50yds)

⊖ ♀(200yds) ▣(¼m) ♫(½m) ▩(½m)

Min£24 Max£72pw (Low)
Min£42 Max£98pw (High)

F **16 Albion Road**
for bookings Mr D A Slack, 7 Lowdale Avenue, Scarborough, N Yorkshire YO12 6JR
☎Scarborough(0723)65197
Five self-contained flats in a large Edwardian terraced house. One flat has a bed-settee in the lounge where the others have a foldaway bed. There is a separate twin-bedded room, bathroom/WC and

separate kitchen. Each flat has two occasional beds available expanding the sleeping to six people. Close to Valley Gardens and the South Cliffs.

Etr–Oct MWB out of season 1wk min, 2wks max, 5units, 1–6persons [◊] [◆] ♩ fridge Electric Gas/elec metered ⊡can be hired ☎(100yds) Airing cupboard on premises Iron in unit Ironing board on premises HCE in unit [Launderette within 300yds] ⊙ [TV] ⊕3pin square ▥ ♨(100yds)
⊖ ♀(200yds) ▨(300yds) ♫(1m) ▦(1m)

Min£45 Max£150pw

F Green Gables Holiday Flats West Bank, Scarborough, N Yorkshire YO12 4DX
☎Scarborough(0834)61005

Ten self-contained flats with modern fittings and furnishings within Green Gables Hotel. Accommodation for up to eight people includes a bed-settee in the lounge and fully equipped bathrooms and kitchens. Located on top floor of hotel with access by lift and stairs. Guests can use hotel facilities.

All year MWB out of season 4days min, 1mth max, 10units, 1–8persons ◊ [◊] [◆] no pets ♩ fridge Gas/elec inclusive ⊡inclusive ☎ [Iron on premises] Ironing board on premises HCE in unit [Launderette on premises] ⊙ ⊛ CTV ⊕3pin square P ♨ ▥ ♨(200yds) ⊡
⊖ ♀(400yds) ▨(1m) ♫(1m) ▦(1m)

F 49 Grosvenor Road for bookings Mrs G Wittering, 54 Deepdale Avenue, Scarborough YO11 2UF
☎Scarborough(0723)66256

Seven self-contained flats in a large town house near the town centre. Four share a common entrance and three have their own individual entrances. Good fittings and furnishings, generally spacious and well appointed.

May–Oct MWB out of season 1wk min, 2mths max, 7units, 4–6persons ◊ ◆ ♩ fridge Electric Elec metered ⊡inclusive ☎ [WM on premises] [SD on premises] [TD on premises] [Iron on premises] Ironing board on premises HCE on premises ⊙ CTV ⊕3pin square ♨(400yds)
⊖ ♀(400yds) ▨(800yds) ▦(600yds)

Min£67.85 Max£134.55pw (Low)
Min£94.30 Max£179.40pw (High)

F 54 Scalby Mills Road for bookings Mr A A Squire, 54 Falsgrave Road, Scarborough, N Yorkshire
☎Scarborough(0723)60542

Large semi-detached house divided into two flats. Conveniently situated for north beach, on the outskirts of town, overlooking golf course. Good, clean standard.

All year MWB out of season 1wk min, 2wks max, 2units, 1–6persons ◊ ◆ no pets ♩ fridge Electric Elec metered ⊡inclusive ☎(300yds) Airing cupboard in unit Iron in unit Ironing board in unit HCE in unit ⊙ CTV P ▥ ♨(300yds)
⊖ ♐ ♀(100yds) ▨(1½m) ♫(1½m) ▦(2m)

Min£50 Max£100pw (Low)
Min£160 Max£190pw (High)

F 11 Valley Bridge Parade for bookings Mrs G Wittering, 54 Deepdale Avenue, Scarborough, N Yorkshire YO11 2UF
☎Scarborough(0723)66256

Four self-contained flats each occupying a single floor of the five-storeyed town house overlooking Valley Bridge close to the central shopping area. First-class fittings and furnishings. Well appointed and well managed.

May–Oct MWB out of season 1wk min, 2mths max, 4units, 4persons ◊ ◆ ♩ fridge Electric Elec metered ⊡inclusive ☎(40yds) HCE ⊙ CTV ⊕3pin square ♨(100yds)
⊖ ♀(300yds) ▨(300yds) ♫(500yds) ▦(300yds)

Min£65.55 Max£88.55pw (Low)
Min£89.70 Max£113.85pw (High)

F 15 Victoria Park for bookings Mr A A Squire, 54 Falsgrave Road, Scarborough, N Yorkshire
☎Scarborough(0723)60542

Large semi-detached house divided into one ground-floor and one first-floor flat with separate entrances. Situated in town in the heart of North Beach holiday facilities and overlooking Peasholme Park, close to cricket ground.

All year MWB out of season 1wk min, 2wks max, 2units, 1–6persons ◊ ◆ no pets ♩ fridge Electric Elec metered ⊡inclusive ☎(30yds) Iron in unit Ironing board in unit HCE in unit ⊙ CTV ⊕3pin square P ▥ ♨(30yds)
⊖ ♐(1m) ♀(50yds) ▨(100yds) ♫(2m) ▦(½m)

Min£50 Max£100pw (Low)
Min£160 Max£180pw (High)

SCILLY, ISLES OF
(No Map)
See **Bryher and St Mary's**

SCORTON
Lancashire
Map 7 SD44

F The Manager Six Arches Caravan Park Scorton, Garstang, Preston, Lancashire PR3 1AL
☎Forton(0524)791683

A block of six brick-built flats within the caravan park, on the banks of the River

Wyre with good views of the Beacon Fells. The flats are of modern design with good furnishings. They are reached by turning E off the A6 by the Little Chef N of Garstang and continuing under the six arches from which the site gets its name.

Mar–Oct 7days min, 6units, 2–6persons ◊ ◆ ♩ fridge Electric Elec metered ⊡can be hired ☎(50yds) [Iron on premises] [Ironing board on premises] HCE in unit [Launderette on premises] ⊙ CTV ⊕3pin square P ▥ ♨ ⊐
⊖ ♀ ▨

Min£40 Max£55pw (Low)
Min£70 Max£100pw (High)

SCRATBY
Norfolk
Map 9 TG51

H Carlton Beach Road Chalet Park, Beach Road
for bookings Hoseasons Holidays, Sunway House, Lowestoft, Suffolk NR32 3LT
☎Lowestoft(0502)62292

Two-storey brick-built homes, modern design, semi-detached, set on a small well-maintained site. On the ground floor there is one double, one twin and one bunk bedded room. The first floor has lounge/dining room, kitchen, combined bath/WC/wash basin. Follow signs to Scratby off B1159, site is ½m on left of Beach Road.

Etr–Oct MWB out of season 4days min, 14units, 2–8persons [◊] [◆] ♩ fridge Electric Elec metered ⊡inclusive ☎(½m) Airing cupboard in unit [Iron on premises] HCE in unit ⊙ TV ⊕3pin square P ♨(200yds) ⊐ Children's play area
⊖ ♀(300yds) ▨(300yds) ♫(300yds)

Ch Mayfair, Beach Road Chalet Park, Beach Road
for bookings Hoseasons Holidays, Sunway House, Lowestoft, Suffolk NR32 3LT
☎Lowestoft(0502)62292

Purpose-built brick/timber semi-detached chalets with small patios set on a well-maintained site. Accommodation has one double, one twin bedroom, combined lounge/kitchen and bathroom/WC. Follow signs to Scratby off B1159, site is ½m on left of Beach Road.

Etr–Oct MWB out of season 4days min, 46units, 2–6persons [◊] [◆] ♩ fridge Electric Elec metered ⊡inclusive ☎(½m) Airing cupboard in unit [Iron on premises] HCE in unit ⊙ TV ⊕3pin square P ♨(200yds) ⊐ Children's play area
⊖ ♀(300yds) ▨(300yds) ♫(300yds)

1982 prices quoted throughout gazetteer

Ch **Summercrest** Summerfields
Holiday Park, Beach Road
for bookings Hoseasons Holidays,
Sunway House, Lowestoft, Suffolk
NR32 3LT
☎Lowestoft(0502)62292

*Purpose-built brick/timber chalet set in
well-maintained grassed area.
Accommodation has one twin bedroom
and one double room, combined
lounge/kitchen/dining room and
bathroom/WC. Follow signs to Scratby off
B1159, site on right of Beach Road.*

Apr–Oct MWB out of season
4 days min, 5 units, 2–6 persons [◇]
[◇] [◆] ◉ fridge Electric
Elec metered ⌷inclusive ☎(200yds)
Airing cupboard in unit [Iron on
premises] HCE in unit ⊙ TV
⊕3 pin square P ♿(200yds)
Children's room, pool

↤ ♿ ♀ 🎞 ♫

Ch **Summer Sands** Summerfields
Holiday Park, Beach Road
for bookings Hoseasons Holidays,
Sunway House, Lowestoft, Suffolk
NR32 3LT
☎Lowestoft(0502)62292

*Purpose-built brick and timber chalets.
Accommodation consists of one
bedroom with double and single beds,
lounge/kitchen/dining room and
combined shower, WC and washbasin.*

Apr–Oct MWB out of season
4 days min, 3 units, 2–5 persons [◇]
[◇] [◆] ◉ fridge Electric
Elec metered ⌷inclusive ☎(200yds)
Airing cupboard in unit Iron on
premises HCE in unit ⊙ TV
⊕3 pin square P ♿(200yds) ⌂

↤ ♿ ♀ 🎞 ♫

Ch **Summersea** Summerfields Holiday
Park, Beach Road
for bookings Hoseasons Holidays,
Sunway House, Lowestoft, Suffolk
NR32 3LT
☎Lowestoft(0502)62292

*Purpose-built brick and timber chalets
set in a well-maintained site with grassed
areas and concrete roads.
Accommodation is one double bedroom,
lounge/kitchen/dining room and
combined bath/WC.*

Apr–Oct MWB out of season
4 days min, 3 units, 2–4 persons [◇]
[◇] [◆] ◉ fridge Electric
Elec metered ⌷inclusive ☎(200yds)
Airing cupboard in unit Iron on
premises HCE in unit ⊙ TV
⊕3 pin square P ♿

↤ ♿ ♀ 🎞 ♫

H **Summer Spray** Summerfields
Holiday Park, Beach Road
for bookings Hoseasons Holidays,
Sunway House, Lowestoft, Suffolk
NR32 3LT
☎Lowestoft(0502)62292

*Brick-built two-storey modern homes set
in well-maintained grassed area.
Accommodation on first floor has one*
*double, one twin and one double and
single bedroom. Ground-floor has
combined lounge/kitchen with bath/WC.
Follow signs to Scratby off B1159 into
Beach Road.*

Apr–Oct MWB out of season
4 days min, 34 units, 2–7 persons [◇]
[◇] [◆] ◉ fridge Electric
Elec metered ⌷inclusive ☎(200yds)
Airing cupboard in unit [Iron on
premises] HCE in unit ⊙ TV
⊕3 pin square P ♿ Children's room

↤ ♿ ♀ 🎞 ♫

H **Summerwave** Summerfields Holiday
Park, Beach Road
for bookings Hoseasons Holidays,
Sunway House, Lowestoft, Suffolk
NR32 2LT
☎Lowestoft(0502)62292

*Brick-built two-storey modern homes set
in a well-maintained site.
Accommodation comprises first-floor
twin bedroom and one double and single
bedroom. Lounge/kitchen/dining room
and combined shower/WC.*

Apr–Oct MWB out of season
4 days min, 4 units, 2–5 persons [◇]
[◇] [◆] ◉ fridge Electric
Elec metered ⌷inclusive ☎(200yds)
Airing cupboard in unit [Iron on
premises] HCE in unit ⊙ TV
⊕3 pin square P ♿ Children's room

↤ ♿ ♀ 🎞 ♫

SCUPHOLME
Lincolnshire
Map 9 TF49

H **Manor Farm House, West Wing**
for bookings C V Stubbs & Sons, Manor
Farm, Calcethorpe, Louth, Lincolnshire
LN11 0RF
☎Louth(0507)604219

*Has a two-storey unit in the W wing of an
attractive modernised 18th-century
farmhouse set in the Lincolnshire
marshes. The large accommodation
comprises combined kitchen/dining
area, separate lounge, one twin-bedded
room and one double bedroom. Located
between the villages of South
Somercotes and South Cockerington and
within easy reach of the nearby resort
towns.*

All year MWB out of season 1 wk min,
1 unit, 4 persons ◇ ◉ fridge 🍳
Elec inclusive ⌷can be hired ☎(2½m)
Airing cupboard in unit HCE in unit TV
⊕3 pin square P 🎞 ♿(2½m)

↤ ♀ (2½m)

Min£65.55 Max£82.80pw (Low)
Min£83.95 Max£106.95pw (High)

1982 prices quoted throughout
gazetteer

SCURLAGE
West Glamorgan
Map 2 SS48

Ch **Georgian Lodge Holiday Homes**
for bookings Hoseasons Holidays,
Sunway House, Lowestoft, Suffolk
NR32 3LT
☎Lowestoft(0502)62292

*Each of the chalets is laid out adjoining
the hotel. Lounge is carpeted and has
bed-settee. Kitchen is fully equipped with
electric appliances. Bathroom. Modern
furnishings and good décor.*

All year MWB out of season 1 wk min,
47 units, 4–6 persons [◇] [◆]
no pets ◉ fridge Electric
Elec metered ⌷inclusive ☎ Airing
cupboard [Iron on premises] [Ironing
board on premises] HCE [Launderette
on premises] ⊙ TV ⊕3 pin square
P 🎞 ♿ ▭

↤ ♀ 🎞

SEATOLLER
Cumbria
Map 11 NY21

C **High Stile Cottage** Top Row
for bookings Mrs P M Brannan, Lingy
Acre, Portinscale, Keswick, Cumbria
☎Keswick(0596)72717

*End-of-terrace stone-built cottage in this
tiny hamlet at the head of the beautiful
Borrowdale Valley. The accommodation
comprises spacious lounge/diner (with
extra divan bed), a modern kitchen on
ground-floor and two twin bedrooms and
bathroom, on the first-floor.*

Apr–Nov 1 wk min, 1 mth max, 1 unit,
2–5 persons ◇ ◆ no pets ◉
fridge Electric Elec metered
⌷not provided ☎(200yds) Airing
cupboard in unit Iron in unit Ironing
board in unit HCE in unit ⊙ TV
⊕3 pin square 1P 1🏠 🎞 ♿(3¼m)

↤ ♀(300yds)

Min£80 Max£100pw (Low)
Min£120 Max£140pw (High)

SEATON
Cornwall
Map 2 SX35

Ch Mr & Mrs M T Davies **Mount Brioni**
22 Looe Hill Road, Seaton, Torpoint,
Cornwall PL11 3JN
☎Downderry(05035)251

*A number of chalets built in a semi-circle
on a terrace around an old house. They
offer a good view over the sea and there
is a small landscaped garden with a
steep drop to the road. 'B' Type chalets
are four units sleeping up to five, situated
on the ground-floor with a sun terrace.
'C1' Type is three units sleeping up to six
persons situated on ground-floor with
private patio. 'C' Type is four units similar
in design to 'C1' Type, but smaller. 'D'
and 'E' Types are attached to the house.
'D' is an upstairs annexe and 'E' is on the
ground-floor of the house with large
attractive rooms.*

Feb-Nov MWB out of season 3days min, 1mth max, 14units, 5–6persons [◇] [◆] no dogs Jun-Aug ◎ fridge Electric Elec metered ☐can be hired ☎ WM on premises [SD on premises] TD on premises Iron on premises Ironing board on premises HCE in unit ⊙ CTV ⊕3pin square P ▥ ⛁(¼m)

⊖ ♀(¼m)

Min£25 Max£55pw (Low)
Min£95 Max£165pw (High)

SEATON
Devon
Map**3** SY28

Ch **CC Ref 633 (A)**
for bookings Character Cottages (Holidays) Ltd, 34 Fore Street, Sidmouth, Devon EX10 8AQ
☎Sidmouth(039 55)77001

A cedarwood chalet-bungalow sited on park 1m from Seaton. Large living room with picture windows and modest furnishings. Two double bedrooms with good divan beds. Well-equipped kitchen with breakfast bar. Concrete approach paths and lawned surround.

All year MWB out of season 1wk min, 6mths max, 1unit, 4–5persons ◆ ◎ fridge Electric Elec metered ☐can be hired ☎ Airing cupboard in unit Iron in unit Ironing board in unit HCE in unit [Launderette] ⊙ [TV] ⊕3pin square ⊕2pin round P ▥ ⛁

⊖ ♀(1m) ▤(1m) ♬(1m)

Min£71 Max£78pw (Low)
Min£91 Max£104pw (High)

F **CC Ref 6039P**
for bookings Character Cottages (Holidays) Ltd, 34 Fore Street, Sidmouth, Devon EX10 8AQ
☎Sidmouth(039 55)77001

Block of well-designed modern flats in quiet residential area. Accommodation consists of good-size lounge/diner with double put-u-up, one twin- and two double-bedded rooms and kitchen. Well-maintained bathroom and WC. Sea views from all flats.

All year MWB out of season 1wk min, 6wks max, 4units, 1–6persons [◆] [◆] ◎ fridge Electric Elec metered ☐not provided ☎(800yds) Airing cupboard in unit HCE in unit ⊙ TV ⊕3pin square P ▥ ⛁(¼m)

⊖ ⛳18(¾m) ♀(¼m) ♬(¼m)

Min£33 Max£42pw (Low)
Min£55 Max£130pw (High)

F **CC Ref 6040P**
for bookings Character Cottages (Holidays) Ltd, 34 Fore Street, Sidmouth, Devon EX10 8AQ
☎Sidmouth(039 55)77001

Block of flats built some 10yrs ago. Accommodation comprises lounge/diner with good-quality furnishings and double put-u-up, two double bedrooms, one with singles and bunk beds, separate bathroom/WC/wash basin, all with modern fittings. Well maintained kitchen. Five minute's walk from seafront.

All year MWB out of season 1wk min, 6wks max, 8units, 1–6persons [◆] [◆] ◎ fridge Electric Elec metered ☐not provided ☎(50yds) Airing cupboard in unit HCE in unit ⊙ TV ⊕3pin square P ▥ ⛁(¼m)

⊖ ⛳18(¾m) ♀(¼m) ♬(¼m)

Min£33 Max£42pw (Low)
Min£55 Max£130pw (High)

F **CC Ref 6041P**
for bookings Character Cottages (Holidays) Ltd, 34 Fore Street, Sidmouth, Devon EX10 8AQ
☎Sidmouth(039 55)77001

Top-floor flat of three-storey hotel property in town centre. Accommodation comprises a double room, one twin and one single room, separate bathroom with WC and wash basin, lounge/diner with double put-u-up, kitchen with built-in units. Very clean and comfortable.

All year MWB out of season 1wk min, 3wks max, 1unit, 1–7persons [◆] [◆] ◎ fridge Electric Elec metered ☐not provided ☎(50yds) HCE in unit [Launderette within 300yds] ⊙ TV ⊕3pin square ▥ ⛁(20yds) Children's room

⊖ ⛳18(½m) ♬(50yds)

Min£26 Max£36pw (Low)
Min£61 Max£91pw (High)

Ch **Tower Country Chalet Park Nos 24, 25, 26 & 29**
for bookings Mr & Mrs W Froom, Middle Mill Farm, Lyme Regis, Dorset DT7 3UB
☎Lyme Regis(02974)2722

Four well-maintained cedarwood chalets in small chalet park. Wood-panelled interiors comprising open plan kitchen, lounge/diner, bathroom, one double and one twin bedroom, also sofa bed in lounge. On main Sidmouth–Seaton road. One mile from beach.

20Mar-Oct MWB out of season 1wk min, 6wks max, 4units, 1–6persons ◆ ◎ fridge Electric Elec metered ☐not provided ☎ Iron in unit Ironing board in unit HCE in unit ⊙ CTV ⊕3pin square 1P ▥ ⛁

⊖ ⛳18(3m) ♀(300yds) ♬(2m)

Min£40 Max£60pw (Low)
Min£70 Max£120pw (High)

SEAVIEW
Isle of Wight
Map**4** SZ69

Ch, B Manager, **Salterns Holiday Bunglaows** Seaview, Isle of Wight PO34 5AQ
☎Seaview(098 371)2330

Large holiday complex consisting of 26 chalets and 51 bungalows, all with kitchens, lounge/diner, showers and WC. Four chalets contain three bedrooms, two units sleep six persons and all the remaining units have two small bedrooms. All units are simply furnished and set in attractive grounds.

15May-25Sep 1wk min, 3mths max, 77units, 2–6persons [◆] no pets ◎ fridge Electric Elec metered ☐not provided ☎ Airing cupboard in unit [Iron on premises] [Ironing board on premises] HCE in unit ⊙ TV ⊕3pin square P

⊖ ♀(300yds) ▤(3m) ♬(3m) 🎥(3m)

Min£44.55 Max£72.45pw (Low)
Min£82.80 Max£112.70pw (High)

SEDBERGH
Cumbria
Map**7** SD69

H **Benson Bank** Hawes Road
for bookings Mrs Stockdale, Bank Cottage Farm, Sedbergh, Cumbria
☎Sedbergh(0587)20429

A large stone-built farmhouse with one twin and two double bedrooms. The accommodation is simple but clean. The farmhouse is situated 1¼m from Sedbergh in a peaceful rural area on the A684 surrounded by magnificent views of hills and fells.

All year MWB 1wk min, 1mth max, 1unit, 6persons no pets ◎ fridge Electric & coal Elec metered ☐not provided ☎(¼m) Airing cupboard in unit HCE in unit ⓦ ⊕3pin square P ⌂ ▥ ⛁(1m) Fishing

⊖ ♀(1m) ▤(1m)

Min£35 Max£60pw

H **The Hylands**
for bookings Mr G D Handley, 31 Allderidge Avenue, Hull HU5 4EG
☎Hull(0482)493875

Large stone-built detached house in attractive gardens, standing in an elevated position ¼m from town centre. Peaceful rural location within N Yorkshire Dales National Park, with magnificent views of surrounding countryside. Comfortable accommodation includes two double and three twin-bedded rooms.

May-Oct 2days min, 3wks max, 1unit, 10persons ◆ ◎ fridge Elec metered ☐not provided ☎(400yds) Airing cupboard in unit Iron in unit HCE in unit TV ⊕3pin square P ▥ ⛁(½m)

⊖ ♀(½m)

Min£50 Max£60pw (Low)
Min£80 Max£300pw (High)

SEDGEBERROW
Hereford & Worcester
Map**4** SP03

C **Forge Cottage**
for bookings Mrs D Stow, Lower Portway Farm, Sedgeberrow, Evesham, Worcestershire
☎Evesham(0386)881298 →

This modernised detached cottage is over 200-years-old and many rooms have the original beamed ceilings. It has a secluded lawned garden adjoining a plum orchard to the rear and side. Accommodation comprises of sitting room, dining room, kitchen and two bedrooms plus bathroom upstairs.

Apr-Oct 1wk min, 3mths max, 1unit, 1–4persons ◇ ◆ no pets ◉ fridge Electric Elec metered ▢ can be hired ☎(200yds) WM in unit SD in unit Airing cupboard in unit Iron in unit Ironing board in unit HCE in unit CTV ⊕3pin square 2P ♨(50yds) ↝Grass ♂ Fishing

↔ ♀(100yds) ▨(3m) ♫(3m) ♨(3m)
Min£55 Max£95pw

F Hall Farm Flats
for bookings Mrs D Stow, Lower Portway Farm, Sedgeberrow, Evesham, Worcestershire
☎Evesham(0386)881298

This large Georgian house has recently been converted to modern flats each having its own entrance. The accommodation varies slightly, depending on the number of occupants but all contain lounges, kitchens and bathroom/WC's.

Apr-Oct MWB 1wk min, 3mths max, 5units, 1–6persons ◇ ◆ no pets ◉ fridge Electric Elec metered ▢ can be hired ☎ Airing cupboard in unit Iron in unit Ironing board in unit HCE in unit [Launderette on premises] CTV ⊕3pin square 8P ↝Grass ♂ Fishing

↔ ♀(100yds) ▨(3m) ♫(3m) ♨(3m)
Min£35 Max£85pw (Low)
Min£50 Max£85pw (High)

H Manor House
for bookings Mrs D Stow, Lower Portway Farm, Sedgeberrow, Evesham, Worcestershire
☎Evesham(0386)881298

This brick built detached manor house stands in its own garden with lawns to front and rear. The house dates from 1572 and most of its rooms are beamed. All accommodation is on the ground-floor (upstairs is closed off) and comprises large lounge with stone fireplace, kitchen, dining room, two bedrooms and bathroom/WC.

Apr-Oct 1wk min, 3mths max, 1unit, 1–6persons ◇ ◆ no pets ◉ fridge Electric Elec metered ▢ can be hired ☎(¼m) WM in unit SD in unit Airing cupboard in unit Iron in unit Ironing board in unit HCE in unit CTV ⊕3pin square 3P 1♨ ♨(60yds) ↝Grass ♂ Fishing

↔ ♀(60yds) ▨(3m) ♫(3m) ♨(3m)
Min£70 Max£120pw

C Manor Lodge
for bookings Mrs D Stow, Lower Portway Farm, Sedgeberrow, Evesham, Worcestershire
☎Evesham(0386)881298

Sedgeberrow
—
Sennen Cove

Small, detached, modernised cottage located in the heart of this peaceful village and comprises of sitting room, dining room, kitchen and bathroom/WC. First-floor has two bedrooms and WC.

Apr-Oct 1wk min, 3mths max, 1unit, 1–4persons ◇ ◆ no pets ◉ fridge Electric Elec metered ▢ can be hired ☎(200yds) WM in unit SD in unit Airing cupboard in unit Iron in unit Ironing board in unit HCE in unit CTV ⊕3pin square 1P 1♨ ♨(25yds) ↝Grass ♂ Fishing

↔ ♀(15yds) ▨(3m) ♫(3m) ♨(3m)
Min£45 Max£80pw

SELKIRK
Borders Selkirkshire
Map12 NT42

C Coach House Court Cottages
for bookings Mrs H Dunlop, Whitmuir Hall, Whitmuir, Selkirk, Selkirkshire TD7 4PZ
☎Selkirk(0750)21728

Six coach house cottages converted from former coach house and stables, standing in wooded grounds of Whitmuir Hall. Red Gauntlet cottage offers open plan lounge/diner/kitchen, two twin bedrooms and bathroom. The other five cottages have the same accommodation with only one twin bedroom and also a shower room. Access off A699 E of junction with A7.

All year MWB out of season 2nights min, 3wks max, 6units, 2–6persons [◇] [◈ ◆] ◉ fridge ▥ Elec metered ▢ inclusive ☎(100yds) [WM on premises] [SD on premises] Airing cupboard in unit Iron on premises Ironing board on premises HCE in unit ⊙ CTV ⊕3pin square 12P ♨(3m) Fishing, outdoor playground, games room

↔ ♙(2m) ♀(3m)
Min£50 Max£110pw (Low)
Min£100 Max£160pw (High)

F Whitmuir Hall
for bookings Mrs H Dunlop, Whitmuir Hall, Whitmuir, Selkirk, Selkirkshire TD7 4PZ
☎Selkirk(0750)21728

Victorian country mansion house in five acres of grounds and split into nine flats. They comprise living room, kitchen and a maximum of three bedrooms. The dining area varies between the kitchen and living room. Most living rooms have a bed-settee. For access drive SE from Selkirk on the A7 for two miles then on to the A699 and follow signs.

All year MWB out of season 3nights min, 3wks max, 9units, 2–8persons ◇ ◆ ◉ fridge ▥ Elec metered ▢ inclusive ☎ [WM on premises] [SD on premises] [TD on

premises] Airing cupboard in unit Iron on premises Ironing board on premises HCE in unit ⊙ CTV ⊕3pin square 15P ▦ ♨(3m)

↔ ♙(3m) ♀(3m) Private loch for coarse fishing Trampoline & table tennis
Min£65 Max£120pw (Low)
Min£100 Max£200pw (High)

SENNEN
Cornwall
Map2 SW32

C Mr A J Loutit Tregiffian Cottages
Tregiffian Hotel, Sennen, Cornwall TR19 7BE
☎Sennen(073687)408

Four units within small complex of converted stone cottages in grounds of small hotel. Granary Cottage is on the first floor and comprises one twin-bedded room, one double, with a double bed-settee in the lounge. There is a separate kitchen and bathroom/WC. Wain Cottage has one twin-bedded room, a small double bedroom, lounge, kitchen and bathroom/WC on ground floor. Forge Cottage comprises two twin-bedded rooms, one double bed-settee in the lounge, separate kitchen and bathroom/WC. Barn Cottage has one twin-bedded room and one double, lounge, kitchen and bathroom/WC.

Mar–Oct MWB out of season 1wk min, 4units, 1–6persons ◇ ◆ ◉ fridge Electric Elec metered ▢ can be hired ☎ SD on premises Iron on premises Ironing board on premises HCE in unit ⊙ ⊛ CTV ⊕3pin square P ▦ ♨(2m)
Max£51.75pw (Low)
Min£151.80 Max£169.05pw (High)

SENNEN COVE
Cornwall
Map2 SW32

C Capstan Cottage
for bookings J A & S D Hedges, Westwards, Bickwell Valley, Sidmouth, Devon
☎Sidmouth(03955)6176

Old-world thatched cottage situated 70yds from seafront and overlooking the sea. Accommodation comprises cosy and attractive sitting room, dining room (both with granite open fireplaces), small well-equipped kitchen, two tastefully decorated bedrooms with double divans and modern bathroom and WC facilities.

All year MWB out of season 1wk min, 6mths max, 1unit, 2–5persons ◇ ◉ fridge Electric Elec inclusive ▢ can be hired ☎ Airing cupboard in unit Iron in unit Ironing board in unit HCE in unit ⊙ CTV ⊕3pin square ⊕2pin round P ♨ ▦ ♨

↔ ♀(¼m)
Min£75 Max£120pw (Low)
Min£150 Max£200pw (High)

C No Place Maria Lane
for bookings J A & S D Hedges,
Westwards, Bickwell Valley, Sidmouth,
Devon
☎Sidmouth(039 55)6176

*Thatched cottage situated on moor
above Sennen Cove. Carpeted living
room, small, well-equipped kitchen,
modern bathroom and WC. Sleeping
accommodation consists of two double
bedrooms, one with wash basin. Fine sea
views and good coastal and cliff walks
and garden.*

All year MWB out of season 1wk min,
6mths max, 1unit, 2–4persons ◆ ◎
fridge Electric Elec inclusive Ⓛcan
be hired ☎ Airing cupboard in unit
Iron in unit Ironing board in unit HCE in
unit ⊙ CTV ③3pin square
⊛2pin round P ♿(½m)

↭ ☕(½m)
Min£75 Max£120pw (Low)
Min£150 Max£200pw (High)

SEVENOAKS
Kent
Map5 TQ55

C Moorings Cottages 99 & 101
Hitchen Hatch Lane
for bookings Moorings Hotel, 97 Hitchen
Hatch Lane, Sevenoaks, Kent TN13 3BE
☎Sevenoaks(0732)452589

*Two semi-detached Victorian cottages in
a small garden plot. Accommodation
comprises two bedrooms, living room,
kitchen and bathroom/WC. The cottages
are situated within 300yds of Sevenoaks
Station with frequent trains to London.*

All year MWB out of season 2wks min in
season 3mths max, 2units,
1–6persons no pets 🥄 fridge 🍴
Gas inclusive Ⓛinclusive ☎ Iron in
unit Ironing board in unit HCE in unit
[Launderette within 300yds] ⊙ CTV
③3pin square P 🅿 ♿(300yds)

↭ ☕(50yds) 🅿(2m) 🎵(2m) 🛒(1m)
Min£138 Max£161pw

SEWERBY
North Humberside
Map8 TA16

C 29 Main Street
for bookings Mrs J D Pallister, 17
Westridge Road, Bridlington, N
Humberside YO15 3PT
☎Bridlington(0262)75564

*This old fisherman's cottage is included
in the list of the Department of the
Environment as a building of special
architectural or historic interest. It has
been brick faced, modernised and
converted into two units. One unit has two
double bedrooms (one with spare divan),
living room, kitchen and shower/WC. The
other unit has one double bedroom, living
room, kitchen and shower/WC.*

All year MWB out of season 1wk min,
2mths max, 2units, 1–5persons ◆ ◎
fridge Electric Elec metered Ⓛcan be
hired ☎(150yds) HCE in unit TV
③3pin square P 🅿 🅿 🛒

Sennen Cove
—
Shanklin

↭ ☕(150yds) 🅿(2m) 🎵(2m) 🛒(2m)
Min£60 Max£75pw (Low)
Max£110pw (High)

C 31 Main Street
for bookings Mrs J D Pallister, 17
Westbridge Road, Bridlington, N
Humberside YO15 3PT
☎Bridlington(0262)75564

*An old brick-faced cottage, listed as a
building of special architectural and
historical interest. Accommodation
comprises three double bedrooms (one
with spare single divan), living room,
kitchen, bathroom and WC.*

All year MWB out of season 1wk min,
3mths max, 1unit, 2–5persons ◆ ◎
fridge Electric Elec metered Ⓛcan be
hired ☎(150yds) HCE in unit TV
③3pin square P 🅿 🅿 🛒

↭ ☕(150yds) 🅿(2m) 🎵(2m) 🛒(2m)
Min£60 Max£75pw (Low)
Max£110pw (High)

B Mrs J Tappenden **40 Sewerby Park
Close**
Sewerby, Bridlington, N Humberside
YO15 1EE
☎Bridlington(0262)77495

*Well-maintained unit contained within a
detached modern bungalow, standing in
a cul-de-sac. Accommodation includes
one twin-bedded room, shower/WC,
living room and kitchenette. Close to
Sewerby Hall Park and Zoo*

Spring Bank Hol–Sep 1wk min,
1mth max, 1unit, 1–2persons, nc
no pets ◎ fridge Electric
Elec metered Ⓛnot provided
☎(300yds) Iron in unit
Ironing board in unit HCE in unit CTV
③3pin square P 🅿 ♿(150yds) 🛒

↭ ☕(100yds) 🅿(2m) 🎵(2m) 🛒(2m)
Min£46 Max£48pw

SHANKLIN
Isle of Wight
Map4 SZ58

B 107 Green Lane
for bookings Alex Greenhill, Tanglin,
Highfield Road, Shanklin, Isle of Wight
☎Shanklin(098 386)3966

*Modern semi-detached bungalow in
quiet residential area about ½m E of town
centre, comprising two double bedrooms,
large lounge/diner, well-equipped
kitchen, separate bathroom with WC.
Well-maintained. Small garden at rear.*

23Apr–Sep MWB out of season
1wk min, 1unit, 1–6persons ◎ fridge
🍴 Elec metered Ⓛcan be hired
☎(200yds) Airing cupboard Iron
Ironing board HCE ⊙ TV
③3pin square 1🅿 🅿 🅿(150yds)
🛒(½m)

Min£90 Max£110pw (Low)
Min£120 Max£185pw (High)

Ch Lower Hyde Leisure Park Lower
Hyde Road, Shanklin, Isle of Wight
PO37 7LL
☎Shanklin(098 386)6131

*Twenty-nine chalets of similar style in a
combined chalet and caravan park. They
are modern and small, with two
bedrooms (double and twin-bedded)
and lounge/diner/kitchenette. The
lounge has a convertible settee, so each
unit can sleep six. Kitchenettes have
immersion heaters.*

26Mar–29Oct MWB in season
3nights min, 4wks max, 29units,
2–6persons [◇ ◆] no pets ◎
fridge Electric Elec metered Ⓛcan be
hired ☎ on premises Ironing
board on premises HCE in unit
[Launderette on premises] ⊙ CTV
③3pin square 30P 🅿 🅿(½m) ⊃
⤴Hard/grass Pitch & putt, take away
food, children's playground

↭ ☕(100yds) 🅿(100yds) 🎵(1m)
🛒(1m)
Min£54 Max£90pw (Low)
Min£120 Max£185pw (High)
See advert on page 228

F Mr A Thompson, **The Priory (Flats),**
Luccombe Road, Shanklin, Isle of Wight
PO37 6RR
☎Shanklin(098 386)2365

*Seven out of nine flats in a large Victorian
house in a quiet rural setting overlooking
the sea. Each flat has one double
bedroom, lounge/diner, well-equipped
kitchenette with microwave ovens and
bathroom. There is a separate television
room for guests use.*

All year MWB out of season 1day min,
2mths max, 7units, 1–4persons [◇ ◆
◆] no pets ◎ fridge/freezer 🍴 & gas
& electric fires Gas/elec metered
Ⓛcan be hired ☎ Iron on premises
Ironing board on premises HCE in unit
[Launderette on premises] ⊙ TV can
be hired ③3pin square 20P 🅿 ♿(½m)
↭ 🚲(½m) ☕(200yds) 🅿(½m)
🎵(½m) 🛒(½m)
Min£50 Max£60pw (Low)
Min£130 Max£160pw (High)
See advert on page 228

F 201 Sandown Road
for bookings Alex Greenhill, Tanglin,
Highfield Road, Shanklin, Isle of Wight
☎Shanklin(098 386)3966

*Two spacious self-contained flats in a
detached Victorian house just E of town
centre, comprising two double
bedrooms, separate bathroom/WC, well
equipped kitchen, lounge/diner and
garden at rear. Both flats are nicely
maintained and comfortably furnished.*

23Apr–Sep MWB out of season
1wk min, 2units, 1–6persons ◎
fridge Elec metered Ⓛcan be hired
☎(100yds) Airing cupboard Iron
Ironing board HCE ⊙ TV
③3pin square 2P 🅿 ♿(75yds)
↭ 🚲(1½m) ☕(½m) 🅿(½m) 🎵(½m)
🛒(½m) →

Min£75 Max£95pw (Low)
Min£105 Max£170pw (High)

F   South Wing Maisonettes
for bookings Mr A Thompson, The Priory,
Luccombe Road, Shanklin, Isle of Wight
PO37 6RR
☎Shanklin(098 386)2365

*A modern extension to this Victorian
house consisting of four maisonettes,
comfortably furnished, each with two
double bedrooms, lounge/diner, well-
equipped kitchen (with microwave oven)
in recess off lounge, and bathroom.
There is a television room for guests use.*

Shanklin — Sheen

All year   MWB out of season   1 day min,
2 mths max, 4 units, 1–4 persons   [◇ ◆
◆] no pets ◎ fridge/freezer ﬛ &
Electric fires   Elec metered   ⌷can be
hired ☎ Iron on premises   Ironing
board on premises   HCE in unit
[Launderette on premises] ⊙ TV can
be hired ⊕3 pin square   20P ▥
♨(¼m)

↔ ◓(¼m) ☗ (200yds) ▨(¼m)
♬(¼m) ▩-(¼m)
Min£85 Max£225pw

SHEEN
Staffordshire
Map 7 SK16

C   Walton Cottage
for bookings Mrs G H Turner, Ashlea, Earl
Sterndale, Buxton, Derbyshire SK17 0BU
☎Longnor(029 883)413

*Surrounded by beautiful countryside, this
tiny cottage has been modernised and
has two bedrooms, bathroom, lounge
and kitchen/diner. It is situated on the
edge of Sheen, which is 300ft above
River Dove between Hartington and
Longnor; this area provides a good base
for touring Staffordshire and South
Derbyshire. Own transport essential.*

All year MWB out of season 3 days min, 4 wks max, 1 unit, 1–5 persons ⊚ fridge Electric Elec inclusive ⬚ not provided ☎(200yds) Airing cupboard in unit HCE in unit ⊕ TV ⊕3pin square P ▥ ⚐(2½m)
⇔ ☗(200yds)
Min £70 Max £80 pw

SHEFFIELD
South Yorkshire
Map **8** SK38

F Mrs V King **Charnwood Apartments**
The Mews, 8 Kenwood Bank, Sheffield S7 1NU
☎Sheffield(0742)57289

Nineteen purpose built apartments in four separate buildings, situated in a pleasant urban area, 1½m from the city centre. All comprise lounge, kitchen, bathroom/shower/WC, with either one, two or three bedrooms sleeping from two to eight persons. Twice weekly cleaning included in rent.

All year MWB 1 day min, 12 wks max, 19 units, 2–8 persons [◇ ◆ ♦] no pets ⚮ fridge ♨ Gas & Elec metered ⬚ inclusive ☎ Iron on premises Ironing board on premises HCE on premises ⊕ CTV ⊕3pin square P ⚐
Min £77 Max £142 pw

SHILBOTTLE
Northumberland
Map **12** NU10

B, C, Ch **Willage Farm**
for bookings Mrs J C M Stoker, Shilbottle Town Foot Farm, Alnwick, Northumberland NE66 2HG
☎Shilbottle(066 575)245

Small farm complex comprising five units. One is a detached stone bungalow with lounge, kitchen, three bedrooms (one double, one twin and one with bunk beds) and bathroom. Two are semi-detached cottages, converted from the original farmhouse. The ground floors have lounge (with bed-settees) and kitchen. Upstairs are two bedrooms, one with bunks, the other with twin beds in one cottage and a double bed in the other. The other two units are Norwegian Pine Chalets with lounge/diner, kitchenette, bathroom/WC and three bedrooms, one with double bed and two with bunks.

All year MWB out of season 2 nights min, 1 mth max, 5 units, 4–6 persons [◇] ◆ ♦ ⚮(in chalets) ⊚(bungalows and cottages) fridge Electric & open fires Gas/Elec inclusive in chalets Elec metered ⬚ not provided ☎ HCE in unit ⊕ CTV ⊕3pin square 5P ▥ ⚐(200yds)
⇔ ⚬⚬(3m) ☗(300yds) 🐾(3m)
Min £45 Max £50 pw (Low)
Min £80 Max £165 pw (High)

SHIPDHAM
Norfolk
Map **5** TF90

C **The Ringers** The Green
for bookings Major G Bowlby, English Country Cottages, Claypit Lane, Fakenham, Norfolk NR21 9AH
☎Fakenham(0328)51155

Once a public house dating from the 13th-century, the property has been completely modernised to form a spacious cottage with exposed beams. Secluded rear garden and lawn at front. Large sitting room, separate dining room, modern kitchen and four bedrooms to sleep six. This conservation-area village lies about 5m S of Dereham.

All year 1 wk summer min, 1 unit, 6 persons ◇ ⊚ fridge ♨ Elec metered ⬚ inclusive ☎ Airing cupboard in unit Iron in unit Ironing board in unit HCE in unit ⊕ TV ⊕3pin square 1P 2⚐ ⚐(50yds)
⇔ ⚬⚬(3m) ☗(100yds)
Min £78 pw (Low)
Min £96 Max £162 pw (High)

SHUCKNALL
Hereford & Worcester
Map **3** SO54

C **2 Quarry Cottages**
for bookings Mr & Mrs E V Sadler, 60 East Road, Stoney Hill, Bromsgrove, Worcester B60 2NS
☎Bromsgrove(0527)73734

5 Miles from Hereford on A4103 Worcester road. This modernised 16th-century stone-faced cottage has ½-acre of garden with fine views of the surrounding Herefordshire countryside. Accommodation consists of kitchen, bathroom/WC, dining room and lounge on ground floor, and one double, one single and one twin bedroom on first floor.

All year MWB out of season 2 days min, 3 wks max, 1 unit, 5 persons ◇ ⊚ fridge Electric Elec metered ⬚ not provided ☎(½m) Airing cupboard in unit Iron in unit HCE in unit TV ⊕3pin square P ⚐(2m)
⇔ ☗(1m)
Min £35 Max £94 pw

SIDBURY
Devon
Map **3** SY19

C **Buckley Hill Cottage** Deepway
for bookings J A & A S D Hedges, Westwards, Bickwell Valley, Sidmouth, Devon
☎Sidmouth(039 55)6176

Delightful olde-worlde cottage with oak beams, large open fireplace and french windows from living room to garden. Kitchen has breakfast bar and dining

room. Four bedrooms plus cot. Modern bathroom and WC, cloakroom and separate WC.

All year MWB out of season 1 wk min, 6 mths max, 1 unit, 2–7 persons ◇ ⊚ fridge Electric Elec inclusive ⬚ can be hired ☎ WM in unit Airing cupboard in unit Iron in unit Ironing board in unit HCE in unit ⊕ TV ⊕3pin square P ▥ ⚐(100yds)
⇔ ☗(1m) ▨(1m) ♫(1m) 🐾(1m)
Min £85 Max £185 pw (Low)
Min £200 Max £315 pw (High)

SIDMOUTH
Devon
Map **3** SY18

C **Pigeon Cottage** Sidbury
for bookings J A & A S D Hedges, Westwards, Bickwell Valley, Sidmouth, Devon
☎Sidmouth(039 55)6176

Terraced thatch and stone cottage in picturesque village three miles from sea. Accommodation comprises sitting-room with inglenook, kitchen, utility room, ground-floor WC, two double bedrooms and bathroom/WC.

All year MWB out of season 1 wk min, 1 unit, 1–4 persons [◇] ◆ ⊚ fridge Electric Elec inclusive ⬚ can be hired ☎(150yds) WM in unit SD in unit Airing cupboard in unit Iron in unit Ironing board in unit HCE in unit ⊕ CTV ⊕3pin square ▥ ⚐(100yds)
⇔ ⚬⚬(3m) ☗(100yds) ▨(3m) ♫(3m) 🐾(3m)
Min £60 Max £95 pw (Low)
Min £125 Max £175 pw (High)

F J A & A S D Hedges **Westwards**
Bickwell Valley, Sidmouth, Devon
☎Sidmouth(039 55)6176

Luxury accommodation on second-floor of large house in secluded valley. Comprises central hall, lounge with sea views, large kitchen/diner with arched window, bedroom with double divan bed, french doors to balcony & garden.

All year MWB out of season 1 wk min, 1 mth max, 1 unit, 2 persons ◇ ⚮ fridge Electric Elec inclusive ⬚ can be hired ☎ WM in unit Airing cupboard in unit Iron in unit Ironing board in unit HCE in unit Launderette within 300 yds ⊕ TV ⊕3pin square ▥ ⚐(300yds)
⇔ ⚬⚬(1½m) ☗(400yds) ▨(400yds) ♫(400yds) 🐾(400yds)
Min £55 Max £85 pw (Low)
Min £100 Max £125 pw (High)

See advert on page 230

B **CC Ref 606 ELP**
for bookings Character Cottages (Holidays) Ltd, 34 Fore Street, Sidmouth, Devon EX10 8AQ
☎Sidmouth(039 55)77001 →

1982 prices quoted throughout gazetteer

Charming modern bungalow on residential site, overlooking Sid Valley, with lawned garden. A high standard of modern furnishings throughout. L shaped living room with dining area, excellent modern kitchen and two double bedrooms, with good divan beds, and modern wardrobes.

All year MWB out of season 1wk min, 6mths max, 1 unit, 4 persons ◇ ◎ fridge ♨ Elec inclusive ⌷ can be hired ☎ Airing cupboard in unit Iron in unit Ironing board in unit HCE in unit ⊕ TV ⊕3pin square ⊕2pin round P ☎ ▥ ♨(½m) ⚲Grass

↩ ⚲(¼m) ▨(¼m) ♫(¼m) ⚑(¼m)
Min£64 Max£92pw (Low)
Min£111 Max£142pw (High)

B CC Ref 608 EL
for bookings Character Cottages (Holidays) Ltd, 34 Fore Street, Sidmouth, Devon EX10 8AQ
☎Sidmouth(039 55)77001

Contemporary bungalow in rural surroundings. Accommodation comprises attractive living room with picture windows, well-equipped kitchen, three good-sized bedrooms, one with H/C washbasin, modern bathroom and WC. High quality furniture and fittings throughout.

All year MWB out of season 1wk min, 6mths max, 1 unit, 5 persons, nc no pets

◎ fridge ♨ Elec inclusive ⌷ can be hired ☎(300yds) WM in unit Airing cupboard in unit Iron in unit Ironing board in unit HCE in unit ⊕ TV ⊕3pin square ⊕2pin round ☎ ▥ ♨(2m)

↩ ⚲(2m) ▨(2m) ♫(2m) ⚑(2m)
Min£60 Max£93pw (Low)
Min£120 Max£173pw (High)

H CC Ref 705L
for bookings Character Cottages (Holidays) Ltd, 34 Fore Street, Sidmouth, Devon EX10 8AQ
☎Sidmouth(039 55)77001

Large, detached house in own grounds overlooking Sidmouth in quiet residential area. Accommodation consists of modern, fitted kitchen, good-sized lounge, dining room, further lounge with TV, laundry room, two twin rooms, one single and one double-bedded room, separate WC and bathroom with wash basin. All furnished to a high standard.

All year MWB out of season 1wk min, 6wks max, 1 unit, 1–8 persons ◇ no pets ◎ fridge ♨ Elec inclusive ⌷ can be hired ☎ WM in unit Airing cupboard in unit Iron in unit Ironing board in unit HCE in unit ⊕ CTV ⊕3pin square P ☎ ▥ ♨(½m)

↩ ♔₁₈(1m) ⚲(⅓m) ▨(⅓m) ♫(⅓m) ⚑(⅓m)
Min£120 Max£175pw (Low)
Min£213 Max£350pw (High)

C CC Ref 723
for bookings Character Cottages (Holidays) Ltd, 34 Fore Street, Sidmouth, Devon EX10 8AQ
☎Sidmouth(039 55)77001

Detached, two-storey cottage 20yds from main street. It has a lounge, small separate kitchen, bathroom with WC and wash basin, stairs to adjoining bedrooms (one double and one twin-bedded room). Clean and compact.

All year MWB out of season 1wk min, 6wks max, 1 unit, 1–4 persons, nc16 no pets ◎ fridge Electric Elec metered ⌷ not provided ☎(20yds) Airing cupboard in unit Iron in unit Ironing board in unit HCE in unit [Launderette within 300yds] TV ⊕3pin square ▥ ♨(20yds)

↩ ♔₁₈(⅓m) ⚲(15yds)
Min£50 Max£73pw (Low)
Min£88 Max£114pw (High)

SILECROFT
Cumbria
Map 6 SD18

C The Cottage Kellet Farm
for bookings Mrs S Mansergh, Kellet Farm, Silecroft, Millom, Cumbria

---

Stoneleigh Country Holidays
(Formerly Leigh Farm Holidays)

Superior chalets — open for inspection.
3 miles Sidmouth. 2 miles Branscombe.
Set in delightful, rural area, with sea views.
Within walking distance of secluded Weston beach.
All electric. *Colour TV. *Shower & toilet to each chalet.
15 March - 15 November.
Parking near chalets. *Regret no pets. *Large play area.

Stamp for further details to Resident owners,
Mr & Mrs F R Salter, Stoneleigh Country Holidays, Weston, Sidmouth, Devon EX10 0PJ.
Tel: (STD 03955) 3619.

Picturesque detached old world cottages in Devon & Cornwall comfortably furnished in character and well equipped. Colour TV, phones, gardens, parking, pets welcome.

SAE please to the owner — Mrs J A Hedges (SC) Westwards, Bickwell Valley, Sidmouth, Devon. Telephone: 03955 (6176).

LA18 4NU
☎Millom(0657)2727

A small 17th-century cottage which was converted and modernised in 1975. Located near the village centre and beach, set in pleasant rural surroundings. Good base for touring the Lake District.

May–Oct MWB out of season
2 days min, 6 mths max, 1 unit,
1–4 persons ◊ ◆ no pets ◎
fridge Electric & coal Elec metered
Ⓛnot provided ☎(30yds) WM in unit
Airing cupboard in unit Iron in unit
Ironing board in unit HCE in unit TV
⊕3 pin square P ▥ ♒(100yds)
⊖ ♨ ♀(100yds) Ⓟ(3m) ♫(3m)
🛥(3m)

Min£45 Max£80pw

H **Hartrees House**
for bookings Mrs S Mansergh, Kellet
Farm, Silecroft, Millom, Cumbria
LA18 4NU
☎Millom(0657)2727

Situated on an unclass road between Silecroft and the beach, this recently converted Victorian semi-detached house of three-storeys, stands in open countryside. There are five bedrooms, all of a good size, and sleeping a total of ten persons. On the ground floor there is a sitting room and kitchen/diner.

May–Oct MWB out of season 1 wk min,
1 mth max, 1 unit, 2–10 persons ◊ ◆
no pets ◎ fridge Electric & open
fires Elec metered Ⓛnot provided
☎(50yds) WM in unit Airing cupboard
in unit Iron in unit Ironing board in unit
HCE in unit ⊕3 pin square P ▥
♒(½m)
⊖ ♨(100yds) ♀(½m)

Min£55 Max£110pw

SKEABOST BRIDGE
Isle of Skye Highland *Inverness-shire*
Map **13** NG44

Ch **Borve Holiday Homes**
for bookings Miss J Nicolson, Morvean,
Borve by Portree, Isle of Skye
☎Skeabost Bridge(047 032)247

Five well-constructed brick-built chalets with lounge/dining room/kitchen, double and twin-bedded rooms. Standing on raised ground with fine views. At junction A856/A850.

All year 1 wk min, 1 mth max, 5 units,
1–5 persons ◊ ◆ ♂ fridge
Electric Gas inclusive Elec metered
Ⓛnot provided ☎(100yds) Iron in unit
Ironing board in unit HCE in unit ⊕
TV ⊕3 pin square P ▥ ♒(4m)
Children's play area
⊖ ♀(1½m)

> 1982 prices quoted throughout
> gazetteer

SKEGNESS
Lincolnshire
Map **9** TF56

Ch **Bahama, Miami & San Diego**
Garden City Bungalow Park, Roman
Bank, Skegness, Lincolnshire
☎Skegness(0754)67201

Situated in a quiet estate about two minutes from the sea. Bahama chalets are brick-built and comprise two bedrooms (one double and one twin), lounge, kitchen/diner and bathroom/WC. Miami chalets are cedarwood and offer similar accommodation to Bahama. San Diego are smaller, flat-roofed cedarwood chalets and comprise a double and a twin bedroom, lounge with kitchenette recess and bathroom/WC. All chalets have bed-settee in the lounge.

All year MWB out of season 2 days min,
1 mth max, 21 units, 1–6 persons [◊
◆] no pets no single-sex groups ◎
fridge Electric Elec inclusive
Ⓛinclusive ☎(150yds) Airing
cupboard in unit [Iron on premises]
[Ironing board on premises] ⊖ CTV
⊕3 pin square 21P ♒(150yds)
⊖ ♨(⅜m) ♀(200yds) Ⓟ(1½m)
♫(1½m) 🛥(1½m)

C Mr & Mrs Jackson **Links Cottage**
Roman Bank, Skegness, Lincolnshire
☎Skegness(0754)4013 or 66202

A white-painted stucco-finished two-storey block, containing seven cottages, which overlooks a large lawned garden backing onto the golf course, with access to the beach. The cottages each have three bedrooms (to sleep six) and are very attractively decorated, and equipped to quality standards throughout.

Whit–Oct 7 units, 1–6 persons ◊ ◆
◎ fridge Gas fires
Gas/elec inclusive Ⓛnot provided
☎(50yds) Airing cupboard in unit Iron
in unit Ironing board in unit HCE in unit
TV ⊕3 pin square 16P ▥ ♒(200yds)
⊖ ♨ ♀(½m) Ⓟ(1m) ♫(1m) 🛥(1m)

B Mr & Mrs M Clark **Merrie Mead
Bungalows** Merrie Mead Drive,
Drummond Road, Skegness,
Lincolnshire PE25 3BS
☎Skegness(0754)4368

Two small, semi detached holiday bungalows adjoining the owners' accommodation and flats. Designed to sleep four in two comfortably fitted bedrooms. A lawned garden is within the small complex with direct access to the beach.

All year MWB out of season 3 days min,
1 mth max, 2 units, 1–4 persons [◊]
[◆] no pets ◎ fridge Electric
Elec metered Ⓛcan be hired
☎(220yds) WM TD Iron on premises
HCE in unit CTV ⊕3 pin square P ▥
♒(220yds)

⊖ ♨(½m) ♀(200yds) Ⓟ(½m)
♫(½m) 🛥(½m)

Min£35 Max£67pw (Low)
Min£70 Max£84pw (High)

F Mr & Mrs M Clark **Merrie Mead Flats**
Merrie Mead Drive, Drummond Road,
Skegness, Lincolnshire PE25 3BS
☎Skegness(0754)4368

Modern two-bedroomed purpose-built flats, each with its own garage beneath. Designed to sleep six (including put-u-up in lounge/diner) they are conveniently situated for shops and beach and have direct access to the beach via the lawned garden.

All year MWB out of season 3 days min,
1 mth max, 3 units, 1–6 persons [◊]
[◆] no pets ◎ fridge Electric
Elec metered Ⓛcan be hired
☎(220yds) WM TD Iron in unit
Ironing board in unit HCE in unit CTV
⊕3 pin square ♒(220yds)
⊖ ♨(½m) ♀(200yds) Ⓟ(½m)
♫(½m) 🛥(½m)

Min£40 Max£80pw (Low)
Min£90 Max£115pw (High)

F Mr & Mrs M Clark **Merrie Mead Flats**
Merrie Mead Drive, Drummond Road,
Skegness, Lincolnshire PE25 3BS
☎Skegness(0754)4368

A large house converted into four spacious self-contained flats with lawned rear garden and direct access to the beach. Equipped to sleep from five to seven, the flats are of varying size, comfortably furnished and in a quiet location. Resident owner.

All year MWB out of season 3 days min,
1 mth max, 4 units, 1–7 persons [◊]
[◆] no pets ♂ fridge Gas
Gas/Elec metered Ⓛcan be hired
☎(220yds) WM TD Iron on premises
Ironing board on premises HCE in unit
CTV ⊕3 pin square ♒ ▥ ♒(200yds)
⊖ ♨(½m) ♀(200yds) Ⓟ(½m)
♫(½m) 🛥(½m)

Min£35 Max£100pw (Low)
Min£95 Max£157pw (High)

SKELTON
North Yorkshire
Map **8** SE55

H **Wide Open Farm**
for bookings Mr G W Proctor, Moor Park,
Skelton Lane, Wigginton, York YO38 RF
☎York(0904)769280

A modernised brick-built farmhouse surrounded by agricultural land, comprises lounge, dining room, kitchen, cloakroom, three first floor bedrooms and a bathroom/WC.

All year MWB out of season 1 wk min,
1 mth max, 1 unit, 1–8 persons ◊ ◎
fridge ♒ Electric & log fires
Elec metered Ⓛnot provided ☎(1½m)
Airing cupboard in unit Iron in unit
Ironing board in unit HCE in unit ⊖
TV ⊕3 pin square P ♒(1½m) →

⊖ ♨
Min£50 Max£70pw (Low)
Min£100 Max£120pw (High)

SKIPNESS
Strathclyde *Argyll*
Map **10** NR95

C East & West High Claonaig
for bookings Mrs M R Oakes, Skipness
Castle, Skipness, Tarbert, Argyll
PA29 6XU
☎Skipness(088 06)207

*Two former estate workers cottages
standing on hillside with magnificent
panoramic views of the coast to Arran.
Accommodation comprises living room,
dining room with open plan kitchen, three
bedrooms and bathroom.*

All year MWB out of season 2wks min,
1wk min in winter, 6wks max, 2units,
1–6persons [◊] ◉ fridge Electric &
coal Elec inclusive high season &
metered low season Ⓛnot provided
☎(200yds) Airing cupboard in unit Iron
in unit Ironing board in unit HCE in unit
⊕3pin square P ⚲(2m)
fishing available
Min£30 Max£115pw (Low)
Max£205pw (High)

C Kibrannan Cottage
for bookings Mrs M R Oakes, Skipness
Castle, Skipness, Tarbert, Argyll
PA29 6XU
☎Skipness(088 06)207

*Originally two farm cottages, Kilbrannan
has been converted into one cottage
which is situated in the village and has
sea view. Two steep spiral staircases
lead to two attic bedrooms with skylights.
Downstairs comprises of small lounge,
kitchen, dining room, one double
bedroom and bathroom.*

All year MWB out of season 1wk min,
6wks max, 1unit, 1–6persons [◊] ◉
fridge Electric & coal Elec inclusive in
summer Elec metered in winter
Ⓛnot provided ☎(150yds) Iron in unit
Ironing board in unit HCE in unit

1982 prices quoted throughout
gazetteer

☎3pin square P ⚲(100yds)
Min£55 Max£200pw

C Meadow View
for bookings Mrs M R Oakes, Skipness
Castle, Skipness, Tarbert, Argyll
PA29 6XU
☎Skipness(088 06)207

*Cottage standing in the coastal hamlet of
Skipness, with fine views across to Arran.
Neatly furnished accommodation
comprises three bedrooms (one double
bed, one with twin beds and one with a
single bed), kitchen/dining room, lounge
with divan, bathroom and WC.*

All year MWB out of season 2wks min,
1wk min in winter, 6mths max, 1unit,
1–6persons [◊] ◉ fridge Electric &
coal Elec inclusive in high season,
metered low season Ⓛnot provided
☎(100yds) Airing cupboard in unit Iron
in unit Ironing board in unit HCE in unit
⊕3pin square P 📺 ⚲(100yds)
Dinghy & fishing available
Min£30 Max£115pw (Low)
Max£205pw (High)

H Pier House
for bookings Mrs M R Oakes, Skipness
Castle, Skipness, Tarbert, Argyll
PA29 6XU
☎Skipness(088 06)207

*Formerly a piermaster's house, this three-
storey building has an unusual setting
nestling beneath cliffs on the seafront,
with panoramic views. Accommodation
comprises six bedrooms sleeping ten,
lounge, dining room, bathroom plus an
outside shower/WC and kitchen.*

All year MWB out of season 2wks min,
1wk min in winter, 6mths max, 1unit,
1–10persons [◊] ◉ fridge Electric
& coal Elec inclusive high season,
metered low season Ⓛnot provided
☎(2m) Airing cupboard in unit Iron in
unit Ironing board in unit HCE in unit
⊕3pin square P ⚲(2m) Dinghy &
fishing
Min£30 Max£120pw (Low)
Max£340pw (High)

SKYE, ISLE OF
Highland *Inverness-shire*
Map **13** NG
**See Carbost, Dunvegan, Isle Ornsay,
Portree, Skeabost Bridge, Staffin**

SMALLRIDGE
Devon
Map **3** SY39

C Lilac Cottage
for bookings Mrs D H Young, Little
Orchard, 26 Clive Road, Esher, Surrey
KT10 8PS
☎Esher(0372)64514

*Detached stone-built old-world cottage
with lawned garden and garage. The
cottage has been carefully modernised
keeping its original character by
restoring the inglenook fireplace and
exposing old beams. Leave A358 at
Weycroft Mill towards Smallridge. In 1m
turn right. Lilac Cottage is 100yds on left.*

All year MWB out of season 4days min,
6mths max, 1unit, 2–6persons ◊ ◉
fridge ♨ Elec metered
Ⓛnot provided Airing cupboard on
premises Iron on premises Ironing
board on premises HCE on premises
☉ ⊛ CTV ⊕3pin square P 🏠 ⚲
⊖ ♨(½m) 📶(1m)
Min£35 Max£80pw (Low)
Min£90 Max£140pw (High)

SOLVA
Dyfed
Map **2** SM72

C Calves Cottage Cerbid
for bookings Mr L Rees, Cerbid Holiday
Cottages, Solva, Haverfordwest, Dyfed
☎Croesgoch(034 83)240

*A charming restored cottage retaining its
own individual style with good views.
Accommodation comprises spacious
living room with open fireplace,
kitchen/diner with dishwasher and
sleeping for eleven, plus cots.*

All year MWB out of season 2days min,
1unit, 1–11persons [◊] ◆ ◉
fridge Electric & log fires
Elec inclusive Ⓛinclusive ☎ WM
TD Airing cupboard in unit Iron in unit
Ironing board in unit HCE in unit ☉

Be Independent with a Cottage and Boat
on Skipness Estates
and Claonaig

Unspoiled, peaceful West Highland Estate with 6 self-catering cottages to let all the
year round. Each with own dinghy except in winter months. Sleep 4-10. Comfortable,
electric kitchen equipment and fires. Most have open fires also. Children welcome,
pets also if controlled. Prices £25-£340 according to season. Magnificent views, sea
from 10 yards to one mile distance. Rocky coast, sandy bay, fishing, walks, golf within
10 miles. Nearby ferries to Arran, Gigha, Jura and Islay.

**Details Mrs M R. Oakes, Skipness House by Tarbert, Arygll
Tel Skipness 207 & 208**

CTV ⊕3pinsquare P 🔲 ♿(3m)
Adventure playground

↔ ♀(3m)

Min£138 Max£345pw (Low)
Min£316 Max£448pw (High)

H   Cerbid House Cerbid
for bookings Mr L Rees, Cerbid Holiday
Cottages, Solva, Haverfordwest, Dyfed
☎Croesgoch(03483)240

*A Georgian farmhouse with extensive
grounds, offering a comfortable family
holiday home with a large farm
kitchen/diner with dishwasher, living
room with log fire, four bedrooms (a
double, a twin, a large single, and a
children's twin-bedded room) and a
bath/WC.*

All year   MWB out of season   2 days min,
1 unit, 2–9 persons   [◇]   ◈   ◆   ◎
fridge   Electric & log fires
Elec inclusive   ▣inclusive   ☎   WM
TD   Airing cupboard in unit   Iron in unit
Ironing board in unit   HCE in unit   ⊖
CTV   ⊕3pinsquare P ♠ 🔲 ♿(3m)
Adventure playground

↔ ♀(3m)

Min£138 Max£345pw (Low)
Min£316 Max£448pw (High)

C   Cerbid Old Farmhouse Cerbid
for bookings Mr L Rees, Cerbid Holiday
Cottages, Solva, Haverfordwest, Dyfed
☎Croesgoch(03483)240

*A traditional 16th-century Welsh-style
farmhouse carefully restored and
retaining interesting features. It has a
spacious living room with open fireplace
and good views, dining area, modern
kitchen with dishwasher and sleeping
accommodation for eight plus cots,*

All year   MWB out of season   2 days min,
1 unit, 1–8 persons   [◇]   ◈   ◆   ◎
fridge   Electric & log fires
Elec inclusive   ▣inclusive   ☎   WM
TD   Airing cupboard in unit   Iron in unit
Ironing board in unit   HCE in unit   ⊖
CTV   ⊕3pinsquare P ♠ 🔲 ♿(3m)
Adventure playground

↔ ♀(3m)

Min£126 Max£310pw (Low)
Min£265 Max£368pw (High)

C   Cwm Eithin Cerbid
for bookings Mr L Rees, Cerbid Holiday
Cottages, Solva, Haverfordwest, Dyfed
☎Croesgoch(03483)240

*A stone cottage converted from a 17th-
century building with a spacious living
room with open fireplace, kitchen/diner
with dishwasher, one double and two
twin-bedded rooms. No steps.*

All year   MWB out of season   2 days min,
1 unit, 1–8 persons   [◇]   ◈   ◆   ◎
fridge   Electric & log fires
Elec inclusive   ▣inclusive   ☎   WM
TD   Airing cupboard in unit   Iron in unit
Ironing board in unit   HCE in unit   ⊖
CTV   ⊕3pinsquare P ♠ 🔲 ♿(3m)
Adventure playground

↔ ♀(3m)

Min£138 Max£345pw (Low)
Min£316 Max£448pw (High)

H   Granary Cerbid
for bookings Mr L Rees, Cerbid Holiday
Cottages, Solva, Haverfordwest, Dyfed
☎Croesgoch(03483)240

*The original granary, now a spacious
house of Welsh stone, in over an acre of
grounds, has a living room with a bay
window and views, pine panelled modern
kitchen/diner with dishwasher and can
sleep up to ten adults.*

All year   MWB out of season   2 days min,
1 unit, 2–10 persons   [◇]   ◈   ◆   ◎
fridge   Electric   Elec inclusive
▣inclusive   ☎   WM TD   Airing
cupboard in unit   Iron in unit   Ironing
board in unit   HCE in unit   ⊖   CTV
⊕3pinsquare P ♠ 🔲 ♿(3m)
Adventure playground

↔ ♀(3m)

Min£138 Max£345pw (Low)
Min£316 Max£448pw (High)

C   No Name Cottage Cerbid
for bookings Mr L Rees, Cerbid Holiday
Cottages, Solva, Haverfordwest, Dyfed
☎Croesgoch(03483)240

*No Name is a fine spacious property with
pleasant country aspects and a gallery
reached by a circular staircase. There is*

*a spacious living room, kitchen/dining
room with dishwasher, a double room,
one twin-bedded room, a three-bedded
room and a single, bathroom/WC and a
cloakroom with shower and WC.*

All year   MWB out of season   2 days min,
1 unit, 1–12 persons   [◇]   ◈   ◆   ◎
fridge   Electric & log fires
Elec inclusive   ▣inclusive   ☎   WM
TD   Airing cupboard in unit   Iron in unit
Ironing board in unit   HCE in unit   ⊖
CTV   ⊕3pinsquare P ♠ 🔲 ♿(3m)
Adventure playground

↔ ♀(3m)

Min£149 Max£368pw (Low)
Min£350 Max£483pw (High)

H   Stable Corner Cerbid
for bookings Mr L Rees, Cerbid Holiday
Cottages, Solva, Haverfordwest, Dyfed
☎Croesgoch(03483)240

*A house of character transformed from a
range of 18th-century stables and barns.
Own lawn and patio. No steps. Large
living room with bay window,
kitchen/dining room with dishwasher,
master bedroom with a four-poster bed.
Children's room with bunks, two twin-
bedded rooms, bathroom/WC and
shower room/WC.*

All year   MWB out of season   2 days min,
1 unit, 1–10 persons   [◇]   ◈   ◆   ◎
fridge   Electric & log fires
Elec inclusive   ▣inclusive   ☎   WM
TD   Airing cupboard in unit   Iron in unit
Ironing board in unit   HCE in unit   ⊖
CTV   ⊕3pinsquare P 🔲 ♿(3m)
Adventure playground

↔ ♀(3m)

Min£138 Max£345pw (Low)
Min£316 Max£448pw (High)

SORN
Strathclyde *Ayrshire*
Map **11** NS53

H   Auchmannoch House
for bookings Mrs E McElroy, Sorn Estate
Office, Sorn Castle, Mauchline, Ayrshire
KA5 6HR
☎Mauchline(0290)51611

*A secluded mansion house at the end of a
300-yard private drive 2½m N of junction
B743/B7037. Accommodation includes →*

five twin bedrooms, a sixth with bunk beds, kitchen, dining room, drawing room and study.

Mar-Oct MWB out of season 1wk min, 32wks max, 1unit, 1–12persons ◈ ◆ ◎ fridge ▦ & open fire Elec metered ◫can be hired ☎ Airing cupboard in unit Iron in unit Ironing board in unit HCE in unit ⊙ [TV] ⊕3pin square P ⌂ ⛟(2m) Fishing & shooting by arrangement

⊖ ♀(2½m) ⊞(2½m)

Min£86.25 Max£106.95pw (Low)
Min£136.85 Max£201.25pw (High)

C Cleugh Cottage
for bookings Mrs E McElroy, Sorn, Estate Office, Sorn Castle, Mauchline, Ayrshire KA5 6HR
☎Mauchline(0290)51611

18th-century sandstone lodge with main road location on steep bank overlooking Cleugh Burn. The accommodation provides sitting room, kitchen/diner and one twin ground-floor bedroom, with a stone spiral staircase leading to two twin bedrooms, bathroom/WC and a separate WC on the first-floor.

Mar-Nov MWB out of season 1wk min, 6mths max, 1unit, 1–6persons ◎ fridge Electric Elec metered ◫can be hired ☎(500yds) Iron in unit Ironing board in unit HCE in unit TV can be hired ⊕3pin square 3P ⛟(½m) Fishing & shooting by arrangement

⊖ ⛳18(3m) ♀(½m) ⊞(½m)

Min£59.80 Max£120.75pw

F East Bothy, Stable Yard
for bookings Mrs E McElroy, Sorn Estate Office, Sorn Castle, Mauchline, Ayrshire KA5 6HR
☎Mauchline(0290)51611

A small first-floor flat in former stables within a courtyard. In Sorn Castle grounds ½m W of Sorn. Comprises sitting room with bed-settee, open-plan kitchen behind serving counter, bathroom and a twin-bedded room.

Mar-Oct MWB out of season 1wk min, 32wks max, 1unit, 1–3persons ◈ ◆ ◎ fridge Electric & open fire Elec metered ◫can be hired ☎ Iron in unit Ironing board in unit HCE in unit ⊙ [CTV] ⊕3pin square P ⌂ ▥ ⛟(½m) Fishing & shooting by arrangement

⊖ ⛳18(2½m) ♀(½m) ⊞(½m)

Min£41.40 Max£48.30pw (Low)
Min£63.25 Max£78.20pw (High)

C Foresters Cottage
for bookings Mrs E McElroy, Sorn Estate Office, Sorn Castle, Mauchline, Ayrshire KA5 6HR
☎Mauchline(0290)51611

The cottage is situated in former stable yard at Sorn Castle on the Sorn Estate. The accommodation consists of lounge, bathroom, kitchen/dining room, one double-bedded room, one twin-bedded room and one with bunk beds.

Mar-Oct MWB out of season 1wk min, 8mths max, 1unit, 1–6persons ◈ ◆ ◎ fridge Electric & open fires Elec metered ◫can be hired ☎ Iron in unit Ironing board in unit HCE in unit ⊙ TV can be hired ⊕3pin round 5P ⛟(½m) Fishing & shooting by arrangement

⊖ ⛳(2½m) ♀(½m) ⊞(½m)

Min£56.35 Max£60.95pw (Low)
Min£90.85 Max£113.85pw (High)

C Golfcourse Cottage
for bookings Mrs E McElroy, Sorn Estate Office, Sorn Castle, Mauchline, Ayrshire KA5 6HR
☎Mauchline(0290)51611

The cottage is situated on a rise, amongst farmland on the Sorn Estate. It sleeps ten persons in one double-bedded room, two twin-bedded rooms and two bunk-bedded rooms. There is a kitchen/dining room, lounge and two bathrooms.

Mar-Oct MWB out of season 1wk min, 8mths max, 1unit, 1–10persons ◈ ◆ ◎ fridge Electric & open fires Elec metered ◫can be hired ☎ Iron in unit Ironing board in unit HCE in unit TV can be hired ⊕3pin square 6P ⛟(½m) Fishing & shooting by arrangement

⊖ ⛳(2½m) ♀(½m) ⊞(½m)

Min£51.75 Max£86.25pw (Low)
Min£102.35 Max£148.35pw (High)

F Grooms Cottage, Stable Yard
for bookings Mrs E McElroy, Sorn Estate Office, Sorn Castle, Mauchline, Ayrshire KA5 6HR
☎Mauchline(0290)51611

In attractive courtyard setting within castle grounds. This ground-floor flat comprises kitchen, living room with bed-settee, hall, bathroom, twin-bedded room with French windows, double room and a further room for three. The estate lies ½m W of Sorn on B743.

Mar-Oct MWB out of season 1wk min, 32wks max, 1unit, 1–8persons [◈] [◆] ◎ fridge Electric & open fires Elec metered ◫can be hired ☎ Iron in unit Ironing board in unit HCE in unit ⊙ [CTV] ⊕3pin round P ⌂ ▥ ⛟(½m) Fishing & shooting by arrangement

⊖ ⛳18(2½m) ♀(½m) ⊞(½m)

Min£56.35 Max£60.95pw (Low)
Min£93.15 Max£120.75pw (High)

C Haggisbank Cottage
for bookings Mrs E McElroy, Sorn Estate Office, Sorn Castle, Mauchline, Ayrshire KA5 6HR
☎Mauchline(0290)51611

The cottage is situated ½m from Sorn village on the Sorn Estate. The accommodation comprises kitchen, lounge/dining room (with open fire), bathroom and three bedrooms (one double-bedded room, one twin-bedded room and one with bunk beds).

Mar-Oct MWB out of season 1wk min, 8mths max, 1unit, 1–6persons ◈ ◆ ◎ fridge Electric & open fires Elec metered ◫can be hired ☎(½m) Iron in unit Ironing board in unit HCE in unit ⊙ TV can be hired ⊕3pin square 4P ⛟(½m) Fishing & shooting by arrangement

⊖ ⛳(½m) ♀(½m) ⊞(½m)

Min£55.20 Max£59.80pw (Low)
Min£89.70 Max£112.70pw (High)

C Holehouse Farmhouse
for bookings Mrs E McElroy, Sorn Estate Office, Sorn Castle, Mauchline, Ayrshire KA5 6HR
☎Mauchline(0290)51611

Converted 18th-century farmhouse with large lawn with fruit trees and bushes to rear. It has a living/dining room with open fireplace, drawing-room, ktichen, two bathrooms, four twin-bedded rooms and one double bedroom. On B743, Sorn–Muirkirk road, one mile E of Sorn.

Mar-Oct MWB out of season 1wk min, 8mths max, 1unit, 1–10persons ◈ ◆ ◎ fridge Electric & open fires Elec metered ◫can be hired ☎ Airing cupboard in unit Iron in unit Ironing board in unit HCE in unit ⊙ [TV] ⊕3pin square 4P ⛟(1m) Fishing & shooting by arrangement

⊖ ⛳18(3m) ♀(1m) ⊞(1m)

Min£64.40 Max£96.60pw (Low)
Min£113.85 Max£171.35pw (High)

C Kilnknowe Cottage
for bookings Mrs E McElroy, Sorn Estate Office, Sorn Castle, Mauchline, Ayrshire KA5 6HR
☎Mauchline(0290)51611

Attractive pair of stone-built Georgian cottages converted into one unit with three twin bedrooms, lounge/dining room, kitchen and bathroom. On the outskirts of Sorn. Fine view of Sorn Castle.

Mar-Oct MWB out of season 1wk min, 8mths max, 1unit, 1–6persons ◈ ◆ ◎ fridge Electric & open fires Elec metered ◫can be hired ☎ Airing cupboard in unit Iron in unit Ironing board in unit HCE in unit ⊙ [TV] ⊕3pin square P ▥ ⛟(¾m) Fishing & shooting by arrangement

⊖ ♀(¾m) ⊞(¾m)

Min£59.80 Max£75.90pw (Low)
Min£97.75 Max£120.75pw (High)

C Ladeside Cottage
for bookings Mrs E McElroy, Sorn Estate Office, Sorn Castle, Mauchline, Ayrshire KA5 6HR
☎Mauchline(0290)51611

Small stone-built converted toll house on the outskirts of Sorn by bridge on B743. It comprises a double bedroom, lounge/diner with convertible settee, kitchen and bathroom.

Mar-Oct MWB out of season 1wk min, 8mths max, 1unit, 1–3persons ◈ ◆

fridge ♨ & open fires
Elec metered ⬜can be hired ☎(½m)
Airing cupboard in unit Iron in unit
Ironing board in unit HCE in unit ⊙
[TV] ⊕3pin square P Fishing &
shooting by arrangement

⊖ ♒(2½m) ☻(½m) ▨(½m)
Min£44.85 Max£51.75pw (Low)
Min£67.85 Max£90.85pw (High)

F West Bothy, Stable Yard
for bookings Mrs E McElroy, Sorn Estate
Office, Sorn Castle, Mauchline, Ayrshire
KA56HR
☎Mauchline(0290)51611

*Small first-floor flat in former stables
within a courtyard in Sorn Castle grounds
½m W of Sorn on B743. Accommodation
comprises sitting room with bed-settee,
kitchen, double bedroom and
bathroom/WC.*

Mar-Oct MWB out of season 1wk min,
8mths max, 1unit, 1–3person [◈] [◆]
♨ fridge Electric & open fires
Elec metered ⬜can be hired ☎ HCE
in unit ⊙ CTV can be hired
⊕3pin square P Fishing & shooting by
arrangement

⊖ ♒(2½m) ☻(½m) ▨(½m)
Min£42.55 Max£49.45pw (Low)
Min£64.40 Max£79.35pw (High)

SOUTHERNESS
Dumfries & Galloway *Kirkcudbrightshire*
Map**11** NX95

B The Estate Office *Southerness
Holiday Village* Southerness, Dumfries
DG28AZ
☎Kirkbean(038788)256

*Twenty chalet-style bungalows
overlooking Solway Firth. They are
collectively sited at the far end of the
predominantly caravan holiday village.
Limited drawer space, coat hangers not
provided. Lounge and kitchenette
combined, and sixth person uses lounge
divan.*

Mar-Oct MWB out of season
3days min, 20units, 2–6persons [◈]
♨ fridge Electric Elec metered
⬜not provided ☎(½m) [Iron on
premises] HCE in unit [Launderette
within 300yds] ⊙ TV can be hired
⊕3pin square P

⊖ ♒ ☻(300yds) ☙(½m)

SOUTH LAGGAN
Highland *Inverness-shire*
Map**14** NN29

Ch Kilfinnan Holiday Cabins Kilfinnan
for bookings Hoseasons Holidays Ltd,
Sunway House, 89 Bridge Road,
Lowestoft, Suffolk NR323LT
☎Wroxham(06053)62292

*Ten wood cabins on W side of Loch
Lochy, 2m S of A82 by single-track road
and forest track. Isolated position on the
edge of forest. Each cabin has its own
balcony and can accommodate up to
eight people.*

Mar-Oct 10units, 8persons [◈]
no pets ♨ fridge Electric

Elec metered ⬜can be hired ☎
Airing cupboard HCE in unit ⊙ TV
⊕3pin square P ☻(2½m) Fishing

SOUTHLEIGH
Devon
Map**3** SY29

F Flats A & B
for bookings Mrs M E Chichester,
Wiscombe Park, Colyton, Devon
☎Farway(040487)252

*Two second-floor flats situated within a
country mansion in a 600-acre country
park, 2m from the A3052. They are
approached by a side door and two
flights of rather steep stairs. Flat A has
kitchen/dining area, bathroom with WC,
living room with double bed-settee, and
two bedrooms (one with three single
beds, the other with a double and a
single). Flat B has a living room with
kitchen area, bathroom with WC, and two
bedrooms (one with three single beds,
the other with a double and a single bed).*

Etr-Oct 1wk min, 1mth max, 2units,
1–6persons ◈ ♨ fridge Electric
Gas & Elec metered ⬜not provided
☎ Airing cupboard in unit Iron in unit
Ironing board in unit HCE in unit ⊙ TV
can be hired ⊕3pin square
⊕3pin round 3P ☙(4m)

⊖ ☻(3m)

F Flat C
for bookings Mrs M E Chichester,
Wiscombe Park, Colyton, Devon
☎Farway(040487)252

*Situated in a country mansion but with a
separate entrance, the flat has
kitchen/dining room and bathroom with
WC on the ground floor. The first floor has
living room and two bedrooms (one with a
double and a single bed, the other with
three singles).*

Etr-Oct 1wk min, 1mth max, 1unit,
1–6persons ◈ ♨ fridge Electric
Elec metered ⬜not provided ☎
Airing cupboard in unit Iron in unit
Ironing board in unit HCE in unit ⊙ TV
can be hired ⊕3pin square
⊕3pin round 3P ☙(4m)

⊖ ☻(3m)

F Flat D (Stable Flat)
for bookings Mrs M E Chichester,
Wiscombe Park, Colyton, Devon
☎Farway(040487)252

*A first-floor flat in a converted stable
block 200yds from the main house. The
accommodation comprises living room,
kitchen/diner, bathroom and WC and two
bedrooms (one with two single beds, the
other with a double bed and a child's
bed).*

Etr-Oct 1wk min, 1mth max, 1unit,
1–5persons ◈ ♨ fridge Electric
Gas/Elec metered ⬜not provided ☎
Airing cupboard in unit Iron in unit
Ironing board in unit HCE in unit ⊙ TV

---

can be hired ⊕3pin square
⊕3pin round 3P ☙(4m)

⊖ ☻(3m)

F Flat E
for bookings Mrs M E Chichester,
Wiscombe Park, Colyton, Devon
☎Farway(040487)252

*First-floor flat comprising lounge with
bed-settee and kitchen at one end,
shower room with WC, and bedroom with
large antique half-tester bed and one
single bed.*

Etr-Oct 1wk min, 1mth max, 1unit,
1–3persons ◈ ♨ fridge Electric
Elec metered ⬜not provided ☎
Airing cupboard in unit Iron in unit
Ironing board in unit HCE in unit ⊙ TV
can be hired ⊕3pin square
⊕3pin round 3P ☙(4m)

⊖ ☻(3m)

C Whitmoor
for bookings Mrs M E Chichester,
Wiscombe Park, Colyton, Devon
☎Farway(040487)252

*The cottage stands completely alone ½m
up the Wiscombe valley. It is stone built
and all the rooms face south; there is a
stream close by. The ground floor
comprises small hall, stone-flagged
lounge with large, open fireplace,
kitchen/dining room (with stone
fireplace) and WC. On the first floor there
are three bedrooms (one with antique
half-tester bed and one single; one twin-
bedded room, and a large bedroom with
three single beds). There is an extra
double bed-settee on the ground floor.*

Etr-Oct 1wk min, 1mth max, 1unit,
1–8persons ◈ ♄ fridge Electric
Gas & Elec metered ⬜not provided
☎ Airing cupboard in unit Iron in unit
Ironing board in unit HCE in unit ⊙ TV
can be hired ⊕3pin square
⊕3pin round 3P ☙(4m)

⊖ ☻(3m)

SOUTHPORT
Merseyside
Map**7** SD31

F Mrs J Gregory **Cairn House**
18 Knowsley Road, Southport,
Merseyside PR90HG
☎Southport(0704)42878

*Two spacious flats on first floor of a large
red-brick house, near the seafront at the
north end of Southport. Each unit
contains one double and one twin-
bedded room. (One flat will also take twin
bunks suitable for children).
Conveniently situated for shopping
centre and resort facilities.*

All year MWB out of season 1wk min,
1mth max, 2units, 2–6persons ◈ ◆
♨ fridge Electric Elec metered
⬜inclusive ☎(400yds) Airing
cupboard in unit HCE in unit TV
⊕3pin square 4P ▥ ☙(200yds) →

1982 prices quoted throughout
gazetteer

235

⊖ ⛳18(½m) ♀(½m) ▣(½m) ♬(½m) 🎥(½m)

Min£65 Max£80pw (Low)
Min£95 Max£110pw (High)

F Mrs O Ward ***Conway Holiday Flats*** 2 Arnside Road, Southport, Merseyside PR9 0QX
☎Southport(0704)37170

A brick-built, semi-detached house with small garden. Situated in quiet road close to town centre shops. The two self-contained flats are clean and adequately furnished.

Allyear MWB out of season 7days min, 2units, 2–3persons no pets ⊘ ◎ fridge Electric & gas fires Gas/Elec metered ▣ can be hired ☎(150yds) Airing cupboard in unit Iron in unit Ironing board in unit HCE in unit [Launderette within 300yds] TV ⊕3pin square P ▥ ⛟(200yds)

⊖ ♀(200yds) ▣(¼m) ♬(¼m) 🎥(1m)

F Mrs M Brown **41 Denmark Road** Churchtown, Southport, Merseyside PR9 7LL
☎Southport(0704)25270

A nicely furnished first floor flat in a semi-detached house, standing in quiet tree-lined road about 1½m N of the town. Long garden at rear. Some way from the sea.

Allyear 1wk min, 4wks max, 1unit, 2persons, nc ⊘ fridge Gas Gas/Elec metered ▣ inclusive ☎(100yds) Airing cupboard in unit HCE in unit [Launderette within 300yds] ⊙ [TV] ⊕3pin square P ▥ ⛟(100yds)

⊖ ♀(150yds) ▣(1½m) ♬(1½m) 🎥(1½m)

F Mrs A Gill **101 Manchester Road** Southport, Merseyside PR9 9BB
☎Southport(0704)42150

A first-floor flat in a detached house built about 100 years ago. The accommodation comprises three bedrooms, all with wash basins, dining room, living room, bathroom and kitchen. Situated on main road some distance from the sea.

Allyear MWB out of season 1wk min, 3mths max, 1unit, 6–10persons [◆] [◆] ◎ fridge ⛓ Elec metered ▣ inclusive ☎(100yds) Airing cupboard in unit Iron in unit Ironing board in unit HCE in unit [Launderette within 300yds] [TV] ⊕3pin square P ▥ ⛟(100yds)

⊖ ♀(100yds) ▣(1m) ♬(1m) 🎥(1m)

Min£50 Max£120pw

F Mrs A Barnard **'Pomme D'Or'** 58 Promenade, Southport, Merseyside PR9 0DY
☎Southport(0704)38003

The first and second floors of this three-storey terraced house on the promenade comprise two self-contained flats at the front and two at the rear. Each flat has one bedroom with double bed plus extra bed space in the lounge. Close to all seaside amenities.

Allyear MWB out of season 1wk min, 4units, 2–5persons ◆ no pets (except dogs) ◎ fridge Electric Elec metered ▣ inclusive ☎ Airing cupboard in unit Iron on premises Ironing board on premises HCE in unit [Launderette within 300yds] TV ⊕3pin square 4P ▥ ⛟(100yds)

⊖ ⛳18(¼m) ♀(100yds) ▣(100yds) ♬(100yds) 🎥(100yds)

Min£45 Max£50pw (Low)
Min£55 Max£60pw (High)

Ch **Pontin's Holiday Village** Ainsdale Beach, Shore Road, Southport, Merseyside PR8 2PZ
☎Southport(0704)77165

Modern self-contained chalet apartments situated on the coast. Each chalet has one or two bedrooms containing two single beds plus a convertible double bed-settee in the lounge and can accommodate up to seven persons.

May–Sep MWB in season 1night min, 768units, 2–7persons ◇ ◆ ◆ no pets ◎ fridge Electric Elec metered ▣ inclusive ☎ [Iron on premises] [Ironing board on premises] HCE in unit [Launderette on premises] ⊙ TV ⊕3pin square P ▥ ▭ Crazy golf

⊖ ♀ ▣ ♬ 🎥

Min£65 Max£120pw (Low)
Min£103 Max£195pw (High)

SOUTH RAYNHAM
Norfolk
Map **9** TF82

F **Vere Lodge, Garden Wing** *for bookings* Major G Bowlby, English Country Cottages, Claypit Lane, Fakenham, Norfolk NR21 8AS
☎Fakenham(0328)51155

A conversion of a former outbuilding into a compact ground-floor apartment adjoining the main house and overlooking the drive, with raised lawns and woodland beyond. The accommodation has been furnished and equipped to high standards. Two bedrooms sleep four.

Allyear 1wk min, 1unit, 1–4persons [◇] ◆ no pets ◎ fridge Electric Elec metered ▣ inclusive ☎(20yds) Iron in unit Ironing board in unit HCE in unit TV ⊕3pin square 6P ▥ ⛟(¾m)

⊖ ♀(¾m)

Min£78pw (Low)
Min£96 Max£162pw (High)

F **Vere Lodge, Dolls House** *for bookings* Major G Bowlby, English Country Cottages, Claypit Lane, Fakenham, Norfolk NR21 8AS
☎Fakenham(0328)51155

A conversion of a small side wing of Vere Lodge into a two-storey compact maisonette. Sleeps four in two double bedrooms (each with wash basin). The Dolls House has the same good quality fitments and furnishings as all the others under this ownership.

Allyear 1wk min, 1unit, 1–4persons [◇] ◆ no pets ◎ fridge ⛓ Elec metered ▣ inclusive ☎(20yds) Iron in unit Ironing board in unit HCE in unit ⊙ TV ⊕3pin square 6P ▥ ⛟(¾m)

⊖ ♀(¾m)

Max£78pw (Low)
Min£87 Max£141pw (High)

C **Vere Lodge Cottages** *for bookings* Major G Bowlby, English Country Cottages, Claypit Lane, Fakenham, Norfolk NR21 8AS
☎Fakenham(0328)51155

Four individual cottages sleeping four or seven adjoining Vere Lodge and its grounds which include seven acres of woods, lawns and flowerbeds. These cottages, of charm and character, have been converted from the Lodge's original outbuildings and have been fitted and appointed to quality standards.

Allyear 1wk min, 4units, 1–7persons [◇] ◆ ◎ fridge ⛓ Elec metered ▣ inclusive ☎ Airing cupboard in unit Iron in unit Ironing board in unit HCE in unit ⊙ TV ⊕3pin square 10P 2⌂ ▥ ⛟(¾m)

⊖ ♀(¾m)

F **Vere Lodge, Possum's Mini** *for bookings* Major G Bowlby, English Country Cottages, Claypit Lane, Fakenham, Norfolk NR21 8AS
☎Fakenham(0328)51155

Once the children's playroom in Vere Lodge, this huge room with high ceiling has been converted to form a unique ground floor mini-apartment with spacious lounge on one side and kitchen/diner on the other. An open-plan staircase leads to a mezzanine floor extending over rear portion of ground floor which contains a gallery twin-bedroom and bathroom. Very luxurious.

Allyear 1wk summer, 1unit, 1–2persons, nc3 ◇ ◆ ◎ fridge ⛓ Elec metered ▣ inclusive ☎(50yds) Airing cupboard in unit Iron in unit Ironing board in unit HCE in unit ⊙ CTV ⊕3pin square 2P ⛟(¾m)

⊖ ♀(¾m)

Max£63pw (Low)
Min£81 Max£126pw (High)

SOUTHWICK
Dumfries & Galloway *Kirkcudbrightshire*
Map **11** NX95

1982 prices quoted throughout gazetteer

C **Burn Cottage** Boreland of Southwick Farm
for bookings G M Thomson & Co, 27 King Street, Castle Douglas, Kirkcudbrightshire
☎Castle Douglas(0556)2701

Secluded stone-built farm cottage positioned by Boreland Burn. Accommodation consists of a double bedroom, a twin room and a single, kitchen, bathroom and living/dining room. Southwick Farm is N of Caulkerbush on B793.

Allyear 1wkmin, 6mthsmax, 1unit, 1–5persons nopets ⌀ fridge Electric Gas/Elec inclusive ⌷notprovided ☎(2m) Airing cupboard in unit Iron in unit Ironing board in unit HCE in unit TV ⊕3pin round P ♨(2m) Fishing
Min£45 Max£105pw

C **Chestnut Cottage** Boreland of Southwick Farm
for bookings G M Thomson & Co, 27 King Street, Castle Douglas, Kirkcudbrightshire
☎Castle Douglas(0556)2701

Comfortable detached farm cottage offering a twin-bedded room, a double room and a single. There is also a living/dining room, kitchen, bathroom and utility room.

Allyear 1wkmin, 6mthsmax, 1unit, 1–5persons ◆ nopets ⌀ fridge Electric Gas/Elec inclusive ⌷notprovided ☎(2m) Iron in unit Ironing board in unit HCE in unit TV ⊕3pinround P ♨(2m) Fishing
Min£45 Max£105pw

C **Hill Cottage** Boreland of Southwick Farm
for bookings G M Thomson & Co, 27 King Street, Castle Douglas, Kirkcudbrightshire
☎Castle Douglas(0556)2701

Pleasant detached farm cottage commanding magnificent views of the Solway Firth. Accommodation comprises a double-bedded room, a twin-bedded and a single room, comfortable, beamed sitting/dining room, bathroom and kitchen.

Allyear 1wkmin, 6mthsmax, 1unit, 1–5persons ◆ nopets ◎ fridge Electric Elec inclusive ⌷notprovided ☎(2m) Iron in unit Ironing board in unit HCE in unit TV ⊕3pinround P ♨(2m) Fishing
Min£35 Max£75pw

SOUTHWOLD
Suffolk
Map5 TM57

F Mr A C Laight **The Craighurst** North Parade, Southwold, Suffolk IP18 6LP
☎Southwold(0502)723115

Three flats situated within a seafront hotel. They comprise one three-bedroomed family flat, one with two bedrooms and one with one bedroom. All have lounge with put-u-up, kitchen/diner, separate shower and WC (except for the one-bedroom flat which has a combined shower/WC).

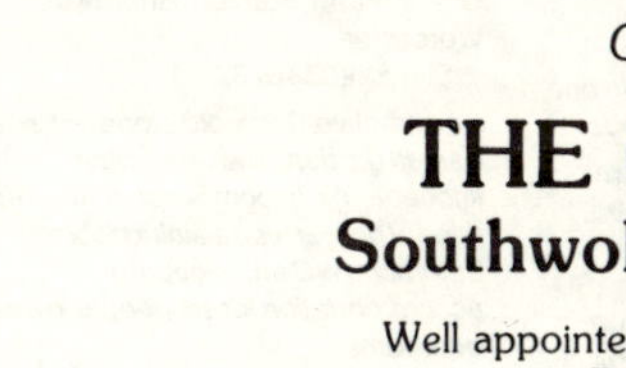

Allyear MWBoutof season 3daysmin, 1mthmax, 3units, 1–7persons ◇ [◆ ◆] ◎ fridge Electric Elecmetered ⌷can be hired ☎ Iron on premises Ironing board on premises HCE in unit ⊖ ⊗ [TVorCTV] ⊕3pinsquare 8P ▥ ♨(¼m) ⇆ ♿(1m) ♀
Min£55 Max£95pw (Low)
Min£100 Max£175pw (High)

SOUTH ZEAL
Devon
Map3 SX69

F Mr & Mrs M W Harbridge **The Old Barn Flats** Poltimore Guest House, South Zeal, Okehampton, Devon
☎Sticklepath(083784)209 →

Ground and second floor flats in converted barn in an attractive setting close to Dartmoor, off the A30. Both comprise lounge, kitchen/diner, two bedrooms and bathroom/WC. Well decorated and furnished.

All year MWB out of season 1wk min, 1mth max, 2units, 1–6persons ◊ ◆ ◉ fridge Electric Elec metered 🔲can be hired ☎(10yds) Airing cupboard in unit Iron in unit Ironing board in unit HCE in unit ☺ CTV ⊕3pin square 3P 📺 ♨(½m)

↔ ☏(10yds) ♫(½m)

Min£25 Max£80pw (Low)
Min£85 Max£110pw (High)

SPARHAM
Norfolk
Map**9** TG01

C Carrstone Cottage
for bookings Major G Bowlby, English Country Cottages, Claypit Lane, Fakenham, Norfolk NR21 8AS
☎Fakenham(0328)51155

A newly modernised end cottage of a row of four with large lawn at rear. The village is just off the A1067 some 10m NE of Norwich. Well furnished sitting room, kitchen/diner, downstairs bath/WC, two twin-bedded rooms and one double-bedded room.

All year 1wk summer, 1unit, 6persons ◊ ◉ fridge ◉ Elec metered 🔲inclusive ☎(1m) Airing cupboard in unit Iron in unit Ironing board in unit HCE in unit TV ⊕3pin square 2P ♨(1m)

↔ ☏(1m)

Max£63pw (Low)
Min£75 Max£114pw (High)

SPARK BRIDGE
Cumbria
Map**7** SD38

H Mrs B Bailey **Dicky Cragg** Down Court, Courtshill Road, Haslemere, Surrey
☎Haslemere(0428)3993

An old store barn converted into two modern open-plan houses and situated on the outskirts of Spark Bridge, three miles south of Coniston Water. Accommodation comprises lounge, kitchen, with open-plan staircase to bedrooms and separate bathroom. One has three bedrooms and the other house has four.

All year MWB out of season 1wk min, 4wks max, 2units, 2–10persons [◊] ◊ ◆ ◉ fridge ♨ Elec inclusive 🔲inclusive ☎ WM on premises SD on premises TD on premises Iron on premises Ironing board on premises HCE in unit ☺ TV ⊕3pin square P ♘ 📺 ♨(2m)

↔ ☏(100yds)

Min£60 Max£90pw (Low)
Min£180 Max£240pw (High)

SPEAN BRIDGE
Highland *Inverness-shire*
Map**14** NN28

C, Ch Pine Cottage Holiday Homes
for bookings Mrs S M Parrish, Pine Cottage, Spean Bridge, Inverness-shire
☎Spean Bridge(039 781)404

The accommodation consists of two aluminium-clad chalets in a tree-studded, secluded, level grass area bordering the River Spean, with splendid views of nearby hills and mountains. Each unit has a small garden area.

All year MWB out of season 1wk min, 2units, 4–5persons ◊ fridge Electric Elec metered 🔲can be hired ☎(400yds) Airing cupboard in unit HCE in unit ☺ TV ⊕3pin square P ♨(400yds)

↔ ☏☺ ☏(½m)

Min£50pw (Low)
Min£90pw (High)

SPINNINGDALE
Highland *Ross-shire*
Map**14** NH78

C Mr A McAdam **Varvels** Spinningdale, Ardgay, Ross-shire IV24 3AE
☎Whiteface(086 288)209

Converted modernised 18th-century stone cottage, with large garden to rear set in small highland village. The ground floor offers sitting room, kitchen/diner and shower room/WC. The first floor consists of one double bedroom, and one room with double room and bunk beds.

Apr–Oct MWB out of season 1wk min, 2wks max, 1unit, 1–6persons ◊ ◆ ♨ fridge ♨ Gas/Elec inclusive 🔲inclusive ☎(200yds) WM in unit SD in unit Airing cupboard in unit Iron in unit Ironing board in unit HCE in unit TV can be hired ⊕3pin square 1P ♨(200yds)

↔ ☏(300yds) Fishing

Min£50 Max£65pw (Low)
Min£70 Max£80pw (High)

SPLAYNE'S GREEN
East Sussex
Map**5** TQ42

C 1 Moonsland Cottage
for bookings Mrs P Welfare, 1 Netherhall Cottage, Fletching Common, Newick, Lewis, E Sussex
☎Newick(082572)2713

A semi-detached cottage built of brick around 1900 and modernised to provide compact kitchen, lounge, diner, double and twin-bedded rooms, and a bathroom/WC. It is situated ½m from Fletching.

All year MWB out of season 1wk min, 1mth max, 1unit, 1–5persons ◊ ◆ no pets ◉ fridge ♨ Elec metered 🔲inclusive ☎(100yds) WM in unit SD

in unit Airing cupboard in unit Iron in unit Ironing board in unit HCE in unit ☺ ❀ CTV ⊕3pin square P ♘ 📺 ♨(½m)

↔ ☏☺(1½m) ☏(½m)

Max£80pw (Low)
Max£110pw (High)

STAFFIN
Isle of Skye Highland *Inverness-shire*
Map**13** NG46

C Mrs A M Gillies **2 Sartle** Staffin, Isle of Skye
☎Staffin(047 062)202

Painted, stone croft cottage on hillside with spectacular hill and cliff backdrop and open views across Staffin Bay to Scottish mainland. Three first-floor bedrooms, a pleasant sitting room, dining room/kitchen and large bathroom with WC on the ground floor. Take A855 from Portree. At the N end of Staffin turn left on Uig via Quirang road. Cottage on right next to petrol pump.

All year MWB out of season 1wk min, 1unit, 1–7persons ◊ ◉ fridge Electric & open fires Elec metered 🔲not provided ☎(½m) Iron in unit Ironing board in unit HCE in unit TV ⊕3pin square 3P 📺 ♨(½m)

↔ ☏(2m)

STANTON
Gloucester
Map**4** SP03

C J W & K J Ryland **Charity Cottage** Charity Farm, Stanton, Broadway, Worcester
☎Stanton(038 673)339

An attractive Cotswold stone cottage with a small garden. The open-plan kitchen/dining room is spacious and well fitted. There is also a sitting room, bathroom/WC and sleeping accommodation for six people in three bedrooms.

All year MWB out of season 1wk min, 1unit, 2–6persons ◊ ◆ ♨ fridge Electric & log fires Gas/elec inclusive 🔲not provided ☎ Airing cupboard in unit Iron in unit Ironing board in unit HCE in unit ☺ TV ⊕3pin square P 📺 ♨ ⌂

↔ ☏☺(3m) ☏(500yds)

Min£92 Max£149.50pw

STARSTON
Norfolk
Map**5** TM28

H Streamlet Farmhouse Harleston
for bookings Major G Bowlby, English Country Cottages, Claypit Lane, Fakenham, Norfolk NR21 8AS
☎Fakenham(0328)51155

Pretty, secluded part 14th-century farmhouse, extensively modernised in 1976/7, standing in ⅓ acre of S facing garden. There are three reception rooms and four bedrooms. Downstairs bathroom.

Apr–Oct 1wk min, 1unit, 1–9persons
◊ ◉ fridge ⧜ Elec metered
⌂inclusive ☎(1m) Airing cupboard in
unit Iron in unit Ironing board in unit
HCE in unit TV ☻3pin square 2P
⚐(1m)

⊷ ⚲(1m)

Min£117 Max£243pw

STAUNTON
Gloucestershire
Map **3** SO51

H **Coach House** The Old Rectory
for bookings Mrs F M Cooke, The Old
Rectory, Staunton, Coleford,
Gloucestershire
☎Dean(0594)33165

*The Coach House, which has recently
been converted and modernised, is
situated in the grounds of the Old Rectory
with use of the garden. It comprises
kitchen/diner, lounge, two bedrooms and
bathroom/WC.*

All year 1wk min, 6mths max, 1unit,
2–4persons [◊] ◊ ◆ ◉ fridge
Electric Elec metered ⌂can be
hired(overseas visitors only) ☎ WM in
unit SD in unit Airing cupboard in unit
Iron in unit Ironing board in unit HCE in
unit TV ☻3pin square 2P ▥
⚐(200yds)

⊷ ⪲(2m) ⚲(200yds) ▦(2m)
Min£50 Max£60pw (Low)
Min£65 Max£70pw (High)

F **Flat 1 & Garden Flat, The Old
Rectory**
for bookings Mrs F M Cooke, The Old
Rectory, Staunton, Coleford,
Gloucestershire
☎Dean(0594)33165

*A maisonette on first- and second-floors
and a smaller flat. Each has a kitchen,
bathroom and two bedrooms. The
maisonette has a sitting/dining room, and
a bed-settee as additional sleeping
accommodation. The smaller flat has a
bed-settee in the sitting room.*

Apr–Sep 1wk min, 6mths max, 2units,
2–5persons [◊] ◊ no pets ◉
fridge Electric Elec metered ⌂can be
hired (overseas visitors only) ☎ Airing
cupboard in unit Iron in unit Ironing
board in unit HCE in unit ⊛ TV
☻3pin square 2P ▥ ⚐(200yds)

⊷ ⪲(2m) ⚲(200yds) ▦(2m)
Min£45 Max£55pw (Low)
Min£60 Max£65pw (High)

STAVELEY
Cumbria
Map **7** SD49

H **Browfoot Dale & Browfoot Fell**
Browfoot Farm, Kentmere Valley
for bookings Windermere Holidays,
Homewood Storrs Park, Windermere,
Cumbria
☎Windermere(09662)4175

*This original 17th-century farmhouse is
now divided into two. Both houses have
two twin-bedded rooms and a third room*

Starston
—
Stepaside

*has bunk beds. The houses retain their
original character and are situated in the
beautiful Kentmere Valley on unclass
road, 2m NW of Staveley village.*

All year MWB out of season 1wk min,
1mth max, 2units, 2–6persons ◊ ◆
no cats ◉ fridge Electric & open
fires Elec metered ⌂not provided ☎
Airing cupboard in unit Iron in unit
Ironing board in unit HCE in unit ⊙
TV ☻3pin square P ⚐(1½m)

⊷ ⚲(1½m)
Min£70 Max£140pw (Low)
Min£110 Max£210pw (High)

H **Low Brow House** Browfoot Farm,
Kentmere Valley
for bookings Windermere Holidays,
Homewood Storrs Park, Windermere,
Cumbria
☎Windermere(09662)4175

*A recently renovated traditional stone-
built Lakeland farmhouse with four
bedrooms – three have twin beds and the
fourth has bunk beds. Situated in the
beautiful Kentmere Valley on unclass
road, 2m NW of Staveley village.*

All year MWB out of season 1wk min,
4wks max, 1unit, 2–8persons ◊ ◆
no cats ◉ fridge Electric & open
fires Elec metered ⌂not provided ☎
Airing cupboard in unit Iron in unit
Ironing board in unit HCE in unit ⊙
TV ☻3pin square P ⚐(1½m)

⊷ ⚲(1½m)
Min£70 Max£140pw (Low)
Min£110 Max£210pw (High)

STEEPLE CLAYDON
Buckinghamshire
Map **4** SP72

B **The Bungalow**
for bookings Mr R J Pike, Hillbrow,
Terrace Road, Dinfield, Berks RG12 5DH
☎Bracknell(0344)25419

*A modern bungalow with open views over
the countryside comprising two
bedrooms and a comfortable lounge.
Within easy reach of village shops.*

All year MWB 1wk min, 3wks max,
1unit, 1–5persons ◉ fridge ⧜
Elec metered ⌂inclusive ☎(120yds)
Airing cupboard on premises Ironing
board on premises HCE TV
☻3pin square 2P ⚐(½m)

⊷ ⚲(½m)
Min£60 Max£110pw

STENNESS
Orkney
Map **16** HY31

H **Blackbraes**
for bookings Mrs V Pirie, Orakirk, Orphir,
Orkney KW17 2RE
☎Orphir(085681)328

*Detached two-storey stone house
formerly a farm set in an isolated position*

---

*off A964 2m S of the junction with the
Stromness – Finstown road. Comprises
dining room, small kitchen, lounge, two
double bedrooms, two twin-bedded
rooms and a bathroom.*

All year 2wks min(summer) 1wk(winter),
1unit, 1–8persons ◊ ◆ no pets ◉
fridge Electric Elec metered
⌂not provided ☎(1m) WM in unit Airing
cupboard in unit Iron in unit Ironing board in
unit HCE in unit ⊛ CTV ☻3pin square
P ▥ ⚐(2m)
⊷ ⚲(2m) ▨(2m)
Min£55 Max£70pw (Low)
Min£65 Max£80pw (High)

C Mrs R Laidlow **Outbrecks** Stenness
by Stromness, Orkney KW16 3EY
☎Stromness(0856)850664

*Originally a farm building and now
tastefully converted into a block of three
cottages set adjacent to the main house.
They comprise two double bedrooms,
living/dining room (with foldaway double
bed), modern kitchen and bathroom with
shower. Situated on A964 ½m S of its
junction with Stromness – Finstown road
and overlooking the islands of Hoy and
Graemsay.*

All year MWB out of season 1wk min,
3units, 2–6persons ◉ fridge ⧜
Elec metered ⌂inclusive ☎(½m)
Airing cupboard in unit Iron in unit HCE
in unit TV can be hired ☻3pin square
P ▥ ⚐(2m)
⊷ ⚲(2m) ▨(3m) Fishing
Min£45 Max£60pw (Low)
Min£70 Max£90pw (High)

STEPASIDE
Dyfed
Map **2** SN01

C **Rose Villa** Pleasant Valley
for bookings Powell's Holidays, High
Street, Saundersfoot, Dyfed
☎Saundersfoot(0834)812791

*Terraced cottage with three bedrooms,
sitting room, kitchen/diner, bathroom and
WC. Cottage stands in a wooded valley
and in quiet location 10 minutes from
Wisemans Bridge. Off A477 Pembroke –
Carmarthen road, at Stepaside turn S to
Wisemans Bridge.*

May–Sep MWB out of season 1wk min,
4wks max, 1unit, 2–8persons [◊] ◆
◉ fridge Electric Elec inclusive
⌂not provided ☎(100yds) Airing
cupboard in unit Iron in unit Ironing
board in unit HCE in unit [Launderette
within 300yds] ⊙ CTV
☻3pin square P ▥ ⚐(300yds)
⊷ ⚲(½m) ▨(3m) ♫(3m)
Min£57 Max£150pw

B **Sea Break** Pleasant Valley
for bookings Powell's Holidays, High →

┌─────────────────────────────┐
│ 1982 prices quoted throughout │
│ gazetteer   │
└─────────────────────────────┘

Street, Saundersfoot, Dyfed
☎Saundersfoot(0834)812791

*A large modern bungalow in a quiet
residential area a short distance from
Wiseman's Bridge. It sleeps up to eight
and has a kitchen, dining room and
lounge with bed-settee.*

May–Sep MWB out of season 1wk min,
4wks max, 1unit, 2–8persons ◆
no pets ◉ fridge ♨ Elec inclusive
🔲 not provided ☎(½m) Airing cupboard
in unit Iron in unit Ironing board in unit
HCE in unit Launderette within 300yds
CTV ⊕3pin square P 🎏 🚌(300yds)
↔ ⛳(½m) 🚾(2m) ♫(2m)

Min£63 Max£168pw

STEYNING
West Sussex
Map**4** TQ11

F Mr & Mrs A Barnicott **Down House
Flats** King's Barn Villas, Steyning,
W Sussex BN4 3FA
☎Steyning(0903)812319

*'One ground and one first-floor flat in
Edwardian house with well-kept gardens
and in rural setting. Ground-floor flat
consists of one double and one twin-
bedded room, lounge/diner, kitchen and
bathroom/WC. First-floor flat has one twin
bedroom, lounge/diner with sofa/bed,
kitchen and bathroom/WC.*

All year MWB 1wk min, 3mths max,
2units, 1–4persons, nc5 ◉ fridge ♨
Gas/Elec inclusive(high season only)
🔲 inclusive ☎ Airing cupboard in unit
Iron in unit Ironing board in unit HCE in
unit ⊕ CTV ⊕3pin square 2P 🎏
🚌(½m)
↔ ⛳(½m)

Min£43 Max£48pw (Low)
Min£68 Max£85pw (High)

C & F Miss J Elsden, **Nash** Horsham
Road, Steyning, W Sussex
☎Steyning(0903)814988

*Three self-contained flats and a small
modernised cottage attached to an old
country house in 8 acres of ground with a
swimming pool and tennis court. The flats
consist of 1–2 bedrooms, lounge/diner,
kitchen, separate bath and WC. The
cottage can accommodate five people in
two bedrooms and also has a
lounge/dining room, kitchen and
bathroom. 1½m N of Steyning (A283) on
the E side off B2135.*

All year MWB 1wk min, 6mths max,
4units, 2–5persons ◆ ◆ no pets
◉ (Aga cooker in cottage) fridge ♨
Elec metered 🔲 can be hired ☎ WM
on premises SD on premises Airing
cupboard on premises Iron on
premises Ironing board on premises
HCE on premises ⊕ TV can be hired
⊕3pin square 22P 🎏 🚌(1¼m) ⌂
⊱Hard
↔ ⛳(1m)

Min£40 Max£120pw

> 1982 prices quoted throughout
> gazetteer

STIBB
Cornwall
Map**2** SS31

C **Grenville & Stowe Cottages**
Houndapitt Farm Holiday Cottages
for bookings Mrs D H W Heard,
61 Kings Hill, Bude, Cornwall
☎Bude((0288)2756

*Originally Houndapitt farmhouse, now
tastefully converted into two self-catering
cottages. Grenville has a large kitchen
with Aga cooker, lounge, dining room
and sleeps up to nine persons. Stowe has
a ground-floor bathroom, kitchen,
lounge, dining room, three bedrooms
sleeping up to seven persons and a small
front garden.*

All year MWB out of season 3days min,
4wks max, 2units, 2–9persons [◇] ◆
◆ ◉ fridge Electric Elec inclusive
🔲 can be hired ☎(100yds) WM on
premises SD on premises Airing
cupboard in unit HCE in unit ⊕ CTV
⊕3pin square P 🚌(100yds)
↔ 🚿(3m) ⛳(100yds) 🚾(3m)

Min£60 Max£80pw (Low)
Min£153 Max£218pw (High)

C **1–8 Houndapitt Farm Holiday
Cottages**
for bookings Mrs D H W Heard,
61 Kings Hill, Bude, Cornwall
☎Bude(0288)2756

*Eight cottages converted from farm
buildings all with lounge/kitchen/diner
and shower room/WC. Three of the
cottages have one double bedroom and
one twin, whilst the other five have two
double and one twin room. Many of the
rooms afford sea views.*

All year MWB out of season 3days min,
4wks max, 8units, 2–7persons [◇] ◆
◆ ◉ fridge Electric Elec inclusive
🔲 can be hired ☎(100yds) WM on
premises SD on premises Airing
cupboard in unit HCE in unit ⊕ CTV
⊕3pin square P 🚌(100yds) Games
room Fishing
↔ 🚿(3m) ⛳(100yds) 🚾(3m)

Min£60 Max£80pw (Low)
Min£153 Max£218pw (High)

STICKLEPATH
Devon
Map**2** SX69

C P J Westcott **Cottages 1–5**
Steddaford Motel, Sticklepath,
Okehampton, Devon
☎Sticklepath(083 784)630

*Five well-converted cottages set around
courtyard attached to licensed
restaurant. Each cottage offers two
double bedrooms, shower, WC, large
lounge and kitchen/diner with breakfast
bar.*

All year MWB 1wk min, 6wks max,
5units, 1–4persons, nc8 ◉ fridge

Electric Elec inclusive 🔲 inclusive ☎
Airing cupboard in unit Iron in unit
Ironing board in unit HCE in unit
[Launderette on premises] ⊕ TV
⊕3pin square 2P 🎏
↔ ♪ (3m) ♫(3m) 🚾(3m)

Min£95 Max£165pw

STIFFKEY
Norfolk
Map**9** TF94

C **Apple Cottage** Bridge Street
for bookings Major G Bowlby, English
Country Cottages, Claypit Lane,
Fakenham, Norfolk NR21 8AS
☎Fakenham(0328)51155

*A beautifully modernised period cottage,
detached and with private garden.
Situated 1m from sea in a village side
street off the A149. Separate sitting and
dining room, ground-floor bathroom,
well-equipped kitchen and three first-
floor bedrooms to sleep six.*

Apr–Oct 1wk min, 1unit, 6persons ◆
◉ fridge Electric Elec metered
🔲 inclusive ☎(100yds) Airing
cupboard in unit Iron in unit Ironing
board in unit HCE in unit TV
⊕3pin square 1P 🚌(100yds)
↔ ⛳(100yds)

Min£114 Max£222pw

C **Cleat Cottage** Cockthorpe
for bookings Mr & Mrs A Bessemer-Clark,
53 Abbotsbury Close, London W14
☎01–603 2591

*Semi-detached flint cottage with fenced
garden located in peaceful hamlet 1½m
from Stiffkey. Accommodation comprises
lounge/diner, kitchen and bathroom/WC
on the ground floor and two
communicating bedrooms (one single,
one twin) and a twin-bedded room
upstairs. Turn off A149 at Stiffkey on to
Binham road then follow signs to
Cockthorpe for 1½m.*

All year MWB out of season 2days min,
4wks max, 1unit, 1–5persons ◉
fridge Electric & open fires
Elec inclusive & metered
🔲 not provided ☎ Airing cupboard in
unit Iron in unit Ironing board in unit
HCE in unit CTV ⊕3pin square 2P
🚌(1m)
↔ ⛳(1m)

Min£60 Max£80pw (Low)
Min£90 Max£125pw (High)

STIRLING
Central *Stirlingshire*
Map**11** NS79

F Vacation Letting Department
University of Stirling Stirling FK9 4LA
☎Stirling(0786)3171 ext2033

*Clean and well-maintained flats on most
attractive University campus. The
accommodation is functional, and there
are up to ten bedrooms per flat. The
University's recreation and leisure
facilities can be used and several well*

---

equipped shops are on the campus.

5Jan–7Feb & 4Jun–10Sep MWB out of
season 1wkmin, 4wksmax, 100units,
1–10persons [◊] nopets
nocaravans ◎ fridge 🍴
Elecinclusive ⌸inclusive ☎ HCEon
premises [Launderette on premises]
☺ ◉3pinsquare P 🎀 ♨ ⌧
↩Hard

⊶ ♿ ♨(½m) 🏊(400yds)
♬(400yds) 🐕(400yds)

Min£57.50 Max£155pw (Low)
Min£69 Max£184pw (High)

STOCKLAND
Devon
Map3 ST20

H CC Ref 640 EP
for bookings Character Cottages
(Holidays) Ltd, 34 Fore Street, Sidmouth,
Devon EX108AQ
☎Sidmouth(039 55)77001

*Rear wing of country house in secluded
position. Modestly furnished entrance
hall, living room and dining area; also has
kitchen with deep sink and oak drainer,
larder, modern bathroom and WC, two
twin-bedded rooms with divans and one
single room with divan.*

Allyear MWBoutofseason 1wkmin,
1mthmax, 1unit, 2–5persons ◆ ◎
fridge Open&electric fires
Elecmetered ⌸can be hired ☎ Airing
cupboard in unit Iron in unit Ironing
board in unit HCE in unit TV
◉3pinsquare ◉2pinround P ♨
♨(6m)

⊶ ♨(1½m)

Min£39 Max£73pw (High)
Min£93 Max£123pw (High)

STOKE FLEMING
Devon
Map3 SX84

F Devon Chalets 1–4
for bookings Mrs F E Brimecombe,
Penhill Coastal Chalets, Shady Lane,
Stoke Fleming, Dartmouth, Devon
TQ60PB
☎Stoke Fleming(080 427)236

Stirling
—
Stoke Lacey

*Four detached, wood built, self-
contained chalets. Each comprise living
room, small kitchen, bathroom/WC and
two bedrooms (one double, one with
bunk beds). WC. Off A379, Dartmouth to
Torcross road, on coastal lane from
village centre.*

Allyear MWB in season 1wkmin,
1mthmax, 4units, 1–4persons [◆]
[◆] nopets ◎ fridge Electric
Elecmetered ⌸can be hired
☎(50yds) Iron on premises Ironing
board on premises HCE in unit
[Launderette within 300yds] CTV
◉3pinsquare P 🎀 ♨(250yds)

⊶ ♨(300yds) 🏊(2m)

Min£30 Max£40pw (Low)
Min£60 Max£85pw (High)

F Penthouse Chalets 15 & 17
for bookings Mrs F E Brimecombe,
Penhill Coastal Chalets, Shady Lane,
Stoke Fleming, Dartmouth, Devon
TQ60PB
☎Stoke Fleming(080 427)236

*Two first-floor flats with balcony
overlooking the sea. They are situated on
a coastal lane off A379, Dartmouth to
Torcross road from village centre. Each
has two bedrooms, one with double, and
one with bunks, living room with studio
couch, kitchenette and bathroom/WC.*

Allyear MWB in season 1wkmin,
1mthmax, 2units, 1–6persons [◆]
[◆] nopets ◎ fridge Electric
Elecmetered ⌸can be hired
☎(50yds) Iron on premises Ironing
board on premises HCE in unit
[Launderette within 300yds] ☺ CTV
◉3pinsquare P 🎀 ♨(250yds)

⊶ ♨(300yds) 🏊(2m)

Min£50 Max£60pw (Low)
Min£85 Max£110pw (High)

Ch Start Bay Chalets 5, 6 & 11–14
for bookings Mrs F E Brimecombe
Penhill Coastal Chalets, Shady Lane,
Stoke Fleming, Dartmouth, Devon
TQ60PB
☎Stoke Fleming(080 427)236

---

*Six detached, wood built, self-contained
holiday chalets on a coastal lane off
A379, Dartmouth to Torcross road, from
village centre. They consist of two
bedrooms, onea double and one with
bunk beds, living room with studio couch,
small kitchen and bathroom/WC.*

Allyear MWB in season 1wkmin,
1mthmax, 6units, 1–6persons [◆]
[◆] nopets ◎ fridge Electric
Elecmetered ⌸can be hired
☎(50yds) Iron on premises Ironing
board on premises HCE in unit
[Launderette within 300yds] CTV
◉3pinsquare P 🎀 ♨(250yds)

⊶ ♨(300yds) 🏊(2m)

Min£35 Max£40pw (Low)
Min£65 Max£90pw (High)

F Swiss Chalets 7–10, 16–18
for bookings Mrs F E Brimecombe,
Penhill Coastal Chalets, Shady Lane,
Stoke Fleming, Dartmouth, Devon
TQ60PB
☎Stoke Fleming(080 427)236

*Four ground floor and two first floor self-
contained flats with living room and
double studio couch, two bedrooms (one
double, one bunk bed), kitchenette and
bathroom with WC. Off A379, Dartmouth
to Torcross road, on coastal lane from
village centre.*

Allyear MWB in season 1wkmin,
1mthmax, 6units, 1–6persons [◆]
[◆] nopets ◎ fridge Electric
Elecmetered ⌸can be hired
☎(50yds) Iron on premises Ironing
board on premises HCE in unit
[Launderette within 300yds] ☺ CTV
◉3pinsquare P 🎀 ♨(250yds)

⊶ ♨(300yds) 🏊(2m)

Min£40 Max£48pw (Low)
Min£70 Max£105pw (High)

STOKE LACEY
Hereford & Worcester
Map3 SO64

C Merryfield Cottage
for bookings Mrs Sadler, Wyvern
Cottages, 60 East Road, Stoney Hill,
Bromsgrove, Worcester
☎Bromsgrove(0527)73734 →

UNIVERSITY OF STIRLING

A detached cottage standing in its own grounds with extensive views across to the Brecon Beacons. Accommodation comprises lounge, dining room, kitchen and bathroom, one twin-bedded room, one double and one single bedroom.

Apr–Oct MWB out of season 1wk min, 4wks max, 1unit, 5persons ◆ ◉ fridge ♨ Elec metered ⬛ not provided ☎(½m) Airing cupboard in unit Iron in unit HCE in unit TV ⊕3pin square 3P ♨(½m)

↩ ⬤(½m)

Min£50 Max£94pw

STONE
Gloucestershire
Map**3** ST69

H Elms Coach House
for bookings Mr L R Duncum, The Elms Guest House, Stone, Berkeley, Gloucestershire
☎Falfield(0454)260279

Modernised coach house situated 1m from M5 (junction 14) motorway. Accommodation comprises one twin-bedded room, one family bedroom, lounge, large kitchen/diner and bathroom. Décor is bright and clean. Residents may use garden of the adjacent 17th-century guest house.

All year MWB out of season 1unit, 5persons ◆ ◉ fridge Electric Elec metered ⬛ can be hired ☎ Airing cupboard Iron Ironing board HCE ⊕ ◈ TV ⊕3pin square P ▥ ♨(50yds)

↩ ⬤

STRAITON
Strathclyde *Ayrshire*
Map**10** NS30

C Balminnoch Cottage
for bookings Mr J Hunter-Blair, Blairquhan Estate Office, Straiton, Maybole, Ayrshire KA197LZ
☎Straiton(06557)239

A fully modernised and extended farm cottage situated 100yds from Balminnoch Farm. It sleeps six in two twin-bedded rooms, and two divan beds in the lounge. There is a bathroom, kitchen/diner and living room. The Estate is on the B741 near the village.

All year MWB out of season 1wk min, 6mths max, 1unit, 1–6persons ◆ ◆ ◉ fridge Electric & open fires Elec inclusive ⬛ not provided ☎(100yds) Iron in unit Ironing board in unit HCE in unit ⊕ ⊕3pin square P ♨(1m) Fishing

↩ ⬤(1m)

Min£71.40 Max£96.30pw (Low)
Min£109 Max£161pw (High)

C Bishopland Lodge
for bookings Mr J Hunter-Blair, Blairquhan Estate Office, Straiton, Maybole, Ayrshire KA197LZ
☎Straiton(06557)239

Stoke Lacey
—
Stratford-upon-Avon

A modernised stone-built cottage dating back to c1800. Accommodation consists of kitchen/dining room, one bedroom with twin beds, living room with three convertible sofas. In a quiet location with fine views of the surrounding countryside.

All year MWB out of season 1wk min, 6mths max, 1unit, 1–5persons ◆ ◆ ◉ fridge Electric & coal Elec metered ⬛ not provided ☎(½m) Iron in unit Ironing board in unit HCE in unit ⊕ ⊕3pin square P ♨ ♨(2m) Fishing

↩ ⬤(2m)

Min£58.30 Max£77.50pw (Low)
Min£87.60 Max£128pw (High)

C Farrer, McIntyre & Wauchope Cottages
for bookings Mr J Hunter-Blair, Blairquhan Estate Office, Straiton, Maybole, Ayrshire KA197LZ
☎Straiton(06557)239

A converted stable with cottages leading off the courtyard, built in 1820–24. Farrer Cottage has a dining room and two bedrooms and sleeps up to eight people. McIntyre has a kitchen/dining room with two bedrooms and sleeps up to six people. Wauchope has a kitchen/dining room and two bedrooms, one leading off the other, sleeping up to five people.

All year MWB out of season 1wk min, 1mth max, 3units, 1–8persons ◆ ◆ ◉ fridge Electric & open fires Elec metered ⬛ not provided ☎ Iron in unit Ironing board in unit HCE in unit ⊕3pin square P ▥ ♨(1m) Fishing

↩ ⬤(1m)

Min£56.50 Max£96.30pw (Low)
Min£111.40 Max£161pw (High)

C Kennedy Cottage
for bookings Mr J Hunter-Blair, Blairquhan Estate Office, Straiton, Maybole, Ayrshire KA197LZ
☎Straiton(06557)239

The cottage is on one side of a courtyard forming part of Blairquhan Castle and dates back to 1575. The cottage itself is fully modernised and decorated to a very high standard. It sleeps seven in two twin-bedded rooms and one double-bedded room and has a lounge with bed-settee, kitchen and bathroom.

All year MWB out of season 1wk min, 1mth max, 1unit, 1–6persons ◆ ◆ ◉ fridge Electric & open fires Elec inclusive ⬛ not provided ☎ Airing cupboard in unit Iron in unit Ironing board in unit HCE in unit ⊕ ⊕3pin square 4P ▥ ♨(1m) Fishing

↩ ⬤(1m)

Min£79 Max£107.40pw (Low)
Min£121.40 Max£180.50pw (High)

C McDowall Cottage
for bookings Mr J Hunter-Blair, Blairquhan Estate Office, Straiton,

---

Maybole, Ayrshire KA197LZ
☎Straiton(06557)239

A late conversion of a garden bothy situated in the garden wall of Blairquhan gardens. The accommodation comprises a double-bedded room, a twin-bedded room, living room with sofa/bed, kitchen and bathroom. The estate is on the B741 near the village.

All year MWB out of season 1wk min, 1mth max, 1unit, 1–5persons ◆ ◆ ◉ fridge Electric & open fires Elec inclusive ⬛ not provided ☎ Iron in unit Ironing board in unit HCE in unit ⊕ ⊕3pin square 6P ▥ ♨(1m) Fishing

↩ ⬤(1m)

Min£66.70 Max£89.20pw (Low)
Min£101 Max£148.50pw (High)

STRATFORD-UPON-AVON
Warwickshire
Map**4** SP25

C Lord Nelson Cottage 35 Great William Street
for bookings Mr & Mrs M V Spencer, Moonraker House, 40 Alcester Road, Stratford-upon-Avon, Warwickshire
☎Stratford-upon-Avon(0789)67115

A converted public house forming part of a line of terraced cottages, in one of Stratford's quaint back streets. The modern interior comprises kitchen/diner, large lounge, bathroom/WC and sleeps up to five persons.

All year 1wk min, 6mths max, 1unit, 1–5persons ◿ fridge ♨ Gas inclusive ⬛ inclusive ☎(250yds) Airing cupboard in unit Iron in unit Ironing board in unit HCE in unit ⊕ CTV ⊕3pin square ◈ ♨(40yds)

↩ ♨(1m) ⬤(250yds) ▥(1m) ♫(300yds) ▣(1m)

C Sandfields Cottage Luddington
for bookings Mrs P Boswell, Sandfields Farm, Luddington, Stratford-upon-Avon, Warwickshire CV37 9SW
☎Stratford-upon-Avon(0789)750202

Semi-detached cottage overlooking farmland and orchards. The downstairs accommodation comprises lounge, kitchen/diner, bathroom and WC. Upstairs there are three bedrooms, one double, one twin-bedded and one with bunks. 2½m W off A439.

All year MWB out of season 2nights min, 1mth max, 1unit, 1–6persons ◆ no pets ◉ fridge Electric Elec inclusive ⬛ inclusive(except sheets & pillowcases) ☎(½m) Airing cupboard in unit Iron in unit Ironing board in unit HCE in unit ⊕ TV ⊕3pin square 2P

↩ ⬤(2m) ▣(2½m) ♫(2½m) ▥(2½m)

Min£74.75 Max£97.75pw

1982 prices quoted throughout gazetteer

242

STRATHYRE
Central *Perthshire*
Map **11** NN51

Ca **Balvaig Log Cabins** Balvaig
Estates Ltd, Strathyre, Perths
☎Strathyre(08774)666

*A group of nine log cabins in varying
designs set in spacious surroundings on
the banks of the River Balvaig. All are
tastefully furnished with full timbered
interior.*

All year MWB out of season 3 days min,
6 wks max, 9 units, 2–8 persons [◇] ◆
◉ fridge Electric Elec metered
Ⓛcan be hired ☎(200yds) Airing
cupboard in unit ⊙ ⊕3 pin square P
Ⅲ ♨(50yds) ✌Hard
⟻ ⚲(200yds) ♫(200yds)
Min£34.50 Max£69pw (Low)
Min£138 Max£184pw (High)

STRATTON
Suffolk
C **Stratton Hall**
see pages 151 & 279

STRETE
Devon
Map **3** SX84

C **CC Ref 426 ELP**
for bookings Character Cottages
(Holidays) Ltd, 34 Fore Street, Sidmouth,
Devon EX10 8AQ
☎Sidmouth(039 55)77001

Strathyre — Sutton St Nicholas

*Semi-detached part thatched cottage
with fine views, lounge, dining room,
large kitchen and three bedrooms
accommodating five. The cottage is
situated on the main road that runs
through the village and is 1m from the
beach.*

All year MWB out of season 1 wk min,
4 wks max, 1 unit, 1–5 persons ◇ [◇]
[◆] ◉ fridge ♨ Electric
Elec metered Ⓛcan be hired
☎(20yds) [Airing cupboard in unit]
Iron in unit Ironing board in unit HCE in
unit ⊙ TV ⊕3 pin square P Ⅲ
♨(20yds)
⟻ ⚲(50yds)
Min£65 Max£84pw (Low)
Min£101 Max£153pw (High)

STRONTIAN
Highland *Argyll*
Map **14** NM86

Ca **Seaview Grazings Holiday Homes**
for bookings Mr Peter Howland, Seaview
Grazings (Strontian) Ltd, Strontian, Argyll
☎Fort William(0397)2496

*Traditional Scandinavian log houses, set
together on uncultivated hillside. Each
one has magnificent loch and mountain
views. They have either two or three good
sized bedrooms, living room with double*

---

*bed-settee and modern, fully fitted
kitchen. They are spacious, very
attractive and equipped to a high
standard, including double glazing
throughout.*

All year MWB out of season 1 wk min,
9 units, 1–8 persons ◇ ◆ ◉ fridge
Electric Elec inclusive Ⓛcan be hired
☎(⅓m) WM in unit Airing cupboard in
unit Iron in unit Ironing board in unit
HCE in unit ⊙ CTV ⊕3 pin square P
♨(⅓m)
⟻ ⚲(⅓m)
Min£80 Max£237pw

SUTTON ST NICHOLAS
Hereford & Worcester
Map **3** SO64

H **Lane Farm Cottage**
for bookings Mr R Andrews, Court Farm,
Sutton St Nicholas, Hereford
☎Sutton St Nicholas(043 272) 224

*An 18th-century, half-timbered stone
farmhouse, ideal for a peaceful holiday.
The ground-floor consists of a
kitchen/diner, lounge, and WC, whilst the
first-floor contains three bedrooms and a
bathroom/WC.*

All year MWB out of season
2 nights min, 6 wks max, 1 unit,
1–6 persons [◇] ◆ ◉ fridge
Electric Elec metered Ⓛcan be hired
☎(⅓m) Airing cupboard in unit Iron in
unit Ironing board in unit HCE in unit →

TV ⊕3pin square 3P ▥ ♣(¼m)
⊖ ♀(¼m)

***H* Watersheep Cottage**
for bookings Mr R Andrews, Court Farm, Sutton St Nicholas, Hereford
☎Sutton St Nicholas(043272) 224
Brick-built semi-detached house located in the heart of a quiet village. Comfortable accommodation comprises of lounge, kitchen/diner, three bedrooms and bathroom/WC. Fishing available at nearby River Lugg.
All year MWB out of season 2nights min, 6wks max, 1unit, 1–6persons [◇] ◈ ◎ fridge Electric Elec metered ◻can be hired ☎(¼m) Airing cupboard in unit Iron in unit Ironing board in unit HCE in unit TV ⊕3pin square 3P ▥ ♣(¼m)
⊖ ♀(¼m)

SWANAGE
Dorset
Map**4** SZ07

***F* Alexander Court**
for bookings Mr & Mrs Fowler, Alexander Court, Grosvenor Road, Swanage, Dorset
☎Swanage(09292)4606
Modern purpsoe-built block of flats in elevated position overlooking town and Swanage Bay. Compact and self-contained with carpeting and modern furniture. Fully equipped to requirements.
All year 1wk min, 1mth max, 6units, 6–8persons ◈ ◆ no pets ◎ fridge ⛭ Elec metered ◻can be hired ☎(100yds) Airing cupboard in unit HCE in unit TV ⊕3pin square P ⌂ ▥ ♣(500yds)
⊖ ♀(500yds) ▨(500yds) ♫(500yds) ⛟(¼m)
Min£30 Max£50pw (Low)
Min£100 Max£200pw (High)

F Mrs D Alexander **Marston Flats** 16 Burlington Road, Swanage, Dorset BH19 1LS
☎Swanage(09292)2221
This detached Purbeck stone and tile-hung gabled house provides three self-contained flats. A fourth flat is occupied by the proprietors. The house is situated in a quiet residential area on a cliff top location. Burlington Road can be found off Ulwell Road. The flats are quite similar with lounge, kitchen, two bedrooms and either a bath or shower with WC. Each has a put-u-up bed in the lounge, so that a total of seven people can be accommodated in each flat. Two flats overlook the sea.
Mar–Oct MWB out of season 2nights min, 4wks max, 3units, 2–7persons, nc3 no pets ◎ fridge Electric Elec metered ◻inclusive ☎(¼m) Airing cupboard in unit Iron in unit Ironing board in unit HCE in unit ⊙ CTV ⊕3pin square P ▥ ♣(¼m)
⊖ ♁18(3m) ♀(250yds) ⛟(¾m)

Min£35 Max£105pw (Low)
Min£145 Max£180pw (High)

***F* Waveney** Park Road
for bookings Mr & Mrs Fowler, Alexander Court, Grosvenor Road, Swanage, Dorset
☎Swanage(09292)4606
Brick and stone Victorian villa in elevated position overlooking town and Swanage Bay, with converted modernised interior. Carpeted, furnishings and equipped to requirements.
All year 1wk min, 1mth max, 7units, 4–10persons ◈ ◆ no pets ♁(2units) ◎(5units) fridge Electric Gas/Elec metered ◻can be hired ☎(100yds) HCE in unit TV ⊕3pin square P ⌂ ▥ ♣(500yds)
⊖ ♀(500yds) ▨(500yds) ♫(500yds) ⛟(¼m)
Min£30 Max£60pw (Low)
Min£100 Max£200pw (High)

TARLAND
Grampian *Aberdeenshire*
Map**15** NJ40

***H* Wardfold**
for bookings Aboyne Estates, Estate Office, Old Station, Dinnet, Aboyne, Aberdeenshire AB3 5LL
☎Dinnet(033985)341
This delightful house was once an inn on an old drove road, and more recently a farmhouse. Four bedrooms, one with bunk beds, living room and separate kitchen. All rooms are lined with dark pine wood and are very spacious. Very pleasant in appearance and comfortably furnished. The house is about 1m S of Tarland and has excellent views of the surrounding countryside.
Mar–Oct 1wk min, 1mth max, 1unit, 1–8persons ◈ ◆ ◎ fridge Elec inclusive ◻can be hired ☎ Iron in unit Ironing board in unit HCE ⊕3pin square P ▥ ♣(1m)
Max£95pw (Low)
Max£128pw (High)

TAVERNSPITE
Dyfed
Map**2** SN21

***H* White Lion**
for bookings Powell's Holidays, High Street, Saundersfoot, Dyfed
☎Saundersfoot(0834)812791
Modern stucco-clad house with fields at rear, situated in a quiet rural area. The property has lounge, dining room, ktichen/diner and four bedrooms (one has a double and bunk beds, two have double beds and cots, and another room has twin beds). The house is situated 1½m E of Tavernspite village on an unclass road.
Apr–Oct MWB out of season 1wk min, 1unit, 10persons [◈] ◎ fridge

Electric Elec inclusive ◻not provided ☎(1½m) Airing cupboard in unit Iron in unit Ironing board in unit HCE in unit ⊙ TV ⊕3pin square P ⌂ ♣(1½m)
⊖ ♀(1½m)
Min£63 Max£168pw

TAYNUILT
Strathclyde *Argyll*
Map**10** NN03

Ch Mrs I Olsen, **Airdeny Chalets,** Airdeny, Taynuilt, Argyll PA35 1HY
☎Taynuilt(08662)648
Wooden chalets designed and built by the owners who also own a nearby Sawmill. Two bedrooms, open-plan living and kitchen areas, shower with WC. High standard of fittings, and visitors generally well looked after. Situated in a quiet setting frequented by deer, facing E to Ben Cruachan (3,600ft). Take the Glen Lonan road at the Taynuit Hotel on the A85, head S for 1m.
Mar–Dec MWB out of season 1wk min, 1mth max, 4units, 1–6persons ◈ ◆ no pets ◎ fridge ⛭ Elec metered ◻not provided ☎(1m) Iron on premises HCE in unit ⊙ ⊕3pin square P ♣(1m)
⊖ ♀(1m)
Max£57pw (Low)
Max£149pw (High)

C Mr & Mrs H A W Baird **Bonawe House Holiday Cottages** Bonawe House, Taynuilt, Oban, Argyll
☎Taynuilt(08662)309
Two recently modernised cottages which were formerly outhouses of Bonawe House. Well equipped, they comprise fitted kitchen, living/dining room and either two or three bedrooms. Bonawe House is reached by a signposted though unclassified road off A85, 1m E of Taynuilt.
All year MWB out of season 1wk min, 2units, 1–6persons ◈ ◆ no pets ◎ fridge Electric Elec inclusive ◻can be hired ☎(300yds) ⊙ CTV ⊕3pin square 8P ♣(¾m) Riding school
⊖ ♀(¾m)
Min£35 Max£145pw (Low)
Min£70 Max£200pw (High)

F Mr & Mrs H A W Baird **Bonawe House Holiday Flats** Bonawe House, Taynuilt, Oban, Argyll
☎Taynuilt(08662)309
Three modernised and well-equipped flats, contained within Bonawe House. Each flat is individually designed and decorated. Located in 10 acres of woodland and gardens, 1m E of Taynuilt.
All year MWB out of season 1wk min, 3units, 1–9persons ◈ ◆ no pets ◎ fridge Electric Elec inclusive ◻can be hired ☎(300yds) Iron in unit Ironing board in unit HCE in unit ⊙ CTV ⊕3pin square 8P ♣(¾m) Riding school
⊖ ♀(½m)

Min£35 Max£145pw (Low)
Min£70 Max£200pw (High)

F Mr H & Miss S Grant **Lonan House** Glen Lonan, Taynuilt, Argyll PA35 1HY ☎Taynuilt(08662)253

A converted country house hotel standing in attractive, landscaped grounds with magnificent scenic views. The flats vary in size but each one is tastefully decorated and furnished. Turn off A85 at Taynuilt along the single track Glen Lonan road; the flats are 1m from Glen Lonan.

All year MWB out of season 1wk min, 4wks max, 8units, 1–6persons [◆ ◆] ◊ ◎ fridge ♨ Elec metered ◻can be hired ☎ Iron on premises Ironing board on premises HCE in unit ⊙ CTV ⊕3pin round 16P ♨(1m)

⊖ ♀(1m)

Min£40 Max£90pw (Low)
Min£60 Max£180pw (High)

TEIGNMOUTH
Devon
Map **3** SX97

F **Campion Flats 2, 3 & 4**
for bookings Mrs S Hawkings, Campion, Buckeridge Avenue, Teignmouth, Devon TQ14 8LX
☎Teignmouth(06267)4574

Three flats on first- and second-floors, two of the flats each have two bedrooms (one double and one with twin beds. Flat 3 has bunk beds) sitting/dining room (Flat 2 has put-u-up) kitchen, bathroom/WC. Flat 4 has one double bedroom, sitting room with foldaway bed, kitchen, dining room and bathroom/WC. Flat 2 is centrally heated throughout.

All year MWB out of season 1wk min, 6mths max, 3units, 2–6persons ◆ ◆ no pets ◎ fridge Electric Elec metered ◻inclusive ☎(300yds) Airing cupboard in unit Iron in unit Ironing board in unit HCE in unit ⊙ CTV ⊕3pin square P ▣ ♨(½m)

⊖ ♂18(1½m) ♀(¾m) ▣(¾m) ♫(¾m) ♞(¾m)

Min£25 Max£55pw (Low)
Min£65 Max£115pw (High)

H **CC Ref 402 ELP**
for bookings Character Cottages (Holidays) Ltd, 34 Fore Street, Sidmouth, Devon EX10 8AQ
☎Sidmouth(03955)77001

A thatched house of character in secluded position, with attractive living room (period furniture), good kitchen, two tastefully decorated bedrooms, combined bathroom and WC, and two beds in living room. Paddock and gardens.

All year MWB out of season 1wk min, 6mths max, 1unit, 2–5persons ◆ ◎ fridge Gas Gas/Elec inclusive ◻not provided ☎(100yds) Airing cupboard in unit Iron in unit Ironing board in unit HCE in unit ⊙ TV ⊕3pin square ⊕2pin round P ▣ ♨(300yds) ✿Grass

⊖ ♀(1½m) ▣(1½m) ♫(1½m) ♞(1½m)

Min£60 Max£86pw (Low)
Min£102 Max£136pw (High)

F **Coachmans Flat**
for bookings Mrs L B Francis, 12 Newton Road, Bishopsteignton, Teignmouth, Devon TQ14 9PN
☎Teignmouth(06267)6656

A spacious ground-floor flat in semi-detached house set back from main Teignmouth–Newton Abbot road. Accommodation comprises large lounge/diner (with divan), one with twin-bedded room, shower room/WC and a modern fitted kitchen. Excellent views of the estuary and hills.

All year 1wk min, 7mths max, 1unit, 3persons [◆ ◆] ◎ fridge ♨ Elec metered ◻inclusive ☎(½m) SD in unit Iron in unit Ironing board in unit HCE in unit ⊙ CTV ⊕3pin square 2P ▣ ♨(½m)

⊖ ♂18(3m) ♀(½m) ▣(2½m) ♫(2½m) ♞(2½m)

Min£50pw (Low)
Min£76pw (High)

F Mr & Mrs F R Bass **Grendons Flats (2, 3, 5 & 6)** 58 Coombe Vale Road, Teignmouth, Devon TQ14 9EN
☎Teignmouth(06267)3667

The house was built in 1870 and is located in the built-up area of Teignmouth ¾m N of town centre. It has a rather difficult approach drive and should be approached from the A379, not from the N. A small, attractive terraced garden is available. Flat 2 is located in an extension, built in 1975 and comprises large sitting/dining room with double bed-settee and kitchenette, bedroom with double bed and bunks, separate bathroom and WC. Flats 3 and 5 are on the first-floor with lounge with double bed-settee, Flat 5 has bedroom with double and bunk beds, Flat 3 has double and two single beds, kitchen and bathroom/WC. Flat 6 has large sitting/dining room with double bed-settee and kitchenette. Separate bathroom/WC and family bedroom with double and bunk beds. Flats 2, 3 and 5 have high chairs provided and also a chargeable baby-sitting service is available.

All year MWB out of season 1wk min, 8mths max, 4units, 1–6persons ◆ ◊(2units) ◎(2units) fridge Electric Gas/Elec metered ◻can be hired ☎(500yds) Airing cupboard in Flat 6 Iron on premises Ironing board on premises HCE on premises [Launderette within 300yds] ⊙ TV ⊕3pin square P ▣ ♨(500yds)

⊖ ♂18(2m) ♀(½m) ▣(½m) ♫(½m) ♞(½m)

Min£43 Max£54pw (Low)
Min£66 Max£104pw (High)

F Mr S H Marshall **Lendrick** Sea Front, Teignmouth, Devon TQ14 8BJ
☎Teignmouth(06267)3009

Seven flats in an end-of-terrace Victorian house overlooking the seafront. They vary in size with one or two bedrooms. All rooms are large, particularly the living rooms, and all flats have kitchens and bathroom/WC or shower units.

All year MWB out of season 1wk min, max by arrangement 7units, 2–8persons no pets ◊ ◎ fridge Electric Gas/Elec metered ◻not provided ☎ Airing cupboard in unit Iron on premises Ironing board on premises HCE in unit [Launderette within 300yds] TV can be hired ⊕3pin square ▣ ♨(50yds)

⊖ ♀ ▣ ♫ ♞

Min£45pw Low)
Min£75pw (High)

F Mrs J Richardson-Brown **Lower Flat** Wytchwood, West Buckeridge, Teignmouth, Devon EX14 8NF
☎Teignmouth(06267)3482

Self-contained first-floor flat with entrance hall, bathroom, sitting room with balcony, kitchen/dining room with french windows to garden, and two bedrooms – one with a double bed and single divan, one with a double bed. Two 'Z' beds are also available. From Exeter on B3192 take first left past cemetery into New Road. Turn first right into Buckeridge Road and then second right (West Buckeridge) to end.

Apr–Sep 1wk min, 7mths max, 1unit, 1–7persons no pets ◊ fridge Gas & Electric Gas/Elec metered ◻can be hired ☎(½m) Airing cupboard in unit Iron in unit Ironing board in unit HCE in unit ⊙ TV ⊕3pin square P ▣ ♨(½m)

⊖ ♂18(3m) ♀(¾m) ▣(¾m) ♫(¾m) ♞(¾m)

Max£80pw (Low)
Max£120pw (High)

B **Redcliff & Seascape**
for bookings Mr & Mrs B S D Coley, Sunningdale, Second Drive, Dawlish Road, Teignmouth, Devon TQ14 8TL
☎Teignmouth(06267)3574

Pair of semi-detached bungalows situated in a private road off the Dawlish road ¾m from town centre. Each contains a kitchen/diner, two double-bedded rooms and one twin-bedded room, lounge, and bathroom with WC.

All year MWB out of season 2days min, 6mths max, 2units, 1–6persons ◆ ◆ ◎ fridge Electric Elec metered ◻inclusive ☎(½m) SD in unit Iron in unit Ironing board in unit HCE in unit ⊙ TV ⊕3pin square 4P ♨(½m) →

1982 prices quoted throughout gazetteer

⊖ δ18(3m) ♀(½m) ▣(½m) ♫(½m) ▣(½m)
Min£60 Max£135pw

F Mrs P R Herring **St Margarets Holiday Flats 1-5 & 9** New Road, Teignmouth, Devon TQ14 8UE
☎Teignmouth(06267)3858

Large 19th-century house converted into flats, situated in an acre of ground ¾m from the seafront. Each has a large sitting room with folding bed, a double bedroom, bathroom/WC and kitchen. Flat 3 sleeps a further two people in another double bedroom.

Allyear MWB out of season 1wkmin, 6mths max, 6units, 2–8persons [◇] ◆ ◆ no pets ◎ fridge Electric Elec metered ▣can be hired ☎(300yds) Iron on premises Ironing board on premises HCE on premises Launderette on premises ⊙ CTV ⊕3pin square P ▲ ▣ ▲(100yds) Games room

⊖ ♀(½m) ▣(½m) ♫(½m) ▣(½m)

TEMPLE CLOUD
Avon
Map **3** ST65

B & C **Barton Springs & Church Farm Cottage**
for bookings Mrs Harris, Hillcrest Farm, Cameley, Temple Cloud, Bristol, Avon
☎Temple Cloud(0761)52423

Modernised stone-built bungalow and semi-detached stone cottage which adjoins the farmhouse. The bungalow has three bedrooms, two double and one twin, (additional bed and cot available) lounge, kitchen and bathroom/WC. The cottage has a split-level interior with reception entrance, stairs to lounge and kitchenette then open staircase to one twin-bedded room, one double-bedded room and bathroom/WC. Quiet setting in valley near historic church.

Allyear MWB out of season 1wkmin, 4wks max, 2units, 2–7persons ◆(in bungalow) no pets ◎ fridge Electric Elec metered ▣not provided ☎(¾m) Airing cupboard in unit Iron in unit Ironing board in unit HCE in unit ⊙ TV & CTV ⊕3pin square 4P ▣ ▲(¾m) Trout fishing

⊖ δ18(3m) ♀(¾m)

Min£45 Max£60pw (Low)
Min£75 Max£130pw (High)

TEMPLECOMBE
Somerset
Map **3** ST72

H ***Manor Farm***
for bookings Mrs M L Hunt, Blackmarsh Farm, Sherborne, Dorset
☎Sherborne(093581)2389

Detached modern stone-built two-storey farmhouse situated on the outskirts of Templecombe. Large spacious accommodation with six bedrooms, large lounge, dining room, modern kitchen, bathroom, shower room and two WCs.

Allyear MWB out of season 1wkmin, 6mths max, 1unit, 2–12persons ◆ ◆ ◎ fridge ▣ Elec metered ▣can be hired ☎(600yds) WM on premises Airing cupboard in unit Iron in unit Ironing board in unit HCE in unit ⊙ CTV ⊕3pin square P ▲ ▲(500yds)

⊖ ♀(500yds)

TENBY
Dyfed
Map **2** SN10

F **Beaufort House** 38 Victoria Street
for bookings Mr & Mrs D R Pennington, 3 Morfa Terrace, Manorbier, Tenby, Dyfed SA70 7TH
☎Manorbier(083482)474

Flats, some with sea views, situated close to the S beach at Tenby. Accommodation varies in size, sleeping up to eight persons in two double or twin bedrooms, or family rooms. Each lounge contains a convertible settee.

May-15Oct MWB out of season 3days min, 1mth max, 4units, 2–8persons [◆ ◆] ◎ fridge Electric Elec metered ▣not provided ☎(300yds) Airing cupboard in some units Iron in unit Ironing board in unit HCE in unit [Launderette within 300yds] ⊙ CTV ⊕3pin square ▣ ▲(400yds)

⊖ ♀(1m) ▣(1m) ♫(1m) ▣(1m)

Min£45 Max£70pw (Low)
Min£80 Max£155pw (High)

F **Flint House** Deer Park
for bookings Mr & Mrs D R Pennington, 3 Morfa Terrace, Manorbier, Tenby, Dyfed SA70 7TH
☎Manorbier(083482)474

Three-storey house on the main road, converted into flats with good décor and furnishings.

Apr-15Oct MWB out of season 1wkmin, 4units, 7persons ◆ ◎ fridge Electric Elec metered ▣not provided ☎(100yds) Airing cupboard in unit Iron in unit Ironing board in unit HCE in unit [Launderette within 300yds] ⊙ CTV ⊕3pin square ▣ ▲ δ

Min£45 Max£65pw (Low)
Min£75 Max£140pw (High)

F **Glentworth House** Southcliffe Street
for bookings Mr & Mrs D R Pennington, 3 Morfa Terrace, Manorbier, Tenby, Dyfed SA70 7TH
☎Manorbier(083482)474

Three-storey end of terrace house converted into four flats, located one block away from the seafront. Accommodation comprises double, twin or family bedrooms to sleep up to seven, lounge with convertible settee, kitchen and bathroom.

Apr-15Oct MWB out of season 3days min, 1mth max, 4units, 2–7persons [◆] ◎ fridge Electric Elec metered ▣not provided ☎(300yds) Airing cupboard in some units Iron in unit Ironing board in unit HCE in unit [Launderette within 300yds] ⊙ CTV ⊕3pin square P ▣ ▲(400yds)

⊖ ♀(1m) ▣(1m) ♫(1m) ▣(1m)

Min£45 Max£65pw (Low)
Min£80 Max£130pw (High)

F Mrs B Holland **Knightston Lodge** New Hedges, Tenby, Dyfed
☎Tenby(0834)2095

Self-contained flats each consisting of kitchen/diner, bathroom, bedroom with double and single beds, and lounge with double foldaway wall bed. About 15 minutes walk from Waterwynch Bay, and approximately 1½m from the resorts of Tenby and Saundersfoot. 2m N A478.

Apr–Oct MWB out of season 1wkmin, 3mths max, 4units, 5persons no pets ◎ fridge Electric Elec metered ▣not provided ☎(100yds) Airing cupboard Iron Ironing board HCE ⊙ TV ⊕3pin square P ▣ ▲(100yds)

⊖ ♀(½m) ▣(½m) ♫(½m) ▣(½m)

Min£30 Max£90pw

B Mrs A Roper **The Firs** Strawberry Lane, Penally, Tenby, Dyfed
☎Tenby(0834)3962

A modern, detached bungalow in an elevated position offering superb panoramic views of the sea. There is ½ acre of landscaped garden. The accommodation comprises lounge/diner, with patio doors, two double and one twin-bedded room, fitted kitchen, bathroom with bidet and separate shower room/WC.

Jun–Sep 1wkmin, 1unit, 6persons ◆ no pets ◎ fridge Electric Elec inclusive ▣not provided ☎(400yds) Airing cupboard in unit Iron in unit Ironing board in unit HCE in unit ⊙ CTV ⊕3pin square P 2▲ ▣ ▲(400yds) δ

⊖ δ18(2m) ♀(400yds) ▣(2m) ♫(2m) ▣(2m)

C & F Mrs J M Wright **The Old Vicarage Hotel** Penally, Tenby, Dyfed
☎Tenby(0834)2773

The Old Vicarage consists of a small cottage and two flats adjoining the main house with access to large walled gardens. Charming small garden cottage with sitting room/dining area, double bedroom with wash hand basin, kitchen and bathroom/WC. Two well-equipped flats both two bedroom, one flat comprising one double room and one with bunks and single bed. There is a sitting room, kitchen/diner, bathroom and WC. The other has one twin-bedded room and a bedroom with three singles, also kitchen, sitting room, dining room, bathroom and WC. The cottage and one

of the flats have convertible single beds in the sitting room (2m SW A4139).

All year MWB out of season 3 days min, 3 units, 2–7 persons ◊ ◆ no pets ◉ fridge ♨ Elec inclusive Ⓛ can be hired (overseas visitors only) ☎(200yds) Airing cupboard in unit Iron in unit Ironing board in unit HCE in unit ☉ TV ⊕3pin square P ▥ ♨(200yds) Children's play area
⊖ ♨(200yds) ♨(2m) ▨(2m) ♫(2m) ♨(2m)

Min£60 Max£110pw(Low)
Min£90 Max£170pw(High)

Powell's Holidays High Street, Saundersfoot, Dyfed
☎Saundersfoot812791
Powell's Holidays have a total of seventeen AA-inspected properties in Tenby. Of these four are houses, two are cottages, seven are bungalows and four are flats.
An entry for one of each type of property follows. For information on the other properties contact Powell's Holidays.

F   Abbey Garden Flat
for bookings Powell's Holidays (address as above)
☎Saundersfoot(0834)812791

First-floor flat in detached dormer bungalow situated 1½m from Tenby. Accommodation comprises kitchen, lounge/diner with bar, bathroom, separate WC, two double bedrooms with additional single beds and one with wash basin and one double bedroom with wash basin.

Apr–Sep MWB out of season 1 wk min, 1 unit, 8 persons no pets ◉ fridge Electric Elec inclusive Ⓛ not provided ☎ Iron in unit Ironing board in unit HCE in unit ☉ CTV ⊕3pin square 1P ▥ ♨(50yds)
⊖ ♨(1½m) ♨(50yds) ▨(1½m) ♫(1½m) ♨(1½m)

Min£69 Max£195pw

C   Myrtle House Penally
for bookings Powell's Holidays (address as above)
☎Saundersfoot(0834)812791

A large cottage, near the centre of Penally, with sea and country views. Accommodation comprises lounge/diner, kitchen, two double bedrooms, one twin-bedded room, one single bedroom and bathroom/WC. There are nine steps up to the cottage.

Apr–Oct MWB out of season 1 wk min, 1 unit, 7 persons ◊ ◆ no pets ◉ fridge Electric Elec inclusive Ⓛ not provided ☎(30yds) Iron in unit Ironing board in unit HCE in unit TV ⊕3pin square ▥ ♨(50yds)
⊖ ♨(1m) ♨(30yds) ♨(2m)

Min£75 Max£216pw

B   3 Seascape Narberth Road
for bookings Powell's Holidays (address as above)
☎Saundersfoot(0834)812791

Tenby
—
Threlkeld

A modern bungalow with lawn and patio, situated on high ground with sea views. Accommodation comprises lounge/diner, kitchen, bathroom/WC, two double bedrooms, one with wash basin and one twin-bedded room.

May–Oct MWB out of season 1 wk min, 6 wks max, 1 unit, 2–6 persons ◊ ◆ no pets ◉ fridge ♨ Electric Elec inclusive Ⓛ not provided ☎(½m) Airing cupboard in unit Iron in unit Ironing board in unit HCE in unit ☉ CTV ⊕3pin square 3P ▥ ♨
⊖ ♨(1m) ♨(½m) ▨(½m) ♫(½m) ♨(½m)

Min£69 Max£195pw

TEWKESBURY
Gloucestershire
Map3 SO83

H   30 St Mary's Lane
for bookings The Landmark Trust, Shottesbrooke, Maidenhead, Berkshire
☎Littlewick Green(062 882)3431

Historic property extended at rear to comprise ground-floor kitchen, dining room, cloakroom with WC and washbasin. Single bedroom and bright spacious sitting room on first floor and second floor has combined bathroom/WC, and family bedroom. On the third floor landing there is a single and twin bedroom.

All year MWB out of season 1 day min, 1 unit, 2–7 persons ◊ ◆ ◉ fridge ♨ Elec inclusive Ⓛ not provided ☎(100yds) Iron in unit Ironing board in unit HCE in unit [Launderette within 300yds] ☉ ⊕3pin square ☎ ▥ ♨(50yds)
⊖ ♨(100yds)

Max£88pw (Low)
Max£180pw (High)

THORNESS BAY
Isle of Wight
Map4 SZ49

Ch   Thorness Bay Holiday Centre
for bookings Hoseasons Holidays, Sunway House, Lowestoft, Suffolk NR32 3LT
☎Lowestoft(0502)62292

A vast holiday complex leading to the Solent Estuary. Of the 132 chalets most can sleep six (including two on convertible settee) and all but twenty-six have gas cookers. All chalets are compact, modern and have simple furnishings and fittings.

3 May–27 Sep MWB out of season 3 days min, 6 mths max, 132 units, 2–6 persons [◊] [◆] ∅ fridge Electric Gas/Elec metered Ⓛ inclusive ☎ HCE in unit [Launderette on premises] TV

1982 prices quoted throughout gazetteer

⊕3pin square P ▥ ♨ ▨ ⌂ Children's playground
⊖ ♨

THORNFORD
Dorset
Map3 ST61

C   No 1 & 2 Trill Cottages
for bookings Mrs M E J Warr, Trill House, Thornford, Sherborne, Dorset
☎Yetminster(0935)872305

Pair of red brick semi-detached cottages in rural setting, comprising lounge, dining room, kitchen, bathroom with WC, all on ground floor. Two twin bedrooms on first floor. Leave Sherborne on A352 (Dorchester road). At town boundary turn right, signposted Thornford.

All year MWB out of season 3 days min, 1 mth max, 2 units, 2–6 persons ◊ ◆ no pets ◉ fridge Electric & open fires Elec metered Ⓛ can be hired ☎(1½m) WM in unit SD in unit Airing cupboard in unit Iron in unit Ironing board in unit HCE in unit ☉ TV ⊕3pin square 6P 1 ▥ ▥ ♨(1½m)
⊖ ♨(1½m)

THORNTON CLEVELEYS
Lancashire
Map7 SD34

F   Mr & Mrs H Studholme Reina 28 Ellerbeck Road, Thornton Cleveleys, Lancashire FY5 1DH

A modest, clean and comfortable flat on the first floor of proprietor's semi-detached house, approx 150yds from the sea. One bedroom sleeps three and a double foldaway bed is in lounge.

All year 1 wk min, 1 unit, 5 persons, nc2 no pets ◉ fridge Electric Elec metered Ⓛ inclusive ☎(100yds) Airing cupboard in unit Iron in unit Ironing board in unit HCE in unit [Launderette within 300yds] ☉ TV ⊕3pin square P ▥ ♨(200yds)
⊖ ♨(100yds) ▨(100yds) ♫(100yds)

Min£48 Max£60pw

THRELKELD
Cumbria
Map11 NY32

F   Netherend & T'Otherend
Guardhouse
for bookings Mrs M Baxter, Gardesse, Guardhouse, Threlkeld, Keswick, Cumbria CA12 4SZ
☎Threlkeld(059 683)671

Stone-built barn converted into two flats to a very high standard. Both flats (one on ground floor and one on first floor) are modern and spacious and have three double-bedded rooms. Located in the tiny hamlet of Guardbridge and an ideal base from which to explore the Lake District.

All year MWB out of season 3 nights min, 1 mth max, 2 units, 6 persons ◊ ◆ ◉ fridge Electric →

Elec metered ⬜not provided ☎(¾m)
Airing cupboard in unit Iron in unit
Ironing board in unit HCE in unit ⊖
[TV] ⊕3pin square 3P ♨(2m)
⊕ δ(¼m) ♀(¾m)

TIDEFORD
Cornwall
Map2 SX35

H Mr R Adlam **Trenance Farm**
Tideford, Saltash, Cornwall
☎Landrake(075538)319

Isolated farmhouse, part of which has been converted and tastefully furnished. Lounge/diner with fitted carpets, open granite fireplace and good three-piece suite. The bedrooms are well decorated and have ample wardrobe space.

Etr–Oct MWB in season 1wk min, 6mths max, 1unit, 2–6persons ◇ ◆ ♦ no pets ◉ fridge Electric Elec inclusive ⬜inclusive ☎ WM Airing cupboard in unit Iron in unit Ironing board in unit HCE in unit ⊖ TV ⊕3pin square ⊕2pin round P ♨ ▥ ♨(2m)

⊕ ♀(2m) ▨(3m)
Min£60 Max£130pw

TINTAGEL
Devon
Map2 SX08

F CC Ref **345E**
for bookings Character Cottages (Holidays) Ltd, 34 Fore Street, Sidmouth, Devon EX108AQ
☎Sidmouth(03955)77001

A brick-built conversion, adjacent to a hotel, containing five flats each sleeping from two to six people. Four have two bedrooms and a bed-settee in the lounge. The fifth has three bedrooms. Each has a kitchen, dining room (or dining area within the kitchen), lounge and bathroom with WC.

All year MWB out of season 1wk min, 1mth max, 5units, 2–6persons [◇] ◆ no pets ◉ fridge Electric Elec metered ⬜can be hired ☎(1m) Airing cupboard in unit Iron in unit Ironing board in unit HCE in unit [Launderette] ⊖ TV ⊕3pin square ⊕2pin round P ♨ ▥ ♨(200yds) ↝Hard

⊕ ♀ ▣ ♫
Min£52 Max£58pw (Low)
Min£102 Max£144pw (High)

C Mrs P K Upright **Halgebron Holiday Cottages** Halgebron, Tintagel, Cornwall
☎Camelford(0840)770667

Four exceptionally fine cottages. Threshings and Chaffcutter are conversions from a stone barn. To obtain the best view the large lounge/diner and open-plan kitchen are on the upper floor. The sleeping accommodation comprises one double room, one twin and one with bunk beds. Cartwheel Cottage is steeped in character, having beams and fireplace. Accommodation comprises lounge, kitchen/diner, small double-bedded room, one family room with double bed and bunks. Granary Cottage is small and a conversion from a stone barn and comprises lounge, kitchen/diner, bedrooms with double bed and bunks and shower/WC. The other cottages have bathroom/WC. Airing cabinet available in units. 1m E off B3263 towards Boscastle.

Mar–Nov MWB out of season 1wk min, 9mths max, 4units, 2–6persons [◇] ◆ ◉ fridge Electric Elec metered ⬜can be hired ☎ Iron in unit Ironing board in unit HCE in unit ⊖ CTV ⊕3pin square P ▥ ♨(1m)

⊕ ♀(½m)
Min£40 Max£60pw (Low)
Min£80 Max£200pw (High)

TINTERN
Gwent
Map3 SO50

C Yew Tree Cottage
for bookings Miss Jennings, Oakwood, St Briavals Common, Lydney, Gloucestershire GL156SJ
☎Dean(0594)530479

Attractive stone-faced cottage in its own garden, with views on all sides including the river. Accommodation comprises spacious lounge with stone fireplace, kitchen with breakfast bar and

ground-floor cloakroom with WC and shower. Upstairs there are four bedrooms (one double, one single, one with two beds and one with twin beds).

Mar–Oct, Xmas & New Year MWB out of season 3days min, 1unit, 2–7persons ◉ fridge ♨ Elec metered ⬜inclusive ☎(½m) WM in unit SD in unit Airing cupboard in unit Iron in unit HCE in unit ⊖ TV ⊕3pin square 4P ♨(1m)
⊕ ♀(100yds)
Min£70 Max£80pw (Low)
Min£110 Max£140pw (High)

TITCHWELL
Norfolk
Map9 TF74

C June Cottage
for bookings Hoseasons Holidays, Sunway House, Lowestoft, Suffolk NR323LT (Mar–Oct) Womack Ringer Ltd, Dodmans Farm, Titchwell, Kings Lynn, Norfolk (Nov–Apr)
☎Lowestoft(0502)62292

Three-storey semi-detached stone-built cottage with a garden and garage, situated 1m from the beach. Accommodation comprises three bedrooms (one double, two twin-bedded), lounge, kitchen and bathroom.

1wk min, 6wks max, 1unit, 1–6persons [◆] ◉ fridge ♨ Elec metered ⬜inclusive ☎(300yds) Airing cupboard in unit Iron in unit HCE in unit TV ⊕3pin square P ♨ ▥ ♨(1½m)
⊕ ♀(20yds)

C May Cottage
for bookings Hoseasons Holidays, Sunway House, Lowestoft, Suffolk NR323LT (Mar–Oct) Womack Ringer Ltd, Dodmans Farm, Titchwell, Kings Lynn, Norfolk (Nov–Apr)
☎Lowestoft(0502)62292

Detached cottage with garden situated in the village of Titchwell adjacent to farm buildings 1m from the sea. Accommodation comprises three bedrooms (one double, one with twin

bunks and one single), lounge, dining room, kitchen and bathroom/WC.

1wkmin, 6wksmax, 1unit, 1–6persons [◇] ◉ fridge ♨ Openfires Elecmetered 🄻inclusive ☎(400yds) Airing cupboard in unit Iron in unit HCE in unit TV ⊕3pinsquare P 🔟 ♨(1½m)

↤ ♀(400yds)

C Orchard Cottage
for bookings Hoseasons Holidays, Sunway House, Lowestoft, Suffolk NR323LT (Mar–Oct) Womack Ringer Ltd, Dodmans Farm, Titchwell, Kings Lynn, Norfolk (Nov–Apr) ☎Lowestoft(0502)62292

Pleasant detached cottage with a secluded garden backing on to an orchard, 1m from the sea. There are three bedrooms (one double, two twin-bedded), lounge, kitchen, cloakroom and bathroom/WC.

Allyear 1wkmin, 6wksmax, 1unit, 1–6persons [◇] ◉ fridge ♨ Openfires Elecmetered 🄻inclusive ☎(½m) Airing cupboard in unit Iron in unit HCEin unit TV ⊕3pinsquare P 🔟 ♨(1½m)

↤ ♀(½m)

TOBERMORY
Isle of Mull Strathclyde Argyll Map13 NM55

Ch Normand Enterprises (Heanish)
Heanish, Tobermory, Isle of Mull PA756PP ☎Tobermory(0688)2097

Ten Norwegian log chalets beside Heanish House in residential area. The chalets are arranged in pairs, connected by a double carport. Each has two very small bedrooms, one with bunks and its own washbasin, and one which can be either bunks or a double bed. There is a spacious living room with two divan beds, and a large modern kitchen. Bedrooms apart, the chalets are large, bright and pleasant.

Allyear MWBoutofseason 1wkmin, 10units, 1–6persons [◇] ◇ ◆ ◉ fridge Electric Elecmetered 🄻inclusive ☎(½m) Airing cupboard in unit Iron on premises Ironing board on premises HCEin unit [Launderette on premises] ⊕ CTVcan be hired ⊕3pinsquare P ♨(½m)

↤ δ₀(400yds) ♀(200yds) 🄿(½m)
Min£69 Max£87pw (Low)
Min£110 Max£156pw (High)

TOMATIN
Highland Inverness-shire Map14 NH82

C Dell Cottage Kyllachy
for bookings Scottish Highland Holiday Homes, 57 Church Street, Inverness IV11DR ☎Inverness(0463)222820

This spacious renovated cottage stands on quiet country road in the valley of the

River Findhorn. The ground-floor accommodation comprises entrance hall, large lounge/diner, kitchen with fridge/freezer and a small sitting room. Upstairs there are four bedrooms (two twin, one single and one with bunks) and a bathroom. 2m SW of Tomatin on unclassified road.

Allyear MWBoutofseason 1wkmin, 1unit, 1–6persons ◉ fridge Electric & open fires Elecmetered 🄻notprovided ☎ SD in unit Airing cupboard in unit Iron in unit Ironing board in unit HCE in unit ⊕3pinsquare 3P 1🛋 ♨(1m)

↤ ♀(2m)
Min£65 Max£120pw

TORLOISK
Isle of Mull Strathclyde Argyll Map13 NM45

C Keepers Cottage
for bookings Mrs G U D Richardson, Torr A'chlachain, Dervaig, Isle of Mull, Argyll PA756QR ☎Dervaig(06884)229

Two-storeyed stone cottage situated in lovely spot on high ground giving superb views of Island of Mull. Comprises sitting/dining room, modern kitchen, bathroom/WC, separate WC and twin-bedded room on ground floor. There is also a single bedroom and twin-bedded room on the first floor. Access by steep staircase–not suitable for the young or elderly. Extremely well maintained throughout.

Mar–Nov MWBoutofseason 1wkmin, 1mthmax, 1unit, 1–5persons, nc10 nocats ◉ fridge Electric Elecmetered 🄻notprovided ☎(100yds) Iron in unit Ironing board in unit HCEin unit ⊕3pinsquare ♨(4m)
Min£45 Max£100pw

TORPOINT
Cornwall Map2 SX45

Ch Whitsand Bay Holiday Park
(Chalets 1–7) for bookings Whitsand Bay Holiday Park, Millbrook, Torpoint, Cornwall ☎Plymouth(0752)822597

Seven identical wooden chalets in middle of holiday park, consisting of lounge, diner with kitchen recess, one double bedroom, one bunk bedroom, and bed-settee. There is a shower room with separate WC adjoining. Well signed from B3247.

Apr–Sep MWBoutofseason 1wkmin, 4wksmax, 7units, 1–6persons [◇ ◆] nopets ◉ fridge Electric Elecmetered 🄻notprovided ☎ [Iron on premises] [Ironing board on premises] [Launderette on premises] ⊕ CTV

⊕3pinsquare 7P 🔟 Games room Children's playground

↤ δ₀(3m) ♀ 🄿 ♫
Min£35 Max£60pw (Low)
Min£70 Max£120pw (High)

TORQUAY
Devon Map3 SX96

F Mr & Mrs T G Whitehouse Abbey View Holiday Flats Rathmore Road, Torquay, Devon TQ26NZ ☎Paignton(0803)559833

Five flats in semi-detached Victorian house, lounge/diner (with folding double beds), kitchen, bath or shower, WC, separate bedroom with double and single beds.

Allyear MWBoutofseason 1wkmin, 3mthsmax, 5units, 2–5persons [◇ ◆] ◉ fridge Electric Elecmetered 🄻can be hired ☎ Airing cupboard in unit Iron on premises Ironing board on premises HCE in unit [Launderette within 300yds] ⊕ CTV ⊕3pinsquare 12P 🔟 ♨(200yds)

↤ δ₀(3m) ♀(200yds) 🄿(½m) ♫(½m) 🕮(½m)
Min£42 Max£82pw (Low)
Min£58 Max£130pw (High)

F Mr & Mrs J Nelson Ashfield Rise Holiday Flats Ruckamore Road, Torquay, Devon TQ26HF ☎Torquay(0803)605156

A pleasantly modernised Victorian building with recently built extension, in quiet position adjacent to a public park. It stands in an elevated position with good views over the town to Tor Bay.

Allyear MWBoutofseason 1wkmin, 1mthmax, 8units, 2–6persons ◇ ◆ nopets ◉ fridge Electric Elecmetered 🄻can be hired ☎(450yds) Iron on premises Ironing board on premises HCE in unit ⊕ [CTV] ⊕3pinsquare P 🔟 ♨(300yds)

↤ ♀(350yds) 🄿(600yds) ♫(½m) 🕮(1m)
Min£54 Max£99pw (Low)
Min£139 Max£207pw (High)

See advert on page 250

F Mr & Mrs M G Britton Aster Apartments Warren Road, Torquay, Devon TQ25TR ☎Shaldon(062687)2634

Thirteen self-contained holiday flats with their own entrances from the main reception hall and stairways. Most have fine views, some have a balcony. On the first-floor there is a double-bedded room which is available with any flat. The flats range in size from being one- to three-bedroomed and can sleep from one to eight persons. Each flat has a hall, living room, separate kitchen, and bathroom. →

1982 prices quoted throughout gazetteer

Torquay

midMar-midJan MWB out of season
1wk min, 16wks max, 13units,
1–8persons [◊ ◆] no pets ◉
fridge Electric Elec metered
⬛inclusive ☎ [WM on premises] [SD
on premises] [TD on premises] Iron on
premises Ironing board on premises
HCE in unit ⊖ CTV ⊕3pin square P
🖾 ♨(½m)
⊖ ♒(2m) ♀(¼m) 🎦(¼m) ♫(½m)
🍴(½m)

Min£45 Max£105pw (Low)
Min£80 Max£195pw (High)

1982 prices quoted throughout
gazetteer

F Mrs J Taylor **The Beacon** 15
Braddons Hill Road East, Torquay,
Devon TQ1 1HA
☎Torquay(0803)23048

*Five flats at ground- and first-floor levels,
all have kitchen, bathroom, WC,
lounge/diner with double wall bed in
each flat. Separate bedroom with double
or double/single/bunks. On high ground
overlooking town.*

Mar-Oct MWB out of season
3days min, 5units, 2–6persons [◊]
◊ ◆ ◉ fridge Electric
Elec metered ⬜can be hired
☎(200yds) Airing cupboard in unit Iron
in unit Ironing board in unit HCE in unit
⊖ TV ⊕3pin square P 🖾
🍴(200yds)
⊖ ♀(500yds) 🎦(500yds)
♫(500yds) 🍴(½m)
Min£50 Max£120pw

H **Blue Tor** Velland Avenue
for bookings Mrs M Whittaker, 43 Petitor
Road, Torquay TQ1 4QF
☎Torquay(0803)38377

250

Modern semi-detached house built in 1970 on a pleasant residential estate some miles from town centre towards Teignmouth. Accommodation comprises dining room, kitchen, lounge with convertible settee, bathroom/WC, and two double bedrooms, one twin-bedded room and one room with bunk beds.

Etr-Nov 1wk min, 2mths max, 1unit, 2–8persons ◊ ◆ ◉ fridge ⋈ Electric Gas & Elec metered ⌁ can be hired ☎(150yds) WM in unit Airing cupboard in unit Iron in unit Ironing board in unit HCE in unit CTV ⊕3pin square 1▥ ▥ ▦(800yds)

⊕ ♨(1½m) ♀(1m) ▨(2m) ♫(2m) ▨(2m)

F Mr & Mrs A Ball **Bronshill Court Holiday Flats** Bronshill Road, Torquay, Devon TQ13HD
☎Torquay(0803)34549

Five flats situated on ground and first-floors of a detached Georgian house, ½m from town centre. Flats have a twin-bedded room plus a double wall bed in lounge/diner (Flat 2 has an additional double bedroom). All have small neat kitchen and bathroom/WC.

Mar-Dec MWB out of season 3days min, 3mths max, 5units, 2–6persons [◊] ◊ ◆ ◉ fridge ⋈ Elec metered ⌁ can be hired ☎ Iron on premises Ironing board on premises HCE on premises TV ⊕3pin square 7P ▥ ▦(500yds) ⊐

⊕ ♨(1m) ♀(½m) ▨(½m) ♫(½m) ▨(½m)

Min£58 Max£68pw (Low)
Min£138 Max£158pw (High)

F Mr & Mrs P W Archer-Moy **Chelston Hall** Old Mill Road, Torquay, Devon TQ26HW
☎Torquay(0803)605520

Good-quality flats in an imposing Victorian house which is set in an elevated position with fine views across the town to Tor Bay. The house stands in its own grounds in a reasonably quiet area yet within easy reach of the town centre and seafront.

All year MWB out of season 3nights min, 6mths max, 9units, 2–8persons [◊ ◆] ◉ fridge Electric Elec metered ⌁ inclusive ☎ Iron in unit Ironing board in unit HCE in unit [Launderette within 300yds] ⊙ CTV ⊕3pin square P ▥ ▦(150yds)

⊕ ♀(100yds) ▨(100yds) ♫(100yds) ▨(2m)

Min£56 Max£65pw (Low)
Min£82 Max£165pw (High)

F Mr & Mrs K Savill **Clovis Holiday Flats** 14 Thurlow Road, Torquay, Devon TQ13EE
☎Torquay(0803)33203

Five flats located in detached Victorian house situated in quiet residential area of Torquay. All flats have bathroom/WC,

---

kitchen, lounge/diner with double wall bed, and bedroom.

All year MWB out of season 1wk min, 5units, 2–6persons ◊ ◉ fridge Electric Elec metered ⌁ can be hired ☎(300yds) Airing cupboard in unit Iron on premises Ironing board on premises HCE in unit [Launderette within 300yds] ⊙ TV ⊕3pin square 8P ▥ ▦(½m)

⊕ ♨(2m) ♀(½m) ▨(½m) ♫(½m) ▨(½m)

Min£24 Max£36pw (Low)
Min£45 Max£160pw (High)

C Mr & Mrs F Matthews **The Cottage & The Coachhouse** Glenfield, Old Torwood Road, Torquay, Devon TQ11PN
☎Torquay(0803)23039

Two cottages, one adjoining the house set in grounds of Victorian house. Cottage comprises kitchen, lounge/diner, bathroom with WC, two twin bedrooms (one on ground-floor), one double and one single bedroom. The Coachhouse consists of lounge/diner, kitchen, bathroom with WC, and one single and two twin bedrooms. Both cottages are traditionally furnished and in pleasant surrounds. Quiet garden.

All year MWB out of season 3days min, 4wks max, 2units, 2–7persons ◊ ◆ no pets ◉ fridge Electric Elec metered ⌁ inclusive ☎(300yds) Airing cupboard in unit HCE in unit [Launderette within 300yds] ⊙ CTV ⊕3pin square 2P ▥ ▦(300yds)

⊕ ♨(3m) ♀(300yds) ▨(500yds) ♫(½m) ▨(1m)

Min£50 Max£100pw (Low)
Min£90 Max£150pw (High)

F Mrs J Hassell **Derwent Hill Superior Holiday Flats** Greenway Road, Torquay, Devon TQ26JE
☎Torquay(0803)22592

Six self-contained flats within an attractive Victorian house set in grounds of one acre, with sea views from most flats. Accommodation comprises lounge with continental wall beds. All flats have separate bedroom with double and twin beds, separate bathroom, WC and kitchen. Situated 1m from town centre and sea.

All year MWB 3days min, 6mths max, 6units, 2–6persons ◊ ◉ fridge Electric Elec metered ⌁ inclusive ☎ Airing cupboard in unit Iron on premises Ironing board on premises HCE in unit [Launderette within 300yds] ⊙ CTV ⊕3pin square 10P 3▥ ▥ ▦(500yds)

⊕ ♨(2½m) ♀(300yds) ▨(300yds) ♫(300yds) ▨(1m)

Min£40 Max£50pw (Low)
Min£55 Max£165pw (High)

F Mr P Jaffa **34 Fleet Street** Torquay, Devon
☎Torquay(0803)25524

Situated over shops in busy shopping area these fully furnished flats include separate bathroom/WC, combined bathroom/WC, and two separate bedrooms.

All year MWB out of season 1wk min, 1mth max, 2units, 6–8persons no pets fridge Electric Elec metered ⌁ can be hired ☎(10yds) Airing cupboard Iron in unit Ironing board in unit HCE in unit [TV] ⊕3pin square ▦

⊕ ♀(200yds) ▨(½m) ♫(½m) ▨(200yds)

F Mr J Fricker **Haldon Court** Haldon Road, Torquay, Devon
☎Torquay(0803)27108

Villa-type house in elevated position within quiet residential area, converted into two ground-floor self-contained flats and three first-floor units. Each has carpeted lounge and bedrooms with modern matching furniture.

All year MWB out of season 1wk min, 1mth max, 5units, 2–6persons [◊] [◆] no pets ◉ fridge Electric Elec metered ⌁ can be hired ☎(½m) Iron on premises Ironing board on premises HCE in unit [Launderette within 300yds] TV ⊕3pin square P ▥ ▦(300yds)

⊕ ♀(½m) ▨(½m) ♫(½m) ▨(½m)

Min£35 Max£63pw (Low)
Min£104 Max£165pw (High)

F Mr & Mrs R S Watts **Kenton Lodge** Croft Hill, (off Abbey Road), Torquay, Devon TQ25NT
☎Torquay(0803)27995

Detached villa on corner site in elevated position with views across Torbay, converted into four flats. Centrally located within easy walking distance of seafront, shops and entertainments. Carpeted flats are light, bright and spacious.

Jan-Oct MWB out of season 1wk min, 1mth max, 4units, 2–6persons ◊ ◆ ◉ fridge ⋈ Elec metered ⌁ can be hired ☎ Airing cupboard in unit Iron on premises Ironing board in unit HCE in unit [Launderette within 300yds] ⊙ TV ⊕3pin square P ▥ ▦(200yds)

⊕ ♀(200yds) ▨(200yds) ♫(200yds) ▨(300yds)

Min£32 Max£180pw

F Mrs S E Hassell **Lauderdale** Torbay Road, Torquay, Devon TQ26QH
☎Torquay(0803)22592

A detached stone-built property now divided into three flats. The building has a sloping lawn in front, is on the sea front, and has good views out to sea. Each flat has a lounge/diner with folding double wall bed, compact kitchen, bathroom and WC. Two flats have a room with a double bed and a single bed. The third flat has two bedrooms, one a double and →

Luxury Holiday Flats

at Torbay, Torquay

LAUDERDALE

Three self-contained centrally heated and spacious Holiday Apartments situated directly on the Sea Front overlooking Corbyn Head and Livermead Beach.

DERWENT HILL

Six self-contained spacious Holiday Apartments situated in a quiet residential area of Torquay with views over Torbay.

Maxton Lodge

Twenty-four self-contained centrally heated luxury Holiday Apartments with heated swimming pool and automatic laundry facilities. Each property has a large garden, ample parking and is situated within reasonable distance of the Sea Front, Torre Abbey Gardens and local shops. Each Apartment has colour television, and is equipped to approved AA and English Tourist Board Standards. Linen is provided. **OPEN THROUGHOUT THE YEAR.** Special short stay terms autumn to spring.

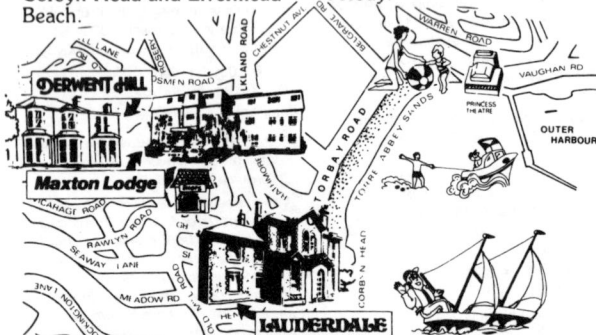

Send for combined colour brochure:
AA2, Maxton Lodge, Rousdown Road, Torquay, Devon TQ2 6PB (or 24 hour Ansaphone (0803) 607811).

252

Torquay

one with twin beds. Use of nearby hotel facilities.

All year MWB out of season 4days min, 6mths max, 3units, 2–6persons [◈] [◆] ◎ fridge ⌘ Elec metered ◫inclusive ☎(½m) Iron in unit Ironing board in unit HCE in unit ⊙ CTV ⊕3pin square P ▥ ⛪(½m)

⇔ ♿(3m) ♀(½m) ◫(1m) ⚑(1m)

Min£65 Max£90pw (Low)
Min£75 Max£235pw (High)

F Mr M J Boxall **Maidencombe Cross Holiday Apartments** Teignmouth Road, Torquay, Devon
☎Torquay(0803)39014

Seventeen flats in large Victorian house, which has recently been extended and stands in 2 acres of private grounds with its own swimming pool. A licenced bar is available to residents. The beach is just a few minutes' walk away.

Etr-Oct MWB out of season 1day min, 17units, 2–7persons ◇ ◈ ◆ ◎ fridge Electric Elec metered ◫can be hired ☎ WM on premises SD on premises [TD on premises] Iron on premises Ironing board on premises HCE in unit ⊙ CTV ⊕3pin square 20P ▥ ⛪(100yds) ⊇

⇔ ♿

Min£40 Max£90pw (Low)
Min£50 Max£225pw (High)

F Mr J K Hassell **Maxton Lodge Holiday Flats** Rousdown Road, Torquay TQ2 6PB
☎Torquay(0803)607811

Twenty-four flats in a residential area about 600yds from the seafront and 100yds from the shops. Well decorated, good fixtures and fittings.

All year MWB 2days min, 24units, 2–7persons ◈ ◆ ◎ fridge ⌘ Elec metered ◫inclusive ☎ SD on premises Airing cupboard in unit Iron on premises Ironing board on premises HCE in unit Launderette on premises ⊙ CTV ⊕3pin square ⊕2pin round P ▥ ⛪(100yds) ⊇

⇔ ♿(3m) ♀(½m) ◫(½m) ♫(½m) ⚑(1m)

Min£55 Max£70pw (Low)
Min£65 Max£195pw (High)

F Mr & Mrs Bradbury ***Moor Haven Holiday Flats*** 43 Barton Road, Torquay, Devon TQ1 4DT
☎Torquay(0803)38567

Twelve purpose-built flats located in a detached building in a residential area, and are well decorated and well equipped with modern furniture and fittings. The grounds contain a heated swimming pool, with patio surround, and lawns. About 1m from the sea and Oddicombe and Watcombe beaches with Babbacombe Downs nearby.

Closed Xmas MWB out of season 1wk min, 6mths max, 12units, 2–6persons [◇] ◈ ◆ no pets ◎ fridge Electric & part gas central heating Elec metered ◫can be hired ☎(50yds) SD TD Airing cupboard in unit Iron on premises Ironing board on premises HCE in unit [Launderette on premises] ⊙ CTV ⊕3pin square P ▥ ⛪(½m) ⊇

⇔ ♀ ◫ ♫ ⚑(½m)

F Mr B Jarvis **Parklands Holiday Flats** Palermo Road, Babbacombe, Torquay, Devon
☎Torquay(0803)34422

Detached villa with modernised extension converted into flats. Pleasant, comfortable and clean. Suburban location with outdoor swimming pool. Near to shops and seafront.

All year MWB out of season 2days min, 1mth max, 6units, 2–6persons [◈ ◆] ◎ fridge Electric Elec metered ◫can be hired ☎(150yds) Iron in unit Ironing board in unit HCE in unit [Launderette within 300yds] ⊙ CTV ⊕3pin square 9P ▥ ⛪(200yds) ⊇→

1982 prices quoted throughout gazetteer

⊖ �(2m)　🚃(20yds)　🚲(2m)　🎵(2m)
🏊(2m)

Min£35 Max£105pw (Low)
Min£95 Max£188pw (High)

F　Mr K J Hughes **Rogana Holiday
Flats** Higher Warberry Road, Torquay,
Devon TQ1 1SQ
☎Torquay(0803)23584

*Seven flats in a detached, Edwardian-
type house standing in its own grounds of
lawns, shrubs and flower beds. Good
décor and furnishings. Within walking
distance of seafront and shops.*

All year　MWB out of season　1wk min,
7units, 2–7persons　[◇]　◆　◉
fridge　Electric　Elec metered
☎(100yds)　Airing cupboard in unit
[Iron on premises]　Ironing board on
premises　HCE in unit　[Launderette on
premises]　⊙　TV　⊕3pin square　P
🚃　🚲

⊖　🚃(100yds)

Min£50 Max£100pw (Low)
Min£70 Max£200pw (High)

F　Mr & Mrs K H Fleming **Rosa Pines**
Higher Warberry Road, Torquay, Devon
TQ1 1RY
☎Torquay(0803)25036

*Mansion in quiet, residential area,
standing in gardens of about 1 acre,
carefully converted into flats. All very
comfortable, well appointed and
comprise lounge, kitchen, shower room,
dining area, and one or two bedrooms. If
travelling from Newton Abbot, on
entering Torquay, turn left at second set
of traffic lights, turn left then first right up
to Westhill Road. At next traffic lights, go
straight on, at next road junction turn right
then sharp left (Quinta Road). At the end
of road turn left then first right into Cedars
Road – at the bottom turn right into Villa
Paradiso. Rosa Pines reception is on the
right about 200yds up Higher Warberry
Road.*

All year　MWB out of season　11units,
2–8persons　[◇]　[◆]　no pets　◉
fridge　Eelctric　Elec metered
🚲inclusive　☎　Iron in unit　Ironing
board in unit　HCE in unit　[Launderette
on premises]　⊙　CTV　⊕3pin square
P　🚃　🚲(1m)　⌐

⊖　🚃(2m)　🚲(2m)　🎵(½m)　🏊(2m)

Min£46 Max£85pw (Low)
Min£115 Max£235pw (High)

F　Wg Cdr & Mrs C C Cooper **St Ronans
Holiday Flats** Middle Warberry Road,
Torquay, Devon TQ1 1RP
☎Torquay(0803)23493

*Five flats in Victorian villa standing in its
own grounds. Most flats have sea views.
Flats 2,3 and 4 have three bedrooms, flat
2B has two bedrooms and flat 7 has one
double bedroom and curtained area with
bunk beds. All flats have kitchen, lounge,
shower or bathroom with WC and wash
hand basin. Most flats have sofa bed in
lounge. Situated in quiet residential area
about 1m from seafront and shops.
Garden.*

Torquay

All year　MWB out of season　1wk min,
8mths max, 5units, 2–10persons　◆
no pets　🌢&◉　fridge　Electric　Gas &
Elec metered　🚲can be hired
☎(200yds)　Airing cupboard in unit　Iron
in unit　Ironing board in unit　HCE in unit
TV　⊕3pin square　9P　🚃　🚲(600yds)

⊖　🚃(2m)　🚃(600yds)　🚲(½m)
🎵(½m)　🏊(1m)

Min£65 Max£90pw (Low)
Min£98 Max£180pw (High)

F　**Sandown Holiday Flats** 27 Ashill
Road, Castle Circus
for bookings Mr C Trethewey, Beech Hill,
Middle Warberry, Torquay, Devon
TQ1 3JB
☎Torquay(0803)26905

*Six flats on ground- and first-floors of a
modern purpose-built detached property
in a residential area. The flats have a
separate and well-equipped kitchen and
bathroom/WC. There is one double- or
twin-bedded room plus a double wall-
bed in lounge. Situated within 500yds of
the main shopping area.*

All year　MWB out of season　1wk min,
1mth max, 6units, 2–4persons　[◇]　◆
◆　no pets　◉　fridge　Electric
Elec metered　🚲can be hired
☎(300yds)　Airing cupboard in unit　Iron
in unit　Ironing board in unit　HCE in unit
Launderette within 300yds　⊙　CTV
⊕3pin square　6P　🚃　🚲(400yds)

⊖　🌢(1m)　🚃(100yds)　🚲(100yds)
🎵(100yds)　🏊(500yds)

Min£49 Max£138pw

Ch　Manager *Sladnor Park*
Maidencombe, Torquay, Devon TQ1 4TF
☎Torquay(0803)34261

*Between Teignmouth and Torquay on
A379 coast road at village of
Maidencombe. A 50-acre estate in
wooded and meadowed valley with open
sea views. Facilities include bar,
restaurant, dancing, shops, outdoor
heated pool and children's pool.
Accommodation comprises one double,
one twin-bedded room,
kitchen/diner/lounge, bathroom/WC in
adjoining ground-floor chalets.*

May–11Oct　MWB out of season
1mth max, 48units　2–5persons　◇
[◇　◆]　no pets　◉　fridge　Electric
Elec inclusive　🚲inclusive　☎　TD in
unit　Airing cupboard in unit　Iron on
premises　Ironing board on premises
HCE in unit　Launderette on premises
⊙　🌀　CTV　⊕3pin square　P　🚃　🚲
⌐　🌢　🏊Hard　Solarium & spa bath

⊖　🚃(1m)　🚲　🚲　🏊

F　Mr D Jordan **South Sands
Apartments** Torbay Road, Torquay,
Devon TQ2 6RG
☎Torquay(0803)23521

*Fifteen ground and first floor flats in a
modern block opposite the beach and*

---

*promenade, located on the main road to
Paignton. All have a modern kitchen,
lounge/diner with wall bed and bathroom
or shower room with WC and washbasin.
Sleeping accommodation varies
between flats sleeping from two to five.
Lawned garden with garden furniture.*

21Mar–Oct　MWB out of season
1 day min, 2mths max, 15units,
2–5persons　◆　◉　fridge　🍴
Elec metered　🚲inclusive　☎　Iron on
premises　Ironing board on premises
HCE in unit　⊙　CTV　⊕3pin square
17P　🚃　🚲(½m)

⊖　🚃(3m)　🚃(20yds)　🚲(20yds)
🎵(20yds)　🏊(1½m)

Min£64 Max£88pw (Low)
Min£120 Max£188pw (High)

See advert on page 253

F　John Phelps Ltd **Sunningdale
Holiday Apartments Type A & B**
Babbacombe Downs Road, Torquay,
Devon TQ1 3LF
☎Torquay(0803)35786

*Villa-type residence set in own grounds
on top of Babbacombe Cliffs with
magnificent sea views. All flats have
kitchen, lounge, bathroom/WC, some
flats have one double bedroom, the
others are two-bedroomed.*

All year　MWB out of season　1wk min,
1mth max, 16units, 2–7persons　◆　◆
no pets　◉　fridge　Electric
Elec metered　🚲inclusive　☎　Airing
cupboard on premises　HCE in unit
[Launderette within 300yds]　⊙　CTV
⊕3pin square　P　🚃　🚲(30yds)

⊖　🚃(3m)　🚃(200yds)　🚲(200yds)
🎵(300yds)　🏊(1½m)

Min£50 Max£120pw (Low)
Min£100 Max£185pw (High)

B　**Sunny Bower** Golden Park Avenue
for bookings Mrs M Whittaker, 43 Petitor
Road, Torquay Devon TQ1 4QF
☎Torquay(0803)388377

*Semi-detached bungalow in residential
district, a few minutes walk from open
countryside. Accommodation comprises
hall, lounge/diner, two bedrooms, one
with additional bunks, and a modern
kitchen/diner.*

Mar–Oct　1wk min, 8mths max, 1unit,
1–8persons　◆　◆　◉　fridge
Electric　Elec metered　🚲can be hired
☎(½m)　Airing cupboard in unit　Iron in
unit　Ironing board in unit　HCE in unit
CTV　⊕3pin square　1P　1🚃　🚲(½m)

⊖　🚃(1m)　🚃(½m)　🚲(2m)　🎵(2m)
🏊(2m)

F　Mr K C Girling **Trinity Mews Holiday
Flats** Trinity Hill, Torquay, Devon
TQ1 2AS
☎Torquay(0803)24245

*Converted Mews with inner courtyard in
central but quiet location comprising
kitchen, lounge, bathroom/toilet, with
seven of the nine flats having two
separate bedrooms. Compact and
comfortably furnished ground and first
floor accommodation.*

All year MWB out of season 3days min, 9units, 2–6persons [◇] ◆ ◆ ◎ fridge Electric (night storage) Elec metered Ⓛinclusive ☎(50yds) [SD on premises] [Airing cupboard on premises] Iron on premises Ironing board on premises HCE in unit ⊙ CTV ⊕3pin square ⌂ ▥ ⛟(50yds) ⊖ ♀(20yds) ▨(100yds) ♬(100yds) ⌘(800yds)

Min£74.75 Max£126.50pw (Low)
Min£149.50 Max£181.25pw (High)

See advert on page 253

F Mr & Mrs A J Dymond **Vansittart Holiday Flats** Higher Erith Road, Torquay, Devon
☎Torquay(0803)35699

Detached Victorian house with seven flats in main building and a further seven in a modern extension. Each has well-equipped kitchen, bathroom, lounge/diner with put-u-up and bedrooms ranging from one twin-bedded room to three bedrooms with double/twin/bunks beds. Located ½m from seafront in residential area.

All year MWB out of season 3days min, 6mth max, 14units, 2–8persons [◆ ◆] No single sex groups ◎ fridge Electric Elec metered Ⓛinclusive ☎ Airing cupboard in unit Iron in unit Ironing board in unit HCE in unit [Launderette within 300yds] ⊙ CTV ⊕3pin square 14P ▥ ⛟(½m) ⊖ ♂(2m) ♀(½m) ▨(½m) ♬(½m) ⌘(½m)

Min£38 Max£96pw (Low)
Min£90 Max£224pw (High)

F **Villa Paradiso** Higher Warberry Road
for bookings Mr & Mrs K H Fleming, Rosa Pines, Higher Warberry Road, Torquay, Devon TQ1 1RY
☎Torquay(0803)25036

Carefully converted mansion in own gardens with heated open-air swimming pool. Some flats have sea views. Accommodation includes entrance hall, lounge, one or two bedrooms, kitchen area, or kitchen with breakfast bar, and fully fitted shower rooms. Well decorated and furnished.

All year MWB out of season 1wk min, 2mths max, 15units, 2–6persons [◇] [◆] [◆] ◎ fridge ⛫ Electric Elec metered Ⓛinclusive ☎ Iron in unit Ironing board in unit HCE in unit [Launderette on premises] ⊙ CTV ⊕3pin square P ▥ ⛟(1m) ⌓ ♀ ⊖ ♂18(2m) ♀(1m) ▨(2m) ♬(½m) ⌘(2m)

Min£46 Max£70pw (Low)
Min£115 Max£200pw (High)

F Mr & Mrs F R Cornelius **York Villa,** York Road, Babbacombe, Torquay, Devon
☎Torquay(0803)37519

Nine flats in modern, well-run, converted Victorian house located on main Babbacombe–Torquay road. Close to shops and Babbacombe Beach.

All year MWB out of season 1wk min, 1mth max, 9units, 2–9persons ◆ ◆ ◎ fridge Electric Elec metered Ⓛcan be hired ☎(30yds) Airing cupboard in unit Iron in unit Ironing board in unit HCE in unit [Launderette within 300yds] ⊙ CTV ⊕3pin square 18P ▥ ⛟(100yds) ⊖ ♀(200yds) ▨(200yds) ♬(200yds) ⌘(1½m)

Min£39 Max£110pw (Low)
Min£98 Max£211pw (High)

TORRINGTON (GREAT)
Devon
Map**2** SS41

Ch Mr Preston **Greenways Valley Holiday Park** Torrington, Devon EX38 7EW
☎Torrington(08052)2153

Chalet bungalows of modern design and furnishings, each comprising kitchen, bathroom/WC, two bedrooms (one with double bed and the other with twin or bunk beds), and lounge (with studio couch). Situated ¾m from Torrington in wooded valley with good views of countryside.

15Mar–Oct MWB out of season 3days min, 3mths max, 14units, 1–7persons [◆] ◎ fridge Electric Elec metered Ⓛnot provided ☎(¾m) Airing cupboard in unit Iron on premises Ironing board on premises HCE in unit ⊙ TV ⊕3pin square 14P ▥ ⛟ ⌓ Children's playground ⊖ ♂9(1m) ♀(1¾m) ⌘(1m)

Min£36.80 Max£80.50pw (Low)
Min£92 Max£102.75pw (High)

TOTLAND BAY
Isle of Wight
Map**4** SZ38

H **Summerhaze** Uplands Road
for bookings Mrs B M Dimmick, Pontivvy Lodge, The Broadway, Totland Bay, Isle of Wight PO39 0BX
☎Freshwater(0983)753384

A well-maintained house set in quiet residential area close to sea and shops. Accommodation consists of one double bedroom, kitchen, lounge/diner and WC on ground-floor, and two twin-bedded rooms and bathroom/WC on the first-floor.

All year MWB 1wk min, 3mths max, 1unit, 2–6persons ◆ no pets ◎ fridge Electric Elec metered Ⓛnot provided ☎(250yds) Airing cupboard in unit Iron in unit Ironing board in unit HCE ⊙ CTV ⊕3pin square ⌂ ▥ ⛟(300yds) Grass ⊖ ♀(400yds) ▨(300yds) ♬(½m)

Min£50 Max£130pw

TOTNES
Devon
Map**3** SX86

C Messrs Hodges & Liddle **Higher Poulston Holiday Cottages** Morleigh Road, Halwell, Totnes, Devon TQ9 7LE
☎Harbertonford(080423)255 or 345

An old stone and slate farm building converted into four cottages and set amidst farmland and rolling hills. The accommodation varies with numbers 1 and 2 having two bedrooms and 3 and 4 having three bedrooms. A small area of field at the rear of the cottages is available for the exclusive use of visitors.

Mar–Nov MWB out of season 1wk min, 8wks max, 4units, 2–8persons ◆ ◆ no pets ◎ fridge Electric Elec metered Ⓛnot provided ☎(1m) Airing cupboard in unit Iron in unit Ironing board in unit HCE in unit ⊙ TV ⊕3pin square 12P ▥ ⛟(1m) ⊖ ♀(1m)

Min£30 Max£85pw (Low)
Min£50 Max£135pw (High)

F **Shippon**
for bookings Mr & Mrs R Miller, Buckyette Farm, Little Hempston, Totnes, Devon
☎Staverton(080426)638

Converted stone-built barn on farm of 40 acres. Offers well furnished accommodation; large lounge with beamed end kitchen area, separate bathroom with WC and wash basin, one double room, one twin and one bunk-bedded room. 4m off A384 Buckfastleigh and Totnes.

end May–Sep MWB out of season 1wk min, 6wks max, 1unit, 1–6persons [◇] ◆ ◆ no pets ◎ fridge Electric Elec metered Ⓛnot provided ☎(20yds) Iron on premises Ironing board in unit HCE in unit TV ⊕3pin square P ▥(except Sun) ⛟(1m) ⊖ ♀(1m)

Min£51.75 Max£59.80pw (Low)
Min£87.40 Max£133.40pw (High)

TREARDDUR BAY
Gwynedd
Map**6** SH27

B **Trearddur Bay Holiday Bungalows** Fron Isalt
for bookings Hoseasons Holidays Ltd, Sunway House, Lowestoft, Suffolk NR32 2LT
☎Lowestoft(0502)62292

Modern, purpose-built brick bungalows, some semi-detached and some in groups of four, consisting of two or three bedrooms, large lounge/diner with bed-settee, kitchen; bathroom and WC. Modern furnishings and well equipped. All are within a short distance of the beach. →

1982 prices quoted throughout gazetteer

All year MWB out of season 3 days min,
6 wks max, 50 units, 1–6 persons ◊ ♦
◉ fridge Electric Elec metered
ⓁInclusive ☎(100yds) Iron on
premises Ironing board on premises
HCE in unit [Launderette on premises]
⊙ CTV ⊕3pin square P
♨(300yds) Children's playground
↮ ☟(200yds) ▥(2m) ♫(2m) 🐾(2m)

TRIMINGHAM
Norfolk
Map9 TG23

B Longhills
for bookings Mrs J Harrison, Hall Farm,
Trimingham, Norwich, Norfolk NR11 8AL
☎Southrepps(026 379)301

Once a shooting lodge, this spacious
bungalow is set on the edge of
woodlands. Situated just off the A148, it is
approached via a quiet caravan park,
which is under the same ownership. The
accommodation comprises three single
and two double bedrooms, large lounge
with dining area and separate
bathroom/WC. An ideal situation for
children, with the sea just ten minutes
away.

May–Sep MWB out of season 1 wk min,
1 mth max, 1 unit, 7 persons ◊ ♦
fridge Electric Gas inclusive
Elec metered Ⓛnot provided ☎(½m)
Airing cupboard in unit Iron in unit
Ironing board in unit HCE in unit TV
⊕3pin round P ♨(¾m)
↮ ☟(¾m)
Min£72.45 Max£84pw

TROUTBECK
Cumbria
Map7 NY40

C Birkhead Cottages
for bookings Miss M R Dawson, Birkhead
Guest House, Troutbeck, Windermere,
Cumbria LA23 1PQ
☎Ambleside(096 63)2288

Situated in the small peaceful village of
Troutbeck. Three tastefully modernised
and furnished stone-built cottages, only a
few minutes drive from Windermere.
Each cottage has two bedrooms and
offers excellent views across the valley to
the fells beyond.

All year MWB out of season 1 wk min,
3 units, 4 persons ◊ ♦ ◉ fridge
Electric Elec metered Ⓛcan be hired
☎(½m) Airing cupboard in unit Iron in
unit Ironing board in unit HCE in unit
⊙ TV ⊕3pin square P ▥ ♨(½m)
↮ ▥(½m) ♫(2½m)
Max£50pw (Low)
Min£70 Max£80pw (High)

TRURO
Cornwall
Map2 SW84

F CC Ref 351 EL Kea
for bookings Character Cottages
(Holidays) Ltd, 34 Fore Street, Sidmouth,
Devon EX10 8AQ
☎Sidmouth(039 55)77001

Trearddur Bay
—
Tyndrum

Modern ground-floor flat situated in a
stone-built cottage on the shoreline of an
inland waterway. There are two
bedrooms (one a double, the other twin-
bedded), separate lounge, dining room,
kitchen and bathroom/WC. From A39
take B3289 signposted Feock and King
Harry Ferry. Pass Punchbowle and Ladle,
take next left to Cowlands and Combe.
Take right turn up unmetalled road
100yds past sharp left bend, ⅓m to
property.

All year MWB out of season 1 wk min,
1 mth max, 1 unit, 1–5 persons, nc4
no pets ♢ fridge Electric
Gas/Elec inclusive Ⓛinclusive
☎(1m) Airing cupboard in unit Iron in
unit Ironing board in unit HCE in unit
⊙ TV ⊕3pin square P ♨(2m)
Boat mooring
↮ ☟(1m)
Min£60 Max£80pw (Low)
Min£100 Max£120pw (High)

**C Mr & Mrs C Ellis Penmount Farm
Country Cottages** Truro, Cornwall
☎Truro(0872)3297

Cornish stone cottages of charm and
character situated in a small farm
complex. They are exceptionally well
furnished and equipped with style and
imagination. Cottages 1, 3, 8 and 10
comprise one double bedroom, one with
one double bed and bunk beds, lounge,
kitchen/diner and bathroom/WC.
Cottages 2 and 9 have one bedroom with
twin beds, one with bunk beds, one
double-bedded room with additional
bunks, lounge, kitchen/diner and
bathroom/WC. Cottages 4 and 7 have
two bedrooms with double beds, one with
bunk beds, lounge, kitchen/diner and
bathroom/WC. Cottages 5 and 6 have
one double bedroom, one bunk-bedded
room, lounge, kitchen/diner and
bathroom/WC.

All year MWB out of season 1 wk min,
10 units, 2–8 persons ◊ ♦ ◉
fridge Electric Elec inclusive
Ⓛinclusive ☎ Iron in unit Ironing
board in unit HCE in unit [Launderette
on premises] ⊙ CTV ⊕3pin square
2P ▥ ♨(2m)
↮ ☍(3m) ▥(3m) ♫(3m) 🐾(3m)

TRUSHAM
Devon
Map3 SX98

F Mr & Mrs I Smart Rydon Farm
Trusham, Newton Abbot, Devon
☎Christow(0647)52260

Self-contained wing of attractive cob
walled thatched farmhouse located at the
end of a ⅜ mile long private road. Situated
in a commanding position overlooking
the Teign Valley. The flat has three
bedrooms, kitchen, beamed lounge with
inglenook, dining room and bathroom
with WC. Leave on the A38 at exit Teign

Valley and follow B3193 for 3m.

Mar–Oct MWB out of season
3 days min, 1 mth max, 1 unit,
2–6 persons ◊ ♦♦ no pets ◉
fridge Electric Elec inclusive
Ⓛinclusive ☎(2m) WM on premises
TD on premises Iron in unit Ironing
board in unit HCE in unit ⊙ CTV
⊕3pin square 4P ▥ ♨(3m)
Barbeque
↮ ☟(2m)

TWITCHEN
Shropshire
Map7 SO37

B Mrs Morgan Llan Farm Twitchen,
Clunbury, Craven Arms, Shropshire
SY7 0HN
☎Little Brampton(058 87)277

Secluded bungalow on a farm, on the
slopes of a partially wooded valley.
Modern furnishings. Leave the Craven
Arms–Clun Road at Puslow on to the
B4385 to Twitchen, where The Llan is
signposted via a narrow metalled road.

All year MWB out of season 1 night min,
1 mth max, 1 unit, 1–7 persons [◊] ◊
◉ fridge ♔ Elec inclusive
Ⓛinclusive ☎(150yds) SD Airing
cupboard in unit Iron in unit HCE in
unit ⊙ TV ⊕3pin square P ▤ ▥
♨(2m)
↮ ☟(3m)
Max£66pw (Low)
Max£89pw (High)

TWYNHOLM
Dumfries & Galloway *Kirkcudbrightshire*
Map11 NX65

C Glenterry Lodge
for bookings G M Thomson & Co, 27 King
Street, Castle Douglas,
Kirkcudbrightshire DG7 1AB
☎Castle Douglas(0556)2701

Small stone built single-storey lodge
cottage standing beside the A75, 2m W
of Twynholm. It is located in an attractive
wooded position and comprises two
double rooms, living room with bed-
settee, kitchen and bathroom.

All year 1 wk min, 1 unit, 1–6 persons
◊ ◉ fridge Electric & open fires
Elec inclusive Ⓛnot provided ☎(2m)
WM in unit SD in unit Iron in unit HCE
in unit TV ⊕3pin square
⊕3pin round P ♨(2m)
↮ ☟(2m)
Min£45 Max£105pw

TYNDRUM
Central *Perthshire*
Map10 NN32

C Crom Allt Cottage
for bookings Mrs Stevenson, Clifton
Coffee House & Craft Centre, Tyndrum,
Perthshire FK20 8RY
☎Tyndrum(08384)271

A small, 200 year old, white painted
cottage located in conservation area.
Accommodation comprises one twin
bedroom, lounge/diner, bathroom and

kitchen. The interior has been tastefully modernised and retains an open fireplace which adds a homely atmosphere. Situated opposite Clifton Coffee House and Craft Centre on the A82.

All year MWB out of season 3 days min, 1 unit, 1–4 persons ◊ ◎ fridge ▯ &
open fire Elec metered
⌸ not provided ☎(60yds) WM in unit
SD in unit Airing cupboard on
premises Iron in unit Ironing board in
unit HCE in unit ⊙ CTV
⊕3 pin square 2P ♣(40yds)
⟷ ☺(¼m) ▨(¼m)
Min£55 Max£65pw (Low)
Min£85pw (High)

TYWYN
Gwynedd
Map **6** SH50

Ch Mr M Short *Plot 66 Erwporthor*
Happy Valley, Tywyn, Gwynedd
☎Tywyn(0654)710175

One of 66 chalets on a 15-acre site, detached cedarwood chalet, well insulated. Nine steps to front door leading into a small kitchen, lounge/diner with bed-settee. One each double and twin bedrooms, bathroom with WC. Between Aberdovey and Tywyn, signposted 'Happy Valley'. Convenient for beaches and mountains.

All year MWB out of season 1 night min, 6 wks max, 1 unit, 1–6 persons [◊ ◆]
◎ fridge Electric Elec metered
⌸ not provided ☎(2m) ⊙ TV
⊕3 pin square 2P ♣(50yds)
⟷ ♨(3m) ☺(2m) ▨(2m) ♫(2m)
🐾(2m)

ULLAPOOL
Highland *Ross & Cromarty*
Map **14** NH19

C Ardmair Bay Chalets Ardmair
for bookings Highland Coastal Estates, Coulmore, Kessock, Inverness-shire
☎Kessock(046373)212

Five timber-built chalets containing open plan lounge/kitchenette (two have separate lounge and kitchen) and three small bedrooms (one double, two twin-bedded). Fine views. 3¾m N A835.

Apr–Oct MWB out of season 1 wk min, 5 units, 1–6 persons ◊ fridge
Electric Elec metered ⌸ can be hired
☎(½m) Airing cupboard in unit HCE in
unit TV ⊕3 pin square P ♣(3m)
Pony trekking, fishing & sea angling
⟷ ☺(3m) ▨(3m)
Min£45.42 Max£71.87pw

C Ardmore
for bookings Highland Coastal Estates, Coulmore, Kessock, Inverness-shire
☎Kessock(046373)212

Reached from A835 from its own steep driveway, this cottage sits on the shore of Loch Broom 1½m NW of Ullapool. It contains sitting/dining room, kitchen, a

double bedroom, and two three-bedded rooms. Commands views of surrounding countryside.

Mar–Nov MWB out of season 1 wk min, 1 unit, 1–8 persons ◎ fridge Electric
Elec metered ⌸ can be hired ☎(1½m)
Airing cupboard HCE TV
⊕3 pin square P ▣(1½m)
⟷ ☺(1½m) ▨(1½m)
Min£69.57 Max£159.27pw

Ch Corry & Corry Point Bungalow
for bookings Highland Coastal Estates, Coulmore, Kessock, Inverness-shire
☎Kessock(046373)212

Two large wooden bungalows each with five bedrooms sleeping nine. Corry has lounge/dining room and kitchen and is set 400yds above Loch Broom. Corry Point has a separate lounge and dining room and is on the lochside. Both are reached by their own access from A835 E of Ullapool.

Mar–Nov MWB out of season 1 wk min, 2 units, 1–9 persons ◎ fridge
Electric Elec metered ⌸ can be hired
☎(1m) HCE in unit TV ⊕3 pin round
P ♣(1m) Pony trekking, fishing & sea angling
⟷ ☺(1m) ▨(1m)
Min£60.27 Max£133.97pw

Ch Corry Hill Bungalow
for bookings Highland Coastal Estates, Coulmore, Kessock, Inverness-shire
☎Kessock(046373)212

A bungalow/chalet containing lounge, kitchenette, one double and two twin bedrooms. The property is reached from the A835, just E of Ullapool on an unclass road signposted 'Braes'. It is two miles from Ullapool and sits on a hillside overlooking Loch Broom.

Apr–Oct MWB out of season 1 wk min, 1 unit, 1–6 persons ◎ fridge Electric
Elec metered ⌸ can be hired ☎(2m)
HCE in unit TV ⊕3 pin square P
♣(2m) Pony trekking, fishing & sea angling
⟷ ☺(2m) ▨(2m)
Min£51.17 Max£108.67pw

B Rhue Baigh Bungalow
for bookings Highland Coastal Estates, Coulmore, Kessock, Inverness-shire
☎Kessock(046373)212

A modern block built and tiled bungalow containing large lounge/diner with convertible sofa, kitchen, two twin-bedded rooms and one double bedroom. It is sited in Rhue Bay which is reached by an unclass road 2m N of Ullapool off A835. Fine views.

Mar–Nov MWB out of season 1 wk min, 1 unit, 1–8 persons ◎ fridge Electric
Elec metered ⌸ can be hired ☎(2m)
Airing cupboard in unit HCE in unit TV

⊕3 pin square P ♣(3m) Pony
trekking, fishing & sea angling
⟷ ☺(3m) ▨(3m)
Min£69.57 Max£159.20pw

Ch Strathain Burn & Strathain Bridge
for bookings Highland Coastal Estates, Coulmore, Kessock, Inverness-shire
☎Kessock(046373)212

Two small timber bungalows/chalets containing a kitchenette, lounge/dining room, one double and two twin-bedded rooms. The chalets are situated at the entrance to Strathain Glen, 2m from Ullapool on A835.

Early May–Sep MWB out of season
1 wk min, 2 units, 1–6 persons ◎
fridge Electric Elec metered ⌸ can be
hired ☎(1m) Airing cupboard in unit
HCE in unit TV ⊕3 pin round P
♣(2½m) Pony trekking, fishing, sea
angling
⟷ ☺(2½m) ▨(2½m)
Min£51.17 Max£108.67pw

ULPHA
Cumbria
Map **7** SD19

H Dunnerdale
for bookings Mrs D Jenner, Travellers
Rest Luxury Holiday Flats, Ulpha,
Broughton-in-Furness, Cumbria
LA206DX
☎Broughton-in-Furness(06576)203

A large house with attractive grounds and set in the Duddon Valley. Ideal accommodation for a large party or family. Comprises four bedrooms, large lounge and spacious kitchen (includes dishwasher).

All year MWB out of season 3 days min, 1 mth max, 1 unit, 2–7 persons ◊ ◆
◎ fridge Electric Elec metered
⌸ can be hired ☎(½m) WM in unit SD
in unit Airing cupboard in unit Iron in
unit Ironing board in unit HCE in unit
⊙ CTV ⊕3 pin square 2P
♣(200yds)
⟷ ☺(3m)
Min£40 Max£100pw

F Miterdale
for bookings Mrs D Jenner, Travellers
Rest Luxury Holiday Flats, Ulpha,
Broughton-in-Furness, Cumbria
LA206DX
☎Broughton-in-Furness(06576)203

Situated in attractive grounds in the peaceful and beautiful Duddon Valley. The Travellers Rest used to be an hotel, part of which has been converted into a very spacious flat comprising two twin bedded rooms, lounge, bathroom and sun lounge all on first floor level. →

Decorated and furnished to a good standard.

All year MWB out of season 3 days min, 1 unit, 2–4 persons ◊ ◆ ◎ fridge ♨ Elec metered ⫿can be hired ☎(¼m) WM in unit SD in unit Airing cupboard in unit Iron in unit Ironing board in unit HCE in unit ☉ CTV ⊕3 pin square 2P ⚲(200yds)

↤ ☏(3m)

Min£30 Max£65pw (Low)
Min£40 Max£90pw (High)

C Wreaks End Cottage
for bookings Mr W M Tyson, Wreaks End House, Broughton-in-Furness, Cumbria ☎Broughton-in-Furness(065 76)216

Large attractive late 18th-century house in pleasant grounds. Extensive views of Coniston and Doddon Fells. Accommodation comprises three bedrooms, bathroom, kitchen and lounge.

Jan–20 Dec MWB out of season 1 mth max, 1 unit, 2–8 persons ◊ no dogs ◉ fridge Electric Elec metered ⫿not provided ☎ Airing cupboard in unit Iron in unit Ironing board in unit HCE in unit ☉ TV ⊕3 pin square P ⚲(1½m)

Min£50 Max£90pw

ULVERSTON
Cumbria
Map 7 SD27

C, F Mr G B Dellows **The Falls**
Mansriggs, Ulverston, Cumbria LA12 7PX
☎Ulverston(0229)53781

Two converted stone-built barns, a cottage and the former dairy of a 17th-century farmstead set in peaceful countryside with views of moorland, mountains and sea. One barn has been converted into a spacious cottage sleeping ten, the other has been made into two flats, each sleeping four. The dairy is now a cottage sleeping four adults and two children. Far Applethwaite is a detached stone cottage sleeping up to four people. The accommodation is of a very high standard and the original character of the property has been maintained. A comprehensive food service is available at extra charge.

All year MWB 1 wk min, 5 units, 2–10 persons [◊] ◊ ◆ calor ⌀ fridge ♨ & log fires Gas/Elec inclusive ⫿inclusive ☎(1½m) WM on premises TD on premises Iron on premises Ironing board on premises HCE in unit ☉ TV ⊕3 pin square 1P ▥ ⚲(1½m)

↤ ☌(2m) ☏(1½m) ☙(1½m)

Min£50 Max£85pw (Low)
Min£125 Max£305pw (High)

UPLYME
Devon
Map 3 SY39

C Hilltop Whalley Lane
for bookings Miss A M Crosse, 14 Miles Road, Clifton, Bristol, Avon BS8 2JW
☎Bristol(0272)736829

Detached cottage in quiet position with lovely views over Uplyme and comprising three bedrooms, sitting room, kitchen and bathroom/WC.

Mar–Oct MWB in season 1 wk min, 1 mth max, 1 unit, 5 persons ◉ fridge Electric Elec metered ⫿inclusive ☎ Airing cupboard on premises Iron on premises Ironing board on premises HCE on premises ☉ [TV] ⊕3 pin square 2P 1⚑ ▥ ⚲(300yds)

↤ ☌(2m) ☏(300yds) ▨(500yds) ♫(1m) ☙(1m)

Min£60 Max£70pw (Low)
Min£75 Max£80pw (High)

C Honeysuckle Cottage Mill Lane
for bookings Mrs D H Young, Little Orchard, 26 Clive Road, Esher, Surrey KT10 8PS
☎Esher(0372)64514

Detached, old world 'picture postcard' cottage in secluded position with own garden and stream. Two twin-bedded rooms and one double bedroom. Low ceilings and oak beams. Combined bathroom and toilet. Lounge with inglenook fireplace and fitted. Modernised kitchen. Leave A3070 Uplyme via Tappers Knapp and turn right into Mill Lane. Honeysuckle is at road's end.

All year MWB out of season 4 nights min, 6 mths max, 1 unit, 2–6 persons, nc5 ◉ fridge ♨ open fires Elec metered ⫿not provided ☎ WM in unit SD in unit Airing cupboard in unit Iron in unit Ironing board in unit HCE in unit ☉ TV can be hired ⊕3 pin square P ⚲(½m)

↤ ☌(1½m) ☏(1½m) ♫(1½m) ☙(1½m)

Min£35 Max£80pw (Low)
Min£90 Max£140pw (High)

F Mr J M Groom **Waterside** Uplyme, Lyme Regis, Dorset
☎Lyme Regis(029 74)2533

A detached half-timbered country residence set in well kept gardens enclosed by shrubs and trees. The Flats are comfortably furnished with tasteful décor and fittings, both have French doors to lawns and gardens and comprise lounge, dining room, kitchen, bathroom/WC and three twin-bedded rooms.

All year MWB out of season 1 wk min, 4 wks max, 2 units, 2–6 persons [◆ ◆] no pets ◉ fridge Electric Elec metered ⫿not provided ☎(½m) Iron in unit Ironing board in unit HCE in

unit ☉ TV ⊕3 pin square ⚑ ▥ ⚲(½m)

↤ ☌(½m) ☏(½m) ▨(1½m) ☙(1½m)

Min£37 Max£44pw (Low)
Min£82 Max£99pw (High)

UPPER SLAUGHTER
Gloucestershire
Map 4 SP12

C Garden Cottage
for bookings Mrs A Turrell, The Manor House, Upper Slaughter, Cheltenham, Gloucestershire GL54 2JG
☎Bourton-on-the-Water(0451)20927

Set in 22 acres of gardens and pasture land, the Garden Cottage enjoys attractive views and the main accommodation is on the first-floor. Small in scale, there is a cosy living room, good kitchen and double bedroom; the bathroom is on ground level. The Manor House is open to the public one afternoon each week, May to September. Use of facilities is reserved first and foremost for those holidaying.

Mar–Oct 1 wk min, 1 unit, 2 persons [◊] [◊] no pets ◉ fridge Electric Elec metered ⫿not provided ☎ Airing cupboard in unit Iron in unit Ironing board in unit HCE in unit ☉ TV ⊕3 pin square P ▥ ⚲(½m) ⊃ ⚲Hard ♞ Games room

Min£60 Max£81pw (Low)
Min£95 Max£114pw (High)

F Granary
for bookings Mrs A Turrell, The Manor House, Upper Slaughter, Cheltenham, Gloucestershire GL54 2JG
☎Bourton-on-the-Water(0451)20927

The Granary is a conversion of the first floor of the stable block. Large living room area with modern furnishings, kitchen, one master bedroom with double bed, one bedroom with twin beds and a bedroom with two bunk beds, small bathroom, separate WC.

Mar–Oct 1 wk min, 1 unit, 6 persons [◊] [◊] no pets ◉ fridge Electric Elec metered ⫿not provided ☎ Airing cupboard in unit Iron in unit Ironing board in unit HCE in unit ☉ TV ⊕3 pin square P ▥ ⚲(½m) ⊃ ⚲Hard Games room

Min£97 Max£147pw (Low)
Min£173 Max£239pw (High)

F Manor House Flat
for bookings Mrs A Turrell, The Manor House, Upper Slaughter, Cheltenham, Gloucestershire GL54 2JG
☎Bourton-on-the-Water(0451)20927

The Manor House Flat is at the top of the main house, traditionally furnished with 16th-century exposed beams and mullion windows and lovely views. Roomy kitchen, dining area and comfortable sitting room, 2 or 3 twin-bedded rooms, bathroom and WC.

Mar–Oct 1 wk min, 1 unit, 4–6 persons [◊] [◊] no pets ◉ fridge ♨ Elec metered ⫿not provided ☎ Airing cupboard in unit Iron in unit

Ironing board in unit HCE in unit ⊙ TV ⊕3pin square P ▥ ♨(½m) ⛵ ⚘Hard Games room

Min£77 Max£147pw (Low)
Min£124 Max£239pw (High)

***C* Studio**
for bookings Mrs A Turrell, The Manor House, Upper Slaughter, Cheltenham, Gloucestershire GL54 2JG
☎Bourton-on-the-Water(0451)20927

The studio is on the other side of the stable block, open plan and at ground level. Sitting room with bed-settee and single divan, kitchen and shower/WC.

Mar–Oct 1wk min, 1unit, 2persons [◇] [◆] no pets ◎ fridge ⚯ Elec metered ▣not provided ☎ Airing cupboard in unit Iron in unit Ironing board in unit HCE in unit ⊙ TV ⊕3pin square P ▥ ♨(½m) ⛵ ⚘Hard Games room

Min£51 Max£66pw (Low)
Min£77 Max£87pw (High)

VENTNOR
Isle of Wight
Map**4** SZ57

***F* Ashcliffe Holiday Flats** The Pitts, Bonchurch
for bookings Mr W Wright, Sandford Park, Holton Heath, Poole, Dorset BH16 6JZ
☎Lytchett Minster(0202)622513

Modernised Victorian house converted into four flats, all of them having combined lounge/diner and separate kitchen. Two flats have three bedrooms, two have two bedrooms. All are quite large and well appointed with modern kitchen equipment, bath and WC.

14May–Sep 3days min, 3mths max, 4units, 1–8persons ◆ ◆ ◎ fridge Electric Elec metered ▣inclusive ☎ Iron in unit Ironing board in unit HCE in unit ⊙ CTV ⊕3pin square P ▥ ♨(½m)

⊖ ♀(200yds) ▤(2m) ♬(2m)

Min£45 Max£65pw (Low)
Min£90 Max£120pw (High)

F Mrs L Watson ***Hawthorne*** St Boniface Road, Ventnor, Isle of Wight PO38 1PN
☎Ventnor(0983)853302

Semi-detached Victorian house, part of which is divided into three self-contained flats. Large simply-furnished rooms. Situated on outskirts of town with access to Downs.

Mid May–Oct MWB out of season 1wk min, 6mths max, 3units, 2–5persons ◆ no pets ◎ fridge Electric Elec metered ▣inclusive ☎(200yds) SD in unit Iron in unit Ironing board in unit HCE in unit TV ⊕3pin square 3P ▥ ♨(400yds) ⚘Hard ♿

⊖ ♀(½m) ▤(½m) ♬(½m) ⛟(1m)

F Mrs M R Jones ***Hillslea House*** Bath Road, Ventnor, Isle of Wight PO38 1JY
☎Ventnor(0983)852259

Victorian house, part of which has been converted into two large modern self-contained flats. Also adjoining the house, are four modern self-contained flats all of which have splendid sea views. All units are spacious and have modern comfortable furnishings.

All year MWB out of season 2days min, 4mths max, 6units, 1–10persons [◇] ◆ ◆ no pets ◎ fridge Electric Elec metered ▣can be hired ☎(400yds) WM on premises SD on premises Iron in unit Ironing board on premises HCE in unit ⊙ [CTV] ⊕3pin square P ▥ ♨(400yds) ⚘(1m) ♿

⊖ ♀(20yds) ▤(20yds) ♬(20yds) ⛟(400yds)

***C* Smugglers Cottage** 10 South Street
for bookings Mrs J Wearing, South Bank, Park Avenue, Ventnor, Isle of Wight PO38 1LD
☎Ventnor(0983)852138

Small semi-detached cottage in elevated position on cliff top with sea views to rear. Modernised accommodation with bright and colourful décor.

All year MWB out of season 6mths max, 1unit, 1–7persons ◆ no pets ♁ fridge Electric & Gas Gas/Elec metered ▣inclusive ☎(400yds) Airing cupboard Iron Ironing board HCE TV ⊕3pin square ▥ ♨(500yds)

⊖ ♀(20yds) ▤(½m) ♬(½m) ⛟(½m)

Min£92pw (Low)
Min£172.50pw (High)

***Ch* Westfield Holiday Centre** Shore Road, Bonchurch, Ventnor, Isle of Wight PO39 1RH
☎Ventnor(0983)852268

A large holiday complex with 98 flats and chalets, a club, indoor pool, putting greens, shop and playground. 61 of the units do not conform to basic requirements. 37 chalets have either a double and two bunk-bedded rooms, or one double and one bunk-bedded room. All have combined lounge/diner, kitchenette and folding double bed except for ten larger ones which have separate lounges.

Etr–Sep MWB out of season 1wk min, 3mths max, 37units, 2–8persons ◇ [◆ ◆] no pets ♁ ◎ fridge Electric Gas inclusive Elec metered ▣can be hired ☎ [WM on premises] [TD on premises] [Iron on premises] HCE in unit ⊙ TV can be hired ⊕3pin square 100P ▥ ♨ ⛵ Putting

⊖ ♀ ▤ ♬ ⛟(1m)

VERYAN
Cornwall
Map**2** SW94

***C* Elerkey Farm House**
for bookings Mr & Mrs J A Hedges, Westwards, Bickwell Valley, Sidmouth, Devon
☎Sidmouth(03955)6176

Charming, well appointed cottage tastefully converted with modern facilities. Accommodation comprises a lounge with inglenook fireplace and small porch to attractive garden, study/bedroom, separate dining room with beams, modern kitchen and utility room, bathroom with bidet and wash basin and separate WC. Two staircases lead to first floor with one double room, one twin-bedded room and one small →

double room, and further WC.

All year MWB out of season 1wk min, 6mths max, 1unit, 8persons ◈ ⊚ fridge ⚱ Electric Elec inclusive Ⓛcan be hired ☎ WM in unit SD in unit Airing cupboard in unit Iron in unit Ironing board in unit HCE in unit ⊙ CTV ⊕3 pin square P ▥ ♨(½m) ⊶ ☎(½m)

Min£85 Max£200pw (Low)
Min£235 Max£350pw (High)

WADEBRIDGE
Cornwall
Map 2 SW97

C Dovecote & The Loft
for bookings Cornish Farm Holidays, Homeleigh Chapel Amble, Wadebridge, Cornwall
☎Wadebridge(020881)2388

Old barn converted into two cottages with stone walls and beams. Accommodation comprises kitchen/diner/lounge, one twin bedroom, one double bedroom with optional bunk beds, and bathroom with shower and WC. Furnished to a very high standard.

Mar–Dec MWB out of season 1wk min, 6wks max, 2units, 1–6persons ◇ ◈ ◆ ⊚ fridge Electric Elec metered Ⓛinclusive ☎(200yds) WM on premises Airing cupboard in unit Iron on premises Ironing board in unit ⊙ CTV ⊕3 pin square 4P ▥

Veryan
—
Wadebridge

♨(200yds) Table tennis
⊶ ⅛(3m) ☎(200yds) ♫(3m) ⬛(3m)
Min£28.75 Max£184pw

C Edmunton Court (Cottages)
for bookings Mrs Harrington, Channel View, Edmunton, Wadebridge, Cornwall
PL27 7JA
☎Wadebridge(020881)2449

Sixteen terraced cottages, 12 of which comprise kitchenette, lounge/diner, double bedroom and twin-bedded room with sofa bed. The other four have lounge, dining room, kitchen, two double and two twin-bedded rooms, bathroom and WC. Set adjacent to paved courtyard with good views over River Camel and Bodmin Moor.

All year MWB out of season 3days min, 3mths max, 16units, 1–8persons ◈ ◆ no pets ⊚ fridge Electric & open fires Elec metered Ⓛcan be hired ☎ Airing cupboard in unit Iron on premises Ironing board on premises HCE in unit ⊙ ⊕3 pin square 16P ▥ ♨(½m) ⊶ ☎ ⬛(2m)

H Edmunton Court (House)
for bookings Mrs Harrington, Channel View, Edmunton, Wadebridge, Cornwall
PL27 7JA
☎Wadebridge(020881)2449

Well-situated detached house built of Cornish stone. Accommodation comprises kitchen, dining room, twin bedroom, double bedroom and bathroom, WC. The lounge is on the first floor and has a single Z bed.

All year MWB out of season 3days min, 3mths max, 1unit, 1–5persons ◈ ◆ no pets ⊚ fridge ⚱ Elec metered Ⓛcan be hired ☎ Airing cupboard in unit Iron on premises Ironing board on premises HCE in unit ⊙ ⊕3 pin square 1P ▥ ♨(½m) ⊶ ☎ ⬛(2m)

F Mr F J Horley, Flats 1, 2 & 3
Wyndhurst, Molesworth Street, Wadebridge, Cornwall
☎Wadebridge(020881)3435

Three flats, one on first and two on second floor of a large Victorian house close to centre of town. Flat 1 comprises lounge/kitchen/diner, two twin bedrooms and one with double and single bed, bathroom and WC. Flat 2 has lounge/kitchen/diner, large bedroom with a double and two single beds (a double sofa-bed in lounge), bathroom and WC. Flat 3 is same as 2 but has no sofa-bed. All flats are well-maintained.

All year MWB out of season 1wk min,
3mths max, 3units, 1–7persons ◇ ◆
◆ ◉ fridge ♯(Flat 1 only) Electric
Elec metered Ⓛcan be hired ☎ Airing
cupboard in unit Iron on premises
Ironing board on premises HCE in unit
[Launderette within 300yds] ⊕ CTV
⊕3pin square 2P ▥ ♨(10yds)
↤ ♒(3m) ♀(10yds) 🐾(½m)
Min£40 Max£120pw

WALKERBURN
Borders *Peeblesshire*
Map**11** NT33

F&H Mrs C S Eaton **Sunnybrae House**
Walkerburn, Peeblesshire EH436AA
☎Walkerburn(089687)501

*The Chapel Suite, the Garden Suite and
the Maisonette are three modern self-
contained apartments in the west wing of
the large mansion set in some four acres
of garden and woodland. The Chapel
Suite is on the ground floor and entry is
by a private door from the garden. It
comprises a spacious open plan lounge,
dining room, kitchen, and two bedrooms
one of which has a shower and one a
bathroom. The Garden Suite is located
on the first floor and it comprises a
lounge, kitchenette, bathroom, a twin
bedroom and a double bedroom. The
Maisonette is contained on the first and
second floors. On the first floor is the
lounge and kitchenette and upstairs is
the shower room, a twin bedroom and a
bedroom with three single beds. The
Lodge stands at the entrance drive, it
comprises open plan lounge and kitchen,
a double bedroom, a small bedroom with
two full size bunk beds and bathroom.*

All year MWB out of season 1wk min,
1mth max, 4units, 4–5persons ◇ ◆
♨(in Lodge) ◉ fridge ♯
Gas/Elec inclusive Ⓛinclusive ☎ Iron
on premises Ironing board on
premises HCE in unit Launderette on
premises ⊕ CTV ⊕3pin square 5P
♨(100yds) Fishing
↤ ♒(2m) ♀(100yds)
Min£35 Max£65pw (Low)
Min£70 Max£145pw (High)

Wadebridge
–
Watchet

WALMER
Kent
Map**5** TR34

F Miss E B Phillips **Clanwilliam House**
1 Marine Road, Walmer, Deal, Kent
CT14 7DN
☎Deal(030 45)4059

*This unit is part of a bungalow on the
Walmer seafront converted from a
Victorian Bathhouse. Comfortable
accommodation comprises three
bedrooms, lounge, kitchen/breakfast
room, sitting/dining room and
bathroom/WC.*

Mar–Oct 2wks min, 8mths max, 1unit,
2–5persons [◇ ◆ ◆] no pets
except dogs ◉ fridge ♯
Elec metered Ⓛcan be hired ☎ SD in
unit Airing cupboard in unit Iron in unit
Ironing board in unit HCE in unit
[Launderette within 300yds] ◉ TV
⊕3pin square ▥ ♨(100yds)
↤ ♀(½m) ▨(1m) ♫(½m) 🐾(½m)
Min£40 Max£65pw (Low)
Min£80 Max£135pw (High)

WASDALE
Cumbria
Map**11** NY10

F **Andrew House, Greendale Holiday
Apartments**
for bookings Mr M D Burnett, Greendale
Holiday Apartments, Wasdale, Seascale,
Cumbria CA20 1EU
☎Wasdale(094 06)243

*Five well equipped flats on ground floor
and first floor of a converted stone barn
standing on an unclass road. 5m E of
Gosforth and ½m from Lake Wastwater in
attractive peaceful surroundings. Three
flats have one twin, one double and one
room with bunks. The other two have two
doubles and one bunk-bedded room*

All year MWB out of season 1wk min,
3wks max, 5units, 4–6persons [◇] ♨
◉ fridge Gas/Elec inclusive Ⓛcan be

---

hired ☎(2m) HCE in unit ◉ TV
⊕3pin square P ♨(5m)
↤ ♀(2m)
Min£90 Max£140pw

F **Stuart House, Greendale Holiday
Apartments**
for bookings Mr M D Burnett, Greendale
Holiday Apartments, Wasdale, Seascale,
Cumbria CA20 1EU
☎Wasdale(094 06)243

*Six newly constructed flats on ground
and first floors of this purpose-built
apartment block. Three flats have one
twin, one double and one small single
room. The other three have one double
and one twin-bedded room. The flats are
situated in a picturesque rural location ½m
from Lake Wastwater.*

All year MWB out of season 1wk min,
3wks max, 6units, 4–5persons ◆ ◉
fridge ♯ Elec inclusive Ⓛcan be
hired ☎(2m) HCE in unit ◉ TV
⊕3pin square P ♨(5m)
↤ ♀(2m)
Min£90 Max£140pw

WATCHET
Somerset
Map**3** ST04

B **Don!ford Holiday Bungalows**
for bookings Bromley Penny Bros, 12
Swain Street, Watchet, Somerset
TA23 0AB
☎Watchet(0984)31232

*Brick-built units in semi-circular
formation. Pleasant situation with good
grass areas, mature shrubs and trees,
with stream running at one side. Good
views of surrounding hills.*

All year MWB out of season 7days min,
4mths max, 18units, 4–5persons [◇]
[◆] ◉ fridge Electric Elec metered
Ⓛnot provided ☎(25yds) Airing
cupboard in unit Iron in unit Ironing
board in unit HCE in unit ◉ CTV
⊕3pin square P ▥ ♨(1m)
↤ ♀(1m) ▨(3m)
Min£28.75 Max£112.70pw

See advert on page 262

WATTEN

WATTEN
Highland *Caithness*
Map**15** ND25

C Achingale Cottage Pennyland
for bookings Mrs B M Oliphant, Bylbster,
Watten, Caithness
☎Watten(095 582)244

*Cottage which has recently been
modernised. It accommodates nine
persons in three double bedrooms and a
convertible settee in the lounge.*

All year MWB out of season 1 wk min,
1 unit, 1–9 persons ◆ no pets ◎
fridge Electric Elec metered
⎣not provided ☎(1m) WM in unit SD
in unit Iron in unit Ironing board HCE
in unit ⊕3 pin square P ♨(1m)
Rough shooting

↩ ♀(½m)

Max£60pw

WEDMORE
Somerset
Map**3** ST44

F Farm House Flat
for bookings Mr & Mrs V & B Carter, Hall
Farm, Sand Road, Wedmore, Somerset
BS28 4BZ
☎Wedmore(0934)712517

*This flat is on two floors with its own
entrance from the garden and comprises
lounge/diner, ground-floor
bathroom/WC. The stairs lead from the
lounge to the first floor which comprises a
bedroom with twin beds. Good standard
of décor and furnishings. Beds for
children available.*

Etr–Oct 1 wk min, 1 mth max, 1 unit,
2 persons ◆ ◆ no pets ◎ fridge
🍳 Elec metered ⎣not provided ☎
SD on premises Airing cupboard in
unit Iron in unit Ironing board in unit
HCE in unit ⊖ TV ⊕3 pin square 1P
🎛 ♨(½m)
↩ ♀(½m)

Min£55pw (Low)
Min£75pw (High)

Watten — Welton Le Wold

C Mr & Mrs V & B Carter **Hall Farm**
Sand Road, Wedmore, Somerset
BS28 4BZ
☎Wedmore(0934)712517

*Converted cider barn with stone-built
exterior, dates back some 200 years.
Accommodation comprises one twin-
bedded room, separate lounge with
put-u-up and dining area, modern fitted
kitchen, bathroom/WC/washbasin. All
very good standard.*

Etr–Oct 1 wk min, 1 unit, 2–4 persons
◊ ◆ ◎ fridge Electric
Elec metered ⎣not provided ☎(½m)
[WM on premises] [SD on premises]
[TD on premises] Airing cupboard in
unit Iron in unit Ironing board in unit
HCE in unit ⊖ ⊕3 pin square P 🎛
♨(½m)
↩ ♀(½m)

Min£60pw (Low)
Min£80pw (High)

WEEK ST MARY
Cornwall
Map**2** SX29

Ca Mr R L Cartwright **Treetops Leisure
Cabins** Week St Mary, Holsworthy,
Devon EX22 6UH
☎Week St Mary(028 884)305

*Twenty-five cedarwood cabins with
cedarwood interiors, set in delightful
north Cornish village not far from the
coast. The cabins either have two or three
bedrooms with divans, or bunk beds,
also a studio couch, kitchen,
lounge/dining room and bathroom.*

May–7 Oct MWB out of season
1 wk min, 1 mth max, 25 units,
4–8 persons [◊] [◈] [◆] no pets
except dogs ◎ fridge Electric
Elec metered ⎣not provided ☎
Airing cupboard in unit Iron on
premises Ironing board on premises
HCE in unit [Launderette on premises]
⊖ TV ⊕3 pin square P 🎛

♨(100yds) ⌐ Games room, restaurant
↩ ♀

Min£30 Max£65pw (Low)
Min£105 Max£140pw (High)

WELTON LE WOLD
Lincolnshire
Map**8** TF28

**C Lincolnshire Wolds Farmyard
Cottage No 3**
for bookings C V Stubbs & Sons, Manor
Farm, Calcethorpe, Louth, Lincolnshire
LN11 0RF
☎Louth(0507)604219

*A semi-detached farm worker's cottage
standing on a farm just off A157,
comprising one single, one family and
one double-bedded room, a combined
kitchen/diner and a separate lounge.*

All year MWB out of season 1 wk min,
1 unit, 6 persons ◆ ◎ fridge
Electric Elec metered except heating
⎣can be hired ☎(1½m) Airing
cupboard in unit HCE in unit TV
⊕3 pin square P ♨(2m)

Min£63.25 Max£103.50pw

H School House
for bookings C V Stubbs & Sons, Manor
Farm, Calcethorpe, Louth, Lincolnshire
LN11 0RF
☎Louth(0507)604219

*An unusual two-storey brick built
building, formerly the village school
house. It stands in the centre of the small
peaceful village. One double, one single,
and one family-bedded room, a lounge,
dining room and kitchen provide ample
accommodation for six.*

All year MWB out of season 1 wk min,
1 unit, 6 persons ◆ ◎ fridge
Electric Elec inclusive ⎣can be hired
☎(1½m) HCE in unit TV ⊕3 pin square
P ♨(3½m)

Min£63.25 Max£103.50pw

1982 prices quoted throughout
gazetteer

WEOBLEY
Hereford & Worcester
Map**3** SO45

***C* Berry Cottage**
for bookings Mrs Sadler, Wyvern Cottages, 60 East Road, Stoney Hill, Bromsgrove, Worcestershire
☎Bromsgrove(0527)73734

Once a small cottage, this has been extended to make a large family home ideal for children with its large lawned garden. On the ground floor there is a lounge, dining room and kitchen. The first floor comprises one double, a twin and a single bedroom and a heated bathroom.

All year MWB out of season 1wk min, 3wks max, 1unit, 6persons ◈ ◎ fridge Electric Elec metered ◫not provided ☎(¼m) Airing cupboard in unit Iron in unit HCE in unit ⊙ TV ⊕3pin square 4P 1🏠 ▥ ♨(¼m) ⇔ ♀(¼m)

Min£35 Max£94pw

WEST AYTON
North Yorkshire
Map**8** SE98

***C* Spikers Hill Cottage** Spikers Hill
for bookings Mrs P Marshall, Spikers Hill Farm, West Ayton, Scarborough, N Yorkshire YO13 9LB
☎Scarborough(0723)862537

One pair of these semi-detached cottages has a double room, single room and a further room with bunk beds, of the other two, cottage No 3 has double and twin bedrooms and cottage No 4 has double and twin bedrooms plus a room with bunk beds. Both have ground-floor lounge and kitchen. All cottages are on a private farm site within North York Moors National Park.

May–Oct MWB out of season 1wk min, 1mth max, 4units, 1–6persons [◈] ◎ fridge Electric Elec metered ◫inclusive ☎(1½m) Airing cupboard in unit Iron on premises Ironing board on premises HCE in unit ⊙(2units) TV(2units) CTV(2units) ⊕3pin square P 🏠 ♨(1½m) ⇔ ♀(1½m) ▨(1½m)

Min£68 Max£82pw (Low)
Min£145 Max£160pw (High)

WESTBY WITH PLUMPTON
Lancashire
Map**7** SD33

***C* Plumpton Grange Cottage**
for bookings Mrs S A Bradley, Plumpton Grange, Westby with Plumpton, Kirkham, Lancashire PR4 3PJ
☎Kirkham(0772)682885

Semi-detached cottage situated in open countryside on a working farm of 57 acres. 5m from Blackpool and Lytham St Annes. Accommodation comprises lounge/dining room, kitchen, shower room, WC and a double-bedded room on ground floor with one double-bedded room and one single on the first floor.

May–Oct MWB out of season 1unit, 2–5persons ◇ ◈ ◆ no pets ◎ fridge Electric Elec metered ◫inclusive ☎(1½m) HCE in unit ⊙ CTV ⊕3pin square P ▥ ♨(1m) ⇔ ♂18(3m) ♀(2m) ▨(3m) ♬(3m)

Min£45 Max£80pw (Low)
Min£115 Max£160pw (High)

WESTHOPE
Hereford & Worcester
Map**3** SO45

***C* Honeycroft** Westhope Hill
for bookings Mrs P Treadgold, Ashcroft, Westhope, Hereford
☎Canon Pyon(043271)336

A recently fully-modernised farm cottage set on an open common with panoramic views. On the ground floor there are two bedrooms (a twin and a double), modern kitchen, lounge, dining room, bathroom/shower with WC and separate WC. Upstairs there are three single beds. Follow signs to Westhope, drive through village, up steep hill and follow signs to cottage.

All year MWB out of season 1wk min, 6mths max, 1unit, 1–8persons ◈ ◎ fridge ▦ Electric & open fires Elec metered ◫inclusive ☎(50yds) Iron in unit Ironing board in unit HCE in unit ⊙ ⊛ CTV ⊕3pin square P ♨(¼m) ⇔ ♀(1½m)

WEST LINTON
Borders *Peeblesshire*
Map**11** NT15

***B* America Cottage**
for bookings Mrs C M Kilpatrick, Slipperfield House, West Linton, Peeblesshire
☎West Linton(0968)60401

A detached bungalow lying in a secluded wooded setting within 100 acres of private grounds with its own Loch. Accommodation comprises lounge with dining area, kitchen, bathroom and three bedrooms. Thoughtfully equipped and well maintained by owner who lives next door.

Apr–Nov MWB out of season 1wk min, 1mth max, 1unit, 2–8persons ◈ ◆ ◎ fridge Electric & coal fires Elec metered ◫can be hired ☎ Wm in unit SD in unit Airing cupboard in unit Iron in unit Ironing board in unit HCE in unit ⊙ TV ⊕3pin square P 🏠 ♨(1m) Fishing ⇔ ♂18(1m) ♀(1m) ▨(1m)

Min £80 Max£150pw

***C* Deanfoot Farm Cottage**
for bookings Miss J Bristow, Thorncroft, Lilliesleaf, Roxburghshire TD6 9JD
☎Lilliesleaf(08357)424

This unit is on a stock-rearing farm complex situated ½m from the small Border village of West Linton. Modernised accommodation comprises dining/sitting room, with open fire, modern kitchen, bathroom, and one double bedroom. Upstairs there is one twin-bedded room (with additional single fold-away bed). Good standard of furnishing and décor throughout.

All year MWB out of season 1wk min, 1mth max, 1unit, 2–5persons ◈ ◎ fridge Electric & coal fires Elec metered ◫can be hired ☎(½m) Airing cupboard in unit Iron in unit HCE in unit TV ⊕3pin square P ♨(½m) ⇔ ♀(½m) ▨(½m)

Min£45 Max£50pw (Low)
Min£65 Max£75pw (High)

***C* Loch Cottage**
for bookings Mrs C M Kilpatrick, Slipperfield House, West Linton, Peeblesshire
☎West Linton(09686)60401

Modernised stone Gamekeeper's cottage adjoining main house, standing in 100 acres of woodland overlooking Slipperfield Loch. Cottage comprises lounge/dining room, modern kitchen and bathroom. Two twin-bedded rooms each on ground and first floors. Access from A702 Edinburgh–Biggar road 1m S of West Linton village.

All year MWB out of season 1wk min, 4wks max, 1unit, 2–4persons ◈ ◆ ◎ fridge Electric Elec metered ◫can be hired ☎ Airing cupboard in unit Iron in unit Ironing board in unit HCE in unit ⊙ TV ⊕3pin square 2P ♨(½m) Trout fishing ⇔ ♂18(1½m) ♀(1½m) ▨(1½m)

Min£60 Max£100pw

WESTON
Devon
Map**3** SY18

***Ch* Stoneleigh Country Holidays**
for bookings Mr & Mrs Salter, Stoneleigh, Weston, Sidmouth, Devon
☎Sidmouth(03955)3619

Modern purpose-built chalets with all modern conveniences, set in a quiet position overlooking sea. All units are comfortably equipped and furnished with separate shower/WC and open-plan kitchen extending into lounge/dining area. Bedroom accommodation varies–sleeping up to nine persons.

15Mar–15Nov MWB out of season 3days min, 1mth max, 27units, 2–9persons [◈] [◆] no pets ◎ fridge Electric Elec metered ◫not provided ☎ [WM on premises] [TD on premises] Iron on premises Ironing board on premises HCE ⊙ →

CTV ③3pin square P 📺 ♨

⇔ ♿(2m) ♀(2m)

Min£46 Max£77.75pw (Low)
Min£92 Max£138pw (High)

WESTON BEGGARD
Hereford & Worcester
Map**3** SO54

C **Lilac Cottage**
for bookings Mrs Sadler, Wyvern
Cottages, 60 East Road, Stoney Hill,
Bromsgrove, Worcester
☎Bromsgrove(0527)73734

*A small semi-detached black and white
period cottage set on the side of a hill and
enjoying extensive views of the Frome
Valley. Accommodation comprises
lounge, kitchen/dining room, combined
bathroom/WC, and one twin- and one
double-bedded room.*

All year MWB out of season 1wk min,
3wks max, 1 unit, 1–4persons ◈ ◉
fridge Electric Elec metered
📵not provided ☎(¼m) Iron HCE
③3pin square 2P ♨(2m)

⇔ ♀(1½m)

Min£35 Max£94pw

WESTON-SUBEDGE
Gloucestershire
Map**4** SP14

F **Canonbourne Flats 4 & 5**
for bookings Mrs D H Young, Little
Orchard, 26 Clive Road, Esher, Surrey
KT108PS
☎Esher(0372)64514

*Two flats in a Georgian house standing in
its own grounds in quiet village. Flat 4 is
on ground floor, comprising one
bedroom (with double bed and cot),
sitting room with two small divans,
kitchen, dining area, bathroom and WC.
Flat 5 is larger and is on the first floor with
kitchen/diner, two bedrooms – one with
double bed and cot, the other with twin
beds, bathroom/WC and drawing room
with two small divans.*

All year MWB out of season
4nights min, 2units, 2–6persons [◇]
◈ ◉ ◔ fridge 🍳
Gas/Elec metered 📵not provided ☎
Airing cupboard in unit Iron in unit
Ironing board in unit HCE in unit ☉
③3pin square 4P 2🏠 ♨(100yds)
✎Hard

⇔ ♿(1½m) ♀(500yds)

Min£25 Max£65pw (Low)
Min£70 Max£115pw (High)

C **Little Tree Lodge**
for bookings Mrs D H Young, Little
Orchard, 26 Clive Road, Esher, Surrey
KT108PS
☎Esher(0372)64514

*Cotswold stone Georgian cottage set in
own garden. A good centre for touring the
Cotswolds and Vale of Evesham. The
accommodation, all on one level,
comprises sitting room with dining
facilities, kitchen, bathroom/WC and two*

Weston
—
Westward Ho!

*bedrooms (one with double bed, one with
two pairs of bunks). On A46
Broadway–Stratford road.*

All year MWB out of season 1wk min,
1unit, 2–6persons ◈ ◆ ◔ fridge
🍳 Gas/Elec metered 📵not provided
☎(1m) Airing cupboard in unit Iron in
unit Ironing board in unit HCE in unit
③3pin square 1P 1🏠 ♨(1m)

⇔ ♿(2½m) ♀(½m)

Min£30 Max£65pw (Low)
Min£80 Max£115pw (High)

WESTON-SUPER-MARE
Avon
Map**3** ST36

F Mr & Mrs B J T Smart **Dalmeny
Holiday Accommodation** 4 Claremont
Crescent, Sea Front, Weston-super-
Mare, Avon
☎Weston-super-Mare(0934)31595

*Flat and flatlet available on the ground
and first floor levels of a large house, on
the seafront. Accommodation comprises
double bedroom, kitchen/dinette/lounge
and bathroom/shower unit. Ground-floor
flat contains a small children's room.*

Etr–Sep 3days min, 2units, 4persons
◈ ◆ no pets ◔(flat 1) ◉(flat 2)
fridge Electric Gas/Elec metered
📵can be hired SD on premises Airing
cupboard in unit HCE in unit ☉ TV
③3pin square ♨

⇔ ♀(200yds) 📮(300yds)
🎵(300yds) 🐕(300yds)

Min£60 Max£90pw

F Mrs S Rose **Merrymead Holiday
Flats (1 & 3)**
1 Ellenborough Park Road, Weston-
super-Mare, Avon BS231XT
☎Weston-super-Mare(0934)29030

*Situated within walking distance of
railway station, town centre and seafront.
Each of the two flats has one bedroom
with double bed, sitting room/diner with a
double bed-settee, small kitchen and
bathroom/WC.*

All year MWB out of season
4nights min, 2units, 2–4persons [◆]
◉ fridge Electric Elec metered
📵can be hired ☎(1m) HCE in unit ☉
TV ③3pin square P 📺 ♨(½m)

⇔ ♿(1½m) ♀(½m) 📮(½m) 🎵(½m)
🐕(½m)

F Mrs L Hetherington **South Crest
Holiday Flats** 23 Atlantic Road, Weston-
super-Mare, Avon BS232DQ
☎Weston-super-Mare(0934)22790

*These three units are on the first, second
and third floors of a large Victorian house;
set on a hillside overlooking the Marine
Lake, with views of Weston Bay and the
Bristol Channel. All have two bedrooms,
lounge, kitchen and bathroom/WC.*

All year MWB out of season 3units,
6–7persons ◇ ◈ ◆ ◉ fridge

Electric & Gas Gas/Elec metered
📵inclusive ☎ WM on premises SD on
premises Airing cupboard in unit Iron
in unit Ironing board in unit HCE in unit
☉ CTV ③3pin square P 📺
♨(350yds)

⇔ ♀ 📮 🎵 🐕

Min£51 Max£73pw (Low)
Min£96 Max£105pw (High)

WESTON-UNDER-REDCASTLE
Shropshire
Map**7** SJ52

C **Church House**
for bookings L W Chesters, Greenacres,
Soulton, Wem, Shropshire
☎Whitchurch(0948)840365

*A half timbered 300-year-old cottage of
character with views. Accommodation
includes two sitting rooms, dining room,
kitchen, two bathrooms with WC, and
three bedrooms (one twin, one double,
and one with a double and a single bed).*

Apr–Oct 6mths max, 1unit,
1–7persons ◈ ◆ ◉ fridge 🍳
Elec metered 📵not provided ☎(½m)
Airing cupboard in unit Iron in unit
Ironing board in unit HCE in unit ☉
TV ③3pin square 2P 📺 ♨(½m)

⇔ ♿(½m) ♀(½m) 📮(½m)

Max£30pw (Low)
Min£65 Max£85pw (High)

WESTWARD HO!
Devon
Map**2** SS42

B, CH & F Mr & Mrs G Gardner
Buckleigh Pines Cornborough Road,
Westward Ho! Devon
☎Bideford(02372)4783

*Two stone built bungalows, four chalets
and three maisonettes situated in small,
well managed, holiday park close to
beaches. They vary in size sleeping 1–8
people, in 2 or 3 bedrooms and a sofa
bed in lounge.*

Apr–Oct MWB out of season
3days min, 28days max, 9units,
1–8persons ◈ ◉ no pets ◔
fridge 🍳 Elec inclusive 📵inclusive
☎ Airing cupboard in unit Iron on
premises Ironing board on premises
HCE in unit [Launderette on premises]
☉ CTV ③3pin square 2P 📺
♨(100yds) ⊃

⇔ ♿(½m) ♀(½m) 📮(3m) 🎵(3m)
🐕(3m)

Min£59 Max£99pw (Low)
Min£109 Max£265pw (High)

B **The Bungalow**
for bookings Mr & Mrs M L Weeks,
Buckleigh Grange Hotel, Buckleigh,
Westward Ho! Devon EX393PU
☎Bideford(02372)4468

*The bungalow stands in a secluded
position in orchard within the hotel
grounds. Accommodation comprises
two twin-bedded rooms and a
convertible settee in the lounge, large
kitchen/diner and bathroom/WC. Guests*

may use the facilities of the hotel.
Ten-minute walk to beach.

Apr–Oct MWB out of season 1wk min,
1unit, 4–6persons ◊ ◆ no pets ◎
fridge Electric Elec metered Ⓛcan be
hired ☎(25yds) Airing cupboard Iron
in unit Ironing board in unit HCE in unit
⊙ TV ③3pin square P 🔲 ⚓(¾m)
🌱Grass ♂
⊖ 🚻(25yds) 📺(¾m) ♬(¾m) 🛁(2m)

B   John Fowler Holiday Bungalows
for bookings John Fowler Holidays,
Marlborough Road, Ilfracombe, Devon
☎Ilfracombe(0271)64135

*These bungalows are in blocks of 2, 3
and 4, well spaced with grassed areas.
There are two bedrooms (one double and
one twin-bedded), with a bed-settee in
the lounge/dining room, kitchen and
bathroom. Beach 100yds.*

Mar–Oct MWB out of season 1wk min,
3wks max, 63units, 2–6persons [◊]
[◆] ◎ fridge Electric Elec metered
Ⓛnot provided Airing cupboard in unit
Iron in unit HCE in unit ⊙ CTV
③3pin square P ♂
⊖ 🚻 📺 ♬(100yds) 🛁(2¼m)
Min£34 Max£171pw

**Ch   Westward Ho! Self Catering
Holiday Centre,** Cornborough Road,
Westward Ho!, Devon
☎Bideford(023 72)3368

Westward Ho!
—
Weybourne

*Concrete-built chalets overlooking
Westward Ho!, part of a large holiday
centre. Accommodation comprises
lounge, diner, small kitchen, one double
bedroom and one with bunks, a bed-
settee in lounge, bathroom/WC.*

Etr–Oct MWB out of season
3days min, 50units, 1–6persons ◊
[◆ ◆] ⚘ fridge Electric
Gas inclusive Ⓛinclusive ☎(200yds)
[SD on premises] [TD on premises]
Airing cupboard on premises [Iron on
premises] [Ironing board on premises]
HCE in unit ⊙ TV ③3pin square
⊕3pin round 10P 40🔥 🔲 ⚓ ⤴
🌱Hard Putting, games room,
restaurant, snack bar
⊖ 🛁(3m) 🚻 📺 ♬ 🛁
Min£35 Max£150pw

WETLEY ROCKS
Staffordshire
Map**7** SJ95

H   Lodge Farm Mill Lane
for bookings Mr P E Meakin, Bramhouse
Farm, Wetley Rocks, Stoke on Trent,
Staffordshire
☎Wetley Rocks(0782)550527

*Large, detached two-storey house in
large gardens on edge of village. It
comprises lounge, kitchen, dining*

---

*room, one twin room, two double rooms
with good furnishings, bathroom/WC.
Wetley Rocks is on A520 5½m S of Leek.
Proceed down Mill Lane past the church
and turn right into lodge gates, house is
on right.*

26Mar–28Sep MWB in season
1wk min, 2wks max, 1unit, 8persons
[◊] ◆ ◆ ◎ fridge 🍴
Elec metered Ⓛnot provided ☎
Airing cupboard in unit Iron in unit
Ironing board in unit HCE in unit ⊙
CTV ③3pin square P 🔥 🔲 ⚓(¾m)
⊖ 🚻(½m) ♬(½m)
Min£65 Max£85pw

WEYBOURNE
Norfolk
Map**9** TG14

C   Old Farm Cottage Station Road
for bookings Mrs J E Paton, 23 The
Greenway, Gerrards Cross,
Buckinghamshire SL9 8LX
☎Gerrards Cross(028 13)84922

*Small modernised flint cottage with oak
beams comprising sitting/dining room,
kitchen, bathroom/WC, one bedroom
with double and single bed and curtain
divider. There is an extra bed on the
landing.* →

1982 prices quoted throughout
gazetteer

27Mar–29Oct MWB out of season
1wk min, 4wks max, 1unit, 1–3persons
◆ no pets ◉ fridge Electric
Elec metered ⌑not provided
☎(200yds) Airing cupboard in unit Iron
in unit Ironing board in unit HCE in unit
TV ⊕3pin square 2P ♨(300yds)

⊷ ♒(3m) ♀(300yds)

Min£48 Max£69pw (Low)
Min£72 Max£117pw (High)

**B 1 & 2 Priory Wood Holiday
Bungalows**
for bookings J M Sharp, 'Robin Hill',
Sheringwood, Sheringham, Norfolk
☎Sheringham(0263)822851

*Two purpose-built holiday bungalows
within a select site of similar properties
overlooking lawns in a quiet rural setting.
Each has two double bedrooms and
large open-plan living area comprising
lounge/diner (with double studio couch)
and kitchen.*

Mar–15Nov MWB out of season
1wk min, 6mths max, 2units,
1–6persons [◇ ◆] ◉ fridge
Electric Elec metered ⌑not provided
☎(100yds) Airing cupboard in unit Iron
in unit Ironing board in unit HCE in unit
[Launderette within 300yds] ⊕ TV
⊕3pin square P 🔲 ♨(100yds)

⊷ ♀(½m)

Min£45 Max£65pw (Low)
Min£75 Max£110pw (High)

WEYMOUTH
Dorset
Map3 SY67

H 4 Birch Way Preston
for bookings Mrs J E Pankhurst, 15 Birch
Way, Weymouth, Dorset DT36JA
☎Preston(0305)832265

*Detached modern house in elevated
position overlooking the bay. It
comprises; lounge, kitchen/diner,
bathroom with WC and three bedrooms
sleeping up to nine people. Situated in
Preston village, a suburb of Weymouth.
(2m N A353).*

All year MWB 1wk min, 4wks max,
1unit, 2–9persons [◇] ◆ ◆ ◉
fridge 🍴 Elec metered ⌑can be
hired ☎(50yds) Airing cupboard in
unit Iron in unit Ironing board in unit
HCE in unit CTV ⊕3pin square P 🔥
🔲 ♨(500yds)

⊷ ♒(3m) ♀(½m) 📺(½m) ♫(3m)
🐾(3m)

Min£69 Max£212.75pw

B 1 Cherry Way Preston
for bookings Mrs J E Pankhurst, 15 Birch
Way, Weymouth, Dorset DT366JA
☎Preston(0305)832265

*Self-contained modern detached
bungalow on a new estate on the outskirts
of Weymouth with views out to sea. It
comprises lounge/diner, kitchen, bath
with WC and three bedrooms. 2m N A353.*

All year MWB 1wk min, 4wks max,
1unit, 2–8persons [◇ ◇] ◆ ◉
fridge Electric Elec metered ⌑can be

hired ☎(500yds) Airing cupboard in
unit Iron in unit Ironing board in unit
HCE in unit CTV ⊕3pin square 🔥
🔲 ♨(500yds)

⊷ ♒(3m) ♀(½m) 📺(½m) ♫(3m)
🐾(3m)

Min£69 Max£212.75pw

F Mr J M Stephens *The Hainings* 26
Preston Road, Weymouth, Dorset
☎Weymouth(0305)833918

*Detached house set back from main road
in quiet suburb. The house is slightly
elevated offering views across common
land and harbour, 400yds from sea.
Located off the A363 at Preston near
Bowleaze Cove. Ground and first-floor
flats have two double bedrooms, lounge
with studio couch, kitchen, bathroom and
WC. Second-floor flat comprises two
double bedrooms, kitchen/diner and
bathroom/WC.*

Apr–Oct MWB out of season 1wk min,
3wks max, 3units, 2–6persons ◆ ◆
no pets ◉ fridge Electric
Elec metered ⌑inclusive ☎(400yds)
Airing cupboard in unit Iron in unit
Ironing board in unit HCE in unit ☺
TV ⊕3pin square 3P 3🔥 🔲
♨(400yds)

⊷ ♒(3m) ♀(500yds) 📺(500yds)
♫(500yds) 🐾(1½m)

F Holmles Holiday Flats
for bookings Mrs P Mason, 13 Grosvenor
Road, Weymouth, Dorset DT47QL
☎Weymouth(0305)782589

*Semi-detached brick gabled villa in
residential area converted into two flats.
Each has lounge/diner, combined
bathroom and WC, kitchen, and bedroom
with double bed and two bunks.
Convertible divan in lounge.*

All year MWB out of season 1wk min,
4wks max, 2units, 2–6persons ◆ ◆
no pets ◉ fridge Electric
Elec metered ⌑can be hired
☎(200yds) Iron in unit Ironing board in
unit HCE in unit [Launderette within
300yds] ☺ CTV ⊕3pin square P
🔲 ♨(200yds)

⊷ ♒(2m) ♀(200yds) 📺(½m)
♫(½m) 🐾(1m)

Min£72 Max£94pw (Low)
Min£92 Max£117pw (High)

F Mr K A Bourne **Ing Ravan Holiday
Flats** 10 Carlton Road North, Weymouth,
Dorset DT47PX
☎Weymouth(0305)786271

*A detached red brick villa close to
seafront and shops, comprising four
ground-floor flats, two first-floor and one
second-floor flat. Each unit consists of
kitchen, lounge, bathroom/WC,
bedrooms and studio couch.*

All year MWB out of season 3days min,
1mth max, 7units, 2–6persons, nc3 ◆
◉ fridge Electric Elec metered

⌑inclusive ☎(100yds) Iron on
premises Ironing board on premises
HCE on premises [Launderette within
300yds] ☺ TV ⊕3pin square P 🔲
♨(100yds)

⊷ ♀ 📺(500yds) ♫(500yds) 🐾(½m)

Min£35 Max£46pw (Low)
Min£69 Max£110pw (High)

B 86 Oakbury Drive Preston
for bookings Mrs J E Pankhurst, 15 Birch
Way, Weymouth, Dorset DT36JA
☎Preston(0305)832265

*A modern detached bungalow on a new
estate on the outskirts of Weymouth with
sea views. It comprises lounge,
kitchen/diner, bathroom and WC, and
three bedrooms. 2m N A353.*

All year MWB 1wk min, 4wks max,
1unit, 2–8persons [◇] ◆ ◆ ◉
fridge Electric Elec metered ⌑can be
hired ☎(500yds) Airing cupboard in
unit Iron in unit Ironing board in unit
HCE in unit CTV ⊕3pin square P 🔥
🔲 ♨(500yds)

⊷ ♒(3m) ♀(½m) 📺(½m) ♫(3m)
🐾(3m)

Min£69pw Max£212.75pw

H 16 Oak Way Preston
for bookings Mrs J E Pankhurst, 15 Birch
Way, Weymouth, Dorset DT36JA
☎Preston(0305)832265

*Situated in Preston village, a suburb of
Weymouth, overlooking the bay. This
modern detached house has lounge,
kitchen/diner, bathroom with WC and
three double bedrooms, plus a single
bed in each. 2m N A353.*

All year MWB 1wk min, 4wks max,
1unit, 2–9persons [◇] ◆ ◆ ◉
fridge Electric Elec metered ⌑can be
hired ☎(75yds) Airing cupboard in
unit Iron in unit Ironing board in unit
HCE in unit CTV ⊕3pin square P 🔥
🔲 ♨(500yds)

⊷ ♒(3m) ♀(½m) 📺(½m) ♫(3m)
🐾(3m)

Min£69pw Max£212.75pw

F Mr J Rose **Panda Holiday Flats**
12 Grosvenor Road, Weymouth, Dorset
DT47QL
☎Weymouth(03057)73817

*Six units within detached villa located in
quiet residential area within walking
distance of seafront and main shopping
area.*

All year MWB out of season 1wk min,
4wks max, 6units, 2–8persons ◆ ◆
◉ fridge Electric Elec metered
⌑can be hired ☎(½m) Airing cupboard
in unit Iron in unit Ironing board in unit
HCE in unit ☺ TV ⊕3pin square P
🔥 🔲 ♨(½m)

⊷ ♒(2m) ♀(½m) 📺(½m) ♫(½m)
🐾(½m)

Min£30 Max£80pw (Low)
Min£95 Max£140pw (High)

F Mr D Archibald **Regent House Flats**
Gordon Place, 28/30 Greenhill,
Weymouth, Dorset
☎Weymouth(0305)786987

*Detached, Georgian house on Sea front
with terraced gardens and direct access
to beach. The flats are on the ground, first
and second floors each with lounge,
kitchen, bath and or shower/WC,
sleeping accommodation varies and all
have a convertible bed settee in lounge.*

All year MWB out of season 1wk min,
1mth max, 6units, 2–8persons [◇ ◆]
◉ fridge Elec metered ⌾can be
hired ☎ Iron in unit Ironing board in
unit HCE in unit [Launderette within
300yds] CTV ⊕3pin square 6P ⑰
⌂(200yds)
↔ ♨(2m) ♀(50yds) ⎗(200yds)
♫(200yds) ⛟(½m)

F Mr D Lloyd-Worth **Seacrest Holiday
Flats** 151 Dorchester Road, Weymouth,
Dorset
☎Upwey(030581)2253

*Three-storey terraced building on main
Dorchester–Weymouth road. Two
ground-floor flats, each having
lounge/diner/kitchen with studio-couch
convertible. One flat has one bedroom
with three single beds and the other flat
has one double bedroom and bunk beds.
Each of the other two flats on the first and
second floors, have separate kitchen,
lounge with convertible bed, and
separate bedroom with double bed and
twin bunks. All with bathroom and WC.*

All year 3days min, 4wks max, 4units,
2–6persons ◇ ◆ ⌀ no pets
fridge Gas Gas metered ⌾inclusive
☎(75yds) Iron in unit Ironing board in
unit HCE in unit [Launderette within
300yds] ⊙ TV ⊕3pin square 4P
⑰ ⌂(150yds)
↔ ♨(1½m) ♀(200yds) ⎗(½m)
♫(½m) ⛟(1½m)

Min£35 Max£45pw (Low)
Min£70 Max£120pw (High)

B **31 Ullswater Crescent** Radlpole
for bookings Mrs J E Pankhurst, 15 Birch
Way, Weymouth, Dorset DT36JA
☎Preston(0305)832265

*A self-contained modern detached
bungalow in the residential area of the
suburb of Radipole. It comprises a
lounge/diner, kitchen, separate bath and
WC, and three bedrooms (three double
and two single beds).*

All year MWB 1wk min, 4wks max,
1unit, 2–8persons [◇] ◆ ◆ ◉
fridge Electric Elec metered ⌾can be
hired ☎(½m) Iron in unit Ironing board
in unit HCE in unit CTV ⊕3pin round
P ⌀ ⑰ ⌂(½m)
↔ ♨(1m) ♀(1½m) ⎗(1½m) ♫(1½m)
⛟(1½m)

Min£69pw Max£212.75pw

F Mrs T M Burt **Venesta Holiday Flats**
23 Dorchester Road, Weymouth, Dorset
DT47JR
☎Weymouth(0305)783042

*Five flats located in semi-basement and
four floors of terraced brick building
situated only two minutes walk from sea
front and five minutes from town centre.
Recently converted, with modern
furnishings and having either one or two
bedrooms.*

May–Oct 3days min, 4wks max, 5units,
2–8persons [◇] ◆ ◆ no pets
fridge Electric Elec metered ⌾can be
hired ☎(250yds) Airing cupboard in
unit Iron in unit Ironing board in unit
HCE in unit [Launderette within
300yds] CTV ⊕3pin square 5P ⑰
⌂(300yds)
↔ ♨(2½m) ♀(200yds) ⎗(500yds)
♫(1m) ⛟(1m)

Min£50 Max£60pw (Low)
Min£105 Max£145pw (High)

WHALLEY
Lancashire
Map**7** SD73

C **Calder Cottage**
for bookings Mrs A Wild, The Marjorie,
Whalley, Blackburn, Lancashire BB69NY
☎Whalley(025482)2152

*An attractive riverside cottage about 250
years old and reputed to have been the
home of one of the Witches of Pendle.
There is a sitting room, dining room with
original stone fireplace, bathroom and
two good bedrooms sleeping up to six.*

All year 1wk min, 1unit, 2–6persons
◇ ◉ fridge Elec metered ⌾can
be hired ☎ WM in unit Sd in unit TD ⌄
on premises Airing cupboard in unit
Iron in unit Ironing board in unit HCE in
unit ⑬ TV ⊕3pin square P ⑰
⌂(500yds) Fishing
↔ ♨(3m) ♀(500yds) ⎗(½m)

Min£60 Max£70pw (Low)
Min£80 Max£95pw (High)

WHARTON
Hereford & Worcester
Map**3** SO55

C **Cooks Folly Cottage**
for bookings Mrs Davis, Wharton Bank
Farm, Wharton, Leominster,
Herefordshire
☎Leominster(0568)2575

*A period cottage set back from the main
road with private gardens, and adjacent
to farm land. On the ground floor are
lounge/dining room, kitchen, bathroom
and WC. A carpeted staircase leads to
one double bedroom, one twin and one
single bedroom.*

Apr–Oct 1wk min, 4wks max, 1unit,
1–5persons ◇ ◉ fridge ♨
Elec metered ⌾can be hired ☎(1m)
Airing cupboard in unit Iron in unit
Ironing board in unit HCE in unit ⊙
TV ⊕3pin square 2P 1⌂ ⑰
⌂(2m) ⌯ ⌆Grass Fishing available

↔ ♨(½m) ♀(½m) ⎗(2m) ♫(2m)
⛟(2m)

Min£50 Max£60pw (Low)
Min£110 Max£120pw (High)

C **Wharton Cottage**
for bookings Mrs Davies, Wharton Bank
Farm, Wharton, Leominster,
Herefordshire
☎Leominster(0568)2575

*A black and white period cottage by a
main road with private gardens.
Accommodation comprises dining room,
lounge with hatch through to kitchen,
separate WC, two double bedrooms, one
twin bedroom, and modern bathroom.*

Apr–Oct 1wk min, 4wks max, 1unit,
1–6persons ◇ ◉ fridge ♨
Elec metered ⌾can be hired ☎ Airing
cupboard in unit Iron in unit Ironing
board in unit HCE in unit ⊙ TV
⊕3pin square 2P 1⌂ ⑰ ⌂(2m)
⌯ ⌆Grass Fishing available
↔ ♨(½m) ♀(½m) ⎗(2m) ♫(2m)
⛟(2m)

Min£50 Max£60pw (Low)
Min£110 Max£120pw (High)

WHEDDON CROSS
Somerset
Map**3** SS93

C **Garage Maisonette**
for bookings Mr & Mrs B Lyons,
Triscombe Farm, Wheddon Cross,
Minehead, Somerset TA247HA
☎Winsford(064385)227

*Converted coachman's cottage on two
floors. Stone built, in grounds of farm.
One room with three single beds and
double bed in partitioned-off sitting room
also double put-u-up in sitting room.
Shower unit and ground-floor WC. 1m
from Wheddon Cross.*

All year MWB out of season 1wk min,
1unit, 1–7persons [◇ ◆] ◉ fridge
Electric Elec metered ☎(1m) Iron in
unit Ironing board in unit HCE in unit
⊙ CTV TV ⊕3pin square ⊕3pin round
P ⌂(1m) ⌆Hard Riding stables
↔ ♀(1m)

Min£47 Max£84pw

F **Jubilee Flat**
for bookings Mr & Mrs B Lyons,
Triscombe Farm, Wheddon Cross,
Minehead, Somerset TA247HA
☎Winsford(064385)227

*Ground-floor flat in stone-built converted
coach house in farm precinct comprising
one twin-bedded and one double room,
lounge with double put-u-up, fitted
kitchen, and shower room. 1m from
Wheddon Cross.*

All year MWB out of season 2days min,
1unit, 1–6persons [◇ ◆] ◉ fridge
Electric Elec charged separately
⌾can be hired ☎ Airing
cupboard in unit Iron in unit Ironing
board in unit HCE in unit ⊙ →

1982 prices quoted throughout
gazetteer

⊕3pinsquare P ⚒(1m) ⤸Hard
⊝ ⚲(1m)
Min£49 Max£88pw

C Rose Cottage
for bookings Mr & Mrs B Lyons,
Triscombe Farm, Wheddon Cross,
Minehead, Somerset TA24 7HA
☎Winsford(064385)227

*Semi-detached stone-built cottage with
two double bedsrooms, one twin and one
single room. Bathroom and WC, separate
kitchen, lounge/dining room, all set on
two floors.*

All year MWB out of season 1wk min,
1unit, 1–9persons [◊ ◆] ◉ fridge
Electric Elec metered ⌷can be hired
☎(1m) Airing cupboard in unit Iron in
unit Ironing board in unit HCE in unit
⊙ CTV ⊕3pinsquare P ⚒(1m)
⤸Hard Riding stables
⊝ ⚲(1m)
Min£49 Max£99pw

F Stable Flat
for bookings Mr & Mrs B Lyons,
Triscombe Farm, Wheddon Cross,
Minehead, Somerset TA24 7HA
☎Winsford(064385)227

*Ground-floor flat which is part of
converted stables. One double room,
one single and one bunk-bedded room.
Double put-u-up in sitting room, kitchen
and bathroom with separate WC.*

All year MWB out of season 1wk min,
1unit, 1–7persons [◊ ◆] ◉ fridge
Electric Elec metered ☎(1m) Airing
cupboard in unit Iron in unit Ironing
board in unit HCE in unit ⊙ CTV
⊕3pinsquare P ⚒(1m) ⤸Hard
Riding stables
⊝ ⚲(1m)
Min£49 Max£88pw

F Steps
for bookings Mr & Mrs B Lyons,
Triscombe Farm, Wheddon Cross,
Minehead, Somerset TA24 7HA
☎Winsford(064385)227

*All facilities on one floor–entrance via
eight steps. One bedroom with double
and single bed, one bedroom with bunk
beds and one single bedroom, kitchen
and bathroom/WC, lounge/dining room
with double put-u-up. Good views.*

All year MWB out of season 1wk min,
1unit, 1–8persons [◊ ◆] ◉ fridge
Electric Elec metered ☎(1m) Airing
cupboard in unit Iron in unit Ironing
board in unit HCE in unit ⊙ CTV
⊕3pinround P ⚒(1m) ⤸Hard
Riding stables
⊝ ⚲(1m)
Min£49 Max£88pw

WHICHAM
Cumbria
Map**6** SD18

Ch Brockwood Park
for bookings Hoseasons Ltd, Sunway
House, Lowestoft, Suffolk NR32 3LT
☎Lowestoft(0502)62292

Wheddon Cross
—
Whitemire Village

*Norwegian timber and cedar wood
lodges set in 26 acres of woodland in the
Whicham Valley. These well-furnished
lodges comprise two or three bedrooms,
lounge, bathroom/WC, four of the lodges
have saunas. Central feature of the site is
the mansion house which comprises a
bar and games room.*

All year MWB out of season 4 days min,
8wks max, 30units, 2–8persons [◊ ◆]
no pets ◉ fridge ♒ Elec inclusive
⌷inclusive ☎ Airing cupboard in unit
Iron on premises Ironing board on
premises HCE in unit [Launderette on
premises] ⊙ TV ⊕3pinsquare 35P
▥ ⚒
⊝ 🛥(2½m) ⚲

WHIMPLE
Devon
Map**3** SY09

B Mrs D Hanson **Lower Southbrook
Farm** Whimple, Exeter, Devon
☎Whimple(0404)822534

*Brick-built converted farm buildings with
lounge/diner and studio couch, one
double bedroom, one room with twin
bunks, kitchen and combined
shower/WC. Leave A30 by unclass road
opposite Bidgood Arms, Rockbeare, the
farm is on the right in ½m.*

Etr–Oct 1wk min, 3wks min, 3units,
2–6persons ◊ ◆ ◆ no pets ◉
fridge Electric Elec metered
⌷not provided ☎ SD in unit Iron in
unit Ironing board in unit HCE in unit
⊙ CTV ⊕3pinsquare ⊕2pinround
P ▥ ⚒(1½m) ⌂
⊝ ⚲(½m) ▦(2m) ♪(2m)
Min£40 Max£104pw

WHITBY
North Yorkshire
Map**8** NZ81

F Mrs J Griffiths **Regent House** 7 Royal
Crescent, Whitby, N Yorkshire
☎Whitby(0947)602103

*Five self-contained flats in a terrace of tall
Regency houses. The ground-floor flat
has one bedroom with double bed, and
bunk beds. Studio couch in lounge. All
other flats have two rooms containing one
double and one single bed, plus a studio
couch in each lounge. All have excellent
fittings and furnishings and good views of
the sea. Lift to all floors.*

All year MWB out of season 1wk min,
1mth max, 5units, 2–8persons ◊ ◉
fridge Electric Elec metered ⌷can be
hired ☎(200yds) Airing cupboard in
unit HCE in unit ⊙ TV
⊕3pinsquare ▥ ⚒(½m)
⊝ ⚲(200yds) ▦(200yds)
♪(200yds) ⛵(½m)
Min£55 Max£70pw (Low)
Min£80 Max£155pw (High)

WHITEBRIDGE
Highland *Inverness-shire*
Map**14** NH41

Ch Highland Lodges
for bookings Highland Lodges, The
Home of Brandon-Bravo Ltd, Beauport
Park, The Ridge, Hastings, Sussex
☎Hastings(0424)53207

*Well serviced and attractive modern
'lodges' with open plan kitchen and living
room and two bedrooms. In a beautiful
setting near a bend of the River Fechlin,
beside General Wade's Bridge. On A862
about 9m NE of Fort Augustus.*

Apr–Oct 1wk min, 11units,
4–6persons ◊ ◉ fridge Electric
Elec inclusive ⌷not provided
☎(100yds) Iron in unit Ironing board in
unit HCE in unit ⊙(7units) ⊛
⊕3pinsquare P ⚒(4m)
⊝ ⚲(200yds)
Min£80.50 Max£109.25pw (Low)
£172.50pw (High)

WHITEMIRE VILLAGE
Grampian *Moray*
Map**14** NH95

C The Denny Darnaway Estate
for bookings Moray Estates Development
Company, Estates Office, Forres, Moray
IV36 0ET
☎Forres(0309)72213

*Delightful cottage in small garden,
situated well off the main road.
Accommodation comprises two
bedrooms (one double bed, one twin-
bedded), lounge/dining room, kitchen,
bathroom and WC.*

Apr–Oct MWB out of season 1wk min,
1unit, 1–4persons ◊ no pets ◉
fridge Electric Elec inclusive ⌷can
be hired ☎(50yds) Iron in unit Ironing
board in unit HCE in unit ⊙ TV
⊕3pinsquare P ▥ ⚒(2m)
Burn fishing
⊝ ⚲(2m)
Min£86.25 Max£97.75pw (Low)
Min£109.25pw (High)

C Glenshiel Darnaway Estate
for bookings Moray Estates Development
Company, Estates Office, Forres, Moray
IV36 0ET
☎Forres(0309)72213

*Semi-detached cottage in a small private
village set amongst woodland.
Accommodation on ground level
comprises two bedrooms (one double,
one twin-bedded), living/dining room,
kitchen and bathroom.*

Apr–Oct MWB out of season 1wk min,
1unit, 1–4persons ◊ no pets ◉
fridge Electric Elec inclusive ⌷can
be hired ☎(50yds) Airing cupboard in
unit Iron in unit Ironing board in unit
HCE in unit ⊙ TV ⊕3pinsquare P
▥ ⚒(2m) Burn fishing
Min£86.25 Max£97.75pw (Low)
Min£109.25pw (High)

C Kistie Darnaway Estate
for bookings Moray Estates Development
Company, Estates Office, Forres, Moray
IV36 0ET
☎Forres(0309)72213

*Small semi-detached cottage standing in
private village amongst woodland and
about 6m SW of Forres. It contains one
bedroom with double bed, living/dining
room, kitchen and bathroom.*

Apr–Oct MWB out of season 1wk min,
1unit, 1–3persons ◆ no pets ◉
fridge Electric Elec inclusive ⬜can
be hired ☎(50yds) Iron in unit Ironing
board in unit HCE in unit ⊙ TV
⊕3pin square P 🔲 ♨(2m) Fishing
Min£74.75 Max£86.25pw (Low)
Min£97.75pw (High)

C The Neuk Darnaway Estate
for bookings Moray Estates Development
Company, Estate Office, Forres, Moray
IV36 0ET
☎Forres(0309)72213

*Detached single-storey stone cottage in
private village surrounded by woodland.
There are two bedrooms (one with twin
beds, one with a single bed),
living/dining room, compact kitchen and
bathroom/WC.*

Apr–Oct MWB out of season 1wk min,
1unit, 1–3persons ◆ no pets ◉
fridge Electric Elec inclusive ⬜can
be hired ☎(50yds) Iron in unit Ironing
board in unit HCE in unit ⊛ TV
⊕3pin square P 🔲 ♨(2m) Fishing
Min£86.25 Max£97.75pw (Low)
Min£109.25pw (High)

H Pinewood Darnaway Estate
for bookings Moray Estates Development
Company, Estates Office, Forres, Moray
IV36 0ET
☎Forres(0309)72213

*Semi-detached cottage in small private
village about 6m SW of Forres.
Accommodation comprises two
bedrooms (one double, one twin-
bedded), living/dining room, kitchen and
bathroom/WC.*

Apr–Oct MWB out of season 1wk min,
1unit, 1–4persons ◆ no pets ◉

fridge Electric Elec inclusive ⬜can
be hired ☎(50yds) Airing cupboard in
unit Iron in unit Ironing board in unit
HCE in unit ⊙ TV ⊕3pin square P
🔲 ♨(2m) Fishing
Min£86.25 Max£97.75pw (Low)
Min£109.25pw (High)

C Stapen Darnaway Estate
for bookings Moray Estates Development
Company, Estates Office, Forres, Moray
IV36 0ET
☎Forres(0309)72213

*Semi-detached cottage in small private
village about 6m SW of Forres. On the
ground floor is one bedroom with a single
bed, living/dining room, kitchen with
small bathroom adjacent. The first floor
contains a twin-bedded room.*

Apr–Oct MWB out of season 1wk min,
1unit, 1–3persons ◆ no pets ◉
fridge Electric Elec inclusive ⬜can
be hired ☎(50yds) Iron in unit Ironing
board in unit HCE in unit ⊙ TV
⊕3pin square P 🔲 ♨(2m) Fishing
Min£74.75 Max£86.25pw (Low)
Min£97.75pw (High)

WHITENESS
Shetland
Map **16** HU34

Ch Mr A G Morrison **Westings Hotel &
Chalets** Wormadale, Whiteness,
Shetland Isles
☎Gott(059584)242

*Ten 'A' frame chalets on elevated hillside
site with superb loch views.
Accommodation comprises ground floor
lounge/diner with double and single
convertible bed settess, very small
kitchenette and shower/WC. A spiral
staircase leads to first floor which is one
long narrow attic room with three single
beds. Located just off A971 at
Wormedale at head of Whiteness Voe.*

All year MWB 3days min, 10units,
1–6persons ◇ [◆ ◆] ◉ fridge
Electric Elec metered ⬜inclusive ☎
SD on premises TD on premises Iron
on premises Ironing board on

premises HCE in unit ⊙ ⊛ CTV
⊕3pin square P ♨(½m) Pony trekking
& fishing

⊖ ♨(3½m)
Max£120.25pw

WHITNEY
Hereford & Worcester
Map **3** SO24

H Wooden House
for bookings Mrs H Williams, Cabalva
Farmhouse, Whitney-on-Wye,
Herefordshire HR3 6EX
☎Clifford(049 73)324

*Detached riverside cedarwood house
built in 1952 with views across river to
Black Mountains. Accommodation
comprises large lounge, dining room,
kitchen, small study/bedroom and
separate WC. The first floor has one
double and two twin-bedded rooms,
bathroom with shower and separate WC.
From Whitney-on-Wye follow A438 to
Clyro, Cabalva is 1m on left.*

All year MWB out of season 3days min,
4wks max, 1unit, 1–7persons ◆ ◆
no pets ◉ fridge Electric & open
fires Elec inclusive ⬜inclusive ☎
Airing cupboard in unit Iron in unit
Ironing board in unit HCE in unit ⊙
CTV ⊕3pin square 2P 1🛏 🔲
♨(2m) Fishing

⊖ ♀(½m) 🅿(2m)

WIDEMOUTH BAY
Cornwall
Map **2** SS20

F Mr D Farrar *Atlantic Court*
Widemouth Bay, Bude, Cornwall
EX23 0DF
☎Widemouth Bay(028885)410

*Isolated converted coastguard building
on clifftop overlooking Widemouth Bay,
ideally situated for cliff walks and beach
activities. High standard of equipment
and good décor.*

Etr–Oct MWB out of season 1wk min,
6mths max, 9units, 2–6persons ◆ ◆ →

> 1982 prices quoted throughout
> gazetteer

---

fridge Electric Elec metered
☐not provided ☎ Airing cupboard on
premises Iron on premises Ironing
board on premises HCE in unit ⊙
CTV can be hired ⊕3pin square
⊕2pin round P Ⅲ ♨(1m)

⊖ ♀ ⊠ ♫

WIGHT, ISLE OF
Map 4 SU SZ

**See Bembridge, Colwell Bay, Culver
Down, Freshwater Bay, Godshill,
Newbridge, Niton, Ryde, St Lawrence,
Seaview, Shanklin, Thorness Bay,
Totland Bay, Ventnor, Wootton Bridge.**

WINCHCOMBE
Gloucestershire
Map 4 SP02

C Badgers Mount
for bookings Mr M G Blanchard,
Cockbury Court Cottages, Winchcombe,
Gloucestershire GL52 4AD
☎Bishops Cleeve (024 267) 4153

*Ground floor accommodation for five
people, described as a garden flat with,
kitchen, spacious lounge, dining area
with open fireplace, and bathroom with
WC. Patio and lawn provides ample
space.*

All year MWB 2 days min, 1 unit,
2–5 persons ◆ no pets ● fridge
♨ open fires Elec inclusive
☐inclusive ☎ Airing cupboard in unit
Iron on premises Ironing board on
premises HCE in unit ⊙ CTV
⊕3pin square P ♨(2m)
⊐(summer only) ✍Hard Croquet

⊖ ♨(½m) ♀(2m)
Min£115 Max£200pw (Low)
Min£230 Max£287pw (High)

C Barn Cottage
for bookings Mr M G Blanchard,
Cockbury Court Cottages, Winchcombe,
Gloucestershire GL52 4AD
☎Bishops Cleeve (024 267) 4153

*Converted from a 16th-century tithe barn.
Cottage sleeps four people and has well
fitted kitchen/diner, sitting room with
open fire (logs supplied in winter).*

All year MWB 2 days min, 1 unit,
2–4 persons ◆ no pets ● fridge

♨ Elec inclusive ☐inclusive ☎
Airing cupboard in unit Iron on
premises Ironing board on premises
HCE in unit ⊙ CTV ⊕3pin square P
♨ ♨(2m) ⊐(summer only) ✍Hard
Croquet

⊖ ♨(½m) ♀(2m)
Min£115 Max£200pw (Low)
Min£230 Max£287pw (High)

C Cockbury Cottage
for bookings Mr M G Blanchard,
Cockbury Court Cottages, Winchcombe,
Gloucestershire GL52 4AD
☎Bishops Cleeve (024 267) 4153

*This is a charming small cottage suitable
for four persons (five by arrangement) in
two bedrooms. Accommodation also
includes a fully fitted kitchen, dining
room, sitting room, cloakroom and
bathroom. Small garden.*

All year MWB 2 days min, 1 unit,
2–5 persons ◆ ● fridge ♨
Elec inclusive ☐inclusive ☎ Iron on
premises Ironing board on premises
HCE in unit ⊙ CTV ⊕3pin square P
♨ ♨(2m) ⊐(summer only) ✍Hard
Croquet

⊖ ♨(½m) ♀(2m)
Min£115 Max£210pw (Low)
Min£240 Max£297pw (High)

C The Gazebo
for bookings Mr M G Blanchard,
Cockbury Court Cottages, Winchcombe,
Gloucestershire GL52 4AD
☎Bishops Cleeve (024 267) 4153

*An unusual building, circular in the main,
built of Cotswold stone with a thatched
roof. The spacious open plan
arrangement includes a dining area,
thatched bar and kitchen, screened
sleeping place. There is a separate
bedroom, two showers and two WCs.*

All year MWB 2 days min, 1 unit,
2–5 persons ◆ no pets ● fridge
♨ Elec inclusive ☐inclusive ☎ Iron
on premises Ironing board on
premises HCE in unit ⊙ CTV
⊕3pin square P ♨(2m)
⊐(summer only) ✍Hard Croquet

⊖ ♨(½m) ♀(2m)
Min£130 Max£230pw (Low)
Min£250 Max£330pw (High)

C Honeysuckle Cottage
for bookings Mr M G Blanchard,
Cockbury Court Cottages, Winchcombe,
Gloucestershire GL52 4AD
☎Bishops Cleeve (024 267) 4153

*A Cotswold stone cottage recently
restored into a spacious holiday home
with a sitting room/diner, modern
bathroom, kitchen and a twin-bedded
room.*

All year MWB 2 days min, 1 unit,
2–3 persons [◇] ◆ ◆ no pets ●
fridge ♨ Elec inclusive ☐inclusive
☎ Airing cupboard in unit Iron on
premises Ironing board on premises
HCE in unit ⊙ CTV ⊕3pin square P
♨(2m) ⊐(summer only) ✍Hard
Croquet

⊖ ♨(½m) ♀(2m)
Min£115 Max£172pw (Low)
Min£195 Max£207pw (High)

F Mr & Mrs M Elliott The Malt House
Corner Cupboard Inn, Winchcombe,
Gloucestershire
☎Winchcombe (0242) 602303

*The Malt House is the self-contained wing
of a 14th-century inn, retaining many
original features including Cotswold
stone walled sitting/dining room. Kitchen,
two bedrooms each with twin beds,
shower/WC and a bed-settee in the
sitting room if required.*

All year MWB 2 nights min, 1 unit,
2–6 persons, nc3 no pets ◢ fridge
♨ Gas/Elec inclusive ☐inclusive
☎(10yds) Iron on premises Ironing
board on premises HCE in unit
[Launderette within 300yds] ⊙ CTV
⊕3pin square 2P ♨(200yds)

⊖ ♨(1½m) ♀
Max£125pw (Low)
Max£200pw (High)

C Mole End
for bookings Mr M G Blanchard,
Cockbury Court Cottages, Winchcombe,
Gloucestershire GL52 4AD
☎Bishops Cleeve (024 267) 4153

A garden bungalow looking towards the water garden and tithe barn. It includes a large lounge/dining area, separate kitchen, one bedroom and a bathroom with WC. Ideal for two people.

All year MWB 2 days min, 1 unit, 2 persons ◆ no pets ◉ fridge ▥ Elec inclusive ▢ inclusive Airing cupboard in unit Iron on premises Ironing board on premises HCE in unit ⊙ CTV ⊕3 pin square P ♨(2m) ⌿(in summer) ⌁Hard Croquet

⟷ ◷⍾(½m) ♀(2m)

Min£110 Max£170pw (Low)
Min£185 Max£200pw (High)

C Tithe Barn
for bookings Mr M G Blanchard, Cockbury Court Cottages, Winchcombe, Gloucestershire GL52 4AD
☎Bishops Cleeve(024 267)4153

A magnificent 16th-century building with exposed beams and oak floor. A large open plan area incorporates a four poster bed, sitting area and a galley kitchen. There is a large separate bathroom with shower and WC. Extra person by arrangement.

All year MWB 2 days min, 1 unit, 2–3 persons [◇] ◆ ⌿ no pets ◉ fridge ▥ Electric Elec inclusive ▢ inclusive ☎ Iron on premises Ironing board on premises ⊙ CTV ⊕3 pin square P ♨(2m) ⌿(in summer) ⌁Hard Croquet

⟷ ◷⍾(½m) ♀(2m)

Min£115 Max£170pw (Low)
Min£195 Max£205pw (High)

WINDERMERE
Cumbria
Map 7 SD49

B Abbotsgarth
for bookings Mr & Mrs P Chance, Beaumont, Thornbarrow Road, Windermere, Cumbria LA23 2DG
☎Winderemere(096 62)5144

Three attractive bungalows built within the grounds of the main house, each with a comfortable lounge with french windows leading to garden. Two bungalows have double bedded rooms, the other has twin beds, all have modern kitchen and an extra folding bed.

All year MWB out of season 2 nights min, 3 wks max, 3 units, 2–3 persons, nc10 no pets ◉ fridge ▥ Elec metered ▢ inclusive ☎ Airing cupboard in unit Iron in unit Ironing board in unit HCE in unit ⊙ ◉ CTV ⊕3 pin square 3P ▥ ♨(200yds)

⟷ ◷⍾(2m) ♀(½m) ▨(1m) ♫(1m) ▇(½m)

Min£50 Max£58pw (Low)
Min£77 Max£118pw (High)

Winchcombe
—
Windermere

F Mr & Mrs F E Coates Applethwaite Holiday Flats, The Heaning, Windermere, Cumbria
☎Windermere(096 62)3453

A large Victorian stone-built house, standing in six acres of grounds, which is divided into six flats (only four are listed). These flats all have lounge, kitchen and shower room/WC. The ground-floor flat has a bunk-bedded room and a fold-away bed in the lounge. One first-floor flat has a fold-away bed and a twin-bedded room; on the second floor one flat has two twin-bedded rooms and another has one twin-bedded room with wash basin, one bunk-bedded room, and a double fold-away bed in the lounge.

All year MWB out of season 3 nights min, 1 mth max, 4 units, 2–6 persons, nc5 no pets ◉ fridge Electric Elec metered ▢ inclusive ☎ Airing cupboard in unit Iron on premises Ironing board on premises HCE in unit [Launderette] ⊙ CTV ⊕3 pin square P ▥ ♨(1m)

⟷ ♀(1m) ▨(1m) ▇(2m)

Min£35 Max£80pw (Low)
Min£73 Max£151pw (High)

F Beaumont Flats 3–6
for bookings Mr & Mrs P J Chance, Beaumont, Thornbarrow Road, Windermere, Cumbria LA23 2DG
☎Windermere(096 62)5144

A late-Victorian stone-built detached house standing in ⅞ acre of gardens with views across to the mountains. Units are very well furnished and equipped. Flats 3 and 4 have lounge and kitchenette. Flat 3 sleeps three persons in double and single bedroom. Flat 4 sleeps four persons in double and twin bedrooms. An extra bed can be supplied. Bath in Flat 4 and shower in Flat 3. Flats 5 and 6 have ground-floor bedroom with double and single beds and shower room; open-plan stairs lead to first-floor kitchenette and lounge. Reached by following Lake Road from Windermere station towards Bowness, turn left into Thornbarrow Road.

All year MWB out of season 2 days min, 3 wks max, 4 units, 2–5 persons, nc10 no pets ◉ fridge ▥ Elec metered ▢ inclusive ☎ Iron on premises Ironing board on premises HCE in unit ⊙ CTV ⊕3 pin square P ▥ ♨(200yds)

⟷ ◷⍾(1½m) ♀(½m) ▨(1m) ♫(1m) ▇(½m)

Min£46 Max£132pw

F 10, 11 & 12 Canterbury Flats
for bookings Mr H E Betham, 41A Quarry Rigg, Lake Road, Windermere, Cumbria LA23 3DT
☎Windermere(096 62)5216/
Canterbury(0227)69803

Modern, comfortably furnished flats built in 1975/6 in grounds of old house in centre of village. Contains three separate bedrooms, one with double and single beds, two with twin beds. Lounge/diner, kitchen, two bathrooms. Close to Bowness Waterfront, steamer pier and shops. Located just off A592. Free use of Stock Park lakeside grounds on West Shore. Accommodation unsuitable for invalids. Rent includes off-peak heating in winter.

All year MWB out of season 2 nights min, 3 units, 2–9 persons [◇ ◆] ◉ fridge Electric Elec metered ▢ inclusive ☎ Airing cupboard in unit Iron in unit Ironing board in unit HCE in unit [Launderette within 300yds] ⊙ CTV ⊕3 pin square 1P ▥ ♨(100yds)

⟷ ◷⍾(2m) ♀(200yds) ♫(½m) ▇(100yds)

Min£110 Max£147pw (Low)
Min£163 Max£225pw (High)

F 19 & 22–27 Canterbury Flats
for bookings Mr H E Betham, 41A Quarry Rigg, Lake Road, Windermere, Cumbria LA23 3DT
☎Windermere(096 62)5216/
Canterbury(0227)69803

Modern, comfortably furnished flats containing two bedrooms, three having twin beds in each room and four having one double and one twin-bedded room. Lounge/diner with open-plan kitchen, bathroom with modern suite. Close to Bowness Waterfront. Free use of Stock Park lakeside grounds on West Shore. Accommodation unsuitable for invalids. Rent includes off-peak heating in winter.

All year MWB out of season 2 nights min, 7 units, 4–7 persons ◇ ◆ no dogs ◉ fridge Electric Elec metered ▢ inclusive ☎ Airing cupboard in unit Iron in unit Ironing board in unit HCE in unit [Launderette within 300yds] ⊙ CTV ⊕3 pin square 1P ▥ ♨(100yds)

⟷ ◷⍾(2m) ♀(200yds) ♫(½m) ▇(100yds)

Min£83 Max£113pw (Low)
Min£124 Max£163pw (High)

F 16A–19A & 21A Canterbury Flats
for bookings Mr H E Betham, 41A Quarry Rigg, Lake Road, Windermere, Cumbria LA23 3DT
☎Windermere(096 62)5216/
Canterbury(0227)69803

Modern, comfortably furnished flats, each containing one bedroom, two having twin beds and three with double bed, lounge/diner, kitchen and bathroom. Extra folding bed and extending settee in all Canterbury Flats. Located just off A592. Free use of Stock Park Lakeside grounds on West Shore. Accommodation unsuitable for invalids.

All year MWB out of season 2 nights min, 5 units, 2–4 persons ◇ ◆ ➔

no dogs ◎ fridge Electric Elecmetered ⬛inclusive ☎ Airing cupboard in unit Iron in unit Ironing board in unit HCE in unit [Launderette within 300yds] ⊖ CTV ⊕3pin square 1P 🔲 🏠(100yds)

⊖ ♿(2m) ♀(200yds) ♫(½m) 🐕(100yds)

Min£69 Max£97pw (Low)
Min£106 Max£131pw (High)

F 32A & 33A Canterbury Flats
for bookings Mr H E Betham, 41A Quarry Rigg, Lake Road, Windermere, Cumbria LA23 3DT
☎Windermere(096 62)5216/ Canterbury(0227)69803

Modern, comfortably furnished flats, each containing one bedroom with double bed, and one with twin beds (extra beds are available). Modern kitchen, lounge and bathroom. Rent includes off-peak heating in winter. Located just off A592. Accommodation unsuitable for invalids.

All year MWB out of season
2nights min, 2units, 2–5persons ◇ ♦
◎ fridge Electric Elecmetered ⬛inclusive ☎ Airing cupboard in unit Iron in unit Ironing board in unit HCE in unit [Launderette within 300yds] ⊖ CTV ⊕3pin square P 🔲 🏠(100yds)

Windermere

⊖ ♿(2m) ♀(200yds) ♫(½m) 🐕(100yds)

Min£73 Max£103pw (Low)
Min£112 Max£145pw (High)

F 40, 40A, 46A, 47 & 47A Canterbury Flats
for bookings Mr H E Betham, 41A Quarry Rigg, Lake Road, Windermere, Cumbria LA233DT
☎Windermere(096 62)5216/ Canterbury(0227)69803

Part of a recent development in the centre of the village; situated on a private road. All flats have twin or double bedrooms and one or two single convertible beds in lounge. Modern comfortable lounges and well-fitted kitchens. Accommodation unsuitable for invalids. Rent includes off-peak heating in winter.

All year MWB out of season
2nights min, 5units, 4–7persons ◇ ♦
◎ fridge Electric Elecmetered ⬛inclusive ☎ Airing cupboard in unit Iron in unit Ironing baord in unit HCE in unit [Launderette within 300yds] ⊖ CTV ⊕3pin square P 🔲 🏠(100yds)
⊖ ♿(2m) ♀(200yds) ♫(½m) 🐕(100yds)

Min£87 Max£122pw (Low)
Min£129 Max£179pw (High)

F Mrs P M Fanstone **Deloraine** Helm Road, Windermere, Cumbria LA23 2HS
☎Windermere(096 62)5557

Edwardian house converted into four flats, situated in a secluded, elevated position overlooking Windermere and the lake, in 1½ acres of garden. 'Brant' being on the ground floor with an entrance hall, dining room with two optional bed spaces, bathroom with shower. Lounge with three beds and bed-settee adjoins the kitchen. This flat is ideal for the disabled. 'Claife' has a long hall, two large bed-sitting rooms each with a double and two single beds, dining room/kitchenette, bathroom and separate WC. 'Scafell' has an entrance hall, kitchen, living/dining room and two chairs that can be converted into beds, plus an additional bed-settee. The bedroom has two single beds and bunk beds. Bathroom/WC. 'Bowfell' has an open-plan lounge/dining/kitchen with two sleeping places. Bedroom has two single beds and bunk beds, bathroom/WC.

All year MWB out of season 3days min, 4units, 2–9persons ◇ ♦ no pets
◎ fridge 🍴 Elecmetered ⬛can be hired ☎ Airing cupboard in 2 units Iron available Ironing board available HCE in unit ⊖ TV ⊕3pin square P 🔲 🏠(½m)
⊖ ♿(2m) ♀(½m) 📺(½m) 🐕(½m)
Min£50 Max£165pw

272

Windermere

C, Ch, F **Dove Nest Holiday Apartments**

for bookings Mrs E Stables, Dove Nest Estate & Farm, Windermere, Cumbria
☎Ambleside(09663)2286

Five luxury flats in main 18th-century house, three modernised cottages and a modernised, stone-built chalet, all of a very high standard. The properties are in a superbly situated 56 acre estate of farmland, woodland and fells overlooking Lake Windermere. Although the A591 divides the estate from the lake, there is a jetty on the foreshore for guests use.

All year MWB 2 nights min, 1 mth max, 9 units, 2–6 persons ◆ ◆ no pets ⊚ fridge 🍴 Elec metered ☐inclusive ☎ Iron on premises Ironing board on premises HCE in unit ⊙ CTV ⊕3 pin square 9P 📺 Sauna, squash & private fishing
⊖ ⚲ ⚭

Min£51.75 Max£166.75pw (Low)
Min£92 Max£230pw (High)

F Mrs M J Riley **Fair Rigg** Ferry View, Bowness-on-Windermere, Windermere, Cumbria LA23 3JB
☎Windermere(09662)3555

A typical Lake District house, stone built, and with good views of mountains and Lake Windermere from the two flats. The flatlet is at the back of the house, also pleasantly situated in rural surroundings 1m from the lakeside village of Bowness. An ideal base from which to enjoy the many attractions of the Lake District. →

1982 prices quoted throughout gazetteer

HOWE FOOT
HOLIDAY & TOURIST FLATS
Bowness-on-Windermere, Cumbria

★ Accommodation for 2-8 persons
★ 5 Ground floor flats
★ Centrally situated for Lake Windermere, shops, buses etc.
★ We provide bed linen, hot and cold water, colour TV
★ Private parking
★ Available long weekends during November to March
★ Ideal for overseas tourists
★ Provisional reservations may be made by phone

Brochure from: Mrs Thexton, Quarry Lodge, Oakthwaite Road, Windermere LA23 2BD
Tel: Windermere (09662) 2792

SO YOU COME TO FALLBARROW TO ENJOY THE LAKE DISTRICT?

In the Wooded Parkland that surrounds your Holiday Home you'll find a friendly Reception & Tourist Information Service, a Shop, Mini-Cinema, Children's Playground and Licensed Bar with Bar Meals. Whilst not 300 yards away there's the village of Bowness with its Restaurants, Shops, Local Inns and Lakeland Crafts.

Within only a few miles there are great mountains, homes of famous authors and poets and a host of other attractions. And still there are those of you who persist in spending your whole holiday on our Waterfront - Boating, Swimming, Fishing, Windsurfing or just relaxing with your holiday novel.

WE USED TO THINK YOU CAME TO FALLBARROW TO ENJOY THE LAKE DISTRICT.
NOW WE KNOW YOU COME TO THE LAKE DISTRICT TO ENJOY FALLBARROW.

FALLBARROW PARK self catering luxury caravans. (We just happen to be on the shore of Lake Windermere.)
Write or telephone for your colour brochure, Fallbarrow Park, Windermere, Cumbria. LA23 3DL. Tel: (096 62) 4427.

273

Mar–Oct 1wkmin, 3wksmax, 3units, 2–4persons, nc10 nopets ◎ fridge Electric Elecmetered ◻inclusive ☎ Airing cupboard in unit Iron in unit Ironing board in unit HCE in unit ⊙ TV ⊕3pinsquare P ▥ ♨(¾m)

⊖ ⛳18(½m) ♀(50yds) ▦(1½m)

Min£40 Max£65pw (Low)
Min£70 Max£95pw (High)

***F* Howe Foot Holiday & Tourist Flats**
Bowness-on-Windermere
for bookings Mrs M Thexton, Hillside, Oakthwaite Road, Windermere, Cumbria
☎Windermere(096 62)2792

Modern flats in an extension built on to the Howfoot Hotel, in a quiet cul-de-sac near to town centre.

Allyear MWB out of season 1wkmin, 7units, 2–7persons ◆ nopets ◎ fridge Electric Elecmetered ◻inclusive ☎ Iron in unit Ironing board in unit HCE on premises [Launderette within 300yds] TV ⊕3pinsquare P ▥ ♨(300yds)

⊖ ♀(¾m) ▦(¼m)

Min£37.95 Max£66.70pw (Low)
Min£75.90 Max£136.85pw (High)
See advert on page 273

***B* Linthwaite Hotel (Bunglaow)**
Bowness-on-Windermere, Windermere, Cumbria LA23 3JA
☎Windermere(096 62)3688

Modern, self-contained bungalow situated in the grounds of Linthwaite Country House Hotel. Accommodation comprises one twin-bedded room with wash basin and WC, one single-bedded room with wash basin, a bathroom and WC combined, comfortable lounge and well equipped kitchen. High standard throughout. Situated off B5284 close to Windermere Golf Course.

Etr–Oct 3daysmin, 1unit, 1–4persons, nc8 nopets ◎ fridge ⚲ Elec inclusive ◻inclusive ☎ Iron on premises Ironing board on premises HCE ⊙ CTV ⊕3pinsquare P ▥ ♨(1m) ⚓ Fishing

⊖ ⛳18(¾m) ♀ ▣(1m) ♬(1m) ▦(1m)

Max£115pw

F Mr R Allman-Smith **Spinnery Cottage Holiday Flats** Fairfield, Brantfell Road, Bowness-on-Windermere, Cumbria LA23 3AE
☎Windermere(096 62)4884

Tastefully converted 200-year-old spinnery in quiet and secluded position a few minutes walk from the lake. Two of the flats are on the ground floor and two on the first floor, all have one bedroom, lounge/diner and kitchen. Three have bathroom/WC and one has shower room/WC.

Allyear MWB out of season 3daysmin, 4wksmax, 4units, 2–4persons ◆ ◆ nopets notrailers ⚲(3) ◎(1) fridge ⚲ Gas & Elec inclusive ◻notprovided ☎(¼m) Airing cupboard on premises Iron on premises Ironing board on premises HCE in unit ⊙ TV ⊕3pinsquare 4P ▥ ♨(¼m)

⊖ ⛳18(2m) ♀(¼m) ▣(¼m) ♬(¼m) ▦(¼m)

Min£40 Max£50pw (Low)
Min£58 Max£115pw (High)

WINTERTON-ON-SEA
Norfolk
Map**9** TG42

***Ch* Winterton Valley Estate** Edward Road
for bookings Hoseasons Holidays, Sunway House, Lowestoft, Suffolk NR32 3LT
☎Lowestoft(0502)62292

Purpose-built wood/brick chalets sited on flat grassed area close to sea/beach. Accommodation is varied in lay-out. There are five basic styles, all have open plan, lounge/kitchen and combined bathroom/WC. Well furnished. Proceed along B1159 turn right into Edward Road, site is 200yds on right.

Apr–Oct MWB out of season 1wkmin, 4wksmax, 30units, 2–6persons [◆] [◆] ◎ fridge Electric Elecmetered ◻inclusive ☎ Airing cupboard in unit [Iron on premises] HCE in unit ⊙ TV ⊕3pinsquare P ♨(200yds) ⛱ Children's play area

⊖ ♀(½m) ▣(½m) ♬(½m)

WITCOMBE
Gloucestershire
Map**3** SO91

***C* 2 The Landers**
for bookings Mrs R E H Saunders, Old Barn, Valley Lane, Upton St Leonards, Gloucestershire GL4 8DR
☎Gloucester(0452)66458

A pretty, black and white, 16th-century cottage situated 4 miles from Gloucester, on the outskirts of Witcombe village. Accommodation consists of two bedrooms, lounge with open fire, kitchen/diner and bathroom/WC. It has its own garden.

Allyear 1wkmin, 1unit, 4persons ◎ fridge Electric & coal fires Elecmetered ◻can be hired (overseas visitors only) ☎(100yds) Airing cupboard in unit Iron in unit Ironing board in unit HCE in unit TV ⊕3pinround 1P 1⌂ ▥ ♨(200yds)

⊖ ⛳18(3m) ♀(¼m)

Min£35 Max£80pw

WITHERIDGE
Devon
Map**3** SS81

***B* Orchard Bungalow**
for bookings Mrs Landshoff, Newland Farm, Witheridge, Tiverton, Devon EX16 8QF
☎Tiverton(0884)860728

Modern detached bungalow located in a fairly isolated position on dairy farm. There are two bedrooms, kitchen/diner, large lounge and bathroom/WC. Large garden and pony available for children.

Allyear MWB out of season 3daysmin, 4mthsmax, 1unit, 1–5persons [◇] ◆ ◎ fridge ⚲ Elec inclusive ◻notprovided ☎(2m) WM in unit SD in unit Airing cupboard in unit Iron in unit Ironing board in unit HCE in unit ⊙ CTV ⊕3pinsquare 2P ▥ ♨(2m)

⊖ ⛳18(2m) ♀(2m)

Min£50 Max£70pw (Low)
Min£75 Max£100pw (High)

WOLFERTON
Norfolk
Map**9** TF62

***C* Downside Cottage**
for bookings Mr Walker, Downside, Wolferton, Kings Lynn, Norfolk
☎Dersingham(0485)40674

Small single-storey detached cottage converted in 1974, forming part of the buildings of the former Royal railway station of Wolferton on the Sandringham estate. The cottage has a lounge/diner with double put-u-up and one double bedroom with shower room. Wooded garden and very quiet rural atmosphere. Lovely local walks and only 1½m from the sea.

Allyear MWB out of season 1nightmin, 1unit, 1–4persons [◇] ◎ fridge Electric Elecmetered ◻notprovided ☎(200yds) Iron in unit HCE in unit TV ⊕3pinsquare P ♨(100yds)

⊖ ♀(3m)

Min£45pw (Low)
Min£75pw (High)

WOOBURN GREEN
Buckinghamshire
Map**4** SU98

***H* Overleigh**
for bookings Mr P G Griffin, Myosotis, Widmoor, Wooburn Green, Buckinghamshire HP10 0JG
☎Bourne End(062 85)21594

Semi-detached country house. Accommodation comprises lounge, dining room, kitchen, bathroom, separate toilet and three bedrooms, two of which have twin beds, the third has one or two single beds. Overlooking the Thames Valley.

Allyear MWB out of season 1wkmin, 6mthsmax, 1unit, 1–6persons ◆ nopets ◎ fridge Electric Elecmetered ◻inclusive ☎ Airing cupboard in unit Iron in unit Ironing board in unit HCE in unit ⊙ CTV ⊕3pinsquare 4P ▥ ♨(1m)

⊖ ⛳18(3m) ♀(¼m) ▦(3m)

Min£130 Max£160pw

1982 prices quoted throughout gazetteer

WOOD DALLING
Norfolk
Map**9** TG12

F **The Little Farmer**
for bookings Mrs E M Smalley, The Old
Jolly Farmers, Wood Dalling, Norwich
NR11 6AQ
☎Saxthorpe(026 387)387

*The stables of this former inn have been
converted into a flat, facing south and
overlooking spacious gardens. The
lounge/bedroom/diner has its own patio
and a divider screens off the bedroom
area, there is a kitchenette, separate WC
and shower.*

All year MWB out of season 3 days min,
4wks max, 1 unit, 1–2 persons no pets
♦ fridge ♨ Gas/Elec metered
Ⓛinclusive ☎(300yds) HCE in unit
TV ⊕3pin square 2P ♨(100yds)
↩Hard

↩ ♀

Min£36 Max£42pw (Low)
Min£52pw (High)

WOODLANDS
Hampshire
Map**4** SU31

C **Merrie Downs**
for bookings Miss E P Davidson, Merrie
Meade, Woodlands Road, Woodlands,
Southampton, Hampshire SO42GE
☎Ashurst(042 129)2830

*An early 19th-century forest cottage
which has been rebuilt and modernised
in quiet residential area on the fringe of
the New Forest, ⅓m off main
Southampton–Cadnam road, 2m E of
Cadnam. Accommodation consists of
two bedrooms, lounge, kitchen/diner and
bathroom/WC.*

Etr–Mar 1wk min, 1mth max, 1unit,
1–4 persons ♦ ♦ fridge ♨
Gas/Elec metered Ⓛcan be hired
☎(⅓m) Iron in unit Ironing board in unit
HCE in unit ⊕ TV ⊕3pin square
⊕2pin round ▥ ♨(150yds)

↩ ♀(⅓m)

Min£50 Max£130pw

WOODTHORPE
Lincolnshire
Map**9** TF47

B **Ash Bungalow**
for bookings C V Stubbs & Sons, Manor
Farm, Calcethorpe, Louth, Lincolnshire
LN11 0RF
☎Louth(0507)604219

*A fairly modern brick-built bungalow in
wooded grounds on B1373. The
accommodation includes two double
and one twin-bedded room, kitchen,
dining area and separate lounge.*

All year MWB out of season 1wk min,
1 unit, 6 persons ♦ ⊚ fridge
Electric Elec inclusive Ⓛcan be hired
☎(500yds) Airing cupboard in unit
HCE in unit TV ⊕3pin square P ▥
♨(1⅓m)

↩ ♀(3⅓m)

Min£74.75 Max£115pw

C **Blue Bell, Cowslip, Foxglove and
Primrose Cottages** Woodland Lane
for bookings C V Stubbs & Sons, Manor
Farm, Calcethorpe, Louth, Lincolnshire
LN11 0RF
☎Louth(0507)604219

*Four modernised, semi-detached, former
farm workers' cottages standing in a
quiet lane on farmland, off B1373. Each
has a kitchen, dining room or dining area,
and a separate lounge. They have either
two or three bedrooms and sleep up to six
persons.*

All year MWB out of season 1wk min,
4units, 4–6 persons ♦ ⊚ fridge ♨
Elec inclusive Ⓛcan be hired ☎(⅓m)
Airing cupboard in unit HCE in unit TV
⊕3pin square P ▥ ♨(1⅓m)

↩ ♀(⅓m)

Min£65.55 Max£92pw (Low)
Min£86.25 Max£115pw (High)

F **Rose Bungalow** Woodland Lane
for bookings C V Stubbs & Sons, Manor
Farm, Calcethorpe, Louth, Lincolnshire
LN11 0RF
☎Louth(0507)604219

*A fairly modern detached bungalow in its
own garden in a quiet lane on farmland,
off B1373. Comprises lounge, dining
room, kitchen, two double and one twin-
bedded room.*

All year MWB out of season 1wk min,
1unit, 6 persons ♦ ⊚ fridge
Electric Elec inclusive Ⓛcan be hired
☎(⅓m) Airing cupboard in unit HCE in
unit TV ⊕3pin square P ▥ ♨(1⅓m)

↩ ♀(1⅓m)

Min£74.75 Max£115pw

WOODY BAY
Devon
Map**3** SS64

F Mrs J Corlett **Martinhoe Manor**
Woody Bay, Parracombe, Devon
EX31 4QX
☎Parracombe(059 83)424

*This beautiful ancient manor, which dates
from the time of the Domesday Book is in
a unique position overlooking the sea and
coastline of Woody Bay and is in 26 acres
of coastal grounds. It is located 3⅓m SW
of Lynton off A39. A private cove, jetty,
and beach are at the bottom of the
garden. Each of the seven flats has a
separate bathroom/WC and
lounge/diner with kitchenette. Five flats
have one double bedroom and one
bedroom with twin and bunk beds. In two
of these units there is also a studio couch.
The garden flat has one double and one
room with twin beds. All bedrooms have
wash basins.*

All year MWB out of season 3 days min,
2mths max, 7 units, 1–8 persons ♦ ♦
⊚ fridge ♨ Elec metered Ⓛcan be
hired ☎ WM on premises SD on
premises Iron on premises Ironing
board on premises HCE in unit ⊖
CTV ⊕3pin square ⊕3pin round P
▥ ♨ ⌂ Stables
Min£57.50 Max£97.75pw (Low)
Min£115 Max£241.50pw (High)

WOOL
Dorset
Map**3** SY88

B **Whitemead Lodge**
for bookings Mrs McCullagh, Frome
Cottage, East Burton Road, Wool, Dorset
☎Bindon Abbey(0929)462241

*Detached Swedish-style bungalow in
rural setting. Accommodation comprises
lounge, kitchen, bathroom/WC, one twin-
bedded room and one with twin beds
plus bunks. A cot is available. Off A352
Dorchester/Wareham Road.*

All year 1wk min, 4wks max, 1unit,
2–6 persons [♦] no pets ⊚ fridge
Electric Elec metered Ⓛcan be hired
(overseas visitors only) ☎(300yds)
HCE in unit [Launderette within
300yds] ⊖ TV ⊕3pin square 2P
♨(100yds)

↩ ♨s(3m) ♀(50yds) ♨(2m)

WOOLACOMBE
Devon
Map**2** SS44

H **CC Ref 527 EL**
for bookings Character Cottages
(Holidays) Ltd, 34 Fore Street, Sidmouth,
Devon EX10 8AQ
☎Sidmouth(039 55)77001

*Dormer-style house within walking
distance of beach. Fine views.
Accommodation includes four
bedrooms, two bathrooms, two WCs,
fitted kitchen and a sitting room/diner.*

All year MWB out of season 1wk min,
6wks max, 1unit, 2–6 persons ♦ ♦
no pets ⊚ fridge Electric
Elec inclusive Electric charged in
winter Ⓛcan be hired ☎(⅓m) WM in
unit Iron in unit Ironing board in unit
HCE in unit TV ⊕3pin square P ▥
♨(⅓m)

↩ ♀(⅓m) ▯(⅓m) ♫(⅓m) ♨(⅓m)
Min£90 Max£136pw (Low)
Min£155 Max£207pw (High)

B The Manager **Golden Coast Holiday
Village** Woolacombe, Devon
☎Woolacombe(0271)870418

*Purpose-built concrete bungalows with
bay windows. Each comprises a large
carpeted lounge with two easy chairs
(adaptable as beds), fitted kitchen,
bathroom/WC, one double-bedded room
and one twin-bedded room. Leisure
amenities are available in the holiday
village. →*

275

Etr–Oct 1wkmin, 4units, 1–6persons
[◆ ◆] nopets ◆ fridge ◻
Elecmetered ⬜notprovided
☎(75yds) Airing cupboard in unit Iron
in unit Ironing board in unit HCE in unit
[Launderette within 300yds] ⊙ TV
⊕3pinsquare P ♨ ⌿ Games room
⊕ ♀ ♬

Min£34.50 Max£57.50pw (Low)
Min£184 Max£247.25pw (High)

C The Manager **Golden Coast Holiday
Village** Woolacombe, Devon
☎Woolacombe(0271)870418

*Purpose-built concrete-and-brick
holiday villas offering a high standard of
accommodation, comprising two
bedrooms (one double and one twin),
lounge/diner with two convertible easy
chairs, kitchen and bathroom/WC.
Leisure amenities are available in the
holiday village.*

Etr–Oct 1wkmin, 51units, 1–6persons
[◆ ◆] nopets ◆ fridge Electric
Elecmetered ⬜notprovided
☎(75yds) Airing cupboard in unit Iron
in unit Ironing board in unit HCE in unit
[Launderette within 300yds] ⊙ TV
⊕3pinsquare P ♨ ⌿ Games room
⊕ ♬

Min£34.50 Max£57.50pw (Low)
Min£184 Max£247.25pw (High)

H Mr D Rigby **Wilmcote** Sunnyside
Road, Woolacombe, Devon EX34 7DG
☎Woolacombe(0271)870445

*House overlooking Woolacombe Bay.
Accommodation comprises
lounge/diner, kitchen and double
bedroom on the ground floor with one
bedroom (one double and one single
bed), bathroom and WC on the first floor.*

All year MWB out of season 1wkmin,
3wks max, 1unit, 1–5persons ◆ ◆
◉ fridge Electric Elecmetered
⬜notprovided ☎(250yds) Airing
cupboard in unit Iron in unit Ironing
board in unit HCE in unit [Launderette
within 300yds] CTV ⊕3pinsquare
⊙ P ▥ ♨(500yds) ⌿ ♂
⊕ ♀(500yds) 🖿(500yds) ♬(500yds)
Min£25 Max£85pw

F **Woolacombe Court Flats**
for bookings Narracott Grand Hotel,
Woolacombe, Devon EX34 7BS
☎Woolacombe(0271)870418

*Modern purpose-built flats in the centre
of Woolacombe. Most have sun
balconies or patios and are fully
equipped with modern furnishings. Each
has a separate bathroom and WC,
compact modern kitchen, lounge/dining
room with convertible settee, one double-
and one twin-bedded room. Use of
nearby hotel amenities.*

All year 1wk min, 8wks max, 15units,
1–6persons [◆] [◆] ◉ fridge ◻
Elecmetered ☎(200yds) Airing
cupboard in unit Iron in unit Ironing
board in unit HCE in unit [Launderette

---

within 300yds] ⊙ TV ⊕3pinsquare
P ▥ ♨(20yds) ▢
⊕ ♀(20yds) 🖿(20yds) ♬(20yds)
Min£57.50 Max£276pw

WOOLFARDISWORTHY
Devon
Map**2** SS32

C Mr & Mrs R Hancock **South View
Farm Cottage** South View Farm,
Woolfardisworthy, Bideford, Devon
☎Clovelly(023 73)397

*Recently converted cottage adjoining
main farmhouse, in quiet North Devon
village. Accommodation comprising
lounge, kitchen/diner, two family
bedrooms comprising a double and a
single in each plus a single room.
Bathroom/WC. Well furnished
throughout.*

All year MWB 3days min, 1unit,
1–7persons [◇] ◆ ◆ nopets ◉
fridge Electric & Aga Elecmetered
⬜can be hired ☎(50yds) Airing
cupboard in unit Iron in unit Ironing
board in unit HCE in unit ⊙ CTV
⊕3pinsquare 2P ▥
⊕ ♙♨(2m) ♨ (50yds)
Max£50pw (Low)
Max£120pw (High)

WOOTTON BRIDGE
Isle of Wight
Map**4** SZ59

H **Laura Cottage** Red Road
for bookings Mrs D Berlow, Witches
Cottage, 11 High Street, Wootton Bridge,
Ryde, Isle of Wight PO33 4PF

*Well-maintained semi-detached house
consisting of two bedrooms, lounge,
dining room, kitchen, bathroom/WC and
conservatory. Set in a quiet road, off the
High Street.*

All year MWB out of season 1wkmin,
3mths max, 1unit, 2–4persons, nc9
[◇] ◉ fridge Electric Elecmetered
⬜included ☎(250yds) Airing
cupboard in unit Iron in unit Ironing
board in unit HCE in unit [Launderette
within 300yds] ⊙ TV can be hired
⊕3pinsquare ♨ ▥ ♨(150yds) ⌿
♐Hard
⊕ ♀(300yds) 🖿(300yds) ♬(300yds)
Min£40 Max£75pw

WORMELOW
Hereford & Worcester
Map**3** SO43

C **Lyston Smithy Cottage**
for bookings Mrs E P Jones, Lyston
Smithy, Wormelow, Herefordshire
HR2 8EL
☎Golden Valley(0981)540368

*A recently converted old blacksmith's
shop, built of stone with original beams.
The accommodation, all on the ground-*

---

*floor, comprises open-plan
kitchen/dining room/lounge, one double
bedroom with private bath and WC and
one twin-bedded room with shower and
WC.*

All year except Xmas MWB 1wk min,
6wks max, 1unit, 1–6persons ◇ ◆
◉ fridge ◻ Elecmetered
⬜inclusive ☎ Airing cupboard in unit
Iron in unit ⊙ CTV ⊕3pinsquare 2P 2♨
♨(½m) Fishing & golf available
⊕ ♀(½m) 🖿(½m) ♬(½m)
Min£30 Max£115pw

WORTHING
Norfolk
Map**9** TF91

C **Riverside Cottages**
for bookings Major G Bowlby, English
Country Cottages, Claypit Lane,
Fakenham, Norfolk NR21 8AS
☎Fakenham(0328)51155

*Modernised cottages converted from an
old wool loft, set in the grounds of the
owner's 18th-century house with 300yds
of river frontage. Cottages accommodate
either four or six persons, and a rowing
boat and games room are available for
residents.*

Apr–Oct MWB 1wk min, 4units,
1–6persons [◇] ◆ ◉ fridge ◻
Elecmetered ⬜inclusive ☎(½m)
Airing cupboard in unit Iron in unit
Ironing board in unit HCE in unit ⊙
TV ⊕3pinsquare 6P 7♨ ▥ ♨(½m)
⊕ ♀(1m)
Min£114 Max£122pw

C **Riverside Cottages, Jacob's
Ladder**
for bookings Major G Bowlby, English
Country Cottages, Claypit Lane,
Fakenham, Norfolk NR21 8AS
☎Fakenham(0328)51155

*Attractive cottage, converted from an old
wool loft, set in the grounds of the owner's
18th-century house. Modern
accommodation includes two bedrooms
to sleep up to five persons. First-floor
balcony commands fine views of the
River Blackwater.*

All year 1wk min, 1unit, 1–5persons
[◇] ◆ ◉ fridge ⬜inclusive
☎(½m) Airing cupboard in unit Iron in
unit Ironing board in unit HCE in unit
⊙ TV ⊕3pinsquare 6P 7♨ ▥
♨(½m) Rowing boat & games room
⊕ ♀(1m)
Max£105pw (Low)
Min£114 Max£222pw (High)

WORTHING
West Sussex
Map**4** TQ10

F Mrs P Mahoney **Chesswood** 56
Homefield Road, Worthing, W Sussex
BN11 2JA
☎Worthing(0903)38512

A detached house, converted into flats, situated in own grounds with lawns, rose beds and large car park, in quiet residential road. The ground-floor flat comprises one twin-bedded room, one with double and single beds, kitchen and bathroom/WC. The first-floor flat comprises one double-bedded room, kitchen/lounge with Wentelbed and bathroom/WC.

All year except Xmas 2units, 2–6persons ⊚ fridge ♨ & Electric Elecmetered ⌷can be hired TV P
Min£50 Max£86pw (Low)
Min£60 Max£86pw (High)

H Hill Top Mill Lane, High Salvington
for bookings Miss B F Green, 35 Storrington Rise, Findon Valley, Worthing, W Sussex BN14 0HT
☎Findon(090671)3823

Pleasant detached house which has lovely views over the downs and sea. Ground floor comprises lounge, small separate dining room, well-equipped kitchen, bathroom and separate WC. On the first floor are two double bedrooms, well furnished but comfortable.
3m N off A24.

All year MWB out of season 1wk min, 5mths max, 1unit, 5persons ◆ ⊚ fridge Electric Elecmetered ⌷can be hired ☎(1m) SD Airing cupboard in unit Iron in unit Ironing board in unit HCE in unit [TV] ⊕3pin square ▦ ≞(½m)
⊛ ♀(1m) ▨(3m) ♫(3m) ▦(3m)
Min£40 Max£120pw

F Berkeley Holiday Suites
for bookings Berkeley Hotel, Marine Parade, Worthing, W Sussex BN11 3QD
☎Worthing(0903)31122

Eighteen self-contained holiday suites in a three storey terraced property. Situated on the corner of Marine Parade and West Street–adjacent to the Berkeley Hotel. Each flat comprises living and cooking area and sleeps from 2–6persons.

All year MWB out of season 1wk min, 4wks max, 18units, 2–6persons [◆ ♦] ⊚ fridge Electric Elecmetered ⌷inclusive ☎ HCE in unit

---

[Launderette on premises] ⊙ CTV
⊕3pin square ≞(100yds)
⊛ ⌂(3m) ♀(50yds) ▨(1m) ♫(½m)
☏(½m)
Min£70 Max£115pw (Low)
Min£120 Max£180pw (High)

F Winslea Holiday Apartments
for bookings Mr H D Potkins, 217–219 Brighton Road, Worthing, W Sussex
☎Worthing(0903)39795

Three houses converted into ten self-contained flats which sleep 2–6 people. The apartments all have a southerly aspect and overlook the sea. Each flat has one or two bedrooms, bathroom, lounge/dining room with kitchenette. Winslea is situated on the sea front, one mile from the town centre.

All year MWB out of season 3days min, 1mth max, 10units, 2–6persons [♦] ⊚ fridge Electric Elecmetered ⌷can be hired ☎(50yds) Iron on premises Ironing board on premises HCE in unit [Launderette within 300yds] ⊙ TV ⊕3pin square P ≞(200yds)
⊛ ⌂(1½m) ♀(20yds) ▨(1m) ♫(1m) ☏(1m)
Min£60 Max£92pw (Low)
Min£76 Max£184pw (High)

WRAMPLINGHAM
Norfolk
Map5 TG10

H Boundary Farm
for bookings Lombe Estate Office, Hall Farm, Great Melton, Norwich NR9 3BW
☎Norwich(0603)810306

This period farmhouse occupies a slightly elevated position facing south overlooking cultivated farmland. On the ground floor accommodation comprises of kitchen, dining room, lounge, bathroom and WC; upstairs is a double bedroom and two twin bedded rooms.

All year 1wk min, 3mths max, 1unit, 1–6persons ⊚ fridge ♨ & Electric Elec inclusive (in summer) ⌷inclusive

---

☎ Airing cupboard in unit Iron in unit Ironing board in unit HCE in unit ⊙ CTV ⊕3pin square 5P ▦ ≞(2m) Coarse fishing
⊛ ♀(1½m)
Min£80 Max£110pw

WROXHAM
Norfolk
Map9 TG21

Ch Melville Bay Chalets Brimbelow Road
for bookings Blakes Chalets Holidays, Wroxham, Norwich, Norfolk NR12 8DH
☎Wroxham(06053)2917

Two cedarwood Swiss/Scandinavian-style chalets in picturesque and peaceful location on bank of River Bure ½m from the centre of Wroxham. Two double-bedded rooms on first floor and one twin on ground floor. Combined bathroom/WC on ground and one separate WC on first floor. Spacious comfortable lounge with picture window overlooking river. Small annexe with twin bunks available. Good quality furnishings and décor throughout. An ideal base for boating or touring holidays.

Mar–mid Oct MWB out of season 1wk min, 2units, 6persons [◆ ♦] ⊚ fridge Electric Elecmetered ⌷inclusive ☎(½m) Airing cupboard in unit HCE in unit ⊙ CTV ⊕3pin square P ▦ ≞(¾m) Boats for hire
⊛ ♀(¾m)
Min£80 Max£165pw (Low)
Min£202 Max£227pw (High)

YARCOMBE
Devon
Map3 ST20

H CC Ref 687
for bookings Character Cottages (Holidays) Ltd, 34 Fore Street, Sidmouth, Devon EX10 8AQ
☎Sidmouth(03955)77001

A 15th-century thatched house with paddock and garden adjacent to River Flagston. Entrance hall, large oak- →

1982 prices quoted throughout gazetteer

---

beamed lounge with inglenook fireplace,
dining room and separate kitchen. Three
double bedrooms, plus cot, h/c wash
basin and one single with h/c wash basin.
Trout fishing available (charged).

All year MWB out of season 1wk min,
6mths max, 1unit, 2–7persons ◆ ◆
◉ fridge Electric Elec inclusive
▣inclusive Airing cupboard in unit Iron
in unit Ironing board in unit HCE in unit
⊙ TV ⊕3pin square ⊕2pin round
P ☎ ♨(2m)
↔ ♀(2m)

Min£84 Max£110pw (Low)
Min£142 Max£194pw (High)

YEALMPTON
Devon
Map2 SX55

C **Longbarn Cottages**
for bookings Mr L I Speare, Torr Farm,
Yealmpton, Plymouth, Devon
☎Plymouth(0752)881281

Farm cottages, with original oak beams,
converted from stone barns.
Accommodation is on two floors and
comprises a large living room with dining
area, separate modern kitchen,
bathroom, and two or three bedrooms.

All year MWB out of season 1wk min,
4wks max, 8units, 1–6persons [◇] ◆
◆ no pets ◉ fridge Electric
Elec metered ▣can be hired
☎(300yds) Airing cupboard in unit Iron
in unit Ironing board in unit HCE in unit
⊙ CTV ⊕3pin square P ▥
♨(300yds) ⌫
↔ ♀(300yds)

YNYS
Gwynedd
Map6 SH44

C **Brynceri & Brynmarch**
for bookings Mr E J Carter, The Pines,
Brockencote, Chaddesley Corbett,
Kidderminster, Worcester
☎Chaddesley Corbett(056283)210

Two semi-detached cottages built of
stone and each comprising lounge,
kitchen/diner, bathroom/WC, a twin-
bedded room and a room with both a
double and a single bed.

Yarcombe
—
York

Mar–Oct 1wk min, 3wks max, 2units,
5persons ◆ ◉ fridge Electric
Elec metered ▣not provided
☎(300yds) Airing cupboard in unit Iron
in unit Ironing board in unit HCE in unit
⊙ CTV ⊕3pin square P ▥
♨(300yds)
↔ ♀(2m)

Min£60 Max£105pw

C Mrs M Jones **Ynys Graiganog** Ynys,
Criccieth, Gwynedd
☎Garn Dolbenmaen(076675)234

Three cottages set in green pastureland
surrounded by woods (facilities for
shooting and fishing). Two cottages are
converted from farm buildings and are
modern, the other is older but in good
condition.

Mar–Nov MWB out of season 3units,
5–12persons [◇] ◆ ◆ ◉ fridge
Electric Elec metered ▣not provided
Airing cupboard in unit Iron on
premises Ironing board on premises
HCE in unit ⊙ TV ⊕3pin square P
▥ Shooting
↔ ♀(2m)

Min£30 Max£50pw (Low)
Min£60 Max£145pw (High)

YORK
North Yorkshire
Map8 SE65

F **Abbey House, Self-catering**
Apartments, 2 St Marys, Bootham, York
☎York(0904)707211

Three flats located in a Victorian terraced
property, near to the town centre. Two of
the flats accommodate two people the
other flat up to four. They all comprise,
lounge, separate dining room and
kitchen plus bathroom/WC.

All year MWB in season 1night min,
6mths max, 3units, 1–4persons [◆]
no pets ◉ fridge Electric
Elec metered ▣inclusive ☎ Airing
cupboard in unit Iron in unit Ironing
board in unit HCE in unit [Launderette
within 300yds] ⊙ CTV
⊕3pin square 1P 1☎ ♨(75yds)

↔ ♨(2m) ♀(100yds) ▨(100yds)
♫(100yds) ☎(2m)

F **Bainton House** 6 St Mary's
for bookings Intermain Leisure Ltd, 7 St
Mary's, Bootham, York YO3 7DD
☎York(0904)36154 (am) & 707211 (pm)

Four flats, two of which sleep four people
in one double-bedded room with two
bed-chairs in the lounge, the other two
flats sleep five people in one double and
one single bed plus two bed-chairs in the
lounge, each have shower/WC.

All year MWB 1night min, 6mths max,
4units, 1–5persons [◆] ◉ fridge
Gas fires Gas/Elec inclusive
▣inclusive ☎ Airing cupboard in unit
Iron in unit Ironing board in unit HCE in
unit [Launderette within 300yds] ⊙
CTV ⊕3pin square 1P 1☎
♨(100yds)
↔ ♨(2m) ♀(100yds) ▨(100yds)
♫(100yds) ☎(2m)

Min£45 Max£85pw (Low)
Min£95 Max£170pw (High)

F **1 Bootham Terrace, (Flats 1–4)**
for bookings Mrs Felicity Walker, 52 North
Lane, Haxby, York YO3 8JP
☎York(0904)768460

Four flats situated in five storey
Edwardian town house near the centre of
the city. They offer different types of
accommodation and are situated
between the basement and the 2nd floor.

All year MWB in season 3days min,
3mths max, 4units, 1–5persons ◆
no pets ⌷ fridge Electric & gas fires
Gas & Elec inclusive ▣inclusive ☎
Iron in unit Ironing board in unit HCE in
unit [Launderette within 300yds] ⊙
CTV ⊕3pin square 5P ♨(50yds)
↔ ♨(3m) ♀(100yds) ▨(500yds)
♫(500yds) ☎(1m)

Min£95 Max£140pw

F **Carlton House** 7 St Mary's
for bookings Abbey House Self Catering
Apartments, 2 St Mary's, Bootham, York
☎York(0904)707211 & Ripon(0765)5133

Three flats within a Victorian terraced
house near to the town centre.
Accommodation comprises one double-
bedded room in the 1st and 2nd floor flats

---

and one twin-bedded room in the ground floor flat, folding beds for two people are available in each of the flats. There is a combined bathroom/WC and a well-equipped kitchen.

All year MWB 1 night min, 6 mths max, 3 units, 1–4 persons ◆ no pets ◉ fridge Electric Elec metered ⌷inclusive ☎ Airing cupboard in unit Iron in unit Ironing board in unit HCE in unit [Launderette within 300yds] ⊕ CTV ⊕3 pin square 1P 1♨ ⛟(100yds)

⊛ ♒(2m) ☎(100yds) ☒(100yds) ♫(100yds) ⛟(2m)

Min£40 Max£60pw (Low)
Min£85 Max£175pw (High)

F Chestnut Flat & Gunnerby House, 5 Bootham Terrace
for bookings Intermain Leisure Ltd, 7 St Mary's, Bootham, York YO3 7DD
☎York(0904)36154 (am) & 707211 (pm)

Two flats located within Victorian terraced property, one sleeps five the other sleeps seven, both have kitchen, bathroom/WC, with divan beds in bedrooms and a bed-settee in the lounge.

All year MWB out of season 1 night min, 6 mths max, 2 units, 1–7 persons [◆] ◉ fridge Gas fires Gas/Elec inclusive ⌷inclusive ☎ Airing cupboard in unit Iron in unit Ironing board in unit HCE in unit [Launderette within 300yds] ⊕ CTV ⊕3 pin square 1P ⛟(30yds)

⊛ ♒(2m) ☎(100yds) ☒(100yds) ♫(100yds) ⛟(2m)

Min£45 Max£85pw (Low)
Min£95 Max£170pw (High)

F Dale House 13 St Mary's
for bookings Abbey House Self Catering Apartments, 2 St Mary's, Bootham, York
☎York(0904)707211 & Ripon(0765)5133

Three flats located within a Victorian terraced house comprising one double-

York

bedded room, one with either twin or bunk beds and folding beds are available in the sitting room, each have bathroom/WC and kitchen.

All year MWB 1 night min, 6 mths max, 3 units, 1–6 persons [◆] no pets ◉ fridge Electric Elec metered ⌷inclusive ☎ Airing cupboard in unit Iron in unit Ironing board in unit HCE in unit [Launderette within 300yds] ⊕ CTV ⊕3 pin square 1P 1♨ ⛟(100yds)

⊛ ♒(2m) ☎(100yds) ☒(100yds) ♫(100yds) ⛟(2m)

Min£40 Max£60pw (Low)
Min£85 Max£175pw (High)

C 537 Huntington Road Huntington
for bookings Mrs L Thorpe, Rosendal, Mill Hill, Huntington Road, Huntington, York YO3 9PY
☎York(0904)769375

Modernised two-storey 19th-century brick built semi-detached cottage on the edge of the village. The accommodation consists of two double-bedded rooms (one having a single bed in addition) bathroom with WC and sitting room/kitchen/dinette. There is also an outside drying area and a well kept front garden.

All year 1 wk min, 1 mth max, 1 unit, 1–5 persons ◆ ◉ fridge ♨ Electric Elec inclusive ⌷can be hired ☎(15yds) SD Airing cupboard in unit Iron in unit Ironing board in unit HCE in unit ⊕ ⊕3 pin square P ♨ ⛟(10yds)

⊛ ☎(200yds) ♫(3m) ⛟(3m)

Min£60 Max£80pw

1982 prices quoted throughout gazetteer

H Holiday Lettings Office, **University of York** Kings Manor, York YO1 2EP
☎York(0904)59861 ext 830

Thirty-four self-contained terraced houses near to the University campus. There are nine single bedrooms on the ground, first and second floors of each house, all with their own wash basins. Each house has a bathroom, separate shower and at least two WC's. There is also a kitchen/diner.

2 Jul–10 Sep 1 wk min, 10 wks max, 34 units, 1–9 persons ◆ ♦ fridge ♨ Gas/Elec inclusive ⌷inclusive ☎ [WM on premises] Iron in unit Ironing board in unit HCE ⊕ TV can be hired ⊕3 pin square 40P ▥ ⛟(½m)

⊛ ♒ ☎ ☒ ♫ ⛟

Min£115 Max£168.25pw

STOP PRESS

STRATTON
Suffolk
Map5 TM23

C 3 Stratton Hall Cottages Stratton Hall Drift
for bookings Mr Dellar, Stratton Hall, Levington, Ipswich, Suffolk
☎Nacton (047388)218

Modern farm cottage on high elevation and with fine views over the River Orwell. Separate dining and sitting rooms, both with open fireplaces. There are three first-floor bedrooms to sleep five. Location is ideal for those requiring a very rural holiday, or for sailing enthusiasts, as cottage is only ½m from Suffolk Yacht Harbour.

All year MWB out of season 3 days min, 4 wks max, 1 unit, 1–5 persons ◆ ◉ fridge Electric Elec metered ⌷not provided ☎(1m) Airing cupboard in unit Iron in unit Ironing board in unit HCE in unit TV ⊕3 pin square P ▥ ⛟(1m)

⊛ ☎(1m)

Min£45 Max£130pw

🅰🅰 GUESTHOUSES, FARMHOUSES AND INNS IN BRITAIN

Details of 3000 comfortable, budget-priced places to stay, all carefully checked by experienced AA inspectors.

AA Farmhouse of the Year — National and Regional winners. Colour photographs and descriptions of the places and the people.

Maps and town plans to help you find the location of your choice.

On sale at AA shops and major booksellers

County List

The following list of towns and villages at which self-catering accommodation listed in this guide are situated. It is arranged in three sections: England, Wales and Scotland. Each country is divided alphabetically into counties (regions in Scotland), under which locations are listed in alphabetical order.

ENGLAND

Avon
Chew Magna
Churchill
Temple Cloud
Weston-super-Mare

Buckinghamshire
Buckingham
Steeple Claydon
Wooburn Green

Cambridgeshire
Cambridge

Cornwall
Bodmin
Boscastle
Bude
Cadgwith
Camelford
Cardinham
Crackington Haven
Crantock
Cury
Downderry
Duloe
Falmouth
Fowey
Godolphin Cross
Goonhavern
Gooseham
Grampound
Gwinear
Gwithian
Hayle
Hellandbridge
Helston
Herodsfoot
Kilkhampton
Lanreath
Launceston
Lelant
Lesnewth
Liskeard
Lizard
Looe
Ludgvan
Marazion
Mawgan Porth
Menheniot
Mevagissey
Minions
Mixtow
Mullion
New Polzeath
Newquay
Padstow
Pelynt
Penzance
Perranporth
Polperro

Polyphant
Polzeath
Porth
Porthleven
Port Isaac
Port Navas
Portwrinkle
Poundstock
Restronguet
Rumford
St Agnes
St Anthony-in-Roseland
St Austell
St Breward
St Clether
St Erth
St Gennys
St Ives
St Just
St Keverne
St Kew
St Mellion
St Minver
St Newlyn East
St Saviours
St Thomas
St Tudy
Seaton
Sennen
Sennen Cove
Stibb
Tideford
Tintagel
Torpoint
Truro
Veryan
Wadebridge
Week St Mary
Widemouth Bay

Cumbria
Ambleside
Arnside
Bassenthwaite
Brampton
Broughton in Furness
Carlisle
Cartmel
Coniston
Gosforth
Grange-over-Sands
Grasmere
Hawkshead
Hesket Newmarket
High Lorton
Kendal
Keswick
Killington
Kirkby Lonsdale
Lamplugh
Lazonby
Low Hesket
Manesty

Nether Wasdale
Newby Bridge
Penton
Seatoller
Sedbergh
Silecroft
Spark Bridge
Staveley
Threlkeld
Troutbeck
Ulpha
Ulverston
Wasdale
Whicham
Windermere

Derbyshire
Ashbourne
Bakewell
Beeley
Buxton
Darley Dale
Edale
Fenny Bentley
Hartington
Hatton
Kniveton
Little Longstone
Litton
Longnor
Matlock
Parwich
Quarnford

Devon
Abbotsham
Ashburton
Ashreigney
Axmouth
Barnstaple
Berrynarbor
Bickleigh
Bideford
Bishopsteignton
Blackborough
Bovey Tracey
Branscombe
Bratton Fleming
Bridgerule
Brixham
Broadhembury
Buckfastleigh
Bucks Cross
Budleigh Salterton
Cadbury
Chagford
Challaborough Bay
Cheriton Bishop
Chillington
Chittlehampton
Christow
Chudleigh
Chudleigh Knighton
Chulmleigh

280

Churston Ferrers
Colaton Raleigh
Colyton
Combe Martin
Copplestone
Cornwood
Dartmouth
Dawlish
Dawlish Warren
Dolton
Drewsteignton
East Portlemouth
East Worlington
Ermington
Exbourne
Exeter
Exmouth
Feniton
Harpford
Hatherleigh
Hemyock
Highampton
Holbeton
Hollocombe
Holsworthy
Horns Cross
Ilfracombe
Ivybridge
Kentisbeare
Kentisburyford
Kenton
Kingsbridge
King's Nympton
Langtree
Littleham
Loddiswell
Loxbeare
Lustleigh
Lydford
Lympstone
Mamhead
Marldon
Metcombe
Mortehoe
Northam
Otterton
Ottery St Mary
Paignton
Parkham
Plymouth
Plymtree
Salcombe
Sampford Peverell
Seaton
Sidbury
Sidmouth
Smallridge
Southleigh
South Zeal
Sticklepath
Stockland
Stoke Fleming
Strete
Teignmouth
Tintagel
Torquay
Torrington (Great)
Totnes
Trusham
Uplyme
Weston
Westward Ho!
Whimple
Witheridge

Woody Bay
Woolacombe
Woolfardisworthy
Yarcombe
Yealmpton

Dorset
Bloxworth
Bournemouth & Boscombe
Bridport
Broadwindsor
Burton Bradstock
Charmouth
Holnest
Lydlinch
Lyme Regis
Marnhull
Milborne
Poole
Swanage
Thornford
Weymouth
Wool

Essex
Clacton-on-Sea
Colchester
Cressing
Orsett

Gloucestershire
Aldsworth
Bledington
Blockley
Bourton-on-the-Hill
Gloucester
Mitcheldean
Newland
Owlpen
Stanton
Staunton
Stone
Tewkesbury
Upper Slaughter
Weston Subedge
Winchcombe
Witcombe

Hampshire
Ashurst
Beaulieu
Hayling Island
Keyhaven
Lymington
Netley Marsh
New Milton
Woodlands

Hereford & Worcester
Abbey Dore
Almeley
Ashton
Bishopstone
Broadway
Carey
Dinmore
Docklow
Droitwich
Eckington

Hereford
How Caple
Inkberrow
Kemerton
Kentchurch
King's Caple
Lea
Ledbury
Leominster
Llangarron
Llangrove
Lyonshall
Madley
Malvern (Great)
Malvern Wells
Old Storridge
Pencoyd
Pencraig
Rock
Ross-on-Wye
Sedgeberrow
Shucknall
Stoke Lacey
Sutton St Nicholas
Weobley
Westhope
Weston Beggard
Wharton
Whitney
Wormelow

Humberside
Bridlington
Foxholes
Gransmoor
Sewerby

Isle of Wight
Bembridge
Colwell Bay
Culver Down
Freshwater Bay
Godshill
Newbridge
Niton
Ryde
St Lawrence
Seaview
Shanklin
Thorness Bay
Totland Bay
Ventnor
Wootton Bridge

Kent
Canterbury
Chillenden
Eastry
Goodnestone
Iden Green
Margate
Northbourne
Sevenoaks
Walmer

Lancashire
Blackpool
Heysham
Lytham St Annes
Morecambe
Scorton
Thornton Cleveleys
Westby with Plumpton
Whalley

County List

Leicestershire
Lyndon
Oakham

Lincolnshire
Calcethorpe
Legbourne
Scupholme
Skegness
Welton-le-Wold
Woodthorpe

London, Greater
Kingston upon Thames
London postal districts
see Gazetteer

Merseyside
Southport

Norfolk
Bacton
Briston
Burgh Castle
California
Cley next the Sea
Clippesby
Happisburgh Common
Hemsby
Hindringham
Holt
Horning
Hoveton St John
Hunstanton
Mundesley-on-Sea
North Creake
North Elmham
Scratby
Shipdham
South Raynham
Sparham
Starston
Stiffkey
Titchwell
Trimingham
Weybourne
Winterton-on-Sea
Wolferton
Wood Dalling
Worthing
Wramplingham
Wroxham

Northumberland
Alwinton
Berwick-upon-Tweed
Byrness
Chathill
Cheswick
Gilsland
Powburn
Shilbottle

Nottinghamshire
Epperstone

Oxfordshire
Bourton
Burford
Duns Tew
Goring-on-Thames
Mapledurham

Shropshire
All Stretton
Ashton-on-Clun
Bicton
Bridgnorth
Church Stretton
Cleeton St Mary
Diddlebury
Hopesay
Leebotwood
Leighton
Llanfair Waterdine
Twitchen
Weston under Redcastle

Somerset
Ashcott
Baltonsborough
Binegar
Burnham-on-Sea
Cheddar
Chilton Polden
Churchingford
Combe St Nicholas
Exford
Ilchester
Keinton Mandeville
Templecombe
Watchet
Wedmore
Wheddon Cross

Staffordshire
Alstonefield
Alton
Basford
Denford
Hollington
Ipstones
Kinver
Leek
Longnor
Rudyard
Sheen
Wetley Rocks

Suffolk
Aldeburgh
Cavendish
Dunwich
Gazely
Kessingland
Kirkton
Levington
Lowestoft
Peasenhall
Southwold
Stratton

Sussex (East)
Bexhill-on-Sea
Brighton
Camber
Eastbourne
Eastdean
Hastings
Newick
Robertsbridge
Splayne's Green

Sussex (West)
Bognor Regis
Cowfold
East Preston
Littlehampton
Middleton-on-Sea
Steyning
Worthing

Tyne & Wear
Elsdon

Warwickshire
Alcester
Canwell
Leamington Spa (Royal)
Little Compton
Stratford-upon-Avon

Wiltshire
Kingston Deverill
Sandy Lane

Yorkshire (North)
Bilton-on-Ainstey
Bishop Monkton
Copmanthorpe
Dunnington
Filey
Fylingdales
Gilling East
Grewelthorpe
Harrogate
Hawes
Hebden
Kirby Hill
Kirkby Malham
Malham
Masham
Pateley Bridge
Primrose Valley
Reighton Gap
Rosedale Abbey
Scarborough
Skelton
West Ayton
Whitby
York

Yorkshire (South)
Sheffield

Yorkshire (West)
Haworth
Leeds

Channel Islands
Alderney

Isle of Man
Douglas
Hilberry
Onchan
Ramsey

Isles of Scilly
Bryher
St Marys

WALES

Clwyd
Colwyn Bay
Derwen
Llangernyw
Prestatyn
Rhyl
Waen-yr-Hydd Foerdref

Dyfed
Aberporth
Aberystwyth
Amroth
Boncath
Borth
Broadhaven
Camrose
Capel Isaac
Cardigan
Cilgerran
Cosheston
Cresselly
Crymmych
Dale
Fishguard
Freshwater East
Haverfordwest
Jeffreston
Keeston
Kilgetty
Landshipping
Laugharne
Little Haven
Llandyssul
Llanstephan
Llwynda Fydd
Llanteg
Ludchurch
Lydstep
Manorbier
Narberth
Newport
Neyland
Oakford
Pantllyn
Pendine
Pontfaen
Ratford Bridge
Rhandirmywn
Sageston
St Davids
St Florence
St Ishmael
Saundersfoot
Solva
Stepsaside
Tavernspite
Tenby

Gwent
Monmouth
Raglan
Tintern

Gwynedd
Aberdaron
Aberdovey
Abersoch
Bangor
Barmouth
Bontddu
Bryncir
Caernarfon

Chwilog
Clynnog Fawr
Criccieth
Deganwy
Edern
Glan Conwy
Harlech
Llandanwg
Llandudno
Llandudno Junction
Llandwrog
Llandy Frydog
Llanengan
Llanfairfechan
Llangybi
Llanrug
Llwygwril
Nantlle
Parc
Pennal
Penrhyndeudraeth
Port Dinorwic
Pwllheli
Trearddur Bay
Tywyn
Ynys

Powys
Brecon
Bronydd
Builth Wells
Churchstoke
Crossgates
Garthmyl
Knighton
Knucklas
Llanfyllin
Llangunllo
Llangynidr
Llanrhaeadr-ym-Mochnant
Llansantffraid-ym-Mechain
Llanwrtyd Wells
Llawr-y-Glyn
Montgomery
Presteigne
Rhayader
Rhosgoch
Whitney

W Glamorgan
Caswell Bay
Horton
Mumbles
Oxwich
Scurlage

SCOTLAND

Borders
Bonchester Bridge
Burnmouth
Coldingham
Denholm
Dryburgh
Greenlaw
Hawick
Jedburgh
Kelso
Kirkton Manor
Lauder

Leadburn
Melrose
Newton St Boswells
Oxton
Peebles
Selkirk
Walkerburn
West Linton

Central
Airth
Callander
Fintry
Port of Menteith
Stirling
Strathyre

Dumfries & Galloway
Annan
Ardwell
Auchenmalg
Borgue
Cairn Ryan
Castle Douglas
Caulkerbush
Corsock
Crocketford
Crossmichael
Dalbeattie
Dalry
Elrig
Gatehouse of Fleet
Gelston
Glen Trool
Haugh of Urr
Kippford
Kirkbean
Kirkcudbright
Kirkpatrick Durham
Langholm
Meoul
Mochrum
Mossdale
New Galloway
Newton Stewart
Parton
Ringford
Rockcliffe
Sandyhills
Southerness
Southwick
Twynholm

Fife
Auchtermuchty
Rathillet
St Andrews

Grampian
Aberdeen
Aboyne
Alford
Alves
Ballater
Banchory
Buckie
Conicavel
Cornhill
Cullen
Dess
Dumphail
Elgin
Findochty

County List

Gartly
Glengairn
Logie-Buchan
Logie-Coldstone
Lumphanan
Montcoffer
Portknockie
Portsoy
Rafford
Redstone
Sandhaven
Tarland
Whitemire Village

Highland
Alcaig
Ardtornish
Aviemore
Ballachulish
Balnain
Banavie
Beauly
Bilbster
Boat of Garten
Carbost (Isle of Skye)
Carrbridge
Contin
Corpach
Culbrokie
Culkein
Culloden Moor
Dingwall
Dornoch
Drumnadrochit
Duirinish
Duisky
Dulnain Bridge
Dunvegan (Isle of Skye)
Evanton
Flichity
Fort William
Gairloch
Garvan
Glenborrodale
Golspie
Invergarry
Invermoriston
Inverness
Isle Ornsay (Isle of Skye)
Kentallen
Kilmorack
Kinlochewe
Kinlochleven
Kirkhill
Lairg
Leckmelm
Lentran
Lethen
Lochinver
Mellon Udrigle
Melvich
Muir of Ord
Nethy Bridge
Newton
Newtonmore
North Kessock
Onich
Portree (Isle of Skye)
Roy Bridge
Salen
Skeabost Bridge (Isle of Skye)
South Laggan
Spean Bridge
Spinningdale

Staffin (Isle of Skye)
Strontian
Tomatin
Ullapool
Watten
Whitebridge

Lothian
Dunbar
Edinburgh
North Berwick

Orkney
Finstown
Orphir
Stenness

Strathclyde
Achnamara
Appin
Ardbrecknish
Arden
Ardfern
Ballantrae
Balvicar
Biggar
Brodick (Isle of Arran)
Carnwath
Carrick Castle
Castle Sween
Clachan Seil
Coll (Isle of)
Connel
Crinan
Cullipool (Isle of Luing)
Dervaig
Dolphinton
Dougarie (Isle of Arran)
Drimnin
Dunsyre
Easdale
Ellary
Girvan
Glasgow
Grantown on Spey
Hollybush
Kilchattan (Isle of Colonsay)
Kilkerran
Kilmarnock
Kilmelford
Kilmore
Kilmory
Kilninver
Kiloran (Isle of Colonsay)
Kiloran Bay (Isle of Colonsay)
Kilsyth
Lamlash (Isle of Arran)
Lendalfoot
Lerags
Lochead
Muasdale
Oban
Ormsary
Port Appin
Port Charlotte (Isle of Islay)
Portsonachan
Rothesay (Isle of Bute)
Scalasaig (Isle of Colonsay)
Skipness
Sorn
Straiton

Taynuilt
Tobermory (Isle of Mull)
Torloisk (Isle of Mull)

Tayside
Aberfeldy
Alyth
Auchterarder
Balgedie
Ballintuim
Bankfoot
Birnam
Blacklunans
Blairgowrie
Bridge of Earn
Butterstone
Calvine
Crieff
Dollerie
Dundee
Dunning
Glenisla
Glenshee (Spittal of)
Inverkeilor
Killiecrankie
Kinloch Rannoch
Kirkmichael
Leysmill
Meigle
Tyndrum

Western Isles
Castlebay (Isle of Barra)
Earsary (Isle of Barra)
Kentangaval (Isle of Barra)

London Postal Districts and ways in & out of London

Aylesbury • Hatfield • A1

M1 & The North • M1 • A41

WHETSTONE N20 • SOUTH GATE N14 • A1000

STANMORE • AA 24 hour

EDGWARE

NORTH FINCHLEY N12 • NEW SOUTHGATE N11

MILL HILL NW7 • NW

N

WOO

↑ N • AA

FINCHLEY N3 • EAST FINCHLEY • MUSWELL HILL N10

Rickmansworth • HENDON NW4 • N2

KINGSBURY NW9 • GOLDERS GREEN NW11 • HIGHGATE N6 • HORN N8 • A1

HARROW • A5 • M1 • A41

A404

Brent Cross Flyover • Road

UPPER HOLLOWAY N19 • AA

WEMBLEY • CRICKLEWOOD NW2 • HAMPSTEAD NW3 • KENTISH TOWN NW5 • HOLLOW N7

Oxford • A40 • GREENFORD • North Circular • KILBURN NW6 • ST JOHNS WOOD NW8 • CAMDEN TOWN NW1 • Road • Euston

A404

WILLESDEN NW10 • A404 • Ring • WC1

HANWELL W7 • WEST EALING W13 • A406 • NTH KEN W10 • W9 • MAIDA HILL • W1

Uxbridge • A4020 • EALING W5 • ACTON W3 • SHEPHERDS BUSH W12 • A40 M • NOTTING HILL W11 • PADDINGTON W2 • Hyde Pk Cnr • WC2

Heathrow Airport • M4 • W • KENSING-TON W8 • Marble Arch • STH KEN SW7 • SW1

Slough & The West • Kew Bridge • HAMMER SMITH W6 • W KEN W14 • WEST-MINSTER • KENNI TON SE11

Staines & The South-West • A4 • CHISWICK W4 • AA • EARLS COURT SW5 • CHELSEA SW3 • A308

Elevated Motorway • A205 • BARNES SW13 • BROMPTON SW10 • SOUTH LAMBETH SW8

FULHAM SW6 • BATTERSEA SW11 • STOC SV

M3 & The South-West • A316 • MORTLAKE SW14 • PUTNEY SW15 • South Circular • Road • A3 • CLAPHAM SW4 • BRIXT SW2

TWICKENHAM • RICHMOND • A306 • WANDSWORTH SW18 • BALHAM SW12

SW • TOOTING SW17 • A24

WIMBLEDON SW19 • A219

AA • TEDDINGTON • A308 • A3 • WEST WIMBLEDON SW20 • STREATHAM SW16 • MITCHAM • Brighton Eastbourne

A308 • A307 • KINGSTON-UPON-THAMES • AA • Dorking Guildford • A24 • Epsom • A217 • Reigate

London Postal Area Boundary
London Postal District Boundaries
Main Roads into and out of London
Signposted North and South Circular
Roads & Ring Road
Other Main Roads

Service Centre **AA**

Scale of Miles
0 1 2 3 4

mbridge
A10

LOWER EDMONTON N9

CHINGFORD E4

UPPER EDMONTON N18

OTTENHAM N17

Epping
Bishops Stortford

A104 M11

WOODFORD E18

A406

Chelmsford
Southend

OUTH TENHAM N15

A503

WALTHAMSTOW E17

A114

GANTS HILL

A12

A12

Romford

OKE INGTON N16

A10

LEYTON E10

LEYTONSTONE E11

CLAPTON E5

E

FOREST GATE E7

MANOR PARK E12

ILFORD

HOMERTON E9

A11

HACKNEY E8

BETHNAL GREEN E2

BOW E3

STRATFORD E15

A117

BARKING

Tilbury
A13

PLAISTOW E13

EAST HAM E6

A13

R THAMES

STEPNEY E1

POPLAR E14

NORTH WOOLWICH E16

THAMESMEAD SE28

ROTHERHITHE SE16

Ring Road

Free Ferry

ABBEY WOOD SE2

Erith
A206

DEPTFORD SE8

CHARLTON SE7

A205

WOOLWICH SE18

NEW CROSS SE14

GREEN WICH SE10

A2

A102M

ar Rd

A202

PECKHAM SE15

BLACKHEATH SE3

WELLING

A207

EAST DULWICH SE22

BROCKLEY SE4

LEWISHAM SE13

A21

A20

South

ELTHAM SE9

A2

FOREST HILL SE23

Rochester
Motorway
Dover

A205

LEE SE12

A20

CATFORD SE6

SE

SYDENHAM SE26

SIDCUP

ANERLEY SE20

A20

Maidstone
Folkestone

TH WOOD 25

A21

BROMLEY
Sevenoaks

Sevenoaks
Hastings

A224

BECKENHAM

© The Automobile Association 1982

287

The National Grid

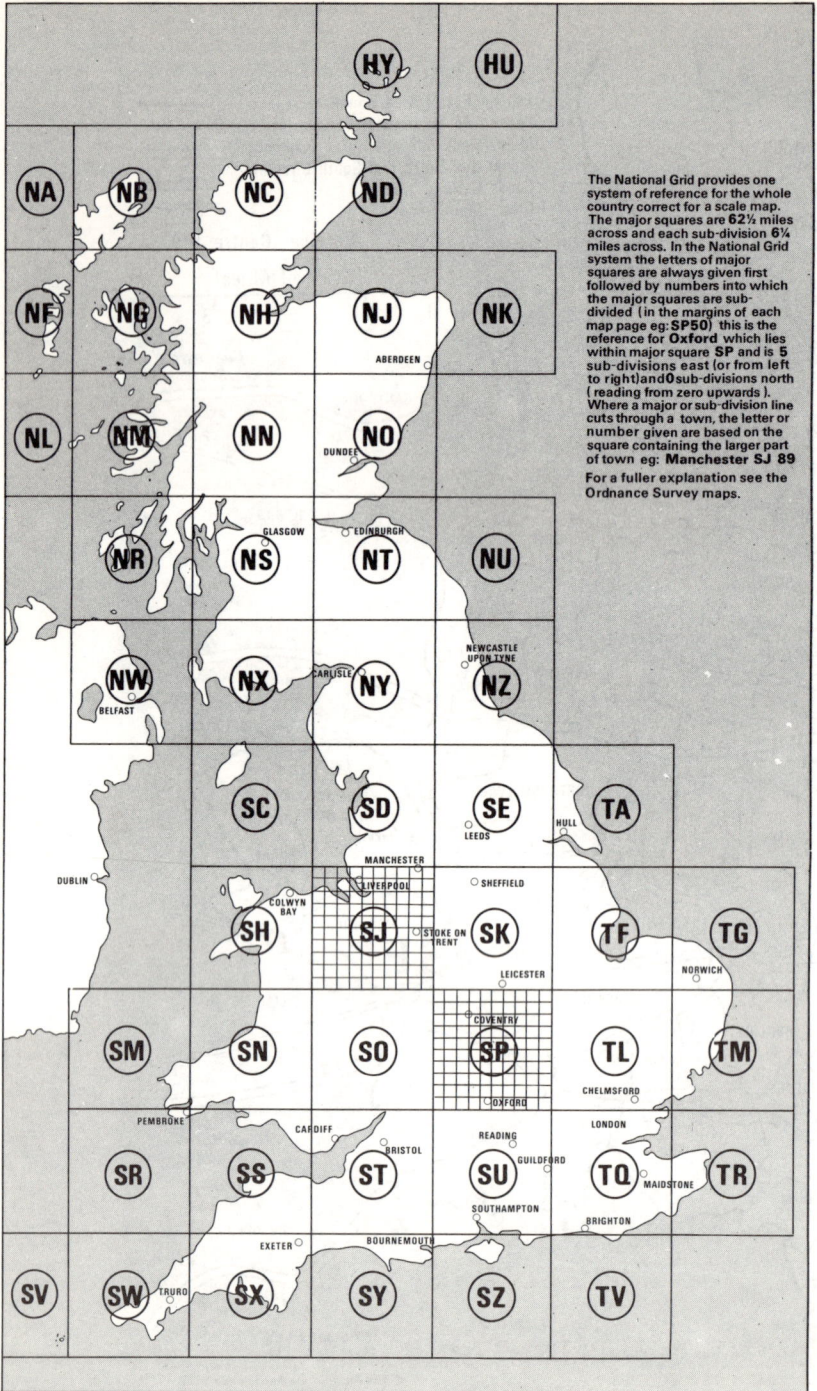

The National Grid provides one system of reference for the whole country correct for a scale map. The major squares are 62½ miles across and each sub-division 6¼ miles across. In the National Grid system the letters of major squares are always given first followed by numbers into which the major squares are sub-divided (in the margins of each map page eg: **SP50**) this is the reference for **Oxford** which lies within major square **SP** and is **5** sub-divisions east (or from left to right) and **0** sub-divisions north (reading from zero upwards). Where a major or sub-division line cuts through a town, the letter or number given are based on the square containing the larger part of town eg: **Manchester SJ 89**

For a fuller explanation see the Ordnance Survey maps.

HY HU

NA NB NC ND

NF NG NH NJ NK
ABERDEEN

NL NM NN NO
DUNDEE

NR NS NT NU
GLASGOW EDINBURGH

NW NX NY NZ
BELFAST CARLISLE NEWCASTLE UPON TYNE

SC SD SE TA
LEEDS HULL
MANCHESTER

SH SJ SK TF TG
COLWYN BAY LIVERPOOL STOKE ON TRENT SHEFFIELD NORWICH
DUBLIN LEICESTER

SM SN SO SP TL TM
COVENTRY CHELMSFORD
PEMBROKE OXFORD

SR SS ST SU TQ TR
CARDIFF BRISTOL READING GUILDFORD LONDON MAIDSTONE
SOUTHAMPTON BRIGHTON

SV SW SX SY SZ TV
TRURO EXETER BOURNEMOUTH

Key to Atlas

16 Orkney and Shetland Islands

Thurso

Wick

Stornoway

13 Portree

14

Banff

15 Peterhead

Inverness

Aberdeen

Fort William

Pitlochry

SCALE

mls 0   30   60
kms 0   50   100

Oban

Perth

Dundee

Stirling

Glasgow

Edinburgh

Largs

Berwick

Campbeltown

Peebles

10

11

12

Ayr

Dumfries

Stranraer

Carlisle

Workington

Douglas

Kendal

Scarborough

Lancaster

York

Blackpool

Leeds

8 Hull

Manchester

Grimsby

9

Liverpool

7

Sheffield

6

Caernarfon

Chester

Stoke

Nottingham

Shrewsbury

King's Lynn

Leicester

Norwich

Aberystwyth

Peterborough

Birmingham

Coventry

Worcester

Northampton

Cambridge

Carmarthen

Hereford

Gloucester

Pembroke

Swansea

Oxford

Chelmsford

5

Cardiff

Bristol

4

Reading

LONDON

Maidstone

2

3

Taunton

Salisbury

Basingstoke

Guildford

Brighton

Exeter

Bournemouth

Truro

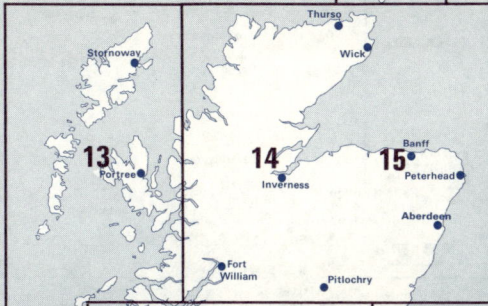

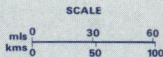

See Page 16 for Channel Islands

Maps produced by

The AA Cartographic Department
(Publications Division), Fanum House,
Basingstoke, Hampshire RG21 2EA

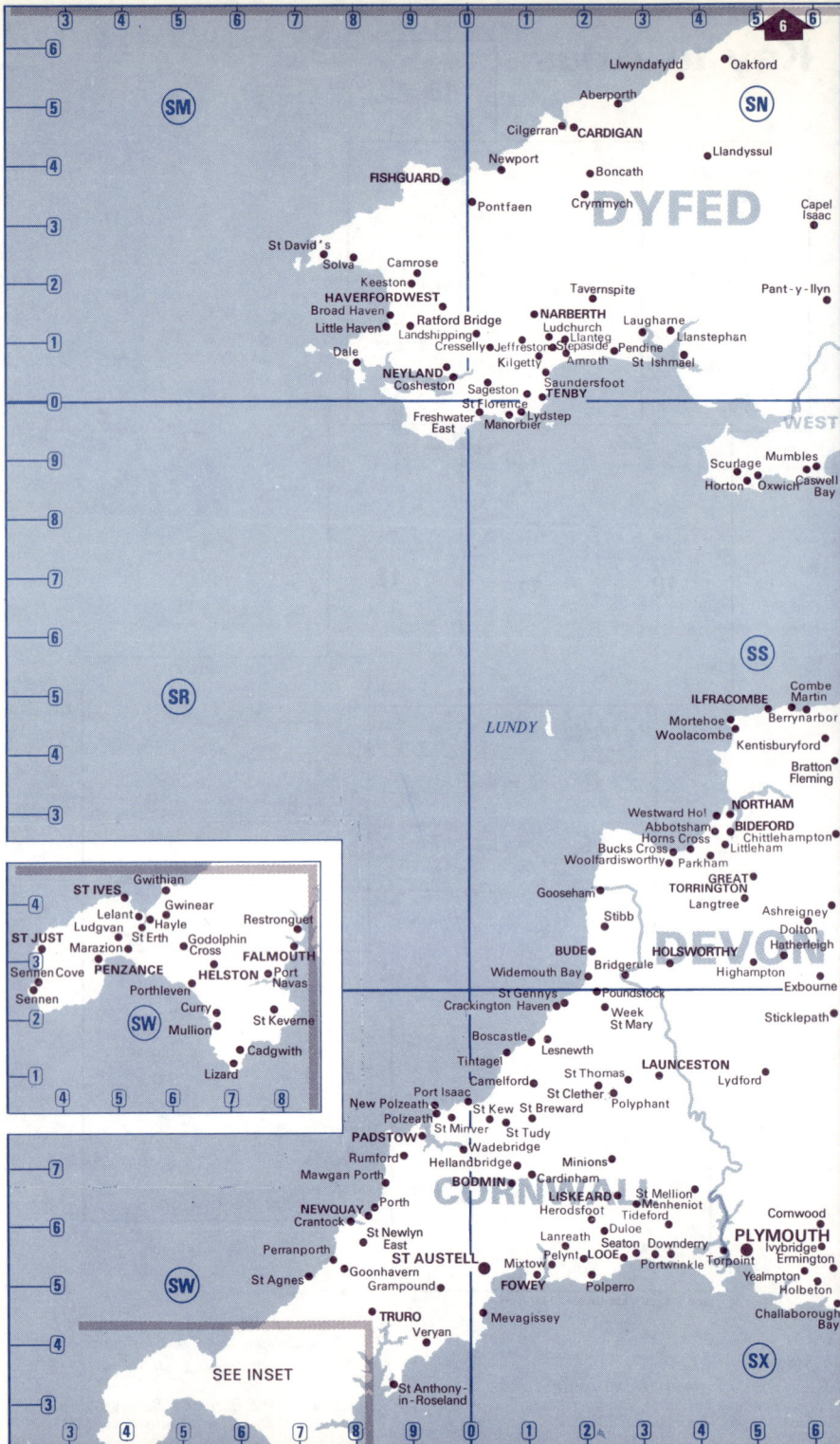

SM

SN

Llwyndafydd Oakford
Aberporth
Cilgerran **CARDIGAN**
Newport
Pontfaen Boncath Llandyssul
Crymmych
DYFED
Capel Isaac

St David's Solva Camrose
Keeston
HAVERFORDWEST
Broad Haven
Little Haven Ratford Bridge Ludchurch
Landshipping **NARBERTH** Laugharne
Dale Cresselly Jeffreston Llanteg Llanstephan
Kilgetty Stepaside Pendine
NEYLAND Amroth St Ishmael
Cosheston Sageston Saundersfoot
St Florence **TENBY**
Freshwater East Lydstep
Manorbier

Tavernspite

Pant-y-llyn

WEST

Scurlage Mumbles
Horton Oxwich Caswell Bay

SR

LUNDY

SS

ILFRACOMBE Combe Martin
Mortehoe Berrynarbor
Woolacombe Kentisburyford
Bratton Fleming
Westward Ho! **NORTHAM**
Abbotsham **BIDEFORD**
Horns Cross Chittlehampton
Bucks Cross Littleham
Woolfardisworthy Parkham
GREAT TORRINGTON
Gooseham Langtree Ashreigney
Stibb Dolton
Hatherleigh
BUDE **HOLSWORTHY**
Widemouth Bay Bridgerule Highampton
St Gennys Poundstock Exbourne
Crackington Haven Week Sticklepath
St Mary
Boscastle Lesnewth
Tintagel St Thomas **LAUNCESTON**
Camelford St Clether Lydford
Port Isaac St Breward Polyphant
New Polzeath St Kew
Polzeath St Minver St Tudy
PADSTOW Wadebridge
Rumford Hellandbridge Minions
Mawgan Porth **BODMIN** Cardinham
NEWQUAY Porth **LISKEARD** St Mellion
Crantock Herodsfoot Menheniot
St Newlyn East Lanreath Tideford Cornwood
Perranporth Duloe **PLYMOUTH**
ST AUSTELL Seaton Downderry Ivybridge
St Agnes Goonhavern Mixtow Pelynt **LOOE** Ermington
Grampound Portwrinkle Torpoint Yealmpton
FOWEY Polperro Holbeton
TRURO Mevagissey Challaborough Bay
Veryan

DEVON

CORNWALL

SX

SEE INSET

St Anthony-in-Roseland

Inset

St Ives Gwithian
Gwinear
Lelant Hayle Restronguet
Ludgvan St Erth
St Just Marazion Godolphin Cross **FALMOUTH**
Sennen Cove **PENZANCE** **HELSTON** Port Navas
Sennen Porthleven
Curry St Keverne
Mullion
Cadgwith
Lizard

SW

For continuation pages refer to numbered arrows

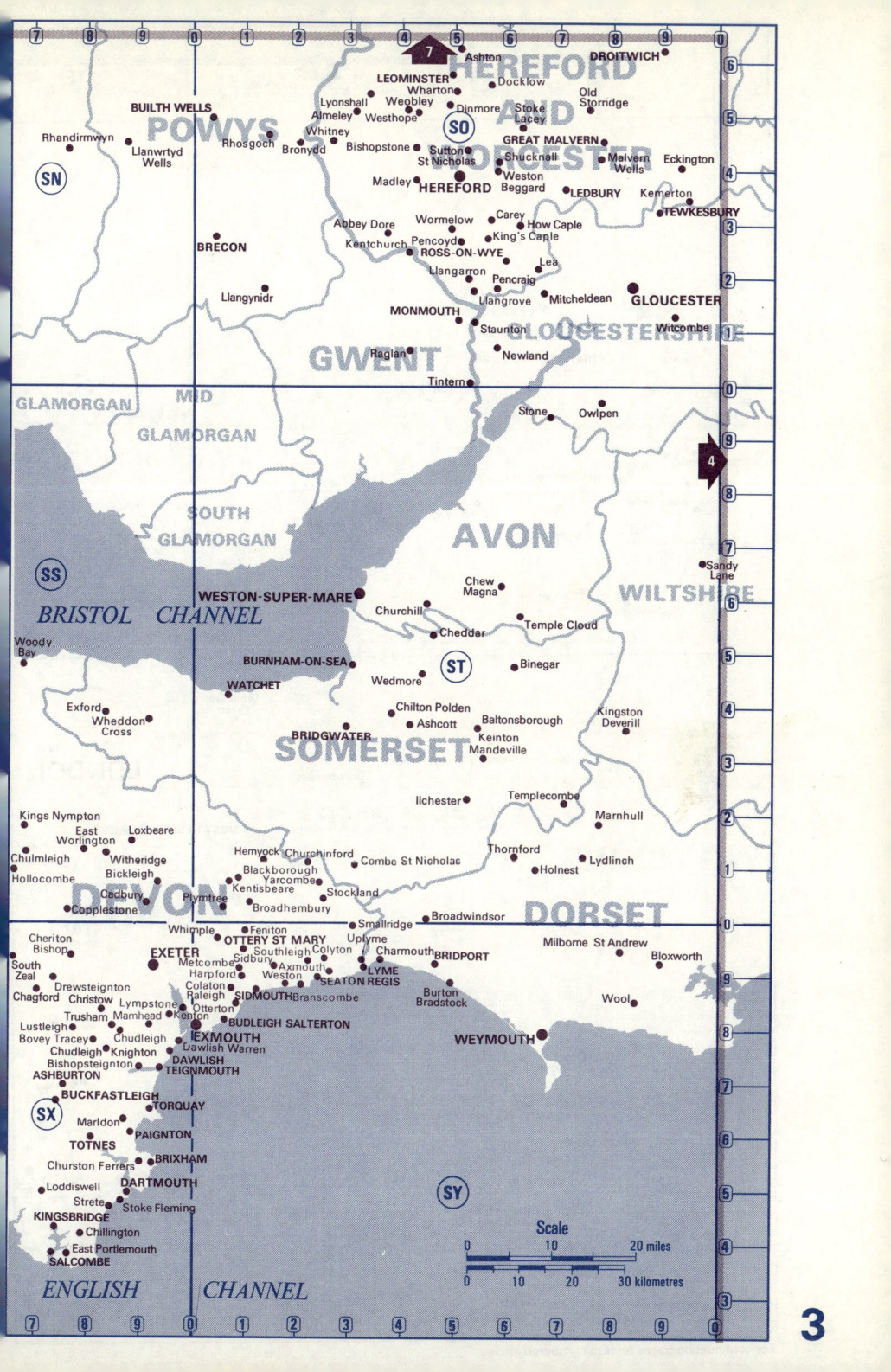

Map grid numbers (top): 7 8 9 0 1 2 3 4 5 6 7 8 9 0

POWYS

SN

Rhandirmwyn
Llanwrtyd Wells
BUILTH WELLS
Rhosgoch
Bronydd
BRECON
Llangynidr

HEREFORD AND MID GLOUCESTER

Ashton
LEOMINSTER
Wharton
DROITWICH
Docklow
Old Storridge
Lyonshall
Weobley
Almeley
Westhope
Whitney
Dinmore
Stoke Lacey
SO
Bishopstone
Sutton St Nicholas
GREAT MALVERN
Shucknall
Malvern Wells
Eckington
Madley
Weston Beggard
HEREFORD
LEDBURY
Kemerton
TEWKESBURY
Abbey Dore
Wormelow
Carey
How Caple
King's Caple
Kentchurch
Pencoyd
ROSS-ON-WYE
Lea
Llangarron
Pencraig
GLOUCESTER
Llangrove
Mitcheldean
MONMOUTH
Llangrove
Staunton
Witcombe
GLOUCESTERSHIRE
Raglan
Newland

GWENT

Tintern

Stone
Owlpen

GLAMORGAN

MID GLAMORGAN

SOUTH GLAMORGAN

AVON

Chew Magna
Sandy Lane
WILTSHIRE

SS

BRISTOL CHANNEL

WESTON-SUPER-MARE
Churchill
Temple Cloud
Cheddar
Woody Bay
BURNHAM-ON-SEA
ST
Binegar
WATCHET
Wedmore
Exford
Wheddon Cross
Chilton Polden
Ashcott
Baltonsborough
Kingston Deverill
BRIDGWATER
Keinton Mandeville

SOMERSET

Kings Nympton
East Worlington
Loxbeare
Ilchester
Templecombe
Marnhull
Chulmleigh
Witheridge
Thornford
Lydlinch
Hollocombe
Bickleigh
Cadbury
Holnest
Hemyock
Churchinford
Combe St Nicholas
Blackborough
Yarcombe
Copplestone
Plymtree
Kentisbeare
Stockland

DEVON

Broadhembury
Smallridge
Broadwinsor
DORSET
Whimple
Feniton
Uplyme
Cheriton Bishop
OTTERY ST MARY
Southleigh
Colyton
Charmouth
Milborne St Andrew
EXETER
Metcombe
Sidbury
Axmouth
BRIDPORT
Bloxworth
South Zeal
Harpford
Weston
LYME REGIS
Drewsteignton
Colaton Raleigh
SEATON REGIS
Chagford
Christow
Otterton
SIDMOUTH
Branscombe
Burton Bradstock
Wool
Trusham
Mamhead
Kenton
Lustleigh
Lympstone
BUDLEIGH SALTERTON
Bovey Tracey
Chudleigh
EXMOUTH
WEYMOUTH
Chudleigh Knighton
Dawlish Warren
Bishopsteignton
DAWLISH
ASHBURTON
TEIGNMOUTH
SX
BUCKFASTLEIGH
Marldon
TORQUAY
TOTNES
PAIGNTON
Churston Ferrers
BRIXHAM
Loddiswell
DARTMOUTH
Strete
Stoke Fleming
KINGSBRIDGE
Chillington
SY
East Portlemouth
SALCOMBE

ENGLISH CHANNEL

Scale

0 10 20 miles

0 10 20 30 kilometres

3

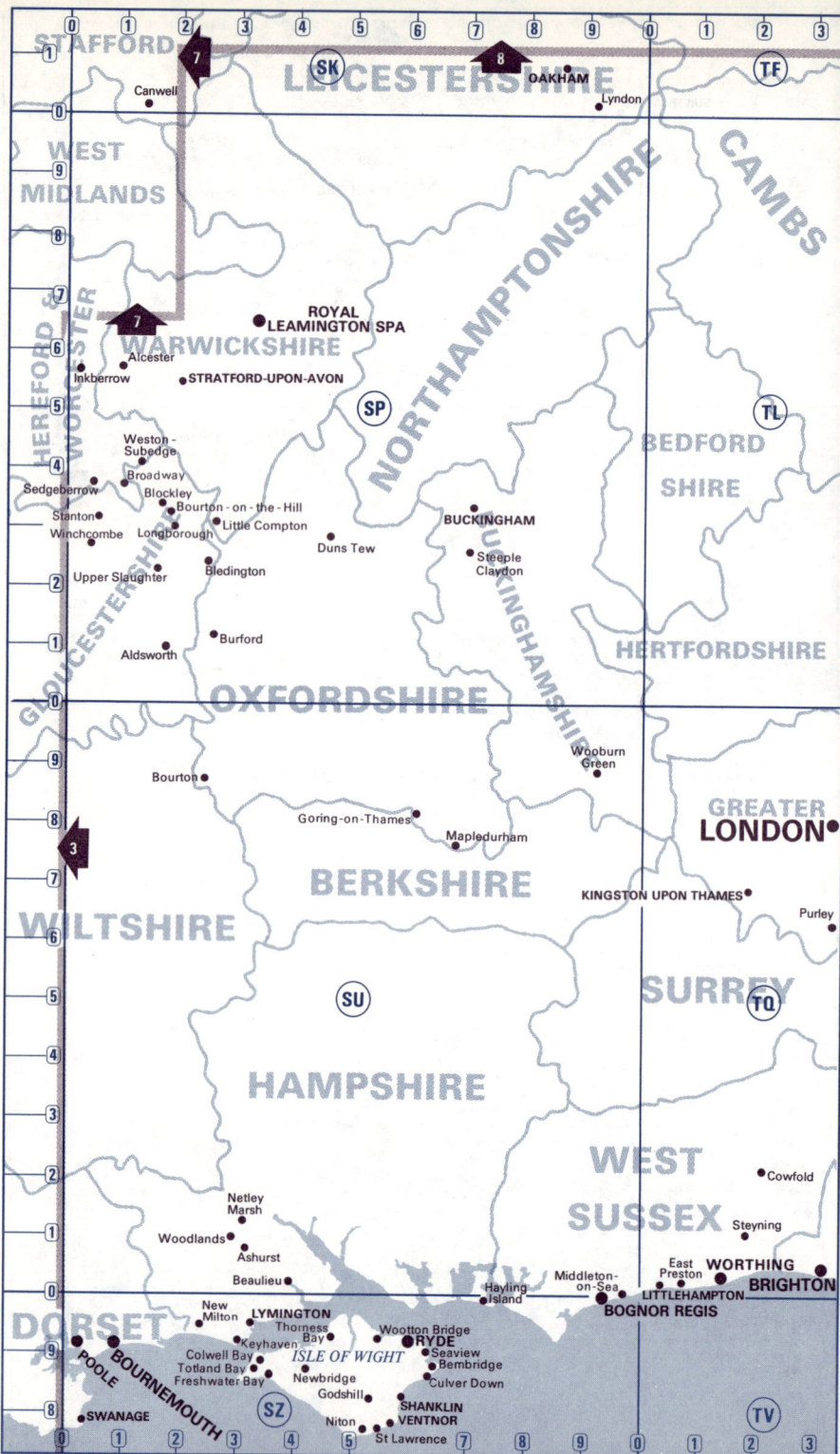

0 1 2 3 4 5 6 7 8 9 0 1 2 3

1

7

SK

8

OAKHAM

TF

Canwell

0

LEICESTERSHIRE

Lyndon

WEST
MIDLANDS

9

8

7

6

7

NORTHAMPTONSHIRE

CAMBS

ROYAL
LEAMINGTON SPA

WARWICKSHIRE

Alcester

Inkberrow

STRATFORD-UPON-AVON

5

SP

TL

BEDFORD
SHIRE

HEREFORD & WORCESTER

Weston-
Subedge

4

Broadway

Sedgeberrow

Blockley

Stanton

Bourton - on - the - Hill

BUCKINGHAM

Winchcombe

Longborough

Little Compton

Duns Tew

Steeple
Claydon

Upper Slaughter

2

Bledington

1

Burford

Aldsworth

GLOUCESTERSHIRE

0

OXFORDSHIRE

HERTFORDSHIRE

9

Wooburn
Green

Bourton

8

Goring-on-Thames

GREATER
LONDON

Mapledurham

3

WILTSHIRE

6

BERKSHIRE

KINGSTON UPON THAMES

7

Purley

5

SU

SURREY

TQ

4

3

HAMPSHIRE

WEST

2

Cowfold

Netley
Marsh

SUSSEX

Steyning

Woodlands

1

Ashurst

East
Preston

WORTHING

Beaulieu

0

Middleton-
on-Sea

BRIGHTON

New
Milton

LYMINGTON

Thorness
Bay

Wootton Bridge

Hayling
Island

LITTLEHAMPTON

BOGNOR REGIS

DORSET

9

Keyhaven

RYDE

Seaview

POOLE

BOURNEMOUTH

Colwell Bay

Totland Bay

Freshwater Bay

Newbridge

ISLE OF WIGHT

Bembridge

Culver Down

Godshill

SHANKLIN

SZ

VENTNOR

8

SWANAGE

Niton

St Lawrence

TV

0 1 2 3 4 5 6 7 8 9 0 1 2 3

4

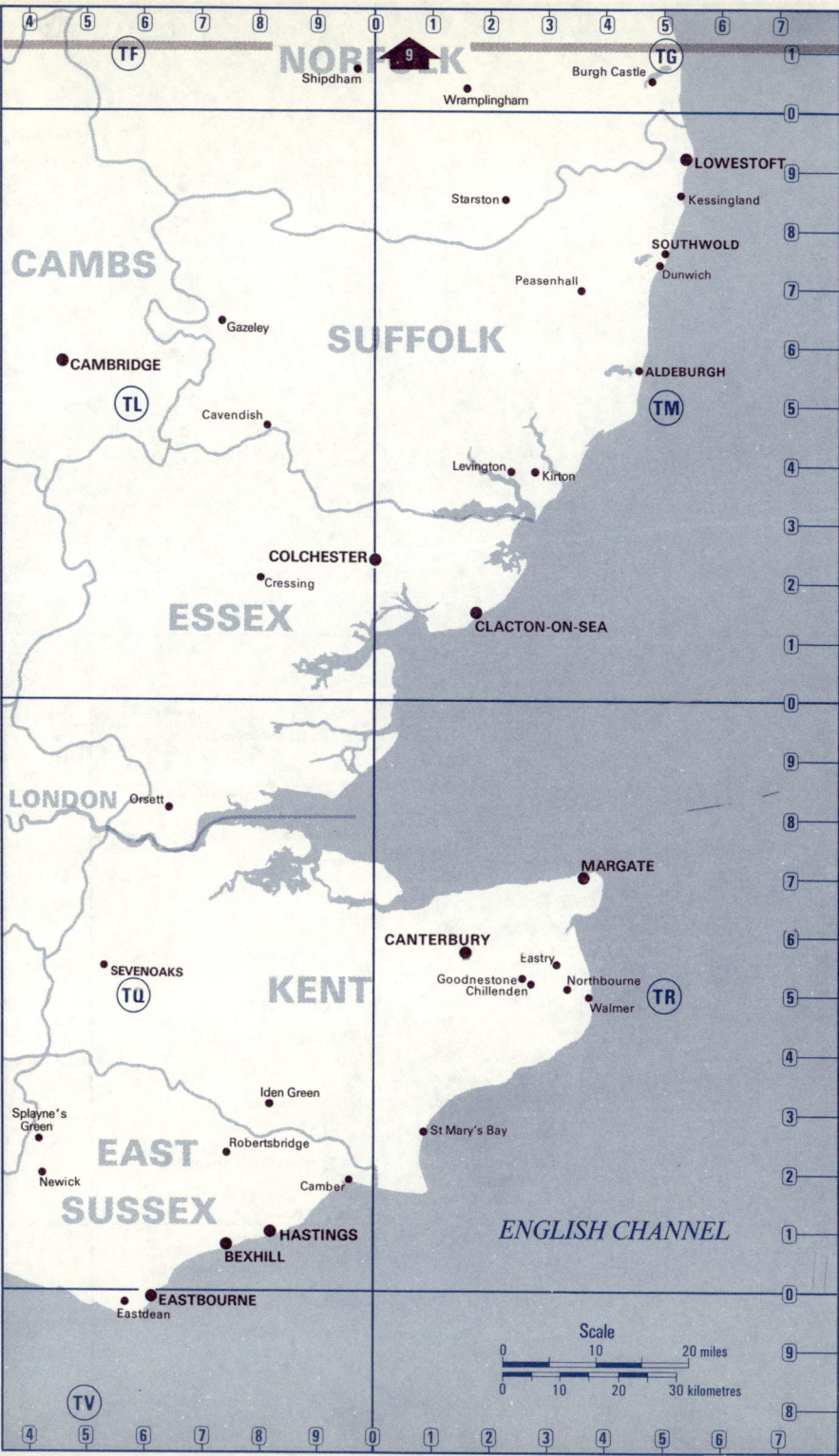

NORFOLK

TF

TG

Shipdham

Wramplingham

Burgh Castle

LOWESTOFT

Starston

Kessingland

SOUTHWOLD

CAMBS

Peasenhall

Dunwich

SUFFOLK

Gazeley

ALDEBURGH

CAMBRIDGE

TL

TM

Cavendish

Levington

Kirton

COLCHESTER

Cressing

ESSEX

CLACTON-ON-SEA

LONDON

Orsett

MARGATE

CANTERBURY

Eastry

SEVENOAKS

Goodnestone

Northbourne

TQ

Chillenden

TR

KENT

Walmer

Iden Green

Splayne's Green

St Mary's Bay

Robertsbridge

Newick

Camber

EAST

SUSSEX

HASTINGS

ENGLISH CHANNEL

BEXHILL

EASTBOURNE

Eastdean

TV

Scale

0   10   20 miles

0   10   20   30 kilometres

5

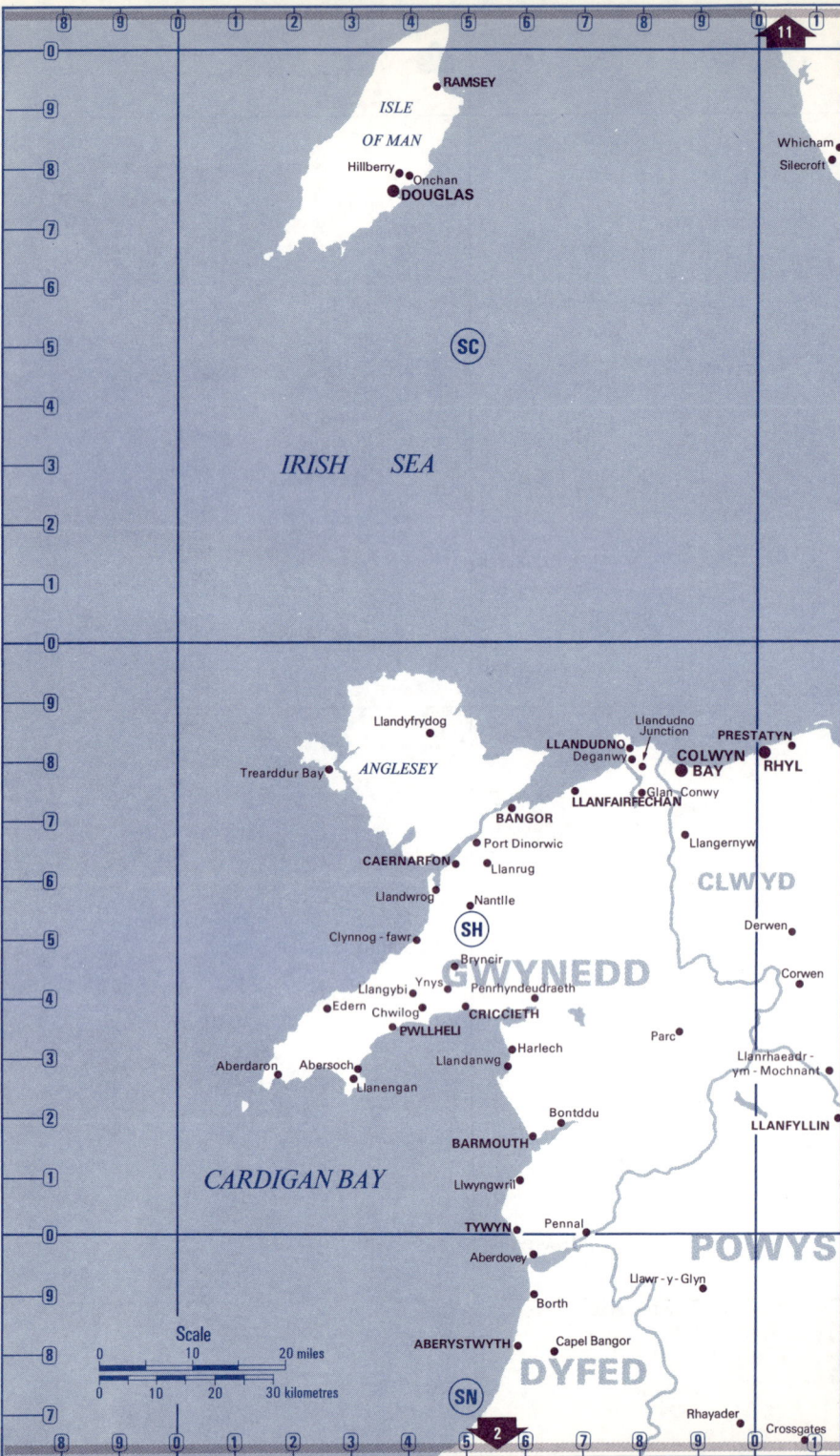

RAMSEY

ISLE
OF MAN

Hillberry
Onchan
DOUGLAS

Whicham
Silecroft

SC

IRISH   SEA

Llandyfrydog

ANGLESEY

Trearddur Bay

Llandudno
Junction

LLANDUDNO
Deganwy

PRESTATYN

COLWYN
BAY

RHYL

Glan - Conwy

LLANFAIRFECHAN

BANGOR

Port Dinorwic

Langernyw

CAERNARFON

Llanrug

CLWYD

Llandwrog

Nantlle

Derwen

Clynnog - fawr

SH

Bryncir

Corwen

GWYNEDD

Ynys

Llangybi

Penrhyndeudraeth

Edern

Chwilog

CRICCIETH

Parc

Llanrhaeadr -
ym - Mochnant

PWLLHELI

Harlech

Aberdaron

Abersoch

Llandanwg

Llanengan

Bontddu

LLANFYLLIN

BARMOUTH

CARDIGAN BAY

Llwyngwril

POWYS

Pennal

TYWYN

Aberdovey

Llawr - y - Glyn

Borth

Scale
10
20 miles

10   20   30 kilometres

ABERYSTWYTH

Capel Bangor

DYFED

SN

Rhayader

Crossgates

2

For continuation pages refer to numbered arrows

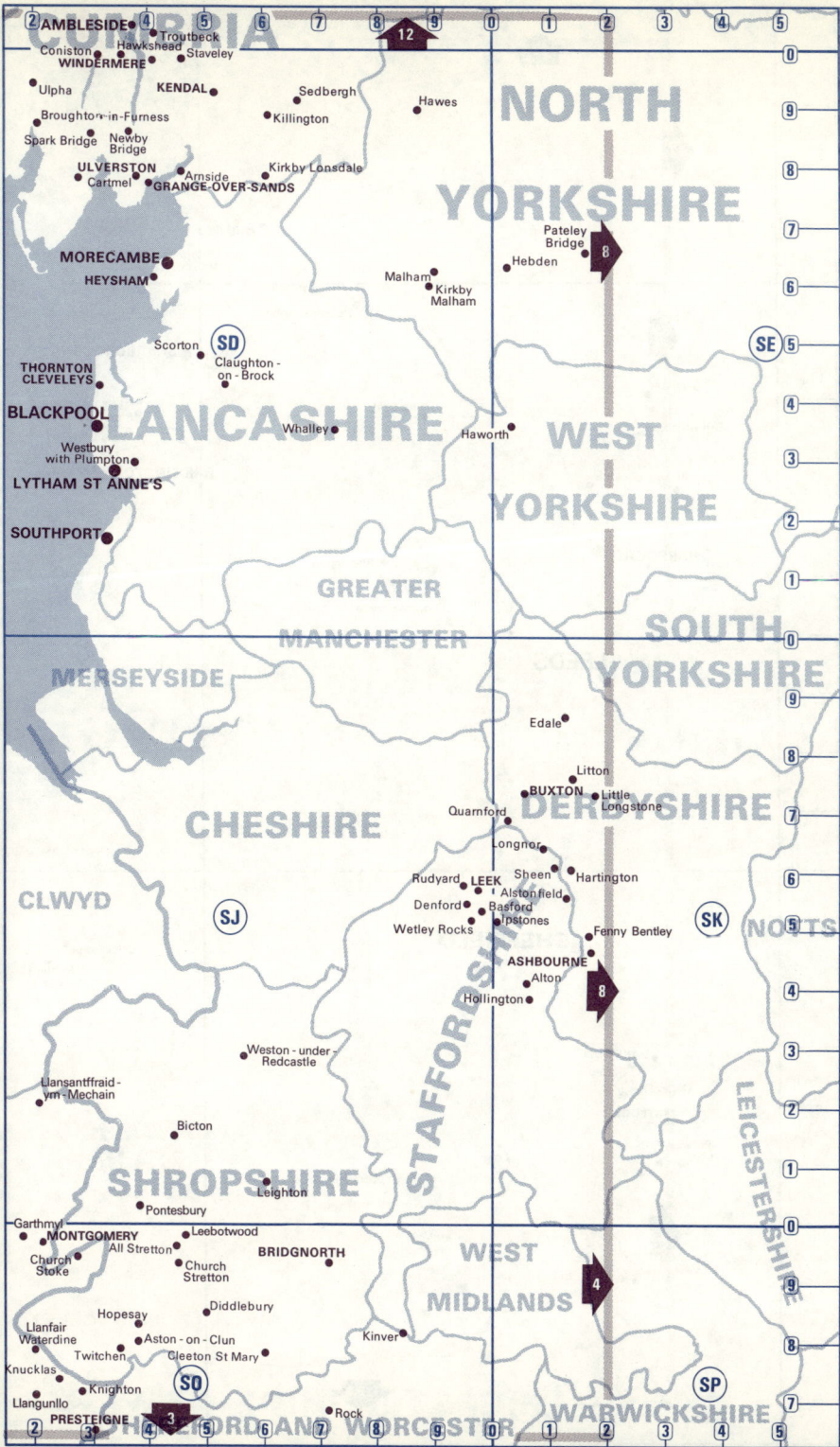

AMBLESIDE
Troutbeck
Coniston
Hawkshead
Staveley
WINDERMERE
Ulpha
KENDAL
Sedbergh
Broughton-in-Furness
Killington
Hawes
Spark Bridge
Newby Bridge
ULVERSTON
Arnside
Kirkby Lonsdale
Cartmel
GRANGE-OVER-SANDS

NORTH YORKSHIRE

MORECAMBE
HEYSHAM

Pateley Bridge
Hebden

Scorton
SD
Claughton-on-Brock

Malham
Kirkby Malham

THORNTON CLEVELEYS

SE

BLACKPOOL
LANCASHIRE
Whalley
Haworth

WEST YORKSHIRE

Westbury with Plumpton
LYTHAM ST ANNE'S

SOUTHPORT

GREATER MANCHESTER

SOUTH YORKSHIRE

MERSEYSIDE

Edale
Litton
BUXTON
Little Longstone
CHESHIRE
Quarnford
DERBYSHIRE

Longnor
Sheen
Hartington
Rudyard
LEEK
CLWYD
Denford
Alstonfield
SJ
Basford
Ipstones
Wetley Rocks
Fenny Bentley
SK
NOTTS

ASHBOURNE
Alton
Hollington
8

Weston-under-Redcastle

Llansantffraid-ym-Mechain

LEICESTERSHIRE

Bicton

SHROPSHIRE
Leighton

Pontesbury

Garthmyl
MONTGOMERY
Leebotwood
All Stretton
WEST MIDLANDS
Church Stoke
Church Stretton
BRIDGNORTH
4

Hopesay
Diddlebury
Llanfair Waterdine
Aston-on-Clun
Kinver
Twitchen
Cleeton St Mary
Knucklas
Knighton
SO
Llangunllo
Rock
SP
PRESTEIGNE
HEREFORD AND WORCESTER
WARWICKSHIRE
STAFFORDSHIRE

7

8

Grid references (top)
0 1 2 3 4 5 6 7 8 9 0 1 2 3

Grid references (left)
4 3 2 1 0 9 8 7 6 5 4 3 2 1 0 9 8 7 6 5 4 3 2 1

Grid references (bottom)
0 1 2 3 4 5 6 7 8 9 0 1 2 3

DURHAM

CLEVELAND

NORTH

YORKSHIRE

WEST

YORKSHIRE

SOUTH

YORKSHIRE

HUMBERSIDE

DERBYSHIRE

NOTTINGHAMSHIRE

LINCOLNSHIRE

STAFFORDSHIRE

LEICESTERSHIRE

12 NZ

12

7

NZ SE TA SK TF

WHITBY
Fylingdales
Rosedale Abbey
West Ayton
SCARBOROUGH
Masham
Gilling East
FILEY
Primrose Valley
Reighton Gap
Grewelthorpe
Foxholes
Bishop Monkton
BRIDLINGTON Sewerby
Pateley Bridge
Gransmoor
HARROGATE
Skelton
Dunnington
SE
YORK
Bilton in Ainstey
Copmanthorpe
LEEDS
SHEFFIELD
Calcethorpe
Welton le Wold
BAKEWELL
Beeley
Darley Dale
MATLOCK
Parwich
SK
Kniveton
Epperstone
TF
7
Hatton
4

For continuation pages refer to numbered arrows

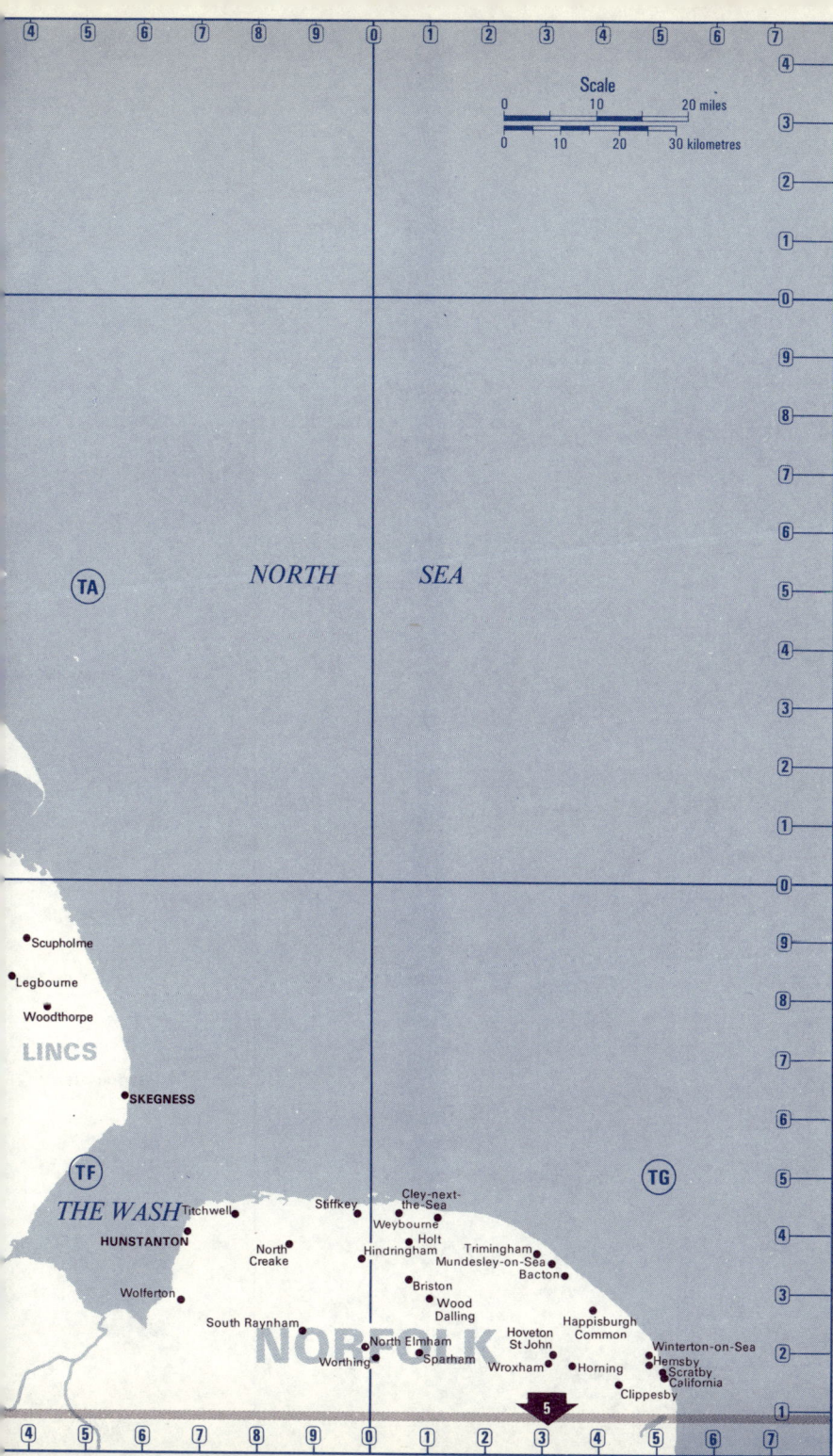

Scale

0   10   20 miles

0   10   20   30 kilometres

NORTH   *SEA*

TA

Scupholme

Legbourne

Woodthorpe

LINCS

SKEGNESS

TF

THE WASH

HUNSTANTON

TG

Titchwell

Stiffkey

Cley-next-the-Sea

Weybourne

Holt

North Creake

Hindringham

Trimingham

Mundesley-on-Sea

Bacton

Wolferton

Briston

Wood Dalling

Happisburgh Common

South Raynham

Hoveton St John

Winterton-on-Sea

North Elmham

Sparham

Hemsby

Scratby

California

NORFOLK

Worthing

Wroxham

Horning

Clippesby

5

9

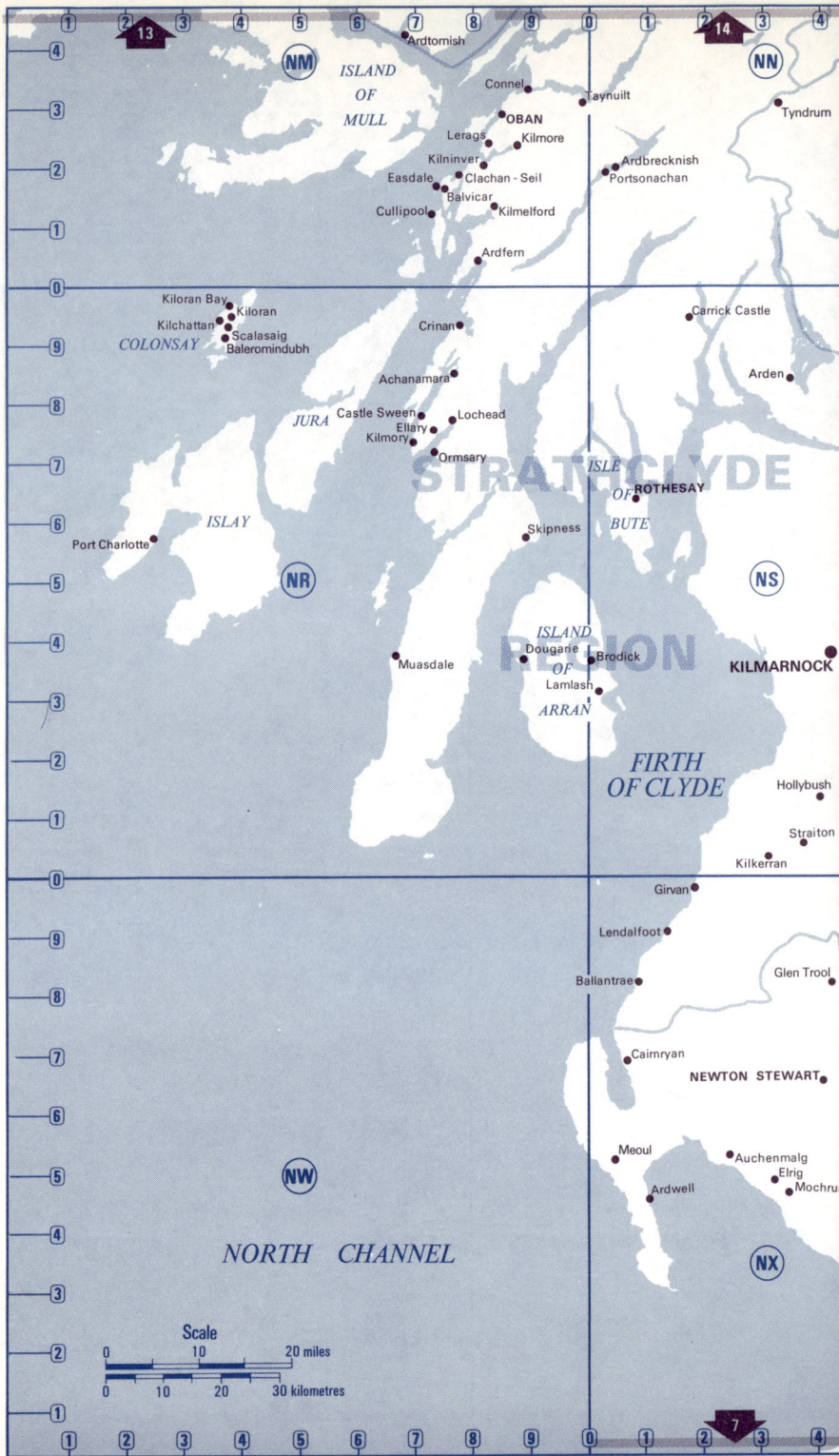

NM   NN

ISLAND OF MULL

Ardtornish
Connel
Taynuilt
Tyndrum
OBAN
Lerags
Kilmore
Kilninver
Ardbrecknish
Easdale
Clachan - Seil
Portsonachan
Balvicar
Cullipool
Kilmelford
Ardfern

Kiloran Bay
Kiloran
Carrick Castle
Kilchattan
Scalasaig
COLONSAY
Baleromindubh
Arden
Crinan

Achanamara

JURA
Castle Sween
Lochead
Ellary
Kilmory
Ormsary

STRATHCLYDE

ISLE OF **ROTHESAY**
BUTE

Skipness

ISLAY

Port Charlotte

NR   NS

ISLAND OF ARRAN

Muasdale
Dougarie
Brodick
REGION
Lamlash
KILMARNOCK

FIRTH OF CLYDE

Hollybush

Straiton
Kilkerran

Girvan

Lendalfoot
Glen Trool

Ballantrae

Cairnryan
NEWTON STEWART

NW

Meoul
Auchenmalg
Elrig
Ardwell
Mochru

NORTH CHANNEL

NX

Scale

0   10   20 miles

0   10   20   30 kilometres

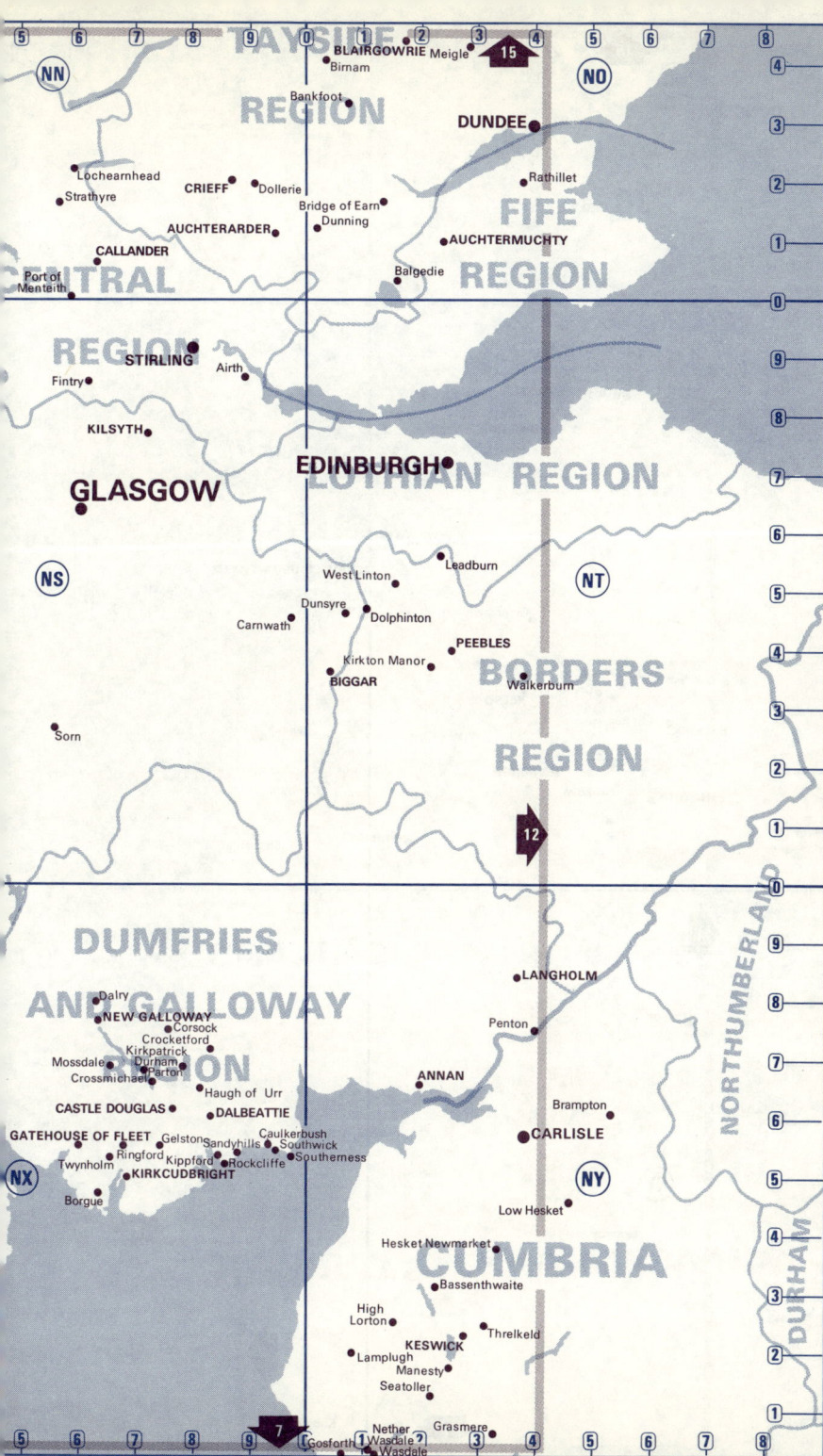

NN

NO

15

BLAIRGOWRIE   Meigle

Birnam

Bankfoot

REGION

DUNDEE

Lochearnhead

Strathyre

CRIEFF   Dollerie

Rathillet

AUCHTERARDER

Bridge of Earn

Dunning

FIFE

CALLANDER

AUCHTERMUCHTY

Port of Menteith

Balgedie

REGION

CENTRAL

REGION

STIRLING   Airth

Fintry

KILSYTH

EDINBURGH

LOTHIAN REGION

GLASGOW

NS

NT

Leadburn

West Linton

Dunsyre

Dolphinton

Carnwath

PEEBLES

Kirkton Manor

BIGGAR

BORDERS

Walkerburn

Sorn

REGION

12

DUMFRIES

LANGHOLM

AND GALLOWAY

Dalry

NEW GALLOWAY

Penton

Corsock

Crocketford

Mossdale   Kirkpatrick

Durham

Crossmichael   Parton

ANNAN

Brampton

Haugh of Urr

CASTLE DOUGLAS   DALBEATTIE

CARLISLE

GATEHOUSE OF FLEET   Gelston

Caulkerbush

Sandyhills   Southwick

NX   Twynholm   Ringford   Kippford   Rockcliffe   Southerness

NY

KIRKCUDBRIGHT

Borgue

Low Hesket

Hesket Newmarket

CUMBRIA

Bassenthwaite

High Lorton

KESWICK   Threlkeld

Lamplugh

Manesty

Seatoller

NORTHUMBERLAND

DURHAM

Grasmere

7

Nether Wasdale

Gosforth   Wasdale

11

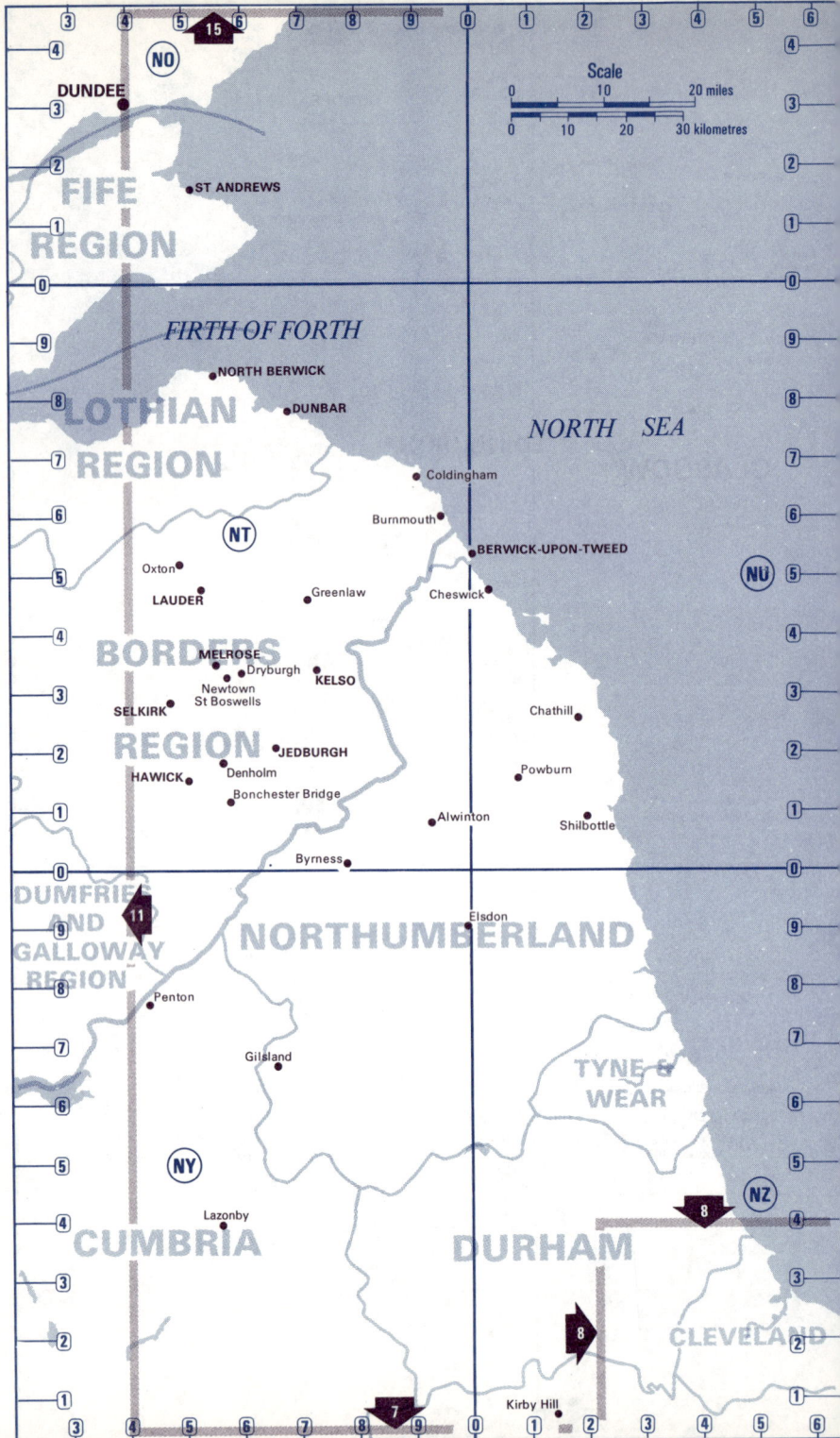

Scale

0	10	20 miles
0	10 20	30 kilometres

NO

DUNDEE

FIFE
REGION

● ST ANDREWS

FIRTH OF FORTH

NORTH SEA

● NORTH BERWICK

LOTHIAN
REGION

● DUNBAR

NT

● Coldingham

● Burnmouth

NU

●BERWICK-UPON-TWEED

Oxton ●
LAUDER ●

● Greenlaw

Cheswick ●

BORDERS

MELROSE ●
● Dryburgh
Newtown ● ●KELSO
St Boswells
SELKIRK ●

● Chathill

REGION

● JEDBURGH

● Powburn

HAWICK ● ● Denholm
● Bonchester Bridge

● Alwinton

Shilbottle ●

Byrness ●

DUMFRIES
AND
GALLOWAY
REGION

11

● Elsdon

NORTHUMBERLAND

● Penton

● Gilsland

TYNE &
WEAR

NY

Lazonby ●

NZ

8

CUMBRIA

DURHAM

CLEVELAND

8

7

● Kirby Hill

15

12

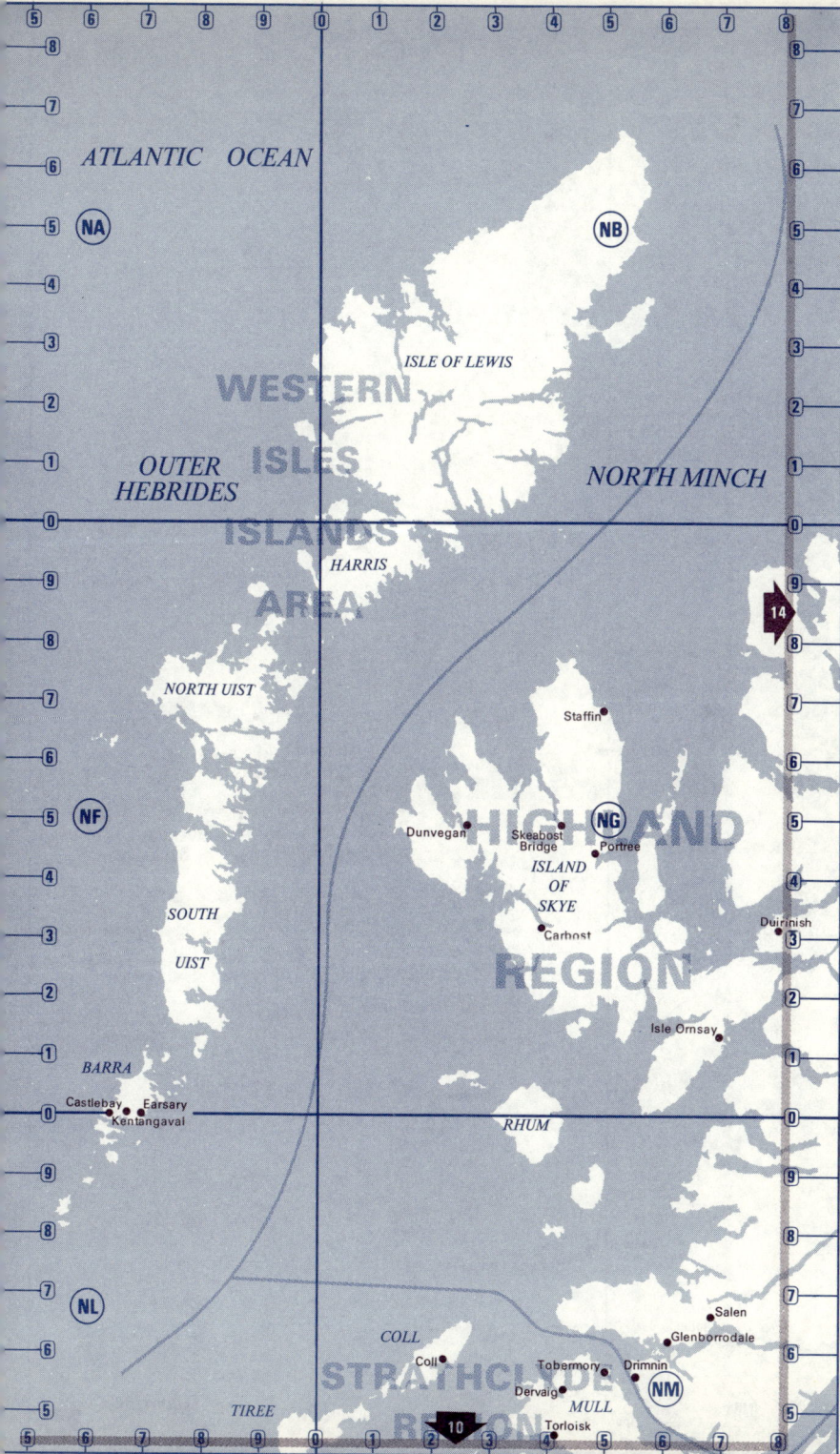

ATLANTIC OCEAN

NA

NB

ISLE OF LEWIS

WESTERN

OUTER
HEBRIDES

ISLES

ISLANDS

AREA

NORTH MINCH

HARRIS

NORTH UIST

14

Staffin

NF

NG
Dunvegan
Skeabost
Bridge
Portree

ISLAND
OF
SKYE

SOUTH

UIST

Carbost

HIGHLAND

REGION

Duirinish

Isle Ornsay

BARRA
Castlebay Earsary
Kentangaval

RHUM

NL

Salen

COLL
Coll
Glenborrodale

STRATHCLYDE
Tobermory
Dervaig
Drimnin

NM

TIREE
MULL
Torloisk

10

WESTERN
ISLES
ISLANDS
AREA

(NB)

(NC)

Melvich

Culkein

Lairg

Mellon Udrigle

Ullapool

Golspie

Leckmelm

Spinningdale

DORNOCH

Gairloch

MORAY

13

Kinlochewe

HIGHLAND

Evanton

DINGWALL

Culbrokie

Logie-Buchan

Contin

Alcaig

Redstone

Whitemire

(NG)

Muir of Ord

Coulmore

Lethen

Conicavel

(NH)

Beauly

INVERNESS

Dunphail

Kilmorack

Kirkhill

Lentran

Culloden Moor

Balnain

Drumnadrochit

Tomatin

GRANTOWN-
ON-SPEY

Flichity

REGION

Dulnain Bridge

Carrbridge

Nethy Bridge

Invermoriston

Boat of Garten

Whitebridge

Aviemore

Newton

Invergarry

Newtonmore

South
Laggan

Spean Bridge

Roy Bridge

Garvan

Corpach

Duisky

Banavie

FORT WILLIAM

Calvine

Strontian

Onich

Kinlochleven

Killiecrankie

Kentallen

Kinloch Rannoch

Ballachulish

TAYSIDE

(NM)

Port Appin

Appin

10

(NN)

ABERFELDY

11

14

For continuation pages refer to numbered arrows

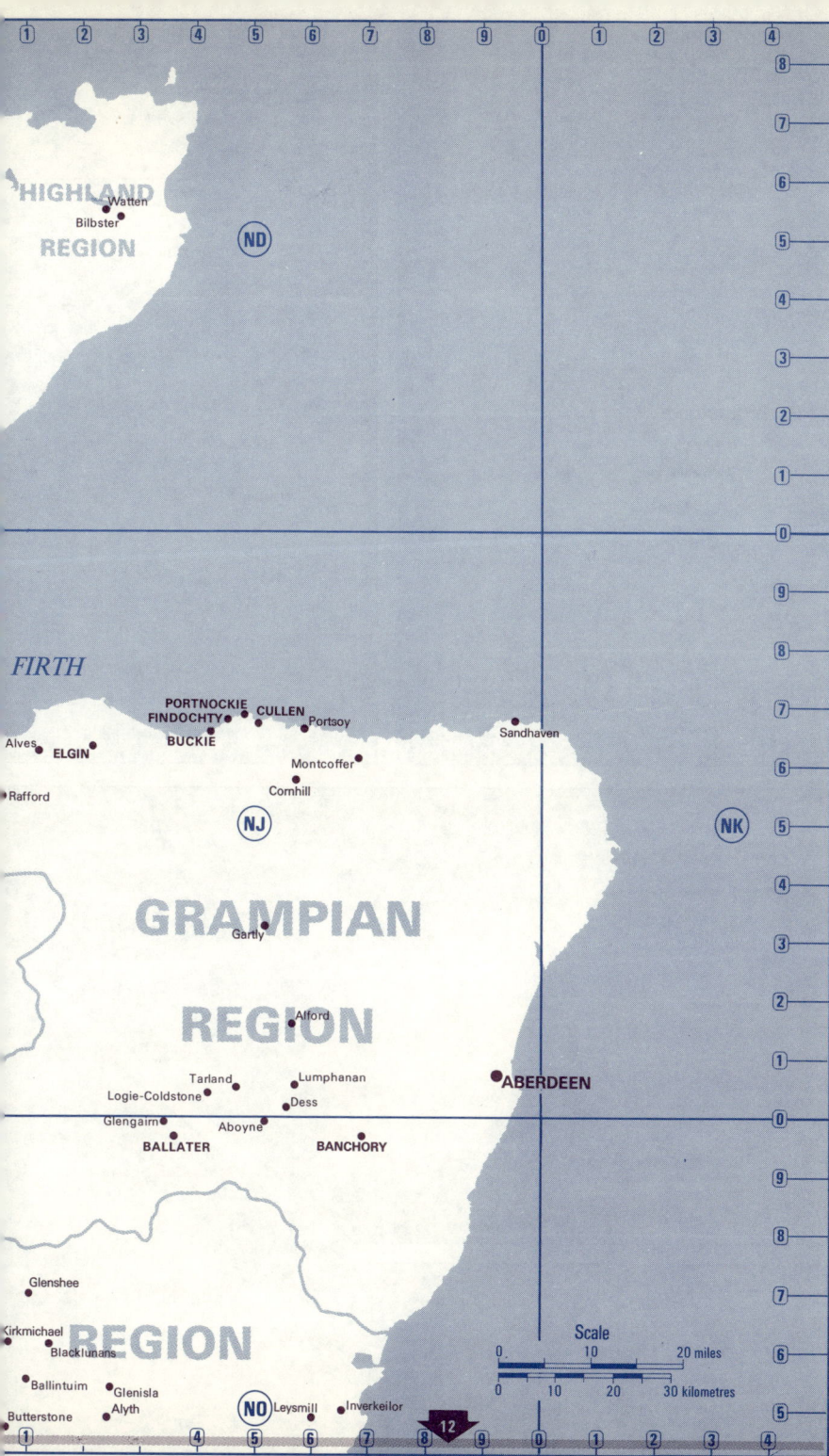

⑦

HIGHLAND
•Watten
Bilbster•

⑥

REGION ND ⑤

⑤

④

③

②

①

⓪

⑨

FIRTH ⑧

PORTNOCKIE ⑦
FINDOCHTY• •CULLEN
BUCKIE •Portsoy Sandhaven•
Alves• ELGIN ⑥
Montcoffer•
•Rafford Cornhill•

NJ NK ⑤

GRAMPIAN ④
•Gartly

③

REGION ②
•Alford

①

Tarland• •Lumphanan ⓪
Logie-Coldstone• •Dess •ABERDEEN
•Glengairn •Aboyne
BALLATER BANCHORY ⑨

⑧

•Glenshee ⑦

Kirkmichael•
•Blacklunans REGION ⑥

•Ballintuim •Glenisla
•Butterstone Alyth• NO •Leysmill •Inverkeilor ⑤

Scale
0   10   20 miles
0   10   20   30 kilometres

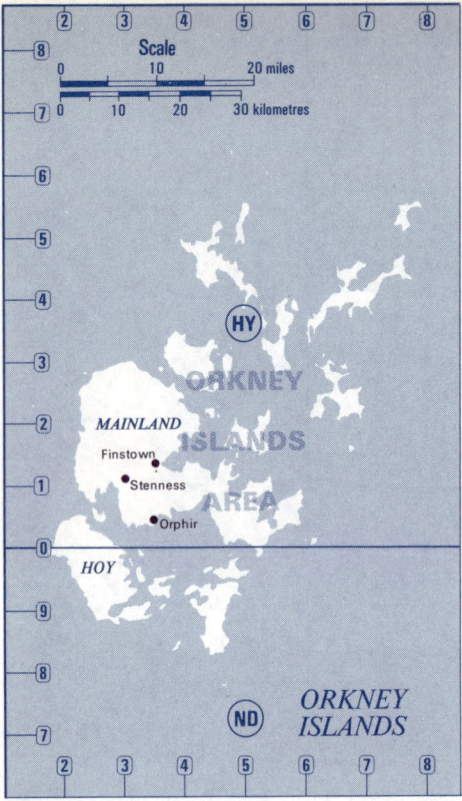

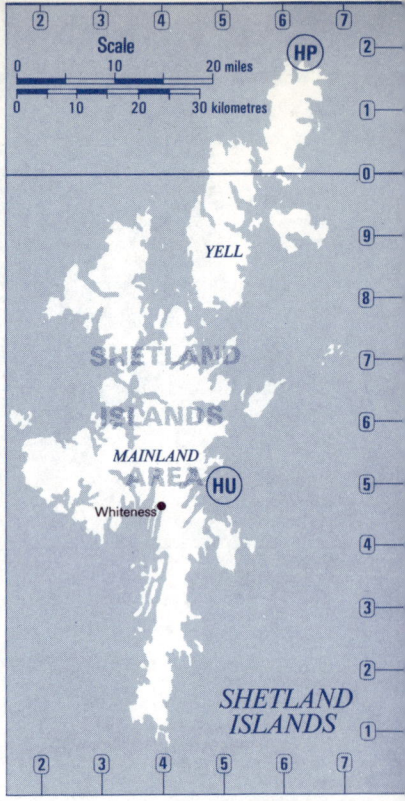

ORKNEY ISLANDS

Scale
0   10   20 miles
0 10   20   30 kilometres

HY

ORKNEY ISLANDS AREA

MAINLAND
Finstown
Stenness
Orphir

HOY

ND

SHETLAND ISLANDS

Scale
0   10   20 miles
0 10   20   30 kilometres

HP

YELL

SHETLAND ISLANDS AREA

MAINLAND
Whiteness

HU

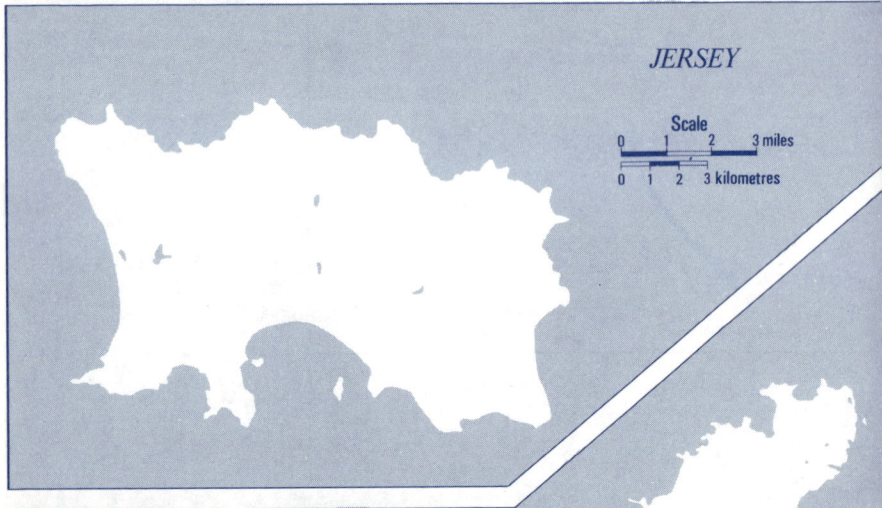

JERSEY

Scale
0   1   2   3 miles
0 1   2   3 kilometres

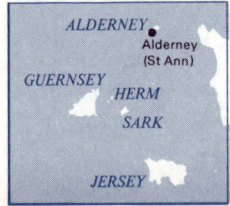

ALDERNEY
Alderney
(St Ann)

GUERNSEY
HERM
SARK

JERSEY

GUERNSEY

St Saviours

Scale
0   1   2   3 miles
0 1   2   3 kilometres